# Defending suspects at police stations

the practitioner's guide to advice and representation

**Ed Cape** is a solicitor and Professor of Criminal Law and Practice at the University of the West of England, Bristol. Formerly a partner in a legal aid practice in Bristol, and a duty solicitor for ten years, Ed writes and researches in the fields of criminal justice policy and procedure and legal services.

**Jawaid Luqmani** is a solicitor specialising in immigration law with Luqmani Thompson & Partners in London. He is a member of the Immigration Law Practitioners Association and served on its Executive Committee between 1997 and 2007. Jawaid was assessor for the Law Society immigration panel (1999–2003) and was appointed to the OISC (Office of the Immigration Services Commission) advisory panel from November 2001 to August 2005. He is an assessor for the Immigration Accreditation and Reaccreditation Schemes. Jawaid contributes regularly to *Legal Action* and lectures on courses for immigration lawyers.

# Defending suspects at police stations

the practitioner's guide to advice and representation

SIXTH EDITION

Ed Cape

with Jawaid Luqmani

Legal Action Group
2011

Sixth edition published in Great Britain 2011
by LAG Education and Service Trust Limited
242 Pentonville Road, London N1 9UN
www.lag.org.uk

© Ed Cape 2011

First published 1993
Second edition 1995
Third edition 1999
Fourth edition 2003
Fifth edition 2006

British Library Cataloguing in Publication Data
a CIP catalogue record for this book is available from the British Library.

This book has been produced using Forest Stewardship Council
(FSC) certified paper. The wood used to produce FSC certified
products with a 'Mixed Sources' label comes from FSC certified
well-managed forests, controlled sources and/or recycled
material.

Print ISBN-978 1 903307 83 0
ebook ISBN-978 1 903307 98 4

Typeset by Regent Typesetting, London
Printed in Great Britain by Hobbs the Printers, Totton, Hampshire

# Preface

It is now just over 25 years since the Police and Criminal Evidence Act 1984 (PACE) and the Codes of Practice came into force. PACE is probably the most important piece of legislation regulating police investigation since the creation of 'modern' policing in the 19th century. Not only did it introduce a statutory right for those held in police custody to consult a lawyer, with a non-means tested legal aid scheme to give it practical effect, but it created a comprehensive, detailed scheme for regulating many police investigative powers. It also provided recognition of the need for transparent and accountable policing, and of the rights of those detained by the police, more than two decades before incorporation of the European Convention on Human Rights by the Human Rights Act 1998. In many respects it has been at the forefront of attempts around the world to ensure that the police are subject to the rule of law.

During those 25 years, the character of policing and of the criminal justice process has significantly changed. Globalisation and technological development has meant that crime, and crime investigation, has become more complex and more transnational. Successive governments have given the police ever-increasing powers. It will surprise many to be reminded that when PACE was enacted the police could take the fingerprints of a person who had not been charged with an offence only on the authority of a superintendent. Now, fingerprinting of those arrested is routine, and in some circumstances a police constable can require a person to provide fingerprints even though the person has not been arrested. Add to that powers to take DNA samples and photographs routinely, to take x-rays and ultrasound scans, to require a person to undergo drug-testing following arrest, and powers to impose conditional bail on a person without charging the person for periods unrestrained by statutory time limits, and you get a sense of how far things have moved in the space of one generation. And with the increasing availability of out-of-court disposals, for many people arrested by the police the criminal justice process is what happens at police stations.

However, whilst the need for good quality and adequately funded legal advice and assistance at police stations has increased, over the past decade the ability of criminal defence lawyers to meet those challenges has been weakened. Fixed fees for police station work mean that many lawyers do not feel able, and are certainly not encouraged, to carry out their work to an appropriate standard. Competitive tendering, still on the government's radar, will reduce client choice and may result in police station work being the loss-leader for those firms desperate for a contract. CDS Direct has meant that suspects arrested for less serious offences have had to accept an inferior, telephone-only, service and there remains the prospect that it will be expanded to cover more serious offences. On top of that, in the Legal Aid, Sentencing and Punishment of Offenders Bill, the government has signalled its intention to introduce both a means and a merits test for police station legal aid.

There is some irony in all of this. The European Court of Human Rights has recognised in a series of judgments that fair trial requires that a suspect has access to a lawyer both before and during police interrogations. This has led to heated debate in many European jurisdictions, but many governments have accepted that they must introduce a legal right to advice and assistance at the investigative stage. The European Union has adopted a 'roadmap' of procedural rights under which member states will have to introduce, amongst others, a right to legal advice and assistance at the police station. PACE led the way, but at the very time that many jurisdictions are looking to see how it is done here, the provision of good quality legal advice at police stations in England and Wales is now threatened as never before.

My original purpose in writing this book was to help criminal defence lawyers to be clear about their role at the police station, and to give them the information – law, guidance and procedures – to enable them to perform it effectively. The role of defence lawyers in the criminal justice process is often undervalued, particularly by politicians and others who want to be seen as tough on crime and who want to reduce spending on legal aid without, apparently, caring about underlying values of respect, fairness and justice. Despite the many challenges, I hope that this book continues to fulfill its purpose.

As always, a book of this kind inevitably relies on the ideas and contributions of many others. Most obviously, I continue to be indebted to Jawaid Luqmani who, as in previous editions, wrote the chapter on advising immigration detainees. I remain grateful for the work done by Gareth Peirce, Roger Ede and Simon Hillyard in reading and commenting upon part or all of the original script. I also thank the many criminal defence lawyers with whom I have worked over the years, those who have attended courses that I have presented, and those who have contacted me directly, for sharing their experiences and helping me to better understand the issues raised by criminal practice at the investigative stage. My thanks also go to my publisher, Esther Pilger, and the staff at the Legal Action Group who continue, often in difficult circumstances, to demonstrate their commitment to improving access to justice. Finally, as they know, none of this would be possible without the support of Liz, Gareth and Matthew.

The law is stated as at 1 August 2011.

Ed Cape
Bristol
1 August 2011

# Contents

# Table of cases

# Table of statutes

# Table of statutory instruments

# Table of European legislation

# Abbreviations

| | |
|---|---|
| ACPO | Association of Chief Police Officers |
| ARC | Application registration card |
| ASBO | Anti-social behaviour order |
| BA 1976 | Bail Act 1976 |
| BIS | Department of Business, Innovation and Skills |
| CCP | Code for Crown Prosecutors |
| CDA 1998 | Crime and Disorder Act 1998 |
| CDS | Criminal Defence Service |
| CIO | Chief immigration officer |
| CLAS | Criminal Litigation Accreditation Scheme |
| CLR | Controlled legal representation |
| CJA 1988 | Criminal Justice Act 1988 |
| CJA 1993 | Criminal Justice Act 2003 |
| CJPA 2001 | Criminal Justice and Police Act 2001 |
| CJPOA 1994 | Criminal Justice and Public Order Act 1994 |
| CPIA 1996 | Criminal Procedure and Investigations Act 1996 |
| CPS | Crown Prosecution Service |
| CYPA 1933 | Children and Young Persons Act 1933 |
| DA 2005 | Drugs Act 2005 |
| DPP | Director of Public Prosecutions |
| DSCC | Defence Solicitor Call Centre |
| DWP | Department for Work and Pensions |
| EA 2003 | Extradition Act 2003 |
| ECHR | European Convention on Human Rights |
| ECO | Entry clearance officer |
| ECtHR | European Court of Human Rights |
| EEA | European Economic Area |
| FACT | Federation Against Copyright Theft |
| FTT | First Tier Tribunal |
| HEO | Higher Executive Officer |
| HMRC | HM Revenue and Customs |
| HRA 1998 | Human Rights Act 1998 |
| IA 1971 | Immigration Act 1971 |
| IAAS | Immigration and Asylum Accreditation Scheme |
| IAC | Immigration and Asylum Chamber |
| IO | Immigration officer |
| IPCC | Independent Police Complaints Commission |
| JSB | Judicial Studies Board |
| LSC | Legal Services Commission |
| MCA 1980 | Magistrates' Courts Act 1980 |
| MCQ | Magistrates' Court Qualification |
| MHA 1983 | Mental Health Act 1983 |
| NAM | New Asylum Model |
| NPIA | National Policing Improvement Agency |
| OISC | Office of the Immigration Services Commissioner |
| PACE | Police and Criminal Evidence Act 1984 |
| PCA | Police Complaints Authority |

| | |
|---|---|
| PCSO | Police community support officer |
| POA 1985 | Prosecution of Offences Act 1985 |
| POCA 2002 | Proceeds of Crime Act 2002 |
| PRA 2002 | Police Reform Act 2002 |
| PSQ | Police Station Qualification |
| PTI | Pre-trial issues |
| RIPA 2000 | Regulation of Investigatory Powers Act 2000 |
| RTA 1988 | Road Traffic Act 1988 |
| SCC 2010 | Standard Criminal Contract 2010 |
| SOA 2003 | Sexual Offences Act 2003 |
| SOCA | Serious Organised Crime Agency |
| SOCPA 2005 | Serious Organised Crime and Police Act 2005 |
| SRA | Solicitors Regulation Authority |
| TA 2000 | Terrorism Act 2000 |
| TICs | Offences to be taken into consideration |
| UKBA | UK Border Agency |

**CHAPTER 1**

# Defending the client

*continued*

1

# Role of the defence lawyer

1.1   The trial, especially jury trial, has traditionally been regarded as the crowning glory of our adversarial criminal justice system. The emphasis placed on the trial justified the view that advising at police stations was relatively unimportant, not requiring the skills or deserving the knowledge and experience expected of courtroom lawyers. In reality, however, what happens at the police station is often more important than what occurs in the courtroom in terms of determining the outcome of the case. Most cases are won or lost at the police station rather than at court. Confessions, sometimes false, are obtained from suspects, evidence is gathered, deals are done, and decisions are made which will inevitably influence the course of subsequent events. The Court of Appeal has described police interrogation and the trial as being 'part of a continuous process in which the suspect is engaged from the beginning'.[1] In a leading case in 2008, the European Court of Human Rights underlined the importance of the investigative stage in the following terms:

> ... the evidence obtained during this stage determines the framework in which the offence charged will be considered at the trial [and at] the same time, an accused often finds himself in a particularly vulnerable position at that stage of the proceedings, the effect of which is amplified by the fact that legislation on criminal procedure tends to become increasingly complex, notably with respect to the rules governing the gathering and use of evidence.[2]

1.2   Defending at police stations is not easy. Clients may be vulnerable, nervous, apprehensive, resentful, angry, rude, or all of these things. Police officers may be unco-operative, secretive, difficult, dismissive or aggressive. The lawyer is on police territory, subject to a police agenda, and is often viewed as an interloper, interfering with both the investigation and the course of justice. On top of this, it may be late at night or in the early hours of the morning, and the lawyer is alone, unsupported by professional colleagues.

1.3   It is essential that lawyers working in this environment are clear about their role, are confident in their knowledge of relevant law and procedure, and possess the skills necessary to be effective. The importance of the lawyer's role is underlined by two Court of Appeal decisions. In the first, *R v Paris, Abdullahi and Miller*,[3] Stephen Miller and his two co-defendants were found guilty of murder largely because of Miller's false confession, made as a result of considerable and illegitimate pressure from the police. As the then Lord Chief Justice Taylor said at the successful appeal: 'Short of physical violence, it was hard to conceive of a more hostile approach by officers to a suspect.' The defendant, during most of the interviews, was

---

1   *R v Howell* [2003] EWCA Crim 1; (2005) 1 Cr App R 1; [2003] Crim LR 405.
2   *Salduz v Turkey* (2008) 49 EHRR 421, at para 54. This principle has, in effect, also been accepted by the United Nations. See *Basic principles on the role of lawyers*, adopted by the Eighth United Nations Congress on the Prevention of Crime and the Treatment of Offenders on 7 September 1990 and welcomed by the General Assembly in Resolution 45/121 of 14 December 1990. For the domestic implications of *Salduz*, see *Cadder v HM Advocate* [2010] UKSC 43.
3   (1993) 97 Cr App R 99; [1994] Crim LR 361.

accompanied by his solicitor and the Court of Appeal was unimpressed: '... the solicitor who sat in on the interviews seemed to have done that and little else. It seemed that his presence might actually have rendered a disservice since the officers might have taken the view that unless and until the solicitor intervened, they could not be criticised for going too far.' The fact that an inactive lawyer can do the client a disservice is also shown by a second case, that of *R v Dunn*,[4] in which it was held that the presence of a lawyer may nullify the otherwise adverse effects for the prosecution of a breach of the Police and Criminal Evidence Act 1984 (PACE) or the Codes of Practice since, in the view of the court, the presence of the lawyer was sufficient to protect the suspect's interests.[5]

1.4     It is for these reasons that this book is called *Defending suspects at police stations*. The proper role of the defence lawyer is not, as some would have it, merely that of an observer.[6] If that were the case, the lawyer could be replaced by a video camera. Neither is it to maintain some kind of balance between police and suspect – it is unlikely that the defence will ever have the powers and resources to match those of the police. Nor is the defence lawyer's function merely, as the Court of Appeal has sometimes implied,[7] that of a provider of legal information. Rather, as Code C states, the 'solicitor's only role in the police station is to protect and advance the legal rights of his client'.[8] In our adversarial system, in which the police actively pursue the interests of the prosecution, the defence lawyer must actively pursue the interests of the suspect or defendant. To the extent that he or she does not do so, the lawyer will, as the Lord Chief Justice indicated in the case of *Paris*, be doing a disservice to the client, becoming in effect an arm of the prosecution.

## Objectives of the defence lawyer

1.5     The defence lawyer, as with any other lawyer, is under a duty to act in the best interests of the client. This duty means that the lawyer must treat the interests of the client as paramount, provided that they do not conflict with the lawyer's professional conduct obligations or the public interest in the administration of justice.[9] While, for example, a client may be advised in strong terms of the advantages of admitting an offence to the police,

4   (1990) 91 Cr App R 237; [1990] Crim LR 572.

5   It is not suggested that the lawyer in this case acted anything other than properly, since she denied that the disputed confession, which the police said was made in her presence, took place at all. For a further discussion of this case, see para 13.32 below.

6   For evidence, from the 1990s, that lawyers frequently took a passive role in police interviews, see M McConville and J Hodgson, *Custodial Legal Advice and the Right to Silence*, Royal Commission on Criminal Justice (RCCJ) Research Study No 16 (HMSO, London, 1993); J Baldwin, *The Conduct of Police Investigations: Records of interview; The defence lawyer's role and Standards of supervision*, RCCJ Research Studies Nos 2, 3 and 4 (HMSO, London, 1992), and M McConville et al, *Standing accused* (Clarendon Press, Oxford, 1994).

7   See, eg, *R v Alladice* (1988) 87 Cr App R 380; [1988] Crim LR 608, and *R v Dunford* (1990) 91 Cr App R 150; [1991] Crim LR 370.

8   Code C Note for Guidance 6D (discussed at para 7.50 below).

9   *SRA Principles 2011*, Principle 4.

whether to do so is a matter for the client and the lawyer should not apply any undue pressure to them to accept the advice.[10] After all, it is the client who has to live with the consequences. If the lawyer feels strongly that the decision of the client is contrary to the advice given, one safeguard is for the lawyer to put the advice in writing and ask the client to read it and sign it. Acting in the client's best interests also involves trying to secure the best possible outcome for the client. This may include advising the client in such a way as to avoid disclosing information or evidence to the police which would be detrimental to the client's interests, trying to persuade the police or prosecutor not to charge, seeking to minimise the length of detention, trying to secure bail, and ensuring that relevant mitigating factors are put forward. The specific objectives of the defence lawyer are summarised below.

## Securing information

1.6 The lawyer should seek to obtain as much relevant information from the police as possible. The police well understand the power of information and, more particularly, the utility of withholding information. It will usually be impossible to advise a client adequately in the absence of information, particularly about the evidence in the hands of the police, but also in relation to the circumstances of the arrest and detention. This takes on added significance in the context of the 'inference from silence' provisions of the Criminal Justice and Public Order Act (CJPOA) 1994, particularly since the Court of Appeal has held that failure of the police to supply information will not necessarily render a decision not to answer police questions reasonable. See further chapters 4 and 5.

## Advising in private

1.7 Giving advice to the client in private is of paramount importance, and is a basic right under PACE s58 and Terrorism Act (TA) 2000 Sch 8 para 7. Police tactics which have the effect of undermining this right should be firmly resisted.[11] See further paras 2.149–2.150 below.

## Advising on matters arising during the period of detention

1.8 In most cases the need for advice is unlikely to be confined to the initial consultation with the client, whether on the telephone or in person. Matters may arise throughout the period that the client is in police custody on which he or she may want or need advice. In particular, advice should not stop when the client enters the police interview or after the lawyer has left the police station. As PACE s58 makes clear, the suspect is entitled to legal advice at any time. Furthermore, the lawyer should not wait until the client

---

10 See the *Code of Conduct for Employees of the Legal Services Commission* (TSO, London, 2001) para 2.2 and Public Defender Service Guidance 1/2002 which, although only directly applicable to PDS lawyers, is relevant for all defence lawyers.

11 It has also been held that this right is capable of enforcement by way of an action for breach of statutory duty (*R v Roques* September 1997 *Legal Action* 23).

asks for advice. There are many occasions when the lawyer should take the initiative.

## Presence at police interviews

1.9   Police interviews are crucial, both to the police and to the client. There are relatively few occasions when a lawyer would be justified in not attending them. The fact that they are tape-recorded or video-recorded is certainly no justification for absence. The fact that the client is intending not to answer questions is an important indication that the lawyer's presence is required. See further chapter 7.

## Safeguarding the client's rights

1.10   Securing police observance of the rights of a suspect under PACE, TA 2000 and the Codes of Practice is not necessarily an easy task since, in particular, PACE and TA 2000 provide no mechanisms for enforcement that can be put into effect at the police station. However, the duty to safeguard a client's rights follows directly from the general duty to act in the client's best interests. If the defence lawyer does not take appropriate action, no one else will.

## Acting ethically

1.11   High ethical standards are important for the defence lawyer, particularly in view of the nature of the work. One aspect of this principle is that the lawyer should do nothing that will compromise the interests of the client. The lawyer is under a professional duty to keep the affairs of the client confidential, and under a duty to pass on to the client all material information regardless of the source of that information. This means that the lawyer must not pass on information about the client to the police unless authorised to do so by the client, and must pass on relevant information to the client even if the police have given the lawyer the information 'in confidence'. See further paras 1.16 and 4.29 below. The principle of acting ethically also means that the lawyer must not compromise himself or herself in relation to the client. The lawyer must be clear, for example, about the difference between pointing out the weaknesses of a client's version of events and helping the client to concoct a story. The former is perfectly proper, the latter probably illegal. The lawyer must always remember that an act performed with intent to impede the apprehension or prosecution of a person who has committed a 'relevant offence' is itself a serious criminal offence.[12] Finally, the lawyer must take care to avoid acting for more than one client where there is a conflict of interests. See further para 5.41 below.

---

12   Criminal Law Act 1967 s4, and see further para 5.35 below. For an example of the difficulties that a lawyer can get into by asserting facts to the police that may not be true, see *R v Williams* [2002] EWCA Crim 2208.

## Dealing with the client

### General approach

1.12    Specific information about dealing with a client at the police station is given throughout this book, but some general points about the lawyer/client relationship are considered here. As noted earlier, the client may be in a variety of emotional states which will require an approach that is both empathetic and inspires confidence. Empathy may be demonstrated by being willing to listen to what the client has to say even if it does not appear directly relevant to the issues. This is not to say that the lawyer should allow the client to ramble on indefinitely, but it will usually be appropriate to allow the client the time and the opportunity to express how and what the client is feeling. In any case, this will then allow the interview to proceed in a calmer and more constructive fashion. At the same time, the lawyer must also take appropriate action to ensure his or her own safety. See further para 5.8 below.

1.13    If the lawyer is to be effective, the lawyer will need to be able to inspire confidence in his or her skills and abilities. An adequate knowledge of the law governing police detention is a pre-requisite but is not, in itself, sufficient. While some might argue that a casual approach, both in dress and manner, means that the lawyer will be 'closer' to the client, in the context of the police station this is often likely to be counter-productive. A lawyer who looks professional and acts professionally, whose demeanour is calm, and who is willing to stand up to the police where necessary, is likely to inspire much greater confidence than one who is casual, uses 'street' language or who is easily knocked off course by confrontation with the police. This is especially important since the police will often be competing with the lawyer in terms of status. If the police are successful, it will be easier for them to influence the suspect in the direction they want, which may entail encouraging the suspect to ignore the lawyer's advice.

### Client care rule

1.14    The lawyer should be aware of the Solicitors' Regulation Authority client care rules.[13] Although certain aspects of the rules are not applicable at the police station, generally the rules may be suitably adapted to police station advice. In order to comply with the rules the lawyer should:

- Tell the client your name and status.
- Identify clearly the client's objectives in relation to the work to be done for the client.
- Give the client a clear explanation of the issues involved and the options available to them.
- Tell the client the likely cost and how it will be met – usually, that advice is provided free under the police station advice and assistance scheme.
- Keep the client informed of progress.

13    *SRA Code of Conduct 2011*, ch 1.

- When the client is to be released from police custody, agree with them the next steps to be taken and inform them of any continuing consequences and write to them confirming the position.

1.15   The lawyer should send the client a 'client care' letter following the client's release from police custody. If the lawyer, or the firm, continues to act for the client in respect of criminal proceedings resulting from the period in the police station, the client care rules should be followed in full.

## Client confidentiality and privilege

1.16   There are a number of important issues regarding the confidentiality of communications between a defence lawyer and the client. The first concerns the professional duty of a solicitor not to disclose communications between himself or herself and the client, and the related question of whether the lawyer can ever be required to divulge such information. The second concerns the power of the police to obtain material which may be privileged. The third issue, which concerns whether the police can listen to communications between a lawyer and client, is dealt with at paras 2.133–2.136 below.

1.17   In relation to the first issue, it is important to distinguish between the duty of confidentiality, which is an obligation governed by the *SRA Code of Conduct 2011*, ch 4, and legal professional privilege, which is an evidential rule governing the question whether a lawyer can be required to divulge information which is otherwise confidential. As noted at para 1.11 above, solicitors and their staff are under a professional duty to keep their clients', and former clients', affairs confidential. No information that has been communicated to the lawyer by or on behalf of a client, including the client's address, may be disclosed to anyone outside the firm without the client's agreement. The duty continues to apply even after the solicitor/ client relationship comes to an end. For problems that may arise where the solicitor/client relationship may be terminated while the lawyer is at the police station, see para 5.36 below.

1.18   The SRA recognises that the duty of confidentiality is overridden in certain circumstances, including:

1) Where disclosure is necessary to prevent the client or a third party committing a criminal act which the solicitor reasonably believes is likely to result in serious bodily harm.

2) In exceptional circumstances involving children where the client is a child and discloses continuing sexual or other physical abuse but refuses to allow disclosure of such information, or where the client is an adult and discloses abuse of a child by them or another adult and refuses to allow disclosure of such information.

3) Where disclosure is required by statute, eg, under the Proceeds of Crime Act (POCA) 2002, or the Money Laundering Regulations. For guidance on the duties of solicitors in respect of reporting terrorism see the Law Society Guidance *Anti-terrorism practice note: the conflicting duties of maintaining client confidentiality and reporting terrorism*.[14]

---

14   Available at www.lawsociety.org.uk/documents/downloads/dynamic/practicenote_terrorismact2000.pdf.

4) Where a court orders confidential information to be disclosed, or issues a warrant which authorises the seizure of confidential information.

These exceptions, and others, are dealt with in more detail in the *Solicitors' Code of Conduct 2007* Guidance to Rule 4 – Confidentiality and disclosure.[15]

1.19 Quite separately from the professional duty of confidentiality, the law recognises that certain communications between a lawyer and the client, or with a third party, should be protected from enforced disclosure, and this is contained within rules concerning legal professional privilege. In some respects these rules cover a narrower range of communications than the duty of confidentiality. Whereas the confidentiality rule covers all confidential information about a client's affairs, legal professional privilege is confined to communications between a lawyer and the client which are made for the purpose of enabling the client to obtain or the lawyer to give legal advice. If a communication is privileged, neither the police nor a court can force either the lawyer or client to divulge the communication.[16] The client, but not the lawyer, can expressly waive privilege and thus allow its disclosure but it is important to note that privilege can be waived by implication; that is, disclosure of some privileged material may result in other material losing its privileged status. If privilege is lost in this way, a court could order disclosure of such material. For a discussion of this in relation to disclosure of legal advice given to a client, see para 5.100 below.

1.20 It follows from the above that the police can never directly force a lawyer to disclose to them information which is covered by legal professional privilege and, in view of the duty of confidentiality, a lawyer must never (subject to the exceptions noted above) volunteer confidential information without the client's consent. However, the police will sometimes seek to persuade a lawyer, possibly in forceful terms, to supply information and/or hand over documents that the lawyer has obtained while acting for a client. If the client consents then, of course, the information can be given or the documents handed over. If the client does not consent, the lawyer should consider the following questions:

1) *Is the information or are the documents covered by the duty of confidentiality?* If the information or documents have been received from the client, they almost certainly will be unless an exception applies (see above). The lawyer should insist on the police obtaining a witness summons or subpoena unless the lawyer has strong prima facie evidence that they have been used by the client to perpetrate a fraud or other crime.[17]

2) *Will I commit an offence if I do not give the information or documents to the police?* Generally, a lawyer will not be committing an offence merely by refusing to hand over information or documents that the

15 See *Solicitors' Code of Conduct 2007*, Guidance to rule 4, paras 9–19. These do not appear in the *SRA Code of Conduct 2011*, but the principles should continue to apply.
16 See *R v Derby Magistrates' Court ex p B and Another* [1995] 4 All ER 526, and *R v Crown Court at Manchester ex p Rogers* [1999] 4 All ER 35; [1999] Crim LR 743. Legal professional privilege also covers communications between a lawyer or client and a third party (eg, a potential witness or expert) where the dominant purpose is preparation for pending or contemplated litigation.
17 *Solicitors' Code of Conduct 2007*, Guidance to rule 4, para 16.

lawyer believes to be covered by the duty of confidentiality. It is highly unlikely that a court would conclude that a lawyer is guilty of wilfully obstructing a constable in such circumstances. There are provisions in the TA 2000 which make it an offence not to disclose to the police a belief or suspicion that a person has committed an offence under TA 2000 ss15–18 (offences relating to terrorist property), where that belief or suspicion is based on information obtained in the course of a trade, profession, business or employment (TA 2000 s19(1) and (2)). Other non-disclosure offences are to be found in TA 2000 ss21A and 38B. Generally, however, disclosure is not required where the information is obtained in circumstances which are covered by legal professional privilege.[18] There are a number of provisions in the POCA 2002 which impose extensive disclosure obligations in relation to the proceeds of crime. In particular, POCA 2002 s328(1) makes it an offence for a person to enter into or become concerned in an arrangement which the person knows or suspect facilitates the acquisition, retention, use or control of criminal property by or on behalf of another person. 'Criminal property' is widely defined to include property that itself constitutes a person's benefit from criminal conduct or which represents such a benefit, wholly or partly and whether directly or indirectly. However, it was held in *Bowman v Fels*[19] that section 328 was not intended to cover or affect the ordinary conduct of litigation by legal professionals, and that even if this conclusion was incorrect, that it did not override the duty of confidentiality or legal professional privilege. Therefore, provided the information is obtained in, or documents are created for the purposes of, the proper conduct of the case, the lawyer will not commit an offence under the Police Reform Act (PRA) 2002 by failing to disclose them.

3) *Do the police have the power to seize documents in my possession?* This may arise in respect of documents in the lawyer's possession while still at the police station, or in respect of documents retained elsewhere, such as in the lawyer's office. Unless the lawyer is himself or herself arrested, the police have no power to seize documents or other material from the lawyer while at the police station.[20] With regard to documents or other material held elsewhere, if such documents or material have been created in the course of a lawyer/client relationship, or have been passed to the lawyer by a client in connection with the matter on which legal advice is sought, it is likely to amount to legally privileged material (unless held with the intention of furthering a criminal purpose) or special procedure material. In this case, the ability of the police to search for or require production of such material is circumscribed by PACE Part II, and generally the police would have to obtain a production order or a search warrant.

---

18  TA 2000 s19(5) and (6). See also the Law Society's *Anti-terrorism practice note*, issued on 19 July 2007, available at www.lawsociety.org.uk/documents/downloads/dynamic/ practicenote_terrorismact2000.pdf.

19  [2005] EWCA Civ 226; [2005] 1 WLR 3083; [2005] 4 All ER 609; [2005] 2 Cr App R 19.

20  For the application of these principles to a statement prepared for the purposes of a police interview, see para 5.157 below.

# Dealing with the police

1.21　Many police officers have a negative attitude towards defence lawyers. This largely results from their 'crime control' values. Their job, as most police officers see it, is to control crime. The best way to control crime is to catch criminals. Anyone, or anything, that interferes with that mission is on the side of the criminal against the police. An important aspect of the police perspective is the need to demand deference from, and to be in control of, those people who they see as 'police property'.[21] By acting for, and speaking on behalf of, such people defence lawyers challenge this perspective. The objective of investigative interviewing have been described by the police as obtaining: 'accurate and reliable accounts from ... suspects about matters under police investigation'.[22] However, the evidence demonstrates that the police are often more interested in securing proof than in discovering truth, and the increasing involvement of Crown prosecutors in crime investigation and charge decisions demonstrates the fact that the police are acting on behalf of the prosecution. Seen from this standpoint, unless defence lawyers can be harnessed to the values of the police, they are bound to interfere with these crime control objectives.[23] Furthermore, the police have developed strategies such as phased (or managed) disclosure and intelligence-led investigation which have the effect, if not the purpose, of making the work of defence lawyers more difficult.

1.22　The defence lawyer, having recognised why the police act as they do towards the lawyer, needs to develop strategies for dealing with such conduct.[24] This may, on occasion, require personal qualities of courage and perseverance. The words of the then Lord Chief Justice, Lord Taylor, in *R v Paris, Abdullahi and Miller*[25] should be borne in mind by all defence lawyers acting at the police station. Having commented on the fact that the lawyer in that case appeared to have done little in the police interview, he went on to say:

> Guidelines for solicitors published by the Law Society provided that a solicitor might need to intervene if the questions were oppressive, threatening or insulting: that a solicitor should intervene if the officer was not asking questions but only making comments or if the questions were improperly put: and that the solicitor should advise the suspect of his right to remain silent if improprieties remained uncorrected or continued. A solicitor fulfilling the exacting duty of assisting a suspect during interviews should follow

---

21　Being 'in control' is very important for the police and much of their behaviour can be understood in these terms. See S Choongh, *Policing as social discipline* (Clarendon, Oxford, 1997).

22　*National Investigative Interviewing Strategy* (NPIA, Wyboston, 2009) p6, available at www.npia.police.uk/en/docs/National_Investigative_Interviewing_Strategy_09.pdf.

23　There have been few recent research studies of the nature of police work and the attitude of police officers to their work, but one that was carried out in the early 1990s still provides valuable insights: M McConville, A Sanders and R Leng, *The case for the prosecution* (Routledge, London, 1991). See also the more recent study, L Skinns, *Police custody: governance, legitimacy and reform of the criminal justice process* (Willan, Abingdon, 2011).

24　For more detailed guidance see E Shepherd, *Police station skills for legal advisers: practical reference* (3rd edn, Law Society, 2004).

25　(1993) 97 Cr App R 99; [1994] Crim LR 361.

the guidelines and discharge his function responsibly and courageously. Otherwise his presence might actually render a disservice.

The defence lawyer should need no further endorsement of the legitimacy of and necessity for a pro-active and interventionist role.

1.23   One matter of general importance is the extent to which defence lawyers can expect the police to respect the confidentiality of consultations with their clients. There is evidence that the police do place listening devices in cells and consultation rooms and record telephone conversations, although not necessarily routinely. For this reason, lawyers should always be aware of the possibility that conversations with their clients may be listened to by the police and, in particular, should never assume that a telephone conversation with a client in a police station is private. They should also warn clients of the possibility that any conversation that they have may be 'bugged'.[26] For the use of covert surveillance in respect of lawyer/client consultations see para 2.135 below.

## Preparing for the defence lawyer's role

### Organisation by the firm

1.24   Effective and efficient organisation is essential for firms providing a service to those detained at the police station because:

- police station work is both individually and organisationally demanding;
- it is unpredictable – clients are often arrested at inconvenient times and frequently in the middle of the night;
- it is required by the Law Society's Practice Management Standards and, for contracted firms, by the Legal Services Commission's (LSC) Standard Criminal Contract (SCC) 2010;
- it may well make the difference between the work being profitable and unprofitable.

In order to satisfy these various requirements, any firm that provides legal advice at the police station must develop structures and procedures to cater for the following.

### Availability 24 hours per day

1.25   Systems are necessary to ensure that a lawyer is available and can be contacted at any time of the day or night in order to deal with police station calls, including back-up arrangements to cater for busy periods.

### Full record-keeping

1.26   Systems are necessary to ensure that all relevant information, from first contact onwards, is recorded in an accessible and retrievable form. This will necessitate appropriate training of all staff, including relevant administrative staff, and the use of pro-formas and checklists (see appendix 3).

---

26  For the bugging of cells see *R v Ali* (1991) *Times* 19 February, *R v Bailey* [1993] 3 All ER 513; [1993] Crim LR 681, *R v Stephen Roberts* [1997] Crim LR 222 and *R v Mason* [2002] Crim LR 841.

A comprehensive and useful pro-forma for police station cases is available from the Public Defender Service.[27]

## Prompt allocation of cases to appropriately qualified staff

1.27 This will involve having systems to ensure that:

- cases are allocated without delay;
- cases are allocated to appropriate staff having regard to the actual or potential seriousness of the case, and the status and experience of the staff member;
- duty solicitor cases are allocated to staff who are appropriately qualified.

## Appropriate supervision

1.28 Three forms of supervision should be considered:

- *Supervision that is available to a police station lawyer at short notice if the lawyer encounters difficulties on which the lawyer needs advice or guidance.* Firms should also consider whether to create protocols giving guidance to police station lawyers on when they should refer to a supervisor while dealing with a case at the police station.
- *Supervision of the conduct of police station cases.* This should involve face-to-face discussion of the way in which a case was conducted, and should be conducted soon after the case to which it related. This form of supervision would only be necessary in respect of a proportion of cases dealt with by each police station lawyer. The purpose is to give the lawyer an opportunity to reflect on the way in which the lawyer dealt with a case and, if necessary, to enable the lawyer to take remedial action.
- *Supervision of file management.*

## Appropriate training

1.29 The need for relevant training is self-evident, and mechanisms should be in place for planning and delivering training for all staff engaged in police station work. Training should cover not only substantive law, procedure and evidence, but also appropriate skills.

## File and case management

1.30 Good file and case management systems are necessary for what is, in many firms, high volume work. Particular attention should be paid to systems that:

- enable files, in particular the most recent, to be retrieved quickly where an existing client has been arrested;
- enable conflict of interests checks to be made without undue delay;
- ensure that information obtained at the police station is available to the court advocate as soon as the client appears in court;
- ensure that information resulting from police station attendance is placed in any subsequent court file.

27  Via www.legalservices.gov.uk/criminal/pds/pds_forms.asp.

*Arrangements with doctors, interpreters, etc*

1.31   Firms should ensure that police station lawyers have up-to-date information on the availability of doctors, interpreters, etc. Firms should consider
making suitable arrangements with such professionals in order to ensure
their availability at short notice.

## Personal organisation

1.32   In addition to the firm being organised appropriately for police station
work, the individual lawyer needs to be organised as well. A number of
matters are relevant here.

*Expertise and skills*

1.33   As noted above, firms should be responsible for ensuring that all staff are
appropriately trained so that they have the necessary knowledge, expertise
and skills to do their job well. It is also the responsibility of individual
police station lawyers to ensure that they are adequately prepared for
defending clients at police stations.

*Dress*

1.34   It may appear unnecessary to deal with what a person wears, but dressing
appropriately is an important consideration for the defence lawyer. Its significance from the police point of view was summed up many years ago by
Walkley in his book *Police interrogation*.[28] He considered the importance of
the relative status of police interviewer and lawyer in terms of influencing
the suspect, stating:

> Many solicitors (although not all) have all the qualities of the proficient inter-
> viewer – articulate, well dressed, well groomed, polite and well prepared
> – and can upstage the interviewer in the status stakes. If the interviewer is
> a bit short on some of these qualities, then it is definitely no contest ... So,
> ideally, the interviewer should certainly look good compared to the lawyer
> – no reason why he should not be better dressed than most of them, he
> probably gets paid more.

While it is not always easy to 'look good', especially in the middle of the
night, failure to do so may well give the police a tactical advantage.

*Comprehensive and legible notes*

1.35   The importance of comprehensive and legible note-taking cannot be over-
stated. The defence lawyer, and all staff involved in any way with a police
station case – such as the person who takes the initial telephone message – must take a contemporaneous note of what is said and done, the
date and time, and the initials or signature of the note-maker. This will
be made easier by the use of a standard police station form.[29] There are
a number of reasons for this. First, it will help ensure that all work done
in respect of a particular case can be included in a claim for work done

28   (Police Review Publishing Company, London, 1988) pp90 and 91.
29   See note 27.

(where an itemised claim can be made). Second, it will facilitate the passing of a case from one lawyer to another. The second lawyer will be able to see, at a glance, what has been done and said before the handover. If it is in the form of a standard case form it will also ensure that the second lawyer is aware of such important details as the review times and when the detention time limit expires. The third reason derives from the fact that events that occur at the police station may well be relevant at trial, and it may be that a member of the firm will be required to give evidence at the trial. For example, in *R v Samuel*[30] the defendant's lawyer was able to give evidence of the times that he had contacted the police station in order to try to gain access to his client and of the conversations that took place, and this was crucial in persuading the court that evidence of the police interviews should have been excluded at trial. The 'right to silence' provisions of the CJPOA 1994 make it even more likely that a defence lawyer will end up giving evidence. Such evidence is likely to be unconvincing if the lawyer has to rely on his or her memory, or on odd scraps of paper on which notes have been made.

1.36    All events must be noted and all conversations with the police and other people recorded, even if they appear insignificant at the time. Indeed, it may be appropriate on occasions to record that nothing was said or done. In *R v Dunn*[31] the lawyer gave evidence that there had been no confession by her client at the end of the police interview, as was alleged by the police (although apparently she was disbelieved by the jury). Thus, in police interviews, the time that the interview ended and the time that the parties left the interview room should be recorded, and the content of any conversation – or the fact that there was no conversation – also noted.

1.37    Guidance concerning what information should be sought is given in subsequent chapters, and in the checklists in appendix 3, but the following lists the kind of information that should be carefully recorded:

- the time and place of all relevant conversations and events;
- the physical and mental state of the client;
- the general conduct of the police and the 'atmosphere' in which the investigation is being conducted;
- anything the police allege has been said by the client before attendance by the lawyer;
- anything the police assert has been said to the client by them, for example, a request to account for an object, etc, and what reply, if any, was made;
- information given by the police to the lawyer;
- requests for information made to the police by the lawyer;
- any request for information to be recorded in the custody record, and any representations made to the custody officer;
- information given to the lawyer by the client;
- the client's apparent understanding of the significance of the allegation, the caution, and the significance of the client's replies or failure to reply;

30  [1988] QB 615; [1988] 2 All ER 135; (1998) 87 Cr App R 232; [1988] Crim LR 299.
31  (1990) Cr App R 237; [1990] Crim LR 572, discussed at para 13.32 below.

- advice given by the lawyer to the client, and the reasons for that advice;
- the wording of any caution or special warning, or explanation of any caution or special warning given, and any response by the client;
- what was said during the course of a police interview;
- anything said at the time of charge/report for summons.

## Tools of the trade

1.38   Lawyers who do police station work should have a 'toolkit' which is easily available and ready to hand for whenever they are called out to a police station. This 'toolkit' should contain the following.

### Sources of reference

1.39   An up-to-date version of PACE and the Codes of Practice is essential (versions that were current at the time of publication can be found in appendices 1 and 2). A reference book containing at least common crimes and defences should also be included. The following should be readily available: the *Director's Guidance on Charging 2011*; the *Code for Crown Prosecutors 2010*; Home Office Circular 16/2008 *Simple Cautioning of Adult Offenders; the Final Warning Scheme: Guidance for the Police and Youth Offending Teams* and Home Office Circular 14/2006 the *Final Warning Scheme*; the *Revised Code of Practice for Conditional Cautions – Adults* 2010 and the *Director's Guidance on Adult Conditional Cautions* (or the current version of these codes and circulars where they have been revised since the date of publication of this book).[32]

### Headed notepaper

1.40   Notepaper may be needed to write a letter to a client to whom access is being denied, to make written representations or a written record of oral representations, or to make a formal complaint. It is important always to keep a copy of any letter or written representation made since it may be needed for future reference or for evidential purposes.

### Writing paper and pen

1.41   The need for this is obvious. A client is unlikely to be impressed by a lawyer who has to ask to 'borrow' some paper or a pen from the police.

### Identification

1.42   A form of identification is useful, particularly if the lawyer is attending at a police station where the lawyer is not known. Non-solicitors doing police station work should carry a letter of authorisation from the firm or solicitor on whose behalf they attend the police station. The contents of such a letter must be taken into account if the police are considering excluding a representative from the police station (Code C para 6.13 and see para 4.6

---

32  Current versions of the *Code for Crown Prosecutors* and the *Director's Guidance* are available via the CPS website, at www.cps.gov.uk/legal_resources.html.

below). In duty solicitor cases, staff undertaking police station advice must carry an identification card as specified by the LSC.[33]

## Legal aid forms

1.43　The 'toolkit' should contain copies of the relevant Criminal Defence Service (CDS) forms, including CDS1 (*Client's Details Form*) and CDS2 (*Application for Advice and Assistance*). Although CDS2 is not needed for claiming payment in respect of police station advice and assistance, it will be needed if any work is to be done that is not covered by the police station scheme.

## Standard case forms

1.44　A standard police station form[34] has a number of functions.

- It acts as a checklist, both helping to ensure that relevant information has been obtained, and prompting the lawyer in relation to events that are coming up, such as review times, or expiry of custody time limits.
- It enables efficient transfer to another lawyer.
- It provides a readily available source of information for use at any subsequent trial.
- It makes the process of billing quicker since all the relevant information is contained in one document.
- It helps satisfy the requirements of the SCC 2010.

1.45　The standard case form should be placed in the case file as soon as it is opened. Other standard forms, and checklists, such as an identification procedure checklist (see appendix 3) should also be included.

## Mobile telephone/tape-recorder/camera

1.46　Mobile telephones cause particular anxiety to some custody officers because of the perception that they may be used to enable the suspect to make unauthorised telephone calls, and officers may ask that telephones be left in the custody suite. While not all custody officers will insist on this, the custody officer should be informed that the lawyer is in possession of a telephone in order to avoid accusations of improper use. Cameras and other image capturing devises (which includes many mobile telephones) can be useful for making a visual record of any injuries to a client, or to make a record of the client's appearance, but the custody officer may have concerns that their use may compromise security. As with mobile telephones, it is advisable for cameras to be declared to the custody officer. Home Office Circular 24/98 *Reducing delays: addressing the reasons for non-compliance with the pre-trial issues (PTI) time guidelines* stated that there is nothing to prevent a solicitor from making his or her own audio recording of a police interview, and the police should refuse a request to do so: 'only if there are individual circumstances specific to the case which may prejudice the course of the investigation'. Again, it is advisable to inform

---

33　SCC 2010, Part A, para 6.56.
34　See note 27.

the custody officer if the lawyer intends to use an audio recording device while at the police station.

*Useful addresses and telephone numbers*

1.47   The kit should include a list of addresses and telephone numbers such as those for police stations in the area, the social services duty team, and other lawyers in the firm. The list should also include details of appropriate doctors, experts and interpreters.

## Qualification for police station advice

### Police station qualification for solicitors

1.48   The Law Society operates a Criminal Litigation Accreditation Scheme (CLAS),[35] consisting of a Police Station Qualification (PSQ) and a Magistrates' Court Qualification (MCQ). The LSC no longer requires solicitors who conduct publicly funded own solicitor cases to have gained the PSQ.[36] However, in duty solicitor cases a solicitor who is not a duty solicitor and who does not have the PSQ cannot accept the initial call from the Defence Solicitor Call Centre (DSCC), provide initial telephone advice, or attend the police station to give advice in person.[37]

### Accreditation for representatives

1.49   Non-solicitors must be registered with the LSC in order for their work to be paid for out of public funds. This is the case in respect of both own solicitor and duty solicitor work.[38] Following registration, and before obtaining accreditation, they are known as probationary representatives. Once they have obtained accreditation, they are known as accredited representatives.[39] The registration arrangements are governed by the LSC's Police Station Register Arrangements 2001 (as amended).[40] The accreditation scheme for non-solicitors is operated by the Solicitors' Regulation Authority (SRA), and consists of three assessments: a portfolio of police station cases, a written test and a critical incidents test.[41] There are no similar requirements for representatives where clients pay privately for police station advice, but the accreditation requirements for publicly funded cases should be treated as a minimum standard (but see para 1.50 below).

1.50   There are a number of limitations and restrictions that apply to representatives. Accredited and probationary representatives are treated as

---

35  Details of the CLAS can be obtained via www.lawsociety.org.uk/productsandservices/ accreditation/accreditationcriminallitigation.page#one.

36  SCC 2010, Part B, para 9.28.

37  SCC 2010, Part B, para 9.28.

38  SCC 2010, Part B, paras 9.26 and 9.27.

39  SCC 2010, Part A, para 1.13.

40  The LSC Police Station Register Arrangements can be obtained via www. legalservices.gov.uk/criminal/stat_material/directions.asp.

41  Details of the accreditation scheme can be obtained at www.sra.org.uk/solicitors/ accreditation/police-station-representatives-accreditation.page.

solicitors for the purposes of PACE Codes C and D, but they can be excluded from a police station in certain circumstances that do not apply to solicitors (Code C paras 6.12–6.14 and Code D para 2.6, and see para 4.4 below). Code C para 6.12 does not include in the definition of 'solicitor' a representative who is neither a probationary nor an accredited representative, and it is unclear whether the police are required to permit access to a suspect by such a person who has been sent to the police station on behalf of a solicitor in a privately funded case.

1.51    In publicly funded cases the SCC 2010 imposes a number of restrictions and obligations. A probationary representative may only provide advice and assistance on behalf of a provider (that is, the firm that has a contract with the LSC) at which his or her supervising solicitor is based, cannot accept the initial call or provide advice or assistance in duty solicitor cases, and cannot provide advice and assistance in respect of an indictable-only case.[42] The provider is responsible for the standard of work of representatives employed by them, and also for those representatives who are not directly employed under a contract of employment, and in the case of the latter there are certain restrictions on claiming for travel time.[43] Before attending a police station the representative must have the telephone number of his or her supervising solicitor and must be able to contact him or her, or another solicitor in the organisation with sufficient experience of police station work, in case the representative needs guidance.[44] Once a case has been concluded, the representative must provide a written report to the conducting solicitor no later than the next working day.[45] A representative must not be employed as a special constable nor in any other capacity that may cause a conflict of interest with his or her work as a representative.[46]

## The Duty Solicitor Scheme

1.52    The police station Duty Solicitor Scheme is regulated by the SCC 2010 under powers granted to the LSC by the Access to Justice Act 1999 s3(4). A duty solicitor is defined as a person who has previously been a member of a Scheme under the Duty Solicitor Arrangements 2008 or an earlier version of those Arrangements, or has been accredited under parts one and two of stage one of the Law Society's Criminal Litigation Accreditation Scheme (CLAS) and undertaken the police station qualification (PSQ) (see para 1.48).[47] As with accredited representatives, duty solicitors must not be special constables.[48] Detailed rules regarding the operation of the scheme are set out in the SCC 2010, Part A, section 6. The obligation to participate in the scheme is imposed on providers who have a contract with the LSC

---

42  SCC 2010, Part B, paras 9.28, 9.35 and 9.36.
43  SCC 2010, Part B, paras 9.29 and 9.30.
44  SCC 2010, Part B, para 9.31.
45  SCC 2010, Part B, para 9.32.
46  SCC 2010, Part B, para 9.37.
47  SCC 2010, Part A, para 1.13.
48  SCC 2010, Part A, para 6.24.

rather than on individual duty solicitors,[49] and duty slots on rota schemes and places on duty solicitor panels are allocated to providers rather than to individual duty solicitors.[50] It is for the LSC to determine whether and where rota and panel schemes should operate, and also to allocate slots on rota schemes.[51]

1.53    Obligations under the SCC 2010 concerning taking duty calls, accepting cases, and attendance at the police station are set out in the relevant sections of chapter 3. Once a request for the duty solicitor has been accepted the provider must normally continue to act for the suspect until the end of the investigation.[52] A duty solicitor case can only be handed back to the DSCC before the end of the investigation if: the duty solicitor is unable to continue to act personally and there is no other suitable person in the organisation who is able to act and it is not possible to instruct and agent; the client removes or rescinds his or her instructions; there is legitimate concern about breach of the professional code of conduct; or the provider confirms that the provider will not claim remuneration in respect of the case.[53] Where a case is handed back to the DSCC the reasons must be clearly recorded on the case file.[54]

## Legal aid

1.54    Those people who are entitled to legal advice and assistance in connection with criminal investigations, which includes those who are arrested and held in custody by police (see para 2.121 below) and HM Revenue and Customs officers (HMRC) (see para 1.65 below), volunteers (see para 2.151 below), persons being interviewed in connection with a service offence (see para 1.71 below), and those detained under TA 2000 Sch 7 (see para 2.121 below), are entitled to legal aid to pay for that advice and assistance without reference to their financial resources.[55]

1.55    The provision of legally-aided advice and assistance is governed by the terms of the LSC's SCC 2010. The contract (together with certain provisions of Code C) imposes significant limitations and conditions both on the right to legal advice at police stations, and on the ability of lawyers to provide it. Reference is made to relevant parts of the contract throughout the book, but three important features are dealt with here: the provisions regarding who initial instructions can be received from in legal aid cases; the CDS Direct scheme; and the 'sufficient benefit' test.

---

49  SCC 2010, Part A, para 6.1.
50  SCC 2010, Part A, para 6.6.
51  SCC 2010, Part A, paras 6.42–6.45.
52  SCC 2010, Part B, para 9.53.
53  SCC 2010, Part B, para 9.54.
54  SCC 2010, Part B, para 9.55.
55  Note that at the date of publication, the Legal Aid, Sentencing and Punishment of Offenders Bill, cl12 contained provision for the introduction of both a means and merits test for police station advice.

## Who instructions can be received from

1.56 Where a suspect who is held in police custody requests legal advice to be paid for by public funds, the police are required to contact the Defence Solicitor Call Centre (DSCC) (Code C Note for Guidance 6B2).[56] The DSCC determines whether the case is covered by the CDS Direct scheme (see para 1.57 below), and if it is not the DSCC then refers the request to the solicitor requested or to the duty solicitor. Generally, payment under the SCC 2010 can only be claimed if the instructions are initially received from the DSCC.[57] However, this rule does not apply where:

- a client attends a police station by prior agreement with the police and requests the solicitor to represent them, although the solicitor must inform the DSCC within 48 hours of the first attendance at the police station, and actually represent him or her at the Police Station; or
- instructions are received from a member of the client's immediate family or a third party of similar status, although the solicitor must report the matter by telephone, fax or email to the DSCC prior to telephoning or attending the client; or
- the solicitor is already at the police station when a suspect requests advice from them, as own solicitor or duty solicitor, although the solicitor must report the matter to the DSCC within 48 hours of receiving instructions.[58]

## The CDS Direct scheme

1.57 The CDS Direct scheme was introduced nationally in 2008.[59] Cases that fall within the scope of CDS Direct are excluded from the scope of the SCC so that solicitors cannot claim for work carried out in respect of such cases other than in the exceptional circumstances set out in the contract. As noted above, when contacted by the police the DSCC determines whether the case is within the scope of the CDS Direct Scheme. If it is, the DSCC will refer the request to CDS Direct to provide advice.

1.58 Cases that fall within the scope of CDS Direct are those where the suspect:

- is detained in respect of a non-imprisonable offence;
- was arrested on a bench warrant for failing to appear and is being held for production before a court, except where the solicitor has clear documentary evidence that would result in the suspect being released from custody (in which case payment for attendance may be allowed provided that the reason is recorded on file;

---

56 Although the LSC appears to accept that the police may pass a request directly to the nominated solicitor, or a duty solicitor, if they are already at the police station since SCC 2010, Part B, para 9.20(c) provides that the solicitor may claim payment for work done in such circumstances provided that the solicitor informs the DSCC within 48 hours of receiving the instructions.

57 SCC 2010, Part B, para 9.18.

58 SCC 2010, Part B, para 9.20.

59 For a critical analysis of CDS Direct see L Bridges and E Cape, *CDS Direct: flying in the face of the evidence* (Centre for Crime and Justice Studies, London, 2008).

- was arrested on suspicion of: driving with excess alcohol and was taken to the police station to provide a specimen (Road Traffic Act (RTA) 1988 s5); failure to provide a specimen (RTA 1988 ss6, 7 and 7A); driving while unfit/drunk in charge of a motor vehicle (RTA1988 s4);
- is detained in relation to breach of police or court bail conditions.[60]

However, a claim for payment may be made in respect of such cases if the sufficient benefit test is satisfied (see para 1.60 below) and one of the following exceptions applies:

- an interview or an identification procedure is to be held;
- the suspect is eligible for assistance from an appropriate adult (see paras 11.13 and 11.66 below);
- the suspect is unable to communicate over the telephone;
- the suspect complains of serious maltreatment by the police;
- the investigation includes another alleged offence which is not within the scope of CDS Direct;
- the solicitor or representative is already at the same police station (in which case the claim cannot exceed the police station telephone advice fixed fee);
- the advice relates to an indictable offence; or
- the request is a 'special request'.[61]

A 'special request' is a request identified to the lawyer as such by the DSCC. Special requests may include, for example, requests where CDS Direct considers that, because of a conflict of interest, the request should be dealt with by a duty or own solicitor, or considers that advocacy assistance is required, or considers that one of the other exceptions specified above applies.[62]

1.59    If any of the exceptional circumstances apply, the solicitor must endorse the file with the reasons for attendance.[63] In addition, a case is not treated as a CDS Direct case if CDS Direct is unable to provide telephone advice, but this does not apply if the reason for this is that the suspect refused to accept advice from CDS Direct.[64] Where CDS Direct refers a case to the suspect's own solicitor (for example, because they are informed that the police do intend to interview the suspect, or discover that the suspect is eligible for assistance from an appropriate adult) it ceases to be a CDS Direct case, and the normal rules apply.[65] Although it is not specifically provided for in the SCC 2010, the definition of 'special request' implies that this is also the case where CDS Direct refer the case to a duty solicitor.

## The sufficient benefit test

1.60    Advice and assistance may only be claimed for under the SCC 2010 if there is sufficient benefit to the client, having regard to the circumstances of the matter, including the personal circumstances of the client, to justify

60  SCC 2010, Part B, para 9.9.
61  SCC 2010, Part B, para 9.10.
62  SCC 2010, Part A, para 1.13.
63  SCC 2010, Part B, para 9.11.
64  SCC 2010, Part B, para 9.12.
65  SCC 2010, Part B, para 9.13.

work or further work being carried out.[66] The sufficient benefit test is automatically satisfied for the purposes of initial advice in respect of a person who has a right to legal advice or who is a volunteer under PACE or the equivalent legislation applying to the armed forces in the case of military investigations. After initial advice has been given, the solicitor must consider whether, and what, further work is justified by reference to there being 'sufficient benefit' for the client.[67] The contract states that the test is satisfied where further legal advice is given to a client immediately following charge. However, it goes on to state that attendance upon the client thereafter while fingerprints, photographs and swabs are taken will not meet the sufficient benefit test except where the client requires further assistance owing to his or her particular circumstances, in which case the relevant factors must be noted on file. It also, in effect, provides that the test would be satisfied where the lawyer remains at the police station in order to make representations about bail, again provided that this justification is noted on file.[68]

## Who does the book apply to?

1.61   This book is primarily concerned with advising a person who has been arrested in connection with a criminal offence and is being held in custody in a police station or other authorised place of detention. The detention and treatment of a client in these circumstances is governed by PACE and Codes of Practice C–F. One of the key definitions in PACE is that concerning 'police detention'. A person is in police detention for the purposes of PACE if the person:

- has been taken to a police station after being arrested for an offence or under TA 2000 s41; or
- is arrested at a police station after attending voluntarily or accompanying a constable to it and he or she is detained there or detained elsewhere in the charge of a constable (PACE s118(2)).

A person is treated as being in police detention if the person is in the custody of a designated civilian detention, investigating or escort office by virtue of the PRA 2002.[69] Furthermore, a person who is arrested and taken to a designated place under the Prevention of Terrorism Act 2005 s5 pending the making of a derogating control order is deemed to be in police detention.[70] A person who is at court after being charged is not in police detention (PACE s118(2)).

1.62   Many of the procedures and police powers in PACE relate only to persons in police detention. However, the right of intimation under PACE s56 (see para 2.116 below) and the right to legal advice under PACE s58 (see para 2.119 below) apply to any person arrested and held in custody at a police station or other premises whether or not the arrest was for an

---

66  SCC 2010, Part A, para 3.10.
67  SCC 2010, Part A, para 3.16.
68  SCC 2010, Part B, para 9.16.
69  Sch 4 paras 22, 34(1) or para 35(3) (PACE s118(2A)).
70  Prevention of Terrorism Act 2005 s5(7)(b).

offence. Furthermore, a volunteer (see para 2.151 below) is always entitled to legal advice. Code C applies to people in custody at a police station in England and Wales whether or not they have been arrested,[71] and it also applies to persons removed to a police station as a place of safety under the Mental Health Act (MHA) 1983 ss135 and 136. However, Code C section 15 (review and extension of detention) applies only to persons in police detention. Code C does not directly govern the treatment of volunteers, but the code should be regarded as establishing minimum standards governing their treatment (see Code C NfG 1A). Persons who are designated civilian officers under PRA 2002 (see para 2.50 below), and those who are accredited under PRA 2002 s41, must have regard to any relevant provision of the PACE Codes in the exercise or performance of their powers (PACE s67(9A)). For the application of Code C where a person is being investigated by others charged with the duty of investigating offences or charging offenders, see below.

## Persons arrested and detained under the Terrorism Act 2000

1.63    Where a person is detained for examination under TA 2000 s53 and Sch 7 (see para 2.29 below), the person's treatment is governed by TA 2000 Sch 8 Part 1. The person is not treated as being in police detention for the purposes of PACE and the PACE Codes of Practice do not apply to the person. There is a separate code of practice for examining officers issued under TA 2000 Sch 14 para 6.[72] A person detained for examination under these provisions may be detained for up to nine hours beginning with the time when the examination began (see para 2.29). The detainee is entitled to have a person informed of his or her detention (TA 2000 Sch 8 para 6) and to consult a solicitor (TA 2000 Sch 8 para 7), but these rights may, in effect, be denied on the authority of a superintendent or above (TA 2000 Sch 8 para 8). A person detained for examination under Sch 7 is entitled to legal aid.[73]

1.64    A person may be arrested under TA 2000 s41(1) on suspicion of being a terrorist (see para 2.27). Where a person is arrested under section 41 the person must be taken to a police station designated by the secretary of state for these purposes (see para 2.56 below). The person is not treated as having been arrested for an offence, but is treated as being in police detention for the purposes of PACE (s118(2)(a)). Code H applies up until the time when a person so detained is charged, released without charge, or transferred to prison (Code H para 1.2). Code C applies if and when

---

71  Code C para 1.10, subject to certain exceptions set out in Code C para 1.12. It was held in *Williamson v Chief Constable of West Midlands Police* [2004] 1 WLR 14 that Code C did not apply to a person detained at a police station following arrest for breach of the peace because such a person was not arrested for an offence, and was therefore not in police detention. However, Code C para 1.10 states that the Code applies to people in custody at police stations 'whether or not they have been arrested'.

72  Terrorism Act 2000 (Code of Practice for Examining Officers) (Revision) Order 2009 SI No 1593.

73  Criminal Defence Service (General) (No 2) Regulations 2001 SI No1437.

the person is charged. Code D does apply to persons arrested under TA 2000 s41, except for those provisions relating to photographs, fingerprints, skin impressions, body samples and impressions of people. PACE Code E does not apply, but there is a separate code of practice governing the audio recording of interviews issued under TA 2000 Sch 8 para 3(1).[74] There are special provisions concerning the length of detention without charge, and review of detention (see paras 2.78 and 2.91 below). A person detained under these provisions has the right to have someone informed of his or her detention (TA 2000 Sch 8 para 6), and the right to consult a solicitor (TA 2000 Sch 8 para 7), but these rights may be delayed on the authority of a superintendent or above (TA 2000 Sch 8 para 8 and see para 2.145 below). In certain circumstances, the police may insist that consultation with a solicitor is carried out in the sight and hearing of a police officer (see para 2.136 below). A person arrested and detained under TA 2000 s41(1) and Sch 8 is entitled to legal aid.

## Persons arrested and detained by HM Revenue and Customs

1.65 PACE s114(2) provides that any provision of PACE relating to the investigation of offences or detention may, by order and with appropriate modifications, be applied to 'relevant investigations' by HMRC officers. A 'relevant investigation' is an investigation conducted by HMRC officers concerning a matter in relation to which HMRC have functions apart from a former Inland Revenue Matter. Most of the relevant provisions of PACE have been applied by virtue of the Police and Criminal Evidence Act 1984 (Application to Revenue and Customs) Order 2007,[75] as amended by the Police and Criminal Evidence Act 1984 (Application to Revenue and Customs) Order 2007 (Amendment) Order 2010[76] ('the 2007 Order'). HMRC officers have a variety of powers of arrest under the Customs and Excise Acts[77] and have powers of detention under PACE s37. A person is in HMRC detention for the purposes of PACE if the person has been taken to a HMRC office after having been arrested for an offence, or is arrested at a HMRC office after attending voluntarily or accompanying an officer to it and is detained there, or elsewhere, in the charge of an officer. A person in HMRC detention may be transferred to police detention, and vice versa (2007 Order article 2(2)). A person in HMRC detention is entitled to legal advice under PACE s58 (and non-means tested legal aid), and is entitled to have a friend or relative informed of the person's arrest and detention under PACE s56.

1.66 The PACE Codes of Practice are specifically applied to HMRC officers by the 2007 Order Sch 1.[78] However, it has been held that they do not

74 Terrorism Act 2000 (Code of Practice on Audio Recording of Interviews) (No 2) Order 2001 SI No189.
75 SI No 3175.
76 SI No 360.
77 As defined in Customs and Excise Management Act 1979 s1(1).
78 And see *R v Sanusi* [1992] Crim LR 43; *R v Weerdesteyn* [1995] Crim LR 239; and *R v Okafor* [1994] 3 All ER 741; (1994) 99 Cr App R 97; [1994] Crim LR 221.

apply where a person was interviewed under the Value Added Tax Act 1994 s60.[79] They also do not apply to the civil investigation of tax fraud procedure.[80] By virtue of the Borders, Citizenship and Immigration Act 2009 s22, the PACE Codes also apply to criminal investigations conducted by designated customs officials relating to a general customs matter or customs revenue matter as they apply to relevant investigations conducted by HMRC officers.

## Persons arrested by SOCA

1.67   The Serious Organised Crime and Police Act (SOCPA) 2005 permits the Director General of the Serious Organised Crime Agency (SOCA) to designate a member of the SOCA staff as a person having the powers of a constable, HMRC officer, and/or an immigration officer (SOCPA 2005 s43(1)). Where a person is designated as having the powers of a constable, the person has all the common law and statutory powers of a constable (SOCPA 2005 s46(2) and (9)), and PACE applies to the person and the exercise of his or her powers.[81] For this purpose PACE is subject to the modifications set out in the Serious Organised Crime and Police Act 2005 (Application and Modification of Certain Enactments to Designated Staff of SOCA) Order 2006[82] Sch 1. The most important modifications are:

- References to 'police officer' and 'officer' are normally to be treated as references to a 'designated person' under SOCPA 2005. One consequence of this is that SOCPA designated persons are governed by the PACE Codes of Practice when exercising their powers as police constables.
- Where authorisation is required for a search under PACE s18, reference to an inspector is replaced by reference to a grade 3 officer.
- References to 'police station', eg, in relation to voluntary attendance (PACE s29), and fingerprints and samples (PACE s63) are to be treated as references to a 'SOCA office'.
- 'SOCA office' means 'a place for the time being occupied by the Serious Organised Crime Agency'.

## Persons investigated by others having a duty to investigate crime

1.68   The provisions of PACE relating to investigation and detention apply only to police officers (and, subject to amendments, Revenue and Customs officers, designated SOCA staff and to investigations under the Armed Forces Act 2006). However, any person who is: 'charged with the duty of investigating offences or charging offenders' must, in the discharge of

---

79  *Khan v Revenue and Customs* [2006] EWCA Civ 89.

80  See HM Revenue and Customs Code of Practice 9 (2009) available at www.hmrc.gov. uk/leaflets/cop9-2009.htm.

81  By virtue of the Serious Organised Crime and Police Act 2005 (Application and Modification of Certain Enactments to Designated Staff of SOCA) Order 2006 SI No 987 art 3.

82  SI No 987.

that duty, have regard to any relevant provisions of the Codes of Practice (PACE s67(9)). This could include officers of the Department for Work and Pensions (DWP), the Serious Fraud Office,[83] or certain local government officers such as trading standards officers[84] and environmental health officers, provided in each case that they do in fact have a duty of investigating offences. Thus, it has been held that Department of Trade and Industry (now the Department of Business, Innovation and Skills (BIS)) inspectors appointed under Companies Act 1985 ss432 and 442 were not investigating officers within section 67(9).[85] A similar conclusion was drawn in respect of local tax inspectors.[86] Prison officers have been treated as persons charged with a duty of investigating offences, but not always.[87]

1.69    It has been held that the Codes apply to commercial investigators interviewing an employee,[88] store detectives[89] and investigators employed by the Federation Against Copyright Theft (FACT),[90] although in each case it is a question of fact whether the relevant personnel are charged with the duty of investigating offences. A senior line manager who interviewed an employee concerning suspicions that he was defrauding the company was treated, on the facts, as not having a duty to investigate offences.[91]

1.70    Where a person is interviewed by a official to whom PACE s67(9) applies, the person is not covered by the police station advice and assistance scheme unless the person is being held in custody at a police station or the interview is conducted in the presence of a police constable although the person will, subject to financial eligibility, qualify for assistance under the means-tested legal advice and assistance scheme.[92]

## Service personnel

1.71    There is an important distinction between investigations conducted by Ministry of Defence police officers and those conducted by service police officers. Ministry of Defence police officers are 'constables'[93] and PACE and the Codes apply to them in the normal way. In respect of investigations by service police officers, PACE s113(1) provides that the secretary of state may, by order, make provisions in relation to the investigation of

83   *R v Director of the Serious Fraud Office ex p Saunders* [1988] Crim LR 837, and *R v Gill* [2003] EWCA Crim 2256.
84   *Dudley MBC v Debenhams* (1994) 159 JP 18; (1994) *Times* 16 August, and *R v Tiplady* (1995) 159 JP 548; (1994) *Times* 23 February.
85   *R v Seelig and Spens* [1991] 4 All ER 429; (1991) 94 Cr App R 17.
86   *R v Doncaster* [2008] EWCA Crim 5.
87   A prison officer was so treated in *R v Devani* [2008] 1 Cr App R 65, but not in *R v Martin Taylor* [2001] EWCA Crim 2922.
88   *R v Twaites and Brown* (1990) 92 Cr App R 106; [1990] Crim LR 863.
89   *R v Bayliss* (1993) 98 Cr App R 235; [1994] Crim LR 687.
90   *Joy v Federation Against Copyright Theft Ltd* [1993] Crim LR 588. See also *Halawa v Federation Against Copyright Theft* [1995] 1 Cr App R 21; [1995] Crim LR 409. The RSPCA has accepted that its officers should comply with the Codes. See *RSPCA v Eager* [1995] Crim LR 59, also reported as *Stilgoe v Eager* (1994) *Times* 27 January.
91   *R v Welcher* [2007] EWCA Crim 480.
92   SCC 2010, Part B, paras 9.56 and 9.117–9.119.
93   Ministry of Defence Act 1987 2(1).

'service offences'[94] which are equivalent to the provisions of PACE Part V (the questioning and treatment of suspects). The Police and Criminal Evidence Act 1984 (Armed Forces) Order 2009[95] applies, with modifications, most of the PACE Part V provisions. A person arrested and held in custody is entitled to consult a legal adviser,[96] although this may be delayed for up to 36 hours in similar circumstances as those that apply under PACE (see para 2.139 below) where the person is in custody in respect of serious service offence.[97] The ordinary PACE Codes of Practice do not apply, but dedicated Codes have been issued under PACE s113(2) and (3).[98] A services person at a services establishment or elsewhere in the UK assisting with an investigation by the services police or suspected of a serious service offence is entitled to legal advice under the police station scheme.[99]

## Immigration detainees

1.72   Where a person has been arrested for an immigration offence, PACE and the Codes of Practice will apply as normal, as will entitlement to advice and assistance under the police station scheme and the duty solicitor scheme. However, the SCC imposes restrictions so that advice and assistance may only be given under the normal police station scheme up to the point that the immigration authorities take over conduct of the investigation and it has been confirmed that no criminal offence or charge is being pursued.[100] See further chapter 12.

## European Arrest Warrant

1.73   Where a person has been arrested under a European arrest warrant under powers granted by the Extradition Act (EA) 2003 Part 4, the person must be taken before an appropriate judge as soon as is practicable (EA 2003 s4(3)), and may be held in custody at a police station until the person is so produced. While at a police station the person is not in police detention (see para 1.61 above), but are covered by dedicated EA 2003 Codes of Practice B, C and D.[101]

---

94  Defined by Armed Forces Act 2006 s50.
95  SI No 1922.
96  The definition of 'legal adviser' in art 2(1) of the 2009 Order excludes non-solicitors or barristers.
97  Police and Criminal Evidence Act 1984 (Armed Forces) Order 2009 SI No 1922 art 9. A 'serious service offence' is defined by art 2(1) to include offences that are equivalent to indictable offences, other service offences that may not be dealt with at a summary hearing by a commanding officer, and certain other specified service offences.
98  Police and Criminal Evidence Act 1984 (Codes of Practice) (Armed Forces) Order 2003 SI No 2315.
99  SCC 2010, Part B, paras 9.59–9.61.
100  SCC 2010, Part B, paras 9.63–9.68.
101  Extradition Act 2003 (Police Powers: Codes of Practice) Order 2003 SI No 3336.

## PACE and the Codes of Practice

1.74  PACE has been amended by numerous subsequent statutes, and the version in appendix 1 contains all amendments up to the date of publication. The PACE Codes of Practice are issued by the Secretary of State under the authority of the PACE ss66 and 67. There are eight Codes of Practice, A to H, set out in appendix 2. Codes A, B and D came into force in their current form on 7 March 2011.[102] However, Code A is to have effect as if paras 2.18A–2.26 (provisions relating to stop and search under TA 2000 s44) were revoked.[103] Code C came into force on 1 February 2008.[104] Codes E and F came into force on 1 May 2010.[105] Code G came into force on 1 January 2006,[106] and Code H on 25 July 2006.[107]

1.75  A failure by a police officer or other person required to have regard to provisions of the codes does not, of itself, render him or her liable to criminal or civil proceedings (PACE s67(10)). However, to the extent that they are relevant, the codes are admissible in evidence in criminal or civil proceedings (PACE s67(11)). See further chapter 13.

---

102 Police and Criminal Evidence Act 1984 (Codes of Practice) (Revisions of Codes A, B and D) Order 2011 SI No 412.

103 Terrorism Act 2000 (Remedial) Order 2011 SI No 631, Sch 2 para 2. The Remedial Order repealed the TA 2000 ss44–47, and introduced a revised power of stop and search governed by a new section 47A, and a new power of the secretary of state to issue a code of practice concerning stop and search powers under section 47A.

104 Police and Criminal Evidence Act 1984 (Codes of Practice) Order 2008 SI No 167.

105 Police and Criminal Evidence Act 1984 (Codes of Practice) (Revisions to Codes E and F) Order 2010 SI No 1108.

106 Police and Criminal Evidence Act 1984 (Codes of Practice) Order 2005 SI No 3503.

107 Police and Criminal Evidence Act 1984 (Code of Practice C and Code of Practice H) Order 2006 SI No 193.

# CHAPTER 2

# Key provisions of PACE, Terrorism Act and the Codes

*continued*

# Introduction

2.1 This chapter sets out some of the key powers, and important terms and phrases, in the Police and Criminal Evidence Act 1984 (PACE), the Terrorism Act (TA) 2000, and the PACE Codes of Practice (and related legislation) and explains their practical significance. The purpose is to provide a ready reference which is of immediate practical use. For a more extended consideration of them, see one of the guides to PACE or police powers.[1]

# Stop and search

2.2 The police have a variety of powers to stop and search people without arresting them. The main general power of stop and search is governed by PACE Part I, but there are other frequently used powers under the Criminal Justice and Public Order Act (CJPOA) 1994 and the TA 2000. Code of Practice A, *Code of Practice for the Exercise by Police Officers of Statutory Powers of Stop and Search*,[2] applies to most police powers of stop and search other than those under Aviation Security Act 1982 s27(2), PACE s6(1) (relating to powers of constables employed by statutory undertakers on the premises of those statutory undertakers), and searches under TA 2000 Sch 7.[3] For a list of powers to which the Code applies, see Code A Annex A. Community support officers do not have powers of stop and search under PACE, but do have powers under other legislation, which are summarised in Code A, Annex C.

2.3 Different police forces make markedly different use of stop and search powers, but nationally about one in ten stops under PACE result in an arrest. Although police station lawyers are not often called upon to advise on stop and search powers, it is important to understand the powers since the legality of an arrest may be affected by the legality of a stop and search that preceded it, and advice concerning a substantive offence allegedly committed in the context of the exercise of stop and search powers, for example, assault on a police officer in the execution of their duty, may be affected by the conduct or legality of the stop and search.

## Powers to stop and search

2.4 PACE Code A para 1.5 provides that a police officer must not search a person where no power to search is applicable, even if the person consents to being searched.[4] Stop and search powers are of two types, those that require reasonable suspicion and those that do not (see Code A paras 2.2–2.29).

---

1 For example, M Zander, *Police and Criminal Evidence Act* 1984 (5th edn, Sweet & Maxwell, London, 2005), although out of date in certain respects.
2 See para 1.74 above.
3 In respect of which there is a separate code of practice issued under TA 2000 Sch 14 para 6. See para 1.63 above and note 8 below.
4 The only exception is where entry to a sports ground or other premises is conditional on consent to being searched.

*Powers requiring reasonable suspicion*

2.5   Reasonable suspicion is required for the exercise of stop and search powers under PACE Part I and TA 2000 s43. Under PACE s1(2) a constable may search any person or vehicle, or anything which is in or on a vehicle, for stolen or prohibited articles, prohibited fireworks, or for an article in relation to which a person has committed, or is committing, or is going to commit an offence under Criminal Justice Act (CJA) 1988 s139 (bladed or sharply-pointed instrument). 'Prohibited articles' are offensive weapons, articles made or adapted for use in the course of or in connection with burglary, theft, taking a conveyance, obtaining property by deception, criminal damage, or intended by the person for such use (PACE s1(7) and (8)). A 'prohibited firework' is a firework possessed in a public place by a person under 18 years or by any person if the firework is of display grade (PACE s1(8B) and (8C)). By PACE s1(3) the constable must have reasonable grounds for suspecting that a relevant article will be found. Under TA 2000 s43 a constable may stop and search a person whom the constable reasonably suspects to be a terrorist to discover whether the person has in the person's possession anything that may constitute evidence that the person is a terrorist.[5] Code A para 2.2 provides that reasonable suspicion must be based on objective facts, information and/or intelligence, although this requirement is qualified by paras 2.3 and 2.6. A person may not be stopped or detained in order to find grounds for a search, but if during an 'ordinary' encounter with a member of the public suspicion emerges, a search may be conducted even though no grounds existed when the person was initially stopped (Code A para 2.11).

*Powers not requiring reasonable suspicion*

2.6   Reasonable suspicion is not required to stop and search a person under a number of statutory powers, including the following:

- CJPOA 1994 s60, which enables a constable in uniform to stop and search persons or vehicles for offensive weapons or dangerous instruments[6] where an inspector or above has given an authorisation under section 60, reasonably believing that incidents involving serious violence may take place or that persons are carrying dangerous instruments or offensive weapons, and that it is expedient to give such authorisation. Under Code A para 2.14A,[7] the selection of persons and vehicles to be stopped and, if appropriate, searched should reflect an objective assessment of the nature of the incident or weapon in question and the individuals and vehicles thought likely to be associated with that incident or those weapons. See further Code A paras 2.12–2.14B.

---

5  'Terrorist' is defined by TA 2000 s40 as a person who has committed an offence under TA 2000 ss11, 12, 15–18, 54 and 56–63, or is or has been concerned in the commission, preparation or instigation of acts of terrorism.

6  Defined as instruments having a blade or which are sharply pointed (CJPOA 1994 s60(11)).

7  This was added following the decision in *Gillan and Quinton v UK* [2010] 50 EHRR 45, although there is some doubt as to whether it goes far enough to avoid violation of European Convention on Human Rights (ECHR) article 8.

- CJPOA 1994 s60AA, which permits a constable in uniform to demand the removal of, and to seize (but not to search for), any item which the constable reasonably believes is being worn wholly or mainly for the purposes of concealing identity. This power is only available if authorisation has been given by an inspector or above under CJPOA 1994 s60 or s60AA(3). See Code A paras 2.15 to 2.18.
- TA 2000 s47A, which permits a constable in uniform to stop and search any person or vehicle where authorisation has been given by an assistant chief constable (or equivalent) or above on the grounds that he or she reasonably suspects that an act of terrorism will take place and considers that such authorisation is necessary to prevent it.[8]
- CJA 1988 s139B, which permits a constable to enter school premises and search the premises or any person on those premises for any bladed or pointed article, or offensive weapon. The officer must have reasonable grounds for believing that an offence under CJA 1988 s139A has been or is being committed, but does not have to have such a belief in relation to any person searched. See Code A paras 2.27 to 2.29.
- Under a warrant issued under Misuse of Drugs Act 1971 s23(3) where the warrant specifically authorises the search of persons found on premises specified in the warrant.

## The conduct of stop and search

2.7   The various statutory powers contain different provisions regarding the conduct of searches (for example, some require the officer to be in uniform and others do not), but Code A sets out minimum requirements that apply to all searches covered by the Code (see para 2.2 above). Reasonable force may be used to carry out a search, but only after it has been established that the person is unwilling to co-operate or resists (PACE s117 and Code A para 3.2). A person may be detained for the purpose of carrying out the search, but the period for which the person is detained must be reasonable and must be kept to a minimum (PACE s1(2)(b) and Code A para 3.3).[9] The search must be conducted at or near the place where the person or vehicle was first detained (Code A para 3.4). However, a place is 'near' if it is within a reasonable travelling distance 'using whatever mode of travel (on foot or by car) is appropriate' (Code A NfG 6). Therefore, a person could be taken to a police station for the search to be conducted if it is near the place where the person was first detained. NfG 6 states that this is the case whether or not the search requires the removal of more than outer clothing. If a search does require the removal of more than

---

8   TA 2000 s44 was repealed, and s47A inserted, by the Terrorism Act 2000 (Remedial) Order 2011 SI No 631, which also provides that Code A is to have effect as if paras 2.18A to 2.26 were revoked, and that the Secretary of State should issue a code specifically dealing with stop and search under this provision. This was a temporary measure in order to comply with the European Court of Human Rights decision in *Gillan and Quinton v UK* (see note 7), and the provisions are expected to be replaced in similar terms by the Protection of Freedoms Bill, when enacted.

9   It was held in *R (on app of Gillan) v Commissioner of Police for the Metropolis and Secretary of State for the Home Department* [2006] UKHL 12 that a 'short detainment' of 20 minutes was acceptable.

outer clothing this cannot be done in public.[10] Therefore, if a search does require the removal of more than outer clothing, and there is no suitable place out of public view nearby, a search cannot be conducted under these powers (see Code A NfG 6).

2.8    Before a search of a person or an attended vehicle is conducted, the officer must take reasonable steps to give the person certain information:

- that the person is being detained for the purposes of a search;
- the officer's name (except in certain terrorist cases) and the name of the officer's police station;
- the legal power of search that is being exercised;
- a clear explanation of the object of the search, the ground for suspicion (where suspicion is required), or the nature of the power and any necessary authorisation (where suspicion is not required));
- their right to a record of the search (PACE s2 and Code A para 3.8).

If the officer is not in uniform the officer must produce documentary evidence that he or she is a constable (eg, a warrant card) (PACE s2(2) and Code A para 3.8). The obligations under PACE s2 are mandatory and failure to comply with them may render the stop and search unlawful.[11] If the person to be searched, or the person in charge of the vehicle to be searched, does not appear to understand what is being said, or there is any doubt about their ability to understand English, the officer must take reasonable steps to bring information regarding their rights to their attention (Code A para 3.11).

## Recording and monitoring

2.9    The officer must make a written record of the stop and search unless it is not practicable to do so (PACE s3). Code A para 4.1 puts this in stronger terms, stating that a record must be made unless there are exceptional circumstances which would make this wholly impracticable. If the search results in an arrest and the person is taken to a police station, the record should be made as part of the person's custody record. Otherwise, the record must normally be made 'on the spot' or, if this is not practicable, as soon as practicable afterwards (PACE s3(2) and Code A para 4.1). If a record is made at the time, the person must be asked if the person wants a copy and if the person does, the person must either be given a copy of the record or a receipt which explains how he or she can obtain a copy (PACE s3(7)–(9) and Code A para 4.2). The information to be included in the record consists of: the identity of the officer making the search; the object of the search and the grounds for making it; the date, time and place when it was made; and, except in the case of a search of an unattended vehicle, the self-defined ethnicity of the person searched or the person in charge

10  PACE s2(9)(a). See Code A para 3.5 for the permissible extent of a search in public.

11  *R v Bristol* [2007] EWCA Crim 3214. The obligation to inform the person of the officer's name and station is mandatory even if they are known to each other (*R (Michaels) v Highbury Corner Magistrates' Court and Crown Prosecution Service* [2009] EWHC 2928 (Admin)). See also *B v DPP* [2008] EWHC 1655 (Admin) in which a stop and search was found to be unlawful where an officer in plain clothes failed to produce his warrant card. If the stop and search is unlawful, the officer will not be acting in the execution of his or her duty.

of the vehicle searched (and, if different, their ethnic origin as perceived by the officer) (PACE s3(6) and (6A) and Code A para 4.3). The obligation to record what, if anything, was found in the search, which was in previous versions of PACE s3, has unfortunately been removed. The obligation to record a 'stop and account' (ie, where an officer requests a person in a public place to account for himself or herself without exercising statutory stop and search powers), has also been removed (Code A para 4.12).

2.10    Supervising officers are required to monitor the use of stop and search powers, and must: 'consider in particular where there is any evidence that they are being exercised on the basis of stereotyped images or inappropriate generalisations' (Code A para 5.1). Any apparent disproportionate use of the powers by particular officers or groups of officers or in relation to specific sections of the community must be identified and investigated (Code A para 5.3).[12] Arrangements must be made for the records to be scrutinised by representatives of the community, and for explanations to be given of the use of the powers at a local level (Code A para 5.4).

## Powers of arrest

2.11    Police powers of arrest without warrant are largely governed by PACE s24, although they also have powers of arrest under a number of other statutes, and also at common law in respect of breach of the peace. In addition, the police have powers of arrest in accordance with warrants issued under the Magistrates' Courts Act (MCA) 1980 s1 or other legislation. PACE Code of Practice G *Code of Practice for the Statutory Power of Arrest by Police Officers* also governs statutory powers of arrest (see para 1.74 above). Generally, the code adds little to the statutory provisions. However, it does stress the importance of the right to liberty,[13] and that exercising the power of arrest 'represents an obvious and significant interference with that right' (Code G para 1.2). It also states that an arrest must be both necessary and proportionate: police officers must: 'consider if the necessary objectives can be met by other, less intrusive means. Arrest must never be used simply because it can be used ... it is essential that it is exercised in a non-discriminatory and proportionate manner' (Code G para 1.3). Thus the less serious the suspected offence, the less likely that arrest rather than, for example, using the summons (or written charge and requisition) procedure, will be justified. This is particularly important because PACE s24 provides the police with powers of arrest in respect of *all* offences.

2.12    This section sets out the major statutory powers of arrest, arrest under warrant, and arrest for breach of the peace, and then deals with some general issues: what constitutes an arrest; use of force; the information to be given on arrest; caution on arrest; the consequences of an unlawful arrest; and action following arrest.

12  Home Office statistics show that stop and search powers are consistently used disproportionately against black and Asian people. See the *Statistics on Race and the Criminal Justice System* series published by the Ministry of Justice, and available at www.justice.gov.uk/publications/raceandcjs-archive.htm.

13  A right under ECHR article 5 (right to liberty and security).

## Police powers of arrest under PACE

2.13   Police officers have powers of arrest without warrant in respect of any offence in three sets of circumstances (PACE s24(1)–(3)). First, they can arrest anyone who is about to commit an offence, or whom they have reasonable grounds for suspecting to be about to commit an offence (PACE s24(1)(a) and (c)). Second, they can arrest anyone who is in the act of committing, or whom they have reasonable grounds for suspecting to be committing, an offence (PACE s24(1)(b) and (d)). Third, if an officer has reasonable grounds for suspecting that an offence has been committed, the officer may arrest any person whom the officer has reasonable grounds to suspect of being guilty of it (PACE s24(2)). Alternatively, if an offence has been committed, a constable may arrest anyone who is guilty of the offence or anyone whom the constable has reasonable grounds for suspecting to be guilty of it (PACE s24(3)).

2.14   The provisions in PACE s24(1)(a) and (b) and (3) give the police powers to arrest a person who is about to commit, is in the act of committing, or has committed, an offence. Provided that this can be proved, for example, by a subsequent conviction of the person for the offence for which the person was arrested, the arrest will have been lawful even if the officer had no, or no reasonable, grounds for suspecting the person at the time of the arrest (subject to the necessity requirement in section 24(4)).[14] However, even if it cannot be proved that an offence was, as a matter of fact, about to be, was being, or had been, committed, an arrest would still be lawful under section 24(1)(c) or (d), (2) or (3) (subject to the necessity requirement) provided that it can be established that the officer had reasonable grounds for suspecting that the person was about to commit or was committing an offence, or had reasonable grounds for suspecting that an offence had been committed and for suspecting that the person the officer arrested had committed the offence. While the reasonable suspicion provisions sound like a due process safeguard preventing arbitrary arrest, in fact they largely operate as a safeguard for the police.

### Reasonable grounds for suspicion

2.15   Where reasonable grounds for suspicion are required, it has been held that whether the officer carrying out the arrest had reasonable grounds for suspicion must be assessed by reference to a mixed subjective/objective test: did the officer actually suspect that the person was guilty of the offence for which the suspect was arrested; and if so, would a reasonable person in possession of the same facts as the officer have suspected the person.[15]

---

14  The police rarely rely on the powers that do not require reasonable suspicion when defending actions for wrongful arrest, although largely for tactical reasons. See *Shields (by his litigation friend, Rebecca Shields) v Chief Constable of Merseyside Police* [2010] EWCA Civ 1281, in which they were encouraged to do so. However, arguably arrest without reasonable suspicion amounts to a breach of ECHR art 5(1)(c) which, in effect, requires reasonable suspicion to justify the interference with liberty represented by an arrest (see para 13.7 below).

15  *Castorina v Chief Constable of Surrey* (1988) 138 NLJ 180. See also *Plange v Chief Constable of South Humberside Police* (1992) *Times* 23 March and *R v Redman* [1994] Crim LR 914.

Unlike Code A in respect of stop and search, Code G does not attempt to define reasonable grounds for suspicion in respect of powers of arrest. In practice, the requirement has often been given such a liberal interpretation by the courts as to provide very little protection against arbitrary arrest.[16] The arresting officer must be in possession of some information giving rise to the suspicion,[17] but the threshold is low.[18] The arresting officer does not have to have identified the precise legal power under which he or she acts.[19] The arresting officer can take a 'broad brush' approach so that it is not necessary for him or her to have identified the specific offence of which the officer is suspicious,[20] although the officer must suspect the existence of facts amounting to an offence of a kind that he or she has in mind.[21] Account can be taken of 'information of particular opportunity for a suspect to have committed an offence',[22] and it has been held that the fact that a small number of people could be identified as the only ones capable of having committed an offence can, in principle, afford reasonable grounds to arrest all of them.[23]

2.16     A major issue concerns arrests that are based on information supplied by someone else, such as a witness, an informant, a store detective, another police officer, or via a computer. A description given by a witness can be sufficient for suspicion to be reasonable, and even a description given in an anonymous telephone call can be sufficient provided that the person arrested corresponds with the information in the message.[24] Information received from a police informant can be sufficient, although it should be treated with considerable reserve.[25] Suspicion based on information contained in a computer entry can support reasonable suspicion even if the information turns out to be incorrect.[26] An instruction or request to arrest made by another police officer, without supporting information, would not be sufficient.[27] How much information has to be given in order to satisfy the reasonable suspicion test would appear to depend on the status and

---

16 Although note *Samuels v Commissioner of Police for the Metropolis* June 1999 *Legal Action* 14 where it was held that the mere fact that a person was walking through an area well-known for burglaries did not provide reasonable grounds for suspicion.

17 *O'Hara v Chief Constable of the Royal Ulster Constabulary* [1997] 1 All ER 129; [1997] Crim LR 432.

18 See, for example, *Armstrong v Chief Constable of West Yorkshire Police* [2008] EWCA Civ 1582, and *Alford v Chief Constable of Cambridgeshire Police* [2009] EWCA Civ 100.

19 *R (Rutherford) v IPCC* [2010] EWHC 2881 (Admin).

20 Thus in *Coudrat v Commissioners of Her Majesty's Revenue and Customs* [2005] EWCA Civ 616 it was held to be sufficient to arrest for 'VAT fraud' without being more specific. Note, however, that if the police wish to exercise a power that is dependent upon the person being under arrest for an indictable offence, a decision as to the precise grounds for the arrest must be made before the power is exercised.

21 *Chapman v DPP* (1988) 89 Cr App R 190.

22 *Al Fayed and others v Commissioner of Police of the Metropolis and others* [2004] EWCA Civ 1579.

23 *Cummings and others v The Chief Constable of Northumbria Police* [2003] EWCA Civ 1844.

24 *Jones v Chief Constable of Bedfordshire* (1999) 30 July (unreported), *King v Gardner* (1979) 71 Cr App R 13, and *DPP v Wilson* [1991] RTR 284.

25 *James v Chief Constable of South Wales* (1991) 6 CL 80.

26 *Hough v Chief Constable of Staffordshire* (2002) *Times* 14 February, CA.

27 *R v Olden* [2007] EWCA Crim 726.

identity of the person providing the information. Even a small amount of information received from a senior police officer is likely to be regarded as sufficient,[28] but it is not enough for the arresting officer to believe that the superior officer is in possession of information that the officer has not disclosed.[29]

2.17    An arrest carried out for an ulterior purpose, for example, to enable the police to install a bugging device in the suspect's house for the purpose of investigating another offence, is lawful provided there are reasonable grounds for suspicion in relation to the offence for which the person was arrested.[30] However, the police must not mislead the suspect as to the true nature of the investigation, for example, by failing to inform a person arrested for burglary that the victim had died.[31]

### Belief that an arrest is necessary

2.18    The powers of arrest under PACE s24(1), (2) and (3) can only be exercised if the arresting officer has reasonable grounds for believing that arrest is necessary for one or more of the reasons set out in PACE s24(5) (PACE s24(4)). It has been held that the necessity for arrest should be assessed by reference to a mixed subjective/objective test: did the officer actually believe that arrest was necessary; if so, would a reasonable person in possession of the same information as the officer have concluded that arrest was necessary; and if so, was the arrest *Wednesbury* reasonable (ie, was the discretion exercised properly having regard only to relevant factors).[32] The requirement of *reasonable belief* that arrest is necessary arguably establishes a higher threshold than that implied by *reasonable suspicion*, although this has not been explicitly considered by the courts. In making the decision on arrest, although the officer does not have to consider that there is no viable alternative to arrest, the officer must make some evaluation of the feasibility of achieving the object of arrest by some alternative means, such as by inviting the person to attend the police station as a volunteer.[33]

2.19    The necessity conditions set out in PACE s24(5), as supplemented by Code G, are as follows:

- To enable the name or address of the person in question to be ascertained (where the constable does not know, and cannot readily ascertain, the person's name or address, or has reasonable grounds for doubting whether a name or address given by the person as their name or address is their real name or address (PACE s24(5)(a) and (b)). Code G states that an address is satisfactory for the purposes of serving a summons if the person will be at it for a sufficiently long period to facilitate service, or that some other person at the address given will

28   *O'Hara v Chief Constable of Royal Ulster Constabulary* [1997] 1 All ER 129; [1997] Crim LR 432, and *O'Hara v UK* [2002] Crim LR 493.
29   *Commissioner of Police for the Metropolis v Raissi* [2008] EWCA Civ 1237.
30   *R v Chalkley and Jeffries* [1998] QB 848; [1998] 3 WLR 146; [1998] 2 All ER 155.
31   *R v Kirk* [2001] 1 WLR 567.
32   *Graham v Chief Constable of West Mercia and others* [2011] EWHC 4 (QB), *Richardson v Chief Constable of West Midlands Police* [2011] EWHC 773 (QB).
33   *Re Alexander and others* [2009] NIQB 20, *Richardson v Chief Constable of West Midlands Police* [2011] EWHC 773 (QB), and see para 2.20 below.

accept service of the summons on their behalf. This condition should not justify an arrest simply because a person does not have proof of their name and address on him or her. It refers to reasonable grounds for doubting the name or address given, which implies that the officer must have some objective reason for doubting the information given.

- To prevent the person causing physical injury to himself or herself or any other person, suffering physical injury, causing loss or damage to property, committing an offence against public decency (which only applies where members of the public going about their normal business cannot reasonably be expected to avoid the person in question), or causing an unlawful obstruction of the highway (PACE s24(5)(c)). Since the officer must have reasonable grounds for believing that a necessity condition renders arrest necessary, and Code G requires officers to consider whether the necessary objective can be achieved by measure short of arrest, the officer should consider whether any of the consequences could be avoided by actions other than arrest.

- To protect a child or other vulnerable person from the person in question (PACE s24(5)(d)). Again, the officer should consider whether the circumstances necessitate arrest or whether protection can be achieved by other means that do not interfere with the liberty of the person.

- To allow the prompt and effective investigation of the offence or of the conduct of the person in question (PACE s24(5)(e)). It is difficult to see how an arrest could be justified by reference to a need to investigate the conduct of the person unless that involves investigation of the offence of which the person is suspected. Code G states that this condition may be satisfied if there are grounds to believe that the person has made false statements or statements that cannot easily be verified, may steal or destroy evidence, may intimidate, threaten or make contact with witnesses, or where it is necessary to obtain evidence by questioning. Furthermore, where a person is suspected of an indictable offence (ie, indictable-only or either-way), Code G states that this condition may justify arrest if there is a need to enter and search premises occupied or controlled by the person (a reference to powers under PACE s18), search the person (a reference to powers under PACE s32), prevent contact with others, or to take fingerprints, footwear impressions, samples or photographs.[34] However, all of these actions, other than conducting an intimate search or taking an intimate sample, can be carried out on the basis of consent of the person concerned, and do not require arrest (but see para 2.20 below). Finally, Code G states that this condition may be satisfied if arrest is necessary to ensure compliance with statutory drug-testing requirements.[35] This condition should not be used to justify arrest where there is no investigative need. In the case of many minor, regulatory or motoring

---

34  Note that the power to take fingerprints, footwear impressions and non-intimate samples without consent from a person in police detention is available where the person is detained in respect of a recordable offence, not necessarily an indictable offence. The power to take photographs without consent from a person in police detention applies in respect of any offence. See generally chapter 6.

35  For police drug-testing powers see para 6.64 below.

offences the taking of fingerprints, photographs or non-intimate samples is not necessary for investigation of the suspected offence. Furthermore, it may be difficult for the police to justify an arrest under this condition where the person is then to be granted 'street bail' (see para 2.45 below), although in these circumstances arrest may be justified under the next condition.

- To prevent any prosecution for the offence from being hindered by the disappearance of the person in question (PACE s24(5)(f)). Code G states that this may arise if there are reasonable grounds for believing that the person will fail to attend court if not arrested, or if the grant of 'street bail' after arrest would be enough to deter the person from trying to evade prosecution. This entails a relatively high test – reasonable grounds for belief – and, therefore, a person should not be arrested merely because the officer suspects that the person may not turn up in court.

2.20   Where a person suspected of an offence voluntarily attends at a police station, it has been the routine practice of the police to arrest the person on arrival at the police station. Routine arrest in such circumstances is not lawful. In *Richardson v Chief Constable of West Midlands Police* the claimant voluntarily attended a police station accompanied by his lawyer in respect of a complaint of assault. He had gone to the police station expecting that he would be arrested and interviewed, but on arrival he confirmed that he was prepared to have a voluntary interview. In seeking to justify his arrest, the police claimed that the arresting officer believed that arrest was necessary because the claimant would interrupt the interview and leave the police station. In finding the arrest to have been unlawful, the court said that there was:

> ... no evidence that [the arresting officer] took into account the circumstances in which the claimant was attending voluntarily at the police station ... no evidence that he made any assessment of the likelihood that the claimant would leave the interview [and he] reached his view based on general propositions ... without taking into account the facts of the particular case.[36]

However, the court came to the opposite conclusion in *Hayes v Chief Constable of Merseyside Police*[37] where there was evidence that the arresting officer had considered alternatives short of arrest, and where there was a danger that evidence might be destroyed or interfered with if the arresting officer had proceeded on a voluntary basis. It should be noted that where a person is dealt with as a volunteer, some of the protective provisions of PACE and Code C do not apply (see para 2.151 below). However, the person may prefer to be dealt with as a volunteer since arrest may have adverse consequences in respect of their employment or travel abroad, and because it may amount to bad character for the purposes of the Criminal Justice Act 2003 ss98–113 (see para 5.170 below). Furthermore, being dealt with as a volunteer will mean that the person will not be locked in a cell.

---

36  *Richardson v Chief Constable of West Midlands Police* [2011] EWHC 773 (QB), para 67.
37  [2011] EWCA Civ 911.

## Civilian powers of arrest

2.21    Civilian powers of arrest are more limited than those of police officers. A
civilian, which for these purposes includes community support officers
and other designated civilians (see para 2.50 below), can arrest in two sets
of circumstances. First, a civilian can arrest a person who is in the act of
committing an indictable offence, or whom the civilian has reasonable
grounds for suspecting to be committing an indictable offence (PACE
s24A(1)). Second, where an indictable offence has been committed, a civilian can arrest a person who is guilty of the offence or whom the civilian
has reasonable grounds for suspecting to be guilty of it (PACE s24A(2)).
Unlike a police officer, a civilian cannot arrest a person for an anticipated
offence. If a civilian arrests a person for an offence the civilian believes has
been committed (as opposed to one that is being committed), the arrest
will be unlawful if it cannot be established that the offence was, in fact,
committed. It can be difficult in practice to determine when an offence is
complete for this purpose. For example, if a store detective arrests a suspected shoplifter as soon as the suspect leaves the shop, it is likely that the
suspect would be regarded as still in the act of committing the offence of
theft. However, if the suspect was arrested 20 minutes later by a security
guard from another shop who had been given a description by the store
detective, it is unlikely that it could be validly maintained that the suspect
was still in the act of committing the offence. The arrest by the security
guard is potentially lawful under PACE s24A(2), but would not be lawful
if it could not be established that an indictable offence had been committed.[38] An arrest by a police officer in these circumstances is likely to be
lawful since PACE s24(2) permits an officer to arrest a person if the officer
has reasonable grounds for suspecting that an offence has been committed. Unlike police powers of arrest, civilians may only arrest for indictable
offences, ie, offences that are triable only on indictment or offences triable
either-way. Therefore, civilians cannot arrest in respect of summary-only
offences.

2.22    The power of arrest under PACE s24A(1) or (2) can only be exercised
if the person making the arrest has reasonable grounds for believing that
arrest is necessary for one or more of the reasons set out in PACE s24A(4),
and it appears to the person that it is not reasonably practicable for a constable to make it instead (PACE s24A(3)). The necessity criteria are more
limited than those relating to arrest by a police officer, and are as follows:

- to prevent the person causing physical injury to himself or herself or
  any other person, or from suffering physical injury (PACE s24A(4)(a)
  and (b));
- to prevent the person causing loss of or damage to property (PACE
  s24A(4)(c));
- to prevent the person making off before a constable can assume responsibility for the person (PACE s24A(4)(d)).

38  See *R v Self* [1992] 3 All ER 476; (1992) 95 Cr App R 42; [1992] Crim LR 572, which
    was decided under the former version of PACE s24, but the same principles apply to
    PACE s24A.

## Arrest for breach of the peace

2.23    An arrest for breach of the peace under common law powers can be made where:

- a breach of the peace is committed in the presence of the person making the arrest; or
- the person effecting the arrest reasonably believes that such a breach will be committed in the immediate future by the person to be arrested; or[39]
- where a breach of the peace has been committed or the person effecting the arrest reasonably believes that a breach has occurred, and it is reasonably believed that a further breach is threatened.

There is a breach of the peace whenever harm is actually done or is likely to be done to a person or, in their presence, to their property or a person is in fear of being harmed through an assault, an affray, a riot, unlawful assembly or other disturbance.[40]

2.24    The power to arrest for an apprehended breach of the peace caused by apparently lawful conduct is exceptional,[41] in the sense that the lawful conduct must be wholly unreasonable and interfere in some way with another person's rights.[42] It was held in *Steel v UK*[43] that an arrest to prevent a breach of the peace did not contravene the ECHR, although it must be proportionate to the aims of preventing disorder and protecting the rights of others. The principles to be followed in 'exercising the now exceptional common law power of arrest' where the conduct is not itself unlawful were set out by the Court of Appeal in *Bibby v Chief Constable of Essex Police*[44] as follows:

- there must be the clearest of circumstances and a sufficiently real and present threat to the peace to justify the extreme step of depriving of their liberty a citizen who was not at the time acting unlawfully;
- the threat must be coming from the person who is to be arrested;
- the conduct must clearly interfere with the rights of others;
- the natural consequence of the conduct must be violence from a third party;
- that violence must not be wholly unreasonable;
- the conduct of the person arrested must be unreasonable.

2.25    Although breach of the peace is a criminal offence for the purposes of ECHR article 5 (*right to liberty and security*) and article 6 (*right to a fair trial*),[45] it is not a criminal offence under domestic law. One consequence of this is that detention at a police station of a person arrested for breach

---

39  *R (Laporte) v Chief Constable of Gloucestershire* [2007] 2 WLR 46. For action short of arrest, such as 'kettling' see *Austin v Commissioner of Police of the Metropolis* [2009] 1 AC 564, and *R (Moos) v Commissioner of Police for the Metropolis* [2011] EWHC 957 (Admin).
40  *R v Howell* [1982] QB 416.
41  *Foulkes v Chief Constable of Merseyside Police* [1998] 3 All ER 705.
42  *Redmond-Bate v DPP* [1999] Crim LR 998.
43  (1998) 28 EHRR 603.
44  (2000) 164 JP 297.
45  *Steel v UK* (1998) 28 EHRR 603.

of the peace is not governed by PACE s37 unless the person is also, or subsequently, arrested for an offence. However, their treatment while held in custody is covered by Code C, although the review of detention provisions strictly do not apply but should be followed as a matter of good practice (see Code C para 1.10 and NfG 15B).[46] A person arrested for breach of the peace may be held in custody at a police station, under common law powers, in order to prevent a breach of the peace. However, for detention to be lawful, fear of a further breach of the peace must be real, and the officer making the decision must have an honest belief, based upon objective and reasonable grounds, that further detention is necessary in order to prevent a breach of the peace. If these conditions are not satisfied, and no other grounds for detention exist, the person must be released.[47]

## Pre-PACE powers of arrest

2.26    PACE abolished most powers of arrest, but Schedule 2 specifically preserves certain powers of arrest under pre-PACE legislation. Preserved powers include the power to arrest under Bail Act (BA) 1976 s7 for absconding or breaching bail conditions, and the power under MHA 1983 to arrest a person who is absent without leave or who has absconded.

## Arrest on suspicion of being a terrorist

2.27    A constable may arrest without warrant a person whom the constable reasonably suspects to be a terrorist (TA 2000 s41(1)). A 'terrorist' is defined as a person who has committed an offence under TA 2000 s11 or s12 (activities in relation to proscribed organisations), ss15–18 (financial activities relating to terrorism), s54 (involvement in weapons training), ss56–63 (various activities relating to terrorism) or s40(1)(b) (where the person is or has been concerned in the commission, preparation or instigation of acts of terrorism) (s40(1)). 'Terrorism' means the use or threat of action where the action falls within TA 2000 s1(2), the use or threat is designed to influence the government or an international governmental organisation or to intimidate the public or a section of the public, and the use or threat is made for the purpose of advancing a political, religious, racial or ideological cause (TA 2000 s1(1)). Action falls within TA 2000 s1(2) if it involves serious violence against a person or serious damage to property, endangers another person's life, creates a serious risk to the health or safety of the public or a section of the public, or is designed seriously to interfere with or seriously disrupt an electronic system. The power of arrest gives a broad discretion to the police since the arresting officer does not have to have a specific offence in mind.

---

46  It was held in *Williamson v Chief Constable of West Midlands Police* [2004] 1 WLR 14 that Code C did not apply to a person detained at a police station following arrest for breach of the peace because such a person was not arrested for an offence, and was therefore not in police detention. However, Code C para 1.10 states that the code applies to people in custody at police stations 'whether or not they have been arrested'.

47  *Chief Constable of Cleveland Police v McGrogan* [2002] EWCA Civ 86.

2.28   Where a person is arrested under TA 2000 s41 the person's detention and treatment are governed by TA 2000 Sch 8 rather than by PACE. The person is not treated as having been arrested for an offence, but is treated as being in police detention by virtue of PACE s118(2)(a). For application of the PACE Codes see para 1.64 above. Where a person is arrested under TA 2000 s41 the person should be taken to a place designated by the secretary of state for the purpose of detention under this section (TA 2000 Sch 8 para 1).

2.29   In addition to the arrest power under TA 2000 s41, an examining officer (which includes a police constable, immigration officer or designated customs officer) may, in respect of a person who is at a port or border area, stop and detain a person if the officer believes that the person's presence there is connected with entering or leaving the country, to enable the examining officer to determine whether the person is or has been concerned in the commission, preparation or instigation of acts of terrorism (TA 2000 s53 and Sch 7 para 2). Such a person may be detained for the purposes of an examination for up to nine hours beginning with the time when the examination began (TA 2000 Sch 7 para 6(4)). Where a person is detained under these powers, the person's treatment is governed by TA 2000 Sch 8 Part 1 (TA 2000 Sch 7 para 6(3)). The person is not treated as being in police detention, and the PACE codes do not apply (see para 1.63 above). Where a person is detained for the purpose of examination, the person should be taken to a place designated by the secretary of state for this purpose (TA 2000 Sch 8 para 1).

## Arrest under warrant

2.30   There are a number of statutes that provide for the issue of a warrant for arrest. The most important of the statutes which authorise arrest under warrant for a criminal offence is the MCA 1980. Section 1 empowers a justice to issue a warrant on the basis of a written information substantiated on oath that a person has, or is suspected of having, committed an offence. Such a warrant may or may not be endorsed for bail. If endorsed for bail, the warrant will (if relevant) specify the amounts in which any sureties are to be bound. If bail is to be granted with sureties, the police must release the offender if the sureties approved by the officer enter into recognisances in accordance with the endorsement. The person bailed is then obliged to appear before a magistrates' court at the time and place named in the recognisance (MCA 1980 s117).

2.31   The power of a magistrates' court to issue a warrant for the arrest of any person who has attained the age of 18 years is limited by MCA 1980 s1(4). The offence concerned must be indictable (see para 2.21 above), or punishable with imprisonment, or the person's address must be not sufficiently established for a summons to be served on the person. A warrant to arrest any person for non-appearance before a magistrates' court must not be issued unless the offence to which the warrant relates is also punishable with imprisonment or where the court, having convicted the defendant, proposes to impose a disqualification upon him. Power is given under MCA 1980 s13 to issue a warrant for the arrest of a person who has failed to appear to answer a summons. Power to issue a warrant for arrest in respect of a person who has been granted bail and who fails to surrender to custody or who, having surrendered to custody, then leaves the court before the case is dealt with, is governed by BA 1976 s7.

## Arrest under PACE s31

2.32 Where a person has been arrested for an offence and is at the police station in consequence of that arrest, and it appears to the police that, if released, the person would be liable to arrest for some other offence, the person must be arrested for that other offence (PACE s31). One effect of this requirement is that the detention time limit runs from the time applicable to the original offence and is not extended by the subsequent arrest (see para 2.71 below). Although powers of arrest are generally discretionary, PACE s31 has the effect of requiring arrest in circumstances where the section applies. However, generally, a person is liable to arrest only if the police have reasonable grounds for suspecting that the person is guilty (for example, under PACE s24(1)–(3)) and arrest is necessary under PACE s24(4) (see para 2.13 above). This gives the police some leeway. They could question a suspect about matters for which the suspect has not been arrested up to the point when (as a result of answers to the questions or otherwise) they form a reasonable suspicion that the suspect is guilty of the other matter(s), at which point the suspect must be arrested for the further offence(s) by virtue of PACE s31. For the obligation to caution the person, see paras 2.43 and 7.6 below.

## Arrest other than for a criminal offence

2.33 In addition to the powers of arrest considered above, police constables and others have a range of powers to arrest people other than in respect of the commission of an offence. For example, they may arrest a person for the purpose of taking fingerprints or samples (PACE s63A(4) and Sch 2A para 17), or for failure to surrender to police bail (PACE s30D or s46A).The police also have powers to arrest a person under the MHA 1983 s136(1), and to arrest youths for breaking conditions of remand (Children and Young Persons Act 1969 s23A).

2.34 Generally, the provisions in PACE Parts IV and V, governing detention, questioning and treatment, relate only to those who are in police detention (see para 1.61 above). The major exceptions to this are the right of intimation under section 56 and the right to legal advice under section 58 which apply whatever the reason for the arrest. However (subject to the exceptions noted in the next paragraph), Code C (except section 15, governing reviews and extension of detention) is expressly applied to people who are in custody, whether or not they have been arrested for an offence, and to those who have been removed to a police station as a place of safety under the MHA 1983 (Code C para 1.10). Therefore, subject to the exceptions noted in para 2.35 below, people arrested for any reason and held in custody in a police station must be treated in accordance with Code C or Code H.

2.35    Code C paras 1.11 and 1.12 provide that the code does not apply to the following groups of people in custody:

1) those who have been arrested on warrants issued in Scotland by officers under CJPOA 1994 s136(2), or arrested or detained without warrant by officers from a Scottish police force under CJPOA 1994 s137(2) (when police powers and suspects' rights are the same as those in Scotland);
2) those arrested under Asylum and Immigration Appeals Act 1999 s142(3) for the purpose of having their fingerprints taken;
3) those whose detention is authorised by an immigration officer under the Immigration Act 1971;
4) convicted or remanded prisoners held in police cells on behalf of the Prison Service under the Imprisonment (Temporary Provisions) Act 1980;
5) those detained for search under stop and search powers, except as required by Code A.

## What is an arrest?

2.36    Despite the fact that the police have long had extensive powers of arrest, the term 'arrest' is not defined by PACE, or by any other legislation, and there is some inconsistency in the case-law. One approach is that a person is arrested if, as a result of what is said or done, the person is under compulsion and is not free to go where the person pleases.[48] Arrest, it is said, is an ordinary English word, and whether or not a person has been arrested depends not on the legality of the arrest but on whether the person has been deprived of his or her liberty to go where the person pleases.[49] A second approach is that context and purpose are relevant. In *Austin v Commissioner of Police of the Metropolis*[50] the House of Lords distinguished between a deprivation of liberty and a restriction of movement. Whether a situation amounts to a deprivation of liberty as opposed to a restriction of movement is a matter of degree and intensity and is highly fact-sensitive. A whole range of factors has to be considered including the individual's specific situation, the context in which the restriction occurs and the purpose of the confinement or restriction. Taking hold of a person's arm for the purpose of simply drawing his attention to what is being said to him, without an intention to detain or arrest, is not an arrest unless it goes beyond what is acceptable by the ordinary standards of everyday life;[51] and the same is true where an officer takes a drunk person by the arm to steady the person for his or her own safety.[52] In *R v Iqbal* it was held that a person who was handcuffed by a police officer and told that he would be arrested later by other officers was not under arrest (although he was unlawfully detained).[53] Under the *Lewis* approach the circumstances in *Iqbal* would clearly have amounted to an arrest, albeit an unlawful arrest because the

48  *Alderson v Booth* [1969] 2 QB 216, *Inwood* (1973) 57 Cr App R 529.
49  *Lewis v Chief Constable of the South Wales Constabulary* [1991] 1 All ER 206.
50  [2009] 1 AC 564.
51  *Mepstead v DPP* (1996) 160 JP 475.
52  *McMillan v CPS* (2008) 172 JP 485.
53  [2011] EWCA Crim 273.

appellant was not told that he was under arrest as required by the PACE s28(1).

2.37    Despite the uncertainty as to the precise meaning of arrest, temporary deprivation of or interference with liberty – such as that under powers of stop and search (see para 2.2 above), or the power of a community support officer to require a person to wait for up to 30 minutes pending the arrival of a constable (see para 2.52 below) – is unlikely to be treated as an arrest either under domestic or ECHR law.

## Use of force

2.38    The power of the police to use force in carrying out an arrest derives from PACE s117, which provides that where any provision of PACE confers a power on a constable and does not provide that the power may be exercised only with the consent of a person other than a police officer, the officer may use reasonable force, if necessary, in the exercise of the power. A civilian designated under the Police Reform Act (PRA) 2002 s38 may, in exercising powers in respect of which the civilian has been designated, use reasonable force in the same circumstances as a constable (PRA 2002 s38(8) and Code C para 1.14). In addition, the Criminal Law Act 1967 s3 empowers any person to use such force as is reasonable in the circumstances in the prevention of crime, or in effecting or assisting in the lawful arrest of an offender or suspected offender or of persons unlawfully at large.

2.39    In determining what force is reasonable, a court may take into account all the circumstances including the nature and degree of the force used, the gravity of the offence for which arrest is to be made, the harm that would flow from the use of force against the suspect, and the possibility of effecting the arrest or preventing the harm by other means.[54] The use of excessive force does not render an otherwise lawful arrest unlawful.[55]

2.40    Handcuffs should be used only where they are reasonably necessary to prevent an escape or to prevent a violent breach of the peace by a prisoner.[56]

## Information to be given on arrest

2.41    A person who is arrested (whether or not for an offence) must, unless the arrest is by way of informing the person that he or she is under arrest, be informed that he or she is under arrest as soon as is practicable after the arrest (PACE s28(1)). If the arrest is by a constable, this requirement applies even if the fact of the arrest is obvious (PACE s28(2)). Failure to inform the person renders the arrest unlawful. If an arrest is unlawful, any subsequent detention may be unlawful (see para 2.44 below).

54  For example, in *Roberts v Chief Constable of Kent* [2008] EWCA Civ 1588 in it was held that reasonable force had been used despite the fact that a police dog had caused serious bite injuries.

55  *Simpson v Chief Constable of South Yorkshire Police* (1991) *Times* 7 March.

56  *R v Lockley* (1864) 4 F & F 155. See the guidance on the use of handcuffs issued by ACPO, available at www.acpo.police.uk/documents/uniformed/2009/Handcuffs_ Guidance_Amended_08x05x09_website.pdf.

2.42    In addition, a person who is arrested must be told of the ground for the arrest, either at the time of the arrest or as soon as is practicable afterwards (PACE s28(3)), and of the reason why arrest was believed to be necessary (Code C NfG 10B, and Code G paras 2.2, 3.3 and NfG 3). This information must also be entered in the officer's pocket book (Code G para 4.1) and, if the suspect is detained in a police station, in the custody record (Code C para 3.4). Enough information must be given to enable the suspect sufficient opportunity to respond.[57] According to Code C NfG 10B and Code G NfG 3, where a person is arrested for an offence the person must be informed of the nature of the suspected offence, and when and where it was allegedly committed. PACE s28(3) expressly provides that failure to do so renders the arrest unlawful.[58] Again, an unlawful arrest may render subsequent detention unlawful. However, an arrest that was unlawful for this reason becomes lawful when grounds for the arrest are given.[59]

## Caution on arrest

2.43    A person who is arrested, or who is further arrested (for example, under PACE s31), must be cautioned at the time of the arrest or as soon as practicable afterwards unless it is impracticable to do so because of the person's condition or behaviour at the time, or the person has already been cautioned immediately before arrest (for example, where the person was initially questioned regarding a suspected offence without being arrested) (Code C para 10.4, Code G para 3.4). The terms of the caution are set out in Code C para 10.4. The alternative caution set out in Code C Annex C para 2 (see para 5.66 below) does not apply unless the person is already in police detention (see para 1.61 above) at the time of the arrest.

## Consequences of an arrest being unlawful

2.44    If an arrest is unlawful, for example, because there was no power of arrest in the particular circumstances or because the person was not told of the fact of or grounds for arrest, subsequent detention at the police station is arguably unlawful since the power to detain a person under PACE s37 (see para 2.53 below) depends on the person having been lawfully arrested. While some forms of unlawful arrest can be 'cured' (see para 2.42 above), this is not the case where, for example, the arrest was not necessary. If the defence lawyer believes an arrest to have been unlawful, the lawyer should consider making representations to the custody officer regarding detention, or bail, at the police station. It was held in *Hutt v Commissioner of Police for the Metropolis*[60] that where a person who has been unlawfully arrested is charged with an offence, bail under PACE s38(1) cannot be

---

57  *Wilson v Lancashire CC Constabulary* (2000) 23 November (unreported), CA. The information does not have to be given by the officer who made the arrest (*Dhesi v Chief Constable of West Midlands Police* (2000) *Times* 9 May).

58  *Ghafar v Chief Constable of West Midlands Police* (2000) 12 May (unreported), CA.

59  *Lewis v Chief Constable of South Wales Constabulary* [1991] 1 All ER 206. In this case, grounds for arrest were given ten and 23 minutes after arrest. See also *DPP v L* [1999] Crim LR 752.

60  [2003] EWCA Civ 1911.

denied. The fact that an arrest was unlawful may amount to a defence against a charge of obstruction or assault arising from the arrest, and this can include an assault on an officer who came to the aid of the officer carrying out the unlawful arrest.[61] An unlawful arrest may also provide grounds for the exclusion of evidence or for a civil action against the police (see chapter 13).

## Action following arrest

2.45    Where a person has been arrested by a police officer in a place other than a police station, or is taken into custody by a police officer after being arrested for an offence by a civilian, the person must normally be taken to a police station as soon as practicable after the arrest (PACE s30(1) and (1A)). However, the person may alternatively be released on bail (known as 'street bail') without first being taken to a police station, to attend at a police station on a future date (PACE s30A).[62] According to Home Office Circular 61/2003, in deciding whether to grant street bail the officer should take into account:

- the severity or nature of the alleged offence;
- the need to preserve evidence;
- the person's fitness to be released;
- the person's ability to understand what is being said or what is happening;
- the likelihood that the person may continue to commit the offence or other offences.

In the case of a juvenile, the police should make telephone contact with the juvenile's parent/carer as soon as practicable after street bail has been granted.[63]

2.46    Street bail may be unconditional or conditional. Such conditions may be imposed as appear to the police officer to be necessary for the purpose of securing surrender, preventing further offences, preventing interference with witnesses or obstruction of the administration of justice, or for the person's own protection (or if the person is under 17 years, for the person's own welfare or in his or her own interests) (PACE s30A(3B)). A surety or security cannot be required, nor a requirement that the person reside in a bail hostel (PACE s30A(3A)). An application to vary or remove conditions may be made to the police (normally the custody officer at the station at which the person is required to surrender) and, thereafter, to a magistrates' court (PACE ss30CA and 30CB).

2.47    Before releasing the person on bail the officer must give the person a notice stating:

- the offence for which the person was arrested;
- the ground on which the person was arrested;

61   *Cumberbatch v CPS; Ali v DPP* [2009] EWHC 3353 (Admin).

62   See Home Office Circular 61/2003 *Criminal Justice Act 2003: Changes Affecting PACE, Section 4 Bail Elsewhere than at a Police Station.* For an analysis of street bail see A Hucklesby 'Not necessarily a trip to the police station: the introduction of street bail' [2004] Crim LR 803.

63   Home Office Circular 61/2003 para B(3)(l).

- if conditions are imposed, the requirements imposed by those conditions and the right to apply for variation of those conditions;
- the fact that the person is required to attend a police station;
- the time and police station where the person is to surrender. However, if the notice does not specify the time and station, the person must subsequently be given a written notice setting out this information (PACE s30B).

The police station that the person is required to attend can be any police station (PACE s30A(5)). There is no statutory limit on the period for which bail may be granted, but Circular 61/2003 suggests a normal maximum of six weeks. The time and place for surrender may subsequently be varied (PACE s30B(6) and (7)), and the requirement to attend may be withdrawn (PACE s30C(1)). When a person answers to street bail, the custody officer must link any documentation held in relation to the arrest with the custody record (Code C para 3.25).

2.48    If the person fails to attend at the specified time the person may be arrested (PACE s30D(1)) and, in any event, may be re-arrested if new evidence justifying a further arrest comes to light after the person's release (PACE s30C(4)). The person may also be arrested if, in the case of conditional street bail, a constable has reasonable grounds for suspecting that the person has broken any of those conditions. If arrested under these provisions, the person must be taken to a police station (which may be the specified police station or any other police station) (PACE s30D). Although breach of conditions, and failure to attend a police station, are not criminal offences, an arrest under these provisions counts as an arrest for an offence for the purpose of PACE ss30 and 31. There is no power of arrest for an anticipated breach of conditions or anticipated failure to surrender. Where a client has been granted street bail, the lawyer should carefully scrutinise the reasons given by the police for why an arrest was necessary since given the willingness of the officer to release the person on bail it may be difficult for them to justify the necessity for the arrest by reference to PACE s24(4) and (5) (see para 2.18 above).

2.49    Taking the person to the police station or releasing the person on street bail may be delayed if the presence of the arrested person is necessary in order to carry out such investigations as it is reasonable to carry out immediately (PACE s30(10)–(11)). This could include a search of premises under PACE s32 (see para 6.100 below), or under PACE s18 (see para 6.104 below). A section 18 search normally requires prior authorisation by an inspector or above, but this may be dispensed with in these circumstances (PACE s18(5)(b) and (5A)), although the officer must then inform an inspector or above that a search has been conducted as soon as practicable after the search has been conducted (PACE s18(6)).

# Powers of designated police civilians

2.50    Certain police powers can be exercised by civilians employed by the police authority and designated by chief police officers as police community support officers (PCSOs), investigating officers, detention officers or escort

officers (PRA 2002 Part 4 and Sch 4).[64] The chief police officer has a qualified discretion as to which powers to grant to such civilians within his or
her force, but there are certain standard powers that apply to community
support officers employed by all police authorities.[65] A list of the discretionary and standard powers of community support officers is set out in
Home Office Circular 33/2007 *Standard Powers and Duties of Police Community Support Officers*, Annex A. The power of PCSOs to detain a person
for up to 30 minutes[66] is a discretionary, and not a standard, power.

2.51    A designated person may only use his or her powers if the person is
wearing an approved uniform (PRA 2002 s42(2)).[67] The person must produce his or her designation to any person in respect of whom the person
uses the powers if so requested (PRA 2002 s42(A1), and if the person is
exercising a non-standard power, he or she must also produce evidence
that he or she has been conferred with the power that being exercised
(PRA 2002 s42(B1)). Where a designated person exercises a power which,
if exercised by a constable, could be accompanied by the use of reasonable force, the person is empowered to use reasonable force (PRA 2002
s38(8) and Code C para 1.14). There are similar offences of assaulting,
obstructing or impersonating designated police civilians as apply to police
officers (PRA 2002 s46). Designated civilians (and other civilian support
staff) must have regard to any relevant provisions of the Codes (PACE s67
and Code C para 1.16).

2.52    The powers of designated civilians are set out in PRA 2002 Sch 4, and
they are, in summary, as follows. Note that in the case of PCSOs some of
the powers listed below are standard powers, whereas others are discretionary and, therefore, may not be available to PCSOs in all police force
areas. In the case of investigating officers, detention officers or escort
officers, all of the powers are discretionary and, therefore, may differ as
between different police forces. Many of the powers are circumscribed by
conditions so, if relevant, a defence lawyer should carefully check whether
the conditions for exercising a power have been met.

## Police community support officers

- Powers to issue certain fixed penalty notices, for example, for disorder,
  riding on a footway, dog fouling, litter.
- Where the PCSO has reason to believe that a person has committed
  a relevant fixed penalty offence, or an offence which appears to have
  caused injury, alarm or distress to another person or the loss of, or
  damage to, another's property:

---

64  There are also powers to designate civilians employed by organisations contracted by
    the authority to supply services as detention officers or escort officer (PRA 2002 s39);
    and powers to accredit civilians under community safety accreditation schemes, and
    who may be granted certain, more limited, powers. See PRA 2002 s41 and Sch 5.
65  PRA 2002 s38A, and Police Reform Act 2002 (Standard Powers and Duties of
    Community Support Officers) Order 2007 SI No 3202.
66  Under PRA 2002 Sch 4 para 2.
67  Although by PRA 2002 s42(2A) an inspector or above may authorise a designated
    investigating officer not to wear a uniform for the purposes of a particular operation.

- the PCSO may require the person to give the PCSO his or her name and address;
- if the person fails to do so, or the designated person suspects the name or address given is false or inaccurate, the PCSO may require the person to wait with the PCSO for up to 30 minutes for the arrival of a constable, although the person can elect to accompany the PCSO to a police station instead of waiting. Failure to comply is a summary offence punishable with a level 3 fine. Where a person has been required to wait, a community support officer has the same powers as a constable under PACE s32 to search the person if the officer has reasonable grounds for believing that the person may present a danger to himself or herself or others, or to search the person for anything which might be used to assist the person to escape from custody, and to seize any relevant items.

- The same powers as a constable in uniform under PRA 2002 s50 to require a person whom he or she has reason to believe to has been acting, or to be acting, in an anti-social manner to give his or her name and address.
- Power to use reasonable force on a person on whom one of the above requirements has been imposed to prevent the person from making off.
- Power to require a person not to consume alcohol in designated places, and to confiscate alcohol from a person under 18.
- The same powers as a constable under PRA 2002 s59 to seize a vehicle being used in a manner causing alarm, distress or annoyance.
- The same powers as a constable to take a photograph away from the police station under PACE s64A(1A).

## Investigating officers

- Applying for, obtaining and executing search warrants under PACE ss8, 15 and 16, and seizing and retaining material found under PACE ss19–22, and under Criminal Justice and Police Act 2001 Part 2.
- Seeking access to excluded and special procedure material under PACE ss9 and 19–22.
- Arresting a person at a police station under PACE s31 (see para 2.32 above). Home Office Circular 67/2002 states that this is to make it easier for designated investigating officers to interview suspects. This is further reinforced by provisions treating the arrest as an arrest by a constable for the purposes of CJPOA 1994 s36 (PRA 2002 Sch 4 para 21), and that the designated investigating officer may ask a suspect to account under CJPOA 1994 ss36 and 37 (PRA 2002 Sch 4 para 23), so that inferences from 'failure to account' may be drawn.
- Receiving detained persons into their custody for the purposes of an investigation.

### Detention officers

- Taking fingerprints under PACE s61, and requiring a person to attend a police station for fingerprints or a sample to be taken under PACE Sch 2A.
- Conducting a non-intimate search, and seizing anything found, under PACE s54.
- Conducting an intimate search under PACE s55.
- Conducting a search to find relevant marks, features or injuries, or to ascertain identity, and to take photographs, under PACE s54A.
- Taking a non-intimate sample without consent under PACE s63.
- Taking photographs under PACE s64A.
- Taking a footwear impression under PACE s61A.

### Escort officers

- Taking a person arrested by a constable to a police station.
- Searching a person in custody at a police station or in police detention otherwise than at a police station, and seizing anything found under PACE s54(6A) and (6B).
- Escorting a person in police detention from one police station to another.

## Power to detain before charge

### Grounds for authorisation of detention

2.53 Following an arrest for an offence at a place other than a police station, the person arrested must normally be taken to a police station as soon as practicable (PACE s30(1), and see para 2.45 above). Where the person arrested is taken to a police station, the custody officer[68] must then determine whether there is sufficient evidence to charge the person, and may detain the person for such time as is necessary to enable the person to do so (PACE s37(1)). If the custody officer decides that there is sufficient evidence to charge the arrested person with the offence for which the person has been arrested, the person must either be charged, or released without charge either on bail or without bail (PACE s37(7)). If, however, the custody officer decides that the officer does not have before him or her sufficient evidence to charge, the arrested person must be released unless the officer has reasonable grounds for believing that detention without charge is necessary:

---

68 An officer designated as a custody officer must be of at least the rank of sergeant, although an officer of any rank can perform the functions if a custody officer is not readily available (PACE s36(3) and (4)). Normally, an officer acting as custody officer must not be involved in the investigation of an offence for which the person in respect of whom the officer is performing such duties is in detention, although there are exceptions (PACE s36(6)). If the person is taken to a non-designated police station (see PACE s35) any officer not involved in the investigation can perform the functions of custody officer (PACE ss36(7)–(7B)).

1) to secure or preserve evidence relating to an offence for which the person is under arrest; or
2) to obtain such evidence by questioning the person (PACE s37(2)).

2.54   These grounds for detention apply to all persons, including juveniles,[69] who have been arrested for an offence, and thus a person arrested for an offence cannot be detained without charge at a police station unless either or both of the grounds are satisfied. A person is deemed to have been arrested for an offence for the purposes of PACE s37 where: the person is arrested under the Road Traffic Act (RTA) 1988 s6D (arrest under the breath-test procedure), or the Transport and Works Act 1992 s30(2) (arrest under the breath-test procedure of a person working on a transport system (PACE s34(7)); the person returns to the police station to answer to bail granted under PACE Part IV or is arrested under PACE s46A for failure to return to the police station to answer to bail; or the person attends the police station having been granted bail under PACE s30A (street bail) or is arrested under section 30D having failed to attend (PACE s34(7)). PACE s37 does not apply to a person arrested other than for an offence, in which case the authority for detention will be governed by the common law, statute or, where a person has been arrested under the authority of a warrant, the warrant itself. Thus PACE s37 does not apply to:

- persons arrested for common law breach of the peace (see para 2.23 above);
- persons arrested under BA 1976 s7;
- persons arrested for breach of an injunction to which a power of arrest is attached; and
- convicted or remanded prisoners who are held in police cells on behalf of the Prison Service (Code C para 1.12(iv)),

although it does apply to prisoners brought to the police station having been arrested for an offence.

2.55   If the custody officer authorises detention[70] the custody officer must:

- open a custody record, and enter certain information such as the offence(s) for which the person has been arrested, and the grounds for the arrest and the detention (PACE s37(4)–(6), Code C paras 2.1 and 3.4, Code H paras 2.2 and 3.4, and see para 2.96 below);
- inform the person of the person's right to legal advice and to have someone informed of the person's arrest (and ask the person whether he or she wishes to exercise those rights), and to consult the Codes of Practice, and give the person a written notice to that effect (Code C, Code H section 3);
- conduct a risk assessment and take any necessary action (Code C, Code H paras 3.6–3.9, and see para 4.23 below);
- if the person is a juvenile, ascertain the person responsible for the juvenile's welfare and inform that person of the arrest and detention

---

69  For instance, a person who appears to be under the age of 17 (PACE s37(15)).
70  Code C para 2.1A states that these duties arise where a person is brought to a police station under arrest, or is arrested at a police station having attended there voluntarily, but in practice they are normally only carried out if detention without charge is authorised.

(Code C para 3.13, Code H para 3.15), and if the juvenile is known to be the subject of a court order under which a person or organisation is responsible for supervising or monitoring the juvenile, inform that person or organisation (Code C para 3.14, Code H para 3.16);

- if the person is a juvenile, mentally disordered or otherwise mentally vulnerable, inform the appropriate adult (Code C para 3.15, Code H para 3.17);
- if the person appears to be deaf or there is doubt about their hearing or speaking ability, or doubt about the person's ability to understand English, and the custody officer cannot establish effective communication, call an interpreter (Code C para 3.12, Code H para 3.24);
- if the person is a national of a foreign country, inform the person of his or her rights of communication with the person's High Commission, embassy or consulate (Code C, and Code H para 3.3 and section 7).

2.56    Where a person has been arrested under TA 2000 s41, the person must be taken as soon as is reasonably practicable to a police station designated by the secretary of state for these purposes (TA 2000 Sch 8 para 1). The decision to detain is governed by TA 2000 Sch 8 Part II which provides that detention must initially be reviewed as soon as is reasonably practicable after arrest (TA 2000 Sch 8 para 21). The review officer can only authorise continued detention if satisfied that it is necessary:

1)  to obtain relevant evidence whether by questioning or otherwise;
2)  to preserve relevant evidence;
3)  pending the result of an examination or analysis of any relevant evidence or of anything the examination or analysis of which is to be or is being carried out with a view to obtaining relevant evidence;
4)  pending a decision whether to apply to the secretary of state for a deportation notice to be served on the detained person;
5)  pending the making of an application to the secretary of state for a deportation notice to be served on the detained person;
6)  pending consideration by the secretary of state whether to serve a deportation notice on the detained person; or
7)  pending a decision whether the detained person should be charged with an offence (TA 2000 Sch 8 para 23).

The review officer is an officer not directly connected with the investigation who, in the case of a review conducted within 24 hours of arrest, is of at least the rank of inspector, and in the case of any other review, is of at least the rank of superintendent (TA 2000 Sch 8 para 24). There is no equivalent to the obligation of a custody officer under PACE s37(7) to make a decision about charge if satisfied that there is sufficient evidence to charge. Under the TA 2000, subject to the overall detention time limits, detention can continue for so long as a review officer is satisfied that one or more of the above conditions applies, provided generally that the officer is satisfied that matters are proceeding diligently and expeditiously (TA 2000 Sch 8 para 23(2) and (3)).

## PACE grounds in practice

2.57   A person arrested for an offence can only be detained without charge if:

1) there is not sufficient evidence to charge the person with the offence for which he or she has been arrested; and

2) detention is necessary for one or both of the two purposes set out in PACE s37(2) (see para 2.53 above).

Despite the clear obligation on the custody officer under PACE s37(1) initially to determine whether there is sufficient evidence to charge, in practice the custody officer normally proceeds to consider the decision whether to detain without enquiring about or considering the strength of the evidence at that stage. It has been held that the custody officer is not required to enquire into the lawfulness of the arrest, but is entitled to assume that it was lawful.[71]

2.58   If the conditions cease to apply, and there are no other grounds on which the person can be detained, the custody officer must immediately release the suspect (PACE s34(2)). In effect, the conditions must continue to be satisfied at each review before charge and where it is proposed to authorise continued detention at the 24-hour stage. In practice, custody officers rarely, if ever, refuse to authorise detention on the grounds that they are not satisfied that the PACE s37 grounds are made out.[72] However, there is some evidence that if the custody officer has doubts about whether the conditions are satisfied, the custody officer may put pressure on the arresting or investigating officers to expedite their inquiries.[73] Furthermore, if the custody officer can be persuaded to proceed straight to charge, inferences under CJPOA 1994 ss34(1)(a), 36 and 37 may be avoided, although inferences under section 34(1)(b) would still be possible. For these reasons, although the custody officer is not under a duty to receive representations in respect of the decision to detain, the lawyer may wish to make representations about the grounds for detention, even if the initial decision to detain has already been taken.

### Is there sufficient evidence to charge?

2.59   The lawyer should first consider whether there is sufficient evidence to charge the person with the offence for which the person was arrested. The phrase 'sufficient evidence to charge' is not defined in PACE or in Code C. In fact, Code C does not provide any guidance on the initial detention decision. The DPP has issued statutory guidance in respect of PACE s37(7) (see para 10.2 below), but this is not binding in respect of a decision under PACE s37(1) and (2).[74] The meaning of 'sufficient evidence to charge' for the purpose of the initial detention decision has received scant judicial

---

71   *DPP v L* [1999] Crim LR 752, *Al Fayed and others v Commissioner of Police for the Metropolis and others* [2004] EWCA Civ 1579.

72   See C Phillips and D Brown, *Entry into the criminal justice system: a survey of police arrests and their outcomes* (Home Office Research Study 185, Home Office, London, 1998), at p49.

73   See D Brown, *PACE ten years on: a review of the research* (Home Office Research Study 155, Home Office, London, 1997), at p59.

74   *R (G) v Chief Constable of West Yorkshire Police* [2008] 1 WLR 550.

attention. In *R v Mehmet*,[75] where the defendant was arrested for, and admitted, possession of an unlawful drug, the Court of Appeal decided that the custody officer was entitled to conclude that there was not sufficient evidence to charge until a forensic analysis has been obtained. However, in *Martin v Chief Constable of Avon and Somerset Constabulary* it was held that the need for analysis did not mean that there was not sufficient evidence to charge.[76] The similar phrase, 'sufficient evidence to prosecute', found in the former PACE Code C para 16.1,[77] has been interpreted as involving some consideration of any explanation, or lack of explanation, coming from the suspect.[78] If this reasoning is applied to the custody officer's decision under PACE s37 it would seem to enable detention to be authorised for interviewing, at least to give the suspect an opportunity of providing an explanation, even where the evidence of guilt at the time the initial detention decision is being made is overwhelming. But, if this is correct, there would be few if any circumstances where detention for questioning under PACE s37(2) could not be justified.

2.60    It seems that the authorities want the expression 'sufficient evidence to charge' to represent a high threshold when it is relevant to the decision whether a person can be detained in order to conduct investigations (ie, under PACE s37(2)), but to represent a low threshold when it is relevant to a decision to charge (ie, under PACE s37(7)). Unless and until the matter is authoritatively decided, if the defence lawyer wishes to avoid detention for questioning, the lawyer should argue that 'sufficient evidence to charge' means sufficient evidence to establish a prima facie case or, at most, sufficient evidence to provide a realistic prospect of conviction (irrespective of any explanation given by the client). See further the discussion at paras 10.6–10.8 below.

2.61    If a person has been arrested for an offence which has little or no 'mental element' (such as minor public order, and strict liability offences), and where the only evidence is that of police officers who witnessed the incident and implicate the suspect, it can be strongly argued that there is sufficient evidence to charge when the person first arrives at the police station. The proper course of action for the custody officer is to make a decision about charge or otherwise under PACE s37(1) and (7) without detaining the person for the purpose of securing evidence.

2.62    Where a person has been arrested for a more serious offence, or in respect of an offence that involves a significant mental element, it will be easier for the custody officer to justify detention even though the apparent evidence is strong. In principle, the only question is whether the custody officer has before him or her sufficient evidence to charge the

75  (1989) 13 June (unreported), *Butterworth's PACE Act Cases*, IV 53.
76  (1997) 29 October (unreported). For further discussion, see E Cape, 'Detention Without Charge: What Does "Sufficient Evidence to Charge" Mean?' [1999] Crim LR 874.
77  Replaced by the phrase 'sufficient evidence to provide a realistic prospect of conviction' in para 16.1 of the current Code C.
78  See *R v Elliott* [2002] EWCA Crim 931 for a review of the relevant cases, and see para 5.77 below for their application to the question whether inferences may be drawn. It should be noted that none of the cases dealt with PACE s37, dealing only with the relevant provisions of Code C.

person with the offence for which the person was arrested, and thus a response from the custody officer that the officer wants to give the suspect the opportunity to comment on the allegation is not relevant. If, in these circumstances, the custody officer does authorise detention, the lawyer may seek to confine any interview to offering the client an opportunity to give an explanation.[79] The custody officer may also be asked what his or her intentions are following any interview. If the officer states that he or she will charge the suspect, it is hard to resist the conclusion that the officer must have had sufficient evidence to charge at the time the person arrived at the police station, and that therefore detention should not be authorised. Even if this argument fails, it may be relevant to the advice to be given to the client concerning strategy in the police interview (see para 5.145 below).[80]

2.63    It should also be noted that PACE s37(7) refers to there being sufficient evidence to charge the person with the offence for which the person has been arrested. Since PACE s37 is in mandatory terms, it should not be legitimate for a custody officer to authorise detention because the officer believes that, although there is sufficient evidence to charge in respect of the offence for which the person was arrested, evidence may subsequently arise which would justify the officer charging the person with a different, perhaps more serious, offence. Code C para 16.1 provides that where a person is detained for more than one offence it is permissible to delay bringing them before the custody officer until the police are ready to charge in respect of all offences. There is here a clear conflict with PACE s37(7) and, as Michael Zander has pointed out, para 16.1 may well be ultra vires, although this does not appear to have been tested in the courts.[81] In any event, para 16.1 only applies where a person has been detained for more than one offence, and the argument here is that the officer should not authorise detention in the first place. The proper course of action would be for the police to consider whether to arrest the suspect for the second offence. In fact, provided there were reasonable grounds for suspicion, the police would be obliged to do so under PACE s31.

2.64    Pursuing this with the custody officer is unlikely to persuade him or her to make a charge decision, but it may reveal the true purpose of the investigation. This, in turn, may prevent the client from being taken by surprise by unforeseen questions, or lines of enquiry, during the police interview.

79  In *R v Coleman, Knight and Hochenberg* (1995) 20 October (unreported) (referred to in *R v Elliott* [2002] EWCA Crim 931), the CA accepted there had been a breach of Code C where the police, having concluded that there was sufficient evidence to successfully prosecute the suspect, nevertheless interviewed him rather than asking him simply whether he had anything to say. See also *R v Dellaway and Moriarty* (2000) 7 April (unreported), CA.

80  In *R v Dervish* [2001] EWCA Crim 2789; [2002] 2 Cr App R 6, a case on inferences rather than PACE s37, the CA accepted that there was a breach of Code C where the suspect was interviewed in circumstances where the police had decided that they would charge him irrespective of what he said in interview.

81  M Zander, *The Police and Criminal Evidence Act 1984* (5th edn, Sweet & Maxwell, London, 2005), at p127, and see para 10.9 below.

## Is detention 'necessary'?

2.65    If the lawyer is satisfied that there is insufficient evidence to charge, the lawyer should go on to consider whether detention is necessary for either or both reasons set out in PACE s37. In principle, the test is quite strong, since not only must the police be seeking to secure or preserve evidence or to obtain it by questioning, but detention must be necessary in order for them to do so. If these objectives can be achieved without the arrested person's detention, then arguably that detention is not necessary. This was emphasised by Douglas Hurd, the Home Office minister at the time of the passage of the Police and Criminal Evidence Bill, who told the House of Commons that the provision required that 'detention is necessary – not desirable, convenient or a good idea but necessary'.[82] In practice it has never been interpreted by custody officers in this way. In *Al Fayed and others v Commissioner of Police for the Metropolis and others*[83] it was held that while the question whether the custody officer has reasonable grounds for their belief that detention is necessary is an objective question, the question of necessity is to be determined by reference to whether the custody officer acted reasonably in determining that detention was necessary. In *Al Fayed* the appellant had attended at the police station voluntarily and indicated that he was willing to be interviewed. Nevertheless, the court found that the decision to arrest, and then to detain, him was reasonable. This should now be considered in the light of the necessity requirement in respect of the decision to arrest. Given that both the arrest decision and the detention decision involve a necessity test, and that the decisions are closely linked, the approach of the court in *Richardson v Chief Constable of West Midlands Police*[84] (see para 2.18 above) should be followed in respect of the detention decision.

2.66    Thus in making the detention decision, the custody officer should have regard to the particular facts of the case, and consider whether the objectives (eg, conducting an interview, taking fingerprints and samples, etc) can be achieved by means that are less intrusive and restrictive than detention. Where the defence lawyer is present at the time the detention decision is taken, and the client is willing, and would prefer, to be treated as a volunteer, the lawyer should consider making representations to this effect. Following the reasoning in *Richardson*, the custody officer might be asked what are the particular features of the case that make detention necessary. If the client has attended the police station as a volunteer, this should strengthen the argument that the client should continue to be treated as a volunteer, and not detained. However, even if the client has been taken to the police station under arrest this does not, in principle, prevent the client from being treated as a volunteer once the client arrives. Alternatively, if it is clear that the client is not willing to answer police questions, it might be argued that the custody officer cannot be satisfied that detention, or continued detention, is necessary for the purpose of obtaining evidence

---

82  Hansard, HC, Standing Committee E, col 1229, 16 February 1984.

83  [2004] EWCA Civ 1579.

84  [2011] EWHC 773 (QB). But see also *Hayes v Chief Constable of Merseyside Police* [2011] EWCA Civ 911.

by questioning, although in view of cases such as *R v McGuinness*[85] and *R v Elliott*[86] this argument is unlikely to be successful. However, if having been detained the person continues to refuse to answer questions, it is arguable that at some stage continued detention for the purpose of obtaining evidence by questioning must become oppressive.

2.67    A detention that is unlawful because there are no grounds to justify it may give rise to a civil action for false imprisonment and trespass to the person, and in appropriate cases it may be advisable to remind the custody officer of this. Furthermore, it may result in evidence obtained during the period of unlawful detention being excluded. See further chapter 13.

## Power to detain after charge

2.68    Where a person (having been arrested for an offence) is charged, the custody officer must order their release from custody, either on bail or without bail, unless certain conditions are satisfied (PACE s38(1)). The relevant law and practical considerations relating to the decision whether to grant bail after charge are dealt with in detail in chapter 10. Note that while a lawyer may wish to make representations, there is no duty on the custody officer to seek them from the suspect or the suspect's adviser. Note also the special rules that apply where a juvenile is denied bail (see para 11.47 below).

## Detention time limits

### Detention under PACE

2.69    The normal maximum period for which a person can be detained without charge is 24 hours commencing with the relevant time. This period may be extended for up to a total of 36 hours from the relevant time on the authorisation of an officer of the rank of superintendent or above if the officer *has reasonable grounds for believing* that:

- detention without charge is necessary to secure or preserve evidence relating to an offence for which the suspect is under arrest, or to obtain such evidence by questioning the suspect;
- the person is under arrest for an indictable offence;[87] and
- the investigation is being conducted diligently and expeditiously (PACE s42(1)).

If the suspect *is* under arrest for an indictable offence a magistrates' court may, on the application of the police, issue a warrant for further detention authorising detention without charge for up to a further 72 hours (PACE ss43 and 44, and see chapter 9).[88]

85    [1999] Crim LR 318.
86    [2003] EWCA Crim 931.
87    See para 2.21 above for definition of indictable.
88    For the significance of the difference between the italicised words see para 2.18 above.

2.70    Time, for the purpose of calculating the period of detention, runs from the 'relevant time', which is generally the time the person arrived at the police station (but see para 2.71 below). Note that, for the purpose of reviews of detention, time does not run from the relevant time but from the time detention was authorised (see para 2.80 below). At the expiry of the maximum period of detention, the person must be charged or released, either on or without bail (PACE ss41(7), 42(10), 43(18)). The maximum period of detention without charge is always subject to the requirement that a person in police detention must be released by the custody officer if the officer is aware that the grounds for detention of that person no longer apply and that there are no other grounds justifying continued detention (PACE s34(2) and Code C para 1.1). Note that PACE s45(2) provides that reference to a period of time is to be treated as approximate. This should be interpreted to allow for 'slippage' measured in minutes rather than anything more substantial (see Code C para 1.1A). Code C NfG 1H states that Code C para 1.1A is intended to cover delays which may occur in processing detainees such as those caused by a large number of detainees being brought to the police station at the same time, interview rooms being full, or by difficulties in contacting lawyers, appropriate adults or interpreters.

### 'Relevant time'

2.71    Generally, the relevant time is the time an arrested person arrives at the first police station the person is taken to, or 24 hours after arrest, whichever is the earlier (PACE s41(2)(a)). However, the following modifications to this rule apply.

1) If the person initially goes to the police station as a volunteer (see para 2.151 below), and is arrested at the police station, the relevant time is the time of the person's arrest (PACE s41(2)(c)).

2) Where a person attends a police station to answer to bail granted under PACE s30A (see para 2.45 above), the relevant time is the time the person arrives at the police station (PACE s41(2)(ca)).

3) If the person, having been detained in respect of one offence, is subsequently re-arrested at the police station in respect of another offence under PACE s31, the relevant time is that relating to the original arrest, so that a re-arrest does not have the effect of prolonging the maximum period of detention (PACE s41(4)).

4) If the person is arrested outside England and Wales, the relevant time is the time the person arrives at the first police station that he or she is taken to in the police area in England and Wales in which the offence for which the person was arrested is being investigated, or 24 hours after the person entered England or Wales, whichever is the earlier (PACE s41(2)(b)).

5) If the person is arrested in police area 1 in connection with an offence for which the person's arrest is sought in police area 2, provided that the person is not questioned in police area 1 in order to obtain evidence concerning the offence, the relevant time is the time the person arrives at the first police station to which he or she is taken in police area 2, or the time 24 hours after the person was arrested, whichever is the earlier (PACE s41(3)). This has the effect of increasing the maximum period

of detention by up to 24 hours. During transit, the person may not be questioned about the offence except to clarify any voluntary statement made by the person (Code C para 14.1). If the person is questioned about the offence in police area 1, the relevant time is calculated in the usual way even if the person is subsequently taken to a police station in police area 2 to be questioned about the same offence.

6) If the person is in police detention in police area 1, and the person's arrest in connection with another offence is sought by police area 2 and the person is taken to police area 2 for the purpose of investigating that other offence without being questioned in police area 1 in order to obtain evidence in connection with that other offence, the relevant time is the time at which the person arrives at the first police station to which the person is taken in police area 2 or the time 24 hours after the person leaves the police station in which the person has been detained in police area 1, whichever is the earlier (PACE s41(5)). This has the effect, where a person is sought by a number of different police forces, of allowing a series of detentions, the relevant time starting afresh in each police area to which the person is taken. During transit, the person may not be questioned about the offence except to clarify any voluntary statement made by the person (Code C para 14.1). Again, if the person is questioned about the offence in police area 1, the relevant time is calculated in the usual way.

7) Where the person is released on bail subject to a duty to attend the police station on a future date under PACE s47(3)(b), if the person is detained when he or she returns to the police station, the relevant time will be that relating to the initial detention. This is the case whether the person returns to the police station under the terms of the person's bail or is arrested under PACE s46A for failure to surrender to police bail (PACE s47(6)). However, if the person is re-arrested other than under PACE s46A, the relevant time will be that relating to the subsequent arrest (PACE s47(7) and see para 10.80 below). For example, PACE s47(2) provides that a person granted bail may be re-arrested if 'new evidence justifying a further arrest has come to light' since the person's release. The precise meaning of this expression is unclear. Where a person is released on bail pending analysis of fingerprints or samples, does it amount to 'new evidence' if the analysis implicates the person? On one view it does since the analysis amounts to new evidence that was not available at the time of the person's release. On the other hand, it could be argued that the evidence was available at the time the person was initially released, but had not been interpreted. Furthermore, if the former argument is correct, it would undermine the provisions regarding the maximum period of detention since it would apply whenever a person was released pending forensic analysis or further investigation. However, it appears that the point has not been judicially decided.

2.72   Generally, time runs continuously from the relevant time during periods that the suspect is in police detention, but does not run during any period when the suspect is on police bail (PACE s47(6) as amended by Police (Detention and Bail) Act 2011 s1(1)). However if, having been detained, the person is in need of medical treatment and as a result is removed to hospital, time spent at the hospital or travelling to or from hospital will not count in calculating the period of detention except for any time spent questioning the suspect for the purpose of obtaining evidence in respect of an offence (PACE s41(6)). A person in police detention at a hospital must not be questioned without the agreement of a responsible doctor (Code C para 14.2), and is entitled to legal advice under PACE s58.

## Detention beyond 24 hours

### a) Grounds and procedure

2.73 The period of detention without charge may be extended for any period up to 36 hours from the relevant time by an officer of the rank of superintendent or above who is in charge of the police station in which the person is detained (PACE s42(1)). If the initial extension is for less than the maximum period, a further extension can be authorised up to the maximum period (PACE s42(2)). Extension of the period of detention can only be authorised if the conditions set out in para 2.69 above are satisfied.

2.74 Authorisation may be granted at any time after the second review of detention (PACE s40 and see below) and before the expiry of 24 hours from the relevant time (PACE s42(4)). If authorisation is granted, the officer must inform the person of the grounds for continued detention (PACE s42(5)), of the right of intimation under PACE s56 and of the right to advice under s58 (if not already exercised) (PACE s42(9)), and record this in the custody record (PACE ss42(5)(b) and 42(9)).

### b) Representations

2.75 Before deciding whether to give authorisation, the officer must give an opportunity to the detained person (unless the detained person is unfit by reason of his or her condition or behaviour), or to the person's solicitor (if available at the time) to make representations (PACE s42(6), (7) and (8)). Unlike reviews under PACE s40, an extension of detention must be dealt with by the officer in person rather than by telephone or video link (Code C NfG 15F). If the detained person is likely to be asleep at the time the decision is made the time should, if the legal obligations and time constraints permit, be brought forward, but the person should not be woken if he or she is asleep (Code C NfG 15C). The meaning of 'available at the time' is not defined in PACE. A former version of Code C defined 'available' in connection with the right to have a solicitor present at a police interview as 'present at the station or on his way to the station or easily contactable by telephone', although this does not appear in the current version. The meaning of 'available at the time' is important since it has been held that PACE s42(6) is mandatory, rendering a purported authorisation following a failure to seek representations invalid.[89] If, after the second review, the lawyer has any concern that the police may seek to extend the period of detention under PACE s42 and wishes to make representations, the lawyer should either leave written representations with the custody officer or,

---

89 *Police v Mudd and McDonough* November 1987 *Legal Action* 19, also reported as *In the matter of an application for a warrant of further detention* [1988] Crim LR 296, although only a magistrates' court decision.

preferably, ask that the custody record be endorsed with a request for the solicitor to be contacted before authorisation is considered.

2.76 Representations at this stage should deal with (as appropriate):

1) Whether there is sufficient evidence to charge. If the custody officer determines that there is sufficient evidence to charge, the suspect must be charged or released (PACE s37(7) and see para 2.59 above and para 10.6 below). In such a case, continued detention without charge could not be justified. Investigating officers sometimes say during interview that they have sufficient evidence to charge but want to give the suspect the opportunity to give their version of events, so the record of any police interview should be checked.

2) Whether detention is necessary to secure, preserve or obtain evidence (see para 2.65 above). This raises questions such as:
   - What is the nature of the evidence that the police hope to secure during the further period of detention?
   - Is it necessary that the person be detained during this period, or could the person be released on police bail?
   - If the person has demonstrated that he or she is unwilling to answer questions, how can further detention to obtain evidence by questioning be justified?

3) Whether the offence for which the person is under arrest is an indictable offence (see para 2.21 above).

4) Whether the investigation is being conducted diligently and expeditiously.[90] If there are periods during which the police appear to be doing nothing, how can this be justified? Although Code C para 12.2 provides that in any period of 24 hours a detained person must usually be allowed a period of at least eight hours for rest, this does not necessarily justify the police in not continuing other aspects of the investigation during this period.

5) The length of the proposed extension of detention, since this should be sufficient for the purpose for which the extension is being granted and no longer.

## Detention beyond 36 hours

2.77 Detention without charge beyond 36 hours from the relevant time can only be authorised by a magistrates' court and only in respect of a person who is under arrest for an indictable offence (see para 2.21 above). See further chapter 9.

## Detention under the Terrorism Act 2000

2.78 The normal maximum period for which a person arrested under TA 2000 s41 can be detained without charge is 48 hours. This may initially be extended by a warrant for further detention for up to a total of seven days, and may be further extended up to a total of 14 days (see para 9.7 below). Where an application is intended to be made for a warrant of further detention, or is made, the person can be detained pending the making of the

---

90 See *R v Chief Constable of Hertfordshire ex p Wiles* [2002] EWHC 387 (Admin).

application or the conclusion of the proceedings (TA 2000 s41(5) and (6)). If the application is refused, the person may still be detained until the expiry of the period of 48 hours (TA 2000 s41(8)). Time runs from the time of the arrest under TA 2000 s41 or, where the person was initially detained for examination under Schedule 7, the time when the examination began (TA 2000 s41(3)).

## Breach of the detention time limit provisions

2.79   If a person is kept in police detention beyond the time allowed by these provisions, the detention will be unlawful unless it is made lawful by any other power to detain. An unlawful detention may provide grounds for civil action for false imprisonment, or for complaint against the police and may, if evidence is obtained during such period, provide grounds for exclusion of that evidence at trial under PACE ss76, 78 or 82(3). Furthermore, there is authority to suggest that failure to abide by the correct procedures, such as seeking representations, renders the detention unlawful.[91] See further chapter 13.

# Review of detention

## Review under PACE

2.80   A person who is in police detention (see para 1.61 above) must have his or her detention reviewed periodically in order to determine whether continued detention is justified. This is so whether or not the person has been charged, but it does not apply to volunteers, to people removed to a police station as a place of safety under the MHA 1983, or to those who have been arrested for something other than an offence, for instance an arrest under a fine default warrant or an arrest for fingerprints or samples PACE Sch 2A, since they are not in police detention (Code C NfG 15B, and see para 1.62 above). However, the detention of such people should still be reviewed periodically as a matter of good practice (Code C NfG 15B). The review provisions do apply to a person detained following an arrest for failure to answer police bail under PACE s46A, or following surrender to bail granted under PACE s30A (street bail), or following an arrest for failure to surrender under PACE s30D, since such a person is deemed to be arrested for an offence (PACE s34(7)). A review must initially be conducted six hours after detention is first authorised, and thereafter at nine-hour intervals, although there is provision for late review. References to periods of time are approximate only (see para 2.70 above). Note that time runs for review purposes from a different time than for the purpose of determining the maximum period of detention. Although the difference may often be only a matter of minutes, if a number of arrested people arrive at the police station at the same time, the difference may be significant. The time that detention is authorised must be noted on the custody record (PACE s37(4)).

---

91   See note 89 above. However, it was held in *DPP v Park* [2002] EWHC 1248 (Admin) that an unlawful detention resulting from failure to charge the accused within the time limit did not render the charges a nullity.

*Review before charge*

2.81    The first review must be carried out no later than six hours after detention was first authorised under PACE s37 (PACE s40(3)(a)). The second and subsequent reviews must be carried out no later than nine hours after the previous review (PACE s40(3)(b)(c)). Reviews must continue to be carried out during any period of extended detention, whether on the authority of a superintendent or a magistrates' court (see para 2.73 and chapter 9).

2.82    A review may be postponed if it is not practicable to carry it out at the due time (PACE s40(4)(a)). PACE specifically provides that there may be a postponement if at the due time:

- the person is being interviewed and the review officer is satisfied that interruption would prejudice the investigation; or
- no review officer is readily available (PACE s40(4)(b)).

2.83    However, there may be other situations where it is not practicable to hold a review at the due time, for example, where there has been a large number of arrests following a public disturbance. A detainee who is asleep need not be woken for a review, but if the detainee is likely to be asleep at the time a review is due to be conducted the reviewing officer should, if legal obligations and time constraints permit, bring the review forward so that the detainee can make representations (Code C NfG 15C). If a review is postponed, it must be carried out as soon as practicable (PACE s40(5)). The timing of subsequent reviews is not affected, and they must be carried out at the time they would have been conducted if there had been no postponement (PACE s40(6)).

2.84    Review before charge is carried out by an officer of at least the rank of inspector, except that continued detention at the 24-hour stage must be authorised by an officer of at least the rank of superintendent (see para 2.73). The primary purpose of the review is to ensure that the grounds for detention continue to apply. This involves consideration of the same factors as those to be taken into account by the custody officer at the time of initial detention. In particular, the review officer must decide whether there is sufficient evidence to charge and if there is not, whether detention is necessary to secure or preserve evidence or to obtain evidence by questioning (PACE s40(8)). If the person has not been charged or released because the person was unfit under PACE s37(9), the review officer must decide whether the person is yet in a fit state (PACE s40(9)). If there is a disagreement between the review officer and a more senior officer about the continued detention of a person in police detention, the review officer must immediately refer the matter to an officer of at least the rank of superintendent who is responsible for the police station concerned (PACE s40(11)). Before conducting a review the review officer must, unless the detainee is asleep, remind the detained person of his or her right to legal advice (Code C para 15.4, and see para 2.75).

2.85    A review (other than a review by a superintendent at the 24-hour stage) may be conducted by video-conferencing facilities where the review officer has access to the use of such facilities enabling the officer to communicate with persons at the police station (PACE s45A(1)). Where such facilities are not available reviews, other than those conducted by a superintendent at the 24-hour stage or by the custody officer following charge, may be conducted by telephone (PACE s40A(1)).[92] The decision whether to conduct a review in person, by telephone or by videoconferencing is a matter for the officer conducting the review. The officer should take into account the needs of the person in custody, and factors such as whether the person is a juvenile, is mentally vulnerable, has received medical attention (other than for a routine minor ailment) or whether 'there are presentational or community issues around the person's detention' (Code C para 15.3C). The precise meaning of the latter is not explained, but presumably means that a review should be conducted in person where the detention of the person is a sensitive matter because, for example, of concerns in the community. If a review is conducted by video-conferencing or telephone there is provision for representations to be made either by means of telephone or video-conferencing or by fax (PACE ss40A(3), (4) and 45A(6), (7)). There is also provision for the record to be made in the custody record by another officer (PACE ss40A(3) and 45A(5)).

### Review after charge

2.86    If the person has been charged, the review requirements set out above continue to apply with the following modifications:

- review is carried out by the custody officer (PACE s40(1)(a));
- the primary purpose of the review is to decide whether the decision to detain in custody rather than to release on bail continues to be justified (PACE s40(10)).

A review after charge must be conducted in person (PACE ss40A(1) and 45A(2)(b)).

### Representations at review

2.87    Before making a decision at review, the review officer must give the detained person (unless asleep or unfit because of their condition or behaviour) and their solicitor and appropriate adult (if relevant, and if available[93] at the time of the review) the opportunity to make oral or written representations about the detention (PACE s40(12), (13), (14) and Code C para 15.3). If the detained person is likely to be asleep at the latest time for review, the review should if practicable be brought forward (see para 2.83 above). The current version of Code C provides that the reviewing officer must give such an opportunity to the suspect and the solicitor. If the solicitor is not likely to be at the police station when the review is conducted, the solicitor should make it clear to the custody officer whether the solicitor wishes to make representations at a future review, and ask that a note be made of this in the custody record. Alternatively, the solicitor could leave written representations (having taken a copy) with the custody officer, with instructions to bring them to the attention of the review officer.

---

92  The former requirement that a telephone review could only be conducted where it was not reasonably practicable for an inspector to be present was removed by an amendment to PACE s40A(1) by CJA 2003 s4.

93  Note the comments about the meaning of 'available' at para 2.75 above.

2.88    Representations at reviews conducted before charge should deal with:

1) Whether there is sufficient evidence to charge. If the custody officer determines that there is sufficient evidence to charge, the officer must do so or release the person (PACE s37(7) and see para 2.53 above). In such a case, continued detention without charge could not be justified.

2) Whether detention is necessary to secure, preserve or obtain evidence (see para 2.65 above).
   - What is the nature of the evidence that the police hope to secure during the further period of detention?
   - Is it necessary for the person to be detained during this period, or could the person be released on police bail?
   - If the person has demonstrated that he or she is unwilling to answer questions, how can detention to obtain evidence by questioning be justified?

3) Whether the investigation is being conducted expeditiously (Code C para 1.1). If there are periods during which the police appear to be doing nothing, how can this be justified? Although Code C para 12.2 provides that in any period of 24 hours a detained person must be allowed a period of at least eight hours for rest, this does not necessarily justify the police in not continuing other aspects of the investigation during this period.

4) Whether a detention limit has expired or is about to expire.

2.89    Representations can be made orally or in writing (PACE s40(13) and see para 2.87 above), although oral representations are preferable where possible. If it is not possible to be at the police station at the appropriate time, then representations could be made over the telephone. A written note must be made in the custody record of the grounds for and extent of any postponement of review (PACE s40(7) and Code C para 15.13), of the fact that the detained person was reminded of their right to advice (Code C para 15.12) and of the outcome of the review (Code C para 15.16). If continued detention is authorised, the review officer must make a note of any comment made by the suspect or their lawyer (Code C para 15.5). The officer must also retain any written representation made (Code C para 15.15). In any event, the lawyer should keep a written record of the representations made and the review officer's comments. The review officer must not put specific questions to the suspect regarding the suspect's involvement in any offence, nor in respect of any comment the suspect may make in response to the decision to keep the suspect in detention (Code C para 15.6).

2.90    Note that the right to make representations is conferred by PACE s40(12) on the detained person's 'solicitor', which is defined for the purposes of Code C as including an accredited or probationary representative included on the register of representatives maintained by the LSC (Code C para 6.12). Once admitted to the police station (see Code C para 6.12A and para 4.4 below), an accredited or probationary representative should be treated in the same way as a solicitor, and this includes the making of representations on review. If a review officer refuses to hear representations from an accredited or probationary representative, the officer should be asked to give reasons for this. If the review officer is still not willing to receive the representative, the instructing solicitor should be contacted and the review officer asked to consider postponing the review to allow time for this. See para 2.82 above regarding postponement of reviews.

## Review under the Terrorism Act 2000

2.91    Where a person has been arrested and detained under TA 2000 s41 (see paras 2.27 and 2.78 above), review of detention is governed by TA 2000 Sch 8 Part II. The first review must be carried out as soon as is reasonably practicable following the arrest (TA 2000 Sch 8 para 21(2)). Subsequent reviews must be conducted at intervals of not more than 12 hours, but reviews are not required after a warrant of further detention has been issued under TA 2000 Sch 8 Part III (TA 2000 Sch 8 para 21(3) and (4), and see chapter 9). A review may be postponed if:

- the detained person is being questioned by police and interruption of the questioning would prejudice the investigation;
- no review officer is readily available; or
- it is not practicable for some other reason to carry out the review (TA 2000 Sch 8 para 22(1)).

If a review is postponed it must be carried out as soon as is reasonably practicable (TA 2000 Sch 8 para 22(2)), but this does not affect the timing of the next review, which must be held not later than 12 hours after the latest time that the postponed review should have been conducted (TA 2000 Sch 8 para 22(3)).

2.92    A review conducted within 24 hours beginning with the time of the arrest is conducted by an officer of at least the rank of inspector. Reviews conducted thereafter must be conducted by an officer of at least the rank of superintendent (TA 2000 Sch 8 para 24). A review officer must not be directly involved in the investigation in connection with which the person is detained (TA 2000 Sch 8 para 24(1)). Where a review is conducted by an officer of lower rank than superintendent and an officer of higher rank gives directions relating to the detained person which are at variance with those of the review officer, the latter must refer the matter immediately to an officer of at least the rank of superintendent (TA 2000 Sch 8 para 25).

2.93    The grounds for continued detention are set out at para 2.56 above. Before deciding whether to authorise continued detention the review officer must give the detained person (unless the person is unfit because of his or her condition or behaviour) or the solicitor an opportunity to make representations, which may be oral or in writing (TA 2000 Sch 8 para 26). If authorising continued detention the review officer must inform the detained person of the person's right to have someone informed of his or her detention under Sch 8 para 6 and the person's right to legal advice under Sch 8 para 7 if they have not yet been exercised or, where relevant, of the fact that they are being delayed (TA 2000 Sch 8 para 27(1)). Where exercise of one or more of these rights has been delayed, the review officer must consider whether the reason(s) for the delay continue to apply and, if the officer decides that they do not, must inform the officer who authorised the delay (unless delay was authorised by the review officer) (TA 2000 Sch 8 para 27(2)).

2.94    The review officer must make a written record of the outcome of the review, together with other relevant information such as the grounds upon which continued detention is authorised, the reason for postponement of the review, and the fact that the detainee has been informed of their rights as required by TA 2000 Sch 8 para 27(1) (TA 2000 Sch 8 para 28(1)). The review officer must inform the detained person whether the officer is authorising continued detention and, if so, the grounds for doing so, and must make the written record in the presence of the detained person, unless the detained person is incapable of understanding what is said to him or her, is violent or likely to become violent, or is in urgent need of medical attention (TA 2000 Sch 8 para 28(2) and (3)). Unlike a PACE review conducted before charge, there is no provision for the review to be conducted by telephone or video-conference facilities (Code H para 14.1).[94]

### Breach of review provisions

2.95    Although the review provisions are expressed in mandatory terms, neither PACE nor TA 2000 provide any direct mechanism for enforcement. Breach of the review provisions, particularly failure to remind the suspect of the suspect's right to advice, may provide grounds for exclusion of evidence under PACE ss76, 78 or 82(3) at a subsequent trial. Breach may also provide grounds for a complaint, and may render the detention unlawful, thus giving rise to a civil action for damages or a criminal action for false imprisonment.[95] It has been held that a late review rendered continued detention unlawful, but that it was arguable that the detention was rendered lawful once the review was conducted.[96]

## Custody records

### Formalities

2.96    A separate custody record must be opened as soon as is practicable for each person who is brought to a police station under arrest, or who is arrested at the police station having attended voluntarily, or who attends at the police station in answer to street bail (Code C para 2.1).[97] This includes a person arrested under TA 2000 s41 (Code H para 2.2). A custody record does not have to be opened in respect of a person who attends voluntarily and who is not arrested. Information that has to be recorded in the custody record (see para 2.101 below) must be recorded as soon as practicable

---

94  Although there is provision for the use of video links in proceedings for a warrant of further detention (Code H NfG 14I).

95  See *R (Craik, Chief Constable of Northumbria Police) v Newcastle upon Tyne Magistrates' Court and others* [2010] EWHC 935 (Admin), although there is no doctrine of vicarious liability in respect of a criminal offence.

96  *Roberts v Chief Constable of Cheshire Constabulary* [1999] 1 WLR 662; [2002] 2 All ER 326, CA. But see *DPP v Park* [2002] EWHC 1248 (Admin).

97  In principle, this applies to all persons brought to the police station under arrest, and not only those whose detention is then authorised. Such a distinction usually has little practical significance because evidence suggests that custody officers rarely, if ever, refuse to authorise detention: see note 72 above.

unless otherwise specified, and entries must be timed and signed by the person making the entry or, where on computer, contain the operator's identification (subject to limited exceptions) (Code C paras 2.1, 2.6 and 2.6A, Code H paras 2.2 and 2.3). The custody officer is responsible for the accuracy and completeness of the record (PACE s39 and Code C para 2.3, Code H para 2.4). If the detained person is transferred to another police station, the custody record or a copy of it must accompany the detained person, and must show the time and reason for the transfer (Code C para 2.3, Code H para 2.4). It is unclear whether a new custody record should be opened where a person is further detained on surrendering to custody following a release on police bail under PACE s47(3) or whether the original custody record should be continued. In any event, time in detention before the release on bail will normally count towards the maximum period of detention (see para 10.82 below).

## Access to the custody record and other information

2.97   A solicitor or appropriate adult must be permitted to see the custody record of a detained person as soon as practicable after their arrival at the police station, and at any other time while the person is detained (Code C para 2.4, Code H para 2.5). The lawyer has no right under the code to insist on an entry being made in the custody record (see further para 2.114 below). As a result of an amendment to PACE s54 by CJA 2003 s8, the former requirement to record in the custody record everything that a person has with him or her when the person is detained is now at the discretion of the custody officer (see Code C, Code H para 4.4). If a record is made, it does not have to be made in the custody record (PACE s54(2A)). However, the detained person should be asked to check any record that is made, and sign it as correct.[98] The purpose of this change was, purportedly, to save police time and it enables the police to place the property in a sealed bag without specifying it on the custody record. The defence lawyer should ask the custody officer what property was taken from the client on arrival at the police station and, in particular, whether it included anything of potential evidential value. The lawyer should also ask whether a record was made and, if so, whether the client was shown it and asked to sign it. If so, it is difficult to see what justification there would be for refusing to permit the lawyer to see the record.

2.98   Where a medical examination by a doctor or other healthcare professional has been requested or conducted, Code C para 9.15 and Code H para 9.17 set out what must be recorded in the custody record:

- the arrangements made for an examination, and any complaint about treatment by police made by the suspect, and any relevant remarks by the custody officer;
- any arrangements made regarding clinical attention under Code C para 9.5 or Code H para 9.6;
- any request for a clinical examination made by the suspect, and arrangements made in response;

98  Home Office Circular 60/2003 para 5.5.

- the injury, ailment, condition or other reason which made it necessary to make any of the above arrangements;
- any clinical directions and advice given to the police by the health-care professional;
- if applicable, the responses received when attempting to rouse a person who is suspected of being intoxicated through drink or drugs, or whose level of consciousness causes concern.

Where a healthcare professional is called in to see a suspect, the custody officer must ask him or her to advise, among other things, about when to carry out an interview (Code C para 9.13, Code H para 9.15). Fitness for interview must be considered by reference to Code C and Code H Annex G, para 7, which states that the healthcare professional's determination and any advice or recommendations should be 'made in writing and form part of the custody record'. Subject to the above, the healthcare professional's own notes do not form part of the custody record, but if the professional's clinical findings are not recorded in the custody record, the record must show where they are recorded (Code C para 9.16, Code H para 9.18). While Code C and Code H do not provide that the suspect or the solicitor have a right to see these if they are not in the custody record, it is difficult to see, subject to practicability, what justification there could be for refusing access to them. This is particularly so if the healthcare professional was called in for therapeutic, as opposed to evidential, reasons.

2.99     The detained person or their legal representative or appropriate adult has a right to a copy of the custody record if a request is made when the person is taken before a court or within 12 months of release from detention. Such request must be satisfied as soon as practicable (Code C para 2.4A, Code H para 2.6). If the police are seeking a warrant of further detention the lawyer should request an up-to-date copy of the custody record. The detained person and their lawyer or appropriate adult also have a right to see the original custody record after the person has left police detention provided reasonable notice is given (Code C para 2.5, Code H para 2.7).

2.100    Note that any audio or video recording made in the custody area does not form part of the custody record (Code C para 2.1, Code H para 2.2). Many police stations have video-recording facilities for custody areas, and some also have video-recording facilities in some or all of the cells. Where they exist, clients should be advised of the potential implications, and the lawyer should consider the evidential potential they may represent which, depending on the circumstances, may be favourable or contrary to the interests of the client.

## Information that must be recorded

2.101    The matters which have to be recorded are extensive, and those required by PACE and Code C include the following.[99] (Note that some recording requirements are noted more than once where they come under more than one heading.)

---

99  The recording requirements under Code H are similar to those in Code C.

## Authorisation of detention

2.102
- The reason and grounds for detention of an arrested person (PACE s37(4), Code C para 3.23).
- The reason for detention of a person charged and not released (PACE s38(3)).
- The reason for imposing or varying bail conditions (BA 1976 s5A(3)).
- The offence for which the person has been arrested and the reasons for the arrest (Code C para 3.4). This should include the reason why arrest was believed to be necessary (See Code C NfG 10B, Code G para 4.3). If the person is answering to street bail, the custody officer should link any documentation held in relation to the arrest with the custody record (Code C para 3.25).
- Grounds for authorising detention beyond 24 hours (PACE s42(5)(b), Code C para 15.16).
- The signature of the detained person confirming receipt of the notice setting out their rights under Code C para 3.2 (Code C para 3.2).
- Any comment made by the detained person in relation to the arresting officer's account of the arrest, or in relation to the decision to detain the detained person (Code C para 3.4).
- The signature of the detained person signifying whether or not the person wishes to receive legal advice at the time of initial detention (Code C para 3.5(b)).
- The decision taken under Code C para 3.5 as to whether the detained person is or might be in need of medical attention, or requires an appropriate adult or help to check documentation (Code C para 3.5(d)).
- Details of special action taken in respect of detainees who are deaf, juvenile, mentally disordered or vulnerable, with a visual handicap, or unable to read (Code C para 3.24).

## Conditions of detention and review

2.103
- The reason for postponement of a review (PACE s40(7), Code C para 15.13).
- The time of and reason for transfer to another police station and time the person is released from detention (Code C para 2.3).
- Details of replacement clothing and meals offered (Code C para 8.9).
- Details of any complaint by a suspect regarding their treatment (Code C para 9.15(a)).
- Arrangements made for examination of a detained person by a healthcare professional, requests made for medical examination by a detained person and arrangements made in response, clinical directions and advice given (including clinical findings or details of where these are recorded), and medication that a detained person had on him or her on arrival at the police station and any medication that the person claims to need but does not have with him or her (Code C paras 9.15 and 9.16).
- The responses received when attempting to rouse a person believed to be intoxicated, under Code C Annex H (Code C para 9.15(f)).
- Consultation with a healthcare professional about medication to be taken or applied in compliance with clinical directions prescribed before detention (Code C para 9.9).

- Times and reasons that the detained person is not in the custody of the custody officer, and the reason for any refusal to deliver a detainee out of that custody (Code C para 12.10).
- The use of any restraints, the reasons for it, and any arrangements for enhanced supervision (Code C para 8.11).
- The fact that a citizen of a Commonwealth or other foreign country has been informed of their rights under Code C s7 (Code C para 7.5).
- The reminder that must be given under Code C para 15.4 before conducting a review or determining whether to extend detention (Code C para 15.12).
- The grounds for and extent of any delay in conducting a review (Code C para 15.13).
- The outcome of each review and application for warrant of further detention (Code C para 15.16).

## Custody records

2.104
- A note of any inspection of the original custody record under Code C para 2.5.
- The fact of and time of any refusal to sign a custody record (Code C para 2.7).

## Legal advice

2.105
- The fact of and time of a request for legal advice, and action taken in response (PACE s58(2), Code C para 6.16).
- The grounds for delay in allowing access to legal advice (PACE s58(9)(b), Code C Annex B para 13).
- The fact that an interview has been conducted in the absence of a solicitor, where the detainee has asked for legal advice, or the fact that a solicitor has been required to leave an interview (Code C para 6.17).
- The signature of the detained person signifying whether or not the person wishes to receive legal advice at the time of initial detention (Code C para 3.5(b)).
- Any reasons given by the detained person for waiving his or her right to legal advice (Code C para 6.5).
- The fact of arrival at the police station of a solicitor wishing to see a detained person, and the decision of the detained person about whether he or she wishes to see the solicitor (Code C para 6.15).
- The reminder that the detained person is entitled to legal advice, which must be given by the review officer before conducting a review or determining whether to extend detention (Code C para 15.12).
- Where a solicitor is initially instructed by a third party and attends the police station, the detained person's signature indicating whether or not he or she wishes to see the solicitor (Code C Annex B para 4).
- Where the right to advice has been delayed, but the grounds for such delay expire within 36 hours (48 hours if the person is detained under the TA 2000), the fact that the detained person has been asked if the person wishes to exercise this right, and the detained person's endorsement about whether he or she then wishes to receive legal advice (Code C Annex B paras 6 and 11).

- The grounds for any action taken under Code C Annex B (Code C Annex B para 13).
- The fact that a detained person is reminded of his or her right to legal advice before being asked to provide an intimate sample (Code D para 6.3).

## Contact with others

2.106
- Details of requests by the detained person to have someone notified of their arrest, details of all letters, messages, telephone calls made or received and visits to the detained person, and refusal by a detained person to have information given to an enquirer (Code C para 5.8).
- The grounds for delaying intimation of arrest (PACE s56(6)(b), Code C Annex B para 6).
- Where the right to intimation has been delayed, but the grounds for such delay expire within 36 hours (48 hours if the person is detained under the TA 2000) the fact that the detained person has been asked if he or she wishes to exercise this right (Code C Annex B paras 6 and 11).
- The grounds for any action taken under Code C Annex B (Code C Annex B para 13).
- The fact that a citizen of a Commonwealth or other foreign country has been informed of his or her rights under Code C s7 (Code C para 7.5).

## Interviews

2.107
- The grounds for commencing the interview of a suspect who has been allowed access to a solicitor before the solicitor arrives (Code C para 6.17).
- Any decision to refuse access to, or to exclude from an interview, a clerk or legal executive (Code C para 6.14).
- The grounds for interviewing a detained person under Code C para 11.18 (urgent interviews of persons under the influence of drink or drugs, of juveniles or mentally disordered or handicapped people in the absence of an appropriate adult, or of those with language or hearing difficulties in the absence of an interpreter) (Code C para 11.20).
- The reasons for not using an interview room and actions taken under Code C para 12.5 in respect of a person who takes steps to prevent himself or herself from being interviewed (Code C paras 3.4 and 12.11).
- The reasons for not tape-recording an interview that should be tape-recorded (Code E para 3.3).

## Juveniles and others at risk

2.108
- Details of special action taken in respect of detainees who are deaf, juvenile, mentally disordered, or with a visual handicap (Code C para 3.24).
- Where a juvenile is kept in a cell, the reasons for this (Code C para 8.10).
- A juvenile's decision not to have an appropriate adult present at an intimate search (although it is not specifically required that this should be in the custody record) (Code C Annex A para 5).

- Action taken to call an interpreter for a detained person who has difficulty understanding English, or who is deaf or who has a speech difficulty (Code C para 13.11).
- The grounds for interviewing a detained person under Code C para 11.18, which relates to urgent interviews of persons under the influence of drink or drugs, juveniles or mentally vulnerable people in the absence of an appropriate adult, or those with language or hearing difficulties in the absence of an interpreter (Code C para 11.20).

## Searches and samples

2.109
- Information relating to the taking of fingerprints, intimate and non-intimate samples, or impressions (PACE s61(7), (7A) and (8), s61A(5) and (6), s62(7), (7A) and (8) and s63(8B) and (9), and Code D para 6.10).
- Information relating to drug testing under PACE ss63B and 63C (PACE s63B(5B) and s63C(4), Code C para 17.12).
- A juvenile's decision not to have an appropriate adult present at an intimate search (although it is not specifically required that this should be in the custody record) (Code C Annex A para 5).
- If an intimate search is carried out, the parts of the person's body that were searched, who carried out the search, who was present, the reasons for and the results of the search, and if carried out by a police officer, the reason why it was impracticable for it to be carried out by a medically-qualified person (Code C Annex A paras 7 and 8).
- If a strip search is carried out, the reasons for this and the result (Code C Annex A para 12).

## Identification procedures

2.110
- The reason why it is not practicable to hold a video identification or an identification parade requested by a suspect (Code D para 3.26).
- The refusal of a detained person to co-operate in an identification parade, group identification or video identification and, if relevant, the grounds for obtaining images in accordance with Code D para 3.20 (Code D para 3.27).
- The reason for taking fingerprints or footwear impressions without consent and of any force used (Code D paras 4.8A, 4.8 and 4.20).
- The fact that the detained person has been told that their fingerprints or footwear impression may be the subject of a speculative search (Code D paras 4.8A and 4.21).
- Information regarding the search, examination or photographing of a person or of any identifying marks found on the person, and any force used (Code D paras 5.17 and 5.18).
- The reasons for taking a sample or impression and, where relevant, its destruction, and any force used (Code D para 6.10).
- The fact that a person has been informed that samples may be the subject of a speculative search (Code D para 6.10).
- The fact that a detained person has been reminded of their right to legal advice before being asked to provide an intimate sample (Code D para 6.11).

- A record of a warning under Code D para 6.3 that refusal to provide an intimate sample without good cause may harm the detained person's case if it comes to trial (Code D para 6.11).

### Bail

2.111 • Where a custody officer grants conditional bail, or varies conditions, the officer must enter a note of the reasons in the custody record and must give the bailed person a copy (BA 1976 s5A).

## Use of the custody record

2.112 The significance of the custody record was summed up by a custody officer who commented, 'If it's not in the custody record, it didn't happen'.[100] It may be used by the police as a mechanism for legitimating events that occur during the period of detention. Equally it may be used by the lawyer in a number of ways that have potential benefit to the client.

2.113 The lawyer should carefully examine the custody record when first attending at the police station,[101] because it will provide valuable information on the police view of the history of the case. It will contain information that may be useful in any negotiations with the police, for example, the grounds on which detention was authorised. It will also contain information that may need to be checked with the client, for example, the address given, the reason for arrest, the time of the request for legal advice, and anything allegedly said by the suspect on arrest or subsequently. Furthermore, it will also contain information that is essential for the lawyer to carry out their duties: the time of arrest, the time of arrival at the police station, the time detention was authorised. Finally, it may contain information that should alert the lawyer to the need to make further enquiries, or the need to be cautious, for example, a deleted or amended entry, or a late entry which, in the circumstances, gives cause for suspicion (see further para 4.20 below). The lawyer should be mindful of the fact that important information, such as property taken from the client on being detained (see para 2.97 above), may be missing from the custody record. In some cases, especially where the investigating officer intends to use the strategy of phased disclosure (see para 4.28 below), the reason for arrest and/or detention that is recorded may be incomplete or misleading.

2.114 The custody record may be used by the lawyer during the period of detention. If significant events occur – if access to advice is denied, representations at review are made, representations about bail after charge are made, or the client complains of unauthorised visits by police officers – the adviser should press to have this noted on the custody record even if this is not formally required by PACE or the Codes of Practice. A written record of such an event may have a significant impact at any subsequent trial. Asking for something to be noted on the custody record may also be an important negotiating tactic. If, for example, access to a client is being denied, a demand that the lawyer's representations be inserted on

100 Reported in K Bottomley et al, 'Safeguarding the rights of suspects in police custody', unpublished paper presented to the British Criminology Conference, Bristol, 1989.
101 See para 2.97 above regarding the lawyer's right to see the custody record.

the record may lead the custody officer to reconsider the decision. The lawyer should keep their own record of such an event, whether or not it is entered in the custody record.

2.115     The custody record may be significant at any subsequent trial. A copy of the custody record should normally be requested if the client is charged or summonsed, and should be carefully scrutinised. For example, the result of the risk assessment conducted under Code C paras 3.6–3.10 may cast doubt on the client's fitness for interview or, of course, may be of assistance to the prosecution. The record may show that a request for legal advice was not acted on – relevant if an application to exclude evidence of a confession is subsequently made. Similarly, the custody record may be important for what it does not contain. Absence of any record that the suspect was reminded of their right to legal advice at review may be critical in an application to exclude evidence. Likewise, absence of any record that the suspect was provided with meals or refreshments. In appropriate cases, prosecution witnesses may be cross-examined on the custody record.

## Right to have someone informed of an arrest

2.116     PACE s56 confers a right, often known as the right of intimation, on a person arrested and detained to have a friend, relative or other person known to the arrested person or who is likely to take an interest in the person's welfare informed of the fact of the arrest as soon as practicable and at public expense. The right applies to any arrested person and not just those arrested for an offence, and may be exercised each time the person is taken to another police station (PACE s56(8), Code C para 5.3). A person detained under TA 2000 s41 or Sch 7 has a similar right (TA 2000 Sch 8 para 6, Code H para 5.3). If the person requested cannot be contacted, up to two alternatives may be nominated, and if they too cannot be contacted the custody officer has a discretion to allow further attempts (Code C, Code H para 5.1). If the detainee does not know anyone to contact, or contact cannot be made with a relative or friend specified, the custody officer should consider any local voluntary organisation that might be able to help (Code C NfG 5C). If a friend, relative or other such person asks the police the whereabouts of the detained person, this information must be given, provided that the person in custody agrees and Code C Annex B does not apply (Code C para 5.5). Furthermore, the person may receive visits at the discretion of the custody officer (Code C para 5.4), and Code C NfG 5B indicates that visits should be allowed when possible.[102] The right of intimation under s56 does not confer a right on the suspect to speak personally to the person contacted (although see para 2.118 below).

2.117     In the case of a person detained for an indictable offence (see para 2.21 above) the right of intimation as set out above may be delayed on the authority of an inspector or above for up to 36 hours, on the same grounds as access to legal advice can be delayed (see para 2.139 below) (PACE s56,

---

102  For persons detained under TA 2000 s41, the guidance is more extensive. See Code H NfG 5B and 5C.

Code C para 5.2 and Annex B). Where a person is detained under TA 2000 s41 or Sch 7, intimation may be delayed for up to 48 hours, on the same grounds as access to legal advice can be delayed (see para 2.145 below) (TA 2000 Sch 8 para 8, Code H para 5.2 and Annex B).

2.118    In addition to the right of intimation, a person arrested and held in custody should be supplied with writing materials and allowed to speak on the telephone for a reasonable time to one person (Code C and Code H para 5.6). However, this may be delayed or denied if the person is detained in respect of an indictable offence (see para 2.21 above) and an officer of the rank of inspector or above considers that sending a letter or making a telephone call may result in any of the consequences set out in Code C or Code H Annex B paras 1 or 2 (interference with evidence connected to an indictable offence, harm to other persons, alerting other suspects, hindering recovery of the value of property that constitutes the benefit from criminal conduct under Proceeds of Crime Act (POCA) 2002 Part 2). Where a person is detained under TA 2000 Sch 7 or s41, access to writing materials, or to a telephone call, may be delayed or denied if it may lead to the consequences set out in Code H Annex B paras 1 or 2 (the same consequences as under paras 1 and 2, plus interference with information gathering about acts of terrorism or alerting others) (Code C and Code H para 5.6). If communication is allowed under Code C or Code H para 5.6, the person must be told that the police can listen in to any telephone call or read any letter, and that information gained could be used in evidence (Code C and Code H para 5.7). Where appropriate, an interpreter may make the telephone call or write the letter on behalf of the detained person (Code C and Code H NfG 5A).

## Right to legal advice

2.119    All persons arrested and held in custody at a police station have a statutory right to consult a solicitor. This is in accordance with the rights guaranteed by ECHR art 6(3)(c) as interpreted by the European Court of Human Rights (ECtHR) in *Salduz v Turkey*.[103] There is statutory provision for delaying access to a solicitor prior to charge provided certain conditions are satisfied, which may have the effect of denying the right altogether. However, this may amount to a breach of article 6(3)(a) (see para 13.10 below). 'Volunteers' also have a right to consult a solicitor.

## Volunteers

2.120    A 'volunteer' (see para 2.151 below) is entitled to legal advice at any time and without hindrance. This is so whether the volunteer is at a police station (Code C NfG 1A) or elsewhere. However, if at a police station, the volunteer does not have to be told of this entitlement unless the volunteer asks (Code C para 3.22) or is arrested or cautioned (Code C para 3.21). If

---

103 (2008) 49 EHRR 421. Note that the right to legal advice 'belongs' to the suspect. PACE s58 does not confer a right on the solicitor to provide it (see *Rixon and others v Chief Constable of Kent* (2000) *Times* 5 April).

arrested, the person must be taken before the custody officer, who must notify the person of his or her rights in the same way as for other detained persons. If cautioned without being arrested, the officer who gives the caution must inform the person, among other things, that he or she is entitled to free and independent legal advice. The officer must also tell the person that the person is entitled to speak to a solicitor on the telephone and must ask the person if he or she wishes to do so (Code C para 3.21).

## Persons under arrest

2.121   A person who has been arrested, whether or not for an offence, and who is being held in custody in a police station or other premises is entitled to consult a solicitor privately at any time (PACE s58(1)). A person detained at a police station under TA 2000 Sch 7 or s41 has the same right (TA 2000 Sch 8 para 7), although there are certain limitations to the right to see the solicitor in private (see para 2.136 below). The police can only delay access to a solicitor in limited circumstances. Access can never lawfully be denied altogether, although it is possible for access to be delayed until the time that a person is charged.

### Information about the right to advice

2.122   Information must be given about the right to independent legal advice, and the fact that such advice is available free of charge:

1) at the time that a person is brought to a police station under arrest, or is arrested having initially attended voluntarily (Code C, Code H para 3.1);
2) immediately before the beginning or re-commencement of any interview at a police station or other authorised place of detention (Code C para 11.2, Code H para 11.3);
3) before conducting a review of detention, or before determining whether to extend the maximum period of detention (Code C para 15.4);
4) after charge or being informed that he or she may be prosecuted, where the police wish to bring to the suspect's attention any statement or the content of any interview, or where they wish to re-interview (Code C paras 16.4 and 16.5);
5) before being asked to provide an intimate sample (Code D para 6.3);
6) before an intimate drug search under s55(1)(b) (Code C Annex A para 2B), or x-ray or ultrasound scan under PACE s55A(1) (Code C Annex K para 3);
7) before conducting an interview after charge (Code C para 16.5);
8) before an identification parade, or group or video identification occurs (Code D para 3.17).

2.123   If a person, on being informed or reminded of their right to legal advice, declines to speak to a solicitor in person, the officer must point out that the right to legal advice includes the right to speak to a solicitor on the telephone. The officer must then ask the person whether the person wishes to speak to the solicitor. If the person declines, the officer must ask the reason why, and any answer must be recorded. However, once it is clear that the suspect does not wish to speak to a solicitor at all, the officer must cease to ask the person the reasons for the decision (Code C para 6.5, Code H para 6.4). Failure to give such information may give cause for complaint, and may lead to exclusion of evidence at a subsequent trial (see chapter 13). The ECtHR has held that the waiver of the right to legal advice: 'must not only be voluntary, but must also constitute a knowing and intelligent relinquishment ... it must be shown that [the suspect] could reasonably have foreseen what the consequences of his conduct would be' (see para 13.11 below).[104] Therefore, if relevant, the defence lawyer should carefully check the circumstance in which a suspect declined legal advice.

## Juveniles and others at risk

2.124    A juvenile or mentally disordered or mentally vulnerable person has a personal right to seek advice, which should not be delayed pending arrival of an appropriate adult. The appropriate adult has an independent right to seek advice (Code C paras 3.19 and 6.5A; Code H paras 3.20 and 6.6). See further chapter 11.

## Police action when a request is made

2.125    Where a request is made for legal advice, the suspect must be permitted to consult a solicitor as soon as practicable, and the custody officer must act without delay to secure its provision (PACE s58(4) and Code C para 6.5, Code H para 6.4) (subject to the power to delay access to a lawyer – see paras 2.139 and 2.149 below). It has been held that a delay of 22 minutes in attempting to contact a lawyer amounted to a breach of PACE s58(4).[105]

2.126    Following the introduction of the Criminal Defence Service (CDS) Direct scheme and the Defence Solicitor Call Centre (DSCC), the duties of the police where a request for legal advice is made differ depending upon whether the suspect is to pay privately for legal advice, or is to rely on legal aid.[106] If the suspect is to pay privately, the suspect must be given the opportunity to consult a specific solicitor or another solicitor from that solicitor's firm, and must be given the opportunity to nominate alternatives if a solicitor is unavailable by these means. If the suspect is to rely on legal aid, the police must contact the DSCC. The DSCC will determine whether the case is covered by the CDS Direct scheme and, if so, will direct the request to CDS Direct. If it is not covered by the CDS Direct scheme, the DSCC will attempt to contact the nominated solicitor (is the suspect has nominated a solicitor or firm) or, alternatively, the duty solicitor (Code C NfG 6B2 and 6D). See further paras 1.56–1.59 above. Apart from carrying out their duties under NfG 6B2, a police officer must not advise the suspect about any particular firm of solicitors (Code C, Code H NfG 6B) and must not attempt to dissuade the person from seeking advice (Code C para 6.4, Code H para 6.3).

104  *Pishchalnikov v Russia*, ECtHR 24 September 2009, No 7025/04.
105  *Gearing v DPP* [2008] EWHC 1695 (Admin).
106  Note that the position following the introduction of the CDS Direct scheme and the DSCC is very unsatisfactory. In particular, Code C does not indicate how the police are to determine whether the suspect intends to pay privately, or what information the police should give about eligibility for legal aid.

2.127   Once a request has been made by the suspect, the suspect must not be interviewed or continue to be interviewed until the suspect has received advice unless (Code C para 6.6, Code H para 6.7):

1) Code C or Code H Annex B applies, which refer to the grounds for delaying access to legal advice under PACE s58 or TA 2000 Sch 8; or

2) an officer of the rank of superintendent or above has reasonable grounds for believing that:
   - delay might lead to interference with, or harm to, evidence connected with an offence; lead to interference or physical harm to other people or serious loss of, or damage to, property; lead to alerting other people suspected of having committed an offence but not yet been arrested for it; or hinder the recovery of property obtained in consequence of the commission of an offence (in which case questioning must cease as soon as sufficient information to avert the risk has been obtained, unless other grounds for continuing the interview in the absence of legal advice apply (Code C, Code H para 6.7); or
   - where a solicitor, including a duty solicitor, has been contacted and has agreed to attend, awaiting their arrival would cause unreasonable delay to the progress of the investigation;[107] or

3) the solicitor requested:
   - cannot be contacted;
   - has previously indicated that he or she does not want to be contacted; or
   - having been contacted, declines to attend,
   and the person has been told of but declines advice from a duty solicitor, provided starting or continuing the interview is authorised by an officer of the rank of inspector or above;[108] or

4) the person who wants legal advice changes their mind, provided agreement to be interviewed without receiving legal advice is recorded in writing or on tape and it is authorised by an officer of the rank of inspector or above. The authorising officer must, before giving authority, enquire into the person's reasons for their change of mind, and the reasons given and the name of the authorising officer must be recorded in the interview record. Authorisation may be given over the telephone provided that the officer is able to satisfy himself or herself of the reasons for the person's change of mind and is satisfied that it is proper for the interview to continue in those circumstances (Code C NfG 6I, Code H NfG 6H).

Where a person is interviewed in the absence of legal advice under 1) or 2) above, inferences from 'silence' cannot be drawn and the person should be cautioned in the terms set out in Code C annex C para 2, rather than the 'normal' caution set out in Code C para 10.5. Evidence of such interviews is admissible at trial in the normal way.[109]

---

107 Note that if an interview is conducted in the circumstances described in 1) or 2), inferences cannot be drawn under CJPOA 1994 s34, s36 or s37 (see para 5.66 below).

108 Note that in these circumstances, the prohibition on drawing inferences does not apply.

109 *R v Ibrahim and others* [2008] EWCA Crim 880, but see para 13.10 below.

2.128    The rule that a person who has requested advice should not be interviewed until he or she has received it does not amount to a requirement that the lawyer must be allowed to be present at any police interview. The right in Code C para 6.8 and Code H para 6.9 to have a solicitor present in interview is subject to the exceptions in Code C para 6.6 and Code H para 6.7 (see para 2.127 above).[110] Therefore, if initial advice is given by the lawyer, either on the telephone or in person, the lawyer should make clear to the custody officer whether the lawyer wishes to be present at any interview, and should ask that this be noted in the custody record. If this is not done there is a danger that the police can argue that advice has been received (albeit on the telephone) and that an interview can thus proceed in the absence of a lawyer.[111] Since an interview may proceed in the absence of legal advice if the suspect changes their mind, any initial telephone advice to the person in custody should include a warning of this possibility (see further para 3.52 below).

2.129    The statutory drink/driving procedure under the RTA 1988 s7 or the Transport and Works Act 1992 s31 does not amount to an interview and, therefore, the suspect has no right to delay the procedure pending legal advice being received.[112]

2.130    If the police proceed with an interview contrary to the above provisions, this may provide grounds for complaint and/or for seeking exclusion of evidence subsequently obtained (see chapter 13).

### 'Arrested and held in custody'

2.131    The right to legal advice applies to persons arrested for offences and also to persons arrested for other reasons, for example, for breach of bail conditions or under the MHA 1983 s136. While the right extends to persons held in custody at places other than a police station, it has been held that it applies only once detention has been authorised under PACE s37. Thus, the right did not apply to a suspect arrested and held in a hotel room.[113] However, where detention has been authorised, the right to advice under

110  It was held in *R v Chief Constable of RUC ex p Begley* [1997] 4 All ER 833, [1997] 1 WLR 1475 that there is no common law right to have a solicitor present in a police interview. However, it has been held by the ECtHR that the right to fair trial under ECHR art 6 does include a right to have a lawyer present in interview where this was a necessary counterweight to the psychologically coercive conditions in an interrogation centre (*Magee v UK* (2001) 31 EHRR 35), and this was reinforced in *Brusco v France* ECHR 14 October 2010 No 1466/07 (and see para 13.10 below).

111  This would also have the effect of permitting inferences. See para 5.66 below.

112  See Code C para 11.1A, and *DPP v Billington and others* [1988] 1 All ER 435; (1988) 87 Cr App R 68; [1997] Crim LR 772, *DPP v Rouse; DPP v Davis* (1992) 94 Cr App R 185; [1991] Crim LR 911, *Campbell v DPP* [2002] EWHC 1314 (Admin), *Kennedy v CPS* [2002] EWHC 2297 (Admin), *Whitley v DPP* [2003] EWHC 2512 (Admin), *CPS v Rice* [2004] EWHC 508 (Admin), *Myles v DPP* [2004] EWHC 594 (Admin), and *Gearing v DPP* [2008] EWHC 1695 (Admin). It was held in *Cowper v DPP* [2009] EWHC 2165 (Admin) that the introduction of the CDS Direct scheme made no difference.

113  *R v Kerawalla* [1991] Crim LR 451, but see the critical commentary at 453. See also *Kircup v DPP* [2004] Crim LR 230. The Court of Appeal took an apparently contrary view in *R v Sanusi* [1992] Crim LR 43. In any event, arguably a person in such circumstances has a common law right to legal advice. See *R v Lemsatef* [1977] 2 All ER 835; (1977) 64 Cr App R 242, and *R v Chief Constable of South Wales ex p Merrick* [1994] 2 All ER 560; [1994] Crim LR 852.

section 58 continues to apply even if the suspect is taken to other premises, for example, for a search to be conducted, or is removed to hospital because of ill health. It also probably continues to apply after charge and first court appearance if the defendant continues to be in custody at a police station and the investigation is continuing.[114]

### 'Solicitor'

2.132   PACE refers only to solicitors, but this is significantly modified by Code C para 6.12 and Code H para 6.13, which defines 'solicitor', for the purposes of the Codes, as meaning a solicitor who holds a current practising certificate or an accredited or probationary representative included on the register of representatives maintained by the Legal Services Commission. 'Solicitor' has the same meaning in Code D (Code D para 2.6), Code E (Code E para 1.5) and Code F (Code F para 1.5). By implication, 'solicitor' does not include a representative (who is neither accredited nor probationary) of a solicitor acting privately, although arguably a solicitor acting privately can send such a representative to advise at the police station if the client consents. Accredited and probationary representatives may be denied access to the police station on the authority of an officer of the rank of inspector or above who considers that their visit will hinder the investigation of crime (Code C para 6.12A, Code H para 6.14, and see para 4.4 below).

### 'Privately'

2.133   Other than in TA 2000 cases (see para 2.136 below), all persons entitled to consult a lawyer are entitled to do so in private. Code C NfG 6J describes the right to consult in private as fundamental, and states that if written or oral communications between the lawyer and their client are compromised by being overheard, listened to, or read, the right is effectively denied. 'Privately' is not defined, and the police have argued that the right to advice in private does not prevent the police from observing the lawyer and client, for example, through glass walls. However, it has been held in relation to lawyer/client consultations at court that '[t]he principle that the defendant is entitled to private and confidential discussions with his legal advisers, unsupervised *and unobserved* by police officers ... is too elementary to require citation of authority' (emphasis added).[115] It is suggested that this principle also applies at the police station.

2.134   Telephone advice raises particular practical problems in terms of privacy, and this has been exacerbated with the introduction of the CDS Direct scheme under which publicly funded legal advice is limited to advice on the telephone in certain circumstances (see para 1.57 above). Code C NfG 6J provides that where a person speaks to a solicitor on the telephone, this should be in private unless impracticable because of the design and layout

---

114  The section 58 right does not apply to a person who has been remanded in custody by magistrates, although the detainee then has a common law right to legal advice (*R v Chief Constable of South Wales ex p Merrick* [1994] 2 All ER 560; [1994] Crim LR 852).

115  *CPS v LR* [2010] EWCA Crim 924, at para 20.

of the custody area or the location of the telephones.[116] This is arguably contrary to PACE s58 under which the right to consult a solicitor privately is not qualified by reference to practicality. It has been held that absence of private facilities for consultations with a solicitor was not contrary to the applicant's ECHR article 6 (right to a fair trial) rights, but it is suggested that this should be revisited in the light of the developing ECtHR case-law on the right to legal advice (see para 13.12 below).[117] Note for Guidance 6J states that the normal expectation is that private facilities will be available unless they are already in use.

2.135   Covert surveillance of private consultations between a lawyer and client at a police station are governed by Regulation of Investigatory Powers Act (RIPA) 2000. It has been held that the power to conduct covert surveillance takes precedence over the right to legal advice in private, although it must be authorised under RIPA 2000 as intrusive surveillance.[118] Even if properly authorised, use at trial of material obtained by such surveillance may breach the person's right to fair trial under ECHR art 6. There is no obligation under RIPA 2000 to inform either the suspect or their lawyer of such covert surveillance, either before or after the event.

2.136   Where a person is detained under TA 2000 Sch 7 or s41, a direction may be given by an Assistant Chief Constable (or Commander) or above that a consultation with a solicitor may be conducted only in the sight and hearing of a 'qualified officer' (TA 2000 Sch 8 para 9(1) and (2), Code H para 6.5). Authorisation may only be given if the officer has reasonable grounds for believing that one of more of the following will be the consequence (TA 2000 Sch 8 para 9(3)):[119]

- interference with or harm to evidence of a serious offence;[120]
- interference with or physical injury to any person;

116  Evidence suggests that most custody offices do not have facilities for private telephone calls. See T Bucke and D Brown, *In police custody: police powers and suspects' rights under the revised PACE Codes of Practice*, Research Study 174 (Home Office, London, 1997), p25.

117  *R (on the application of M) v Commissioner of Police for the Metropolis* [2002] Crim LR 215, but see the critical commentary. See also R Pattenden and L Skinns, 'Choice, privacy and publicly funded legal advice at police stations' (2010) 73 *Modern Law Review* 3, 349. For a report of a successful action for breach of statutory duty where the police insisted on being present when a suspect spoke to his solicitor on the telephone, see *Roques v Metropolitan Police Commissioner* (1997) September *Legal Action* 23.

118  *Re Mc E; In re M; In re C (AP) and another (AP)* [2009] UKHL 15. See the Regulation of Investigatory Powers (Extension of Authorisation Provisions: Legal Consultation) Order 2010 SI No 461.

119  In *Brennan v UK* [2002] Crim LR 216 the ECtHR, while not holding that these restrictions interfered with the right to fair trial under ECHR article 6(3)(c), emphasised the need for compelling reasons for the interference with the right to advice, such as evidence that the lawyer would collaborate with the suspect. See Home Office Circular 40/2003 which provides that authorisation should only be granted if it is proportionate to do so in the light of all the circumstances. The officer should consider whether the suspect has been initially co-operative and making admissions (which 'may indicate that the suspect is in need of legal advice and as such required uninhibited access to his solicitor') and whether the suspect could be considered vulnerable. See also Code H NpG 6I.

120  TA 2000 Sch 8 para 8(9) provides that a 'serious offence' is an indictable offence (see para 2.21 above) or any offence mentioned in TA 2000 s40(1)(a) or attempt or conspiracy to commit such an offence.

- the alerting of persons who are suspected of having committed a serious offence but who have not been arrested for it;
- the hindering of the recovery of property obtained as a result of a serious arrestable offence or in respect of which a forfeiture order could be made under TA 2000 s23;
- interference with the gathering of information about the commission, preparation or instigation of acts of terrorism;
- the alerting of a person and thereby making it more difficult to prevent an act of terrorism;
- the alerting of a person, thereby making it more difficult to secure a person's apprehension, prosecution or conviction in connection with the commission, preparation or instigation of an act of terrorism;
- hindering the recovery of the value of the property constituting a benefit from their criminal conduct (which is to be decided in accordance with POCA 2002 Part 2).

A 'qualified officer' is a uniformed officer of at least the rank of inspector, who has no connection with the detained person's case (TA 2000 Sch 8 para 9(4)). A direction ceases to have effect once the reason for giving it ceases to subsist (TA 2000 Sch 8 para 9(5)).

### 'At any time'

2.137    A person entitled to legal advice is entitled to receive it at any time. Subject to the power of the police to delay access to advice under PACE s58 and TA 2000 Sch 8 (see paras 2.139 and 2.145 below), this right is not qualified in any way and may be exercised at any time.

2.138        The fact that a person is entitled to legal advice at any time may assist a lawyer who is experiencing difficulty in speaking to their client either in person or on the telephone. PACE does not limit the right by any consideration of practicality or convenience. There may be difficulty, however, if the right to receive advice at any time is used during the course of a police interview to prevent the interview from proceeding effectively (see further para 7.50 below).

## Delaying access to advice – valid reasons

### Grounds for delay – detention under PACE

2.139    Where an arrested person held in police custody requests a lawyer, the police may only delay access if:

- the person is detained in respect of an indictable offence (see para 2.21 above);
- the person has not been charged; and
- delay is authorised by an officer of the rank of a superintendent or above (PACE s58(6), Code C Annex B).

Note, however, that in some circumstances an interview may proceed before advice has been received (see para 2.127 above). There is no power to delay access to legal advice where a person is detained in respect of a summary-only offence, or where a person has been arrested otherwise than for an offence.

2.140    The maximum period of delay is 36 hours from the relevant time (see para 2.71 above), and the right may be delayed only for as long as necessary (PACE s58(5), Code C Annex B para 6), which should be determined according to the reason why delay was authorised. If the grounds for delay cease to exist the person must, as soon as practicable, be asked if the person wishes to consult a solicitor, and appropriate action must then be taken. If the police seek a warrant of further detention under PACE s43, the person must be allowed access to a solicitor in reasonable time before the hearing, even if this is within the 36-hour period (Code C Annex B para 7).

2.141    Provided that the other conditions are satisfied, an officer of the rank of superintendent or above may authorise delay if the officer has reasonable grounds for believing that exercise of the right (PACE s58(8), Code C Annex B paras 1 and 2):

- will lead to interference with or harm to evidence connected with an indictable offence or interference with or physical injury to other people (PACE s58(8)(a));
- will lead to the alerting of other people suspected of having committed such an offence but not yet arrested for it (PACE s58(8)(b));
- will hinder the recovery of property (PACE s58(8)(c)); or
- will hinder the recovery of the value of the property by which the person has benefited as a result of their criminal conduct (which is to be decided in accordance with POCA 2002 Part 2) (PACE s58(8A)).

2.142    POCA 2002 Part 2 concerns confiscation of the value of a benefit derived from criminal conduct and requires a Crown Court in certain circumstances to make a confiscation order in respect of a person who is convicted of an offence in proceedings before the Crown Court, or is committed for sentence to a Crown Court under the Powers of Criminal Courts (Sentencing) Act 2000 or under POCA 2002 s70.

2.143    The grounds for delaying access to advice under s58 are strictly phrased, since the officer concerned must have reasonable grounds for believing that access to legal advice *will* lead to one of the prohibited consequences. This is reinforced by Code C Annex B para 3 which provides:

> Authority to delay a detainee's right to consult privately with a solicitor may be given only if the authorising officer has reasonable rounds to believe the solicitor the detainee wants to consult will, inadvertently or otherwise, pass on a message from the detainee or act in some other way which will have any of the consequences specified under paragraphs 1 or 2.

2.144    Code C Annex B NfG B3 makes it clear that a decision to delay access to a specific solicitor will be a rare occurrence which will apply only when it can be shown that the suspect is capable of misleading that particular solicitor and there is more than a substantial risk that the suspect will succeed in causing information to be conveyed which will lead to one or more of the specified consequences. If a decision to delay access to a particular solicitor is made, the detainee must be allowed to choose another solicitor (Code C Annex B para 3). Thus, it will be unusual for the police to be able to justify delaying access to a particular solicitor and almost inconceivable that they could justifiably delay access to any solicitor.[121] It has been held that in order to comply with ECHR article 6, delaying access to legal advice requires 'compelling reasons' and, even if justified, use of the interview in evidence may amount to as breach of the right to fair trial.[122]

### Grounds for delay – detention under the Terrorism Act 2000

2.145　Where a person is detained under TA 2000 Sch 7 or s41 (see para 2.56 above), the police may only delay access to a solicitor if the person has not been charged with an offence and delay is authorised by an officer of at least the rank of superintendent (TA 2000 Sch 8 para 8(1)(b), Code H para 6.4 and Annex B). Note that in some circumstances an interview may proceed before advice has been received (see para 2.127 above). Where a person is detained under Sch 7, the period of delay may be up to the maximum period of detention under that Schedule (see para 1.63). Where a person is detained under TA 2000 s41, the maximum period of delay is 48 hours from the time of arrest or, where the person was detained under Sch 7 when the person was arrested, from the time when the person's examination under that Schedule began (TA 2000 Sch 8 para 8(2)). Any authorised delay may only be for as long as is necessary, and if the grounds cease to exist the detainee must, as soon as practicable, be asked if he or she wishes to consult a solicitor (TA 2000 Sch 8 para 8(8), Code H Annex B para 6). If the police seek a warrant of further detention under Sch 8 Part III, the detained person must be allowed access to a solicitor for a reasonable time before the hearing, even if this is within the 48-hour period (Code H Annex B para 7).

2.146　Delay in access to a solicitor may only be authorised if the officer has reasonable grounds for believing that exercise of the right at the time that the person desires to exercise it (TA 2000 Sch 8 para 8(3)–(5), Code H Annex B paras 1 and 2):

- will lead to interference with or harm to evidence of a serious offence;[123]
- will lead to interference with or physical injury to any person;
- will lead to the alerting of persons who are suspected of having committed a serious offence but who have not been arrested for it;
- will hinder the recovery of property obtained as a result of a serious offence or in respect of which a forfeiture order could be made under TA 2000 s23;

---

121　The leading case is *R v Samuel* [1988] QB 615; [1988] 2 All ER 135; (1988) 87 Cr App R 232; [1988] Crim LR 299. For a case which held that delaying access was proper see *R v Governor of Pentonville Prison ex p Walters* (1987) *Times* 9 April, although this was decided before the current version of Code C came into force and the facts were rather unusual. Other than in cases of detention under the terrorism provisions the evidence suggests that the formal power to delay access to legal advice is almost never used. See D Brown, *PACE ten years on: a review of the research* (Home Office Research Study 155, Home Office, London, 1977), p118 and T Bucke and D Brown, *In police custody: police powers and suspects rights under the revised PACE Codes of Practice* (Home Office Research Study 174, Home Office, London 1997) p23.

122　*Cadder v Her Majesty's Advocate* [2010] UKSC 43, and see para 13.10 below.

123　TA 2000 Sch 8 para 8(9) provides that a 'serious offence' is an indictable offence (see para 2.21 above) or any offence mentioned in TA 2000 s40(1)(a) or attempt or conspiracy to commit such an offence.

- will lead to interference with the gathering of information about the commission, preparation or instigation of acts of terrorism;
- will lead to the alerting of a person and thereby making it more difficult to prevent an act of terrorism;
- will lead to the alerting of a person, thereby making it more difficult to secure a person's apprehension, prosecution, or conviction in connection with the commission, preparation or instigation of an act of terrorism;
- hindering the recovery of the value of the property constituting a benefit from their criminal conduct (which is to be decided in accordance with POCA 2002 Part 2).

The grounds for delaying access to a solicitor are strictly phrased, although more extensive than under the equivalent provisions in PACE (see para 2.139 above).

### Representations against delaying access

2.147   The police are not under a duty to receive representations regarding the decision to delay access to a solicitor and, by its very nature, the decision will normally be taken without the solicitor knowing that the client has been arrested and detained. Evidence obtained following wrongful denial of access will not necessarily be excluded at trial (but see paras 13.10 and 13.47), so it is important that if a solicitor is aware that the decision has been made, or is being contemplated, the solicitor should make representations to the appropriate officer, which may relate to:

1) whether the offence for which the person is detained is an indictable offence, or other relevant offence where a person is detained under TA 2000;
2) whether others are aware of the person's arrest because, if they are, the involvement of a lawyer is unlikely to have any adverse effect;[124]
3) what grounds the officer has for believing that the lawyer concerned will conduct himself or herself in such a way as to lead to one of the prohibited consequences;
4) what grounds the officer has for believing that the suspect is capable of misleading the lawyer, and for believing that there is a substantial risk that the suspect will succeed in causing the lawyer to convey information that will lead to one or more of the specified consequences (ie, those set out at paras 2.141 or 2.146 above); and
5) whether the suspect has been asked if he or she wants to speak to the duty solicitor.

2.148   If these representations fail, the police should be asked to deliver a letter to the client explaining that the police are preventing access and advising the client to ask to speak to a duty solicitor (specimen letter 1, appendix 4). All representations, together with the time they were made and the responses given, should be carefully noted. In *R v Samuel*[125] the solicitor who had

---

124 See *R v Davison* [1988] Crim LR 442, where the court disapproved of delay in access to a solicitor after the defendant had spoken to his wife on the telephone from the police station.

125 [1988] QB 615; [1988] 2 All ER 135; (1988) 87 Cr App R 232; [1988] Crim LR 299.

sought access gave evidence of the times he had tried to speak to his client, and this almost certainly had an effect on the outcome.

## Delaying access to advice – invalid reasons

2.149   It is the experience of many lawyers that the police use informal or unlawful methods of deterring or preventing access to legal advice. Some of these ploys are dealt with in greater length in chapters 3 and 4, but the following is a summary of the more common reasons given by the police for delaying or denying access, all of which are contrary to specific provisions of Code C.

1) The lawyer may advise the person not to answer questions. Although, in the past, this was the reason for much of the reluctance of police officers to allow access to legal advice, it is specifically prohibited by Code C and Code H Annex B para 4 and is probably now less significant in view of the 'silence' provisions of the CJPOA 1994. The lawyer was initially asked to attend by someone else and the suspect has not asked for the lawyer. In this case, the suspect must be informed of the lawyer's presence and must be asked to sign the custody record to signify whether or not the suspect wishes to see the lawyer (Code C, Code H Annex B para 4).

2) The suspect has declined advice. Where a lawyer attends the police station, the suspect must, unless an interview in the absence of legal advice has been authorised (see para 2.127 above), be informed of the lawyer's arrival and must be asked whether the suspect would like to see the lawyer. This is the case whether or not the suspect is then being interviewed, and even if the suspect has declined advice or, having initially requested it, subsequently agreed to being interviewed without it. The solicitor's attendance and the decision must be noted on the custody record, although it does not have to be signed by the suspect (Code C para 6.15, Code H para 6.17). Strictly, this provision, and the one above, only applies where the lawyer actually attends the police station (as opposed to telephoning the police station) (see further para 3.22 below).

3) There is a conflict of interests (see para 5.40 below). Code C confirms that conflict is a question of professional ethics for the lawyer to decide, not the police, although it provides that if waiting for a lawyer to give advice may lead to unreasonable delay to the interview of another, the provisions of Code C para 6.6(b) may apply (see para 2.127 above) (Code C NfG 6G, Code H NfG 6F).

4) The suspect is a juvenile, mentally disordered or mentally handicapped and the presence of an appropriate adult is awaited. All persons arrested and held in custody have a right to advice irrespective of age or other circumstances. If such a person requests advice, it must be acted on in the usual way (see para 2.125 above). Code C para 6.5A and Code H para 6.6, which state that in the case of a juvenile 'an appropriate adult should consider whether legal advice from a solicitor is required', may be misinterpreted. The purpose of this provision is to make it clear that if a juvenile has declined legal advice, the appropriate adult should, nevertheless, consider whether legal advice is required.

5) An accredited or probationary representative has been denied access to the police station. In this case, the employing solicitor must be notified and given the opportunity to make alternative arrangements (Code C para 6.14, Code H 6.16).

6) The lawyer has been excluded from interview for 'misconduct'. In this case, the suspect must be given the opportunity to consult another lawyer before the interview continues (Code C para 6.10, Code H 6.11).

2.150   If an invalid reason has been used to justify delaying or denying access to a lawyer, this may provide grounds for a complaint and/or grounds for any evidence subsequently obtained to be excluded at trial. See further chapter 13.

## Volunteers

2.151   A volunteer is a person who, for the purpose of assisting with an investigation, attends voluntarily at a police station or at any other place where a constable is present or accompanies a constable to a police station or any such other place without having been arrested (PACE s29). The term does not include a person being interviewed by someone other than a police officer unless the interview is in the presence of a constable. However, it is wide enough to include witnesses, victims and even appropriate adults. A volunteer is entitled to leave at any time unless and until arrested, and must be informed that he or she is under arrest if a decision is made to prevent the volunteer leaving at will (PACE s29, Code C para 3.21). For arrest and detention of a person who attends at a police station as a volunteer see paras 2.20 and 2.65 above.

2.152   A volunteer is entitled to legal advice at any time and to communicate with anyone outside the police station (Code C NfG 1A). Although a volunteer does not normally have to be informed of the right to advice, if the volunteer is subsequently arrested, the volunteer must be informed of this right in the usual way. If a volunteer is cautioned, which he or she must be if there are grounds to suspect that the volunteer has committed an offence (Code C para 10.1), the volunteer must be informed of his or her right to advice (Code C para 3.21 and see para 2.120 above). This is also the case if a volunteer asks about entitlement to advice (Code C para 3.22). Legal advice may be provided under the police station scheme if the volunteer attends at a police station, or elsewhere where a police constable is present, for the purpose of assisting with an investigation.[126] If the person is subject to a non-police investigation, the person may be entitled to legal aid under the free-standing legal advice and assistance scheme.[127] A witness is not entitled to legal aid unless there is a 'complicating factor'.[128]

2.153   Many of the provisions of PACE and the Codes do not apply to volunteers, for example, those relating to review and those relating to treatment of detained persons (see para 1.62 above). However, Code C NfG 1A provides that volunteers at police stations should be treated with no less consideration than those who are in custody.

126  Standard Criminal Contract (SCC) 2010, Part B, paras 9.1 and 9.56.
127  SCC 2020, Part B, para 9.117.
128  SCC 2010, Part B, paras 9.3 and 9.4.

# CHAPTER 3

# Dealing with the initial call

*continued*

# Introduction

3.1    The way in which the lawyer deals with the initial call concerning a person who has been arrested and detained will often determine whether the intervention will be successful, and whether the client will be satisfied with the lawyer's handling of the client's case. Generally, the first indication that a person has been arrested and wants legal advice will be a telephone call from the Defence Solicitor Call Centre (DSCC). Sometimes, however, the first contact will be made by a friend or relative, either by telephone or by calling at the office or, where the suspect is not under arrest, by the suspect himself or herself. To some extent, different considerations apply depending on who makes the initial contact. This chapter is concerned with the initial call, whoever it comes from, and goes on to deal with the first contact with the police and the client.

3.2    As noted in para 1.36 above, careful recording of events is an important task for the defence lawyer and all staff that deal with a case, and the recording of some information is mandatory under the Standard Criminal Contract (SCC) 2010. This chapter makes extensive reference to information that should be sought, and advice that should be given by the defence lawyer, and this should always be recorded.

## Call from the DSCC

3.3    Generally, where a suspect who is held in police custody requests legal advice to be paid for from public funds, the police are required to contact the DSCC. The DSCC then directs the request to Criminal Defence Service (CDS) Direct (if the case is covered by the CDS Direct scheme), or to the nominated solicitor or firm, or to the duty solicitor (see paras 1.54–1.59 and 2.126 above).

### Restrictions and obligations

3.4    No claim for payment for police station advice and assistance can be made under the police station scheme unless the initial instructions came from the DSCC. This is subject to limited exceptions: where a client attends a police station by prior agreement with the police (see para 3.12 below); where the instructions are received from a third party (see para 3.17 below); or where the lawyer is already at the police station when the client requests advice from him or her (see para 3.30 below).[1] Where a case is covered by the CDS Direct scheme, the fact that the suspect has refused advice from CDS Direct does not enable a lawyer to provide advice and assistance under the police station scheme.[2] However, if CDS Direct refer a case to the suspect's own solicitor, it ceases to be a CDS matter, and the normal rules regarding police station advice and assistance apply.[3]

---

1    SCC 2010, Part B, paras 9.18–9.20.
2    SCC 2010, Part B, para 9.12.
3    SCC 2010, Part B, para 9.13.

3.5      In all cases under the police station scheme, payment relies on the sufficient benefit test having been satisfied. It is automatically satisfied in a case referred to the lawyer by the DSCC in respect of the initial advice, but after that the lawyer must consider whether, and what, further work is justified by reference to the test (see para 1.60 above).

3.6      The lawyer must record and keep on file details of the reference number provided by the DSCC, and the file must also contain a note of the time at which the call was accepted and the time at which first contact was made with the client.[4] Having been accepted, the case must be retained until the end of the investigation. However, a duty solicitor case may be handed back to the DSCC if:

a)  the lawyer is unable to continue to act personally and there is no other suitable person in the firm able to act, and the lawyer is unable to instruct a suitable agent;
b)  the client removes or rescinds his or her instructions;
c)  the firm is unable to act because of legitimate concerns about a breach of the professional code of conduct; or
d)  the lawyer confirms that he or she will not make a claim under the police station scheme.[5]

## Duty solicitor cases

3.7      The Duty Solicitor Scheme Rules are set out in the SCC 2010, Part A, section 6 (see para 1.52 above). SCC 2010, Part B, section 9 sets out a number of obligations in duty solicitor cases. Cases referred by the DSCC to a duty solicitor on rota duty must be accepted unless the nominated duty solicitor is already engaged with another client at a police station or at a hearing of an application for a warrant of further detention or an extension of such a warrant, or at an armed forces custody hearing, or if a conflict of interest arises.[6] In these circumstances, the firm must accept the case provided that it has a duty solicitor available who can accept it without delay and, if necessary, attend the police station within 45 minutes.[7] If the duty solicitor is already at the police station when a person requests the duty solicitor, the solicitor must inform the DSCC when the solicitor accept the request for advice.[8] A firm must use all reasonable endeavours to accept panel and back-up cases referred by the DSCC.[9]

3.8      A duty solicitor must inform a client that the client is not obliged to instruct the duty solicitor.[10] If the person wants another solicitor to act, the duty solicitor must not do so unless the named solicitor is unavailable and the person asks the duty solicitor to act on that occasion.[11]

---

4  SCC 2010, Part B, paras 9.21 and 9.25.
5  SCC 2010, Part B, paras 9.53–9.55.
6  SCC 2010, Part B, para 9.48.
7  SCC 2010, Part B, para 9.50.
8  SCC 2010, Part B, para 9.49.
9  SCC 2010, Part B, para 9.51.
10  SCC 2010, Part A, para 6.57.
11  SCC 2010, Part A, para 6.58.

## Use of representatives

3.9　The accreditation scheme for police station representatives is explained at para 1.49 above. A representative must be competent to undertake cases assigned to him or her, and must also be appropriately supervised.[12] Under the police station advice and assistance scheme (ie, other than in privately funded cases), in own solicitor cases the initial call from the DSCC can be taken, and advice and assistance provided (by telephone or in person), by accredited or probationary representatives who are registered with the LSC. In duty solicitor cases, accredited (but not probationary) representatives may be used to accept the initial call from the DSCC, and to provide advice and assistance provided (by telephone or in person). Probationary representatives are not permitted to provide advice in respect of indictable-only offences.[13] Non-duty solicitor staff may be used to receive calls from the DSCC in duty solicitor cases provided prior written approval has been obtained from the LSC.[14]

# Call from the client

3.10　The initial contact will rarely come from a client in police custody. Most clients who want legal advice and assistance will rely on the police station legal advice and assistance scheme and, as explained at para 3.4 above, this normally requires the case to be referred by the DSCC. However, a client in police custody who intends to pay privately may be permitted to contact the lawyer directly, and a client who is not in custody may, or course, do so.

## Client in police custody

3.11　Where a person has been arrested and detained, and intends to pay privately for legal advice, the custody officer may allow the person to telephone the lawyer directly. Subject to the right to delay access under Annex B, suspects must be informed that they may communicate with a solicitor at any time, including by telephone (Code C para 6.1, and see para 2.137 above). Advising clients by telephone is dealt with at para 3.25 below, but the lawyer should bear the following points in mind if contacted directly by a client in this way:

1) The telephone call may be overheard by police officers (see para 2.134 above), and anything said by the lawyer or any information requested from the suspect must take this into account.

2) If the lawyer gives advice on the telephone and also intends to attend in person, the custody officer should be informed of this together with the expected time of arrival. Failure to do so could enable the police to

---

12　See generally SCC 2010, Part A, section 6, and Part B, para 9.30 in respect of representatives who are not directly employed by the firm under a contract of employment.
13　SCC 2020, Part B, paras 9.26–9.28, and para 9.35.
14　SCC 2010, Part B, para 9.52.

argue that since the suspect has received advice, the suspect can legitimately be interviewed in a lawyer's absence (see para 2.128).

3) If the suspect has been arrested on suspicion of an excess alcohol offence, the police are not required to delay taking specimens until the lawyer arrives, and refusal to supply a specimen pending the arrival of the lawyer may amount to the offence of refusing to supply a specimen (see para 2.129 above).

## Client at liberty

3.12    The initial contact may be made by a client who has not been arrested but who is aware that the police are looking for him or her and/or wish to interview him or her, or by a client who is on police bail. In the former case, the lawyer should take initial instructions from the client in a similar way to the instructions taken from a client who is in custody (see chapter 5), but there are also other considerations. Probably the most important question is whether the client should surrender himself or herself to the police. Ultimately this is a matter for the client, and it would be a serious breach of professional duty for the lawyer to contact the police to indicate the client's whereabouts without the client's consent.

3.13    Clients should normally be advised that it is in their interests to attend the police station voluntarily, since the police may agree to this being done by appointment at a mutually convenient time. Such an arrangement could be beneficial because the time would then be known in advance, it would enable the client to make any suitable domestic arrangements, and it would ensure that a lawyer could accompany the client to the police station. It may also avoid an arrest at an inconvenient time or in embarrassing circumstances or, given the necessity requirement for arrest, avoid arrest (see para 2.20 above) or detention (see para 2.65 above) altogether. It would also give the lawyer the opportunity to try to discover more about the reasons why the police wish to arrest and/or interview the client, including what evidence they have, thus enabling both lawyer and client to prepare more effectively in advance of any police interview. Care should be taken in contacting the police, since if they suspect that the client is with the lawyer, they may arrive to arrest the client within a short period of time. If the police are not willing to come to an arrangement for attendance at the police station, it may be advisable for the lawyer to attend at the police station with the client as soon as possible. The client's voluntary attendance will still be relevant to the necessity of arrest or detention, and may assist the client in any bail application at a later stage.

3.14    If the client agrees to attend at the police station, he or she should be advised on what is likely to happen. Unless the police have indicated otherwise, the client should normally be advised that he or she may be arrested and detained on attendance at the police station. Among other things, the client must expect to be searched and have personal possessions removed (Code C, Code H section 4). Clients will also be asked to give their name and address. If there are any problems with accommodation these should, if possible, be sorted out before attending at the station so that this cannot be used as a reason for treating arrest as necessary or for withholding bail in the event of the client being charged. On detention, the client will be informed of his or her rights, including the right to legal advice (Code C, Code H section 3), and should be advised to confirm his or her wish to receive that advice. Finally, the client should be warned that although the police may be ready to proceed straight to an interview, if arrested the client is likely to be detained in a cell either before or after it. Many people are unaware of how long they can be detained in a police station, and advice should also be given on this.

3.15 Contact may be made by a person who has previously been arrested and then been granted 'street bail' (see para 2.45 above) or bail without charge (see para 10.73 below). In these circumstances the lawyer should take initial instructions in a similar way to the instructions taken from a client who is in custody (see chapter 5), and also ascertain the date on which, and the police station at which, the client is to surrender. Note that the police may vary the time and place for surrender, and may withdraw the requirement to surrender (see para 2.46 above and para 10.80 below).

3.16 Where a person is advised in either of these circumstances, advice and assistance may be claimed as free-standing advice and assistance, although the means test will apply and there are limitations where the person has received advice and assistance in connection with the same matter in the previous six months.[15] If the lawyer attends the police station with the client, the lawyer may be paid under the police station advice and assistance scheme provided that the attendance is by prior agreement with the police, and that the lawyer informs the DSCC within 48 hours of the first attendance.[16]

## Call from a third party

3.17 The initial contact may be from a relative, friend or acquaintance of the person who has been arrested. The person may have been present at the arrest or may have heard about it from others. The person may have been asked by the arrested person to contact a lawyer, or the person may have done so on his or her own initiative. Whatever the situation, it must be remembered that it is the *suspect* who is the client, or potential client, and not the person who has contacted the lawyer. Nevertheless, that person may be a useful source of information. See checklist 1 for the information that should be sought from the third party.

3.18 If, as a result of the contact by the third party, advice is given to a client in police custody, payment may be claimed under the police station advice and assistance scheme provided that the lawyer reports the matter to the DSCC prior to telephoning or attending the client.[17]

15 SCC 2010, Part B, paras 9.117–9.144.
16 SCC 2010, Part B, para 9.20(a).
17 SCC 2010, Part B, para 9.20(b).

## Instructions from a third party

3.19   It is well established that a third party can retain a lawyer on behalf of an arrested person[18] subject to the lawyer being satisfied that the instructions arise from a genuine concern for the suspect's welfare, and subject to the instructions being confirmed by the suspect. Two common problems that may be encountered where instructions are received from a third party are dealt with below.

### 'The suspect has not asked for a solicitor'

3.20   Where the lawyer is initially contacted by a third party, the police may try to deter the lawyer from speaking to the suspect by maintaining that the suspect has not asked for a lawyer. Code C, Code H Annex B para 4 provides that access to a solicitor may not be delayed on the ground that the solicitor has 'been asked to attend the police station by someone else' provided that the suspect then wishes to see the solicitor. The suspect must be told that the lawyer has come to the police station and must be asked to sign the custody record to signify whether or not the suspect wishes to see the lawyer. This is reinforced by Code C para 6.15 and Code H para 6.17 which provide that the detained person must be told of the arrival of the solicitor even if he or she has declined advice or, having initially asked for it, has agreed to be interviewed without it. In the past, where the suspect was being interviewed by police when the lawyer arrived, custody officers sometimes refused to interrupt the interview to inform the suspect of the lawyer's arrival. Code C para 6.15 and Code H para 6.17 now provide that the suspect must be informed of the lawyer's arrival, whether or not the suspect is being interviewed.

3.21   If the lawyer attends the police station and is refused access on the ground that the suspect has declined advice, the solicitor should consider asking the custody officer to pass a letter to the suspect (specimen letter 1, appendix 4). The lawyer should also consider asking to see the custody record to confirm that the refusal of legal advice has been recorded.

3.22   Strictly, Code C, Code H Annex B para 4 is confined to the situation where a solicitor actually attends the police station in person, although it may also be of assistance in persuading the police to allow access on the telephone. At the very least, the lawyer should ask the custody officer to go to the suspect while the lawyer is on the telephone, to ask whether or not the suspect wishes to speak to the lawyer. Any reply should be noted.[19]

---

18   *R v Sally Jones* [1984] Crim LR 357, and see Code C, Code H Annex B para 4.

19   In *R v Chahal* [1992] Crim LR 124 the Court of Appeal upheld the trial judge's refusal to exclude admissions in circumstances where the police had failed to inform the suspect that a solicitor instructed by his family had telephoned the police station. In *R v Franklin* (1994) *Times* 16 June, on the other hand, the court held that admissions should have been excluded. In this case, the solicitor actually attended the police station, and there were other relevant differences. Chahal was described as an experienced businessman whereas Franklin was described as a young unemployed man who had never previously been in a police station.

*'The suspect has asked for another solicitor'*

3.23   A further possibility is that the police will say that the suspect has instructed another lawyer. Code C para 6.15 and Code H para 6.17 do not directly deal with this situation, although the wording implies that the suspect should, nevertheless, be informed of the lawyer's arrival. Clearly, the wishes of the suspect are paramount, although it may be advisable to contact the other lawyer to ensure that he or she has been instructed.

---

### Checklist 1: Instructions from a third party

1 Date and time of call
2 Name of person taking the call

*Details of third party*
3 Name
4 Address
5 Telephone number
6 Relationship to person arrested

*Details of arrested person*
7 Name
8 Address
9 Telephone number
10 Any aliases used
11 Any vulnerabilities, medication, etc
12 Whether the suspect requested legal advice

*Details of the incident*
13 Reason for the arrest
14 Time and place of arrest
15 Circumstances of the arrest
16 Involvement of the third party (if any)
17 Details of other persons arrested
18 Details of any other witnesses

*Details of the detention*
19 Police station suspect taken to
20 Name(s) of officer(s) involved

*Initial advice given*
21 Advice given to third party
22 Action taken in response to third party contact

A full and accurate note must be taken of all information obtained and advice given, which should be timed and dated.

---

## Details of the third party

3.24   The name, address and telephone number of the third party should be obtained so that the suspect can be informed and so that the lawyer can let him or her know whether access to the suspect has been secured (but see para 3.28 below). Details of the third party's relationship to the suspect may also assist in obtaining access.

## Details of the arrested person

3.25   It is, of course, essential to obtain the name and address of the arrested person and, if possible, his or her age. Difficulties may arise if the person uses one or more aliases, since the lawyer must avoid inadvertently alerting the police to this possibility. If the initial contact with the police station where the suspect is believed to be is met with the response that the person named is not there, it may be wise for another member of the firm to make a second enquiry referring to another name used by the suspect. Clearly, reference to both names in the same telephone conversation should be avoided. Such an approach, at this stage, is not unethical since it does not involve the lawyer in knowingly misleading the police. It is helpful to know whether the suspect asked the third party to instruct a lawyer, since if the suspect did, this should ease access. The third party may also possess other important information about the arrested person, such as any vulnerability, medication, etc.

## Details of the incident

3.26   The third party can be an important source of information. The third party may have been present at the time of arrest and may know something of the apparent reasons for it and the circumstances surrounding it. He or she may also know whether anyone else has been arrested and/or details of any relevant witnesses.

3.27   Care is necessary if there is a possibility that the third party might be implicated in the alleged offence or that the police might believe this to be so. The third party should be questioned about this. The lawyer is under no obligation to inform the custody officer of the identity of the person from whom the lawyer has received initial instructions. Equally, if the third party is possibly implicated, the lawyer must be wary of telling the third party anything other than that the detained person has been contacted. In any event, if the suspect does instruct the lawyer, information should only be given to the third party if the client consents to such disclosure.

## Advice and action taken

3.28   The lawyer may advise the third party in general terms and should also tell the third party what action is intended. However, in view of the duty of confidentiality, the lawyer should not offer to inform the third party of details about the client's case unless the client gives authority for such information to be given.

## Finding the client

3.29   Apart from the use of an alias (see para 3.25 above), the lawyer may encounter other problems in finding the suspect. Where a person is arrested away from a police station he or she will normally be taken to the local station, but there are a number of reasons why this may not happen, or may not happen immediately. The local station may not be a designated police station (see para 3.31 below), and so the suspect may be taken to another police station that is designated. It may be that the suspect has been arrested for an offence allegedly committed in another police division, in which case the suspect may be taken to a police station in that division. Alternatively, the suspect may have been arrested in connection with an offence allegedly committed in another police area. In this case the suspect may be taken to a police station in that other police area, although he or she will normally be taken to a police station in the area of the arrest before transfer to the police area where the interview is to take place. Finally, it may be that the suspect is not being detained at a police station at all, for example, where the arrest has been made by an HR Revenue and Customs (HMRC) officer or the suspect is a member of the armed services detained by the services police. Checklist 2 may help in finding the suspect.

---

**Checklist 2: Finding the client**

1) Contact the custody officer at the police station where it is believed that the suspect has been taken. Where an enquiry about the whereabouts of a suspect is made by a person with an interest in the suspect's welfare, that information must normally be given, provided the suspect agrees (Code C, Code H para 5.5).

2) If the custody officer is not willing to give the required information, it may be that a decision has been made to hold the suspect incommunicado under Police and Criminal Evidence Act 1984 (PACE) s56 or the Terrorism Act (TA) 2000 Sch 8 para 8 (see para 2.117 above). This presents a difficulty, since from the police point of view disclosing to the lawyer that the person has been detained may defeat the purpose of the action they have taken. The lawyer may wish to give an undertaking not to disclose the whereabouts of the suspect to a third party. The lawyer should also ask whether a decision to delay access to legal advice under PACE s58 or TA 2000 Sch 8 has been taken (see paras 2.139 and 2.145 above), since if it has not, the police will be under a duty to inform the suspect of the lawyer's interest, although strictly only if the lawyer attends in person (see para 3.22 above).

3) If the custody officer says that the person is not detained at that police station, the custody officer should be asked whether the person has been at that station and, if so, where the person has been taken. If this still draws a blank, the custody officer should be asked whether he or she is aware of an arrest having taken place recently and whether he or she is expecting a suspect to be brought into the police station in the near future. It may assist if the names of any officers involved in the arrest are known.

4) If this still does not work, it is worth asking the custody officer to check the custody records, since although the custody officer should be aware of who is, or has been, in custody, there may have been a recent change of shift or there may be a temporary custody officer. If this still does not work, the custody officer should be asked to inform the lawyer if and when the person is brought in. If the suspect is not located but there is still reason to believe that the suspect is in custody, checks should be made at regular intervals.

5) If all of the above fail, the lawyer should consider telephoning other stations and going through the same process. Depending on the circumstances, the lawyer may also consider contacting HMRC offices or other police forces such as the British Transport Police.

A full and accurate note should be kept of all information sought and obtained, including the date, time and name and status of officers spoken to.

## Call from the police

3.30 Normally, the initial call will only come from the police where the suspect intends to pay privately for legal advice (see para 2.126 above). In cases where the suspect relies on the police station legal advice and assistance scheme, a lawyer cannot be paid under the scheme unless the request for legal advice is made via the DSCC (see para 3.4 above). This is subject to an exception where the lawyer is already at the police station when the client requests advice from the lawyer, in which case the lawyer must report the matter to the DSCC within 48 hours of receiving instructions.[20]

3.31 It is worth noting here that each designated[21] police station must have at least one custody officer, who must be of at least the rank of sergeant, although an officer of any rank may perform the functions of a custody officer if one is not readily available (PACE ss35 and 36).[22] While acting as custody officer, the officer must not be involved in the investigation of an offence for which the suspect concerned is in police detention.[23] If the station is not a designated police station, the functions of a custody officer may be carried out by an officer of any rank who is not involved in the investigation or, failing this, by any police officer (PACE s36(7)). A person may not be detained at a non-designated station for more than six hours (PACE s30(6)). A person arrested under TA 2000 s41 must be detained in a place designated by the secretary of state (TA 2000 Sch 8 para 1).

## Initial contact with the custody officer

3.32 The initial contact with the custody officer[24] provides the opportunity to gather important information, which will be needed in order for a decision to be made on how to proceed. In particular, it will help in deciding

---

20 SCC 2010, Part B, para 9.20(c).
21 That is, designated by the chief officer of police under PACE s35.
22 See *Vince and Another v Chief Constable of the Dorset Police* [1993] 2 All ER 321.
23 Subject to exceptions in PACE s36(6).
24 Reference is made here to the custody officer, but although certain duties under PACE are specifically assigned to a custody officer as defined in PACE (see para 3.31 above) in practice many functions associated with persons in police detention are carried out by detention officers or other civilian officers. There is evidence that such civilians sometimes perform functions reserved to custody officers. See L Skinns, *Police custody: governance, legitimacy and reform of the criminal justice process* (Willan, Abingdon, 2011), ch3.

whether to attend the police station, and will help to indicate whether there are likely to be difficulties, such as a police decision to delay access to a lawyer. Sometimes a custody officer will say that he or she does not know much about the case and therefore cannot give details. Most of the information to be obtained at this stage should be in the custody record, but the custody officer may be reminded that, under PACE Part IV, legal responsibility for ensuring that the grounds for detention exist and continue to exist in respect of any person in police detention rests on the custody officer (see PACE ss34 and 37 in particular). Therefore, if the officer is not aware of crucial information about the case, the officer may be asked how he or she can satisfy these statutory duties.[25] Although custody work may be carried out by designated officers (see para 2.52 above) or other civilians, the custody officer remains legally responsible (Code C para 1.15, Code H para 1.19).

3.33    Checklist 3 below sets out the information that should be sought from the custody officer. The nature and extent of information to be obtained at this stage will vary, depending on the circumstances of the case. However, it must be sufficient to enable the lawyer to make an informed decision on:

- whether and when to attend the police station (see para 3.58 below);
- whether there is, or is a risk of, a conflict of interests (see para 5.40 below);
- whether, given the nature of the case, the lawyer has the necessary knowledge and experience to be able to deal with the matter. It may be that the lawyer should do some preliminary research before attending the police station or should consider referring to someone else in the firm;
- whether anything has occurred that may be of particular legal or evidential significance.

---

**Checklist 3: Obtaining information from the custody officer on the telephone**

*Details of the suspect*
1 Name
2 Address
3 Date of birth
4 Gender
5 Whether a risk assessment has been conducted, and its outcome
6 Whether juvenile/vulnerable/other special needs (for example, interpreter)
7 Identity of appropriate adult and whether contacted (if relevant)

*Police and investigation details*
8 Name of custody officer
9 Station where held and custody record number
10 Name of officer in case/arresting officer

---

25  An investigation by the Police Complaints Authority (PCA) in 1998 found that almost a quarter of custody officers had received no special training. See *Custody officer training: investing in safety* (PCA, London, 1998).

11 Whether client arrested or a volunteer
12 Time and place of arrest
13 Time of arrival at station
14 Time detention authorised
15 Reason for and circumstances of arrest, and why arrest necessary
16 Details of alleged offence(s)
17 Whether an indictable offence
18 Any exceptional police procedure (delay in advice/delay in informing relative or friend/intimate body search/drug test/identification procedure)
19 Reason for detention
20 Time solicitor requested
21 Reason for delay in contacting solicitor (if relevant)
22 Reason for proceeding without solicitor (if relevant)
23 Whether interviewed yet (if so, why)
24 Whether and when interview likely to take place
25 Whether search made/proposed and/or samples taken/proposed, and result
26 Any significant statement or silence
27 Any other person(s) arrested/sought by police

*Charge/release (if relevant)*
28 If charged:
    time of charge
    nature of charge(s)
    bailed/detained in custody
29 If bailed following charge:
    date/time/place of court appearance
    any conditions attached to bail
30 If not bailed:
    reason for refusing bail
    date/time/place of court appearance
    police attitude to bail from the court
31 If not charged:
    whether released unconditionally/reported for summons/bailed
    if reported for summons, what offence(s) anticipated
32 If bailed without charge:
    reason for police bail
    date/time/place of surrender

*Action*
33 Arrange telephone access to client
34 Confirm with custody officer:
    expected time of arrival
    that the officer will contact the lawyer if plans change that the client
    will not be interviewed before the lawyer arrives
    that above will be noted on custody record

A full and accurate note must be taken of all information requested and obtained, and the source of that information, which should be timed and dated.

# The suspect

## Name and address

3.34 The name and address and age of the suspect should be confirmed, together with gender if there is any doubt.

## Juvenile or mentally disordered or vulnerable

3.35 If the person in detention is a juvenile, or mentally disordered or vulnerable, or vulnerable for other reasons, special provisions will apply and special care will be necessary (see chapter 11). On detaining a person, the custody officer must carry out a risk assessment as soon as practicable, and the results together with any action taken must be entered in the custody record (see para 4.23 below). If no specific risks have been identified, that must be noted in the custody record (Code C, Code H para 3.8).

## Whether under the influence of drink or drugs

3.36 As noted above, when a suspect is booked in at the police station the custody officer must conduct a risk assessment and take appropriate action. If the lawyer is informed that the suspect is under the influence of drink or drugs, the lawyer must decide whether it is possible or necessary to speak to the suspect on the telephone. Sometimes the custody officer will refuse to bring the suspect to the telephone for this reason. There is no provision in PACE or the Codes empowering the police to delay access to legal advice because the suspect is under the influence of drink or drugs, although clearly in certain situations it would be inappropriate for advice to be given over the telephone. On the other hand, as Code C NfG 9C makes clear, a person who appears to be drunk may be ill, injured or suffering from the effects of drugs.

# Police details

## Names of officers concerned

3.37 The need to record the name of the custody officer and the police station concerned is self-evident. It is also important to obtain the name of the officer in charge of the case. Although the custody officer may change at the end of a shift, the officer in charge is likely to remain the same throughout the investigation. In more serious cases there may well be a senior officer in charge of the case as a whole, with individual officers assigned to particular suspects. It is important to know whether this is the case and, if so, the names of both officers. It may be that any representations should be made to the officer in overall charge since the more junior officer may simply not have the authority to make a particular decision. A junior officer cannot be relied on to relay representations to the officer making the decision accurately or with the force with which the lawyer would wish to make them.

## Status of the client

3.38   It is important to establish the status of the client, that is, whether the client is under arrest or a volunteer, since this will determine whether the client has an absolute right to legal advice and whether the client is subject to a maximum period of detention. Where relevant, a check should be made on whether the person is detained under PACE or under TA 2000 (see para 2.53 above). If the client is a volunteer (see para 2.151 above), much of the information in the checklist will not be relevant unless the client is subsequently arrested, but it will still be necessary to ascertain the name of the officer in the case, and details about interviews and searches.

## Time and place of arrest

3.39   Information about the time and place of arrest will help in assessing a number of things. If there is a significant lapse of time between the arrest and the time of arrival at the police station, an explanation should be sought. PACE s30 provides that, following an arrest away from a police station, the person must be taken to a police station as soon as practicable (see para 2.45 above).[26] However, this is subject to a power of delay if the person's presence elsewhere is necessary to carry out 'such investigations as it is reasonable to carry out immediately' (see para 2.49 above). This may include a search or taking the suspect to the scene of the alleged crime, but in any event PACE s30(11) provides that the reason for delay must be recorded when the suspect arrives at the police station. The lawyer will, therefore, want to know why the suspect was not taken to the police station immediately following arrest. The lawyer should enquire whether the suspect has made a 'significant statement or silence' (see para 5.113 below), and should ask whether the suspect was interviewed before arriving at the police station. By Code C para 11.1 this should not normally happen, although the Code does provide for exceptions (see para 4.44 below). If relevant, the lawyer should ask the custody officer to confirm that the suspect will not be asked to sign a pocket book or other document purporting to record an earlier statement or 'silence' other than in the presence of the lawyer.

## Time of arrival at police station

3.40   The time of arrival at the police station will normally determine when the detention time limit expires, although it will differ if the suspect was arrested at the police station having attended voluntarily or was arrested in another police area (see paras 2.69 and 2.78 above). A note should be made of the time of arrival at the police station, but it may be advisable for the lawyer subsequently to check that the lawyer's calculation of the time the detention time limit expires agrees with that of the custody officer.

---

26   Where a person is arrested under TA 2000 s41, a similar obligation applies by virtue of TA 2000 Sch 8 para 1(4).

## Time detention was authorised

3.41 Where a person is detained under PACE, the time that detention was authorised will determine the timing of reviews (see para 2.80 above). Where a person is detained under TA 2000 s41, the timing of reviews is governed by the time of arrest (see para 2.91 above).

## Reasons for arrest and detention

3.42 With regard to the reason(s) for arrest, it is necessary both to find out the initial reason for arrest and the offence for which the person has been detained. Normally the offence will be the same, but it may be that, having been arrested for one offence, the suspect is further arrested before arrival or while at the police station. Note that PACE s31 provides that where a person is at a police station having been arrested for an offence, if the person would be liable to arrest for another offence when released, then the person must be arrested for that other offence (see para 2.32 above).

3.43 Ascertaining the reason for arrest will help in determining whether that arrest was lawful (see para 2.11 above). If the arrest was unlawful, the detention may be unlawful. The lawyer may wish to seek the suspect's release on this basis, but care will be needed since grounds for arrest may be 'discovered' even though such grounds were not considered at the time of arrest or, where relevant, the information required under PACE s28 may be given, rendering the arrest lawful (see para 2.44 above). In such a situation, therefore, it would be important to try to ascertain as much detail as possible about the ground for arrest before arguing that it was unlawful.

3.44 Ascertaining the offence in respect of which the suspect is detained is necessary in order to determine whether the suspect is being detained under PACE or TA 2000 and, if the former, whether the suspect is being detained in respect of an indictable offence (see para 2.21 above), and also whether it is a recordable offence (see Code D NfG 4A for definition). This is important because the type of offence for which the suspect has been detained will determine what powers the police have. It will also enable the lawyer to decide whether he or she has sufficient knowledge or experience to deal with the case, and whether he or she needs to check the law in relation to the offence(s).

3.45 A person arrested for an offence may only be detained in a police station without charge if the conditions under PACE s37(2) are satisfied. The custody officer will normally recite PACE s37(2) in whole or in part, although the custody officer should give the grounds for his or her belief rather than merely reciting the statutory authority for detention. Note that the grounds under section 37(2) relate only to those arrested for an offence. PACE s51 specifically provides that powers to detain in custody under the Immigration Act 1971, the TA 2000 and under legislation relating to the armed forces, are unaffected by PACE Part IV. Furthermore, the police also have certain powers to detain people other than in respect of an offence, for example, under the Mental Health Act 1983 s136 (removal to a place of safety), under the Bail Act 1976 s7 (breach of bail conditions), under a warrant issued by a court (for example, for failure to surrender to custody following a grant of bail) or under a power of arrest in civil proceedings.[27] In such cases PACE s37 does not apply, although the lawyer should ensure that proper grounds for the detention do exist. For powers to detain in a police station see para 2.53 above.

### Time of request for legal advice

3.46    The time that the suspect requested a lawyer may be relevant, particularly if the lawyer has been contacted some time after the original request was made. If this is the case, the lawyer should find out the reason for the delay. Where legal advice is requested, the custody officer must normally 'act without delay to secure the provision of such advice' (Code C para 6.5, Code H para 6.4 and see para 2.125 above). Lawful delay under PACE and the TA 2000 is dealt with at paras 2.139 and 2.145 above, and is relatively unusual. It may be that the reason for delay is legitimate, or may not be the fault of the police – for example, it may result from the DSCC or from an inappropriate referral to CDS Direct – but whatever the cause, prompt contact with the suspect is important since the suspect may well have been adversely affected by, and is unlikely to know the reason for, the delay. A careful note should be made of the time the lawyer was first contacted and a check should be made of whether the police have taken any significant step between the time that legal advice was requested and the time the lawyer was first contacted.

3.47    Generally, once a request for advice has been made, the suspect cannot be interviewed, or continue to be interviewed, until the suspect has received advice (see para 2.127 above). If the custody officer maintains that one of the exceptions to the general rule did apply, the officer should be carefully questioned about the reasons for this and the authorisation given, and a careful note made of the answers. If the person detained made admissions during any interview carried out under one of the exceptions, then whether the exception did in fact apply or whether, alternatively, the questioning went beyond that allowed for in the exceptions, will be relevant to the question of admissibility of evidence of the admissions at any subsequent trial (see para 4.35 below). Inferences cannot be drawn from 'silence' where a suspect who has requested legal advice is denied access to a lawyer before being interviewed (see para 5.66 below).

### Whether the client has been interviewed or questioned

3.48    It is important to find out whether the client has been interviewed. Such an interview may be entirely proper, since the suspect may not have requested legal advice until after the interview had taken place. Nevertheless, if the client has been interviewed, the lawyer should ask for information about the content of the interview, although such a request may be better directed at the officers who conducted the interview. It is also important to find out whether an interview is to be held and, if so, when this is likely to take place. The lawyer should ask whether the suspect has already made any 'significant statement or silence' (see para 5.113 below), whether or not in the context of a formal interview. Such a statement or

---

27  In all these cases, the person detained is entitled to legal advice, since PACE s58 applies to all people arrested and held in custody, and not just those detained under Part IV. Where a person is detained under TA 2000 s41, the right to legal advice is governed by TA 2000 Sch 8 para 7. See para 2.119 above.

silence may, or may not, be admitted at any subsequent trial and the lawyer will need to take account of it when advising the suspect.

### Whether a search has been conducted

3.49 It is important to find out whether a search of the suspect's person, or of premises, has been conducted or is intended. Police powers of search are dealt with in chapter 6. At this stage, the lawyer should ascertain the power under which the search was carried out, or is intended to be carried out and, where appropriate, on whose authority. Note, in particular, that a search of property under PACE s32(2)(b) or s18 may only be conducted where the person has been arrested for an indictable offence (see para 2.21 above). Furthermore, where a search has already been carried out, the custody officer should be asked whether anything significant was found or seized, although this question may be better directed at the officer in charge of the case. If a search of premises is intended, the lawyer must decide whether to be present.

### Whether others are sought or have been arrested

3.50 The lawyer should ask whether any other person has been arrested or is sought by the police in connection with the offence for which the client has been arrested. If there is more than one person in custody, it may be that two or more of them will request the same lawyer to act for them. Conflict of interests is dealt with at para 5.40 below. If other people are being sought in respect of the offence, the lawyer must take care not to take any action that would hinder their arrest, either intentionally or unintentionally.

## Charge or release

3.51 It is relatively uncommon for a lawyer to be contacted for the first time at the time of release or shortly after release from detention. If this does occur, a careful check on when legal advice was requested should be made and, if so, the time of the request and the reasons for delay in contacting the lawyer. In any event, it will be necessary to find out whether the suspect has been charged and, if so, what the charges are, whether the suspect has been bailed from the police station (and any conditions that may have been imposed) and, if not, what the police attitude to bail from the court will be. Whether or not bailed, the lawyer should ascertain the time, date and place of the first court appearance. If the suspect has been released on bail without charge (see para 10.73 below), the time, date and place of surrender should be ascertained so that arrangements can be made for attendance by the lawyer.

## Initial contact with the client

3.52 SCC 2010, Part B para 9.23 provides that the first contact with the client should be made within 45 minutes of first notification that a client has been arrested and has requested advice. A note of the time at which the call was accepted, and the time at which first contact was made with the client, must be noted in the lawyer's file. If contact is not made within 45 minutes, the reason for this must also be noted in the file.[28] It is important to do this, particularly since when lawyers are notified by the DSCC of the request for advice, they often experience difficulty in getting through on the telephone to the police station.

## Confidentiality of the telephone conversation

3.53    Security and privacy should always be considered when speaking to a suspect on the telephone (see paras 2.134 and 2.135). At the beginning of the conversation it is advisable to ask the suspect whether the conversation is taking place within the presence or hearing of a police officer, especially since many police stations do not have private telephone facilities. If necessary, the lawyer should ask to speak to the police officer and remind the officer of the right to privacy. If there is any doubt, the lawyer should advise the suspect not to speak other than to answer questions which should be capable of being answered by 'yes' or 'no' and which should not prompt any incriminating response. If the lawyer is concerned that the police might be listening in to the conversation covertly, the conversation should be kept to a minimum and a prompt visit made to the police station. In appropriate cases the client should also be warned that the police may 'bug' the client's cell.

## Initial advice

3.54    Having spoken to the custody officer, the lawyer should normally speak to the client on the telephone immediately afterwards. By this stage, the client may have spent some time in custody and may be afraid, vulnerable, angry or just bored. In any of these states of mind the client could be susceptible to an approach from the police to 'crack on with the interview' instead of waiting for the lawyer. Relying on the custody officer to pass on a message that the lawyer has telephoned and will be attending in person in due course is not adequate. The custody officer may forget, be too busy, or may want the suspect to think that the lawyer has not been in contact. If a request to speak to the client on the telephone is resisted by the custody officer, the officer should be reminded that Code C, Code H para 6.1 provide that, subject to the power to delay access to advice under PACE s58(8), (8A) and TA 2000 Sch 8 para 8: 'all detainees must be informed that they may at any time consult and communicate privately with a solicitor, whether in person, in writing or by telephone'.

### Initial advice by a duty solicitor

3.55    A duty solicitor (or an accredited representative[29]) is required to give initial advice to the suspect on the telephone unless he or she is already at or

---

28  SCC 2010, Part B para 9.25. The contract provides that the 45-minute target must be met in at least 80 per cent of matters (para 9.24).

29  See para 3.9 above regarding the use of accredited representatives in duty solicitor cases.

close to the police station and can advise the client in person without delay or the police refuse to permit the suspect to speak to the duty solicitor on the telephone. The only exception to the obligation to speak to the suspect in person arises if the suspect is incapable of speaking to the lawyer, for example, by reason of drunkenness or violent behaviour, or because an interpreter is required. In this case, the duty is postponed, but the lawyer must make arrangements to provide initial advice as soon as the suspect is capable of speaking to him or her.[30] This will inevitably mean that the lawyer must rely on the custody officer to inform him or her when the suspect is in a fit state to speak, or is otherwise able to do so. It is advisable to ask that the custody record be endorsed with a request to this effect. For the obligation to inform the suspect that he or she is not obliged to use a duty solicitor, see para 3.8 above.

### Objectives of the initial telephone contact

3.56 The objectives of the initial telephone contact with the suspect are set out in checklist 4 below.

3.57     If the lawyer is not going to attend in person, the suspect should be given appropriate advice, which will depend on the reason for the suspect's detention and the proposed or likely action on the part of the police. Whether or not the lawyer intends to attend in person, the suspect should be reminded that he or she is entitled to legal advice at any time (under PACE s58 and Code C, Code H para 6.1), and that he or she can insist on being able to speak to the lawyer at any stage of the detention.

---

**Checklist 4: Initial telephone conversation with client**

1) Confirm that the suspect does want legal advice, and does want it from the lawyer concerned (or the lawyer's firm).
2) Inform the client of the lawyer's status, and confirm that legal advice is free (unless the client has chosen to instruct the lawyer privately).
3) If appropriate, inform the client of the lawyer's role and, in particular, that the lawyer's role is to act in the client's best interests.
4) Obtain initial information from the client, the client's understanding of the reason for the arrest, and any particular concerns or complaints that the client may have. The lawyer may at this stage be asked to contact a third party to inform him or her of the suspect's arrest. In principle, there is no reason why this should not be done, but care must be taken to ensure that this message is not used to pass on information to a person evading arrest or which might result in evidence or proceeds not being recovered or which might otherwise lead to interference with the course of justice. If in any doubt, the lawyer should agree to contact the third party only on the understanding that the lawyer will first tell the custody officer what is intended.
5) Decide whether, and when, to attend in person (see para 3.58 below).
6) Give initial advice to the suspect, including advice about whether it would be advisable for the lawyer to attend in person. If the lawyer

---

30 SCC 2010, Part B para 9.43.

does intend to attend, or to arrange for attendance, in person the lawyer should usually advise the suspect not to answer police questions,
and not to sign any documents, until the suspect has received advice
in person. However, in drink/driving cases the suspect should not normally be advised to refuse to give a sample pending arrival of the lawyer (see para 2.129 above). If attendance is to be delayed, the suspect
should be warned of possible attempts by the police to persuade the
suspect to proceed with an interview in the absence of the lawyer.

A full and accurate note should be taken of all information obtained and
advice given, which should be timed and dated.

## Deciding whether to attend

3.58    The decision whether to attend is one of the more difficult decisions for a
lawyer doing police station work. The information obtained by this stage
may be insufficient to make a fully informed decision, and even if the
custody officer has been co-operative, the information received must be
treated cautiously because it may be incomplete or misleading, or the position may change rapidly. The decision is also difficult because the lawyer
may have competing demands on his or her time, or may be making the
decision in the early hours of the morning when the only thing the lawyer
really wants to do is to stay in bed!

3.59    In the past, some lawyers believed that if the client was not going to
answer questions in interview, there was no need for the lawyer to attend.
This belief is, and was, wrong. A suspect who refuses to answer questions is likely to be regarded as antagonistic by the police and is likely to
be subjected to greater pressure from them. If the suspect then makes
admissions under such pressure, it is less likely that those admissions will
be excluded at trial because it will be argued that the suspect has received
advice, albeit only by telephone. In any event, in view of the 'silence' provisions of the Criminal Justice and Public Order Act (CJPOA) 1994 ss34, 36
and 37, whether to advise a client not to answer questions is a complex and
critical decision which should not normally be made on the telephone.

3.60    Another belief, although less prevalent now, is that there is no need for
the lawyer to attend if the interview is to be tape-recorded. This is based on
the fallacy that the role of the lawyer is simply to act as an observer. There
are many occasions when a suspect will require advice during a police interview. In any case, tape-recording does not appear to inhibit some police
officers from acting inappropriately, and pressure may be exerted before
the tape is switched on.[31]

3.61    It is important, therefore, for the lawyer to have guidelines to assist him
or her in making the decision, and checklist 5 is designed to assist in making the appropriate decision. It must be remembered that one of the main
aims of police detention and interrogation is to persuade the suspect to talk.
The Court of Appeal has even stated that provided PACE and the Codes
of Practice are observed, the police are entitled to try to obtain admissions

---

31   For a graphic illustration of this, see M McConville, 'Videotaping interrogation: police
behaviour on and off camera' [1992] Crim LR 532.

from the suspect.[32] The presence of a lawyer at the police station and at the police interview may, therefore, be of critical importance.

### Circumstances where attendance will not be paid for

3.62   Restrictions on payment for attendance on a client at a police station are set out in paras 1.56–1.60 above. In all cases, the sufficient benefit test must be satisfied, although provided that the attendance is for the purpose of providing legal advice to a client, and the advice could not reasonably be given over the telephone, the test will be satisfied in respect of the initial attendance.

### Mandatory attendance

3.63   The starting-point for deciding whether to attend is the SCC 2010, Part B paras 9.39–9.41 which are binding on duty solicitors and own solicitors providing services under the contract. In the absence of exceptional circumstances, once a case has been accepted attendance in person is mandatory:

a)   to provide advice and to attend all police interviews with the client where the client has been arrested in connection with an offence;
b)   at an identification parade, group identification or confrontation; and
c)   where the suspect complains of serious maltreatment by the police.

Attendance at a video identification is not mandatory under the contract, although it may be claimed for provided it is justified. The contract does not specify what constitutes exceptional circumstances, but may include where a client specifically instructs the lawyer not to attend. If they do arise, the lawyer must record on file the decision not to attend, including details of the exceptional circumstances and the reasons for the decision.

3.64       The provision of advocacy assistance at a warrant of further detention hearing is not mandatory, even for a duty solicitor. However, if the client is a services person requiring advocacy assistance within England and Wales at a custody hearing before a judicial officer under the Armed Forces Act 2006, the SCC 2010 para 9.60 provides that a duty or own solicitor must attend personally upon the client to provide advice and assistance including advocacy assistance.

### Discretionary attendance

3.65   Where attendance in person is not mandatory, a lawyer providing services under the SCC 2010 has a discretion to attend in person. Whether such attendance will be paid for under the contract will depend upon whether the sufficient benefit test is satisfied (see para 1.60 above) and whether the case falls within the restrictions on payment for attendance in person (see paras 1.56 to 1.59 above).

### Clients under the influence of drink or drugs

3.66   A difficult problem arises where the lawyer is told by the custody officer that the suspect is unfit to be interviewed because the suspect is drunk

---

32  *R v Oliphant* [1992] Crim LR 40.

or suffering from the effects of drugs. An initial question is whether the suspect is really intoxicated through drink or drugs, or appears to be so as a result of causes other than alcohol or drugs. Code C, Code H NfG 9C provides a reminder that a person who appears to be drunk or who is behaving abnormally may be ill or injured or may be suffering from the effects of drugs. If there is any doubt, the police should call in a healthcare professional as a matter of urgency.

3.67    When a person is initially detained at a police station, the custody officer must conduct a structured risk assessment, which includes an assessment of whether drug or alcohol abuse is 'an immediate factor in the treatment/ handling of the detainee' (Code C, Code H paras 3.5 to 3.11).[33] If the person is suspected of being intoxicated through drink or drugs, or the person's level of consciousness causes concern, the person must, subject to clinical directions, be visited and roused at least every half hour and have his or her condition assessed in accordance with Code C, Code H Annex H, and clinical treatment must be arranged if appropriate (Code C para 9.3, Code H para 9.4). If a healthcare professional is called in, the professional must be asked for his or her opinion about the detainee's fitness for detention, fitness for interview, and the need for safeguards (Code C para 9.13 and Code H para 9.15). Therefore, if the lawyer has reason for doubting that the condition of the suspect is one of simple intoxication, the lawyer should press the custody officer to call in a healthcare professional, and attend in person if not satisfied with the response. A healthcare professional does not have to be called by the police if the suspect is simply intoxicated, but does have to be called (or in urgent cases, the suspect taken to hospital or to a medical practitioner) if the suspect:

- appears to be suffering from physical illness;
- is injured (unless a minor injury);
- appears to be suffering from a mental disorder; or
- otherwise appears to need medical attention (Code C para 9.5 and Code H para 9.6).

This obligation applies even if the suspect has not requested clinical attention and whether or not the suspect has already received clinical attention elsewhere (Code C para 9.5A, Code H para 9.7).

3.68    It would not normally be appropriate for the police to interview a suspect who is intoxicated. Before every interview the custody officer must determine whether the suspect is fit to be interviewed, by reference to the factors set out in Code C, Code H Annex G. Where necessary, the decision should be taken in consultation with the officer in charge of the investigation and with the healthcare professional (see further para 5.22 below). If the lawyer believes that his or her client is not fit to be interviewed, the lawyer should consider calling an independent medical practitioner. Code C para 9.8 and Code H para 9.10 provides that a suspect is entitled to be examined by a medical practitioner of the suspect's own choice, although at the suspect's expense.[34]

---

33  See Home Office Circular 32/2000 *Detainee Risk Assessment and Revised Prisoner Escort Record (PER) Form*, para 22.

34  Any cost may be claimable as a disbursement provided it is reasonably incurred. See para 5.24 below.

## Checklist 5: Deciding whether to attend the police station

1) The lawyer should normally attend if:

the suspect has been arrested for an offence and is going to be interviewed;

the police are intending to conduct an identification procedure;

the client complains of serious maltreatment by the police;

the client is a youth or a person at risk.

2) If 1) above does not apply, the lawyer should still consider attending if:

the client is apparently drunk or under the influence of drugs (unless satisfied that the police have taken all appropriate action);

the alleged offence (or circumstances, if the client has been arrested for other than an offence) is serious or may have serious consequences;

there are important issues concerning searches of person or property;

there are important issues concerning the taking of samples;

an interview has been conducted, but advice is necessary at the time of charge;[36]

the circumstances of the client indicate that attendance is necessary – for example, the client is unfamiliar with police processes, or the client is particularly upset or nervous;

detention is likely to be lengthy;

the lawyer is not satisfied that advice by telephone can be given with sufficient confidentiality;

the lawyer is not satisfied that he or she can adequately communicate with the client by telephone;

representations need to be made to the police and these cannot adequately be made by telephone, e-mail or fax.

3) Attendance may not be necessary or justified where the client:[37]

has been arrested for a road traffic offence (including excess alcohol);

has been arrested on warrant and no further offence is suspected;

has been arrested for breach of bail and no further offence is suspected;

has been arrested under a civil order or warrant.

Always consider whether attendance is mandatory and, if not, whether the sufficient benefit test is satisfied. Consider whether professional obligations to the client require attendance even though payment may not be made under the Standard Criminal Contract.

A full and accurate note must be taken of all information obtained, advice given, reason for not attending (where attendance is mandatory) and reason for attending (where attendance is not mandatory).

---

35  In a duty solicitor case, advice on the implications of the caution that will be given on charge is mandatory, although the lawyer must consider whether this requires attendance in person, or whether it is possible to give confidential telephone advice (SCC 2010, Part B Para 9.43(b)).

36  Which may, in any event, be covered by the CDS Direct scheme. See para 1.57 above.

### Deciding when to attend

3.69   Having decided to attend, the lawyer must also decide when to attend. This will depend on a variety of factors including:

- how long the client has been at the police station;
- whether the client appears to be distressed and/or vulnerable; and
- when the police are intending to interview, conduct an identification procedure, etc.

The SCC 2010, Part B para 9.17 provides that where the time for a police interview of identification procedure has been fixed, the lawyer must attend in sufficient time to undertake reasonable steps that directly relate to the interview or identification procedure. This, of course, includes consultation with the client. The lawyer should discuss the decision whether and when to attend with the client, and should try to ensure that the client understands both the decision and the reasons for it. It is important to remember that the police may give the client the impression that delay in dealing with the client's case is the fault of the lawyer, which may make the client susceptible to proceeding to an interview without waiting for the lawyer to attend.[37]

## Informing the custody officer of the lawyer's intentions

3.70   The lawyer should inform the custody officer of his or her intentions regarding attendance. Where the lawyer has spoken to the suspect on the telephone, the lawyer should not ask the suspect to pass a message on to the police. The suspect may get it wrong or the custody officer may take no notice of what is said. If the lawyer is not intending to attend in person, it is a matter of courtesy to inform the custody officer so that the police can proceed to interview if that is their intention. If the lawyer wishes to attend, the lawyer should inform the custody officer of the lawyer's intentions for a number of reasons.

3.71        First, the lawyer may wish to delay the visit until nearer the estimated time of a police interview. In this case, the lawyer will need to establish from the custody officer when the interview is likely to take place and to inform the custody officer that the lawyer intends to attend in person nearer the time. The custody officer should be asked to note this on the custody record and be asked to inform the lawyer of any change of plan. The suspect should be told of the lawyer's intentions, and if the delay is likely to be, or turns out to be, prolonged, the lawyer should consider attending to give initial advice in person. The longer the client is in custody, the more vulnerable the client is likely to become, particularly to a suggestion by the police that the delay may be shortened if the client agrees to be interviewed in the lawyer's absence. Where the lawyer is acting as a rota duty solicitor and the interview (or identification procedure) is postponed to a time when the lawyer is no longer on duty (or, if as a panel duty solicitor, until a time when it is no longer convenient to act as duty solicitor), the lawyer

---

37  For evidence of this, see L Skinns, '"Let's get it over with": early findings on the factors affecting detainees' access to custodial legal advice' (2009) 19 (1) *Policing and Society* 58-78.

is required to make arrangements to ensure that the suspect continues to receive advice either by another duty solicitor or by acting as the client's own solicitor.[38]

3.72    Second, Code C para 6.6 and Code H para 6.7 provide, subject to exceptions, that a person who wants legal advice may not be interviewed or continue to be interviewed until the person has received such advice. Where a suspect has been given legal advice on the telephone and the custody officer is not aware that the lawyer intends to attend in person, the custody officer could argue that the interview can proceed in the lawyer's absence since the suspect has 'received' advice. By the same argument, despite the general prohibition on inferences being drawn from 'silence' where a suspect who has asked for legal advice is interviewed without having received it,[39] there is a risk that inferences could be drawn. However, this justification would be difficult to sustain if the police know that the lawyer intends to attend the police station.

3.73    Third, Code C para 6.6(b)(ii) and Code H para 6.7(b)(ii) provide that an interview can proceed in the absence of a lawyer, on the authority of an officer of the rank of superintendent or above, if waiting for the lawyer to arrive would cause unreasonable delay to the process of the investigation. However, Code C and Code H NfG 6A provides that if the lawyer says that he or she is on the way to the station or that he or she will set off immediately, it will not normally be appropriate to begin an interview before the lawyer arrives. Although the NfG states that the officer should ask the lawyer for an estimate of the time of arrival at the station, the lawyer should ensure that he or she informs the custody officer of the estimated time of arrival, whether or not he or she is asked.

3.74    Fourth, if the lawyer has other commitments which would result in the lawyer's attendance being delayed, the lawyer should seek agreement with the custody officer that this will be acceptable. The effect of Code C para 6.6(b)(ii), Code H para 6.7(b)(ii), and NfG 6A is that if the delay is unacceptable to the police, they should inform the lawyer how long they will be prepared to wait before commencing an interview so that alternative arrangements for the suspect to receive advice in person can be made. Again, the lawyer should speak to the client on the telephone so that the client is made fully aware of any delay.

3.75    The custody officer should be asked to note on the custody record the decisions taken regarding attendance and also to note, where relevant (as it usually will be), that the lawyer has requested that the client should not be interviewed or asked to sign any police document until the time of the lawyer's attendance.

38  SCC 2010, Part B para 9.43(c).
39  CJPOA 1994 ss34(2A), 36(4A) and 37(3A), and see para 5.66 below.

# CHAPTER 4

# Action on arrival at the police station

*continued*

# Introduction

4.1 The action taken by a defence lawyer on arrival at the police station can significantly affect the whole case, and may determine whether it is successful from the defence point of view. A thorough, diligent and skilful approach may well improve the client's position, resulting in the client being released without charge, in the police evidence being less strong than it otherwise would have been, or in crucial evidence in mitigation being put forward at an early stage. On the other hand, a lawyer who simply 'goes through the motions', facilitating the police processes, might as well don a police uniform. While the lawyer will frequently encounter no particular difficulty, the lawyer may be met with obstructiveness or prevarication which may or may not be deliberate or legitimate. It is worth remembering that the police often regard the presence of a lawyer as a potential hindrance to their work, and research has shown that they do resort to informal ploys in an attempt to keep lawyers away, or at least to try to minimise their impact.[1] Police behaviour of this kind, even if detected, will not necessarily result in the exclusion of any evidence obtained. Even if the police have acted, and continue to act, entirely properly, an appropriate adversarial stance on the part of the defence lawyer will be the best way of protecting the client's interests.

4.2 This chapter deals first with problems of obtaining access to a client in police detention and suggests ways of dealing with them. It then goes on to deal with obtaining the information from the police that will be necessary for the lawyer to be able to advise the client properly. As always, the lawyer should keep a careful note of all relevant action taken and information obtained, together with relevant times.

# Problems in obtaining access

## Denial of access under PACE and the Terrorism Act 2000

4.3 The powers of the police to delay access to legal advice under Police and Criminal Evidence Act 1984 (PACE) s58 and the Terrorism Act (TA) 2000 Sch 8, which are relatively rarely exercised, and guidance on what representations to make in this situation, are dealt with at paras 2.139–2.148 above.

## Exclusion of representatives

4.4 Legal advisers who are not solicitors may be dealt with less favourably than solicitors by the police, who sometimes use the difference in status to undermine the advice given by them or to influence them into accepting a course of action that they would not otherwise wish to accept. It is important, therefore, to know precisely what different powers the police have in

---

1 See A Sanders and L Bridges, 'Access to legal advice and police malpractice' [1990] Crim LR 494–509 and, for more recent evidence, L Skinns, *Police custody: governance, legitimacy and reform in the criminal justice process* (Willan, Abingdon, 2011) especially chs 4 and 5.

relation to non-solicitors compared with solicitors. It is also important to be clear about who does and does not qualify as a solicitor for the purposes of the Codes of Practice (see para 2.132 above). Although probationary and accredited representatives come within the definition of 'solicitor' for the purposes of the Codes of Practice, they are subject to powers to exclude them from police stations (see para 4.6 below). The Codes make no reference to representatives who are neither probationary nor accredited. While the SCC 2010 does not permit payment for police station work carried out by such persons, there appears to be no reason in principle why a solicitor acting on a private basis could not use a representative who is not registered with the Legal Services Commission (LSC). However, it may be argued that since PACE s58 specifically refers to the right to consult a solicitor, and Code C defines the meaning of the term for the purposes of the Code, the police would be entitled to refuse access to a non-solicitor who is neither a probationary nor an accredited representative.

4.5    Although PACE s58 and TA 2000 Sch 8 para 7(1) refer only to the right to consult a solicitor, a solicitor may send a probationary or accredited representative to the police station to provide advice on the solicitor's behalf (Code C para 6.12A, Code H para 6.14). Generally, the additional powers police have to exclude representatives apply only at the stage of admission to the police station. Once admitted, they are to be dealt with as if they were solicitors (Code C para 6.12A, and Code H para 6.14). However, for police tactics in respect of representatives during police interviews see para 7.50 below.

4.6    The power to exclude a representative from the police station is governed by Code C para 6.12A and Code H para 6.14, which enable an officer of the rank of police inspector or above to refuse a representative admission to the station if the officer considers that such a visit will hinder the investigation of crime. This is a decision for individual officers, although they may receive guidance from senior officers.[2] Thus, senior officers could warn of the possible unsuitability of certain representatives, but it would be for individual inspectors to make a decision on exclusion in any particular case. Hindering the investigation of crime does not include giving proper advice to a detained person in accordance with Code C NfG 6D or Code H NfG 6C. It is unclear precisely what is meant by the phrase 'refuse admission to the station', but in practice it is likely to mean admission beyond the waiting area into the 'non-public' part of the station. In exercising his or her discretion to exclude, the officer should, in particular, take the following into account (Code C para 6.13, Code H para 6.15):

1) whether the identity and status of the representative has been established;

2) whether the representative is of suitable character to provide legal advice, which is unlikely if the representative has a criminal record, unless for a minor offence and not of recent date;[3] and

---

2  *R v Chief Constable of Avon and Somerset ex p Robinson* [1989] 1 WLR 793; [1989] 2 All ER 15; (1989) 90 Cr App R 27; [1989] Crim LR 440.

3  See *R v Chief Constable of the Northumbria Constabulary ex p Thompson* [2001] 4 All ER 354 in which it was held that it was the responsibility of the employing solicitor, and not the police, to determine whether a representative was sufficiently independent.

3) any other matters in any written letter of authorisation provided by the solicitor on whose behalf the representative is attending the station.

4.7   Code C para 6.13 and Code H para 6.15 make no reference to the qualifications or experience of the representative, and lack of qualifications or experience are not grounds for exclusion. However, the SCC 2010 imposes requirements regarding suitability and supervision of non-solicitors conducting police station work. Lawyers employing representatives should ensure that they are properly trained, and should provide them with guidance on the type of case they are permitted to deal with, the circumstances in which they should seek advice or assistance from a solicitor, and the mechanisms for contacting a solicitor at short notice. Representatives must provide a written report to the conducting solicitor once the attendance at the police station has been concluded, and no later than the next working day.[4]

4.8   If the police decide to refuse access, they must inform the solicitor who employs the representative (as well as the suspect), and must give the solicitor the opportunity to make alternative arrangements (Code C para 6.14, Code H para 6.16). The solicitor should seek reasons, preferably in writing, for the refusal of access and check that the decision was made by an officer of the appropriate rank. If necessary, the matter should be taken up at a more senior level, since if the representative is refused access on one occasion, there is a danger that the representative will be refused admission again in the future.

## Acting for more than one client

4.9   Acting for more than one client in respect of the same or a connected allegation may present a conflict of interests, and the lawyer may have to make a difficult ethical decision about whether the lawyer can advise all or any of the suspects. Guidance on what may amount to a conflict of interests, and how conflicts and potential conflicts should be dealt with, is given at para 5.40 below. The police will sometimes seek to deny a lawyer access to one or more suspects on the ground that there is a conflict of interests. Code C NfG 6G and Code H NfG 6F confirm that a solicitor may advise more than one client in an investigation and '[a]ny question of conflict of interest is for the solicitor under their professional code of conduct'. It is, therefore, the lawyer's decision and not that of the police.

4.10   However, the NfG goes on to state that if waiting for the solicitor may lead to unreasonable delay, authority under Code C para 6.6(b) (or Code H para 6.7(b)) may be given for an interview to proceed without the suspect having received advice. This will not be relevant since the same officers will be interviewing all suspects. However, the lawyer should check, particularly in more serious cases where a number of officers are involved in the investigation, when the interviews are to be conducted so that the lawyer can arrange for another lawyer to attend if necessary. Code C para 6.6(b) and Code H para 6.7(b) enable the superintendent to give authority for the interview to proceed in the lawyer's absence only if 'awaiting their

---

4   SCC 2010, Part B paras 9.26–9.38.

arrival' would cause unreasonable delay. It could be argued, therefore, that since the lawyer is at the station, albeit advising another suspect, the power to proceed in the absence of the lawyer does not apply.

## Juvenile clients

4.11    Where the suspect is a juvenile, the police may seek to deny the lawyer access on the grounds that either the appropriate adult has not yet been contacted or that the appropriate adult has not asked for or confirmed the request for legal advice. The right to legal advice under PACE s58 and TA 2000 Sch 8 is not limited to adults and there is no authority for delaying access on the ground that the suspect is a juvenile. The same applies to mentally disordered or mentally vulnerable suspects. See further para 2.124 above and chapter 11.

## 'The suspect no longer wants a solicitor'

4.12    Having initially requested legal advice, a suspect may later change his or her mind and agree to proceed with a police interview without having received it. Code C para 6.6(d) and Code H para 6.7(d) permit an interview to proceed in these circumstances provided that the suspect agrees in writing or on tape and an inspector or above, having enquired about the suspect's reasons for his or her change of mind, authorises an interview to proceed. The change of mind may have been genuine, but on the other hand it may have been induced by a variety of factors. Research has found that the police sometimes use the prospect of further delay to persuade a suspect to agree to being interviewed without having received the advice the suspect initially wanted.[5]

4.13    If a lawyer arrives at the station to see a client the detained person must, unless Annex B applies (ie, access to a solicitor is delayed under PACE s58(8) or TA 2000 Sch 8 para 8), be informed of the presence of the lawyer and must be asked if the person would like to see the lawyer (Code C para 6.15, Code H para 6.17).[6] This applies whether or not the suspect has already declined advice or, having asked for it, has changed his or her mind. The fact of the lawyer's attendance and the decision of the suspect must be noted in the custody record.

4.14    Therefore, if on arrival at the station the lawyer is told that the client no longer wants to see the lawyer, the custody officer should be asked to confirm that the suspect has been informed of the lawyer's arrival and that the suspect has been asked whether he or she wishes to see the lawyer. The lawyer should consider asking the custody officer to hand a letter to the suspect, advising the suspect to ask to see the lawyer (specimen letter 1 appendix 4). Strictly, there is no right to demand this, but it may help allay fears that the significance of the lawyer's visit has not been properly conveyed to the client. If the custody officer maintains that the suspect still does not wish to see the lawyer, the lawyer should consider asking to see the custody record to check that this has been properly recorded.

5   See note 1 above.
6   See paras 2.139 and 2.145 above.

The suspect does not have to endorse the decision on the custody record personally, unlike the position where the lawyer has been instructed by a third party (see para 3.20 above).

## 'The interview has already started'

4.15 The custody officer may say that the client is being interviewed, and the custody officer does not want to interrupt it. Code C para 6.15 and Code H para 6.17 explicitly provide that, whether or not the client is being interviewed, the client must be told of the lawyer's arrival and asked whether he or she would like to see the solicitor.

4.16 Where the interview is interrupted and the suspect wants the lawyer to be present, the police may press for the interview to proceed without an opportunity being given to advise the suspect in private. This should be strongly resisted. The lawyer should insist on speaking to the client in private, an absolute right under PACE s58, before agreeing to the interview being re-commenced. In addition to the information the lawyer would usually seek to gather at the initial stage (see para 4.19 below), the suspect and the interviewing officer should be asked what has been said in the interview so far. If the interview has been tape-recorded the lawyer should consider asking to listen to it. If it has been recorded in writing, a request should be made to see the written record. If the police seek to prevent the lawyer from seeing the client in private, the lawyer should normally make representations to the custody officer (or superior officer) and advise the client not to answer questions in the meantime.

## 'The suspect wants another solicitor'

4.17 On arrival at the police station, the lawyer may be told that the client has asked for another lawyer. This should not happen in a publicly funded case where the lawyer has been contacted by the DSCC (see para 3.3 above), but may happen if the lawyer was instructed by a third party and has gone to the police station without first speaking to the suspect on the telephone. In this case, it will be advisable to contact the other lawyer to ensure that he or she has been instructed. If, however, the lawyer has already spoken to the suspect on the telephone and agreed to attend, it should give cause for concern. If the suspect has not yet seen the other lawyer, it will be advisable to try to see the suspect to confirm the position. If the custody officer is not willing to allow this, the lawyer is faced with the problem that PACE s58 gives the right to legal advice to the suspect as opposed to giving the lawyer a right of access to give advice.[7] The police may treat it simply as a matter of competition between lawyers in which the suspect has the right to make the decision. On the other hand, in some cases the police may encourage the use of another lawyer if that lawyer is regarded as more compliant. In the absence of a right to see the suspect in the police station, there is little the lawyer can do other than to take it up with the suspect, and possibly the other lawyer, at a later stage, and keep a careful note of what is said and done.

7 *Rixon v Chief Constable of Kent* (2000) *Times* 11 April.

## 'The officer in the case is not here'

4.18   The custody officer may try to avoid taking responsibility for deciding whether to allow the lawyer access to the client by stating that the officer in the case is out, possibly conducting a search or interviewing witnesses, and that a decision on access cannot be made until the officer returns. PACE Part IV, especially s39, firmly places legal responsibility for the treatment of suspects on the custody officer. Furthermore, since access to a lawyer can only be delayed on the authority of an officer of the rank of superintendent or above under PACE s58(8) or TA 2000 Sch 8 para 8, if such authority has not been given the custody officer has no power to delay access.

## Obtaining information from the police

4.19   On arrival at the police station the lawyer should normally:
- inform the custody officer of the lawyer's status;
- request sight of the custody record;
- seek information from the custody officer;
- seek information from the officer in charge of the case or interviewing officer.

This should normally be done before seeing the client, but if carrying out any of these functions is likely to involve any significant delay, the lawyer should have a preliminary consultation with the client.

## Information from the custody record

4.20   A solicitor is entitled to consult the client's custody record as soon as is practicable after arrival at a police station, and at any other time while the client is detained (Code C para 2.4, Code H para 2.5). Although custody records cannot be presumed to be accurate, they contain information which may be of great value to the defence lawyer.[8] Given the circumstances, there is a danger that the lawyer may skim-read the record and miss important detail. The lawyer should ensure, therefore, that the lawyer takes sufficient time to read it and take a careful note of the contents. This should be checked against what the lawyer has already been told, and against the relevant police powers, and it may prompt questions to the custody officer, the officer in the case and the client. Particular attention should be paid to the matters set out in checklist 6.

---

8  For an explanation of what constitutes the custody record and what must be recorded in it, see para 2.96 above.

**Checklist 6: Reading the custody record**

1) The custody record number
2) The name and address of the suspect
3) The grounds and reasons for arrest
   - Is this the same as the information already given to the lawyer?
   - What is the statutory or common law authority for the arrest?
   - Why was arrest necessary?
   - Is the arrest lawful?
   - Is it an indictable offence?
   - Is it indictable-only? This is relevant, in particular, to probationary representatives
4) The age of the suspect
   - If the suspect is under 17 years, what action has been taken in respect of an appropriate adult?
5) The time that a solicitor was requested
   - What time was this acted on by the police?
   - If there is a significant time lapse, why is this?
6) The time of arrest and the time of arrival at the police station
   - If there is a significant time difference, why is this?
7) The time detention was authorised and grounds for detention being authorised
   - Are the grounds for detention lawful?
   - Is there sufficient evidence to charge?
8) The property found on the suspect, if recorded. This may give an important indication of evidence in relation to the offence for which the suspect has been arrested (for example, large sums of money, bunches of keys, self-sealing bags, etc), or of other offences about which the police may want to question the suspect.
9) Any indication that the suspect is, or may be, mentally disordered or mentally vulnerable, and the results of the risk assessment conducted by the custody officer
   - If so, what action has been taken in respect of an appropriate adult?
   - Has a healthcare professional been called?
10) Any indication that the suspect is, or may be, unfit through drink or drugs
   - If so, has a healthcare practitioner been called?
   - If a healthcare practitioner has already examined the client, what was the purpose of the examination and what was the result?
11) Whether a property search been authorised
   - If so, on what authority and for what purpose?
   - What, if anything, has been seized?
12) Whether the suspect has been asked to sign a police officer's notebook
   - If so, why was the suspect asked to do so before the lawyer's arrival?
   - What was in the officer's notebook?
13) Whether an interview has been conducted
   - If so, why was an interview conducted at that stage?
   - Was it conducted contrary to Code C para 6.6 or para 11.1?
   - What was said in the interview?

14) Any authorities given or decisions taken in respect of the taking of samples, fingerprints, photographs or drugs-testing
   • Have these been conducted?
   • What was the result?
   • Why were they authorised/conducted before the arrival of the lawyer?
15) Actions taken in respect of the risk assessment required under Code C para 3.6
16) Any unusual entries – for example, late entries, deleted entries

A full and accurate note must be taken of all information obtained and further enquiries made, which should be timed and dated.

## Information from the custody officer

4.21    Having seen the custody record, the lawyer should check with the custody officer whether there have been any changes in the information obtained earlier in the initial telephone call, request any further information in checklist 3 which was not obtained in the initial conversation, and raise any questions arising from the custody record. It will often be advisable to ask the custody officer what he or she knows of the circumstances of the arrest and the evidence, since the custody officer may be more forthcoming than the officer in the case, and it may be instructive to compare this information with that subsequently given by the officer in the case. Furthermore, given the significance of previous convictions (see para 5.170 below), the custody officer should be asked for any information he or she has regarding the client's previous convictions. This is information that the custody officer is required to obtain as part of the risk assessment described below.

4.22    The custody officer should be asked about the risk assessment that the custody officer must carry out in respect of all suspects when they are being booked in at the police station (Code C, Code H para 3.6). If there are any indications that the suspect is injured, ill, or suffering from the effects of alcohol or drugs, the lawyer should seek to ensure that appropriate action has been taken, and make suitable representations where necessary. This is important not only in relation to the general welfare of the client, and whether the client is fit to be detained and/or interviewed, but also because evidence shows that actions taken by the custody officer can be critical in preventing self-harm by suspects at risk while in police custody.[9] The lawyer should also ask whether there are any indications that the suspect might present a risk to the safety of the lawyer (see para 5.8 below).

---

9   See T Bucke, et al, *Near misses in police custody: a collaborative study with forensic medical examiners in London*, IPCC Research and Statistics Series, Paper 10 (Independent Police Complaints Commission, London, 2008); and see generally Association of Chief Police Officers (ACPO), *Guidance on the safer detention and handling of persons in police custody* (Centrex, Bedford, 2006).

4.23 The requirement to conduct a risk assessment means that the custody officer must consider whether a detainee is likely to present specific risks to custody staff or to himself or herself. This includes a check on the police national computer, which must be done as soon as practicable. The risk assessment must be carried out in a structured way. Guidance on risk assessment is set out in Home Office Circular 32/2000, of which the following should be noted.

- A risk assessment must be made in respect of all persons entering police custody.
- The results of the risk assessment must be set out in the custody record, indicating either that no risks have been identified or indicating the risks that have been identified and the responses to the questions that must be asked of persons entering police custody under Code C and Code H para 3.5. This is also required by Code C and Code H para 3.8.
- Risk assessment is an ongoing process and assessments must be reviewed if circumstances change (see Code C, Code H para 3.10).
- Risk categories include medical or mental conditions, medication issued, special needs, intoxication, violence, escape risk, suicide or self-harm, injuries, vulnerability and force/restraint/spray used. If appropriate, the custody officer should consult with others, such as a healthcare professional, and is responsible for implementing the response to any specific risk identified (Code C, Code H para 3.9).

4.24 If a person is suspected of being intoxicated through drink or drugs, or the person's level of consciousness causes concern, the person must (subject to clinical directions) be visited and roused at least every half hour, and have his or her condition assessed in accordance with Code C and Code H Annex H. If a suspect appears to be suffering from a physical illness or from a mental disorder, is injured, or appears to need clinical attention, the custody officer must ensure that the person receives appropriate clinical attention (Code C para 9.5, Code H para 9.6). The custody officer must also consider the need for clinical attention where a person is suffering the effects of alcohol or drugs (Code C para 9.5B, Code H para 9.8). If a healthcare professional is called in, the healthcare professional must be asked for his or her opinion about any risks or problems which the police need to take into account when making decisions about detention, when to carry out an interview (if relevant), and the need for safeguards (Code C para 9.13, Code H para 9.15). Before any interview, the custody officer must assess whether the detainee is fit to be interviewed (see para 5.22).

## Information from the officer in the case

4.25 In order to advise effectively, the lawyer should attempt to obtain a clear idea of what evidence the police have. Unfortunately, the police are under a very limited legal obligation to disclose information relevant to the suspected offence. They are under no statutory obligation to disclose information apart from the grounds for arrest, and the grounds for detention, and the courts have only been willing to extend the obligation to disclose the contents of a previous interview where this is necessary to enable the lawyer to advise the client about whether or not to consent to a caution.[10] It has been held that the 'silence' provisions of Criminal Justice and Public Order Act (CJPOA) 1994 do not impose any obligation on the police to give full disclosure before a police interview.[11]

4.26    Despite these limited obligations, the lawyer should normally seek as much information as possible about the allegation and the available evidence from the police. This is necessary for a number of reasons.

1) Advice to the client is more likely to be correct, and effective, if it is based on full information.

2) If the client is advised to answer police questions, it is necessary to consider what facts the client may rely on at trial and, therefore, what information the client should give to the police in interview.

3) The courts have held that although a complete absence of information from the police may justify a failure to tell the police about facts that will be relied on at trial, a failure by the police to give all available information is unlikely to do so.[12]

4) Intelligence-led policing, and techniques of targeting suspects, are likely to produce information that is not readily apparent, and may not be used as evidence at any trial, but which may be highly relevant to advising the client.

5) Information may be obtained at the police station stage which, lawfully or not, may not subsequently be disclosed under the provisions of the Criminal Procedure and Investigations Act (CPIA) 1996.[13]

If the information obtained from the police is incorrect or misleading, it may provide grounds for the exclusion of evidence of a subsequent interview where the lawyer relied on that information as a basis for advising the client.[14]

4.27    The information that the lawyer is able to obtain will depend in part on the officer he or she is dealing with, but also on the lawyer's own negotiation skills (see para 4.55 below). In a more serious case, the officer assigned to the client may not be the officer in charge of the case, and it may be advisable to try to speak to the latter since the officer dealing with

---

10  *DPP v Ara* [2001] 4 All ER 559. For an analysis of this case see J Azzopardi, 'Disclosure at the police station, the right of silence and *DPP v Ara*' [2002] Crim LR 295. Where an identification procedure is to be held, the police must disclose the first description of the suspect given by a witness who attends the procedure. For an argument that European Convention on Human Rights article 6 (right to a fair trial) imposes a disclosure obligation, see R Toney, 'Disclosure of evidence and legal assistance at custodial interrogation: what does the European Convention on Human Rights require?', (2001) 5 *International Journal of Evidence and Proof* 1, p39.

11  *R v Imran and Hussain* [1997] Crim LR 754. See also *R v Nottle* [2004] EWCA Crim 599 and *R v Farrell* [2004] EWCA Crim 597. In *R v Thirlwell* [2002] EWCA Crim 2703, the Court of Appeal held that, where a person had been arrested on suspicion of murder, the police were under no obligation to disclose provisional medical evidence of the cause of death.

12  See, in particular, *R v Condron* [1997] 1 WLR 827; [1997] 1 Cr App R 185; [1996] Crim LR 215; and *R v Argent* [1997] 2 Cr App R 27; [1997] Crim LR 346.

13  See R Ede and E Shepherd, *Active Defence* (Law Society, London, 2000), especially chapter 9.

14  *R v Mason* [1987] 3 All ER 481; (1988) 86 Cr App R 349; [1987] Crim LR 757.

a particular suspect may be under instructions to give limited information and may not know all of the relevant facts. Any information obtained should be treated with caution for it may be partial, incomplete or exaggerated (see further para 4.54 below).

4.28 Many police forces use a strategy of 'phased disclosure' (otherwise known as drip-feed or managed disclosure), especially in more serious cases, by which the disclosure of information to the suspect and the lawyer is actively managed. In some investigations the police may appoint a 'disclosure officer'[15] whose function is to consider and advise the interviewing officers on what disclosure to make as the investigation and interviews progress. In some cases the custody officer may be aware of the disclosure strategy, and may be working with the officers in the case to keep relevant information out of the custody record. One of the main purposes of a phased disclosure strategy is to preserve the element of surprise and to encourage the suspect to answer questions without being aware of the extent of the information known by the police, while disclosing enough information to persuade a court, if relevant, that inferences from silence should be drawn. Sometimes the fact that such a strategy is being employed is obvious, because the lawyer may be handed a written document headed something like 'Disclosure 1', but this is not always the case. If the lawyer suspects that the police are using a phased disclosure strategy the lawyer should:

- ask the police directly whether they are using a phased disclosure strategy;
- ask the police if they have any evidence that they have not disclosed;
- note carefully what information is disclosed and at what time; and
- reconsider the advice whether to answer questions on each occasion that disclosure is made.

While complete lack of disclosure before an initial interview may be treated by a court as sufficient justification to prevent inferences from silence, the more information that is disclosed the less likely it will be that a court will accept this justification for failure to tell the police of relevant facts.

4.29 Sometimes an officer may give the lawyer certain information but then ask the lawyer to withhold it from the client. Lawyers have a general duty to pass on material information to their clients.[16] Therefore, if the officer seeks to prevent information from being passed on, the lawyer would normally have to inform the officer that the lawyer has no choice but to pass it on to the client. Alternatively, an officer may say that he or she will give information to the lawyer on condition that the lawyer does not tell the client. In this situation the lawyer should normally inform the officer that the lawyer cannot accept information on such a condition. However, there are exceptions to the general rule. First, the Solicitors Regulation Authority (SRA) recognises that a lawyer does not have to pass on information that could harm the client because of the client's mental or physical condition. Second, under the Proceeds of Crime Act (POCA) 2002, and other similar legislation, to make a disclosure that is likely to prejudice an investigation

---

15 Not to be confused with a disclosure officer appointed for the purposes of CPIA 1996.
16 *SRA Code of Conduct 2011*, ch 4.

concerning the recovery of the proceeds of crime constitutes the offence of 'tipping off', although a lawyer normally has a defence if the disclosure was to a client in connection with the giving of legal advice.[17] If in doubt, the lawyer should contact the SRA professional ethics helpline for advice.[18]

4.30    Generally, the lawyer should try to obtain or confirm the information in checklist 7 from the officer in the case, and compare it with information obtained from the custody officer and client. Some of the matters are dealt with in greater detail after the checklist.

---

### Checklist 7: Information from the officer in the case

1) The reason for and circumstances of the arrest, and reason why arrest was necessary.
2) Details of the suspected offence(s) for which the client was originally arrested.
3) Details of any other suspected offence(s) and whether the client has been, or is to be, re-arrested under PACE s31 in respect of such offences.
4) Whether any other person has been arrested in connection with the offence(s), and whether that other person implicated the client.
5) Whether any other person is being sought in connection with the offence(s).
6) Whether the client has been interviewed and, if so, why and what was said.
7) Whether the client has made any admissions, or any significant statement or silence, outside the context of an interview.
8) Whether any question has been put to the client under CJPOA 1994 s36 or s37 and any reply made.
9) Details of the evidence the police have that allegedly implicates the client.
10) Whether a search of property has been conducted.
    - If so, whether anything of evidential significance has been found.
    - If not, whether and when it is proposed to carry out a search. In both cases, the legal authority for the search should be ascertained and checked against the offence for which the client has been arrested.
11) Whether it is intended to carry out any other procedure such as:
    - removal of clothing;
    - an intimate or non-intimate search;
    - taking an intimate or non-intimate sample;
    - taking a handwriting sample;
    - conducting an identification procedure;
    and the reasons for and legal authority for such procedures.
12) What other investigations are being conducted or are intended.
13) Whether the client has any previous convictions or other forms of previous misconduct.
14) The purpose of any forthcoming interview.

---

17  See, eg, POCA 2002 ss330–333, and see para 1.20 above.
18  Available via www.sra.org.uk/solicitors/advice-support.page.

15) Whether the officer has any other relevant information that has not been disclosed to the lawyer and, if relevant, whether a strategy of phased disclosure is being used.

16) The officer's view of the client's fitness for interview and whether the client may come within the categories requiring an appropriate adult.

17) Whether the officer has sufficient evidence to charge (if relevant), and what is likely to happen after the interview.

18) (Where appropriate) The attitude of the officer to diversion from prosecution.

19) Whether the officer is aware of any indications that the client may present a risk to the safety of the lawyer.

A full and accurate note must be taken of all information sought and obtained, together with relevant times.

## The circumstances of the arrest

4.31    It is important to probe the reason for and the circumstances of the arrest, and the reasons why arrest was necessary, since this may disclose information about the true nature of the investigation, the legality of the arrest (see para 2.13 above), and of detention (see para 2.53 above), and information that may be relevant to and/or explain the attitude of the police to the client. For example, a client who resisted arrest, or who in some other way contested the authority of the police, is likely to be dealt with more harshly. It may also be important to question the officer about how the client came to be arrested. In many cases this will be obvious, but in others, seeking to establish how or why the client came to be arrested may disclose the existence of evidence or information that has not been revealed, for example, the involvement of an informer or undercover officer, or some form of surveillance.

## The suspected offence

4.32    It is important to confirm what the suspected offence(s) is (are). This should lead the lawyer to consider:

1) the category of the offence(s), for example, indictable or summary-only, and the consequences, for example, whether the arrest was lawful, etc;

2) what the police/prosecution will have to establish in order to prove the offence;

3) what evidence the police appear to have, and/or what evidence they might seek, in order to prove the offence;

4) whether the evidence that the police appear to have is sufficient to charge the suspect without conducting an interview (see para 2.59 above);

5) whether the police may be considering, or may subsequently consider, whether to investigate the client for, or seek to charge the client with, other offences instead of or in addition to the offence(s) for which the client has been arrested. For example, following an arrest for assault

occasioning actual bodily harm the police may consider common assault or, on the other hand, Offences Against the Person Act 1861 s18 or s20 wounding or grievous bodily harm;

6) what defence(s) may be available to the client;

7) whether a simple caution (or reprimand or warning in the case of a juvenile) or a conditional caution may be considered;

8) what information should subsequently be sought from the client.

## Other people arrested

4.33   If other people have been arrested in connection with the same offence(s), one question that arises is the significance of what they have told the police, particularly insofar as it may implicate the client. If a co-suspect, in the absence of the client, makes a confession in a police interview that also implicates the client, it is well established that evidence of this statement cannot be used by the prosecution as evidence against the client at a subsequent trial.[19] It may amount to evidence against the co-suspect, but not against the client. However, although evidence of the statement cannot be used at trial against the client, the co-suspect himself or herself could give evidence against the client at a subsequent trial. This can happen if the co-suspect is not prosecuted or, having been prosecuted, the case is discontinued for some reason, or if prosecuted and the co-suspect pleads guilty before the trial of the client. In these circumstances, the co-suspect can be called as a prosecution witness. Alternatively, if the co-suspect is prosecuted and pleads not guilty, he or she can give evidence against the client when giving evidence on his or her own behalf.

4.34   At the police station it will normally be impossible accurately to predict what will happen in respect of the co-suspect. However, it cannot be assumed that the fact that a co-suspect has implicated the client will necessarily have an adverse effect on the client at any trial.

## Admissions or 'silences' already made by the client

4.35   Whether evidence of a confession, or 'significant silence' (see para 4.50), made by the client before receiving advice from the lawyer is likely to be admitted at trial will be impossible to predict with certainty at the police station. However, it is important that the lawyer is aware of what may happen regarding any prior confession or 'silence' at the trial stage since this will affect the advice to be given to the client. The lawyer should consider:

• whether the suspect should have been cautioned and, if so, whether the suspect was cautioned;

• whether the confession (or silence) was made in the context of an 'interview';

---

19  See, eg, *R v Rhodes* (1959) 44 Cr App R 23. But note *R v Hayter* [2005] UKHL 6; [2005] 1 WLR 605; [2005] 2 All ER 209; [2005] 2 Cr App R 3; [2005] Crim LR 720 in which it was held that where a co-defendant's guilt had been established by his own out of court confession, that finding of guilt could be used as evidence against the defendant.

- whether, if it did come within the definition an 'interview', it should have been conducted at that stage; and
- whether it was properly recorded.

In questioning the officer in the case, the lawyer will want to try to establish precisely what was said to the client by that, or any other, officer, the circumstances and purpose of such question(s), and the alleged response (if any) of the client. However, the lawyer should avoid alerting the officer to any actual or potential procedural errors (for example, a failure to caution) or requirements (for example, the obligation under Code C and Code H para 11.4 to put a significant statement or silence to a suspect at the beginning of an interview).

### Admissions and confessions

4.36 The terms 'admission' and 'confession' can, in practice, be used interchangeably. Generally, evidence of a confession, such as evidence from the police officer who heard it or a tape-recording of it, will be admissible at trial (PACE s76(1)).[20] However, whether in a particular case a confession will be admitted will in part depend on whether it was made in the context of a police 'interview'. 'Confession' is defined, for the purpose of determining whether it is governed by PACE s76, as including: 'any statement wholly or partly adverse to the person who made it, whether made to a person in authority or not' (PACE s82(1)). It includes direct or indirect statements by the suspect that the suspect committed the offence, mixed statements such as 'I hit him, but it was in self-defence', and also statements that, although not amounting to a direct admission of involvement, are detrimental to the suspect in the light of other available evidence. However, a statement that is intended to be exculpatory or neutral at the time that it is made does not amount to a confession even it is adverse by the time of the trial.[21]

### 'Interview' and the obligation to caution

4.37 'Interview' is defined as:

> [T]he questioning of a person regarding their involvement or suspected involvement in a criminal offence or offences which, under paragraph 10.1, must be carried out under caution ... Procedures undertaken under the Road Traffic Act 1988, section 7 or the Transport and Works Act 1992, section 31 do not constitute interviewing for the purpose of this Code (Code C para 11.1A).[22]

A caution must be given where a person is questioned about his or her involvement or suspected involvement in an offence (or questioned further

---

20 Although this is subject to PACE s76(2), and the discretion to exclude prosecution evidence under s78. See paras 13.34 and 13.42 below.

21 For example, a statement by the accused to the police that the accused was not present at the scene of a crime, which by the time of the trial the prosecution can prove, or the accused accepts, was false. See *R v Hasan* [2005] UKHL 22; [2005] 2 AC 467; [2005] 2 WLR 709; [2005] 4 All ER 685; [2005] 2 Cr App R 314.

22 Where a person is arrested under TA 2000 s41, interview is defined as 'the questioning of a person arrested on suspicion of being a terrorist which, under *paragraph 10.1*, must be carried out under caution' (Code H para 11.1).

where the answers given to previous questions provide the grounds for suspicion) if there are grounds to suspect the person of that offence, and the person's answers or silence may be given in evidence (Code C, Code H para 10.1). Although the Codes do not expressly say so, the courts have interpreted the provision so that a caution only has to be given where there are reasonable grounds for suspicion.[23] Code C para 10.1 (but not Code H para 10.1) goes on to explain that a caution need not be administered if the questions are put for other purposes (see para 4.42 below). If a caution is not administered in circumstances where it is required, this may lead to exclusion of evidence obtained under PACE s76 or s78, but it may not, especially if the suspect's lawyer is present (see para 13.48 below).

4.38    Therefore, questions put to an arrested person about the offence for which the person has been arrested, or any other offence of which the person is suspected, will amount to an interview. Similarly, questions put to a person who has not been arrested about an offence of which he or she is suspected will also be an interview, provided that there are reasonable grounds for that suspicion. If an officer, without suspecting the person, puts questions to the person about an offence and, as a result of the answers to those questions (or some other reason, such as evasiveness or refusal to answer), the officer forms a suspicion that the person is involved in an offence, the person must be cautioned before further questions are put to him or her about the offence, and such further questioning will amount to an interview.[24]

### Was the confession made in an interview?

4.39    It is important to recognise that the definition of an interview given above is not confined to a formal police interview that takes place in an interview room at a police station. Any 'questioning of a person regarding their involvement or suspected involvement in a criminal offence' which is required to be carried out under caution amounts to an interview, wherever it takes place,[25] even if it consists of only one question and answer.[26] This would include questions put by a custody officer if those questions

---

23  See *R v James* [1996] Crim LR 650. In *R v Miller* [2007] EWCA Crim 1891 it was held that a caution should have been given where, on finding a butterfly knife during a drug search, the officer asked the person why he had it with him. The contrary conclusion was drawn where questions were put to a TIE (trace, interview and elimination) individual, where there were conflicting accounts of his possible involvement and the police were not sure if he was the person who was the last to be seen with the victim (*R v Shillibier* [2006] EWCA Crim 793). See also *Hughes v DPP* [2010] EWHC 515 (Admin).

24  See *R v Senior* [2004] EWCA Crim 454; [2004] 3 All ER 9; [2004] 2 Cr App R 12, *R v Perpont* [2004] EWCA Crim 2562, *Ridehalgh v DPP* [2005] EWHC 1100 (Admin), and *Sneyd v DPP* [2006] EWHC 560 (Admin).

25  Thus, questioning that should have been carried out under caution ought to be treated as an interview even if, as a matter of fact, it was not carried out under caution.

26  See *R v Ward* (1994) 98 Cr App R 337, where it was held that it was the nature of the question, rather than its length, that was relevant. For a useful illustration of this point see *R v Miller* [1998] Crim LR 209.

concern involvement or suspected involvement in a criminal offence.[27] It has been held that a 'co-operation conversation' conducted by customs officers with a suspect, designed to encourage the suspect to provide information rather than for the purposes of gathering evidence against the suspect, was not an interview, although the inducement offered in return for co-operation meant that the conversation could not be used in evidence against the suspect.[28]

4.40    Questions put to a person in the street or in a police car have, in the past, caused the courts some difficulty in deciding whether they amounted to an interview. This was, in part, a result of the confusing definition contained in previous versions of Code C. This has been largely remedied in the current version of the Code. Where a person has been cautioned (whether or not the person had been arrested), or where a person ought to have been cautioned because there are reasonable grounds to suspect the person of an offence, and the person is questioned regarding involvement or suspected involvement in a criminal offence, such questioning will amount to an interview (Code C paras 10.1 and 11.1A). For example, questioning of a person in the street following his or her arrest for a drugs offence concerning three polythene wraps that the person had been seen to throw away was held to amount to an interview.[29] Similarly, questions put to a person in a police car, following arrest for having an offensive weapon in a public place, about why the person was carrying a flick-knife, were held to amount to an interview.[30]

4.41    However, questions are necessary for a conversation to amount to an interview, so it will not be an interview if a suspect 'blurts out' a confession unprompted by any question, provided that the police do not then proceed to ask questions.[31] Questions put by a police officer during an undercover operation are not likely to amount to an interview provided that the officer does not ask the questions for the sole purpose of gathering evidence rather than as part of the purpose of the transaction itself (see para 13.53 below).[32] Asking a person under arrest to account for an object,

27  See *R v Oransaye* [1993] Crim LR 772, in which questioning by a custody officer about money found in the defendant's possession when being booked in was held to be an interview. Note that Code C para 3.4 specifically provides that a custody officer must not ask questions regarding a suspect's involvement in an offence, nor in respect of any comments made by the suspect in response to the arresting officer's account of the arrest or in response to the decision to detain, because of the danger that it will amount to an interview. See also *R v Weerdesteyn* [1995] 1 Cr App R 405; [1995] Crim LR 239.

28  *R v de Silva* [2002] EWCA Crim 2673; [2003] 2 Cr App R 5; [2003] Crim LR 474.

29  *R v Goddard* [1994] Crim LR 46.

30  See *R v Hunt* [1992] Crim LR 582, and see *R v Miller* at note 26 above which concerned similar facts.

31  See *R v Younis and Ahmed* [1990] Crim LR 425, *R v Menard* (1994) *Times* 23 March; and *R v Doyle* [2002] EWCA Crim 1176.

32  See *R v Bryce* [1992] 4 All ER 567; (1992) 95 Cr App R 320; [1992] Crim LR 728, *R v Christou and Wright* [1992] QB 979; [1992] 4 All ER 559; [1992] 3 WLR 228; (1992) 95 Cr App R 264; [1992] Crim LR 729, *R v McCarthy* [1996] Crim LR 818, *R v Edwards* [1997] Crim LR 348, and *R v Rajkuma* [2003] EWCA Crim 1955. For useful surveys of this difficult area, see S Sharpe, 'Covert police operations and the discretionary exclusion of evidence' [1994] Crim LR 793, G Robertson, 'Entrapment Evidence: manna from heaven or fruit of the poisoned tree?' [1994] Crim LR 805 and S Sharpe, *Judicial discretion and criminal investigation* (Sweet & Maxwell, London, 1998).

substance or mark or to account for his or her presence at the place where the person was arrested will almost certainly amount to an interview (see para 5.87 below).

4.42    Code C para 10.1 gives examples of questioning that would not require a caution and which, therefore, would not amount to an interview. These are:

- Questions put solely to establish a person's identity or ownership of a vehicle.
- Questions put to obtain information in accordance with any relevant statutory requirement, for example, under Road Traffic Act (RTA) 1988 s165 (which empowers a police constable to require certain people driving, or believed to have driven, motor vehicles to supply their name and address).[33]
- Questions put in furtherance of the proper and effective conduct of a search. For example, questioning during a search about whether articles discovered belong to the suspect will not amount to an interview. However, questioning that goes further, for example, about whether drugs found were intended to be supplied to others, would almost certainly amount to an interview.[34]
- Questions seeking verification of a written record in accordance with Code C para 11.13 (see para 5.113 below).

In addition, questions put in examining a person in accordance with TA 2000 Sch 7 do not amount to an interview (see para 1.63 above).

4.43    If the conversation did not amount to an interview, evidence of any confession made will generally be admissible subject to the requirements regarding recording and verification (see para 4.49 below). If the conversation did amount to an interview, the next question in determining whether evidence of it is likely to be admitted at trial is whether it was permissible to conduct an interview at that stage.

### Should an interview have been conducted?

4.44    Generally, once a decision to arrest a person has been made, the suspect must not be interviewed about the offence except at a police station or other authorised place of detention (Code C para 11.1, Code H para 11.2). Note that this applies once a 'decision to arrest' has been made, as opposed to an arrest itself, so that it may be relevant to establish when a police officer made the decision to arrest since the officer may not have acted on that decision immediately. Therefore, if a decision to arrest has been made, a person should not be interviewed at home, in the street, or in the police car on the way to the station. The general prohibition on interviewing away from the police station is subject to an exception if delay would be likely to:

---

33  It has been held that the statutory 'drink-driving' procedure under the RTA 1988 is not an interview. See *DPP v Rouse; DPP v Davis* [1991] Crim LR 911, also reported as *DPP v D (a Juvenile); DPP v Rouse* (1992) 94 Cr App R 185.

34  See Code B paras 6.12 and 6.12A, and *R v Langiert* [1991] Crim LR 777, *R v Khan* [1993] Crim LR 54, and *R v Raphaie* [1996] Crim LR 812.

1) lead to interference with or harm to evidence, or interference with or physical harm to other people, or serious loss of, or damage to, property; or

2) lead to the alerting of other people suspected of committing an offence but not yet arrested for it; or

3) hinder the recovery of property obtained in consequence of the commission of the offence (Code C para 11.1, Code H para 11.2).

If an interview is carried out under this exception, it must cease once the relevant risk has been averted or the necessary questions have been put in order to attempt to avert that risk.

4.45    If the suspect was interviewed contrary to Code C para 11.1 or Code H para 11.2, a court may exclude evidence of any confession made during it (under PACE s76 or s78), although other factors will also be relevant, such as whether it was recorded, whether the suspect was given an opportunity to verify the record, whether the suspect was aware of his or her right to silence and whether the suspect is a juvenile or a person at risk. Evidence of an interview conducted under one of the exceptions outlined above will probably be admitted.[35] Note that the provisions on accounting for an object, substance or mark, etc, or for presence, under CJPOA 1994 ss36 and 37 do not authorise the police to interview a suspect away from the police station.

4.46    If it was permissible to conduct an interview away from the police station, a further question is whether the formalities in Code C have been complied with.

## Have the interviewing requirements been complied with?

4.47    Certain requirements set out in Code C and Code H apply only to interviews conducted in police stations or other authorised place of detention (Code C paras 11.2, 11.4 and the whole of section 12, and Code H paras 11.2, 11.4 and the whole of section 12), but others apply to interviews wherever they are conducted. The requirements are dealt with more fully at para 7.5 below, but a number of points should be noted at this stage.

1) Code C para 11.15 provides that while juvenile and mentally vulnerable suspects should not be interviewed in the absence of an appropriate adult, this is subject to an exception where they are interviewed away from the police station under the provisions of Code C para 11.1 (see para 4.44 above), or in the police station under Code C para 11.18 (urgent interviews). Code H para 11.9 contains similar provisions. See further chapter 11.

2) If the interview took place before the suspect was taken to a police station, the police are not under a duty to inform the suspect that he or she is entitled to legal advice. It has been held that an arrested person is not entitled to legal advice under PACE s58 until detention has been authorised under PACE s37,[36] although arguably such a person, and

35  See *R v Ibrahim, Omar, Osman and Mohamed* [2008] EWCA Crim 880. This case concerned a 'safety' interview at a police station under TA 2000 Sch 8 paras 7–9 (subsequently replaced by Code H para 6.7), but the same principles are likely to apply to a 'safety' interview conducted away from a police station.

36  *R v Kerawalla* [1991] Crim LR 451, and *Kircup v DPP* [2003] EWHC 2354 (Admin); [2004] Crim LR 230.

a person who has not been arrested, has a common law right to legal advice (see para 2.131 above).

3) Whether or not the interview took place at a police station, the police must make an accurate record of it (Code C para 11.7).[37] If it was not practicable for the record to be made during the interview, it must be made as soon as practicable after the interview (Code C para 11.8).

4) Whether or not the record is made during the interview, the suspect must, unless it is impracticable, be given the opportunity to read the interview record (unless it was tape-recorded, in which case the verification arrangements in Codes E or F will apply) and to sign it as correct or to indicate the respects in which the suspect considers it inaccurate (Code C para 11.11).

4.48   At the beginning of an interview the interviewing officer must, following the caution, put to the suspect any significant statement or silence which occurred in the presence and hearing of a police officer or civilian interviewer before the start of the interview, and which has not been put to the suspect in the course of a previous interview (Code C, Code H para 11.4). This requirement applies whether or not the statement or silence occurred within the context of an interview (see para 4.37 above for definition). The recording and verification requirements noted above (if made in the context of an interview) and below (if not made in the context of an interview) would apply to such a statement or silence.

### Recording and verifying 'non-interviews'

4.49   As noted earlier, a confession made outside the context of an interview (see para 4.37 above for definition) will generally be admitted at trial provided it is recorded and verified in a similar manner to that provided for interviews (Code C para 11.13). As with interviews conducted before arrival at the police station, Code C and Code H para 11.4 provide that any such statement or silence must be put to the suspect at the beginning of any subsequent interview. See further para 5.113 below.

### Significant silences

4.50   A 'significant silence' is defined as a failure or refusal to answer a question, or answer satisfactorily, when under caution, which might give rise to an inference under CJPOA 1994 (Code C para 11.4A, Code H para 11.5). This means that Code C and Code H para 11.4 do not require the police to put a 'silence' to a suspect in interview where that 'silence' was made in circumstances where inferences could not be drawn. Inferences cannot be drawn where a suspect is interviewed in circumstances where the suspect has not been given an opportunity to consult a solicitor (see para 5.66 below). A failure to respond to a request to account under CJPOA 1994 s36 or s37 should only amount to a 'significant silence' if the suspect was asked to account in an interview at a police station (see para 5.90 below).

---

37   Code H para 11.8 provides that interview records should be made in accordance with the Code of Practice issued under to the TA 2000 Sch 8 para 3 where the interview takes place at a designated place of detention.

## The effect of 'tainted' interviews on subsequent interviews

4.51  The foregoing sections deal with the question of the likely admissibility of a prior statement or silence and the effect that this might have on advice on whether to answer questions in a subsequent interview. This section deals with a further issue – whether an improperly conducted interview (or non-interview) might affect the admission in evidence of a subsequent interview that is properly conducted. The effect on a subsequent interview of an earlier 'tainted' interview will depend on how reliable or fair the subsequent interview is in the light of the tainted interview.

4.52  In order for a subsequent, properly conducted, interview to be excluded as a result of an earlier, inadmissible, interview there must be a clear connection between them.[38] The courts will consider whether the arrangements for the second or subsequent interview gave the accused a sufficient opportunity to exercise an informed and independent choice about whether to repeat or retract what was said in the excluded interview or to say nothing.[39] In *R v McGovern*,[40] the Court of Appeal held that evidence of a confession made in a second interview should have been excluded because it was a direct consequence of a confession made in an initial interview held when access to a solicitor had been improperly denied. If the suspect receives advice from a lawyer before the subsequent interview, it is likely that a court will not regard it as being tainted by the first, and is likely to admit it in evidence. However, this may not be the result if the court takes the view that despite legal advice the suspect did not have the opportunity to make an informed and independent choice. Thus, in *McGovern* the Court of Appeal held that the second interview should have been excluded, despite the fact that the suspect received advice from a solicitor before, and at, that interview because the tainted interview was still operative, partly because the solicitor had not been told that the suspect had been denied access to a lawyer before the initial interview.[41]

4.53  In the cases cited in the previous paragraph, the accused had made admissions in the subsequent interviews. A question that appears to be undecided is whether inferences should be drawn where, in the second interview, the suspect remains silent. If the factors that rendered the initial interview inadmissible are still operative at the time of the subsequent interview, or if the suspect did not have the opportunity before the second interview of exercising an informed and independent choice (for example, because the suspect did not have legal advice), arguably no adverse inferences should be drawn.

---

38  *R v Gillard and Barnett* (1992) 92 Cr App R 61; [1991] Crim LR 280. See also *Y v DPP* [1991] Crim LR 917, *R v Geddis* (1992) *Times* 28 December, *R v Conway* [1994] Crim LR 838, *R v Glaves* [1993] Crim LR 685, and *R v Ahmed* [2003] EWHC Crim 3627.

39  *R v Neil* [1994] Crim LR 441.

40  (1990) 92 Cr App R 228; [1991] Crim LR 124.

41  For a useful discussion of the relevant cases, see P Mirfield, 'Successive confessions and the poisonous tree' [1996] Crim LR 554. For a more recent example, where evidence of a second interview was excluded, where the first interview had been conducted in the absence of a caution, see *R v Webster* (2000) 12 December (unreported).

## Evidence implicating the suspect

4.54   The officer in the case should be asked for full information concerning the case, and a full and careful note should be taken of the response. Officers will frequently not disclose all relevant information in sufficient detail, and will usually need to be prompted. The lawyer should be careful to devote sufficient time to this since information obtained may be crucial to advising the client appropriately, and to the future conduct of the defence, and it may lead to the disclosure of information that might otherwise never be disclosed. The officer should be specifically asked whether he or she has any relevant information that the officer has not disclosed. The information that should be sought is set out in checklist 8.

---

**Checklist 8: Summary of police evidence to be requested**

1) A history of the case, or 'case narrative',[42] including whether and how the case was reported to the police or whether and why the police initiated the investigation, how the client came to be arrested and what happened on arrest, and what has happened in the case so far from the officer's point of view.

2) What investigations have been made at the crime scene (if relevant), including who has attended (arresting and other officers, scene of crime officers, forensic specialists, etc).

3) What relevant communications have taken place (for example, between members of the public and the police, and between police officers), what was said, and how this has been recorded. Where appropriate, the lawyer should ask to see or hear records made.[43]

4) Who has been interviewed in relation to the case, and who has made a statement. The lawyer should ask to see relevant statements. Where appropriate, a detailed note should be taken of descriptions given of relevant events and relevant people, especially possible suspects.

5) What searches have been conducted, samples taken, photographs or other recordings made. The lawyer should ask to see the product of such activities.

6) What relevant real evidence or objects the police have in their possession (for example, weapons, documents, clothing, CCTV recordings, etc). Again, where appropriate, the lawyer should ask to see such items.

7) What forensic examinations or tests have been conducted, and the results of such examinations or tests.

8) What other investigations, forensic tests, etc, are planned.

9) What information the officer has concerning the client's previous convictions or other forms of previous misconduct.

A full and accurate note must be taken of all information sought and obtained, together with relevant times.

---

42  See R Ede and E Shepherd, *Active Defence* (Law Society, London, 2000), chapter 9.

43  Note that the Sexual Offences (Protected Material) Act 1997 imposes certain restrictions on the use made by a solicitor of material disclosed in respect of certain sexual offences. However, these restrictions only apply to material disclosed by a prosecutor (as distinct from disclosure by a police officer).

## Dealing with reluctance or refusal to disclose evidence

4.55   As stated at para 4.25, the police are under no legal obligation to provide information regarding the evidence, and they may be reluctant to give any useful information at all. Code C para 11.1A states that an interview 'is the questioning of a person regarding their involvement or suspected involvement in a criminal offence'. The lawyer can argue, therefore, that he or she cannot properly advise the client in relation to that alleged involvement if the police are not willing to tell the lawyer about the evidence indicating the client's involvement.

4.56   If the officer refuses to give information which is requested, the lawyer should consider what strategy to adopt. This will depend on the extent, and importance, of the information that the officer has refused to disclose. The lawyer should consider the following strategies.

1) Persisting with the request for information. An officer who initially refuses to provide information may do so without thinking about why he or she is doing so, and faced with a tenacious lawyer may decide that refusal is not worth the aggravation.

2) Telling the officer that the lawyer will stop the interview whenever the officer introduces evidence of which the lawyer has not been told or, where appropriate, allowed to see.

3) Informing the officer that the lawyer will have no alternative but to advise the client not to answer questions at all.

4) Informing the officer that the courts have held that inferences cannot be drawn if the police have disclosed insufficient information to enable the solicitor usefully to advise the client.[44]

5) If a Crown prosecutor is in attendance at the police station, or on call, asking to speak to the Crown prosecutor.

4.57   Such strategies may lead the officer to disclose the relevant information. If they fail, the lawyer should consider advising the client not to answer questions in the police interview, and use the interview to obtain information about the allegation. In this case, the lawyer should explain at the commencement of the interview that in view of the lack of disclosure the lawyer is unable to give meaningful advice to the client or that the lawyer is now advising the client not to answer questions because the police have failed to disclose sufficient information (see further para 5.111 below). After the police interview, the lawyer can then advise the suspect whether to request a second interview during which the suspect will answer questions. There is no right to insist on a second interview. However, if a second interview is refused, the lawyer should advise the client whether to make a written statement either in the presence of a police officer or, if this is also refused, to the lawyer. Having taken a copy, the lawyer can then hand it to the police. This may be advisable where, for example, the suspect has a defence which it is important to place on record at an early stage, but which the suspect should not divulge in detail until the suspect knows the full extent of the allegations against him or her, or where

---

44   See, in particular, *R v Argent* [1997] 2 All ER 27; [1997] 2 Cr App R 27; [1997] Crim LR 346; and *R v Roble* [1997] Crim LR 449.

inferences from failure to give information to the police under the CJPOA 1994 would be particularly damaging (see para 5.149 below).

## The dangers of incomplete information

4.58   Any information that the officer gives concerning evidence against the suspect should be treated cautiously for a number of reasons. In some cases the information may be exaggerated in order to encourage the suspect to confess on the basis that the suspect is 'bang to rights'. It is common, for example, for the police to say that a suspect has been identified when in fact a witness has simply given a description which the police think fits the suspect. Whether the witness would pick out the suspect in an identification procedure is another matter altogether. Alternatively, the strength of the evidence may be underplayed by the officer in order to lull the suspect into a false sense of security so that the suspect becomes careless. In particular, the officer may withhold some vital pieces of information from the lawyer in order to trap the suspect by introducing it during the interview, or in the hope that the suspect will assert facts that subsequently appear to be unsustainable in the light of that information. While the PEACE model of police interviewing does encourage the interviewing officer to consider the likely effect of giving insufficient information to the lawyer, it does not go so far as to encourage full disclosure.[45]

## The evidential status of the information

4.59   Consideration must be given to whether any of the apparent evidence may be inadmissible or excluded at trial. For example, the evidence of a very young child may not be admissible, and a confession made by a co-defendant will not be admissible as evidence against the client. Similarly, it may be that a potential witness may not be compellable as a witness and/or may be reluctant to give evidence (see para 5.50 below).

## The purpose of the interview

4.60   It is important to ask the officer to explain the purpose of any intended police interview. In many cases, the officer may simply say that it is to give the opportunity to the suspect to give his or her version of events. This is unlikely to be the case. Since the police are engaged in an adversarial process, they are likely to view the interview as an opportunity to secure evidence which will be of use to them. Occasionally, the police may genuinely view the interview as an opportunity for the suspect to give an innocent explanation, but this is relatively unusual.

---

45   PEACE stands for Planning and preparation; Engage and explain; Account, clarify and challenge; Closure; Evaluation (see para 7.19). The PEACE model of investigative interviewing was set out in *A practical guide to investigative interviewing* (National Crime Faculty, Bramshill, 2000). See now the NPIA *National Investigative Interviewing Strategy 2009*, available at www.npia.police.uk/en/13001.htm.

4.61    Establishing the purpose of the interview is important for a number of reasons.

1) It will help to establish the nature of the questioning, the likely length of the interview, and whether the police are considering questioning the suspect about matters other than those for which the suspect has been arrested. In the latter case, it may be appropriate to try to negotiate separate interviews for separate matters.

2) In those cases where there is likely to be more than one interview, the police may have different objectives in each interview, which may be part of a formal phased disclosure strategy (see para 4.28 above). The first interview may be used to establish the general response of the suspect, for example, whether the suspect admits the offence or whether the suspect will be putting forward a particular defence, which will be useful to the police in determining what lines of enquiry to pursue. In a subsequent interview, the police interviewer may seek greater detail in respect of anything said by the suspect in the first interview, and may seek to exploit any inconsistencies between what the suspect says in the respective interviews, or between what the suspect has said and what any witnesses have said. The lawyer will need to consider appropriate strategies. The lawyer may, for example, want to consider using the first interview to put the police on notice of a particular defence or may want to use it as a way of gathering information about the police case. In any event, the lawyer should advise the client that anything said in the first interview may not only be of evidential significance, but may be used against the client in a subsequent interview. Discrepancies and inconsistencies may be used by the police to try to undermine what the suspect says in the second or subsequent interview, or to seek to demonstrate that the suspect has lied.

3) Probing the purpose of the interview may lead the officer to disclose information not previously disclosed, or may lead the officer to disclose that he or she believes that there is sufficient evidence to charge and/or that the police intend to charge the suspect irrespective of what is said in the interview. In these circumstances, the lawyer should consider what course of action to take. If the lawyer believes that an interview would be to the advantage of the client (for example, enabling the client to put forward a defence at an early stage), the lawyer should allow the interview to proceed. If, on the other hand, the lawyer is of the view that a police interview would not be to the client's advantage (for example, because the client is not going to answer questions and the lawyer wants to try to avoid adverse inferences at trial), there are two arguments for moving to a decision about charge without interview. The first involves making representations to the custody officer that since the officer in the case accepts that there is sufficient evidence to charge, PACE s37 requires the officer to proceed to make a decision about charge (see para 2.59 above). The second is that the combined effect of Code C paras 11.6 (Code H para 11.7) and 16.1 requires the officer to take the suspect to the custody officer for a decision about charge (see para 10.4 below). In such circumstances, the lawyer should consider making representations to the custody officer that further detention

without charge is unlawful and/or indicating at the beginning of the interview that the lawyer is advising the suspect not to answer questions because the lawyer believes that the interview is being conducted contrary to PACE s37 and/or Code C paras 11.6 and 16.1 (see further para 5.149).

## Previous misconduct

4.62   The previous misconduct provisions under Criminal Justice Act 2003 are explained at para 5.170 below. As a result of these provisions, the police often include questions about previous misconduct in interviews of suspects. In order to be able to advise the client appropriately, the officer in the case should normally be asked whether he or she intends to ask such questions, unless the lawyer has good reason to believe that this would prompt the officer to ask questions that the officer had not previously considered. The lawyer should ask:

- what information the police have about the client's previous convictions or other misconduct, including the source and extent of that information, and the precise details;
- what the specific purpose of the questions is; and
- under what 'gateway' of admissibility they are relevant.

The lawyer should also consider suggesting that such questions be asked in an interview separate from that dealing with the substantive offence(s).

## What will happen after the interview?

4.63   The interviewing officer will often have a fairly firm idea of what will happen after the police interview. In most cases, especially in less serious cases, there is likely to be only one police interview,[46] and the officer may well have decided that charge is likely to follow. Probing the officer for this information may also result in further information about the future course of the investigation, further police interviews, timescale, the likely attitude to bail, or the potential for a caution or other form of diversion from prosecution. It should also prompt the lawyer to consider whether he or she should initiate any action such as securing the attendance of a doctor or other expert, or interviewing witnesses.

---

46   One study found that there was only one police interview in 90 per cent of cases. See T Bucke and D Brown, *In police custody: police powers and suspects' rights under the revised PACE Codes of Practice*, Research Study 174 (Home Office, London, 1997), p31.

# CHAPTER 5

# Advising the client

*continued*

# Introduction

5.1    This chapter assumes that the lawyer has arrived at the police station and has successfully negotiated his or her way past the custody officer and is now seeing the client for the first time. This may not be the first time that the lawyer has spoken to the client. The client may be an existing or former client and, in any event, the lawyer will normally have spoken to the client on the telephone before attending the police station.

5.2        The chapter deals with the following issues:

1) The lawyer's role.
2) The initial interview with the client:
   - initial introduction;
   - taking initial instructions;
   - assessing fitness to be interviewed.
3) Issues arising from instructions received:
   - admissions of guilt;
   - suspicion of guilt;
   - inconsistent instructions;
   - an intention to mislead the police;
   - an intention to give a false identity.
4) Conflict of interests.
5) Advising the client:
   - advice on the legal position;
   - the legal consequences of 'silence';
   - advice on whether to answer police questions;
   - strategies for avoiding or minimising inferences.
6) The relevance of previous misconduct.
7) Preparing the client for the police interview.

# The lawyer's role

5.3    Whether or not the client has been in police custody before, the client is likely to be in a vulnerable state of mind, perhaps through fear or anxiety, or simply because the client wants to get out of the police station as soon as possible. In either case, the client may be less coherent than usual and is likely to be susceptible to pressure. Such considerations make it important for the lawyer to be absolutely clear about his or her role, sympathetic to the plight of the suspect, careful not to impose his or her views on the suspect, and willing to take appropriate action to ensure that the client's wishes and decisions are respected.

5.4        Although giving advice will sometimes simply involve the giving of information or outlining options, this will often be insufficient. The client may need careful guidance through the range of options open to them and sometimes may be unable to decide which option to follow. On occasions this will be directly expressed by the client in the form of a question to the lawyer such as, 'Well, what would you do?'. Strictly speaking, decisions should be made by the client, but it must be recognised that sometimes decisions are, in effect, made by the lawyer, whether directly or as a result of the way in which the options are presented to the client. Such a role places great responsibility on the lawyer, particularly where there is more than one appropriate course of action. Two things should be considered. First, having made clear to the client the possible consequences flowing from a particular decision, the lawyer may wish to write them down and ask the client to sign the record acknowledging that the consequences have been explained. Second, where the suspect is heavily reliant on the lawyer for advice to the point where the lawyer is making a decision, again this should be committed to writing and suitably endorsed by the client. In any event, the lawyer should make a careful note of the advice given and the reasons for that advice. This is especially important where the advice of the lawyer and/or the decision of the client may lead to a court considering whether to draw inferences under the Criminal Justice and Public Order Act (CJPOA) 1994. In recording the reasons for advice, the lawyer should be careful to note relevant factors such as the extent of the information disclosed by the police, the view taken by the lawyer of that information, and any factors affecting the physical or psychological state of the client.

5.5    Another responsibility resting upon the lawyer is to seek to ensure that any decision of the client is respected by the police. In chapter 7 it will be seen, for example, that this may well lead to the lawyer intervening during the course of an interview. It may also mean that the lawyer will have to take action outside the context of the interview, particularly if the decision is likely to be unpopular with the police. For example, if the suspect decides that he or she does not want to give an intimate sample, or does not wish to give a handwriting sample, the lawyer will need to be vigilant to see that this decision is not undermined by the police. Since the lawyer will not be able to remain at the station throughout the period of detention, the suspect must be warned about action the police may take once the lawyer has left the station.

5.6    The lawyer, whether solicitor or representative, also needs to give consideration at this stage to the 'client care' rules in the *SRA Code of Conduct* (see para 1.14 above). These provide that solicitors must tell a client the likely cost and how it will be met. If, as is usually the case, the solicitor is acting under the terms of the Standard Criminal Contract (SCC) 2010, or is employed by the Public Defender Service, the issue of costs is usually straightforward since advice and assistance is available free and without reference to financial means to persons arrested and held in custody at a police station and to volunteers.[1] If, however, the solicitor intends to charge on a private basis, the solicitor is under a professional obligation to discuss with the client whether the client may be eligible for legal aid and should apply for it,[2] and must also give a clear indication of fees and other charges.[3] The Code of Conduct also requires solicitors to inform clients in writing of the system for dealing with complaints. A suspect at a police

---

1   See para 1.54 above, and note the limitations imposed by the CDS Direct Scheme (at para 1.57 above), and the sufficient benefit rule (at para 1.60 above).
2   *SRA Code of Conduct 2011*, ch 1, IB (1.16).
3   *SRA Code of Conduct 2011*, ch 1, IB (1.14) and (1.15).

station is not likely to be too concerned about the lawyer's complaints system, and it would be sufficient to give information about the complaints handling procedure in a letter to the client following charge and/or release.[4]

## Initial consultation

5.7 The initial consultation with the client is important for a number of reasons. It will present the lawyer with the opportunity to provide support and reassurance to the client, and to instil confidence in the lawyer's ability to deal with the case efficiently and effectively. The lawyer must ensure that the consultation is carried out in private (see para 2.133 above). If private facilities are not provided, the lawyer should make representations to a senior officer, and make a note of the details of any obstruction and of any representations made. If private facilities are still not granted, the lawyer should not proceed with the consultation, but should explain the situation to the client and advise them to say nothing until private facilities are provided.

5.8 The lawyer should take appropriate action to ensure his or her own safety. Enquires should have been made of the custody officer and the officer in the case to check whether there were any risk indicators of this kind (see para 4.22). If there were, the lawyer should discuss with the custody officer what action should be taken; for example, stationing an officer outside the consultation room. Home Office Circular 034/2007 states that lawyers 'should not expose themselves to unnecessary risk simply for the sake of expediency'. It also provides that police cells and secure visits rooms should not be offered for the purpose of a consultation other than as a last resort and provided arrangements are in place to deal with any identified risks which may affect the safety of the lawyer.[5] If necessary, the lawyer should insist on appropriate facilities and arrangements before proceeding with a consultation.

5.9 A suggested structure for the initial consultation is set out in checklist 9. For a checklist of information to be given and obtained, see checklist 10 in appendix 3. Generally, the consultation should be carried out in the order suggested. It is particularly important that advice is given after instructions are taken. If it is not conducted in this order, the client may conclude that the advice is being given so that the client can adjust the instructions accordingly, which is close to colluding with the client to put forward a false defence.

---

4 *SRA Code of Conduct 2011*, ch 1, O (1.9).
5 See Home Office Circular 034/2007, *Safety of solicitors and accredited and probationary representatives working in custody suites at police stations.*

---

**Checklist 9: Structure of initial consultation**

1) Explain who you are, your status, the fact that legal advice and assistance is free (if appropriate), and how the consultation will be conducted.

2) Seek out any immediate preoccupations or specific needs – for example, medication, food, concern about children, etc – and take appropriate action.

3) Take client's background details. This may help the client to settle down and develop confidence in you, and enables you to assess the client. However, it may be more appropriate to do this later in the interview, particularly if the client is known to you.

4) Tell the client what information you have obtained from the police, give an outline of what the prosecution would have to prove (if appropriate), and (where appropriate) an initial indication of the apparent strength of the police case.

5) Take the client's account of the relevant circumstances, including the circumstances of the arrest and whether the client has already said anything relevant to the police.

6) Give advice on the client's legal position.

7) Give advice on whether the client should answer questions in the police interview.

8) Give advice (as appropriate) on search, samples, identification procedures, etc.

9) Brief the client on the conduct of the police interview and your role during the interview.

10) Prepare the client for the police interview.

---

## Initial introduction

5.10    On introducing themselves, the lawyer should explain his or her status[6] and reassure the client that anything said is confidential and will not be passed to the police, or anyone else, without the client's permission. This is particularly important in the case of duty solicitors, since some suspects believe that they are associated with the police. In these circumstances, it is advisable to explain that the duty solicitor is a private or public defender service solicitor who happens to be on duty at that time. The lawyer should also make it clear whether he or she is a solicitor or representative. There is evidence that some representatives do not do so. This not only amounts to a deception upon the client, but may prove counter-productive. One tactic sometimes adopted by the police to try to undermine legal advice that they do not like is to attack the credibility of the lawyer. If the client has been misled into believing that the lawyer is a solicitor, the client may well have their confidence shaken if a police officer points out that the lawyer is 'only a clerk'. If, however, the lawyer has been clear about his or her status from the beginning, such a tactic is less likely to succeed.

---

6  In duty solicitor cases SCC 2010, Part B para 9.46 provides that before advice is given, the client must be informed of the status of the duty solicitor or representative.

5.11    The client should be reassured at an early stage that the client is covered by the police station legal advice and assistance scheme and that the client will not have to pay for work done in relation to detention at the police station (assuming that this is the case). If the lawyer intends to charge privately, the lawyer must tell the client that the client is entitled to legal aid and must give the client information about costs (see para 5.6 above). Although Codes C and H provide that detained persons must be told that legal advice is free (Code C, Code H para 3.1) and this must be confirmed in writing (Code C, Code H para 3.2), evidence suggests that some suspects are still not aware that it is free.[7] Furthermore, if the client is a volunteer, the police do not have to inform the client of the right to advice, and that it is free, unless the client is cautioned or arrested (Code C para 3.21) or asks (Code C para 3.22).

5.12    At this stage it may be very difficult to predict the future course of events. The suspect, however, is likely to want to know when the police are going to interview the suspect, how long the suspect will be in police custody, whether the suspect is likely to be charged, whether the suspect is likely to get bail from the police station, or what sort of sentence the suspect might get. In less serious cases some of this information may be known with some degree of certainty, and the officer in the case may have already given an indication. In other cases, while the lawyer may have some idea, accurate answers may simply not be possible. The lawyer may feel able to give some indication to the client, but this involves a difficult balancing act. An over-optimistic assessment may well result in a dissatisfied client, but if the lawyer is too pessimistic the client may feel unduly pressured into making unwarranted statements to the police. It will be possible, however, even in this kind of case, for the lawyer to give some useful information such as the likely length of detention without charge and the likely course of events while in police custody.

5.13    One issue that has presented difficulties is whether the lawyer can or should provide the client with any material benefit such as money, food or cigarettes. The Law Society has stated that making a gift to a person with the intention of persuading them to become or remain a client was a breach of professional standards; and that the only form of gift that is acceptable is refreshments or cigarettes for immediate consumption in the presence of the lawyer.[8] Although this was stated some time ago, the same principles apply today.

## Taking initial instructions

5.14    In order to advise the client, it is necessary to obtain information from the client not only about the alleged offence(s), but also about the circumstances of the arrest, whether the client has made any admissions or there has been a significant silence, the client's personal circumstances and the client's criminal history (if any). See further appendix 3 checklist 10.

---

7  Although the written notice given to detained persons states that advice is free, there is evidence to suggest that many suspects did not understand earlier versions. See G Gudjonsson *The psychology of interrogations and confessions* (Wiley, Chichester, 2003) especially p71.

8  See (1994) LS Gaz 22 June p34.

5.15     The initial consultation should commence with questions about any immediate pre-occupations or worries that the client has (for example, concerns about medication, or who will collect the children from school), since they may prevent the client from paying adequate attention to the process, or from dealing with the situation appropriately. The lawyer should use this initial contact with the client to assess the client's physical and psychological state and to identify any particular problems such as literacy difficulties or the effects of alcohol or drugs.[9] The lawyer should expect that this process will take some time, and any pressure from the police to proceed to the police interview quickly should be firmly resisted.[10]

5.16     After the preliminary matters have been dealt with, the lawyer should tell the client what the lawyer has been told about the allegation. This helps the client to focus on the information that might be relevant. It often needs to be emphasised to the client, however, that this information may be incomplete and that, of course, it represents only one side of the story. The client can then be asked what he or she has to say about the allegation. In the first instance, it is usually appropriate to give the client freedom to tell the story in the client's own words and in terms of what the client thinks is relevant, perhaps taking only a few notes of key issues. This having been done, the lawyer can then take the client back over the story, exploring in more detail those aspects which are most significant in terms of the elements of the alleged offence, possible defences and potential evidence. It is important at this stage to take a careful note of what the client says.

5.17     The importance of going through this kind of process cannot be over-emphasised. The client cannot be expected to know what is legally or evidentially important about the case, but will have his or her own ideas about what is important. For example, a person arrested for assault may feel considerably aggrieved and may describe his or her actions as having been in self-defence. A more careful examination may show that while the person was provoked, the provocation fell short of that which is required for the defence of self-defence to be successful. Furthermore, since explaining an event often involves a degree of interpretation of what happened and what the client felt during an event that may have only taken a few seconds or minutes, the way that the client explains what happened may determine the whole course of subsequent events and, most importantly, whether the client is charged and subsequently convicted. In many cases, evidence of an offence is not simply 'out there' waiting to be collected. Rather, the police go through a process of constructing a case against the suspect, and

---

9  For guidance on factors relevant to fitness for interview, see Code C, Code H Annex G, and for the observation list that the police must use where the suspect's condition causes concern, see Code C, Code H Annex H. For a useful, practical guide to assessing client vulnerability see E Shepherd, *Police station skills for legal advisers: practical reference* (Law Society, London, 2004) p306.

10  In a study for the Royal Commission on Criminal Justice in the early 1990s, it was found that in nearly half the cases, the initial consultation between client and lawyer took less than ten minutes. It was also noted that the police generally expected the consultation to be brief because, by the time the lawyer attended, they were ready to interview the suspect. See M McConville and J Hodgson, *Custodial legal advice and the right to silence* (HMSO, London, 1993) especially ch 4.

the police interview is part of that 'construction' process.[11] For this reason, the police interview may be crucial in determining not simply whether the suspect is ultimately found guilty, but in creating evidence that might not otherwise have existed. For example, suppose a person is found in possession of a baseball bat and is arrested for the offence of having an offensive weapon in a public place. A baseball bat is not offensive per se, but may be an offensive weapon if the suspect intended to use it for the purpose of causing injury. Therefore, whether an offence has been committed will depend on the suspect's state of mind, the primary evidence of which is likely to be what the suspect says his or her intention was. If the suspect is asked whether he or she would use it to defend himself or herself if attacked, and the answer is in the affirmative, the suspect has helped 'construct' the case against him or her. In such a case, the client will need to be closely questioned by the lawyer about the client's state of mind, and possible intentions, so that the client can be advised about whether to answer questions in the police interview.

5.18    In seeking information about the alleged offence from the client, the lawyer must have in mind the key elements of the offence concerned. The identity of the offender, whether the physical acts involved in the offence were performed, and the necessary 'mental elements' are all relevant here and the lawyer needs to find out what the client has to say about them. Possible defences such as self-defence, provocation and alibi must also be explored. Similarly, the client may have knowledge of the potential evidence. Were there any witnesses, who were they and what connection do they have with the suspect or the victim? Are there any reasons why the evidence is likely to be unreliable or less convincing than it might otherwise seem? It is for the lawyer to pursue these issues, since the suspect may simply be unaware of their significance.

5.19    Having explored the allegation with the client, the lawyer should ask the client whether he or she has said anything of relevance to the police and, if so, what the client said, from the time of the client's first contact with the police. The lawyer may have been told by the police that admissions or damaging statements have already been made and, if so, the lawyer will need to ask the client about them. If the police have not disclosed such information, the client should always be asked and it is often helpful specifically to tell the client that anything the client has said may potentially be used in evidence. There is nothing worse than being told by a client that he or she had nothing to do with the offence and advising the client to answer questions, only to find in interview that the police say that the client admitted the offence in the police car on the way to the station. Therefore, the client must be asked whether he or she remembers saying anything to the police at any stage that might have a bearing on the question of guilt. Since any significant 'silence' (as well as statements) should be put to the client at the beginning of the police interview, and may lead to adverse inferences being drawn at trial, the client should also be asked whether any questions have been put to the client by police officers (and possibly others, such as store detectives) and what, if any, reply the client

11  For an explanation of 'case construction' see M McConville, A Sanders and R Leng, *The case for the prosecution* (Routledge, London, 1991).

gave. In addition, the lawyer should check with the client what was found in the client's possession either at the time of arrest or when booked in at the police station and, if a search of property has been conducted, whether the client is aware of anything being found during the search.

5.20    The lawyer should seek information from the client about the circumstances of the arrest. In particular, the client should be asked what information the police gave about the grounds and reasons for the arrest, and why arrest was necessary, what (if any) property was found at the time, whether anyone else was arrested, and whether there was any struggle or argument then or subsequently. The latter will be significant because it may determine the police attitude to the client, and may also lead the police to re-arrest and/or charge the suspect in relation to the incident. Furthermore, in some cases it may not be obvious why the client was arrested, which may indicate the involvement of an informant or some kind of covert police operation. Where relevant, this should be discussed with the client, who should be asked whether he or she has any knowledge of what led to the client's arrest.

5.21    Finally, it is important during the initial interview to obtain information about the client's personal circumstances, including whether the client has previously been arrested for and/or convicted of an offence. This information is useful since it may give some clue to the client's familiarity with the interview process, which may affect the advice to be given. It may give an indication of whether the client is likely to be questioned about previous convictions in the police interview (see para 5.170), and will be relevant to the question of whether a simple or conditional caution (or reprimand or warning) is a realistic possibility if the offence is admitted. It will also give an early indication of whether there are likely to be problems regarding bail if the client is charged.

## Assessing fitness to be interviewed

5.22    One objective of the initial consultation with the client is to assess their fitness to be interviewed by the police. The lawyer should have obtained information about the risk assessment that must be carried out by the custody officer and ascertained what action, if any, has been taken in respect of any risk identified (see para 4.23 above). The custody officer, where necessary in consultation with the officer in charge of the investigation and the healthcare professional, must assess whether a detainee is fit to be interviewed before every interview conducted at a police station (Code C, Code H para 12.3). According to the Codes, fitness for interview involves two distinct sets of risks:

- the risk that conducting an interview could significantly harm the detainee's physical or mental state; or
- the risk that anything said by the detainee in an interview might be considered unreliable in subsequent court proceedings because of their physical or mental state.

Code C, Code H Annex G sets out guidance on how fitness is to be assessed, and provides that if a healthcare professional is consulted, he or she should:

- consider the functional ability of the suspect, and not simply give a medical diagnosis;
- advise on the need for an appropriate adult to be present;
- advise on whether re-assessment of fitness for interview will be necessary if the interview lasts beyond a specified time;
- advise on whether a specialist opinion is required;
- be asked to quantify the risks involved in interviewing.

The circumstances in which a healthcare professional should be called in are set out in Code C paras 9.5–9.8 and Code H paras 9.6–9.10. The healthcare professional's determination and any advice or recommendation must be entered in the custody record (Code C, Code H Annex G para 7).

5.23    It is for the custody officer to decide, having regard to any information from the healthcare professional, whether or not to allow an interview to proceed, and to decide what safeguards are needed (Code C, Code H Annex G para 8). The custody officer must not allow a detainee to be interviewed if the officer considers it would cause significant harm to the detainee's physical or mental state (Code C, Code H para 12.3). Suspects in any of the following categories must not be interviewed unless a superintendent or above considers that delay will lead to the consequences set out in Code C para 11.1(a)–(c), or Code H para 11.2(a)–(c), and is satisfied that the interview would not significantly harm the person's physical or mental state:

a) a juvenile or person who is mentally disordered or otherwise mentally vulnerable (see chapter 11), if an appropriate adult is not present at the interview;

b) any other person who at the time of the interview appears unable to:
- appreciate the significance of questions and their answers; or
- understand what is happening because of the effects of drink, drugs or any illness, ailment or condition;

c) a person who has difficulty understanding English or has a hearing disability, if an interpreter is not present at the interview (Code C paras 11.18 and 12.3, Code H paras 11.11 and 12.3).

If a suspect within these categories is interviewed, the interview must cease once sufficient information has been obtained to avert the specified consequences (Code C paras 11.19 and 12.3, Code H paras 11.12 and 12.3), and a record must be made of the grounds for the decision to interview (Code C paras 11.20 and 12.3, Code H paras 11.13 and 12.3).

5.24    The lawyer should find out whether their client's fitness to be interviewed has been assessed and, if so, what the result was. However, it is the lawyer's responsibility to make their own assessment of the client's fitness for interview. The lawyer may have concerns about fitness that have not been identified by the custody officer or the healthcare professional. If the police insist on proceeding, the lawyer may wish to advise the client not to answer questions. However, there is a danger that in deciding whether inferences under CJPOA 1994 can be drawn a court would prefer the opinion of the healthcare practitioner to that of the lawyer,[12] so the

---

12  See *R v Condron* [1997] 1 Cr App R 185; [1996] Crim LR 215.

lawyer should consider speaking to the healthcare professional to try to persuade them that the client is not fit to be interviewed. If the healthcare professional is not a doctor, the lawyer should consider asking the custody officer to call one in. The custody officer must seek the advice of a doctor if a safe and appropriate care plan cannot be provided (Code C para 9.8, Code H para 9.10). If this fails, the lawyer should consider seeking an independent medical opinion. A suspect has a right to be examined by a doctor of the suspect's own choice at his or her expense (Code C para 9.8, Code H para 9.10). For lawyers acting under the SCC 2010 the cost can be claimed under the contract provided it is incurred in the best interests of the client, is reasonably incurred, and the cost is reasonable.[13]

5.25    A comprehensive guide to assessment of clients at the police station can be found in *Police station skills for legal advisers: practical reference*.[14] It sets out a number of tests that a lawyer can use to assess aspects of a client's condition such as memory, co-ordination and literacy. It also states that in making an assessment the lawyer should consider information obtained by:

- asking others who should or could know (for example, custody officer, relatives);
- listening to the way in which the client is talking (for example, slurring speech, talking very quickly or slowly, loss of control);
- finding out details of medication prescribed (whether or not taken);
- visual monitoring of the client (for example, to detect shaking, condition of the eyes, sweating);
- conducting simple tests (for example, to assess memory, co-ordination or literacy).

To this list should be added:

- asking the client whether he or she has been taking any non-prescribed drugs and/or alcohol.

The lawyer should also take a careful note of his or her observations and the information gathered.

5.26    A suspect who is unfit to be interviewed as a result of the effects of drink or drugs may become fit as the effects wear off. However, depending upon the nature of the disorder or vulnerability, a mentally disordered or mentally vulnerable suspect may not become fit for interview, or the risks may be appropriately dealt with by medication or a safeguard such as an appropriate adult. Therefore, the suspect's condition may not provide grounds for delaying an interview provided appropriate safeguards are implemented. If the lawyer believes that the client is or may be mentally disordered or vulnerable, but this has not been identified by the police, the lawyer should, subject to the instructions of the client, inform the custody officer. If the police are informed in good faith that a suspect may be suffering from mental disorder or otherwise be mentally vulnerable, the suspect must be treated as such (Code C para 1.4, Code H para 1.10, and see para 11.58 below).

---

13  SCC 2010, Part A, para 5.39.
14  E Shepherd, *Police station skills for legal advisers: practical reference* (Law Society, London, 2004) p306.

5.27    A potentially more contentious problem arises if the lawyer believes that the client is not fit to be interviewed for other reasons. The client may be extremely tired, or may be distracted as a result of the arrest and detention, or may be preoccupied by worries such as a sick relative or who is looking after their young child. In each case, the lawyer should seek to deal with the problem, since otherwise the client may be particularly prone to confessing falsely in order to get out of the stressful situation.[15] If the client is tired, the lawyer should direct the custody officer's attention to Code C and Code H para 12.2 which provides, subject to exceptions, that in any period of 24 hours the detained person must be allowed a continuous period of eight hours' rest, free from questioning. Although it states that this should usually be at night, it also provides that account must be taken of when the suspect last slept or rested. It is also worth noting the provisions for breaks in interview provided by Code C and Code H para 12.8. If the client is suffering from serious stress as a result of the arrest and detention, the lawyer should consider trying to delay a police interview until the client has become calmer. If the police are reluctant to do this, the lawyer should consider advising the client to request a medical examination. If a suspect makes such a request, a healthcare professional must be called as soon as practicable to assess the suspect's clinical needs (Code C para 9.8, Code H para 9.10). If the client is distracted for other reasons, it may be possible for the client to be reassured, for example, that his or her child is being looked after by a person acceptable to the client. In some circumstances it may be appropriate to suggest to the police that the client be released on bail for a short period to enable arrangements to be made. There will, however, be some cases where the police wish to proceed despite the doubts and representations of the lawyer. In this case, the lawyer should consider asking for his or her representations regarding the condition of the client to be entered on the custody record, and to make them again at the commencement of the interview so that a contemporaneous record of them is made.

5.28    The lawyer should also be aware of other difficulties the client might face besides unfitness. The Codes require special care to be taken in respect of those who are, or who appear to be, blind or seriously visually handicapped, deaf, unable to read, unable to speak or who have difficulty in speaking because of a speech impediment (Code C para 1.6, Code H para 1.12, and Codes C and H section 13). Similarly, special provisions apply if the client has difficulty in understanding English (Code C, Code H section 13). See further chapter 11.

## Issues arising from the instructions received

5.29    A number of issues may arise during the initial interview that will require consideration or action before the police interview. For guidance on the potential obligations on the lawyer to disclose information received from

---

15    See further paras 5.128 and 7.39 below. For an excellent study of factors inducing false confessions, see G Gudjonsson *The psychology of interrogations and confessions: a handbook* (Wiley, Chichester, 2003).

a client, especially in respect of terrorism and the proceeds of crime, see para 1.16 above.

## Admission of guilt

5.30    The fact that a client says that he or she committed the offence does not mean that the client should be advised to answer police questions and admit their guilt. Even if the client is in fact guilty, the police may not have sufficient evidence to charge or successfully prosecute without a confession. This approach is well established,[16] although it is coming under concerted attack from both the government and some senior judges who argue that times have changed and those who are guilty should have to assist the prosecution by admitting their guilt.[17] However, it accords with the privilege against self-incrimination and the presumption of innocence and these are principles that defence lawyers should seek to uphold.

5.31    The client's belief that he or she committed an offence does not necessarily mean that the client is, in fact, guilty. There is ample evidence that some people confess to crimes they did not commit, and that they do so for a variety of reasons associated with their own circumstances or mental state, or the way in which the police interview them.[18] In one case, for example, a suspect whose memory was adversely affected by drug addiction responded to police suggestions that they had evidence of her guilt by saying that she must have done it.[19] However, a suspect's belief in his or her guilt may result from a mistaken understanding of the law. The suspect may, for example, believe that he or she is guilty of theft because the suspect has taken something that belongs to another person. The lay person is likely to be unfamiliar with the concept of dishonesty as defined for the purposes of the Theft Act 1968, and be unaware of the requirement that there must be an intention to permanently deprive.

5.32    The lawyer can play a crucial role in preventing false confessions. If the client says that he or she is guilty, the client should be carefully questioned by the lawyer both in order to establish the facts and to establish the client's understanding of the law. It may then become clear that the client is not guilty or that the client has a defence to the allegation, and must be advised accordingly.

## Suspicion about guilt

5.33    The most frequent question asked of the criminal lawyer is, 'How can you defend a person if you know that the person is guilty?'. The short answer is that if a client does not tell the lawyer that the client is guilty, or provide

16  For an illustration, see *R v Calderdale Magistrates' Court ex p Donahue and Cutler* [2001] Crim LR 141, in which it was held to be quite proper, in the context of proceedings in a magistrates' court, for the defence not to indicate a plea until the prosecution had disclosed video evidence.

17  See, for example, the judgments in *R v Howell* [2003] EWCA Crim 1; [2005] 1 Cr App R 1; [2003] Crim LR 405, and *R v Hoare and Pierce* [2004] EWCA Crim 784; [2005] 1 WLR 1804; [2005] 1 Cr App R 22; [2005] Crim LR 567.

18  See G Gudjonsson *The psychology of interrogations and confessions* (Wiley, Chichester, 2003).

19  *R v Brady* [2004] EWCA Crim 2230.

the lawyer with instructions that demonstrate the client's guilt, the lawyer cannot know that the client is guilty. Whether the client is guilty is for a court, and not the lawyer, to decide. This is not to say that the lawyer may not have very great suspicion of guilt. The instructions given by the client may sound highly improbable, or the client may simply refuse to tell the lawyer anything at all. In either case, the role of the lawyer is to act in the best interests of the client. In the case of instructions that do not appear credible, the lawyer should question the client, perhaps asking the kind of questions that are likely to be asked in the police interview. In the final analysis, the lawyer must advise on the basis of what the client tells the lawyer, whatever the lawyer's suspicions. These principles would also apply if the client had previously told the police that he or she were guilty, provided that the client now tells the lawyer that he or she is not. The client should be advised, in appropriate terms, of the dangers of lying in the police interview. Demonstrable lies can be used to devastating effect by the prosecution at trial, and can also lead to inferences under CJPOA 1994 s34 (see para 5.67 below) and, where relevant, the client should be advised of this.

### Inconsistent instructions

5.34   If the lawyer goes through the process of taking instructions as set out para 5.14 above, it may be that the client's story will change in a material way during the course of the consultation. This may because the client's recollection has genuinely changed or is unclear or, of course, because the client has realised that there are gaps or inconsistencies in his or her story. The fact of inconsistent instructions is not, of itself, a reason for the lawyer to refuse to act. Only where it is clear that the client is attempting to put forward false evidence should the lawyer stop acting. It will normally be appropriate for the lawyer to question the client closely, but the lawyer must avoid assisting the client in concocting a defence. The lawyer's questions must be directed at establishing the instructions rather than to pointing out weaknesses so that the client can plug the gap.

### Intention to mislead police

5.35   It is a fundamental ethical rule that a lawyer must not, knowingly and actively, assist their client to mislead the police. This rule is derived from a number of sources. First, the *Solicitors' Code of Conduct 2007* provides that a solicitor acting in litigation must never deceive or knowingly or recklessly mislead the court, or knowingly allow the court to be misled.[20] Although the lawyer is not 'acting in litigation' at the police station stage, and would not be involved in deceiving or misleading a court directly, it is likely in many cases that a known deception at this stage would lead to a known deception of a court. This rule applies as much to representatives as it does to the solicitors that employ them. Second, the Criminal Law Act 1967 s4 provides that:

20   *SRA Code of Conduct 2011*, ch 5, O (5.1) and O (5.2).

Where a person has committed a relevant offence, any other person who, knowing or believing him to be guilty of an offence ... does without lawful authority or reasonable excuse any act with intent to impede his apprehension or prosecution, shall be guilty of an offence.[21]

5.36    A number of practical considerations follow from this ethical rule.

1) If a client tells the lawyer that he or she is guilty, or gives instructions that demonstrate his or her guilt, the lawyer should, subject to the matters considered at para 5.30 above, advise the client of the advantages and disadvantages of admitting guilt in the police interview (see para 5.139 below).

2) If the client tells the lawyer that he or she intends to lie to the police, the lawyer should advise the client of the possible adverse consequences of doing so. If the client persists with this stated intention, the lawyer must withdraw. However, in doing so, the lawyer must be careful not to inform the police of the reason for withdrawal, because this would contravene the principle of client confidentiality.

3) The lawyer must advise the client on whether he or she should deal with the police interview by refusing to answer questions. It is perfectly proper for a lawyer to advise a client to make no comment in interview even if the lawyer knows that the client is guilty. However, a further problem may arise here if the client, having accepted the advice not to answer police questions, starts to answer questions in the police interview in a way which the lawyer knows to be untrue. In such circumstances, it would normally be wrong for the lawyer to withdraw immediately, since this would be likely to have the effect of informing the police by implication that the suspect is not telling the truth (which would be a breach of confidence). The lawyer may remain in the interview until it has finished, and then advise the client that the lawyer will have to withdraw. A careful note should be taken of the reasons for, and circumstances of, the withdrawal.

4) Many lawyers will, at an early stage in the initial interview, advise the client that if the client tells the lawyer that he or she is guilty, then the lawyer will not be able to continue to act for the client if the client subsequently wishes to deny the offence to the police. Opinions differ about whether this is appropriate. On the one hand it is argued that it is a practical strategy designed to enable the lawyer to continue to act. On the other hand, since it may not be so much a statement of fact as an implied encouragement to lie to the lawyer (and, ultimately, to the court) it may be regarded as unethical. The author favours the latter view. The professional obligation of the lawyer is to advise and assist the client in the client's best interests, and does not extend to assisting the client to present a false defence.

5.37    The principle of not knowingly misleading the police applies equally to the case of a client who tells the lawyer, or gives instructions that demonstrate, that the client is innocent but that the client intends to admit guilt to the police. In this case, the client should be informed of the disadvantages of

---

21  A 'relevant offence' is one for which sentence is fixed by law, or that carries at least five years' imprisonment (Criminal Law Act 1967 s4(1A)).

such a course of action (particularly that it will be virtually impossible to convince a court that the client is not guilty) and that the client risks prosecution for wasting police time or perverting the course of justice. If the client insists on proceeding on this basis, although there is no absolute duty to withdraw,[22] the lawyer should consider withdrawing, and must do so if the lawyer knows that the client is admitting guilt in order to protect the person who did commit the offence.

### Intention to give a false identity

5.38    A similar problem may arise where the client has given a false name to the police or pretends to be someone else. While it is the case that people can call themselves what they like, the solicitor must consider why the client has given the police a false or different name. If the purpose is to avoid the police finding out that the client has previous convictions or that the client is wanted on warrant for another alleged crime, then the lawyer must not assist the client in pursuing this deception.[23] The client should be advised of the likelihood of his or her true identity being established, for example, by fingerprints. The client should also be advised of other possible consequences such as prosecution for wasting police time or perverting the course of justice.[24] If the client is not willing to give his or her true identity to the police, the lawyer should withdraw, but again must avoid disclosing the reason for withdrawal to the police.

5.39    The lawyer should also be cautious if the client, while not giving a false name, has given a false date of birth or address. The lawyer has to tread a careful path which may be illustrated in the following way. If, within the knowledge of the lawyer, the client has given a false address for the purpose of supporting a false identity or to avoid their address being searched because there is stolen property there, the lawyer cannot continue to act if the client wishes to persist in the deception. If the client intends to refuse to answer questions about their address, the lawyer can continue to act. However, in practice, if the client has initially given an address to the police and subsequently refuses to answer questions in relation to his or her address, the police will suspect that it is false. Likewise with a name or date of birth. Thus, in most circumstances, either the client will have to agree to disclose his or her true name, address and date of birth or the lawyer will have to withdraw.

---

22  The *SRA Code of Conduct 2011* makes no reference to this issue.

23  *SRA Code of Conduct 2011*, ch 5, O (5.2) and IB (5.5).

24  In *R v Sookoo* [2002] EWCA Crim 800, the Court of Appeal held that in the absence of aggravating features, giving a false identity to the police should be charged as wasting police time rather than perverting the course of justice, and imposed a three-month custodial sentence.

# Conflict of interests

## Principles

5.40    A lawyer owes a number of important duties to a client.

1) A solicitor must act in the best interests of each client.[25]

2) A solicitor and his or her firm must keep the affairs of clients and former clients confidential except where disclosure is permitted or required by law or by the client or former client.[26]

3) A solicitor is under a duty (subject to important exceptions) to pass on to his or her client all relevant information which is relevant to the matter, irrespective of the source of the information.[27]

5.41    A conflict of interests arises whenever a solicitor or firm acts for more than one client in circumstances where one or more of the above duties conflicts with the other(s), or there is a significant risk that they may do so. At the police station, a lawyer must not normally act for two or more clients if there is a conflict, or a significant risk of a conflict, of interests between them.[28] If, having accepted instructions, a conflict arises between two or more clients, the lawyer must normally cease to act for both (all) clients, although the lawyer may continue to act for one of them provided that the lawyer is not in possession of relevant confidential information concerning the other(s) which was obtained when acting for the other client(s).

## Practice

5.42    The above principles can raise considerable practical difficulties when advising at the police station, particularly where more than one client, or potential client, is detained in respect of the same or a related matter. Although a pragmatic solution may often be found, the principles must always be observed. The following factors should be taken into account (and see checklist 11).

1) The issue of conflict is for the lawyer to resolve, not the police (see Code C NfG 6G, Code H NfG 6F).

2) Firms must have a system for checking for actual or potential conflicts of interest, preferably one that can be used at short notice.

3) Where two or more potential clients are arrested in respect of the same, or a connected, matter, the lawyer should always consider the potential for a conflict of interests before seeing the second or subsequent suspect. The risk of a conflict is especially high where the first client implicates the second while denying or minimising his or her own involvement. Information obtained from the police may also indicate a risk of conflict, for example, where two people have been arrested but the evidence suggests that only one could have been responsible.

---

25  *SRA Principles 2011*, principle 4.
26  *SRA Code of Conduct 2011*, ch 4, and see para 1.16 above.
27  *SRA Code of Conduct 2011*, ch 4, and see para 4.29 above.
28  *SRA Code of Conduct 2011*, ch 3, and for exceptions see O (3.6) and O (3.7).

4) In principle, the lawyer is under a duty to tell each client all relevant information, including what other clients have said. However, the duty of confidentiality always overrides the duty of disclosure.[29] Therefore, disclosure of information obtained from a client to a second or subsequent client would require permission of the client from whom the information had been obtained. The lawyer must approach this with extreme caution even if the first client is willing to give permission, since passing information from one client to another may assist him or her falsely to put forward the same story to the police. In some circumstances this could amount to an offence such as that under Criminal Law Act 1967 s4 (see para 5.35 above).

5) It is quite proper to give a second client relevant information that has been obtained from the police while acting for the first client, including information obtained during a police interview. Again, the lawyer must be alert to the danger of assisting the client to concoct a story. However, in certain, exceptional, circumstances information should not be passed on to the client (see para 4.29 above).

6) If a conflict, or significant risk of a conflict, becomes apparent after seeing the second or subsequent client, the lawyer must consider whether he or she should withdraw from both (or all) cases. In the case of an actual conflict, generally the lawyer must withdraw from both (or all) cases.[30] The critical question is whether the obligation to act in a client's best interests can be fulfilled having regard to whether the duty of full disclosure conflicts with the duty of confidentiality. However, if the lawyer concludes early on in an interview with the second client that there is likely to be a conflict, it may well be possible to withdraw from acting for that second client while continuing to act for the first.

7) If the lawyer does have to withdraw from acting for a client, the duty of confidentiality requires that the lawyer does not disclose the reason for withdrawal either to the police or to another client.

---

**Checklist 11: Dealing with more than one client in respect of the same or a related offence**

1) Take instructions from Client 1. Tell him or her that you have also been asked to act for Client 2 and ask whether Client 1 is aware of any conflict or potential conflict of interests. If Client 1 says that there is, you cannot act for Client 2, although you should take action to ensure that Client 2 is able to secure access to legal advice.

2) If Client 1 says that he or she is aware of no conflict or potential conflict, consider for yourself whether the instructions given by Client 1 disclose a conflict or potential conflict, and if you conclude that they do, you cannot act for Client 2.

---

29  *SRA Code of Conduct 2011*, ch 4.
30  *SRA Code of Conduct 2011*, ch 3.

3) If you are satisfied that there is no conflict or potential conflict, advise Client 1 that if you receive information that is confidential to Client 1 but which is relevant to Client 2, you will have to disclose that information to Client 2, and will seek permission from Client 1 to disclose that information if the situation arises. If Client 1 does not agree to this, you cannot act for Client 2.

4) If Client 1 is content with this approach, see Client 2 and advise him or her that you are acting for Client 1, and that if there is a conflict or potential conflict of interests, you cannot act for Client 2. Ask Client 2 if he or she is aware of a conflict or a potential conflict with Client 1. If Client 2 says that there is, tell Client 2 that you cannot act for him or her, although you can take action to secure legal advice for him or her.

5) If Client 2 says that he or she is not aware of a conflict, or potential conflict, inform Client 2 that if he or she gives you any information, or you subsequently receive information, that is relevant to Client 1 you will have to disclose it to Client 1. If Client 2 does not agree to this, you cannot act for Client 2.

6) If Client 2 is content with this, take instructions from Client 2. In view of the danger of concoction, do not give any information to Client 2 that you have obtained from Client 1 before you have taken instructions from him or her.

7) Consider whether the instructions obtained from Client 2 disclose a conflict or potential conflict of interests. If they do, you cannot continue to act for Client 2, and must also consider whether you can continue to act for Client 1 having regard to the principles set out in paras 5.40 and 5.41 above.

8) Continue to keep the issue of conflict of interests under review, and if a conflict of interests becomes apparent, consider whether you should cease to act for either or both clients.

Keep a full and accurate note of what is said to the clients, and their responses, and consider asking them to endorse the notes.

5.43 A different form of conflict may arise if a client asks the lawyer to pass messages to a third party, either another client at the police station or someone outside of the police station. While a lawyer has a duty to act in the best interests of a client, this is obviously constrained by both ethical and legal rules. Many requests from a client detained in a police station to pass a message to someone outside the police station are perfectly legitimate. For example, a client may want a relative to be told about the client's arrest by the lawyer rather than by the police. However, the potential for abuse is self-evident. If the lawyer has any doubts about the purpose of a request, the lawyer should either refuse to accept the message, or suggest that it only be passed on with the agreement of the custody officer.

## Advising the client

5.44 Once the lawyer has taken initial instructions from the client and considered, where relevant, the client's fitness to be interviewed and any actual or potential conflict of interests, the lawyer must consider what advice to give concerning:

- the client's legal position (see para 5.48 below);
- the consequences of lying to the police (see para 5.46 below);
- whether the client should answer police questions (see para 5.102 below) or make a statement (see para 5.157 below);
- the relevance of previous convictions and other forms of misconduct (see para 5.170 below);
- whether to consent to fingerprints and photographs (see paras 6.3 and 6.10 below);
- whether to consent to, or ask for, an identification procedure (see para 8.23 below);
- whether to consent to intimate or non-intimate samples (see paras 6.37 and 6.56 below);
- search of the person (see paras 6.16 and 6.77 below) and property (see para 6.98 below).

5.45 The lawyer should try to ensure that the client understands not only what the advice is, but also the reasons why the advice is given. This is particularly important where the advice advocates a certain course of action as opposed simply to outlining the options open to the client. A careful note of the advice given, and the reasons for the advice, must be taken. The lawyer should consider whether to ask the client to sign a statement that the client has received and understood the advice. This may be particularly important if the advice is not to answer police questions, or if the client does not want to accept the advice given by the lawyer.

5.46 Where appropriate, it is important that the lawyer explains to the client the possible consequences of lying in a police interview. This, of course, has to be approached with suitable diplomacy, but there are many occasions when the client's version of events sounds inherently improbable or lacks credibility for some other reason.[31] While it would not normally be appropriate for the lawyer to tell the client that he or she does not believe the client's version of events, it is possible to impress on the client the dangers of not telling the truth without directly indicating that the lawyer thinks the client is lying. Of course, lying will not necessarily have adverse consequences for the client. However, if the client is prosecuted and pleads not guilty and the prosecution is able to establish that the client did lie to the police, or if the defence put forward at trial is significantly different to that put forward in the police interview, this may be used not only to attack the defendant's credibility but also as evidence supportive of guilt. Furthermore, if the defence at trial differs from that put forward to the police, inferences may be drawn under CJPOA 1994 s34 since the defendant will be relying on facts at trial not mentioned to the police on being questioned.

31 For guidance where the lawyer knows that the client intends to lie to the police, see para 5.35 above.

5.47      In order to be able to give effective advice to a client, especially as to what strategy to adopt in the police interview, the lawyer requires a good understanding of the client's legal position, the potential implications of the client's previous misconduct, and the legal consequences of failure to answer questions and, more specifically, the consequences of failure to tell the police about matters that may become relevant at trial. Thus, the remainder of the chapter is structured as follows:

- advising the client on his or her legal position;
- the legal consequences of 'silence';
- advice on whether to answer police questions;
- strategies to avoid or minimise adverse inferences;
- the relevance of previous misconduct;
- preparing the client for interview.

## Advice on the client's legal position

5.48    Before considering and giving advice to the client on what strategy to adopt in relation to the police interview, the lawyer should consider and advise the client on his or her legal position. This involves consideration of:

- the offence or offences of which the client is suspected;
- the apparent strength of the evidence in relation to that offence or those offences;
- the defences that may be available;
- the possible outcomes of detention at the police station.

### The suspected offence(s)

5.49    The lawyer should consider the offence or offences that the client has been arrested for, and also what other offences may be suggested by the police and/or by the evidence. This involves considering what the prosecution would have to prove, both in terms of the actus reus (the act or omission) and the mens rea (the mental element). The lawyer should be familiar with the elements of the offences that are frequently encountered, but if in any doubt the lawyer should check them before giving advice. It is important that the lawyer does not ignore this or guess what the relevant elements of the offence(s) are, since otherwise the advice given may well be incorrect. Establishing the elements of the alleged offence(s) is an essential step before going on to consider the strength of the evidence in respect of those elements.

### The strength of the evidence

5.50    Advising on the strength of the prosecution evidence is often difficult because the lawyer cannot be sure that the lawyer has been given full information about the evidence the police have, the police may have exaggerated or minimised it, there is often uncertainty about what other evidence the police are seeking or may obtain, and it may not be possible to predict with any certainty whether the evidence would be admitted by a court. The lawyer should consider the following factors:

a) What is known about evidence from witnesses – have they been interviewed, has the lawyer seen their witness statements, what is the status of such witnesses (for example, are they likely to be co-defendants)?

b) What other forms of evidence are there – do the police have evidence resulting from searches or samples, or from speculative searches of fingerprint, DNA and other databases, what evidence do they have from a scene-of-crime investigation, do the police have documentary evidence?

c) What other evidence are the police likely to seek or obtain in a case of this nature – which witnesses are the police likely to interview, what searches are they likely to conduct, what samples are they likely to take, what other forms of evidence are the police likely to seek (for example, bank records, communication records such as those relating to telephone or computer use), what forensic examinations are they likely to conduct?

d) What evidence would the lawyer expect in a case of this nature – are the police likely to have relied on information from an informant, are they likely to have conducted some form of surveillance, what kind of police records are likely to exist (for example, crime reports, communications, information from databases)?[32]

e) Is the evidence likely to be admitted at trial and what is its likely effect?

5.51 Evidential rules that may affect the strength of the police case primarily concern corroboration, competence and compellability, and admissibility. It is often difficult at the police station stage to assess with any certainty how evidential rules will apply to a particular case at the trial stage, but they do need to be considered in formulating advice to be given to the client.

## Corroboration

5.52 The general rule is that a defendant can be convicted on the basis of any admissible evidence (for example, a confession) even though it is not corroborated (ie, supported) by other evidence, provided that the court is nevertheless satisfied of guilt beyond reasonable doubt. There are a few, relatively minor, exceptions where a person cannot be convicted in the absence of corroborating evidence.[33] Of more practical importance are cases where the court must be warned of the dangers of convicting a person on the basis of certain evidence that is not supported by other evidence. The most important of these are a) the evidence of a mental patient of bad character,[34] b) confessions by mentally handicapped persons,[35] and c) the

32 For a detailed explanation of police investigative methods, see R Ede and E Shepherd, *Active Defence*, (Law Society, London, 2000).
33 See, for example, Perjury Act 1911 s13, Road Traffic Regulation Act 1984 s89(2) and Criminal Attempts Act 1981 s2(2)(g).
34 See *R v Spencer* [1987] AC 128.
35 By PACE s77 a judge in a trial on indictment must warn the jury of the special need for caution before convicting a person on the basis of their confession if the case depends wholly or mainly on the confession, the accused is mentally handicapped, and the confession was not made in the presence of an independent person.

evidence of an identification witness.[36] The requirement that a judge give a corroboration warning in respect of the evidence of an accomplice and the evidence of the complainant of a sexual offence was abolished by CJPOA 1994 s32, but a warning may still be given if the judge concludes that an accomplice may have a motive for falsely incriminating the accused or exaggerating the accused's role in the offence.[37] In any case, where the prosecution case is likely to rest wholly or mainly on such evidence, the lawyer must carefully consider whether evidence derived from the police interview with the suspect might provide the supporting evidence.

## Competence and compellability

5.53    Some potential witnesses are not able to give evidence for the prosecution (ie, they are not competent), and others may be competent but cannot be required to give evidence for the prosecution (ie, they are not compellable). A co-defendant is not competent to give evidence for the prosecution unless they cease to be a co-defendant for these purposes, usually by the prosecution deciding not to proceed against them, by securing separate trials or by the co-defendant pleading guilty before the trial. Note, however, that a co-defendant can give evidence on his or her own behalf which may implicate the client. Other witnesses who may not be competent to give evidence are those who are mentally ill and very young children. The most important example of a competent witness who nevertheless cannot be compelled to give evidence for the prosecution is the defendant's spouse or civil partner. However, the spouse or civil partner is compellable where the defendant is accused of assault on or injury or threat of injury to the spouse or civil partner, or assault or a sexual offence on a person under 16 years.[38]

5.54    Therefore, if significant evidence is likely to come from a witness who is not, or may not be, competent or compellable, refusal to answer police questions may be appropriate at this stage. This may also be the case if, despite the witness being technically competent and compellable, the witness is likely to be reluctant or unwilling to give evidence despite any adverse consequences. Examples here include close friends or relatives of the accused, and members of certain religious sects.

## Rules on admissibility

5.55    Certain evidence may not be admissible at trial. The admissibility of evidence of the defendant's own confession or admissions is discussed at paras 4.35 above, and 13.34 and 13.42 below. Evidence of a confession by a co-suspect that implicates the defendant is not admissible against the latter (see para 4.33 above). The admissibility of identification evidence is dealt with in chapter 8 and para 13.50 below). The evidential rules concerning hearsay evidence were considerably revised by Criminal Justice Act

---

36  When the Turnbull guidelines apply. See *R v Turnbull* [1977] QB 224.
37  See *R v Makanjuola* [1995] 1 WLR 1348.
38  The law on competence and compellability has been the subject of significant legislative development in recent years, and reference should be made to an up-to-date text on evidence.

(CJA) 2003 Part 11 Chapter 2, as were those concerning evidence of previous misconduct (see para 5.170 below). The court has a discretion under Police and Criminal Evidence Act 1984 (PACE) s78(1) to exclude any prosecution evidence if it would have such an adverse effect on the fairness of the proceedings that it ought not be admitted (see para 13.42 below).

## Available defences

5.56    Defences are broadly of two types. The first type essentially consists of the assertion that the prosecution cannot prove the elements of the offence beyond reasonable doubt, and includes defences which consist of the accused asserting that he or she was not present at the time of the offence, that identity cannot be established, or that the accused did not have the requisite mens rea (see para 5.49 above). The second type, often described as a positive or assertive defence, is where the accused claims a defence based upon a common law or statutory rule. An example is the defence of self-defence – the accused accepts that he or she did assault the complainant but the circumstances were such that this was legally justified (as a result of the rule that permits a person to use reasonable force to defend himself or herself against attack). Generally, the accused bears an evidential burden in respect of an assertive defence. This means that in order to make the defence a live issue at trial the accused must adduce sufficient evidence to satisfy the judge that it should be treated as a potential defence. Once the accused has done so, the accused must be found not guilty unless the prosecution can disprove the defence beyond reasonable doubt.

5.57    The lawyer must consider what defences may be available to the client. This involves careful consideration of whether there is a specific common law or statutory defence,[39] the type and elements of the defence, whether there is evidence (or whether evidence is likely to be available) to establish the defence, and where the burden of proof lies. With regard to the latter, the general rule is that the legal (or persuasive) burden of proof rests with the prosecution – in order to secure a conviction, the prosecution must prove beyond reasonable doubt all the elements of the offence and, in effect, disprove the defence. For example, in a prosecution for assault in which the accused satisfied the evidential burden in respect of the defence of self-defence, the prosecution must prove the elements of assault and demonstrate beyond reasonable doubt that the accused did not act in self-defence. If the court concludes that the accused may have acted in self-defence, it must acquit the accused. However, there are both common law rules and statutory defences which have the effect of placing the legal burden of proving a defence (on a balance of probabilities) on the accused in the case of certain offences (sometimes described as reverse-onus clauses or defences). In such cases, if the prosecution can prove the elements of the offence beyond reasonable doubt, they will succeed unless the accused

---

39  Especially in respect of offences with which the lawyer is not familiar. The Court of Appeal has been critical of defence lawyers acting in relation to immigration document offences who have not advised their clients in respect of the statutory defences available (*Mohamed v The Queen; MV v The Queen; Mohamed v The Queen; and Nofallah v The Queen* [2010] EWCA Crim 2400).

can persuade the court that the defence is more likely than not to be true. For example, in a prosecution under CJA 1988 s139, if the prosecution can prove beyond reasonable doubt that the accused did have a bladed article in a public place, they will succeed unless the accused can satisfy the court that it was more likely than not that the accused had a good reason or lawful authority.

5.58    In some cases where the legal burden of proof is apparently imposed on the accused the courts have concluded, as a result of the Human Rights Act (HRA) 1998 and the European Convention on Human Rights (ECHR) article 6 (right to a fair trial), that it amounts only to an evidential and not a legal burden. Determining where the burden of proof lies may be relevant to the advice to be given on the appropriate strategy to adopt in the police interview, particularly because inferences from silence may be more damaging where a legal burden, as opposed to an evidential burden, of proof is placed on the accused. Some examples of cases where the courts have determined the nature of the burden on the accused are set out below.[40]

a)  Cases where the courts have held that a legal burden on the accused to establish a defence does not infringe ECHR article 6:
   - Health and Safety at Work Act 1974 s40 (proving that it was not reasonably practicable to do more than was in fact done to satisfy the duty of care under ss3 and 33).[41]
   - CJA 1988 s139 (proving that the accused had a good reason or lawful authority for having a bladed article in a public place).[42]
   - Road Traffic Act (RTA) 1988 s5 (establishing that at the time the accused is alleged to have committed the offence of driving or being in charge of a motor vehicle, there was no likelihood of the accused driving while the proportion of alcohol in their breath, blood or urine exceeded the prescribed limit).[43]
   - Road Traffic Offenders Act 1988 s15 (proving that the accused had consumed alcohol after the offence and before providing a specimen).[44]
   - Road Traffic Offenders Act 1988 s37(3) (proving that the accused had a provisional licence and that the accused was driving in accordance with its conditions).[45]
b)  Cases where the courts have held that a burden should be treated as an evidential and not legal burden:
   - Terrorism Act (TA) 2000 s11(2) (proving that an organisation that the accused belongs or professes to belong to was not proscribed when the accused belonged to it and that the accused had not taken part in its activities while it was proscribed).[46]

---

40  See generally I Dennis, 'Reverse Onuses and the Presumption of Innocence: In Search of Principle' [2005] Crim LR 901.
41  *Davies v Health and Safety Executive* [2002] EWCA Crim 2949.
42  *Lynch v DPP* [2002] 2 All ER 854; [2002] Crim LR 320, and *R v Matthews* [2003] EWCA Crim 813.
43  *Parker v DPP* (2001) 165 JP 213, *R v Sheldrake* [2004] UKHL 43.
44  *R v Drummond* [2002] Crim LR 666.
45  *DPP v Barker* [2004] EWHC 2502 (Admin).
46  *Attorney-General's Reference (No 4 of 2004)* [2004] UKHL 43.

- Misuse of Drugs Act 1971 s28(2) and s28(3)(b)(i) (proving that the defendant did not believe, suspect or have reason to suspect that the substance was a controlled drug contrary to section 5(3)).[47]
- Prevention of Corruption Act 1916 (proving that a gift was not made corruptly for the purposes of an offence under Public Bodies Corrupt Practices Act 1889 s1(2).[48]

## Powers of the police and possible outcomes

5.59 Depending upon the circumstances, it may be appropriate to consider and to advise the client about:

- the powers that the police have to gather evidence (for example, searches, samples, fingerprints, photographs);
- the length of time the police can detain without charge;
- the powers of the police to detain or release following charge;
- the powers of the police to grant, and likelihood of them granting, bail without charge;
- the possibility of diversion from prosecution, such as simple or conditional caution;
- possible sentences, and possible sentence-discount resulting from an admission.

# The legal consequences of 'silence'

5.60 Before the CJPOA 1994, the 'right to silence' was regarded as a well-entrenched principle of law, although it was by no means uncontested. Despite the fact that the Royal Commission on Criminal Justice recommended that there be no change to the common law position, believing that the possibility of an increase in the conviction of the guilty was outweighed by the risk of more convictions of the innocent,[49] shortly after its report was published the government announced its intention to 'abolish' the right to silence. Thus, CJPOA 1994 ss34, 36 and 37 came into force on 10 April 1995.[50] These three sections are examined below (see para 5.67 below onwards), but a number of contextual matters should be noted.

5.61 First, the right to silence was not, strictly, abolished. Silence, or refusal to answer police questions, remains a viable, and indeed, appropriate option in many cases. Rather, the issue is the use that the prosecution can make of such silence or refusal at any trial. Furthermore, a defendant cannot be convicted (or have a case to answer, or have a case committed or transferred to the Crown Court) solely on the basis of an inference drawn

---

47  *R v Lambert* [2001] UKHL 37.
48  *R v Webster* [2010] EWCA Crim 2819.
49  Royal Commission on Criminal Justice, Report (HMSO, London, 1993), p54.
50  CJPOA 1994 s35 also enables a court to draw inferences from the failure of a defendant to give evidence at their trial, but is not dealt with further here. The provisions are applied to courts-martial and other related proceedings by CJPOA 1994 s39 and the Criminal Justice and Public Order Act 1994 (Application to the Armed Forces) Order 2009 SI No 990.

from silence.[51] There must be some other evidence tending to show that the person is guilty.

5.62      Second, quite separately from the CJPOA 1994, there are a number of statutory and other obligations on persons to provide information or otherwise co-operate in connection with the investigation of crime, in respect of which failure or refusal may amount to an offence or have other adverse consequences. These include the following.

1) Refusal to give an intimate sample may result in adverse inferences (see para 6.40 below).

2) Failure to submit to a drugs test may amount to an offence (see para 6.71 below).

3) In some circumstances, failure to provide information is a criminal offence. Following the case of *Saunders v UK*,[52] in which it was held that the use of evidence obtained as a result of compulsory questioning contravened ECHR article 6(1), the Youth Justice and Criminal Evidence Act 1999 s59 and Sch 3 prohibited the use of information obtained as a result of compulsory disclosure under a number of statutory powers, mostly concerning financial investigations, as evidence against the person from whom it was obtained.[53] However, the evidential use of information obtained from some forms of compulsory questioning has not been treated as breaching article 6(1). In particular, it has been held that compulsory questioning under RTA 1988 s172, requiring the registered keeper of a motor vehicle to supply information identifying the driver of a vehicle, does not breach article 6(1).[54]

4) The Proceeds of Crime Act (POCA) 2002 imposes potentially extensive obligations to disclose to the authorities knowledge or suspicion that a person is in some way dealing with criminal property, and failure to do so may amount to a criminal offence (see para 1.20 above).

5.63      Third, the common law position continues to apply where the statutory provisions do not apply or the conditions for drawing inferences are not satisfied, for example, where questioning was not conducted under caution (see para 5.74 below).[55] The common law position is that generally failure or refusal to answer questions does not amount to evidence against the person concerned, unless it can be said that the defendant was on 'equal terms' with the questioner. Therefore, where the CJPOA 1994 conditions are not satisfied, failure to answer questions put by a police officer, or someone in a similar position, is unlikely to lead to adverse inferences

---

51  See CJPOA 1994 s38(3).

52  (1997) 23 EHRR 313.

53  Insurance Companies Act 1982, Insolvency Act 1986, Company Directors Disqualification Act 1986, Building Societies Act 1986, Financial Services Act 1986, Banking Act 1987, CJA 1987, Companies Act 1989, Friendly Societies Act 1992.

54  See *Stott (PF, Dunfermline) and another v Brown* [2001] 2 All ER 97, *DPP v Wilson* [2002] RTR 37 and *Charlebois v DPP* [2003] EWHC 54 (Admin). In *O'Halloran and Francis v UK* [2007] Crim LR 897 the ECtHR confirmed that this did not breach the ECHR art 6(1). See also *R v Hertfordshire County Council ex p Green Environmental Industries* [2002] 2 AC 412; [2000] 2 WLR 373; [2000] 1 All ER 773, concerning a notice issued under Environmental Protection Act 1990 s71(2).

55  This was confirmed in *R v Johnson; R v Hind* [2005] EWCA Crim 971.

being drawn at any trial.[56] However, failure to answer some questions where other questions are answered can have an adverse effect on the defendant at trial. In some situations, the questions not answered should be edited out so that the jury or magistrates do not hear them. However, this will not always achieve the desired result. Although a jury should be told that in circumstances where CJPOA 1994 ss34, 36 and 37 do not apply that a suspect need not answer questions, a jury or bench is likely to make its own judgment about why certain questions have not been answered.[57]

5.64    Fourth, the European Court of Human Rights (ECtHR) has held that CJPOA 1994 s34 does not, per se, contravene ECHR article 6(1). In *Condron v UK*[58] the court held that while it would be incompatible with article 6 to base a conviction solely or mainly on the accused's silence, silence could be taken into account in assessing the persuasiveness of the prosecution evidence where the situation clearly called for an explanation from the accused. While the courts must be cautious in invoking silence against the accused, whether it breaches article 6 depends upon the circumstances, having regard to:

- the situations in which an inference can be drawn;
- the weight attached to inferences by the court in its assessment of the evidence; and
- the degree of compulsion inherent in the situation.

The fact that the accused was advised by a lawyer to remain silent must be given appropriate weight by the court, but it does not prevent inferences from being drawn (see further para 5.96 below).[59]

5.65    Fifth, different courts and judges have drawn very different conclusions as to the purpose of the silence provisions in the CJPOA 1994 which, in addition to the differing reactions of juries and magistrates, make it difficult to predict with any degree of accuracy whether, and what, inferences will be drawn. One line of cases, exemplified by *R v Howell*[60] and *R v Hoare and Pierce*,[61] reflects the view that suspects are under an obligation to put forward their defence from the time of their first interview following arrest, and that the silence provisions are designed to enforce this. Thus Auld LJ said in *Hoare and Pierce*:

> Section 34 is concerned with flushing out innocence at an early stage or supporting other evidence of guilt at a later stage, not simply with whether a guilty defendant is entitled, or genuinely or reasonably believes that he is entitled, to rely on legal rights of which his solicitor has advised him.

---

56  See, eg, *R v Gilbert* (1977) 66 Cr App R 237, *R v Raviraj* (1987) 85 Cr App R 93, *R v Hubbard* [1991] Crim LR 449, *R v Forbes* [1992] Crim LR 593 and *R v Chandler* [1976] 3 All ER 105; (1976) 63 Cr App R 1.

57  See *R v Mann* (1972) 56 Cr App R 750, *R v Henry* [1990] Crim LR 574 and *R v Welch* [1992] Crim LR 368.

58  (2002) 31 EHRR 1; [2000] Crim LR 679.

59  See also *Murray v UK* (1996) 22 EHRR 29, *Averill v UK* (2001) 31 EHRR 36; [2000] Crim LR 682, and *Beckles v UK* (2001) 31 EHRR 1; [2002] Crim LR 917. In fact the Court of Appeal has given little weight to the fact that silence was on legal advice.

60  [2003] EWCA Crim 1; [2005] 1 Cr App R 1; [2003] Crim LR 405.

61  [2004] EWCA Crim 784; [2005] 1 WLR 1804; [2005] 1 Cr App R 22. See also *R v Essa* [2009] EWCA Crim 43.

Another line of cases, of which *R v Brizzalari*[62] and *R v Beckles*[63] are leading examples, view the silence provisions as being directed at non-disclosure of positive defences and ambush defences. In *Brizzalari*, Hedley J, giving the judgment for the court, said:

> ... the mischief at which [CJPOA 1994 s34] was primarily directed was the positive defence following a 'no comment' interview and/or the 'ambush' defence ... [and] we would counsel against the further complicating of trials and summings-up by invoking this statute unless the merits of the individual case require that it should be done.

In *Beckles*, Woolf LCJ doubted whether the silence provisions should have been invoked in circumstances where the accused had told the police the substance of his defence on being arrested. He went on to say:

> This last point, coupled with the fact that he had made it clear that he was prepared to give evidence as to the advice he had received (albeit that this was not pursued by the advocates), suggest that a section 34 direction may not have been appropriate in this case at all, because the evidence before the jury was consistent with the Appellant having acted genuinely on the advice of his solicitor. His being silent could not result in the prosecution being ambushed or taken by surprise.

5.66   Finally, inferences cannot be drawn under CJPOA 1994 ss34, 36 and 37 if the accused was at an authorised place of detention[64] at the time of failure to mention facts subsequently relied upon, and the accused had not been allowed an opportunity to consult a solicitor before being questioned, charged or informed that the accused may be prosecuted (CJPOA 1994 ss34(2A), 36(4A) and 37(3A)). Therefore, inferences under these provisions cannot be drawn if access to legal advice is delayed under PACE s58(8) or TA 2000 Sch 8 para 8, or if a superintendent or above authorises an interview to proceed under Code C para 6.6(b) without the suspect having received legal advice (see paras 2.127 and 2.139). In such circumstances, the suspect must be given a different caution which makes no reference to adverse consequences of silence (see Code C, Code H Annex C para 2). Where the solicitor nominated by the suspect cannot be contacted or refuses to come to the police station, and the suspect refuses the services of a duty solicitor, the prohibition on inferences from failure to mention relevant facts in a subsequent interview does not apply (see Code C, Code H Annex C). One question arising from these provisions for which there is no clear answer is whether the restriction on drawing inferences would apply where, although a solicitor was not present at the interview, the suspect had received advice on the telephone. For this reason, as noted in para 3.72 above, it is very important for the lawyer, when giving initial telephone advice, to ensure that the custody officer is aware that the lawyer intends to attend the police station in person, and to agree the arrangements for the visit.

---

62   [2004] EWCA Crim 310. See also *R v Johnson* [2005] EWCA Crim 3540.
63   [2004] EWCA Crim 2766; [2005] 1 WLR 2829; [2005] 1 All ER 705; [2005] 1 Cr App R 23.
64   'Authorised place of detention' means a police station or any other place prescribed for the purpose of that provision by order made by the secretary of state (CJPOA 1994 s38(2A)).

## CJPOA 1994 s34

5.67 CJPOA 1994 s34 is directed at enabling a court to draw inferences where a defendant relies on facts in his or her defence that the defendant did not tell the police about at the time that he or she was being questioned under caution or charged. It is important to note that it is not silence, or failure to answer a question or questions, per se which may have adverse consequences.[65] Rather, it is the failure to mention facts that are subsequently relied on in that person's defence. For example, if a defendant relies at trial on an alibi defence but did not tell the police about the alibi when being questioned or when charged then, assuming that all of the conditions are satisfied, the court may draw 'proper' inferences from that failure. Furthermore, inferences may be drawn even though the defendant answered all questions put to him or her by the police. This may happen if the defendant lied during the police interview or gave evasive answers.[66]

5.68 In order to take proper account of CJPOA 1994 s34 when formulating advice at the police station it is necessary to be clear about the circumstances in which the section will apply, and its relationship to other relevant aspects of law, especially PACE and the Codes of Practice. CJPOA 1994 s34 enables a court to draw 'proper' inferences where evidence is given that the accused:

a) at any time before the accused was charged with the offence, on being questioned under caution by a constable trying to discover whether or by whom the offence had been committed, failed to mention any fact relied on in his or her defence in those proceedings; or

b) on being charged with the offence or officially informed that the accused might be prosecuted for it (which includes reporting with a view to a caution, reprimand or warning),[67] failed to mention any such fact, being a fact which in the circumstances existing at the time the accused could reasonably have been expected to mention (CJPOA 1994 s34(1)).

Inferences cannot be drawn where the accused was at an authorised place of detention (for example, a police station) at the time of the failure to mention facts subsequently relied upon, and the accused had not been allowed an opportunity to consult a solicitor before being questioned, charged or informed that he or she may be prosecuted (see para 5.66 above). Where the conditions for drawing inferences are satisfied, they may be drawn in deciding whether to commit or transfer a case to the Crown Court, in determining whether there is a case to answer, and in determining guilt (CJPOA 1994 s34(2)).[68]

---

65 See *T v DPP* [2007] EWHC 1793 (Admin) in which the magistrates' court wrongly drew inferences from a failure to answer police questions.

66 Although in such cases, at trial the judge should normally give a s34 direction or a *Lucas* direction concerning lies, and not both (*R v Rana* [2007] EWCA Crim 2262).

67 Or, when CJA 2003 Part 4 is fully in force, reporting with a view to a written charge.

68 Inferences can also be taken into account in deciding whether to grant an application under Crime and Disorder Act (CDA) 1998 Sch 3 para 2 (application to dismiss a charge sent for trial under CDA 1998 s51) (CJPOA 1994 s34(2)(b)).

*In what circumstances can an inference be drawn?*

5.69   An inference from 'silence' under CJPOA 1994 s34 may only be drawn where all of the conditions set out in section 34(1) have been satisfied, as follows.[69]

### There must be proceedings for an offence

5.70   CJPOA 1994 s34 only applies in criminal proceedings. It does not apply, for example, to proceedings for disqualification of a company director.[70]

### The failure to mention facts must occur no later than charge

5.71   The failure to mention a fact must occur when the suspect is being questioned under caution or when the suspect is charged or informed that he or she might be prosecuted. The wording of the section is such that a court could draw an inference from failure to mention a fact on being questioned even though the suspect did subsequently mention it on being charged. This could be important, for example, where a suspect gives a 'no comment' interview but makes, or hands in, a statement at charge. While handing in a statement at that stage may prevent an inference that the defence was fabricated after charge, it may not prevent an inference that the defendant was not prepared at an early stage to subject his or her defence to scrutiny in a police interview (see further para 5.85 below). Conversely, inferences from failure to mention a relevant fact at the time of charge could be drawn where, for example, a statement is handed in at the beginning of a police interview, but evidence is disclosed by the police during the interview that has not been taken into account in the statement (see para 5.73 below). However, some cases have suggested that inferences should not be drawn where the accused did give information to the police about the accused's defence before being formally interviewed, and before obtaining legal advice, even though the accused then remained silent in interview.[71]

5.72       Failure to mention a fact after charge cannot lead to inferences being drawn. This would be significant where the relevance of a particular fact (for example, that the suspect was present at a certain place at a particular time) only became apparent after charge.[72] Note, however, that the fact that a person has been charged with one offence does not prevent inferences being drawn from failure to mention a fact in respect of an offence for which the person has not yet been charged.

---

69  *R v Argent* [1997] 2 All ER 27; [1997] 2 Cr App R 27; [1997] Crim LR 346.

70  See *R v Secretary of State for Trade and Industry ex p McCormick* (1998) *Times* 10 February. See also *Secretary of State for Trade and Industry v Crane and Another* (2001) *Times* 4 June.

71  *R v Beckles* [2004] EWCA Crim 2766; [2005] 1 WLR 2829; [2005] 1 All ER 705; [2005] 1 Cr App R 23, and *R v Johnson* [2005] EWCA Crim 3540.

72  See *R v N* [1999] Crim LR 61; (1998) *Times* 13 February, where the defendant did not give an explanation of how the victim's nightdress had come to have a semen stain on it in circumstances where the police had not known, at the time of the police interview, that this was the case, and had therefore not questioned him about it. In order for inferences to be drawn, the prosecution would have to prove that the defendant knew of the relevant facts at the time of interview or charge (*R v B* (MT) [2000] Crim LR 181).

## The failure must occur during questions under caution or at charge

5.73 The failure to mention relevant facts must occur 'on being questioned under caution' (CJPOA 1994 s34(1)(a)), or 'on being charged' (or on officially being informed that the person might be prosecuted) (CJPOA 1994 s34(1)(b)). If a defendant did not mention relevant facts in the police interview, the prosecution is likely to concentrate on inferences under section 34(1)(a). If, on the other hand, the defendant did mention relevant facts during the police interview, there will usually be no conceivable 'proper inference' to be drawn from the fact that the defendant did not repeat those facts on being charged. The only exception to this might be where the defendant had not been questioned, where the questioning had been defective in that a caution had not been administered (see below), or where the accused did mention relevant facts in the interview, but the police subsequently made further disclosure. In *R v Dervish*,[73] inferences were drawn under section 34(1)(b) where evidence was disclosed by the police during the interview which had not been taken into account in the statement that the accused had handed in. The court observed that the accused could have made a statement at the time of charge in respect of that information, which would have prevented inferences under this subsection. Alternatively, following further disclosure by the police, a supplementary statement could be handed in by the suspect. Apart from these exceptions, in most circumstances it would be arguable that it would not be reasonable to have expected the defendant to have mentioned relevant facts at the charge stage (see para 5.84 below).

5.74 CJPOA 1994 s34(1)(a) only applies in respect of questioning that is under caution. Therefore, if no caution is administered, through inadvertence or otherwise, no inference can be drawn from failure to mention a fact in response to such questioning. A number of issues arise in this connection.

1) *Was the person properly cautioned?* The caution which must normally be given prior to police questioning is:

> You do not have to say anything. But it may harm your defence if you do not mention when questioned something which you later rely on in court. Anything you do say may be given in evidence. (Code C para 10.5, Code H para 10.4.)

The caution on being charged, set out at Code C para 16.2, is almost identical. For the caution to be given where a person is questioned in circumstances where inferences cannot be drawn, see para 5.66 above. Minor variations in the wording of the caution will not constitute a breach provided that the sense of the caution is preserved (Code C para 10.7, Code H para 10.6).[74]

2) *Should a caution have been administered?* A person must be cautioned, where there are grounds to suspect them of an offence, before any questions are put to them regarding their involvement or suspected involvement in that offence if the suspect's answers or silence could be given in evidence in a criminal prosecution (Code C, Code H para 10.1,

---

73 [2001] EWCA Crim 2789; [2002] 2 Cr App R 6.
74 See *R v Saunders (Rosemary)* [1988] Crim LR 521.

and see paras 4.37 and 4.42 above). If there is any break in questioning, the interrogating officer must ensure that the person is aware that he or she is still under caution (Code C para 10.8, and Code H para 10.7). Furthermore, a person must normally be cautioned on being arrested (Code C, Code H para 10.3).

3) *Did the questioning amount to an interview?* Most questioning in circumstances where a person has been cautioned is likely to constitute an interview (see para 4.37 above).

4) *Should an interview have been conducted?* Where a decision to arrest a person has been made, the person should not normally be interviewed except at a police station (see para 4.44 above). Evidence of an interview conducted contrary to Code C or Code H may be excluded at trial by virtue of PACE s76 (if it led to a confession) or s78 (if it led to a confession or other evidence the prosecution wish to use, including inferences from 'silence').[75]

5.75   Any alleged 'significant statement or silence' made before the lawyer reached the police station should be considered in the light of the discussion above. Evidence of such a statement or silence may be excluded at trial if it was obtained in breach of the cautioning or interviewing provisions, and this will therefore affect the advice to be given regarding police interviews at the police station. Alternatively, it could be argued that even if the evidence is not excluded, a defendant could not reasonably be expected to have mentioned a fact in the context of an interview conducted contrary to Code C. See further para 5.84 below.

### The questioning must be directed to trying to discover whether or by whom the alleged offence was committed

5.76   Although CJPOA 1994 s34(1)(a) refers to questioning by a constable,[76] section 34 also applies in relation to questioning by other persons charged with the duty of investigating offences or charging offenders (CJPOA 1994 s34(4)). This is the same wording as is used in PACE s67(9), which concerns the application of the Codes of Practice (see paras 1.65–1.66, and 1.68–1.69 above). If questioning is carried out by a person charged with the duty of investigating offences or charging offenders and a caution is administered, inferences are possible if the other conditions of section 34 are satisfied. If a caution is not administered, or if the questioning is by a person who does not come within section 34(4), no inferences are possible under section 34, and the common law rules apply (see para 5.63 above).

5.77   In order for the inference provisions of CJPOA 1994 s34(1)(a) to apply, the questioning must be directed at trying to discover whether or by whom the offence had been committed. This has been considered by the Court

---

75   See, eg, *R v Weekes* (1993) 97 Cr App R 222; [1993] Crim LR 211, and *R v Oransaye* [1993] Crim LR 772; and see generally paras 13.34 and 13.42 below.

76   'Constable' includes police officers of all ranks, and also includes constables of forces whose powers are limited by reference to their purpose, or their geographical area, such as British Transport Police or Ministry of Defence Police, although probably only when acting within their jurisdiction. A designated civilian investigating officer (see para 2.50 above) is not a constable, but is a person charged with the duty of investigating offences.

of Appeal in a number of cases, with differing results. In *R v Pointer*[77] the police had conducted an undercover operation in which, the prosecution alleged, undercover officers purchased, or tried to purchase, unlawful drugs from the appellant. The court held that since the interviewing officer believed that he had sufficient evidence for a successful prosecution before the interview, he could not have been trying to discover whether or by whom an offence had been committed, and therefore the section 34 conditions had not been satisfied. However, in *R v Elliott*[78] the court reviewed the authorities and concluded that even where the interviewing officer believed that there was sufficient evidence to justify charging the suspect, Code C paras 11.4 and 16.1 (of the version of Code C applicable before 1 April 2003) did not prevent the officer from interviewing the suspect since it would give the opportunity for an innocent explanation or a defence to be proffered. For the same reason, the condition that questioning be directed to trying to discover whether or by whom the offence had been committed was satisfied. This interpretation is reinforced by para 11.6 of the current Code C which permits questioning to continue until the officer in charge of the investigation is satisfied that all the questions the officer considers relevant to obtaining accurate and reliable information have been put to the suspect.[79] It would seem, therefore, that if the police have already made up their mind to charge the suspect before the interview commences, inferences should not be drawn, but that if they still have an open mind despite the fact that there is sufficient evidence to charge, inferences can be drawn.

### The fact not mentioned is relied on by the defence at trial

5.78    According to the Court of Appeal in *R v Argent*[80] this part of CJPOA 1994 s34(1) involves two questions of fact: a) is there some fact which the defendant has relied on in their defence; and b) did the defendant fail to mention it when the defendant was being questioned or on being charged?

5.79    *'Relied on in their defence'* The lawyer at the police station has to consider what facts are likely to be relevant at trial, and what matters the defendant may seek to rely on. In any particular case, this will depend on what information has been gained from the police and client (and any other source), the substantive criminal law and any relevant rules of evidence. This is an important task, and one that is not made easier by the elastic interpretation given to the expression 'any fact relied on in his defence' by the Court of Appeal in *Argent*. A 'fact' is not limited to events or acts, but can be an assertion that 'something is actually the case', as where a person accused of conspiracy gives in evidence an explanation for their association with their alleged co-conspirators.[81]

---

77  [1997] Crim LR 676.
78  [2002] EWCA Crim 931. See also *R v Hoare and Pierce* [2004] EWCA Crim 784; [2005] 1 WLR 1804; [2005] 1 Cr App R 22.
79  Note that there is some inconsistency between Code C para 11.6 and para 16.1, and that it may also be arguable that if the custody officer is aware that there is sufficient evidence to charge, continued detention is unlawful. See paras 2.59 above and 5.146 below.
80  [1997] 2 All ER 27; [1997] 2 Cr App R 27; [1997] Crim LR 346.
81  *R v Milford* [2001] Crim LR 330.

5.80   Clearly, a fact is relied on by the accused if the accused gives or calls evidence about that fact. However, it has been held that a defendant may be treated as having relied on a fact even if the defendant does not give or call evidence. Merely putting the prosecution to proof is unlikely to be treated as relying on a fact, but cross-examination of prosecution witnesses which involves asserting the existence of facts may well be so treated.[82] Offering a hypothesis about facts put in evidence by the prosecution has been held not to amount to relying on a fact, and neither does a bare admission made in cross-examination.[83]

5.81   Note that even if an inference cannot be drawn under section 34 because it cannot be said that the defendant relied on a fact, an inference may in some circumstances still be drawn under CJPOA 1994 s36 or s37 (see para 5.87 below).

5.82   *'Failed to mention any fact'* Whether a suspect did mention a fact to the police may be disputed, and will be for the court to decide on hearing evidence. It has been suggested that in some circumstances, a police officer might maintain that a suspect had not mentioned a fact when in fact the suspect had done so, since this could lead a court to draw adverse inferences. If the alleged 'silence' occurred before the suspect arrived at the police station, the failure to answer questions would have to be put to the suspect at the beginning of the interview in the police station (see para 5.113 below).

5.83   The courts have accepted that a defendant does mention a fact if the defendant hands in a statement setting out the fact to the police at the time of questioning or charge.[84] This is also the case if the defendant orally asserts facts to the police in interview but does not answer questions.[85] See further para 5.149 below.

### The accused could reasonably have been expected to mention the fact

5.84   CJPOA 1994 s34(1) refers to facts which the defendant could reasonably have been expected to mention in the circumstances existing at the time and, therefore, requires the court to assess reasonableness in the light of those circumstances, rather than with the benefit of hindsight. It would seem that the test of reasonableness is a mixed subjective/objective test. The court must have regard to 'the actual accused with such qualities, apprehensions, knowledge and advice as he is shown to have had at the time',[86] but is a matter for the jury 'in the exercise of their collective common-sense'.[87] Ultimately, what is reasonable depends upon what is expected of suspects in an adversarial system, and on the purpose of s34,

82   See *R v Bowers* [1998] Crim LR 817, *R v Moshaid* [1998] Crim LR 420, *R v Reader, Connor and Hart* (1998) 7 April (unreported), and *R v Webber* [2004] UKHL 1; [2004] 1 WLR 404; [2004] 1 All ER 770; [2004] 1 Cr App R 40.
83   *R v Nickolson* [1999] Crim LR 61, *R v Betts and Hall* [2001] EWCA Crim 224; [2001] 2 Cr App R 257; [2001] Crim LR 754, and *R v Milford* [2001] Crim LR 330.
84   *R v McGarry* [1999] 1 WLR 1500; [1998] 3 All ER 805; [1999] 1 Cr App R 377; [1999] Crim LR 316. See also *R v Ali* [2001] EWCA Crim 863 and *R v Knight* [2003] EWCA Crim 1977; [2004] 1 WLR 340; [2004] 1 Cr App R 9; [2003] Crim LR 799.
85   *R v Ashton* [2002] EWCA Crim 2782.
86   *R v Argent* [1997] 2 Cr App R 27; [1997] Crim LR 346.
87   *R v Hoare and Pierce* [2004] EWCA Crim 784; [2005] 1 WLR 1804; [2005] 1 Cr App R 22.

and as noted at para 5.65 above, the courts have disagreed on this. In view of this, there can be no absolute rules about what is, or is not, reasonable, but a number of factors must be taken into account.

1) *Understanding of the caution* It is unlikely to be reasonable to expect a person to have mentioned a fact if the person genuinely could not understand the caution, or any explanation given by the police officer under Code C NfG 10D.[88] If the relevant caution was given in the absence of the lawyer, it is important to find out precisely what the officer did say, whether the officer gave an adequate explanation of its meaning, and whether the client understood it. An argument that the defendant did not understand the caution is likely to be unsuccessful if the defendant was in receipt of legal advice at the time. Nevertheless, many suspects, especially those who are mentally disordered or mentally vulnerable, have great difficulty in understanding, or may not be able to understand at all, the meaning and significance of the caution.[89] If the lawyer is concerned that the client does not understand the caution, the lawyer should tell the interviewing officer at the commencement of the police interview. This may subsequently help to persuade a court that inferences under CJPOA 1994 s34 should not be drawn.[90]

2) *Legal advice* See para 5.96 below.

3) *Age, health and mental disorder* In deciding whether it is reasonable for a defendant to have mentioned a fact subsequently relied upon at trial, the court should take account of the age of the defendant, and whether the defendant is mentally disordered, mentally vulnerable or unable to understand the significance of failure to mention a fact for some other reason, such as substance abuse, bereavement, severe stress, etc. It should be noted that Code C, Code H NfG 11C states that juveniles and mentally disordered or vulnerable people may be particularly prone to providing information which is unreliable, misleading or self-incriminating. By analogy, it could also be argued that they may be particularly prone to failing to recognise that a particular fact is, or may be, relevant to their defence. In *R v Howell*[91] the court indicated that mental vulnerability, confusion, intoxication and shock could mean that it would not be reasonable to expect the suspect to have mentioned facts, although the fact that the suspect was suffering from the effects of drugs or alcohol has not prevented courts from drawing inferences from silence in a number of cases.[92] It is important in such cases for the lawyer to try

88 Which requires the officer giving the caution to explain it in their own words if the suspect does not understand it.
89 Research has demonstrated that even when administered in ideal conditions, only ten per cent of people fully understand the caution even though 96 per cent claim to understand it. See G Gudjonsson, *The psychology of interrogations and confessions: a handbook* (Wiley, Chichester, 2003) p73.
90 Although see *R v V* [2005] EWCA Crim 581 in which it was held that the judge was right to leave inferences to the jury even though the defendant's solicitor gave evidence that he advised silence because he believed that his client was unable to understand the caution, and the defendant gave evidence that he did not understand it.
91 [2003] EWCA Crim 1; [2003] Crim LR 405.
92 See, eg, *R v Condron* [1997] 1 Cr App R 185; [1996] Crim LR 215 and *R v Kavanagh* (1997) 7 February (unreported).

to obtain medical evidence at the time of the suspect's unfitness to be interviewed (see para 5.21 above).

4) *Inadmissible evidence* It can be argued that it would not be reasonable for a defendant to mention a fact in response to information given, or material provided, by the police which is itself inadmissible. For example, if a suspect is shown, or informed of, a statement of a co-suspect that implicates the suspect, it is arguable that it would not be reasonable to expect the suspect to have mentioned a fact in response since the statement itself would be inadmissible at trial as evidence against the suspect.

5) *Unfair or unlawful police conduct* If prosecution evidence (including failure to mention a fact) is obtained as a result of unfair or unlawful police conduct, the defence lawyer should argue for its exclusion at trial under PACE s76 or s78 (see paras 13.34 and 13.42 below). However, even if such evidence is not excluded it may be argued that it would not be reasonable to expect a defendant to have mentioned a fact in the context of such police behaviour.[93]

6) *Complexity of the evidence or age of the allegation* The Court of Appeal has held that a lawyer could be regarded as having a good reason for advising a client not to answer questions where the material in the hands of the police is complex, or relates to incidents so long ago that no sensible immediate response is feasible.[94] It would follow that it would not be reasonable to expect the suspect to mention facts in such circumstances. However, it may become reasonable if the police give the suspect sufficient time or sufficient notice of the allegation to enable a sensible response to be made.

7) *The apparent strength of the police case* It is arguably not reasonable to expect a suspect to respond to police questioning where the evidence in the hands of the police is so weak as not to deserve an explanation. In *R v Argent*[95] the trial judge excluded evidence of the first police interview where the defendant had been arrested on the basis of one anonymous telephone call. The Court of Appeal took the view that the judge had probably gone too far in excluding the evidence for this reason, but it certainly would have been arguable that it would not have been reasonable to expect the suspect to have answered police questions at that stage. Similarly, in *R v McGarry*,[96] where the police had arrested the defendant on a 'fishing expedition', the prosecution did not seek to rely on inferences from his failure to answer police questions, and this was not criticised by either the trial judge or the Court of Appeal. Conversely, if the prosecution evidence is, or is likely to be, strong a court is likely to take the view that this is a situation calling for an explanation from the suspect.[97]

---

93  See cases such as *R v Paris, Abdulahi and Miller* (1993) 97 Cr App R 99; [1994] Crim LR 361, and *R v Glaves* [1993] Crim LR 685.

94  *R v Roble* [1997] Crim LR 449. See also *R v Howell* [2003] EWCA Crim 1; [2003] Crim LR 405.

95  [1997] 2 All ER 27; [1997] Crim LR 346.

96  [1998] 3 All ER 805.

97  See, eg, *Condron v UK* (2001) 31 EHRR 1; [2000] Crim LR 679 and *R v Howell* [2003] EWCA Crim 1; [2003] Crim LR 405.

### What inferences may be drawn?

5.85   If the conditions for an inference to be drawn are satisfied, a jury must be directed that they must only draw an inference where they are satisfied that the accused had no innocent explanation or none that would stand up to scrutiny.[98] Having decided to draw an inference, the jury or court must decide what inference to draw, and the only guidance from CJPOA 1994 s34 itself is that the inference must be 'proper'. The Judicial Studies Board states that possible inferences include:

- the fact now relied on is true but the defendant, for reasons of his or her own, chose not to reveal it;
- the fact now relied on is irrelevant;
- the fact now relied on is of more recent invention;
- the defendant's present answer to the prosecution case is fabricated;
- the defendant is guilty.[99]

What inference is drawn is very much dependent on the facts, and on the particular jury (or magistrates or district judge), and it is possible that no inference is drawn even though the conditions for doing so are satisfied.

5.86   The damage that inferences may do to a defence put forward at trial will depend on a number of factors, in particular, the strength of the other evidence presented at trial. Inferences may, of course, be crucial. A defence of self-defence, for example, may be considerably undermined even if the prosecution evidence consists primarily of the evidence of the complainant. It must be remembered, however, that answering police questions may also damage the defence if, for example, alibi witnesses named to the police do not give evidence for the defence, or inconsistencies are exploited by the prosecution. See further para 5.102 below.

## CJPOA 1994 ss36 and 37

5.87   The CJPOA 1994 ss36 and 37 enable a court to draw inferences from the failure of a defendant, following their arrest, to account for an object, substance or mark, etc, or to account for their presence at a place at or about the time a crime was committed. In some cases, a defendant may be at risk of inferences under either or both of these sections and under CJPOA 1994 s34. There are many similarities between the three sections, including the fact that inferences cannot be drawn where the accused was at an authorised place of detention when asked to account and had not been given an opportunity to consult a solicitor.[100] Before examining the provisions in detail, it is worth noting the major differences between them.

---

98   *R v Betts and Hall* [2001] 2 Cr App R 257; [2001] Crim LR 754, and see Judicial Studies Board *Crown Court Bench Book: Directing the Jury* (JSB, London 2010) p264.

99   Judicial Studies Board *Crown Court Bench Book: Directing the Jury* (JSB, London 2010) p261. It must be doubted whether it is legitimate for a direct inference of guilt to be drawn.

100   CJPOA 1994 s36(4A) and s37(3A), and see para 5.66 above.

- Section 34 applies where the suspect has been cautioned, but not necessarily arrested,[101] whereas sections 36 and 37 only apply where the suspect has been arrested.
- Sections 36 and 37 apply whether or not a fact is relied upon in a person's defence, whereas section 34 applies only in respect of failure to mention a fact relied upon in the person's defence.
- Section 34 applies to questioning by police constables and others having a duty to investigate offences or charge offenders, whereas sections 36 and 37 apply only to questions put by police constables, designated civilian investigating officers (see para 2.50 above) and HM Revenue and Customs (HMRC) officers (s36(1) and (5), and s37(1) and (4)).
- Under sections 36 and 37, inferences may not be drawn unless the constable or officer has explained why the substance, etc, or the presence of the suspect, is attributable to the suspect's participation in the offence (sections 36(1) and 37(1)), and the effect of failure or refusal (sections 36(4) and 37(3)), whereas under section 34 only a caution is required.

## CJPOA 1994 s36

5.88    Section 36(1) provides that a court can draw proper inferences where:

a) a person is arrested by a constable, and there is:
   i)   on his or her person; or
   ii)  in or on his or her clothing or footwear; or
   iii) otherwise in his or her possession; or
   iv)  in any place in which he or she is at the time of arrest,
   any object, substance or mark, or there is any mark on any such object; and

b) that or another constable investigating the offence reasonably believes that the presence of the object, substance or mark may be attributable to the participation of the person arrested in the commission of an offence specified by the constable; and

c) the constable informs the person arrested that he or she so believes, and requests the person to account for the presence of the object, substance or mark; and

d) the person fails or refuses to do so.

### For what purposes can an inference be drawn?

5.89    Inferences under CJPOA 1994 s36 can be drawn for the same purposes as under CJPOA 1994 s34 (see para 5.68 above). However, since the power to draw inferences under s36 arises where there has been a failure to account (whereas under section 34 it only arises where the defendant has relied on a fact not previously mentioned), it is quite clear that an inference can be drawn in determining whether to commit for trial, and in determining whether the defendant has a case to answer, irrespective of any defence that might be put forward.

---

101 Although generally, where a person has been cautioned, the person should not normally be interviewed except at a police station. See para 4.35 above.

### In what circumstances can an inference be drawn?

5.90   In addition to the legal advice requirement (see para 5.87 above), an inference from 'silence' under CJPOA 1994 s36 will only be possible where all of the conditions set out in section 36(1) and (4) are satisfied.

1) *Arrest* The defendant must have been arrested by a constable (or HMRC officer), although not necessarily for the offence in respect of which the constable has the necessary belief.[102] It is likely that the arrest must be a lawful arrest, so that failing to account following an unlawful arrest should not lead to inferences being drawn (see paras 2.11 to 2.43 above).

2) *Presence of an object, substance or mark* There must, as a matter of fact rather than belief, be an object, substance or mark on the suspect's person, in or on his or her clothing, in his or her possession, or in any place in which he or she was at the time of arrest. Inferences will not be possible if the object, etc, was found elsewhere.[103] The reference to clothing or footwear in CJPOA 1994 s36(1)(a)(ii) includes its condition as well as any object, substance or mark in or on it (CJPOA 1994 s36(3)).

3) *Reasonable belief by the constable* The constable (or designated civilian or HMRC officer) conducting the interview, or another constable investigating the offence, must have a reasonable belief that the presence of the object, etc, may be attributable to the participation of the arrested person in the commission of an offence specified by the constable (not necessarily the offence for which the person was arrested). The term 'reasonable' has, in relation to arrest, been held to require that the officer actually held the requisite belief and that the belief was reasonable according to the standards of the ordinary person (see para 2.15 above). If the prosecution cannot establish that the belief was reasonable, or that the officer specified the relevant offence, inferences could not be drawn under CJPOA 1994 s36.

4) *Request to account for the presence of the object, etc* CJPOA 1994 s36(1)(c) requires that the officer informs the arrested person of their relevant belief and requests the suspect to account for the presence of the object, substance or mark. This is supplemented by section 36(4), which provides that inferences cannot be drawn unless the accused was told in ordinary language by the constable when making the request what the effect would be if the accused failed or refused to comply with the request. These requirements are set out in, and extended by, Code C para 10.11 and Code H para 10.10 which provide that, in order for an inference to be drawn, the constable must inform the suspect in ordinary language:
   - what offence the constable is investigating;
   - what fact the constable is asking the suspect to account for;

---

102  However, in this case if the person is at a police station the person should normally have been re-arrested by virtue of PACE s31 before the request is put to the person.
103  For example, in possession of the complainant. *See R v Abbas and another* [2010] All ER (D) 79 (Jan).

- that the constable believes this fact may be due to the suspect's taking part in the commission of the offence in question;
- that a court may draw a proper inference if the suspect fails or refuses to account for the fact about which the suspect is being questioned; and
- that a record is being made of the interview and that it may be given in evidence if the suspect is brought to trial.

Unlike with the caution under Code C para 10.5 and Code H para 10.4, there is no set form of words, and it may be relevant to ascertain precisely what was said by the police officer, and whether the client understood what was said to them. Although the CJPOA 1994 does not explicitly provide that s36 only applies to the situation where a suspect is asked to account in an interview at a police station or other authorised place of detention, this is clearly implied by the first sentence of Code C para 10.10 and Code H para 10.9. The drafting of section 36 means that while the belief as to the relevance of the object, substance or mark etc, may be held either by the officer conducting the interview or another officer, inferences may only be drawn when the request to account is made by the officer who arrested the suspect.

5) *Failure or refusal to account for the object* Unlike under CJPOA 1994 s34, there is no reasonableness requirement. Simple failure or refusal to account for the object, etc, reasonable or otherwise, will enable the court to draw inferences.[104] However, the court may take into account the reason for failure or refusal to account in deciding what inference is proper. Whether a person 'refused' to account will usually be a fairly clear-cut question of fact. 'Failure' to account may be more difficult to determine, especially where the suspect has given a partial account, and raises similar issues to those in respect of section 34 (see para 5.84 above). It has been held that the presence of heroin and a substantial amount of money in a safe found at the accused's premises was not 'accounted' for by a bare statement that the accused was a heroin user.[105]

## What inferences may be drawn?

5.91    If the conditions for an inference to be drawn are satisfied, a jury should be directed that they must only draw an inference where they are satisfied that the accused had no innocent explanation or none that would stand up to scrutiny (see para 5.85 above). As noted above, although there is no reasonableness requirement under s36, a court should take into account the reasonableness of the failure or refusal to account in deciding what inference is proper.[106]

---

104  Although it can be argued that the approach of the European Court of Human Rights to CJPOA 1994 s34 in *Condron v UK* (2001) 31 EHRR 1; [2000] Crim LR 679 would require a court to give due weight to the fact that a failure or refusal to account had been as a result of legal advice.

105  *R v Compton and others* [2002] EWCA Crim 2835.

106  See Judicial Studies Board *Crown Court Bench Book: Directing the Jury* (JSB, London 2010) p268.

## CJPOA 1994 s37

5.92   Section 37(1) provides that a court may draw proper inferences where:

a)   a person arrested by a constable was found by the constable at a place at or about the time the offence for which the person was arrested is alleged to have been committed; and that or another constable investigating the offence reasonably believes that the presence of the person at that place and at that time may be attributable to the person's participation in the commission of the offence; and

b)   the constable informs the person that he or she so believes, and requests the person to account for that presence; and

c)   the person fails or refuses to do so.

### For what purpose can an inference be drawn?

5.93   Inferences under section 37 can be drawn for the same purposes as under section 36 (see para 5.89 above).

### In what circumstances can an inference be drawn?

5.94   In addition to the legal advice requirement (see para 5.87 above), an inference from 'silence' under CJPOA 1994 s37 will only be possible where all of the conditions set out in section 37(1) and (3) are satisfied.

1)   *Arrest* The condition is the same as for section 36 (see para 5.90), except that under section 37 the arrest must be for the offence in respect of which the suspect is being asked to account.

2)   *At a place at or about the time the offence was committed* 'Place' is defined to include any building or part of a building, any vehicle, vessel, aircraft or hovercraft and any other place whatsoever (CJPOA 1994 s38(1)). It is likely that the reference to 'place' is a reference to any place, and not necessarily the place where the alleged offence was committed, provided that the person was found there at or about the time the offence was allegedly committed (and provided the person's presence may be attributable to his or her participation in the alleged offence (see 3 below)). The expression 'at or about the time' the offence was committed clearly leaves room for interpretation and will, in part, depend on the circumstances of the alleged offence.

   The section refers to a person being found by the constable who arrested the person at the relevant time and place. Therefore, it will not apply where a person is asked to account for his or her presence at a place where the person was seen by some other person (for example, a store detective). However, such a failure to account may come within CJPOA 1994 s34 if the conditions for the drawing of an inference under that section are satisfied. Furthermore, inferences may be drawn at common law from unexplained presence at a particular place at a particular time.[107]

3)   *Reasonable belief by the constable* The issues are similar to those in respect of CJPOA 1994 s36 (see para 5.90 above), except that the belief must be in relation to the offence for which the person was arrested.

107  See *R v Morgan* [1993] Crim LR 87.

4) *Request to account for presence, etc* The issues are similar to those in respect of CJPOA 1994 s36 (see para 5.90 above).

5) *Failure or refusal to account* The issues are similar to those in respect of CJPOA 1994 s36 (see para 5.90 above).

### What inferences may be drawn?

5.95   The inferences that may be drawn are the same as for CJPOA 1994 s36 (see para 5.91 above).[108]

## Legal advice and waiver of privilege

### Legal advice

5.96   The early cases on the silence provisions of the CJPOA 1994 held that a mere assertion by the accused that he or she was advised not to answer questions was unlikely to be sufficient to prevent inferences from being drawn, and this is still the case.[109] In *Condron v UK*[110] the ECtHR treated the presence of a solicitor during the police interview as an important safeguard against any compulsion to speak. It followed that: 'the very fact that an accused is advised by his lawyer to maintain his silence must ... be given appropriate weight by the domestic court', and therefore the jury should not have been left to draw an adverse inference notwithstanding that it may have been satisfied that the explanation given by the accused (that the accused was relying on legal advice) may have been plausible. This was followed by *R v Betts and Hall*,[111] in which the Court of Appeal held that if the fact of legal advice is a plausible reason for not mentioning relevant facts then inferences must not be drawn.

5.97   However, the argument that inferences should not be drawn where the accused relied on the advice of their lawyer to remain silent presented the courts with a dilemma, summed up by Woolf LCJ in *R v Beckles*:

> Where the reason put forward by a defendant for not answering questions is that he is acting on legal advice, the position is singularly delicate. On the one hand the Courts have not unreasonably wanted to avoid defendants driving a coach and horses through section 34 and by so doing defeating the statutory objective. Such an explanation is very easy for a defendant to advance and difficult to investigate because of legal professional privilege. On the other hand, it is of the greatest importance that defendants should be able to be advised by their lawyer without their having to reveal the terms of that advice if they act in accordance with that advice.[112]

In this context, the cases following *R v Betts and Hall*, and the Judicial Studies Board Specimen Directions fail to stress the importance of legal advice in determining whether inferences should be drawn. The Specimen

---

108   And see Judicial Studies Board *Crown Court Bench Book: Directing the Jury* (JSB, London 2010) p271.

109   *R v Condron* [1997] 1 Cr App R 185; [1996] Crim LR 215 and *R v Argent* [1997] 2 Cr App R 27; [1997] Crim LR 346.

110   [2000] Crim LR 679.

111   [2001] 2 Cr App R 257; [2001] Crim LR 754.

112   [2004] EWCA Crim 2766; [2005] 1 All ER 705, para 43.

Directions[113] suggest that a judge should tell the jury that a suspect has a choice whether to accept or reject legal advice, although they give no indication of the basis on which a suspect is expected to make such a choice.

5.98    The current approach, based on the decisions in *R v Howell*,[114] *R v Hoare and Pierce*[115] and *R v Beckles*,[116] can be summarised as follows:

1) Where an accused gives evidence that he or she remained silent on the advice of his or her solicitor, the question for the jury or court is whether, in the circumstances existing at the time, it is reasonable to expect the accused to have mentioned the relevant fact or facts.

2) The fact that the court or jury accepts that the accused genuinely relied on legal advice not to tell the police about facts on which the accused subsequently relied in his or her defence does not mean that they have to conclude that it was reasonable for the accused not to mention those facts. They may, for example, conclude that it was not reasonable to rely on that advice, or that the accused relied on the advice because it suited the accused's purpose, for example, to hide the fact that the accused had no innocent explanation.

3) A court or jury may be more likely to conclude that reliance on legal advice not to put forward relevant facts was reasonable if there were 'soundly based objective' or 'good' reasons for that advice. The following may be regarded as 'good reasons':
   • little or no disclosure by the police so that the solicitor cannot usefully advise the client;
   • the case is so complex, or relates to matters so long ago, that no sensible immediate response is feasible;
   • the suspect has substantial difficulty in responding as a result of factors such as ill-health, mental disability, confusion, intoxication or shock.

4) A court or jury is less likely to conclude that reliance on legal advice was reasonable if the advice was not based on 'good' reasons. The following are unlikely to be regarded as 'good reasons':
   • a belief by the solicitor that the detention is unlawful;
   • the absence of a written statement from the complainant;
   • a belief that the complainant may withdraw the complaint;
   • a belief that the police intend to charge whatever the suspect says in interview.

5.99    The defence lawyer is, therefore, placed in considerable difficulty in formulating advice whether or not to remain silent. The Court of Appeal has clearly attempted to persuade lawyers that they must only advise silence for reasons that would be approved of by the court. However, the courts

---

113  The specimen directions have been superseded by the Crown Court Bench Book, but the specimen directions on inferences under CJPOA 1994 s34 are reproduced in appendix 2. See Judicial Studies Board *Crown Court Bench Book: directing the jury* (JSB, London 2010) p394.

114  [2003] EWCA Crim 1; [2003] Crim LR 405.

115  [2004] EWCA Crim 784; [2005] 1 WLR 1804; [2005] 1 Cr App R 22.

116  [2004] EWCA Crim 2766; [2005] 1 All ER 705. See also *R v Essa* [2009] EWCA Crim 43, and Judicial Studies Board *Crown Court Bench Book: directing the jury* (JSB, London 2010) p259.

have not been entirely consistent in determining what are 'good' reasons for advice and, in any event, the obligation of the lawyer is to advise the client in their best interests which may well lead to silence being advised for reasons that would not be approved of by a court. Nevertheless, the lawyer must always be clear in his or her own mind why he or she is advising a particular course of action, such as silence, and should both explain the rationale to the client and keep a careful record. The client should also not be left with the impression that advice to remain silent will necessarily prevent inferences from being drawn.

## Waiver of privilege

5.100   As noted above, the reasons for advice to remain silent may be relevant to the question whether a court should draw inferences from silence. However, if either the accused or the accused's lawyer explains the grounds or reasons for the advice, this is likely to amount to a waiver of privilege. Confidential communications between solicitors and their clients concerning legal advice are usually legally privileged, meaning that neither can be required to disclose to the prosecution, or to the court, the content of those consultations.[117] If privilege is waived, this enables the accused (or his or her lawyer if the accused gives evidence) to be cross-examined about what was said and this, of course, may be damaging to the interests of the accused. The following principles can be drawn from the relevant cases:

- If the accused simply gives evidence that he or she was advised to remain silent, this will not amount to a waiver of privilege.[118]
- If the accused, or the accused's lawyer, tells the police during the police interview (or at any other time), or gives evidence of, the grounds or reasons for the advice, this will almost certainly amount to a waiver of privilege.[119] Note that a lawyer's opening statement in a police interview can be adduced in evidence by the prosecution at trial.[120]
- If privilege is waived the accused (and the accused's lawyer if giving evidence) may be asked what else was said in the consultation, including whether there were any other reasons for advice to remain silent, although this is not necessarily the case.[121]

5.101   Normally, therefore, the solicitor should not tell the police nor state in the police interview the reason(s) for advice given to the client. This is the case even if the reasons given for the advice do not refer to anything said by the client to the lawyer. For example, where a lawyer told the police that he had advised his client not to answer questions because he had not been given sufficient information by the police, and that he understood that there was forensic evidence and possibly relevant CCTV footage, this was

---

117  See para 1.19 above and *R v Derby Magistrates' Court ex p B* [1996] 1 AC 487.
118  *R v Condron* [1997] 1 WLR 827; [1997] 1 Cr App R 185; [1996] Crim LR 215.
119  *R v Bowden* [1999] 1 WLR 823; [1999] 4 All ER 43; [1999] 2 Cr App R 176; *R v Loizou* [2006] EWCA Crim 1719; *R v Seaton* [2010] EWCA Crim 1980.
120  *R v Fitzgerald* (1998) 6 June (unreported) CA.
121  In *R v Seaton* [2010] EWCA Crim 1980 the court said that waiver may well not open up everything said to cross-examination, and that the test is 'fairness and/or the avoidance of a misleading impression' (at para 43(d)).

held to amount to a waiver of privilege.[122] Although there is no specific authority on the point, it should not amount to a waiver of privilege for the lawyer to tell the police that the lawyer has advised the client not to answer questions and, separately and without reference to the advice, to inform them of facts relevant to that decision, for example, a belief on the part of the lawyer that the detention or interview is unlawful or contrary to Code C or Code H. Similarly, it should not amount to a waiver of privilege if the solicitor advises the client in the police interview not to answer questions provided that no reference is made to information obtained or advice given during a privileged conversation with the client. Thus, 'I now advise my client not to answer questions because you have given me no disclosure' or 'In view of the lack of disclosure I am unable to advise my client' should not amount to a waiver. On the other hand, saying 'I now advise my client not to answer questions because my client has told me that he does not want to name the person who is in fact responsible for the offence' will amount to a waiver.

## Advice on whether to answer police questions

5.102  Advising a client on whether to answer police questions is normally the most important, and the most difficult, task for the lawyer at the police station. Anything said by a suspect in the context of a police interview at which the suspect's lawyer was present will almost certainly be admitted at trial. On the other hand, things that are not said in the interview may, as a result of CJPOA 1994 ss34, 36 and 37, have a critical impact on both the decision whether to initiate criminal proceedings and on the outcome of any trial. Furthermore, the lawyer has to give advice in circumstances where the lawyer normally has limited information, and is uncertain about both the possible prosecution evidence and about the position of the client.

5.103  Advice should always be given on the basis of a considered balancing of the risks of answering questions set against the risks of not answering questions, having regard to the fact that the burden of proving guilt rests on the prosecution (subject to the exceptions noted at para 5.57 above). The client should, as far as possible, be made aware of the possible benefits and risks of any course of action considered, but where appropriate the lawyer should give positive advice, and, if necessary, in strong terms. Despite the fact that the Court of Appeal has attempted to limit the circumstances in which a lawyer advises a client to remain silent (see para 5.98 above), the lawyer's professional obligation is to advise a client in the client's best interests.

5.104  This is particularly important in the context of CJPOA 1994 ss34, 36 and 37. While a client must be informed of the possible consequences of failure to mention a fact or failure to account, and the fact that legal advice to remain silent will not necessarily prevent inferences from being drawn, the lawyer must seek to minimise any adverse consequences. If the lawyer considers that a particular course of action is in the interests of the client,

122 *R v Hall-Chung* [2007] EWCA Crim 3429.

it is the lawyer's duty to give such advice, and to act in a manner designed both to ensure that any decision of the client is respected, and (as far as legitimately possible) that inferences will not be drawn or that they will not be adverse to the client. It is important to recognise that many clients at the police station are not in a position to make a decision without considerable guidance from his or her lawyer. This may be because of factors such as age, mental capacity or psychological state, but it may also be because of the pressures resulting from arrest and detention. The lawyer is the legal expert and, as with any professional, should expect to give (and should be expected to give) such guidance and protection.

5.105    In considering, and giving, advice about whether to answer questions in interview, the lawyer should, in particular:

- consider the possible impact of all three sections of CJPOA 1994 (ie, ss34, 36 and 37) and whether the pre-conditions for drawing inferences are likely to be satisfied (see paras 5.60 to 5.99 above);
- consider whether the client has allegedly made a 'significant statement or silence' at any prior time, and what impact this may have (see para 5.113 below);
- remember that one consequence of a client not answering questions in the police interview is that the police may not have sufficient evidence to charge them with any offence;
- consider how to avoid, or minimise, the impact of inferences at trial, including what should be said by the lawyer in any opening statement in the police interview (see paras 5.143–5.169, and para 7.48 below); and
- take a careful note of the advice given to the client and the reasons for that advice.

5.106    The major factors, in addition to the possible adverse consequences of 'silence', that should be considered in formulating advice to the client regarding the police interview are set out in paras 5.107–5.142 below. The weight to be attached to each of these factors will vary, depending on the circumstances of the case, and the strategies that may be available to prevent or minimise inferences.

## The police case

5.107    Seeking information from the police about the evidence in their possession is dealt with in chapter 4. The lawyer must be cautious in making judgments about the police case because it may have been exaggerated or, on the other hand, crucial information may have been withheld (see para 4.58) above.[123]

5.108    The police are only under a limited obligation to provide disclosure prior to interview (see para 4.25 above). In *R v Argent*[124] the appellant argued that the police had not given the solicitor sufficient information to enable him to advise his client. The police had provided limited disclosure,

---

123  In *R v Farrell* [2004] EWCA Crim 597 it was held that it was not necessarily wrong for the police to hold back information before interviewing a suspect because disclosing it might handicap legitimate police enquiries.
124  [1997] 2 Cr App R 27; [1997] Crim LR 346.

and the Court of Appeal took the view that the appellant could have given basic facts to the police, such as the fact that he had left the scene before the incident occurred and was not involved in any violence, even if he had not received full disclosure from the police. In *R v Howell*[125] it was held that the fact that the police did not have a written statement from the complainant did not amount to a 'good' reason for advising the client to remain silent. However, in such circumstances the lawyer will need to consider why there is no written statement, and what other evidence has been disclosed. The Court of Appeal also stated in *Howell* that a belief that the complainant may withdraw the complaint was not a 'good' reason for silence. Whether a 'withdrawal' of a complaint will, in practice, prevent a prosecution proceeding will depend upon the nature and seriousness of the allegation and the other evidence in the case. In many circumstances, such a belief may justify advice to remain silent, although the suspect must be advised that if the complainant does not withdraw the complaint or the prosecution proceeds on the basis of other evidence, inferences are likely to be drawn.

5.109    The lawyer must carefully consider how far it is appropriate to press the police to supply information about the evidence in advance of the interview. Pressing too hard may result in information being given which would make it difficult to justify the client not answering questions for this reason. However, failure to seek information from the police may result in the interviewing officer responding to an opening statement by an offer of more information. In terms of the impression it may make on a court in considering inferences to be drawn, failure to answer questions following an offer of further information is likely to have an adverse effect on the client's case. In most circumstances, the lawyer should seek as much information as possible from the police.

5.110    Having assessed the information obtained from the client and the police, and having considered the likely admissibility of the potential evidence (see paras 5.50–5.55 above), the lawyer will be in a position to make a preliminary assessment of the strength or weakness of the police case. Where the evidence of guilt is, or is likely to be, strong, a court is likely to take the view that this is a situation calling for an explanation from the suspect. In such circumstances, adverse inferences flowing from silence may not add very much to the prosecution case, although they are likely to damage a positive defence put forward at trial. Therefore, if the client is to be advised to remain silent in the police interview the lawyer should consider what strategies might be adopted that would minimise the effect of inferences. In particular, regard should be had to whether there is already sufficient evidence to charge (see para 2.59 above) or whether the interviewing officer believes that there is already sufficient evidence to establish the guilt of the suspect (see paras 5.77 above and 7.69 below), and also to whether a statement should be handed in to the police (see para 5.149 below). If the lawyer does succeed in persuading the police not to interview, the lawyer must still consider whether the client should state any facts on being charged to avoid inferences being drawn under CJPOA 1994 s34(1)(b) (see para 5.73 above).

125 [2003] EWCA Crim 1; [2005] 1 Cr App R 1; [2003] Crim LR 405.

5.111    If the police have disclosed little or no information about the accusation, or it appears uncertain (eg, there is uncertainty about relevant dates or times), or the evidence is weak, answering questions will often be inadvisable (see para 5.84), although given the danger of inferences, the lawyer should consider whether a statement should be handed in. If the suspect is not going to answer questions, the lawyer's opening statement might include the following:

> I now advise my client not to answer questions, since the information you have given me raises no reasonable suspicion that my client has committed an offence [and/or] the allegation is so vague and uncertain that I cannot advise my client what facts may become relevant at trial if they are charged. [Or] The information that you have disclosed is so minimal that I am unable to give sensible advice to my client about answering police questions.

## Legality of arrest, detention and questioning

5.112    The lawyer should carefully consider the legality of the arrest (see para 2.11 above) and the legality of the detention (see para 2.53 above). If the arrest or detention is unlawful a court may be persuaded that evidence of the interview should not be admitted (see paras 13.34 and 13.42 below), so that the prosecution would be unable to establish that the accused failed to mention relevant facts, etc. Alternatively, even if the interview is admitted, the court may be persuaded that it would not be reasonable to expect the accused to have mentioned facts on which the accused relies at trial. Where the lawyer believes that the client's detention is unlawful, but that belief is not subsequently upheld by a court, the fact that advice to remain silent is based upon that belief should be taken into account by the court in determining whether the accused acted reasonably in failing to mention relevant facts, but it does not necessarily render silence reasonable.[126] The lawyer should normally make representations as to the unlawfulness of arrest or detention to the officer in charge of the investigation and/or the custody officer, and should always keep a careful record of the reasoning, representations and responses. As noted at para 7.69 below, the police are given a great deal of latitude in determining whether interviewing should cease, and it will be difficult to argue that an interview breaches Code C para 11.6 or Code H para 11.7 unless it is clear that the police have decided to charge whatever is said in interview[127] or they have asked all relevant questions of the suspect (see para 5.145 below).

---

126  *R v Hoare and Pierce* [2004] EWCA Crim 784; [2005] 1 WLR 1804; [2005] 1 Cr App R 22.

127  In *R v Howell* [2003] EWCA Crim 1; [2005] 1 Cr App R 1; [2003] Crim LR 405 the Court of Appeal said that the fact that the lawyer believed that the suspect would be charged in any event was not a 'good' reason for advice to remain silent. Nevertheless, in practice it may be appropriate for the lawyer to advise silence in such circumstances, but the argument that inferences should not be drawn will be stronger if there is evidence that the police have already decided to charge, eg, a statement to that effect by the officer in the case or the custody officer.

## Prior comments and silences of the client

5.113    An important consideration in formulating advice concerning the police interview is whether the client has, or is alleged by the police to have, made a significant statement or silence at some prior stage. A significant statement is defined by Code C para 11.4A and Code H para 11.5 as: 'one which appears capable of being used in evidence against the suspect, in particular a direct admission of guilt'.[128] It does not include anything said by the suspect as part of the conduct constituting the alleged offence.[129] A significant silence is defined as 'a failure or refusal to answer a question or to answer satisfactorily when under caution which might, allowing for the restrictions on drawing inferences from silence ... give rise to an inference under the CJPOA 1994, Part III' (see para 5.60 above). Where there has been a significant statement or silence which occurred in the presence and hearing of a police officer or other police staff before the start of the interview, and which has not been put to the suspect in the course of a previous interview, the interviewing officer must, at the beginning of an interview, ask the suspect whether the suspect confirms or denies the statement or silence and whether the suspect wishes to add anything to it (Code C, Code H para 11.4). A written record should have been made of any interview, whether or not conducted at a police station (Code C para 11.7(a)).[130] Furthermore, a written record should have been made of any relevant comments made by the suspect outside an interview, solicited or not (Code C para 11.13), although under Code C there is no obligation on an officer to record a significant silence or, as important, the questions that led to the silence. Note that the obligation to put a significant statement or silence to a suspect applies whether it occurred before arrival at the police station or at the police station but outside the context of an interview.

5.114    Where there is an alleged significant statement or silence, the lawyer must consider:

- what comment, if any, the client should make in respect of the significant statement or silence;
- what impact the alleged significant statement or silence has on the decision whether the client should answer questions in the interview;
- in the case of a significant silence, whether the client should answer any question(s) which allegedly resulted in the silence if they are repeated in the police interview.

To a certain extent, significant statements raise different considerations to significant silences, so they are dealt with separately below.

---

128  Note that an exculpatory statement that could be used at trial to show that the suspect was lying would also amount to a significant statement (*R v Park* (1993) 99 Cr App R 270; [1994] Crim LR 285).

129  For example, as part of conduct amounting to disorderly conduct contrary to the Public Order Act 1986 s5 (*DPP v Lawrence* [2007] EWHC 2154 (Admin)).

130  Code H para 11.8 provides that interview records should be made in accordance with the Code of Practice issued under TA 2000 Sch 8 para 3 where the interview takes place at a designated place of detention.

## Significant statements

5.115   If the client denies having made the alleged statement, the client should normally be advised to say so, even if the client is not going to answer questions generally in the interview. If a defendant relies at trial on an assertion that he or she did not make such a statement, a failure to make the denial at this stage would almost certainly lead to adverse inferences being drawn under CJPOA 1994 s34. If the lawyer is concerned that the client would find it difficult to comment on the alleged statement and then remain silent for the rest of the interview, there is no reason why the lawyer should not indicate to the police that the client does not accept that the statement was made, or include a denial in a prepared statement. A comment on an alleged statement or silence would normally be appropriate even if the lawyer believes that it was made in the context of an interview that should not have been conducted (see para 4.44 above), although this should also normally be indicated. If the officer, in accordance with the requirement under Code C para 11.11 or para 11.13, asks the client to verify the written record of the alleged statement, an endorsement should be made in similar terms.

5.116   If the statement that is denied was allegedly made in response to a question put by the police officer, the officer may repeat the question in the interview in the hope that, even if evidence of the original question and response is excluded, either the suspect will now answer it or, if not, the court could be asked to draw inferences from failure to do so. Therefore, the client will need advice on how to respond.

5.117   It may help to illustrate this process with an example. Suppose the police allege that, following an arrest for having an offensive weapon in a public place, they asked the suspect in the street why the suspect was carrying the weapon, and that the suspect responded by saying that he kept it for protection. In instructions to the lawyer, the client denies having said this. The alleged conversation is almost certainly an interview within Code C para 11.1A and, in view of Code C para 11.1, almost certainly should not have been conducted at that time. Evidence of such an unlawfully conducted interview may be excluded by a court under PACE s78, although since PACE s78 is discretionary it is possible that the court will not exclude it. It was suggested above that when the conversation is put to the client in interview, the alleged statement by the suspect should be denied and, normally, the illegality of the interview asserted. This response will, if anything, bolster an argument in court that evidence of the conversation should be excluded. However, if the court does not exclude it, the client can deny having responded in the manner alleged, and will then be able to point to his consistent denial at the interview in the police station. Of course, the interviewing officer could simply repeat the question in the interview, but the officer is likely to do so in any event.

5.118   If the client accepts that he or she did say what the police allege the suspect said, the first issue to be considered is whether the statement was made in the context of an interview that should not have been conducted (see para 4.44 above). If it was made in that context, it would normally be advisable for the client to make no comment when the significant statement is put to the suspect, but for the lawyer to indicate that he or she believes the street interview to have been unlawfully conducted. If at trial the court cannot be persuaded to exclude evidence of the street interview, and if the client then relies in his or her defence on the fact that it was not true, arguably an inference should not be drawn from the failure to mention this in interview since, in view of the lawyer's advice that the street interview was unlawful, it would not be reasonable to expect the defendant to have mentioned it. This is likely to be better than the client, in the police station interview, admitting making the statement but denying its truth, since it would then be more difficult to seek exclusion of the original statement.

5.119　If the statement was not made in the context of an unlawfully conducted interview, it will then be relevant whether the client accepts the statement as being true. If the client accepts that he or she said it but denies that it was true, it will normally be appropriate to state this, since otherwise it will be difficult to challenge it at trial. If, however, the client admits that he or she made the statement and accepts that it is true, then clearly the client should not comment upon it unless the client intends to admit the offence or wish to show that the statement is consistent with innocence.

5.120　The impact that the prior statement has on the decision whether to answer questions generally in the police interview will depend, in part, on whether that statement is likely to be admitted in evidence at trial, the nature of the statement, and the strength of the other evidence. Certainly, if the prior statement is not likely to be admitted at trial, and there is little or no other evidence, the client should not normally answer questions in interview unless the client wishes to admit the offence.

## Significant silences

5.121　A significant silence is likely to be a failure or refusal to answer a specific question or questions put to the client before arriving at the police station or outside the context of the formal police interview. However, Code C para 11.4A and Code H para 11.5 also include a failure to answer a question satisfactorily. CJPOA 1994 ss36 and 37 refer to failure to 'account' (for an object, substance or mark, or for presence at or about the time of an offence), which could include a failure to answer satisfactorily.[131] However, whether an answer is 'satisfactory' is a matter of degree and perspective, since a satisfactory answer from the defence point of view may not be one that a police officer finds satisfactory. In this case, when the alleged significant silence is put to the suspect in the police interview, the lawyer may wish to point out that he or she does not regard the answer given as unsatisfactory and therefore that there is no significant silence.

5.122　The potential areas of dispute include both the question(s) put to the client and the client's alleged failure or refusal to answer, or failure to answer satisfactorily. If the client denies that a question (or questions) was put to him or her, this should normally be asserted by the client, or by the lawyer on the client's behalf, in order to try to avoid adverse inferences

---

131　In *R v Compton* [2002] EWCA Crim 2835 it was held, where the drugs and a large amount of money was found near to the accused, that they were not accounted for by a mere statement by the accused that he was a heroin user.

at trial. This is the case even if the question should not have been put because it would have amounted to an unlawful interview. However, in such circumstances the lawyer should also consider stating that in his or her view the interview was unlawful. The officer may, of course, repeat the question in the interview, and the client will require advice on whether to answer it at this stage.

5.123    If the client accepts that he or she was asked the question, but maintains that he or she did answer it, whether the client should now assert this will depend on whether the alleged answer was incriminating (which is probably unlikely, as otherwise the officer would want to use the answer as evidence against the suspect) and whether the conversation amounted to an interview that should not have been conducted by virtue of Code C para 11.1 or Code H para 11.2. As stated at para 5.90 above, most questions consisting of a request to account for a substance, etc, or presence, put following an arrest but before arrival at the police station, will amount to an interview which should not have been conducted at that stage. The lawyer must also consider whether, if it is a situation where CJPOA 1994 s36 or s37 may apply, the requirements of those sections and the requirements of Code C para 10.11 or Code H para 10.10 have been satisfied (see paras 5.90 and 5.94 above). If the client did answer the question in a way that was, and is, consistent with innocence, it will normally be advisable for the client to so assert at this stage, even if the question was originally asked in the context of an unlawfully conducted interview. If the answer was incriminating, clearly it should not now be asserted. If, however, the question was asked in the context of an unlawfully conducted interview or did not comply with the relevant requirements (see above), the lawyer should normally make this clear in order to try to avoid adverse inferences being drawn from the alleged failure to answer the question.[132] In either case, the client will need advice on how to respond if the question is repeated in the interview.

5.124    If the police version of the question(s) and the failure or refusal to answer is accepted by the client, it must first be considered whether the client should now answer the question and explain why it was not answered before. If the client is to answer questions in the police interview, then it will normally be advisable for the client to comment on and, if possible, explain his or her previous failure to answer the question in order to try to avoid an adverse inference being drawn from his or her prior silence. If the conversation amounted to an unlawfully conducted interview or if the relevant requirements were not satisfied (see above), the lawyer should make this clear, again, in order to prevent an adverse inference being drawn from the original failure to answer. If the client is not going to answer questions in the police interview, then it will not normally be appropriate to comment on the prior silence. Even if the prior silence was in the context of an unlawfully conducted interview, there is probably little advantage in pointing this out at this stage since it will only put the officer on notice and give the officer a reminder to rectify it in the interview.

---

132 Although probably only in very general terms, in order not to alert the officer to problems that may be cured by repeating the question in the proper form in the interview.

## Likely fairness of the interview

5.125   Whether the police interview is likely to be conducted in a fair manner may be difficult to judge, but relevant factors will include prior knowledge of the officers who will be interviewing the suspect and the nature and circumstances of the alleged offence. Certain police officers have a reputation for being aggressive in interview or for resorting to underhand tactics, despite the presence of lawyers. Experienced lawyers will build up their own knowledge of officers in the police stations with which they are familiar, and defence lawyers should be encouraged to share this information with each other. Such knowledge of the officers concerned will be a factor to be taken into account together with the other factors identified. Likewise, the nature and circumstances of the alleged offence may have an impact on the way in which the police interview is likely to be conducted. This will be particularly so if the allegation is of assault on a police officer, or it is a serious offence where the police may be under some pressure to achieve a 'result'. In these circumstances, the lawyer must be careful to avoid undue pressure being placed upon the client, and advising the client not to answer questions may be one way of achieving this. It may also be the case that an interview that starts off being conducted fairly degenerates so that it becomes unfair.

5.126   A suitable statement might be:

> I am now advising my client not to answer further questions, since your style of interviewing is such that my client is unnecessarily distressed [or] is unable properly to explain their position [or] is being intimidated.

If this is done during the course of the police interview, it should not amount to a waiver of privilege since there is no reference to a privileged conversation (see para 5.100 above). Having made the statement, the lawyer should normally then have a private consultation with the client to explain the reasons for the intervention. On resumption of the interview, the lawyer should then state that he or she has advised the client not to answer further questions, without giving reasons for that advice.

5.127   Another way in which the interview process might be unfair is if the nature of the questioning is likely to relate to memory of fine detail, particularly where the client has not had an opportunity to refresh their memory, for example, by looking at documents (see para 5.84 above). In these circumstances it may be advisable for the client not to answer questions at least until the client has had the opportunity to refresh his or her memory or to examine the documents concerned. The opening statement in such circumstances should not normally include reasons for the advice, but the lawyer should separately make representations to the officer concerned, for example, that time should be allowed to examine relevant documents.

## State of the client

5.128   The question of whether a suspect is fit to be interviewed at all is dealt with at para 5.22 above. The question here is whether, assuming that he or she is fit to be interviewed, the client is in a position to be able to deal with the interview either by answering questions or by not doing so. This is very much a matter for the judgment of the lawyer and, where appropriate, should be discussed with the client. Some people would be unable to deal with the pressure inherent in an interview where they are not answering questions. Others might find this relatively easy, whereas they may not be able to answer police questions without becoming belligerent or careless. It is perfectly legitimate for a guilty client to refuse to answer questions, and this may be such a client's only option if the client wishes the lawyer to remain in the interview but has already told the lawyer that he or she is guilty (see para 5.30 above). Conversely, a client who has asserted his or her innocence may be best advised not to answer questions if the client is likely to become confused or to confess falsely. Although false confessions probably occur more often in the absence of a lawyer, research suggests that certain types of people, or people in certain types of situations, are particularly prone to false confessions.

5.129 The noted forensic psychologist, Gisli Gudjonsson, has suggested a number of factors that tend to make a suspect vulnerable to falsely confessing:

- an inability to handle interrogation pressure;
- unfamiliarity with police procedures and the process of detention and interrogation;
- specific fears, such as a fear of a police officer or a fear of being locked up;
- physical discomfort, pain or exhaustion;
- a mental state that interferes with the suspect's ability to make a rational decision, such as extreme anxiety, depression or bereavement;
- a failure to consider seriously enough the long-term consequences of making a false confession;
- a propensity to tell lies to escape from stress;[133]
- an inability to recall events, or lack of confidence in one's ability to do so. This may be specifically related to alcohol or drug abuse, or other interference with the functioning of the brain such as a head injury or emotional trauma;
- an inability to detect discrepancies between what the suspect observed and what the suspect has subsequently been told, whether by the police or others;
- factors associated with mental states such as severe anxiety or confusion, or feelings of guilt or bereavement.[134]

Furthermore, if the suspect is likely to become aggressive, or overly cynical or sarcastic, the lawyer should remember that at trial this may look or sound like evidence of guilt.

5.130 However, the state of the client and their fitness for interview must be approached with some caution by the lawyer. The Court of Appeal in *R v Argent*[135] said that in considering reasonableness, the circumstances of the

---

133 In *R v Brine* [1992] Crim LR 122 it was accepted that a confession should have been excluded where a propensity to lie under pressure resulted from mild paranoid psychosis.

134 G Gudjonsson 'Interrogation and false confessions: vulnerability factors' (1992) 47 *British Journal of Hospital Medicine* 8, and see generally G Gudjonsson, *The psychology of interrogations and confessions: a handbook* (Wiley, Chichester, 2003).

135 [1997] 2 Cr App R 27; [1997] Crim LR 346.

suspect must be taken into account (see para 5.84 above). However, in a number of cases, the fact that the suspect was suffering from the effects of drugs was not sufficient to remove the issue of inferences from the jury, particularly where the forensic medical examiner had certified the suspect fit to be interviewed.[136] In formulating advice, the lawyer must consider whether answering questions will present a greater danger than the possibility of inferences. Consideration should also be given to obtaining a second medical opinion (see para 5.24 above).

5.131    Given the dangers of waiver of privilege (see para 5.100 above), it will normally be better not to explain reasons for advice in the opening statement, but to make appropriate representations to the relevant officer outside of the police interview. For example, the lawyer may suggest a postponement of the interview and, if relevant, a temporary release on bail, to enable the problem to be sorted out.

## The client's case

5.132    Where the instructions obtained from the client and/or the lawyer's assessment of the legal position demonstrate that the client has a defence, the lawyer must consider the dangers of not putting it forward in interview, particularly in terms of the potential damage from inferences and the general impact on credibility from failing to put forward a defence at the investigative stage. If putting forward the defence in police interview is appropriate, the lawyer should go on to consider what strategy (eg, answering questions or making a written statement) would be most appropriate. See further para 5.160 below.

5.133    If the client has a specific defence, there will be advantages to this being placed on record at an early stage, either in the hope that the police will decide not to prosecute or with a view to strengthening that defence for the purposes of a trial. Furthermore, failure to mention a specific defence at this stage is likely to lead to adverse inferences being drawn if that defence is subsequently relied on at trial. The two most obvious defences in this category are those of alibi and self-defence, but there is a need for caution in respect of both. Potential alibi witnesses have an unfortunate propensity to fail to confirm the suspect's whereabouts at the crucial time or to be unwilling to become involved at all. The problem is this. On the one hand, it would sound very convincing at trial for the defendant to be able to say that he or she gave the names and addresses of his or her alibi witnesses at the earliest opportunity. On the other hand, if the police do go to see a potential alibi witness while the suspect is still in custody, the witness may very well be unco-operative because of the witness's own view of or relationship with the police, or may simply not support the version of events given by the suspect.

5.134    One possibility is for the lawyer to visit the witness before the witness's name is given to the police. In this case, the lawyer must be careful to find out what the witness has to say, and whether the witness would be willing to confirm this to the police, and at all costs must avoid passing on

---

136  See *R v Condron* [1997] 1 Cr App R 185; [1996] Crim LR 215, and *R v Kavanagh* (1997) 7 February (unreported).

information that the client has given to the lawyer. Interviewing a witness in these circumstances is not within the scope of police station attendance under the SCC 2010, but could be paid as free-standing legal advice and assistance, provided the witness satisfies the means test.[137] Another possibility is for the client to indicate the fact, and general nature of, the alibi without specifying the detail. This may be done in the form of a written statement rather than by answering questions. However, this may not prevent inferences from being drawn at trial.[138] Alternatively, the lawyer may take a full statement from the client regarding the alibi, and reserve its use for trial should it become necessary (see further para 5.165 below). Note that if the client does answer questions regarding an alibi in the police interview, or a statement is handed to the police outlining the alibi, this could be used against the client if the defence at trial differs.

5.135    With regard to the defence of 'self-defence', the client's understanding of it may well be at variance with its legal meaning. Broadly, the force used must be reasonable in the sense that it was proportional to the threat as perceived by the defendant. This is judged objectively, although the court must make allowances for the stress inherent in the circumstances.[139] There is no duty to retreat, although the possibility of retreat is relevant in judging the reasonableness of the force used.[140] Furthermore, although a 'pre-emptive strike' to ward off an anticipated attack may amount to self-defence, this again must be judged by whether it was reasonable in the circumstances.[141] Although putting the defence forward at the earliest opportunity can be advantageous, the lawyer should gather as much information as possible from the police including, if possible, sight of the witness statements and any CCTV record. The lawyer should also question the client carefully to ensure that the client's version of events does indeed constitute a legal defence. If there is serious doubt resulting from lack of information from the police, or from the version of events given by the client, the lawyer may conclude that the possible adverse consequences of an interview in which the client answers police questions may be worse than adverse inferences which may be drawn at trial under CJPOA 1994 s34. This is particularly so given the confusing evidence that often surrounds a fight and the tendency of the police to treat the original complainant as the innocent party. As with an alibi defence, the lawyer should consider what strategy to adopt to try to avoid or minimise adverse inferences (see further para 5.143 below).

137 See SCC 2010, Part B para 9.117, although para 9.120 provides that advice and assistance to a witness may only be provided under the scheme if there is a complicating factor.

138 In *R v Lewis* [2003] EWCA Crim 223, it was held that the fact that the accused had, in general terms, told the police in his first interview of his alibi of which he gave evidence at trial, did not prevent inferences from being drawn from failure to mention facts in support of the alibi. However, the police had, in a second interview, asked him detailed questions about his alibi and, had they not done so, the court may have taken a different view.

139 See Criminal Justice and Immigration Act 2008 s76 and, eg, *R v Shannon* (1980) 71 Cr App R 192.

140 See *R v Bird* [1985] 2 All ER 513; (1985) 81 Cr App R 110, and *R v McInnes* [1971] 3 All ER 295; (1971) 55 Cr App R 551.

141 See *Beckford v The Queen* [1988] 3 All ER 425; (1987) 85 Cr App R 378.

5.136    In those cases where the burden of proof in establishing a defence is on the accused (see para 5.57 above), inferences resulting from failure to mention the facts on which the defence is based in the police interview (by answering questions or by handing in a statement) are likely to be particularly damaging.

5.137    Note that in view of the previous misconduct provisions of the CJA 2003, special care is needed in putting forward a defence in the police interview that involves an assertion of good character, or in casting imputations on the character of another person (see para 5.170 below).

## Specific reasons for not answering questions

5.138    In addition to the other factors dealt with here, there are some specific reasons why a client may not wish to answer police questions despite being innocent. These include a desire to protect others, fear of reprisals and embarrassment about the allegations. In each case, the client should be advised of the potential adverse consequences of failure to answer questions, which may include a police assumption that the client is guilty, as well as the possibility of adverse inferences being drawn at trial. Nevertheless, the lawyer or, more likely, the client may still believe that answering questions would have worse consequences than not doing so. In these circumstances it may be difficult for the lawyer to protect the client against adverse inferences being drawn. If the lawyer informs the police that the lawyer has advised the client not to answer questions because, for example, the fear of reprisals outweighs the danger of inferences, this is likely to amount to a waiver of privilege (see para 5.100 above). The best course of action may be for a statement to be drafted which is not handed in to the police, although this may not have the effect of preventing inferences from being drawn (see para 5.165 below).

## Advantages of admitting guilt

5.139    If, having regard to the relevant law, the client's instructions indicate that the client is guilty of the alleged offence(s), the lawyer should consider the strength of the police evidence. A guilty client may feel it important to admit guilt to the police and this is, of course, the client's decision, but the lawyer's function is to advise the client whether from a legal point of view it is in the client's best interests to do so. If the evidence of the client's guilt is weak or there are particular difficulties of the kind discussed at paras 5.50–5.55 above, the client must be advised that one of the options is to refuse to answer questions and to wait to see if the prosecution can prove its case. Refusing to answer questions at the police station will not normally irrevocably determine the subsequent course of the client's approach to the case, whereas a confession at this stage will make it very difficult, if not impossible, for the client to plead not guilty at trial even if the prosecution case turns out to be weak or seriously flawed.

5.140    If the prosecution evidence does appear to be strong, there may be advantages to the client admitting guilt at the interview. CJA 2003 s144 requires a court to take into account the stage of the proceedings at which an offender indicated their intention to plead guilty and the circumstances in which the indication is given. Broadly speaking, the earlier the intention to plead guilty was made clear, and the less strong the police evidence of guilt, the greater the sentence discount should be. The *Sentencing Guidelines* state that a court may consider it to have been reasonable (thus attracting the maximum discount) for a defendant to have indicated his or her willingness to plead guilty in police interview, although the court would need to be satisfied that the defendant and the defendant's lawyer had been given sufficient information about the allegation.[142] Generally, therefore, indicating a willingness to plead guilty at the police station (rather than at an early court hearing) will normally make no difference to sentence, although it may do so where it leads to:

- the curtailment of an otherwise lengthy and costly investigation;
- the recovery of property that otherwise would not have been recovered;
- a significant reduction in the risk to, or suffering experienced by, a victim;
- the arrest of other suspects;
- the release of other persons suspected of the crime;
- the police accepting that the suspect played a minor role in the crime; or
- a charge for a less serious offence than might have been warranted by the circumstances.

Even if one or more of these factors applies, the client should be made aware that the impact on sentence of an admission of guilt is uncertain.

5.141    In addition to the factors relevant to sentence listed above, admission of the offence in interview could have two other possible advantages for the client. First, it might assist with a subsequent bail application, particularly where property has been recovered. The fact of co-operation with the police may, in particular, persuade the custody officer or the magistrates' court that there are no substantial grounds for believing that the suspect would interfere with witnesses or the course of justice if released on bail. However, again the client should be warned that this could not be guaranteed, and that this uncertain advantage might be outweighed by other more certain disadvantages. Second, admission of guilt might be advisable where it may lead to the police or prosecutor proceeding by way of a caution, reprimand or warning, or to a conditional caution, rather than prosecution. Even here, the lawyer would have to weigh up the likelihood of diversion from prosecution against the possibility of an acquittal in the absence of an admission. See further paras 10.46, 10.56, and 11.30 below.

5.142    A further area of difficulty relates to offences to be taken into consideration (TICs). Over the years the practice has developed of defendants accused of a number of crimes asking the court to take into account offences with which the defendant has not been charged for the purpose of sentencing. The advantage to the defendant is that he or she is likely to receive a lesser sentence than if the defendant were separately charged

---

142  See Sentencing Guidelines Council *Sentencing Guidelines 2007 Part 1 Annex 1*.

with each of the offences.[143] For the police it improves their clear-up rate with very little effort. The problem at the police station stage is that whatever the interviewing officer says about treating offences as TICs, this cannot be guaranteed, and once the client has admitted the offences there is nothing to stop the police from charging the client with all the offences. Therefore, the client must be warned of this possibility. Furthermore, TICs can tip the balance so that a court can impose a custodial or a community sentence where it would not have had the power to do so in the absence of a TIC.[144] Although the matter will often be difficult to judge at the police station stage, if there is any reason to suggest that a TIC may tip the balance in this way, the client should be advised of this danger.

## Strategies to avoid or minimise adverse inferences

5.143　In considering the appropriate advice as to whether a client should answer questions in the police interview, the lawyer should consider the various strategies that may have the effect of avoiding or minimising adverse inferences under CJPOA 1994. They are also, of course, relevant once a decision has been made that the client will not answer questions. A distinction should be made between strategies that may avoid inferences altogether and strategies that, while not avoiding inferences, may lead to inferences that are less damaging to the defence than they might otherwise have been. Of course, no strategy can be guaranteed to be successful, and the client must be made aware of the risks attached to any suggested course of action. The strategies that are available or appropriate in any particular case will depend on all the circumstances, including both the instructions obtained from the client, and the degree of confidence that the lawyer has in those instructions.

### Strategies that may avoid inferences

5.144　Strategies to avoid adverse inferences will be relevant if the lawyer considers that:

- one or more of the conditions necessary for inferences to be drawn under CJPOA 1994 s34, s36 or s37 are not, or will not be, satisfied; or
- factors exist which may lead to evidence of the police interview(s) not being admitted.

The lawyer should consider the following strategies.

#### Arguing no power to detain or interview

5.145　If the lawyer is aware that the police case is apparently strong, it may be appropriate to make representations to the interviewing officer, or the

---

143　In *R v Miles* [2006] EWCA Crim 256 it was stated that TICs will often add nothing, or relatively little, to the sentence for the substantive offence(s), but may do so if, for example, they show a pattern of criminal behaviour which suggests careful planning or deliberate criminality, offences committed on bail or a return to crime immediately after being given a non-custodial sentence.

144　CJA 2003 ss148(2) and 153(2). TICs count as an 'associated offence' for the purposes of assessing seriousness.

custody officer, that an interview should not be conducted. While such representations are unlikely to succeed, the fact that such representations are made may assist in avoiding adverse inferences at trial. There is some difficulty with this argument in view of the line of cases starting with *R v McGuinness*.[145] However, there are two reasons why, if a person is interviewed in such circumstances, evidence of the interview may be excluded under PACE s78, with the result that inferences could not be drawn under CJPOA 1994 s34(1)(a).

5.146    First, if the custody officer is aware that there is sufficient evidence to charge, PACE s37(7) requires the officer to charge or release without delay. The meaning of 'sufficient evidence to charge' is dealt with at para 10.6. Detention for the purposes of interviewing the suspect in such circumstances is, arguably, unlawful.

5.147    Second, if the police intend to charge whatever is said in interview, the custody officer should proceed to deal with them under PACE s37(7), and if they do not do so detention is, again, arguably unlawful.[146] Furthermore, if an interview is conducted in such circumstances, it can be argued that inferences should not be drawn under CJPOA 1994 s34(1)(a) since the officer would not be trying to discover whether or by whom the offence was committed (see para 5.77 above). If appropriate, the lawyer should consider: a) informing the custody officer of the evidence showing that there is sufficient evidence to charge; and/or b) asking the officer in the case questions such as whether he or she believes that there is sufficient evidence to charge, whether the officer believes that the client is guilty of the offence, what other evidence the officer would expect to obtain, and what the officer intends to do after the interview.

5.148    Note, however, that if an interview is successfully avoided, this would not prevent inferences from being drawn under CJPOA 1994 s34(1)(b), and the lawyer should consider whether to advise the client to make an oral statement, or to hand in a written statement, at charge.

### Making a prepared statement

5.149    The use of prepared statements as a way of potentially avoiding adverse inferences under CJPOA 1994 is now well established,[147] but the strategy needs to be approached with care. Although the early cases on prepared statements adopted a fairly liberal approach, especially as to how much information had to be included to avoid inferences, the subsequent approach of the courts has been to limit their utility from the defence point of view. The reason why a prepared statement may avoid adverse Inferences is that an inference can only be drawn where a fact is relied on at trial which was not mentioned to the police in interview or at charge (CJPOA 1994 s34), or where an accused refuses or fails to account (CJPOA 1994 ss36

---

145  [1999] Crim LR 318, and see paras 2.59 above and 10.4 below.

146  See *R v Mulayim Dervish* [2001] EWCA Crim 2789; [2002] 2 Cr App R 6 in which it was held that where it was established that the police intended to charge irrespective of what was said in interview, the interview was conducted in breach of the former Code C paras 11.4 and 16.1.

147  See *R v McGarry* [1998] 3 All ER 805; [1999] Crim LR 316, *R v Ali* [2001] EWCA Crim 863, and *R v Knight* [2003] EWCA Crim 1977; [2004] 1 WLR 340; [2004] 1 Cr App R 9; [2003] Crim LR 799.

and 37). Mentioning facts, or providing an account, in a prepared statement is treated in the same way as if the information had been provided in response to police questions. Inferences under the CJPOA 1994 may be drawn from failure or refusal to provide the information specified in those sections, not from failure to answer police questions.[148] Furthermore, as the Court of Appeal said in *R v Knight*, 'the aim of s34(1)(a) does not distinctly include police cross-examination of a suspect upon his account over and above the disclosure of that account. Had that been intended, it seems to us that parliament would have used significantly different language'.[149] Therefore, once a statement has been given by the suspect, while the police may seek to question him or her on it, the suspect is under no obligation to answer such questions.

5.150   The strategy of making a prepared statement should be considered where there are good reasons for informing the police of facts that are likely to be relied on by the defence at trial (or for providing an account), but there are reasons why the client should not be subjected to the risks associated with police questioning – for example, because the client is nervous, the client may not respond well to police questioning, the facts are complicated, or because police disclosure has been limited or partial. In considering whether and how to use a prepared statement, the following factors should be considered.

### The implications of making a statement

5.151   While a prepared statement may avoid inferences at trial, it will have the effect of 'fixing' the suspect with the defence. If the defence advanced at trial differs in a significant way from the statement, the prosecution are likely to use this against the accused.[150] The defendant may then try to 'blame' the lawyer for the 'inaccuracies' in the statement, although this is unlikely to be successful.[151] A prepared statement will give the police and prosecution early warning of the defence, which may be used as the basis for asking further questions in interview or for gathering further evidence, and may lead the police or prosecution to adjust their case against the accused accordingly. Furthermore, the statement may give the police sufficient evidence to charge, and may enable the prosecution to establish a prima facie case in circumstances where otherwise this may not have been possible. For example, if the client is suspected of assault, and there is a question about whether the police can establish identity, handing in a statement putting forward self-defence will provide the necessary evidence of identity. The lawyer will have to balance the disadvantages of this against those that follow from the use of any other strategy.

5.152   It is important, therefore, that the lawyer explains to the client the implications of making a prepared statement, ensures that the statement accurately reflects the client's instructions, and that the client reads the statement (or has it read to them) before it is given to the police. It is also

---

148  *R v Knight* [2003] EWCA Crim 1977; [2004] 1 WLR 340; [2004] 1 Cr App R 9; [2003] Crim LR 799, and *T v DPP* [2007] EWHC 1793 (Admin).
149  *R v Knight* [2003] EWCA Crim 1977 at para 11.
150  See, for example, *R v Alagaratnam* [2010] EWCA Crim 1506.
151  See, for example, *R v Seaton* [2010] EWCA Crim 1980.

advisable for the statement to include a declaration, signed by the client, such as: 'This is my statement. I have read the statement [The statement has been read to me], and I agree with its contents. I have not been told what to say.'

## How much information to include in the statement

5.153   In the early case of *R v McGarry*[152] the court accepted that a statement that contained the key elements of the defence, without setting out full details, was sufficient to avoid inferences. However, the cases since then have emphasised that while a statement prevents inferences in respect of facts set out in the statement, it does not prevent inferences from being drawn from failure to mention facts in the statement that are subsequently relied on at trial. For example, in *R v Lewis*[153] the fact that basic information regarding an alibi had been given to the police in interview did not prevent inferences from being drawn from failure to mention various details concerning the alibi which were subsequently relied on at trial.[154]

5.154   Therefore, care must be taken to anticipate the facts that are likely to be relied upon at trial, and also to respond to any request to account under CJPOA 1994 s36 or s37 (see para 5.87 above), and to deal with these in the statement. If there is more than one interview, or the police are using a strategy of 'phased disclosure' (see para 4.28 above), the statement should be reviewed in the light of any information disclosed by the police during the course of a prior interview, or between interviews, and consideration given to handing in a supplementary statement.

5.155   Provided that the facts subsequently relied upon at trial are adequately covered, a statement handed to the police during a police interview should have the effect of avoiding inferences under CJPOA 1994 s34(1)(a), or under ss36 or 37. However, a statement submitted during an interview will not necessarily prevent inferences being drawn under section 34(1)(b). Normally, the courts appear reluctant to draw inferences under section 34(1)(b), especially where facts have been disclosed in interview, but it could be relevant if information is disclosed by the police in the interview that is not adequately covered in the statement (see para 5.73 above). In these circumstances, the lawyer should consider whether a supplementary statement should be handed in to the police.

## When to submit a statement

5.156   Careful thought must be given to when a prepared statement should be given to the police. It follows from the wording of CJPOA 1994 s34(1)(a) that in order to avoid inferences under that subsection the statement must be handed in or read out during the interview. If a prepared statement is given to, or read out to, the police at the beginning of an interview, information may be disclosed by the police during the interview which renders the statement inadequate. On the other hand, waiting until the end of the

---

152   [1998] 3 All ER 805; [1999] Crim LR 316.
153   [2003] EWCA Crim 223.
154   See also *R v Ali* [2001] EWCA Crim 863, *R v Knight* [2003] EWCA Crim 1977; [2004] 1 WLR 340; [2004] 1 Cr App R 9; [2003] Crim LR 799, *R v Turner (Dwaine)* [2003] EWCA Crim 3108, and *R v Mohammad* [2009] EWCA Crim 1871.

interview may mean that the opportunity to hand it in or read it out during the interview is lost. In a straightforward case, where the lawyer is satisfied that the police have made adequate disclosure, it will normally be appropriate to submit the statement at the beginning of the interview. However, in a more complex case or where the police have given no, or limited, disclosure, it may be better to hand the statement to the police towards the end of the interview. In this case, before the interview ends, the lawyer should tell the police that before it is concluded he or she wishes to have a private consultation with the client. The statement should then be drafted in consultation with the client, and handed in to the police at the resumed interview. If the police try to end the interview before the statement is submitted, the interviewing officer should be reminded that under Code C para 11.6 they are, in effect, obliged to give a suspect the opportunity to give an innocent explanation.

### Handing in or reading out a statement

5.157    It has been held that an oral statement of facts by the suspect, who then refuses to answer questions, amounts to mentioning facts for the purpose of CJPOA 1994 s34.[155] However, unless the client is particularly confident, it would normally be more advisable to hand in a written statement. It is normally better to hand the statement to the police rather than to read it out in the interview. If, before handing it in, the lawyer considers that the statement that has been prepared omits relevant information or includes information that should not be disclosed to the police, the statement should be re-drafted during a private consultation with the client. Prepared statements are covered by legal professional privilege, and the police have no right to seize them (see para 1.16 above). If the interviewing officer makes a serious attempt to seize the statement, the lawyer should ask to speak to a senior officer and, as a last resort, should ask that the statement be placed in a sealed envelope with the condition that it only be opened on the order of a court.

### Answering some questions and not others

5.158    Generally, a client should be advised either to answer all questions or none. Answering only some questions is not normally an appropriate strategy because of the potential adverse effects on credibility of the defence at trial (see para 5.63 above). Where a client is advised to answer police questions, but the client indicates that he or she is not willing to answer questions concerning certain matters (assuming that they are relevant and proper questions), it may be more advisable to submit a statement covering the relevant facts.

### Refusal to be interviewed

5.159    It would not normally be appropriate to advise a client to refuse to be interviewed unless the lawyer is strongly of the view that the client is not fit to be interviewed (see para 5.22 above). However, clients do occasionally decide for themselves that they are not prepared to leave their cell for the

---

155   *R v Ashton and others* [2002] EWCA Crim 2782.

purpose of an interview, and the police should not use force to take them to an interview room.[156] Such a refusal may have the effect of preventing an interview from taking place, although Code C and Code H para 12.5 states that in these circumstances, the suspect should be cautioned and told that the suspect's failure or refusal to co-operate may not prevent an interview taking place in the cell and that evidence of such an interview may be given in evidence. If an interview does take place in the cell, the normal principles regarding inferences from silence apply. If an interview does not take place, inferences cannot be drawn under CJPOA 1994 s34(1)(a)[157] but may still be possible under s34(1)(b).

## Strategies to minimise inferences

5.160   If the circumstances are such that it will not be possible to prevent the prospect of inferences under the CJPOA 1994, the lawyer should consider what action may be taken at the police station stage which could help persuade a court that:

- the suspect could not reasonably have been expected to mention facts to the police that are relied upon at trial; or
- any inference to be drawn should be less damaging than it might otherwise have been.

The lawyer should consider the following strategies.

### Telling the police about the reasons for the advice

5.161   Explaining, in the police interview, the grounds for advice to remain silent can, in principle, help to minimise the risk of inferences since it has been held in a number of cases that 'good' reasons for advice to remain silent may persuade a court that it is not reasonable to expect the accused to have mentioned relevant facts (see para 5.98 above). However, this will almost certainly amount to a waiver of privilege and, furthermore, any explanation given may be used against the accused if the defence at trial is incompatible with the explanation given.[158] In some circumstances it may be appropriate to give advice not to answer questions in the police interview, and provided no reference is made to a privileged conversation in so doing, privilege should not be waived. Alternatively, it may be possible to separate the advice from the reasons for it, for example, by making representations to the officer in the case or the custody officer as to the relevant issue and, in the interview, simply stating that the client has been advised not to answer questions. In circumstances where there has been no, or very limited disclosure, by the police, informing the interviewing officer that given the lack of disclosure the lawyer has not been able to give

---

156 Code C para 12.5A, which deals with such circumstances, does not suggest that the police can use force. This is supported by *R v Jones and Nelson* (1999) *Times* 21 April which found that the use of force on a suspect to enable a confrontation to take place was unlawful.

157 *R v Johnson; R v Hind* [2005] EWCA Crim 971.

158 *R v Fitzgerald* (1998) 6 June (unreported).

sensible advice to the client will not amount to a waiver of privilege. See further paras 5.100 and 5.101 above.

5.162 In view of the dangers of waiver of privilege, the lawyer should only give an explanation of the reasons for the advice if:

- the lawyer is confident that any defence disclosed by the explanation will be consistent with any defence put forward at trial; and
- waiver of privilege would not lead to disclosure of information that would be adverse to the client.

However, even if these conditions are satisfied, careful consideration should be given to whether to give reasons for the advice in interview since it is not always possible to predict whether waiver of privilege may have a damaging effect on the client's case.[159] It may be better for the lawyer to take a careful note of the advice given, the reasons for it, and the time and date the advice was given (which the lawyer should do in any event). If, at trial, it is apparent that waiver of privilege will not cause difficulty for the client, the lawyer could then give evidence of the reasons for the advice given, and use the note to refresh his or her memory.

### Asking whether the interviewing officer has disclosed all available evidence

5.163 Asking the officer whether he or she has disclosed all relevant information may lead the officer to disclose further information, in which case the lawyer will want a further private consultation in order to reconsider his or her advice to the client regarding the interview strategy. If the officer says that there is information that has not been disclosed, but the officer refuses to give further information, the lawyer may use the interview as a means of discovering that further information. The lawyer should then reconsider his or her advice, and consider whether to ask for a further police interview at which the client answers questions or hands in a statement.

### Stating that the client does not understand the caution

5.164 This strategy is only appropriate if the client genuinely does not understand the implications of the caution, for example, if the client is very young or has limited intellectual capacity. If it appears to the interviewing officer that the suspect does not understand the caution given, the suspect must explain it in his or her own words (Code C NfG 10D, Code H NfG 10C), and the lawyer should check that the explanation given accurately reflects the caution. Research has shown not only that the caution is too complex for most suspects to understand, but that many police officers do not understand it either.[160] The lawyer should also prepare the client so

159 In *R v Bowden* [1999] 1 WLR 823; [1999] 4 All ER 43; [1999] 2 Cr App R 176 damage was caused to the defendant's case because waiver of privilege enabled the prosecution to cross-examine him about what he had not said to his solicitor at the police station, ie, that his mother had paid for a holiday which the prosecution alleged had been paid for out of the proceeds of a robbery.

160 See G Gudjonsson, *The psychology of interrogations and confessions: a handbook* (Wiley, Chichester, 2003) p72.

that the client does not agree that he or she understands the explanation given unless the client genuinely does so.[161]

### Taking a statement that is not handed to the police

5.165 This strategy was, in effect, suggested by the Court of Appeal in *R v Condron*[162] in which it held that an inference that a defence had been fabricated could be avoided if the accused adduced evidence that information about the defence had been given to a solicitor at or about the time of the police interview.[163] Crucially, it held that doing so would not amount to a waiver of privilege (see para 5.100 above). Such a strategy would not necessarily prevent any inference from being drawn, since it has been made clear in subsequent cases that other inferences are possible: that the defendant had fabricated the defence before the police interview but was not sufficiently confident of it to expose it to police questioning, or that the defendant had not thought up all of the details of the defence at the time of the police interview.[164] Nevertheless, it provided a useful means of trying to limit inferences in circumstances where they could not be avoided altogether.

5.166 While is may still be the best available strategy in any particular circumstances, more recent cases have limited its usefulness. First, in *R v Seaton*[165] the Court of Appeal held that if a defendant gives evidence that the defendant provided his or her lawyer with an account of the defendant's defence at the police station, this will normally amount to a waiver of privilege. Second, if at trial the prosecution avoid alleging recent fabrication, as in *R v Howell*,[166] the accused may not be able to adduce evidence of the statement made to the lawyer since it will amount to a previous consistent statement.[167]

5.167 Nevertheless, taking a statement that is not handed in to the police may be an appropriate strategy where the lawyer takes the view that a statement should not be handed in because of doubts about the instructions received or about information that has not been disclosed by the police, and that these considerations outweigh the advantages of other strategies, particularly that of making a prepared statement. The lawyer should take as full a statement as possible from the client and ensure that it is checked and signed by the client. The lawyer should also anticipate whether the client is likely to be asked to account under CJPOA 1994 s36 or s37 (see para

---

161 Research conducted by Gudjonsson has also shown that many people claim to understand the caution when, in fact, they do not. A defendant's lack of understanding of the caution may still not prevent inferences from being left to the jury. See *R v V* [2005] EWCA Crim 581.

162 [1997] 1 WLR 827; [1997] 1 Cr App R 185; [1996] Crim LR 215.

163 This may amount to hearsay evidence, normally requiring notice of intention to adduce. See the analysis in E Cape, 'Police station law and practice update' (2009) October *Legal Action* 12.

164 See *R v Daniel* [1998] Crim LR 818, *R v Randall* (1998) 3 April (unreported), and *R v Beckles and Montague* [1999] Crim LR 148, and see para 5.85 above.

165 [2010] EWCA Crim 1980.

166 [2003] EWCA Crim 1; [2005] 1 Cr App R 1; [2003] Crim LR 405.

167 However, see *R v Athwal and others* [2009] EWCA Crim 789 in which it was held that a previous consistent statement is admissible hearsay (subject to the power of the judge to exclude it) by virtue of CJA 2003 s120(2).

5.87 above) and include relevant information in the statement. The client should be advised of the implications of using this strategy, in particular, that a court may subsequently see the statement and that it may not have the effect of preventing damaging inferences.

### Handing in a statement in interview or at charge

5.168　Handing in a statement during a police interview was described at para 5.157 above as a strategy designed to prevent inferences from being drawn. As explained, however, this may fail if the defence put forward at trial goes beyond the facts set out in the statement. In these circumstances, while not preventing inferences, such a statement may minimise the inferences drawn in the same way as a statement that is not handed to the police. The lawyer should also anticipate whether the client is likely to be asked to account under CJPOA 1994 s36 or s37 (see para 5.87 above) and include relevant information in the statement.

5.169　Alternatively, a statement may be handed in at charge. This may be particularly useful if the lawyer believes that the police will not have enough evidence to charge. As noted at para 5.151 above, a statement given to the police during the interview may give them enough evidence to charge. Thus, the lawyer may consider advising a 'no comment' interview, and submitting a statement only if the police do decide to charge. The police can only interview after charge for limited reasons, such as clearing up an ambiguity in the statement (Code C para 16.5), and inferences cannot be drawn from failure to mention facts after charge. However, while inferences cannot be drawn under CJPOA 1994 s34(1)(b) (assuming that the defence put forward at trial is consistent with the statement), inferences can be drawn under CJPOA 1994 s34(1)(a), and these may damage the client's defence.

## The relevance of previous misconduct

5.170　The previous misconduct provisions of the CJA 2003 ss98–113 mean that what the suspect says in a police interview, or in a statement handed in to the police, may allow the prosecution to introduce evidence of bad character or to cross-examine the accused as to bad character at trial. If such evidence is admitted, it may be used to show that the defendant had the propensity to commit the offence of which the defendant is accused and/ or to attack the credibility of the defendant's evidence. As a result of these provisions, questions relating to bad character may be introduced into police interviews. The provisions are complex, and it is not appropriate to provide a full guide to them here. However, in advising clients at police stations, lawyers should be particularly aware of the following.

5.171　Evidence of the defendant's bad character is admissible if:

a) all parties to the proceedings agree to the evidence being admissible;

b) the evidence is adduced by the defendant himself or herself, or is given in answer to a question asked by the defendant in cross-examination and intended to elicit it;

c) it is important explanatory evidence;

d) it is relevant to an important matter in issue between the defendant and the prosecution;

e) it has substantial probative value in relation to an important matter in issue between the defendant and the co-defendant;

f) it is evidence to correct a false impression given by the defendant; or

g) the defendant has made an attack on another person's character (CJA 2003 s101(1)).

These are known as the character 'gateways', and gateways c)–g) are further defined in CJA 2003 ss102–106. Broadly, if one or more of the gateways is satisfied, evidence of previous misconduct of the accused will be admissible and/or the accused can be cross-examined on it. Where evidence of previous misconduct is admissible under gateways d) and g) the court must not admit that evidence if it appears to the court that to admit it would have such an adverse effect on the fairness of the proceedings that the court ought not to admit it (CJA 2002 s101(3)). There is no similar provision in respect of the other gateways, although the court has a general discretion to exclude prosecution evidence under PACE s78 (see para 13.42 below).

5.172    'Bad character' is widely defined to mean evidence of, or of a disposition towards, misconduct of the accused (CJA 2003 s98), and 'misconduct' means the commission of an offence or other reprehensible behaviour (CJA 2003 s112(1)). Clearly, previous convictions comes within the definition, but so too could previous arrests, cautions,[168] previous unproven allegations, or the use of unlawful drugs.[169] It could also include conduct that, while reprehensible, is not criminal, such as misconduct at work.

5.173    Information given by a suspect in a police interview could be used by the prosecution to establish previous misconduct. The police could, of course, simply ask the accused whether he or she has previous convictions. They are likely to be in possession of such information already, but may not know about other forms of previous misconduct. They may wish to question the suspect about the circumstances of any previous convictions. In *R v Hanson, Gilmore and Pickstone*[170] it was held that in order to decide on admissibility it will sometimes be necessary to look beyond the mere fact of conviction to the surrounding circumstances, for example, to see if there was a similar pattern of behaviour. If the suspect answers such questions, the prosecution may be able to adduce evidence of previous misconduct in circumstances where they otherwise would not be able to do so. Furthermore, even in the absence of a direct question, a suspect could disclose information that amounts to an admission of previous misconduct. For example, if a suspect tells the police that he or she is a drug addict, this may be admitted if it is relevant to an important matter

---

168  *R v Olu, Wilson and Brooks* [2010] EWCA Crim 2973, although it was held in that case that an accused could, for the purpose of the misconduct provisions, adduce evidence that the accused was not guilty of the offence.

169  *R v Highton, Nguyen and Carp* [2005] EWCA Crim 1985.

170  [2005] EWCA Crim 824; [2005] 1 WLR 3169; [2005] 2 Cr App R 21. See also *R v Humphris* [2005] EWCA Crim 2003, *R v Ainscough* [2006] EWCA Crim 694, and *R v K* [2008] EWCA Crim 3177.

in issue between the suspect and the prosecution.[171] Therefore, where a suspect is answering police questions, or hands in a statement, the lawyer must carefully consider whether any admission of previous bad character is necessary.

5.174 Two of the character gateways specifically refer to things said or done by a suspect at a police station (s101(2)(f) and s101(7)(g)), so that what a suspect says in a police interview (or in a prepared statement) may have the effect of opening the gateway to the introduction of previous misconduct. The CJA 2003 s101(1)(f) permits the prosecution to adduce evidence to correct a false impression given by the defendant. A defendant gives a false impression if the defendant is 'responsible for the making of an express or implied assertion which is apt to give the court or jury a false or misleading impression' about himself or herself (CJA 2003 s105(1)(a)). There are a number of ways in which a defendant may make such an assertion, and one is if he or she makes the assertion on being interviewed by the police, or on being charged (or officially informed that he or she may be prosecuted) and evidence of the assertion is given in the proceedings (CJA 2003 s105(2)(b)). Thus the conditions are only satisfied if evidence of the assertion is given at trial, but once the assertion has been made by the suspect in the police interview, the suspect has no control over whether the prosecution will seek to use it, and (assuming the other conditions are satisfied) the court has no specific power to prevent them from doing so.[172]

5.175 The scope of this provision is potentially very wide. Clearly a suspect gives a false impression if the suspect wrongly tells the police that he or she has no previous convictions.[173] The suspect may also do so if he or she wrongly tells the police that the suspect has never been arrested for a similar offence before. The false impression need not relate to previous contact with the police or the courts. An assertion by the suspect that he or she has a good work record, or a high reputation in the community, when this is demonstrably false, can satisfy the conditions.[174] Again, therefore, if the suspect is answering police questions, or handing in a statement, the suspect must be carefully advised about the dangers of making such assertions.

5.176 The second of the two gateways that specifically refers to what may be said or done at a police station is CJA 2003 s101(1)(g), which enables evidence of the defendant's bad character to be adduced where the defendant

---

171 For example, in *R v Highton, Nguyen and Carp* [2005] EWCA Crim 1985, in a prosecution for cultivating cannabis, the prosecution sought to admit evidence of an admission by one of the accused in interview that he was a heroin addict in order to demonstrate that he must have known that the plants being cultivated were cannabis. On the facts, the Court of Appeal held that the evidence should not have been admitted (since the accused accepted that he knew it must have been an unlawful drug), but it is clear that in principle such evidence could have been admitted.

172 CJA 2003 s101(3) does not apply, although the court does have a discretion to exclude any prosecution evidence under PACE s78.

173 As in *R v Ullah* [2006] EWCA Crim 2003.

174 In *R v Weir and others* [2005] EWCA Crim 2866; [2006] Crim LR 433 seeking to demonstrate that the accused had a good reputation as a priest was held to satisfy section 101(1)(f). See also *R v Renda and others* [2005] EWCA Crim 2826, and *R v Chable* [2009] EWCA Crim 496.

has made an attack on another person's character. Attacking another person's character means giving evidence that the other person has committed an offence or has behaved, or is disposed to behave, in a reprehensible way (s106(2)). There are a number of ways in which a defendant may make such an attack, including if the defendant makes it on being interviewed by the police, or on being charged (or officially informed that the defendant may be prosecuted) and evidence of the attack is given in the proceedings (CJA 2003 s106(1)(c)). As with giving a false impression, having made an attack, a suspect has no control over whether the prosecution will seek to use it against him or her at trial, although CJA 2003 s101(3) does apply (see para 5.171 above).[175]

5.177    The potential adverse effects of CJA 2003 s101(1)(g) are much wider than those of section 101(1)(f). The conditions may be satisfied if the suspect asserts that a co-suspect or, indeed, any other person committed the offence of which the suspect is suspected, and this is so even if that other person is not named. The conditions could also be satisfied if the suspect accuses the police of misconduct, such as having assaulted him or her during the course of arrest. The provisions create particular difficulty where the suspect seeks to place blame on the victim or complainant. For example, where a person has been arrested for assault, an assertion that person acted in self-defence will almost inevitably involve an assertion that the complainant assaulted that person or, at least, acted in a reprehensible manner.[176]

5.178    In some cases, if the suspect is to answer questions or hand in a statement, there will be no alternative but to provide information that may mean that the conditions for admission of evidence of bad character are satisfied. It will normally not be possible to put forward a defence of self-defence without casting imputations on the complainant, and a defence to assault on police may inevitably mean that the suspect alleges that the police assaulted him or her. Since, if such a defence is put forward at a trial, the gateway will be opened anyway, it will often be better to assert the defence in the police interview because otherwise inferences under CJPOA 1994 s34 may be even more damaging. However, the various courses of action must be carefully thought through, and the client advised of the potential consequences. Where appropriate, the client should be advised not to make unwarranted or unnecessary allegations or comments.[177]

5.179    Guidance on preparing for an interview where questions about previous bad character may be asked is given at para 4.62 above, but the

---

175  It was held in *R v Nelson* [2006] EWCA Crim 3412 that the prosecution should not be permitted to adduce evidence of an attack on the character of a person (who did not appear as a witness) where it was irrelevant to the facts in issue. It was not proper, said the court, 'for the prosecution to seek to get such comments before a jury simply to provide a basis for satisfying gateway (g)'.

176  *R v Lamaletie and Royce* [2008] EWCA Crim 314. See also *R v O* [2009] EWCA Crim 2235.

177  In *R v Renda and others* [2005] EWCA Crim 2826; [2006] 2 All ER 553; [2006] 1 Cr App R 24, during the course of the police interview one of the appellants, who had been arrested for rape, described the complainant as 'a slag' who had had sex with most of the men in the pub. It was held that this was enough to satisfy the section 101(1)(g) conditions so that the prosecution could introduce evidence of his previous bad character.

question remains whether a client should be advised to answer questions about character if they are put by the police. In some circumstances it may be to the client's advantage to answer questions about previous bad character, or to deal with it in a prepared statement, particularly where this would demonstrate that there is no particular connection between the previous bad character and the client's credibility or the client's propensity to commit the offence of which he or she is now suspected. However, there will often be no advantage to the client answering such questions even if the client does answer questions about the suspected offence. Although the issue has not yet been addressed by the courts, it is unlikely in most circumstances that inferences could be drawn from a failure or refusal to answer questions about previous misconduct.

## Preparing the client for interview

5.180 The police interview is almost certainly the most crucial event during the period of a person's detention at a police station. Having listened carefully to what the client has to say, and having advised the client on his or her position and the approach that should be taken, the lawyer must then prepare the client for the coming event. The client may never have been through a police interview before, but even if the client has, time spent at this stage may make the difference between the interview proceeding in accordance with the advice given and complete disaster. Quite literally, it may make the difference between a conviction and an acquittal.

5.181 It is important that the client understands what to expect during a police interview, and the lawyer should explain in general terms how the interview is likely to be conducted. This will include who is likely to be present, how the room will be arranged, where the lawyer will be, how long it may last, and what may happen at the end of the interview. Of course, some of this may not be known, but the client should be given the best indication possible. Most interviews are audio-recorded, so the lawyer should explain how this will be done, and what will happen to the record of the interview. If the interview is to be visually recorded, the client should be advised of the potential impact of visual cues. If it is not to be audio or visually recorded, then the system of contemporaneous recording that is likely to be used should be explained. The purpose and content of an opening statement to be made by the lawyer should be discussed with the client.

5.182 The client should also be advised how to behave during the interview. The client's general demeanour will be important, particularly if the interview is to be visually recorded. If the client is to answer questions, the client should be advised to try to avoid sarcastic comments, 'clever' answers, and above all, losing his or her temper. All of these would be likely to come over very badly, particularly if a court were subsequently to hear or see the recording of the interview. It may be remembered that in the notorious case involving Winston Silcott[178] the apparently crucial piece of evidence leading to his initial conviction was his alleged comment: 'You

178 See, eg, the report at (1991) *Guardian* 19 March.

ain't got any evidence. Those kids will never go to court. You wait and see. No one else will talk to you. You can't keep me away from them.' It may help to remind the client that the police may use tactics precisely designed to get the client to make off-hand remarks or to lose his or her temper. The lawyer should tell the client that the client is entitled to ask for legal advice in private at any time during the course of the interview. Although the police often do not like this happening, PACE s58(1) and TA 2000 Sch 8 para 7 are absolutely clear that the suspect is entitled to 'consult a solicitor privately *at any time*' (emphasis added) (see para 2.137 above). Conversely, the client cannot expect the lawyer to prompt him or her, or to answer questions on the client's behalf.

5.183    It should also be made clear to the client that anything the client says within the hearing of the police may be used as evidence. Some people believe that it is only what they say during the course of the interview that is important in this respect, and that once the recording mechanism is switched off, they can make admissions with impunity. This belief may be encouraged by the police. This is clearly not the case. Code C para 11.13 explicitly refers to comments made by a suspected person, including un-solicited comments, outside the context of an interview, which may be relevant to the offence. There have been a number of reported cases where alleged 'off the record' remarks have resulted in conviction, even though the police breached the recording requirements.[179] Therefore, the client should be left in no doubt that there is no such thing as an 'off the record' conversation with a police officer.

5.184    The client should be prepared for interviewing tactics that might be employed by the police, and the lawyer should explain the purpose behind them. How to deal with these tactics during the course of the interview is covered in chapter 7, but such tactics are less likely to be successful if the client expects and recognises them. Attempts to undermine advice and to drive a wedge between lawyer and client are not uncommon, as are trick questions and questions designed to put pressure on the suspect, and they are not necessarily contrary to the provisions of Code C or Code H. The client must also be advised how to respond to any request by the police under Code C or Code H para 11.4 to comment on any earlier significant statement or silence (see para 5.113 above), how to respond to any specific request to account for an object, etc, or presence under CJPOA 1994 ss36 and 37 (see para 5.87 above), and how to respond to any questions about previous misconduct (see para 5.179 above).

5.185    If the client has decided not to answer police questions, the client should be given practical advice on how to do this, and should be prepared for tactics designed to get him or her to talk. Many people find it difficult, if not impossible, simply to sit and say nothing when faced with a series of questions. For this reason, the client may be best advised to say 'no com-ment' to each question, although the client can confirm his or her name and address at the outset. It may also be advisable to warn the client that

---

179 See, in particular, *R v Dunn* (1990) 91 Cr App R 237; [1990] Crim LR 572 where evidence of the comments was admitted despite breaches of the Codes and despite denials of the comments by both the defendant and his co-accused and their lawyer who was present.

he or she may feel a strong impulse to say something and that, if necessary, the client should ask to speak to the lawyer in private.

5.186    One way in which the police try to get suspects to talk is to start by asking some seemingly innocuous questions, or by trying to engage the suspect in seemingly friendly or light-hearted conversation. Furthermore, some police forces have prepared scripts for use when faced with a 'no comment' interview, referring to their desire to give the suspect an opportunity to tell the suspect's side of the story. Other tactics include seeking to undermine the advice given by the lawyer by commenting on the lawyer's status (particularly if he or she is a representative), by referring to the view expressed by some judges that suspects do not have to follow their lawyer's advice, or by referring to the supposed views of the Law Society. As stated earlier, informing the client of such possibilities will probably reduce their likely effectiveness. Finally, the 'right to silence' provisions of the CJPOA 1994 are likely to be used by some officers to try to persuade the client to talk. The caution may, in effect, be used as a threat. Despite the inferences that may follow from failure to answer questions, the aim of some police officers is still to get the suspect to talk. The certainty of a confession is better, from the police point of view, to the unknown effects of an inference. The client must be fully prepared for such a tactic.

5.187    Another tactic, although not necessarily deliberately employed by the interviewing officer, is to ask during the course of the interview whether the client is willing to take part in an identification procedure. While this is unlikely to affect the admissibility of the interview, it may be better that during the interview the client refrains from answering the question, since having answered one question, it may be more difficult for the client to revert to not answering subsequent questions. One method of dealing with this is for the lawyer to indicate on the client's behalf whether he or she would be willing to participate.

5.188    By this stage, the client should be fully prepared, or as prepared as the client will ever be, for the interview with the police, but it may be advisable to deal with a few final matters. First, the client should be given the opportunity to ask the lawyer any questions. The client may have a remaining concern which he or she has not yet had the opportunity of raising. Second, the client should be told (where appropriate) that there may be subsequent police interviews and, particularly if it is to be a 'no comment' interview, that the client should be wary of the police subsequently coming to see him or her in the absence of the lawyer (see paras 7.74 and 10.104 below). Finally, the client should be reminded that he or she may interrupt the interview at any stage in order to seek further legal advice in private.

# CHAPTER 6

# Fingerprints, photographs, samples and searches

*continued*

# Introduction

6.1 This chapter deals with the police powers to:

- take fingerprints;
- take photographs;
- conduct searches and examinations to establish identity;
- take footwear impressions;
- take intimate and non-intimate samples;
- conduct drug-testing procedures;
- conduct searches, including search of the person and search of premises.

It does not cover search warrants and orders under the Police and Criminal Evidence Act 1984 (PACE) ss8 and 9, or other legislation. Identification procedures are dealt with in chapter 8.

# Fingerprints, photographs and footwear impressions

6.2 The powers of the police to take, use and retain biometric samples and impressions, footwear impressions and photographs, both with or without consent, have grown significantly in the last decade. Some powers apply in respect of suspects in police detention,[1] but others may be exercised in respect of people who are not in police detention, although there are extensive powers to require a person to attend a police station for the purposes of taking fingerprints, with a power of arrest in default (PACE s63A(4) and Sch 2A). In addition to the statutory provisions, the powers are governed by Code D. The taking of fingerprints and photographs is routinely carried out by the police, partly for evidential purposes but also to enable them to conduct speculative searches and to populate their databases. Therefore, a lawyer should advise the client about these powers in the initial interview so that the client is aware that his or her fingerprints and a photograph will be taken, and the use that may be made of them.

## Fingerprints

### *Power to take fingerprints under PACE*

6.3 'Fingerprints' are defined as any record, produced by any method, of the skin pattern and other physical characteristics or features of a person's fingers or palms (PACE s65(1)). The police can always take a person's fingerprints if 'appropriate consent' is given, although in the case of a person at a police station (not necessarily in police detention), such consent must be in writing (PACE s61(2) and Code D para 4.2). 'Appropriate consent', in the case of a person aged 17 years or more, is the consent of that person; for a juvenile under 14 years it is the consent of a parent or guardian;[2] and

---

1 The provisions refer to a person who is 'detained at a police station', which is likely to be a reference to a person who is in police detention (see para 1.61 above).

2 Or local authority or voluntary organisation if the juvenile is in their care (Code D NfG 2A).

for a juvenile aged 14 years or more it means the consent of both the juvenile and a parent or guardian (PACE s65(1) and Code D para 2.12). Section 65 and Code D refer to the parent or guardian rather than the appropriate adult, and Code D Note for Guidance NfG 2A indicates that if he or she is not present (for example, because another person is acting as appropriate adult), consent can be given by telephone, but he or she must be given full information and must be allowed to speak to the juvenile and the appropriate adult if he or she wishes. The consent of a mentally disordered or mentally vulnerable person must be given in the presence of the appropriate adult (Code D para 2.12). In both cases, the fingerprints should be taken in the presence of the appropriate adult (Code D para 2.15).

6.4　　Fingerprints can be taken without consent in the following circumstances:

1) The fingerprints of a person detained at a police station in consequence of arrest for a recordable offence[3] may be taken without consent provided that the person has not had his or her fingerprints taken in the course of the investigation of that offence by the police (PACE s61(3)). The latter proviso does not apply if the fingerprints taken on a previous occasion do not constitute a complete set of fingerprints or some or all of them are not of sufficient quality to allow for satisfactory analysis, comparison or matching (PACE s61(3A)). Authorisation by a senior officer is not required.

2) The fingerprints of a person detained at a police station may be taken without consent if the person has been charged with a recordable offence, or informed that he or she will be reported for such an offence[4] and the person's fingerprints have not been taken during the course of the investigation (PACE s61(4)). This is subject to the same proviso as in 1) above. The fingerprints of a person not detained at a police station may be taken without consent if the person has been charged with a recordable offence (of informed that he or she will be reported for such an offence), and the person has not had his or her fingerprints taken in the course of the police investigation; or they have had his or her fingerprints taken but the exception to the proviso in 1) above applies (PACE s61(5B)). Authorisation is not required.

3) The fingerprints of a person who has answered to bail at court or a police station may be taken without consent at the court or police station on the authorisation of the court or of an inspector or above, which may be given if the person answering to bail has answered it for a person whose fingerprints have been taken and there are reasonable grounds to believe that he or she is not the same person, or the person who has answered to bail claims to be a different person from a person whose fingerprints were taken on a previous occasion (PACE s61(4A) and (4B)). Authorisation may be given orally or in writing, but if orally, must be confirmed in writing as soon as practicable (PACE s61(5)).

---

3 Regulations governing recordable offences are issued under PACE s27(4). All imprisonable offences are recordable offences, as are a small number of non-imprisonable offences. See Code D NfG 4A for an explanation.

4 With a view to summons, caution, final warning or reprimand.

4) A person's fingerprints can be taken without consent if the person has been arrested for a recordable offence and released and, in the case of a person who is on bail, the person has not had his or her fingerprints taken in the course of the police investigation; or the person has had his or her fingerprints taken but the exception to the proviso in 1) above applies (PACE s61(5A)). Authorisation is not required.

5) A person's fingerprints can be taken without consent if the person has been convicted of a recordable offence, has been cautioned in respect of a recordable offence and admit the offence at the time of the caution, or has been warned or reprimanded under Crime and Disorder Act 1998 s65 for a recordable offence (PACE s61(6)). This is subject to the condition that the person has not had his or her fingerprints taken since the conviction, caution, reprimand or warning, or the person has but the exception to the proviso mentioned in 1) above is satisfied. Authorisation by an inspector or above is required, which may only be given if satisfied that taking the fingerprints is necessary to assist in the prevention or detection of crime (PACE s61(6)–(6ZC)).

6) A person's fingerprints may be taken without consent if a constable reasonably believes that the person is committing or attempting to commit, or has committed or attempted to commit, an offence and the name of the person is unknown to and cannot readily be ascertained by the constable, or the constable has reasonable grounds for doubting whether the name given by the person is the person's real name (PACE s61(6A) and (6B)). Note that this power can be exercised without the person being arrested, and in respect of any offence, not necessarily a recordable offence.

In addition, there are powers to take fingerprints from a person who has been convicted of an offence in a foreign jurisdiction, provided certain conditions are satisfied (PACE s61(6D)–(6G)).

6.5    Where fingerprints are taken without consent under section 61, before they are taken the person must be informed of the reason for taking the fingerprints, the power under which they are taken and, where authorisation is necessary, that authorisation has been given (PACE s61(7) and Code D para 4.7). In the case of a person detained at a police station, the fact that this information has been given must be noted in the custody record (PACE s61(8) and Code D para 4.8A). Where fingerprints are taken (with or without consent) at a police station, or other place in the case of powers under section 61(4A) or (6A), the person must be told that their fingerprints may be made the subject of a speculative search, and this must be recorded as soon as practicable (PACE s61(7A)). If fingerprints are taken without consent, a police constable or designated civilian detention officer may use reasonable force in order to take them (PACE s117 and Police Reform Act (PRA) 2002 s38(8) and Sch 4 para 29).

## Speculative searches, retention and destruction

6.6    Where fingerprints have been taken under any of the powers set out in para 6.4 above (other than under PACE s61(4A)), they may be checked against other fingerprints held by or on behalf of a relevant law enforcement authority[5] or held in connection with or as a result of an investigation of an offence (a 'speculative search') (PACE s63A).[6] Where fingerprints are taken under other powers, or with consent, they may be the subject of a speculative search only if the person consents in writing (PACE s63A(1C)), but once consent has been given it cannot be withdrawn (PACE s63A(1D)).

6.7     Provisions governing retention and destruction of fingerprints are set out in PACE s64 and Code D annex F. Section 64 was to have been repealed and replaced by complex new provisions in Crime and Security Act 2010 s14. However, these provisions are not now going to be brought into force, and further new provisions on retention and destruction are contained in the Protection of Freedoms Bill (2011).

### Power to take fingerprints under Terrorism Act 2000

6.8     Where a person is detained for examination under Terrorism Act (TA) 2000 Sch 7 or on suspicion of being a terrorist under TA 2000 s41, fingerprints may be taken by a constable with appropriate consent[7] or, where the person is detained at a police station, on the authority of a superintendent or above, or if the person has been convicted of a recordable offence (TA 2000 Sch 8 para 10(4)). Where authorisation is required to take fingerprints from a person arrested under section 41 it may be given if the officer reasonably suspects the person has been involved in a terrorist offence mentioned in TA 2000 s40(1)(a), and reasonably believes that fingerprints will tend to confirm or disprove the person's involvement. In any other case, authorisation may only be given if the officer is satisfied that the taking of the fingerprints is necessary in order to assist in determining whether the person falls within TA 2000 s40(1)(b) (ie, is or has been concerned in the commission, preparation or instigation of acts of terrorism). If authorisation is given orally, it must be confirmed in writing as soon as is reasonably practicable (TA 2000 Sch 8 para 10(7)). For limitations on the use of fingerprints taken under these provisions, and the power to conduct speculative searches, see TA 2000 Sch 8 para 14. For the information that must be given to the person before fingerprints are taken, see Sch 8 para 11.

### Advising on fingerprints

6.9     It will be evident from the above that the police have very extensive powers to take fingerprints without consent. In the case of a client who is in police detention following arrest, the only real limitation on the police power to take his or her fingerprints is that the offence for which the client has been arrested is a recordable offence. Having checked that it is, the client should be advised that resistance is pointless and could result in a charge of obstruction or assault on a police officer (or designated civilian)[8] in the execution of their duty.

---

5   For definition, see PACE s63A(1A) and (1B).
6   For a case reviewing the nature of fingerprint evidence and the standards to be applied, see *R v Smith* [2011] EWCA Crim 1296.
7   Which has the same meaning as under PACE s65 (TA 2000 Sch 8 para 15(1)) (see para 6.3 above).
8   PRA 2002 s46(1) makes it an offence to assault a designated person in the execution of his or her duty.

# Photographs

## *Power to take photographs*

6.10 The police have extensive statutory powers to photograph persons detained at a police station with or without their consent. PACE s64A(1) provides that a person detained at a police station (see para 6.2 above) may be photographed with appropriate consent (see para 6.3 above), or without appropriate consent if it is withheld or it is not practicable to obtain it. There are no other pre-conditions for the exercise of this power. Furthermore, a person who is not at a police station may be photographed with appropriate consent, or without appropriate consent if it is withheld or it is not practicable to obtain it, where the person has been:

- arrested by a constable for an offence;
- taken into custody by a constable after being arrested for an offence by a person other than a constable;
- made subject to a requirement to wait with a community support officer under the PRA 2002 Sch 4 para 2(3) or (3B);
- given a direction by a constable under Violent Crime Reduction Act 2006 s27;
- given a penalty notice by a constable in uniform under Criminal Justice and Police Act (CJPA) 2001 Chapter 1 Part 1, or a penalty notice by a constable under Education Act 1996 s444A, or a fixed penalty notice by a constable in uniform under Road Traffic Offenders Act 1988 s54;
- given a notice in relation to a relevant fixed penalty offence (within the meaning of PRA 2002 Sch 4 para 1) by a community support officer, or in relation to a relevant fixed penalty offence (within the meaning of PRA 2002 Sch 5A para 1) by an accredited person (PACE s64A(1A) and (1B)).

Code D NfG 5E gives examples of when it would not be practicable to obtain consent, including that the person is drunk or otherwise unfit to give consent, that there are reasonable grounds to suspect that if the person became aware that a photograph was to be taken the person would take steps to prevent this, that in order to take a suitable photograph it is necessary to take it covertly and, in the case of a juvenile, that his or her parent or guardian cannot be contacted in sufficient time to allow the photograph to be taken. The power under PACE s64A(1) is in addition to the power to photograph any identifying mark found in an examination under section 54A (see para 6.18 below). Code D para 5.19 provides that the powers to take photographs of detained persons also apply to volunteers, but force may not be used (Code D para 5.21).

6.11 The photograph must be taken by a constable (PACE s64A(3)), and reasonable force can be used (PACE s117 and see Code D NfG 5F). The person may be required to remove any item or substance worn on or over the whole or part of the face or head, and the constable or designated civilian may remove it themselves if the requirement is not complied with (PACE s64A(2)). The term 'photograph' includes any process by means of which a visual image may be produced and includes both still and moving images (PACE s64A(6 and (6A))). Where a person is to be photographed under this power the person must be told the purpose of the photograph, and the purposes for which the photograph may be used, disclosed or retained (Code D para 5.16). This information must be given before the photograph is taken, unless it is taken covertly. The documentation requirements are set out in Code C para 5.17.

6.12    The power to photograph a person detained under TA 2000 Sch 7 or s41 is even more extensive than under PACE. An authorised person (including a constable and an examining officer) may take any steps that are reasonably necessary for photographing a detained person (TA 2000 Sch 8 para 2). No authorisation is necessary.

### Retention, use and destruction

6.13    Where a photograph is taken under PACE s64A it may be used by, or disclosed to, any person for any purpose related to the prevention or detection of crime, the investigation of an offence or the conduct of a prosecution (PACE s64A(4)(a)). 'Crime' includes conduct that constitutes a criminal offence in any part of the United Kingdom or any other country, and conduct that would be a crime if it took place in the United Kingdom (PACE s64A(5)(a)). References to an investigation and to a prosecution include any criminal investigation outside the United Kingdom and to a prosecution brought outside of the United Kingdom (PACE s64A(5)(b)).

6.14    Photographs taken under PACE s64A do not have to be destroyed, but may only be used for a purpose set out in PACE s64A(4)(a) (PACE s64A(4)(b)). A photograph of a volunteer must, subject to any retention requirement under the Criminal Procedure and Investigations Act 1996, be destroyed (together with any negatives and copies) unless the person is charged or informed that he or she may be prosecuted for a recordable offence, prosecuted for a recordable offence, cautioned (or warned or reprimanded) for a recordable offence, or the person has given consent to retention (Code D para 5.22). Where the destruction obligation applies, the person must be given an opportunity to witness the destruction (Code D para 5.23).

### Advising on photographs

6.15    It will be seen from the above that the police have extensive powers to take photographs with or without consent, and there is no requirement that the offence concerned be a recordable offence. The client should be advised that resistance could result in a charge of obstruction or assault on a police officer (or designated civilian)[9] in the execution of the officer's duty. There is no reference in PACE s64A to the parts of the body that may be photographed, although the reference to removal of a face or head covering in PACE s64A(2) implies that, although a photograph could be taken of more than merely a person's face or head, a person could not be required to remove other forms of clothing to facilitate the taking of a photograph. However, the police do have powers to photograph other parts of the body under PACE s54A, although only in respect of a person who is detained in a police station (see para 6.16 below). A client who is a volunteer should

---

9  PRA 2002 s46(1) makes it an offence to assault a designated person in the execution of their duty.

be advised of the destruction and use provisions, and should be advised that if the client gives consent it is likely that it cannot subsequently be withdrawn.[10]

## Search and examination to ascertain identity

### Power to search and examine

6.16 An inspector or above may authorise a person detained in a police station (see para 6.2 above) to be searched or examined, or both:

- for the purpose of ascertaining whether the person has any mark that would tend to identify him or her as a person involved in the commission of an offence (PACE s54A(1)(a)); or
- for the purpose of facilitating the ascertainment of the person's identity (PACE s54A(1)(b)).

A 'mark' includes features (for example, moles, scars, tattoos) and injuries, and a mark is an 'identifying mark' if its existence facilitates the ascertainment of the person's identity or their identification as a person involved in the commission of an offence (PACE s54A(12)). Establishing a person's identity includes showing that he or she is not a particular person (PACE s54A(11)(a)). A person taken to a police station in order to be searched under a stop and search power (see para 2.2 above) is not a person detained at a police station for these purposes (Code D para 5.1).

6.17 Authorisation may only be given for a search or examination under PACE s54A(1)(a) if appropriate consent (see para 6.3) above has been withheld or it is not practicable to obtain such consent (PACE s54A(2)). Code D NfG 5D gives examples of when it would not be practicable to obtain consent, including that the person is drunk or otherwise unfit to give consent, that there are reasonable grounds to suspect that if the person became aware that a search or examination was to be conducted the person would take steps to prevent this, and, in the case of a juvenile, that his or her parent or guardian cannot be contacted in sufficient time to allow the search or examination to be carried out or the photograph to be taken. Authorisation may only be given under PACE s54A(1)(b) if the person has refused to identify himself or herself, or the officer has reasonable grounds for suspecting that the person is not who the person claims to be (PACE s54A(3)). Authorisation may be oral or in writing, but if given orally, must be confirmed in writing as soon as practicable (PACE s54A(4)). Code D para 5.19 provides that the powers to search or examine detained persons also apply to volunteers, but force may not be used (Code D para 5.21). Where a person is to be searched, examined or photographed under this power the person must be told the purpose of the search, examination or photograph, the grounds on which authority has been given, and the purposes for which any photograph taken may be used, disclosed or retained (Code D para 5.16). This information must be given before the search, examination or photograph unless the photograph is to be taken covertly. The documentation requirements are set out in Code D para 5.17.

---

10 Although unlike with fingerprints, there is no statutory provision to this effect (see para 6.6 above).

6.18    Any identifying mark found on a search or examination under PACE s54A can be photographed, either with the appropriate consent (see para 6.3 above), or without it if it is withheld or it is not practicable to obtain it (PACE s54A(5) and see Code D NfG 5D). A photograph includes any process by means of which a visual image may be produced (PACE s54A(11)(b)). A search or examination may only be conducted, or a photograph taken, by a constable or designated civilian officer of the same sex as the person searched, examined or photographed, and reasonable force may be used (PACE s54A(6) and (7)). An intimate search (see para 6.84 below) cannot be conducted under PACE s54A, and if the search or examination involves the removal of more than outer clothing it must be treated as a strip search and conducted in accordance with Code C Annex A para 11, or Code H Annex A para 12 (Code D para 5.10, and see para 6.83 below).

6.19    The power to search and examine a person detained under TA 2000 Sch 7 or s41 is even more extensive than under PACE. An authorised person (including a constable and an examining officer) may take any steps that are reasonably necessary for the purpose of identifying a detained person (TA 2000 Sch 8 para 2). No authorisation is necessary.

### Retention, use and destruction

6.20    The provisions on retention, use and destruction of photographs taken under PACE s54A are the same as those under PACE s64A (see para 6.13 above).

### Advising on searches and examinations to establish identity

6.21    Although PACE s54A gives the police extensive powers to search and examine detained persons, the lawyer should carefully consider whether the conditions set out in PACE s54A(1)–(3) are satisfied. Note that there is no requirement that the offence concerned be a recordable offence. Where the conditions are satisfied the client should be advised that refusal of consent will not prevent a search or examination from taking place, and that resistance could result in a charge of obstruction or assault on a police officer (or designated civilian)[11] in the execution of his or her duty. A client who is a volunteer should be advised of the destruction and use provisions, and should be advised that if the client gives consent it is likely that it cannot be subsequently withdrawn.[12]

## Footwear impressions

### Power to take footwear impressions

6.22    The police can take a footwear impression from a person if appropriate consent (see para 6.3 above) is given which, if the person is at a police station when consent is given, must be in writing (PACE s61A(1) and (2)

---

11  PRA 2002 s46(1) makes it an offence to assault a designated person in the execution of his or her duty.

12  Although unlike with fingerprints, there is no statutory provision to this effect (see para 6.6 above).

and Code D para 4.16). A footwear impression can be taken without appropriate consent if:

- the person is detained at a police station (see para 6.2 above) in consequence of an arrest for a recordable offence, or the person has been charged with, or informed that he or she will be reported for, a recordable offence;[13] and
- the person has not had an impression taken of his or her footwear in the course of the investigation of that offence by the police (PACE s61A(3)).

In relation to the latter, if the person has already had an impression taken of his or her footwear in the course of the investigation, a further impression may be taken if the previous impression was incomplete or is not of sufficient quality to allow for satisfactory analysis, comparison or matching (PACE s61A(4)). The power to take an impression may be exercised by any police constable (PACE s61A(7)). The meaning of 'impression of footwear' is not defined.

6.23   Before an impression is taken, whether with or without consent, the person must be informed of the reason the impression is to be taken, and that it may be retained and made the subject of a speculative search (unless destruction is required (PACE s61A(5), Code D para 4.19 and Annex F Part (a)). Where the person is detained at a police station, this must be recorded in the custody record (Code D paras 4.20–4.21).

### Speculative searches, retention and destruction

6.24   The provisions are the same as for fingerprints (see paras 6.6 and 6.7 above).[14]

### Advising on footwear impressions

6.25   The position is essentially the same as for fingerprints (see para 6.9 above).

## Samples and skin impressions

6.26   Four kinds of sample are dealt with in this section: intimate samples and dental impressions, non-intimate samples and skin impressions, handwriting samples, and samples in road traffic cases.

## Intimate samples

6.27   The power to take intimate samples is governed by PACE s62 and Code D section 6. An 'intimate sample' is defined as a sample of blood, semen or any other tissue fluid, urine or pubic hair, a dental impression or a swab taken from any part of a person's genitals (including pubic hair) or from a person's body orifice other than the mouth (PACE s65(1)). However, despite the reference to urine and blood samples, the taking of such

---

13  See note 3 above.
14  For the problems of analysis of footwear impressions, see *R v T* [2010] EWCA Crim 2439.

samples under the Road Traffic Act (RTA) 1988 or the Transport and Works Act 1992 is unaffected by this section (PACE s62(11) and see para 6.60 below).[15]

### Power to take intimate samples under PACE

6.28   An intimate sample may only be taken if the following conditions are satisfied:

1) Authorisation is given by an officer of the rank of inspector or above under PACE s62(1)(a), (1A)(a) or (2A)(b). Authorisation may be given orally or in writing, but if orally, must be confirmed in writing as soon as practicable (PACE s62(3)). Authorisation may only be given if:

   - in the case of a person in police detention (see para 1.61 above) the officer has reasonable grounds for suspecting the person's involvement in a recordable offence[16] and for believing that the sample will tend to confirm or disprove involvement (s62(1) and (2));
   - in the case of a person who is not in police detention but from whom, in the course of investigation of an offence,[17] two or more non-intimate samples suitable for the same means of analysis have been taken which proved to be insufficient, the officer has reasonable grounds for suspecting the person's involvement in a recordable offence and for believing that the sample will tend to confirm or disprove involvement (PACE s62(1A) and (2));[18]
   - in the case of any person,[19] two or more non-intimate samples suitable for the same means of analysis have been taken under PACE s63(3E) (persons convicted of offences outside England and Wales) which have proved insufficient (PACE s62(2A)).

And:

2) Appropriate consent (see para 6.3 above) is given (PACE s62(1)(b), (1A) or (2A)). The consent requirement means that an intimate sample may never be taken in the absence of consent, although refusal may result in adverse inferences (see para 6.40 below).

And:

3) Before the sample is taken, the person is informed of the reason for taking the sample, the fact that authorisation has been given and the provision under which it was given and, if the sample is taken at a police station, the fact that it may be the subject of a speculative search

---

15  For a useful discussion of the relationship between intimate and non-intimate samples see D Miers, 'Taking samples under the Police and Criminal Evidence Act 1984' (1995) *Journal of Clinical Forensic Medicine* 2, 93–102.

16  See note 3 above.

17  Note that the words 'an offence' are used rather than 'the offence', which implies that the non-intimate samples may have been taken in respect of an offence other than that for which an intimate sample is required (see note 29 below).

18  An insufficient sample is one that is insufficient with regard to quantity or quality, or as a result of loss, damage or use, has become insufficient or unavailable. See PACE s65(1) and (2), and Code D para 6.2(b) and NfG 6B.

19  There is no reference in this subsection to whether or not the person is in police detention, so presumably it applies whether or not the person is in police detention.

(PACE s62(5) and (6)). Although not a statutory requirement the person should, in addition, be cautioned (see para 6.31 below).

6.29   Where the conditions for taking an intimate sample are satisfied, it may be taken in any prison or other institution to which the Prison Act 1952 applies (PACE s63A(3)). This would seem to be confined to powers under PACE 62(1A) or (2A), since the powers under section 62(1) can only be exercised if the person is in police detention (see para 1.61 above). Powers to require a person to attend a police station for the purpose of taking an intimate sample are governed by PACE s63A(4) and Sch 2A. These provisions only grant powers to require a person to attend a police station, and do not confer any extra powers to take an intimate sample. Therefore, even if the person is required to attend for the purpose of taking an intimate sample, or is arrested in default, a sample cannot be taken unless the necessary conditions are satisfied and appropriate consent is given.

6.30   An intimate sample, other than a sample of urine (which may be taken by a police officer) or a dental impression (which can only be taken by a registered dentist), may only be taken by a registered medical practitioner or registered healthcare professional (PACE s62(9) and (9A)).

6.31   PACE s62(10) provides that where a person refuses without good cause to consent to an intimate sample, a court may draw 'proper' inferences (see para 6.40 below). Before an intimate sample is requested, the person must be cautioned in the following terms:

> You do not have to provide this sample/allow this swab or impression to be taken, but I must warn you that if you refuse without good cause, your refusal may harm your case if it comes to trial (Code D para 6.3 and NfG 6D).

6.32   If the suspect is in police detention and not legally represented, the suspect must be reminded of his or her entitlement to free legal advice, or if the sample is being taken under PACE s62(1A) (see para 6.28) and the person is attending the police station voluntarily, the right to free legal advice must be explained (Code D para 6.3). If the person has been arrested under the provisions in PACE Sch 2A (see para 6.29 above), then although the person is not in police detention, he or she is entitled to legal advice under PACE s58, since he or she is a 'person arrested and held in custody'. A record must be made of the authorisation, the grounds for giving that authorisation, the fact of consent, the reminder of the right to legal advice, and the fact that a speculative search may be conducted and, where the person is detained at a police station, the record must be made in the custody record (PACE s62(7) and (8) and Code D paras 6.3, 6.10 and 6.11).

## Speculative searches

6.33   The power to conduct a speculative search in respect of an intimate sample is the same as for fingerprints (see para 6.6 above).

## Retention, use and destruction

6.34   The provisions are the same as for fingerprints (see paras 6.6 and 6.7 above).

*Power to take intimate samples under TA 2000*

6.35   An intimate sample can be taken from a person who is detained under TA 2000 Sch 7 or s41 if the person is detained in a police station, appropriate consent[20] is given in writing, and it is authorised by a superintendent or above. A superintendent may only give authority if:

- in the case of a person detained under TA 2000 s41, the officer reasonably suspects that the person has been involved in an offence under the provisions mentioned in TA 2000 s40(1)(a) and the officer reasonably believes that the sample will tend to confirm or disprove the person's involvement, or
- in any case, the officer is satisfied that the taking of the sample is necessary in order to assist in determining whether the person falls within TA 2000 s40(1)(b) (ie, is or has been concerned in the commission, preparation or instigation of acts of terrorism) (TA 2000 Sch 8 para 10(5) and (6)).

Where two or more non-intimate samples suitable for the same means of analysis have been taken from a person under TA 2000 Sch 8 para 10 and those samples have proved insufficient and the person has been released from detention, an intimate sample can be taken if appropriate consent is given and it is authorised by a superintendent or above. The superintendent must be satisfied that taking a sample is necessary for the same reasons as under TA 2000 Sch 8 para 10(6).

6.36   An intimate sample, other than a sample of urine (which may be taken by a police constable) or a dental impression (which can only be taken by a registered dentist), may only be taken by a registered medical practitioner (TA 2000 Sch 8 para 13(2) and (3)). Refusal without good cause to provide a sample can result in inferences being drawn (TA 2000 Sch 8 para 13(1)). For limitations on the use of samples taken under these provisions, and the power to conduct speculative searches, see TA 2000 Sch 8 para 14. For the information that must be given to the person before samples are taken, see TA 2000 Sch 8 para 11.

*Advising on intimate samples*

6.37   In advising the client, the lawyer must consider all of the conditions set out in para 6.28 above, or the equivalent provisions in TA 2000. With regard to authorisation under PACE s62(2) the lawyer should first consider whether the offence suspected is a recordable offence,[21] and whether a sample will tend to confirm or disprove involvement (or whether the person falls within TA 2000 s40(1)(b)). The officer should be asked whether the police are in possession of any forensic samples and the nature of such samples. If they do not possess them, it may be argued that the taking of an intimate sample cannot fulfil this requirement. If this is the case, the lawyer may consider advising the suspect to withhold consent (but see para 6.40 below). Similarly, the lawyer must consider whether the nature of the alleged offence is

20   Which by TA 2000 Sch 8 para 15 has the same meaning as under PACE. See para 6.3 above.
21   See note 3 above.

such that an intimate sample is likely to have probative effect. For example, in an allegation of rape, a sample of semen will not tend to confirm or disprove the allegation if the client has admitted intercourse at the relevant time. If authority has already been given, the lawyer should ask to see the written authority (if given in writing, see paras 6.28 and 6.35 above), and should check the grounds on which authority has been given.

6.38    Where the person has been requested to return to the police station or is arrested under PACE Sch 2A, consideration must be given to whether the police have the power to take an intimate sample since, even if the suspect consents, it can only be taken if the conditions set out in para 6.28 above are satisfied. If the person attends voluntarily in response to a request, or is arrested under Schedule 2A, a sample cannot be taken under PACE s62(1) because the person is not in police detention since the person has not been arrested for an offence. If the person attends voluntarily and is then arrested, it could be argued by the police that the person is then in police detention, since PACE s118(2)(b) (arrest after attending voluntarily) does not refer to arrest for an offence. However, the structure of PACE s118(2) clearly implies that section 118(2)(b) refers to arrest for an offence, and normally arrest for an offence would not be justified in these circumstances.

6.39    If the only available power to take an intimate sample is under PACE s62(1A) or (2A), or TA 2000 Sch 8 para 12, it must be remembered that these provisions require that the police have previously taken at least two non-intimate samples. Therefore, if the police originally took an intimate sample, or only one non-intimate sample, that has proved insufficient (PACE s65(1) and (2)), they have no power to take an intimate sample. The police may be able to rectify this by their power to take non-intimate samples under PACE s63(3A) which, if the sample then proved insufficient, may enable an intimate sample to be taken under PACE s62(1A). The police cannot short-circuit this by simply asking the person to consent to an intimate sample, since the conditions in PACE s62 must always be satisfied. Code D NfG 6C provides that nothing in Code D para 6.2 prevents intimate samples being taken with consent for elimination purposes. The meaning of this is not defined, but is likely to refer to a sample taken in order to establish that the person is not a suspect, as opposed to seeking to establish that a suspect is, or may be, guilty. This is unlikely to be the case where the person has been required to attend or been arrested under Schedule 2A. Note that as a result of the definition of 'insufficient' in PACE s65(1) and (2), the powers under PACE s63A will be available if the sample had been lost, damaged or destroyed.

6.40    If authority is given for the taking of an intimate sample and the lawyer is satisfied that the statutory conditions are satisfied, the client will require advice on whether to give consent. PACE s62(10) and TA 2000 Sch 8 para 13 provide that if consent is refused without good cause, the court or jury in subsequent proceedings may draw such inferences from the refusal as appear proper. Before being asked to provide an intimate sample, the person must be warned that refusal may be so treated (Code D para 6.3 and NfG 6D). It is difficult to accurately predict how a refusal to give consent to a sample being taken will be interpreted at the trial stage, and a client should always be warned of the dangers of refusal. Three factors need to be considered.

6.41 The first factor is relevant if the refusal is based on legal advice. What inferences can a court or jury properly draw if the evidence is that the refusal resulted from the advice given by the lawyer? Unlike inferences under Criminal Justice and Public Order Act (CJPOA) 1994 s34 there is no reasonableness requirement, but section 62(10) only permits inferences if consent was refused without good cause. It can be argued that legal advice not to consent should amount to good cause. Even if it does not, it may be argued that refusal to give consent on advice should not be taken as an indication of guilt. In the case of a juvenile, refusal to give consent by a parent or guardian may also present difficulties to a court in determining whether and what inference to draw. On the other hand, irrespective of the strict legal provisions regarding inferences, if a jury or court is made aware that consent was refused it may well lead them to place less credibility on the defence put forward at trial.

6.42 The second factor concerns the question of what other evidence the police have, or might secure. It will often not be easy to assess this for the reasons discussed at para 4.25 above. However, if there is no other evidence, or that other evidence is weak, a refusal may not in itself add very much to the overall weight of evidence. For example, if the case involves identification, and the client has not been picked out in an identification procedure and there is no other evidence, not only may there be no other evidence to be corroborated by the fact of refusal to allow a sample to be taken, but allowing a sample to be taken may actually provide the police with the evidence they need to be able to prosecute the client successfully. It is not improper for a lawyer who knows the client to be guilty to advise the client to refuse consent for a sample to be taken. However, it should be noted that if the police are seeking an intimate sample for the purposes of DNA analysis, as is often the case, they are likely to be able to achieve the same result by taking a non-intimate sample, which they may take whether or not the suspect consents (see para 6.48 below). If this is the case, the suspect would be at risk of inferences being drawn without any advantage resulting from refusal to consent.

6.43 The third factor concerns the feelings of the client and is related to the question of whether the client has 'good cause' to refuse consent. The client may be embarrassed, worried about being roughly treated, scared of needles, or have religious objections. With regard to embarrassment or a fear of rough treatment, a number of provisions of PACE and Code D may be relevant. Intimate samples other than of urine may only be taken by a medical or dental practitioner, as appropriate (see para 6.36 above). Where the taking of a sample requires the removal of clothing in circumstances likely to cause embarrassment to the person, no person of the opposite sex other than a medical practitioner or nurse may be present (unless in the case of a juvenile, or a mentally disordered or mentally vulnerable person, he or she specifically requests the presence of a particular adult of the opposite sex who is readily available), nor may anyone whose presence is unnecessary (Code D para 6.9). In most cases this will mean that no more than one police officer, or possibly two if necessary in the interests of security, should be present.

6.44   In the case of a juvenile, removal of clothing in these circumstances may only take place in the absence of the appropriate adult if the juvenile requests this in the presence of the appropriate adult and the appropriate adult agrees (Code D para 6.9). This would seem to mean that a juvenile could insist on a particular adult of the opposite sex being present (provided the adult is readily available) and/or that the appropriate adult should not be present. For example, a juvenile in the care of a local authority might want his or her parent to be present rather than the social worker who is acting as appropriate adult. It appears to be an anomaly that the person could insist on the presence of a parent if the parent is of the opposite sex, but not if they are both of the same sex.

6.45   In the case of a mentally disordered or mentally vulnerable person, it would seem that the appropriate adult should be present, since Code D para 2.15 provides that an appropriate adult must be present for any procedure involving the 'participation of a person' who is mentally disordered or otherwise mentally vulnerable. Code C Annex A para 12 and Code H Annex A para 6 provide that an intimate search of such a person should only be carried out in the presence of an appropriate adult of the same sex unless the person specifically requests otherwise, but there is no similar provision in relation to the taking of intimate samples.

6.46   Given the above provisions, it is unlikely that embarrassment or fear of the way in which the person might be treated would amount to good cause for the purposes of PACE s62(10), particularly if the client has received legal advice. With regard to other reasons for refusal of consent, the difficulty for the lawyer in advising the client is that it would be impossible to predict accurately how a court would view the refusal. There are no reported cases on this point, although it may be instructive to consider decisions made under RTA 1988 s7 and its predecessors, which provides for the defence of 'reasonable excuse' to a prosecution for failure to provide a specimen. It was held in *Kemp v Chief Constable of Kent*[22] that the question of whether circumstances were capable of amounting to a reasonable excuse was a question of law, whereas whether those circumstances did in fact provide a reasonable excuse was a matter of fact. Generally, the excuse must arise out of a physical or mental inability to provide a specimen or a substantial risk to health resulting from providing a specimen.[23] It has been held that a fear of AIDS is not a reasonable excuse, but that a medically recognised phobia may be so.[24] If a client puts forward such reasons for wanting to refuse consent, the client should be carefully questioned in order to try to determine the basis for the view, and an accurate note taken of what the client says. It may also be advisable, subject to agreement of the client, to inform the police of the reasons and ask that they be noted on the custody record. In any event, the lawyer should warn the client that a court may not accept that the reasons for refusing consent amount to good cause.

22  [1987] RTR 66.
23  *R v Lennard* [1973] 1 WLR 483.
24  See *Fountain v DPP* [1988] Crim LR 123 and *De Freitas v DPP* [1993] RTR 98 respectively.

## Non-intimate samples and skin impressions

6.47   Non-intimate samples and skin impressions are governed by PACE s63, TA 2000 Sch 8 para 10, and Code D section 6. A 'non-intimate sample' is defined as a sample of hair other than pubic hair,[25] a sample taken from a nail or under a nail, a swab taken from any part of the body other than a part from which a swab taken would be an intimate sample (see para 6.27 above), saliva or a skin impression (PACE s65(1)). A skin impression is any record, other than a fingerprint, of the skin pattern and other physical characteristics or features of the whole or any part of a person's foot or any other part or their body (s65(1)). The definition is such that it includes ear impressions.[26] Although PACE s63 is headed 'other samples', it is confined to non-intimate samples as defined by PACE s65, and does not cover non-body samples such as handwriting.

### Power to take non-intimate samples under PACE

6.48   The major difference between the powers to take intimate and non-intimate samples concerns the question of consent. Unlike intimate samples, a non-intimate sample may always be taken with appropriate consent (see para 6.3 above) in writing (PACE s63(1) and (2) and Code D para 6.5). If consent is given the offence concerned does not have to be a recordable offence. If appropriate consent is not given, a non-intimate sample can be taken:

1) From a person in police detention (see para 1.61 above) in consequence of their arrest for a recordable offence,[27] provided that the person has not had a non-intimate sample of the same type and from the same part of the body taken from them in the course of investigation of the offence, or has had such a sample taken but it proved insufficient (PACE s63(2A)–(2C)).[28] No authorisation is required.

2) From a person who is being held in custody by the police on the authority of a court, and an inspector or above authorises it to be taken (PACE s63(3)). Authorisation may only be granted if the officer has reasonable grounds:
   • for suspecting the person's involvement in a recordable offence; and
   • for believing that the sample will tend to confirm or disprove that involvement (PACE s63(4)).

   Authorisation cannot be given for a non-intimate sample consisting of a skin impression if a skin impression of the same part of the body has

---

25   Note that a plucked hair, as well as a cut hair, is a non-intimate sample (unless it is a pubic hair) (Code D para 6.1(b)). Where hair samples are taken for the purpose of DNA analysis (as opposed to, for example, making a visual match), the suspect must be permitted, within reason, to choose the part of the body from where the hairs are to be taken (Code D NfG 6A).

26   The scientific analysis of ear impressions has caused significant difficulty. See *R v Dallagher* [2002] Crim LR 821; and *R v Kempster* [2008] EWCA Crim 975 in which the science was reviewed.

27   See note 3 above.

28   For the meaning of 'insufficient' see note 18 above.

already been taken from the person in the course of the investigation of the offence, and the impression taken has not proved insufficient (PACE s63(5A)). Authorisation under PACE s63(4) maybe given orally or in writing, but if orally, must be confirmed in writing as soon as practicable (PACE s63(5)).

3) From a person who has been arrested for a recordable offence and released and:

- in the case of a person who is on bail, the person has not had a non-intimate sample of the same type and from the same part of the body taken in the course of the investigation of the offence, or
- in any case, the person has had a non-intimate sample taken in the course of that investigation but it was not suitable for the same means of analysis or it proved insufficient (PACE s63(3ZA)).

No authorisation is required.

4) From a person who has been charged with a recordable offence or informed that he or she will be reported for such an offence (with a view to summons, caution, warning or reprimand), and either the person has not had a non-intimate sample taken in the course of investigation of the offence, or the person has had a non-intimate sample taken but either it was not suitable for the same means of analysis or, though so suitable, the sample proved insufficient (PACE s63(3A)).[29] No authorisation is required.

5) From a person who has been convicted of a recordable offence, or cautioned for a recordable offence which, at the time of the caution, the person had admitted, or been reprimanded or warned for a recordable offence (PACE s63(3B)). The power to take a non-intimate sample under this provision only applies if a non-intimate sample has not been taken from the person since the person was convicted, cautioned, warned or reprimanded, or it has been taken but was not suitable for the same means of analysis or it proved insufficient (PACE s63(3BA). Authorisation is required from an inspector or above, who may only give authorisation if satisfied that it is necessary to assist in the prevention or detection of crime (PACE s63(3BB) and (3BC)).

6) The person is imprisoned or detained following an acquittal on grounds of insanity or a finding of unfitness to plead (or similar) (PACE s63(3C)).

In addition, there are powers to take a non-intimate sample from a person who has been convicted of an offence in a foreign jurisdiction, provided certain conditions are satisfied (PACE s63(3E)–(3H)).

6.49 Where the conditions for taking a non-intimate sample are satisfied, it may be taken in any prison or other institution to which the Prison Act 1952 applies (PACE s63A(3)). However, this would not apply to the powers described in 1) or 2) above since for these powers to be exercised the person must either be in police detention or held in custody by the

---

29 Note that it refers to whether samples have been taken in the investigation of 'the' offence, ie, the one for which the person has been charged or informed that he or she will be reported. Contrast this with the power to take an intimate sample under PACE s62(1A) (see note 17 above).

police on the authority of a court, and this would usually exclude detention in a prison. Where the power to take a non-intimate sample is provided by PACE s63(3B) in respect of a person who is detained under Mental Health Act 1983 Part III pursuant to a hospital order, interim hospital order or transfer direction imposed following conviction for a recordable offence, or by PACE s63(3C), the sample may be taken in the hospital where the person is detained (PACE s63A(3A)). Where the power to take a non-intimate sample is provided by PACE s63(3B) in respect of a person detained in pursuance of directions of the secretary of state under Powers of Criminal Courts (Sentencing) Act 2000 s92, the sample may be taken at the place where the person is detained (PACE s63A(3B)).

6.50    Where a non-intimate sample is taken without appropriate consent, before the sample is taken the person must be informed of the reason for taking the sample, the power under which it is to be taken and, where authorisation is required, the fact that it has been given (PACE s63(6)). If the person is at a police station, whether with or without appropriate consent, the person must be told that the sample may be the subject of a speculative search (PACE s63(8B)). In each case, the relevant matters must be recorded, and if at a police station, the record must be made in the custody record (PACE s63(8), (8B) and (9)). Since a non-intimate sample can be taken without consent, there is no provision for the person to be warned of the evidential consequences of failure to consent. A non-intimate sample may be taken by a constable (PACE s63(9ZA)) or a designated civilian officer (PRA 2000 Sch 4 para 31).

6.51    Powers to require a person to attend a police station for the purpose of taking a non-intimate sample are governed by PACE s63A(4) and Sch 2A. The power to take a non-intimate sample under PACE s63(2A)–(2C) would not apply to a person who voluntarily attended the police station or who was arrested in default; the person is not in police detention since he or she has not been arrested for an offence. However, many of the other powers to take a non-intimate sample set out in para 6.48 above would apply to such a person.

### Speculative searches

6.52    The power to conduct a speculative search in respect of a non-intimate sample is the same as for fingerprints (see para 6.6 above).

### Retention, use and destruction

6.53    The provisions are the same as for fingerprints (see paras 6.6 and 6.7 above).

### Power to take non-intimate samples under TA 2000

6.54    Where a person is detained under TA 2000 Sch 7 or s41, a non-intimate sample may be taken by a constable with appropriate consent in writing, on the authority of a superintendent or above, or if the person has been convicted of a recordable offence on or after 10 April 1995 (TA 2000 Sch 8 para 10(3) and (4)). Where authorisation is required, a superintendent may only give it if:

- in the case of a person detained under TA 2000 s41, the officer reasonably suspects that the person has been involved in an offence under the provisions mentioned in TA 2000 s40(1)(a) and the officer reasonably believes that the sample will tend to confirm or disprove the person's involvement; or
- in any case, the officer is satisfied that the taking of the sample is necessary in order to assist in determining whether the person falls within TA 2000 s40(1)(b) (ie, is or has been concerned in the commission, preparation or instigation of acts of terrorism) (TA 2000 Sch 8 para 10(5) and (6)).

6.55    For limitations on the use of samples taken under these provisions, and the power to conduct speculative searches, see TA 2000 Sch 8 para 14. For the information that must be given to the person before samples are taken, see TA 2000 Sch 8 para 11.

### Advising on non-intimate samples

6.56    The police have extensive powers to take non-intimate samples, although in most cases the power can only be exercised in relation to a recordable offence, and a number of the powers require authorisation. Having checked the power under which the police intend to proceed, and that the relevant conditions are satisfied, the lawyer should normally advise the client that he or she has little alternative but to submit to the sample being taken. There is no provision in PACE s63 (as there is for intimate samples) for a court to draw adverse inferences from a refusal to allow a sample to be taken, but if the conditions for taking a sample are satisfied and the suspect does not co-operate, reasonable force may be used in order to obtain the sample (PACE s117). Furthermore, resistance could result in a charge of obstruction of or assault on a police constable (or designated civilian) in the execution of their duty.

## Handwriting samples

6.57    PACE does not deal with handwriting samples, which is somewhat surprising since they are often requested by the police.[30] The use of disputed handwriting as evidence is governed by Criminal Procedure Act 1865 s8, which permits evidence of handwriting to be admitted at trial, but the taking of handwriting samples is not regulated. This lack of statutory authority creates difficulty for the lawyer in advising the client whether to co-operate in the taking of such samples. In particular, it is unclear whether a refusal to cooperate can lead to adverse inference being drawn at trial.

6.58    It was seen in the section on advising clients whether to answer police questions (see para 5.63 above) that at common law, the failure of a person to answer police questions could not be used as evidence against the person at trial. There is a strong argument that the question of samples[31] is analogous with silence, that is, people cannot be required to incriminate

---

30  Although PACE s76(4) permits part of an excluded confession to be admitted to establish that an accused writes in a particular way.
31  Except intimate samples, which are governed by PACE s62(10).

themselves, whether by words or actions. The initial difficulty with this argument lies in the case of *R v Smith (Robert William)*[32] in which the analogy was rejected in relation to a hair sample, and it was held that a suspect's refusal to allow the police to take a sample of his hair was evidence capable of amounting to corroboration. It has been suggested that this case is authority for the proposition that refusal, in the presence of a solicitor, of a police request for a sample, handwriting or participation in an identification procedure may be capable of amounting to corroboration.[33] However, *Smith* was decided before PACE came into force. The particular facts of the case would now be covered by PACE s63, and reasonable force could have been used to take the sample since the accused was suspected of involvement in robbery, a recordable offence. More importantly, it could be argued that since that case, parliament has considered the question and chosen not to provide for inferences to be drawn other than in the case of intimate samples under PACE s62. If it were the general common law position that refusal to allow a sample to be taken could result in adverse inferences at trial, there would have been no need for the special statutory provision in PACE s62(10).

6.59    However, it has to be accepted that the position is uncertain as there is no reported case on the point since PACE came into force. In terms of advising a client faced with a request for a sample not covered by PACE or the RTAs, the advice should be that there may be some danger in refusing to co-operate but that the dangers are likely to be minimal. Even if adverse inferences could be drawn at trial, such a danger may well be outweighed by the danger of providing the sample. This is particularly so in the case of handwriting, since forensic handwriting analysis cannot be regarded as an exact science. Furthermore, one way of reducing any danger of adverse inferences is for the lawyer to ensure that he or she advises the suspect before responding to the request, and that if the suspect decides to refuse to co-operate, the suspect should say that he or she is not willing to provide the sample on legal advice. In this way, the primary inference to be drawn should be that the suspect was acting on advice.[34] The lawyer should keep a careful note of the advice, and of the thinking behind it, since this may become relevant at trial.

## Road Traffic Act samples

6.60    As was noted at para 6.27 above, blood and urine samples taken for the purpose of the drink/driving procedures under the RTA 1988 are excluded from the provisions relating to intimate samples by PACE s62(11). Samples of breath would not come under either PACE s62 or s63 in any event.

6.61    The major question that arises at the police station is whether the suspect should be advised to provide a sample. Failure without reasonable excuse to provide a sample is an offence under RTA 1988 s7(6), on conviction

---

32  (1985) 81 Cr App R 286.
33  Law Society, *Advising a suspect in the police station* (Law Society, London, 1991) at p25.
34  But see the discussion regarding the impact of legal advice on inferences under CJPOA 1994 s34 at para 5.96 above.

for which the defendant will usually be disqualified from driving. It has been held that it is not a reasonable excuse to refuse to give a sample until the person has consulted a solicitor, although the person should be permitted to consult a solicitor briefly if the solicitor is immediately available.[35] Medical reasons for not giving a sample will not normally amount to a reasonable excuse unless the act of giving a sample, or attempting to give a sample, would be injurious to health (see para 6.46 above). For this reason, even if the lawyer suspects that the procedure may be unlawful, the lawyer should advise the suspect that failure to provide a specimen is likely to lead to prosecution and disqualification.

6.62    The current prescribed limits are 35 micrograms of alcohol in 100 ml of breath, 80 mg of alcohol in 100 ml of blood, and 107 mg of alcohol in 100 ml of urine. The sample taken at the police station will normally be of breath. However, in two situations the sample may be of blood or urine. First, if the breath specimen contains no more than 50 micrograms of alcohol in 100 ml of breath, the suspect can require the police to take a further sample of blood or urine (RTA 1988 s8(2)). The suspect will normally be best advised to take advantage of this opportunity, since the blood or urine sample may show a lower reading. Second, a constable may require a sample of blood or urine rather than of breath if:

1) the constable has reasonable cause to believe that for medical reasons a specimen of breath cannot be provided or should not be required; or

2) at the time of the request a device for taking a breath sample is not available or it is not practicable to use such a device (for example, it is broken);

3) the suspected offence is one under RTA 1988 s4 (driving or being in charge of a motor vehicle when under the influence of drink or drugs) and the constable has been advised by a medical practitioner that the condition of the suspect might be due to some drug (RTA 1988 s7(3)).

6.63    In these circumstances, it is for the officer to decide whether the sample should be of blood or of urine, unless the constable has been advised by a medical practitioner that for medical reasons a specimen of blood cannot or should not be taken (RTA 1988 s7(4)). However, the officer must give the suspect the opportunity to express a preference before the officer decides which form of sample to require.[36] Therefore, if the suspect does not wish to give a blood sample, he or she should say so at this stage, and if there is a medical reason for the suspect's preference, this should be made known to the doctor who is called to take a blood sample.

## Drug-testing for class A drugs

### Power to test for class A drugs

6.64    The power to test people in police detention (see para 1.61 above) for class A drugs is governed by PACE ss63B and 63C, and by Code C section 17.

---

35  See *Kennedy v DPP* [2002] EWHC 2297 (Admin), and *Whitley v DPP* [2003] EWHC 2512 (Admin), and cases cited at para 2.129 above.

36  *DPP v Warren* [1992] Crim LR 200.

The powers are not available in all police stations, and in some stations they are only available in respect of suspects who have attained the age of 18 years, whereas in others drug-testing following charge (but not before charge) is possible in respect of suspects who are between the ages of 14 and 17 years.[37]

6.65    Where a person is in police detention (in a police station in which the powers are available) a sample of urine or a non-intimate sample may be taken from the person for the purpose of ascertaining whether the person has any specified class A drug in his or her body provided that the person has been brought before a custody officer (PACE s63B(5D)) and the conditions set out below are satisfied. The conditions are:

- either the arrest condition or the charge condition is met; and
- both the age condition and the request condition are met; and
- the notification condition is met in relation to the arrest condition, the charge condition or the age condition (as relevant) (PACE s63B(1)).

6.66    The *arrest condition* is satisfied if the suspect has been arrested for, but not charged with, a trigger offence or any offence where an inspector or above, having reasonable grounds for suspecting that the misuse by that person of any specified class A drug caused or contributed to the offence, authorises a sample to be taken (PACE s63B(1A)). The *charge condition* is satisfied if the suspect has been charged with a trigger offence or any offence where an inspector or above, having reasonable grounds for suspecting that the misuse by that person of any specified class A drug caused or contributed to the offence, authorises a sample to be taken (PACE s63B(2)). If a sample is taken in respect of which the arrest condition was satisfied, no further sample can be taken under PACE s63B during the same continuous period of detention unless the suspect remains in police detention in respect of another offence in respect of which the arrest condition is satisfied (PACE s63B(5B) and (5C) and Code D para 17.9). A 'specified class A drug' and 'trigger offence' have the same meanings as in Criminal Justice and Court Services Act 2000 Part III, and the trigger offences are set out in Code C NfG 17E.

6.67    The *age condition* is, where the arrest condition is met, that the person has attained the age of 18, and where the charge condition is met, that the person has attained the age of 14 (PACE s63B(3)). The *request condition* is simply that a police officer has requested the suspect to give the sample (PACE s63B(4)). Before requesting a sample, the suspect must be warned that failure without good cause to provide the sample requested renders the suspect liable to prosecution (PACE s63B(5) and Code C NfG 17A). Failure without good cause to provide a sample is an offence punishable, on summary conviction, with up to three months' imprisonment and/or a fine not exceeding level 4 (PACE s63B(8) and s63C(1)). If the suspect does refuse to provide a sample, the police cannot use force to obtain one (Code C para 17.14). The suspect must also be told the purpose of taking the sample, that authorisation has been given (where required), and of the suspect's right to have someone informed of his or her arrest, to legal

37  See Home Office Circulars 3/2006, 7/2007 and 4/2009.

advice and to consult the Codes of Practice (Code C para 17.6). Where the suspect is a juvenile, the making of the request, the warning that refusal may amount to an offence, and the taking of a sample must be in the presence of an appropriate adult (PACE s63B(5A) and Code C para 17.7). The *notification condition* is that the relevant chief officer has been notified by the secretary of state that appropriate arrangements have been made for the police area as a whole, or for the particular police station in which the suspect is in police detention (PACE s63B(4A)).

6.68     The authorisation (where authorisation is required) and grounds for suspicion, the warning as to the consequences of refusal, and the time at which the sample is given, must be recorded in the custody record (PACE s63C(3) and (4) and Code C para 17.2). Where a suspect aged 18 years or older has tested positive for a specified class A drug under PACE s63B the police may, before the suspect is released, impose a requirement that the suspect attend an initial assessment of the suspect's drug misuse and to remain for the duration of the assessment, and also to attend a follow up assessment. Where the suspect is tested before charge, the requirement can be imposed even if the suspect is not subsequently charged with an offence. Failure to attend or to remain at the assessment, or to attend a follow up assessment, is an offence carrying imprisonment up to 51 weeks and/or a fine not exceeding level 4 (Drugs Act (DA) 2005 s12(3), (4) and s14(3), (4)). When such a requirement is imposed, the suspect must be told of the time and place for the assessment and be warned that failure without good cause to attend and to remain renders the suspect liable for prosecution (DA 2005 s11(2), (3) and s13(4), (5), and Code C para 17.18). The suspect must also be given a written notice containing this information (Code C para 17.19) and the process must be entered in the custody record (Code C para 17.20).

6.69     Where the arrest condition is met, a suspect can be detained for up to 24 hours from the relevant time (see para 2.70 above) in order for a sample to be taken, even though the custody officer would otherwise have decided that the suspect should be released on bail under PACE s37(2) (bail without charge), or under PACE s37(7)(a) (release without charge and on bail with a view to a Crown Prosecutor making the charge decision) or PACE s37(7)(b) (release without charge and on bail but not for that purpose) (PACE s37(8A) and (8B) and Code C para 17.10). Where the arrest condition (but not the charge condition) is satisfied in respect of one offence (offence 1) and the suspect's release would be required before a sample could be taken but for the suspect's continued detention in respect of an offence that does not satisfy the arrest condition (offence 2), the suspect may have a sample taken while he or she continues to be detained provided that it is taken within 24 hours of the suspect's arrest for offence 1 (PACE s63B(5C) and Code C para 17.10). Thus, if a person is charged with an offence that did satisfy the arrest condition, and a sample could not be taken before the suspect was charged, but the suspect continues to be detained in respect of an offence that does not satisfy the arrest condition, a sample may be taken during that period of further detention, provided that it is taken within 24 hours of the arrest for the first offence. Where a sample may be taken from a person under PACE s63B, but the person is charged before a sample is taken and the custody officer would otherwise release the person on bail under PACE s38, the custody officer may authorise the person's detention for up to six hours from the time of charge in order for a sample to be taken (PACE s38(1)(a)(iiia) and (2) and Code C para 17.10).

6.70     A sample taken under PACE s63B cannot be used for any purpose other than to ascertain whether the person concerned has a specified class A drug present in his or her body (Code C para 17.16(a)). Although it must be retained until the person has made his or her first appearance at court (Code C para 17.16(b)), it cannot be used for the purpose of prosecuting the person for an offence, other than those offences mentioned below. Information obtained from a sample taken under these powers may be disclosed for any of the following purposes:

- for the purpose of informing a decision as to bail, whether by the police or by a court;
- for the purpose of informing a decision about the imposition of a conditional caution;
- for the purpose of informing any decision about the supervision of the person in police detention, in custody or on bail;
- following conviction, for the purpose of informing any decision about sentence, and any decision about supervision or release;
- for the purpose of a drugs assessment which the suspect is required to attend by the police by virtue of DA 2005 s9(2) (initial assessment) or s10(2) (follow-up assessment);
- for the purposes of a prosecution under DA 2005 s12(3) (for failure to attend or remain at an initial assessment) or s14(3) (for failure to attend or remain at a follow-up assessment); and
- for the purpose of ensuring that appropriate advice and treatment is made available to the person concerned (PACE s63B(7)).

## Advising on drug-testing

6.71     Where the conditions for drug-testing under PACE s63B are satisfied, the lawyer should advise the client about the drug-testing process and the possible consequences of failure to comply. Force cannot be used to drug-test under PACE s63B, but the client may commit an offence if the client does not permit a sample to be taken, and if the client is charged with such an offence, this may in itself adversely affect the prospects of bail following charge. If a sample is taken and the test is positive for a specified class A drug (heroin, cocaine and crack cocaine), the suspect can be required to attend an initial assessment. If the suspect is unwilling to attend or otherwise to co-operate with a drugs assessment, or to attend a follow up assessment, the suspect must be advised that this may amount to an offence and may also mean that bail is not granted, either by the police or by a court.[38]

---

38   See Bail Act 1976 s3(6C)–(6E) and Sch 1 para 6.

# Searches

## Search of the person away from the police station

*Power to search the person*

6.72 Police powers of search of the person are complex and various, and this book does not attempt to provide a comprehensive treatment of such powers. The police have power to search a person who has not been arrested without the person's consent under a number of powers, including PACE Part I, CJPOA 1994 s60, TA 2000 ss43 and 44 and Misuse of Drugs Act 1971 s23 (see para 2.2 above).

6.73 Where a person is arrested other than at a police station, the person may be searched if the officer has reasonable grounds for believing that the person may present a danger to himself or herself or others (PACE s32(1)). In addition, the person may be searched for anything which might be used to assist the person in escaping from lawful custody or which might be evidence relating to an offence (PACE s32(2)(a)). The officer must have reasonable grounds for believing that the person may have such an item concealed on him or her. Any item found in such a search may be seized by the officer if the officer has reasonable grounds for believing that the person searched might use it to cause physical injury to himself or herself or others (PACE s32(8)), or (providing it is not an article subject to legal privilege) has reasonable grounds for believing that the person might use it to assist the person to escape, or that it is evidence of an offence, or has been obtained in consequence of the commission of an offence (PACE s32(9)). It was held in *Tomlinson v DPP*[39] that whether an officer had reasonable grounds for a search was a two-stage question. The first question is whether the officer had grounds from a subjective point of view (ie, did the officer believe there were grounds for a search?). If the answer is 'no', the search is unlawful. If the answer is 'yes', the second question is whether the belief was reasonable from an objective point of view (ie, would a reasonable person in possession of the same information as the officer have had such a belief?). Only if both questions can be answered in the affirmative will the search be lawful.

6.74 A search under PACE s32 must only be conducted to the extent that is reasonably required for the purpose of discovering the thing or evidence concerned (PACE s32(3)). It does not enable the officer to require the person to remove any of his or her clothing (other than an outer coat, jacket or gloves) in public,[40] but it does enable the officer to search the person's mouth which, it would seem, could be in public and using reasonable force if the person refuses the request (PACE s32(4)). It would seem that the power of search under PACE s32(1) applies whether or not the arrest was for an offence, and unlike search of premises under PACE s32(2)(b) (see para 6.100 below) there is no requirement that the arrest be for an indictable offence.

---

39 (1992) May *Legal Action* 21.
40 Although note the power under CJPOA 1994 s60AA to remove items that conceal identity (see para 2.6 above).

### Advising on search of the person

6.75    Following a search it may be alleged that the suspect had items of evidential value on him or her when arrested. The lawyer should, therefore, check with the custody officer and the arresting officer or officer in charge of the case on arrival at the police station to see whether any such item has been found. Instructions should then be taken from the suspect to find out, among other things, whether the suspect accepts that the item was found in his or her possession and how the item came to be there. The lawyer will also need to consider whether the search was lawful, since this may affect the advice to be given, particularly in relation to whether the client should answer questions in interview.

6.76    In practice, it will be very difficult to make an accurate assessment at this stage of whether the search was lawful, and even more difficult to predict whether any unlawfulness would result in a court refusing to admit evidence obtained from such a search. The common law position is that the fact that an item was found as a result of an unlawful search will not render evidence of it having been found inadmissible at trial.[41] The common law rule is subject to PACE s78, which gives a discretion to a court to refuse to admit prosecution evidence if it appears, having regard to all the circumstances including the circumstances in which the evidence was obtained, that the admission of such evidence would have such an adverse effect on the fairness of the proceedings that it ought not to be admitted. Although there have been no reported cases on the admission of evidence obtained by an illegal search under PACE s32, it is likely that evidence would be admitted despite the fact that it was obtained in an unlawful search unless, perhaps, it could be shown that the police knew that they were acting unlawfully.[42] In consequence, it is likely that even if the lawyer believes that a search may have been unlawful, this will have little effect on the advice to be given regarding whether to answer police questions. The lawyer should consider advising the client regarding any civil claim that the client may have and about whether a complaint is appropriate (see chapter 13).

## Search of the person at the police station after arrest

### Power to search at the police station

6.77    This section deals with searches carried out at the police station, other than intimate searches which are dealt with at para 6.84 below. Where a person is taken to a police station having been arrested (whether or not for an offence)[43] elsewhere or after being committed to custody by an order

---

41  See *Kuruma v R* [1955] 1 All ER 236; [1955] 2 WLR 223, and *Jeffrey v Black* [1978] 1 All ER 555; (1978) 66 Cr App R 81; [1977] Crim LR 555.

42  See *R v Wright* [1994] Crim LR 55 (unlawful search purportedly conducted on PACE s18, and *Khan v UK* [2000] Crim LR 684 (which suggested that evidence would not be excluded even if it amounted to a breach of the right to private life under European Convention on Human Rights article 8). However, note *R v Olden* [2007] EWCA Crim 726 in which it was held that evidence seized in an unlawful property search should have been excluded.

43  Including a person arrested under TA 2000 s41, but not a person detained for examination under TA 2000 Sch 7 in respect of whom there are separate powers of search under Sch 7 paras 7 and 8.

or sentence of a court, or is arrested (whether or not for an offence) at the police station,[44] the custody officer is under a duty to ascertain everything the person has with them (PACE s54(1) and Code C, Code H para 4.1). In order to do so, the person may be searched if the custody officer considers this is necessary in order to ascertain what property the person has, but only to the extent that the custody officer considers necessary for that purpose (PACE s54(6) and Code C, Code H para 4.1). Furthermore, a person who is in police detention (see para 1.61 above) may be searched at any time in order to ascertain whether the person has with him or her anything which could be used to cause physical injury to himself or herself or others, to damage property, to interfere with evidence or to assist the person to escape (PACE s54(6A)). An intimate search cannot be carried out under this provision (PACE s54(7)), but a strip search can be conducted if the custody officer considers it to be necessary in order to remove an article which the detained person would not be allowed to keep and the officer reasonably considers that the person might have concealed such an article (Code C Annex A para 10, Code H Annex A para 11 and see para 6.83 below).

6.78    The officer can seize and retain anything found in such a search, subject to the proviso that clothes and personal effects can only be seized if the officer:

1) believes that the person from whom they are seized may use them:
   • to cause physical injury to himself or herself or others;
   • to damage property; or
   • to interfere with evidence; or
   • to assist the person to escape; or

2) has reasonable grounds for believing that they may be evidence relating to an offence (PACE s54(3), (4), (6B) and (6C) and Code C, Code H para 4.2).

'Personal effects' are defined as those items which a person may lawfully need or use or refer to while in detention, but not cash or other items of value (Code C, Code H para 4.3). Therefore, a suspect should normally be allowed to keep his or her watch, glasses and belt. Generally, the suspect must be told of the reason for seizure unless the suspect is violent or likely to become violent, or the suspect is incapable of understanding what is said to him or her (PACE s54(5) and Code C, Code H para 4.2).

6.79    A search can only be carried out by a police constable or civilian detention officer[45] of the same sex as the suspect (PACE s54(8) and (9)). It is now a matter for the custody officer to decide whether to record any or all of the things that the person had with him or her, and if the officer does make a record it does not have to be in the custody record (PACE s54(2) and (2A) and Code C, Code H para 4.4, and see para 2.97 above). However, if the person is not allowed to keep any article of clothing or personal effects, the reason must be recorded (Code C, Code H para 4.5), although it appears that this does not have to be in the custody record.

---

44  Or is detained at a police station having answered to police bail, or having been arrested under PACE s46A having failed to answer to police bail (PACE s54(1)(b)).
45  PRA 2002 Sch 4 para 26, which grants powers of search and seizure under PACE s54.

6.80    In addition to the power of search under PACE s54, s54B gives the power to any police officer to search, at any time, a person who is in a police station to answer to live link bail (see para 10.87 below), and any article in the possession of such a person (s54B(1)). The officer may seize and retain, or cause to be seized an retained, any thing in the possession of the person which they believe ought to be seized on the grounds that: it may jeopardise the maintenance of order in the police station; may put the safety of any person at the police station at risk; or may be evidence of, or in relation to, an offence (s54(B)(2) and (3)). A search must be by an officer of the same sex as the person being searched, and an intimate search cannot be conducted under this section.

## Advising on search at the police station

6.81    A search will normally already have been carried out before the lawyer arrives at the police station and, therefore, the scope for intervention by the lawyer is limited. The lawyer should ask whether a record was made and, if so, whether it was made in the custody record, and should ask to see the record.[46] This is important, since the property that the person had with them at the time of the search may be the subject of questions in the police interview (for example, money, keys, etc). Since the power to search on arrival at the station is very broad, it is unlikely to have been unlawful (but see the discussion on strip searches at para 6.83 below). However, it is worth noting that Code C NfG 4A emphasises that PACE s54 does not require every detained person to be searched and, in particular, that a search may not be necessary if it is clear that the person will only be detained for a short period and is not to be placed in a cell.

6.82    Exceptionally, the police may wish to carry out a search while the lawyer is at the police station, for example, where the lawyer has accompanied the client to the station, or where the police are exercising their power to search under PACE s54(6A). Generally, since the search is likely to be lawful, the client should be advised to co-operate. The police are entitled to use reasonable force in order to carry out the search (PACE s117). The lawyer should insist on being present if the client so wishes, which the client is entitled to demand since PACE s58(1) provides that a person arrested and held in custody is entitled to consult a solicitor at any time.

## Strip searches

6.83    A strip search is a search that is not an intimate search, but which involves the removal of more than outer clothing (ie, coat, gloves, scarf, shoes and socks, etc) (Code C Annex A para 9, Code H Annex A para 10). If a strip search is carried out, the reasons for the search and its result must be recorded (Code C Annex A para 12, Code H Annex A para 13). It was recognised in the pre-PACE case of *Lindley v Rutter*[47] that strip searches 'involve an affront to the dignity and privacy of the individual', and Donaldson LJ

---

46  If a record made is not in the custody record the lawyer has no right to see it, but as noted in para 2.96 above it is difficult to see what legitimate reason there could be to refuse such a request.

47  [1981] QB 128.

said that removal of a brassiere would require considerable justification. It was seen earlier that a strip search can be carried out if the custody officer considers it to be necessary to remove an article which the detained person would not be allowed to keep (see para 6.77 above), and it is likely that this refers to the items specified in PACE s54(4) (see para 6.78 above). In addition, the officer must reasonably consider that the person might have concealed such an article (Code C annex A para 10, Code H annex A para 11). The lawyer should, therefore, ask the officer to justify the decision to carry out a strip search in terms of what it is the officer expects to find, and on what grounds the officer believes the person to be in possession of such items. If the lawyer forms the view that the search is or may be unlawful, the lawyer should make appropriate representations, including an indication that the client will be advised about the possibility of taking civil action for assault, and ask that they be noted on the custody record. However, if the officer insists on carrying out the search, the client should normally be advised that while the client should not consent to the search, he or she should not actively resist it. Active resistance could result in a successful prosecution for obstruction or assault if a court were subsequently to find that the search was lawful. Subject to the client's wishes, the lawyer should insist on being present, although if not of the same sex as the client, the lawyer should arrange for the attendance of a lawyer who is of the same sex. Note that a search or examination to ascertain identity under section 54A (see para 6.16 above) that involves the removal of more than outer clothing must be conducted in accordance with Code C Annex A para 11 or Code H Annex A para 12 (Code D para 5.10).

## Intimate searches, x-rays and ultrasound scans

### Power to carry out an intimate search

6.84 An 'intimate search' is defined as a search which consists of the physical examination of a person's body orifices other than the mouth (PACE s65(1)). 'Body orifice' is not defined, but includes the ears, nose, anus and vagina. Physical insertion into a body orifice would amount to an intimate search, as would any application of force to an orifice or its immediate surroundings, such as the removal of something within an orifice.[48] The definition of an intimate search is not coextensive with those parts of a body from which an intimate sample may be taken, since an intimate sample includes the taking of samples from parts of the body other than orifices.

6.85 An intimate search can only be carried out if an officer of the rank of inspector or above authorises it, for which purpose the officer must have reasonable grounds for believing that:

1) a person who has been arrested and is in police detention (see para 1.61 above) may have concealed on him or her anything which:
   - the person could use to cause physical injury to himself or herself or others; and
   - the person might use for this purpose while in police detention or in the custody of a court (PACE s55(1)(a)); or

---

48  See Code C, Code H Annex A para 11(e), which also implies that touching an orifice in these circumstances would amount to an intimate search.

2) such a person:
- may have a class A drug concealed on him or her; and
- was in possession of it with the appropriate criminal intent (see para 6.92 below) before the person's arrest (PACE s55(1)(b)).

Code C, Code H Annex A NfG A1 and A2 provide that the authorising officer must first try to obtain the relevant article by seeking to persuade the detainee to hand it over and, if this fails, the officer must review all relevant factors before authorising an intimate search.

6.86    Authorisation may be given orally or in writing, but if orally, it must be confirmed in writing as soon as practicable (PACE s55(3)). Note that there is no requirement that the person be suspected of involvement in a recordable offence,[49] although the conditions for conducting a search under PACE s55(1)(b) would inevitably involve suspicion of a recordable offence. In order for authorisation to be given, the officer must have reasonable grounds for believing that the item cannot be found without the person being intimately searched (PACE s55(2)). It will be seen that the circumstances in which an intimate search may be carried out are extremely limited, which may explain why in one research study intimate searches were found to have been carried out in only 17 out of more than 10,000 cases.[50]

6.87    An intimate search must not be carried out in conducting a search or examination under PACE s54A (search or examination to establish identity). Consent is not required for a search under PACE s55(1)(a), but appropriate consent (see para 6.3 above) in writing is required for a search under PACE s55(1)(b) (a drug offence search). If consent to a search under PACE s55(1)(b) (but not under PACE s55(1)(a)) is refused without good cause, proper inferences can be drawn (PACE s55(13A) and see para 5.85 above). Assuming that the requirements of CJPOA 1994 s36 have been satisfied (see para 5.88 above), an inference could be drawn from failure or refusal to account for an object or substance found in an intimate search, since the object is likely to be regarded either as 'on his person' (CJPOA 1994 s36(1)(a)(i)) or 'otherwise in his possession' (CJPOA 1994 s36(1)(a)(iii)).

6.88    Anything found in an intimate search may be seized and retained if the custody officer:

1) believes that the person from whom it is seized may use it:
- to cause physical injury to himself or herself or others;
- to damage property;
- to interfere with evidence; or
- to assist the person to escape; or
2) has reasonable grounds for believing that it may be evidence relating to an offence (PACE s55(12)).

The power to seize and retain the item applies even if the item found was not the item or in the same class of item for which the intimate search was carried out.

---

49  See note 3 above.
50  T Bucke and D Brown, *In police custody: police powers and suspects' rights under the revised PACE Codes Of Practice,* (Home Office Research Study No 174) (Home Office, London, 1997), at p49.

## Power to take and x-ray or ultrasound scan

6.89 An x-ray and/or ultrasound scan can be taken where an inspector or above authorises it, for which purpose the officer must have reasonable grounds for believing that a person who has been arrested and who is in police detention (see para 1.61 above):

1) may have swallowed a class A drug; and
2) was in possession of it with the appropriate criminal intent (see para 6.92 below) before their arrest (PACE s55A(1)).

The power can only be exercised with the appropriate consent (see para 6.3 above), but refusal of consent may result in proper inferences (PACE s55A(9) and see para 5.85 above).

## Advising on intimate searches, x-rays and ultrasound scans

6.90 Although an authorising officer is not under a specific duty to receive representations from the lawyer, the lawyer should seek to establish what grounds the officer has for the belief that the grounds are satisfied. Since the officer must have reasonable grounds for the belief that the person has concealed or swallowed a relevant item, the officer must be capable of stating what those grounds are. Clearly, a simple recitation of the statutory grounds is not sufficient, since the officer must be able to articulate the basis on which he or she believes the grounds to be satisfied. The basis for the belief does not have to consist of evidence that would necessarily be admissible in court, but it would have to give cause for more than mere suspicion or even reasonable suspicion.

6.91 As noted above, the powers can only be exercised if the authorising officer has reasonable grounds for the belief. In the case of an intimate search, the reasonableness of the belief relates not only to the grounds for the search but also to whether an intimate search is the only way of finding out whether the person is secreting the item concerned. If the officer is reluctant to state the basis for the belief, the lawyer could argue that the officer cannot reasonably believe that an intimate search is the only way of finding the item (and that, therefore, the search would be unlawful), since if the officer were to say what it is he or she is looking for and why he or she believes it to be concealed, the lawyer could advise the client to produce it (if, indeed, the client has concealed the item). Furthermore, if it is likely that the item would be naturally expelled within a reasonable period of time, the officer cannot be satisfied that it cannot be found without an intimate search, although in these circumstances an x-ray or ultrasound scan could be carried out.

6.92 For the purposes of a search under section 55(1)(b), class A drug has the meaning assigned to it by Misuse of Drugs Act 1971 s2(1)(b) (PACE s55(17)). The officer must believe that the person was in possession of it 'with the appropriate criminal intent before the arrest', which means an intent to commit an offence under:

1) Misuse of Drugs Act 1971 s5(3) (possession of controlled drugs with intent to supply another); or
2) Customs and Excise Management Act 1979 s68(2) (exportation, etc, with intent to evade a prohibition or restriction) (PACE s55(17)).

This ground is, therefore, very restrictive, and a mere belief that the person is a known drug-user or drug-dealer would not be sufficient to warrant authorisation being given. The officer would have to have reasonable grounds for believing that the person had the concealed drugs on him or her, or had swallowed them, and that the person was intending to supply or export those drugs.

6.93    If authorisation is given for an intimate search under PACE s55(1)(a) (but not under PACE s55(1)(b) or an x-ray or scan under PACE s55A), the police can use reasonable force in order to carry out the search (PACE s117). Whereas a search under PACE s55(1)(b), or an x-ray or ultrasound scan under PACE s55A, can only be conducted by a suitably qualified person, ie, a registered medical practitioner or a registered nurse (PACE s55(4) and (17) and s55A(4) and (10)), a search under PACE s55(1)(a) can be carried out by a constable if an inspector or above considers that it is not practicable for it to be carried out by a suitably qualified person. If the search is to be carried out by a suitably qualified person, the person could not lawfully use force and it would seem that the wording of PACE s117 is such that an officer present at such a search could not use force himself or herself since the officer would not be carrying out the search. This is only relevant to a search under PACE s55(1)(a) since searches under PACE s55(1)(b) and x-rays or scans can only be conducted with the appropriate consent.[51] If it is clear that the police intend to carry out such a search, the lawyer should advise the client to indicate that the client does not consent to the search, but to offer no resistance, for to do so could result in a charge of obstruction or assault. If the search is unlawful, a court may not admit evidence of anything so obtained. Although it was suggested in the discussion at para 6.76 above that unlawfulness of a search will usually not render inadmissible evidence found as a result, it may be that a court would exclude evidence under PACE s78 if it was obtained when the police were clearly put on notice that such a search was unlawful. The argument is stronger given the gross intrusion of privacy that such a search would constitute. The lawyer should also advise the client whether a civil action against the police for assault would be appropriate.

6.94    If a search under PACE s55(1)(a) is not to be carried out by a suitably qualified person, it must be carried out by a police constable or civilian detention officer (PRA 2002 Sch 4 para 28) of the same sex as the suspect (PACE s55(5), (6) and (7) and Code C Annex A paras 2 and 6). Whether it is impracticable for the purposes of section 55(5) would depend on the circumstances of the case, but Code C Annex A para 3A provides that a search by a person other than a medical practitioner or nurse must only be considered as a matter of last resort and when the authorising officer is satisfied that the risks associated with allowing the item to remain with the detainee outweigh the risks associated with removing it. Furthermore, Note for Guidance A4 provides that a search in these circumstances must only be used if other approaches have failed, and the authorising officer is satisfied that the detainee might use the article to cause physical injury to themselves or to another and that the injury likely to be caused is

51  Although it could still be relevant if the suspect is under 14 years where the suspect's parent or guardian consents but the suspect does not.

sufficiently severe to justify it being carried out by a non-medical person. If the authorising officer has any doubts, he or she should seek the advice of a superintendent or above (Code C Annex A NfG A5). An intimate search carried out under PACE s55(1)(a) may only take place at a hospital, surgery, other medical premises or a police station (PACE s55(8) and Code C Annex A para 4).

6.95    If the intimate search is to be carried out under PACE s55(1)(b), or an x-ray or ultrasound scan is to be taken under PACE s55A(1), it must be carried out by a registered medical practitioner or registered nurse, and cannot be carried out by a police officer or civilian detention officer (PACE s55(4) and s55A(4), and Code C Annex A para 4). There is no requirement that the medical practitioner or nurse be of the same sex. A drug search, x-ray or ultrasound scan may only be carried out in the same premises as for a search under PACE s55(1)(a), except that it cannot be carried out in a police station (PACE s55(9) and s55A(4), and Code C Annex A para 4).

6.96    If the person concerned is a juvenile or mentally disordered or otherwise mentally vulnerable person, and the intimate search is carried out at a police station, it should only be carried out in the presence of an appropriate adult of the same sex unless the person specifically requests the presence of a particular adult of the opposite sex who is readily available. In the case of a juvenile, the search may only take place in the absence of an appropriate adult if the juvenile makes this request in the presence of the appropriate adult and the appropriate adult agrees (Code C Annex A para 5). Subject to the above provision, no person of the opposite sex may be present at the search, and no one else should be present whose presence is unnecessary (Code C Annex A para 6). Generally, therefore, only those police officers who are carrying out the search (where this is permitted) and the minimum number of officers necessary for the purposes of security, should be present.

6.97    Subject to the wishes of the client, the lawyer should insist on being present. Such presence can be justified by virtue of PACE s58(1), which provides that a person arrested and held in custody is entitled to consult a solicitor at any time. This would apply even if the search is carried out away from the police station, since PACE s58 refers to the person being held in custody 'in a police station or other premises'. If the lawyer is of the opposite sex to the client, then, by virtue of Code C Annex A para 6, the lawyer will have to arrange for the presence of a lawyer of the same sex. Arguably, in the case of a juvenile or mentally disordered or mentally vulnerable person who is searched at a police station (where this is permitted), a lawyer of the opposite sex could be present if the person specifically requests the presence of the lawyer (Code C Annex A para 5), although this would not normally be appropriate.

## Search of premises

6.98    The powers of the police to enter and search premises are both extensive and various. An entry on to and search of premises is always permissible with the consent of a person entitled to grant entry, although consent should be obtained in writing if practicable (Code B section 5). The police may enter and search premises without consent on the authority of a warrant from a court, or without a warrant under a number of statutory powers including PACE ss17, 18 and 32 and under numerous other statutes. This section is confined to the powers to search premises at the time of arrest under PACE s32, and after arrest under PACE s18.

6.99    Generally, powers of search and seizure under PACE are limited to police constables, but the PRA 2002 Sch 4 grants certain powers relating to search and seizure to designated civilian investigating officers. However, any power that includes a power to use force to enter any premises is only exercisable by a designated civilian if he or she is in the company, and under the supervision, of a constable, or the entry is for the purpose of saving life or limb or preventing serious damage to property (PRA 2002 s38(9)).

### Search of premises on arrest

6.100    Where a person is arrested at a place other than a police station, a constable has power to enter and search any premises in which the arrested person was when the person was arrested or immediately before he or she was arrested, for evidence relating to the offence for which the person had been arrested (PACE s32(2)(b)). This power is only available where the person is arrested for an indictable offence. 'Premises' are defined as including any vehicle, vessel, aircraft, hovercraft, offshore installation, renewable energy installation, tent or moveable structure (PACE s23). Where the premises concerned consist of two or more separate dwellings (for example, a multi-occupied house), the power to search is limited to any dwelling in which the arrest took place or in which the person arrested was immediately before their arrest, and any parts of the premises which the occupier of any such dwelling uses in common with the occupiers of any other dwellings comprised in the premises (PACE s32(7)). Where the premises consist of self-contained dwellings, it is clear that the search must be confined to the dwelling occupied by the arrested person, together with any common parts such as stairways and corridors. If the premises consist of shared accommodation, where each occupier has his or her own room, perhaps with shared use of some rooms such as kitchen, living room and toilet, the police should not enter those rooms exclusively occupied by the other flat-sharers.[52] The power of search applies whether or not the person arrested owns, controls or occupies the premises. Therefore, if the person is arrested at a friend's house, the police would have power to search it provided the other conditions are satisfied.

6.101    Section 32(2)(b) refers to the premises where the person was at the time of arrest 'or immediately before he was arrested'. Where the person is arrested in premises, this will present no problem, but 'immediately before' requires interpretation. In has been held that, in contrast to a search under PACE s18, s32 is an immediate power and the police cannot return to search the premises several hours after the arrest.[53] It is probable that

---

52  See *Thomas v DPP* [2009] All ER (D) 245 (Oct), a case concerning entry and search under PACE s17(1)(b).

53  *R v Badham* [1987] Crim LR 202. In *Hewitson v Chief Constable of Dorset Constabulary* [2003] EWHC 3296 (Admin) it was indicated that a gap of two hours and ten minutes between the arrest and the search was too long for a search to be carried out under PACE s32.

once a person has been taken to a police station, a section 32 search can-not be carried out, although a section 18 search may be possible (see para 6.104 below).

6.102  In order to carry out such a search the officer must have reasonable grounds for believing that there is evidence for which a search is permit-ted on the premises (PACE s32(6)). Furthermore, the power to search is only a power to search to the extent that is reasonably required for the purpose of discovering any such evidence (PACE s32(3)). Therefore, the nature of the search must relate to the kind of evidence the officer believes to be on the premises, having regard to the offence for which the person has been arrested. For example, an arrest on suspicion of a recent burglary could justify a search of the premises for the items stolen. On the other hand, if the person is arrested for an assault, a search would be hard to justify except, perhaps, to look for any weapon used. Furthermore, once found, no further search would be justified.

6.103  The police may use reasonable force to carry out the entry and search (PACE s117). There are no specific powers of seizure under PACE s32(2)(b), but s19 provides that a constable who is lawfully on any premises has power:

1) to seize anything which is on the premises if the constable has reason-able grounds to believe that it has been obtained in consequence of the commission of an offence, or that it is evidence in relation to an offence, and that it is necessary to seize it in order to prevent it being concealed, lost, altered or destroyed (PACE s19(2) and (3));

2) where the constable has similar reasonable grounds, to require that in-formation which is stored in any electronic form and is accessible from the premises be produced in a form in which it can be taken away and which is in a visible and legible form or in a form (such as a disk) from which a visible and legible version can be produced (PACE s19(4)).

The power of seizure under PACE s19(2) and (3) includes the premises themselves if they are readily moveable, eg, a car or caravan. However, it does not extend to seizing things that are not on the premises, such as a car parked in a car park adjacent to the premises.[54] Items which the constable has reasonable grounds for believing to be subject to legal pro-fessional privilege must not be seized (s19(6)). However, this must be in-terpreted by reference to the CJPA 2001, s50. This enables a constable to seize the whole or part of a suspect item so as to remove it from the premises for the purpose of determining whether it falls within the power, provided that it is not reasonable practicable to do this on the premises. Note the procedural requirements governing section 32 searches in Code B sections 6–9.

### Search of premises after arrest

6.104  A police constable, or a designated civilian investigating officer,[55] can enter and search any premises occupied or controlled by a person who is

54  *Wood v North Avon Magistrates' Court* [2009] EWHC 3614 (Admin).
55  PRA 2002 Sch 4 para 18.

under arrest[56] for an indictable offence provided that they have reasonable grounds for suspecting that there is on the premises evidence, other than items subject to legal privilege, relating to that offence or to some other indictable offence which is connected with or similar to that offence (PACE s18(1)). The power to search is only a power to search to the extent that is reasonably necessary for the purpose of discovering such evidence (PACE s18(3)).

6.105    Generally, an entry and search under PACE s18 can be carried out only if it is authorised in writing by an officer of the rank of inspector or above (PACE s18(4)). However, a constable can conduct a search without authorisation and before taking the arrested person to the police station, or before releasing the person on 'street bail' (see para 2.45 above), if the presence of that person at a place other than a police station is necessary for the effective investigation of the offence (PACE s18(5) and (5A)). In such a case, the officer must inform an inspector or above of the search as soon as practicable afterwards (PACE s18(6)). It would be possible, provided that the various conditions were satisfied, for both a section 32 search and a section 18 search to be carried out before the person is taken to the station – for example, where the person is arrested at a friend's house, and a search is conducted there and at the suspect's own home. However, neither power of search is available unless the person is arrested for an indictable offence, and thus where a person is arrested for a summary-only offence the police do not have power to enter and search premises for evidence.[57]

6.106    Even if authorised under section 18(4), section 18 powers cannot be exercised unless the officer conducting the search has reasonable grounds for suspecting that there is evidence on the premises relating to that offence or to some other indictable offence which is connected with or similar to that offence (PACE s18(1)).[58] 'Reasonable grounds for suspecting' implies a mixed subjective/objective test.[59] The evidence concerned must relate to the offence for which the person has been arrested or to some other indictable offence which is 'connected with or similar to' the offence for which the person has been arrested. For example, if a person has been arrested for burglary of a dwelling-house which is situated in a road where there have been a number of other burglaries within the previous few days, all with the same method of entry, this could justify a search for property stolen from the other dwellings, since they could be said to be 'connected'. However, the officer must have reasonable grounds for suspecting the presence of such evidence, and a search of premises occupied by a person

---

56  The premises must as a fact, or perhaps as a matter of mixed fact and law, be occupied or controlled by the person under arrest: reasonable suspicion that the person occupies or controls them is not enough (*Khan v Commissioner of Police of the Metropolis* [2008] EWCA Civ 723, and see Code B para 4.3).

57  Although the police do have certain powers of entry and search under PACE s17, eg, to effect an arrest in respect of certain specified offences that are not indictable offences.

58  Research evidence suggests that even this minimal requirement is often ignored by the police, and that speculative searches are not unusual. See D Brown *PACE ten years on: a review of the research*, Home Office Research Study 155 (Home Office, London, 1997).

59  See, in relation to arrest, para 2.15 above.

arrested when attempting to burgle a dwelling-house would not be justi-fied simply because the police believe that the person may have committed other burglaries.

6.107     A search under PACE s18 extends to premises occupied or controlled by the arrested person. 'Premises' has the same meaning as for section 32 searches (see para 6.100). 'Occupied' denotes at least some degree of per-manency and would not include premises that were simply being visited by the arrested person at the time of his or her arrest, but would include temporary accommodation occupied by the arrested person, such as a hotel room. 'Controlled' would include management as well as ownership, for example, a shop owned or managed by the arrested person. While it is clear that a section 18 search could be carried out at residential premises rented by an arrested tenant, the question arises of whether those premis-es could be searched if the person arrested was the landlord. It is certainly arguable that the landlord does not 'control' the premises, since generally the landlord will have no right to enter the premises without permission of the tenant. The position is less clear if the premises are let on some sort of licence, and a hotel room would almost certainly be regarded as 'controlled' by the hotel owner or manager. There is no similar provision in section 18 to that in PACE s32(7) regarding premises consisting of two or more separate dwellings (see para 6.100), although it is likely that the same principles would apply.

6.108     A constable may use reasonable force to carry out an entry and search under section 18 (PACE s117). The officer may seize and retain anything for which he or she may search under section 18(1), and in addition, the powers of seizure under PACE s19 apply (see para 6.103 above). Note the procedural requirements governing section 18 searches in Code B sec-tions 6–9.

## Advising on search of premises

6.109   A client at the police station may require legal advice on a number of aspects relating to search of premises. If a search has already been car-ried out (particularly if it was carried out at the time of the arrest), if it was carried out with some degree of force or if damage was done on gain-ing entry, the client may well feel angry and believe that the search must have been unlawful. With regard to damage, Code B para 6.13 provides that before leaving premises entered by force, the officer in charge must satisfy himself or herself that they are secure. If the client is concerned about this, the lawyer could ascertain what arrangements were made and consider whether they are satisfactory. The lawyer may also seek to check that the damage has been recorded on the record of the search (see Code B para 8.1).

6.110     The legality of the search may have a bearing on whether any evidence obtained is likely to be admissible at trial. This, in turn, may affect the advice the lawyer gives to the client at the police station, particularly regard-ing whether the client should answer police questions. The effect of the illegality of search of the person is discussed at para 6.76 above and simi-lar principles apply to search of premises. Answering questions regarding any item found in such a search may render pointless any application to exclude evidence of the item being found. However, a failure to answer questions may lead to inferences under CJPOA 1994 ss34 and 36, and it is unlikely that a court would direct that inferences should not be drawn merely on the basis that a search was believed to be unlawful. Advice may also be necessary regarding a possible formal complaint or civil action in respect of an illegal search (see chapter 13).

6.111    It was suggested at para 4.35 above that the lawyer should establish at an early stage whether the client has already made any comment or admissions. This is particularly important if a search of premises was carried out at which the client was present, since anything allegedly said may form the basis for questions in the police interview and may, subject to what is said below, be used in evidence at trial. As with other comments allegedly made by the suspect outside the context of an interview at the police station, the lawyer must make an assessment of whether evidence of such statements is likely to be admissible at trial since this will affect the advice to be given, particularly with regard to whether the client should answer police questions in interview.

6.112    Generally, once a decision has been made to arrest a person, the person must not be interviewed except at a police station (Code C para 11.1, Code H para 11.2, and see para 4.44 above). If an interview is conducted contrary to this provision, it may be possible to exclude evidence of the interview at trial under PACE s76 or s78. Questioning will not amount to an interview if the questions are put only as part of the proper and effective conduct of a search.[60] The police should confine questions to whether any article they discover is property claimed by the suspect and, if so, whether it is property that could amount to evidence of an offence. The police must not use a search to ask questions on unconnected matters.[61]

6.113    If a conversation during the search did not amount to an interview, it is not caught by the prohibition in Code C para 11.1, and evidence of what was said is likely to be admitted at trial, although as with any relevant comment, a written record should be made and where practicable the suspect must be given an opportunity to verify the record (Code C para 11.13). If this is not done, a court may refuse to admit evidence of the conversation, whether or not it amounted to an interview. As with items found during a search, it may be advisable that the client does not answer questions in interview if the lawyer has reason to believe that anything said during the course of the search may not be admitted at trial (see para 6.110 above).[62]

---

60  An interview is defined by Code C para 11.1A as questioning of a person regarding their involvement or suspected involvement in an offence and which by virtue of Code C para 10.1 is required to be carried out under caution. Para 10.1 provides that a caution is not necessary where questions are put in the furtherance of the proper and effective conduct of a search. See also Code B paras 6.12 and 6.12A, and para 4.37 above.

61  *R v Langiert* [1991] Crim LR 777, although in this case the evidence was not in fact excluded. See also *R v Khan* [1993] Crim LR 54, *R v Joseph* [1993] Crim LR 206 and *R v Raphaie* [1996] Crim LR 812.

62  See, for example *R v Chung* (1991) 92 Cr App R 314; [1991] Crim LR 622, *R v Williams (Violet)* [1989] Crim LR 66 (where evidence of questioning during a search was excluded), and *R v White* [1991] Crim LR 779, and *R v Courtney* [1995] Crim LR 63 (where it was not).

6.114 If the police are proposing to carry out a search of premises, the lawyer should consider its legality. It is likely that a proposed search at this stage would be under section 18, and the lawyer should consider in particular:

- whether the client is under arrest for an indictable offence;
- whether the premises to be searched are occupied or controlled by the client;
- whether there are reasonable grounds for suspecting that there is on those premises evidence relating to the offence for which the person is under arrest, or some other connected or similar indictable offence; and
- whether the search has been properly authorised.

6.115 If the lawyer believes the search to be unlawful, the lawyer should make representations to the authorising officer to this effect. Whether or not it is likely to be lawful, if authorisation for a search is given the lawyer should check (if appropriate) whether the client has a key in his or her possession or whether someone else can provide access, in order to avoid unnecessary damage caused by a forced entrance. The lawyer should also consider whether he or she should attend at the search. Neither PACE nor Code B require that either the suspect or the lawyer be given the opportunity to attend, although Code B para 6.11 states that if the occupier wishes a friend, neighbour or other person to witness the search, this must be allowed unless the officer in charge has reasonable grounds for believing that this would seriously hinder the investigation or endanger the officers concerned or other people and provided it does not cause unreasonable delay. Therefore, if the client is the occupier, arguably the lawyer can insist on being present.

# CHAPTER 7

# The police interview

*continued*

7.67      Style of questioning
          *The principles of investigative interviewing*

**7.68      The end of the interview**

7.69      At what stage should interviewing cease?

7.74      What should the lawyer do at the end of the interview?

# Introduction

7.1 The police interview is without doubt the crucial event during the course of a person's detention in a police station. As McConville et al have pointed out, 'interrogation is the central investigative strategy'.[1] This is not surprising, since if the police can obtain a confession during an interview, it reduces the investigative work they have to do and makes a successful prosecution more likely. Even where the police have carried out extensive investigations before arrest or interview, emphasis is still likely to be placed on the interview. In a pre-PACE (Police and Criminal Evidence Act 1984) study, Baldwin and McConville found that in nearly a third of cases, admissions by the defendant were crucial to the prosecution case, and of those who had made written confessions only a small minority were acquitted. They concluded that 'to obtain a written confession from a suspect is tantamount to securing his conviction'.[2] More recent research shows that more than half of suspects provide some form of admission to the police,[3] and the majority of those who confess go on to plead guilty or are convicted following a trial.

7.2 At the same time, it has come to be recognised that police interviews can produce false evidence, either because suspects falsely confess or because the police falsely maintain that the suspect has confessed.[4] A series of notorious miscarriages of justice in the 1970s and 1980s, such as the Guildford Four', the 'Birmingham Six', the 'Tottenham Three', Judith Ward, the Darvell brothers, Stefan Kiszko, David McKenzie, the 'Cardiff Three', and cases involving the West Midlands Serious Crime Squad, all involved false confession evidence of one type or other. While many of these cases were originally investigated prior to the introduction of PACE, there is plenty of evidence that the problem has not gone away.[5] Moreover, it has also come to be recognised that certain psychological conditions, or certain external factors, can mean that some suspects falsely confess even if the police conduct themselves properly.[6]

7.3 Although most of the cases referred to above involved confessions made in the absence of a lawyer, there is evidence that even if a lawyer is present a suspect may still make a false confession, particularly if the lawyer is too passive. This is graphically illustrated by the case of *R v Paris, Abdullahi*

1 M McConville, A Sanders, and R Leng *The case for the prosecution* (Routledge, London, 1991), at p57. See also S Moston, G Stephenson and T Williamson 'The effect of case characteristics on suspects' behaviour during police questioning' (1992) 32 *British Journal of Criminology* 1.

2 J Baldwin and M McConville *Confessions in Crown Court trials*, Royal Commission on Criminal Procedure, Research Study No 5 (HMSO, London, 1980), p19.

3 C Phillips and D Brown *Entry into the criminal justice system: a survey of police arrests and their outcomes*, Home Office Research Study 185 (Home Office, London, 1998) at p71.

4 See, eg, the Royal Commission on Criminal Justice, *Report* (HMSO, London, 1993), p57.

5 See, eg, *R v Ridley* (1999) 17 December (unreported), *R v Smith* [2003] EWCA Crim 927, *R v Brady* [2004] EWCA Crim 2230.

6 See G Gudjonsson *The psychology of interrogations and confession: a handbook* (Wiley, Chichester, 2003) and paras 7.41–7.46 below.

*and Miller*[7] (the 'Cardiff Three' case), in which Miller finally (falsely) confessed to murder during 13 hours of interviews conducted over a four-day period in the presence of his lawyer. In allowing the appeal, the Court of Appeal held that Miller's confession should have been excluded under PACE s76(2) because the police adopted hostile and intimidating techniques amounting to oppression The solicitor should, said the court, have intervened when improper questions were put, and to the extent that he did not, may have helped lead the police to believe that they were doing nothing wrong.[8]

7.4    This chapter deals with the formal requirements applicable to police interviews and examines the police objectives in interview. It goes on to deal with the role and objectives of the defence lawyer in the police interview and with intervention in police interviews. It finishes with the point at which interviewing should cease. Note that Police Reform Act (PRA) 2002 s38 and Sch 4 enable interviewing to be conducted by a designated civilian investigating officer, who is specifically empowered to arrest for a further offence under PACE s31 (PRA 2002 Sch 4 para 21), to receive into his or her custody a person in police detention (PRA 2002 Sch 4 para 22), and to require a person to account under Criminal Justice and Public Order Act (CJPOA) 1994 ss36 and 37 (PRA 2002 Sch 4 para 23).

## Formal requirements of police interviews

7.5    The meaning of the term 'interview' is set out at para 4.37 above. An interview at a police station at which a lawyer is present will undoubtedly come within the definition. A number of formalities must normally be complied with. These are listed in the box below and are thereafter dealt with more fully.

---

**The formal requirements of police interviews**

1) The suspect must be cautioned.
2) The suspect must be reminded of his or her right to legal advice.
3) The interview must normally be recorded contemporaneously.
4) At the beginning of the interview, the police interviewer must put to the suspect any significant statement or silence which occurred before the interview commenced.

---

### Cautioning

7.6    A person who is suspected of an offence must be cautioned before being questioned for the purpose of obtaining evidence (Code C, Code H para 10.1, and see para 4.37 above), and must be reminded of the caution on

---

7   (1992) 99 Cr App R 99, [1994] Crim LR 361. It was not until July 2003 that the real murderer was finally convicted.
8   See also *R v Glaves* [1993] Crim LR 685, in which the Court of Appeal commented: 'It behoved the solicitor representing the appellant to ensure that there was somebody present who would interfere if questioning apparently went too far'.

the re-commencement of an interview where there has been a break (Code C para 10.8, Code H para 10.7). Failure to do so may result in evidence obtained being excluded at trial, although this is less likely if a lawyer is present.[9] The caution should be in the following terms: 'You do not have to say anything. But it may harm your defence if you do not mention when questioned something which you later rely on in court. Anything you do say may be given in evidence' (Code C para 10.5, Code H para 10.4).[10] While minor deviations are permissible, the sense of the caution must be preserved (Code C para 10.7, Code H para 10.6).[11] If the suspect does not understand the caution, the officer should explain it (Code C NfG 10D, Code H NfG 10C). The lawyer should already have explained the caution to the suspect and if the lawyer is concerned that the client does not understand it, the lawyer should usually state this in the police interview. Any explanation given by the officer should be carefully noted, since officers are prone to imply that inferences will (as opposed to may) be drawn if the suspect refuses to answer questions. If the lawyer is still concerned that the suspect does not understand the caution, the lawyer should (if appropriate, after a further private consultation with the client) confirm that the suspect does not understand. The lawyer must be aware of the dangers of a client telling the police that he or she does understand the caution when he or she does not, or does not fully, understand it (see para 5.84 above). The lawyer should not normally indicate to the police that the client does understand the caution.

## Reminder of the right to legal advice

7.7    The suspect must be reminded of their right to legal advice at the commencement or re-commencement of any interview at a police station or other authorised place of detention, and this reminder should be recorded in the interview record (Code C para 11.2, Code H para 11.3).

## Contemporaneous record

7.8    A contemporaneous record of a police interview must normally be made (Code C para 11.7).[12] While it is permissible for the record to be made at a later time in some circumstances, this is unlikely to apply to an interview conducted in a police station (Code C para 11.7(c)). If, for some reason, a contemporaneous record is not made, a record of the interview must be

---

9  See *R v Armas-Rodriguez* [2005] EWCA Crim 1081; and see para 13.48 below).

10  Where, in exceptional circumstances, the police are permitted to interview a suspect who has asked to speak to a solicitor without them having received legal advice, or after charge, the caution is different. See Code C paras 10.6, 16.5 and Annex C and para 5.66 above. Note that in *R v Pall* [1992] Crim LR 126 it was held that while Code C does not require a caution if a statement is taken after charge, it should nevertheless be given.

11  *R v Saunders (Rosemary)* [1988] Crim LR 52. Where an interpreter is used, precise interpretation is not necessary provided that the essential features of the caution are adequately conveyed to the suspect (*R v Koc* [2008] EWCA Crim 77).

12  Where a person is detained under TA 2000 s41, Code H para 11.8 provides that interviews conducted at a designated place of detention must be recorded in accordance with the Code of Practice issued under TA 2000 Sch 8 para 3.

made as soon as practicable after completion of the interview (Code C para 11.8). If the interview is audio-recorded, the provisions of Code E apply (see para 7.10 below), and where it is visually recorded, the provisions of Code F apply (see para 7.11 below). Where, exceptionally, the record is made in writing, the suspect must be given the opportunity to read it (unless it is impracticable) and to sign it as correct or to indicate the respects in which the suspect considers it to be inaccurate (Code C para 11.11 and see para 7.16 below). Failure by the police to comply with the recording and checking requirement may lead a court to refuse to admit evidence of what was said, although this is less likely if a lawyer was present.[13]

## Significant statement or silence

7.9   At the beginning of an interview carried out at a police station, the interviewing officer must, after cautioning the suspect, put to the suspect any significant statement or silence which occurred in the presence and hearing of a police officer or civilian interviewer before the start of the interview, and which has not been put to the suspect in the course of a previous interview which occurred before his or her arrival at the police station, and must ask the suspect whether he or she confirms or denies the earlier statement or silence and whether he or she wishes to add anything (Code C, Code H para 11.4, and see paras 5.113–5.114 above).

## Audio and visual recording of police interviews

7.10   The audio-recording of police interviews is governed by Code C para 11.7 and Code E. There is a separate code for the audio-recording of interviews of persons examined under Terrorism Act (TA) 2000 Sch 7 or arrested under s41, and PACE Code E does not apply to such interviews. Interviews conducted at a police station in the following circumstances must be audio-recorded:

- interviews of a person cautioned under Code C section 10 in respect of any indictable offence, including an offence triable either-way;
- interviews that take place in respect of an indictable offence after charge or after the person has been told that he or she may be prosecuted;[14]
- where an interviewer wants to tell a person, after the person has been charged or informed that he or she may be prosecuted for an indictable offence, about any written statement or interview with another person (Code E para 3.1).

Interviews conducted in other circumstances, for example, in respect of a non-indictable offence, may be audio-recorded (Code E NfG 3A), and in practice they normally are so recorded. Where audio-recording is mandatory, a custody officer may authorise an interviewing officer not to audio-record an interview where it is not reasonably practicable because of failure of or unavailability of recording equipment, or where it is clear that no prosecution will ensue (Code E para 3.3).

13   *R v Dunn* (1990) 91 Cr App R 237; [1990] Crim LR 572 and see para 13.32 below.
14   Which may only take place in limited circumstances. See Code C para 16.5 and para 10.28 below.

7.11   Visual recording of interviews is not mandatory in any police force area, but where visual recording facilities are available and a police officer chooses to use them, the officer must comply with Code F. Note that there is a separate code for visual recording of interviews of persons examined under TA 2000 Sch 7 or arrested under s41.

7.12   Occasionally, a client is reluctant or unwilling to be interviewed if it is to be audio or visually recorded, but is willing to be interviewed if the interview is recorded in writing. Codes E and F para 4.8 effectively permit a suspect to object and provide that in these circumstances the interview must be recorded in writing. However, the police are permitted to proceed with audio or visual recording if the interviewing officer reasonably considers that they may proceed to put questions to the suspect with the recording equipment still operating. This would seem to be designed to allow the officer to test out how serious the suspect is about not wanting the interview to be recorded, so if a client does not want to be so recorded the client should be advised to remain silent until the officer has made clear that the recording equipment is not operating.

7.13   The lawyer may need to explain the arrangements for sealing and securing the master recording and the advisability of signing the master recording label (see Codes E and F para 4.18). The lawyer will also be asked to sign the label, and there is no reason why the lawyer should not do so providing he or she is content that the procedure has been satisfactorily followed. If there is a break in the interview during which the suspect leaves the interview room, the fact of the break, the reason for it and the time must be recorded. The recording media should then be removed and sealed (Code E para 4.12A, Code F para 4.12). If, however, the break is to be short and both the police officer and the suspect are to remain in the interview room, it is permissible for the recording equipment to be turned off and for the re-commenced interview to continue to be recorded using the same recording media (Code E para 4.13, Code F para 4.13). Neither Code E nor Code F deal with the situation where the police leave and the suspect remains in the room, but it is suggested that in these circumstances the same procedure that applies when the suspect leaves the room should be followed. Note that these provisions are modified where interviews are recorded using a secure digital network (see Codes E and F section 7).

7.14   The client should be advised of the possible consequences of an audio or visually recorded interview being heard or seen by a court. Everything said while the machine is switched on is recorded and, unless inaudible, may be transcribed. Therefore, the client should not treat the interview as if it were a private conversation, and should be made aware that the court may pick up cues from the way in which things are said. In the case of visually recorded interviews, there is the added dimension of non-verbal cues, such as facial expressions or physical gestures, which may have an adverse effect on the client's interests.

7.15   During the course of an audio or visually recorded interview the lawyer should attempt, as far as possible, to take a verbatim note of what is said. This is often difficult because of the speed with which people usually speak, but the lawyer should at least try to accurately record what the client says. There are a number of reasons for this.

1) It is a practical demonstration that the lawyer is taking an active part in the interview, which is important for both the client and the police to recognise.

2) If the lawyer confines the taking of notes to what he or she regards as the important parts of the interview, this may give valuable information to an observant police officer, who may recognise that certain lines of enquiry that they had not previously considered important may be worth pursuing.

3) Particularly during a lengthy interview, or where there is more than one interview, the interviewing officer may refer back to an earlier part of the interview, or to an earlier interview, in order to try to show, for example, that the client is being inconsistent. The interviewing officer may not take any notes during the course of the interview, and referring back to the recording of an earlier part of the interview, or to an earlier interview, may not be feasible. The lawyer may, from their own record, be able to correct the officer. Similarly, what is said in interview may be relevant to other matters, such as an application to extend detention beyond 24 hours.

4) Although the suspect or the suspect's lawyer is normally entitled to be provided with access to, or a copy of, the recording after charge or after being informed that he or she will be prosecuted (Code E paras 4.19 and 7.13, Code F para 4.19), it may not be received for some time. A record of what was said may well be required during this time, for example, in relation to a bail application or in order to advise on plea.

5) The summary of the record of the interview subsequently prepared by the officer may not accurately reflect the content of the interview.[15] The lawyer's notes of the interview will provide a quick reference to check the fairness of the summary, and will safeguard against difficulties caused by faulty or inaudible recordings.

## Police interviews recorded in writing

7.16   If, exceptionally, an interview is not audio or visually-recorded, it must normally be contemporaneously recorded in writing. This will frequently consist of one officer conducting the interview while another writes down what is said. Such interviews are usually slow and laborious, and often the result does not amount to a verbatim record of what has been said. They may be punctuated by statements like, 'Stop writing, and let's make this clear before we go on', which may come from the police, the suspect or the lawyer. Thus a degree of negotiation occurs. While this does not necessarily work to the disadvantage of the suspect, the lawyer must take care to see that it does not. If the suspect is speaking too fast for what he or she says to be accurately recorded, the lawyer should ask the suspect to slow down.

---

15  Research conducted shortly after audio-recording was introduced, one-quarter of tape summaries provided a 'reasonable outline of the salient details', and one-half either omitted so much detail that they did not provide a fair summary or were misleading, distorted or of poor quality. See J Baldwin and J Bedward, 'Summarising tape recordings of police interviews' [1991] Crim LR 671–679.

7.17    As with audio or visually recorded interviews, the lawyer should take their own note of what is said and in this case it should, as far as possible, be a verbatim account. At the end of the interview the suspect must, unless it is impracticable, be given an opportunity to read through the interview record and to sign it as correct or to indicate the respects in which the suspect considers it to be inaccurate (Code C para 11.11).[16] There is a temptation, particularly after a long interview or one conducted late at night, for the suspect to sign the record without reading it properly. This is potentially very damaging, since once it is signed the suspect will have little chance of persuading a court that it is inaccurate. The lawyer should also be aware that the client may not be able to read or the client's reading ability may be limited, a fact that the client may be reluctant to admit. For this reason, it may be appropriate for the lawyer to read the interview record out loud, although if the police are aware of a suspect's reading difficulty the senior interviewer present should do so (Code C para 11.11). The client should be advised to sign the record of the interview only if the client is absolutely satisfied that it is an accurate account of what was said. If the client is not satisfied, the record should be endorsed accordingly. If the difference is minor, the interviewing officer may be willing to amend the written record. If, however, the disagreement is more significant and the police will not agree to change it even after reference to the lawyer's own notes, the client should fully explain in writing what the client disagrees with and what he or she believes the record should show. Furthermore, if the client wishes to add anything to the record (and this is something on which the lawyer may wish to give the client advice), this should be added. Only when these things have been done should the client sign the interview record. Code C para 11.12 provides that the lawyer must be given an opportunity to read and sign the record. While the lawyer should read it, the lawyer should not sign it unless absolutely satisfied that it is an accurate record of the interview.

## Police objectives in interview

7.18    As noted at para 7.1 above, the police interview of the suspect is frequently the focus of a police investigation. While 'interview' is defined in Code C as 'the questioning of a person regarding his involvement or suspected involvement in a criminal offence or offences' (Code C para 11.1A), in practice interviewing officers view the process in a more one-sided fashion. McConville et al described police interviews as an 'instrument for creating evidence', in which the police hold the balance of power. It involves a relationship often characterised by 'dealing', 'trading' and 'bargaining'. Most importantly, rather than being an investigation designed to establish 'the truth', the police interview is often used as a mechanism for justifying and helping to prove that the police's belief that the suspect is guilty is correct. Issues raised by the suspect that interfere with this belief are often regarded as 'irrelevant red herrings to be ignored or argued away'.

16  See, eg, *R v Parchment* [1991] Crim LR 626, *R v Walsh* (1989) 91 Cr App R 161; [1989] Crim LR 822 and *R v Waters* [1989] Crim LR 62.

Inconsistencies may be exploited in order to demonstrate that the suspect is lying.[17]

7.19    This is not how the police characterise the purpose or process of police interviewing. The *National Investigative Interviewing Strategy* is based on the PEACE interview framework.[18] 'PEACE' stands for:

- *Planning and preparation* The interviewer should consider whether and why an interview is necessary, the timing of the interview, and what the objectives are. This entails considering what is known by the police about the suspect, what evidence is available, and what needs to be proved.
- *Engage and explain* This is the first of the three stages of an interview, and involves establishing a relationship with the suspect and explaining the purpose of the interview, the suspect's rights, the ground rules and relevant procedures.
- *Account, clarification and challenge* The second stage of an interview, which involves asking or persuading a suspect to provide an account in relation to the allegation(s), seeking clarification, and challenging the suspect in respect of any part of their account that conflicts with other evidence obtained. The PEACE model distinguishes between co-operative and unco-operative interviewees, and indicates the importance of putting all relevant questions to a suspect even if the suspect is not answering questions, in order to try to ensure that adverse inferences may be drawn at trial.
- *Closure* The third and final stage of a police interview requires the officer to consider whether the interview has covered all of the relevant issues, to summarise the interviewee's account, and to explain what is going to happen next.
- *Evaluation* After completion of the interview the police interviewer(s) should consider what information has been obtained in the interview, compare it with other information received and what has to be proved, and consider what further action is to be taken.

7.20    There are five levels of interview training, and most interviewing officers will probably only have completed the first one or two levels. An indication that the interviewing officer is using their PEACE interview training is the use of a written 'Interview Plan' containing prompts for 'Points to prove', 'Defences', 'Purpose [of the interview]' and 'Relevant issues' which is further divided into 'Facts already established' and 'Facts to be determined'. However, while an interviewing officer may emphasise his or her desire to 'seek the truth', nothing can detract from the fact that the officer is seeking evidence for the prosecution.

17  *The case for the prosecution* (note 1 above), at pp57, 61 and 76.
18  Published jointly by ACPO and the National Policing Improvement Agency, and available at www.npia.police.uk/en/docs/National_Investigative_Interviewing_ Strategy_09.pdf. See generally T Williamson (ed) *Investigative interviewing: rights, research, regulation* (Willan, Cullumpton, 2006).

## Police tactics in interview

7.21   The police approach differs in detail from case to case, and from officer to officer, but despite the fact that the PEACE training material encourages officers to approach interviews with an open mind, experience suggests that police officers often do not do so, and may well use tactics designed to obtain a confession. In some police force areas interviewing officers read out, and hand to the suspect, a notice indicating that the suspect is likely to receive a sentence discount if the suspect makes admissions in the police interview (see para 5.140 above). They may also ask questions about the suspect's previous convictions or other misconduct (see paras 4.62 and 5.170 above). Some specific police interview tactics are dealt with in the section on 'Intervening during interviews' at para 7.49 below, but some more general issues are dealt with here.

### *Undermining the lawyer's advice*

7.22   The interviewing officer may try to undermine the status of the lawyer or the lawyer's advice, or the relationship between lawyer and client, particularly if the officer believes that the lawyer has advised the client in a way which the officer sees as contrary to their interests. The interviewing officer may seek to achieve this by simple strategies such as introducing the lawyer to the client, or by ensuring that the officer selects the seating position in the interview room so that there is no eye contact between lawyer and client. The lawyer should be aware of such strategies, and take appropriate action to avoid any adverse effects.

7.23   If the lawyer is an accredited or probationary representative, the police may try to undermine the lawyer's status by referring to that fact in interview. Although accredited and probationary representatives are defined as solicitors for the purposes of the Codes,[19] the significance of this may not be apparent either to the police officer or to the client. The lawyer should explain his or her status in the initial consultation with the client, and this may help to minimise the impact of such a tactic (see para 5.10 above). If it is encountered, the lawyer (or the lawyer's firm) should consider taking the matter up with the chief constable.

7.24   The interviewing officer may try to undermine the lawyer's advice by telling the suspect that he or she is not obliged to accept advice to remain silent. The lawyer should deal with this in the following way:

- Before the interview, warn the client that the interviewing officer may use this tactic, explaining the officer's aim – to make the client lose faith in the legal advice given – and what the lawyer will do if the officer attempts to do so.
- During the interview, if the officer attempts to use this tactic, intervene immediately to inform the officer that: a) should the case go to trial, it will be for the court to decide on the merits of the legal advice given to the client and the client's decision; and b) the court will draw its own conclusions as to the appropriateness of the officer's conduct.

19   Code C para 6.12, and see para 2.132 above.

## Seating arrangements

7.25   The way in which seating is arranged in the interview room may both undermine the status of the lawyer and effectively marginalise the lawyer, so that the suspect 'forgets' that the lawyer is there. In the past some interview rooms had a seat in the corner, behind and out of sight of the suspect, with the label 'solicitor' on it, although this practice appears to have ceased. Ideally, the lawyer should indicate where the lawyer and the client are to sit. The best seating position for the lawyer is next to the client, but placed so that the lawyer can have eye contact with both the client and the interviewing officer. In this way the lawyer can establish his or her presence and be able to observe any non-verbal communication between the officer and the client.

7.26   If the police try to insist on the lawyer sitting in a place which marginalises the lawyer, he or she should consider advising the client not to answer questions until the matter is resolved. It may be advisable for the lawyer to see the client in private, if he or she has not already been warned of this possibility, so that the lawyer can explain what is going on, because it will not necessarily be obvious to the client. Another tactic the lawyer may consider is to sit where requested by the police until the recording device is switched on, and then move to where he or she wishes to sit. It will then be more difficult for the interviewing officer to make an issue of it. There is no reference in Code F (visual recording of interviews) to seating position, but the fact that the interview is being visually recorded should not be used as a reason to prevent the lawyer sitting in an appropriate position.

## 'Phased' or 'managed' disclosure

7.27   The police strategy of phased or managed disclosure, and the suggested pre-interview response of the defence lawyer, is explained at para 4.28 above. In the interview the lawyer should consider asking the interviewing officer:

- whether a phased disclosure strategy is being used or, where this is clear, asking the officer to confirm that the strategy is being used;
- to confirm what information has been disclosed to the suspect or the lawyer;
- to indicate whether the officer has information concerning the alleged offence that the officer has not disclosed;
- to disclose the information that the officer has not yet disclosed;
- to confirm whether the officer intends to introduce into the interview information or allegations that the officer has not disclosed.

This may persuade the interviewing officer to make further disclosure. Even if it does not, it helps to establish evidence of the level of police disclosure made and whether the police are deliberately withholding information, which may assist the accused in any subsequent argument as to inferences from 'silence'.

## The 'no comment' interview

7.28   The lawyer should be prepared for particular challenges if the client is not going to answer police questions. Since the police want confessions, and confessions cannot be obtained if the client will not answer questions, the police may try to step up the pressure on the suspect. Code C, Code H para 12.5 specifically provides that the police do not require a suspect's consent or agreement to be interviewed even if the suspect chooses not to answer questions.[20] Police interview training materials do not now appear to be publicly available, but material that was published at the turn of the century stated that interviewing officers should not be put off by an indication that the suspect will not answer police questions, or by 'no comment' answers. It encouraged officers faced with a suspect who refused to answer questions to continue to ask 'all the relevant questions', bearing in mind that failure to do so may result in a court deciding that no inferences can be drawn. Specifically, it suggested that the interviewing officer might need to ensure that 'the suspect is fully aware of any incriminating evidence which has been disclosed and has not misunderstood its implications'.[21]

7.29    Thus, the police may still proceed with an interview of a suspect who does not intend to answer questions, whether or not a prepared statement has been submitted (see para 5.149). While it may be legitimate in such circumstances for the police to ask some questions, at some point such an interview may become oppressive if its purpose is to break down the suspect so that the suspect speaks against his or her will. Although it may be difficult to gauge the point at which an interview becomes oppressive, the lawyer should certainly intervene if the interviewer goes beyond putting relevant questions, becomes repetitive, or if the client becomes distressed.

7.30    Some police forces use pre-prepared pro-forma to be produced when the interviewing officer is faced with a suspect who is not answering questions. In some cases they are used even to the extent of being inserted into an otherwise handwritten summary of the interview record. Typical of such pro-formas is the suggestion that the officer only wishes to see fair play, to ensure that the truth comes out, and is unbiased. Thus, one such pro-forma contained the following:

> I must outline my position in this enquiry. We have received a complaint of (offence) and it is alleged that you are responsible. My position is one of impartiality. I am here to seek the truth. My job is to gather all the information available in this matter and present it to the Crown Prosecution Service, and it is they who will make the final decision whether or not to prosecute in this matter. Have you any information you can now furnish me with which would ultimately assist the Crown Prosecution Service in making a decision not to prosecute in this matter?[22]

While such statements may lack a certain degree of honesty, they are generally not contrary to PACE or the Codes of Practice. The most effective safeguard is to warn the client of the possible use of such a ploy during the initial consultation (see para 5.184 above).

20  Although para 12.5 goes on to indicate that a suspect cannot be forced to go to an interview room.
21  *A practical guide to investigative interviewing* (Central Police Training and Development Authority (Centrex), 2000), pp61 and 86.
22  Quoted from a pro-forma used at one time by officers in the Avon and Somerset Constabulary.

7.31    One further tactic is to suggest to the suspect that a failure to reply to questions implies that the suspect is guilty. The danger of such a suggestion is not the effect that it might have on magistrates or a jury. Rather, its danger lies in the fact that the suspect may feel forced to say something, or something other than 'no comment'. For this reason, the lawyer should intervene immediately, making it clear that the client is acting on legal advice, or that there are many reasons, consistent with innocence, why a person may remain silent in interview.

7.32    In a case where the police have seized property belonging to the suspect, they may imply that it cannot be returned until its true ownership has been established. This may be an astute tactic, particularly if they know that it is something valued by the suspect. The lawyer should intervene to reassure the client that the matter can be dealt with later, outside the context of the interview. Again, it is less likely to have an adverse impact if the client has received advice from the lawyer on this matter before the police interview begins.

7.33    Another tactic used for this purpose is for the police to try to get the suspect into the 'habit' of talking, for example, by starting the interview by completing the antecedent forms that are usually completed after an interview. The lawyer should try to persuade the officer not to do this by reference to Code C para 11.1A, which provides that an interview is the questioning of the suspect regarding an offence. Questions about antecedents do not relate to an offence. If the officer persists, the lawyer should consider advising their client not to answer the questions. There is, in any event, no obligation on the client to assist the police in completing the antecedent forms.

## The lawyer's objectives in the police interview

7.34    As was suggested at para 1.3 above, defence lawyers need to be clear about their role. This is particularly true with regard to police interviews, not simply in view of their importance, but also because there are various factors that potentially inhibit the lawyer. Not only do interviews take place on police territory and according to a police agenda, but interviews are often highly emotionally charged, with police officers giving clear signals that they are in control and that lawyers are there on sufferance, as long as they 'behave'. In these circumstances, it is helpful for lawyers to have in mind the definition of the lawyer's role set out in Code C Note for Guidance 6D (and Code H NfG 6C) and the objectives set out below, which supplement the general requirement that lawyers must act in the best interests of their clients.

> The solicitor's only role in the police station is to protect and advance the legal rights of their client. On occasions this may require the solicitor to give advice which has the effect of the client avoiding giving evidence which strengthens a prosecution case. The solicitor may intervene in order to seek clarification, challenge an improper question to their client or the manner in which it is put, advise the client not to reply to particular questions, or if they wish to give their client further legal advice (Code C NfG 6D).

> ### The defence lawyer's objectives
> 1) The lawyer is there to ensure that the client does his or her best in interview, whether or not the client is answering questions.
> 2) The lawyer should ensure that an accurate account is kept of the interview, and that the lawyer keeps his or her own record.
> 3) The lawyer must seek to ensure that the police act fairly at all times and observe the requirements of PACE and the Codes of Practice.
> 4) The lawyer must protect the client from unnecessary pressure and distress and, in particular, must protect vulnerable clients.

7.35 Underlying these objectives should be the clear understanding that the courts are likely to regard the lawyer as a sufficient protection for the client so that the lawyer's mere presence will, except perhaps in more extreme cases such as *R v Paris, Abdullahi and Miller*,[23] vitiate the effect of any unfairness or breach of PACE or the Codes by the police. Therefore, lawyers must actively pursue these objectives – otherwise their presence will be of no positive effect and may even harm the interests of the client. In seeking to meet these objectives, the lawyer should have regard to a number of specific matters.[24]

## Ensuring that the police act fairly

7.36 In ensuring that the police act fairly and in accordance with PACE and the Codes, the lawyer must be aware of the specific requirements of Code C relating to interviews, in particular the following.

1) In any period of 24 hours, the suspect must be allowed a continuous period of eight hours' rest, usually at night, free from interviewing or interruption, subject to limited exceptions. The rest period should usually be at night, but account should be taken of when the detainee last slept or rested (Code C, Code H para 12.2).
2) The suspect must be fit to be interviewed, subject to exceptions in cases of urgency (Code C, Code H para 12.3).[25] The custody officer must consider the risks to the detainee's physical and mental state if an interview takes place, the risk that the interview may be considered unreliable by a court, and must also determine what safeguards are needed if an interview is to proceed (see para 5.22 above).
3) The interview should, as far as practicable, take place in an interview room which must be adequately heated, lit and ventilated (Code C, Code H para 12.4), and the suspect must not be required to stand during the interview (Code C, Code H para 12.6).
4) Subject to limited exceptions, there must be breaks in interviewing at recognised meal times (or at other times that take account of when

23 (1993) 97 Cr App R 99, [1994] Crim LR 361, and see para 7.3 above.
24 For a comprehensive account of the lawyer's objectives and appropriate actions in police interviews see E Shepherd *Police station skills for legal advisers: practical reference* (Law Society, London, 2004) ch 14.
25 See *R v Crampton* (1990) 92 Cr App R 369; [1991] Crim LR 277 (fitness to be interviewed of drug addict suffering from withdrawal symptoms).

the suspect last had a meal), and also short breaks for refreshment at intervals of approximately two hours (Code C, Code H para 12.8).[26]

The lawyer must also act promptly to deal with police tactics that are unfair. See 'Intervening during interviews' at para 7.49 below.

## Ensuring that clients do their best in interview

7.37    Where the client does not intend to answer police questions, the lawyer should seek to ensure that this decision is respected. Tactics designed to undermine the decision should be firmly resisted (see para 7.28 above). If the client starts to answer questions, the client should be reminded of his or her right to remain silent and, if necessary, the interview should be interrupted so that a private consultation can take place.

7.38    Where the client has decided to answer police questions, the lawyer should take any necessary action to see that the client's version is coming out, both clearly and in full. There are two aspects to this. First, the lawyer should listen carefully to what is being said so that if it is unclear or ambiguous, the lawyer can intervene to enable the client to clarify his or her position. It is not being suggested that the lawyer should try to take over the questioning, or that the lawyer should answer questions on behalf of the suspect. In fact, to do the latter could justify the lawyer's removal from the interview (see Code C NfG 6D, and para 7.50 below). However, it is legitimate for the lawyer to ask a question, or perhaps to summarise what the lawyer believes the client means to say and to ask the client if that is so. In many cases, such intervention may be accepted, or even welcomed, by the police officer. If the police do object, they should be reminded that Code C para 11.6 and Code H para 11.7 require the officer to allow the suspect an opportunity to give an innocent explanation and that the lawyer is helping to achieve that requirement. The second aspect applies at the end of the interview. If it appears that the officer is preparing to wind up the process, and the lawyer knows that the interview has not covered all the matters that should have been dealt with, the lawyer should ask appropriate questions to elicit the necessary information. It may be that the interview has not adequately dealt with a defence, such as self-defence, which it is important to establish at this stage. If the client is admitting the offence, there may be important mitigating factors that the client has not been given the opportunity of fully explaining, or the client may wish to express regret. For guidance on strategy where a prepared statement has been, or is intended to be, submitted see para 5.149 above.

## Protecting the client

7.39    Finally, the lawyer should take care to protect the client, especially if the client is vulnerable for one reason or another. The specific issues relating to juveniles and mentally disordered and mentally vulnerable suspects are

---

26  See *R v Trussler and another* [1988] Crim LR 446 (failure to allow rest periods); *R v Gopee and Gopee* (1992) 89 LS Gaz 24 (three-hour interview without a break, where suspect had not eaten for four hours before commencement of interview).

dealt with in chapter 11. This section deals with the factors that may make a confession more likely.

## Propensity to confess

7.40 Gudjonsson,[27] and Phillips and Brown,[28] have examined in detail the factors that are associated with confessions. While the factors are complex, and interrelated, some are worthy of particular note:

- Some studies suggest that younger suspects are more likely to confess than older suspects.
- Evidence suggests that suspects confess more readily to certain types of offences, such as property offences and, in particular, sexual offences.
- Suspects with no previous convictions are more likely to confess than those with previous convictions, although possibly those who have confessed before confess more easily.
- Women are significantly more likely to make admissions than men.
- Admission rates vary considerably between police stations.

## False confessions

7.41 Four general categories of false confession have been identified: the 'voluntary false confession', the 'coerced-compliant confession', the 'coerced-internalised confession',[29] and the 'coerced-passive confession'.[30]

7.42 *Voluntary false confessions* occur without any externally imposed pressure or coercion, and may be associated with circumstances where a person attends voluntarily at a police station and tells the police that he or she has committed a particular crime. It is commonly believed that such confessions do not occur, but it is clear that this view is incorrect, although how often they occur is unknown. Gudjonsson gives four reasons why a person might make a voluntary false confession:

1) in order to draw attention to himself or herself, driven by a 'morbid desire for notoriety';
2) a need for punishment because of guilt in relation to a connected or unconnected matter, or because of generalised feelings of guilt;
3) a belief in guilt because of a delusion, often (but not necessarily) associated with a serious psychiatric illness;
4) in order to protect the real culprit.

Eric Shepherd adds a further reason:

5) in order to deter the police from investigating some other, more serious, offence.[31]

---

27 G Gudjonsson *The psychology of interrogations and confession: a handbook* (Wiley, Chichester, 2003).

28 C Phillips and D Brown, *Entry into the criminal justice system: a survey of police arrests and their outcomes, Home Office Research Study* 185 (Home Office, London, 1998), especially p72.

29 Largely based on Gudjonsson's work.

30 Suggested by M McConville et al *The case for the prosecution* (Routledge, London, 1991) p68.

31 E Shepherd *Police station skills for legal advisers: practical reference* (Law Society, London, 2004).

7.43   *Coerced-compliant confessions* result from the nature of the interrogation. While a suspect knows that he or she is not guilty, the suspect confesses as a result of the coercive nature of the questioning coupled with a belief that the suspect will achieve some advantage from confessing. If the suspect thinks of the long-term consequences at all, he or she may believe that the truth will come out later or that the suspect's lawyer will be able to sort it out. The advantages that a suspect may perceive include the following.

1) *Being able to end the interview, or to leave custody, after confessing* Code C para 11.5 provides that unless a suspect directly asks, a police officer must not try to obtain answers to questions by indicating what action the police will take if questions are answered.[32] However, the interviewing officer may suggest, directly or indirectly, that a confession may lead to certain consequences, or encourage the suspect to believe this.

2) *Being able to cope with the pressures of the situation* Such pressures may be many and varied, and may be internal as well as external. A confession is likely to please the interviewer, which in itself will relieve the pressure, but may also bring with it the prospect of more favourable treatment, such as refreshments, a visit or a telephone call. If a client is clearly distressed, the lawyer must consider intervening. This is not always easy, since the police are likely to believe that distress is a sign of guilt, and that it may be a prelude to a confession. However, distress may occur for a number of reasons unconnected with guilt.

3) *Avoidance of being locked up in custody* This may be of particular importance to suspects in certain situations. They may have a job to go to, an appointment to keep, a phobia about being confined in a locked cell, or they may have young children about whose care they are concerned (see para 5.27 above).

7.44   *Coerced-internalised confessions* occur where a suspect believes, or comes to believe, in his or her own guilt, even if only temporarily. Gudjonsson suggests that this is related to two distinct conditions. The first occurs where the suspect has no memory of the incident which, in particular, may result from amnesia or alcohol- or drug-induced memory failure. Typically, the suspect may then think, 'If the police say I did it, I must have done it'.[33] Although generally suspects must not be interviewed if they are unfit through drink or drugs to the extent that they are unable to appreciate the significance of the questions put or their own answers (see para 5.22 above), this kind of internalised confession can occur when the suspect is not under such influence at the time of interview but was, or may have been, at the time of the incident. The second type of coerced-internalised confession occurs where a suspect, while having a clear recollection that he or she did not commit the offence, submits to a manipulative interviewing process which leads the suspect to distrust his or her own recollection.

32  Although where failure by the suspect to co-operate may have an effect on their immediate treatment (eg, where refusal to provide a name and address when charged may lead to further detention), the officer may inform the person of any relevant consequences (Code C para 10.9, Code H para 10.8).

33  For an example see *R v Brady* [2004] EWCA Crim 2230, where an innocent person whose memory was adversely affected by drug addiction admitted to a robbery of which she had no recollection because the police said that they had evidence that she had committed it.

7.45     *Coerced-passive confessions* occur where the interrogation induces a suspect to: 'adopt the *confession form* without necessarily adopting or even *understanding* the substance of what has been accepted or adopted' (original emphasis). An example would be where the interviewing officer persuades a suspect to accept a hypothetical possibility as a fact, eg, 'If you were attacked, you would have used the knife, wouldn't you?'.

## The commencement of the interview

7.46     At the beginning of the interview, the interviewing officer must identify himself or herself (Code C, Code H para 12.7) and the suspect must be cautioned and reminded of the right to legal advice (Code C paras 10.1 and 11.2, Code H paras 10.1 and 11.3). If the lawyer believes that the client does not understand the caution the lawyer should say so (see para 7.6 above). The officer must also put to the suspect any significant statement or silence which occurred before his or her arrival at the police station (Code C, Code H para 11.4, and see para 5.113 above).

7.47     The lawyer should make an opening statement,[34] adapting the following suggested statement to the circumstances.

---

**Defence lawyer's opening statement**

1) My role is to protect and advance my client's legal rights. I will continue to advise my client throughout the interview where this is necessary.
2) I want you to address my client and myself throughout the interview with appropriate formality.
3) [On my advice, my client is intending to answer questions.] or [I am advising my client not to answer questions in this interview.] Please do not try to undermine my client's decision in any way. If you do, I will intervene.[35]
4) So that there is no room for doubt, I will [also] intervene if:
   - my client asks for legal advice;
   - you refer to evidence, or produce evidence, in respect of which you have not given me adequate information or access;
   - you try to put pressure on my client;
   - a break in the interview is necessary.
5) Before the interview, you gave me the following information ...
6) Please tell me:
   - what is the purpose of this interview;
   - whether you have evidence or information relating to the alleged offence that you have not told me about;
   - whether you consider that you have sufficient evidence to charge my client;
   - what you intend to do after the interview has finished.[36]

---

34 Suggested in E Shepherd *Police station skills for legal advisers: practical reference* (Law Society, London, 2004) p260.

35 See paras 5.100 and 5.161 above on the dangers of waiving privilege. Adapt this part of the opening statement as appropriate if insufficient police disclosure has been given to enable sensible advice to be given, or if a statement is to be handed in.

36 See para 5.145 above.

7.48   An opening statement is a useful device for laying down ground rules for the interview and for establishing the fact that the presence of the lawyer is to be an active one. Intervening will be much easier if the interviewing officer has been warned to expect it. It is also useful, where the lawyer suspects that full disclosure has not been given, to ensure that the fact of lack of disclosure is recorded, especially where the police are using a strategy of phased disclosure (see para 7.27 above). In view of the dangers of waiver of privilege, reasons for advice to remain silent should not usually be given (see paras 5.100 and 5.161 above).

## Intervening during interviews

7.49   In this section guidance is given on the powers of the police to exclude lawyers from police interviews and on intervention in police interviews. It is essential that the lawyer takes a careful note of any intervention that he or she makes and the reasons for it. If no intervention is made, the lawyer should make a note to this effect. Such a record may be important in the event of any complaint about the conduct of the lawyer or if the lawyer subsequently has to give evidence concerning the conduct of the interview.

### Power to exclude the lawyer

7.50   Codes of Practice C and H make it clear that a lawyer can only be required to leave an interview if the lawyer's conduct is such that the interviewing officer is unable properly to put questions to the suspect (Code C para 6.9, Code H para 6.10). Code C NfG 6D and Code H NfG 6C indicate that, in carrying out his or her role, the lawyer may intervene in a police interview in order to seek clarification, or to challenge an improper question, or the manner in which it is put, or if the lawyer wishes to give the client further advice. It goes on to provide that the power to exclude the lawyer will only arise if the lawyer's approach or conduct prevents or unreasonably obstructs proper questions being put or the response from being recorded. The examples of misconduct warranting removal given in the Note for Guidance are answering questions on a suspect's behalf or providing written replies for the suspect to quote.[37] Other examples might include conveying the answers to be given by gestures to the client, interrupting to such an extent that the interviewing officer is unable to put questions to the client, or using threatening or offensive words or behaviour. In any event, such behaviour is likely to be counterproductive, even if the police officer is also acting in such a manner. It will be better to 'let the interview record speak for itself' or, if the behaviour is non-verbal and the interview is being audio-recorded or the non-verbal behaviour would not be captured by visual recording (where the interview is being visually recorded), for the lawyer to say something like, 'For the purposes of the recording the officer is standing over my client in a threatening manner'. In most

---

37   This is not a reference to handing in a prepared statement, but drafting answers for the client to quote in response to specific questions.

situations, the lawyer should ask the officer to stop the offending behaviour and, if necessary, should terminate the interview so that the issue can be dealt with outside the context of the interview and so that, if necessary, the custody officer can be involved.

7.51 It can be seen that the lawyer must go a long way in terms of intervening in an interview before it would be legitimate for the police to consider ejecting him or her, and in most circumstances if the lawyer is acting professionally, exclusion could not be appropriate.[38] Representatives face particular difficulty since although once inside the police station there are no additional powers to eject them over and above those relating to solicitors (see para 4.4 above), they are particularly vulnerable to police threats to do so.

7.52 If the police officer is acting in a grossly improper way, or the lawyer feels in danger of losing his or her temper, the lawyer should suggest to the client that the lawyer wishes to advise the client in private, which is always legitimate by virtue of PACE s58(1). In this way, the heat can be taken out of the situation and, if necessary, there will be time for the lawyer to regain composure.

## Procedure for exclusion

7.53 The interviewing officer cannot himself or herself take the decision to remove the lawyer. Code C para 6.10 and Code H para 6.11 provide that before exclusion the officer must consult with a superintendent or above, or an inspector or above if a superintendent is not readily available. It is only that officer who can decide whether or not the interview can continue in the presence of the lawyer and that officer can only take that decision after speaking to the lawyer. Furthermore, Code C NfG 6E and Code H NfG 6D provide that the officer must be in a position to satisfy a court that the decision was properly made and in order to do this, may need personally to witness what is happening. Therefore, if the lawyer believes that his or her conduct has been entirely proper and that it is the interviewing officer who is acting improperly, the lawyer should consider asking the superintendent to sit in on the interview. However, before doing so, the lawyer should check with the client, since the client may object or may want time to calm down.

7.54 If the lawyer is ejected, the suspect must be given an opportunity to consult another lawyer and to have that lawyer present at the resumed interview (Code C para 6.10, Code H para 6.11).

7.55 If such an incident does occur, whether or not the lawyer is ultimately asked to leave, the lawyer should take a careful note of what occurred as soon as possible, for this may be relevant at trial, or at any disciplinary proceedings taken against either the police officer or the lawyer. Code C para 6.11 and Code H para 6.12 require the officer taking the decision to exclude the lawyer to consider reporting the matter to the Law Society and, in the case of a duty solicitor, to the Legal Services Commission. If this is

---

38 But note that PACE s58 grants the right to legal advice to the suspect, as opposed to giving a right to a particular lawyer to give advice (*Rixon and others v Chief Constable of Kent* (2000) *Times* 11 April).

likely, it may be better that the lawyer (or if a representative, the employing solicitor) takes the initiative and reports the matter to these bodies themselves.

## When should the lawyer intervene?

7.56   The opening statement set out at para 7.47 above sets out some of the circumstances in which the lawyer should intervene. Some of these, and some others, are now dealt with in more detail.

### Breach of PACE or the Codes of Practice

7.57   If there is any apparent breach of PACE or the Codes of Practice, then unless the breach is very minor the lawyer should normally intervene. It has been suggested that it may be better to make no comment and to raise the breach at trial in order, for example, to seek the exclusion of damaging statements by the suspect. However, such a strategy is unlikely to be successful. If the suspect confesses or makes admissions as a result, the suspect may feel under pressure to plead guilty. Furthermore, other than in extreme circumstances,[39] it is highly unlikely that a court would exclude evidence obtained in the presence of a lawyer as a result of a breach of PACE or the Codes and of which the lawyer was aware (see para 13.32 below).

7.58   If the interviewing officer gives an incorrect or misleading explanation of the caution, perhaps in response to the client or lawyer indicating that the client does not understand the caution, the lawyer should point out that it is incorrect or misleading (see para 7.6 above). However, the lawyer should not normally attempt to explain it to the client in the police interview. If the interviewing officer fails to administer the caution, this is unlikely to lead to exclusion of evidence of a police interview at which a lawyer was present.

7.59   As an exception to the general rule, if the interviewing officer fails to give the special warning under Code C para 10.11 or Code H para 10.10 in circumstances where inferences may be drawn from failure to account under CJPOA 1994 s36 or s37, the lawyer should not intervene. Failure to give the suspect the information required by CJPOA 1994 s36(1)(c) or s37(1)(c) will mean that inferences could not be drawn under these sections (see para 5.90 above).

### The client starts answering questions

7.60   The tactics employed by the police to try to persuade a suspect to answer questions are dealt with at para 7.28 above. The point to be made here is that if a client who has made a clear decision not to answer questions starts to do so in the police interview, the lawyer should intervene promptly. Even if the client has been carefully advised about the police interview, on commencing it or during the course of it the lawyer may find the pressure to answer too great. Of course, if a client changes his or her mind, the lawyer should not try to prevent the client from doing so, but should ensure

39  See, eg, *R v Paris, Abdullahi and Miller* (1993) 97 Cr App R 99; [1994] Crim LR 361.

that this is a deliberate and informed decision. If the client appears to be about to answer a question, the lawyer should remind the client of his or her decision not to do so. It may be that this will be sufficient, but if not, the lawyer should consider suggesting that the interview be interrupted for the purpose of giving legal advice. The interviewing officer may very well be annoyed by this, but a suspect in this situation is always entitled to receive legal advice (PACE s58(1)).

## Unfair interrogation

7.61   PACE and the Codes provide very little guidance on the question of what may amount to unfair interrogation. Code C and Code H provide rules for the general well-being of the suspect while in the police station, and for the proper treatment of the suspect while in interview (see para 7.36 above), but say nothing of the nature of the interviewing other than to provide that oppression must not be used (Code C para 11.5, Code H para 11.6). PACE s76 provides that a confession is not admissible if (when raised by the defence) the prosecution cannot prove that it was not obtained by oppression or in circumstances likely to render it unreliable. PACE s78 gives a court a discretion to exclude evidence if to admit it would have an adverse effect on the fairness of the proceedings. However, apart from oppression, which is partially defined by PACE s76(8), the sections do not offer any further guidance. Some indication of the courts' approach to unfair interrogation may be obtained from the many cases decided under these two sections (see para 13.28 below).

7.62     There is little agreement about what is and is not acceptable in a police interrogation, other than in respect of behaviour which is clearly oppressive. Fundamental questions remain unanswered, such as how long the police can continue questioning when the suspect is not answering, to what extent the police can continue asking the same or similar questions if they are not getting the answers that they want, to what extent the interviewing officer can raise his or her voice and use bad language, whether the police can legitimately seek to direct the suspect in terms of where the suspect sits, who the suspect looks at, etc, and to what extent the police can use tricks and subterfuge (see para 7.68 below). The lawyer must, therefore, intervene using as his or her guide the professional obligation to act in a client's best interests. The following account of unfair forms of interrogation is offered as guidance. A court would not necessarily exclude evidence obtained as a result of such forms of interrogation nor, indeed, conclude that they are unfair. In view of this, intervention by the lawyer is even more important.

7.63     Unfair interrogation may take a number of forms. First, it may be that a *specific question* is unfair because, for example, it has been put in a confusing or an ambiguous way. Second, the *form of the question* may be unfair because, for example, it is a leading question. Third, the *style of the questioning* may be unfair because, for example, it is bombastic and bullying. The lawyer must be prepared to deal with each kind of unfairness. Failure to do so may result in damaging admissions being made that are likely to be admitted at trial however unfair the questioning was. If the lawyer does intervene, the lawyer must consider the possible impact of a refusal to answer the question in view of CJPOA 1994 ss34, 36 and 37 (see para 5.60 above), and must keep a careful note of the advice given and the reasons for that advice, since it may become relevant at trial.

## Unfair questions

7.64   Specific questions may be unfair for a number of reasons.

1) *Multiple questions* These are questions that consist of a number of questions rolled into one. They are potentially misleading because an answer intended to be an answer to one part of the question may, at the time or subsequently, be taken to be an answer to another part of the question. For example, the answer 'yes' to the question, 'You had the knife on you to use in case there was any trouble. You took the knife out with you when you left your house, didn't you?' may be intended by the suspect to relate to the second question but may be interpreted as an answer to the first.

2) *Ambiguous questions* These are questions that can have more than one meaning. The danger lies in the fact that an answer may be based on one meaning, but be taken by others to be based on another meaning. This may occur particularly where the police officer is using a word or phrase that is a legal term, but which is not necessarily understood as such by the suspect. The question 'Did you know it is wrong to steal?' may, in certain circumstances, be ambiguous because it confuses the distinction between taking something and stealing it, and because an affirmative answer may be taken to imply an acceptance by the suspect that it correctly describes their conduct.

3) *Irrelevant questions* An irrelevant question is one that has no logical connection with the offence for which the suspect has been arrested and detained. While an irrelevant question may not, in itself, be unfair or prejudicial, it may fit within a pattern of questioning that is. For example, questions about family or friends may be asked in order to try to get the suspect into the 'habit' of answering questions. They may be used to lull the unwary suspect into a false sense of security, and to break down adversarial barriers. While the lawyer may feel that a degree of latitude is acceptable, the lawyer should be wary of the purpose of such questions and intervene if necessary. If the officer objects to such intervention, it should be pointed out that Code C para 11.1A provides that an interview is the: 'questioning of a person regarding his involvement or suspected involvement in a criminal offence or offences'. Irrelevant questions, it can be argued, do not relate to involvement in an offence. Questions about previous convictions or other misconduct may, depending on the circumstances – including the nature of the offence and the nature of the questions put – be regarded as irrelevant. For guidance on questioning about bad character see paras 4.62 and 5.170 above.

4) *Questions concerning other offences* One particular form of irrelevant question is that relating to offences other than that for which the suspect has been arrested and detained. It may be that the suspect wants to admit to other offences so that they can be taken into consideration

when the matter comes to court. In this case, there will be no objection to such a question. However, questions about other offences may be introduced for the purpose of seeing whether the suspect will admit to them, even though the police have no evidence of involvement. They may also be asked in order to put pressure on the suspect. If the suspect believes that the police want to question the suspect about offences that are more serious or more extensive than those for which the suspect has been arrested, the suspect may confess to the offence(s) for which he or she has been arrested in order to 'take the heat off' and to lead the police away from pursuing the other matters.

The Codes of Practice do not specifically prevent questions about offences for which the suspect is not under arrest. Intervention by the lawyer will often lead to the response, 'This is my interview, and I'll ask what questions I like'. However, PACE s31 provides that where a person has been arrested and detained, if it appears that the person would be liable to arrest for some other offence on release, the person must also be arrested for that offence. Therefore, if the officer begins to ask questions about an offence for which the suspect is not under arrest, the lawyer should ask whether the officer intends to arrest the suspect under PACE s31. If the answer is yes, then once that arrest has taken place, questioning about that offence will be legitimate.[40] However, if there is no intention to arrest, presumably this will be because the officer does not have reasonable grounds for suspecting commission of the offence by the suspect. This being the case, further questioning about such an offence should be resisted. If the officer persists, the suspect should be advised not to answer such questions.

5) *Hypothetical questions* A hypothetical question may be asked by the interviewing officer in order to try to establish a particular mental state, or to trap a suspect into accepting and responding to evidence that may not exist. With regard to the former, a suspect found with a knife in a public place might be asked, 'What would you have done if you were attacked?', in order to show that the suspect intended to use the knife to cause injury. In relation to the latter, a suspect arrested for burglary may be asked, 'What would you say if the fingerprints found at the scene of the burglary turned out to be yours?'. In this situation, the lawyer should ask whether the police are in possession of such evidence before the client answers. It has been held that hypothetical questions, of the first type at least, are permissible.[41] Nevertheless, the dangers of a suspect answering a hypothetical question may be such that the suspect should be advised not to answer.

6) *Questions concerning co-suspects* Questions concerning others arrested in connection with the same offence may be of two types. The interviewing officer may ask about the involvement in the alleged offence of the other person(s) arrested, or the officer may ask the suspect to comment on what other co-suspects have said. In either case, it should

---

40  However, the lawyer will usually wish to terminate the interview in order to obtain more information from the officer about the alleged offence(s) and to advise the client before recommencing the interview.

41  *R v Stringer* [2008] EWCA Crim 1222.

be remembered that evidence implicating a co-defendant contained in a confession is not admissible at trial as evidence against the co-defendant (see paras 4.33 and 5.53 above).

With regard to questions concerning the involvement of a co-suspect, if the suspect is answering questions in interview, the suspect will have to decide whether to answer such questions. In many cases, a suspect will not wish to implicate a co-suspect, either because of some perceived obligation towards that person or through fear. The suspect may require advice about the advantages of implicating a co-suspect, particularly if that person is more culpable. On the other hand, an over-readiness to blame another for the commission of an offence may also have disadvantages.

Care should be taken where the police ask the suspect to comment on a statement or record of interview of a co-suspect. While it is not prohibited by Code C, the lawyer should consider why it is being done. In a case where the suspect is denying the offence, or is not answering questions, the production of the record of an interview with a co-suspect may be designed to secure a confession, particularly if the co-suspect has clearly implicated the suspect. If the interview record shows that the co-suspect has implicated the suspect, while exonerating themselves, it may be produced in the hope that the suspect will at least do the same. Such differences may then be exploited further so that either or both suspects may be led to confess, or at least to make damaging admissions.

While it would seem that the lawyer cannot object to the introduction into the interview of an interview record of another suspect, the lawyer should ask to see it and it may be advisable for the lawyer to advise the suspect in private on how to respond before the interview proceeds further.

7) *Questions based on dubious or non-existent evidence* Questions may be based, either expressly or impliedly, on evidence that does not in fact exist. This may involve deliberate misrepresentation by the police, or may be inadvertent, as where the officer himself or herself has been misinformed about the existence of evidence. In *R v Mason*[42] a confession obtained in the presence of a solicitor after the police falsely informed the suspect that his fingerprint was found on a piece of a bottle used to cause a fire, was subsequently ruled to be inadmissible.[43] This is probably one of the few situations where evidence obtained in breach of PACE or the Codes, or as a result of other misconduct, is likely to be excluded despite the fact that it occurred in the presence of the lawyer. The fact that evidence does not exist is unlikely to be known to the lawyer at the time. A lawyer should certainly resist any attempt to solicit

---

42  [1987] 3 All ER 481, [1987] Crim LR 757.

43  However, the fact that the lawyer was also deceived is likely to have been an important factor. In *R v Maclean and Kosten* [1993] Crim LR 687, it was noted by the Court of Appeal that not every trick will result in exclusion of evidence, although in *R v Imran and Hussain* [1997] Crim LR 754, the Court of Appeal held that there was a duty on the police not to actively mislead a suspect. See also *R v Christou and Wright* (1992) 95 Cr App R 264, *R v Woodall* [1989] Crim LR 228 and *R v Beales* [1991] Crim LR 118.

co-operation in a police deception of a suspect. If the lawyer does have any suspicion about the existence of evidence implied by a question, the lawyer should raise this with the officer before the suspect answers it and, if appropriate, ask to see the evidence. In due course, the lawyer should check whether evidence supposedly in existence at the time of the interview is subsequently forthcoming at trial.

Exaggeration of the strength of evidence is probably more likely than misrepresentation of its existence.[44] The suspect may be told, for example, that there are several witnesses who have identified the suspect, when in fact what they have done is to give a description which may (or may not) fit the suspect. Any representation by the police about the existence of evidence should be treated with caution. If appropriate, the lawyer should question the officer about the precise nature of the evidence, and ask to see it, before the suspect answers the question in interview.

8) *Questions that amount to an inducement to confess* Interviewing officers should not ask questions that are designed, or are likely, to have the effect of inducing the suspect to confess by indicating what may or may not happen if the suspect answers a question or questions, or fails to do so. The police must not 'indicate, except in answer to a direct question, what action will be taken on the part of the police if the person being interviewed answers questions, makes a statement or refuses to do either' (Code C para 11.5, Code H para 11.6). A confession obtained by inducement should be excluded under PACE s76(2)(b), but exclusion is less likely if obtained in the presence of a lawyer (see para 13.37 below). One form of inducement that the courts may accept as legitimate, however, is an indication that an admission will result in a sentence discount (see para 5.140 above).

During the police interview, therefore, the lawyer should be aware of any improper inducement made and should intervene if necessary. References by the interviewing officer to bail, to the nature of charges that may be forthcoming, to the possibility of a caution[45] or to the fact that others may be arrested and interviewed, should all be watched out for.[46] As noted above, Codes C and H provide that if the suspect does ask the interviewing officer what action will be taken in the event of the suspect answering questions, making a statement or refusing to do either, then the officer may inform the suspect what action the police propose to take, provided that such action is itself proper. If the suspect does ask a specific question, the lawyer should listen carefully to the answer given and, if necessary, should intervene to correct any false impression given. It may even be advisable to intervene before the

---

44  For an account of how and why this happens, see E Shepherd 'Ethical Interviewing' (1991) 7 *Policing* 1 pp42–60.

45  In *R v Commissioner of Police for the Metropolis ex p U; R v Durham Constabulary ex p R* [2003] EWHC 2486 (Ch) it was held that the offer of a caution amounted to an unlawful inducement. This decision was overturned by the House of Lords in *R (on app of R) v Durham Constabulary and another* [2005] UKHL 21; [2005] 1 WLR 1184; [2005] 2 All ER 369, but that part of the decision still stands.

46  Even a reference to interviewing further witnesses has been held to be an improper inducement (*R v Howden-Simpson* [1991] Crim LR 49).

officer answers and to tell the suspect that the lawyer will advise about this when the interview has been completed.

An improper inducement does not necessarily involve the police in stating what action they intend to take. It may be more subtly, and perhaps unintentionally, offered by an expression of concern. In one instance, for example, a young single parent had been arrested and her baby left with a relative. During the course of the interview the woman became very distressed and the interviewing officer repeatedly asked her if she was worried about her baby and what she was going to do with her baby if she was kept in police custody for any length of time. In the circumstances, there was clearly a risk that such questions would induce the suspect to confess, and the solicitor rightly intervened. If the officer had really been concerned, it would have been appropriate to stop the interview or to release the suspect on bail so that she could make suitable arrangements for her child (see para 5.27 above).

It should be remembered that inducements may be made outside of the context of the interview and at a time when the lawyer is not present.[47] The offer of bail, food and cigarettes, or social visits may all be made, directly or indirectly, conditional on 'co-operation', and the lawyer should be conscious of this when advising the client. It may even be that there has been no specific attempt by the police to offer such an inducement. It is commonly believed (and is often true) that co-operation with the police, particularly in the form of a confession, will ease the passage through the period of detention and will, in its turn, induce the police to look more favourably on the suspect when it comes to the issue of bail.

## The form of questions

7.65   Quite apart from the unfairness of particular questions, the form or structure of a question or series of questions may make it more likely that the suspect answers them in the way the police want. While all the types of question specified below are permitted under PACE and the Codes of Practice, the lawyer should be aware of their potential for unfairness, and should be ready to intervene if necessary.

7.66   McConville et al identified four forms of question which 'overtly manipulate the suspect's decision-making'.[48]

1) *Leading questions* These are questions that suggest the desired answer. An example would be, 'You did intend to steal the watch, didn't you?'. While such questions are prohibited during evidence-in-chief in a trial, they are permissible during an interrogation. However, they may lead to unfairness precisely because they lead to the suspect giving a particular answer, while deterring other answers. Police training materials have strongly suggested that interviewers should avoid using leading questions, except when summarising or confirming information that has already been given, because of the danger of misleading the suspect

---

47   See M McConville et al *The case for the prosecution* (Routledge, London, 1991) p60.
48   M McConville et al *The case for the prosecution* (Routledge, London, 1991) p69.

or planting a false memory.[49] They are particularly dangerous when questioning young children and those who are mentally vulnerable.[50]

2) *Statement questions* These are statements put in the form of a question which the suspect is invited to adopt or defied to contradict. An example would be, 'What you did is, you went into town to meet your girlfriend, saw the car, noticed the expensive stereo, and thought you'd have it out quick. The owner then came along, so you hit him and ran off. That's right, isn't it?'. As with leading questions, it is quite clear what answer is wanted, and it discourages other answers or explanations.

3) *Legal-closure questions* These questions appear to invite the suspect to give information but, unknown to the suspect, have the effect of forcing that information into a legally significant category. This commonly occurs with an offence like theft, where the suspect admits taking the item but without accepting that the suspect was acting dishonestly or that he or she intended to deprive the owner permanently. The police response may well then be, 'So what you are saying is that you stole the item?'. While appearing simply to confirm what the suspect has said, it introduces the legal concept of theft, which does not accord with a simple taking of goods. In this way, the suspect is led into accepting that he or she stole the item. The lawyer should be particularly alert when the interviewing officer appears to re-state what has been said, and should object if the re-statement does not accurately reflect what the suspect said.[51]

4) *Imperfect syllogistic questions* Despite the name, the concept is relatively simple. This form of question seeks to persuade the suspect to accept a disputed fact (which is likely to be damaging to them) by persuading them that it logically follows from another fact or facts that have been accepted by the suspect. It may be illustrated by the following exchange.

> Officer:  You accept that you had been drinking, don't you?
> Suspect: Yes.
> Officer:  And that you sat down next to the shop?
> Suspect: Yes.
> Officer:  And you have said that you didn't see anyone else?
> Suspect: Yes.
> Officer:  And that the shop window was broken when you woke up?
> Suspect: Yes.
> Officer:  So it must have been you that smashed it, mustn't it?

Of course, it does not logically follow that the suspect smashed the window, but the suspect may be led in this way into accepting that he or she did. This form of questioning may be particularly effective from the police point of view where the suspect's recollection is unclear

---

49 *A practical guide to investigative interviewing* (Central Police Training and Development Authority (Centrex), 2000), p32.

50 In *R (M) v (1) Leicester Constabulary (2) CPS* [2009] EWHC 3640 (Admin) the court expressed concern about the use of leading questions during the interview of a juvenile, making the point that questions put to juveniles should be short and clear.

51 The PEACE interview framework encourages interviewing officers to summarise what a suspect has said in the interview (see para 7.19 above).

(perhaps through drink or drugs), or where for other reasons the suspect is susceptible to confession, albeit false. Again, the lawyer should be alert to the dangers of this form of question, and should intervene if necessary.

## Style of questioning

7.67  The way in which questioning is conducted may have a significant impact on the outcome, and may have the effect of inducing an unwilling suspect to talk, or to make a false confession. Indeed, the style of questioning may specifically result from the officer's intention to produce such an effect. It must be remembered that the officer will frequently be working from an assumption that the suspect is guilty.

1) *Domineering and bullying questioning* There is plenty of evidence, both anecdotal and from research, that certain officers most of the time, and many officers some of the time, will resort to a style of questioning that is domineering, insulting, offensive, threatening or bullying.[52] This is contrary to *The principles of investigative interviewing*, published by the Association of Chief Police Officers (ACPO) and the National Policing Improvement Agency in 2007,[53] which are set out below.

---

**The principles of investigative interviewing**

i.   The aim of investigative interviewing is to obtain accurate and reliable accounts from victims, witnesses or suspects about matters under police investigation.

ii.  Investigators must act fairly when questioning victims, witnesses or suspects. Vulnerable people must be treated with particular consideration at all times.

iii. Investigative interviewing should be approached with an investigative mindset. Accounts obtained from the person who is being interviewed should always be tested against what the interviewer already knows or what can reasonably be established.

iv.  When conducting an interview, investigators are free to ask a wide range of questions in order to obtain material which may assist an investigation.

v.   Investigators should recognise the positive impact of an early admission in the context of the criminal justice system.

vi.  Investigators are not bound to accept the first answer given. Questioning is not unfair merely because it is persistent.

vii. Even when the right to silence is exercised by a suspect, investigators have a responsibility to put questions to them.

---

52  See, eg, *R v Paris, Abdullahi and Miller* (1992) 97 Cr App R 99; [1994] Crim LR 361, and M McConville et al *The case for the prosecution* (Routledge, London, 1991) p66. For an account of an 'unpleasant, hectoring and abusive' interview conducted by a detective inspector, see M McConville 'Videotaping interrogations: police behaviour on and off camera' [1992] Crim LR 532–548, especially pp542–544.

53  Available at www.npia.police.uk/en/docs/National_Investigative_Interviewing_Strategy_09.pdf.

Two important questions for the defence lawyer are, how far is an interviewing officer legally permitted to go, and when and how should the lawyer intervene. Code C para 11.5 and Code H para 11.6 provide that, 'No police officer may try to obtain answers to questions or to elicit a statement by the use of oppression'. This reflects PACE s76, which provides that a confession is inadmissible in evidence if the prosecution cannot prove that it was not obtained by oppression (PACE s76(2)(a)). 'Oppression' is defined to include torture, inhuman or degrading treatment, and the use or threat of violence (whether or not amounting to torture) (PACE s76(8)). Confession evidence is also inadmissible unless the prosecution can prove that it was not obtained in circumstances likely to render it unreliable (PACE s76(2)(b)). Furthermore, courts have a discretion under PACE s78 to exclude prosecution evidence if, having regard to all the circumstances including the circumstances in which it was obtained, admitting the evidence would have such an adverse effect on the fairness of the proceedings that the court ought not to admit it. While the Court of Appeal has refrained from laying down rules, it is possible to derive some guidance on the interpretation of these provisions from decided cases. 'Oppression' was defined by the Court of Appeal in *R v Fulling*[54] as 'the exercise of authority or power in a burdensome, harsh or wrongful manner; unjust or cruel treatment of subjects, inferiors, etc, the imposition of unreasonable or unjust burdens'. In a later case, evidence of a confession was rejected where it was obtained in an interview in which the suspect was 'hectored and bullied from first to last'.[55] However, in *R v Emmerson*[56] the Court of Appeal held that questioning that was rude and discourteous, with a raised voice and some bad language, and that gave the impression of impatience and irritation, was not oppressive. Useful guidance, derived from the Crown Court case of *R v West*[57] was given in *A practical guide to investigative interviewing*.[58] For example, an interviewing officer must never use abusive language and should never raise his or her voice or shout. While the officer may point out that the suspect is telling lies, it might be oppressive if this is repeated or shouted. Furthermore, if a suspect breaks down in the course of a police interview the suspect should be offered a break in the interview, although if: 'the officer suspects that it is a mere sham he should put it specifically to the suspect to give him an opportunity to answer that'.

Bullying or offensive behaviour by the interviewing officer is less likely to be regarded as amounting to oppression, and is less likely to lead to exclusion of evidence, if it was conducted in the presence of a lawyer.[59] This does not mean, of course, that such behaviour will not have

54  [1987] 2 All ER 65; (1987) 85 Cr App R 136; [1987] Crim LR 492.
55  *R v Beales* [1991] Crim LR 118.
56  (1991) 92 Cr App R 284.
57  (1988) unreported.
58  *A practical guide to investigative interviewing* (Central Police Training and Development Authority (Centrex), 2000), p146.
59  See *R v Dunn* (1990) 91 Cr App R 237; [1990] Crim LR 572 (and see discussion at para 13.32 below); but contrast *R v Paris, Abdullahi and Miller* (1992) 97 Cr App R 99; [1994] Crim LR 361.

an adverse impact on the suspect simply because a lawyer is present. Indeed, its impact may be even greater if the lawyer is seen by the suspect to be intimidated himself or herself, or is thought to be colluding with or indifferent towards such behaviour. The lawyer should normally intervene at an early stage, although the point of intervention requires careful judgment. Some suspects will not be unduly concerned about bad language or raised voices, whereas others will be intimidated by it. Generally, however, intervention should be sooner rather than later. Oppressive and similar forms of conduct can only be designed to obtain a confession. The officer should be reminded that Code C and Code H, and the *Principles of investigative interviewing*, require a police officer to act fairly, and that the stated purpose of an interview is to: 'obtain accurate and reliable accounts from ... suspects', not a confession. Furthermore, if the suspect is vulnerable for any reason, the suspect must be treated with 'particular consideration at all times'. If the officer persists with such behaviour, the lawyer should consider interrupting the interview in order to advise the client in private and allow time for tempers to cool. If, however, the behaviour persists the lawyer should consider approaching the custody officer, or a more senior officer, with a view to another officer taking over the interview. The lawyer should also consider advising the client about lodging a formal complaint.

2) *Failure to allow exculpatory statements* A bullying or threatening style is not the only style of questioning that can lead to unfairness. The officer may encourage statements by the suspect that are harmful to the suspect's interests, but move on quickly whenever the suspect tries to explain his or her behaviour in terms that may provide a defence or important mitigation. If this is the case, the lawyer should ensure that the suspect has the opportunity to bring out such issues, either at the time or before the end of the interview.

3) *Topic hopping* This is a more generalised form of the kind of questioning described in 2) above. As *A practical guide to investigative interviewing* recognised,[60] changing topics before a suspect has had the chance to think about his or her response or say all that the suspect would wish to say is distracting and may cause confusion.

4) *Maximising and minimising consequences* This style of questioning is particularly likely where the suspect is not answering questions, but the officer believes that the suspect may be persuaded to speak. It consists of maximising the advantages and minimising the disadvantages of a confession. The officer may seek to persuade the suspect that confessing could be in the suspect's interests, and/or that the consequences of confessing may not be as bad as the suspect believes. This tactic may contravene Code C para 11.5 or Code H para 11.6, which provide that interviewing officers must not indicate what action the police will take if the person answers questions or gives a statement. Even if it does not, it may still amount to an improper inducement. The lawyer should intervene if this is the case, or if what is said by the officer in any way misrepresents the truth.

---

60 *A practical guide to investigative interviewing* (Central Police Training and Development Authority (Centrex), 2000) p32.

# The end of the interview

7.68 Two separate, but interrelated, issues are involved here. First, at what stage should police interviewing cease? Second, what should the lawyer do at the conclusion of any police interview? A further question, of whether a suspect can be interviewed after charge, is dealt with at para 10.28 below.

## At what stage should interviewing cease?

7.69 In the case of most suspects, there is only one police interview.[61] Code C para 11.6 (and Code H para 11.7) sets out the circumstances in which an interview, and interviewing, must stop, but the following provisions are of general relevance.

- In any period of 24 hours, a detained person must be allowed a continuous period of at least eight hours for rest, free from questioning, travel, etc. The rest period should usually be at night, but account must be taken of when the suspect last slept or rested (Code C, Code H para 12.2).
- There must be breaks in interviewing at recognised meal times, and also short breaks for refreshment at intervals of approximately two hours, subject to exceptions if the break would involve a risk of harm to others or damage to property, or would unnecessarily delay the suspect's release from custody, or would otherwise prejudice the outcome of the investigation (Code C, Code H para 12.8).
- Suspects must not be interviewed if the custody officer considers that an interview would cause significant harm to the detainee's physical or mental state (Code C, Code H para 12.3, and see para 5.22 above). Therefore, an interview should cease if the suspect becomes unfit during the course of an interview.

7.70 Code C and Code H give the police a significant degree of latitude in terms of determining when interviewing should cease. Code C para 11.6 and Code H para 11.7 provide that interviewing must stop when:

a) *The officer in charge of the investigation is satisfied that all the questions the officer considers relevant to obtaining accurate and reliable information about the offence have been put to the suspect* The Code provides that this includes allowing the suspect an opportunity to give an innocent explanation, and for the interviewer to test the accuracy and reliability of the explanation by asking further questions. Whether or not the suspect is answering questions, this provision is intended to enable the interviewer to continue asking questions until the interviewer has asked all questions that he or she believes to be relevant (although see para 7.72 below). If the suspect puts forward an explanation, it enables the officer to ask questions in order to test that explanation, for example, by reference to other evidence or by reference to what else the suspect

---

61 Research from the 1990s shows that there is more than one interview in only one case in ten. See T Bucke and D Brown *In police custody: police powers and suspects' rights under the revised PACE Codes of Practice, Home Office Research Study* 174 (Home Office, London, 1997), at p31.

has said. If the suspect is not answering questions, the provision is designed to enable the interviewer to ask all relevant questions, which is likely to assist in persuading a court in a subsequent trial that the accused did not act reasonably in failing to mention a fact relied upon in the accused's defence, an explanation for which should have been prompted by the questions asked (see para 5.84 above).

b) *The officer in charge of the investigation has taken account of any other available evidence* This appears to be designed to enable the police to have regard to other evidence that they have secured, or to seek other evidence (for example, in response to any explanation provided or assertion made by the suspect in interview), before concluding interviewing.

c) *The officer in charge of the investigation, or in the case of a detained suspect, the custody officer, reasonably believes there is sufficient evidence to provide a realistic prospect of conviction for the offence in respect of which the suspect is being interviewed* A 'realistic prospect of conviction' reflects the evidential sufficiency test in the Code for Crown Prosecutors, which makes clear that the test involves consideration of what the defence case may be and how it is likely to affect the prosecution case. It further states that the test is an objective one: is a jury or court, properly directed in accordance with the law, more likely than not to convict the defendant of the alleged charge?

7.71 The structure of Code C para 11.6 and Code H para 11.7 is such that interviewing does not have to cease until all three conditions are satisfied. Thus, even if the interviewing officer is satisfied that that there is a realistic prospect of conviction, it permits interviewing to continue if the officer is not satisfied that all relevant questions have been asked, or that not all available evidence has been taken into account. However, the effect of the Code provisions is less straightforward than might appear for a number of reasons:

1) If it can be established that the police intend to prosecute whatever further questions are put, or whatever the suspect might say in interview, it can be argued that a decision regarding prosecution should be made without further interviewing (see para 5.145 above).

2) Code C para 16.1 provides that when the officer in charge of the investigation reasonably believes there is sufficient evidence to provide a realistic prospect of conviction, the officer must inform the custody officer without delay, who must then decide whether to charge the detainee. This suggests that the decisive factor in determining whether interviewing should cease is the sufficiency of the evidence, and that once the officer is satisfied that it provides a realistic prospect of conviction, interviewing must cease even if the officer is not satisfied that all relevant questions have been put to the suspect or that all available evidence has been taken into account.

3) There is a contradiction between Code C paras 11.6 and 16.1 in that the latter states that it is the officer in charge of the investigation who must determine whether the evidence is such that there is a realistic prospect of conviction, whereas the former provides that in the case of a detained suspect this decision is for the custody officer. It is probable that the intention was to place initial responsibility on the officer in

charge of the investigation to decide whether the realistic prospect of conviction test is satisfied, in which case the custody officer should be informed who must then consider whether he or she is also so satisfied. However, the current version of Code C is unclear in this respect, but given the statutory responsibility placed on custody officers by PACE s37, a charge decision must be made if the custody officer is satisfied that there is a realistic prospect of conviction.

4) There is arguably a conflict between Code C para 11.6 and PACE s37(7). The latter provides that if the custody officer determines that the officer has before him or her sufficient evidence to charge the person arrested with the offence for which the person was arrested, a decision about charge must be made. 'Sufficient evidence to charge' is not defined in PACE, but the *Director's guidance on charging* provides that the applicable standard is normally sufficient evidence to provide a realistic prospect of conviction. There is nothing in either PACE s37(7) or the *Director's guidance* that permits the police to carry on questioning after the 'sufficient evidence to charge' threshold has been met (see para 10.6 below).

7.72   In practice, it is often difficult for the lawyer to judge whether the stage has been reached when interviewing should cease since the lawyer will often not be fully aware of the evidence in the possession of the police. The lawyer may, in any event, be content for an interview to proceed in circumstances where it should stop if the client is answering questions in order to establish the client's defence or in order to lay the grounds for an effective mitigation. However, if the lawyer is of the view that continued interviewing is not in the client's best interests – for example, because the client is in danger of adversely affecting his or her position by what the client says or because continued interviewing may make adverse inferences more likely – the lawyer should carefully consider whether the conditions for bringing interviewing to an end are satisfied and to make appropriate representations. If the lawyer believes that there is sufficient evidence to charge, the lawyer should consider interrupting the interview and making representations to the custody officer by reference to the factors set out in para 7.71 above.

7.73   Where a suspect has been arrested and detained for more than one offence, Code C para 16.1 provides that it is permissible for the interviewing officer to delay taking the suspect before the custody officer until the conditions have been met in respect of all of the offences. As Professor Zander has pointed out, Code C para 16.1 cannot be reconciled with PACE s37(7) and, in his view, the former may be ultra vires.[62] While a custody officer, and still less an interviewing officer, is unlikely to be impressed by argument about the ultra vires nature of Code C para 16.1, the lawyer could seek to bring interviewing to an end by persuading the custody officer that his or her duty to charge or otherwise under PACE s37(7) has arisen and cannot be delayed. If interviewing does continue beyond the time when it should cease, it will be possible to argue that any resulting confession or other evidence adverse to the suspect should be excluded

62  M Zander *The Police and Criminal Evidence Act 1984* (5th edn, Sweet & Maxwell, London, 2005), at 150.

at trial under PACE s76 or s78 (see para 13.28 below). Furthermore, the police may be liable for false imprisonment if the detention goes beyond that permitted by PACE (see para 13.25 below).

## What should the lawyer do at the end of the interview?

7.74  At the end of a police interview the lawyer should:

1) Ensure that the recording and checking requirements have been complied with (see paras 7.13 and 7.17 above).

2) Take a careful note of the time that the interview ended, the time that the various parties left the interview room, and the content of any conversation during this period. This would help to prevent any allegation by the police that the suspect confessed after the tape was turned off from being accepted by a court.[63]

3) Ask the officer how the investigation is to proceed after the interview. The information is necessary in order to enable the lawyer to advise the suspect on the future course of events, and it is normally helpful to obtain this information in the presence of the suspect.

4) Consider whether to ask the police to pursue any particular lines of enquiry. If the suspect has put forward a defence in the police interview, or the lawyer is aware that the client has a defence that is capable of further investigation by the police, the lawyer should consider asking the officer in the case what action the officer intends to take to investigate these and, where appropriate, to press the officer to undertake such investigation. If the officer appears reluctant to do so, the officer should be reminded of the Code of Practice issued under Criminal Procedure and Investigations Act 1996 s23, para 3.4 of which provides that in conducting an investigation the 'investigator should pursue all reasonable lines of enquiry, whether these point towards or away from the suspect'. The lawyer should keep a careful note of any such representations since they may be relevant at trial.

5) Arrange to speak to the client in private and:
   - Evaluate the interview, in particular, whether the point has been reached when the police should make a decision about charge, and whether the client should request a further police interview. This may be necessary, for example, in order to deal with any matters missed in the interview or, where the client did not answer questions and the interview was used to obtain information about the police case, where it is now advisable to answer questions. Consideration should also be given to whether it is appropriate to submit a written statement, or a supplementary statement (see para 5.149 above).
   - Advise on the likely course of the investigation and detention. It is important that the suspect has as accurate an idea as possible about the likely course of the remaining period of detention in order to allay any unjustified fears and to minimise risks of the suspect

---

63  Which occurred in *R v Dunn* (1990) 91 Cr App R 237; [1990] Crim LR 572; and see para 13.32 below.

becoming vulnerable to pressure. In particular, if the suspect has denied the offence in interview or made a 'no comment' interview, the suspect should be warned that the police may visit him or her in the absence of the lawyer in order to persuade the suspect to talk or confess. The importance of giving this warning is demonstrated by the facts of and decision in *R v Williams*.[64] In this case, the defendant was arrested for burglary and was interviewed in the presence of his lawyer, making no admissions. After the lawyer left the police station, the interviewing officers paid an hour-long 'social visit' to the suspect in the cells. Subsequently, he agreed to be interviewed in the absence of his lawyer and confessed. The Court of Appeal upheld the conviction, finding that there had been no breach of PACE. In appropriate cases the client should also be warned of the possibility that he or she may be the subject of covert surveillance.

- Consider, in the context of CJPOA 1994 s34 what, if anything, should be said at the time of charge, or whether a statement should be handed in at the time of charge (see paras 5.73 and 5.149 above).
- Take instructions on and give advice in respect of bail without or following charge (see paras 10.73 and 10.92 below).
- Remind the suspect that he or she has a right under PACE s58 to legal advice at any time during the period of detention, and tell the suspect how to exercise that right.

64  (1992) *Times* 6 February.

# CHAPTER 8

# Identification procedures

*continued*

# Introduction

8.1 This chapter deals with visual identification and recognition procedures, and also with voice identification. Other methods of identification such as fingerprints, footwear impressions, body samples, and examination to establish identity, are dealt with in chapter 6. The current version of Code D makes a fundamental distinction between the procedures to be followed in respect of visual identification by eye-witnesses and those to be followed in cases of recognition. However, this distinction is not satisfactory, and may cause some confusion as to the circumstances in which they apply (see para 8.5 below).There is no code covering procedures to be followed in respect of voice identification, but they are dealt with in this chapter because there is limited reference to voice identification in Code D.

8.2 It has long been recognised by the courts that visual identification evidence is problematic, and may be unreliable, even where a witness honestly believes that the he or she has made a correct identification. As a result, not only must the correct identification procedure be observed in accordance with Code D, but in a trial on indictment the jury court must be warned of the dangers inherent in evidence of identification. This is known as a 'Turnbull warning' after the case of *R v Turnbull*.[1]

8.3 The consequence of this for the lawyer at the police station is that the lawyer must be diligent in ensuring that the appropriate method of identification is conducted and that it is properly conducted. If the lawyer is unhappy about any aspect of the procedure, the lawyer should make appropriate representations at the time. The lawyer should also keep a careful note of such concerns, of representations made, and of the police response, since these may be relevant both to the question of whether the identification evidence should be admitted at trial at all and, if it is admitted, to the direction to be given to a jury. As with intervention during the course of interviews, if the lawyer acquiesces in an identification procedure about which the lawyer has reservations, the evidence of identification may be admitted on the basis that the presence (and implied consent) of the lawyer nullifies the effect of any breach of Code D.

8.4 There is no specific provision in the Police Reform Act 2002 granting powers to designated civilian officers in relation to the identification procedures dealt with in this chapter. The arrangements for, and the conduct of, identification procedures are the responsibility of an 'identification officer' who must be an inspector or above. However, generally the identification officer may delegate these functions to another police officer or to a civilian on condition that the officer provides effective supervision (Code D para 3.11). Code D does not affect the powers under Terrorism Act 2000 Sch 8 to take photographs, fingerprints, body samples and impressions, but the Code does apply to visual identification procedures.

---

1 [1977] QB 224; [1976] 3 All ER 549; (1976) 63 Cr App R 132. For a comprehensive guide to identification law and practice see P Bogan, *Identification: investigation, trial and scientific evidence* (Legal Action Group, London, 2004). See also R Wilcock, R Bull and R Milne, *Witness identification in criminal cases: psychology and practice* (Oxford University Press, Oxford, 2008).

## Identification or recognition?

8.5     In a departure from previous versions, the current version of Code D makes a distinction between identification and recognition. The procedures in Code D section 3(A) apply when an eye-witness has seen the offender committing the crime or in any other circumstances which tend to prove or disprove the involvement of the person the witness saw in the crime (Code D para 3.0). This section of the code sets out the procedures to be followed to test the ability of that eye-witness to identify a person suspected of involvement in the offence as the person the witness saw on the previous occasion (see para 8.8 below). The procedures in Code D section 3(B) apply when, for the purposes of obtaining evidence of recognition, any person (including a police officer) views the image of another person in a film, photograph or other visual medium, and is asked whether the person recognises that individual as someone who is known to him or her (Code D para 3.34, and see para 8.75 below). It is clear that section 3(A) applies to an eye-witness who may be able to identify the offender, and that section 3(B) applies to a person who is not an eye-witness who may be able to recognise the offender from a visual image shown to him or her. What is not clear is which section applies to an eye-witness who may recognise the person the eye-witness saw committing the offence. Code D para 3.34 refers to 'any person' and does not appear to confine section 3(B) to those who are not eye-witnesses. Code D NfG 3AA states that the procedures in section 3(A) should not be used to test whether a witness can recognise a person as someone the witness knows and where the witness would be able to give evidence of recognition along the lines of 'On (describe date, time, location) I saw an image of an individual whom I recognised as AB'. In such cases, the Note states, the procedures in section 3(B) should be used. This begs the key question, since until the witness has viewed the image it will not be known whether the witness will be able to say that he or she recognises the person in the image. It also has the potential to lead to an unreliable identification – an identification procedure under section 3(A) may usefully and fairly test whether an uncertain recognition by an eye-witness is accurate, whereas the procedures under section 3(B) cannot.

8.6         While the police are under no obligation to consult a suspect or their lawyer as to which procedures to follow, where a suspect disputes a purported recognition by an eye-witness the lawyer should, if necessary, consider making representations to the police to use section 3(A) procedures rather than section 3(B) procedures. There is support for this argument in the case-law.[2] While it has been held that an identification procedure is not required where a witness recognises a suspect in the sense that the witness knows the suspect from previous contact with the suspect,[3] if the recognition is less certain – and particularly if the suspect disputes the purported recognition – it has been held that the identification procedures

---

2   Although note that all of the cases referred to here were decided before the current versions of Code D came into force.

3   *H v DPP* [2003] EWHC 133 (Admin).

do apply. In *R v Fergus*[4] it was held that an identification parade should have been held where the witness had only seen the suspect once before and had been told his name by a third party. In *R v Harris*,[5] although categorising the case as one of recognition rather than identification, the court held that an identification procedure should have been held where the suspect disputed the purported recognition, which was based on contact at school two years before the incident.

8.7    It has been held that the identification procedures in Code D (ie, those in section 3(A) of the current version) do not apply where the witness has merely given a description of the clothing worn by the suspect and has not described the suspect's features.[6] However, this case was decided in the context of a former version of Code D, and it may be that under the current version an identification procedure should be held in such circumstances if the identifying witness expresses an ability to identify the suspect or there is a reasonable chance of them being able to do so (Code D para 3.12(ii)).[7]

## Identification procedures under Code D section 3(A)

8.8    The procedures to be followed in respect of identification by eye-witnesses are set out in Code D section 3(A) and Annexes A–E. The code distinguishes between cases where the suspect's identity is not known and those where it is known and, in the latter case, between cases where the suspect is known and available and cases where the suspect is known but is not available. It is important to determine which of these applies since this will determine which form of identification is applicable. A suspect is 'known' if there is sufficient information known to the police to justify the arrest of a particular person for suspected involvement in the offence (Code D para 3.4). This is the case whether or not the suspect has actually be arrested.[8] A suspect is 'available' where he or she is immediately available or will be within a reasonably short time, and is willing to take an effective part in an identification procedure which it is practicable to arrange (Code D para 3.4).

8.9    The description of a suspect as first given by a potential witness must normally be recorded before the witness takes part in an identification procedure (Code D para 3.1). A copy of the record must, where practicable, be shown to the suspect or the suspect's lawyer before a video identification, identification parade, group identification or confrontation is conducted.

---

4  [1992] Crim LR 363; and see *R v Byrne* [2004] EWCA Crim 979. Contrast *R v C; R v B* (2003) 4 March (unreported), where the evidence was treated as recognition rather than identification even though the witnesses knew the names of the suspect only because they had been told them by others; and see also *Folan v R* [2003] EWCA Crim 908.

5  [2003] EWCA Crim 174.

6  See *D v DPP* (1998) *Times* 7 August, and *Parry v DPP* (1998) 12 October, unreported, CA.

7  Although see *R v Haynes* [2004] EWCA Crim 390.

8  See *R v Nunes* [2001] EWCA Crim 2283 (where the suspect had been arrested), and *R v Preddie* [2011] EWCA Crim 312 (where the suspect had been stopped by police with a view to arrest). For borderline cases see *R v Haynes* [2004] EWCA Crim 390, and *B v DPP* [2006] EWHC 660 (Admin).

If it has not already been disclosed, the lawyer should request a copy of the description as soon as it becomes apparent that identification may be in issue. The lawyer should carefully examine the witness description, noting in particular the circumstances of the view and the nature and extent of the description given, and should ask the police whether it fully reflects the description given by the witness. In *R v Nolan*,[9] an identification was held to have been properly admitted even though the witness description provided to the defence lawyer omitted the fact that the witness had told the police that she had only seen the offender from the back.

## Cases where the suspect's identity is not known

### Street identification

8.10    Where the identity of the suspect is not known, a witness may be taken to a particular neighbourhood or place to see whether the witness can identify the person he or she saw in relation to the alleged crime. Code D para 3.2 provides that while the rules governing formal identification procedures do not directly apply to a street identification, the principles should be followed as far as practicable. It goes on to provide the following examples of the appropriate procedures to be followed:

a)  where it is practicable to do so, a record should be made of the witness's description of the suspect before asking the witness to make an identification;

b)  care must be taken not to direct the witness's attention to any individual unless, taking into account all the circumstances, this cannot be avoided;

c)  where there is more than one witness, every effort should be made to keep them separate and witnesses should be taken to see whether they can identify a person independently;

d)  once there is sufficient information to justify the arrest of a particular individual for suspected involvement in the offence, eg, after a witness makes a positive identification, other witnesses should not be asked to make a street identification, and the case should be treated as one where the suspect is known and available;

e)  the officer or civilian support staff accompanying the witness must record, in his or her pocket book, the action taken as soon as, and in as much detail as, possible.

### Showing photographs or other visual images

8.11    Where the identity of the suspect is not known or, if known, the suspect is not available, the police may show a witness photographs or other visual images in accordance with Code D Annex E (Code D para 3.3). In the case of a suspect who is known, but who is not available because, for example, the suspect refuses to co-operate, the identification officer can make arrangements for a video or group identification (Code D para 3.21). It is suggested that if it is practicable to do so, such a procedure should be used in preference to the showing of photographs or visual images.

9  [2002] EWCA Crim 464.

8.12 The showing of photographs or other visual images under Code D Annex E is quite separate from the procedure to be followed under Code D section 3(B) in potential recognition cases (see para 8.75 below). Although Annex E is entitled 'Showing photographs', and largely refers to photographs, the procedures should also be followed where other visual images are shown to a witness. The showing of photographs and other visual images must be supervised and directed by an officer of the rank of sergeant or above, who must confirm that the first description of the suspect by the witness has been recorded before the witness is shown the photographs. If this cannot be confirmed, the showing of photographs must be postponed, presumably in order for this to be done (Code D Annex E paras 1 and 2). Annex E provides, in particular, that:

1) Only one witness at a time may be shown photographs and the witness must not be allowed to communicate with other witnesses in the case.
2) The witness must be shown at least 12 photographs at a time which should, as far as possible, all be of a similar type.
3) The witness must be told that a photograph of the person the witness saw may not be among them, and the witness must not be prompted or guided in any way.
4) The witness must be told that he or she should not make a decision until he or she has viewed at least 12 photographs.
5) If a witness makes a positive identification from photographs, unless the person identified is otherwise eliminated from the enquiries or is not available, other witnesses must not be shown photographs. The identifying witness and any other witnesses must be asked to attend a video identification, identification parade or group identification unless there is no dispute about the identification of the suspect.
6) Where the use of a computerised or artist's composite or similar likeness has led to there being a known suspect who can be asked to participate in a video identification, identification parade or group identification, that likeness must not be shown to other potential witnesses.
7) The officer in charge of an investigation must inform the identification officer whether a witness to a video identification, identification parade or group identification has previously been shown photographs or computerised or artist's composite or similar likeness and, if this is the case, the suspect and the lawyer must be informed before the identification procedure takes place. There is no requirement for this to be done before a confrontation, but it is suggested that this requirement should also apply.

## Implications for legal advice

8.13 A defence lawyer is unlikely to be involved at the stage of an investigation where the police carry out a street identification or show photographs or other visual images to a witness, although the lawyer may be in the latter case where the suspect has been arrested but refuses to co-operate in another form of identification. When advising in respect of an identification procedure described in para 8.20 below the lawyer should, where appropriate, ask whether there has been a street identification or whether any witness has been shown photographs or other visual images, and seek

detailed information about the procedure used, and whether any identification was made. Note in particular that once a positive identification
has been made by means of a street identification, or once a positive identification has been made from photographs, other witnesses should not
normally take part in a street identification or be asked to view photographs (Code D para 3.2(d) and Annex E para 6). There is no prohibition
on the identifying witness taking part in a further identification procedure, although the lawyer should consider whether it would serve a useful purpose (see para 8.19 below). Where a witness has previously been
shown photographs or other visual images the suspect and the suspect's
lawyer must be told before the further identification procedure is carried
out (Code D Annex E para 9). There is no similar provision in respect of a
street identification, but the suspect will almost certainly be aware of it. If
it appears that the provisions of Code D have not been observed, appropriate representations should be made, and a careful note taken of both the
representations and any reply. For the effect of any breach on admissibility
of the identification evidence at trial, see para 13.50 below.

## Cases where the suspect is known but not available

8.14    If a suspect is known but is not available (see para 8.8 above), or has ceased
to be available (because, for example, the suspect has withdrawn consent),
the identification officer (Code D para 3.11) may make arrangements for
a video identification (if necessary using still images rather than moving
images), a group identification, or the showing of photographs or other
visual images (Code D paras 3.3 and 3.21). Any suitable moving or still
image may be used for a video identification, and these may be obtained
covertly if necessary (but see para 8.34 below). A video or group identification may also be used where, in the case of a juvenile suspect, the consent
of the juvenile's parent or guardian to an identification procedure is either
refused or reasonable efforts to obtain consent have failed.

8.15        Code D does not explicitly deal with the situation where a video or
group identification has been conducted under Code D para 3.21 and the
suspect subsequently becomes available. It would seem that an identification procedure should be held in respect of the witness who was asked to
make an identification under para 3.21 if the conditions set out in Code
D para 3.12 are satisfied (see para 8.18 below), but the key issue will be
whether such a procedure would serve a useful purpose. In many circumstances, if the witness has picked out the suspect in a procedure conducted
under para 3.21, there would be no useful purpose in conducting another
form of identification procedure. If there are other witnesses who have not
taken part in an identification procedure under para 3.21, the usual rules
under Code D para 3.12 will apply.

8.16        If a video or group identification has been conducted under para 3.21,
the lawyer should carefully consider whether the conditions for conducting a procedure under this provision were satisfied. Particular attention should be paid to the image of the suspect used, and whether there
were any significant differences between this image and the images of
the comparators used (for example, whether they were all still or moving
images, the background of the images, etc).

## Cases where the suspect is known and available

8.17 Where a suspect is known and available (see para 8.8 above), the police must decide whether to hold an identification procedure and select the form of procedure to be used.

### When must an identification procedure be held?

8.18 The circumstances in which an identification procedure must be held are set out in Code D para 3.12, as follows. Where:

(i) an eye witness has identified a suspect or purported to have identified them prior to the conduct of a video or group identification or identification parade; or

(ii) there is a witness available who expresses an ability to identify the suspect, or where there is a reasonable chance of the witness being able to do so, and they have not been given an opportunity to identify the suspect in a video or group identification or identification parade;

and the suspect disputes being the person the witness claims to have seen, an identification procedure must be held unless it is not practicable or it would serve no useful purpose in proving or disproving whether the suspect was involved in committing the offence.

If these conditions are not satisfied an identification procedure may, nevertheless, be held if the officer in charge of the investigation considers that it would be useful (Code D para 3.13).

8.19 Thus, the conditions that make the holding of an identification procedure mandatory are as follows:

1) *A witness has identified a suspect etc* There must be a eye-witness who has identified or purported to have identified a suspect. See para 8.5 above for the distinction between identification and recognition.[10] Provided the other conditions are satisfied, an identification procedure must be held even though the witness has identified or purported to identify the suspect in a procedure conducted under Code D para 3.2 (suspect's identity is not known) or under Code D para 3.21 (suspect is known but not available). In relation to the former, Code D para 3.2(d) states that once there is sufficient evidence to justify the arrest of a particular person the provisions set out from para 3.4 onwards (ie, the provisions that are applicable when a suspect is known and available) apply. Furthermore, in relation to both, para 3.12(i) and 3.12(ii) are expressed in the alternative, so that (assuming the other conditions are satisfied) an identification procedure must be held if either of them are satisfied. Unlike para 3.12(ii), para 3.12(i) makes no reference to the witness having previously been given the opportunity to identify the suspect. However, the fact of a prior identification may mean that no useful purpose would be served by holding an identification procedure if the only witness is one who has already identified the suspect in another procedure (see 5) below).

---

10 If there is no identification but, for example, an accumulation of circumstantial evidence that points to the identity of the suspect, Code D does not apply (*Alabusheva v DPP* [2007] EWHC 264 (Admin)).

2) *A witness expresses an ability to identify the suspect, etc* This is unfortunately worded since it is not an ability to identify 'the suspect' that is the issue but an ability to identify the person seen by the witness in relation to the alleged offence. This condition makes the holding of an identification procedure mandatory in circumstances where, although the witness does not express an ability to make a positive identification, there is a reasonable chance of the witness being able to do so. In *R v Nolan*,[11] for example, the witness had told the police that she had only seen the gunman from the back. However, the police thought that she was frightened and that she had seen more than she had told the police. The case was decided on an earlier version of Code D, but it would seem that in similar circumstances under the current Code D, the holding of an identification procedure would, assuming that the other conditions were satisfied, be mandatory.

3) *The suspect disputes being the person* This will clearly apply if the suspect denies having been present at the relevant time. It will also be relevant if the suspect accepts that he or she was present but denies participation.[12] It would not normally apply if the suspect merely disagrees with the suspect's level of involvement in the alleged offence since the issue would be one of participation rather than identification. If the suspect does dispute being the person the witness claims to have seen, it is important that this is made known to the police before charge. If identification is disputed for the first time after charge it may be that a court will permit some other form of identification such as a dock identification (but see para 8.77 below).[13]

4) *An identification is not impracticable* The cases on practicability were decided before the development of video identification and were principally concerned with the practicability of holding an identification parade. Given the widespread availability of video identification, and the development of image libraries, it is now more difficult for the police to maintain that all forms of identification procedure would be impracticable. The police must make their decision regarding practicability on reasonable grounds, and must take all reasonably practicable steps to investigate the possibility of holding a video identification before moving to another form of identification.[14] However, a procedure may be impracticable if the suspect has distinctive features that cannot be effectively disguised.[15]

---

11  [2002] EWCA Crim 464.

12  *R v Hope, Limburn and Bleasdale* [1994] Crim LR 118; and *R v K* [2003] EWHC 351 (Admin).

13  *Karia v DPP* [2002] EWHC 2175 (Admin).

14  *R v Britton and Richards* [1989] Crim LR 144. The decision was made at a time when identification parades were the primary form of procedure, but the same principles should apply to video identification.

15  In *R v Martin* [2002] EWCA Crim 251, (2002) *Times* 5 March, it was held that the use of make-up, etc, was not inherently unfair, but care was needed to ensure that its use could not be detected by the witness. The wearing of hats should be avoided if possible, but there may be circumstances where their use would enhance the fairness of the procedure.

5) *Serving a useful purpose* Even if all of the other conditions are satisfied, an identification procedure does not have to be held if it would serve no useful purpose in proving or disproving whether the suspect was involved in committing the alleged offence. This condition is likely to cause difficulty both to the police and to defence lawyers, and ultimately for the courts. In *R v Forbes*[16] the House of Lords, in interpreting a former version of Code D, attempted to reduce the discretion of the police to decline to hold an identification parade on the ground that they did not think it would serve a useful purpose. In their Lordships' view, the code was intended as 'an intensely practical document giving police officers clear instructions on the approach that they should follow in specified circumstances'. However, subsequent amendments to Code D explicitly re-introduced the 'useful purpose' provision.

The police are most likely to decide that an identification procedure would serve no useful purpose where there has already been a street identification or other form of identification of the suspect. However, as noted in 1) above, the wording of Code D para 3.12(i) suggests that a further identification procedure may be required in such circumstances, so the key question in such cases will be whether a further procedure will serve a useful purpose. This is principally a matter for the identification officer (Code D para 3.11), but if the defence lawyer believes that it would be in the interests of the client for an identification procedure to be held, the lawyer should seek to persuade the officer that a formal procedure would serve a useful purpose.

The decision on whether an identification procedure would serve a useful purpose is clearly fact-sensitive, but some useful guidance on interpretation of the provision may be gained from the case-law. It was held in *R v Callie*[17] that the 'useful purpose' provision does not permit the police to carry out a proportionality exercise. The relevant question is whether an identification procedure might produce relevant evidence. The fact that one witness has made a positive identification does not mean that inviting other witnesses to view an identification procedure would not serve a useful purpose.[18] In *R v Harris*[19] the Court of Appeal decided that a formal identification procedure would have served a useful purpose in circumstances where the accused disputed 'recognition' by the complainants who had attended the same school some years earlier. The court made the important point that in these circumstances there was a useful purpose from the defence point of view because there was a real possibility that one or both of the complainants would not have picked the defendant out at an identification parade.

16  [2001] 1 AC 473; [2001] 2 WLR 1; [2001] 1 All ER 686; [2001] 1 Cr App R 31.
17  [2009] EWCA Crim 283.
18  *R v Gojra* [2010] EWCA Crim 1939.
19  [2003] EWCA Crim 174. This was decided under the version of Code D that came into force in April 2002, which also provided that an identification procedure need not be held if it would serve no useful purpose.

*Selecting the identification procedure*

8.20   Where the conditions for conducting an identification procedure are satisfied the suspect must initially be offered a video identification unless:

a) a video identification is not practicable; or

b) an identification parade is both practicable and more suitable than a video identification; or

c) the officer in charge of the investigation considers that a group identification is more satisfactory than a video identification or an identification parade and the identification officer considers it practicable to arrange (Code D para 3.14).

In making the decision about which procedure to offer to the suspect, the identification officer and the officer in charge of the investigation should consult each other, but para 3.14 makes it clear that video identification is the preferred option.

8.21   The suspect is entitled to legal advice as to whether to accept the procedure offered, and may also consult with the appropriate adult (if relevant, and if the adult is present). If the suspect refuses the procedure offered, the suspect must be asked to state the reasons for refusal. The suspect and the lawyer may make representations as to why another procedure should be used, and the identification officer must then offer that procedure or, if the officer decides it is not suitable and practicable, must record the reasons for refusal to offer the procedure preferred by the suspect (Code D para 3.15).

8.22   It can be seen, therefore, that it is up to the police to decide which procedure is to be used but they must listen to, and record, representations if the suspect wants a procedure other than that initially offered. It should be noted that only an identification parade requires active consent and co-operation of the suspect. A video identification can be arranged using images of the suspect that are not taken under identical conditions as the images of the comparators if the suspect fails or refuses to co-operate (Code D Annex A para 3). A group identification can take place without consent of the suspect, covertly if necessary (Code D Annex C para 2). The identification officer may arrange for a confrontation to take place, in accordance with Code D Annex D, if none of the other formal methods of identification are practicable (Code D para 3.23). There is no express provision for inferences to be drawn from failure or refusal to co-operate with a particular form of identification but evidence of failure or refusal to co-operate could be given in evidence (Code D para 3.17(v)), and the court could draw its own conclusions from that failure or refusal.

*Should the suspect ask for an identification procedure?*

8.23   The conditions that make the holding of an identification procedure mandatory (see para 8.18 above) leave the police with considerable discretion, for example, as to whether it would serve a useful purpose. If the conditions are not satisfied, the police have the discretion to conduct an identification procedure if the identification officer considers that it would be useful (Code D para 3.13). Failure to hold a procedure where the conditions are satisfied may result in other evidence of identification being excluded at trial (see para 8.83 below). Therefore, advice on whether to request an identification procedure can have a significant impact on the subsequent course of the investigation and the eventual outcome.

8.24     The lawyer will need to take account of what is known about the facts of the case, and should ask for a copy of the original description given to the police by any potential identification witness. The lawyer is entitled to see this (see para 8.9 above), although while Code D para 3.1 states that it must be given to the suspect or the suspect's lawyer before an identification procedure is conducted, it does not specifically state that it must be given before a decision about whether to hold a procedure has been taken. The lawyer should also ask the police whether any identification witness has been shown photographs or video or other film (see para 8.11 above). If any material has been released to the media by the police for the purpose of recognising or tracing the suspect, the suspect or the lawyer must be allowed to view it before any identification procedure is carried out, provided that it is practicable and would not unreasonably delay the investigation (Code D para 3.29). The lawyer should also consider what, if any, other form of identification evidence will be available if a formal identification procedure is not held. If a successful prosecution is likely to be dependant upon adequate identification evidence, and none is likely to be available, it is unlikely to be in the suspect's interests to ask for an identification procedure to be held where it is not being proposed by the police. In considering whether other identification evidence is likely to be available, the lawyer should consider, in particular, the possible availability of CCTV footage.

8.25     If the suspect is reasonably confident that he or she will not be picked out, then it is likely to be advisable to request an identification procedure. It is important, even here, however, that the suspect is warned of the potential danger of being identified. A firm identification in a formal identification procedure by one or more witnesses is likely to weigh against the suspect very heavily at trial. If the police appear reluctant to hold an identification procedure, the lawyer should consider whether to advise the client to request one. It may be that the police are unsure of their identification witness(es) and are hoping for a confession that would render it unnecessary. It may be that they do not want to go to the trouble of arranging an identification procedure and are hoping to get by without one. Alternatively, the police may not have adequate evidence to link the suspect with the crime, and the defence lawyer will not want to prompt an identification procedure which might give the police the very evidence that they need.

8.26     It follows that in advising their client about whether to request an Identification procedure, the lawyer must take account of what information he or she has about the nature of the identification evidence and what method of identification the police are considering. The lawyer should seek details of how many potential identification witnesses there are, whether they say they have seen the suspect before, what description they gave to the police, and the circumstances of the alleged identification. This information will enable the lawyer to make informed judgments concerning the factors referred to above.

*Should the suspect co-operate with a police request for an identification procedure?*

8.27   This section is concerned with whether the suspect should co-operate with a proposed identification procedure, and whether the lawyer should make representations about the form of identification procedure offered. With regard to the former, it was noted in para 8.22 above that only an identification parade requires the active co-operation of the suspect and a failure to co-operate can be given in evidence. Other forms of identification can be carried out without the consent of the suspect. Therefore, it would normally be appropriate to advise a client to co-operate with an identification procedure proposed by the police since if the suspect does not, the police may be able to conduct an identification procedure in any event, and evidence of the refusal or failure to co-operate may disadvantage the client at trial.

8.28         However, before advising the client to consent to an identification procedure the lawyer should consider what information is available, particularly as to the description given by the identifying witness(es). As noted at para 8.24 above, Code D para 3.1 does not specifically provide that the witness description must be supplied prior to a decision about an identification procedure (as opposed to the conduct of an identification procedure) and some police officers take the view that it does not have to be supplied until shortly before the procedure is conducted. If it has not been supplied, the lawyer should ask for the original description before giving advice to the client as to co-operation with an identification procedure. The lawyer should also ask whether any further relevant information has been obtained since the original description was given. If the police fail to disclose any, or adequate, information, the lawyer may decide that in view of the lack of information he or she is not in a position to advise the client about whether to co-operate with the identification procedure. If this is the case, bearing in mind the dangers to the suspect of failing to co-operate, the lawyer should make clear to the police that the lawyer cannot advise the client on whether to co-operate with an identification procedure because of the refusal of the police to provide any (or adequate) information. The lawyer should try to ensure that this is accurately recorded on the custody record.

8.29         The police will normally offer a video identification in preference to another form of identification procedure. Some lawyers believe that there are fewer witness identifications in video identifications than in identification parades, although research evidence indicates that there is little difference between the two.[20] Given the availability of image databanks, it is certainly easier, in video identifications, to ensure that the comparators are sufficiently similar to the suspect. For these reasons, it will normally be appropriate for the lawyer to advise the client to co-operate with a video identification rather than to seek another form of identification. If the choice is between an identification parade and a group identification, most lawyers would probably advise co-operation with the former. A

---

20  See R Wilcock, R Bull and R Milne *Witness identification in criminal cases: psychology and practice* (Oxford University Press, Oxford, 2008) p127.

group identification may take a variety of forms, and is less controllable than a video identification or identification parade. Furthermore, while a group identification should normally be held away from a police station (and for this reason some lawyers regard it as potentially fairer than a parade in a station), it may be held inside a police station on grounds of security, safety or practicality (Code D Annex C para 37). Although a group identification should, as far as possible, follow the principles and procedures governing parades (Code D Annex C para 1), a group identification conducted in a police station may simply be a watered-down version of a parade with, perhaps, fewer people taking part. The potential for unfairness may, therefore, be greater but it is likely to be difficult successfully to discredit the identification at trial if the lawyer acquiesced in it. A group identification may be particularly problematic if the suspect is distinctive-looking for some reason, since the suspect is more likely to stand out in a crowd than in a video identification or identification parade composed of similar-looking people.

## Video identification

8.30 Video identification is governed by Code D paras 3.5 and 3.6, and Annex A, and is the responsibility of an identification officer (Code D para 3.11). Witnesses are shown images of the suspect together with those of at least eight other people who, as far as possible, resemble the suspect in age, height, general appearance and position in life (Code D Annex A para 2). Moving images must be used unless the suspect is known but not available (see para 8.13 above), or the identification officer does not consider that replication of a physical feature can be achieved or that it is not possible to conceal the location of the feature on the image of a suspect if moving images are used (Code D para 3.5). As far as possible, all persons on the set of images should be filmed in the same positions or carrying out the same sequence of movements, and under identical conditions (Code D Annex A para 3).

### Can the police insist on a video identification?

8.31 The police can, in effect, insist on a video identification. It is for the identification officer, in consultation with the officer in charge of the investigation, to determine which form of identification procedure to offer to the suspect (Code D para 3.14). Although the suspect can make representations that another form of identification be used (Code D para 3.15), a video identification can still be held if the identification officer decides that an alternative procedure is not suitable and practicable. If the suspect then refuses to co-operate, the police can proceed with an identification procedure provided that they have or are able to obtain a suitable image (Code D para 3.21). The image of the suspect may be taken covertly if the police believe this to be necessary (see para 8.34 below).

## Can the suspect demand a video identification?

8.32   The suspect cannot insist on a video identification, although this will normally be the method of identification offered by the police. Video identification procedures may have advantages for some suspects. A nervous suspect may find it easier to be filmed than to stand on a parade. Also, with the development of image databases, it is easier to arrange for the images to look similar to the suspect than it is to arrange for suitable members of the public to stand on an identification parade.

## Conduct of a video identification

8.33   Before a video identification takes place, the identification officer must explain to the suspect a number of things about the conduct of the procedure, as set out in Code D para 3.17. The information to be given to the suspect must be recorded in a written notice which must be handed to the suspect, and which the suspect must be given the opportunity of reading. The suspect must then be asked to sign a copy of the notice to indicate the suspect's willingness to co-operate (Code D para 3.18). The lawyer should ensure that he or she is present while this is done, and that the client fully understands what is being agreed to. If necessary, the notice should be read over to the suspect.

8.34   The duties under Code D paras 3.17 and 3.18 may be performed by a custody officer rather than an inspector if it is proposed to hold the identification procedure at a later date and an inspector is not available to act as an identification officer before the suspect leaves the police station (Code D para 3.19). If the identification officer and the officer in charge of the investigation have reasonable grounds for suspecting that if the suspect is given the information and notice under these provisions the suspect would take steps to avoid being seen by a witness in an identification procedure, the identification officer can arrange for a suitable image to be taken of the suspect for possible use in a video identification, and give the notice and information to the suspect after that has been done (Code D para 3.20). Note that, although not mentioned in Code D, covertly recording a suspect's image may amount to a breach of the suspect's right to private life under European Convention on Human Rights article 8 unless properly authorised as 'directed surveillance' under the Regulation of Investigatory Powers Act 2000 ss26 and 28.[21]

8.35   The suspect or the lawyer must, where practicable, be given a copy of the original description given by an identifying witness (see para 8.9 above). They must also be told whether a witness has been shown photographs or other visual images by the police before the identity of the suspect became known (see para 8.11 above). If any relevant material has been released to the media for the purposes of recognising or tracing the suspect, which has been broadcast or published, the suspect or the solicitor must be allowed to view it before a video identification is conducted (Code D para 3.29).

21   *Perry v UK* (2004) 39 EHRR 3; (2003) *Times* 26 August.

8.36    The suspect or the lawyer, friend or appropriate adult must be given
a reasonable opportunity to see the complete set of images to be used in
the identification procedure before they are shown to any witness (Code
D Annex A para 7). While this provides for the suspect *or* the lawyer to
view the images, the lawyer should normally view the images together
with the client. The set of images must show at least eight other people
(or 12 if there are two suspects of roughly similar appearance to be shown
on the same set of images) who as far as possible resemble the suspect
in age, height, general appearance and position in life (Code D Annex A
para 2, and see para 8.51 below). If the suspect has an unusual physical
feature (eg, a facial scar or tattoo) the police may take steps to replicate or
conceal it, and if this is done the reasons for so doing must be recorded
(Code D Annex A paras 2A and 2B). The lawyer should satisfy himself or
herself that the images are sufficiently similar, and should ensure that
there is nothing about the set of images, such as posture, lighting or background, that marks out the suspect's image as different from those of the
comparators (see Code D Annex A para 3). Particular attention should
be paid to whether any attempt to mask or replicate an unusual physical
feature is satisfactory.[22] If the suspect or the lawyer has objections to the
set of images, such steps as are practicable must be taken to remove the
grounds for objection (Code D Annex A para 7). If this is not practicable,
the officer must explain why.[23] The lawyer should, therefore, make appropriate representations, bearing in mind that the officer may respond either
by proceeding with the video identification or by abandoning it and proceeding with another form of identification if it becomes impracticable to
hold it.

8.37    Provided it is practicable, the lawyer must be given reasonable notification of the time and place it is intended to conduct the video identification
in order that the lawyer may attend. If the lawyer is not present, the viewing of the set of images by the witness(es) must be recorded on video. For
obvious reasons, the suspect cannot be present at the video identification
(Code D Annex A para 9). Witnesses must not be able to communicate
with each other before seeing the set of images, and must not be able to
overhear a witness who has seen them (Code D Annex A para 10). The lawyer should satisfy himself or herself that the arrangements are adequate
to prevent this. No officer involved with the investigation may take part
in the procedure and, in particular, officers must not view the set of images before they are shown to any witness (Code D para 3.11, and Annex
A para 15). The identification officer must not discuss with a witness the
composition of the set of images or indicate whether a previous witness
has made an identification (Code D Annex A para 10). Further, the identification officer must avoid directing the witness's attention to any person
on the film or give any other indication of the suspect's identity (Code D

22  See *R v Pecco* [2010] EWCA Crim 972, in which the suspect had a tattoo on her neck
    which was not concealed in the image used for the video identification, and where the
    comparators did not have such a tattoo.
23  In *R v Middleton* [2005] EWCA Crim 692 failure by the police to comply with Code D
    Annex A para 7 did not result in exclusion of the video identification evidence since,
    the court stated, the suspect and the lawyer do not have an unfettered right to object
    to the images to be used in the video identification.

Annex A para 13).[24] If the witness has previously made an identification from a photograph or similar, the witness must not be reminded of it, nor must the witness be reminded of any description of the suspect.

8.38    Before viewing the set of images, the witness must be told that the person the witness saw may or may not appear in the images shown, and that if the witness cannot make a positive identification he or she must say so. Furthermore, the witness must be informed that he or she can ask to see a particular part of the set of images again or to have a particular image frozen, and that there is no limit on the number of times the witness may ask to see the set of images or any part of them. However, the witness must be asked to refrain from making any positive identification or saying that he or she cannot make a positive identification until the witness has seen the entire set of images at least twice (Code D Annex A para 11). Where the images have been adapted to conceal or replicate an unusual physical feature (see para 8.35 above) and a witness asks to view an image without the feature being concealed or replicated, the witness may be allowed to do so (Code D Annex A para 2C). However, if this results in the comparators not being sufficiently similar, this may amount to a breach of Code D Annex A para 2.[25] Having seen the set of images at least twice, and having indicated that the witness does not wish to see it again, the witness must then be asked whether the person the witness saw on the earlier occasion was shown on the set of images (see para 8.54 below). If the answer is in the affirmative, the witness must be shown the image of the person identified and asked to confirm it (Code D Annex A para 12). Each witness must be asked whether he or she has seen any broadcast or published image, or description, of suspects relating to the offence, and each answer must be recorded (Code D Annex A para 14).

8.39    There is no specific provision in Code D Annex A that, where there is more than one witness, the position of the suspect in the order of images can, or should, be altered after each witness has viewed the set of images. Compare this with identification parades (see para 8.49 below). However, it may be advisable for the lawyer to request such a change in the order of images, if this is possible. Furthermore, Annex A does not provide for the situation where a witness makes an identification after the viewing has ended. For the lawyer, similar considerations apply as for identification parades (see para 8.57 below). However, since a video identification can proceed in the absence of consent of the suspect, a witness could be allowed to view the set of images again even though the suspect or the lawyer does not consent. In this case, appropriate representations should be made to the identification officer.

8.40    As with other identification procedures, the lawyer should take a careful note of the whole process, including the overall time spent, whether and for how long the witness lingered over any particular image, any request to see a particular image, any request to see an image without a feature being concealed or replicated, any other conversation during the course of

24  '... a witness should not be told whether an identification is right or wrong until after the witness has made any further statement that the witness may wish.' Per Lord Bingham CJ, *R v Willoughby* [1999] 2 Cr App R 82.
25  *R v Marcus* [2004] EWCA Crim 3387.

the viewing, and the precise words used if the witness identifies any of the people in the set of images.[26] Although Code D Annex A makes no specific provision for representations to be made, the lawyer should make appropriate representations if the provisions have not been properly complied with or if, for any other reason, the process was potentially unfair to the suspect.

8.41    The police must make arrangements for all relevant material contained in the set of images to be kept securely, and their movements accounted for (Code D Annex A para 15). In most circumstances the police will be able to retain photographs and other visual images taken of a suspect for the purpose of a video identification (Code D paras 3.30 and 3.31).

## Identification parades

### Parade arrangements

8.42    Identification parades are governed by Code D paras 3.7 and 3.8, and Annex B, and since they are now relatively unusual it is a good idea for the lawyer to remind himself or herself of the provisions before any parade takes place. The lawyer needs to pay particular attention to the physical arrangements for the parade and the information that is to be given by the police to the suspect.[27] Parades can take place in a normal room or one equipped with one-way screens. In the latter case, the parade must be conducted in the presence of the suspect's lawyer, friend or appropriate adult (Code D Annex B para 2). In all cases, a video recording or colour photograph of the parade must normally be made or taken (Code D Annex B para 23). Use and retention of any images is governed by Code D paras 3.30 and 3.31. Care must be taken to ensure that the parade is not rendered unfair:

1) by contact between the witnesses;
2) by contact between witnesses and the suspect or others standing on the parade before it begins; or
3) as a result of intervention by the officers involved in the investigation (see Code D para 3.11 and Annex B para 14).

8.43    With regard to 1) and 2) the lawyer should satisfy himself or herself so far as possible that the arrangements by which the various parties are to arrive at, and remain at, the station are satisfactory. If the suspect has been released on police bail pending the parade, the lawyer should ensure that there is no risk of the suspect being seen by potential witnesses. Thus, their respective arrival times and, if possible, their point of entry to the station, should be quite separate. Furthermore, witnesses should not see any of the other members, or potential members, of the parade, and

---

26  A qualified identification, such as 'I think it's him' or 'I can't be quite certain' may have some probative value, although a person should not be convicted on qualified identification evidence alone (*R v George* [2003] Crim LR 282).

27  For an identification parade checklist and report form, see checklist 13 in appendix 3. For an examination of issues concerning identification parades, see I McKenzie 'Psychology and legal practice: fairness and accuracy in identification parades' [1995] Crim LR 200; and R Wilcock, R Bull and R Milne *Witness identification in criminal cases* (Oxford University Press, Oxford, 2008) especially ch 7.

the lawyer should check that the witnesses are not within sight when the potential members of the parade arrive. The lawyer should normally ask to check the route to be taken by the witnesses from the room where they are kept waiting to the parade room, to ensure that they will not have the opportunity of seeing any member of the parade en route. Witnesses must not have contact with other witnesses who have already seen the parade, or have an opportunity to overhear them (Code D Annex B para 14), so the lawyer should check that once witnesses have seen the parade, they are kept well away from those witnesses still to view it.

8.44    The conduct of a parade is the responsibility of the identification officer, and no officer involved with the investigation may take part in the identification procedure (Code D para 3.11). Officers involved in the investigation must not take any witness to the parade,[28] including the victim,[29] although it appears that it is permissible for such an officer to take the suspect to the parade.[30] The lawyer may, therefore, consider asking where the investigating officers will be during the parade, and who will be escorting the witnesses to the parade.

8.45    If the lawyer is not happy with the arrangements for the parade, the lawyer should make appropriate representations and make a careful note of the response. In many cases, any cause for objection can be removed so that the parade can satisfactorily proceed. However, if this is not the case, the lawyer will have to consider whether to advise the suspect to withdraw consent to the parade, which can only proceed with the suspect's consent.[31] Such a decision will require careful consideration. If the lawyer acquiesces in a breach of the Codes or in a procedure which is otherwise unfair, the court of trial may decide to admit the evidence. On the other hand, a refusal of consent could lead to another, less fair, form of identification and could have adverse consequences for the suspect at trial (see para 8.22 above). If, despite any breach, the suspect decides to proceed with the parade, the lawyer should ensure that the identification officer has made a written note of the representations made.

## Preparing the client for the parade

8.46    An identification parade that is conducted strictly in accordance with the provisions of Code D Annex B can still lead to an unreliable identification as a result of the actions of the suspect. The suspect must, therefore, be carefully advised on his or her conduct during the parade. Many suspects will not have been on a parade before, and they should be told what is likely to happen, and how long it is likely to take. Parades, especially at the preparation stage, can be long-winded and tedious, and suspects should be prepared for this. They should also be prepared for the fact that they are likely to feel nervous during the parade. This in itself, if apparent to

---

28   *R v Gall* (1990) 90 Cr App R 64; [1989] Crim LR 745.
29   *R v Ryan* [1992] Crim LR 187.
30   *R v Terrence Jones* [1992] Crim LR 365.
31   An identification parade can only be conducted if the suspect is 'available', which means that the suspect is willing to take an effective part in the procedure (see para 8.9 above).

the witness(es), could result in the suspect being identified, and the lawyer should be prepared to discuss appropriate strategies with the client.

8.47    It is important that the suspect looks 'right' in the parade. If the suspect has been in custody for some time, or if the suspect was arrested in the early hours of the morning, he or she may look untidy and dishevelled and, if male, may be unshaven. The objective is that the suspect should look as similar as possible to the other members of the parade. If, as is likely, the others do not look like this, the lawyer should ensure that the suspect is given the opportunity and the facilities to clean up and to make himself or herself look reasonably tidy.

8.48    Suspects should be advised on how to conduct themselves during the parade. Their stance should be as relaxed as possible, although they should be advised to take their cue from the other members of the parade. They should be told that the witness may well stand and stare at them for some time. Ideally, they should simply look straight in front of them, without following the witnesses as they move. They should not look at the lawyer. If the parade is to be conducted with one-way screens, suspects should be advised about the effect of the screens, that they may be unaware of where the witness is, and that they should not move until they are told the witness has left the room.

8.49    Suspects should be told that they may choose where they stand in the line-up, and that if there is more than one witness, they may change position after each witness has left the room (Code D Annex B para 13). Furthermore, they should be prepared for the possibility that they are asked to speak, to move or to adopt a particular posture (see para 8.54 below). They should be advised that if this does occur they should comply with the request and to leave any objection to the lawyer, since to object at the time (if only by facial expression) will make it more likely that they are identified. Finally, they should be advised that if they have any objection before the parade begins, or are unhappy about the way in which the parade was conducted, they should discuss this with the lawyer so that representations can be made to the police at the time.

## Conduct of the parade

8.50    An identification parade must consist of at least eight people (in addition to the suspect) who so far as possible resemble the suspect in age, height, general appearance and position in life (Code D Annex B para 9). Only one suspect may stand on a parade, unless there are two suspects who look sufficiently similar, in which case they can both be part of the same parade provided that there are at least 12 other people on the parade. In no circumstances can more than two suspects stand on the same parade. Suspects may select their own positions in the line, and if there is more than one witness, they may change position after each witness has left the room (Code D Annex B para 13).

8.51    One of the most difficult tasks for the lawyer is to decide whether the other members of the parade do look sufficiently similar to the suspect. The lawyer should pay particular attention to features such as height, hair (colour, length and style), baldness, facial hair, eye colour, build, racial characteristics, jewellery and clothing (including footwear). If necessary, the members of the parade can be asked to alter their appearance. For example, they may all be asked to wear hats to hide their hair colour, or plasters to obscure tattoos or other marks (see Code D Annex B para 10, and para 8.55 below).[32] What is 'sufficiently similar' is frequently difficult to judge, but the views of the suspect are obviously important here. The lawyer should also take account of any information about the description originally given by witnesses to the police so that the lawyer can seek to ensure that any features noted by the witnesses are also to be found in the other members of the parade.

8.52    When the suspect is brought to the room where the parade is to take place, the suspect must be asked whether he or she has any objections to the arrangements for the parade. If practicable, steps must be taken to remove any grounds for objection (Code D Annex B para 12). If the suspect or the lawyer believes that one or more of the members of the parade are not sufficiently similar, the lawyer should seek their replacement by others who are more similar. In doing so the lawyer must try to gauge how far the identification officer is prepared to go, and how long the officer is prepared to allow the process of forming the parade to continue. This may involve a careful process of negotiation, balancing the need to ensure that the parade members are sufficiently similar against the fact that the identification officer will at some point decide that a parade is not practicable and move to an alternative form of identification. It may be in the suspect's interests for a parade to become impracticable if the alternative is likely to be a group identification in circumstances that are more favourable to the suspect, but this requires careful judgment and full consultation with the client. Note that whereas it has been held that the lawyer is entitled to seek time to find appropriate people to stand on a parade,[33] the lawyer has no right to substitute someone of the lawyer's choice for a person already obtained by the police.[34]

8.53    If the identification officer does decide that a parade has become impracticable because of the difficulty of finding suitable people to stand on it, the lawyer should take a note of the reasons given by the officer, the attempts made to find people, and any suggestions for forming a suitable parade made by the lawyer. Once the line-up has been finalised, the lawyer should take a note of the appearance of the members of the parade, noting in particular any features that are significantly different to those of the suspect.

8.54    Witnesses must be brought to the parade one at a time. A note should be made of the number of the officer bringing the witness to the parade. Immediately before they inspect the parade, the identification officer must tell witnesses that the person that they saw may or may not be on the parade and that if they cannot make a positive identification, they should say so.

---

32  *R v Marrin* [2002] EWCA Crim 251 endorsed the use of make-up and props, but warned that care must be taken to ensure that they do not direct attention to the suspect. Hats might be used, but should be avoided if possible if they had not been worn during the offence. See also para 8.36 above regarding replicating or concealing unusual physical features in video identifications.

33  *R v Britton and Richards* [1989] Crim LR 144.

34  *R v Thorne* [1981] Crim LR 702.

Witnesses must then be asked to look[35] at each member of the parade at least twice, taking as much care and time as they wish. The officer must ask each witness, having done so, whether the person they saw on the earlier relevant occasion is on the parade (Code D Annex B para 17). The officer must avoid directing the witness's attention to any person on the film or give any other indication of the suspect's identity (see para 8.37 above). In some police force areas, if a witness makes an identification, it is standard practice for the witness to be asked what he or she had seen the person identified do on the relevant occasion. This is not provided for in Annex B, although it has been held that the answer given by the witness is admissible in evidence.[36] The lawyer should consider objecting to such a question on the ground that it is not mandated by Annex B. A note of precisely what is said to the witness by the identification officer should be taken. Any material departure from the requirements of para 17 should be noted and appropriate representations should be made at the end of the parade (see para 8.56 below). The exact words of the answer given by the witness must be noted, since they may well disclose any uncertainty. 'I think it is number 8' is obviously less strong an identification than, 'It is number 8' (see para 8.40 above). The identification officer's record of what was said and done should be checked at the time. If possible, this should be agreed but, if this is not possible, the lawyer must make appropriate representations and ensure that they are noted by the officer.

8.55    If the witness wishes to hear any member of the parade speak, adopt a particular posture or see the member move, the identification officer must ask the witness whether he or she can make an identification on the basis of appearance only, before complying with the request. If it is a request to hear a parade member speak, the officer must remind the witness that the parade members have been selected on the basis of physical appearance alone. Only then should members of the parade be asked to comply with the request (Code D Annex B para 18). The lawyer should normally object to such a request precisely because the parade was not arranged with this in mind (see para 8.79 below). If intervention is necessary, it must be done speedily and without identifying the suspect. If the identification officer proceeds with the request from the witness, the lawyer should ensure that all members of the parade do what has been requested, but any other representations may be best left until after the witness has left the room. Where props have been used to disguise a particular feature (see Code D Annex B para 10, and para 8.54 above), a witness may ask that a person on the parade remove it (Code D Annex B para 19). The lawyer can do little in such circumstances since to object may direct attention to the suspect. All relevant conversation must be carefully noted and, if appropriate, representations should be made to the identification officer after the witness has left the room. After the procedure each witness must

---

35  Under a previous version of Code D, the officer was required to tell witnesses to walk along the parade at least twice, and the current requirement must be regarded as a retrograde step. The current version of Code D therefore legitimates the kind of procedure that was held to be contrary to Code D in *R v Quinn* [1995] Crim LR 56. The lawyer should carefully observe the witness to try to establish whether they have complied with the identification officer's request.

36  *R v Lynch* [2001] EWCA Crim 3035.

be asked whether he or she has seen any broadcast or published films or photographs or any description of suspects relating to the offence, and the replies must be recorded (Code D Annex B para 21).

8.56    Once the last witness has left the room, the suspect must be asked whether the suspect wishes to comment on the conduct of the parade (Code D Annex B para 22). If the lawyer has any reservations or objections to the way in which the parade was conducted, the lawyer should make these known to the identification officer and ensure that they are accurately recorded. Such representations might include anything in relation to the conduct of the parade itself, or other matters such as whether the suspect has seen a witness on a previous occasion. In *R v Ogundipe*,[37] for example, the Court of Appeal was critical of the conduct of a parade in which noise and laughter from waiting volunteers could be heard.

8.57    If a witness makes an identification after the parade has ended, the suspect and lawyer must be told, and consideration must given to allowing the witness a second opportunity to identify the suspect (Code D Annex B para 20). The Code does not make it clear whether this should be in a differently-constituted parade, although this would not be appropriate since the identity of the suspect would become obvious. In any event, the lawyer should carefully examine the reasons given for such a request and, in particular, ask whether the witness spoke to any other witness, or any officer involved in the investigation, after viewing of the parade. If there is any risk that such contamination has taken place, the lawyer may advise the client not to agree to a further parade, and make the reasons clear to the identification officer.

## Group identification

8.58    Group identifications are governed by Code D paras 3.4 and 3.16, and Annex C. A group identification can take a variety of forms, ranging from a less formal kind of identification parade (perhaps containing fewer than eight members of the public) conducted in the police station, to a street scene which a witness is asked to observe. They must be conducted, as far as possible, in accordance with the principles and procedures for identification parades 'so that the conditions are fair to the suspect in the way they test the witness's ability to make an identification' (Annex C para 1). This includes the requirement that no officer involved with the investigation may take part in the procedures (Code D para 3.11). Before conducting a group identification, a record of the original description given by identifying witnesses must, if practicable, be shown to the suspect or the lawyer (Code D para 3.1). A group identification may be video recorded if this is practicable. Alternatively, a video recording or colour photograph must also be taken of the scene of the group identification immediately after it has been held or, if this is impracticable, at some later time (Code D Annex C paras 8 and 9). Use, retention and destruction of images of the suspect captured under these provisions are dealt with in Code D paras 8.30 and 8.31.

---

37  [2001] EWCA Crim 2576.

8.59    It is for the identification officer to decide where a group identification is to be held. In making the decision, the officer may take into account any representations made by the suspect, appropriate adult, lawyer or friend. A group identification should normally be held in a place where other people are either passing by, or waiting around informally, in groups so that the suspect is able to join them and is capable of being seen by the witness(es) at the same time as they can see other members of the group. The Code gives examples such as people leaving an escalator, pedestrians walking through a shopping centre and passengers on railway and bus stations waiting in queues or groups (Code D Annex C para 4). A group identification should not normally be conducted in a police station (Code D Annex C paras 3 and 37). If a group identification is to be conducted covertly (Code D para 3.21), the choice of location may be more limited, and Code D Annex C para 5 suggests that suitable locations might be along regular routes travelled by the suspect, including buses or trains or public places frequented by the suspect. In choosing a location, the officer must have regard to the general appearance and number of people likely to be present and must, in particular, reasonably expect that, over the period the witness observes the group, the witness will be able to see from time to time a number of people whose appearance is broadly similar to that of the suspect (Code D Annex C para 6). Clearly, the lawyer should take these factors into account in making any representation to the identification officer and in considering whether the proposed location is satisfactory.

## Can the police insist on a group identification?

8.60    The police can, in effect, insist on a group identification. It is for the identification officer, in consultation with the officer in charge of the investigation, to determine which form of identification procedure to offer to the suspect (Code D para 3.14). A group identification can be offered in preference to other forms of identification procedure if the officer in charge of the investigation considers it more satisfactory than a video identification or identification parade, and the identification officer considers it practicable to arrange (Code D para 3.16). Although the suspect can make representations that another form of identification be used (Code D para 3.15), the final choice rests with the police, and a group identification can be conducted covertly if the suspect is not available (Code D para 3.21, and see paras 8.8 and 8.34 above). Force cannot be used to make a suspect participate in a group identification.[38]

8.61    The question of practicability in relation to identification procedures generally is dealt with at para 8.19 above. Having decided that a video identification or identification parade is not practicable, or that a group identification is more satisfactory, the police should consider whether a group identification is practicable (Code D para 3.16). Whether a group identification is practicable in a situation where the other two forms of identification procedure are not will depend in part on the form that the group identification is to take and the circumstances of the case. In

38  See *R v Jones and Nelson* (1999) *Times* 21 April, which concerned a confrontation, but the same principles apply.

*R v Ladlow, Moss, Green and Jackson,*[39] where there were 11 witnesses to a fight, following which 21 suspects had been arrested, the court held that the police should not have moved straight to a confrontation after deciding that a parade was impracticable (since it could have involved up to 231 parades on a bank holiday), without considering the practicability of a group identification. It is not clear, however, that a group identification in those circumstances would have been any more practicable than a parade. In some situations, the lawyer may prefer a group identification to a parade (see para 8.64 below) but, if not, the lawyer should carefully consider the police justifications for not proceeding with a video identification or a parade, and why a group identification is practicable whereas neither of those methods is.

8.62    If the police request a group identification, in considering whether the suspect should consent, the lawyer should have regard to the possible adverse consequences of failure to consent. The issues here are similar to those relating to identification generally (see para 8.27 above). However, since a group identification can take a variety of forms, the lawyer should consider the potential for unfairness of the form of group identification being suggested by the police. If this leads the lawyer to advise the suspect to refuse consent, the lawyer should make clear to the police the precise reasons for refusal. In appropriate circumstances, the lawyer may wish to propose an alternative form of group identification which would be fairer to the suspect.

## Can the suspect demand a group identification?

8.63    The suspect cannot insist on a group identification. The police will normally offer a video identification, and although the suspect or the lawyer can make representations as to why another form of identification should be used (Code D para 3.15), in most circumstances it would be difficult to justify a group identification in preference to a video identification. If, however, the police have rejected a video identification and are proposing to hold an identification parade, it may be possible for the suspect to achieve a group identification since a parade can only be held if the suspect consents. For a discussion of the relative merits of parades and group identification, see para 8.29 above.

8.64    In considering advice on whether the suspect may refuse to co-operate in an identification parade in order to achieve a group identification, consideration must be given to whether a refusal to give consent to a parade can have adverse effects at trial. Evidence of failure or refusal to consent to or co-operate in a video identification or identification parade can be given in evidence (Code D para 3.17, and see para 8.22 above), but it should be noted that even if there is a danger of adverse comment at trial, the scope for such comment is limited if the suspect is willing to consent to a group identification. Nevertheless, the suspect should be advised of the potential dangers. If the suspect does not wish to give consent to a video identification or identification parade but does wish to consent to a group identification this should be made absolutely clear to the identifica-

---

39  [1989] Crim LR 219, although now such a case would almost certainly have been dealt with by way of a video identification.

tion officer to forestall the danger of the officer assuming consent is withheld to both and thus moving directly to a confrontation. If the problem with other forms of identification procedure is practicability rather than consent, and the suspect wants a group identification in preference to a parade, the lawyer should be prepared to argue that a group identification is practicable. This will be particularly relevant where the police do not have suitable video images or are having difficulty in finding sufficiently similar-looking people to stand on the parade.

## The conduct of a group identification

8.65    Code D Annex C provides detailed guidance on how a group identification should be conducted. The provisions are not set out here, but it should be noted that they deal separately with group identifications involving moving groups and stationary groups, those conducted with and without the suspect's consent, identifications involving prison inmates, and group identifications in police stations. With regard to the latter, a group identification should only be conducted in a police station for reasons of safety or security or because it is impracticable to hold it elsewhere (Code D Annex C para 37).

8.66    Since group identifications must, as far as possible, be conducted according to the same principles and procedures as for identification parades, much of what is said about the conduct of parades is relevant here (see para 8.50 above). Group identifications are often less controllable than parades and, therefore, the lawyer should be particularly alert to anything that might make the identification unfair. The lawyer should note in particular:

- the relative position of the witness and suspect;
- how many other people were in the vicinity, and how many of those people were similar in looks to the suspect;
- the length of time the procedure took;
- what was said by the witness if the witness made an identification.

After the procedure has been completed, the lawyer should, in consultation with the client, make appropriate representations to the identification officer, and ensure that they are recorded in writing.

## Confrontation

8.67    Confrontations are governed by Code D para 3.23 and Annex D. A confrontation is defined as a procedure whereby the suspect is directly confronted by a witness. Confrontations have significant potential to lead to an unsafe identification since the witness will know that the person the witness is asked to look at is a suspect. A defence lawyer should, therefore, try to avoid a confrontation taking place. Although the Court of Appeal has decided that identification evidence based on confrontation should be excluded where the confrontation should not have taken place,[40] it may be

---

40  See, eg, *R v Britton and Richards* [1989] Crim LR 144, and *R v Ladlow, Moss, Green and Jackson* [1989] Crim LR 219.

admitted where the suspect demands a confrontation in the presence of the lawyer.[41] Furthermore, it is likely that evidence of a confrontation conducted contrary to Code D would be admitted at trial if it was conducted with the knowledge and acquiescence of the lawyer.[42] Therefore, if the police are proposing to hold a confrontation in contravention of Code D, it is important that the lawyer explains to the identification officer why a confrontation should not be held, and ensures that these representations are noted in writing. As with other forms of identification, the suspect or the lawyer must, where practicable, be supplied with a copy of the first description given by an identifying witness before a confrontation takes place (Code D Annex D para 2, and see para 8.9 above). After the procedure, each witness must be asked whether he or she has seen any broadcast or published films or photographs or any description of suspects relating to the offence, and the replies must be recorded (Code D Annex D para 7).

## Can the police insist on a confrontation?

8.68    A confrontation may only be held if none of the other formal methods of identification are practicable (Code D para 3.23), although this may be subject to any demand for a confrontation by the suspect.[43] If this condition is satisfied, the police may proceed with a confrontation, whether or not the suspect consents, although the police are not permitted to use force to make the suspect take part, or to make their face visible.[44]

8.69    Evidence of a confrontation 'engineered' by the police may not be admitted at trial.[45] Furthermore, a confrontation should not be held in preference to another form of identification procedure simply because the witness concerned happens to be a police officer.[46]

## Can a suspect demand a confrontation?

8.70    Strictly, a suspect cannot require the police to hold a confrontation. It may be possible to 'engineer' a confrontation by refusing consent to any other form of identification, but the police may be able to conduct a video identification or group identification in the absence of consent or co-operation (Code D para 3.21, and see para 8.14 above). Determined opposition to other forms of identification procedure, coupled with a demand by the suspect for a confrontation,[47] may achieve a confrontation, but it is unlikely to be in the interests of the suspect for a confrontation to be held in view of its inherent unfairness. Therefore, a lawyer would rarely, if ever, advise such a course of action.

41  *R v Miller* (1991) 23 March (unreported).
42  See *R v Dunn* (1990) 91 Cr App R 237; [1990] Crim LR 572, and see para 13.32 below.
43  See *R v Miller* (1991) 23 March (unreported).
44  *R v Jones and Nelson* (1999) *Times* 21 April, and Code D Annex D para 3.
45  *R v Nagah* [1991] Crim LR 55.
46  *R v Samms, Elliot and Bartley* [1991] Crim LR 197 and see Code D NfG 3A.
47  See *R v Miller* (1991) 23 March (unreported).

## Conduct of a confrontation

8.71 Where a confrontation is to be conducted it must be arranged by an identification officer (Code D para 3.11). No officer involved in the investigation may take part (Code D paras 3.11 and 3.23). It has been held to be a significant breach of Code D for an officer involved in the investigation to accompany the witness to the confrontation.[48] However, the court decided that, as there was no evidence of unfairness to the defendant, the trial judge has been entitled to admit evidence of the confrontation. The lawyer should, therefore, check the arrangements for the confrontation with the identification officer, including who is to take the witness(es) to it.[49]

8.72 Before the confrontation takes place, the identification officer must tell the witness that the person the witness saw may or may not be the person the witness is to confront, and that if the witness cannot make a positive identification he or she should say so (Code D Annex D para 1). The suspect must be confronted independently by each witness, who must be asked, 'Is this the person?'. If the witness identifies the person but is unable to confirm the identification the witness must be asked how sure he or she is that the person is the one the witness saw on the earlier occasion (Code D Annex D para 5). The confrontation must take place in the presence of the suspect's lawyer, interpreter or friend, unless this would cause unreasonable delay (Code D Annex D para 4). It must normally be conducted in a police station, either in a normal room or one equipped with a screen. In the latter case, it must be conducted with a solicitor, friend or appropriate adult present or be recorded on video (Code D Annex D para 6). It is clear, therefore, that a confrontation should not take place in a cell unless, perhaps, this is justified by the refusal of the suspect to leave the cell or by the suspect's violent behaviour.

8.73 The lawyer should take a careful note of precisely what is said by the participants in the confrontation, and take a particular note of what is said by the witness (see para 8.54 above). The lawyer should also note who is present, who conducted the witness to the confrontation and, particularly if there is more than one witness, check whether there was any opportunity for the witnesses to talk with each other before, during or after the confrontation.

8.74 After the procedure, each witness must be asked whether he or she has seen any broadcast or published films or photographs or any description of suspects relating to the offence, and the replies must be recorded (Code D Annex D para 7).

---

48 *R v Ryan* [1992] Crim LR 187.
49 One reason for the finding that there had been no unfairness in *Ryan* was the fact that the lawyer had asked the officer whether he had said anything about the appellant, and that he was also present at the confrontation so that he could have overheard anything said by the police officer to the witness. This reinforces the need to try to avoid such incidents by advance preparation.

## Recognition procedures under Code D section 3(B)

8.75   Code D section 3(B) (ie, paras 3.34–3.37) applies when, for the purposes of obtaining evidence of recognition, a person (including a police officer) views the image of an individual in a film, photograph or other visual medium and is asked whether the person recognises that individual as someone who is known to him or her (Code D para 3.34). The procedure is to be distinguished from the showing of photographs or other visual images to eye-witnesses where a suspect is not known (see para 8.11 above). Although the Code is not clear on the point, it is suggested that the procedure under section 3(B) should not be adopted in the case of disputed recognition of a known suspect by an eye-witness (see Code D para 3.3, and paras 8.5 and 8.6 above). The procedure to be adopted under Code D section 3(B) must, as far as possible, follow the principles applicable to a video identification if the suspect is known, or identification by photographs if the suspect is not known (Code D para 3.35, and see paras 8.33 and 8.12 above respectively).[50]

8.76   Procedures under Code D section 3(B) will normally be carried out before a defence lawyer is involved or, at least, without consulting them. A possible exception is in the case of disputed recognition of a known suspect. In these circumstances, the lawyer should consider whether an identification procedure under Code D section 3(A) (for example, a video identification) would be preferable. If so, the lawyer should make representations to this effect (see para 8.6 above). If the police proceed to show photographs or other visual images to an eye-witness in such circumstances, and then propose to hold a video identification (or identification parade or group identification) to be viewed by that witness, the lawyer should consider whether to object, having regard in particular to whether such an identification procedure would serve a useful purpose (see para 8.19 above). Prior to any such identification procedure the police should inform the suspect or their lawyer of the fact that a witness has been shown photographs or other visual images.[51]

## Identification procedures after charge

8.77   Whereas Code C prohibits (subject to exceptions) further questioning regarding an offence once a person has been charged with the offence (Code C para 16.5), Code D makes no reference to identification procedures after charge. It would seem that the power of the police to hold a procedure and the right of the suspect to request a procedure apply equally

---

50   The provisions in Code D para 3.36 largely deal with the concerns of the Court of Appeal expressed in *R v Smith* [2009] 1 Cr App R 521, which involved a police officer being asked to view CCTV footage to see if the officer could recognise an offender. For other cases involving police officers who were asked if they recognised an offender, see *R v McGrath* [2009] EWCA Crim 1758, and *R v Moss* [2011] EWCA Crim 252.

51   Code D Annex E para 9 requires this where photographs or other visual images have been shown under Code D paras 3.3, and Code D para 3.35 requires the same principles to be applied to the showing of photographs or other visual images under Code D Section 3(B).

before and after charge.[52] The suspect may wish to consider requesting a procedure even after charge if, for some reason, a procedure was not held before charge or if a witness has only come forward after charge.

8.78    If the police ask the suspect to co-operate with an identification procedure after the suspect has been charged, it may be because they are genuinely unsure of the suspect's guilt or, perhaps more likely, because they wish to strengthen the evidence that they have against the suspect. For this reason, such a request requires careful consideration, particularly given the possible adverse consequences of not co-operating. Since Code C para 16.1 requires the officer in charge of an investigation to be satisfied that there is sufficient evidence for a prosecution to succeed before bringing the suspect before the custody officer with a view to charging, it could be argued that the suspect should not be required to undergo further attempts to bolster the prosecution evidence. By analogy with interviews, there comes a point at which the investigative process should stop (at least insofar as it requires the co-operation of the suspect) and that point is at the stage of charging the suspect. If a procedure is held after charge, the police may be able to justify interviewing the suspect following the procedure under Code C para 16.5 on the basis that information has come to light since charge (that is, the fact that the suspect has been identified) which, in the interests of justice, should be put to the suspect. Note that inferences under Criminal Justice and Public Order Act (CJPOA) 1994 s34, s36 or s37 could not be drawn from silence in such an interview (see para 5.72 above).

## Voice identification

8.79    Code D is primarily concerned with visual identification, and the rules governing the conduct of various methods of identification make it clear that the aim is to achieve fairness in respect of *visual* identification.[53] Code D makes no provision for cases in which an attempted identification is to be made on the basis of voice alone, but Code D Annex B para 18 does permit a witness at an identification parade to ask a member of the parade to speak, and lawyers should treat such requests with great caution (see para 8.55 above). The lack of regulation of voice identification is unfortunate since there is clear evidence of the risks of mistaken identification.[54]

8.80    One approach is for the Code D provisions regarding visual identification to be adapted in order to hold a 'voice identification parade'. In

---

52 This is implied in *R v Joseph* [1994] Crim LR 48. See also *R v Collins* (1996) 23 July (unreported).

53 It was confirmed in *R v Deenik* [1992] Crim LR 578 that identification of a suspect's voice was not directly covered by Police and Criminal Evidence Act 1984 (PACE) or Code D.

54 See *R v Gummerson and Steadman* [1999] Crim LR 680, *R v Roberts* [2000] Crim LR 183, *R v O'Doherty* [2002] Crim LR 761, *R v Chenia* [2002] EWCA Crim 2345; [2004] 1 All ER 543; [2003] 2 Cr App R 6, and *R v Flynn* [2008] 2 Cr App R 266. For a discussion of the issues concerning voice identification see D Ormerod, 'Sounds familiar? – voice identification evidence' [2001] Crim LR 595 and D Ormerod, 'Sounding out expert voice identification' [2002] Crim LR 771.

*R v Hersey*[55] the police held such a parade in which the suspect and 11 volunteers read out a piece of text. Evidence of the witness's identification of the suspect's voice was admitted at trial, a decision upheld by the Court of Appeal. In 2003 the Home Office issued Circular 57/2003 *Advice on the use of voice identification parades* which stated that the Home Office was working on the development of reliable procedures for voice identification, although no further guidance appears to have been issued. The Circular stated that the police should not attempt to conduct 'live' voice identification procedures. Instead, the police should use a procedure involving recorded voices of both the suspect and foils.[56]

8.81    If faced with a request by police for a 'live' voice identification procedure, whether or not within the terms of Code D Annex B para 18, the lawyer should carefully consider whether it is in the suspect's interests to consent to such a procedure. Refusal to co-operate with a voice identification procedure cannot lead to adverse inferences under the CJPOA 1994. Although evidence of refusal to co-operate in a 'live' procedure may be admissible, in view of the uncertainty about voice identification it is unlikely that this would have adverse consequences for the suspect. If the lawyer does advise the client to refuse to co-operate, the reasons for this advice should be carefully recorded.

## Intervention in the case of breach of Code D

8.82    Breach of Code D may occur where the police fail to hold an identification procedure in circumstances where they should do so or where, in conducting an identification procedure, they fail to observe the requirements of Code D. Breach does not automatically lead to exclusion of identification evidence, but it may be excluded under PACE s78 (see para 13.50 below).

8.83    The courts have not always been consistent in their approach to exclusion of identification evidence under PACE s78 where there has been a breach of Code D. However, since the case of *R v Popat*[57] the courts have generally adopted the approach that in considering whether to exclude identification evidence, the key consideration is not whether the police have complied with the detailed rules set out in Code D, but whether the overall purpose of the Code – securing fair identification practices leading to reliable identification evidence – has been respected. While the provisions of Code D are mandatory, a breach of a particular provision of Code D may not frustrate the overall purpose of the Code. Therefore, if a breach does not fundamentally undermine the overall purpose, it may be dealt with by appropriate directions to the jury rather than exclusion of evidence. Such directions should make clear to the jury that the suspect

55 [1998] Crim LR 281. See also *R v Davies* [2004] EWCA Crim 2521.

56 In *R v Flynn* [2008] 2 Cr App R 266 the Court of Appeal provided a critical assessment of the problems of voice identification, stating that it was more likely to be reliable when carried out by experts using acoustic and spectrographic techniques, and sophisticated auditory techniques, than by lay witnesses (including police officers).

57 [1998] Crim LR 825; (1998) *Times* 10 April. *Popat* was disapproved of in *R v Forbes* [2001] 1 AC 473; [2001] 2 WLR 1; [2001] 1 All ER 686; [2001] 1 Cr App R 31, but in respect of other aspects of the decision.

has lost the benefit of the safeguards provided by the Code, and that they should take that fact into account in their assessment of the whole case.[58] See further para 13.50 below.

8.84     Therefore, the defence lawyer cannot rely on a breach of Code D procedures leading to exclusion of evidence thereby obtained. Consequently, the lawyer should normally intervene if the police fail to comply with the provisions of Code D in a way which is, or is potentially, damaging to the client's interests. Equally, the lawyer should intervene if the lawyer is aware of police conduct which, while in conformity with Code D, is or may be unfair.

58   *R v Forbes* [2001] 1 AC 473. See also *R v Charles* [2001] EWCA Crim 1698, *R v Williams* [2003] EWCA Crim 3200, *R v Donald* [2004] Crim LR 841, and *R v Hassan* [2004] EWCA Crim 1478.

# CHAPTER 9

# Warrant of further detention

# Introduction

## Detention under PACE

9.1　Detention without charge up to 36 hours from the relevant time is dealt with at paras 2.69–2.76 above. Detention without charge beyond 36 hours is only possible in respect of a person who was arrested for an indictable offence (ie, indictable-only or either-way) and on the authority of a warrant of further detention issued by a magistrates' court. Warrants of further detention are governed by Police and Criminal Evidence Act 1984 (PACE) ss43–45.

9.2　A suspect who is brought before a court on the hearing of an application for a warrant of further detention is entitled to be legally represented at the hearing and, if the suspect is not represented but wishes to be, the hearing must be adjourned in order for this to be arranged (PACE s43(3)). A suspect who is the subject of an application for a warrant of further detention is entitled to police station legal aid for the purposes of the application, and the sufficient benefit test (see para 1.60 above) is deemed to be satisfied.[1] Advocacy assistance, and reasonable preparation and follow-up work, may be conducted and claimed for under the Standard Criminal Contract (SCC) 2010.[2] The lawyer who is advising a client at the police station should, given the obligation under the contract to continue to act for the client until the end of the investigation,[3] provide advocacy assistance in respect of the application. The relevant duty solicitor scheme is the police station scheme rather than the court scheme. A duty solicitor's representative who is not a solicitor cannot be heard at the hearing of a warrant application since he or she does not have a right of audience.

9.3　A person detained for an indictable offence may be denied access to a lawyer for up to 36 hours from the relevant time, provided that certain conditions are satisfied (see para 2.138 above). In theory, a suspect whose continued detention has been authorised by a court under PACE s43 may still be denied access to a lawyer for any period up to the expiry of 36 hours from the relevant time. However, if the suspect received legal advice in respect of the application for a warrant, it would be virtually impossible for a superintendent to be satisfied that one or more of the grounds for delaying access to legal advice under PACE s58(8) is satisfied.

9.4　An application for a warrant of further detention provides the lawyer with an opportunity to obtain information from both the client and the police. If the lawyer has been advising the client at the police station in respect of the matter which is the subject of an application, the lawyer will be in possession of much of the information needed to deal with the application. It may be, however, that the lawyer is only requested, or an earlier request for legal advice by the suspect complied with, at this stage. If this is the case, the lawyer should seek the information from the client set out in chapter 5. In addition, the lawyer should seek information from the client about what has occurred while the suspect has been in police

---

1　SCC 2010, Part B, para 9.146.
2　SCC 2010, Part B, paras 9.145–9.157.
3　SCC 2010, Part B, para 9.53.

detention. In particular, the lawyer will want to know whether any admissions have been made, and will also want to assess whether the police have acted in breach of PACE or the Codes of Practice. Particular attention should be paid to why a lawyer was not involved at an earlier stage.

9.5 The lawyer should also seek information from the police in advance of the application hearing. PACE s43(2) provides that the suspect must be provided with a copy of the information supporting the police officer's sworn application for the warrant, and the information must state (PACE s43(14)):

- the nature of the offence for which the person has been arrested;
- the general nature of the evidence on which that person was arrested;
- what enquiries relating to the offence have been made and what further enquiries are proposed; and
- the reasons for believing that continued detention is necessary for the purpose of such further enquiries.

9.6 In addition to a copy of the information, the lawyer should seek a copy of the custody record. Code C para 2.4A provides that where a suspect leaves police detention or is taken before a court, the suspect or the suspect's legal representative is entitled to a copy of the custody record, as soon as practicable after the request is made.[4] The custody record may, in particular, indicate whether PACE and the Codes have been complied with and whether any aspect of the detention has been unlawful.

## Detention under the Terrorism Act 2000

9.7 A person detained under Terrorism Act (TA) 2000 s41 may be detained for up to 48 hours from the time of arrest (see para 2.67 above). The person can be detained beyond this period, for up to a total of 14 days beginning with the time of arrest, only if a judicial authority grants a warrant of further detention.[5] The rules and processes are similar to applications under PACE, including the provisions regarding legal aid, subject to the following modifications.

9.8 Application for a warrant of further detention is made to a judicial authority (a specially designated district judge) (TA 2000 Sch 8 para 29(4)(a)). The application must be made before the expiry of 48 hours from the time of arrest, or within six hours of the end of that period, but the judicial authority must dismiss an application under the latter provision if they consider that it would have been reasonably practicable to have made it within 48 hours (TA 2000 Sch 8 para 30). The person to whom the application relates must be given a notice stating that an application is to be made, the times at which it is to be made and heard, and the grounds upon which further detention is sought (TA 2000 Sch 8 para 31).

9.9 The person to whom the application relates must be given an opportunity to make oral or written representations to the judicial authority and is

---

4 This is in addition to the right to see the custody record under Code C para 2.4.
5 The power to extend detention up to 28 days in TA 2000 Sch 8 para 36(3)(b)(ii) was subject to a 'sunset' clause, and the power has not been renewed, so that the maximum period is now 14 days. When the Protection of Freedoms Bill (2011) clause 57 is enacted, this reduction will be made permanent.

entitled to be legally represented (TA 2000 Sch 8 para 33(1)). However, the judicial authority may exclude from any part of the hearing the person to whom the application relates and anyone representing himself or herself (TA 2000 Sch 8 para 33(3)). TA 2000 Sch 8 does not set out any conditions or criteria for the exercise of this power, nor does it require that reasons be given. Furthermore, the officer making the application may apply to the judicial authority for an order that specified information upon which the officer intends to rely be withheld from the person to whom the application applies and from that person's representative (TA 2000 Sch 8 para 34(1)). To make an order, the judicial authority must have reasonable grounds for believing that if the information was disclosed, one or more of the consequences set out in para 34(2) or (3) would occur (TA 2000 Sch 8 para 34(2)).

9.10    A judicial authority may only issue a warrant of further detention if satisfied that there are reasonable grounds for believing that further detention is necessary:

- to obtain relevant evidence (whether by questioning or otherwise);
- to preserve evidence; or
- pending the result of an examination or analysis of any relevant evidence, or of anything the examination or analysis of which is to be or is being carried out with a view to obtaining relevant evidence,

and that the investigation is being conducted diligently and expeditiously (TA 2000 Sch 8 para 32(1) and (1A)). 'Relevant evidence' means, in relation to the person to whom the application relates, evidence that relates to the person's commission of an offence under any of the provisions mentioned in TA 2000 s40(1)(a), or which indicates that he or she is a person falling within TA 2000 s40(1)(b) (ie, is or has been concerned in the commission, preparation or instigation of acts of terrorism) (TA 2000 Sch 8 para 32(2)).

9.11    The remainder of the chapter deals with warrants of further detention under PACE, but the same principles apply to applications under TA 2000, subject to appropriate modifications.

## Application process

9.12    An application for a warrant of further detention has to be made on oath by a constable and must be supported by an information (PACE s43(1)). The requirements regarding the content of the information are set out at para 9.5 above. A copy of the information must be supplied to the suspect (PACE s43(2)), who must be brought before the court for the hearing (PACE s43(2)) and who is entitled to legal representation (PACE s43(3)). The application is heard by a magistrates' court, which is defined as a court consisting of two or more justices of the peace sitting otherwise than in open court (PACE s45(1)).

## Lawfulness of the detention

9.13    In order for a warrant to be issued, the detention itself must be lawful. The detention, or continued detention, may be unlawful if:

1) The original arrest was unlawful, for example, because it was made in the absence of reasonable grounds or was not necessary (see paras 2.15 and 2.18 above), or the arresting officer failed to give reasons (see para 2.42 above).

2) There are no grounds for detention, or continued detention, without charge under PACE s37 or any other provision. In particular, if the custody officer is satisfied that there is sufficient evidence to charge, the suspect must be charged or released (see para 2.53 above).

3) The decision to detain beyond 24 hours was made unlawfully. It has been held that a court had no jurisdiction to grant a warrant of further detention where the detention was unlawful because the decision to extend the period of detention beyond 24 hours by a superintendent had been made without giving an opportunity to the suspect or the solicitor to make representations, as is required by PACE s42(6).[6]

4) The conditions for interviews to be ended and for a decision regarding charge are satisfied (see paras 7.69 above and 10.4 below).

## Time limits

9.14 An application can be made at any time before the expiry of 36 hours from the relevant time (see para 2.70 above), and thus can be made before the expiry of the initial 24-hour detention time limit.[7] For the purpose of calculating the time limit, the time of the application is the time that the constable makes the application on oath and gives evidence.[8] The time limit may be extended for a further six hours (that is, up to the expiry of 42 hours from the relevant time) if it is not practicable for the court to sit before the expiry of 36 hours, but it will sit during the six hours following the expiry of 36 hours (PACE s43(5)(b)(ii)). However, the 36-hour time limit is a strict one, and the court must dismiss an application if it appears that it would have been reasonable for the police to make the application before the expiry of 36 hours (PACE s43(7)). In *R v Slough Justices ex p Stirling*,[9] the application was lodged nine minutes before the expiry of 36 hours, but the application was not made until one-and-a-half hours later (when the magistrates returned from lunch). It was held that the court should have dismissed the application since the application could reasonably have been made before the 36-hour time limit expired. Code C NfG 15D provides that an application should usually be made between 10 am and 9 pm, and if possible during usual court hours. PACE s45(2) provides that any reference to a period of time is to be treated as approximate only, so that an application made within minutes of the expiry of the time limit will probably be accepted, but the cut-off point is uncertain.

6 *Police v Mudd and McDonough* November 1987 *Legal Action* 19, also reported as *In the matter of an application for a warrant of further detention* [1988] Crim LR 296. Note that it is a decision of a stipendiary magistrate and, although of persuasive authority, is not binding on other courts.

7 Note that time during which a person has been released on police bail does not count for the purpose of calculating the period from the relevant time (see para 2.72 above).

8 *R v Sedgefield Justices ex p Milne* (1987) 5 November (unreported), Lexis No CO/1318/87.

9 [1987] Crim LR 576.

## Issue of a warrant

9.15    The court may issue a warrant of further detention if it is satisfied that there are reasonable grounds for believing that further detention is justified (PACE s43(1)).[10] The period of the warrant should be such period as the court thinks fit, having regard to the evidence before it, up to a maximum of 36 hours (PACE s43(11) and (12)). If the suspect is to be transferred to another police area, the court must have regard to the distance and the time the journey would take in fixing the period (PACE s43(13)).

9.16    A warrant can be extended for up to a further period of 36 hours if an application is made in the proper form (see para 9.12 above) and the court is satisfied that further detention is justified. However, this is subject to an overall maximum period of detention of 96 hours from the relevant time (PACE s44(3)). Successive applications for extension of the warrant can be made, subject to the overall maximum period of detention. Under no circumstances can a suspect be detained without charge for longer than 96 hours from the relevant time.

9.17    A suspect who is the subject of a warrant of further detention must still have their detention reviewed in the usual way (see para 2.80 above), and must be released before the expiry of the warrant if the grounds for detention cease to apply (PACE s34(2)). In any event, unless the warrant is extended, the suspect must be released or charged on or before expiry of the warrant (PACE s43(18)).

## Refusal of a warrant

9.18    If the court is not satisfied that further detention is justified, it must either refuse the application or adjourn the hearing of it until a time not later than 36 hours after the relevant time (PACE s43(8)). If the court adjourns, the suspect can be kept in police detention during the period of adjournment (PACE s43(9)). If the 36 hours has expired at the time of the application, and it appears to the court that it would have been reasonable for the application to have been made before the expiry of that period, the court must dismiss (PACE s43(7)). If a warrant is refused, the police can continue to detain the suspect without charge up to 24 hours from the relevant time, or 36 hours from the relevant time if authorised by a superintendent under PACE s42, provided that grounds for detention without charge still exist under PACE s37 (PACE s43(16)). Furthermore, if a warrant is refused, no further application for a warrant of further detention can be made unless supported by evidence that has come to light since the court's refusal (PACE s43(17)).

9.19    A question that arises is whether the police could, on the refusal of a warrant, extend the period of detention without charge by arresting the person for a further offence. Generally this would not be possible, since PACE s31 provides that where a person has been arrested for an offence and it appears to a constable that, if released, the person would be liable to arrest for some other offence, the person must be arrested for that other offence as well. PACE s41(4) then provides that where a person has been

---

10  For the definition of 'justified' see para 9.23 below.

arrested under PACE s31, the relevant time (see para 2.71 above) is the relevant time for the original offence. However, PACE s31 only applies where the person is at a police station in consequence of the arrest for the original offence.[11] It could be argued, therefore, that the police could prolong the period of detention if they were to re-arrest the person while they are still at court.[12] However, even if such an argument were upheld, any evidence obtained during the prolonged period of detention might be excluded under PACE s78 since the further detention would clearly be contrary to the spirit of PACE s41.

## Hearing of the application

9.20　Applications for a warrant of further detention are relatively rare, and courts may be keen, particularly if the hearing is outside usual court hours, to deal with the matter as quickly as possible. This can result in pressure being placed on the lawyer to rush the preparation stage so that the hearing can commence. Such pressure should be resisted, and the magistrates may need to be reminded of the important issues at stake. Particular pressure may be applied if the time limit for making the application is about to expire since, as seen at para 9.14, the critical time is the time that the police officer makes the application and gives evidence on oath. Because the suspect is entitled to legal representation under PACE s43(3), the lawyer is in a relatively strong position to hold out for more time to prepare. If the time taken by the defence to prepare results in the application being made outside the 36-hour limit, the question will arise as to whether the court can still admit the application under PACE s43(5)(b)(ii) (see para 9.14 above). In making the decision about practicality, the court must have regard to PACE s43(7), which provides that it must dismiss the application if it appears that it would have been reasonable for the police to make the application before the time expired. Since the police should have anticipated that the defence would need a reasonable period for preparation, it can be argued that the court cannot be so satisfied.

9.21　　The issues of the legality of the detention, of whether the formal requirements have been satisfied (ie, supplying a copy of the information to the suspect and their physical presence), and of time limits may be taken as preliminary points. If they are successful, the application cannot proceed further. If there are no such preliminary points, or the defence lawyer cannot persuade the court to uphold them, the court will proceed to hear the substantive application. In order for a warrant to be issued under PACE s43 (or to be extended under PACE s44) the conditions in PACE s43(4) must be satisfied (see para 9.23 below). The burden of establishing these conditions is clearly on the prosecution.

---

11　The suspect is still in police detention as defined by PACE s118(2), but s31 only applies where the suspect is 'at a police station'.

12　A similar ploy used in relation to custody time limits has been accepted by the Divisional Court as starting time limits afresh, even though the new charge arose from the same facts as the original charge (*R v Waltham Forest Magistrates' Court ex p Lee and Lee* [1993] Crim LR 522).

9.22    In considering an application for a warrant of further detention, a court cannot draw inferences from silence or failure to account under Criminal Justice and Public Order Act (CJPOA) 1994 ss34, 36 and 37, since an application for a warrant of further detention is not included in the list of stages of proceedings where the sections apply (CJPOA 1994 ss34(2), 36(2) and 37(2)). The power of a court to draw inferences from failure to give evidence or to answer any question under CJPOA 1994 s35 also does not apply.[13]

## Is further detention justified?

9.23    The general requirement for a warrant to be issued or extended is that the court must be satisfied that there are reasonable grounds for believing that the further detention of the suspect is justified (PACE ss43(1) and 44(1)). The term 'justified' is defined so that the court must be satisfied in relation to all of the following three factors (PACE s43(4)).

### To secure, preserve or obtain evidence

9.24    The court must be satisfied that detention without charge 'is necessary to secure or preserve evidence relating to an offence for which he is under arrest or to obtain such evidence by questioning him' (PACE s43(4)(a)). This is the same test as applies at the time of initial detention and at the 24-hour stage (see para 2.65 above). At the hearing, the police officer(s) should be cross-examined, and appropriate representations made, in relation to the following questions.

1) *Why the suspect needs to be detained for this purpose* The section requires that detention be necessary, not merely convenient. Why is it that the suspect cannot be released and questioned outside of police detention, or released while the police are gathering other evidence? Is there any evidence to suggest that the suspect will abscond or seek to interfere with witnesses or evidence, or otherwise interfere with the course of the investigation?

2) *Whether the suspect has been charged* It is clear from PACE s43(4) that if the suspect has been charged with an offence, an application for a warrant of further detention in respect of that offence cannot be entertained. If the suspect has been arrested and detained in respect of more than one offence, and has been charged in respect of one or more of the offences, it is doubtful whether the court can issue a warrant in respect of the offence(s) for which the suspect has not been charged. The reason is that once a suspect has been charged, PACE s38 provides that the custody officer must release the suspect unless the conditions for withholding bail are satisfied, and if this is so, PACE s46 provides that the suspect must be brought before a court as soon as practicable.[14] An

---

13  See, in particular, CJPOA 1994 s35(3)).
14  Although if bail is not granted, it would seem that there is nothing to stop the police from interviewing a suspect about matters for which the suspect has not been charged during the period before the suspect is produced in court. The restriction on questioning after charge in Code C para 16.5 applies only to questioning in respect of the matter for which the person has been charged.

application for a warrant would not count as a production before the court for these purposes. The proper course in these circumstances would be for the police to produce the suspect under PACE s46 in respect of the matter for which the suspect has been charged, to oppose bail, and then to ask for a remand to a police station for up to three days under Magistrates' Court Act 1980 s128(7).[15]

3) *Whether the suspect should have been charged already* PACE s37(7) provides that a custody officer must make a decision about charge if the officer has before him or her sufficient evidence to charge the person. See the discussion of what amounts to 'sufficient evidence to charge' at para 10.4 below. If the evidence given at the hearing of the application discloses that there is sufficient evidence to charge, then in view of PACE s37(7) the court will have no power to issue the warrant. If the suspect has been arrested and detained in respect of more than one offence, Code C para 16.1 provides that it is permissible to delay bringing the suspect before the custody officer until there is sufficient evidence in respect of all the offences. Therefore, the police could apply for a warrant in respect of one offence even though there is sufficient evidence to charge in relation to another offence. Note, however, that this aspect of para 16.1 may be ultra vires (see para 7.73 above).

4) *What evidence the police intend to secure or preserve during the period of the warrant* While a court may be reluctant to require the police to divulge their plans in precise detail, the police should be prepared to indicate the nature of the evidence they hope to obtain, how they intend to obtain it and how long this is likely to take. Does this involve interviewing witnesses and, if so, are they likely to be available? Will it involve seeking information that may be held electronically and, if so, when will it be possible to obtain it? For example, if the application is being heard on a Friday night, it may be impossible to obtain information from banks and building societies until the following Monday morning – outside the 36-hour initial maximum period of the warrant. It may be that the police wish to carry out tests on materials such as suspected drugs. If so, who will this be done by and when will it be done?

5) *What evidence the police hope to obtain by questioning the suspect* If the suspect has been answering questions in interview, the police should be asked what other matters they want to put to the suspect. This may, of course, depend on what other evidence they hope to obtain but, again, it may be appropriate for the lawyer to explore why the suspect needs to be in detention for this purpose. If the suspect has not been answering questions in interview, and has indicated firmly that he or she does not intend to answer them, it can be argued that this ground for issuing a warrant cannot be satisfied. Although the fact that a suspect does not intend to answer questions does not alter the police's entitlement to put questions, this cannot be authority for continuing detention which has as its sole or primary purpose the undermining of the suspect's right to silence.

15 Or in the case of certain drugs offences, remand for up to 192 hours under Criminal Justice Act 1988 s152 as amended by Drugs Act 2005 s8.

### Under arrest for an indictable offence

9.25   The suspect must be under arrest for an indictable offence (ie, indictable-only or either-way) (PACE s43(4)(b)). Whether an offence is indictable will usually be straightforward. However, the police may lawfully arrest a person without precisely specifying the offence for which the person is arrested (see para 2.15 above). In order to make an application for a warrant of further detention, the police must have specified the offence with sufficient precision to establish that it is an indictable offence.

### Diligent and expeditious investigation

9.26   Further detention is only justified if 'the investigation is being conducted diligently and expeditiously' (PACE s43(4)(c)). A mere assertion by the police that this is so is not sufficient since, by PACE s43(1), the court must have reasonable grounds for believing that further detention is justified and, therefore, must have reasonable grounds for believing that the condition in PACE s43(4)(c) is satisfied. The expression 'diligently and expeditiously' involves the idea that the police are carrying out the investigation as quickly as possible and are approaching it in a careful and industrious manner. From the suspect's point of view, there are often periods when the police appear to be doing little or nothing to progress the investigation and, if relevant, this needs to be dealt with in cross-examination of the police. Furthermore, it may appear that the police are only dealing with one issue at a time, when they could be pursuing various lines of enquiry simultaneously. To some extent this obviously depends on investigative resources, but again this may be an area worth pursuing in cross-examination. Although Code C sections 8, 9, 11 and 12 place limits on the times during which, and the periods for which, the suspect can be interviewed, they do not provide that the investigation should not proceed by other means during those fallow times. If, for example, the investigating officers went home at 6 pm and did not return until 8 am the next morning, during which time nothing was done to progress the investigation, it should be difficult for the police to satisfy the court as to diligence and expedition. Such lack of progress should not be justified by the fact that the suspect 'was having his lie down'.

## Period of the warrant

9.27   The foregoing paragraphs indicate the range of issues that may be included in a defence submission that a warrant of further detention should not be issued. The court may need to be reminded that it must be satisfied that there are reasonable grounds for believing that further detention is justified, and that for this to be the case, all three of the criteria in PACE s43(4) must be satisfied. If the court is so satisfied, the remaining issue is the period of the warrant. If possible, a defence submission as to the period of the warrant should only be made once the court has decided that a warrant is to be issued.

9.28   A warrant can be issued for such period as the court thinks fit, having regard to the evidence before it, subject to a maximum of 36 hours

(PACE s43(11) and (12)). This clearly means that the period should not automatically be 36 hours, but should relate to what the police intend to do to progress the investigation. Inevitably, this will require the court to make an informed guess, but since the decision involves loss of liberty the court should be urged to issue the warrant for the minimum appropriate period. Since the police can, subject to the overall time limit, make an application to extend the warrant under PACE s44, the investigation would not be jeopardised by the issuing of a warrant for a shorter rather than a longer period.

# CHAPTER 10

# The decision to charge and afterwards

*continued*

# Introduction

10.1    In its white paper *Justice for All*[1] the then government signalled its intention to shift primary responsibility for charging decisions from the police to the Crown Prosecution Service (CPS) and also to enhance the role of Crown prosecutors in advising the police on their investigations. The purpose of this change was to encourage more focused police investigations, to help ensure that charge decisions are appropriate, and to reduce the number of cases discontinued by the prosecution. The policy (known as statutory charging) was put into effect by amendments to Police and Criminal Evidence Act 1984 (PACE), and by giving statutory responsibility to the Director of Public Prosecutions (DPP) for issuing guidance on charging. However, the coalition government intends to transfer many charging decisions back to the police. As a result, the law and practice concerning charging is in a state of flux, and the applicable law and guidance varies in different police force areas. Responsibility for making decisions regarding alternatives to charging, such as simple and conditional cautions, rests with either the police or a Crown prosecutor, depending on the out-of-court disposal concerned. Responsibility for making decisions regarding bail following charge remains with the custody officer.

10.2    The detailed provisions relevant to the decision to charge, out-of-court disposals and bail are set out in this chapter, but to help make sense of the detailed provisions a broad outline of the charge decision process is provided here. Responsibility for determining whether there is sufficient evidence to charge, and for deciding what action should then be taken, is placed on the custody officer by PACE s37(7). In making those decisions, the custody officer must have regard to guidance issued by the DPP under PACE s37A (PACE s37A(3)). This guidance is known as the *Director's Guidance on Charging*,[2] and it sets out the tests for determining whether there is sufficient evidence to charge, and also sets out the offences and circumstances in respect of which the custody officer or a Crown prosecutor[3] respectively have responsibility for making a charge decision. In cases or circumstances where a Crown prosecutor must make a charge decision, the police must supply information to the prosecutor, and the prosecutor must decide whether there is sufficient evidence to charge and, if so, must decide whether the person should be charged and what the person should be charged with (PACE s37B(1)–(3)). The prosecutor must then notify his or her decision to an officer dealing with the case, and if the decision is

---

1   Cm 5563, July 2002, chapter 3.

2   The most recent version of the *Guidance* was issued in January 2011, and is available at www.cps.gov.uk/publications. It now incorporates guidance on the streamlined process, which was originally issued as separate guidance, but is subject to a phased roll-out as specified in the Schedule to the *Guidance*. References in this chapter are to the *Guidance* issued in January 2011 (the fourth edition). For police force areas where the revised *Guidance* is not in force reference should be made to the *Guidance* issued in February 2007 (the third edition, also available at www.cps.gov.uk/publications). In January 2010, the Revenue and Customs Prosecution Office became a specialist division in the CPS, but there is separate guidance on charging for revenue and customs cases.

3   PACE s37B refers to decisions to be made by the DPP, but in practice they are normally taken by a Crown prosecutor.

that the person should be charged, the custody officer must then charge, or arrange to be charged, the person accordingly (PACE s37A(4)–(7)). If the person is in police detention at the relevant time, the person may be charged in the normal way, but if the person is not in police detention (because, for example, he or she has been granted bail without charge), the person may be charged by means of the written charge and requisition procedure (PACE s37B(8)).[4]

10.3     Statutory charging has impacted on defence lawyers in a number of ways. Negotiations concerning charge, where the charge decision is to be made by a Crown prosecutor, are often difficult or impossible since prosecutors are usually unwilling to speak to defence lawyers at the police station. The previous New Labour government indicated that it would pilot arrangements whereby Crown prosecutors could initiate discussions with defence lawyers concerning charge,[5] but in the event a national scheme was not established. Nevertheless, the defence lawyer should, where appropriate, ask to speak to the Crown prosecutor making the charge decision and should ask for written representations to be given to the prosecutor where he or she refuses to speak to the defence lawyer. Statutory charging also means that suspects and their lawyers often have to wait while the case is being considered by the prosecutor, and such delays can often be lengthy. The Standard Criminal Contract (SCC) 2010 requires duty solicitors, in respect of cases they have accepted, to provide advice where a client is to be charged, and to consider attending at the time of charge: 'bearing in mind whether it is possible to give confidential telephone advice and the possible consequences of not making a statement when charged'.[6] Although not binding in own solicitor cases, these obligations on duty solicitors should be regarded as establishing a minimum standard applicable in all cases.

## Decision regarding charge

### When must a decision be made?

10.4     The point at which a decision must be made regarding charge is governed by a number of provisions in PACE (or the Terrorism Act (TA) 2000) and Code C.[7] The latest time at which a decision about charge must be made is, in effect, at the expiry of the detention time limit. In the case of PACE detentions, this is 24 hours from the relevant time, or later if extended by a superintendent or magistrates' court (see paras 2.69–2.77 above). Where a person is detained under the TA 2000, it is 48 hours from the time of arrest, or later if extended by a judicial authority (see para 2.78 above). In practice, a decision about charge will usually have been made before the

---

4  The written charge and requisition procedure, which is governed by Criminal Justice Act (CJA) 2003 ss29 and 30, is intended to replace the summons procedure for public prosecutions. It is now available in all police force areas.

5  See *A fairer deal for legal aid*, Cm 6591, July 2005, para 4.9.

6  SCC 2010, Part B, para 9.43.

7  Note that Code H does not contain separate provisions regarding charge, but confirms that charging is governed by PACE and Code C section 16.

detention time limit expires, but if no decision has been made by this time the suspect must be released, either on bail or unconditionally.

10.5      By PACE s37(7), if the custody officer determines that the officer has before him or her sufficient evidence to charge an arrested person with the offence for which the person was arrested, the suspect must be:

a) released without charge and on bail, or kept in police detention, for the purpose of enabling a Crown prosecutor to make a charge decision (PACE s37(7)(a)(i) and (ii));

b) released without charge and on bail, but not for that purpose (eg, where, although the custody officer has determined that there is sufficient evidence to charge, the police want to gather more evidence) (PACE s37(7)(b));[8]

c) released without charge and without bail (PACE s37(7)(c)); or

d) charged (PACE s37(7)(d)).

PACE s37(7) is in mandatory terms and contains no provision for delay in making a decision as to the appropriate course of action. Where, under the *Director's Guidance on Charging*, the custody officer is required to refer the matter to a Crown prosecutor for a charge decision, the suspect is to be detained for no longer than is reasonably necessary to decide on how the suspect is to be dealt with (Code C NfG 16AB). Unreasonable delay is likely to render the detention unlawful even if it is within the maximum period of detention. If the suspect is unlikely, if charged, to be granted bail the delay in making a charge decision may not prolong the suspect's detention. If, however, the suspect is likely to be granted bail, the defence lawyer may argue that prolonged, and possibly unlawful, delay can be avoided by releasing the suspect on bail under PACE s37(7)(a)(i) or (b).

## Sufficient evidence to charge

10.6      A key issue in determining when a charge decision under PACE s37(7) must be made is the meaning of 'sufficient evidence to charge'. When the custody officer determines that the officer has before him or her sufficient evidence to charge, the officer must deal with the suspect in accordance with PACE s37(7)(a) to (d). The phrase 'sufficient evidence to charge' is not defined in PACE itself, and is subject to different interpretations in Code C and in the *Director's Guidance on Charging*. Code C para 16.1 does not use the phrase 'sufficient evidence to charge', but states that when the officer in charge of an investigation reasonably believes there is sufficient evidence to provide a 'realistic prospect of conviction' the officer must, without delay, inform the custody officer. This implies that a decision under PACE s37(7) must be made *as soon as* the custody officer is in possession of information that leads the officer to conclude that there is sufficient evidence to charge, and that the relevant test is the 'realistic prospect of conviction' test.[9]

---

8  For bail without charge, see para 10.73 below.

9  For the point at which interviewing must cease see para 7.69 above. For the contradictions between Code C para 11.6 and para 16.1, see para 7.71 above. For consideration of the meaning of 'sufficient evidence to charge' for the purpose of determining whether a person arrested and taken to a police station should be detained for investigation see para 2.59 above.

10.7     The *Director's Guidance on Charging* sets out two different tests for determining whether there is sufficient evidence to charge – the 'full code test' and the 'threshold test'.[10] The full code test is the normal test to be applied in determining whether there is sufficient evidence to charge. The threshold test may only be applied in exceptional circumstances.

1) *The full code test* The full code test is set out in the *Code for Crown Prosecutors*[11] (CCP) and consists of an evidential stage and a public interest stage, although only the former is relevant to the initial decision to be made by the custody officer under PACE s37(7). The officer must be satisfied that there is enough evidence to provide a realistic prospect of conviction, taking into account what the defence case may be and how it is likely to affect the prosecution case. The CCP states that this is an objective test and means that a court, properly directed on the law, would be more likely than not to convict the defendant of the offence alleged. In deciding whether there is enough evidence, the officer must consider whether the evidence can be used and is reliable. Whether evidence can be used depends upon whether, having regard to evidential rules, it is likely to be admitted. In determining whether it is reliable, the officer should take into account:

   • whether there is evidence that might support or detract from the reliability of any confession made;
   • any explanation provided by the suspect, and whether a court is likely to find it credible taking into account the evidence as a whole;
   • where identification is likely to be disputed, whether the evidence of identification is likely to be strong enough;
   • the likely credibility and accuracy of witnesses, having regard to any motive they may have or relevant previous convictions.[12]

2) *The threshold test* The threshold test may be applied by the custody officer in determining whether a case should be referred for a charge decision to a Crown prosecutor under PACE s37(7)(a) where the suspect presents a substantial bail risk if released and not all the evidence is available at the time when he or she must be released from custody unless charged.[13] In order to satisfy the threshold test there must be: a) reasonable suspicion that the suspect has committed the offence; and b) reasonable grounds for believing that the continuing investigation will provide sufficient evidence to satisfy the full code test within a reasonable time (see para 10.17 below).

### Representations by the defence lawyer

10.8     If the lawyer concludes that it is in the client's interests for a decision about charge to be made, for example, because detention has been lengthy and/or there is evidence to justify charging and the lawyer wishes to avoid further interviews, the lawyer should consider the following:

---

10  *Director's Guidance on Charging* paras 8 and 12.
11  Issued under Prosecution of Offences Act (POA) 1985 s10, and available at www.cps. gov.uk/publications/code_for_crown_prosecutors/.
12  CCP paras 4.5–4.7.
13  *Director's Guidance on Charging* paras 4, 5 and 12.

- If it is clear that the police have decided to charge the client in any event, the custody officer must proceed to make a charge decision under PACE s37(7), and further detention without charge is likely to be unlawful.[14]
- If it appears that the police have sufficient evidence to provide a realistic prospect of conviction but the interviewing officer cites Code C para 11.6 as authority for allowing further questioning of the client, the lawyer should cite Code C para 16.1 as authority for the requirement that the interviewing officer must take the suspect before the custody officer without delay. If the interviewing officer refuses to do so, the lawyer should consider making appropriate representations to the custody officer and asking them to determine that there is sufficient evidence to charge.
- If it appears that there is sufficient evidence to charge (which will depend on which test under the *Director's Guidance on Charging* is relevant – see para 10.7 above), but the custody officer is reluctant to make a decision, the lawyer should make representations that under PACE s37(7) and the *Director's Guidance*, the officer must make a decision.

If it appears that there is insufficient evidence to charge, and there is unlikely to be sufficient evidence in the near future, the lawyer should consider making representations to the custody officer that charge be refused or that the client be released on bail under PACE s34(5) (which cannot be made subject to conditions) or s37(2) (which can be made subject to conditions) pending further enquiries (see para 10.73 below). All representations, and responses, should be recorded, and the lawyer should also ask that they be entered on the custody record.

## Detention for more than one offence

10.9   PACE s37(7) does not deal with the situation where a suspect is detained in respect of more than one offence. Code C para 16.1 provides that where a person is detained in respect of more than one offence, it is permissible for the investigating officer to delay bringing the person before the custody officer until the investigating officer believes that there is sufficient evidence to provide a realistic prospect of conviction in respect of all the offences.[15] There are two possible arguments here from the defence point of view. First, this provision may be ultra vires since PACE s37(7) is in clear mandatory terms (see para 7.73 above). Second, even if Code C para 16.1 is valid, while it may be used by the interviewing officer to justify a decision not to take the suspect before the custody officer until a later stage, if the custody officer becomes aware (for example, because the lawyer has informed him or her) that there is sufficient evidence to provide a realistic prospect of conviction, the custody officer is bound by the terms of PACE s37(7).

14   See *R v Elliott* [2002] EWCA Crim 931; and *R v Mulayim Dervish* [2001] EWCA Crim 2789; [2002] 2 Cr App R 6.
15   Although the suspect must not be further questioned about any offence in respect of which the conditions in Code C para 11.6 are satisfied.

10.10    Arguably, if released the suspect should not be at risk of arrest for the offence for which questioning was not completed, since PACE s31 provides that if the suspect was liable to arrest for that offence while detained in respect of the other matter for which the suspect was originally arrested, the arrest must take place while in detention. However, it should be noted that while there is a prohibition on re-arrest following release at the expiry of 24 hours (PACE s41(9)), 36 hours (PACE s42(11)), a warrant of further detention (PACE s43(19)), or having been released on police bail[16] (unless new evidence justifying a further arrest has come to light since the suspect's release), there is no similar provision preventing re-arrest where a person is released in the circumstances being considered here. It may be, therefore, that the argument is of more practical use in seeking to speed up the process rather than in trying to secure the immediate release of the suspect, since the latter might simply result in the suspect being re-arrested.

## Who makes the decision on charge?

10.11   As noted in para 10.5 above, it is the custody officer's responsibility under PACE s37(7) to decide whether there is sufficient evidence to charge, but the decision as to charge (or an alternative to charging) may be that of a custody officer or a Crown prosecutor under the terms of the *Director's Guidance on Charging*.

10.12   A Crown prosecutor must make the charge decision in respect of all indictable-only offences, and any either-way offence in respect of which, under the *Director's Guidance*, a custody officer is not permitted to make a charge decision (see below). In cases where more than one charge may be appropriate, and at least one of them must be referred to a prosecutor for a charge decision, all matters must be referred to the prosecutor.

10.13   A custody officer may make the charge decision (under PACE s37(7)(d)) in respect of any summary-offence (including criminal damage where the value of the loss or damage is less than £5,000) irrespective of likely plea. A custody officer may also make a charge decision in respect of an either-way offence where it is anticipated that the suspect will plead guilty and it is suitable for sentence in a magistrates' court, provided that it is not:

- a case requiring the consent to prosecute of the DPP or a law officer;
- a case involving death;
- connected with terrorist activity or official secrets;
- classified as a hate crime or domestic violence under CPS policies;
- an offence of violent disorder or affray;
- an offence involving causing grievous bodily harm or wounding, or actual bodily harm;
- an offence under the Sexual Offences Act 2003 (SOA) 2003 committed by or upon a person under 18 years; or
- an offence under the Licensing Act 2003.[17]

---

16  Subject to the power to arrest for failure to answer to police bail under PACE s46A.
17  *Director's Guidance on Charging* para 19.

The *Director's Guidance* provides that a case may be considered suitable for sentencing in a magistrates' court unless the loss or damage relating to the charge is more than £5,000 or would exceed that sum if more than one offence is charged (or taken into consideration); or the overall circumstances of the offence are so serious that the court may decide that a sentence of more than six months' imprisonment justifies sending the case to the Crown Court; or the offence has been committed while the suspect was subject to a Crown Court order then in force.[18]

10.14   A custody officer may also, provided that it is authorised by an inspector or above, charge a person with an offence that under the *Director's Guidance* should normally be referred to a Crown prosecutor for a charge decision where the continued detention of the suspect after charge is justified and it is not possible to obtain a prosecutor's authority for the charge before the expiry of any relevant detention time limit. In making a charge decision under this provision, the custody officer may decide to charge on the basis of the threshold test (see para 10.17 below), and must refer the case to a Crown prosecutor as soon as possible after charge and no later than the time proposed for the suspect's first court appearance.[19]

## The tests for deciding on charge

### The full code test

10.15   The decision regarding charge, whether made by a custody officer or by a Crown prosecutor, must normally be made in accordance with the full code test set out in the CCP.[20] The full code test consists of two stages, the evidential stage and the public interest stage. The test to be applied at the evidential stage is set out at para 10.7 above. It has been held that in deciding whether there is a realistic prospect of conviction, rather than take a statistical approach the prosecutor (and the same would apply to a custody officer) should imagine himself or herself to be the fact finder and ask whether, on balance, the evidence is sufficient to merit a conviction taking into account what the he or she knows about the defence case.[21] Note that in cases where trafficking of human beings is an obvious possibility the police should make appropriate enquiries which the prosecutor should take into account in deciding whether a person should be charged.[22]

10.16   The public interest stage of the test must only be applied after the prosecutor or custody officer has determined that the evidential stage is satisfied. Where the evidential test is satisfied, a prosecution should usually proceed unless there are public interest factors that outweigh those in favour of prosecution, or the prosecutor or custody officer is satisfied that the public interest may be properly served by offering the offender the

18  *Director's Guidance on Charging* para 22.
19  *Director's Guidance on Charging* para 24.
20  *Director's Guidance on Charging* paras 8 and 12.
21  *R (FB) v DPP* [2009] 1 Cr App R 580.
22  *R v LM* [2011] 1 Cr App R 135, and see the *CPS Policy for prosecuting cases of human trafficking*, available via www.cps.gov.uk/publications, and the CPS legal guidance *Human trafficking and smuggling*, available via www.cps.gov.uk/legal/.

opportunity to have the matter dealt with by an out-of-court disposal.[23] The following examples of relevant factors are given in the CCP.[24]

*A prosecution is more likely to be needed if:*

- a conviction is likely to result in a significant sentence;
- a conviction is likely to result in an order of the court in excess of that which a prosecutor is able to secure through a conditional caution;
- the offence involved the use of a weapon or the threat of violence;
- the offence was committed against a person serving the public (eg, a member of the emergency services, a police or prison officer, or a nurse);
- the suspect was in a position of authority or trust and the suspect took advantage of it;
- the suspect was a ringleader or an organiser of the offence;
- there is evidence that the offence was premeditated;
- there is evidence that the offence was carried out by a group;
- the victim was vulnerable, had been put in considerable fear, or suffered personal attack, damage or disturbance;
- the offence was committed in the presence of, or in close proximity to, a child;
- the offence was motivated by any form of discrimination against the victim's ethnic or national origin, gender, disability, age, religion or belief, political views, sexual orientation, or gender identity, or the suspect demonstrated hostility towards the victim based on any of those characteristics;
- there is a marked difference between the actual or mental ages of the suspect and the victim and the suspect took advantage of this;
- the suspect's previous convictions or the previous out-of-court disposal which the suspect has received are relevant to the present offence;
- the suspect is alleged to have committed the offence in breach of an order of the court;
- there are grounds for believing that the offence is likely to be continued or repeated;
- the offence was committed in order to facilitate more serious offending; or
- a prosecution would have a significant positive impact on maintaining community confidence.

*A prosecution is less likely to be needed if:*

- the court is likely to impose a nominal penalty;
- the seriousness and the consequences of the offending can be appropriately dealt with by an out-of-court disposal which the suspect accepts and with which s/he complies;
- the suspect has been subject to any appropriate regulatory proceedings, or any punitive or relevant civil penalty which remains in place or which has been satisfactorily discharged, which adequately addresses the seriousness of the offending and any breach of trust involved;

---

23  CCP para 4.12.
24  CCP paras 4.16–4.20.

- the offence was committed as a result of a genuine mistake or mis-understanding;
- the loss or harm can be described as minor and was the result of a single incident, particularly if it was caused by a misjudgment;
- there has been a long delay between the alleged offence taking place and the date of the trial, unless the offence is serious, the delay has been caused wholly or in part by the suspect, the offence has only recently come to light, the complexity of the offence has meant that there has been a long investigation, or new investigative techniques have been used to re-examine previously unsolved crimes and, as a result, a suspect has been identified;
- a prosecution is likely to have an adverse effect on the victim's physical or mental health, having regard to the seriousness of the offence and the views of the victim about the effect of a prosecution on their phys-ical or mental health;
- the suspect played a minor role in the commission of the offence;
- the suspect is, or was at the time of the offence, suffering from signifi-cant or physical ill health, unless the offence is serious or there is a real possibility that it may be repeated;
- the suspect has put right the loss or harm that was caused (but a sus-pect must not avoid prosecution solely because the suspect pays com-pensation or repays the sum of money he or she unlawfully obtained);
- a prosecution may require details to be made public that could harm sources of information, international relations or national security.

## The threshold test

10.17 Exceptionally, a prosecutor may charge on the basis of the threshold test if satisfied that: there is insufficient evidence available to apply the eviden-tial stage of the full code test; there are reasonable grounds for believing that further evidence will become available within a reasonable period of time; the seriousness or the circumstances of the case justifies the making of an immediate charging decision; and there are continuing substantial grounds to object to bail in accordance with the Bail Act (BA) 1976 and, in all the circumstances of the case, an application to withhold bail may be properly made.[25] For circumstances in which a custody officer may charge on the basis of the threshold test see para 10.14 above. The threshold test may not be used to charge a summary-only offence that does not carry imprisonment.[26]

10.18 If the relevant conditions for applying the threshold test are satisfied, consideration must then be given to the evidential and public interest stages. The evidential stage of the threshold test is in two parts. First, the prosecutor (or custody officer where he or she is permitted to charge on the basis of the threshold test) must be satisfied that there is at least a reasonable suspicion that the person to be charged has committed the offence. As will be evident, this is no different than the level of suspicion normally required for the original arrest (see para 2.15 above). Second, if so satisfied, the prosecutor (or custody officer) must be satisfied that there are reasonable grounds for believing that the continuing investigation will provide further evidence, within a reasonable period of time, so that all the evidence taken together is capable of establishing a realistic prospect of conviction in accordance with the full code test. In applying the second part of the test, the prosecutor must take into account a range of factors: the nature, extent and admissibility of any likely further evidence and the impact it will have on the case; the charges that all the evidence will support; the reasons why the evidence is not already available; and the time required to obtain the further evidence and whether any consequential delay is reasonable in all the circumstances. This potentially gives the prosecutor (or custody officer) a great deal of latitude to speculate, and importantly the *Director's Guidance on Charging* states that the further evidence 'must be identifiable and not merely speculative'.[27] The public interest stage is the same as for the full code test, taking into account the information available at the time the charge decision is made (see para 10.16 above).[28]

10.19   If the prosecutor decides that the threshold test is not satisfied, the suspect cannot be charged and the case must be referred back to the custody officer. The custody officer will then have to decide whether the suspect can continue to be detained without charge (which will in part depend on the detention time limit), released on bail under PACE s34(5) (which could not be subject to conditions) or PACE s37(2) (which could be made subject to conditions), or released unconditionally.[29] If the prosecutor decides that the threshold test is satisfied, the suspect may be charged, and the evidence must be regularly assessed to ensure that the charge is still appropriate and that continued objection to bail is justified. The full code test must be applied as soon as is reasonable practicable and in any event before any contested hearing (presumably a substantive hearing, and not a bail hearing), and at the very latest before the expiry of any relevant custody time limit.[30] For action to be taken where a suspect is charged by a custody officer on the basis of the threshold test, see para 10.14 above.

## Charges that require consent

10.20   The institution of proceedings for certain offences, or for offences in certain circumstances, requires the consent of either the Attorney-General or the DPP or, in some cases, some other person such as a relevant government minister. While consent of the Attorney-General must be provided

---

27   *Director's Guidance on Charging* para 15. Note that a previous version of the threshold test was disapproved of as a test for determining whether to charge in *G v Chief Constable of West Yorkshire Police* [2006] EWHC 3485 (Admin). The revised test does require the prosecutor or custody officer to consider that further evidence will be forthcoming within a reasonable period, but it remains to be seen whether this will be sufficient to satisfy the courts.

28   *Director's Guidance on Charging* para 15.

29   *Director's Guidance on Charging* para 16.

30   *Director's Guidance on Charging* para 17. The reference to a custody time limit is a reference to time limits under POA 1985 s22, and not detention time limits under PACE.

by that office-holder, consent of the DPP may be given on his or her behalf by a Crown prosecutor (POA 1985 s1(7)). CPS guidance, *Consents to prosecute*, states that a prosecutor must specifically consider the case and decide whether proceedings should be instituted. However, it appears that lack of consent does not prevent a person from being charged with such an offence, nor prevent the person from being remanded in custody or on bail (POA 1985 s25(2)). Annex 1 of *Consents to prosecute* contains a useful list of prosecutions requiring consent by the Attorney-General or the DPP.[31]

## Charging the suspect

### Negotiating the charge

10.21 The lawyer should consider whether, and if so how, to negotiate regarding possible charges. Custody officers and Crown prosecutors have broad discretionary powers as to the appropriate course of action, and there is no obligation on them to charge a suspect simply because the threshold or full code tests have been satisfied (CCP para 4.10). There are practical difficulties in negotiating with a Crown prosecutor since, as noted at para 10.3 above, such prosecutors are usually unwilling to speak to the defence lawyer directly. Where a prosecutor is to make the charge decision, the lawyer should consider asking the relevant police officer to include any written representations in the pre-charge report that the officer must give to the prosecutor.

10.22 In addition to evidential and public interest considerations (see paras 10.15 and 10.16 above), the following provisions of the CCP may be relevant to the representations that may be made:

- Charges should be selected which: reflect the seriousness and extent of the offending; give the court adequate powers to sentence and impose appropriate post-conviction orders; and which enable the case to be presented in a clear and simple way. As the CCP states: '[t]his means that prosecutors may not always choose or continue with the most serious charge where there is a choice'.[32]
- A prosecutor (or custody officer) should not proceed with more charges than are necessary just to encourage an accused to plead guilty to a few, nor proceed with a more serious charge just to encourage an accused to plead guilty to a less serious one.[33]
- In making a charge decision, consideration should be given to alternatives to prosecution.[34]

However, care must be taken where the lawyer would wish to indicate that the client would admit a lesser offence than that likely to be charged, or would be willing to admit an offence on a certain factual basis, since

31 Available via www.cps.gov.uk/legal.
32 CCP paras 6.1 and 6.2.
33 CCP para 6.3.
34 CCP paras 7.1–7.8.

any communication to this effect would not be privileged and could be adduced at any subsequent trial.[35]

10.23    Negotiation regarding the charging decision is important because the decision made may well affect the police attitude to bail which, in turn, will affect the court's attitude to bail. Furthermore, the emphasis on speed of processing cases once they reach court means that there may be limited scope for negotiation after the charge decision has been taken. In considering what representations to make, the lawyer should take account of:

1) Whether the custody officer or Crown prosecutor may be persuaded to deal with the matter other than by charging the suspect. Custody officers must take alternatives to prosecution into account in deciding whether to refer a case to a Crown prosecutor or in making a charge decision (Code C NfG 16A). A prosecutor must consider an out-of-court disposal if it is appropriate to the circumstances of the case (*Director's Guidance on Charging* para 10).

2) What charge(s) would be appropriate. Custody officers and Crown prosecutors have a large degree of discretion in determining what charges are appropriate for any given set of facts, and there are CPS charging standards and policies in respect of many offences.[36] Factors to consider include: the mode of trial implications of a particular charge; the possibility of an alleged offence(s) being treated as an offence to be taken into consideration (see para 5.142 above); the fact that a conviction or caution (or reprimand or warning in the case of a juvenile) for many (although not all) sexual offences will result in the offender being placed on the sex offenders register (see para 10.51 below).

3) The sentence implications of particular charges. The 'dangerous offenders' provisions in the CJA 2003 Part 12 Chapter 5 mean that persons aged 18 years or over convicted of certain specified violent or sexual offences may be made the subject of an extended sentence. The specified offences are set out in CJA 2003 Sch 15. They are too extensive to set out here but, for example, assault occasioning actual bodily harm (Offences Against the Person Act 1861 s47) is specified, whereas common assault is not, unless it is racially or religiously aggravated. Putting a person in fear of violence under the Protection from Harassment Act 1997 s4 is a specified offence, whereas putting a person in fear of violence under the Public Order Act 1986 s4 is not. Certain firearms offences, and certain drugs or domestic burglary offences where the suspect has previous convictions for similar offences, may be subject to a mandatory minimum sentence (see the box below).

---

35  *R v Hayes* [2004] EWCA Crim 2844; [2005] 1 Cr App R 33.
36  Available at www.cps.gov.uk/legal/index.html.

---

**Mandatory minimum sentences**

*Certain firearms offences*
Subject to exceptions, a person who commits an offence under Firearms Act 1968 s5(1)(a), (ab), (aba), (ac), (ad), (ae), (af) or (c), or under s5(1A)(a) (possession, purchase, acquiring, manufacturing, selling or transferring of certain forms of firearm or other weapons), is subject to a mandatory custodial sentence of five years (where the person was aged 18 years or over when he or she committed the offence) or three years (where the person was at least 16 years but under 18 years at the time when he or she committed the offence) (Firearms Act 1968 s51A). Minding a firearm for another person contrary to the Violent Crime Reduction Act 2006 s28 is subject to a similar mandatory minimum sentence (Powers of Criminal Courts (Sentencing) Act 2000 s91).

*Drug trafficking offences*
Subject to exceptions, a person who, at the time that the person commits a class A drug trafficking offence, is aged 18 years or over and already has two separate convictions for class A drug trafficking, is subject to a mandatory minimum custodial sentence of seven years. A 'drug trafficking offence' is defined by Drug Trafficking Act 1994 s1(3) as including production, supply, possession with intent to supply, importing or exporting a controlled drug (Powers of Criminal Courts (Sentencing) Act 2000 s110).

*Domestic burglary*
Subject to exceptions, a person who, at the time that he or she commits an offence of domestic burglary (ie, a burglary committed in respect of a building or part of a building which is a dwelling), is aged 18 years or over and already has two separate convictions for domestic burglary, is subject to a mandatory minimum custodial sentence of three years (Powers of Criminal Courts (Sentencing) Act 2000 s111).

---

## The process of charging

10.24   Responsibility for charging rests with the custody officer. If a Crown prosecutor has made the charge decision, he or she must notify an officer involved in the investigation of the case (PACE s37B(4)). The person to be charged must, if still in police detention, be charged in accordance with the prosecutor's decision. If the person has been released on bail, the person must be charged when he or she returns to the police station to answer bail or by means of the written charge and requisition procedure (PACE s37B(6) and (8)).[37]

10.25   The process of charging is often little more than a formality, although the lawyer should consider the potential for inferences to be drawn under the Criminal Justice and Public Order Act (CJPOA) 1994 s34(1)(b) (see

---

37  Under CJA 2003 s29.

paras 5.68 and 5.73 above).[38] A person charged at a police station must be cautioned in the following terms (Code C para 16.2):[39]

> You do not have to say anything. But it may harm your defence if you do not mention now something which you later rely on in court. Anything you do say may be given in evidence.

The person must also be given a written notice showing particulars of the offence(s) for which the person is charged, including the name of the officer in the case (or warrant number in cases where Code C para 2.6A or Code H para 2.8 apply), the police station and reference number for the case, and confirmation of the caution. As far as possible, the particulars of the charge must be stated in simple terms, but they must show the precise offence with which the person is charged (Code C para 16.3). If the person does not understand English, the person must be promptly informed of the charge in a language that he or she understands (European Convention on Human Rights (ECHR) article 5(2)).

10.26   Before the charging process commences, the lawyer should advise the client about whether the client should say anything on being charged and whether to hand in a written statement (see paras 5.73 and 5.169 above). If a written statement is to be handed in, it will normally not be appropriate to say anything further. If a written statement is not to be handed in, this will normally be in circumstances where the suspect has said all that the suspect should say while being questioned, or where it has been decided that the suspect should say nothing at all. In these circumstances, there would be little point in the client saying anything at charge unless there are specific reasons why the client should say something orally rather than hand in a written statement. It may be appropriate, for example, for the client simply to deny the offence on being charged, although the evidential value of this is limited.

10.27   The lawyer should always discuss with the client whether the lawyer should be present at the time of charge, and if the lawyer is not to be present the client should be clearly advised on what the client should do and say at charge. Duty solicitors are under an obligation, where a client is to be charged with an offence, to advise the client on the implications of the caution at charge, and must consider whether to attend at the time of charge having regard to whether it is possible to give confidential advice by telephone and the possible consequences of not making a statement when being charged.[40] This should be standard practice in own solicitor cases as well.

---

38  Note that where a person is charged under the written charge and requisition procedure, inferences may be drawn from 'silence' when the person is officially told that he or she is being reported to the CPS with a view to a written charge.

39  Unless they have not been given the opportunity to consult a solicitor, in which case they must be cautioned in the terms set out in Code C Annex C para 2 (see para 5.66 above).

40  SCC 2010, Part B para 9.43(b).

## Questioning after charge

### *Questions about the offence charged*

10.28   The police may wish to question a person after the person has been charged with an offence for a number of reasons. If the person handed in a statement, or made an oral statement, at the time of charge the police may want to question him or her about it. Where a person has been charged on the basis of the threshold test (see paras 10.14 and 10.17 above), the police may want to interview the person following the further investigations they must carry out. Generally, the police are not permitted to interview a person about an offence with which the person has been charged or informed that he or she may be prosecuted for it (Code C para 16.5).[41] This would seem to extend to preventing an interview about an offence that is closely related to that with which the person has been charged or informed that he or she may be prosecuted for it.[42] There are two exceptions to the general prohibition on further interviewing.

10.29     First, if the police wish to bring to the suspect's notice a written statement or interview record of another person, they may do so, but must not invite comment other than to caution the suspect (Code C para 16.4). In most circumstances, the suspect should be advised not to comment unless the content of the statement or interview record changes the basis for the advice originally given to the suspect by the lawyer. In this case, the lawyer should speak to the suspect in private so that advice can be given on whether to respond.

10.30     Second, a person may be interviewed about an offence with which the person has been charged or informed that he or she may be prosecuted for it if is necessary:

- for the purpose of preventing or minimising harm or loss to some other person or to the public; or
- to clear up an ambiguity in a previous answer or statement; or
- in the interests of justice for the person to have put to him or her, and to have an opportunity to comment on, information concerning the offence which has come to light since the person was charged or told that he or she might be prosecuted (Code C para 16.5).

10.31   Before showing the person charged a written statement or interview record under Code C para 16.4, or before interviewing under Code C para

---

41  Strictly, Code C para 16.5 prohibits the interview of a 'detainee' after the detainee has been charged. It might be argued that the prohibition does not apply to a person who has been released on bail or produced in court following charge, since the person is no longer in police detention as defined by PACE s118(2). Even if this is correct, the person would not have to co-operate with such questioning, and inferences could not be drawn from 'silence' in response to such questioning. There is provision in Counter-Terrorism Act 2008 Part 2 permitting police questioning after charge for a terrorist offence or an offence that appears to have a terrorist connection, but this had not been implemented at the date of publication.

42  It has been held to be a breach of Code C para 16.5 for a person to be interviewed about an offence of driving while under the influence of alcohol where they had already been informed that they would be charged with the offence of being in charge of a motor vehicle while under the influence of alcohol (*Charles v DPP* [2010] RTR 402).

16.5, the person must be cautioned that he or she does not have to say anything but that anything the person does say may be given in evidence. This caution differs from the caution that must usually be given before or at charge[43] because inferences under CJPOA 1994 ss34, 36 or 37 cannot be drawn from failure to mention facts after charge. Failure to give the caution as required arguably amounts to a significant and substantial breach, which may result in exclusion under PACE s78 of evidence so obtained.

10.32   There is no specific power to detain a person for questioning under Code C paras 16.4 or 16.5. Therefore, if the person has been granted bail following charge, the police will only be able to conduct such questioning if the person agrees to stay at the police station for this purpose. If the suspect has not been granted bail, the police may interview under these provisions during the period between charge and production in court.

10.33   If the police indicate their desire to put further questions while the lawyer is present, the lawyer should establish why the police wish to do so, and the nature of the proposed questioning. The client should normally be advised in private before any further interview takes place. Whether the client should be advised to answer further questions will depend on the circumstances (for general principles, see para 5.102 above), although as noted above, inferences under CJPOA 1994 cannot be drawn from failure to mention a fact, or failure or refusal to account, at this stage. If there is a genuine ambiguity in a previous answer or statement, it may well be in the suspect's interests for this to be clarified, although the suspect should be warned that questions may go further than that required to resolve the ambiguity. If they do, the lawyer should intervene to ensure that the questions are kept to those permitted by Code C para 16.5. The lawyer should consider whether it would be more appropriate to hand in a statement rather than submit to further questioning. If the suspect has previously admitted the offence in interview, there may be mitigation advantages to providing information that will prevent further loss or that will lead to the recovery of goods. If the reason for the further questioning is the emergence of new information, the lawyer will want to know the nature of such information so that the suspect may be advised whether to answer such questions.

10.34   If the police wish to put further questions after the lawyer has left the police station, the usual rules regarding the right to legal advice apply (see para 2.119 above). However, the police may allege that the suspect asked for a further interview following the departure of the lawyer. If true, it would be relatively easy for the police to justify further questions under Code C para 16.5. It has been held that in such circumstances it is preferable for the lawyer to be present, although absence of the lawyer did not amount to a breach of PACE or the Codes as they then stood.[44] Under the current Code C para 6.5, not only would the suspect have to be reminded of the right to legal advice, but would also have to be reminded that he or she could speak to the lawyer on the telephone, and asked why he or she does not wish to have legal advice if it is refused (see also Code C paras

43  See Code C Annex C.
44  *R v Williams* (1992) *Times* 6 February.

16.4(b) and 16.5(b)). In any event, before leaving the police station the lawyer should routinely advise the client of the danger of such interviews, and may consider asking the custody officer to record in the custody record a request to be notified if any further interview is to take place.

### Questions about other matters

10.35 The police may wish to interview a suspect about matters other than the offence(s) with which the suspect has been charged. They may wish to interview about other offences allegedly committed by the suspect, or may be seeking specific or general intelligence. They may even wish to recruit the suspect as an informant.

10.36 The question arises as to whether the police have power to detain the suspect in order to interview for such purposes. A suspect who has been charged and granted bail can, of course, voluntarily agree to remain at the police station. Where the police wish to interview a suspect who does not agree to remain, they may be able to prolong detention by arresting the suspect on suspicion of another offence(s) by virtue of PACE s31 (see para 2.32 above). However, the position is unclear. Section 31 provides that the police must arrest a person who is: 'at a police station in consequence of [the original] arrest' if the person would be liable to arrest on release. This suggests that the person could be arrested after the person has been charged in respect of the offence for which he or she was originally arrested. However, PACE s38 provides that following charge, the custody officer must order the release of the suspect unless one or more of the conditions for withholding bail applies. It could be argued that this implies that a person should not be arrested and detained in respect of another offence following charge in respect of the original offence. However, since a person granted bail after charge in respect of the original offence could be arrested when the person leaves the police station,[45] it may be preferable for the person to be arrested while at the police station under the provisions of PACE s31 because the detention time limit will run from the relevant time relating to the original arrest (by virtue of PACE s41(4)). In principle, the same argument applies to a person who has been charged but refused bail, although the police may simply seek to interview the person during the period between charge and production in court. There is nothing to prevent the police from doing this although, as noted below, the lawyer may wish to ascertain whether the police are prepared to arrest in respect of the new allegation(s).

10.37 If, after charge, the police say that they wish to interview the suspect about an offence other than that for which the suspect has been charged, the lawyer should consider asking the police whether they intend to arrest by virtue of PACE s31. If the police say that they do not intend to arrest, this is likely to mean that they have insufficient information to amount to

---

45 Although arguably this would be unlawful if the conditions for arrest were satisfied while the person was in the police station since the requirement to arrest under s31 is in mandatory terms. However, 'liable to arrest' may not mean simply that there are sufficient grounds for arrest. A police officer may decline to arrest even if there are sufficient grounds, either at all, or because the officer wishes to arrest at a later date in order, for example, to give an opportunity to gather further evidence.

reasonable grounds for suspicion. If, alternatively, the police respond by arresting the suspect, the lawyer and client will have a clearer idea of the basis on which the police wish to conduct the interview.

10.38   If the police wish to interview the suspect after charge for intelligence-gathering purposes or in order to see if the suspect might act as an informant,[46] arrest under PACE s31 would not be possible. Therefore, they could only conduct such an interview if the suspect agrees to remain at the police station for this purpose or if, having been charged, bail was denied. In the latter case, an interview could be conducted in the period between charge and production in court.

### Questions concerning the proceeds of crime

10.39   Confiscation of the proceeds of crime, together with powers to enquire into and restrain a person's assets and income where it is suspected that they are the proceeds of crime, is governed by the Proceeds of Crime Act (POCA) 2002.[47] The Serious Organised Crime Agency (SOCA) has responsibility for recovering unlawfully obtained assets, and the police, HM Revenue and Customs (HMRC) and the CPS have a statutory duty to co-operate with the agency. SOCA and other agencies have a wide range of powers to investigate, to search and seize, to apply for civil recovery orders, and to tax in relation to the proceeds of crime. Restraint orders, which prohibit a specified person from dealing with any realisable property held by the person and enable such property to be seized, may be made by the Crown Court in a number of circumstances. These include where a criminal investigation has been commenced, or criminal proceedings have been started, and there is reasonable cause to believe that the alleged offender has benefited from his or her criminal conduct. Some powers apply irrespective of whether the person has been convicted of a criminal offence. The Crown Court may order confiscation of the assets of a person convicted of or sentenced for an offence, or committed to the Crown Court for consideration of such an order, where it is satisfied that the person has a 'criminal lifestyle' or in respect of the benefit obtained by the person's 'criminal conduct'. The POCA 2002 also creates a number of money laundering offences.[48]

10.40   The question that arises at the police station is whether the suspect should respond to questions purportedly put under the Police Reform Act 2002, and designed to obtain information about the financial resources of the suspect. Code C para 11.6 provides that the conditions under that paragraph that determine when interviewing should cease (see para 7.70

---

46   Note that the recruitment of informants is governed by Regulation of Investigatory Powers Act (RIPA) 2000 Part II and the Covert Human Intelligence Sources Code of Practice.

47   It replaced the confiscation provisions of the CJA 1988 and Drug Trafficking Act 1994, although these Acts are still mentioned in Code C para 11.6. Useful CPS guidance to the asset recovery provisions can be accessed via www.cps.gov.uk/legal/.

48   Note that a number of these offences potentially affect defence lawyers, including failure to disclose information about money laundering activities of a client and tipping-off. See the Law Society *Anti-money laundering* Practice Note, available at www.lawsociety.org.uk/productsandservices/practicenotes/aml.page.

above) do not prevent suspects being invited to complete a formal question-and-answer record under the proceeds of crime legislation after the interview concerning the alleged offence has concluded. Whether such questioning takes place before or after charge, a significant issue is whether information supplied by the suspect for confiscation purposes could be used by the police as evidence in respect of the offence charged or to be charged. There is limited protection of information supplied by a person (preventing its use in criminal proceedings against them) under POCA 2002 s18 and Sch 6, but this is unlikely to apply to questioning at the police station stage. Therefore, it should be assumed that any information supplied by the suspect in respect of the proceeds of crime, whether or not it is supplied to officers unconnected with the investigation of the offence, may be used as evidence in respect of the offence itself. For this reason, it will normally not be in the suspect's interests to provide such information while at the police station. A refusal would not have adverse evidential consequences in respect of the criminal proceedings, and it is not an offence to fail to provide such information. It may be advisable, however, for the suspect to indicate that he or she will consider the matter further once released from detention, when the suspect has had the opportunity to take full legal advice on the matter.

## Alternatives to charging

10.41 There is a range of alternatives to charging a person even in circumstances where the relevant conditions for charge are satisfied (see para 10.15 above). These include out-of-court disposals such as simple cautions (or reprimands and warnings in respect of juveniles), conditional cautions and penalty notices for disorder, and other courses of action such as reporting for summons, no further action and police bail without charge. Police forces often have their own policies on use of these alternatives, and police officers often have a 'patchy knowledge' of the range of disposals and of the relevant criteria.[49] It is important, therefore, for the defence lawyer to know what alternatives are available in the circumstances of any particular case.

### Reporting for summons

10.42 As an alternative to charging, the suspect may be reported for summons. This means that the decision whether to proceed against the suspect will be taken at a later date and, if the police do proceed, they will lay an information with a view to a summons being issued by a magistrates' court. This may be served personally on the suspect, or by post. Alternatively, a Crown prosecutor (and certain other public prosecutors) may institute proceedings by issuing a 'written charge' and 'requisition' to the suspect.[50]

49 See the report of the joint inspection by HM Inspectorate of Constabulary and HM CPS Inspectorate, *Exercising discretion: the gateway to justice*, 2011, available via www. hmic.gov.uk/publication/exercising-discretion-the-gateway-to-justice/

50 Governed by the CJA 2003 Part 4. It is now available in all police force areas. See Criminal Justice Act 2003 (Commencement No 26) Order 2011 SI No 2188.

The main difference to the summons procedure is that a written charge can be issued directly by the prosecutor without a requirement to make an application to a magistrates' court. The summons procedure tends to be used in respect of less serious offences, or in respect of certain types of offence (such as traffic offences). There is no reason, in principle, why the summons or written charge procedure cannot be used in respect of more serious offences although in practice their use is limited by the fact that the accused cannot be kept in custody pending the first court appearance. Where the summons or written charge procedure is to be used, or is to be considered, the police may release the suspect unconditionally, or on bail under PACE s37(7)(a)(i) (see para 10.73 below).

10.43   If the suspect is reported for summons or with a view to a written charge, the suspect should be advised that if a summons or written charge and requisition is subsequently served the suspect will be under a duty to attend court on the date specified in the summons. Failure to do so would not amount to an offence, but could result in the court issuing a warrant for the suspect's arrest. The suspect should also be advised to contact the lawyer if and when a summons or written charge is served on the suspect so that initial instructions can be taken and, if appropriate, an application for legal aid made.

10.44   The general prohibition on further questioning after charge also applies where the suspect has been informed that he or she may be prosecuted for the offence (see para 10.28 above). The suspect should be advised that if, nevertheless, the police subsequently seek to question the suspect further, the suspect should ask to speak to the lawyer before answering any such questions.

## 'Simple' cautions

10.45   There are two forms of caution: 'simple' cautions (previously known as police cautions, dealt with here), and conditional cautions (see para 10.56 below). Simple cautions are only available in respect of persons aged at least 18 years of age. Suspects under the age of 18 years may be dealt with by way of a reprimand or warning (see para 11.30 below). Unlike conditional cautions, which are statutory, simple cautions are non-statutory, and are currently governed by Home Office Circular 16/2008 *Simple cautioning of adult offenders.*[51] Generally, the decision whether to offer a simple caution is for the police. However, a decision to offer a simple caution for an indictable-only offence must be referred to a Crown prosecutor.[52] A Crown prosecutor may also direct that a person be offered a simple caution (PACE

51  At the date of publication, the Ministry of Justice had established a pilot project for the use of simple cautions in respect of certain specified immigration status offences where the offender agrees to be removed from the UK and otherwise meets eligibility criteria. For details see *Simple cautions for foreign national offenders pilot policy statement*, available at www.legalservices.gov.uk/Simple_cautions_for_foreign_national_offenders_pilot_-_policy_statement.pdf, and the Law Society Practice Note *Cautioning foreign nationals for document offences*, available via www.lawsociety.org.uk/productsandservices/practicenotes.page.
52  *Director's Guidance on Charging* para 23, and CCP para 7.5.

s37B(6).[53] Note that in addition to the simple caution scheme, there is an Association of Chief Police Officers (ACPO) Cannabis Warning Scheme that may result in an 'informal' warning for a person found in possession of a small amount of cannabis.[54]

## Criteria for a simple caution

10.46 In determining whether a simple caution is appropriate, Circular 16/2008 provides that the following factors must be taken into account:

1) Whether the suspect has made a clear and reliable admission of the offence, either verbally or in writing.[55] The Circular states that an admission corroborated by some other evidence is sufficient evidence to provide a realistic prospect of conviction. Corroboration could be obtained from information in a crime report or obtained during the course of the investigation. A simple caution will not be appropriate where the suspect has not made a clear and reliable admission of the offence (eg, if intent is denied or there are doubts about the suspect's mental health or intellectual capacity, or where a statutory defence is offered[56]). The admission must be made before the suspect is offered a caution.[57] If the admission is made outside the context of a formal interview, a written record of it must be made and the suspect must be invited to sign the record to confirm its accuracy.[58]

2) Whether there is a realistic prospect of conviction were the person to be prosecuted in accordance with the full code test set out in the CCP (see para 10.7 above). For this purpose, a clear, reliable admission corroborated by some other 'material and significant evidential fact' will be sufficient.

3) Whether it is in the public interest to use a simple caution as the appropriate means of disposal. Officers should take into account the public interest principles set out in the CCP[59] (see para 10.16 above).

4) Whether a simple caution is appropriate to the offence and the offender having regard to the ACPO Gravity Factors Matrix.

If all of the above requirements are met, a simple caution may be the appropriate disposal but regard must be had to other possible out-of-court disposals, particularly a conditional caution.[60] However, before a decision to caution is made the police must attempt to establish the views of the victim, the nature and extent of any harm or loss and its significance having

53  See also CCP para 7.6.
54  Details are available at www.acpo.police.uk/documents/crime/2009/200901CRICAN01.pdf.
55  There have been a number of cases, particularly involving sexual offences, where the courts have subsequently decided that an admission that resulted in a caution was not 'clear and reliable'. See, for example, *R (Wyman) v Chief Constable of Hampshire Constabulary* [2006] EWHC 1904 (Admin).
56  Circular 16/2008 para 16.
57  Circular 16/2008 para 18. And see *R (R) v Durham Constabulary* [2005] 1 WLR 1184.
58  Circular 16/2008 para 19.
59  Circular 16/2008 para 9.
60  Circular 16/2008 paras 10 and 12.

regard to the circumstances of the victim, and whether the offender has made any form of reparation or paid any compensation. It is clear, however, that a caution can be offered even if the victim objects.[61]

10.47   Circular 16/2008 gives guidance on interpreting these criteria in respect of three specific types of offence.

- *Violence against the person* Generally, a simple caution is not appropriate for the most serious violence against the person. However, where an offence of personal violence is not accompanied by any aggravating factor and where the victim does not support a prosecution, a simple caution may be appropriate.[62]
- *Domestic violence* Positive action is recommended in cases of domestic violence to ensure the safety and protection of victims and children while allowing the criminal justice system to hold the offender to account. A positive action approach considers the incident in its entirety, not just the oral and written evidence of the victim. Where a positive action policy has been adhered to and officers still have difficulty in securing a charge or summons, forces need to have a system in place to ensure that simple cautions are considered in preference to a decision to take no further action.[63]
- *Harassment (racial or other)* In deciding whether to offer a simple caution, officers should be aware that it will render all conduct on which the caution is based inadmissible as evidence of a course of conduct should this continue subsequently, and that since a restraining order may only be issued by a court, the only way of protecting a victim against future conduct would be by seeking an anti-harassment injunction from a civil court. In cases of aggravated harassment, a prosecution should be pursued. Therefore, the views of the victim should be fully considered, and a simple caution should only be offered where the police are confident that the harassment will not continue.[64]

## Consent of the suspect

10.48   A simple caution cannot be imposed on a person who refuses to accept it (Circular 16/2008 para 16). If a Crown prosecutor directs the police to offer a caution, and this proves not to be possible (eg, because the suspect refuses to accept it) the suspect must instead be charged with the offence (PACE s37B(6) and (7)).

## Repeat cautions

10.49   A simple caution cannot normally be offered to a suspect who has previously been cautioned (including a previous conditional caution) However, a second or subsequent caution may be appropriate if:

a) there has been a sufficient lapse of time to suggest that a previous caution has had a significant deterrent effect;

---

61  Circular 16/2008 paras 20–22.
62  Circular 16/2008 para 56.
63  Circular 16/2008 paras 57 and 58.
64  Circular 16/2008 paras 59 and 60.

b) the current offence is trivial or unrelated to the offence for which the previous caution was imposed; or

c) it is part of a mixed disposal.

The Circular gives as an example of a mixed disposal case where a person who is arrested for being drunk and disorderly is found in possession of a set of keys which the person admits he or she intended to use in order to steal from cars. A fixed penalty notice could be imposed for the drunk and disorderly offence, and a caution for the 'going equipped' offence.[65] A previous conviction does not necessarily prevent a caution from being offered for an offence that is not related to the offence for which the previous conviction was received, although there should be a significant time lapse between the two.[66] If the suspect has previously received a reprimand or final warning as a juvenile, a caution should not usually be offered for a subsequent offence unless at least two years has elapsed[67].

## Decision-making

10.50 Other than in the case of an indictable-only offence (see para 10.45 above) the decision to impose a caution should usually be referred for approval to a sergeant or above (not necessarily a custody officer) who is not involved in the investigation.[68] However, in cases that must be referred to a Crown prosecutor for a charge decision (see para 10.12 above), the prosecutor has a duty to consider whether a caution should be offered (PACE s37B(3)).

## Consequences of a simple caution

10.51 A caution should be administered by a suitably trained person to whom authority to administer cautions has been delegated. Unlike a conditional caution, no conditions can be attached, but the offender should be asked to sign a form, which sets out the offender's personal details and details of the offence, accepting the terms of the caution (Circular 16/2008 para 44). Although a caution is not a criminal conviction, if it is imposed for a recordable offence it will be entered on the Police National Computer and forms part of the offender's criminal record. It may, therefore, be cited in any subsequent court proceedings, may be used as evidence of previous misconduct where this is permitted (see para 5.170 above),[69] and may also prevent a further caution being offered in the future (see para 10.49 above). Fingerprints and other identification data can be taken and retained (if the caution is for a recordable offence, see paras 6.4 and 6.48 above)), and in the case of a relevant sexual offence the offender is placed on the sex offenders register for two years (see para 10.23 above). If a simple caution is imposed on a person employed in a notifiable occupation the police

---

65 Circular 16/2008 paras 15 and 54.
66 Circular 16/2008 para 23.
67 Circular 16/2008 para 23.
68 Circular 16/2008 para 27.
69 A defendant may challenge evidence of previous misconduct based on a caution by adducing evidence to show that he or she was not guilty of an offence, but this is unlikely to be successful if the defendant was in receipt of legal advice when he or she accepted the caution (*R v Olu, Wilson and Brooks* [2010] EWCA Crim 2975).

should disclose the caution to the employer in accordance with Home Office Circular 6/2006, *The notifiable occupations scheme: revised guidance for police forces.* A simple caution imposed for certain offences may also have adverse implications for people who work with children or vulnerable adults.[70] Simple cautions are covered by the Rehabilitation of Offenders Act 1974, and are immediately spent when administered. Normally, a person cannot be prosecuted for an offence in respect of which the person has been cautioned (but see paras 10.85 and 10.86 below).

### Advising on simple cautions

10.52    A number of issues arise for the lawyer in respect of simple cautions, many of which are also relevant to other out-of-court disposals. First, the possibility of a caution may affect the advice to be given about whether the suspect should answer questions in interview and, in particular, whether the suspect should make admissions (see para 5.102 above). This needs to be approached with care. It was held in *R (R) v Durham Constabulary*[71] that the police must not induce an admission by offering a caution, and the lawyer must ensure that they do not do what the police are prohibited from doing. However, the lawyer is likely to know whether a caution is a potential disposal and may have already have canvassed the possibility with the officer in the case. The lawyer should take instructions from the client regarding the alleged offence, and consider whether the criteria for a caution are satisfied, before discussing with them the possibility of a caution. Particular attention should be paid to whether the instructions from the client amount to a 'clear and reliable' admission of guilt, and to what other evidence of guilt the police have.[72] In addition, the client should be advised that if the client admits the offence, the police may proceed to charge rather than caution.

10.53    Second, in circumstances where the police have not suggested that they are considering a caution, the lawyer should consider whether to try to persuade the police to caution rather than charge. This will only be appropriate where the client has admitted or is willing to admit the offence, and where the lawyer is satisfied that the other conditions for a caution are satisfied, and is satisfied that the client understands the consequences of a caution. Failure to persuade the police to caution is not necessarily the end of the matter since, if it is a case that must be referred to a Crown prosecutor to make a charge decision (see para 10.12 above), the prosecutor has an independent duty to consider whether a caution should be offered (see para 10.45 above).

10.54    Third, in circumstances where the police are offering a caution, the client will need advice on whether to consent. Again, the lawyer should

70  Circular 16/2008 paras 38 and 39.
71  [2005] 1 WLR 1184.
72  There have been a number of appeals, particularly in respect of sexual offences, where a caution (or reprimand or warning) was accepted when there was no clear and reliable admission (see, for example, *R (Wyman) v Chief Constable of Hampshire Constabulary* [2006] EWHC 1904 (Admin)), or where there was insufficient evidence to give a realistic prospect of conviction (see, for example, *R (Mohammed) v Chief Constable of West Midlands* [2010] EWHC 1228 (Admin).

take into account whether the client has admitted or is willing to admit the offence, and whether the lawyer is satisfied that the other conditions for a caution are satisfied, and is satisfied that the client understands the consequences of a caution. The lawyer should also consider any danger that, having secured an admission, the police change their mind and proceed to charge.[73] Most importantly, if the client has instructed the lawyer that the client is not guilty, the lawyer should try to persuade the client not to admit to the offence simply because a caution appears to be an easy way out. Note that where the police interviewed the client in the absence of the lawyer, and the lawyer is asked to advise on whether the client should accept a caution, the police should disclose the interview to the lawyer in order to enable the lawyer to give such advice.[74]

10.55    The decision regarding a caution is often not an easy one, either for the suspect or the lawyer, for although theoretically there may not be a realistic prospect of conviction, regard must be had to the willingness of some courts to convict on less than convincing evidence. In any event, the lawyer should emphasise to the client the potential adverse consequences of accepting a caution (see para 10.51 above). Care is also needed because of the advantages to the police of securing a caution in circumstances where, in the absence of an admission, they do not have sufficient evidence to provide a realistic prospect of conviction. Offering a caution may mean that they get some kind of 'result', whereas if they cannot obtain an admission they may simply not have enough evidence to proceed at all. Moreover, if the officer in the case 'offers' a caution, the officer does not have the power to decide whether a caution or prosecution should follow. The lawyer should, therefore, seek confirmation from the appropriate officer before giving advice to the client in these circumstances.[75]

## Conditional cautions

10.56    Conditional cautions for those aged 18 years or more are governed by CJA 2003 Part 3 and the *Revised code of practice for conditional cautions – adults* (the *Conditional caution code*) issued under the CJA 2003 s25.[76] In addition, the DPP has issued the *Director's Guidance on Adult Conditional Cautions* (the *Director's Guidance*) under powers granted by PACE s37A.[77] As well as having a statutory basis, conditional cautions differ from simple cautions in that they may require the offender to engage in some kind of activity

73  Although the danger of this is ameliorated by the decision in the *Durham Constabulary* case, considered at para 10.52 above.

74  *DPP v Ara* [2001] 4 All ER 559.

75  It was held in *Omar v Chief Constable of Bedfordshire Constabulary* [2002] EWHC 3060 (Admin) that prosecution for an offence for which a person had been cautioned would not be an abuse of process provided that they had not been induced to make an admission and that they had not been expressly told that they would not be prosecuted. In *Jones v Whalley* [2005] EWHC 931 (Admin) a similar decision was made in respect of a private prosecution. See paras 10.85 and 10.86 below.

76  The current Code was brought into force by Criminal Justice Act 2003 (Conditional Cautions: Code of Practice) Order 2010 SI No 133.

77  Available at www.cps.gov.uk/publications/directors_guidance/adult_conditional_cautions.html.

and/or pay a sum of money, and breach can result in the offender being prosecuted for the original offence. Where a person has been drug-tested under PACE s63B, information from the sample can be used for the purpose of informing a decision about the imposition of a conditional caution (see para 6.70 above).

### Criteria for a conditional caution

10.57    A conditional caution may be imposed on a person aged 18 or over (see para 11.42 below for those under 18 years) only in respect of offences listed in the *Director's Guidance* Annex A.[78] In order for a conditional caution to be imposed, five requirements must be satisfied (CJA 2003 ss22(1) and 23).

1) The *authorised person* has evidence that the offender has committed an offence.
2) The *relevant prosecutor* decides there is sufficient evidence to charge and that a conditional caution should be given. The prosecutor must apply the full code evidential test and the public interest test (see para 10.15 above).
3) The offender admits the offence to the *authorised person*. The admission does not have to be made before a relevant prosecutor decides whether a conditional caution is appropriate, but it must be made (or repeated) at the time the caution is given (*Conditional Caution Code* para 4.2).
4) The *authorised person* explains the effects of the conditional caution to the offender and warns the offender that failure to comply with any of the conditions renders him or her liable to being prosecuted for the original offence.
5) The offender signs a document which contains details of the offence, an admission that the offender committed it, the offender's consent to the conditional caution, and the conditions that are attached to the caution.

An *authorised person* is a constable, a designated civilian investigating officer or a person authorised for this purpose by the relevant prosecutor (CJA 2003 s22(4)). A *relevant prosecutor* means the Attorney-General, Director of the Serious Fraud Office, DPP, secretary of state, the Director of Revenue and Customs Prosecutions, or a person specified in an order made by the secretary of state (CJA 2003 s27). It will be seen from this that it is a prosecutor and not a police officer who decides whether a conditional caution should be offered to the suspect.

---

78  In *R (Guest) v DPP* [2009] 2 Cr App R 426 a conditional caution imposed for an offence not listed in Annex A was quashed.

## What conditions can be imposed?

10.58   Any condition can be imposed provided it has the purpose of:

a)  facilitating the rehabilitation of the offender;
b)  ensuring that the offender makes reparation for the offence; and or
c)  punishing the offender (CJA 2003 s22(3)).[79]

Rehabilitation may involve conditions directed at helping: 'to modify the behavior of the offender, serve to reduce the likelihood of re-offending or help to reintegrate the offender into society'.[80] This could include a requirement to take part in drug or alcohol misuse programmes, or to take part in schemes tackling other addictions or personal problems, such as gambling or debt management.[81] Reparation may involve conditions which: 'serve to repair the damage done either directly or indirectly'.[82] This could include conditions that require apologising, repairing or otherwise making good any damage caused, provided that this is acceptable to the victim. It could also require financial compensation to be paid. Where the offending has resulted in damage to community property, reparation may take the form of unpaid work to repair that damage or of a payment to an appropriate local charitable or community fund.[83] In those areas where the power to punish the offender is in force, a financial penalty may be imposed only where the conditional caution is imposed in respect of an offence specified in, and subject to a maximum set out in, an order of the secretary of state.[84] Conditions that impose restrictions on the offender, such as a prohibition on contacting individuals, visiting certain locations, or participating in particular activities, can be used provided that they contribute towards rehabilitation, reparation or punishment.[85]

10.59   Conditions must be appropriate, proportionate and achievable.[86] Punitive conditions should only be used where there are no appropriate reparative or rehabilitative conditions, or where such conditions would not provide a proportionate response to the offending behaviour.[87] Offenders must be able to complete the conditions satisfactorily within a reasonable time. In the case of cautions imposed for a summary-only offence, this should be within 16 weeks of the date of commission of the offence, and this should also be the normal period for either-way offences. Prosecutors should take into account the circumstances of the offender such as

---

79  The power to punish the offender is not currently available in all police areas. At the date of publication it was in force in Cambridgeshire, Merseyside, Norfolk, Hampshire and Humberside (Police and Justice Act 2006(Commencement No 11) Order 2009 SI No 1679, and (Commencement No 12) Order 2009 SI No 2774). The maximum penalty depends on the offence, and ranges between £50 and £150.
80  *Conditional Caution Code* para 6.1.
81  *Conditional Caution Code* para 6.2.
82  *Conditional Caution Code* para 6.1.
83  *Conditional Caution Code* para 6.3.
84  See Criminal Justice Act 2003 (Conditional Cautions: Financial Penalties) Order 2009 SI No 2773.
85  *Conditional Caution Code* para 6.5.
86  *Conditional Caution Code* para 7.1.
87  *Conditional Caution Code* para 7.2.

the offender's physical and mental capacity. Financial conditions must be commensurate with the offender's means.[88]

### Consent of the suspect

10.60   A conditional caution cannot be imposed without the informed, written consent of the suspect (see para 10.57 above).

### Repeat cautions

10.61   Simple cautions (or reprimands and warnings) and conditional cautions doe not form a hierarchy in which the former will inevitably be followed by the latter if the person reoffends. A previous caution does not preclude a subsequent conditional caution,[89] and nor does a previous conviction.[90] A second conditional caution is also not precluded, but should not generally be offered in the absence of exceptional circumstances indicating that it may be appropriate.[91] A previous failure to comply with a conditional caution will normally mean that a further conditional caution should not be offered.[92]

### Decision-making

10.62   The decision to offer a conditional caution is that of a Crown prosecutor rather than a police officer (see para 10.57 above). However, custody officers have responsibility for identifying cases that may be suitable for a conditional caution and, in such a case, should refer it to a prosecutor with a view to the prosecutor making such a decision.[93] Since custody officers have the power to charge in respect of cases that are most likely to be suitable for a conditional caution (see para 10.13 above), if they are unwilling to deal with the case by way of a simple caution, and the defence lawyer believes that a conditional caution is both possible and in the client's interests, the lawyer should seek to persuade the custody officer to refer the case to the Crown prosecutor for this purpose.

### Consequences of a conditional caution

10.63   The offender will, of course, be required to satisfy the conditions imposed under the terms of the caution. Fingerprints and other identification data can be taken and retained, and in the case of a relevant sexual offence the offender is placed on the sex offenders register for two years (see para 10.23 above). Although a conditional caution is not a criminal conviction, if it is imposed for a recordable offence it is entered on the Police National Computer and forms part of the offender's criminal record. Thus it may be cited in any subsequent court proceedings, and whether recordable or not may be used as evidence of previous misconduct where this is permitted

---

88   *Conditional Caution Code* paras 7.2–7.9.
89   *Director's Guidance* para 4.2.
90   *Director's Guidance* para 4.3.
91   *Director's Guidance* para 4.2.
92   *Director's Guidance* para 4.3.
93   *Director's Guidance* para 3.2.

(see para 5.170 above). There is no specific reference in the *Conditional Caution Code* regarding notification of a conditional caution imposed on a person in a notifiable occupation, or on a person who works with children or vulnerable adults, but it is likely that the position is the same as for simple cautions (see para 10.51 above). Conditional cautions are covered by the Rehabilitation of Offenders Act 1974, and are spent at the end of the 'relevant period for the caution', that is, normally three months of the date on which it was given. As noted at para 10.49 above, a conditional caution may prevent a caution from being offered in the future. Normally, a person cannot be prosecuted for an offence in respect of which the person has received caution. However, it has been held that where a conditional caution was given contrary to the *Director's Guidance*, it could be quashed, leaving open the possibility of prosecution for the original offence.[94]

10.64    Although failure to comply with the conditions is not an offence, it does render the offender liable to prosecution for the original offence (CJA 2003 s24(1)). If a constable has reasonable grounds for believing that the offender has failed, without reasonable cause, to comply with the conditions the constable can arrest the offender without a warrant (CJA 2003 s24A(1)). Following arrest, the offender may be charged with the original offence (assuming that it is within any relevant time limit), released without charge to enable a charge decision to be made, or released without charge and without bail (with or without variation of the conditions attached to the caution) (CJA 2003 s24A(2)).On prosecution for the original offence, the document that the offender signed (see para 10.57 above) will be admissible in evidence (CJA 2003 s24(2)).

## Advising on conditional cautions

10.65    Many of the considerations that apply when advising on simple cautions also apply to advice on conditional cautions (see paras 10.52–10.55 above). The client should be specifically advised of the consequences of non-compliance, and the other consequences set out in paras 10.63 and 10.64. Given that Crown prosecutors usually refuse to speak to defence lawyers at police stations, negotiations regarding a conditional caution are difficult, if not impossible. As noted in para 10.62 above, a conditional caution may be an appropriate disposal in cases where the custody officer does not have to refer the case to a Crown prosecutor for a charge decision so, where appropriate, the defence lawyer should specifically request the custody officer to refer the case to the prosecutor for this purpose. If the custody officer refuses to do so, and proceeds to charge the suspect, a prosecutor will have to decide whether continued prosecution is appropriate,[95] so the defence lawyer should consider making appropriate further representations at that stage.[96]

94  *R (G) v DPP* [2009] EWHC 594 (Admin).

95  CCP paras 3.3 and 7.1.

96  Note that communications with the CPS are not privileged so that an admission contained in any letter seeking to persuade the CPS to conditionally caution a client may be adduced in evidence if a prosecution proceeds. See *R v Hayes* [2004] EWCA Crim 2844.

## Fixed penalty notices

10.66    Fixed penalty notices are most frequently used in respect of road traffic offences under the Road Traffic Offenders Act 1988 Part 3. However, they are available for a range of other offences under a variety of statutes and, in particular, may be used in respect of certain theft, criminal damage and drugs offences. Since they will normally be imposed in circumstances where a suspect has not requested legal advice, they are only dealt with in outline here.

10.67    Under the Criminal Justice and Police Act (CJPA) 2001 ss1 and 2, a fixed penalty notice can be issued in respect of specified offences. These include: being drunk on a highway, other public place, or licensed premises (Licensing Act 1872 s12); disorderly behaviour while drunk in a public place (CJA 1967 s91); wasting police time or giving a false report (Criminal Law Act 1967 s5(2)); theft, limited by guidance to a maximum value of £100 (Theft Act 1968 s1); destroying or damaging property, limited by guidance to a maximum value of £300 (Criminal Damage Act 1971 s1(1)); behaviour likely to cause harassment, alarm or distress (Public Order Act 1986 s5); and possession of cannabis and related offences (Misuse of Drugs Act 1971 s5(2)). Home Office guidance provides that only one penalty notice should be issued for retail theft, and that a notice should not be issued for retail theft or criminal damage to a person who is a known substance misuser.[97]

10.68    Where a police officer has reason to believe that a person has committed a listed offence the officer may give the person a penalty notice (CJPA 2001 s2(1)). Unless at a police station, the officer must be in uniform (CJPA 2001s2(2)). The notice must state the alleged offence, provide reasonable information about the circumstances of the alleged offence, specify the 'suspended enforcement period' and explain its effect, state the amount of the penalty and where it can be paid, and inform the recipient of their right to ask to be tried for the alleged offence and explain how that right may be exercised (CJPA 2001 s3). The amount of the penalty depends on whether the offence is listed in Part I or Part II of Schedule 1 to the Penalties for Disorderly Behaviour (Amount of Penalty) Order 2002, and is either £80 or £50 respectively for a person aged 16 or over, and £40 or £30 respectively for a person aged under 16 years.[98] If the penalty is paid within the suspended enforcement period (ie, 21 days beginning with the date on which the order was given), no proceedings may be brought for the offence (CJPA 2001 s5). The recipient of the notice can ask, during the suspended enforcement period, to be tried and in this case proceedings may be commenced against him or her (CJPA 2001 s4). If the recipient of the notice does not ask to be tried and does not pay the penalty during the suspended enforcement period, a sum equal to one and half times the amount of the penalty may be registered against him or her as a fine (CJPA 2001 s8).

97  Guidance on the use of fixed penalty notices is available at www.homeoffice.gov.uk/ police/penalty-notices/.

98  See the Penalties for Disorderly Behaviour (Amount of Penalty) Order 2002 SI No 1837, and the Penalties for Disorderly Behaviour (Amount of Penalty)(Amendment) Order 2009 SI No 83.

10.69     A penalty notice is not a conviction, and does not amount to an admission of guilt nor to proof that a crime has been committed.[99] Where a fixed penalty notice has been imposed, prosecution for an offence arising from the same circumstances is permissible if evidence of a more serious offence than that for which the penalty was imposed comes to light.[100]

10.70     There are similar provisions under the Anti-social Behaviour Act 2003 in respect of offences listed in section 44(1) of that Act, although in this case penalty notices are issued by an authorised officer of a local authority rather than a police officer. Most other fixed penalty provisions are to be found in environmental protection legislation.

## No further action

10.71   It is relatively rare for the police, having sufficient evidence to charge a person, to decide to take no action against the person[101] and performance management and targets mean that the police may be under some pressure to charge or caution in these circumstances. However, there is no legal rule that requires a prosecution or caution simply because there is sufficient evidence to charge, and in some cases formal action may not be appropriate. This is most likely in the case of a juvenile suspect or a suspect who is mentally disordered or vulnerable (see further chapter 11). See also the public interest factors for and against prosecution in the CCP (set out at para 10.16 above).

10.72     In practice, a decision to take no further action and to release unconditionally is likely only if the police do not have sufficient evidence to charge and believe that they are unlikely to have such evidence in the foreseeable future. In these circumstances, the suspect should be advised that the police may arrest the suspect again in respect of the same matter, although this is only likely if they do obtain further evidence.

## Release on police bail without charge

10.73   The police have a variety of powers and duties to grant bail to suspects who have been arrested for an offence and detained at a police station under PACE, but who have not been charged. They do not have power to bail without charge a person arrested and detained under the TA 2000 s41.[102] For the power to grant bail to an arrested person without taking the person to a police station, see para 2.45 above.

### Powers and duties to grant bail without charge

10.74   Bail from a police station without charge is often known as 'section 47(3) bail' but in fact there are a number of different bail powers in Part IV

99  *R v Hamer* [2011] 1 WLR 528.
100  *R v Gore* [2009] 1 WLR 2454.
101  It has been persuasively argued that the police often use arrest as a mechanism of 'social discipline' in which prosecution may be less important than the disciplinary effects of the arrest itself. See S Choongh, *Policing as social discipline* (Clarendon, Oxford, 1997).
102  *R (I) v City of Westminster Magistrates' Court* [2008] EWHC 2146 (Admin).

of PACE. Section 34(2) provides that where a custody officer becomes aware, in relation to a person in police detention (see para 1.61 above), that grounds for detention have ceased to apply and the officer is not aware of any other grounds to justify detention, the officer must order the immediate release of the detained person from custody (unless it appears to the officer that the person was unlawfully at large when arrested, PACE s34(4)). Such release must be without bail unless it appears to the custody officer that there is a need for further investigation of any matter in connection with which the person was detained at any time during the period of detention or that in respect of any such matter proceedings may be taken against the person (or, if a juvenile, that the juvenile may be reprimanded or warned under the Crime and Disorder Act (CDA) 1998 s65), in which case the release may be on bail (PACE s34(5)).

10.75   Where a person arrested either without warrant or under a warrant not endorsed for bail is taken before a custody officer under PACE s37(1), and the officer determines that the officer does not have before him or her sufficient evidence to charge, the person must be released either without bail or on bail unless the officer has reasonable grounds for believing that detention is necessary for one or more of the specified grounds (see para 2.53 above). If the officer determines that there is sufficient evidence to charge, the detainee must be dealt with in accordance with PACE s37(7) (see para 10.5 above).

10.76   If the officer conducting a review of detention under PACE s40 (see para 2.80 above) concludes that detention can no longer be justified by reference to the conditions in PACE s37, the officer must release the suspect with or without bail (PACE s40(8)). Where a detained person has not been charged at the expiry of 24 hours after the relevant time, the person must be released with or without bail unless further detention is authorised under PACE s42 or s43 (PACE s41(7)). A similar provision applies at the expiry of the 36-hour time limit (s42(10)), or where an application for a warrant or extension of a warrant of further detention is refused (unless the 36 hours or the existing warrant has not expired (PACE s43(15), (16) and s44(7), (8)), or where a warrant expires (PACE s43(18)). There is no similar provision where an extended warrant expires, although it is probable that the same principles must apply.[103]

10.77   Where a custody officer determines that there is sufficient evidence to charge a suspect the officer may release the suspect on bail with a view to a charge decision being made by a Crown prosecutor (PACE s37(7)(a)(i), and see para 10.5 above). Alternatively, having determined that there is sufficient evidence to charge, the custody officer may release the suspect without charge and on bail, but not for the purpose of a charge decision being made (PACE s37(7)(b)). The purpose appears to be to permit the police to continue with their investigation of the offence for which the suspect was arrested and detained even though the custody officer has determined that there is sufficient evidence to charge (but para 10.81 below).

---

103  Note that if a detention time limit has expired it is difficult to see why the police should then have the power to release the suspect on bail, as opposed to unconditionally, since they would not have the power to detain the suspect on their surrender to bail unless new evidence justified their further arrest.

### Power to impose conditions

10.78  A release on bail under PACE Part IV (which includes all of the powers to grant bail referred to in paras 10.74–10.77 above, but not bail granted without taking the suspect to a police station),[104] is deemed to be a release on bail in accordance with the BA 1976 ss3, 3A, 5 and 5A, as those sections apply to bail granted by a constable. However, conditions can be attached to bail granted without charge only where it is granted under PACE s37 (PACE s47(1A)).[105] Such conditions can be imposed as appear necessary for the purpose of ensuring that the person surrenders to custody, does not commit an offence on bail, does not interfere with witnesses or otherwise obstruct the course of justice, and/or for the person's own protection (or where the person is under 17 years, for the person's own welfare or in his or her own interests) (PACE s47(1A), and BA 1976 ss3(6) and 3A(5)). Any condition may be imposed other than a condition that the person reside in a bail hostel, make himself or herself available for the purposes of a court report, or attend an interview with a lawyer (BA 1976 s3A(2)). It has been held in relation to a court's power to impose bail conditions that in considering whether and what conditions to impose, the court must perceive a real and not merely fanciful risk of the relevant outcome,[106] and it is suggested that the same principle must apply to a decision by a police officer. See further paras 10.95–10.97 below. An application to vary or remove conditions may be made to a custody officer or to a magistrates' court (see para 10.99 below).

### Consequences of bail without charge

10.79  There is no time limit under PACE on the period for which bail without charge can be granted, and no limit on the number of times that bail may be renewed. It would seem that the courts will only intervene in exceptional circumstances and there appear to be no reported decisions where the courts have done so.[107]

10.80  A person who has been released on bail under PACE Part IV may be re-arrested if new evidence justifying a further arrest comes to light after release (PACE s47(2) and see para 2.71 above). Where a person has been released on conditional bail, the person may be arrested by a constable having reasonable grounds for suspecting that the person has broken any of the conditions (PACE s46A(1A)). Further, a person granted bail to return to a police station (whether conditional or not) is under a duty to do so, and may be arrested if the person fails to attend the police station at the appointed time (PACE s46A(1)). The person must then be taken to the police

---

104  For the power to attach conditions to bail granted without taking the suspect to a police station, see para 2.46 above.

105  Confirmed in *R (Torres) v Commissioner of Police of the Metropolis* [2007] EWHC 3212 (Admin), although it was held that bail could be granted under PACE s37(2) in all circumstances where it could be granted under PACE s34(5).

106  *R v Mansfield Justices ex p Sharkey* [1985] QB 613.

107  See *R (C) v Chief Constable of A* [2006] EWHC 2352 (Admin). Note that it has been argued that police bail without charge, particularly where granted with conditions, may breach the right to liberty under ECHR article 5. See E Cape and R Edwards (2010) 'Police bail without charge: the human rights implications', *Cambridge Law Journal* 69(3), 423–465.

station at which he or she was required to surrender as soon as is practicable (PACE s46A(1A)), and the person is treated as having been arrested for an offence for the purposes of PACE s30 (duty to take arrested person to a police station) and s31 (arrest for further offence) (PACE s46A(2) and (3)). If the person had been released under PACE s37(7)(a) and the Crown prosecutor has not made a charge decision under PACE s37B, the custody officer may either charge the person or release him or her on bail again (PACE s37C(2) and (3)). The duty to attend at the police station on the appointed date is subject to the power of a custody officer to give notice in writing to the person that the person's attendance is not required (PACE s47(4)). Unlike under the BA 1976 s7(3), there is no power of arrest in respect of an anticipated breach of conditions or anticipated failure to surrender. Breach of conditions is not an offence, but failure without reasonable cause to surrender to custody is an offence (BA 1976 s6, as applied by PACE s47(1)).

10.81    Where a person returns to the police station in accordance with the person's bail (or fails to surrender and is arrested and taken to the police station), the custody officer may authorise the person's further detention only if the grounds in PACE s37 are satisfied (as a result of PACE s34(7)). This does not apply where the person was released on bail under PACE s37(7)(a), in which case the person may be kept in police detention to enable a charge decision to be made in accordance with PACE ss37B or 37C (PACE s37D(4)). Where the person was released on bail under PACE s37(7)(b) (see para 10.77 above) the person may be kept in police detention to enable a charge decision to be made or for the purpose of determining a new date for surrender to bail (PACE s37D(4A)). However, it is difficult to see how the person could be lawfully detained for the purpose of further investigation or in order to interview the person since a pre-condition for the person having been released on bail under PACE s37(7)(b) is that the custody officer had determined that there was sufficient evidence to charge him or her. That precludes detention for the purpose of investigation under PACE s37(2).

10.82    Normally, time spent in police detention before the initial release on bail counts for the purpose of calculating the maximum period of detention without charge, whether or not the person surrendered as required, or failed to surrender and was arrested under PACE s46A(1) (PACE s47(6)).[108] However, if the person has been arrested under PACE s 47(2) (see para 10.80 above) the detention clock starts again (PACE s47(7)).

## Advising in respect of bail without charge

10.83    The powers to grant bail without charge, taken together with the powers to impose conditions, give the police a great deal of flexibility in conducting investigations. Given the detention time limits, the defence lawyer may seek to use this to the advantage of the client in securing the client's release on bail, especially where the investigation cannot be proceeded with quickly. As noted at para 10.77 above, release on bail is possible even if the custody officer has determined that there is sufficient evidence to

---

108 Any period during which the person was released on bail does not count for the purpose of calculation the maximum period of detention (PACE s47(6)).

charge, and in appropriate cases a release on bail in these circumstances may give the lawyer the opportunity to secure evidence of assistance to the client or to seek to make representations to the prosecutor. On the other hand, as noted at para 10.79 above, there is no time limit on bail, or limit on the number of occasions on which bail can be renewed.

10.84   When the suspect is released on police bail, the suspect must be given a notice specifying the date and time on which he or she must surrender, and the police station at which he or she must attend (which may be different from that from which the suspect was bailed). It is normally advisable for the lawyer to arrange to meet the client shortly before the time given for surrender, and to advise the client to ensure that if they do not meet before the client's further detention that the client makes it clear to the police that the client wants legal advice. It is always worth checking with the police before the time for surrender to ensure that the suspect has not, in the meantime, been notified that he or she does not need to attend, and to check what action the police intend to take on the suspect's surrender. In view of the potential for inferences under CJPOA 1994 s34(1)(b), the lawyer should always consider whether to attend, even if it is understood that the client is simply to be charged without further interview (see para 10.27 above). On attending with the suspect, the lawyer should ensure that time already spent in police detention in connection with the matter is correctly taken into account (see para 10.82 above).

## Challenges to charge decisions

### Decisions to charge

10.85   Where a charge decision has been made by the police rather than a Crown prosecutor, the decision must be reviewed by a prosecutor prior to the first hearing. The case should be continued only if the relevant tests under the CCP are satisfied.[109] Even if the charge decision was made by a Crown prosecutor, the prosecutor has a duty to keep prosecution decisions under review, and to take into account any change of circumstances. In doing so, the prosecutor should take into account any information or evidence supplied on behalf of the accused (CCP paras 3.3–3.6). Generally, a decision to prosecute cannot be challenged by way of judicial review by the accused since it can be challenged within the trial process itself, notably by an application to stay proceedings on the grounds of abuse of process. Arguments relating to abuse of process may and should be raised in the course of the criminal trial itself save in wholly exceptional circumstances.[110] However, it has been held that a decision to prosecute rather than caution is susceptible to judicial review at the instance of the accused, but the courts are reluctant to intervene in a decision unless breach of an authority's clear and settled policy is established.[111] Note that a decision not to prosecute

109  *Director's Guidance on Charging* para 25.
110  *R (Pepushi) v CPS* (2004) *Times* 21 May; *R v DPP ex p Kebilene* [2000] 2 AC 326.
111  *R v Chief Constable of Kent and CPS ex p GL* (1991) 93 Cr App R 416), *R v Metropolitan Police Commissioner ex p Thompson* [1977] 1 WLR 1519, and *R (Mondelly) v Metropolitan Police Commissioner* (2007) 171 JP 121.

may be challenged by way of judicial review by the complainant, although the courts are generally reluctant to intervene.[112] Note also that the decision of the police or a Crown prosecutor not to prosecute does not prevent a private prosecution, and a private prosecutor is not bound by the CCP full code test.[113]

### Decisions to caution, reprimand or warn

10.86    A decision to caution may be challenged by way of judicial review by the person cautioned if it is made in breach of settled policy, such as where no clear and reliable admission was made.[114] Note that a decision to caution rather than prosecute may be challenged by the complainant by way of judicial review. If the complainant launches a private prosecution after the offender is cautioned it may be stayed for abuse of process, but a stay will not necessarily be ordered.[115]

## Bail or detention after charge

10.87    Where a person arrested for an offence otherwise than under a warrant endorsed for bail is charged with an offence, the custody officer must, subject to CJPOA 1994 s25 (see para 10.101 below), release the person from detention either on bail or without bail, unless one or more of the conditions in PACE s38 is satisfied (PACE s38(1)).[116] If released, the person will be given a date for the court appearance which, by PACE s47(3A), must normally be no later than the first sitting of the relevant magistrates' court after the person is charged.[117] Alternatively, in areas where the 'virtual court' provisions are in operation, the custody officer may bail the person to attend a police station pursuant to a live link direction under the CDA 1998 s57C.[118] If the person charged is not released, the first appearance in court is governed by PACE s46, which generally provides that the person

---

112  See, for example, *R v DPP ex p Manning* [2001] QB 330.

113  *R (Charlson) v Guildford Magistrates' Court* [2006] 1 WLR 3494.

114  *R (Wyman) v Chief Constable of Hampshire Constabulary* [2006] EWHC 1904 (Admin)). See also *R (Mohammed) v Chief Constable of West Midlands* [2010] EWHC 1228 (Admin) where, on the facts, an unlawfully administered caution for a sexual offence amounted to a breach of the rights of the recipient under ECHR article 8.

115  Compare *Jones v Whalley* [2007] 1 AC 63, in which a private prosecution was stayed, and *Hayter v L* [1998] 1 WLR 854, in which it was not. For a successful challenge by a complainant of a decision to give a conditional caution, see *R (Guest) v DPP* [2009] 2 Cr App R 426.

116  If the person was arrested on a warrant endorsed for bail, release will be determined by the terms of the warrant. Where a person is charged under CJA 2003 s87(4) (charge under the re-trial for certain serious offence provisions of CJA 2003 Part 10), the person cannot be released without bail, and if the person is granted bail, must be bailed to the Crown Court and not a magistrates' court (CJA 2003 s88(1)).

117  Although by PACE s47(3A)(b) it can be later if the designated officer for the relevant local justice area has notified the police that the appearance cannot be accommodated until a later date.

118  See PACE s47(3) as amended by Police and Justice Act 2006 s46.

must be brought before a magistrates' court as soon as practicable[119] and not later than the first sitting after charge.[120] This will normally mean that the suspect must be produced in court no later than the day following the date of charge, excluding Christmas day, Good Friday or a Sunday.[121]

## Drug testing and bail

10.88 The drug testing powers, both before and following charge, are dealt with at paras 6.64–6.71 above. Information from a drug test can be used to inform the decision as to bail (PACE s63B(7)), which includes both the decision whether bail should be granted and, if it is, the decision about any conditions to be imposed. Where a sample could be taken under PACE s63B and the custody officer determines that the person should be released under PACE s37(2) or s37(7)(a) or (b), the person can continue to be detained for up to 24 hours from the relevant time (see para 6.69 above) to enable a sample to be taken (PACE s37(8A) and (8B)). Furthermore, where such a sample could be taken, but the person is charged before a sample is taken and the custody officer would otherwise release them on bail under PACE s38, the officer can authorise the person's detention for up to six hours from the time of charge in order for a sample to be taken (PACE s38(1)(a)(iiia) and (2) and Code C para 17.10).

## Making representations regarding the bail/detention decision

10.89 The decision whether to bail a person after the person has been charged is a very important one, not least because for many suspects, getting out of the police station may be more important at that stage than the eventual result of the proceedings. It is also important because it has been shown that the police decision about bail is the single most important influence on whether a court will grant bail.[122] If the police grant bail, the court will normally do so. If, on the other hand, the police withhold bail, then the court is more likely to come to the same decision despite the accused's prima facie right to bail under the BA 1976. It is also likely that, where bail is granted subject to conditions, the court will be heavily influenced by the police decision on what conditions to impose. Note that the bail decision is

119 For interpretation of 'as soon as is practicable' see *Nikonovs v Governor of HM Prison Brixton and the Republic of Latvia (interested party)* [2005] EWHC 2405 (Admin).

120 Except where the person is charged under CJA 2003 s87(4) (charge under the re-trial for certain serious offence provisions of CJA 2003 Part 10), in which case the person must be brought before a Crown Court as soon as practicable and no later than 24 hours after he or she is charged (CJA 2003 s88(2)). In terrorism cases the person must usually be produced before Bow Street Magistrates' Court (see Management of Terrorism Cases: A Protocol issued by the President of the Queen's Bench Division, 18 January 2006).

121 On Saturdays, justices should be available to deal with cases arising after completing the list of cases before them (*R v Clerk to the Justices, Teesside Magistrates' Court ex p H* (2000) 19 October (unreported)).

122 See, eg, F Simon and M Weatheritt, *The use of bail and custody by London magistrates' courts before and after the Criminal Justice Act* (HMSO, London, 1984), p15.

that of the custody officer even in cases where the charge decision is made by a Crown prosecutor.

10.90   It is, therefore, vitally important for the lawyer to try, where appropriate, to persuade the custody officer to grant bail, with or without conditions. Although there is no specific duty on them under PACE or Code C to receive representations, most of the criteria for denying bail under PACE s38 require the custody officer to have reasonable grounds for his or her belief. It may be argued that the custody officer cannot do so if the officer knows that the lawyer has a relevant representation to make to which the officer is not prepared to listen. One problem, particularly in a busy custody office, is that it is easy for the custody officer to go through the motions of listening to the lawyer's representations without, in reality, considering the arguments put forward. Since the custody officer is, in effect, performing a quasi-judicial role, the investigating officer and the lawyer should make representations to the custody officer regarding bail in each other's presence.[123] The custody officer must give reasons for imposing conditions (although not for granting unconditional bail or for withholding bail), which must be noted in the custody record, and a copy of that note must be given to the defendant (BA 1976 s5A(2) and (3)).

10.91   The nature of the representations to be made by the lawyer will depend on the circumstances and on the lawyer's judgment about the way in which the custody officer is likely to be thinking. If the primary issue is whether bail should be granted at all, the officer should be asked to consider PACE s38(1) (see para 10.103 below) and which of the criteria may be satisfied. This will enable the lawyer to concentrate on the issues of primary concern, and will also enable the lawyer to argue (as appropriate) that the concerns could be adequately dealt with by the imposition of appropriate conditions. If the issue is whether any conditions should be imposed, and if so what form they should take, clearly the lawyer should consider, and direct the custody officer's attention to, the criteria for the imposition of conditions (and for the taking of a security or surety) under BA 1976 s3A(5) (see paras 10.93–10.97 below). The lawyer should, where relevant, already have discussed possible conditions with the client. Conditions should be both realistic and proportionate to the risk and, as noted at para 10.96 below, the perceived risk must be a real one and not purely speculative. If the conditions imposed are onerous, it may be that the client will indicate that he or she does not intend to keep to them. It has been held, in relation to court bail, that in such circumstances the defendant should be given the opportunity to comply with the conditions, and it is suggested that the same principle applies to police bail.[124] However, it would normally be better for the client to agree with the conditions, and then seek review by another custody officer or a court (see para 10.99 below).

---

123 Note that it has been held to be an abuse of process for the investigating officer to oppose bail following charge where the officer had promised that, if the suspect voluntarily returned to the UK and surrendered to the police, bail would be granted (*R (Hauschildt) v Highbury Corner Magistrates' Court* [2007] EWHC 3494 (Admin)).

124 *R v Bournemouth Justices ex p Cross and Others* (1988) *Times* 24 October; (1989) 153 JP 440.

## Bail after charge

10.92 A release on bail under PACE s38(1)[125] is deemed to be a release on bail granted in accordance with BA 1976, ss3, 3A, 5 and 5A, as they apply to bail granted by a constable (PACE s47(1)), and the 'normal powers to impose conditions of bail' (as defined in BA 1976 s3(6)) applying (PACE s47(1A)). On granting bail a custody officer can require a security or surety, or impose a condition or conditions, or a combination of these.

### Securities

10.93 A security – that is, money or some other valuable item such as jewellery or a passport given by the suspect or on the suspect's behalf before being released – may be required if it appears necessary for the purpose of preventing the person from absconding (BA 1976 ss3(5) and 3A(5)).[126]

### Sureties

10.94 A surety is, in effect, a promise by a person (other than the suspect) to forfeit a sum of money if the suspect fails to surrender to custody at the appointed time. One or more sureties can be required if it appears necessary to ensure that the person surrenders to custody (BA 1976 s3(4) and 3A(5)).[127] In the case of a person under 17 years of age, if a parent or guardian consents to be a surety for the juvenile, the surety may be required to ensure that the juvenile complies with any condition imposed on him or her (see below). However, a parent or guardian cannot be so bound if the juvenile will reach 17 years before the date on which the juvenile is due to surrender, nor be bound to any condition to which the juvenile does not consent. In any event, the person cannot be bound in a sum greater than £50 (BA 1976 s3(7)). In practice, sureties are rarely required by the police when granting bail.

### Conditions

10.95 A custody officer cannot attach conditions to bail unless it appears to the officer necessary to do so:

a) for the purpose of preventing the person from failing to surrender to custody; or

b) for the purpose of preventing the person from committing an offence while on bail;

---

125 This includes section 38(1) as applied by section 40(10) (ie, where bail is considered in respect of a person whose detention is under review at some time following charge).

126 The former condition that a security could only be required if it appeared likely that the person would not remain in Great Britain no longer applies. Although BA 1976 s3A(5) states that a security can be required if it is necessary for any of the purposes mentioned in para 10.95 below, section 3(5) restricts their use to ensuring surrender to custody.

127 Although BA 1976 s3A(5) states that a surety can be required if it is necessary for any of the purposes mentioned in para 10.95 below, section 3(4) restricts their use to ensuring surrender to custody.

c) for the purpose of preventing the person from interfering with witnesses or otherwise obstructing the course of justice, whether in relation to himself or herself or any other person; or

d) for the person's own protection or, in the case of a juvenile, for the juvenile's own welfare or in his or her own interests (BA 1976 s3A(5)).

If one or more of these requirements is satisfied, the custody officer may impose any relevant condition that a court could impose other than:

- a condition that the defendant reside at a bail hostel;
- a condition designed to ensure that the person co-operates with the preparation of a court report;
- a condition that the person attends an interview with the lawyer;
- electronic monitoring;
- medical examination in the case of a person charged with murder; or
- drugs assessment and follow-up (BA 1976 s3A(2) and (5)).

10.96   The custody officer is not required to have substantial grounds for believing in the necessity of any conditions, only that such conditions 'appear' to be necessary for one of the specified purposes. The question arises as to what grounds the officer is required to have for their belief. It has been held that a court, in considering conditions, must perceive a real and not merely a fanciful risk that the defendant will not surrender to custody,[128] and it is suggested that the same principle should apply to custody officers in respect of all of the relevant purposes of bail conditions. Therefore, the officer must be able to point to a concrete reason why a condition is necessary, and how it relates to one or more of the statutory purposes. The lawyer should consider how any proposed condition relates to the statutory purposes, whether it is realistic and whether it is proportionate to the perceived risk. It has been held that although a condition not to drive is lawful, the fact that it may have unjust results by, in effect, extending a subsequently imposed period of disqualification, should be considered.[129]

10.97   In view of the wide powers to impose conditions, it is not possible to provide an exhaustive list of possible conditions. Below is a list of commonly imposed conditions, by reference to the criteria for imposing conditions under the BA 1976 s3A.

a) Failing to surrender to custody
   - Security
   - Reporting to a police station
   - Residence at a particular address
   - Not to leave Great Britain (possibly combined with a condition of surrender of passport)

b) Committing an offence while on bail
   - Not to go to a particular place or area (licensed premises, shopping centre, address of victim, etc)

---

128  *R v Mansfield Justices ex p Sharkey* [1985] QB 613, [1985] 1 All ER 193.
129  *R v Kwame* (1975) 60 Cr App R 65.

- Curfew[130]
- Not to drive
- Residence at a place some distance from scene of alleged crime

c) Interference with witnesses or obstruction of course of justice
- Not to contact, directly or through others, named witnesses
- Not to go within a specified distance of address of witness

d) Own protection (or welfare)
- Residence at a particular address
- Not to go to a particular place or area
- Curfew

### Enforcement of bail

10.98 Police bail granted under PACE s38 is enforceable in the same way as bail granted by a court. Failure to surrender to custody at the appointed time without reasonable cause is an offence under BA 1976 s6, and the suspect may be arrested if the suspect fails to surrender or if a police officer has reasonable grounds for believing that the suspect is not likely to surrender to custody (BA 1976 s7). Breach of bail conditions is not an offence, but a person released on bail subject to conditions may be arrested if a constable has reasonable grounds for believing that the person is likely to breach any of the conditions, or for suspecting that the person has broken any of the conditions. Furthermore, if the person was released subject to a surety, the person may be arrested if the surety notifies the police in writing that the person is unlikely to surrender to custody and that the surety wants to be relieved of the obligations as surety (BA 1976 s7(3)). The court at which the suspect is due to appear may extend bail by fixing a later time at which the suspect is to surrender, whether or not bail was granted subject to a surety (Magistrates' Courts Act (MCA) 1980 s43(1) as amended by PACE s47(8)(a)).

## Review of bail decisions

10.99 If the custody officer grants bail subject to conditions, whether without charge or following charge, the suspect may make an application to the same or another custody officer serving at the same station for the conditions to be varied. That officer may vary or remove conditions, but may also impose new conditions including more onerous conditions (BA 1976 s3A(4)). There is no prescribed procedure for making such an application. The suspect may, alternatively or in addition, make an application to a magistrates' court for variation of the conditions (MCA s43B(1)). As with application to a custody officer to review conditions, an application requires careful consideration since the court has the power to impose conditions that had not been imposed or impose more onerous conditions

---

130 It was held in *R v Chorley Justices ex p* CPS [2002] EWHC 2162 (Admin); (2002) *Times* 22 October, that where a curfew condition is imposed, a further condition requiring the person to present himself or herself at the door of the person's home during the curfew to a police officer could be imposed.

(PACE s47(1D) and (1E)). An application to a magistrates' court must be made in writing not less than 24 hours before the hearing and must: contain a statement of the grounds upon which it is made; specify the offence with which the suspect was charged before the suspect's release on bail; state the reasons given by the custody officer for imposing or carrying the conditions of bail; state the variation or conditions proposed; give details of the address at which the suspect would reside if the court imposed a condition of residence; and state the name and address of any surety provided by the suspect before the suspect's release on bail. In considering variation or removal of conditions, a court can take into account a police officer's opinion that the suspect may not surrender to custody even though the sources of the information giving rise to the officer's opinion has not been disclosed.[131]

10.100   Note that where a custody officer has granted conditional or unconditional bail, a prosecutor may apply to the court for a condition to be imposed or varied, or for bail to be denied (BA 1976 s5B(1)). However, an application can only be made if it is based on information that was not available to the officer granting bail when the decision was first made (BA 1976 s5B(3)).

## Detention in custody after charge

### The 'right to bail'

10.101   Where a person is charged with an offence, the person must be released pending his or her first court appearance unless one or more of the criteria in PACE s38(1) is satisfied.[132] The presumption of bail is subject to two significant restrictions. First, a custody officer cannot grant bail to a person charged with murder (PACE s38(1)(c)). Second, where the suspect is charged with any of the following offences, and the suspect already has a conviction[133] for any of those offences in any part of the UK (or a conviction for culpable homicide), bail may only be granted if the custody officer is satisfied that there are exceptional circumstances which justify the grant of bail (CJPOA 1994 s25).[134] The offences concerned are:

- attempted murder;
- manslaughter;

---

131 *R (Ajaib) v Birmingham Magistrates' Court* [2009] EWHC 2127 (Admin).

132 It was held in *Hutt v Commissioner of Police for the Metropolis* [2003] EWCA Civ 1911 that if the arrest leading to the detention was unlawful, bail could not be denied under PACE s38(1). This probably does not apply where the nature of the illegality was such that it could be, or has been, 'cured', eg, where failure to give the required information under PACE s28 is 'cured' by the arrested person subsequently being given this information.

133 Including a finding of not guilty by reason of insanity, a finding under Criminal Procedure (Insanity) Act 1964 s4A(3) (unfitness to plead) that a person did the act or made the omission charged against the person, or conviction for an offence for which the person was absolutely or conditionally discharged (CJPOA 1994 s25(5)).

134 It was held in *R v Harrow Crown Court ex p R* [2003] EWHC 868 (Admin); (2003) *Times* 29 May that CJPOA 1994 s25 does not violate ECHR article 5 (right to liberty and security) provided that it is not construed too narrowly.

- rape (under SOA 1956 s1 or SOA 2003 s1, or under the law of Scotland or Northern Ireland);
- assault by penetration (SOA 2003 s2);
- causing a person to engage in sexual activity without consent where the activity caused involved penetration within subsection (4)(a)–(d) (SOA 2003 s4);
- rape of a child under 13 (SOA 2003 s5);
- assault of a child under 13 by penetration (SOA 2003 s6);
- causing or inciting a child under 13 to engage in sexual activity, where an activity involving penetration within subsection (2)(a)–(d) was caused (SOA 2003 s8);
- sexual activity with a person with a mental disorder impeding choice, where the touching involved penetration within subsection (3)(a)–(d) (SOA 2003 s30);
- causing or inciting a person with a mental disorder impeding choice, to engage in sexual activity, where an activity involving penetration within subsection (3)(a)–(d) was caused (SOA 2003 s31); or
- an attempt to commit any of these offences (other the first three listed above) (CJPOA 1994 s25(2)).

10.102  Where the previous conviction was for any of the offences listed above or culpable homicide in any part of the United Kingdom, the restriction only applies if the person received a custodial sentence (CJPOA 1994 s25(3A)).[135] No guidance is given in the CJPOA 1994 to the meaning of 'exceptional circumstances' or to the relationship between CJPOA 1994 s25 and PACE s38. It would seem that the custody officer would still have to be satisfied that one or more of the PACE s38 conditions applies before withholding bail, but in practice, it is highly unlikely that a custody officer would grant bail in the circumstances covered by CJPOA 1994 s25.

## Grounds for withholding bail

10.103  In the case of an adult, the PACE s38(1) criteria are as follows:

1) The suspect's name or address cannot be ascertained, or the custody officer has reasonable grounds for doubting whether the name or address given by the suspect is real (PACE s38(1)(a)(i)). The expression 'cannot be ascertained' imposes a strict test and more or less equates with a refusal by the suspect to give such details, and where there is no other information about the suspect's name or address. Doubt about the suspect's true name or address has to be reasonable, and the lawyer will want to know the grounds for such a belief. Mere suspicion is not enough. Doubt may occur where, for example, documents are found on the suspect containing a name different from that given. It may be that the suspect can offer an explanation, although the suspect should be warned that any statement made at this stage could provide evidence to the police in respect of the offence for which the suspect has been charged or any other offence. Sometimes the police may have

---

135  Section 25(3B) also applies the restrictions where the previous conviction was by a court in another European Union member state, subject to modifications.

visited the address given by the suspect and been told that the suspect is not known and/or does not live there. Again, there may be a rational explanation for this that can be safely disclosed to the police.

2) The custody officer has reasonable grounds for believing that the person arrested will fail to appear in court to answer bail (PACE s38(1)(a)(ii)). In considering this ground the custody officer must have regard to the following factors (PACE s38(2A)):

- the nature and seriousness of the offence, and the probable penalty;
- the character, antecedents, associations and community ties of the defendant;
- the defendant's record in respect of previous grant of bail;
- the strength of the evidence;
- any other relevant consideration.

The officer must have reasonable grounds for his or her belief, and the lawyer should seek to ascertain what those grounds are. The grounds may derive from the nature and seriousness of the offence charged or from a record of previous failure to surrender to custody. The lawyer should consider whether those grounds are reasonable and, if they are, whether they may be suitably catered for by the imposition of conditions.

3) Where the person was arrested for an imprisonable offence, the custody officer has reasonable grounds for believing that the detention of the person is necessary to prevent the person from committing an offence (PACE s38(1)(a)(iii)). There is room for confusion over this ground, since it is stated to apply to a person arrested for an imprisonable offence, rather than to a person charged with an imprisonable offence. It is suggested that the wording follows from the general structure of the section, and that it should only be applied where a person is charged with such an offence. This provision is similar to that relating to bail from a court under BA 1976 Sch 1 Part I para 1(2)(b).[136] In considering this ground, the custody officer must have regard to the same factors as under 2) above. Particular factors that will be relevant to whether a defendant may commit offences while on bail include a history of offending which is persistent and repetitive (where the current alleged offence is part of the same pattern), previous offending on bail, the fact that the current alleged offence was committed while on bail,[137] and factors in the current alleged offence (for example, a history of bad feeling between the defendant and the victim) that might suggest further offending. Since the officer must believe that detention is necessary to prevent the defendant from offending, it follows that the

---

136 However, under BA 1976 a court must have substantial grounds for believing that the defendant would commit an offence while on bail, whereas under PACE the custody officer must have reasonable grounds for believing that detention is necessary to prevent this.

137 Note that one ground on which a court may withhold bail where a person is charged with an imprisonable indictable offence is that it appears to have been committed while the person was on bail for another offence, but this is not the case under PACE s38(1).

officer would have to be satisfied that the imposition of appropriate conditions would not be adequate to prevent offending.

4) In a case where a sample may be taken under PACE s63B (see para 10.88 above), the custody officer has reasonable grounds for believing that the detention of the person is necessary to enable the sample to be taken (PACE s38(1)(a)(iiia)). In this case the suspect cannot be kept in police detention after the end of the period of six hours beginning when the person was charged with the offence (PACE s38(2)).

5) Where the person was arrested for a non-imprisonable offence, the custody officer has reasonable grounds for believing that detention is necessary to prevent the person from causing physical injury to any other person or from causing loss of or damage to property (PACE s38(1)(a)(iv)). In considering this ground, the custody officer must have regard to the same factors as under 2) above, particularly in establishing 'reasonable grounds'. The comments regarding the requirement for a belief that detention is 'necessary' in 3) above also apply here. In some respects, fear of future injury, loss or damage is similar to fear of offences being committed. However, there may be a fear of offences in circumstances where it would not be possible for the custody officer to maintain that this amounted to a fear of injury, loss or damage. In any event, it should only be in rare circumstances that a person is denied bail when charged with a non-imprisonable offence.[138]

6) The custody officer has reasonable grounds for believing that detention is necessary to prevent the person from interfering with the administration of justice or with the investigation of offences or of a particular offence (PACE s38(1)(a)(v)). In considering this ground, the custody officer must have regard to the same factors as under 2) above. Note the comments on 'reasonable grounds' in 2) above, and on the requirement for a belief that detention is 'necessary' in 3) above.

7) The custody officer has reasonable grounds for believing that detention is necessary for the person's own protection (PACE s38(1)(a)(vi)). Once again, note the comments on 'reasonable grounds' in 2) above, and the comments regarding the requirement for a belief that detention is 'necessary' in 3) above. This ground may be relevant either because the suspect is at risk from others (perhaps because of the nature of the alleged offence), or because the suspect is vulnerable (perhaps through age or mental disorder), or because the suspect has threatened to injure himself or herself. In the former case, the lawyer should explore whether the suspect could move to another address, if only temporarily, away from the area of hostility. If appropriate, this could be made a condition of bail. In the case of vulnerability, if the problem is lack of any, or appropriate, accommodation it may be possible to make arrangement for the suspect to be suitably housed (see para 11.78 below regarding mentally disordered or mentally handicapped suspects).

---

138 In fact, PACE s38(1)(a)(iv) refers to a person having been arrested for (as opposed to charged with) an offence which is not imprisonable. See the comments regarding this distinction under 3) above.

# Leaving the police station

10.104   The actions to be taken by the lawyer before leaving the police station will depend on the stage the investigation has reached and whether the client has been charged. If the client has not been charged, the lawyer should review the matters set out in para 7.74 above in order to check whether any further action should be taken at this stage. If the client has been charged, the lawyer should consider whether it is appropriate to ask the police to pursue any particular lines of enquiry given their obligation under the to pursue all reasonable lines of enquiry including those that may point away from the suspect (under the Criminal Procedure and Investigations Act 1996 Code of Practice para 3.4).

10.105   If the suspect has been charged and bailed to court, the lawyer should ensure that the client is clear about any bail conditions, the client's obligation to surrender to custody and the consequences of not doing so, and the arrangements for representation in the court proceedings. If the client has been given a long bail date, it may be appropriate for an appointment to be made at the lawyer's office.

10.106   If the client has been charged and detained in custody, the lawyer should normally see the client again before leaving the station. First, it will frequently be helpful for the lawyer to take initial instructions relevant to any bail application to be made at the first court appearance. The lawyer should, by this stage, know what the police objections to bail are, and although the prosecutor will not necessarily adopt the same approach, the police view is clearly important. If bail with conditions, or with a surety or security, is possible, instructions can be taken about what conditions would be acceptable to the suspect, what might be available as a security, and/or who might be available as a surety. For a checklist of information to be obtained in respect of a bail application, see appendix 3 checklist 12.

10.107   A second reason for seeing the client at this stage is to ensure that the client understands what is going on, and what is likely to happen, including the timescale. If the suspect is to be produced in court the following morning, the client needs to know this. It should not be assumed that the police will tell the client, or that the client will understand or believe what he or she is told by the police. Detainees may want to make arrangements for fresh clothes, food or reading material to be brought in. Usually there will be no objection from the police to such arrangements. Suspects are normally entitled to speak on the telephone to a person nominated by the person (Code C, Code H para 5.6), although visits are at the custody officer's discretion (Code C, Code H para 5.4).

10.108   Suspects should be told that they continue to be entitled to legal advice at any time. Furthermore, particularly if they have refused to answer police questions or if they have denied the allegation, they should be warned of the possibility that they will be visited by the officer in the case after the lawyer has left. Unfortunately, the courts do not always disapprove of such visits, even where the suspect subsequently agrees to be interviewed without the lawyer present, and then proceeds to make admissions. In *R v Williams*,[139] for example, the Court of Appeal held that a judge was

139 (1992) *Times* 6 February.

entitled to accept that an hour-long 'social visit' by the investigating officers to the suspect in his cell, followed by an interview in the absence of his lawyer during which the suspect made damaging admissions, was perfectly proper and not in breach of the Codes of Practice. The court did say, however, that such visits should usually be avoided.[140] Whether the police will take any notice of this view may be doubted, and the suspect should be strongly advised that in the event of such a visit, a request to see the lawyer should be made. The suspect should also be warned in appropriate cases of the possibility that the police may conduct covert surveillance of the suspect's cell, a practice that has come to light in a number of cases, or that the police may recruit cell-mates or others in detention to act as informants.[141]

140  See also *R v Marshall* (1992) *Times* 28 December, where it was held that evidence of a confession made in a subsequent interview with a 'borderline subnormal' suspect should have been excluded.

141  See *R v Ali* (1991) *Times* 19 February, *R v Bailey* [1993] 3 All ER 513; [1993] Crim LR 681, *R v Mason* [2002] Crim LR 841, *PG and JH v UK* [2002] Crim LR 308 and see para 13.62. In *R v Allan* [2004] EWCA Crim 2236; [2005] Crim LR 716 it was held that the use of a fellow prisoner as an informant to obtain admissions infringed the defendant's common law right to silence and the privilege against self-incrimination. The RIPA 2000 Covert Surveillance Code of Practice para 5.4 indicates that surveillance of police cells is to be treated as 'intrusive surveillance', which requires authorisation at chief constable level (RIPA 2000 ss26 and 32).

# CHAPTER 11

# Juveniles, persons at risk and other special groups

*continued*

# Introduction

11.1 This chapter deals with issues that that specifically relate to suspects who are juveniles, mentally disordered or vulnerable, or potentially vulnerable for other reasons such as hearing, sight or language difficulties, or who are foreign nationals. Both Police and Criminal Evidence Act 1984 (PACE) and the Codes of Practice contain specific provisions regarding juveniles. PACE makes no reference to mentally disordered suspects, and limited reference to mentally handicapped suspects,[1] but the Codes do contain provisions for mentally vulnerable suspects. The Codes also contain specific provisions for suspects in the other special groups referred to above.

11.2 Lawyers will need to consider how they should take into account the special needs of clients from the groups considered in this chapter. The need for special consideration is recognised, to an extent, by the Standard Criminal Contract (SCC) 2010 which provides that payment for personal attendance at the police station may be claimed where the client is eligible for assistance from an appropriate adult, or requires an interpreter, even in circumstances where a claim for personal attendance would not otherwise be met.[2]

# Juveniles

## General considerations

11.3 Crime and Disorder Act (CDA) 1998 s37(1) provides that: 'the principal aim of the youth justice system is [to] prevent offending by children and young persons'. Defence lawyers, in common with all others who carry out functions in relation to the youth justice system, have a statutory duty to have regard to that aim (CDA 1998 s37(2)). However, the lawyer's professional obligation to act in the client's best interests remains paramount.[3]

11.4 CDA 1998 s38 requires local authorities, in co-operation with the police, probation service and health authorities, to ensure that the following youth justice services are available in their area at the pre-court stage:

- appropriate adult services;
- a final warning scheme and related services;
- bail support;
- placement of those remanded to local authority accommodation.

11.5 In addition, local authorities must publish youth justice plans setting out how youth justice services are to be provided (CDA 1998 s40(1)), and must appoint one or more youth offending teams to co-ordinate and provide youth justice services (CDA 1998 s39). Defence lawyers should ensure that

1 The only reference is in PACE s77 which provides for a warning to be given to a jury of the special need for caution where a case is substantially dependent on a confession by a mentally handicapped person made in the absence of an independent person.
2 SCC 2010, Part B, para 9.10 and see para 1.58 above.
3 See generally, the special edition of the Law Society's *Criminal Practitioners Newsletter*, 'Youth court cases: defence good practice', April 2002; and M Ashford, A Chard and N Redhouse, *Defending young people* (3rd edn LAG, London, 2006).

they are familiar with the services and schemes available in their area. Information is also available from the Youth Justice Board, and it has published national standards which require youth offending team managers to develop integrated remand management structures that include provision for appropriate adults, and for providing accommodation where it is required under PACE s38(6) in respect of a juvenile who had been denied bail following charge.[4]

## Definition of 'juvenile'

11.6    Anyone who appears to be under the age of 17 must be treated as a juvenile in the absence of clear evidence to the contrary for the purposes of PACE and the Codes of Practice (PACE s37(15), Code C para 1.5, Code H para 1.11 and Code D para 2.4). The actual age of the suspect is irrelevant, so that even if a suspect is 17 years old or older, but the available evidence points to the suspect being younger, the suspect must be treated as a juvenile unless and until evidence to the contrary is available. If the lawyer is aware that the client is a juvenile, the lawyer should normally advise the client to disclose his or her true age. If the client is not willing to do so, the lawyer should consider withdrawing for the same reasons as those that apply where a client gives a false name and/or address (see para 5.38 above).

11.7    Although for most purposes in the criminal justice system 17-year-olds are not treated as adults, this is not the case for those detained at a police station (PACE s37(15)). Therefore, 17-year-olds are to be treated as adults in the police station, although they will normally appear in a youth court if charged or summonsed for an offence. However, a 17-year-old is a young person for the purposes of reprimands and final warnings (see para 11.30 below), and youth conditional cautions (see para 11.42 below).

## Police powers

11.8    The minimum age of criminal responsibility is ten years[5] and a child under that age should neither be arrested nor held in police detention. Generally, police powers in respect of person between the ages of 10 and 16 years are the same as for adults. However, note the following powers in respect of children and young persons, some of which also apply to children under 10 years.

1) A child under 18 years may be kept under police protection at a police station, as a place of safety, where a police officer has reasonable cause to believe that the child would be likely to suffer significant harm if not removed to suitable accommodation (Children Act 1989 s46(1)). The child can be kept under police protection for up to 72 hours, although if the child is taken to a police station the child must be moved to local authority or other suitable accommodation as soon as reasonably practicable (Children Act 1989 s46(3)(f)).

---

4 Available via www.justice.gov.uk/index.htm. See also the duties under Children Act 2004 s11, and for application to the police *(1) Adam Castle (2) Rosie Castle (3) Sam Eaton v Commissioner of Police of the Metropolis* [2011] EWHC 2317 (Admin).

5 Children and Young Persons Act (CYPA) 1933 s50.

2) A court can make a child safety order in respect of a child under 10 years who has committed an act which, if the child had been 10 or over, would have constituted an offence (CDA 1998 s11). However, the police have no powers of arrest in relation to child safety orders.

3) Where a local authority has designated premises or a superintendent or above has authorised use of the power (CDA 1998 s16(1) and (2)), a police constable who has reasonable cause to believe that a child or young person found by the constable in a specified area during a specified period is of compulsory school age[6] and is absent from school without lawful authority, may remove the child or young person to the designated premises or to the school from which the child or young person is absent (CDA 1998 s16(3)).

## Persons who must be informed

11.9 The police have a duty to inform a number of people of the arrest and detention of a juvenile, which is in addition to the suspect's right of intimation under PACE s56 (see para 2.116 above).[7]

1) Where a child or young person is in police detention, the police must take such steps as are practicable to ascertain the identity of the person responsible for the child's or young person's welfare (CYPA 1933 s34(2)). If the child or young person is in the care of the local authority, it is the authority rather than the parent or guardian who should be informed (CYPA 1933 s34(8)). Unless it is impracticable, that person (or authority) must be informed that the child or young person has been arrested, why he or she has been detained and the place of detention. This must be done as soon as is practicable (CYPA 1933 s34(3) and (4) and Code C para 3.13, Code H para 3.15).

2) If the child or young person is known to be subject to a supervision order as defined in the Children Act 1989 Part IV, the responsible officer must be given the same information as in 1) above as soon as reasonably practicable (CYPA 1933 s34(7) and Code C para 3.14, Code H para 3.16). There is a similar requirement to inform the local authority where it is known that the child or young person is being provided with accommodation by or on behalf of a local authority under the Children Act 1989 s20 (CYPA 1933 s34(7A)).

3) The appropriate adult, who may or may not be the parent or guardian, must be informed of the grounds for detention and the place of detention as soon as practicable, and must be asked to come to the police station (Code C para 3.15, Code H para 3.17, and see para 11.13 below).[8]

4) Where a suspect is a ward of court, the police should notify the parent or foster parent with whom the ward is living or other appropriate adult

---

6 A person ceases to be of compulsory school age at the end of the school year in which the person attains the age of 16 years (Education Act 1996 s8).

7 CYPA 1933 s34(9) makes it clear that the right of intimation is separate from and in addition to the police duty to inform certain people of the juvenile's arrest and detention.

8 It was held in *DPP v Evans* [2003] Crim LR 338 that the police were not required to delay a breath test procedure to enable an appropriate adult to be present.

(as above) and, if practicable, the reporting officer (if one has been appointed). The latter should, if practicable, be invited to attend the police interview or nominate a third party to attend on his or her behalf. A record of the interview, or a copy of any statement made by the ward, should be supplied to the reporting officer. If the ward has been interviewed without the reporting officer knowing, the police should inform the reporting officer at the earliest opportunity, and he or she must also be informed if the police wish to conduct further interviews with the ward.[9]

11.10   The lawyer should check with the custody officer to see who has been informed and, in particular, whether the appropriate adult is at the police station and, if not, what steps are being taken to secure the appropriate adult's presence. There is no provision for delay in informing the persons specified above even if the juvenile is being held incommunicado under PACE s56 or legal advice is being delayed under PACE s58 (Code C, Code H Annex B NfG B1).

## Juvenile's right to legal advice

11.11   The right to legal advice under PACE s58 and Terrorism Act (TA) 2000 Sch 8 para 7 (see para 2.119 above) applies to juveniles in the same way as it does to adults. PACE s58(4) and TA 2000 Sch 8 para 7 provide that where a person makes a request to consult a solicitor the person must be permitted to do so as soon as practicable, and there is no provision for action on the request to be delayed until the request has been confirmed with the appropriate adult. Code C para 6.5A and Code H para 6.6 state that in the case of a juvenile an appropriate adult should consider whether legal advice from a solicitor is required. However, it is clear from the context that this is intended to apply to the situation where the juvenile has refused legal advice, and thus should not be used to delay contacting a lawyer where a juvenile has requested legal advice. Any apparent delay in contacting a lawyer should be investigated.

11.12   Since there is no provision for the police to delay contacting an appropriate adult, once an appropriate adult has been contacted it would be difficult for the police to justify delaying access to a lawyer under PACE s58(8) or TA 2000 Sch 8 para 8(1) (see paras 2.139 and 2.145 above). Unless the police have specific evidence which leads them to believe that the lawyer requested is dishonest, once the appropriate adult has been contacted (or any other person that the police are required to inform), the fact of detention has been disclosed and it will be difficult for a superintendent to maintain that contact with a lawyer will lead to one of the prohibited consequences. It has been held that it would be difficult for a superintendent to have a reasonable fear in respect of contact with a lawyer where the suspect had already spoken to his wife twice on the telephone, and a similar principle should apply to contact with an appropriate adult.[10]

9  Consolidated Criminal Practice Direction Part I para I.5.
10  *R v Davison* [1988] Crim LR 442.

## The appropriate adult

11.13   Where a juvenile has been detained, the police must contact an appropriate adult as soon as is practicable and ask the adult to attend the police station (see para 11.9 above). Local authorities have a duty to secure the provision of sufficient appropriate adults for their area (CDA 1998 s38), and responsibility is also placed on youth offending team managers to ensure that appropriate adults are available (see para 11.5 above). PACE envisages that appropriate adults should play a key role during the detention of a juvenile, although evidence suggests that they frequently do not understand their role, are often passive, and may have an adverse impact on the interests of the person they are supposedly there to protect.[11] Lawyers should be aware of the fact that appropriate adults normally do not owe a duty of confidentiality to the juvenile, but the presence of an appropriate adult at a consultation between the lawyer and the client does not destroy legal professional privilege (see para 11.23 below).

### Appropriate people

11.14   The appropriate adult may be:

- the juvenile's parent or guardian (or care authority if the juvenile is 'in care');[12]
- a local authority social worker; or
- failing either of the above, another responsible adult aged 18 or over who is not a police officer nor employed by the police (Code C para 1.7, Code H para 1.13 and Code D para 2.6).

In respect of the last, it was held in *R v Palmer*[13] that a 17-year-old attending on his 16-year-old brother could not be an appropriate adult because he was not 18 or over and was too close in age. In *R v Morse and others*[14] it was indicated that the suspect's father, who had a low IQ, was virtually illiterate and who was probably incapable of appreciating the gravity of the situation, was not suitable.[15]

11.15   The definition of who may be an appropriate adult amounts to a hierarchy. The appropriate adult should, if possible, be a parent or guardian (or representative of the care authority) and only if they are unavailable or inappropriate should it be a social worker, finally moving to the third category if both the others are unavailable or inappropriate. In relation to

---

11   For a summary of research conducted in the 1990s see D Brown, *PACE ten years on: a review of the research*, Home Office Research Study 155 (Home Office, London, 1997). The Home Office publishes a *Guide for appropriate adults* (available at www. homeoffice.gov.uk/publications/police/operational-policing/appropriate-adults-guide), which encourages a more active role, and there is a National Appropriate Adult Network which is concerned to improve standards (see www.appropriateadult. org.uk/).

12   The term 'in care' applies to all cases in which a juvenile is 'looked after' by a local authority under the terms of the Children Act 1989 (Code C para 1.7(a)(i), Code H para 1.13(a)(i)). This includes those in respect of whom a care order has been made, and those who are 'accommodated' by a local authority.

13   September 1991 *Legal Action* 21.

14   [1991] Crim LR 195.

15   But see *R v W and another* [1994] Crim LR 130, where, on the particular facts of the case, a mother was held to be suitable despite being psychotic.

availability, no guidance is given in the Codes about what efforts should be made by the police and what kind of delay should be countenanced. The custody officer will have to take into account the detention time limits and the general requirement that all persons in custody must be dealt with expeditiously. A balance is necessary between the need to protect the juvenile by ensuring the attendance of an appropriate person and the disadvantages of prolonged detention in a police station.

## Inappropriate people

11.16   Even if a potential appropriate adult is available, the adult may not be suitable. The following are either unsuitable to act as appropriate adults or are prohibited from doing so.

### Estranged parents

11.17   A parent who is estranged from the juvenile, and whose presence is expressly and specifically objected to by the juvenile, should not act as the appropriate adult (Code C, Code H NfG 1B). In *DPP v Blake*,[16] a confession was excluded where it had been obtained in the presence of the juvenile's father whom she had specifically rejected in favour of her social worker who was unavailable.

11.18      The question of estrangement is not necessarily an easy one, either for the custody officer or the lawyer. Parents are frequently annoyed or angry with their children at the police station, irrespective of whether the juvenile is guilty of the offence for which the juvenile has been detained. The determining factor has to be the attitude of the juvenile – does the juvenile 'expressly and specifically' object to the parent's presence?

### Interested parties

11.19   A potential appropriate adult may have an involvement with the case that renders them inappropriate or ineligible.

1) *Persons suspected of involvement* A person, including a parent or guardian, should not be the appropriate adult if the person is suspected of involvement in the offence, is the victim, is a witness, is involved in the investigation or has received admissions before attending to act as the appropriate adult (Code C, Code H NfG 1B). The meaning of 'involved in the investigation' is unclear, but could include a person who, while not a victim or witness, reported the offence. The exclusion of a person who has received admissions is also not without difficulty. The purpose of this provision (as with that relating to social workers – see below) must be to try to ensure that the adult advises the child fairly and does not simply pressure the child into confessing to the police. This could be important, for example, if a parent has unfairly pressured the juvenile into making admissions to them. It could have the effect of reinforcing an untrue confession. Alternatively, it may be that the juvenile quite truthfully admitted the offence to his or her parent, and that it is perfectly in order for the parent to accompany the child when interviewed by the police. Even then, however, the parent is likely to be

unaware of the strength of the evidence in the hands of the police, and an uninvolved adult might advise the juvenile quite differently. Note that the restriction only applies where the person received admissions *before* attending to act as appropriate adult.

2) *Social workers* If the juvenile has admitted the offence to, or in the presence of, a social worker or member of a youth offending team other than while they are acting as the appropriate adult, another appropriate adult should be appointed 'in the interests of fairness' (Code C, Code H NfG 1C). A social worker would also be inappropriate if involved in the same ways as applies to others (see 1) above). It has been held that a social worker who reported the offence to the police and who would be seen by the juvenile as being 'on the side of the police' probably should not have acted as the appropriate adult.[17]

### Solicitors

11.20  If it is proving difficult to secure the attendance of an appropriate adult, the police may ask the lawyer to act as the appropriate adult. Indeed, the juvenile himself or herself may be keen for the lawyer to do so because it raises the prospect of being released earlier than otherwise might be the case. However, there are difficulties, not only in terms of potential conflict of role, but also because it may not hasten the juvenile's release unless the lawyer is willing to accept responsibility for the juvenile after release, which is usually not advisable. Codes C and H specifically provides that a lawyer who is at the police station in a professional capacity cannot act as the appropriate adult (Code C, Code H NfG 1F).[18]

### Role of the appropriate adult

11.21  The role of the appropriate adult is not specified in general terms in the PACE Codes, but the Home Office *Guide for appropriate adults* states the following:

> You are *not* simply an observer. Your role is to assist the detainee to ensure that they understand what is happening at the police station during the interview and investigative stages. In particular you should:
> - support, advise and assist the detainee
> - ensure that the police act fairly and respect the rights of the detainee
> - help communication between the detainee, the police and others
> You are *not* there to provide the detainee with legal advice.

The role of the appropriate adult during police interviews is set out in similar terms in Code C para 11.17 and Code H para 11.10. Generally, a juvenile must not be interviewed by the police or asked to provide a written statement in the absence of the appropriate adult, unless to avoid an immediate risk of harm to persons or serious loss or serious damage to property (Code C paras 11.1 and 11.15, Code H paras 11.2 and 11.9). The appropriate adult also has specific roles in relation to legal advice, searches and samples, and identification procedures (see paras 11.22, 11.52 and 11.54 below).

---

17  *DPP v Morris* (1990) 8 October (unreported).

18  This prohibition also applies to an independent custody visitor (formerly known as 'lay visitor') who is present at the station in that capacity.

11.22    For the lawyer, the appropriate adult can be a useful ally, but the adult's presence may also cause some difficulty for a number of reasons. It was noted above that a juvenile suspect has a right to legal advice in the same way as an adult. The appropriate adult can ask for legal advice on behalf of the detainee (Code C para 3.19, Code H para 3.20), and this is so even if the juvenile has declined legal advice (Code C para 6.5A, Code H para 6.6). This could cause a problem if the adult requests legal advice but the juvenile does not wish to receive it, since the lawyer should not impose himself or herself on an unwilling client. In such circumstances, the lawyer could treat the appropriate adult as the client.[19] A more common difficulty occurs where the adult is hostile to the lawyer requested by the juvenile. The lawyer should remember that his or her client is the juvenile and not the adult. This may mean, in an extreme case, that the lawyer should seek the exclusion of the adult.

11.23    An important question is whether an appropriate adult can disclose, or can be required to disclose, what is said in the adult's hearing during a consultation between the lawyer and the client. With regard to the latter, it has been held that the presence of an appropriate adult does not destroy legal professional privilege.[20] Therefore, an appropriate adult cannot be required, by the police or by a court, to disclose what is said during a lawyer/client consultation. However, there is a separate question of whether the appropriate adult can voluntarily disclose what is said, and here the position is less certain.[21] Even if a social worker is bound by a duty of confidentiality, a parent is not, and in any event the law will provide scant protection if the appropriate adult proceeds to tell the police what the adult has heard.

11.24    As a result, the lawyer should initially speak to the client in the absence of the appropriate adult in order to advise the client of the risk of disclosure, and to ask the client whether he or she wants the adult to be present during the consultation (see Code C, Code H NfG 1E). If the client does wish the adult to be present, the lawyer should consider asking the adult to give an undertaking that he or she will not pass on to the police any information divulged during the consultation. Such an undertaking is unenforceable, but may serve to underline the importance of confidentiality to the appropriate adult.

## Special considerations when advising juveniles

### Taking instructions from and advising juveniles

11.25    A particular effort may be needed to establish a rapport with a juvenile client since, for the juvenile, the lawyer may be just another adult authority

19  Since the appropriate adult has attended voluntarily at the police station for the purpose of assisting with an investigation, the adult should qualify for advice under the police station advice and assistance scheme on the basis that the adult is a volunteer under PACE s29 (see para 2.151 above).

20  *A Local Authority v B* [2008] EWHC 1017 (Fam).

21  In *A Local Authority v B* the court held that the local authority that employed the social worker who acted as appropriate adult could not use the information so obtained in order to assess the needs of the family.

figure who is not to be trusted. Although not necessarily the case, a juvenile may be particularly nervous, scared and vulnerable and in need of support and guidance. Equally, the juvenile may fail to understand the seriousness of his or her predicament, or may believe that anything the juvenile says at the police station can be 'undone' later. In the consultation with a juvenile client the lawyer should:

- start by seeking basic information about the client and the client's circumstances;
- be aware of indications of learning disability, such as the type of school attended and (if appropriate) ask if anyone helps the client with his or her reading;
- take time to prepare the client for the police interview, telling the client how it will be conducted, how long it will last and who will be present;
- carefully explain the caution and its implications and, if necessary, ask the client to explain it back to the lawyer;
- if advice to make no comment in the police interview is accepted, consider conducting a practice interview with the client.[22]

## Legal incapacity

11.26   A child under the age of ten years is deemed unable to commit a crime (see para 11.8 above). At common law, a child between the ages of 10 and 14 was presumed not to be able to commit a crime (the presumption of doli incapax). This presumption could be rebutted by the prosecution by adducing evidence that the child knew that what he or she did was gravely or seriously wrong. The presumption of doli incapax was abolished by CDA 1998 s34.[23] However, the age and maturity of a juvenile suspect may still be relevant to issues such as intention, recklessness and dishonesty, and the juvenile's age may be relevant to whether the juvenile is capable of committing certain offences (such as some sexual offences).

## Changing age

11.27   It was noted at paras 11.6 and 11.7 above that the age of a suspect will determine whether the suspect is treated as a juvenile at the police station, the court in which suspect will appear if charged, and the range of sentences available. Generally, a person under the age of 18 years must first appear in a youth court unless the person is jointly charged with an adult. If the person has his or her 18th birthday before the date on which the person is first due to appear in court, the person should appear in the adult rather than the youth court. If the person is charged with an either-way offence and has his or her 18th birthday before plea is entered, the person has the right to elect trial in the Crown Court even though he or she has appeared in the youth court.

11.28       With regard to sentencing powers that depend upon age, generally the relevant date is the date of conviction and not the date of the offence or

---

22  See the Law Society's *Criminal Practitioners Newsletter*, 'Youth court cases: defence good practice', April 2002.
23  Confirmed in *R v JTB* [2009] UKHL 20.

first court appearance.[24] However, a defendant who was 17 years at the date of commission of the offence and 18 years at the date of conviction should receive a sentence that he or she was likely to have received if sentenced on the date of commission of the offence.[25]

## Police interviews

11.29   Code C, Code H NfG 11C states the following:

> Although juveniles ... are often capable of providing reliable evidence, they may, without knowing or wishing to do so, be particularly prone in certain circumstances to provide information that may be unreliable, misleading or self-incriminating. Special care should therefore always be exercised in questioning such a person, and the appropriate adult should be involved if there is any doubt about a person's age, mental state or capacity. Because of the risk of unreliable evidence it is also important to obtain corroboration of any facts admitted whenever possible.

This underlines the importance of the lawyer being vigilant during the police interview in order to detect unfair, inappropriate or oppressive questioning, and the lawyer should intervene where necessary to protect the juvenile's interests. Juveniles should be interviewed using short, clear questions in order to avoid ambiguous statements or admissions.[26] It has been held that hypothetical questions are permissible, but in the case of juvenile or vulnerable suspects such questions should be approached with care.[27] For intervention in interviews generally see para 7.49 above.

## Reprimands and final warnings

11.30   Reprimands and warnings, which replace simple cautions for persons under the age of 18 years, are governed by the CDA 1998 ss65 and 66. Extensive guidance is set out in *Final Warning Scheme: Guidance for the Police and Youth Offending Teams* (the Guidance)[28] as updated by Home Office Circular 14/2006 *The Final Warning Scheme*. See also the National Standards for Youth Justice Services, National Standard 2.[29] The Guidance makes it clear that the police retain a discretion to take informal action short of a reprimand, in the form of 'firm advice'. However, the Guidance states that informal action (rather than a reprimand or warning) should only be taken in exceptional circumstances where the police consider that it will be sufficient to prevent future offending. This will usually only be appropriate in cases involving very minor non-recordable offences[30] or:

24   That is, where the person is being sentenced for the offence for the first time. It may be different where the person is being re-sentenced following discharge, revocation or breach. For more detailed consideration of issues relating to age, see M Ashford, A Chard and N Redhouse, *Defending young people* (3rd edn LAG, London, 2006).

25   See *R v Ghaffoor* [2002] Crim LR 339, and *R v Jones* [2003] EWCA Crim 1609.

26   *R (M) v (1) Leicestershire Constabulary (2)CPS* [2009] EWHC 3640 (Admin).

27   *R v Stringer* [2008] EWCA Crim 1222.

28   Home Office/Youth Justice Board November 2002, available via www.justice.gov.uk/about/yjb/.

29   Available via www.yjb.gov.uk/en-gb/practitioners/MonitoringPerformance/NationalStandards/.

30   For definition, see PACE s27(4) and Code D NfG 4A.

'anti-social behaviour where the behaviour falls short of being "criminal"'. The meaning of the latter is unclear since in such circumstances criminal proceedings are not possible in any event. The reprimand and warning scheme is not confined to recordable offences (Guidance para 4.17).

11.31    The CDA 1998 provides that the decision to issue a reprimand or final warning must be made by a 'constable'. This continues to be the case in respect of either-way and summary-only offences but, as with simple cautions, decisions in respect of indictable-only offences must be taken by a Crown prosecutor (see para 10.45 above). Non-police agencies do not have the power to issue a reprimand or warning. Such agencies should consider whether a reprimand or warning should be given rather than prosecution in accordance with the same criteria as set out in CDA 1998 and the Guidance[31] and, where appropriate, should contact the police in order for them to administer a reprimand or warning (Guidance para 12.21 and Annex H).

### Conditions for a reprimand or warning

11.32    In order for a reprimand or warning to be given, the following conditions must be satisfied:

a)    a constable must have evidence that the child or young person has committed an offence;

b)    the constable must consider that the evidence is such as to give a realistic prospect of conviction;

c)    the child or young person must admit to the constable that he or she has committed the offence;

d)    the child or young person must not previously have been convicted of an offence; and

e)    the constable must be satisfied that a prosecution would not be in the public interest (CDA 1998 s65(1)).

With regard to c) above, the admission must be a clear and reliable admission to all elements of the offence.[32] With regard to d) above, this has been modified in respect of those areas where youth conditional cautions are available (see para 11.42 below) so that a reprimand or warning may not be given where the young person has previously been given a conditional caution. Further, in those areas, CDA 1998 s65(1)(e) is substituted by a requirement that the constable does not consider that the offender should be prosecuted or given a youth conditional caution.[33]

11.33    The conditions, although similar to those for simple cautions, differ in two significant respects. First, while a simple or conditional caution may be given even if the person has a previous conviction, a reprimand or warning cannot. Second, there is no requirement for the juvenile (or the juvenile's parent or guardian) to consent to a reprimand or warning (Guidance para 4.13). It has been held that since a warning does not amount to the determination of a criminal charge, the lack of a requirement of

---

31  *R (on the application of H) v London Bus Services* [2002] EWHC 224 (Admin).

32  *R (M) v Leicestershire Constabulary* [2009] EWHC 3640 (Admin).

33  See Criminal Justice and Immigration Act 2008 (Commencement No 12) Order SI No 2780.

consent does not breach European Convention on Human Rights (ECHR) article 6 (right to fair trial).[34]

## Decision to reprimand, warn or charge

11.34    Where the above conditions are satisfied, the following factors should be taken into account by the police officer in deciding whether to reprimand, warn or charge a child or young person:

1) A child or young person may be reprimanded provided that he or she has not previously been reprimanded or warned (CDA 1998 s65(2)). It follows that a child or young person may only be reprimanded once, and that a final warning prevents a future reprimand.

2) A child or young person may be warned if he or she:
   - has not previously been reprimanded, but the constable considers the offence to be so serious as to require a warning (CDA 1998 s65(4));
   - has not previously been warned; or
   - has previously been warned no more than once, but the current offence was committed more than two years after the date of the previous warning and the constable does not consider the offence to be so serious as to require him or her to be charged (CDA 1998 s65(3)). A child or young person cannot be warned more than twice in any circumstances.

3) A caution administered before CDA 1998 ss65 and 66 came into force is treated as a reprimand, and a second or subsequent caution is treated as a warning (CDA 1998 Sch 9 para 5).

4) In addition to the relevance of the child or young person's previous offending history, the key factor in deciding whether he or she should be reprimanded, warned or charged is the seriousness of the offence, both in terms of the nature of the offence and the surrounding circumstances. In determining seriousness, the police officer should take into account the Association of Chief Police Officers (ACPO) Gravity Factor Matrix (which is set out in Home Office Circular 14/2006) under which a score is determined ranging from 1 to 4, leading to the following recommended action:
   - 4    Always charge.
   - 3    Usually warn for a first offence. If offender does not qualify for a warning, then charge. Only in exceptional circumstances should a reprimand be given. Decision-maker needs to justify reprimand.
   - 2    Usually reprimand for a first offence. If offender does not qualify for a reprimand but qualifies for a warning then give a warning. If offender does not qualify for a warning then charge.
   - 1    Always the minimum response applicable to the individual offender, ie, reprimand, warning or charge.

5) Where there is more than one offender, each must be considered separately, and different disposals may be justified (Guidance para 4.29).

---

34  *R (on app of R) v Durham Constabulary and Another* [2005] UKHL 21; [2005] 1 WLR 1484; [2005] 2 All ER 369, confirmed by the European Court of Human Rights (ECtHR) in *R v UK* (2007) 44 EHRR SE17.

6) Where there is more than one offence, a final warning may be given provided, overall, it is an appropriate and proportionate response (Guidance para 4.30). If they arise from one incident, the most serious should be considered and the gravity factors applied to that offence, although the other offences may aggravate or mitigate the gravity factors (Guidance para 4.31).

7) Where the offence concerned is a breach of an anti-social behaviour order (ASBO) the police, in consultation with the youth offending team, should make an assessment of both the seriousness of the breach and of the young person's offending history. Where breach of the ASBO is effectively a first offence, a warning may be appropriate provided the breach was not a flagrant one. If it was a flagrant breach, the person should usually be charged 'unless there were some very unusual circumstances'.[35]

8) Juveniles involved in prostitution should normally be dealt with as victims of abuse and be diverted away from the criminal justice system altogether. However, in exceptional cases where diversion has repeatedly failed, the police may (after consultation with other agencies) initiate criminal proceedings or administer a final warning.[36]

Where a child or young person is charged with a criminal offence, a court will not normally require the police or the CPS to reconsider imposing a reprimand or warning,[37] and a court is unlikely to interfere even if the officer making the decision made an error in applying the Gravity Factor Matrix.[38]

### Decision-making

11.35 Other than in respect of indictable-only offences, responsibility for making decisions under the statutory scheme is that of the police. In straightforward cases where there are no risk factors, or where the juvenile is only in the area temporarily, a reprimand or warning can be given straightaway (Guidance para 9.1). However, the police may ask the local youth offending team to carry out an assessment before making a decision, especially where consideration is being given to imposing a final warning (Guidance para 3.1). Bail may be granted for this purpose under PACE s34(2) and (5), or s37(7).

### The process of giving a reprimand or warning

11.36 Reprimands and warnings can only be given by a police constable (CDA 1998 s65)[39] but there is no restriction on the rank of the officer concerned. In the case of an offender under 17 years, the reprimand or warning must

---

35 Home Office Circular 14/2006 para 5.
36 Guidance paras 12.17–12.18.
37 *R (F) v CPS* (2004) 168 JP 93.
38 *R (D) v Commissioner of Police for the Metropolis* [2008] EWHC 442 (Admin).
39 All police officers hold the rank of constable. There is no provision for designated civilian officers under Police Reform Act 2002 to administer reprimands and warnings.

be given in the presence of an appropriate adult (CDA 1998 s65(5)(a)).[40] In the case of a final warning, a youth offending team officer should normally also be present, but the officer is not a replacement for the appropriate adult.[41] There is no statutory obligation for reprimands or warnings of 17-year-olds to be given in the presence of an appropriate adult.

11.37     The form of a reprimand or warning is governed by CDA 1998 s65(5)(b) and (6), and is set out in further detail in the Guidance paras 9.11 and 9.12. Broadly, the officer giving a reprimand or warning must specify the offence(s), explain that it is a serious matter, and explain the consequences (see below). This must be done orally, and supplemented with a written explanation.

### The consequences of a reprimand or warning

11.38     When a warning (but not a reprimand) is administered, the police must refer the child or young person to a youth offending team (CDA 1998 s66(1)).[42] The youth offending team must then make an assessment of them and, unless it considers it inappropriate to do so, must arrange for the child or young person to participate in an intervention programme (CDA 1998 s66(2)). Therefore, a warning will normally result in the child or young person being required to participate in some activity determined by the youth offending team. There is no enforcement provision in the CDA 1998 for failure to participate in, or breach of, a rehabilitation programme (but see below).

11.39     Reprimands and warnings do not count as convictions, but they, or any report on failure to participate in a rehabilitation programme, can be cited in criminal proceedings in the same circumstances as convictions can be cited (CDA 1998 s66(5), and see para 10.51 above). They are covered by the Rehabilitation of Offenders Act 1974, and are spent when administered. If the offence is one that is covered by the Sexual Offences Act 2003 Part 2, the offender will be placed on the sex offenders register for a period of two and a half years. This must be explained to the offender on being given the reprimand or warning.

11.40     Where a person who has been given a final warning under CDA 1998 s65 is convicted of another offence committed within two years of the warning, the court cannot impose a conditional discharge unless it is of the opinion that there are exceptional circumstances relating to the offence or the offender which justify such a course of action (CDA 1998 s66(4)). This does not apply if the offender has been reprimanded rather than warned. Fingerprints and other identification data can be taken and retained where the reprimand or warning is in respect of a recordable offence (see paras 6.4 and 6.48 above).

---

40  'Appropriate adult' is defined by CDA 1998 s65(7) in similar terms to the definition in Code C para 1.7.

41  Guidance paras 9.4 and 9.15.

42  CDA 1998 s39 requires all local authorities to establish one or more youth offending teams. See para 11.5 above.

*Advising on reprimands and warnings*

11.41   Most of the considerations relevant to advice in respect of cautions are also relevant to advice regarding reprimands and warnings (see para 10.52 above). However, since consent is not required the scope for negotiation is less than for an adult in similar circumstances. It should be remembered that a warning may lead to the client being required to undergo an intervention programme in circumstances where, if charged, the CPS may not have proceeded with the prosecution or where, if convicted, the penalty would not have been so onerous. Also, as noted earlier, a reprimand or a warning may prevent a future reprimand or warning, and a warning may prevent a court imposing a conditional discharge in future. Therefore, in circumstances where a reprimand or warning is likely to be given if the offence is admitted, these additional considerations should be taken into account in formulating advice on whether to admit the offence.

## Youth conditional cautions

11.42   Conditional cautions may be offered to 16- and 17-year-olds in those areas where the scheme has been brought into effect.[43] The scheme and requirements are broadly the same as for adults (see para 10.56 above). However, they are governed by CDA 1998 ss66A–66G rather than by the Criminal Justice Act (CJA) 2003.There is also a separate code of practice issued under CDA 1998 s66G, the *Code of Practice for Youth Conditional Cautions for 16 and 17 year olds*,[44] and separate guidance issued by the Director of Public Prosecutions (DPP) under PACE s37A, the *Director's Guidance on Youth Conditional Cautions*.[45]

## Charging

11.43   Generally, subject to the provisions on reprimands and warnings, the considerations and processes relating to decisions to charge are the same for juveniles as they are for adults (see chapter 10). The *Director's Guidance on Charging* (see para 10.2 above) makes no special reference to charge decisions regarding juveniles. The Code for Crown Prosecutors requires prosecutors to have regard to the principal aim of the youth justice system, to prevent offending by children and young people, and to consider the interests of the youth when deciding whether it is in the public interest to prosecute. Custody officers should have regard to the same principles.

## Choice between bail and custody

11.44   With one addition, if a juvenile is charged with an offence, the decision whether to grant bail (conditional or unconditional) or to keep the juvenile in police detention pending the first court appearance is subject to the

43   See Criminal Justice and Immigration Act 2008 (Commencement No 12) Order 2009 SI No 2780 for those areas in which they were available at the date of publication.

44   Brought into effect by Crime and Disorder Act 1998 (Youth Conditional Cautions: Code of Practice) Order 2010 SI No 127.

45   Available via http://cps.gov.uk/publications/directors_guidance/index.html.

same conditions as for adults (see para 10.87 above).[46] The additional criterion is that a juvenile can be kept in detention if the custody officer has reasonable grounds for believing that the juvenile ought to be detained in his or her own interests (PACE s38(1)(b)(ii)). The expression 'own interests' is not defined and is open to broad interpretation, so that the custody officer may argue that it includes situations where the juvenile is homeless, or is a traveller, or is living in conditions of which the custody officer does not approve and which the officer believes to be contrary to the juvenile's interests.

11.45    Where a juvenile is kept in police detention after charge,[47] the juvenile must be dealt with in accordance with PACE s38(6)–(7). Section 38(6) provides that the custody officer must arrange for the juvenile to be transferred to local authority accommodation unless he or she certifies:

a)  that, by reason of such circumstances as are specified in the certificate, it is impracticable to do so; or

b)  in the case of an arrested juvenile who has attained the age of 12 years, that no secure accommodation is available and that keeping the juvenile in other local authority accommodation would not be adequate to protect the public from serious harm from the juvenile.

Despite the fact that PACE s38(6) means that transfer to local authority accommodation should be the norm, there is evidence of widespread non-compliance, so that juveniles who have been charged are frequently detained at the police station pending their first court appearance.

11.46    With regard to practicability, Code C NfG 16D provides that neither the juvenile's behaviour nor the nature of the offence with which the juvenile is charged provides grounds for the custody officer to retain the juvenile in police detention rather than to arrange a transfer to local authority accommodation. A custody officer may argue that he or she is justified in deciding that transfer would not be practicable if he or she believes that the accommodation to be provided by the local authority would not be secure.[48] However, NfG 16D provides that lack of secure local authority accommodation does not make it impracticable for the custody officer to transfer the juvenile, and notes that the availability of secure accommodation is only a factor in relation to a juvenile aged 12 or over where the local authority accommodation would not be adequate to protect the public from serious harm from the juvenile. Home Office Circular 78/1992 *Criminal Justice Act* 1991: *Detention, etc, of Juveniles* states that 'impractical' means circumstances where transfer would be physically impossible by reason of, for example, floods, blizzards, or the impossibility, despite repeated efforts, of contacting the local authority. Presumably, it would also include circumstances where the local authority fails or refuses to

---

46  Except that detention for the purpose of administering a drug test under PACE s38(1)(a)(iiia) applies only if the juvenile has attained the minimum age (PACE s38(1)(b)(i)). See para 6.67 above.

47  But not if detained under some other power, eg, a warrant not backed for bail, or following arrest for common law breach of the peace or for breach of bail conditions.

48  By reference to *R v Chief Constable of Cambridgeshire Constabulary ex p Michel* [1991] 2 WLR 1226; [1991] 2 All ER 777; (1991) 91 Cr App R 325; [1991] Crim LR 382.

provide accommodation.[49] Furthermore, NfG 16D provides that the obligation to transfer a juvenile to local authority accommodation applies as much to a juvenile charged during the daytime as to a juvenile who is to be held overnight, subject to the requirement to bring a person charged and kept in police detention or detained in local authority accommodation under these provisions before a court as soon as is practicable (PACE s46(1) and (2)).[50]

11.47    In the case of juveniles between the ages of 12 and 16, the custody officer can take into account the lack of secure accommodation where keeping the suspect in other local authority accommodation would not be adequate to protect the public from the risk of serious harm from them (PACE s38(6)(b)). It is understood that this subsection was intended to apply only to juveniles of that age who were charged with violent or sexual offences.[51] However, somewhat strangely, PACE s38(6A) provides that: 'any reference, in relation to an arrested juvenile charged with a violent or sexual offence, to protecting the public from serious harm from him shall be construed as a reference to protecting members of the public from death or serious personal injury, whether physical or psychological, occasioned by further such offences committed by him'. Therefore, the possibility of keeping a juvenile in police custody after charge under PACE s38(6) is not confined to those charged with a violent or sexual offence. Furthermore, the justification of: 'protecting the public from serious harm' is defined only in respect of those charged with a violent or sexual offence. It is suggested, however, that this definition gives an indication of the gravity of the threat of harm to the public that would be required in order to keep a juvenile charged with any other offence in police detention.[52]

11.48    Note that although PACE s38(6)(b) refers to the non-availability of *secure* accommodation, the police cannot insist that the local authority places the juvenile in secure accommodation even if it is available. 'Secure accommodation' has a technical meaning, and a local authority cannot restrict the liberty of a juvenile in its care otherwise than in approved secure accommodation. However, a local authority may decide to hold a juvenile placed with it under PACE s38(6) in secure accommodation for up to 72 hours within any 28-day period.[53] The authority may only do so if it appears that non-secure accommodation is inappropriate because:

49  The Youth Justice Board's National Standards require youth offending team managers to develop a strategy which includes facilities to accommodate young people under PACE s38(6).

50  In *R (on app of M) v Gateshead Metropolitan Borough Council* [2006] EWCA Civ 221 it was held that local authorities should have a reasonable system in place to enable them to respond to requests under PACE s38(6), but that they were not under an absolute duty to provide secure accommodation. Where the request was made at 0020 hours, with a view to the juvenile being produced in court at 1000 hours the same day, it was wholly impracticable for the local authority to provide accommodation.

51  A 'violent offence' means murder or an offence specified in CJA 2003 Sch 15 Part 1. A 'sexual offence' means an offence specified in CJA 2003 Sch 15 Part 2 (PACE s38(6A)).

52  A view supported by Home Office Circular 78/1992 at para 10.

53  Children (Secure Accommodation) Regulations 1991 SI No 1505 (Secure Accommodation Regs) reg 10(1).

1) the juvenile is likely to abscond from other accommodation; or
2) the juvenile is likely to injure himself or herself or other people if kept in other accommodation.[54]

11.49    Where the custody officer is considering keeping a juvenile in police detention under PACE s38(6)(b), the lawyer will want to know what grounds there are for believing that the public would be at risk of serious harm if the juvenile were placed in non-secure accommodation. This will involve consideration of the nature of the harm feared and what evidence there is that the juvenile would inflict such harm. However, it is likely that the custody officer would be justified in keeping the juvenile in detention if there are grounds for fearing serious harm to the public, even if the risk of such harm is small.[55] For example, the risk of a juvenile accused of arson absconding and causing another fire may be small, but the danger to the public if the juvenile did so would be very serious.

11.50    If a juvenile is kept in police detention under PACE s38(6)(a) or (b), the custody officer must certify the reasons, and this certificate must be produced to the court before which the juvenile first appears (PACE s38(7)).

## Miscellaneous issues

### Interviews on school premises

11.51    Juveniles should not be interviewed by the police at school other than in exceptional circumstances, and then only if the school principal or his or her nominee agrees. In these circumstances, every effort must be made to contact both the juvenile's parents or other person responsible for the juvenile's welfare, and the appropriate adult (if different), and reasonable time must be allowed to enable the person who is to act as the appropriate adult to be present. However, if waiting would cause unreasonable delay, the principal or his or her nominee can act as the appropriate adult unless the juvenile is suspected of an offence against the educational establishment (Code C para 11.16). The juvenile is entitled to legal advice since the juvenile is a volunteer as defined by PACE s29, but the juvenile does not have to be told of the right to advice (see para 2.120 above). This contrasts with a volunteer interviewed at a police station who does have to be informed of the right to legal advice if the volunteer is cautioned (Code C para 3.21) or if he or she asks (Code C para 3.22).

### Searches

11.52    A search carried out at the time of initial detention, or during detention, under PACE s54 (see para 6.77 above) does not have to be carried out in the presence of the appropriate adult, unless it is a strip search. In this case, unless it is urgent, if the strip search involves exposure of intimate parts of the body, it must only take place in the presence of an appropriate adult unless the juvenile requests, in the presence of the appropriate

---

54  Secure Accommodation Regs reg 6.
55  See, eg, *R v Birch* (1989) 11 Cr App R(S) 202, a case on an analogous point under Mental Health Act (MHA) 1983 ss37 and 41.

adult, that the search be conducted in their absence, and the appropriate adult agrees. A record must be made of the juvenile's decision, signed by the appropriate adult (Code C Annex A para 11(c), Code H Annex A para 12(c)).

11.53   An intimate search under PACE s55 (see para 6.84 above) must generally only be conducted in the presence of the appropriate adult, who must be of the same sex unless the juvenile specifically requests a particular adult of the opposite sex who is readily available. However, an intimate search can be carried out in the absence of the appropriate adult if the juvenile signifies in the presence of the appropriate adult that the juvenile prefers it to be conducted in the adult's absence, and the adult agrees. A record must then be made of the decision and signed by the adult (Code C Annex A para 5, Code H Annex A para 6).

## Identification and other procedures

11.54   Where an identification or other evidential procedure requires appropriate consent, such consent must be obtained from both the juvenile and the juvenile's parent or guardian[56] (as opposed to the appropriate adult) unless the juvenile is under 14 years, in which case consent of the parent or guardian is sufficient (PACE s65(1) and Code D para 2.12, and see para 6.3 above). If the parent or guardian is not acting as the appropriate adult he or she does not have to be present in order to give consent, but must be given an opportunity to speak to the juvenile and the appropriate adult if he or she wishes (Code D NfG 2A). If the only obstacle to conducting a video identification, identification parade or group identification is that a parent or guardian refuses consent, or cannot be contacted after making reasonable efforts to do so, the juvenile may be treated as known but not available (see para 8.14 above). Identification procedures that require appropriate consent are:

- fingerprints, subject to exceptions (see para 6.3 above);
- photographs, subject to exceptions (see para 6.10 above);
- searches and examinations to ascertain identity, subject to exceptions (see para 6.16 above);
- footwear impressions (see para 6.22 above);
- x-rays and ultrasound scans (see para 6.89 above);
- intimate samples under PACE s62 (see para 6.27 above);
- non-intimate samples under PACE s63, subject to exceptions (see para 6.47 above);
- video identifications, identification parades and group identifications, subject to exceptions (see chapter 8);
- drug-testing procedures under PACE s63B (see para 6.64 above).

11.55   Samples of handwriting are not specifically covered by PACE or the Codes of Practice (see para 6.57 above). In practice, they cannot be obtained without the consent of the suspect, but it seems unlikely that consent of the parent or guardian is necessary.

---

56  Or, if the juvenile is in the care of a local authority or voluntary organisation, that authority or organisation (Code D NfG 2A).

*Detention in a cell*

11.56   A juvenile must not be placed in a police cell unless no other secure accommodation is available and the custody officer considers that it is not practicable to supervise the juvenile if he or she is not placed in a cell, or the custody officer considers that a cell provides more comfortable accommodation than other secure accommodation in the police station. Often, there is little to distinguish a cell from a juvenile detention room. In any event, juvenile suspects must be kept separate from adult suspects (CYPA 1933 s31, Code C para 8.8, Code H para 8.9).

# Mentally disordered and mentally vulnerable people

11.57   Special provision is made in Codes C and D in respect of mentally disordered and mentally vulnerable people and others whose understanding is limited by reason of mental incapacity. A useful summary of the Code C provisions may be found in Code C Annex E. Guidance is available in Home Office Circular 66/1990 *Provision for mentally disordered offenders,*[57] and also in Home Office Circular 7/2008 *Police stations as places of safety.* Circular 66/90 summarising the relevant legal powers and draws attention to 'the desirability of ensuring effective co-operation between agencies to ensure that the best use is made of resources and that mentally disordered persons are not prosecuted where this is not required by the public interest'. Circular 7/2008 states that, other than in exceptional circumstances, a police station is not a suitable place of safety for detaining a person under MHA 1983 s136. However, mentally disordered and vulnerable people continue to be routinely detained in police stations, both as suspects and under the MHA 1983.

## Determining whether a suspect is mentally disordered or vulnerable

11.58   If a police officer has any suspicion, or is told in good faith, that a person of any age may be mentally disordered or otherwise mentally vulnerable, in the absence of clear evidence to dispel that suspicion, the person must be treated as such for the purposes of Codes C, D and H (Code C para 1.4, Code D para 2.3, Code H para 1.10). 'Mental disorder' is defined by MHA 1983 s1(2) as 'any disorder or disability of the mind'.[58] A person with a learning disability[59] is not considered as suffering from a mental disorder for certain purposes under the MHA 1983 unless that disability is associated with abnormally aggressive or seriously irresponsible conduct

57   Supplemented by Home Office Circular 12/1995 *Mentally disordered offenders: inter-agency working.* Note that Circular 66/1990 is, in certain respects, out-of-date and, in particular, does not take account of the Criminal Procedure (Insanity and Unfitness to Plead) Act 1991.

58   Note that the version of Code C in force at the date of publication refers, at NfG 1G, to the definition of mental disorder prior to amendment of MHA 1983 s1 by Mental Health Act 2007.

59   Defined by MHA 1983 s1(4) as a state of arrested or incomplete development of the mind which includes significant impairment of intelligence and social functioning.

(MHA 1983 s1(2A)). The person may, however, be mentally vulnerable for the purposes of Code C and D. Dependence on alcohol or drugs is not considered to be a disorder or disability of the mind for the purposes of determining whether a person is mentally disordered (MHA 1983 s1(3)). Nevertheless, a person who is so dependant may be mentally vulnerable. The term 'mentally vulnerable' applies to any detainee who, because of his or her mental state or capacity, may not understand the significance of what is said, of questions or of his or her replies (Code C NfG 1G). Where the custody officer has any doubt about the mental state or capacity of a detainee, the detainee must be treated as mentally vulnerable and an appropriate adult must be called (Code C, Code H NfG 1G).

11.59    It is clear from the above that it does not have to be positively established that a suspect is mentally disordered or otherwise mentally vulnerable in order for the suspect to have to be treated as such – 'any suspicion' is sufficient to trigger the obligation. At the time of authorising detention, the custody officer must determine whether the suspect is, or might be, in need of medical treatment or attention and whether, among other things, the suspect requires help to check documentation (Code C, Code H para 3.5(c)). The custody officer must also conduct a risk assessment (Code C, Code H paras 3.6–3.10, and see para 4.22 above). This involves assessing where the detainee is likely to present specific risks to custody staff or to themselves. Guidance on risk assessments is set out in Home Office Circular 32/2000 *Detainee risk assessment and revised prisoner escort record form*, which makes clear that risk categories include medical or mental conditions, medication issued, drugs and alcohol 'issues', special needs, violence, escape risk, suicide or self harm, injuries and vulnerabilities.

11.60    Having conducted the risk assessment, the custody officer must then decide on the appropriate response to any risk identified. If the person appears to be suffering from a mental disorder or is otherwise in need of clinical attention, the custody officer must make sure that the person receives appropriate clinical attention as soon as is reasonably practicable or, in urgent cases, immediately (Code C para 9.5, Code H para 9.6). The custody officer may fulfil this obligation by calling in an appropriate healthcare professional.[60] Where a healthcare professional is called in, the custody officer must ask the healthcare professional for his or her opinion about any risks or problems which the police need to take into account when making a decision about continued detention, when to carry out an interview and the need for appropriate safeguards (Code C para 9.13, Code H para 9.15). For fitness for detention and fitness for interview, see para 5.22 above.

## The lawyer's assessment

11.61    It is important to remember that custody and other police officers are not medically trained and frequently do not make appropriate judgments

---

60 Defined as a clinically qualified person working within the scope of practice as determined by their relevant professional body. Whether they are 'appropriate' depends on the circumstances of the duties they carry out at the time (Code C, Code H NfG 9A).

concerning whether suspects are suffering from a mental disorder or vulnerability.[61] Defence lawyers should always be aware of the possibility that a client may be mentally disordered or otherwise mentally vulnerable. The lawyer should look out for the following signs:

1) apparent lack of comprehension;
2) lack of coherence;
3) unexpected levels of agitation, anger or other emotions;
4) physical signs such as lack of co-ordination, drowsiness or body movements;
5) unexpected patterns of behaviour;
6) reference by the client to medication or hospitalisation.[62]

11.62   If the lawyer is concerned that the client may be mentally disordered or vulnerable, the lawyer should usually pursue the matter with the client by asking questions such as whether the client:

1) is, or has recently been, on medication and, if so, what for;
2) has recently been in hospital and, if so, what for;
3) is currently, or has recently been, a hospital or clinic outpatient;
4) received special education;
5) attends any kind of day centre;
6) has contact with a social worker or community psychiatric nurse.

11.63   If the lawyer concludes that the client may be mentally disordered or vulnerable, the question arises whether the lawyer should tell the police of his or her knowledge or suspicions. If the suspect consents this will present no problem, but there may be difficulties if the suspect does not give consent. If the lawyer's knowledge or belief arises from previous professional contact with the suspect or from something told to the lawyer by the suspect, the information should not be passed on to the police.[63] If, however, the belief is based on the observations of the lawyer, this is almost certainly not covered by the duty of confidentiality. In either case, the lawyer should normally discuss his or her suspicions with the suspect before deciding whether to say anything to the police, although there will be times when the lawyer will form the opinion that this would be unwise, for example, if the lawyer is concerned about his or her own safety. If the police are not notified, and they had no reason to believe that the suspect was mentally disordered or vulnerable, while arguably any confession obtained from a mentally disordered or vulnerable suspect is likely to be unreliable for the

---

61  See G Gudjonsson et al, *Persons at Risk during interviews in police custody: the identification of vulnerabilities*, RCCJ Research Study No 12 (HMSO, London, 1993). Note also *Mentally disordered offenders: inter-agency working* (a booklet on best practice issued with Home Office Circular 12/1995) at p31, which states that defence lawyers 'need to be diligent to make sure that "borderline" mentally vulnerable people ... are identified so that proper safeguards under PACE Code C can be implemented'.

62  For further guidance on this and acting for mentally disordered clients generally, see D Postgate and C Taylor, *Advising mentally disordered offenders* (Law Society, London, 2000). This is now out of print, but a second edition is due to be published. For a comprehensive guide to assessing a client's vulnerability at the police station see E Shepherd, *Police station skills for legal advisers: practical reference* (Law Society, London, 2004) Key Topic 4.

63  See para 1.16 above.

purposes of PACE s76, an application at trial to exclude evidence of the confession made in the absence of an appropriate adult may not succeed.[64] If the lawyer does tell the police of his or her belief the police must treat the suspect as mentally disordered or vulnerable (Code C para 1.4, Code H para 1.10).

11.64 A suspicion that a client is mentally disordered or vulnerable may only become apparent during the course of a police interview. In this case, the lawyer should normally stop the interview and speak to the client in private so that a decision can be made about whether to inform the police. Again, if the officer is given such information in good faith, the officer must act on the information given and treat the suspect as mentally disordered or vulnerable.

## Right to legal advice

11.65 A suspect who is, or who is being treated as, mentally disordered or vulnerable has the same right to legal advice as any other person who is in police custody (see para 2.119 above). The appropriate adult also has a right to seek legal advice on behalf of the suspect (Code C para 3.19, Code H para 3.20), but if the suspect requests advice, the appropriate action must be taken straightaway and must not be delayed until the appropriate adult arrives. For guidance on circumstances where the suspect and the appropriate adult take differing views about asking for legal advice see para 11.22 above. Since there is no provision for the police to delay contacting an appropriate adult, once an appropriate adult has been contacted it would be difficult for the police to justify delaying access to a lawyer under PACE s58(8) or TA 2000 Sch 8 para 8 (for the reasons given at para 11.12 above).

## The appropriate adult

### *Informing the appropriate adult*

11.66 If, as a result of the risk assessment conducted under Code C, Code H para 3.6 or otherwise, a police officer forms any suspicion, or is told in good faith, that a suspect may be mentally disordered or otherwise mentally vulnerable, the custody officer must identify and inform an appropriate adult and ask him or her to come to the police station (Code C para 3.15, Code H para 3.17). There is no provision for delaying informing the appropriate adult even if the suspect is being held incommunicado under PACE s56 or TA 2000 Sch 8 para 8, or access to legal advice is delayed under PACE s58 or TA 2000 Sch 8 para 8 (Code C, Code H Annex B NfG B1). Having concluded that a suspect may be mentally disordered or vulnerable, custody officers may decide not to call an appropriate adult on the ground that they believe that the suspect is capable of understanding questions. This is a misinterpretation of the relevant provisions.[65]

---

64 See, eg, *R v Campbell* [1995] 1 Cr App R 522; [1995] Crim LR 157.
65 See *R v Aspinall* [1999] Crim LR 741.

## Appropriate people

11.67   The appropriate adult may be:

- a relative, guardian or other person responsible for the care or custody of the suspect;
- someone who has experience of dealing with mentally disordered or mentally vulnerable people but who is not a police officer or employed by the police (for example, an approved social worker as defined by the MHA 1983 or a specialist social worker); or
- failing either of the above, some other responsible adult aged 18 or over who is not a police officer or employed by the police (Code C para 1.7(b), Code D para 2.6 and Code H para 1.13).

11.68   As with appropriate adults for juveniles, this list amounts to a hierarchy, although Code C, Code H NfG 1D provide that in certain (unspecified) circumstances it may be more satisfactory if the appropriate adult is someone experienced or trained in the care of mentally disordered or vulnerable people rather that a person lacking such qualifications. However, the Codes make it clear that the suspect's wishes should, if practicable, be respected.

## Inappropriate people

11.69   The provisions governing those who should not act as appropriate adults are generally the same as for juveniles (see para 11.16 above).

## Role of the appropriate adult

11.70   The role of the appropriate adult, and the assistance the adult may give or the difficulties that the adult may present to the lawyer, are similar to those as for juveniles (see para 11.21 above). If a confession made by a mentally handicapped person, on which the case against the person wholly or substantially rests, is made in the absence of an 'independent person', a jury must be warned of the dangers of convicting in reliance on it (PACE s77).[66] PACE s77 does not apply where the suspect is mentally disordered, although a judge always has a discretion to give such a warning, and a confession may be excluded as oppressive, unreliable or unfair under PACE s76 or s78.

# Special considerations for the lawyer

## Interviews

11.71   The lawyer should act with special care when dealing with people who are, or may be, mentally disordered or mentally vulnerable. It is significant that in a number of well-known miscarriage of justice cases the defendant was described as being, or verging on being, mentally disordered or handicapped, although in none of these cases did this appear to have been identified at the time of the defendant's detention.[67] The relevance of Code C and Code H NfG 11C – which warn that such people may be prone

---

66  PACE s77 refers to an independent person rather than an appropriate adult. See also *R v Lamont* [1989] Crim LR 813, and *R v McKenzie* [1993] 1 WLR 453; (1993) 96 Cr App R 98.
67  See, eg, *R v Paris, Abdullahi and Miller* (1993) 97 Cr App R 99; [1994] Crim LR 361.

to giving information that is unreliable, misleading or self-incriminating and requires that special care be taken when questioning them – will not necessarily be appreciated or taken into account by the police.

11.72    In most cases where a suspect is suspected of being mentally disordered or vulnerable a healthcare professional will have to be called in by the police (see para 11.60 above). The practitioner may be of some assistance to the lawyer, although not necessarily so. First, it must be remembered that the practitioner may not be bound by the same duty of confidentiality as the lawyer, and anything disclosed may not be covered by legal professional privilege.[68] Second, although the Codes do not specifically say so, the practitioner's role is primarily to assess the suspect's medical condition on behalf of the police. Third, the practitioner called will be paid by the police, and may be directly employed by them, and experience suggests that practitioners do not always play a helpful role from the defence point of view. Healthcare practitioners called in to the police station do not always understand the meaning and significance of 'fitness to be detained', 'fitness to be interviewed', or the definition of mental disorder and vulnerability, although Code C and Code H Annex G should assist in determining fitness to be interviewed. The suspect has a right to be examined by a medical practitioner of the suspect's own choice, but at his or her own expense (Code C para 9.8, Code H para 9.10). The cost, provided it is reasonable and was incurred in the best interests of the client, may be claimed under the SCC 2010.[69]

### Mental Health Act 1983 s136

11.73    It is important to establish at an early stage whether the person has been arrested for an offence, or detained under MHA 1983 s136. Section 136 gives a constable power to remove a person from a public place to a place of safety if the constable considers that the person is suffering from a mental disorder and is in immediate need of care and control. This power exists irrespective of whether the person is suspected of having committed an offence, and irrespective of the person's age. The person may be detained for up to 72 hours for examination by a doctor and interview by an approved mental health practitioner in order that suitable arrangements can be made for the person's treatment or care (MHA 1983 s136(2)). A police station is a 'place of safety' although it should not be treated as suitable other than in exceptional circumstances involving the risk or threat of serious harm posed by the person to themselves or others. Wherever possible, the person should be detained in a hospital rather than a police station.[70] A person who is initially taken to a police station as a place of safety can be taken to another, more suitable, place of safety during the 72-hour period (MHA 1983 ss135(3A) and 136(3), (4)).

---

68  See *R v McDonald* [1991] Crim LR 122. See para 11.23 above in relation to appropriate adults for juveniles. Arguably, if a healthcare practitioner is present during a lawyer/ client consultation, this should not destroy privilege. However, anything disclosed to the healthcare professional by the suspect in the absence of the lawyer is unlikely to be covered by privilege.

69  SCC 2010 Part B, para 5.39.

70  Home Office Circular 7/2008 para 2.2.

11.74    Code C applies to people detained under MHA 1983 s136, except for para 15 (concerning reviews and extension of detention) (Code C para 1.10). A person detained under section 136 is entitled to legal advice. If the assessment is to take place at the police station, an approved social worker and registered medical practitioner must be called to the station as soon as possible. Once the person has been assessed and suitable arrangements made for the person's treatment or care, of if a registered medical practitioner determines that the person is not mentally disordered, the person can no longer be detained under section 136 (Code C para 3.16).

11.75    It is possible for a person to be under arrest for an offence and detained under MHA 1983 s136 at the same time. If this is the case, the police or prosecutor may be persuaded not to initiate any criminal proceedings if suitable arrangements can be made either under the MHA 1983 or on a voluntary basis. As noted at para 11.57 above, Home Office Circular 66/1990 refers to the desirability of ensuring that mentally disordered persons are not prosecuted where this is not required by the public interest. The *Director's Guidance on Charging* makes no specific reference to mentally disordered or vulnerable suspects, but the Code for Crown Prosecutors public interest test provides that one factor against prosecution is that the defendant is, or was at the time of the offence, suffering from significant mental ill health. However, the seriousness of the alleged offence must be taken into account, and prosecutors 'must balance a suspect's mental or physical ill health with the need to safeguard the public or those providing care services to such persons'[71] (see para 10.16 above).

### Cautions, reprimands and warnings

11.76    There is no special provision for mentally disordered or vulnerable people in either the legislation relating to conditional cautions, or reprimands or warnings, or in the relevant circulars, codes or guidance. However, as noted at para 11.75 above, the CCP public interest test involves consideration of the mental condition of the suspect. Home Office Circular 66/1990 makes it clear that diversion from prosecution should be considered wherever possible in the case of mentally disordered persons. The Circular requires that consideration be given:

- to cautioning the suspect if the criteria are met; or
- if the cautioning criteria are not met, to whether any action needs be taken against the person, particularly where it appears that prosecution is not required in the public interest in view of the nature of the offence; or
- to finding alternatives to prosecution, such as admission to hospital under MHA 1983 s2 or s3, or to guardianship under s7, or informal support in the community by social services.[72]

11.77    Clearly, the additional possibility of a simple caution, conditional caution, or reprimand or warning in the case of a juvenile, or no formal action, should be taken into account when advising the client whether to answer police questions. The lawyer may also refer to the Home Office Circular

71  CCP para 4.17(g).
72  Home Office Circular 66/1990 para 4(iii).

and the public interest test when seeking to persuade the custody officer or prosecutor to take action other than charging the suspect. In the case of a juvenile it may be appropriate to press for an assessment by the youth offending team so that such issues can be adequately considered.

## Bail or custody?

11.78    PACE s38 contains no specific reference to mentally disordered or vulnerable suspects (see para 10.87 above) but Home Office Circular 66/1990 emphasises that, where a decision to charge has been made, a mentally disordered or mentally handicapped person has the same right to bail as other suspects.[73] There may, however, be particular concerns arising from the suspect's mental state or from associated problems such as homelessness. This could potentially justify a decision not to grant bail for the suspect's own protection, or in order to prevent injury or damage, or absconding. In these circumstances, the Circular suggests that suitable arrangements be made with health, probation and social services departments to ensure that support can be provided, or admission to a hospital or hostel be arranged where appropriate and available. Any such arrangements could be reinforced by appropriate bail conditions (see para 10.92 above). In many areas such facilities are unlikely to be available, particularly at short notice. If the suspect is kept in police detention, the lawyer should make appropriate preparations for any bail application to the court, bearing in mind the additional powers of the court in respect of people who are mentally disordered.

## Miscellaneous issues

### Searches

11.79    A search carried out at the time of initial detention, or during detention, under PACE s54 (see para 6.77 above) does not have to be carried out in the presence of the appropriate adult, unless it is a strip search. In this case, if the strip search involves exposure of intimate parts of the body it must, except in cases of urgency, be conducted in the presence of an appropriate adult. It would appear that, unlike in the case of juveniles (see para 11.53 above), there is no provision for a mentally disordered or vulnerable suspect to dispense with attendance of the appropriate adult (Code C Annex A para 11(c), Code H Annex A para 12(c)). An intimate search (see para 6.84 above) may take place only in the presence of an appropriate adult of the same sex unless the suspect specifically requests the presence of a particular adult of the opposite sex who is readily available (Code C Annex A para 5, Code H Annex A para 6). It is probable that this means that the search can only take place in the presence of an appropriate adult.

### Identification and other procedures

11.80    Where an identification or other evidential procedure requires consent, consent is only valid if given in the presence of the appropriate adult (Code

---

73   Home Office Circular 66/1990 para 4(v).

D para 2.12). There is no provision for consent to be given on behalf of the suspect by the appropriate adult. For procedures requiring consent, and for comment on handwriting samples, see paras 11.54 and 11.55 above.

## Other special groups

11.81   If a person appears to be blind, seriously visually impaired, deaf, unable to read or speak or has difficulty orally because of a speech impediment, the person must be treated as such for the purposes of the Code in the absence of clear evidence to the contrary (Code C para 1.6, Code H para 1.12, and Code D para 2.5). The lawyer should be vigilant to ensure that appropriate action is taken. It has been held, for example, that where the police were not aware that the suspect was deaf, and had no doubts about the person's hearing ability, there was no breach of the Code when the suspect was treated as if he or she was not deaf.[74] If the lawyer is aware, or has doubts, about whether the suspect comes within one of these categories, the lawyer should initially speak to the client in private to establish whether the lawyer's belief or suspicion is correct. Since to a large extent, the special provisions of the Codes are protective, the suspect should normally be advised to make the problem known to the police. The major exception to this is in the case of suspects who might have problems with their immigration status, or asylum-seekers who may not want his or her embassy or consulate informed (see Code C, Code H para 7.4). See further chapter 12.

### Communication difficulties

#### Provisions of the Codes

11.82   If a suspect appears to be deaf or there is doubt about the suspect's hearing or speaking ability or ability to understand English, and the custody officer cannot establish effective communication, the officer must call an interpreter as soon as practicable to assist in the action required by Code C, Code H paras 3.1–3.5 (Code C para 3.12, Code H para 3.14). All reasonable attempts should be made to make clear to the suspect that an interpreter will be supplied at public expense (Code C, Code H para 13.8). The notice of entitlements required to be given to a suspect by Code C, Code H para 3.2 should be available in Welsh, the main ethnic minority languages and the principal European languages 'whenever they are likely to be helpful', and audio versions should also be available.[75]

---

74   *R v Clarke* [1989] Crim LR 892.

75   Code C, Code H NfG 3B. Note that the ECHR article 5(2) requires that an arrested person must be informed promptly, in a language which the person understands, of the reasons for the person's arrest and of any charge against him or her. Note also that the EU Directive on Interpretation and Translation requires member states to introduce laws and procedures, no later than 27 October 2013, that ensure, among other things, that a suspect has a right to free interpretation at the police station, and translation of essential documents (Directive 2010/64/EU, 20 October 2010). PACE, Code C and certain other legislation will require some modification in order to comply with the Directive.

11.83    Where a suspect has difficulty understanding English, the police interviewer does not speak the suspect's language, and the suspect wants an
interpreter to be present, the suspect must not be interviewed in the absence of an interpreter except where the urgent interview provisions of
Code C paras 11.1, and 11.18 to 11.20 apply (Code C, Code H para 13.2). If
the interview is not audio or video-recorded, the interviewing officer must
ensure that the interpreter makes a note of the interview at the time in the
language of the suspect and certifies its accuracy, and the suspect must be
given the opportunity to read it and certify it as correct or indicate the respects in which the suspect considers it to be inaccurate (Code C, Code H
para 13.3 and Code E NfG 4C). Where a statement is made in a language
other than English, the statement must be taken down in the language in
which it is made and the person making it must be asked to sign it. An
English translation must be made in due course (Code C, Code H para
13.4). If, after a suspect has been charged, the officer wishes to bring to
the suspect's attention a written statement made by another person or a
record made of an interview with another person, the officer may read it to
the suspect if the suspect cannot read it (Code C paras 16.4 and 16.4A).

11.84    Where the suspect requests legal advice and cannot communicate with
the lawyer, an interpreter, who must not be a police officer or civilian support staff, must be called (see para 11.87 below).[76]

11.85    Where an identification procedure requires information to be given to
or sought from a suspect, and there is doubt about the suspect's ability to
understand English and the officer cannot establish effective communication, the information must be given or sought through an interpreter
(Code D para 2.14). Where an identification parade is held, once it is
formed, the whole parade must take place in the presence and hearing of
an interpreter (Code D Annex B para 8). If a witness makes an identification after an identification parade has ended, the suspect and the suspect's
interpreter, if present, must be informed (Code D Annex B para 20).

### Practical considerations

11.86    Where an interpreter is required, there is no provision for delay in requesting one, or for conducting interviews in the absence of an interpreter
other than in the case of urgent interviews (Code C Para 11.18(c), Code H
para 11.11(c)). Where an interpreter does attend, it will be difficult for the
police to justify holding the suspect incommunicado under PACE s56 or
TA 2000 Sch 8 para 8 or delaying access to legal advice under PACE s58 or
TA 2000 Sch 8 para 8.[77]

11.87    The Law Society has issued a practice note, *Use of interpreters in criminal
cases*, which provides that:

•    the lawyer must ensure that the client's interpretation needs are met;
•    the lawyer must decide whether the interpreter arranged by the police
     can also act as the interpreter for the lawyer/client consultation;

---

76    Code C, Code H para 13.9. Note that the EU Directive specifically provides for free
      interpretation of lawyer/client communications where this is necessary to safeguard
      the fairness of the proceedings (article 2(2)).
77    See, in relation to juveniles, para 11.12 above.

- the lawyer should use a different interpreter if the interpreter arranged by the police cannot meet all of the client's needs, there are multiple suspects, or the client knows the interpreter arranged by the police;
- other relevant factors for the lawyer to consider include whether the suspected offence is particularly sensitive and/or serious or there is a particular risk that the interpretation may be challenged, and whether community relations are such that the client has little confidence in the relationship between the interpreter and the police;
- if the lawyer decides to use the interpreter arranged by the police, the lawyer should explain the position to the client and obtain the client's consent and arrange for the interpreter to sign an undertaking as to confidentiality.[78]

The cost of a separate interpreter, provided it is reasonable and is incurred in the best interests of the client, may be claimed under the SCC 2010.[79] Note that the presence of an interpreter at a consultation between the lawyer and the client does not destroy legal professional privilege.[80]

11.88   Interpreters can be a source of difficulties for the lawyer, particularly where it is not feasible to use a second interpreter for the consultation. The onus is on the custody officer to obtain an interpreter (Code C para 3.12, Code H para 3.14), and although Code C, Code H para 13.1 requires chief officers of police to ensure that there are appropriate arrangements in place for the provision of suitably qualified interpreters, they may not be available in any particular case. Since an interpreter obtained by the police will be paid by them, the problem of lack of independence from the police is obvious. This problem is not necessarily solved by using friends or relatives of suspects as interpreters, since their connection with the suspect may lead them to give a less than accurate account of what the suspect says. Similarly, if the interpreter comes from the same local community, the suspect may be reluctant to talk freely to that person.

11.89   Even if the interpreter is suitably independent, the lawyer should try to satisfy himself or herself that the interpreter has a sufficient knowledge of both languages. The fact that the suspect and the interpreter may have a common national origin does not guarantee that they will speak the same language. Many countries have populations speaking diverse languages, and even if there is an 'official' language, only the formal form of the language may be learnt by some inhabitants who would not fully understand the language when spoken colloquially.

## Deafness and hearing and speech difficulties

11.90   Many of the issues relating to interpretation for a person who does not speak or understand English are also relevant where the suspect is deaf or has hearing or speech difficulties.

---

78  Available at www.lawsociety.org.uk/productsandservices/practicenotes/interpreters. page. For information about qualified interpreters, see the National Register of Public Service Interpreters at www.nrpsi.co.uk/.
79  SCC 2010 Part B, para 5.39.
80  *R (Bozkurt) v South Thames Magistrates' Court* [2001] EWHC 400 (Admin).

11.91    If a suspect appears to be deaf the suspect must be treated as such for the purposes of the code in the absence of clear evidence to the contrary (Code C para 1.6, Code D para 2.5 and Code H para 1.12). If a suspect appears to be deaf or there is doubt about the suspect's hearing or speaking ability and the custody officer cannot establish effective communication, the custody officer must call an interpreter as soon as practicable and ask the interpreter to give the suspect the information required in Code C, Code H paras 3.1 to 3.5 (Code C para 3.12, Code H para 3.14). Such a person must not be interviewed in the absence of an interpreter unless the person agrees in writing or an urgent interview is conducted under Code C para 11.1 or paras 11.18–11.20, or Code H para 11.11 (Code C para 13.5, Code H para 13.2). Similarly, if the suspect is a juvenile and the suspect's parent or guardian who is present as an appropriate adult appears to be deaf or there is doubt about the person's hearing or speaking ability, an interpreter should be called to attend the interview unless the person agrees in writing to the interview proceeding in the absence of an interpreter or an interview is conducted under the urgent interview provisions (Code C, Code H para 13.6). All reasonable attempts should be made to make clear to the suspect that an interpreter will be provided at public expense (Code C, Code H para 13.8).

11.92    If the suspect requests legal advice and cannot communicate with the lawyer, an interpreter, who must not be a police officer or civilian support staff, must be called for the purpose of obtaining legal advice (Code C, Code H para 13.9). See further paras 11.86 and 11.87 above.[81]

11.93    Where the suspect is deaf or is suspected of having impaired hearing, and the interview is audio-recorded, the interviewer must also take a contemporaneous note of the interview in accordance with the requirements of Code C (Code E para 4.7). The suspect must then be given the opportunity to read the interview record (Code C para 11.11). Note that the Law Society has issued a practice note, *Police interviews involving sign language interpreters* which states that where a police interview involves a sign language interpreter the lawyer should insist that it is video-recorded, and in such a way that images of both the suspect and the interpreter are captured.[82]

11.94    If any identification procedure requires information to be given to or sought from a suspect who appears to be deaf or if there is doubt about the suspect's hearing or speaking ability and the officer cannot establish effective communication, the information must be given or sought through an interpreter (Code D para 2.14). Where an identification parade is held, once it has been formed, everything must take place in the presence and hearing of the suspect and of any interpreter who is present (Code D Annex B para 8). If a witness makes an identification after the parade has ended, the suspect, and the suspect's interpreter if present, must be informed (Code D Annex B para 20).

81  For information about qualified sign language interpreters see the Signature Directory, available at www.signature.org.uk/.
82  Available via www.lawsociety.org.uk/productsandservices/practicenotes.page.

## Blindness, visual handicap and reading difficulties

11.95    If a suspect appears to be blind or seriously visually impaired, the suspect must be treated as such for the purpose of the Code in the absence of clear evidence to the contrary (Code C para 1.6, Code D para 2.5 and Code H para 1.12). If a suspect is blind or seriously visually handicapped, or is unable to read, the custody officer must ensure that the suspect's solicitor, relative, appropriate adult or some other person likely to take an interest in the suspect (and who is not involved in the investigation) is available to help in checking any documentation. Where Code C or Code H require written consent or a signature, the person who is assisting may be asked to sign instead of the suspect, if the suspect desires this (Code C para 3.20, Code D para 2.13 and Code H para 3.21).

11.96    If a police interview is recorded in writing, the senior police officer present must read it over to the suspect and ask the suspect whether he or she would like to sign the record as correct or make his or her mark or to indicate the respects in which the suspect considers it inaccurate. The officer must then indicate on the interview record what has occurred (Code C para 11.11). There is no special provision in Codes E and F in relation to the signing of the label of an audio or video-recorded interview, but it is suggested that a third party present in the interview should be asked to sign the label and that the interviewer should record what has occurred. Where the suspect makes a written statement in accordance with Code C or Code H Annex D and the suspect cannot read, the senior officer present must read it over to the suspect and ask the suspect whether he or she would like to correct, alter or add anything and to sign or make his or her mark at the end. The officer must then certify what has occurred on the statement itself (Code C, Code H Annex D para 12).

11.97    If, after the suspect is charged, the officer wishes to bring to the suspect's notice a statement made by another person or the content of an interview with another person, if the suspect cannot read, the officer may read it to the suspect (Code C para 16.4A).

## Foreign nationals

11.98    A citizen of an independent Commonwealth country or a national of a foreign country (including the Republic of Ireland) must be informed as soon as practicable of his or her right to communicate at any time with the citizen's High Commission, embassy or consulate, and of the citizen's right to have his or her High Commission, embassy or consulate told of his or her whereabouts and the grounds for detention (Code C, Code H paras 3.3 and 7.1). In *R v Van Axel and Wezer*,[83] a confession of a Dutch national was excluded where it had been obtained without the Dutch Embassy having been informed and after the defendant had been given out-of-date information about his rights in Dutch. It has been held that the right to consular access cannot be withheld even if the suspect is being held incommunicado under PACE s56.[84] A request for consular access must be acted on as soon as practicable (Code C, Code H para 7.1).

83   September 1991 *Legal Action* 12.
84   *R v Bassil and Mouffareg* December 1990 *Legal Action* 23.

11.99　　　If a citizen of an independent Commonwealth country or a national of a foreign country with which a bilateral consular convention or agreement is in force[85] is detained, the appropriate High Commission, embassy or consulate must be informed as soon as practicable (Code C, Code H para 7.2). However, if the suspect is a political refugee or seeking political asylum, this information should be given only at the express request of the suspect (Code C, Code H para 7.4). Consular officials may visit suspects out of the hearing of police officers and may arrange legal advice (Code C, Code H para 7.3).

11.100　　The exercise of these rights may not be delayed or prevented, even where the suspect is being held incommunicado under PACE s56 or TA 2000 Sch 8 para 8, or where legal advice is delayed under PACE s58(8) or TA 2000 Sch 8 para 8 (Code C, Code H NfG 7A).

---

85　For a list, see Code C, Code H Annex F, although this appears to be out of date.

# CHAPTER 12

# Immigration detainees

*continued*

**12.108    The role of the embassy**

**12.110    Brief synopsis**
Checklist 15: Questions to ask an immigration detainee
*Flow chart for detained clients*

# Introduction

12.1    This chapter attempts to give criminal practitioners a basic understanding of how to assist people in detention with immigration-related problems, when encountered in police stations, and also to try to identify issues that, for detainees, are likely to be most relevant both at the time of detention and immediately thereafter.

12.2    A comprehensive understanding of the immigration process is beyond the scope of this chapter, and the principal aim is to enable the practitioner to assist the detainee to identify the range of options that may be open to him or her.

12.3    One practical problem for practitioners in the field of immigration, and consequently also for those practising in criminal work where there is an immigration component, is that the relevant provisions are not contained within one piece of legislation, but are governed by an ever-growing series of statutes, immigration rules, statutory instruments and other delegated legislation, defining the terms on which processes for appeals and bail are to be governed. Furthermore, there are a number of Home Office policies and concessions which are not formally codified, but may exist either in response to parliamentary questions or by way of press releases and which, consequently, are not subject to parliamentary scrutiny. To complicate matters further, some of the policies and concessions, such as those relating to unaccompanied minors, may be limited to a class of persons who applied at a particular time and the concession granted for a limited and specific purpose.[1]

12.4    The statutes empower the secretary of state, immigration officers (IOs) or entry clearance officers (those carrying out functions at embassies and consular officers abroad) to make decisions to grant or refuse applications. The immigration rules set out the criteria governing how those applications for entry clearance, for leave to enter, or for permission to remain are to be determined. The most recent set of consolidated rules took effect from 1 October 1994 (Statement of Changes of Immigration Rules HC 395). These have been substantially amended several times since that consolidation. The Home Office website maintains a relatively current version of the immigration rules which incorporates the amendments[2] although it should be noted that the website version can be a few days out of date and there have occasionally been problems in the past with the accuracy of the information, as the web version has not always accurately replicated the wording of the rules as published.

12.5    Despite the many legislative changes, there has been no consolidating statute, and hence it remains necessary to examine legislation dating back to the Immigration Act (IA) 1971 which contains many of the provisions relating to the powers of detention and sets out the classes of persons who

---

1   Persons seeking asylum who are unaccompanied are presently granted leave for a period of 3 years or until they reach 17 years 6 months, whichever is the shorter: Asylum Policy Unit Notice 3/2007, available at www.ukba.homeoffice.gov. uk/sitecontent/documents/policyandlaw/asylumpolicyinstructions/apunotices/ amendmenttodlpolicyasc.pdf?view=Binary.

2   Available at http://ukba.homeoffice.gov.uk/policyandlaw/immigrationlaw/ immigrationrules/.

are likely to be afforded an entitlement to apply for immigration bail. A draft consolidating bill was discussed by the previous administration but never fully published.

12.6     Detention at a police station under the immigration legislation may have resulted from a raid carried out by IOs alone or in concert with the police. Alternatively, it may follow after a person has been arrested for a criminal matter when the person's status was called into question. The police may have little subsequent interest in the initial arrest (which may have been for a relatively minor offence), and the only obligation upon them would be to ensure that the detainee's treatment in detention is broadly consistent with the Police and Criminal Evidence Act 1984 (PACE) until such time as the detainee is released from custody or transferred into alternative immigration detention. Increasingly, detainees are being held specifically in relation to immigration offences relating to their mode of entry to the UK and lack of formal documentation (see para 12.31 below).

12.7     If the police do proceed to investigate an alleged offence, then the provisions of PACE will apply as they would to other detainees. The immigration investigation may be deferred until after the criminal investigation has been concluded, although it is becoming increasingly common for detainees to be subject to parallel investigations. It should be noted that if the person is released without charge in relation to the criminal matter, that does not necessarily secure the person's release from custody since the immigration service may and often do exercise powers to authorise continued detention. A further limited power of arrest also arises enabling a designated IO to detain an individual at a port of entry for up to three hours where the officer believes that an individual has committed a criminal (non-immigration) offence or is subject to an arrest warrant.[3]

12.8     There has been some debate about whether PACE and the Codes of Practice apply to immigration detainees in police stations. The general view is that while matters are being investigated and could constitute a criminal offence (including an immigration offence), PACE and the Codes will apply. They may cease to apply from the time that it is clear that the person is being detained solely in respect of, and having been served with, a notice under the immigration legislation,[4] or where the person has been arrested on the authority of an IO solely for the purposes of having his or her fingerprints taken (Code C para 1.12 (ii)). However, even though the full provisions of PACE will not apply, the provisions as to conditions of detention and treatment while at the police station under Code C sections 8 and 9 will continue to apply.

12.9     Furthermore, under Immigration and Asylum Act 1999 s145, when exercising any power to arrest, question, search the person, enter or search premises, or seize property found on a person, an IO must have regard to the PACE Code. In addition, where certain functions are carried out by designated customs officials (which includes certain IOs) they are obliged

---

3   UK Borders Act 2007 s2(1).
4   Code C para 1.12 (iii).

to apply PACE orders[5] in respect of, among other matters, detention in UK Border Agency (UKBA) offices or premises.[6]

12.10    Within the context of immigration powers that are exercisable, different roles are played by those carrying out immigration functions under the overall responsibility of the Secretary of State for the Home Department through the UKBA.

## The role of entry clearance officers

12.11    Many people seeking entry to the UK require prior entry clearance in order to do so, commonly referred to as a visa. The entry clearance officer (ECO) will consider an application made at a post abroad and if satisfied, may grant the application, and if not will refuse the application. Persons entering the UK in the absence of an appropriate entry clearance are liable to be returned to the country from which they embarked and may be detained pending the determination of the removal arrangements, but such detention would be authorised in the UK by an IO rather than by the police.[7]

12.12    The existence of carrier liability sanctions to penalise airlines, passenger ferries and travel operators, together with the introduction of the 'points-based' system has significantly reduced the number of such individuals gaining entry to the UK.

## The role of immigration officers

12.13    In broad terms, IOs are responsible for dealing with and determining cases involving persons from abroad who arrive in the UK seeking lawful entry. The individual may have recently arrived at a port, or may have made an application at a port of entry and be awaiting consideration of the application, for example asylum, where the decision will not necessarily be made within a few hours or even days. In the immigration context, the grant of leave to enter or leave to remain is key. An individual who has arrived in the UK but who has not yet been given leave to enter, will need such leave from an IO even if, as with asylum claims, the IO may have little, if anything, to do with the assessment of the asylum case itself. In theory, under the New Asylum Model (NAM) all elements of decision-making, including service of the decision to grant or refuse leave to enter, is to be made by the same NAM 'case owner'. In practice, however, this does not always happen. As it is normally an IO who will have responsibility for the decision as to leave to enter, the IO will also have responsibility for those persons identified as being illegal entrants. The IO's powers extend not only to the grant or refusal of leave, but also to the power to authorise detention or release (temporary admission), and if the latter, to imposing conditions on that release.[8]

---

5  Police and Criminal Evidence Act 1984 (Application to Revenue and Customs) Order 2007 SI No 3175 and the Police and Criminal Evidence (Application to Revenue and Customs) Order (Northern Ireland) 2007 SR 464.

6  Borders, Citizenship and Immigration Act 2009 s22.

7  IA 1971 Sch 2 para 16(2).

8  IA 1971 Sch 2 para 21.

12.14   In addition to IOs working within the various ports of entry in the UK, there are also IOs operating within designated enforcements units such as that at Croydon. Furthermore, with a policy directed at pushing border controls offshore, there are also 'juxtaposed controls' operating outside the UK, enabling powers to be exercised by IOs, including power to take fingerprints in controlled zones within France.[9] While in France, they do not operate as ECOs but instead carry out functions (which include powers to arrest and detain) as if they were in the UK.

## The role of the secretary of state

12.15   In cases where an individual had previously been granted lawful leave to enter or remain in the UK, any after-entry decisions in respect of that individual will be taken by the secretary of state through the UKBA. This may include the decision to grant or refuse an extension of time to remain in the UK, or a decision to allow or refuse permission for the individual to remain in a different capacity from that under which the individual initially sought and obtained leave to enter.

12.16   The secretary of state has power to make a decision to deport, whether following a recommendation from a court or otherwise, or where the secretary of state deems it to be conducive to the public good. The power to deport also extends to dependant family members such as a spouse or civil partner, or a minor child of the individual who faces deportation. In: 'automatic deportation cases the Secretary of State has not merely a power, but a duty, to make a deportation order' (see para 12.24 below). The secretary of state also has the power to sign a deportation order, and to revoke a deportation order that has been signed.

12.17   The secretary of state also has responsibility for determining applications for asylum under the Convention Relating to the Status of Refugees 1951 (the Refugee Convention), or where it is alleged that removal would constitute a breach of an individual's human rights under the European Convention on Human Rights (ECHR). Further, the secretary of state has responsibility for considering applications made for citizenship.

12.18   The decisions of the UKBA are carried out at a variety of offices, the central unit being based at Croydon, although there are also regional offices in Belfast, Birmingham, Glasgow, Leeds and Liverpool.

## Illegal entrants

12.19   An illegal entrant is a person who has entered or sought to enter the UK unlawfully, or who has gained or attempted to gain entry through his or her deception, or through the deception of another party. A person who arrives on a false passport would be an obvious example of someone who is an illegal entrant, as would someone who seeks to arrive in a clandestine manner without going through immigration control at all. The Court of Appeal has gone so far as to state that if a person requiring leave to

---

9   Nationality, Immigration and Asylum Act 2002 (Juxtaposed Controls) Order 2003 SI No 2818 as amended by Nationality, Immigration and Asylum Act 2002 (Juxtaposed Controls) (Amendment) Order 2006 SI No 2908.

enter was not given that leave, even where an error was made by an IO as to whether the person required such leave, the person can be classified as an illegal entrant.[10] If it is clear that deception had been used in gaining the original leave to enter, then any leave granted is treated as being void ab initio and consequently any subsequent permission to remain, or decisions made thereafter (in ignorance of the facts), do not prevent the individual from later being treated as an illegal entrant.

## Overstayers

12.20    An overstayer is a person who, having previously lawfully entered the UK, has remained beyond the time permitted either by an IO or (in the event of an extension), by the secretary of state. The initial entry for such an individual would have been lawful, and the fact that the person overstayed does not mean that the person's presence in the UK throughout his or her residence here is deemed to be unlawful, merely that period from when there was no lawful leave.

## Persons in breach of their conditions

12.21    This might include a person who has overstayed, since one of the conditions of leave will relate to the period of time granted, but it will also include those persons who breach some other condition, for example, the condition prohibiting them from taking up employment. Persons granted entry as students are permitted to take up employment during term time of up to 20 hours a week. Any work in excess of this period during term time will be a breach of the conditions of leave.

12.22        Whether an individual has been identified as an illegal entrant, an overstayer or in breach of his or her conditions of leave, the person will be liable to administrative removal in accordance with Immigration and Asylum Act 1999 s10 and would not automatically benefit from an appeal right exercisable prior to removal. The entitlement to appeal before removal will apply to some people in each of the categories, but only if the grounds of appeal are that the removal would be a breach of the individual's rights under the Refugee Convention, the ECHR or European Community law.[11]

## Deportees

12.23    As observed at para 12.16 above, those who face deportation include those who have been recommended for deportation, as well as those in respect of whom the secretary of state has made a decision that their removal is conducive to the public good. This can include persons who have been lawfully given settlement rights in the UK as well as family members. Persons who are subject to deportation action (as opposed to administrative removal under Immigration and Asylum Act 1999 s10 – see para 12.22) are entitled to bring an appeal prior to removal. Where a recommendation for deportation is made by a criminal court, the appeal right may be

10  *R v SSHD ex p Rehal* (1989) Imm AR 576.
11  Nationality Immigration and Asylum Act 2002 s92(4).

within the criminal courts' jurisdiction, but where the removal potentially engages either the ECHR or the Refugee Convention, the decision on that application (if refused) will trigger an appeal to the immigration courts.

## Automatic deportation

12.24   Individuals who are foreign nationals and have been convicted in the UK and sentenced to terms of imprisonment of 12 months or more,[12] or who commit an offence which is specified by the secretary of state as being particularly serious[13] are subject to automatic deportation, whereby the secretary of state must make a deportation order.[14]

12.25   There are limited exceptions where such an order does not need to be made:

- persons that would be exempt due to meeting certain specific require-ments (Commonwealth or Irish nationals resident on 1 January 1973);
- where removal would breach the Refugee Convention or the ECHR;
- where the person is under 18 on the date of conviction;
- where removal would be a breach of European Community law;
- where there are extant extradition proceedings;
- where the removal would contravene the Council of Europe Conven-tion on Action against Trafficking in Human Beings; or
- where the individual is subject to certain orders under the Mental Health Act 1983.[15]

12.26   In theory, where an order is signed, no appeal right is available. In practice the appeal is against whether the section should apply at all by reason of the exceptions.[16]

## Powers of arrest and detention for offences

12.27   IA 1971 s28A(1) empowers a police constable or an IO to arrest, without warrant, on reasonable grounds for suspicion any person who has com-mitted or attempted to commit any of the following offences:

- knowingly entering the UK in breach of a deportation order or without leave;[17]
- knowingly overstaying or breaching a condition of leave;[18]
- overstaying as a seaman or crew member;[19]

---

12   UK Borders Act 2007 s32(2).
13   UK Borders Act 2007 s32(3), although it should be noted that the designation of offences by the secretary of state under the Nationality, Immigration and Asylum Act 2002 (Specification of Particularly Serious Crimes) Order 2004 SI No 1910 was declared ultra vires by the Court of Appeal in *EN (Serbia) v SSHD* [2009] EWCA Civ 630, an appeal to the Supreme Court was pending at the time of writing.
14   UK Borders Act 2007 s32(5).
15   UK Borders Act 2007 s33.
16   Nationality, Immigration and Asylum Act 2002 s82(3A)(a).
17   IA 1971 s24(1)(a).
18   IA 1971 s24(1)(b).
19   IA 1971 s24(1)(c).

- failing to comply with a restriction on temporary admission such as residence, reporting or taking up employment without reasonable excuse;[20]
- obtaining leave to enter or remain, or avoiding, delaying or revoking enforcement action, by deception.[21]

12.28 In addition, IA 1971 s28A also empowers an IO, having reasonable grounds to believe that an offence has been committed, to arrest in respect of the following:

- being knowingly concerned in facilitating the commission of a breach of immigration law by a non EU national where the person facilitating knows or has reasonable cause for believing that his or her act does so facilitate and that the individual is not an EU national;[22]
- knowingly and for gain facilitating the arrival in the UK of a person whom the individual knows or has reasonable cause to believe to be an asylum-seeker;[23]
- knowingly facilitating the breach of a deportation order in respect of an EU national;[24]
- knowingly facilitating the arrival, entry or stay of an individual in respect of whom the secretary of state has made an exclusion order on the grounds that it is conducive to public good;[25]
- obstructing an IO or other person in the execution of his or her duties under the Act where it is impractical to serve a summons because of a lack of certainty about an individual's address, or where arrest is otherwise necessary to prevent the individual causing or suffering physical injury or causing loss or damage to property;[26]
- making, altering, possessing without reasonable excuse, using or attempting to use with an intention to deceive, a false registration card issued to persons who have made claims for asylum (application registration card (ARC));[27]
- possessing a genuine or replica immigration stamp without reasonable excuse.[28]

12.29 IOs are empowered to enter premises in order to search for and arrest those suspected of having committed offences.[29] This power to search also relates to business premises,[30] with such power being exercisable upon the belief that the individual is on the premises, not because it is believed that the individual owns or has a financial interest in the premises.

20  IA 1971 s24(1)(e).
21  IA 1971 s24A(1).
22  IA 1971 s25.
23  IA 1971 s25A.
24  IA 1971 s25B(1).
25  IA 1971 s25B(3).
26  IA 1971 s26(1)(g).
27  IA 1971 s26A(3).
28  IA 1971 s26B.
29  IA 1971 Sch 2 paras 25A and 25B.
30  IA 1971 s28CA(1).

12.30    IOs also have arrest powers exercisable without a warrant, where in the exercise of their duties they have a reasonable suspicion that a person has committed, or has attempted to commit, a variety of additional offences, including: conspiracy to defraud, bigamy, perjury, theft, obtaining property, services or a pecuniary advantage by deception, handling stolen goods and forgery.[31]

12.31    In addition to the increase in powers given to IOs, more individuals are potentially subject to the criminal law in this area. Asylum and Immigration (Treatment of Claimants, etc) Act 2004 s2 makes it an offence to arrive in the UK without proper documentation, regardless of the purpose for which entry is being sought. Following the instructions of an agent to destroy the passport or using a false passport for any part of the journey will not necessarily constitute a defence.[32] However, if no passport is used for the totality of the journey, then a section 2 offence is not committed.[33] Those who are charged with the offence may need urgent immigration advice if they are also seeking asylum in the UK, since the consequence of failure to produce a passport, or destruction of a passport or ticket without reasonable explanation, may be to damage the individual's credibility in the context of the asylum claim.[34]

12.32    An IO or a police constable also has power to arrest without warrant a person who has unreasonably refused to assist in the person's own departure from the UK, such as by refusing to attend an interview or complete an application form for a passport or return travel document.[35]

## Powers of administrative detention

12.33    As noted above, even if a potential criminal investigation (whether for an immigration offence or otherwise) has been concluded, the person will not necessarily be released and their detention can be authorised by an IO or by the secretary of state in respect of deportees. Furthermore, the grant of bail by a magistrates' court in connection with any pending criminal action will not result in the automatic release of the person, who may be required to apply to an immigration judge[36] of the First Tier Tribunal (Immigration and Asylum Chamber) for bail, which is subject to a different process and is determined by reference to different criteria than those that apply in criminal proceedings (see para 12.95 below).

12.34    The power administratively to detain, whether before, during or after any criminal detention, applies to the following class of persons:

---

31  Asylum and Immigration (Treatment of Claimants, etc) Act 2004 s14.
32  Asylum and Immigration (Treatment of Claimants, etc) Act 2004 s2(7)(b)(iii).
33  *Soe Thet v DPP* [2006] EWHC 2701 (Admin).
34  Asylum and Immigration (Treatment of Claimants, etc) Act 2004 s8(1).
35  Asylum and Immigration (Treatment of Claimants, etc) Act 2004 s35(5).
36  Following the Asylum and Immigration Tribunal (Judicial Titles) Order 2005 SI No 227, legally qualified personnel determining appeals and bail hearings were designated as immigration judges (having previously been known as adjudicators or members of the tribunal).

- persons arriving in the UK, pending a decision as to whether or not they should be given leave to enter, or where their leave has been suspended, pending a decision as to whether the leave should be cancelled;[37]
- persons refused leave to enter the UK, pending the setting of removal directions;[38]
- persons treated as illegal entrants or suspected of being illegal entrants, pending the setting of removal directions;[39]
- persons in breach of landing conditions or who are suspected of having obtained leave by deception.[40]

These powers may be exercised by the secretary of state as well as by an IO.[41]

12.35    Further detention powers are exercisable only by the secretary of state in respect of the following:

- persons liable to deportation following a recommendation by a criminal court, even where granted bail by a criminal court pending appeal against conviction or against the recommendation;[42]
- persons served with a decision to deport, pending the making of the deportation order;[43]
- persons in respect of whom a deportation order has been signed, pending removal;[44]
- persons in respect of whom consideration is being given as to whether or not the automatic deportation provisions apply to them following completion of a term of imprisonment[45] or once an automatic deportation order has been made.[46]

12.36    It must be remembered that the power to detain consequently applies not only to those persons in respect of whom a decision has already been made, but also to those in respect of whom a decision has yet to be made. The adviser needs to make clear to the client that detention does not necessarily mean that all is lost, and that there may be remedies to pursue regarding release, and regarding the individual's circumstances more generally.

12.37    It is unlikely that the person will remain at the police station for very lengthy periods. After five days, any further detention must be either in a prison, a removal centre or another designated place. In the case of those in respect of whom a removal direction has been issued, the maximum period is extended to seven days.[47]

---

37  IA 1971 Sch 2 para 16.
38  IA 1971 Sch 2 para 16.
39  IA 1971 Sch 2 para 16(2).
40  Immigration and Asylum Act 1999 s10(7).
41  Nationality Immigration and Asylum Act 2002 s62.
42  IA 1971 Sch 3 para 2(1) and (1A).
43  IA 1971 Sch 3 para 2(2).
44  IA 1971 Sch 3 para 3.
45  UK Borders Act 2007 s 36(1).
46  UK Borders Act 2007 s36(2).
47  Immigration (Places of Detention) Directions 1999 and see Enforcement Instructions and Guidance manual chapter 55.5.3 which requires detention in a police cell for more than two nights to be authorised by an officer of the rank of Inspector or Senior Executive Officer.

## Awaiting a decision

12.38   In some cases, the person detained will already have made an application to the Home Office and be awaiting a decision. This may be someone who had leave and who has applied for an extension of stay. The fact that many weeks or months have passed since the date on which the person made the application to the Home Office does not mean that the person inadvertently become an overstayer if no decision is made by the Home Office. IA 1971 s3C specifically provides that a person who has made a valid application either for an extension of the person's existing leave, or for leave in a different capacity, has the original leave and conditions (apart from the one concerning time) extended by operation of law, until either the application is withdrawn, or any appeal relating to it is disposed of, provided that during that time the individual does not leave the UK. As a consequence individuals in this capacity ought not to be detained. However, if an application was made to the Home Office, but after the person's leave had expired, then although the person may not necessarily be removed until after the person's application has been considered, he or she can be detained.

12.39   If an individual is initially detained in respect of a non immigration-related matter, that might trigger some action in respect of the pending application, although it should be observed that in such circumstances the outcome tends to be negative rather than positive. It will often be the making of the decision that triggers detention, since there is an increasing trend for the secretary of state to detain individuals for the purposes of serving refusal decisions. This is particularly so for those where the decisions would not be appealable from within the UK.

## Immigration decisions

12.40   Not all immigration decisions attract a right of appeal, and in some cases, although there is a right of appeal, it is not exercisable from within the UK before removal. Consequently it will be important for the adviser to try to assist the detainee in determining whether there is an appealable decision exercisable prior to removal since this is likely to impact on, among other things, whether it is sensible to remain detained, particularly as in many cases the individual may be advised that the individual can be more swiftly removed if he or she agrees to a voluntary departure.

12.41   In broad terms, decisions that attract a right of appeal prior to removal from the UK include:

- refusal of a certificate of entitlement to the right of abode;
- refusal to vary a person's leave resulting in the person having no leave;
- variation of that leave with the consequence that the person has no leave;[48]

---

48  An appeal right will only be available in these two scenarios where the application is made while the individual had current leave. If the individual applied as an overstayer or with no leave, then the refusal would not attract an entitlement to an in country appeal right – see *R (Daley-Murdock) v SSHD* [2011] EWCA Civ 161.

- revocation of indefinite leave if the individual is liable to deportation but cannot be deported for legal reasons, or where the individual obtained leave to remain indefinitely by deception but cannot be removed for legal or practical reasons, or where the individual or the person on whom the individual is dependant ceases to be a refugee, having acquired a new (non-British) nationality or availing himself or herself of the protection of the state from which the individual had previously claimed to fear persecution;
- a decision to make a deportation order, including cases where the deportation order is made under the automatic deportation regime;[49]
- a decision to refuse leave to enter where the individual had prior entry clearance which has not been cancelled and where the person is seeking leave to enter in the capacity for which the entry clearance was granted;[50]
- a decision refusing leave to enter to a person holding a work permit where the person is either a British overseas territories citizen, a British overseas citizen, a British national (overseas), a British protected person or a British subject;[51]
- a person making an asylum or human rights claim in the UK;[52]
- a European Economic Area (EEA) national or the family member of an EEA national alleging a breach of a European Community law right regarding entry or residence in the UK.[53]

12.42 In respect of asylum claimants or those who argue that their removal would breach their human rights, a refusal does not attract a right of appeal from within the UK if either the claim was certified by the secretary of state as being clearly unfounded on the grounds that it raises no legitimate Refugee Convention or human rights element,[54] or where the secretary of state seeks to remove the person to a safe third country.[55]

12.43 In such a case a challenge might be pursued by way of judicial review of the certificate, or of the decision to remove to a safe third country. Specialist advice would need to be sought swiftly in such a case, as expressing an intention to apply for judicial review will not operate to prevent or delay removal.[56]

12.44 In considering whether or not to make a deportation order, the immigration rules require the secretary of state to start from the presumption that the public interest requires deportation. The secretary of state

---

49 All of these categories are set out at Nationality Immigration and Asylum Act 2002 s92(2).
50 Nationality Immigration and Asylum Act 2002 s92(3).
51 Nationality Immigration and Asylum Act 2002 s92(3D). Many territories retain historical links with the UK through the Commonwealth. Although they have a slightly favoured position on some aspects of immigration control, generally possession of a passport from one of these territories will have little impact on improving the individual's chances of being able to remain in the long term.
52 Nationality Immigration and Asylum Act 2002 s92(4)(a).
53 Nationality Immigration and Asylum Act 2002 s92(4)(b).
54 Nationality Immigration and Asylum Act 2002 s94(2).
55 Asylum and Immigration (Treatment of Claimants, etc) Act 2004 Sch 3.
56 Enforcement Instructions and Guidance chapter 60 Judicial review and Injunctions para 5.

will thereafter consider whether the relevant factors in a particular case outweigh this initial presumption, and it is clear that it would only be in exceptional cases, which would otherwise be a breach of either the Refugee Convention or the ECHR, that such a presumption would be outweighed.[57]

12.45   Where automatic deportation applies, then subject to considering whether a relevant exception applies, no such balancing exercise is required, as the secretary of state must make such an order.[58]

12.46   In the context of deportation decisions which follow serious criminal offences committed in the UK, the Court of Appeal has accepted that the secretary of state has a wide margin of discretion in assessing what is in the public interest.[59]

12.47   While the starting point for considering deportation under the rules will be that the presumption is in favour of deportation, it is unclear whether that balancing exercise will also be tipped in favour of the state when assessing whether deportation would amount to a breach of ECHR article 8.[60]

12.48   It will be critical for the practitioner to be able correctly to identify whether the detainee is likely to benefit from an appealable decision exercisable prior to removal. If there is no entitlement to appeal, then the prospects for temporary release and bail are reduced, and the possibility of pursuing any other remedies, such as through representations (see para 12.95 below) may be severely limited.

## Mandatory bans on return

12.49   One aspect that will need to be considered at a very early stage is whether the client has any intention to return to the UK in the future. If a person is an overstayer, illegal entrant, used deception or breached a condition attached to the person's leave, then the person faces the prospect of a mandatory ban on returning to the UK for a specified period of time. The ban will not apply to those seeking to return where they were under 18 years when they most recently breached immigration law, or where they are seeking to return to join a family member in the UK,[61] nor where they have overstayed for not more than 28 days and leave voluntarily at their own expense.[62] In other cases, the ban will be for a period between one and ten years depending on their level of co-operation, and where deception had been used in respect of any earlier application.[63]

---

57  HC 395 para 364.
58  HC 395 para 364A.
59  *N (Kenya) v SSHD* [2004] EWCA Civ 1094.
60  In *RU (Bangladesh) v SSHD* [2011] EWCA Civ 651 the Court of Appeal opined that in automatic deportation cases, greater weight should be attached in assessing proportionality, but accepted that the matter would need to be determined in another case.
61  HC 395 para 320(7C).
62  HC 395 para 320(7B)(d)(i).
63  HC 395 para 320(7B).

# Immigration appeals

12.50　As observed above, not all decisions attract a right of appeal from within the UK.[64] Those that do are subject to strict rules about time limits for bringing appeals, and the grounds upon which it can be argued that a decision should be overturned.

12.51　　The time limit for bringing an appeal is ten days from the date the decision is served for persons in the UK, but only five days in the case of persons detained under the Immigration Acts.[65] For those who are detained, notice should either be lodged with the First Tier Tribunal (FTT) (the decision will invariably contain details for serving the notice, including a fax number), or on the person having custody of the individual.[66] Although there is scope for late notice of appeals to be lodged, time will only be extended where the tribunal is satisfied that, by reason of special circumstances, it would be unjust not to do so.[67] The fact that someone is detained is unlikely, in normal circumstances, to be a special circumstance, per se, since the time limit is specifically shortened under the procedure rules for those who are detained.[68]

12.52　　Any appeal that is brought will be limited to grounds specified by statute. Nationality, Immigration and Asylum Act 2002 s84 specifies that an appeal must be brought on one or more of the grounds listed:

- the decision is not in accordance with the immigration rules;
- the decision is unlawful as being a breach of Race Relations Act 1976 s19B;
- the decision is unlawful as being contrary to Human Rights Act 1998 s6;
- the decision breaches the appellant's European Community law rights;
- the decision is not in accordance with the law;
- the person making the decision should have exercised discretion differently;
- removal would breach the UK's obligations under either the Refugee Convention or the ECHR.

12.53　Cases are heard initially by an immigration judge in the FTT (or a panel of two in deportation appeals following a conviction) and either party may request permission to appeal from that determination if it believes that the FTT may have made an error of law.[69] Any such request must be made within five working days of the receipt of the immigration judge's decision, and a decision as to whether or not to grant permission to appeal is initially considered by the FTT. If that application is refused, a dissatisfied party may renew an application for permission to appeal to the Upper Tribunal itself.[70]

---

64　See para 12.40 above and Nationality, Immigration and Asylum Act 2002 ss92 and 94, and Asylum and Immigration (Treatment of Claimants, etc) Act 2004 Sch 3.
65　Asylum and Immigration Tribunal (Procedure) Rules 2005 SI No 230 r7.
66　Asylum and Immigration Tribunal (Procedure) Rules 2005 r6(3).
67　Asylum and Immigration Tribunal (Procedure) Rules 2005 r10(5).
68　*MK (Iran) v SSHD* [2007] EWCA Civ 554.
69　Asylum and Immigration Tribunal (Procedure) Rules 2005 r24.
70　Tribunal Procedure (Upper Tribunal) Rules 2008 SI No 2698 r21(2).

12.54    The FTT may, as an alternative to granting or refusing permission, order a review of the decision provided that it is satisfied that the original decision contained an error of law.[71]

12.55    Legal aid is only available on a retrospective cost basis for the making of an application for permission to appeal to the Upper Tribunal if granted either by the FTT or by the Upper Tribunal. This applies only where the request for permission to appeal is made by the individual and not where the Home Office seeks permission. In that event, the normal costs provisions under public funding apply (see para 12.106 below regarding funding).

12.56    Most clients are unlikely to be detained in a police station throughout the appeal process. However, it is possible that the practitioner will be contacted for advice by an individual who has been detained following the rejection of the initial appeal and who may seek advice as to any onward appeal, for which the time limit is only five days.[72]

12.57    It is understood that many criminal practitioners already have difficulty in being able to refer cases on to immigration specialists. With the advent of retrospective costs orders, it is likely to be particularly difficult to refer a case which has reached this stage in the appeals process. Further legal aid changes that were proposed in the Legal Aid, Sentencing and Punishment of Offenders Bill 2011[73] include the removal of significant areas from the scope of funding altogether and will, if enacted, make finding representatives willing to assist even more difficult in the future.

12.58    While most in-country appeals will be dealt with subject to the time limits and provisions above, cases which raise issues of national security or relations between the UK and other states are likely to be dealt with instead through appeals to the Special Immigration Appeals Commission.[74] The number of appeals proceeding under this mechanism instead of the usual appeals process is very small. If there is an issue of particular sensitivity, it is essential that the lawyer should seek to refer the case to a specialist practitioner without delay. The mechanism of the appeals process particular to that scheme is beyond the scope of this chapter. Similarly, there are also asylum appeals dealt with under what is known as the detained fast track process. Invariably such appeals will emanate from persons detained solely under Immigration Act powers at a designated detention centre. Since the likelihood of such individuals being at police stations is extremely small, the procedure will not be examined here, save to say that the time limits and appeals mechanism are accelerated.[75]

## Asylum/human rights cases

12.59    With increasing numbers of criminal investigations regarding mode of entry and lack of documentation, an increasing number of detainees

---

71  Asylum and Immigration Tribunal (Procedure) Rules 2005 r26(1).
72  Asylum and Immigration Tribunal (Procedure) Rules 2005 r24(2).
73  HC Bill 205, introduced 21 June 2011.
74  Established by virtue of Special Immigration Appeals Commission Act 1997.
75  Asylum and Immigration Tribunal (Fast Track Procedure) Rules 2005 SI No 560.

are being processed through the criminal justice system without being afforded an opportunity to present their asylum claims at an early stage. It is understood that the Home Office has had concerns about spurious asylum claims being made (and sometimes, it believes, even encouraged by representatives) at the last moment largely to frustrate removal. It is crucial for the lawyer to be aware of the tension that exists between bringing a claim that may lack merit, and the danger in not pursuing a claim until after it is too late. As immigration law and practice is increasingly growing in complexity, many lawyers at the police station may be faced with hard choices about how best to advise. The Legal Services Commission (LSC) has introduced a telephone advice scheme for the provision of immigration-only advice to those held in police stations or short-term detention facilities on a nationwide basis. This scheme is, in part, a response to the difficulties faced by criminal practitioners who may feel uneasy about offering advice which may have a potentially detrimental impact on whether an individual can or should bring such a claim. If clients are clear that they do wish to present a claim for asylum, wherever possible the lawyer should try to refer the case on to an immigration practitioner.

12.60    For those practitioners advising detainees in relation to documentation offences, the impact of a conviction on the client's credibility both in the assessment of the client's claim by the Home Office as well as the assessment of the client's credibility on an appeal must be considered. Admission of the offence may be the best way of avoiding a lengthy sentence,[76] but there may well be serious consequences in relation to the asylum claim. Wherever possible in such cases, the lawyer advising at the police station should try to enlist the assistance of an immigration practitioner, even if the criminal lawyer continues representing the individual in relation to the criminal charge.[77]

## Access to detainees

12.61    Generally there will be no difficulty in securing access to an immigration detainee at a police station, since the police will normally have no reason to object to legal advice being received, particularly if they believe that it will speed up the process of emptying the cell. Their function is restricted to acting as jailor for the immigration service once any immigration decision has been served. There are some restrictions on access to

---

76   *R v Lu Zhu Ai* [2005] EWCA Crim 396, the Court of Appeal indicated that a sentence of nine months would probably be excessive and substituted that sentence for one of five months for a male adult aged 26. In *R v Bei Bei Wang* [2005] EWCA Crim 293, the Court of Appeal concluded that a sentence of two months would be appropriate for a person who was aged 18 who had an extant claim for asylum and had pleaded guilty at the first opportunity.

77   Many criminal practitioners will be all too well aware of the criticism inherent in the judgement of Lord Justice Hughes in *LM and others v R* [2010] EWCA Crim 2327 as to the lack of familiarity within the profession in that case with the Council of Europe Convention on Action Against Trafficking in Human Beings . If in doubt it may be wise to seek specialist advice, as the range of potential defences to document offences was certainly expanded following the decision of the House of Lords in *R v Asfaw* [2008] UKHL 31.

advice where offences are still being investigated, particularly if the matter which led to the detention is alleged to have a national security and/or terrorism element. The current policy set out in the Enforcement Instructions and Guidance[78] makes it plain that where a person is being held at a police station for immigration matters, the individual is entitled to contact a representative.[79]

12.62    Given that the client may not have English as a first language, the lawyer is frequently dependant on the police or the immigration service, and on friends or relatives of the detainee, for relevant information. In some cases the lawyer at the police station may discover that the client already has an adviser assisting in connection with the immigration matter.

12.63    Immigration and Asylum Act 1999 s91 makes it a criminal offence for any person to provide immigration advice to another, unless the adviser (or his or her employer) is either a member of a designated professional body (such as the Law Society or the Bar Council), or the adviser is regulated or exempted by the Office of the Immigration Services Commissioner (OISC).

12.64    The range of organisations regulated or exempted by the OISC is broad and, as with most professionals, the quality of advice given varies. There may be some cases in which an OISC adviser will indicate that the adviser cannot assist further because of the detention (advisers are regulated at differing levels and some may be prohibited from dealing with detention and bail issues). In other cases, the client will indicate a level of dissatisfaction with the original adviser. Despite the unhappiness of the client, it may be detrimental to the client's interests for the police station lawyer to accept responsibility for the case in place of a previous representative, particularly as the time limits are short.[80]

12.65    If access to a detainee is refused on the basis that the initial instructions came from a third party, then the custody officer should be reminded of the provisions of Code C Annex B para 4. Although in theory it would be open to a custody officer to take the view that Code C does not apply to an immigration detainee, other than provisions as to conditions of detention and medical treatment under Code C paras 8 and 9, the present position as to entitlement to legal advice is clear from the Enforcement Instructions and Guidance.[81]

## Advising the client before the interview

12.66    Before advising the client the lawyer should, if possible, speak to the IO in order to establish what information the immigration authorities already have about the client. At the very least, the lawyer should try to ascertain this before the immigration interview takes place. The lawyer should

---

78  See www.ukba.homeoffice.gov.uk/policyandlaw/guidance/enforcement/.

79  Enforcement Instructions and Guidance chapter 38.2. This also includes the right to contact a representative from an immigrant welfare organisation.

80  The pool of potential referrals was further reduced by the introduction of compulsory accreditation for those undertaking asylum and immigration work (the Immigration and Asylum Accreditation Scheme).

81  Enforcement Instructions and Guidance chapter 38.2; and see para 12.81 below.

also ask to see any documents that have been taken from the client such as a passport, residence document or other identity document (such as an asylum application registration card) and any prior correspondence with the immigration authorities. This might include details of a previous immigration adviser who may not have been alerted to the fact of the client's detention, and who may be able to shed some light on the matter that would assist the lawyer at the police station, even if the immigration adviser does not take over the conduct of the matter at that stage.

12.67    Although the IO is not obliged to provide the lawyer with full details, a lack of co-operation would be a matter worth commenting on in an interview, particularly where it is clear that there are no existing criminal proceedings.[82]

12.68    At the initial interview with the client before an immigration interview is conducted, the lawyer should try to ascertain as much detail and information about the client as possible (see appendix 3 checklist 15). This will assist in determining whether the client is likely to be liable to administrative removal, and therefore (absent a human rights, asylum or EU law element) to be unable to exercise an appeal before removal,[83] or to deportation action, in which case an appeal before removal should be available. The lawyer should also be aware that where an appeal is pursued, and is unsuccessful, this will not prevent the operation of a mandatory ban if the client is already an overstayer. The question of whether an appeal can be brought will also be of relevance to the question of whether it is likely that an application for immigration bail would have a realistic prospect of success. Where information has already been gleaned from an IO prior to the meeting, the lawyer should still seek instructions from the client, since the information disclosed by the immigration service may not be accurate, and because the lawyer should formulate his or her advice on the basis of information and instructions obtained from the client. It is possible that the information obtained from the client will conflict with that obtained from the IO, and reaching a conclusion about merits and whether an appeal exists may be premature until the conflict of information has been discussed with the client.

12.69    However, some clients believe that their best strategy is to provide a 'revised' version of their immigration history. This may not be because of any inherent desire to deceive or to avoid responsibility, but may arise from advice proffered within communities, or from the fear of being returned to another country, or from a desire to protect friends or family who are also in the UK and whose immigration status may be precarious. In the event of receiving conflicting information, the practitioner should advise the client of information held by the immigration service, so that the client is forewarned that if the client chooses to present a revised version he or she may be disbelieved.

12.70    As with any detainee, gaining the trust and confidence of the client will be critical to being able to give proper informed advice and to enable the client to select realistic solutions as to how best to proceed. The lawyer should be aware that in some cases there will be little that can be achieved

82  Enforcement Instructions and Guidance chapter 42.2.
83  Nationality, Immigration and Asylum Act 2002 s92(4).

other than reducing the amount of time needlessly spent in detention, when in reality there is no prospect of being able to avoid the inevitability of administrative removal or enforcement of a deportation order.

12.71    It is for this reason that the lawyer should try to take as full an account as possible of all aspects of the individual's circumstances. For example, it may be that while the client is an illegal entrant, having arrived some years earlier, the client has subsequently formed a relationship with a person settled here and may have a child born in the UK.[84] Although liability to removal as an illegal entrant will not normally attract an appeal right,[85] it may be argued that removal in these circumstances would be a breach of the individual's human rights in that removal would interfere with the right to family life under ECHR article 8. In assessing the question of proportionality of any family life issue, regard must also be had to the impact on family members by any proposed deportation or removal.[86] The IO's file may not have details of the individual's family circumstances, and at the very least this information should be emphasised. These factors may not ultimately make a difference to the outcome of the IO's decision as to whether or not removal should proceed, but they provide a basis upon which the individual may be able to assert an entitlement to bring an appeal against the decision.[87] It is also possible that, while an appeal is lodged, representations can be simultaneously submitted to the immigration service regarding the family ties and the impact that removal would have in causing a break-up of any family unit. Furthermore, these factors may be relevant to whether the individual would remain detained while pursuing a remedy.

12.72    At the very least, these aspects should be explored as a means of establishing the relative merits of remaining in the UK to contest proceedings, albeit with the possibility of detention in the interim, or accepting that on the facts of the particular case an appeal would be unlikely to succeed. In such an event, the main issue may relate to seeking to minimise the impact of a mandatory ban on any prospective return to the UK in the future. Although the lawyer at the police station may not have sufficient knowledge as to whether a case is ultimately likely to succeed, the lawyer can at least advise the client of possible remedies to pursue. However, bare assertion that the removal will be a breach of the right to family life will not necessarily mean that an appeal before an immigration judge would succeed. Similarly, the fact that the UKBA may not accept that removal would be a breach does not mean that an immigration judge would reach the same conclusion especially it is less clear that the assessment of whether there would or would not be a breach of article 8 is weighted in favour of the secretary of state as it is under the immigration rules.[88]

12.73    For this reason, as a rule of thumb, remaining silent during an immigration interview is unlikely to be advantageous since if there is new

---

84   In *ZH (Tanzania) v SSHD* [2011] UKSC 4 the Supreme Court accepted that where a child was British, the best interest of that child would be highly relevant in an assessment of proportionality when considering removal of a parent.

85   Immigration and Asylum Act 1999 s10.

86   *Beoku-Betts v SSHD* [2008] UKHL 39.

87   Nationality Immigration and Asylum Act 2002 s92(4).

88   HC 395 para 364.

information to present, the failure to present it at the earliest opportunity may mean that the chance of mounting a successful appeal is lost, or delay may lead to adverse inferences being drawn at a subsequent appeal, given that the client would have had the opportunity of raising the matters with an IO before a decision being taken on whether to proceed with removal action.

12.74    In other cases, remaining silent would almost certainly be fatal to the prospects of success. For example, persons alleging that their removal would engage the Refugee Convention are already likely to be facing hurdles regarding credibility for not having made an application for asylum at an earlier stage,[89] and waiting until after an interview to assert a fear of return would compound the problem even further.[90]

12.75    In contrast to criminal proceedings, since very few of those detained will have effective appeals against administrative removal, failing to respond to questions put in an immigration interview is unlikely to be productive where it is clear that there is no likelihood of further criminal charges being brought. There will be no trial at which inferences from silence can be drawn, since failing to allege a breach of the individual's human rights will mean that removal will take place without an appeal. While there is no requirement to answer questions put by an IO regarding a person's immigration status, the issue for the adviser to consider is what might be lost by failing to speak.

12.76    If the client has indicated that his or her primary reason for seeking to avoid removal is that the client has a fear that if returned to the client's home country that the client would face serious harm and the client wishes to make an asylum or human rights claim, then it would be sensible for the adviser to indicate that to the IO either in advance, or at the commencement of the interview. It is not normally appropriate for a full asylum interview to be conducted at a police station given the importance of the issues and the fact that the client may benefit from specialist advice in this area. The IO may conduct a shortened interview to determine how best to proceed with the asylum claim (a screening interview), but invariably would not seek to conduct a full asylum interview but instead refer the matter to the Home Office. In the unlikely event that an IO insists on proceeding with a substantive interview on the asylum claim, the lawyer should ask for the interview to be delayed and to be given an opportunity to speak to a senior IO.

12.77    If the possibility of bringing criminal charges has not yet been ruled out and any interview is conducted under caution, then the advice to the detainee would be no different from that given to any other persons interviewed under caution, even if the interview is being conducted by an IO (see generally chapter 5).[91] This will include documentation offences even

---

89  Asylum and Immigration (Treatment of Claimants, etc) Act 2004 s8(6).

90  See also HC 395 para 339L (iv) in respect of those seeking humanitarian protection.

91  Enforcement Instructions and Guidance chapter 37.2.12 are that in straightforward cases where no criminal proceedings are being used, the use of a 'caution +2' should be used making it clear that the individual is not under arrest and is free to leave although in practice this is likely to have little impact on the detainee's willingness to co-operate given that the detainee is not in reality free to leave detention if that detention has been authorised under the Immigration Acts.

where the client has indicated a desire to claim asylum. While it may be sensible to make no comment so as to avoid the client implicating himself or herself in terms of the commission of an offence (overstaying and illegal entry are offences), at the conclusion of the interview the client should provide details of the client's personal or other circumstances if it is sought to rely on information that would trigger an in-country appeal right. Alternatively, if the initial interview is conducted under caution, it may be sensible to request that at its conclusion a further interview be conducted, not under caution, so as to enable the client to provide that information relevant to a potential 'family life' human rights claim.[92]

12.78    As with any detainee, the presence of a lawyer ought to have a positive impact on the ability of the client to handle the interview, but this can only be achieved if a relationship of trust is built with the client in what will inevitably be strained circumstances. The lawyer should emphasise the confidentiality of the instructions, and should seek to ensure that the client is not under the misconception that a willingness on the client's part to endure lengthy detention will mean that the immigration service will be more likely to accept that the client is telling the truth. The lawyer should also point out that whereas in criminal proceedings the burden of proof rests on the prosecution, in the immigration context the burden of establishing an entitlement to reside, or that the person was granted lawful entry, that the person has not overstayed, or that the person is British,[93] will be on the individual. It is also important for the lawyer to explain the lawyer's ethical duties and that were the client to make statements in interview which the lawyer knew to be false, the lawyer may have to withdraw from the interview.

12.79    If the client does not speak English the lawyer should attempt to secure the attendance of an independent interpreter. Although an interpreter will be arranged by the police or the immigration service, it would not be appropriate for that interpreter to be used for the purpose of obtaining client instructions and advising the client. The LSC recognises the need to maintain the impartiality of advice given, and has agreed that the costs of an independent interpreter can be met as a disbursement.[94]

12.80    It would be sensible to alert the IO, as well as the custody officer, where an independent interpreter is to be used to monitor what is being said during interview. Unless there are specific issues about the conduct of a particular interpreter in the past, or the fact that the interpreter is related to the detainee, there would normally be no difficulty. If the IO or the custody officer objects, the lawyer should ask for the reasons for the objections, and note any response.

92  Enforcement Instructions and Guidance chapter 37.15 envisages such material not being disclosed on tape but that it should be recorded and the detainee afforded the opportunity to raise such issues.

93  IA 1971 s3(8).

94  Police Station and Duty Solicitor Costs Assessment Manual para 7.11.2.

## Attending the interview

12.81   Wherever possible, the lawyer should attend any interview conducted by an IO. This should help to ensure that the client is more at ease and consequently feels more able to reveal any relevant information that may affect the outcome of any enforcement decision. As with any other police station interview, the lawyer's presence should ensure that the client does not feel bullied or intimidated during the interview and is afforded the opportunity to respond to questions properly put. There is no statutory right to have a lawyer present where the interview solely relates to the issue of administrative removal. However, the Enforcement Instructions and Guidance manual make it plain that a person is permitted to seek legal advice,[95] and denial of legal advice for the purposes of such an interview or preventing an adviser from attending is a rare occurrence. However, the absence of a lawyer will not invalidate any decision made on the basis of information obtained in such an interview.[96]

12.82   Enforcement interviews are normally now tape recorded when conducted in a police station provided such facilities exist and are working.[97]

12.83   If the questions asked in the interview have not enabled the detainee to state everything that the lawyer believes to be relevant, the lawyer should ask the IO to permit the client to put forward any additional information. This is important given that the consequences of a decision which does not attract an appeal may result in swift removal from the UK without any prior judicial scrutiny of the detainee's circumstances.

## Advising the client after the interview

12.84   In some cases, an immigration interview may already have been conducted by the time the lawyer is able to see the client. However, the lawyer may still have an important role to play, particularly in terms of assessing whether or not an appeal right exists and, if so, the (short) time limits within which the right must be exercised. Any papers served on the client should be carefully examined since the decision as to how the individual is to be dealt with by the immigration authorities is likely to be made shortly after the interview. If the client was not forthcoming during the interview, either because the client chose to remain silent, or because the client was not afforded an opportunity to put the client's family or other circumstances to the interviewing officer, then it would be appropriate for written representations as to those circumstances to be sent urgently by fax to the relevant immigration office, the details of which should be apparent from any notices served on the client. This might affect whether a client would have a right of appeal exercisable prior to removal although, as observed above, the delay in submitting the information after interview may raise serious credibility problems at appeal.

95  Enforcement Instructions and Guidance chapter 38.2.
96  *R v Secretary of State for the Home Department ex p Vera Lawson* [1994] Imm AR 58.
97  Enforcement Instructions and Guidance chapter 37.7.

12.85    If such issues are raised at interview or through representations, then the client is likely to be served with a 'one stop' notice and the client is required to set out in detail his or her grounds for remaining in the UK.[98] The onus remains on the individual to show that removal would be unlawful. The time limit for the return of the one stop notice is ten days, and the secretary of state has the power to certify that the matter should not proceed to an appeal if the one stop notice is not returned in time, or if the matters could have been raised in response to an earlier notice,[99] or, where relevant, an earlier appeal.[100] For the lawyer, it is imperative to impress upon the client the need to comply with any time limit.

12.86    It may also be appropriate to contact the family members of the detainee after the interview to keep them apprised of the situation. The family members may also be at risk of enforcement action, in which case they should be advised to seek advice, or it may be that they have rights of residence in the UK. In any event, they are likely to want to be informed about whether anything can be done for the detainee. If the detainee has raised new issues at the interview relating to family members, it would be appropriate to ask for evidence of the relationship to be provided, such as a marriage or civil partnership certificate, or a child's birth certificate. Given the tight time limits for appeals, and one stop notices, it is important that the process of evidence-gathering begin as soon as possible.

12.87    Many defence lawyers are understandably reluctant to engage too deeply with the client's immigration case once work at the police station has been concluded. This may be because of the potential complexity, and because there remains some uncertainty about whether any work done beyond the police station will be remunerated, bearing in mind the requirement to be accredited under the Law Society's Immigration and Asylum Accreditation Scheme.[101] Wherever possible, the lawyer should try to refer the client on to an immigration specialist given that time limits are tight and, if further action is required, the work is likely to be time-consuming. If the lawyer has advised the client that there may be an appealable decision, it would be unwise to offer a definitive view on the prospects of success, bearing in mind that the client may unwittingly spend longer in detention pursuing an appeal where the prospects are poor, and may face a longer mandatory ban, or may be inadvertently persuaded to abandon an appeal that might have succeeded.

12.88    If in real doubt, given the tight time limits, where there is a right of appeal it may be safer for it to be exercised, and for the client to be referred on to an immigration adviser so that, if relevant, the immigration adviser can assess at an early stage whether it is appropriate to pursue or abandon the appeal. This at least has the advantage of avoiding complications that may arise from an attempt to lodge an appeal out of time. The reality, however, is that for many criminal practitioners, finding an immigration adviser ready, willing and able to accept the referral is proving increasingly difficult, particularly if at the time of the referral the client is still at

98  Nationality Immigration and Asylum Act 2002 s120.
99  Nationality Immigration and Asylum Act 2002 s96(2).
100  Nationality Immigration and Asylum Act 2002 s96(1).
101  Standard Civil Contract (SCC) 2010 Immigration Specification 8.16.

the police station, since the client may be relocated anywhere within the country while an appeal or other representations are pursued. Additionally, since October 2010, the LSC have operated through procurement areas, for which only limited scope exists to assist clients residing out of the area of the practitioner,[102] and for those transferred to removal centres under the detained fast track process, exclusive contracting arrangements rule out the possibility of a practitioner who does not have such a contract.[103]

## Temporary admission/release

12.89 As observed at para 12.33 above, power to detain exists in a number of circumstances, even where there is no question of pursuing a criminal investigation. With the power to detain, there is also a corresponding power to release. There is no obligation on an IO or the secretary of state to keep the person in detention in such cases. 'Temporary admission' is the phrase used in relation to those who have yet to be granted leave to enter, which includes illegal entrants. 'Temporary release' is the phrase used in respect of those who have previously been granted lawful leave to enter, but where that leave has since expired, or where a decision to deport is made. The fact that an individual is released from the police station and given temporary admission does not mean that the individual is being given leave to enter, nor does it mean that the individual is any more likely to be given leave in the future. It is merely a decision not to keep the person in detention at that time. An individual who makes an application to remain in the UK on some other basis while on temporary admission is not entitled to insist on the application being determined, and the individual would not be able to assert that any refusal of an application would give rise to a right of appeal. The exception to this is if the application to remain engages the Refugee Convention or the ECHR, in which case refusal will usually trigger an appeal.[104]

12.90 Conditions may be attached to the decision to grant temporary admission/release, such as a condition of residence, a condition requiring the person to report to an immigration reporting centre, or to the police, or a condition preventing the person from taking up employment, or from residing in a particular area.[105]

12.91 The instructions given to immigration service staff suggest that detention should be used sparingly and for the shortest period necessary.[106] According to those instructions, factors influencing a decision whether or not to detain include:

- the likelihood of the person being removed and the likely timescale of the removal;
- evidence of previous absconding;

---

102 SCC 2010 Immigration Specification 8.20.
103 SCC 2010 Immigration Specification 8.5, although there are limited exceptions for existing clients, or close relatives of existing clients.
104 Nationality, Immigration and Asylum Act 2002 s83(2).
105 IA 1971 Sch 2 para 21(2) and 21(2B).
106 Enforcement Instructions and Guidance Manual Chapter 55.1.3.

- evidence of any previous breach of conditions of temporary admission/ release;
- whether or not there has been an attempt to breach the immigration law;
- whether there is a history of previous non-compliance (such as overstaying);
- ties such as family members, and whether there is a permanent address;
- whether there is a realistic prospect of challenging the negative decision, eg, by an appeal;
- whether there is a history of the individual having undergone torture;
- whether there is a history of physical or mental ill health;
- whether the individual is believed by the immigration service to be under 18;
- whether there is a risk of offending or harm to the public.[107]

12.92    The lawyer should consider making representations both orally and in writing to seek to secure the client's immediate release after the conclusion of the interview. Any decision on whether to keep the person in detention will normally be taken by a more senior officer than the one conducting the interview, usually a chief immigration officer (CIO) or Higher Executive Officer (HEO) within the UKBA.[108] Detention must be regularly reviewed and for those held at police stations in excess of two nights, the guidance is explicit in stating that such detention must be authorised by an IO of at least the rank of inspector, or a senior executive officer at the Home Office.[109] However, were there to be a breach of the procedure for review or authorisation, where detention would otherwise have been authorised, the failure to adhere to the correct policy and procedure would not necessarily result in release and is likely to be remedied by no more than nominal damages.[110]

12.93    A CIO also has power to agree to grant temporary admission subject to satisfactory sureties.[111] For a client who has access to friends or family who are in a position to offer substantial sums (presently in the region of £2,000), such an approach may be a speedier alternative than waiting for a bail hearing to be fixed. If this is not possible or if, despite the availability of willing sureties, the CIO is not persuaded to release the client, then a bail application should be considered.

## Applications for bail

12.94    The First Tier Tribunal (Immigration and Asylum Chamber) has jurisdiction to grant bail to most people detained under Immigration Act powers.[112] For persons newly arrived in the UK held pending a decision

---

107  Enforcement Instructions and Guidance Manual chapter 55.3.1.
108  Enforcement Instructions and Guidance Manual chapter 55.5.
109  Enforcement Instructions and Guidance Manual chapter 55.13.2.
110  *Walumba Lumba v SSHD* [2011] UKSC 12.
111  IA 1971 Sch 2 para 22 (1A).
112  IA 1971 Sch 2 paras 22, 29 and 34.

on whether or not they should be given leave to enter, the opportunity to apply for bail arises only after they have been in the UK for seven days.[113]

12.95 Unlike those appearing before criminal courts, there is no statutory presumption in favour of bail, and the Bail Act 1976 criteria do not apply. The relevant criteria in deciding whether to grant or refuse bail will be: the reasons why the individual is detained; the length of past detention and the likely length of future detention; and the likelihood of the individual complying with bail.[114]

12.96 The obligation is on the individual, or the individual's representative, to request a bail hearing and while there is no requirement on the immigration authorities for the detainee to be brought before a court to have the individual's detention reviewed, there is an obligation on the immigration service to ensure that regular reviews are carried out,[115] but in theory there is no upper limit to the length of time for which an individual can be detained.[116]

12.97 In order to initiate an application for bail, it is necessary for the detainee or the detainee's representative to lodge with the FTT a notice for bail on the prescribed form.[117] This can be sent by fax and should be sent to the appropriate hearing centre. This is not necessarily the closest to where the detainee is being held, and often the only way of establishing the relevant centre is to contact the enquiry unit on 0300 123 1711. The FTT is then required to forward details of the application to the secretary of state and to fix a bail hearing date.[118] In theory a bail hearing will be fixed within three working days from the date on which the FTT receives the application form, although in practice this target date is regularly not met.[119] The notices of hearing are generally sent from the tribunal by fax. The secretary of state is required to file reasons for objecting to bail and serve the same on the detainee or their representative no later than 2pm (14.00 hours) on the working day prior to the bail hearing.[120]

12.98 If bail is granted, an immigration judge may impose conditions such as requirements of residence, electronic tagging, reporting and sureties. If bail is refused, there is nothing to prevent a further application being made, although unless there has been a significant development in the case, or a period of time has elapsed (especially if action ought to have been taken by the immigration authorities to progress the individual's case), the prospects of securing bail at a second or subsequent bail hearing are limited. Bail guidance for immigration judges is issued from time

---

113 IA 1971 Sch 2 para 22(1B).
114 Bail Guidance for Immigration Judges para 4, see below 12.98.
115 Enforcement Instructions and Guidance Manual chapter 55.8.
116 Save for the limited possibility of applying for habeas corpus or judicial review if the detention can be said to be truly excessive or no longer justifiable where there is no realistic prospect of removal.
117 Form B1 as required by Asylum and Immigration Tribunal (Procedure) Rules 2005 SI No 230 r38(1).
118 Asylum and Immigration Tribunal (Procedure) Rules 2005 r39(1).
119 In material produced by the tribunal for the period April to December 2010, the three-day deadline was met in 50.4 per cent of cases, an improvement over the 45.3 per cent figure for the previous year.
120 Asylum and Immigration Tribunal (Procedure) Rules 2005 r39(2)(a).

to time, and most recently by the president of the FTT Immigration and Asylum Chamber (IAC) in July 2011.[121]

## Further action

12.99   The lawyer who advised at the police station should try to refer the case to an immigration specialist adviser. Urgent steps to be taken may include contacting family members, making representations about issues not dealt with in the interview or about factors that should lead to the client being served with a one stop notice, or advising on the (tight) time limits and the opportunities for bail. Where the case cannot be referred on, the lawyer may want to consider which if any of those steps can be undertaken by them. As observed above, in practice there is difficulty in identifying firms that are willing to undertake such cases, particularly given the restrictions on public funding. Two national organisations – Refugee Migrant Justice (RMJ) (formerly the Refugee Legal Centre) and the Immigration Advisory Service (IAS) – both went into administration[122] and as a consequence this places further pressure on the capacity of other firms and organisations able to provide this advice, even before the anticipated changes to scope under legal aid (see para 12.57 above).

12.100   It may also be important to try to track down the client's whereabouts if the client is no longer at the police station. Custody officers may assume that if the detainee is transferred out of the police station by the immigration service, the individual has been removed from the UK. This may be incorrect given the limits on the length of time that individuals can be detained at a police station and the requirements relating to the seniority of officers who can authorise continued detention.[123]

12.101   Any person aged 17 or over who is not a British citizen may be recommended for deportation by a criminal court as part of a sentence imposed if the offence for which the person is convicted carries a term of imprisonment, irrespective of whether a custodial sentence is actually imposed.[124] The power arises in relation to any offence and is not limited to cases with an immigration element. Notice of the possibility of such a recommendation must be served at least seven days before the date on which the sentence is imposed. This is usually done at the police station. If the notice has not been served and the court is considering imposing a recommendation, then it may adjourn the criminal proceedings for the appropriate notice to be served.[125]

12.102   Given that the automatic deportation provisions apply to persons aged 18 or over as at the date of conviction, it is increasingly less relevant whether or not a recommendation is made in terms of whether removal will follow a conviction where the sentence imposed is 12 months or more.[126]

---

121   See www.justice.gov.uk/downloads/guidance/courts-and-tribunals/tribunals/immigration-and-asylum/lower/bail-guidance-immigration-judges.pdf.

122   RMJ June 2010, IAS July 2011.

123   Enforcement Instructions and Guidance chapter 55.8; and see para 12.92 above.

124   IA 1971 s3(6).

125   IA 1971 s6(2).

126   UK Borders Act 2007 s32(5).

# Legal aid

12.103  Where advice is being given to a person arrested in respect of an offence, whether an immigration offence or otherwise, the SCC 2010 will apply as normal. Failure by a duty solicitor to accept such a case referred while on rota could lead to suspension or removal from the scheme.[127]

12.104  Where the detainee is not subject to any ongoing investigation of a criminal charge, the position is less clear. Under the SCC 2010, it is unlikely that significant work would be permitted in an immigration matter given the requirement to be accredited under the Immigration and Asylum Accreditation scheme, although the definition of immigration offence for the purposes of the SCC is widely defined.[128] There are certainly matters in respect of which advice will be required at the police station itself, if only to identify the range of options that may be open and the limitations of any potential remedies for a particular detainee.

12.105  As to any significant work beyond the police station, this is almost certainly now out of scope given the requirement to be accredited under the Immigration and Asylum Accreditation Scheme (IAAS).[129] Where it is not possible to refer a detainee on to an immigration adviser, arguably work done simply for the purposes of securing an appeal, or securing a bail hearing, should be remunerated, albeit that the criminal lawyer would not be entitled to remuneration for attendance at an immigration appeal or a bail hearing under the legal aid criminal or civil contracts. The LSC suggests in response to an enquiry by the author that, once a case has been transferred to the immigration authorities, the lawyer should refer the matter back to the DSCC subject to limited exceptions.[130]

12.106  For lawyers working in firms that also hold an immigration contract, public funding is available for the conduct of the initial appeal and any application for bail, subject to meeting a means and merits test under controlled legal representation (CLR). Where the legally aided party resists a subsequent appeal brought by the secretary of state, CLR will continue to apply. For cases in which the legally aided party has requested permission to appeal the original decision, funding is subject to the retrospective costs regime.[131]

12.107  Funding for work done on progressing an immigration application is available under Legal Help, again subject to means and merits and in most cases under the fixed fee scheme.[132] Where appropriate, such suppliers are also able to undertake applications for judicial review or habeas corpus under emergency civil legal aid certificates, in some cases by exercising devolved powers. All of the current provisions as to the availability of funding will need to be considered in the light of any changes made to the scope of work remaining within the legal aid provisions (see para 12.57 above).

---

127  Duty Solicitor Arrangements 2008 para 5.4.
128  SCC Specification Part A para 1.13.
129  SCC Specification 8.11.
130  SCC Specification Part B paras 9.63–9.69.
131  SCC Specification 8.99.
132  SCC Specification 8.63.

## The role of the embassy

12.108   Citizens of independent Commonwealth countries or nationals of any foreign country held in a police station have the right to contact their High Commission, embassy or consulate.[133] Many clients are unwilling to contact their own national authorities, fearing potential reprisals. There has also been a tendency on the part of some consular officials to advise their own nationals to leave the country without exercising any potential remedies that may be open to them. If contact with consular staff has been made, and advice given, the lawyer ought to check whether the advice was appropriate, having regard to the individual circumstances of the detainee. The lawyer can check with the custody officer as to whether any such contact has been made, since it should have been recorded.[134]

12.109   For nationals of certain countries listed in PACE Code C Annex F, bilateral conventions or agreements exist whereby notification of arrest and detention of a national will automatically be given to the relevant consular official,[135] except in cases where the individual held is a refugee or an asylum-seeker, in which case contact should only be made with the specific consent of the detainee.[136] Although Code C does not refer to persons claiming that their removal would be a breach of their human rights, it would be prudent to ask the police not to make contact with consular officials in such cases.

## Brief synopsis

12.110   • Wide powers of arrest and detention for both immigration and non-immigration offences.
   • Detention at a police station where authorised by an IO will largely mirror PACE requirements.
   • Interviews by IOs may be a mixture of those under caution, caution +2 and non-caution.
   • Care will be needed to determine whether an individual can or cannot pursue an appeal, and whether such an appeal can be pursued from within the UK.
   • Advice will need to be given that while bail can be sought, it may not be granted and there are limitations on what the police station adviser can do beyond advising at the police station itself.
   • Legal aid restrictions currently prevent representation either at bail or at an appeal unless the police station adviser is accredited under the IAAS. Further legislative proposals envisage the removal of advice for work relating to matters beyond the detention issue as to the substance of any appeal.

133  Code C para 7.1, and see Enforcement Instructions and Guidance manual para 55.18.
134  Code C para 7.5.
135  Code C para 7.2.
136  Code C para 7.4.

- Asylum and protection based human rights claims, applications to remain on the basis of family life, European Community law rights will in general enable an appeal to be brought prior to removal. In cases raising no such issue, an appeal is less likely to be available.
- Even where asylum or human right claims are pursued, power exists to prevent appeal rights from being pursued prior to removal.

---

**Checklist 15: Questions to ask an immigration detainee**

1. Full name including any aliases previously used.
2. Date of birth.
3. Nationality; and if different, country of birth.
4. Current address (other than detention), and addresses for last six months.
5. Contact details of relative or friend.
6. Date and place of most recent travel.
7. Whether travelling on own passport on arrival.
8. Were any questions asked at airport by immigration; and if so, details.
9. Were any answers given then inaccurate; and if so, details.
10. If the client had to apply for entry clearance, were answers given then inaccurate; and if so, details.
11. Has the client instructed previous lawyer or adviser; and if so, how recently?
12. If so, why does the client not wish to continue with previous adviser?
13. Has the client been served with any papers?
14. Does the client need interpreter; if so, what language and dialect?

*In-country clients with leave:*
15. If the client was given lawful leave, when does it/did it expire?
16. If the client made application for extension, what was the date submitted and does client have proof of sending?
17. Does the client have a UKBA reference number (usually letter of alphabet for surname followed by 6–7 digits)?
18. If not retained by immigration service, what is the whereabouts of the client's passport?

*If entered illegally or in breach of landing conditions:*
19. What are the client's present family circumstances, including long-term relationships?
20. Where relevant, what is the immigration status of family members?
21. If any children were born in the UK, what was the immigration status of the other parent at the time of birth?
22. Are immigration authorities aware of family circumstances; and if so, when were they told about them?
23. How has the client been supporting herself or himself to date?
24. If the client is returned, what does the client think will happen:
    a. to the family group in the UK?
    b. to the client themselves?
25. If the client expresses anxiety about what will happen to him or her, what evidence is there to justify the anxiety?

26. If the client has overstayed for less than 28 days, or if the client is in breach of the client's landing conditions, is it sensible to consider seeking to leave as soon as possible?
27. Is it likely that if removed the client would wish to return to the UK lawfully in the future?

*If an appeal right given exercisable prior to removal:*
28. Has the client already lodged an appeal notice?
29. Does the client have community ties other than as identified above?
30. Does the client have any physical or mental health issues?
31. Does the client have friends willing and able to stand surety?
32. If so, what is their immigration status?
33. If not already doing so before detention, could the client reside with surety?
34. Has the client ever failed to attend any court in the UK previously?

*If no present appeal right is available, but answers to 22–25 above indicate there may be asylum/human rights issues:*
35. Why were family details not disclosed to immigration authorities earlier?
36. If fear of serious ill harm/persecution on return exists, why was an application to the UKBA not made earlier?
37. What evidence can be gathered to support either asylum/human rights element, as it will be needed urgently?

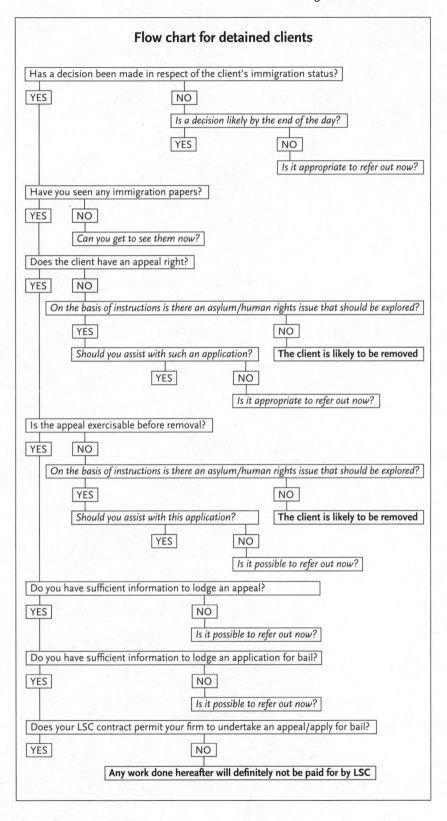

# Flow chart for detained clients

Has a decision been made in respect of the client's immigration status?

YES     NO

*Is a decision likely by the end of the day?*

YES     NO

*Is it appropriate to refer out now?*

Have you seen any immigration papers?

YES     NO

*Can you get to see them now?*

Does the client have an appeal right?

YES     NO

*On the basis of instructions is there an asylum/human rights issue that should be explored?*

YES     NO

*Should you assist with such an application?*     **The client is likely to be removed**

YES     NO

*Is it appropriate to refer out now?*

Is the appeal exercisable before removal?

YES     NO

*On the basis of instructions is there an asylum/human rights issue that should be explored?*

YES     NO

*Should you assist with this application?*     **The client is likely to be removed**

YES     NO

*Is it possible to refer out now?*

Do you have sufficient information to lodge an appeal?

YES     NO

*Is it possible to refer out now?*

Do you have sufficient information to lodge an application for bail?

YES     NO

*Is it possible to refer out now?*

Does your LSC contract permit your firm to undertake an appeal/apply for bail?

YES     NO

**Any work done hereafter will definitely not be paid for by LSC**

# CHAPTER 13

# Complaints and enforcement

## Introduction

13.1    One of the more difficult problems for the defence lawyer is how to deal effectively with police conduct that is illegal, unfair or improper. Clients may feel aggrieved about the way they have been dealt with and may complain of incivility at one end of the scale, or serious assault or dishonesty at the other. Lawyers themselves may witness behaviour that is unacceptable, or may believe that the police are ignoring or misunderstanding legal or other provisions. One of the weaknesses of the Police and Criminal Evidence Act 1984 (PACE) and the Terrorism Act (TA) 2000 is that they provide no mechanisms for enforcement that are effective at the time that the problem is encountered. Those remedies that do exist, primarily formal complaint, civil action, abuse of process and exclusion of evidence, come into effect only after the event, by which time the damage is likely to have been done. Judicial review of police and prosecution decisions may be available, but the Divisional Court is generally reluctant to intervene in respect of decisions made at the early stages of the criminal process.

13.2         For this reason, the lawyer will often have to rely on his or her skills of persuasion and negotiation.[1] This is frequently not easy, since the lawyer is on police territory, with their permission, and in a situation where the police can ultimately use their proprietorial or law enforcement powers to remove a lawyer who is proving to be a nuisance. An argument with a police officer may quickly result in the lawyer being surrounded by other officers who, whatever their motives, may appear very intimidating. In this context, the lawyer must exploit what few aids to enforcement there are. In particular, it will often be appropriate to ask the custody officer to make a note in the custody record. This may at least show them that the lawyer is taking the matter seriously. There is, however, no right to insist on an entry being made. In the event of a refusal, the lawyer should make a note of the cause for complaint, and the fact of refusal to enter it on the custody record, and sign and date it. The lawyer should also consider asking the custody officer to place a copy with the custody record, although with computerised systems this may not be possible.

13.3         The other action the lawyer can take at the police station is to refer the matter to an officer of higher rank. There is no specific provision for this in PACE, TA 2000 or the Codes, but in practice an inspector is likely to be on duty, and there will always be an officer in charge of the station, usually at the level of superintendent. An officer of higher rank may be more amenable to arguments based on statutory provisions or the Codes, or other legal authority, and the lawyer should, if possible, prepare such arguments carefully. Given the natural propensity for senior officers to support their staff, the lawyer should endeavour to prepare an argument so constructed that the senior officer would not, by agreeing with the lawyer, be seen to be critical of their junior officer.

---

1   E Shepherd, *Police station skills for legal advisers: practical reference and accreditation manual* (Law Society, London, 2004), deals extensively with the skills of negotiation and assertion, and also the skills of interviewing and advising. See also R Ede and E Shepherd, *Active defence* (Law Society, London, 2000).

13.4     However, it will often not be possible for matters of concern to the lawyer to be dealt with on the spot in this way. The matter may be one where
there is a conflict over the facts, and in this situation a senior officer is
highly unlikely to decide in favour of the suspect and the lawyer. It may be
one that arose before the lawyer arrived at the police station, for example,
a complaint by the suspect that the suspect was assaulted at the time of
arrest or on the way to the station. The remainder of this chapter deals
with the some of the major enforcement mechanisms that take effect after
the event: formal complaint, civil and criminal action against the police,
abuse of process applications and exclusion of evidence. It begins with
brief consideration of the Human Rights Act (HRA) 1998, particularly as
it relates to the police station.[2]

## The Human Rights Act 1998

13.5    It is unlawful for a public authority, including the police and Crown Prosecution Service (CPS), to act in a way which is incompatible with a right
under the European Convention on Human Rights (ECHR) (HRA 1998
s6). Rights under the HRA 1998 are enforceable by taking proceedings in
an appropriate court or by relying on the right in any legal proceedings,
including criminal proceedings (HRA 1998 s7). An application may be
made to the European Court of Human Rights (ECtHR) only once all domestic remedies have been exhausted.

13.6    The most significant ECHR rights applicable to suspects at the police
station are:

- article 3 (*prohibition of torture, degrading and inhuman treatment*);
- article 5 (*right to liberty and security*);
- article 6 (*right to a fair trial*);
- article 8 (*right to respect for private and family life*); and
- article 10 (*freedom of expression*).

The HRA 1998 may enable a number of aspects of arrest, detention and
evidence-gathering to be challenged. In some cases, the effect of the Act is
to strengthen a claim for which there is an existing remedy; for example,
a claim for wrongful arrest on the grounds that the police officer did not
have reasonable suspicion that an offence had been committed. In other
cases, the effect will be to enable a challenge to be made to police conduct
that is apparently lawful, for example, delaying access to a lawyer under
PACE s58(8). The HRA 1998 may also be relevant to an application to stay
proceedings for an abuse of process or to exclude evidence under PACE
s76 or s78. Set out here is a brief survey of aspects of police investigation
that may be susceptible to challenge under the HRA 1998.

---

2   For fuller treatment of complaints and criminal and civil action against the police see
J Harrison, S Cragg and H Williams, *Police misconduct: legal remedies* (4th edn, LAG,
London, 2005).

## Arrest

13.7    ECHR article 5(1) prohibits deprivation of a person's liberty except, among other things, by means of a lawful arrest effected for the purpose of bringing the person before a competent legal authority on reasonable suspicion of having committed an offence or when it is reasonably considered necessary to prevent the person from committing an offence.[3] Most powers of arrest under PACE and other legislation require the officer to have reasonable grounds for suspicion, and although the domestic courts have set a low standard for the level of suspicion required, this has been held to be sufficient by the ECtHR.[4] PACE s24(1)(a), (b) and (3)(a) do not require reasonable suspicion (see para 2.14 above). This may not satisfy the requirements of article 5(1)(c), but the provisions do not appear to have been challenged by reference to the ECHR. The ECtHR has considered the power of arrest for breach of the peace, and held that the definition of breach of the peace is sufficiently certain to meet the requirements of article 5, but that arrest for breach of the peace may contravene article 5 if its effect is to deprive a person of his or her right of freedom of expression under article 10 and is disproportionate to the perceived risk.[5] PACE Code G takes article 5 into account by requiring that in exercising powers of arrest, officers must act in a proportionate manner, and should consider whether the: 'necessary objectives can be met by other, less intrusive means'.

13.8    ECHR article 5(2) provides that the person arrested must be: 'informed promptly, in a language which he understands, of the reasons for his arrest and any charge against him'. This is broadly reflected by PACE s28(1) (see para 2.41 above), although section 28(1) requires the information to be given as soon as is practicable after the arrest which, in a particular case, may not be the same as 'promptly'.[6] Difficulties may arise if the person arrested does not understand English. Article 5(2) requires the information to be given in a language the arrested person understands, whereas PACE s28(1) makes no reference to the language in which the information must be given. With regard to what information must be given, a simple reference to the statutory provision under which a person is arrested will generally not be sufficient.[7] Rather, the person must be informed of the facts which form the foundation of the decision to arrest.[8]

---

3   'Reasonable suspicion' means the existence of facts or information that would satisfy an objective observer that the person concerned may have committed the offence (*Fox, Campbell and Hartley v UK* (1991) 13 EHRR 157).

4   *O'Hara v UK* (2002) 34 EHRR 32; [2002] Crim LR 493.

5   *Steel v UK* (1999) 28 EHRR 603; [1998] Crim LR 893. See also *McLeod v UK* (1999) 27 EHRR 493, which considered breach of the peace in relation to ECHR article 8. Note that the ECtHR takes its own, 'autonomous', view of what amounts to criminal proceedings, and proceedings for breach of the peace were deemed to be criminal even though they are not criminal proceedings under domestic law.

6   Although in *Fox, Campbell and Hartley v UK* (1991) 13 EHRR 157 the ECtHR held that determining the content and promptness of the information conveyed regard must be had to the particular facts of the case.

7   *Fox, Campbell and Hartley v UK* (1991) 13 EHRR 157.

8   *X v Germany* (1978) 16 DR 111.

## Detention following arrest

13.9    ECHR article 5(3) provides that a person arrested or detained in criminal proceedings must be brought promptly before a judge or other judicial officer, and is entitled to trial within a reasonable time or release (which may be subject to conditions) pending trial. It was held in *Michalko v Slovakia*[9] that article 5(3) is concerned with two separate stages – the early stage following arrest, and the period pending eventual trial before a criminal court. In relation to the first, the presumption must be in favour of release, and when deciding whether a person should be released or detained the authorities are obliged to consider alternative measures of ensuring the defendant's appearance at court. Under PACE, a person who has been arrested but not charged must be brought before a court within 36 hours (see para 2.66). A person detained without charge under TA 2000 Sch 8 must be produced before a judicial authority within 48 hours (see para 2.78 above). The ECtHR has not laid down a precise definition of 'promptly', but in *Brogan v UK*[10] the court found that a delay of four days and six hours did not satisfy the requirement. Generally, the provisions under PACE and the TA 2000 regarding the maximum period of detention without charge satisfy article 5(3). However, this may not be the case where a person is released on bail without charge, especially if bail is subject to onerous conditions.[11] The restriction on the grant of bail after charge under Criminal Justice and Public Order Act (CJPOA) 1994 s25[12] is probably in compliance (see para 10.101 above). The inability of a custody officer to grant bail to a person charged with murder may not be, although provided bail is considered by a court within a reasonable time following charge, this will probably be sufficient.[13]

## Access to a lawyer

13.10   ECHR article 6(3)(c) provides that everyone charged with a criminal offence has a right to legal assistance. In *Murray v UK*[14] the ECtHR held that where the attitude of the accused during police questioning can have consequences at trial, article 6 will usually require that the accused is allowed access to a lawyer at that stage. This resulted in the amendment of CJPOA 1994 ss34, 36 and 37 so that inferences from 'silence' cannot be drawn where a person in police detention asks for, but is not allowed to consult, a solicitor before being interviewed (see para 5.66 above). Since

---

9   (1988) 11 EHRR 117.

10   ECtHR 21 December 2010 No 35377/05.

11   For an analysis of whether police bail without charge may breach rights under articles 5, 8 or 10 see E Cape and R Edwards, (2010) 'Police bail without charge: the human rights implications', *Cambridge Law Journal* 69(3), 423–465.

12   Which was amended following an adverse decision in *Caballero v UK* [1999] Crim LR 228.

13   By Coroners and Justice Act 2009 s115, only a Crown Court judge can grant bail to a person charged with murder. There are provisions governing the maximum period within which the decision must be made (section 115(3)).

14   (1996) 22 EHRR 29. See also *Averill v UK* (2001) 31 EHRR 36; [2000] Crim LR 682, and *Magee v UK* (2001) 31 EHRR 35; [2000] Crim LR 681.

*Murray,* the right to legal assistance at the police station has been developed in a large number of ECtHR decisions following *Salduz v Turkey.*[15] Essentially, a suspect arrested and detained by the police has a right to legal assistance and, although this is not absolute, it can only be interfered with if it is demonstrated in the light of the particular circumstances of the case that there are compelling reasons to restrict access. Even if there are such reasons, the use of evidence obtained in circumstances where access to legal assistance has been denied may breach the right to fair trial under article 6(1). Therefore, delaying access to a lawyer under PACE s58(8) and TA 2000 Sch 8 (see paras 2.139 and 2.145 above) may, depending on the circumstances, contravene article 6 rights, as may the use of evidence obtained in an interview conducted in circumstances where access to a lawyer has not been permitted or where an interview is held in the absence of lawyer with a suspect who wants legal advice (see para 2.127 above).[16]

13.11    The ECtHR has held that while the right to legal assistance can be waived, any waiver must not only be voluntary, but: 'must also constitute a knowing and intelligent relinquishment ... it must be shown that [the suspect] could reasonably have foreseen what the consequences of his conduct would be'.[17] Code C requires a custody officer to ask a suspect who declines legal advice why the suspect has refused, but does not require the officer to explain to the suspect the consequences of waiving their right (see para 2.123 above). Arguably, this does not go far enough to satisfy the 'knowing and intelligent relinquishment' requirement, although this will depend upon the particular circumstances.

13.12    In *S v Switzerland,*[18] the right to private consultation with a lawyer was described by the ECtHR as: 'one of the basic requirements of a fair trial in a democratic society'. In *Brennan v UK,*[19] the ECtHR held that although the right to private consultation could be restricted for good cause, in the absence of good cause it would amount to breach of article 6 without the need to demonstrate an actual adverse effect. Interference with the right to private consultation may also amount to a breach of the right to private life under article 8.[20] Under PACE and the TA 2000 a suspect has the right to consult a solicitor *in private,* but this is subject to certain legal limitations and, where legal advice is provided by telephone, certain practical limitations (see paras 2.133–2.136 above).

## The 'right to silence'

13.13    See the references to ECtHR case-law in paras 5.60–5.66 above.

15  ECtHR 27 November 2008 No 36391/02.
16  *Sebalj v Croatia* ECtHR 28 June 2011 No 4429/09.
17  *Pishchalnikov v Russia* ECtHR 24 September 2009 No 7025/04, para 101. See also *Plonka v Poland* ECtHR 31 March 2009 No 20310/02.
18  (1992) 14 EHRR 670, and see the critical commentary at [2002] Crim LR 215.
19  (2002) 34 EHRR 18; [2002] Crim LR 216.
20  *Heino v Finland* ECtHR 15 February 2011 No 56720/09.

## Ill-treatment in police custody

13.14    ECHR article 3 provides that no one shall be subjected to torture or to inhuman or degrading treatment or punishment. Code C para 11.5 and Code H para 11.6 provide that no interviewer may try to obtain answers or elicit a statement by the use of oppression, and Code C, Code H section 8 sets out the minimum requirements regarding the conditions of detention. Therefore, provided that the police comply with these provisions, there should be no question of breach of article 3. The ECtHR has held that to admit evidence obtained in breach of article 3 would amount to a breach of article 6,[21] and this is reflected in PACE s76(2) (see para 13.34 below). It should be noted that it is well-established by ECtHR jurisprudence that where a person is taken into police custody in good condition, but is found to be injured on release, the onus is on the state to provide a plausible explanation as to how the injuries were caused.[22]

## Complaints against the police

13.15    The scheme for dealing with complaints against the police is governed by Police Reform Act (PRA) 2002 Part II and Sch 13.[23] Under the PRA 2002 a complaint is one that is made about the conduct of a person serving with the police (PRA 2002 s12(1)). This includes members of a police force, civilian employees who are under the direction and control of a chief officer[24] and special constables (PRA 2002 s12(7)). The scheme does not cover complaints about the direction or control of a police force (PRA 2002 s14). The scheme covers complaints by:

- members of the public who claim to be the person in relation to whom the conduct took place;
- members of the public who claim to have been adversely affected by the conduct;
- members of the public who claim to have witnessed the conduct; and
- persons acting on behalf of any of the above (PRA 2002 s12(1)).

In most cases, the actions of individual officers in relation to a particular suspect will be susceptible to complaint. Indeed, complaint may be the only action available to the suspect where the behaviour complained of does not amount to a criminal or civil wrong, and the suspect is not prosecuted or is prosecuted and pleads guilty. Breach of PACE or the Codes of Practice does not, in itself, render the officer concerned liable to criminal or civil action (PACE s67(10)), although such breaches are admissible in any such proceedings. Although disciplinary action may be taken against an officer for breach of PACE or the Codes of Practice, neither a lawyer nor a member of the public can initiate such action.

21  *Austria v Italy* (1963) 6 YB 740.
22  See, eg, *Aksoy v Turkey* (1996) 23 EHRR 553 and *Selmouni v France* (2000) 29 EHRR 403.
23  For a full explanation of the complaints procedure see J Harrison, S Cragg and H Williams, *Police misconduct: legal remedies* (note 2 above) ch 4.
24  This includes designated civilian officers. See para 2.50 above.

## Whose complaint is it?

13.16   If a complaint is to be considered, the initial decision to be made is whether the complaint should come from the lawyer or from the client. A lawyer can make a complaint on behalf of the client, or make a complaint on his or her own account if the conduct directly related to the lawyer or if the lawyer witnessed the conduct or was adversely affected by it. If the lawyer makes a complaint on his or her own behalf, this may deflect unwelcome pressure from the client. However, it would normally be advisable for the lawyer to complain personally only where the behaviour directly concerns the lawyer, as where the officer conducting an interview improperly seeks to undermine the lawyer by questioning the lawyer about his or her qualifications. Otherwise, if the lawyer does make a complaint, it should generally be made on behalf of the client.

## How to complain

13.17   A complaint may be made orally or in writing, although it is always advisable for it to be made in writing or, if made orally, to be confirmed in writing (see specimen letter 5, appendix 5). It may be made to the Independent Police Complaints Commission (IPCC), to the relevant police authority, or to the chief officer of police (PRA 2002 Sch 3 para 2). A complaint does not have to be given to any particular officer, but if made at the police station it should normally be presented to the custody officer (unless the custody officer is the subject of the complaint, in which case it would be better to present it to a more senior officer). It should be addressed to the chief officer of police for the relevant police area.

13.18      Where a complaint is made while the client is still at the police station, the lawyer should, in particular, consider:

1) Including a request that any interview of the complainant, whether while the complainant is detained or subsequently, should only take place after having given due notice to the lawyer and in the lawyer's presence.

2) Whether the suspect should decline to be interviewed about the complaint while still detained at the police station. The police sometimes imply that if a complaint is to be pursued, the complainant must be interviewed about it while still detained. This is not so. Code C para 9.2 and Code H para 9.3 do provide that where a detained person makes a complaint, a report must be made to an inspector or above who is not connected with the investigation, but there is no requirement for immediate investigation either in Code C or PACE. Normally, particularly if a civil action against the police might be considered (see para 13.24 below), the suspect should be advised to decline to be interviewed about the complaint at the police station. The major exception to this would be where a complaint has been made for tactical purposes, and there is good reason to believe that the matter might be resolved with the intervention of a senior officer.

3) If the client complains of physical injury having been caused, whether a doctor should be called. Code C para 9.2 provides that where a complaint concerns a possible assault or the possibility of the unnecessary

or unreasonable use of force, an appropriate healthcare professional must be called as soon as practicable. However, if the police call in a healthcare professional, the client should be advised not to discuss the circumstances of the injury with him or her, and the lawyer or client should arrange for an examination by an independent doctor as soon as possible.[25] The complainant is under no obligation to see a police healthcare professional if one is called. Where an independent doctor is called in to examine the client at the police station, the doctor's fee may be claimed as a disbursement under the Standard Criminal Contract (SCC) 2010 provided that it is incurred in the best interests of the client and is reasonably incurred.[26] In more minor cases, it may be more practical, where the suspect is likely to be released relatively soon, for the suspect to be advised to see his or her own doctor as soon as possible after release.

## How a complaint should be dealt with by the police

13.19   As noted above, if a complaint about the police is made by or on behalf of a detained person about the person's treatment since arrest, a report must be made to an inspector or above as soon as practicable. It is suggested that this should also apply where the complaint is about treatment immediately before, or on, arrest. The police are also under a duty to take any steps that appear desirable for the purpose of obtaining or preserving evidence relating to the conduct complained of (PRA 2002 Sch 3 para 1). On receiving the complaint, the police must determine whether they are the appropriate authority and, if not, must notify the complainant (PRA 2002 Sch 3 para 2). If the police decide not to take action under PRA 2002 Sch 3 para 2, they must notify the complainant, who can then appeal to the IPCC. Thereafter, what happens will depend in part on whether or not the complaint is considered suitable for local resolution. A complaint is suitable for local resolution if the appropriate authority is satisfied that the conduct complained of would not, if proved, justify the bringing of any criminal or disciplinary proceedings, or the IPCC approves the use of local resolution (PRA 2002 Sch 3 para 3). If it is suitable for local resolution, the police must seek to resolve it in this way by asking the complainant if he or she is willing to accept local resolution (PRA 2002 Sch 3 para 6(2)). It will be appropriate for some complaints to be dealt with by local resolution, particularly if the behaviour complained of is not very serious. The PRA 2002 provides for the secretary of state to issue regulations setting out the procedures to be followed when a complaint is to be dealt with by local resolution (PRA 2002 Sch 3 para 8(2)). However, the regulations that have been issued merely refer to procedures approved by the IPCC.[27] The complainant has a right of appeal to the IPCC in respect of the conduct of

---

25  J Harrison, S Cragg and H Williams, *Police misconduct: legal remedies* (note 2 above) p77.

26  SCC 2010 Part B, para 5.39.

27  See Police (Complaints and Misconduct) Regulations 2004 SI No 643. Further information can be obtained from the IPCC website at www.ipcc.gov.uk/en/Pages/complaints.aspx.

a local resolution (PRA 2002 Sch 3 para 9). Clients should be warned that they may be approached by an officer following their release who may try to persuade them to deal with the complaint in this way. The lawyer should consider advising the client not to speak to the police about the complaint except in the lawyer's presence. At any such interview, the police station legal advice scheme will not apply, although the client may be eligible for assistance under free-standing advice and assistance if the client satisfies the financial eligibility criteria.

13.20　If the police decide that they do not have to, or do not need to, refer the complaint to the IPCC under PRA 2002 Sch 3 para 2, and that the complaint is not suitable for local resolution, or the complainant is not willing to accept this, the chief officer must appoint an officer from his or her own, or another, force to investigate the complaint (PRA 2002 Sch 3 para 16). This officer will want to interview the complainant, although this is unlikely to be until some time after the complainant has been released from police custody. As indicated above, the complainant should agree to be interviewed by the officer only in the presence of the lawyer. The complainant should, in particular, be advised to be wary of any attempt to dissuade the complainant from proceeding with the complaint.[28] Certain more serious complaints must be referred to the IPCC and the IPCC has discretionary power to require that any other complaint is referred to them (PRA 2002 Sch 3 para 4). In such cases, the IPCC will determine the form that the investigation is to take (having regard to the seriousness of the case and the public interest), which may be an investigation by the police, an investigation conducted by the IPCC itself, or an investigation by the police under the supervision or management of the IPCC (PRA 2002 Sch 3 Part III).

## Whether to make a complaint

13.21　The question remains whether the suspect should make a complaint against the police while the suspect is still in police detention. This entails considering whether a complaint is appropriate at all and, if it is, whether it should be made before leaving custody or subsequently. In advising a client, the following factors may indicate that making a complaint would be appropriate:

1) A complaint may be the only form of action open to the client if the police behaviour concerned is unlikely to give rise to criminal or civil liability, taking into account the problems of proving that the behaviour did occur.

2) Making a formal complaint may help the client feel better, and may help the client feel that something is being done about the conduct that has caused the problem. Against this, however, must be set the possible adverse consequences (see para 13.22 below), and the fact that only a small percentage of complaints are upheld.

---

28　Under the previous complaints system, about 40 per cent of complaints were withdrawn, and there was evidence that while some withdrawals were justified, others resulted from improper pressure from the police. See, eg, M Maguire and C Corbett, *A study of the police complaints system* (HMSO, London, 1991), ch 7.

3) Where the behaviour concerned may be relevant at trial, a failure to complain at the earliest opportunity may have an adverse impact. For example, if the client maintains at trial that the reason for confessing shortly after the arrest was because of an assault by the arresting officers, the prosecutor, on any application to have the confession excluded, is likely to suggest that a failure to complain at the time is evidence of fabrication.

4) As noted earlier, where a complaint is received, steps must be taken to obtain or preserve evidence. This may be important where there is potential evidence that may disappear or deteriorate over time. For example, if the complainant alleges assault by an unidentified officer, identification procedures undertaken at an early stage may be important.

13.22 There are, however, a number of factors that may weigh against making a complaint while the suspect is in police custody:

1) While in police custody the client is particularly vulnerable. First, especially in the case of more serious complaints or where feelings are 'running high', the suspect is at risk of police pressure such as prolonging detention, delays in responding to calls from the cell, insults, threats or even assault. Second, in certain circumstances, it may make the likelihood of prosecution greater. For example, if the suspect complains of assault by the police at the time of arrest, the police may take pre-emptive action by bringing a charge of assault on police against the suspect. In this way, any injuries to the suspect can be explained by the need for restraint.

2) If the conduct concerned may give rise to a civil action against the police, for example, in respect of an assault by the police, a complaint can have an adverse effect on the civil proceedings, although this danger is now limited. It was formerly the case that the police had access to statements and documents arising from the investigation of a complaint in preparing their defence to civil proceedings, but that access was denied to the plaintiff on the grounds that the documents were covered by public interest immunity. However, in *R v Chief Constable of West Midlands Police ex p Wiley*,[29] it was held that public interest immunity does not apply to such documents as a class, although it might in particular circumstances. The result is that police officers can still have access to the documents in preparing their defence in civil proceedings, but that the claimant is also normally entitled to access to them.[30] The complaints regime under the PRA 2002 imposes a number of disclosure requirements on both the IPCC and the police.

3) A complaint may alert the police to the defence the client will use at the trial of the criminal case against the client. In many cases, this will be obvious anyway but the danger can be limited by giving only brief details of the behaviour complained of while at the police station.

---

29 [1994] 3 WLR 433; [1994] 3 All ER 420.
30 See further J Harrison, S Cragg and H Williams, *Police misconduct: legal remedies* (note 2 above) chs 4 and 12.

4) Even if a complaint is upheld, there is no provision for financial compensation to be paid to the complainant, although occasionally ex gratia payments are made.

## Criminal prosecution of the police

13.23   Police officers are, in principle, subject to the criminal law in the same way as anyone else. However, in practice, a suspect would face considerable difficulty in trying to initiate criminal proceedings against a police officer, either himself or herself or by reporting the matter to the police. In the case of a private prosecution, no legal aid is available to the complainant other than under free-standing legal advice and assistance. For these reasons, the prospect of a criminal prosecution of a police officer is of limited relevance to the lawyer advising at the police station. As noted above, breach of PACE or the Codes of Practice does not of itself give rise to criminal liability (PACE s67(10)).[31]

## Civil actions against the police

13.24   Although breach of PACE or the Codes of Practice does not of itself give rise to civil liability (PACE s67(10)), a breach may be relevant in determining whether the police are liable in civil proceedings. The Codes are admissible in any civil proceedings and, if relevant, are to be taken into account by the court (PACE s67(11)).[32]

13.25   Note, in particular, potential claims for the following:

1) *False imprisonment* is form of trespass to the person involving the complete deprivation of liberty without lawful excuse. False imprisonment could result, for example, from an unlawful arrest, unlawful stop and search or drug search, detention contrary to PACE s37, improper authorisation of continued detention at the 24-hour stage, or improper detention beyond a relevant time limit.[33]

2) *Trespass to the person* consists of an assault or battery. It could result from an unlawful search or detention, or where unreasonable force is used.[34]

---

31  See further J Harrison, S Cragg and H Williams, *Police misconduct: legal remedies* (note 2 above) ch 5.

32  See generally J Harrison, S Cragg and H Williams, *Police misconduct: legal remedies* (note 2 above) chs 6–10.

33  See, eg, *Roberts v Chief Constable of the Cheshire Police* [1999] 2 All ER 326, in which it was held that a suspect was unlawfully detained where a review was not conducted at the relevant time.

34  See, eg, *Chief Constable of Thames Valley Police v Hepburn* [2002] EWCA Civ 1841; (2002) *Times* 19 December, where a person was unlawfully detained following the execution of a search warrant that did not include a power to search persons. Note that there are certain restrictions on claims for trespass to the person where the claimant was convicted of an imprisonable offence on the same occasion as that on which the act is alleged to have been done (Criminal Justice Act 2003 s329); and see *Adorian v CPM* [2010] EWHC 3861 (QB).

3) *Trespass to land* is an unjustified direct physical intrusion onto land in possession of another. It could result from an unlawful search or entry on to property to effect an arrest, etc.

4) *Malicious prosecution* requires proof that:
   - there has been a prosecution which has caused them damage;
   - the prosecution was instituted or continued by the police;
   - the prosecution terminated in favour of the plaintiff;
   - the prosecuting police officer acted without reasonable and probable cause;
   - the prosecuting police officer acted maliciously.

5) *Negligence or breach of statutory duty* Negligence involves a breach of a duty of care owed to another and could result, for example, from a failure to take adequate care of a vulnerable suspect, or causing injury or damage in conducting a search of a person or property or carrying out an arrest. Breach of statutory duty does not simply consist of breach of a statutory provision, but involves the idea that parliament intended a piece of legislation to confer a cause of action on members of a protected class.[35]

13.26 Civil action against the police has a number of advantages over making a complaint or criminal proceedings. Full legal aid may be available, and a successful action may result in financial damages, sometimes quite substantial, being paid to the applicant. Guidance on quantum was set out in *Thompson v Commissioner of Police of the Metropolis*.[36] The standard of proof is 'on a balance of probabilities', so that success is more likely than in criminal proceedings, which require the case to be proved beyond reasonable doubt.

13.27 As noted above, the lawyer should always consider the possibility of civil proceedings, including judicial review,[37] when advising a client whether to make a complaint against the police, although civil action is not covered by the SCC 2010. A stated intention to advise a client to initiate a civil action may, in appropriate cases, be helpful when negotiating with the police, particularly with more senior officers. The lawyer should be particularly careful to take full contemporaneous notes where civil action by the client is a possibility.

---

35  It was held in *Cullen v Chief Constable of the Royal Ulster Constabulary* [2003] 1 WLR 1763 that failure to inform a suspect why legal advice was being denied did not give rise to this form of tortious liability, although a minority of the judicial committee of the House of Lords were of the view that the statutory provision was of such importance that it should be actionable without proof of harm.

36  [1997] 2 All ER 774.

37  See J Harrison, S Cragg and H Williams, *Police misconduct: legal remedies* (note 2 above) p595.

## Exclusion of evidence

13.28    Probably the strongest means of enforcement in respect of police conduct is an application to stay proceedings as an abuse of process,[38] or the exclusion of improperly obtained evidence under PACE ss76 and 78. PACE s82(3) also preserves the common law discretion of a court to exclude evidence, but in practice PACE ss76 and 78 have rendered the common law powers almost redundant. There is also special provision for the evidential use of confessions obtained from mentally handicapped people (PACE s77 and see para 11.1 above). Of course, exclusion of evidence does not directly affect police conduct, and it will only be of direct relevance if criminal proceedings are initiated against a suspect who then pleads not guilty. Nevertheless, the defence lawyer at the police station should be aware of the exclusionary provisions for a number of reasons, dealt with below. The intention here is not to provide a full explanation of the exclusionary provisions, but rather to indicate their utility from the point of view of the lawyer advising at the police station.[39]

13.29    If the lawyer is aware that evidence may potentially be excluded, the lawyer should take this into account when advising the suspect, and may use this possibility when negotiating with the police. For example, if an initial interview has been conducted in breach of PACE or the Codes of Practice, the lawyer should consider not only whether evidence of the initial interview might be excluded, but also whether it might lead to evidence of a subsequent interview being excluded. In either case, this will be a relevant factor in considering whether to advise the client to answer questions in the interview at which the lawyer is present. If the oppression or other factor that caused the original confession is still operative at the time of the subsequent interview, the evidence of that interview will be inadmissible, or should be excluded, on the same grounds. If the factor is no longer directly operative in the subsequent interview, and the subsequent interview is properly conducted, evidence of that interview may still not be admitted if the first interview 'tainted' the second or subsequent interview. The fact that the suspect has received legal advice before the second interview will not necessarily remove the 'taint'. See further para 4.51 above.

13.30    The lawyer should be particularly vigilant if the lawyer is aware of breaches of PACE or the Codes of Practice, and should ensure that he or she takes a full, contemporaneous note of the conduct concerned. If the conduct subsequently provides grounds for an application to exclude evidence, the lawyer may have to give evidence, which will be more credible if a clear contemporaneous note has been taken.

13.31    Not every breach of PACE or the Codes of Practice will result in the exclusion of evidence.[40] Conversely, evidence may be excluded even where there has been no breach. It was held in *R v Brine*,[41] that use of PACE s78

---

38    Abuse of process is not further considered here. See, eg, C Wells *Abuse of process: a practical approach* (LAG, London, 2006) ch 2.

39    For fuller consideration of PACE ss76 and 78 see, eg, M Zander, *The Police and Criminal Evidence Act 1984* (5th edn, Sweet & Maxwell, London, 2005).

40    See, eg, *Watson v DPP* [2003] EWHC 1466 (Admin).

41    [1992] Crim LR 122.

(and the principle probably also applies to PACE s76(2)(b) but not to (a)) is not confined to circumstances involving improper conduct by the police. In that case, the court heard that the defendant was suffering from mild paranoid psychosis, the effect of which was that he was likely to tell lies, that is falsely confess, under stress. The Court of Appeal held that evidence of his confession should have been excluded even though the police were unaware of his condition.[42]

13.32    If the lawyer is aware of a breach of PACE or the Codes of Practice, or of other improper conduct, in his or her presence, the lawyer should normally intervene at the time.[43] If the lawyer fails to intervene at the time, evidence obtained by even a clear and substantial breach may not be excluded at trial. In *R v Dunn*,[44] the prosecution alleged that the defendant, who had denied the offence in interview, admitted it in the presence of his lawyer during the signing of the interview notes. In breach of Code C, the alleged confession was not recorded contemporaneously and the defendant was not shown a note of it. The defendant denied at trial that the conversation had ever taken place, and this was supported by his lawyer, a solicitor's representative. The alleged confession was not excluded, and he was found guilty. The Court of Appeal held that the trial judge had rightly decided that the lawyer was present to protect the defendant's interests, that intervention by her would have been possible, and that her presence would have inhibited the police from fabricating the evidence. The trial judge said that he would have excluded the evidence had the lawyer not been present. The lawyer, of course, denied the conversation took place, but the court held that it was for the jury to decide whether it believed her, which it obviously did not. It follows from this decision that failure by the lawyer to intervene could jeopardise the chances of exclusion of improperly obtained evidence.

13.33    This will not always be so. In *R v Paris, Abdullahi and Miller*[45] the Court of Appeal held that evidence of a confession in interview should have been excluded even though a solicitor was present. However, this was an extreme case where Miller was described as being on the borderline of mental handicap and where the court said that it was hard to conceive of a more hostile and intimidating approach to a defendant by the police officers interviewing him. The court also castigated the solicitor, supporting the Law Society's advice that the lawyer should intervene if questioning is oppressive, threatening or insulting, and that the suspect should be advised to remain silent if improprieties remained uncorrected or continued. If the lawyer failed to do this, said the court, the lawyer's presence might actually render the suspect a disservice since the police may take the lack of intervention as an indication that their conduct was not improper.

---

42  However, contrast *R v Campbell* [1995] Crim LR 157, where the confession of a mentally handicapped defendant obtained in the absence of an appropriate adult was admitted in circumstances where the police were unaware of the defendant's handicap at the time of interview.

43  As an exception to the normal rule, the lawyer should not intervene if an interviewing officer fails to give a special warning under Code C para 10.11 or Code H para 10.10 (see para 7.59 above).

44  (1990) 91 Cr App R 237; [1990] Crim LR 572.

45  (1993) 97 Cr App R 99; [1994] Crim LR 361. See also *R v Glaves* [1993] Crim LR 685.

## PACE s76(2)

13.34    PACE s76 is concerned only with confession evidence, which includes any statement wholly or partly adverse to the person who made it (PACE s82(1)).[46] The general rule is that evidence of a confession is admissible in any proceedings (PACE s76(1)). However, PACE s76(2) provides as follows:

> If, in any proceedings where the prosecution proposes to give in evidence a confession made by an accused person, it is represented to the court that the confession was or may have been obtained –
> (a) by oppression of the person who made it; or
> (b) in consequence of anything said or done which was likely, in the circumstances existing at the time, to render unreliable any confession which might be made by him in consequence thereof,
> the court shall not allow the confession to be given in evidence against him except in so far as the prosecution proves to the court beyond reasonable doubt that the confession (notwithstanding that it may be true) was not obtained as aforesaid.[47]

13.35    PACE s76(2) creates two grounds for the exclusion of confession evidence, which are dealt with below, but a number of general points should first be made:

1) Once a representation[48] has been made to the court that a confession was, or may have been, obtained in one of the prohibited ways, evidence of the confession cannot be adduced unless the prosecution establish beyond reasonable doubt that it was not so obtained. See, for example, *R v Harvey*,[49] *R v Davison*[50] and *R v Paris, Abdullahi and Miller*.[51]

2) It is irrelevant for the purpose of deciding whether to exclude the confession that the confession is or might be true. Thus, in *R v Cox*,[52] the Court of Appeal held that evidence of a confession of a mentally handicapped defendant made in the absence of an appropriate adult should have been excluded even though the defendant admitted the offence to the trial court. The correct question to ask, said the Court of Appeal, was not whether the confession was likely to be true, but whether it was likely to be unreliable.

---

46  It was held in *R v Hasan* [2005] UKHL 22 that whether a statement is to be treated as a confession is to be decided in the light of the circumstances when the statement was made and not at the time that it falls to be considered. Thus if the accused makes an apparently exculpatory or neutral statement in the police interview, a court will have no power to exclude it under PACE s76 (although it may do so under section 78) even though by the time of the trial it is adverse to the accused – because, for example, the prosecution can then prove that the statement was untrue.

47  Note that PACE s76A enables a confession made by a co-defendant to be admitted on behalf of another person charged in the same proceedings (because, for example, it strengthens the case of that person or undermines the case of the co-accused), subject to similar provisions regarding oppression and unreliability.

48  A 'representation' does not have to be evidence adduced. Representations made to the court by defence counsel are sufficient (*R v Dhorajiwala* [2010] EWCA Crim 1237).

49  [1988] Crim LR 241.

50  [1988] Crim LR 442.

51  (1993) 97 Cr App R 99; [1994] Crim LR 361.

52  [1991] Crim LR 276. See also *R v Kenny* [1994] Crim LR 284, and *R v Mushtaq* [2005] UKHL 25; [2005] 1 WLR 1513; [2005] 3 All ER 885; [2005] 2 Cr App R 32.

3) Evidence obtained as a result of a confession that is excluded at trial may be admitted, although the prosecution is not allowed to adduce evidence that it was discovered as a result of the confession (PACE s76(4)–(6)). Thus, if a confession which is subsequently excluded enables the police to recover stolen property, evidence may be given at the trial of the finding of the property, but evidence may not be given that the police knew where to look because of the confession.

## Oppression

13.36 'Oppression' is defined to include torture, inhuman or degrading treatment, and the use or threat of violence (whether or not amounting to torture) (PACE s76(8)). This definition is not exhaustive and other forms of behaviour may be treated as amounting to oppression. In *R v Fulling*,[53] the Court of Appeal held that the word 'oppression' should be given its ordinary dictionary meaning, namely the: 'exercise of authority or power in a burdensome, harsh, or wrongful manner; unjust or cruel treatment of subjects, inferiors, etc; or the imposition of unreasonable or unjust burdens'. It also held that the expression would almost certainly involve some impropriety on behalf of the interrogator. In *R v Paris, Abdullahi and Miller*,[54] the Court of Appeal accepted that a series of interviews totalling 13 hours over five days, where the defendant, although accompanied by his solicitor, was bullied and hectored, and where, short of physical violence: 'it was hard to conceive of a more hostile and intimidating approach', was oppressive. Similarly, in *R v Beales*,[55] an interview in which the defendant was: 'hectored and bullied from first to last' was held to be oppressive. On the other hand, in *R v Emmerson*,[56] rude and discourteous behaviour on the part of the interrogator was held not to amount to oppression. In *R v Ridley*,[57] it was held that a three-hour interview of an accused who was described as naïve, conducted in a manner that was tendentious, persistent, aggressive and prurient, should have been excluded on the grounds of oppression. For exclusion to follow, there must be a causal, or possible causal, link between the oppression and the confession.[58]

## Unreliability

13.37 The unreliability provision in PACE s76(2)(b) does not require any impropriety on the part of the police.[59] There must, however, be a causal connection between what was 'said or done' and the confession, as where a

53 [1987] 2 All ER 65; (1987) 85 Cr App R 136; [1987] Crim LR 492.
54 (1993) 97 Cr App R 99; [1994] Crim LR 361.
55 [1991] Crim LR 118.
56 (1991) 92 Cr App R 284; [1991] Crim LR 194. See also *R v L* [1994] Crim LR 839, in which evidence of aggressive questioning was not excluded, and *R v Heron* (1993) (not fully reported, but see M Zander, *The Police and Criminal Evidence Act 1984* (5th edn, Sweet & Maxwell, London, 2005) p350.
57 (1999) 17 December (unreported).
58 *R v Parker* [1995] Crim LR 233.
59 *R v Fulling* [1987] 2 All ER 65; (1987) 85 Cr App R 136; [1987] Crim LR 492.

suspect confesses as a result of an inducement.[60] What was 'said or done' refers to the police and not to what was said or done by the suspect[61] so that, for example, the mere fact that the suspect was withdrawing from the effects of drugs would not in itself come within the subsection,[62] although the circumstances might render the result unfair within section 78. It is likely that the expression includes things not said or done. The expression 'the circumstances existing at the time' includes the circumstances of the suspect, and whether or not the police were aware of them. Thus, the fact that the suspect had a mental age of eight years could be relevant.[63] The following are examples of the kind of conduct that may, or may not, result in exclusion of a confession.

### Denying access to a lawyer

13.38   Wrongly denying access to lawyer has resulted in exclusion of a confession under PACE s76(2), although normally when associated with other improprieties. See, for example, *R v Davison*,[64] *R v McGovern*[65] and *R v Moss*.[66] However, denial of access to a lawyer has more often been dealt with under PACE s78, and denial in itself will not result in exclusion. See, for example, *R v Oliphant*.[67]

### Failure to secure attendance of appropriate adult

13.39   In circumstances where an appropriate adult should be called in (see paras 11.13 and 11.66 above), failure to do so, or calling a person who is inappropriate, may result in exclusion of a confession. See, for example, *R v Dutton*,[68] *R v Cox*[69] and *R v W*[70] where no appropriate adult was called, and *DPP v Blake*,[71] *R v Morse*[72] and *R v Palmer*,[73] where inappropriate adults were in attendance.

### Misleading the suspect

13.40   Although often dealt with under PACE s78 (see para 13.56 below), a confession may be excluded under PACE s76(2)(b) where the suspect is

---

60  *R v Delaney* (1988) 88 Cr App R 338; [1989] Crim LR 139. See also *R v Barry* (1991) 95 Cr App R 384. It was held in *R v Samuel* [2005] EWCA Crim 704 that there is a distinction between making a confession 'in consequence' of something said or done (which did engage section 76(2)(b)) and making a confession 'in the light of' something said or done (which did not).

61  *R v Goldenberg* (1988) 88 Cr App R 285; [1988] Crim LR 678.

62  *R v Crampton* (1990) 92 Cr App R 369; [1991] Crim LR 277.

63  *R v Everett* [1988] Crim LR 826.

64  [1988] Crim LR 442.

65  (1990) 92 Cr App R 228; [1991] Crim LR 124.

66  (1990) 91 Cr App R 371; (1990) 140 NLJ 665.

67  [1992] Crim LR 40.

68  (1988) *Independent* 5 December.

69  [1991] Crim LR 276.

70  [2010] EWCA Crim 2799.

71  (1989) 89 Cr App R 179.

72  [1991] Crim LR 195.

73  September 1991 *Legal Action* 21.

misled by the police about the existence of evidence – for example, that the suspect has been identified where this is not so.[74]

### Conditions of detention and interview

13.41 A confession may be excluded where the provisions of Code C regarding the conditions of the suspect's detention or interview are contravened, for example, inadequate rest periods[75] or inadequate refreshment,[76] although there would normally have to be an accumulation of breaches to result in exclusion.

## PACE s78

13.42 PACE s78(1) provides for the exclusion of any form of prosecution evidence,[77] including confession evidence:

> In any proceedings, the court may refuse to allow evidence on which the prosecution proposes to rely to be given if it appears to the court that, having regard to all the circumstances, including the circumstances in which the evidence was obtained, the admission of the evidence would have such an adverse effect on the fairness of the proceedings that the court ought not to admit it.

13.43 Section 78 provides a court with a sufficiently broad discretion to exclude evidence even though it was not obtained in breach of PACE or the Codes of Practice.[78] Conversely, breach of PACE or the Codes will not necessarily result in exclusion of the evidence thereby obtained. Although the Court of Appeal has been reluctant to lay down guidelines for the interpretation of PACE s78 generally, for a breach of PACE or the Codes to result in exclusion of evidence, it must be a significant and substantial breach and must have such an adverse effect that justice demands its exclusion.[79] Where these conditions are satisfied, it is likely that the evidence will be excluded.[80] This may be illustrated by two cases involving confessions obtained following the wrongful denial of legal advice: *R v Samuel*[81] and *R v Alladice*.[82] In *Samuel*, the solicitor gave evidence that he would probably have advised his client before the interview in which he confessed (he had been interviewed a number of times previously) not to answer questions. The Court of Appeal decided that the confession evidence should not have been admitted. The court came to the opposite conclusion in *Alladice*, where the defendant gave evidence that although he wanted his solicitor present, he was well aware of his right to remain silent. Both

---

74 *R v Blake* [1991] Crim LR 119.
75 *R v Trussler* [1988] Crim LR 446.
76 *R v Gopee and Gopee* (1992) LSG 24 June, p32.
77 Including evidence of a significant silence under CJPOA 1994 s34, s36 or s37, and evidence of lies told by the accused.
78 *R v Brine* [1992] Crim LR 122.
79 See *R v Walsh* (1989) 91 Cr App R 161; [1989] Crim LR 822, and *R v Keenan* [1989] 3 All ER 598; (1989) 90 Cr App R 1; [1989] Crim LR 720.
80 *R v Allen* [2001] EWCA Crim 1607.
81 See [1988] 2 All ER 135; (1988) 87 Cr App R 232; [1988] Crim LR 299.
82 (1988) 87 Cr App R 380; [1988] Crim LR 608.

cases involved a significant and substantial breach, but while in *Samuel* the court concluded that this breach adversely affected the accused, in *Alladice* it concluded that there was no adverse effect.

13.44    The significance of the breach does not, in itself, determine whether evidence will be excluded. Thus evidence obtained in breach of defendant's rights under the ECHR will not necessarily be excluded. In *R v Khan*,[83] the House of Lords held that in considering exclusion of evidence under PACE s78 breach of ECHR rights was of no greater significance than breach of domestic law. Since breach of domestic law does not necessarily lead to exclusion so obtained, breach of a convention right should not do so either. This was effectively upheld by the ECtHR in *Khan v UK*,[84] where the court held that although the evidence had been obtained in breach of the right to private life under ECHR article 8, the right to fair trial under article 6 did not necessarily require that the evidence so obtained be excluded. It could be argued that the ECHR, incorporating as it does rights that are fundamental, should weigh very heavily in a court's mind in considering exclusion under PACE s78. However, it may take some years, if at all, for such a view to develop.[85]

13.45    What follows is intended to give some indication of the kinds of conduct and breaches that may, or may not, result in exclusion of evidence under PACE s78. However, it must be remembered that the courts are not always consistent in terms of the underlying principles informing their decisions on exclusion of evidence under PACE s78, decisions are very fact-sensitive, and the Court of Appeal is reluctant to interfere with the decisions of trial judges.[86]

## Withholding information on suspects' rights

13.46    Evidence of an admission made in interview may be excluded if the suspect is misled about his or her rights, as in *R v Beycan*,[87] where the defendant was led to believe that interviews were usually conducted in the absence of a lawyer. A similar result may follow from a failure to inform a suspect of the suspect's right to advice,[88] although not if the suspect then 'genuinely' agrees to speak to the police.[89]

## Wrongful denial of legal advice

13.47    As noted at para 13.38 above, wrongful denial of access to a lawyer may result in exclusion of evidence under PACE s76(2)(b) but this is more likely under PACE s78.[90] Evidence is unlikely to be excluded if denial of

83  [1996] 3 WLR 162; [1996] Crim LR 733.
84  (2001) 31 EHRR 45; [2000] Crim LR 684.
85  See the critical commentary on *Khan v UK* in the *Criminal Law Review* report, and D Ormerod 'ECHR and the exclusion of evidence: trial remedies for article 8 breaches' [2003] Crim LR 61.
86  *R v Jelen* (1989) 90 Cr App R 456.
87  [1990] Crim LR 185.
88  *R v Williams (Violet)* [1989] Crim LR 66.
89  *R v Hughes* [1988] Crim LR 519.
90  *R v Samuel* [1988] QB 615; [1988] 2 All ER 135; (1988) 87 Cr App R 232; [1988] Crim LR 299.

advice is treated by the court as having no adverse effect on the fairness of the proceedings. See, for example, *R v Alladice*,[91] *R v Walsh*[92] and *R v Dunford*.[93] These cases were all decided before the ECtHR decisions on the right to legal advice noted at para 13.10 above, but the key issue continues to be whether denial of access to legal advice had such an adverse effect on the fairness of the proceedings that the evidence so obtained should be excluded. Note that incompetent legal advice at the police station may result in exclusion under PACE s78, although there is in practice a heavy burden on the accused in demonstrating the adverse effects on fairness of such incompetence.[94]

### Failure to caution the suspect

13.48 A person must be cautioned before any questions about an offence are put to the person if there are grounds to suspect him or her of having committed the suspected offence, whether or not this takes place at a police station[95] (see para 4.37 above). Generally, where the courts conclude that a caution ought to have been given, and was not, they are likely to decide that evidence of what was said should be excluded.[96] However, this is not always the case, especially where the suspect could be expected to have been aware of his or her rights or if the suspect was in receipt of legal advice.[97] The courts generally pay close attention to whether a caution was required. It was noted at para 4.37 above that the courts have limited the obligation to caution in circumstances where there are *reasonable* grounds for suspicion. It has also been decided that a caution is not necessary in advance of questioning about a particular offence if the suspect was cautioned about another matter shortly before, unless the suspect is further arrested.[98] Furthermore, it has been held that a caution was not necessary where a suspect, on being questioned by the police about a particular offence, started to tell them about a completely different matter of which the police had no knowledge.[99] While Code C provides that minor deviations from the wording of the caution are permissible provided the sense of the caution is preserved (Code C para 10.7), it was held in *R v Ibrahim, Omar, Osman*

---

91  (1988) 87 Cr App R 380; [1988] Crim LR 608.

92  [1989] Crim LR 822.

93  (1990) 91 Cr App R 150; [1991] Crim LR 370. See also *R v Anderson* [1993] Crim LR 447.

94  See E Cape 'Incompetent police station advice and the exclusion of evidence' [2002] Crim LR 471, and *R v Wahab and Cromer* [2002] EWCA Crim 1570.

95  Code C, Code H para 10.1.

96  *R v Hunt* [1992] Crim LR 582. See also *R v Okafor* [1994] 3 All ER 741; (1994) 99 Cr App R 97; [1994] Crim LR 221, *R v Oransaye* [1993] Crim LR 772, *R v Allen* [2001] EWCA Crim 1607, *R v Senior* [2004] EWCA Crim 454; [2004] 3 All ER 9; [2004] 2 Cr App R 12 and *R v Miller* [2007] EWCA Crim 1891.

97  *R v Hoyte* [1994] Crim LR 215, *R v Armas-Rodriguez* [2005] EWCA Crim 1081, and *R v Devani* [2007] EWCA Crim 1926.

98  *R v Oni* [1992] Crim LR 183 and *R v Pall* [1992] Crim LR 126. But contrast *R v Kirk* [1999] 4 All ER 698, which held that where the police have arrested for one offence, but question about another, more serious, offence they must, at least, ensure that the suspect is aware of the true nature of the investigation.

99  *R v Purcell* [1992] Crim LR 806.

*and Mohamed* that administering the wrong caution would not necessarily lead to exclusion of evidence of the subsequent interview.[100]

## Conduct and recording of interviews

13.49   Evidence has been excluded where the recording requirements of Code C have not been complied with. The courts have recognised that the provisions in Code C dealing with the recording of interviews and other relevant conversations (see paras 4.49 and 7.8) were designed to prevent 'verballing' or suspicion of 'verballing'. Thus, in cases like *R v Canale*,[101] *R v Keenan*,[102] *R v Walsh*,[103] *R v Joseph*[104] and *R v Rowe*,[105] the Court of Appeal held that evidence of interviews that were not contemporaneously recorded should not have been admitted in evidence. However, exclusion will not always follow where there has been such a breach, as was seen in *R v Dunn* (see para 13.32 above), and in the somewhat surprising decision in *R v White*.[106] Evidence of an interview conducted contrary to the provisions of Code C para 11.1 and Code H para 11.2 (that, following a decision to arrest, the interview must normally be conducted in a police station) will normally be excluded (see para 4.44 above). Similarly, an interview conducted in breach of PACE s37 or Code C paras 11.4 or 16.1 may be excluded.[107]

## Identification procedures

13.50   Failure to hold an identification procedure in breach of Code D has, in the past, frequently resulted in exclusion of other identification evidence obtained, particularly evidence from a confrontation.[108] However, this was not always the case, especially where the court was of the view that, in the circumstances, another form of identification had not worked to the disadvantage of the defendant.[109] In *R v Popat*,[110] the Court of Appeal held that decisions on exclusion should be based on whether, overall, the identification process was fair and reliable, rather than on whether the detailed rules of Code D had been complied with. This was overruled in relation to other aspects of the decision by *R v Forbes*.[111] However, *Forbes* reinforced the point that courts should be concerned with whether the overall purpose of Code D had been respected. While the provisions of

---

100  [2008] EWCA Crim 880.
101  [1990] 2 All ER 187; (1990) 91 Cr App R 1; [1990] Crim LR 329.
102  [1989] 3 All ER 598; (1989) 90 Cr App R 1; [1989] Crim LR 720.
103  [1989] Crim LR 822.
104  [1993] Crim LR 206.
105  [1994] Crim LR 837.
106  [1991] Crim LR 779. See also *R v Courtney* [1995] Crim LR 63, *R v Dures, Williams and Dures* [1997] Crim LR 673, and *R v Heera* [2010] EWCA Crim 1779.
107  *R v Coleman, Knight and Hochenberg* (1996) 20 October, CA (unreported), briefly considered at (1998) NLJ 3 July.
108  *R v Conway* (1990) 91 Cr App R 143; [1990] Crim LR 402, and *R v Britton and Richards* [1989] Crim LR 144.
109  *R v Penny* (1991) 94 Cr App R 345; [1992] Crim LR 184.
110  [1998] Crim LR 825; (1998) *Times* 10 April.
111  [2001] 1 AC 473; [2001] 2 WLR 1; [2001] 1 All ER 686; [2001] 1 Cr App R 31; [2001] Crim LR 649.

Code D are mandatory, a breach of a particular provision of the Code may not frustrate the overall purpose. In such circumstances a judge may admit the evidence of identification and direct the jury that there had been a breach, pointing out the consequences of that breach and that the accused had lost the possible benefit of the Code provisions (see the cases referred to at para 8.83 above).

13.51    There is extensive case-law on evidence of visual identification, the distinction between recognition and identification, and the Code D identification procedures (see generally chapter 8). Examples of post *Forbes* cases where it was held that identification evidence did not need to be excluded include *Marsh v DPP*[112] (breach of the obligation to take an original description from the witness), and *R v B*[113] (witness not told to view the array in a video identification at least twice). Cases where it was held that the trial judge should have excluded the identification evidence include *R v Pecco*[114] (distinguishing marks on the suspect not adequately disguised), and *R v Preddie*[115] (street identification of a known suspect). The courts are particularly likely to exclude identification evidence where they conclude that the police deliberately tried to circumvent the provisions of Code D.[116]

### Questioning during a search of property

13.52    Where a search is carried out at which the suspect is present, questions should be confined to whether any article that is discovered, which the police are entitled to seize and retain, is property claimed by the suspect and, if it is, whether it is property that could amount to evidence of an offence (see para 6.112). If it goes further, it could be excluded.[117] If the right to delay taking the suspect to the police station while the search is being carried out (PACE s30(10)) is abused by the police or customs officers who use the opportunity to conduct an irregular interview, evidence of the interview should be excluded.[118]

### Entrapment

13.53    Entrapment is not a defence but, depending on the facts, may lead to exclusion of evidence under PACE s78, although in some circumstances it is more appropriate for an application to be made to stay proceedings on the ground of abuse of process.[119] It is important to distinguish between cases where a person is effectively incited to commit an offence, and those where the police use undercover strategies to secure evidence of a crime already committed. Only the former can properly be described as entrapment, although both the case-law and commentary is often confused by use of the

---

112  [2006] EWHC 1525 (Admin).
113  [2008] EWCA Crim 1524.
114  [2010] EWCA Crim 972.
115  [2011] EWCA Crim 312.
116  *R v Nagah* (1990) 92 Cr App R 344; [1991] Crim LR 55.
117  *R v Langiert* [1991] Crim LR 777. See also *R v Raphaie* [1996] Crim LR 812.
118  *R v Khan* [1993] Crim LR 54.
119  See *R v Loosely* [2001] 1 WLR 2060 for guidance on which is appropriate. For the treatment of entrapment by non-state agencies see *R v Shannon* [2000] Crim LR 1001 and *R v Hardwicke* [2001] Crim LR 220.

term to describe both. In *R v Smurthwaite and Gill*,[120] the Court of Appeal identified five factors as being relevant to the question of whether such evidence should be excluded, although it did not specify how the factors were to be interpreted or what weight was to be placed on them:

1) Was the officer acting as an agent provocateur in the sense that the officer was enticing the defendant to commit an offence that the defendant would not otherwise have committed?
2) What was the nature of the entrapment?
3) Is the evidence of admissions or of the offence itself?
4) How active or passive was the officer?
5) Is there an unassailable record of what occurred, or is it strongly corroborated?

Predisposition of the accused to commit a crime is not the deciding factor. A critical factor is whether the police did no more than present the accused with an unexceptional opportunity to commit a crime,[121] although the court will be concerned to examine whether the conduct of the police was so seriously improper as to bring the administration of justice into disrepute.

13.54   Two contrasting cases may help to illustrate the approach to entrapment. In *R v Christou and Wright*,[122] the police set up a bogus jeweller's shop in order to recover stolen property and to collect evidence against the thieves and handlers. Admissions obtained in the course of conversations with the suspects when they went to the shop to sell stolen property were held to have been properly admitted.[123] In *R v Bryce*,[124] an undercover police officer contacted the suspect to ask if he could supply a stolen car, and it was held that admissions obtained during the course of this transaction should not have been admitted since it amounted to an interrogation with the effect, if not the design, of using an undercover pose to circumvent Code C.

13.55   The ECtHR has accepted that the use of undercover agents is legitimate, but has held that it should be subject to adequate safeguards and must not lead to the incitement of crime.[125] For a useful illustration of conduct that may or may not amount to incitement, see *R v Loosely*.[126]

---

120 [1994] 1 All ER 898; (1994) 98 Cr App R 437; [1994] Crim LR 53.
121 *R v Loosely* [2001] 1 WLR 2060. See also *R v M* [2011] EWCA Crim 648.
122 [1992] 4 All ER 559; (1992) 95 Cr App R 264; [1992] Crim LR 729.
123 See also *Ealing LBC v Woolworth PLC* [1995] Crim LR 58, *R v Morley* [1994] Crim LR 919, *R v Pattemore* [1994] Crim LR 836, *R v Edwards* [1997] Crim LR 348, and *R v Mann and Dixon* [1995] Crim LR 647. See A Ashworth, 'Re-drawing the boundaries of entrapment' [2002] Crim LR 161, D Ormerod and A Roberts, 'The trouble with Teixeira: developing a principled approach to entrapment' (2000) 6 *International Journal of Evidence and Proof* 1, 38, S Sharpe, 'Covert police operations and the discretionary exclusion of evidence' [1994] Crim LR 793, and G Robertson, 'Entrapment evidence: manna from heaven, or fruit of the poisoned tree?' [1994] Crim LR 805.
124 [1992] 4 All ER 567; (1992) 95 Cr App R 320; [1992] Crim LR 728. See also *R v Smith* [1995] Crim LR 659 and *R v Rajkuma* [2003] EWCA Crim 1955.
125 *Teixeira de Castro v Portugal* [1998] Crim LR 751. This was distinguished in *Nottingham CC v Amin* [2000] 1 WLR 1071; [2000] 2 All ER 946; [2000] 1 Cr App R 426; [2000] Crim LR 174.
126 [2001] 1 WLR 2060. See also *R v Byrne* [2003] EWCA Crim 1073.

## Deception

13.56 If a suspect is deceived by the police into believing in the existence of evidence that does not in fact exist, evidence of admissions made in consequence may not be admitted, especially if the suspect's lawyer is also deceived.[127] Exclusion may also follow where the suspect 'deceives' himself or herself, as where the suspect misunderstands the nature of a police inquiry and believes that the suspect is simply assisting with an investigation of the death of a friend, as a witness and not a suspect.[128] However, a deception practised by the police in the form of 'bugging' a police interview room is unlikely to result in exclusion of evidence so obtained.[129] Indeed, the courts seem generally reluctant to exclude evidence obtained by trickery or deception. Thus, in *R v Maclean and Kosten*,[130] evidence obtained by pretending that a courier had been involved in a car accident was not excluded. Nor was evidence excluded in *Williams v DPP*,[131] where the police had left a van apparently unattended in the hope that someone might try to steal from it.

## Inducements

13.57 Code C para 11.5 provides that an officer conducting an interview must not: 'indicate, except to answer a direct question, what action will be taken by the police if the person being questioned answers questions, makes a statement or refuses to do either'. To do so may amount to an inducement to confess, and any confession so obtained may be excluded. In *R v Howden-Simpson*,[132] a confession was excluded where a choirmaster accused of theft of money belonging to the choristers was told that if he admitted the offence the police would proceed on only two charges, but that if he did not do so, they would interview all the choristers and charge him separately in respect of each one. Indicating that a caution (or reprimand or warning) will be given if the suspect confesses may amount to an inducement.[133]

127 *R v Imran and Hussain* [1997] Crim LR 754, and *R v Mason* [1987] 3 All ER 481; (1988) 86 Cr App R 349; [1987] Crim LR 757.

128 *R v Williams* [1991] Crim LR 708.

129 *R v Ali* (1991) *Times* 19 February, *R v Bailey* [1993] 3 All ER 513; [1993] Crim LR 681, *R v Roberts* [1997] Crim LR 222, *R v Mason and others* [2002] Crim LR 841, *R v Khan* [1997] AC 558; [1996] 3 WLR 162; [1996] Crim LR 733, and *R v Parker* [1995] Crim LR 233. However, these cases were all decided before the enactment of Regulation of Investigatory Powers Act 2000 and an important issue now would be whether any covert surveillance was properly authorised (see para 10.108 above).

130 [1993] Crim LR 687.

131 [1993] 3 All ER 365; (1993) 98 Cr App R 209; [1993] Crim LR 775. See also *R v Cadette* [1995] Crim LR 229, and *R v Chalkley and Jeffries* [1998] QB 848; [1998] 3 WLR 146; [1998] 2 All ER 155; [1998] 2 Cr App R 79; [1999] Crim LR 214.

132 [1991] Crim LR 49.

133 See *R (R) v Durham Constabulary* [2005] 1 WLR 1184, and para 10.46 above.

# APPENDICES

# Extracts from legislation[1]

**Police and Criminal Evidence Act 1984    502**

**Criminal Justice and Public Order Act 1994 ss34–38    587**

# Police and Criminal Evidence Act 1984

## PART I:  POWERS TO STOP AND SEARCH

### Power of constable to stop and search persons, vehicles etc

1(1) A constable may exercise any power conferred by this section–

   (a) in any place to which at the time when he proposes to exercise the power the public or any section of the public has access, on payment or otherwise, as of right or by virtue of express or implied permission; or

   (b) in any other place to which people have ready access at the time when he proposes to exercise the power but which is not a dwelling.

 (2) Subject to subsection (3) to (5) below, a constable–

   (a) may search–

     (i)  any person or vehicle;

     (ii) anything which is in or on a vehicle,

for stolen or prohibited articles, any article to which subsection (8A) below applies or any firework to which subsection (8B) below applies; and

   (b) may detain a person or vehicle for the purpose of such a search.

 (3) This section does not give a constable power to search a person or vehicle or anything in or on a vehicle unless he has reasonable grounds for suspecting that he will find stolen or prohibited articles, any article to which subsection (8A) below applies or any firework to which subsection (8B) below applies.

 (4) If a person is in a garden or yard occupied with and used for the purposes of a dwelling or on other land so occupied and used, a constable may not search him in the exercise of the power conferred by this section unless the constable has reasonable grounds for believing–

   (a) that he does not reside in the dwelling; and

   (b) that he is not in the place in question with the express or implied permission of a person who resides in the dwelling.

 (5) If a vehicle is in a garden or yard occupied with and used for the purposes of a dwelling or on other land so occupied and used, a constable may not search the vehicle or anything in or on it in the exercise of the power conferred by this section unless he has reasonable grounds for believing–

   (a) that the person in charge of the vehicle does not reside in the dwelling; and

   (b) that the vehicle is not in the place in question with the express or implied permission of a person who resides in the dwelling.

 (6) If in the course of such a search a constable discovers an article which he has reasonable grounds for suspecting to be a stolen or prohibited article, an article to which subsection (8A) below applies or a firework to which subsection (8B) below applies, he may seize it.

 (7) An article is prohibited for the purposes of this Part of this Act if it is–

   (a) an offensive weapon; or

   (b) an article–

     (i)  made or adapted for use in the course of or in connection with an offence to which this sub-paragraph applies; or

     (ii) intended by the person having it with him for such use by him or by some other person.

 (8) The offences to which subsection (7)(b)(i) above applies are–

   (a) burglary;

   (b) theft;

   (c) offences under section 12 of the Theft Act 1968 (taking motor vehicle or other conveyance without authority);

   (d) fraud (contrary to section 1 of the Fraud Act 2006); and

   (e) offences under section 1 of the Criminal Damage Act 1971 (destroying or damaging property).

(8A) This subsection applies to any article in relation to which a person has committed, or is committing or is going to commit an offence under section 139 of the Criminal Justice Act 1988.

(8B) This subsection applies to any firework which a person possesses in contravention of a prohibition imposed by fireworks regulations.
(8C) In this section–
  (a) 'firework' shall be construed in accordance with the definition of 'fireworks' in section 1(1) of the Fireworks Act 2003; and
  (b) 'fireworks regulations' has the same meaning as in that Act.
  (9) In this Part of this Act 'offensive weapon' means any article–
  (a) made or adapted for use for causing injury to persons; or
  (b) intended by the person having it with him for such use by him or by some other person.

**Provisions relating to search under section 1 and other powers**
2(1) A constable who detains a person or vehicle in the exercise–
  (a) of the power conferred by section 1 above; or
  (b) of any other power–
    (i) to search a person without first arresting him; or
    (ii) to search a vehicle without making an arrest,
  need not conduct a search if it appears to him subsequently–
    (i) that no search is required; or
    (ii) that a search is impracticable.
  (2) If a constable contemplates a search, other than a search of an unattended vehicle, in the exercise–
  (a) of the power conferred by section 1 above; or
  (b) of any other power, except the power conferred by section 6 below and the power conferred by section 27(2) of the Aviation Security Act 1982–
    (i) to search a person without first arresting him; or
    (ii) to search a vehicle without making an arrest,
  it shall be his duty, subject to subsection (4) below, to take reasonable steps before he commences the search to bring to the attention of the appropriate person–
    (i) if the constable is not in uniform, documentary evidence that he is a constable; and
    (ii) whether he is in uniform or not, the matters specified in subsection (3) below;
  and the constable shall not commence the search until he has performed that duty.
  (3) The matters referred to in subsection (2)(ii) above are–
  (a) the constable's name and the name of the police station to which he is attached;
  (b) the object of the proposed search;
  (c) the constable's grounds for proposing to make it; and
  (d) the effect of section 3(7) or (8) below, as may be appropriate.
  (4) A constable need not bring the effect of section 3(7) or (8) below to the attention of the appropriate person if it appears to the constable that it will not be practicable to make the record in section 3(1) below.
  (5) In this section 'the appropriate person' means–
  (a) if the constable proposes to search a person, that person; and
  (b) if he proposes to search a vehicle, or anything in or on a vehicle, the person in charge of the vehicle.
  (6) On completing a search of an unattended vehicle or anything in or on such a vehicle in the exercise of any such power as is mentioned in subsection (2) above a constable shall leave a notice–
  (a) stating that he has searched it;
  (b) giving the name of the police station to which he is attached;
  (c) stating that an application for compensation for any damage caused by the search may be made to that police station; and
  (d) stating the effect of section 3(8) below.
  (7) The constable shall leave the notice inside the vehicle unless it is not reasonably practicable to do so without damaging the vehicle.
  (8) The time for which a person or vehicle may be detained for the purposes of such

a search is such time as is reasonably required to permit a search to be carried out either at the place where the person or vehicle was first detained or nearby.

(9) Neither the power conferred by section 1 above nor any other power to detain and search a person without first arresting him or to detain and search a vehicle without making an arrest is to be construed–

(a) as authorising a constable to require a person to remove any of his clothing in public other than an outer coat, jacket or gloves; or

(b) as authorising a constable not in uniform to stop a vehicle.

(10) This section and section 1 above apply to vessels, aircraft and hovercraft as they apply to vehicles.

### Duty to make records concerning searches

3(1) Where a constable has carried out a search in the exercise of any such power as is mentioned in section 2(1) above, other than a search–

(a) under section 6 below; or

(b) under section 27(2) of the Aviation Security Act 1982,

a record of the search shall be made in writing unless it is not practicable to do so.

(2) If a record of a search is required to be made by subsection (1) above–

(a) in a case where the search results in a person being arrested and taken to a police station, the constable shall secure that the record is made as part of the person's custody record;

(b) in any other case, the constable shall make the record on the spot, or, if that is not practicable, as soon as practicable after the completion of the search.

(3) [Repealed.]

(4) [Repealed.]

(5) [Repealed.]

(6) The record of a search of a person or a vehicle–

(a) shall state–

(i)   the object of the search;

(ii)  the grounds for making it;

(iii) the date and time when it was made;

(iv)  the place where it was made;

(v)   except in the case of a search of an unattended vehicle, the ethnic origins of the person searched or the person in charge of the vehicle searched (as the case may be); and

(b) shall identify the constable who carried out the search.

(6A) The requirement in subsection (6)(a)(v) above for a record to state a person's ethnic origins is a requirement to state–

(a) the ethnic origins of the person as described by the person, and

(b) if different, the ethnic origins of the person as perceived by the constable.

(7) If a record of a search of a person has been made under this section, the person who was searched shall be entitled to a copy of the record if he asks for one before the end of the period specified in subsection (9) below.

(8) If–

(a) the owner of a vehicle which has been searched or the person who was in charge of the vehicle at the time when it was searched asks for a copy of the record of the search before the end of the period specified in subsection (9) below; and

(b) a record of the search of the vehicle has been made under this section,

the person who made the request shall be entitled to a copy.

(9) The period mentioned in subsections (7) and (8) above is the period of 3 months beginning with the date on which the search was made.

(10) The requirements imposed by this section with regard to records of searches of vehicles shall apply also to records of searches of vessels, aircraft and hovercraft.

### Road checks

4(1) This section shall have effect in relation to the conduct of road checks by police officers for the purpose of ascertaining whether a vehicle is carrying–

(a) a person who has committed an offence other than a road traffic offence or a vehicle excise offence;

    (b) a person who is a witness to such an offence;
    (c) a person intending to commit such an offence; or
    (d) a person who is unlawfully at large.
 (2) For the purposes of this section a road check consists of the exercise in a locality of the power conferred by section 163 of the Road Traffic Act 1988 in such a way as to stop during the period for which its exercise in that way in that locality continues all vehicles or vehicles selected by any criterion.
 (3) Subject to subsection (5) below, there may only be such a road check if a police officer of the rank of superintendent or above authorises it in writing.
 (4) An officer may only authorise a road check under subsection (3) above–
    (a) for the purpose specified in subsection (1)(a) above, if he has reasonable grounds–
      (i) for believing that the offence is an indictable offence; and
      (ii) for suspecting that the person is, or is about to be, in the locality in which vehicles would be stopped if the road check were authorised;
    (b) for the purpose specified in subsection (1)(b) above, if he has reasonable grounds for believing that the offence is an indictable offence;
    (c) for the purpose specified in subsection (1)(c) above, if he has reasonable grounds–
      (i) for believing that the offence would be an indictable offence; and
      (ii) for suspecting that the person is, or is about to be, in the locality in which vehicles would be stopped if the road check were authorised;
    (d) for the purpose specified in subsection (1)(d) above, if he has reasonable grounds for suspecting that the person is, or is about to be, in that locality.
 (5) An officer below the rank of superintendent may authorise such a road check if it appears to him that it is required as a matter of urgency for one of the purposes specified in subsection (1) above.
 (6) If an authorisation is given under subsection (5) above, it shall be the duty of the officer who gives it–
    (a) to make a written record of the time at which he gives it; and
    (b) to cause an officer of the rank of superintendent or above to be informed that it has been given.
 (7) The duties imposed by subsection (6) above shall be performed as soon as it is practicable to do so.
 (8) An officer to whom a report is made under subsection (6) above may, in writing, authorise the road check to continue.
 (9) If such an officer considers that the road check should not continue, he shall record in writing–
    (a) the fact that it took place; and
    (b) the purpose for which it took place.
(10) An officer giving an authorisation under this section shall specify the locality in which vehicles are to be stopped.
(11) An officer giving an authorisation under this section, other than an authorisation under subsection (5) above–
    (a) shall specify a period, not exceeding seven days, during which the road check may continue; and
    (b) may direct that the road check–
      (i) shall be continuous; or
      (ii) shall be conducted at specified times,
    during that period.
(12) If it appears to an officer of the rank of superintendent or above that a road check ought to continue beyond the period for which it has been authorised he may, from time to time, in writing specify a further period, not exceeding seven days, during which it may continue.
(13) Every written authorisation shall specify–
    (a) the name of the officer giving it;
    (b) the purpose of the road check; and
    (c) the locality in which vehicles are to be stopped.

(14) The duties to specify the purposes of a road check imposed by subsections (9) and (13) above include duties to specify any relevant indictable offence.

(15) Where a vehicle is stopped in a road check, the person in charge of the vehicle at the time when it is stopped shall be entitled to obtain a written statement of the purpose of the road check if he applies for such a statement not later than the end of the period of twelve months from the day on which the vehicle was stopped.

(16) Nothing in this section affects the exercise by police officers of any power to stop vehicles for purposes other than those specified in subsection (1) above.

### Reports of recorded searches and of road checks

5(1) Every annual report–
  (a) under section 22 of the Police Act 1996; or
  (b) made by the Commissioner of Police of the Metropolis,
  shall contain information–
    (i) about searches recorded under section 3 above which have been carried out in the area to which the report relates during the period to which it relates; and
    (ii) about road checks authorised in that area during that period under section 4 above.

(1A) [Repealed.]

(2) The information about searches shall not include information about specific searches but shall include–
  (a) the total numbers of searches in each month during the period to which the report relates–
    (i) for stolen articles;
    (ii) for offensive weapons or articles to which section 1(8A) above applies; and
    (iii) for other prohibited articles;
  (b) the total number of persons arrested in each such month in consequence of searches of each of the descriptions specified in paragraph (a)(i) to (iii) above.

(3) The information about road checks shall include information–
  (a) about the reason for authorising each road check; and
  (b) about the result of each of them.

### Statutory undertakers etc

6(1) A constable employed by statutory undertakers may stop, detain and search any vehicle before it leaves a goods area included in the premises of the statutory undertakers.

(1A) Without prejudice to any powers under subsection (1) above, a constable employed by the British Transport Police Authority may stop, detain and search any vehicle before it leaves a goods area which is included in the premises of any successor of the British Railways Board and is used wholly or mainly for the purposes of a relevant undertaking.

(2) In this section 'goods area' means any area used wholly or mainly for the storage or handling of goods; and 'successor of the British Railways Board' and 'relevant undertaking' have the same meaning as in the Railways Act 1993 (Consequential Modifications) Order 1999.

(3) [Repealed.]

(4) [Repealed.]

### Part I–supplementary

7(1) The following enactments shall cease to have effect–
  (a) section 8 of the Vagrancy Act 1824;
  (b) section 66 of the Metropolitan Police Act 1839;
  (c) section 11 of the Canals (Offences) Act 1840;
  (d) section 19 of the Pedlars Act 1871;
  (e) section 33 of the County of Merseyside Act 1980; and
  (f) section 42 of the West Midlands County Council Act 1980.

(2) There shall also cease to have effect–
  (a) so much of any enactment contained in an Act passed before 1974, other than–

   (i)  an enactment contained in a public general Act; or
   (ii) an enactment relating to statutory undertakers,
as confers power on a constable to search for stolen or unlawfully obtained goods; and
   (b) so much of any enactment relating to statutory undertakers as provides that such a power shall not be exercisable after the end of a specified period.
(3) In this Part of this Act 'statutory undertakers' means persons authorised by any enactment to carry on any railway, light railway, road transport, water transport, canal, inland navigation, dock or harbour undertaking.

## PART II: POWERS OF ENTRY, SEARCH AND SEIZURE
### Search warrants
### Power of justice of the peace to authorise entry and search of premises
8(1) If on an application made by a constable a justice of the peace is satisfied that there are reasonable grounds for believing–
   (a) that an indictable offence has been committed; and
   (b) that there is material on premises mentioned in subsection (1A) below which is likely to be of substantial value (whether by itself or together with other material) to the investigation of the offence; and
   (c) that the material is likely to be relevant evidence; and
   (d) that it does not consist of or include items subject to legal privilege, excluded material or special procedure material; and
   (e) that any of the conditions specified in subsection (3) below applies in relation to each set of premises specified in the application,
he may issue a warrant authorising a constable to enter and search the premises.
(1A) The premises referred to in subsection (1)(b) above are–
   (a) one or more sets of premises specified in the application (in which case the application is for a 'specific premises warrant'); or
   (b) any premises occupied or controlled by a person specified in the application, including such sets of premises as are so specified (in which case the application is for an 'all premises warrant').
(1B) If the application is for an all premises warrant, the justice of the peace must also be satisfied–
   (a) that because of the particulars of the offence referred to in paragraph (a) of subsection (1) above, there are reasonable grounds for believing that it is necessary to search premises occupied or controlled by the person in question which are not specified in the application in order to find the material referred to in paragraph (b) of that subsection; and
   (b) that it is not reasonably practicable to specify in the application all the premises which he occupies or controls and which might need to be searched.
(1C) The warrant may authorise entry to and search of premises on more than one occasion if, on the application, the justice of the peace is satisfied that it is necessary to authorise multiple entries in order to achieve the purpose for which he issues the warrant.
(1D) If it authorises multiple entries, the number of entries authorised may be unlimited, or limited to a maximum.
(2) A constable may seize and retain anything for which a search has been authorised under subsection (1) above.
(3) The conditions mentioned in subsection (1)(e) above are–
   (a) that it is not practicable to communicate with any person entitled to grant entry to the premises;
   (b) that it is practicable to communicate with a person entitled to grant entry to the premises but it is not practicable to communicate with any person entitled to grant access to the evidence;
   (c) that entry to the premises will not be granted unless a warrant is produced;
   (d) that the purpose of a search may be frustrated or seriously prejudiced unless a constable arriving at the premises can secure immediate entry to them.

(4) In this Act 'relevant evidence', in relation to an offence, means anything that would be admissible in evidence at a trial for the offence.

(5) The power to issue a warrant conferred by this section is in addition to any such power otherwise conferred.

(6) This section applies in relation to a relevant offence (as defined in section 28D(4) of the Immigration Act 1971) as it applies in relation to an indictable offence.

(7) Section 4 of the Summary Jurisdiction (Process) Act 1881 (execution of process of English courts in Scotland) shall apply to a warrant issued on the application of an officer of Revenue and Customs under this section by virtue of section 114 below.

### Special provisions as to access

9(1) A constable may obtain access to excluded material or special procedure material for the purposes of a criminal investigation by making an application under Schedule 1 below and in accordance with that Schedule.

(2) Any Act (including a local Act) passed before this Act under which a search of premises for the purposes of a criminal investigation could be authorised by the issue of a warrant to a constable shall cease to have effect so far as it relates to the authorisation of searches–

(a) for items subject to legal privilege; or

(b) for excluded material; or

(c) for special procedure material consisting of documents or records other than documents.

(2A) Section 4 of the Summary Jurisdiction (Process) Act 1881 (which includes provision for the execution of process of English courts in Scotland) and section 29 of the Petty Sessions (Ireland) Act 1851 (which makes equivalent provision for execution in Northern Ireland) shall each apply to any process issued by a [circuit judge] *judge*[2] under Schedule 1 to this Act as it applies to process issued by a magistrates' court under the Magistrates' Courts Act 1980 (c 43).

### Meaning of 'items subject to legal privilege'

10(1) Subject to subsection (2) below, in this Act 'items subject to legal privilege' means–

(a) communications between a professional legal adviser and his client or any person representing his client made in connection with the giving of legal advice to the client;

(b) communications between a professional legal adviser and his client or any person representing his client or between such an adviser or his client or any such representative and any other person made in connection with or in contemplation of legal proceedings and for the purposes of such proceedings; and

(c) items enclosed with or referred to in such communications and made–

(i) in connection with the giving of legal advice; or

(ii) in connection with or in contemplation of legal proceedings and for the purposes of such proceedings,

when they are in the possession of a person who is entitled to possession of them.

(2) Items held with the intention of furthering a criminal purpose are not items subject to legal privilege.

### Meaning of 'excluded material'

11(1) Subject to the following provisions of this section, in this Act 'excluded material' means–

(a) personal records which a person has acquired or created in the course of any trade, business, profession or other occupation or for the purposes of any paid or unpaid office and which he holds in confidence;

(b) human tissue or tissue fluid which has been taken for the purposes of diagnosis or medical treatment and which a person holds in confidence;

(c) journalistic material which a person holds in confidence and which consists–

---

2  Words 'circuit judge' in square brackets repealed and subsequent word in italics substituted by the Courts Act 2003 s65, Sch 4 para 5. Not yet in force: see Courts Act 2003 s110(1).

(i) of documents; or

(ii) of records other than documents.

(2) A person holds material other than journalistic material in confidence for the purposes of this section if he holds it subject–

(a) to an express or implied undertaking to hold it in confidence; or

(b) to a restriction on disclosure or an obligation of secrecy contained in any enactment, including an enactment contained in an Act passed after this Act.

(3) A person holds journalistic material in confidence for the purposes of this section if–

(a) he holds it subject to such an undertaking, restriction or obligation; and

(b) it has been continuously held (by one or more persons) subject to such an undertaking, restriction or obligation since it was first acquired or created for the purposes of journalism.

## Meaning of 'personal records'

12 In this Part of this Act 'personal records' means documentary and other records concerning an individual (whether living or dead) who can be identified from them and relating–

(a) to his physical or mental health;

(b) to spiritual counselling or assistance given or to be given to him; or

(c) to counselling or assistance given or to be given to him, for the purposes of his personal welfare, by any voluntary organisation or by any individual who–

(i) by reason of his office or occupation has responsibilities for his personal welfare; or

(ii) by reason of an order of a court has responsibilities for his supervision.

## Meaning of 'journalistic material'

13(1) Subject to subsection (2) below, in this Act 'journalistic material' means material acquired or created for the purposes of journalism.

(2) Material is only journalistic material for the purposes of this Act if it is in the possession of a person who acquired or created it for the purposes of journalism.

(3) A person who receives material from someone who intends that the recipient shall use it for the purposes of journalism is to be taken to have acquired it for those purposes.

## Meaning of 'special procedure material'

14(1) In this Act 'special procedure material' means–

(a) material to which subsection (2) below applies; and

(b) journalistic material, other than excluded material.

(2) Subject to the following provisions of this section, this subsection applies to material, other than items subject to legal privilege and excluded material, in the possession of a person who–

(a) acquired or created it in the course of any trade, business, profession or other occupation or for the purpose of any paid or unpaid office; and

(b) holds it subject–

(i) to an express or implied undertaking to hold it in confidence; or

(ii) to a restriction or obligation such as is mentioned in section 11(2)(b) above.

(3) Where material is acquired–

(a) by an employee from his employer and in the course of his employment; or

(b) by a company from an associated company,

it is only special procedure material if it was special procedure material immediately before the acquisition.

(4) Where material is created by an employee in the course of his employment, it is only special procedure material if it would have been special procedure material had his employer created it.

(5) Where material is created by a company on behalf of an associated company, it is only special procedure material if it would have been special procedure material had the associated company created it.

(6) A company is to be treated as another's associated company for the purposes of this section if it would be so treated under section 449 of the Corporation Tax Act 2010.[3]

### Search warrants–safeguards

15(1) This section and section 16 below have effect in relation to the issue to constables under any enactment, including an enactment contained in an Act passed after this Act, of warrants to enter and search premises; and an entry on or search of premises under a warrant is unlawful unless it complies with this section and section 16 below.

(2) Where a constable applies for any such warrant, it shall be his duty–
  (a) to state–
     (i)   the ground on which he makes the application; ...
     (ii)  the enactment under which the warrant would be issued; and
     (iii) if the application is for a warrant authorising entry and search on more than one occasion, the ground on which he applies for such a warrant, and whether he seeks a warrant authorising an unlimited number of entries, or (if not) the maximum number of entries desired;
  (b) to specify the matters set out in subsection (2A) below; and
  (c) to identify, so far as is practicable, the articles or persons to be sought.

(2A) The matters which must be specified pursuant to subsection (2)(b) above are–
  (a) if the application relates to one or more sets of premises specified in the application, each set of premises which it is desired to enter and search;
  (b) if the application relates to any premises occupied or controlled by a person specified in the application–
     (i)   as many sets of premises which it is desired to enter and search as it is reasonably practicable to specify;
     (ii)  the person who is in occupation or control of those premises and any others which it is desired to enter and search;
     (iii) why it is necessary to search more premises than those specified under sub-paragraph (i); and
     (iv)  why it is not reasonably practicable to specify all the premises which it is desired to enter and search.

(3) An application for such a warrant shall be made ex parte and supported by an information in writing.

(4) The constable shall answer on oath any question that the justice of the peace or judge hearing the application asks him.

(5) A warrant shall authorise an entry on one occasion only unless it specifies that it authorises multiple entries.

(5A) If it specifies that it authorises multiple entries, it must also specify whether the number of entries authorised is unlimited, or limited to a specified maximum.

(6) A warrant–
  (a) shall specify–
     (i)   the name of the person who applies for it;
     (ii)  the date on which it is issued;
     (iii) the enactment under which it is issued; and
     (iv)  each set of premises to be searched, or (in the case of an all premises warrant) the person who is in occupation or control of premises to be searched, together with any premises under his occupation or control which can be specified and which are to be searched; and
  (b) shall identify, so far as is practicable, the articles or persons to be sought.

(7) Two copies shall be made of a warrant (see section 8(1A)(a) above) which specifies only one set of premises and does not authorise multiple entries; and as many copies as are reasonably required may be made of any other kind of warrant.

3   Words 'section 449 of the Corporation Tax Act 2010' substituted by the Corporation Tax Act 2010 s1177, Sch 1 Pt 2 para 193. This amendment has effect for corporation tax purposes for accounting periods ending on or after 1 April 2010 (see the Corporation Tax Act 2010 s1184(1)(a)); and for income tax and capital gains tax purposes for the tax year 2010–11 and subsequent tax years (see the Corporation Tax Act 2010 s1184(1)(b)).

(8) The copies shall be clearly certified as copies.

**Execution of warrants**

16(1) A warrant to enter and search premises may be executed by any constable.

(2) Such a warrant may authorise persons to accompany any constable who is executing it.

(2A) A person so authorised has the same powers as the constable whom he accompanies in respect of–

(a) the execution of the warrant, and

(b) the seizure of anything to which the warrant relates.

(2B) But he may exercise those powers only in the company, and under the supervision, of a constable.

(3) Entry and search under a warrant must be within three months from the date of its issue.

(3A) If the warrant is an all premises warrant, no premises which are not specified in it may be entered or searched unless a police officer of at least the rank of inspector has in writing authorised them to be entered.

(3B) No premises may be entered or searched for the second or any subsequent time under a warrant which authorises multiple entries unless a police officer of at least the rank of inspector has in writing authorised that entry to those premises.

(4) Entry and search under a warrant must be at a reasonable hour unless it appears to the constable executing it that the purpose of a search may be frustrated on an entry at a reasonable hour.

(5) Where the occupier of premises which are to be entered and searched is present at the time when a constable seeks to execute a warrant to enter and search them, the constable–

(a) shall identify himself to the occupier and, if not in uniform, shall produce to him documentary evidence that he is a constable;

(b) shall produce the warrant to him; and

(c) shall supply him with a copy of it.

(6) Where–

(a) the occupier of such premises is not present at the time when a constable seeks to execute such a warrant; but

(b) some other person who appears to the constable to be in charge of the premises is present,

subsection (5) above shall have effect as if any reference to the occupier were a reference to that other person.

(7) If there is no person present who appears to the constable to be in charge of the premises, he shall leave a copy of the warrant in a prominent place on the premises.

(8) A search under a warrant may only be a search to the extent required for the purpose for which the warrant was issued.

(9) A constable executing a warrant shall make an endorsement on it stating–

(a) whether the articles or persons sought were found; and

(b) whether any articles were seized, other than articles which were sought and, unless the warrant is a warrant specifying one set of premises only, he shall do so separately in respect of each set of premises entered and searched, which he shall in each case state in the endorsement.

(10) A warrant shall be returned to the appropriate person mentioned in subsection (10A) below–

(a) when it has been executed; or

(b) in the case of a specific premises warrant which has not been executed, or an all premises warrant, or any warrant authorising multiple entries, upon the expiry of the period of three months referred to in subsection (3) above or sooner.

(10A) The appropriate person is–

(a) if the warrant was issued by a justice of the peace, the designated officer for the local justice area in which the justice was acting when he issued the warrant;

(b) if it was issued by a judge, the appropriate officer of the court from which he issued it.

(11) A warrant which is returned under subsection (10) above shall be retained for 12 months from its return–
  (a) by the designated officer for the local justice area, if it was returned under paragraph (i) of that subsection; and
  (b) by the appropriate officer, if it was returned under paragraph (ii).
(12) If during the period for which a warrant is to be retained the occupier of premises to which it relates asks to inspect it, he shall be allowed to do so.

### Entry and search without search warrant

### Entry for purpose of arrest etc

**17**(1) Subject to the following provisions of this section, and without prejudice to any other enactment, a constable may enter and search any premises for the purpose–
  (a) of executing–
    (i) a warrant of arrest issued in connection with or arising out of criminal proceedings; or
    (ii) a warrant of commitment issued under section 76 of the Magistrates' Courts Act 1980;
  (b) of arresting a person for an indictable offence;
  (c) of arresting a person for an offence under–
    (i) section 1 (prohibition of uniforms in connection with political objects) of the Public Order Act 1936;
    (ii) any enactment contained in sections 6 to 8 or 10 of the Criminal Law Act 1977 (offences relating to entering and remaining on property);
    (iii) section 4 of the Public Order Act 1986 (fear or provocation of violence);
    (iiia) section 4 (driving etc when under influence of drink or drugs) or 163 (failure to stop when required to do so by constable in uniform) of the Road Traffic Act 1988;
    (iiib) section 27 of the Transport and Works Act 1992 (which relates to offences involving drink or drugs);
    (iv) section 76 of the Criminal Justice and Public Order Act 1994 (failure to comply with interim possession order);
    (v) any of sections 4, 5, 6(1) and (2), 7 and 8(1) and (2) of the Animal Welfare Act 2006 (offences relating to the prevention of harm to animals);
  (ca) of arresting, in pursuance of section 32(1A) of the Children and Young Persons Act 1969, any child or young person who has been remanded or committed to local authority accommodation under section 23(1) of that Act;
  (caa) of arresting a person for an offence to which section 61 of the Animal Health Act 1981 applies;
  (cb) of recapturing any person who is, or is deemed for any purpose to be, unlawfully at large while liable to be detained–
    (i) in a prison, remand centre, young offender institution or secure training centre, or
    (ii) in pursuance of section 92 of the Powers of Criminal Courts (Sentencing) Act 2000 (dealing with children and young persons guilty of grave crimes), in any other place;
  (d) of recapturing any person whatever who is unlawfully at large and whom he is pursuing; or
  (e) of saving life or limb or preventing serious damage to property.
(2) Except for the purpose specified in paragraph (e) of subsection (1) above, the powers of entry and search conferred by this section–
  (a) are only exercisable if the constable has reasonable grounds for believing that the person whom he is seeking is on the premises; and
  (b) are limited, in relation to premises consisting of two or more separate dwellings, to powers to enter and search–
    (i) any parts of the premises which the occupiers of any dwelling comprised in the premises use in common with the occupiers of any other such dwelling; and

(ii) any such dwelling in which the constable has reasonable grounds for believing that the person whom he is seeking may be.

(3) The powers of entry and search conferred by this section are only exercisable for the purposes specified in subsection (1)(c)(ii) or (iv) above by a constable in uniform.

(4) The power of search conferred by this section is only a power to search to the extent that is reasonably required for the purpose for which the power of entry is exercised.

(5) Subject to subsection (6) below, all the rules of common law under which a constable has power to enter premises without a warrant are hereby abolished.

(6) Nothing in subsection (5) above affects any power of entry to deal with or prevent a breach of the peace.

### Entry and search after arrest

18(1) Subject to the following provisions of this section, a constable may enter and search any premises occupied or controlled by a person who is under arrest for an indictable offence, if he has reasonable grounds for suspecting that there is on the premises evidence, other than items subject to legal privilege, that relates–

(a) to that offence; or

(b) to some other indictable offence which is connected with or similar to that offence.

(2) A constable may seize and retain anything for which he may search under subsection (1) above.

(3) The power to search conferred by subsection (1) above is only a power to search to the extent that is reasonably required for the purpose of discovering such evidence.

(4) Subject to subsection (5) below, the powers conferred by this section may not be exercised unless an officer of the rank of inspector or above has authorised them in writing.

(5) A constable may conduct a search under subsection (1)–

(a) before the person is taken to a police station or released on bail under section 30A, and

(b) without obtaining an authorisation under subsection (4),

if the condition in subsection (5A) is satisfied.

(5A) The condition is that the presence of the person at a place (other than a police station) is necessary for the effective investigation of the offence.

(6) If a constable conducts a search by virtue of subsection (5) above, he shall inform an officer of the rank of inspector or above that he has made the search as soon as practicable after he has made it.

(7) An officer who–

(a) authorises a search; or

(b) is informed of a search under subsection (6) above, shall make a record in writing–

(i) of the grounds for the search; and

(ii) of the nature of the evidence that was sought.

(8) If the person who was in occupation or control of the premises at the time of the search is in police detention at the time the record is to be made, the officer shall make the record as part of his custody record.

### Seizure etc

### General power of seizure etc

19(1) The powers conferred by subsections (2), (3) and (4) below are exercisable by a constable who is lawfully on any premises.

(2) The constable may seize anything which is on the premises if he has reasonable grounds for believing–

(a) that it has been obtained in consequence of the commission of an offence; and

(b) that it is necessary to seize it in order to prevent it being concealed, lost, damaged, altered or destroyed.

(3) The constable may seize anything which is on the premises if he has reasonable grounds for believing–

(a)  that it is evidence in relation to an offence which he is investigating or any other offence; and

(b)  that it is necessary to seize it in order to prevent the evidence being concealed, lost, altered or destroyed.

(4)  The constable may require any information which is stored in any electronic form and is accessible from the premises to be produced in a form in which it can be taken away and in which it is visible and legible or from which it can readily be produced in a visible and legible form if he has reasonable grounds for believing–

(a)  that–

(i)   it is evidence in relation to an offence which he is investigating or any other offence; or

(ii)  it has been obtained in consequence of the commission of an offence; and

(b)  that it is necessary to do so in order to prevent it being concealed, lost, tampered with or destroyed.

(5)  The powers conferred by this section are in addition to any power otherwise conferred.

(6)  No power of seizure conferred on a constable under any enactment (including an enactment contained in an Act passed after this Act) is to be taken to authorise the seizure of an item which the constable exercising the power has reasonable grounds for believing to be subject to legal privilege.

### Extension of powers of seizure to computerised information

20(1)  Every power of seizure which is conferred by an enactment to which this section applies on a constable who has entered premises in the exercise of a power conferred by an enactment shall be construed as including a power to require any information stored in any electronic form and accessible from the premises to be produced in a form in which it can be taken away and in which it is visible and legible or from which it can readily be produced in a visible and legible form.

(2)  This section applies–

(a)  to any enactment contained in an Act passed before this Act;

(b)  to sections 8 and 18 above;

(c)  to paragraph 13 of Schedule 1 to this Act; and

(d)  to any enactment contained in an Act passed after this Act.

### Access and copying

21(1)  A constable who seizes anything in the exercise of a power conferred by any enactment, including an enactment contained in an Act passed after this Act, shall, if so requested by a person showing himself–

(a)  to be the occupier of premises on which it was seized; or

(b)  to have had custody or control of it immediately before the seizure,

provide that person with a record of what he seized.

(2)  The officer shall provide the record within a reasonable time from the making of the request for it,

(3)  Subject to subsection (8) below, if a request for permission to be granted access to anything which–

(a)  has been seized by a constable; and

(b)  is retained by the police for the purpose of investigating an offence,

is made to the officer in charge of the investigation by a person who had custody or control of the thing immediately before it was so seized or by someone acting on behalf of such a person, the officer shall allow the person who made the request access to it under the supervision of a constable.

(4)  Subject to subsection (8) below, if a request for a photograph or copy of any such thing is made to the officer in charge of the investigation by a person who had custody or control of the thing immediately before it was so seized, or by someone acting on behalf of such a person, the officer shall–

(a)  allow the person who made the request access to it under the supervision of a constable for the purpose of photographing or copying it; or

(b)  photograph or copy it, or cause it to be photographed or copied.

(5)  A constable may also photograph or copy, or have photographed or copied, anything

which he has power to seize, without a request being made under subsection (4) above.

(6) Where anything is photographed or copied under subsection (4)(b) above, the photograph or copy shall be supplied to the person who made the request.

(7) The photograph or copy shall be so supplied within a reasonable time from the making of the request.

(8) There is no duty under this section to grant access to, or to supply a photograph or copy of, anything if the officer in charge of the investigation for the purposes of which it was seized has reasonable grounds for believing that to do so would prejudice–
   (a) that investigation;
   (b) the investigating of an offence other than the offence for the purposes of investigating which the thing was seized; or
   (c) any criminal proceedings which may be brought as a result of–
       (i) the investigation of which he is in charge; or
       (ii) any such investigation as is mentioned in paragraph (b) above.

(9) The references to a constable in subsections (1), (2), (3)(a) and (5) include a person authorised under section 16(2) to accompany a constable executing a warrant.

**Retention**

22(1) Subject to subsection (4) below, anything which has been seized by a constable or taken away by a constable following a requirement made by virtue of section 19 or 20 above may be retained so long as is necessary in all the circumstances.

(2) Without prejudice to the generality of subsection (1) above–
   (a) anything seized for the purposes of a criminal investigation may be retained, except as provided by subsection (4) below,–
       (i) for use as evidence at a trial for an offence; or
       (ii) for forensic examination or for investigation in connection with an offence; and
   (b) anything may be retained in order to establish its lawful owner, where there are reasonable grounds for believing that it has been obtained in consequence of the commission of an offence.

(3) Nothing seized on the ground that it may be used–
   (a) to cause physical injury to any person;
   (b) to damage property;
   (c) to interfere with evidence; or
   (d) to assist in escape from police detention or lawful custody,
   may be retained when the person from whom it was seized is no longer in police detention or the custody of a court or is in the custody of a court but has been released on bail.

(4) Nothing may be retained for either of the purposes mentioned in subsection (2)(a) above if a photograph or copy would be sufficient for that purpose.

(5) Nothing in this section affects any power of a court to make an order under section 1 of the Police (Property) Act 1897.

(6) This section also applies to anything retained by the police under section 28H(5) of the Immigration Act 1971.

(7) The reference in subsection (1) to anything seized by a constable includes anything seized by a person authorised under section 16(2) to accompany a constable executing a warrant.

*Supplementary*

**Meaning of 'premises' etc**

23 In this Act–
   'premises' includes any place and, in particular, includes–
       (a) any vehicle, vessel, aircraft or hovercraft;
       (b) any offshore installation;
       (ba) any renewable energy installation;
       (c) any tent or movable structure;

'offshore installation' has the meaning given to it by section 1 of the Mineral Workings (Offshore Installations) Act 1971;

'renewable energy installation' has the same meaning as in Chapter 2 of Part 2 of the Energy Act 2004.

## PART III: ARREST

### Arrest without warrant: constables

24(1) A constable may arrest without a warrant–

(a) anyone who is about to commit an offence;

(b) anyone who is in the act of committing an offence;

(c) anyone whom he has reasonable grounds for suspecting to be about to commit an offence;

(d) anyone whom he has reasonable grounds for suspecting to be committing an offence.

(2) If a constable has reasonable grounds for suspecting that an offence has been committed, he may arrest without a warrant anyone whom he has reasonable grounds to suspect of being guilty of it.

(3) If an offence has been committed, a constable may arrest without a warrant–

(a) anyone who is guilty of the offence;

(b) anyone whom he has reasonable grounds for suspecting to be guilty of it.

(4) But the power of summary arrest conferred by subsection (1), (2) or (3) is exercisable only if the constable has reasonable grounds for believing that for any of the reasons mentioned in subsection (5) it is necessary to arrest the person in question.

(5) The reasons are–

(a) to enable the name of the person in question to be ascertained (in the case where the constable does not know, and cannot readily ascertain, the person's name, or has reasonable grounds for doubting whether a name given by the person as his name is his real name);

(b) correspondingly as regards the person's address;

(c) to prevent the person in question–

(i) causing physical injury to himself or any other person;

(ii) suffering physical injury;

(iii) causing loss of or damage to property;

(iv) committing an offence against public decency (subject to subsection (6)); or

(v) causing an unlawful obstruction of the highway;

(d) to protect a child or other vulnerable person from the person in question;

(e) to allow the prompt and effective investigation of the offence or of the conduct of the person in question;

(f) to prevent any prosecution for the offence from being hindered by the disappearance of the person in question.

(6) Subsection (5)(c)(iv) applies only where members of the public going about their normal business cannot reasonably be expected to avoid the person in question.

### Arrest without warrant: other persons

24A(1) A person other than a constable may arrest without a warrant–

(a) anyone who is in the act of committing an indictable offence;

(b) anyone whom he has reasonable grounds for suspecting to be committing an indictable offence.

(2) Where an indictable offence has been committed, a person other than a constable may arrest without a warrant–

(a) anyone who is guilty of the offence;

(b) anyone whom he has reasonable grounds for suspecting to be guilty of it.

(3) But the power of summary arrest conferred by subsection (1) or (2) is exercisable only if–

(a) the person making the arrest has reasonable grounds for believing that for any of the reasons mentioned in subsection (4) it is necessary to arrest the person in question; and

(b) it appears to the person making the arrest that it is not reasonably practicable for a constable to make it instead.

(4) The reasons are to prevent the person in question–
   (a) causing physical injury to himself or any other person;
   (b) suffering physical injury;
   (c) causing loss of or damage to property; or
   (d) making off before a constable can assume responsibility for him.

(5) This section does not apply in relation to an offence under Part 3 or 3A of the Public Order Act 1986.

25 [Repealed.]

### Repeal of statutory powers of arrest without warrant or order

26(1) Subject to subsection (2) below, so much of any Act (including a local Act) passed before this Act as enables a constable–
   (a) to arrest a person for an offence without a warrant; or
   (b) to arrest a person otherwise than for an offence without a warrant or an order of a court,
shall cease to have effect.

(2) Nothing in subsection (1) above affects the enactments specified in Schedule 2 to this Act.

### Fingerprinting of certain offenders

27(1) [Repealed.]
 (1A) [Repealed.]
 (1B) [Repealed.]
  (2) [Repealed.]
  (3) [Repealed.]
  (4) The Secretary of State may by regulations make provision for recording in national police records convictions for such offences as are specified in the regulations.
 (4A) [Repealed.]
  (5) Regulations under this section shall be made by statutory instrument and shall be subject to annulment in pursuance of a resolution of either House of Parliament.

### Information to be given on arrest

28(1) Subject to subsection (5) below, where a person is arrested, otherwise than by being informed that he is under arrest, the arrest is not lawful unless the person arrested is informed that he is under arrest as soon as is practicable after his arrest.

(2) Where a person is arrested by a constable, subsection (1) above applies regardless of whether the fact of the arrest is obvious.

(3) Subject to subsection (5) below, no arrest is lawful unless the person arrested is informed of the ground for the arrest at the time of, or as soon as is practicable after, the arrest.

(4) Where a person is arrested by a constable, subsection (3) above applies regardless of whether the ground for the arrest is obvious.

(5) Nothing in this section is to be taken to require a person to be informed–
   (a) that he is under arrest; or
   (b) of the ground for the arrest,
if it was not reasonably practicable for him to be so informed by reason of his having escaped from arrest before the information could be given.

### Voluntary attendance at police station etc

29 Where for the purpose of assisting with an investigation a person attends voluntarily at a police station or at any other place where a constable is present or accompanies a constable to a police station or any such other place without having been arrested–
   (a) he shall be entitled to leave at will unless he is placed under arrest;
   (b) he shall be informed at once that he is under arrest if a decision is taken by a constable to prevent him from leaving at will.

### Arrest elsewhere than at police station

30(1) Subsection (1A) applies where a person is, at any place other than a police station–

(a) arrested by a constable for an offence, or

(b) taken into custody by a constable after being arrested for an offence by a person other than a constable.

(1A) The person must be taken by a constable to a police station as soon as practicable after the arrest.

(1B) Subsection (1A) has effect subject to section 30A (release on bail) and subsection (7) (release without bail).

(2) Subject to subsections (3) and (5) below, the police station to which an arrested person is taken under subsection (1A) above shall be a designated police station.

(3) A constable to whom this subsection applies may take an arrested person to any police station unless it appears to the constable that it may be necessary to keep the arrested person in police detention for more than six hours.

(4) Subsection (3) above applies–

(a) to a constable who is working in a locality covered by a police station which is not a designated police station; and

(b) to a constable belonging to a body of constables maintained by an authority other than a police authority.

(5) Any constable may take an arrested person to any police station if–

(a) either of the following conditions is satisfied–

  (i) the constable has arrested him without the assistance of any other constable and no other constable is available to assist him;

  (ii) the constable has taken him into custody from a person other than a constable without the assistance of any other constable and no other constable is available to assist him; and

(b) it appears to the constable that he will be unable to take the arrested person to a designated police station without the arrested person injuring himself, the constable or some other person.

(6) If the first police station to which an arrested person is taken after his arrest is not a designated police station, he shall be taken to a designated police station not more than six hours after his arrival at the first police station unless he is released previously.

(7) A person arrested by a constable at any place other than a police station must be released without bail if the condition in subsection (7A) is satisfied.

(7A) The condition is that, at any time before the person arrested reaches a police station, a constable is satisfied that there are no grounds for keeping him under arrest or releasing him on bail under section 30A.

(8) A constable who releases a person under subsection (7) above shall record the fact that he has done so.

(9) The constable shall make the record as soon as is practicable after the release.

(10) Nothing in subsection (1A) or in section 30A prevents a constable delaying taking a person to a police station or releasing him on bail if the condition in subsection (10A) is satisfied.

(10A) The condition is that the presence of the person at a place (other than a police station) is necessary in order to carry out such investigations as it is reasonable to carry out immediately.

(11) Where there is any such delay the reasons for the delay must be recorded when the person first arrives at the police station or (as the case may be) is released on bail.

(12) Nothing in subsection (1A) or section 30A above shall be taken to affect–

(a) paragraphs 16(3) or 18(1) of Schedule 2 to the Immigration Act 1971;

(b) section 34(1) of the Criminal Justice Act 1972; or

(c) any provision of the Terrorism Act 2000.

(13) Nothing in subsection (10) above shall be taken to affect paragraph 18(3) of Schedule 2 to the Immigration Act 1971.

### Bail elsewhere than at police station

30A(1) A constable may release on bail a person who is arrested or taken into custody in the circumstances mentioned in section 30(1).

(2) A person may be released on bail under subsection (1) at any time before he arrives at a police station.

(3) A person released on bail under subsection (1) must be required to attend a police station.

(3A) Where a constable releases a person on bail under subsection (1)–
   (a) no recognizance for the person's surrender to custody shall be taken from the person,
   (b) no security for the person's surrender to custody shall be taken from the person or from anyone else on the person's behalf,
   (c) the person shall not be required to provide a surety or sureties for his surrender to custody, and
   (d) no requirement to reside in a bail hostel may be imposed as a condition of bail.

(3B) Subject to subsection (3A), where a constable releases a person on bail under subsection (1) the constable may impose, as conditions of the bail, such requirements as appear to the constable to be necessary–
   (a) to secure that the person surrenders to custody,
   (b) to secure that the person does not commit an offence while on bail,
   (c) to secure that the person does not interfere with witnesses or otherwise obstruct the course of justice, whether in relation to himself or any other person, or
   (d) for the person's own protection or, if the person is under the age of 17, for the person's own welfare or in the person's own interests.

(4) Where a person is released on bail under subsection (1), a requirement may be imposed on the person as a condition of bail only under the preceding provisions of this section.

(5) The police station which the person is required to attend may be any police station.

### Bail under section 30A: notices

30B(1) Where a constable grants bail to a person under section 30A, he must give that person a notice in writing before he is released.

(2) The notice must state–
   (a) the offence for which he was arrested, and
   (b) the ground on which he was arrested.

(3) The notice must inform him that he is required to attend a police station.

(4) It may also specify the police station which he is required to attend and the time when he is required to attend.

(4A) If the person is granted bail subject to conditions under section 30A(3B), the notice also–
   (a) must specify the requirements imposed by those conditions,
   (b) must explain the opportunities under sections 30CA(1) and 30CB(1) for variation of those conditions, and
   (c) if it does not specify the police station at which the person is required to attend, must specify a police station at which the person may make a request under section 30CA(1)(b).

(5) If the notice does not include the information mentioned in subsection (4), the person must subsequently be given a further notice in writing which contains that information.

(6) The person may be required to attend a different police station from that specified in the notice under subsection (1) or (5) or to attend at a different time.

(7) He must be given notice in writing of any such change as is mentioned in subsection (6) but more than one such notice may be given to him.

### Bail under section 30A: supplemental

30C(1) A person who has been required to attend a police station is not required to do so if he is given notice in writing that his attendance is no longer required.

(2) If a person is required to attend a police station which is not a designated police station he must be–
   (a) released, or
   (b) taken to a designated police station,
   not more than six hours after his arrival.

(3) Nothing in the Bail Act 1976 applies in relation to bail under section 30A.

(4) Nothing in section 30A or 30B or in this section prevents the re-arrest without a

warrant of a person released on bail under section 30A if new evidence justifying a
further arrest has come to light since his release.

**Bail under section 30A: variation of conditions by police**

30CA(1)Where a person released on bail under section 30A(1) is on bail subject to
conditions–
- (a) a relevant officer at the police station at which the person is required to attend,
or
- (b) where no notice under section 30B specifying that police station has been given
to the person, a relevant officer at the police station specified under section
30B(4A)(c),

may, at the request of the person but subject to subsection (2), vary the conditions.

(2) On any subsequent request made in respect of the same grant of bail, subsection
(1) confers power to vary the conditions of the bail only if the request is based on
information that, in the case of the previous request or each previous request, was
not available to the relevant officer considering that previous request when he was
considering it.

(3) Where conditions of bail granted to a person under section 30A(1) are varied under
subsection (1)–
- (a) paragraphs (a) to (d) of section 30A(3A) apply,
- (b) requirements imposed by the conditions as so varied must be requirements that
appear to the relevant officer varying the conditions to be necessary for any of
the purposes mentioned in paragraphs (a) to (d) of section 30A(3B), and
- (c) the relevant officer who varies the conditions must give the person notice in
writing of the variation.

(4) Power under subsection (1) to vary conditions is, subject to subsection (3)(a) and (b),
power–
- (a) to vary or rescind any of the conditions, and
- (b) to impose further conditions.

(5) In this section 'relevant officer', in relation to a designated police station, means a
custody officer but, in relation to any other police station–
- (a) means a constable who is not involved in the investigation of the offence for
which the person making the request under subsection (1) was under arrest
when granted bail under section 30A(1), if such a constable is readily available,
and
- (b) if no such constable is readily available–
  - (i) means a constable other than the one who granted bail to the person, if such
a constable is readily available, and
  - (ii) if no such constable is readily available, means the constable who granted
bail.

**Bail under section 30A: variation of conditions by court**

30CB(1)Where a person released on bail under section 30A(1) is on bail subject to conditions, a magistrates' court may, on an application by or on behalf of the person, vary
the conditions if–
- (a) the conditions have been varied under section 30CA(1) since being imposed
under section 30A(3B),
- (b) a request for variation under section 30CA(1) of the conditions has been made
and refused, or
- (c) a request for variation under section 30CA(1) of the conditions has been made
and the period of 48 hours beginning with the day when the request was made
has expired without the request having been withdrawn or the conditions having been varied in response to the request.

(2) In proceedings on an application for a variation under subsection (1), a ground may
not be relied upon unless–
- (a) in a case falling within subsection (1)(a), the ground was relied upon in the request
in response to which the conditions were varied under section 30CA(1), or
- (b) in a case falling within paragraph (b) or (c) of subsection (1), the ground was
relied upon in the request mentioned in that paragraph,

but this does not prevent the court, when deciding the application, from considering different grounds arising out of a change in circumstances that has occurred since the making of the application.

(3) Where conditions of bail granted to a person under section 30A(1) are varied under subsection (1)–

(a) paragraphs (a) to (d) of section 30A(3A) apply,

(b) requirements imposed by the conditions as so varied must be requirements that appear to the court varying the conditions to be necessary for any of the purposes mentioned in paragraphs (a) to (d) of section 30A(3B), and

(c) that bail shall not lapse but shall continue subject to the conditions as so varied.

(4) Power under subsection (1) to vary conditions is, subject to subsection (3)(a) and (b), power–

(a) to vary or rescind any of the conditions, and

(b) to impose further conditions.

### Failure to answer to bail under section 30A

30D(1) A constable may arrest without a warrant a person who–

(a) has been released on bail under section 30A subject to a requirement to attend a specified police station, but

(b) fails to attend the police station at the specified time.

(2) A person arrested under subsection (1) must be taken to a police station (which may be the specified police station or any other police station) as soon as practicable after the arrest.

(2A) A person who has been released on bail under section 30A may be arrested without a warrant by a constable if the constable has reasonable grounds for suspecting that the person has broken any of the conditions of bail.

(2B) A person arrested under subsection (2A) must be taken to a police station (which may be the specified police station mentioned in subsection (1) or any other police station) as soon as practicable after the arrest.

(3) In subsection (1), 'specified' means specified in a notice under subsection (1) or (5) of section 30B or, if notice of change has been given under subsection (7) of that section, in that notice.

(4) For the purposes of–

(a) section 30 (subject to the obligations in subsections (2) and (2B)), and

(b) section 31,

an arrest under this section is to be treated as an arrest for an offence.

### Arrest for further offence

31 Where–

(a) a person–

(i) has been arrested for an offence; and

(ii) is at a police station in consequence of that arrest; and

(b) it appears to a constable that, if he were released from that arrest, he would be liable to arrest for some other offence,

he shall be arrested for that other offence.

### Search upon arrest

32(1) A constable may search an arrested person, in any case where the person to be searched has been arrested at a place other than a police station, if the constable has reasonable grounds for believing that the arrested person may present a danger to himself or others.

(2) Subject to subsections (3) to (5) below, a constable shall also have power in any such case–

(a) to search the arrested person for anything–

(i) which he might use to assist him to escape from lawful custody; or

(ii) which might be evidence relating to an offence; and

(b) if the offence for which he has been arrested is an indictable offence, to enter and search any premises in which he was when arrested or immediately before he was arrested for evidence relating to the offence.

(3) The power to search conferred by subsection (2) above is only a power to search to the extent that is reasonably required for the purpose of discovering any such thing or any such evidence.

(4) The powers conferred by this section to search a person are not to be construed as authorising a constable to require a person to remove any of his clothing in public other than an outer coat, jacket or gloves but they do authorise a search of a person's mouth.

(5) A constable may not search a person in the exercise of the power conferred by subsection (2)(a) above unless he has reasonable grounds for believing that the person to be searched may have concealed on him anything for which a search is permitted under that paragraph.

(6) A constable may not search premises in the exercise of the power conferred by subsection (2)(b) above unless he has reasonable grounds for believing that there is evidence for which a search is permitted under that paragraph on the premises.

(7) In so far as the power of search conferred by subsection (2)(b) above relates to premises consisting of two or more separate dwellings, it is limited to a power to search–
  (a) any dwelling in which the arrest took place or in which the person arrested was immediately before his arrest; and
  (b) any parts of the premises which the occupier of any such dwelling uses in common with the occupiers of any other dwellings comprised in the premises.

(8) A constable searching a person in the exercise of the power conferred by subsection (1) above may seize and retain anything he finds, if he has reasonable grounds for believing that the person searched might use it to cause physical injury to himself or to any other person.

(9) A constable searching a person in the exercise of the power conferred by subsection (2)(a) above may seize and retain anything he finds, other than an item subject to legal privilege, if he has reasonable grounds for believing–
  (a) that he might use it to assist him to escape from lawful custody; or
  (b) that it is evidence of an offence or has been obtained in consequence of the commission of an offence.

(10) Nothing in this section shall be taken to affect the power conferred by section 43 of the Terrorism Act 2000.

33 [Repealed.]

## PART IV: DETENTION

### *Detention–conditions and duration*

#### Limitations on police detention

34(1) A person arrested for an offence shall not be kept in police detention except in accordance with the provisions of this Part of this Act.

(2) Subject to subsection (3) below, if at any time a custody officer–
  (a) becomes aware, in relation to any person in police detention, that the grounds for the detention of that person have ceased to apply; and
  (b) is not aware of any other grounds on which the continued detention of that person could be justified under the provisions of this Part of this Act,
  it shall be the duty of the custody officer, subject to subsection (4) below, to order his immediate release from custody.

(3) No person in police detention shall be released except on the authority of a custody officer at the police station where his detention was authorised or, if it was authorised at more than one station, a custody officer at the station where it was last authorised.

(4) A person who appears to the custody officer to have been unlawfully at large when he was arrested is not to be released under subsection (2) above.

(5) A person whose release is ordered under subsection (2) above shall be released without bail unless it appears to the custody officer–
  (a) that there is need for further investigation of any matter in connection with which he was detained at any time during the period of his detention; or
  (b) that, in respect of any such matter, proceedings may be taken against him or he

may be reprimanded or warned under section 65 of the Crime and Disorder Act 1998,

and, if it so appears, he shall be released on bail.

(6) For the purposes of this Part of this Act a person arrested under section 6D of the Road Traffic Act 1988 or section 30(2) of the Transport and Works Act 1992 is arrested for an offence.

(7) For the purposes of this Part a person who–
   (a) attends a police station to answer to bail granted under section 30A,
   (b) returns to a police station to answer to bail granted under this Part, or
   (c) is arrested under section 30D or 46A,

is to be treated as arrested for an offence and that offence is the offence in connection with which he was granted bail.

But this subsection is subject to section 47(6) (which provides for the calculation of certain periods, where a person has been granted bail under this Part, by reference to time when the person is in police detention only).

(8) Subsection (7) does not apply in relation to a person who is granted bail subject to the duty mentioned in section 47(3)(b) and who either–
   (a) attends a police station to answer to such bail, or
   (b) is arrested under section 46A for failing to do so,

(provision as to the treatment of such persons for the purposes of this Part being made by section 46ZA).[4]

### Designated police stations

35(1) The chief officer of police for each police area shall designate the police stations in his area which, subject to sections 30(3) and (5), 30A(5) and 30D(2), are to be the stations in that area to be used for the purpose of detaining arrested persons.

(2) A chief officer's duty under subsection (1) above is to designate police stations appearing to him to provide enough accommodation for that purpose.

(2A) The Chief Constable of the British Transport Police Force may designate police stations which (in addition to those designated under subsection (1) above) may be used for the purpose of detaining arrested persons.

(3) Without prejudice to section 12 of the Interpretation Act 1978 (continuity of duties) a chief officer–
   (a) may designate a station which was not previously designated; and
   (b) may direct that a designation of a station previously made shall cease to operate.

(4) In this Act 'designated police station' means a police station designated under this section.

### Custody officers at police stations

36(1) One or more custody officers shall be appointed for each designated police station.

(2) A custody officer for a police station designated under section 35(1) above shall be appointed–
   (a) by the chief officer of police for the area in which the designated police station is situated; or
   (b) by such other police officer as the chief officer of police for that area may direct.

(2A) A custody officer for a police station designated under section 35(2A) above shall be appointed–
   (a) by the Chief Constable of the British Transport Police Force; or
   (b) by such other member of that Force as that Chief Constable may direct.

(3) No officer may be appointed a custody officer unless the officer is of at least the rank of sergeant.

---

4  Subs (8) inserted by the Police and Justice Act 2006 s46(1), (2). Date in force (in relation to the local justice area of Lambeth and Southwark): 1 April 2007 (SI 2007/709 art 3(n)). Date in force (in relation to certain local justice areas): 14 November 2008 (SI 2008/2785 art 2). Date in force for remaining purposes: to be appointed: see the Police and Justice Act 2006 s53(1)(a).

(4) An officer of any rank may perform the functions of a custody officer at a designated police station if a custody officer is not readily available to perform them.

(5) Subject to the following provisions of this section and to section 39(2) below, none of the functions of a custody officer in relation to a person shall be performed by an officer who at the time when the function falls to be performed is involved in the investigation of an offence for which that person is in police detention at that time.

(6) Nothing in subsection (5) above is to be taken to prevent a custody officer–
    (a) performing any function assigned to custody officers–
        (i)  by this Act; or
        (ii) by a code of practice issued under this Act;
    (b) carrying out the duty imposed on custody officers by section 39 below;
    (c) doing anything in connection with the identification of a suspect; or
    (d) doing anything under sections 7 and 8 of the Road Traffic Act 1988.

(7) Where an arrested person is taken to a police station which is not a designated police station, the functions in relation to him which at a designated police station would be the functions of a custody officer shall be performed–
    (a) by an officer who is not involved in the investigation of an offence for which he is in police detention, if such an officer is readily available; and
    (b) if no [such officer] *such person* is readily available, by the officer who took him to the station or any other officer.[5]

(7A) Subject to subsection (7B), subsection (7) applies where a person attends a police station which is not a designated station to answer to bail granted under section 30A as it applies where a person is taken to such a station.

(7B) Where subsection (7) applies because of subsection (7A), the reference in subsection (7)(b) to the officer who took him to the station is to be read as a reference to the officer who granted him bail.

(8) References to a custody officer in section 34 above or in the following provisions of this Act include references to an officer other than a custody officer who is performing the functions of a custody officer by virtue of subsection (4) or (7) above.

(9) Where by virtue of subsection (7) above an officer of a force maintained by a police authority who took an arrested person to a police station is to perform the functions of a custody officer in relation to him, the officer shall inform an officer who–
    (a) is attached to a designated police station; and
    (b) is of at least the rank of inspector,
that he is to do so.

(10) The duty imposed by subsection (9) above shall be performed as soon as it is practicable to perform it.

(11) [Repealed.]

### Duties of custody officer before charge

37(1) Where–
    (a) a person is arrested for an offence–
        (i)  without a warrant; or
        (ii) under a warrant not endorsed for bail,
    (b) [Repealed.]
the custody officer at each police station where he is detained after his arrest shall determine whether he has before him sufficient evidence to charge that person with the offence for which he was arrested and may detain him at the police station for such period as is necessary to enable him to do so.

(2) If the custody officer determines that he does not have such evidence before him, the person arrested shall be released either on bail or without bail, unless the custody officer has reasonable grounds for believing that his detention without being charged is necessary to secure or preserve evidence relating to an offence for which he is under arrest or to obtain such evidence by questioning him.

---

5  Words 'or a staff custody officer' in subs 7(a) inserted by the Serious Organised Crime and Police Act (SOCPA) 2005 s121(1), (4)(a)(i). Not yet in force: see SOCPA 2005 s178(8). Words 'such officer' in subs 7(b) repealed and subsequent words in italics substituted by SOCPA 2005 s121(1), (4)(b). Not yet in force: see SOCPA 2005 s178(8).

(3) If the custody officer has reasonable grounds for so believing, he may authorise the person arrested to be kept in police detention.

(4) Where a custody officer authorises a person who has not been charged to be kept in police detention, he shall, as soon as is practicable, make a written record of the grounds for the detention.

(5) Subject to subsection (6) below, the written record shall be made in the presence of the person arrested who shall at that time be informed by the custody officer of the grounds for his detention.

(6) Subsection (5) above shall not apply where the person arrested is, at the time when the written record is made–
   (a) incapable of understanding what is said to him;
   (b) violent or likely to become violent; or
   (c) in urgent need of medical attention.

(7) Subject to section 41(7) below, if the custody officer determines that he has before him sufficient evidence to charge the person arrested with the offence for which he was arrested, the person arrested–
   (a) shall be–
      (i) released without charge and on bail, or
      (ii) kept in police detention,
   for the purpose of enabling the Director of Public Prosecutions to make a decision under section 37B below,
   (b) shall be released without charge and on bail but not for that purpose,
   (c) shall be released without charge and without bail, or
   (d) shall be charged.

(7A) The decision as to how a person is to be dealt with under subsection (7) above shall be that of the custody officer.

(7B) Where a person is dealt with under subsection (7)(a) above, it shall be the duty of the custody officer to inform him that he is being released, or (as the case may be) detained, to enable the Director of Public Prosecutions to make a decision under section 37B below.

(8) Where–
   (a) a person is released under subsection (7)(b) or (c) above; and
   (b) at the time of his release a decision whether he should be prosecuted for the offence for which he was arrested has not been taken,
   it shall be the duty of the custody officer so to inform him.

(8A) Subsection (8B) applies if the offence for which the person is arrested is one in relation to which a sample could be taken under section 63B below and the custody officer–
   (a) is required in pursuance of subsection (2) above to release the person arrested and decides to release him on bail, or
   (b) decides in pursuance of subsection (7)(a) or (b) above to release the person without charge and on bail.

(8B) The detention of the person may be continued to enable a sample to be taken under section 63B, but this subsection does not permit a person to be detained for a period of more than 24 hours after the relevant time.

(9) If the person arrested is not in a fit state to be dealt with under subsection (7) above, he may be kept in police detention until he is.

(10) The duty imposed on the custody officer under subsection (1) above shall be carried out by him as soon as practicable after the person arrested arrives at the police station or, in the case of a person arrested at the police station, as soon as practicable after the arrest.

(11)-(14)[Repealed.]

(15) In this Part of this Act–
   'arrested juvenile' means a person arrested with or without a warrant who appears to be under the age of 17;
   'endorsed for bail' means endorsed with a direction for bail in accordance with section 117(2) of the Magistrates' Courts Act 1980.

**Guidance**

37A(1) The Director of Public Prosecutions may issue guidance–
    (a) for the purpose of enabling custody officers to decide how persons should be dealt with under section 37(7) above or 37C(2) or 37CA(2) below, and
    (b) as to the information to be sent to the Director of Public Prosecutions under section 37B(1) below.
  (2) The Director of Public Prosecutions may from time to time revise guidance issued under this section.
  (3) Custody officers are to have regard to guidance under this section in deciding how persons should be dealt with under section 37(7) above or 37C(2) or 37CA(2) below.
  (4) A report under section 9 of the Prosecution of Offences Act 1985 (report by DPP to Attorney General) must set out the provisions of any guidance issued, and any revisions to guidance made, in the year to which the report relates.
  (5) The Director of Public Prosecutions must publish in such manner as he thinks fit–
    (a) any guidance issued under this section, and
    (b) any revisions made to such guidance.
  (6) Guidance under this section may make different provision for different cases, circumstances or areas.

**Consultation with the Director of Public Prosecutions**

37B(1) Where a person is dealt with under section 37(7)(a) above, an officer involved in the investigation of the offence shall, as soon as is practicable, send to the Director of Public Prosecutions such information as may be specified in guidance under section 37A above.
  (2) The Director of Public Prosecutions shall decide whether there is sufficient evidence to charge the person with an offence.
  (3) If he decides that there is sufficient evidence to charge the person with an offence, he shall decide–
    (a) whether or not the person should be charged and, if so, the offence with which he should be charged, and
    (b) whether or not the person should be given a caution and, if so, the offence in respect of which he should be given a caution.
  (4) The Director of Public Prosecutions shall give notice of his decision to an officer involved in the investigation of the offence.
 (4A) Notice under subsection (4) above shall be in writing, but in the case of a person kept in police detention under section 37(7)(a) above it may be given orally in the first instance and confirmed in writing subsequently.
  (5) If his decision is–
    (a) that there is not sufficient evidence to charge the person with an offence, or
    (b) that there is sufficient evidence to charge the person with an offence but that the person should not be charged with an offence or given a caution in respect of an offence,
a custody officer shall give the person notice in writing that he is not to be prosecuted.
  (6) If the decision of the Director of Public Prosecutions is that the person should be charged with an offence, or given a caution in respect of an offence, the person shall be charged or cautioned accordingly.
  (7) But if his decision is that the person should be given a caution in respect of the offence and it proves not to be possible to give the person such a caution, he shall instead be charged with the offence.
  (8) For the purposes of this section, a person is to be charged with an offence either–
    (a) when he is in police detention at a police station (whether because he has returned to answer bail, because he is detained under section 37(7)(a) above or for some other reason), or
    (b) in accordance with section 29 of the Criminal Justice Act 2003.
  (9) In this section 'caution' includes–
    (a) a conditional caution within the meaning of Part 3 of the Criminal Justice Act 2003,

(aa) a youth conditional caution within the meaning of Chapter 1 of Part 4 of the Crime and Disorder Act 1998 and[6]

(b) a warning or reprimand under section 65 [of the Crime and Disorder Act 1998] *of that Act.*[7]

## Breach of bail following release under section 37(7)(a)

37C(1) This section applies where–

  (a) a person released on bail under section 37(7)(a) above or subsection (2)(b) below is arrested under section 46A below in respect of that bail, and

  (b) at the time of his detention following that arrest at the police station mentioned in section 46A(2) below, notice under section 37B(4) above has not been given.

  (2) The person arrested–

    (a) shall be charged, or

    (b) shall be released without charge, either on bail or without bail.

  (3) The decision as to how a person is to be dealt with under subsection (2) above shall be that of a custody officer.

  (4) A person released on bail under subsection (2)(b) above shall be released on bail subject to the same conditions (if any) which applied immediately before his arrest.

## Breach of bail following release under section 37(7)(b)

37CA(1) This section applies where a person released on bail under section 37(7)(b) above or subsection (2)(b) below–

  (a) is arrested under section 46A below in respect of that bail, and

  (b) is being detained following that arrest at the police station mentioned in section 46A(2) below.

  (2) The person arrested–

    (a) shall be charged, or

    (b) shall be released without charge, either on bail or without bail.

  (3) The decision as to how a person is to be dealt with under subsection (2) above shall be that of a custody officer.

  (4) A person released on bail under subsection (2)(b) above shall be released on bail subject to the same conditions (if any) which applied immediately before his arrest.

## Release on bail under section 37

37D(1) Where a person is released on bail under section 37, 37C(2)(b) or 37CA(2)(b) above, a custody officer may subsequently appoint a different time, or an additional time, at which the person is to attend at the police station to answer bail.

  (2) The custody officer shall give the person notice in writing of the exercise of the power under subsection (1).

  (3) The exercise of the power under subsection (1) shall not affect the conditions (if any) to which bail is subject.

  (4) Where a person released on bail under section 37(7)(a) or 37C(2)(b) above returns to a police station to answer bail or is otherwise in police detention at a police station, he may be kept in police detention to enable him to be dealt with in accordance with section 37B or 37C above or to enable the power under subsection (1) above to be exercised.

  (4A) Where a person released on bail under section 37(7)(b) or 37CA(2)(b) above returns to a police station to answer bail or is otherwise in police detention at a police station, he may be kept in police detention to enable him to be dealt with in accordance with section 37CA above or to enable the power under subsection (1) above to be exercised.

  (5) If the person mentioned in subsection (4) or (4A) above is not in a fit state to enable

---

6  Subs (9)(aa) inserted by the Criminal Justice and Immigration Act (CJIA) 2008 s148, Sch 26 Pt 2 para 20(1)(a). In force (for certain purposes): 16 November 2009 (SI 2009/2780 art 2(1)(b), (d), (2)). Date in force for remaining purposes: see CJIA 2008 s153(7).

7  Subs (9)(b) words 'of the Crime and Disorder Act 1998' in square brackets repealed and subsequent words in italics substituted by CJIA 2008 s148, Sch 26 Pt 2 para 20(1)(b). In force (for certain purposes): 16 November 2009 (SI 2009/2780 art 2(1)(b), (d), (2)). Date in force for remaining purposes: see CJIA 2008 s153(7).

him to be dealt with as mentioned in that subsection or to enable the power under subsection (1) above to be exercised, he may be kept in police detention until he is.

(6) Where a person is kept in police detention by virtue of subsection (4), (4A) or (5) above, section 37(1) to (3) and (7) above (and section 40(8) below so far as it relates to section 37(1) to (3)) shall not apply to the offence in connection with which he was released on bail under section 37(7), 37C(2)(b) or 37CA(2)(b) above.

### Duties of custody officer after charge

38(1) Where a person arrested for an offence otherwise than under a warrant endorsed for bail is charged with an offence, the custody officer shall, subject to section 25 of the Criminal Justice and Public Order Act 1994, order his release from police detention, either on bail or without bail, unless–

(a) if the person arrested is not an arrested juvenile–

  (i) his name or address cannot be ascertained or the custody officer has reasonable grounds for doubting whether a name or address furnished by him as his name or address is his real name or address;

  (ii) the custody officer has reasonable grounds for believing that the person arrested will fail to appear in court to answer to bail;

  (iii) in the case of a person arrested for an imprisonable offence, the custody officer has reasonable grounds for believing that the detention of the person arrested is necessary to prevent him from committing an offence;

  (iiia) in a case where a sample may be taken from the person under section 63B below, the custody officer has reasonable grounds for believing that the detention of the person is necessary to enable the sample to be taken from him;

  (iv) in the case of a person arrested for an offence which is not an imprisonable offence, the custody officer has reasonable grounds for believing that the detention of the person arrested is necessary to prevent him from causing physical injury to any other person or from causing loss of or damage to property;

  (v) the custody officer has reasonable grounds for believing that the detention of the person arrested is necessary to prevent him from interfering with the administration of justice or with the investigation of offences or of a particular offence; or

  (vi) the custody officer has reasonable grounds for believing that the detention of the person arrested is necessary for his own protection;

(b) if he is an arrested juvenile–

  (i) any of the requirements of paragraph (a) above is satisfied (but, in the case of paragraph (a)(iiia) above, only if the arrested juvenile has attained the minimum age); or

  (ii) the custody officer has reasonable grounds for believing that he ought to be detained in his own interests;

(c) the offence with which the person is charged is murder.

(2) If the release of a person arrested is not required by subsection (1) above, the custody officer may authorise him to be kept in police detention but may not authorise a person to be kept in police detention by virtue of subsection (1)(a)(iiia) after the end of the period of six hours beginning when he was charged with the offence.

(2A) The custody officer, in taking the decisions required by subsection (1)(a) and (b) above (except (a)(i) and (vi) and (b)(ii)), shall have regard to the same considerations as those which a court is required to have regard to in taking the corresponding decisions under paragraph 2(1) of Part I of Schedule 1 to the Bail Act 1976 (disregarding paragraph 2(2) of that Part).

(3) Where a custody officer authorises a person who has been charged to be kept in police detention, he shall, as soon as practicable, make a written record of the grounds for the detention.

(4) Subject to subsection (5) below, the written record shall be made in the presence of the person charged who shall at that time be informed by the custody officer of the grounds for his detention.

(5) Subsection (4) above shall not apply where the person charged is, at the time when the written record is made–
   (a) incapable of understanding what is said to him;
   (b) violent or likely to become violent; or
   (c) in urgent need of medical attention.
(6) Where a custody officer authorises an arrested juvenile to be kept in police detention under subsection (1) above, the custody officer shall, unless he certifies–
   (a) that, by reason of such circumstances as are specified in the certificate, it is impracticable for him to do so; or
   (b) in the case of an arrested juvenile who has attained the age of 12 years, that no secure accommodation is available and that keeping him in other local authority accommodation would not be adequate to protect the public from serious harm from him,
   secure that the arrested juvenile is moved to local authority accommodation.
(6A) In this section–
   'local authority accommodation' means accommodation provided by or on behalf of a local authority (within the meaning of the Children Act 1989);
   'minimum age' means the age specified in section 63B(3)(b) below;
   'secure accommodation' means accommodation provided for the purpose of restricting liberty;
   'sexual offence' means an offence specified in Part 2 of Schedule 15 to the Criminal Justice Act 2003;
   'violent offence' means murder or an offence specified in Part 1 of that Schedule;
   and any reference, in relation to an arrested juvenile charged with a violent or sexual offence, to protecting the public from serious harm from him shall be construed as a reference to protecting members of the public from death or serious personal injury, whether physical or psychological, occasioned by further such offences committed by him.
(6B) Where an arrested juvenile is moved to local authority accommodation under subsection (6) above, it shall be lawful for any person acting on behalf of the authority to detain him.
(7) A certificate made under subsection (6) above in respect of an arrested juvenile shall be produced to the court before which he is first brought thereafter.
(7A) In this section 'imprisonable offence' has the same meaning as in Schedule 1 to the Bail Act 1976.
(8) In this Part of this Act 'local authority' has the same meaning as in the Children Act 1989.

## Responsibilities in relation to persons detained

39 (1) Subject to subsections (2) and (4) below, it shall be the duty of the custody officer at a police station to ensure–
   (a) that all persons in police detention at that station are treated in accordance with this Act and any code of practice issued under it and relating to the treatment of persons in police detention; and
   (b) that all matters relating to such persons which are required by this Act or by such codes of practice to be recorded are recorded in the custody records relating to such persons.
(2) If the custody officer, in accordance with any code of practice issued under this Act, transfers or permits the transfer of a person in police detention–
   (a) to the custody of a police officer investigating an offence for which that person is in police detention; or
   (b) to the custody of an officer who has charge of that person outside the police station,
   the custody officer shall cease in relation to that person to be subject to the duty imposed on him by subsection (1)(a) above; and it shall be the duty of the officer to whom the transfer is made to ensure that he is treated in accordance with the provisions of this Act and of any such codes of practice as are mentioned in subsection (1) above.

(3) If the person detained is subsequently returned to the custody of the custody officer, it shall be the duty of the officer investigating the offence to report to the custody officer as to the manner in which this section and the codes of practice have been complied with while that person was in his custody.

(4) If an arrested juvenile is moved to local authority accommodation under section 38(6) above, the custody officer shall cease in relation to that person to be subject to the duty imposed on him by subsection (1) above.

(5) [Repealed.]

(6) Where–
   (a) an officer of higher rank than the custody officer gives directions relating to a person in police detention; and
   (b) the directions are at variance–
      (i)  with any decision made or action taken by the custody officer in the perform-ance of a duty imposed on him under this Part of this Act; or
      (ii) with any decision or action which would but for the directions have been made or taken by him in the performance of such a duty,
the custody officer shall refer the matter at once to an officer of the rank of super-intendent or above who is responsible for the police station for which the custody officer is acting as custody officer.

(7) [Repealed.]

### Review of police detention

40(1) Reviews of the detention of each person in police detention in connection with the investigation of an offence shall be carried out periodically in accordance with the following provisions of this section–
   (a) in the case of a person who has been arrested and charged, by the custody offi-cer; and
   (b) in the case of a person who has been arrested but not charged, by an officer of at least the rank of inspector who has not been directly involved in the investigation.

(2) The officer to whom it falls to carry out a review is referred to in this section as a 'review officer'.

(3) Subject to subsection (4) below–
   (a) the first review shall be not later than six hours after the detention was first authorised;
   (b) the second review shall be not later than nine hours after the first;
   (c) subsequent reviews shall be at intervals of not more than nine hours.

(4) A review may be postponed–
   (a) if, having regard to all the circumstances prevailing at the latest time for it speci-fied in subsection (3) above, it is not practicable to carry out the review at that time;
   (b) without prejudice to the generality of paragraph (a) above–
      (i)  if at that time the person in detention is being questioned by a police officer and the review officer is satisfied that an interruption of the questioning for the purpose of carrying out the review would prejudice the investigation in connection with which he is being questioned; or
      (ii) if at that time no review officer is readily available.

(5) If a review is postponed under subsection (4) above it shall be carried out as soon as practicable after the latest time specified for it in subsection (3) above.

(6) If a review is carried out after postponement under subsection (4) above, the fact that it was so carried out shall not affect any requirement of this section as to the time at which any subsequent review is to be carried out.

(7) The review officer shall record the reasons for any postponement of a review in the custody record.

(8) Subject to subsection (9) below, where the person whose detention is under review has not been charged before the time of the review, section 37(1) to (6) above shall have effect in relation to him, but with the modifications specified in subsection (8A).

(8A) The modifications are–

    (a) the substitution of references to the person whose detention is under review for references to the person arrested;

    (b) the substitution of references to the review officer for references to the custody officer; and

    (c) in subsection (6), the insertion of the following paragraph after paragraph (a)– '(aa) asleep;'.

  (9) Where a person has been kept in police detention by virtue of section 37(9) or 37D(5) above, section 37(1) to (6) shall not have effect in relation to him but it shall be the duty of the review officer to determine whether he is yet in a fit state.

 (10) Where the person whose detention is under review has been charged before the time of the review, section 38(1) to (6B) above shall have effect in relation to him, with the modifications specified in subsection (10A).

(10A) The modifications are–

    (a) the substitution of a reference to the person whose detention is under review for any reference to the person arrested or to the person charged; and

    (b) in subsection (5), the insertion of the following paragraph after paragraph (a)– '(aa) asleep;'.

 (11) Where–

    (a) an officer of higher rank than the review officer gives directions relating to a person in police detention; and

    (b) the directions are at variance–

       (i) with any decision made or action taken by the review officer in the performance of a duty imposed on him under this Part of this Act; or

      (ii) with any decision or action which would but for the directions have been made or taken by him in the performance of such a duty,

the review officer shall refer the matter at once to an officer of the rank of superintendent or above who is responsible for the police station for which the review officer is acting as review officer in connection with the detention.

 (12) Before determining whether to authorise a person's continued detention the review officer shall give–

    (a) that person (unless he is asleep); or

    (b) any solicitor representing him who is available at the time of the review,

an opportunity to make representations to him about the detention.

 (13) Subject to subsection (14) below, the person whose detention is under review or his solicitor may make representations under subsection (12) above either orally or in writing.

 (14) The review officer may refuse to hear oral representations from the person whose detention is under review if he considers that he is unfit to make such representations by reason of his condition or behaviour.

### Use of telephone for review under s40

40A(1) A review under section 40(1)(b) may be carried out by means of a discussion, conducted by telephone, with one or more persons at the police station where the arrested person is held.

  (2) But subsection (1) does not apply if–

    (a) the review is of a kind authorised by regulations under section 45A to be carried out using video-conferencing facilities; and

    (b) it is reasonably practicable to carry it out in accordance with those regulations.

  (3) Where any review is carried out under this section by an officer who is not present at the station where the arrested person is held–

    (a) any obligation of that officer to make a record in connection with the carrying out of the review shall have effect as an obligation to cause another officer to make the record;

    (b) any requirement for the record to be made in the presence of the arrested person shall apply to the making of that record by that other officer; and

    (c) the requirements under section 40(12) and (13) above for–

      (i) the arrested person, or

     (ii) a solicitor representing him,

to be given any opportunity to make representations (whether in writing or orally) to that officer shall have effect as a requirement for that person, or such a solicitor, to be given an opportunity to make representations in a manner authorised by subsection (4) below.

(4) Representations are made in a manner authorised by this subsection–
   (a) in a case where facilities exist for the immediate transmission of written representations to the officer carrying out the review, if they are made either–
      (i)  orally by telephone to that officer; or
      (ii) in writing to that officer by means of those facilities;
   and
   (b) in any other case, if they are made orally by telephone to that officer.

(5) In this section 'video-conferencing facilities' has the same meaning as in section 45A below.

## Limits on period of detention without charge

41(1) Subject to the following provisions of this section and to sections 42 and 43 below, a person shall not be kept in police detention for more than 24 hours without being charged.

(2) The time from which the period of detention of a person is to be calculated (in this Act referred to as 'the relevant time')–
   (a) in the case of a person to whom this paragraph applies, shall be–
      (i)  the time at which that person arrives at the relevant police station; or
      (ii) the time 24 hours after the time of that person's arrest,
      whichever is the earlier;
   (b) in the case of a person arrested outside England and Wales, shall be–
      (i)  the time at which that person arrives at the first police station to which he is taken in the police area in England or Wales in which the offence for which he was arrested is being investigated; or
      (ii) the time 24 hours after the time of that person's entry into England and Wales,
      whichever is the earlier;
   (c) in the case of a person who–
      (i)  attends voluntarily at a police station; or
      (ii) accompanies a constable to a police station without having been arrested,
      and is arrested at the police station, the time of his arrest;
   (ca)in the case of a person who attends a police station to answer to bail granted under section 30A, the time when he arrives at the police station;
   (d) in any other case, except where subsection (5) below applies, shall be the time at which the person arrested arrives at the first police station to which he is taken after his arrest.

(3) Subsection (2)(a) above applies to a person if–
   (a) his arrest is sought in one police area in England and Wales;
   (b) he is arrested in another police area; and
   (c) he is not questioned in the area in which he is arrested in order to obtain evidence in relation to an offence for which he is arrested;
   and in sub-paragraph (i) of that paragraph 'the relevant police station' means the first police station to which he is taken in the police area in which his arrest was sought.

(4) Subsection (2) above shall have effect in relation to a person arrested under section 31 above as if every reference in it to his arrest or his being arrested were a reference to his arrest or his being arrested for the offence for which he was originally arrested.

(5) If–
   (a) a person is in police detention in a police area in England and Wales ('the first area'); and
   (b) his arrest for an offence is sought in some other police area in England and Wales ('the second area'); and
   (c) he is taken to the second area for the purposes of investigating that offence,

without being questioned in the first area in order to obtain evidence in relation to it,

the relevant time shall be–

    (i) the time 24 hours after he leaves the place where he is detained in the first area; or

    (ii) the time at which he arrives at the first police station to which he is taken in the second area,

whichever is the earlier.

(6) When a person who is in police detention is removed to hospital because he is in need of medical treatment, any time during which he is being questioned in hospital or on the way there or back by a police officer for the purpose of obtaining evidence relating to an offence shall be included in any period which falls to be calculated for the purposes of this Part of this Act, but any other time while he is in hospital or on his way there or back shall not be so included.

(7) Subject to subsection (8) below, a person who at the expiry of 24 hours after the relevant time is in police detention and has not been charged shall be released at that time either on bail or without bail.

(8) Subsection (7) above does not apply to a person whose detention for more than 24 hours after the relevant time has been authorised or is otherwise permitted in accordance with section 42 or 43 below.

(9) A person released under subsection (7) above shall not be re-arrested without a warrant for the offence for which he was previously arrested unless new evidence justifying a further arrest has come to light since his release; but this subsection does not prevent an arrest under section 46A below.

### Authorisation of continued detention

42(1) Where a police officer of the rank of superintendent or above who is responsible for the police station at which a person is detained has reasonable grounds for believing that–

    (a) the detention of that person without charge is necessary to secure or preserve evidence relating to an offence for which he is under arrest or to obtain such evidence by questioning him;

    (b) an offence for which he is under arrest is an indictable offence; and

    (c) the investigation is being conducted diligently and expeditiously,

he may authorise the keeping of that person in police detention for a period expiring at or before 36 hours after the relevant time.

(2) Where an officer such as is mentioned in subsection (1) above has authorised the keeping of a person in police detention for a period expiring less than 36 hours after the relevant time, such an officer may authorise the keeping of that person in police detention for a further period expiring not more than 36 hours after that time if the conditions specified in subsection (1) above are still satisfied when he gives the authorisation.

(3) If it is proposed to transfer a person in police detention to another police area, the officer determining whether or not to authorise keeping him in detention under subsection (1) above shall have regard to the distance and the time the journey would take.

(4) No authorisation under subsection (1) above shall be given in respect of any person–

    (a) more than 24 hours after the relevant time; or

    (b) before the second review of his detention under section 40 above has been carried out.

(5) Where an officer authorises the keeping of a person in police detention under subsection (1) above, it shall be his duty–

    (a) to inform that person of the grounds for his continued detention; and

    (b) to record the grounds in that person's custody record.

(6) Before determining whether to authorise the keeping of a person in detention under subsection (1) or (2) above, an officer shall give–

    (a) that person; or

(b) any solicitor representing him who is available at the time when it falls to the officer to determine whether to give the authorisation,

an opportunity to make representations to him about the detention.

(7) Subject to subsection (8) below, the person in detention or his solicitor may make representations under subsection (6) above either orally or in writing.

(8) The officer to whom it falls to determine whether to give the authorisation may refuse to hear oral representations from the person in detention if he considers that he is unfit to make such representations by reason of his condition or behaviour.

(9) Where–

(a) an officer authorises the keeping of a person in detention under subsection (1) above; and

(b) at the time of the authorisation he has not yet exercised a right conferred on him by section 56 or 58 below,

the officer–

(i)   shall inform him of that right;

(ii)  shall decide whether he should be permitted to exercise it;

(iii) shall record the decision in his custody record; and

(iv)  if the decision is to refuse to permit the exercise of the right, shall also record the grounds for the decision in that record.

(10) Where an officer has authorised the keeping of a person who has not been charged in detention under subsection (1) or (2) above, he shall be released from detention, either on bail or without bail, not later than 36 hours after the relevant time, unless–

(a) he has been charged with an offence; or

(b) his continued detention is authorised or otherwise permitted in accordance with section 43 below.

(11) A person released under subsection (10) above shall not be re-arrested without a warrant for the offence for which he was previously arrested unless new evidence justifying a further arrest has come to light since his release; but this subsection does not prevent an arrest under section 46A below.

## Warrants of further detention

43(1) Where, on an application on oath made by a constable and supported by an information, a magistrates' court is satisfied that there are reasonable grounds for believing that the further detention of the person to whom the application relates is justified, it may issue a warrant of further detention authorising the keeping of that person in police detention.

(2) A court may not hear an application for a warrant of further detention unless the person to whom the application relates–

(a) has been furnished with a copy of the information; and

(b) has been brought before the court for the hearing.

(3) The person to whom the application relates shall be entitled to be legally represented at the hearing and, if he is not so represented but wishes to be so represented–

(a) the court shall adjourn the hearing to enable him to obtain representation; and

(b) he may be kept in police detention during the adjournment.

(4) A person's further detention is only justified for the purposes of this section or section 44 below if–

(a) his detention without charge is necessary to secure or preserve evidence relating to an offence for which he is under arrest or to obtain such evidence by questioning him;

(b) an offence for which he is under arrest is an indictable offence; and

(c) the investigation is being conducted diligently and expeditiously.

(5) Subject to subsection (7) below, an application for a warrant of further detention may be made–

(a) at any time before the expiry of 36 hours after the relevant time; or

(b) in a case where–

(i) it is not practicable for the magistrates' court to which the application will be made to sit at the expiry of 36 hours after the relevant time; but

(ii) the court will sit during the 6 hours following the end of that period,
at any time before the expiry of the said 6 hours.

(6) In a case to which subsection (5)(b) above applies–
    (a) the person to whom the application relates may be kept in police detention until the application is heard; and
    (b) the custody officer shall make a note in that person's custody record–
        (i) of the fact that he was kept in police detention for more than 36 hours after the relevant time; and
        (ii) of the reason why he was so kept.

(7) If–
    (a) an application for a warrant of further detention is made after the expiry of 36 hours after the relevant time; and
    (b) it appears to the magistrates' court that it would have been reasonable for the police to make it before the expiry of that period,
the court shall dismiss the application.

(8) Where on an application such as is mentioned in subsection (1) above a magistrates' court is not satisfied that there are reasonable grounds for believing that the further detention of the person to whom the application relates is justified, it shall be its duty–
    (a) to refuse the application; or
    (b) to adjourn the hearing of it until a time not later than 36 hours after the relevant time.

(9) The person to whom the application relates may be kept in police detention during the adjournment.

(10) A warrant of further detention shall–
    (a) state the time at which it is issued;
    (b) authorise the keeping in police detention of the person to whom it relates for the period stated in it.

(11) Subject to subsection (12) below, the period stated in a warrant of further detention shall be such period as the magistrates' court thinks fit, having regard to the evidence before it.

(12) The period shall not be longer than 36 hours.

(13) If it is proposed to transfer a person in police detention to a police area other than that in which he is detained when the application for a warrant of further detention is made, the court hearing the application shall have regard to the distance and the time the journey would take.

(14) Any information submitted in support of an application under this section shall state–
    (a) the nature of the offence for which the person to whom the application relates has been arrested;
    (b) the general nature of the evidence on which that person was arrested;
    (c) what inquiries relating to the offence have been made by the police and what further inquiries are proposed by them;
    (d) the reasons for believing the continued detention of that person to be necessary for the purposes of such further inquiries.

(15) Where an application under this section is refused, the person to whom the application relates shall forthwith be charged or, subject to subsection (16) below, released, either on bail or without bail.

(16) A person need not be released under subsection (15) above–
    (a) before the expiry of 24 hours after the relevant time; or
    (b) before the expiry of any longer period for which his continued detention is or has been authorised under section 42 above.

(17) Where an application under this section is refused, no further application shall be made under this section in respect of the person to whom the refusal relates, unless supported by evidence which has come to light since the refusal.

(18) Where a warrant of further detention is issued, the person to whom it relates shall be released from police detention, either on bail or without bail, upon or before the expiry of the warrant unless he is charged.

(19) A person released under subsection (18) above shall not be re-arrested without a warrant for the offence for which he was previously arrested unless new evidence justifying a further arrest has come to light since his release; but this subsection does not prevent an arrest under section 46A below.

### Extension of warrants of further detention

44(1) On an application on oath made by a constable and supported by an information a magistrates' court may extend a warrant of further detention issued under section 43 above if it is satisfied that there are reasonable grounds for believing that the further detention of the person to whom the application relates is justified.

(2) Subject to subsection (3) below, the period for which a warrant of further detention may be extended shall be such period as the court thinks fit, having regard to the evidence before it.

(3) The period shall not–
(a) be longer than 36 hours; or
(b) end later than 96 hours after the relevant time.

(4) Where a warrant of further detention has been extended under subsection (1) above, or further extended under this subsection, for a period ending before 96 hours after the relevant time, on an application such as is mentioned in that subsection a magistrates' court may further extend the warrant if it is satisfied as there mentioned; and subsections (2) and (3) above apply to such further extensions as they apply to extensions under subsection (1) above.

(5) A warrant of further detention shall, if extended or further extended under this section, be endorsed with a note of the period of the extension.

(6) Subsections (2), (3), and (14) of section 43 above shall apply to an application made under this section as they apply to an application made under that section.

(7) Where an application under this section is refused, the person to whom the application relates shall forthwith be charged or, subject to subsection (8) below, released, either on bail or without bail.

(8) A person need not be released under subsection (7) above before the expiry of any period for which a warrant of further detention issued in relation to him has been extended or further extended on an earlier application made under this section.

### Detention before charge–supplementary

45(1) In sections 43 and 44 of this Act 'magistrates' court' means a court consisting of two or more justices of the peace sitting otherwise than in open court.

(2) Any reference in this Part of this Act to a period of time or a time of day is to be treated as approximate only.

### Use of video-conferencing facilities for decisions about detention

45A(1) Subject to the following provisions of this section, the Secretary of State may by regulations provide that, in the case of an arrested person who is held in a police station, some or all of the functions mentioned in subsection (2) may be performed (notwithstanding anything in the preceding provisions of this Part) by an officer who–
(a) is not present in that police station; but
(b) has access to the use of video-conferencing facilities that enable him to communicate with persons in that station.

(2) Those functions are–
(a) the functions in relation to an arrested person taken to, or answering to bail at, a police station that is not a designated police station which, in the case of an arrested person taken to a station that is a designated police station, are functions of a custody officer under section 37, 38 or 40 above; and
(b) the function of carrying out a review under section 40(1)(b) above (review, by an officer of at least the rank of inspector, of the detention of person arrested but not charged).

(3) Regulations under this section shall specify the use to be made in the performance of the functions mentioned in subsection (2) above of the facilities mentioned in subsection (1) above.

(4) Regulations under this section shall not authorise the performance of any of the functions mentioned in subsection (2)(a) above by such an officer as is mentioned in subsection (1) above unless he is a custody officer for a designated police station.

(5) Where any functions mentioned in subsection (2) above are performed in a manner authorised by regulations under this section–

   (a) any obligation of the officer performing those functions to make a record in connection with the performance of those functions shall have effect as an obligation to cause another officer to make the record; and

   (b) any requirement for the record to be made in the presence of the arrested person shall apply to the making of that record by that other officer.

(6) Where the functions mentioned in subsection (2)(b) are performed in a manner authorised by regulations under this section, the requirements under section 40(12) and (13) above for–

   (a) the arrested person, or

   (b) a solicitor representing him,

to be given any opportunity to make representations (whether in writing or orally) to the person performing those functions shall have effect as a requirement for that person, or such a solicitor, to be given an opportunity to make representations in a manner authorised by subsection (7) below.

(7) Representations are made in a manner authorised by this subsection–

   (a) in a case where facilities exist for the immediate transmission of written representations to the officer performing the functions, if they are made either–

      (i) orally to that officer by means of the video-conferencing facilities used by him for performing those functions; or

      (ii) in writing to that officer by means of the facilities available for the immediate transmission of the representations;

     and

   (b) in any other case if they are made orally to that officer by means of the video-conferencing facilities used by him for performing the functions.

(8) Regulations under this section may make different provision for different cases and may be made so as to have effect in relation only to the police stations specified or described in the regulations.

(9) Regulations under this section shall be made by statutory instrument and shall be subject to annulment in pursuance of a resolution of either House of Parliament.

(10) Any reference in this section to video-conferencing facilities, in relation to any functions, is a reference to any facilities (whether a live television link or other facilities) by means of which the functions may be performed with the officer performing them, the person in relation to whom they are performed and any legal representative of that person all able to both see and to hear each other.

### *Detention–miscellaneous*

### Detention after charge

46(1) Where a person–

   (a) is charged with an offence; and

   (b) after being charged–

      (i) is kept in police detention; or

      (ii) is detained by a local authority in pursuance of arrangements made under section 38(6) above,

he shall be brought before a magistrates' court in accordance with the provisions of this section.

(2) If he is to be brought before a magistrates' court in the local justice area in which the police station at which he was charged is situated, he shall be brought before such a court as soon as is practicable and in any event not later than the first sitting after he is charged with the offence.

(3) If no magistrates' court in that area is due to sit either on the day on which he is charged or on the next day, the custody officer for the police station at which he was charged shall inform the designated officer for the area that there is a person in the area to whom subsection (2) above applies.

(4) If the person charged is to be brought before a magistrates' court in a local justice area other than that in which the police station at which he was charged is situated, he shall be removed to that area as soon as is practicable and brought before such a court as soon as is practicable after his arrival in the area and in any event not later than the first sitting of a magistrates' court in that area after his arrival in the area.

(5) If no magistrates' court in that area is due to sit either on the day on which he arrives in the area or on the next day–
   (a) he shall be taken to a police station in the area; and
   (b) the custody officer at that station shall inform the designated officer for the area that there is a person in the area to whom subsection (4) applies.

(6) Subject to subsection (8) below, where the designated officer for a local justice area has been informed–
   (a) under subsection (3) above that there is a person in the area to whom subsection (2) above applies; or
   (b) under subsection (5) above that there is a person in the area to whom subsection (4) above applies,
   the designated officer shall arrange for a magistrates' court to sit not later than the day next following the relevant day.

(7) In this section ' the relevant day'–
   (a) in relation to a person who is to be brought before a magistrates' court in the local justice area in which the police station at which he was charged is situated, means the day on which he was charged; and
   (b) in relation to a person who is to be brought before a magistrates' court in any other local justice area, means the day on which he arrives in the area.

(8) Where the day next following the relevant day is Christmas Day, Good Friday or a Sunday, the duty of the designated officer under subsection (6) above is a duty to arrange for a magistrates' court to sit not later than the first day after the relevant day which is not one of those days.

(9) Nothing in this section requires a person who is in hospital to be brought before a court if he is not well enough.

### Persons granted live link bail[8]

46ZA(1) This section applies in relation to bail granted under this Part subject to the duty mentioned in section 47(3)(b) ('live link bail').

(2) An accused person who attends a police station to answer to live link bail is not to be treated as in police detention for the purposes of this Act.

(3) Subsection (2) does not apply in relation to an accused person if–
   [(a) at any time before the beginning of proceedings in relation to a live link direction under section 57C of the Crime and Disorder Act 1998 in relation to him, he informs a constable that he does not intend to give his consent to the direction;][9]
   (b) [at any such time,][10] *at any time* before the beginning of proceedings in relation to a live link direction under section 57C of the Crime and Disorder Act 1998 in relation to the accused person, a constable informs him that a live link will not be available for his use for the purposes of that section;
   (c) [proceedings in relation to a live link direction under that section have begun but

---

8   Inserted by the Police and Justice Act 2006 s46(1), (3). In force (in relation to the local justice area of Lambeth and Southwark): 1 April 2007 (SI 2007/709 art 3(n)); (in relation to certain local justice areas): 14 November 2008 (SI 2008/2785 art 2). Not yet in force (for remaining purposes): see the Police and Justice Act 2006 s53(1)(a).

9   Subs (3)(a) repealed by the Coroners and Justice Act 2009 ss107(1), (2)(a)(i), 178, Sch 23 Pt 3. In force (in relation to certain specified local justice areas): 14 December 2009 (SI 2009/3253 art 3(1)(b), (2)); for transitional provisions see art 4(4)(a), (5). Not yet in force (for remaining purposes): see the Coroners and Justice Act 2009 s182(5).

10  Words 'at any such time,' in square brackets repealed and subsequent words in italics substituted by the Coroners and Justice Act 2009 s107(1), (2)(a)(ii). In force (in relation to certain specified local justice areas): 14 December 2009 (SI 2009/3253 art 3(1)(b), (2)); for transitional provisions see art 4(4)(a), (5). Not yet in force (for remaining purposes): see the Coroners and Justice Act 2009 s182(5).

he does not give his consent to the direction]¹¹; or
(d) the court determines for [any other reason]¹² *any reason* not to give such a direction.
(4) If [any of paragraphs (a) to (d) of subsection (3) apply]¹³ *paragraph (b) or (d) of subsection (3) applies* in relation to a person, he is to be treated for the purposes of this Part–
(a) as if he had been arrested for and charged with the offence in connection with which he was granted bail, and
(b) as if he had been so charged at the time when that paragraph first applied in relation to him.
(5) An accused person who is arrested under section 46A for failing to attend at a police station to answer to live link bail, and who is brought to a police station in accordance with that section, is to be treated for the purposes of this Part–
(a) as if he had been arrested for and charged with the offence in connection with which he was granted bail, and
(b) as if he had been so charged at the time when he is brought to the station.
(6) Nothing in subsection (4) or (5) affects the operation of section 47(6).

**Power of arrest for failure to answer to police bail**
46A(1) A constable may arrest without a warrant any person who, having been released on bail under this Part of this Act subject to a duty to attend at a police station, fails to attend at that police station at the time appointed for him to do so.
(1ZA)¹⁴ The reference in subsection (1) to a person who fails to attend at a police station at the time appointed for him to do so includes a reference to a person who–
(a) attends at a police station to answer to bail granted subject to the duty mentioned in section 47(3)(b), but
(b) leaves the police station at any time before the beginning of proceedings in relation to a live link direction under section 57C of the Crime and Disorder Act 1998 in relation to him[, without informing a constable that he does not intend to give his consent to the direction]¹⁵.
(1ZB)¹⁶ The reference in subsection (1) to a person who fails to attend at a police station at the time appointed for the person to do so includes a reference to a person who–
(a) attends at a police station to answer to bail granted subject to the duty mentioned in section 47(3)(b), but

11 Subs (3)(c) repealed by the Coroners and Justice Act 2009 ss107(1), (2)(a)(iii), 178, Sch 23 Pt 3. Date in force (in relation to certain specified local justice areas): 14 December 2009 (SI 2009/3253 art 3(1)(b), (2)); for transitional provisions see art 4(4)(a), (5). Not yet in force (for remaining purposes): see the Coroners and Justice Act 2009 s182(5).
12 Subs (3)(d) words 'any other reason' in square brackets repealed and subsequent words in italics substituted by the Coroners and Justice Act 2009 s107(1), (2)(a)(iv). Date in force (in relation to certain specified local justice areas): 14 December 2009 (SI 2009/3253 art 3(1)(b), (2)); for transitional provisions see art 4(4)(a), (5). Not yet in force (for remaining purposes): see the Coroners and Justice Act 2009 s182(5).
13 Words 'any of paragraphs (a) to (d) of subsection (3) apply' in square brackets repealed and subsequent words in italics substituted by the Coroners and Justice Act 2009 s107(1), (2)(b). In force (in relation to certain specified local justice areas): 14 December 2009 (SI 2009/3253 art 3(1)(b), (2)); for transitional provisions see art 4(4)(a), (5). Not yet in force (for remaining purposes): see the Coroners and Justice Act 2009 s182(5).
14 Inserted by the Police and Justice Act 2006 s46(1), (4). In force (in relation to the local justice area of Lambeth and Southwark): 1 April 2007: (SI 2007/709 art 3(n)); (in relation to certain local justice areas): 14 November 2008 (SI 2008/2785 art 2). Not yet in force (for remaining purposes): see the Police and Justice Act 2006 s53(1)(a).
15 Words ', without informing a constable that he does not intend to give his consent to the direction' in square brackets repealed by the Coroners and Justice Act 2009 ss107(1), (3), 178, Sch 23 Pt 3. In force (in relation to certain specified local justice areas): 14 December 2009 (SI 2009/3253 art 3(1)(b), (2)); for transitional provisions see art 4(4)(b), (5). Not yet in force (for remaining purposes): see the Coroners and Justice Act 2009 s182(5).
16 Inserted by the Coroners and Justice Act 2009 s108(2). In force (in relation to certain specified local justice areas): 14 December 2009 (SI 2009/3253 art 3(1)(c), (2)). Not yet in force (for remaining purposes): see the Coroners and Justice Act 2009 s182(5).

(b) refuses to be searched under section 54B.

(1A) A person who has been released on bail under section 37, 37C(2)(b) or 37CA(2)(b) above may be arrested without warrant by a constable if the constable has reasonable grounds for suspecting that the person has broken any of the conditions of bail.

(2) A person who is arrested under this section shall be taken to the police station appointed as the place at which he is to surrender to custody as soon as practicable after the arrest.

(3) For the purposes of–
   (a) section 30 above (subject to the obligation in subsection (2) above), and
   (b) section 31 above,
   an arrest under this section shall be treated as an arrest for an offence.

### Bail after arrest

47(1) Subject to the following provisions of this section, a release on bail of a person under this Part of this Act shall be a release on bail granted in accordance with sections 3, 3A, 5 and 5A of the Bail Act 1976 as they apply to bail granted by a constable.

(1A) The normal powers to impose conditions of bail shall be available to him where a custody officer releases a person on bail under section 37 above or section 38(1) above (including that subsection as applied by section 40(10) above) but not in any other cases.
   In this subsection, 'the normal powers to impose conditions of bail' has the meaning given in section 3(6) of the Bail Act 1976.

(1B) No application may be made under section 5B of the Bail Act 1976 if a person is released on bail under section 37, 37C(2)(b) or 37CA(2)(b) above.

(1C) Subsections (1D) to (1F) below apply where a person released on bail under section 37, 37C(2)(b) or 37CA(2)(b) above is on bail subject to conditions.

(1D) The person shall not be entitled to make an application under section 43B of the Magistrates' Courts Act 1980.

(1E) A magistrates' court may, on an application by or on behalf of the person, vary the conditions of bail; and in this subsection 'vary' has the same meaning as in the Bail Act 1976.

(1F) Where a magistrates' court varies the conditions of bail under subsection (1E) above, that bail shall not lapse but shall continue subject to the conditions as so varied.

(2) Nothing in the Bail Act 1976 shall prevent the re-arrest without warrant of a person released on bail subject to a duty to attend at a police station if new evidence justifying a further arrest has come to light since his release.

(3) Subject to subsections (3A) and (4) below, in this Part of this Act references to 'bail' are references to bail subject to a duty–
   (a) to appear before a magistrates' court at such time and such place as the custody officer may appoint;
   (b) to attend at such police station as the custody officer may appoint at such time as he may appoint for the purposes of–
      (i) proceedings in relation to a live link direction under section 57C of the Crime and Disorder Act 1998 (use of live link direction at preliminary hearings where accused is at police station); and
      (ii) any preliminary hearing in relation to which such a direction is given; or
   (c) to attend at such police station as the custody officer may appoint at such time as he may appoint for purposes other than those mentioned in paragraph (b).

(3A) Where a custody officer grants bail to a person subject to a duty to appear before a magistrates' court, he shall appoint for the appearance–
   (a) a date which is not later than the first sitting of the court after the person is charged with the offence; or
   (b) where he is informed by the designated officer for the relevant local justice area that the appearance cannot be accommodated until a later date, that later date.

(4) Where a custody officer has granted bail to a person subject to a duty to appear at a police station, the custody officer may give notice in writing to that person that his attendance at the police station is not required.

(5) [Repealed.]

(6) Where a person who has been granted bail under this Part and either has attended at the police station in accordance with the grant of bail or has been arrested under section 46A above is detained at a police station, any time during which he was in police detention prior to being granted bail shall be included as part of any period which falls to be calculated under this Part of this Act and any time during which he was on bail shall not be so included.

(7) Where a person who was released on bail under this Part subject to a duty to attend at a police station is re-arrested, the provisions of this Part of this Act shall apply to him as they apply to a person arrested for the first time; but this subsection does not apply to a person who is arrested under section 46A above or has attended a police station in accordance with the grant of bail (and who accordingly is deemed by section 34(7) above to have been arrested for an offence) or to a person to whom section 46ZA(4) or (5) applies.

(8) In the Magistrates' Court Act 1980–

(a) the following section shall be substituted for section 43–

'**43  Bail on arrest**

(1) Where a person has been granted bail under the Police and Criminal Evidence Act 1984 subject to a duty to appear before a magistrates' court, the court before which he is to appear may appoint a later time as the time at which he is to appear and may enlarge the recognizances of any sureties for him at that time.

(2) The recognizance of any surety for any person granted bail subject to a duty to attend at a police station may be enforced as if it were conditioned for his appearance before a magistrates' court for the petty sessions area in which the police station named in the recognizance is situated.'; and

(b) the following subsection shall be substituted for section 117(3)–

'(3) Where a warrant has been endorsed for bail under subsection (1) above–

(a) where the person arrested is to be released on bail on his entering into a recognizance without sureties, it shall not be necessary to take him to a police station, but if he is so taken, he shall be released from custody on his entering into the recognizance; and

(b) where he is to be released on his entering into a recognizance with sureties, he shall be taken to a police station on his arrest, and the custody officer there shall (subject to his approving any surety tendered in compliance with the endorsement) release him from custody as directed in the endorsement.'.

### Early administrative hearings conducted by justices' clerks

47A Where a person has been charged with an offence at a police station, any requirement imposed under this Part for the person to appear or be brought before a magistrates' court shall be taken to be satisfied if the person appears or is brought before a justices' clerk in order for the clerk to conduct a hearing under section 50 of the Crime and Disorder Act 1998 (early administrative hearings).

### Remands to police detention

48 In section 128 of the Magistrates' Courts Act 1980–

(a) in subsection (7) for the words 'the custody of a constable' there shall be substituted the words 'detention at a police station';

(b) after subsection (7) there shall be inserted the following subsection–

'(8) Where a person is committed to detention at a police station under subsection (7) above–

(a) he shall not be kept in such detention unless there is a need for him to be so detained for the purposes of inquiries into other offences;

(b) if kept in such detention, he shall be brought back before the magistrates' court which committed him as soon as that need ceases;

(c) he shall be treated as a person in police detention to whom the duties under section 39 of the Police and Criminal Evidence Act 1984 (responsibilities in relation to persons detained) relate;

(d) his detention shall be subject to periodic review at the times set out in section 40 of that Act (review of police detention).'.

## Police detention to count towards custodial sentence

49 [Repealed.]

## Records of detention

50(1) Each police force shall keep written records showing on an annual basis–
(a) the number of persons kept in police detention for more than 24 hours and subsequently released without charge;
(b) the number of applications for warrants of further detention and the results of the applications; and
(c) in relation to each warrant of further detention–
    (i) the period of further detention authorised by it;
    (ii) the period which the person named in it spent in police detention on its authority; and
    (iii) whether he was charged or released without charge.

(2) Every annual report–
(a) under section 22 of the Police Act 1996; or
(b) made by the Commissioner of Police of the Metropolis,
shall contain information about the matters mentioned in subsection (1) above in respect of the period to which the report relates.

## Savings

51 Nothing in this Part of this Act shall affect–
(a) the powers conferred on immigration officers by section 4 of and Schedule 2 to the Immigration Act 1971 (administrative provisions as to control on entry etc);
(b) the powers conferred by virtue of section 41 of, or Schedule 7 to, the Terrorism Act 2000 (powers of arrest and detention);
(c) ...
    or
(d) any right of a person in police detention to apply for a writ of habeas corpus or other prerogative remedy.

52 [Repealed.]

## PART V: QUESTIONING AND TREATMENT OF PERSONS BY POLICE

### Abolition of certain powers of constables to search persons

53(1) Subject to subsection (2) below, there shall cease to have effect any Act (including a local Act) passed before this Act in so far as it authorises–
(a) any search by a constable of a person in police detention at a police station; or
(b) an intimate search of a person by a constable;
and any rule of common law which authorises a search such as is mentioned in paragraph (a) or (b) above is abolished.

(2) [Repealed.]

### Searches of detained persons

54(1) The custody officer at a police station shall ascertain everything which a person has with him when he is–
(a) brought to the station after being arrested elsewhere or after being committed to custody by an order or sentence of a court; or
(b) arrested at the station or detained there, as a person falling within section 34(7), under section 37 above *or as a person to whom section 46ZA(4) or (5) applies.*[17]

(2) The custody officer may record or cause to be recorded all or any of the things which he ascertains under subsection (1).

---

17 Words 'or as a person to whom section 46ZA(4) or (5) applies' in italics inserted by the Police and Justice Act 2006 s46(1), (6). In force (in relation to the local justice area of Lambeth and Southwark): 1 April 2007 (SI 2007/709 art 3(n)) ; (in relation to certain local justice areas): 14 November 2008 (SI 2008/2785 art 2). Not yet in force (for remaining purposes): see the Police and Justice Act 2006 s53(1)(a).

(2A) In the case of an arrested person, any such record may be made as part of his custody record.
(3) Subject to subsection (4) below, a custody officer may seize and retain any such thing or cause any such thing to be seized and retained.
(4) Clothes and personal effects may only be seized if the custody officer–
  (a) believes that the person from whom they are seized may use them–
    (i) to cause physical injury to himself or any other person;
    (ii) to damage property;
    (iii) to interfere with evidence; or
    (iv) to assist him to escape; or
  (b) has reasonable grounds for believing that they may be evidence relating to an offence.
(5) Where anything is seized, the person from whom it is seized shall be told the reason for the seizure unless he is –
  (a) violent or likely to become violent; or
  (b) incapable of understanding what is said to him.
(6) Subject to subsection (7) below, a person may be searched if the custody officer considers it necessary to enable him to carry out his duty under subsection (1) above and to the extent that the custody officer considers necessary for that purpose.
(6A) A person who is in custody at a police station or is in police detention otherwise than at a police station may at any time be searched in order to ascertain whether he has with him anything which he could use for any of the purposes specified in subsection (4)(a) above.
(6B) Subject to subsection (6C) below, a constable may seize and retain, or cause to be seized and retained, anything found on such a search.
(6C) A constable may only seize clothes and personal effects in the circumstances specified in subsection (4) above.
(7) An intimate search may not be conducted under this section.
(8) A search under this section shall be carried out by a constable.
(9) The constable carrying out a search shall be of the same sex as the person searched.

### Searches and examination to ascertain identity

54A(1) If an officer of at least the rank of inspector authorises it, a person who is detained in a police station may be searched or examined, or both–
  (a) for the purpose of ascertaining whether he has any mark that would tend to identify him as a person involved in the commission of an offence; or
  (b) for the purpose of facilitating the ascertainment of his identity.
(2) An officer may only give an authorisation under subsection (1) for the purpose mentioned in paragraph (a) of that subsection if–
  (a) the appropriate consent to a search or examination that would reveal whether the mark in question exists has been withheld; or
  (b) it is not practicable to obtain such consent.
(3) An officer may only give an authorisation under subsection (1) in a case in which subsection (2) does not apply if–
  (a) the person in question has refused to identify himself; or
  (b) the officer has reasonable grounds for suspecting that that person is not who he claims to be.
(4) An officer may give an authorisation under subsection (1) orally or in writing but, if he gives it orally, he shall confirm it in writing as soon as is practicable.
(5) Any identifying mark found on a search or examination under this section may be photographed–
  (a) with the appropriate consent; or
  (b) if the appropriate consent is withheld or it is not practicable to obtain it, without it.
(6) Where a search or examination may be carried out under this section, or a photograph may be taken under this section, the only persons entitled to carry out the search or examination, or to take the photograph, are constables.
(7) A person may not under this section carry out a search or examination of a person of the opposite sex or take a photograph of any part of the body of a person of the opposite sex.

(8) An intimate search may not be carried out under this section.

(9) A photograph taken under this section–

    (a) may be used by, or disclosed to, any person for any purpose related to the prevention or detection of crime, the investigation of an offence or the conduct of a prosecution; and

    (b) after being so used or disclosed, may be retained but may not be used or disclosed except for a purpose so related.

(10) In subsection–

    (a) the reference to crime includes a reference to any conduct which–

        (i) constitutes one or more criminal offences (whether under the law of a part of the United Kingdom or of a country or territory outside the United Kingdom); or

        (ii) is, or corresponds to, any conduct which, if it all took place in any one part of the United Kingdom, would constitute one or more criminal offences;

    and

    (b) the references to an investigation and to a prosecution include references, respectively, to any investigation outside the United Kingdom of any crime or suspected crime and to a prosecution brought in respect of any crime in a country or territory outside the United Kingdom.

(11) In this section–

    (a) references to ascertaining a person's identity include references to showing that he is not a particular person; and

    (b) references to taking a photograph include references to using any process by means of which a visual image may be produced, and references to photographing a person shall be construed accordingly.

(12) In this section 'mark' includes features and injuries; and a mark is an identifying mark for the purposes of this section if its existence in any person's case facilitates the ascertainment of his identity or his identification as a person involved in the commission of an offence.

(13) Nothing in this section applies to a person arrested under an extradition arrest power.

### Searches of persons answering to live link bail

54B(1) A constable may search at any time–

    (a) any person who is at a police station to answer to live link bail; and

    (b) any article in the possession of such a person.

(2) If the constable reasonably believes a thing in the possession of the person ought to be seized on any of the grounds mentioned in subsection (3), the constable may seize and retain it or cause it to be seized and retained.

(3) The grounds are that the thing–

    (a) may jeopardise the maintenance of order in the police station;

    (b) may put the safety of any person in the police station at risk; or

    (c) may be evidence of, or in relation to, an offence.

(4) The constable may record or cause to be recorded all or any of the things seized and retained pursuant to subsection (2).

(5) An intimate search may not be carried out under this section.

(6) The constable carrying out a search under subsection (1) must be of the same sex as the person being searched.

(7) In this section 'live link bail' means bail granted under Part 4 of this Act subject to the duty mentioned in section 47(3)(b).

### Power to retain articles seized[18]

54C(1) Except as provided by subsections (2) and (3), a constable may retain a thing seized under section 54B until the time when the person from whom it was seized leaves the police station.

---

18 Inserted by the Coroners and Justice Act 2009 s108(1). In force (in relation to certain specified local justice areas): 14 December 2009 (SI 2009/3253 art 3(1)(c), (2)). Date in force (for remaining purposes): to be appointed: see the Coroners and Justice Act 2009 s182(5).

(2) A constable may retain a thing seized under section 54B in order to establish its lawful owner, where there are reasonable grounds for believing that it has been obtained in consequence of the commission of an offence.

(3) If a thing seized under section 54B may be evidence of, or in relation to, an offence, a constable may retain it–

(a) for use as evidence at a trial for an offence; or

(b) for forensic examination or for investigation in connection with an offence.

(4) Nothing may be retained for either of the purposes mentioned in subsection (3) if a photograph or copy would be sufficient for that purpose.

(5) Nothing in this section affects any power of a court to make an order under section 1 of the Police (Property) Act 1897.

(6) The references in this section to anything seized under section 54B include anything seized by a person to whom paragraph 27A of Schedule 4 to the Police Reform Act 2002 applies.

### Intimate searches

55 (1) Subject to the following provisions of this section, if an officer of at least the rank of inspector has reasonable grounds for believing–

(a) that a person who has been arrested and is in police detention may have concealed on him anything which–

(i) he could use to cause physical injury to himself or others; and

(ii) he might so use while he is in police detention or in the custody of a court; or

(b) that such a person–

(i) may have a Class A drug concealed on him; and

(ii) was in possession of it with the appropriate criminal intent before his arrest,

he may authorise an intimate search of that person.

(2) An officer may not authorise an intimate search of a person for anything unless he has reasonable grounds for believing that it cannot be found without his being intimately searched.

(3) An officer may give an authorisation under subsection (1) above orally or in writing but, if he gives it orally, he shall confirm it in writing as soon as is practicable.

(3A) A drug offence search shall not be carried out unless the appropriate consent has been given in writing.

(3B) Where it is proposed that a drug offence search be carried out, an appropriate officer shall inform the person who is to be subject to it–

(a) of the giving of the authorisation for it; and

(b) of the grounds for giving the authorisation.

(4) An intimate search which is only a drug offence search shall be by way of examination by a suitably qualified person.

(5) Except as provided by subsection (4) above, an intimate search shall be by way of examination by a suitably qualified person unless an officer of at least the rank of inspector considers that this is not practicable.

(6) An intimate search which is not carried out as mentioned in subsection (5) above shall be carried out by a constable.

(7) A constable may not carry out an intimate search of a person of the opposite sex.

(8) No intimate search may be carried out except–

(a) at a police station;

(b) at a hospital;

(c) at a registered medical practitioner's surgery; or

(d) at some other place used for medical purposes.

(9) An intimate search which is only a drug offence search may not be carried out at a police station.

(10) If an intimate search of a person is carried out, the custody record relating to him shall state–

(a) which parts of his body were searched; and

(b) why they were searched.

(10A) If the intimate search is a drug offence search, the custody record relating to that person shall also state–

(a) the authorisation by virtue of which the search was carried out;

(b) the grounds for giving the authorisation; and

(c) the fact that the appropriate consent was given.

(11) The information required to be recorded by subsections (10) and (10A) above shall be recorded as soon as practicable after the completion of the search.

(12) The custody officer at a police station may seize and retain anything which is found on an intimate search of a person, or cause any such thing to be seized and retained–

(a) if he believes that the person from whom it is seized may use it–

    (i)   to cause physical injury to himself or any other person;

    (ii)  to damage property;

    (iii) to interfere with evidence; or

    (iv) to assist him to escape; or

(b) if he has reasonable grounds for believing that it may be evidence relating to an offence.

(13) Where anything is seized under this section, the person from whom it is seized shall be told the reason for the seizure unless he is–

(a) violent or likely to become violent; or

(b) incapable of understanding what is said to him.

(13A) Where the appropriate consent to a drug offence search of any person was refused without good cause, in any proceedings against that person for an offence–

(a) the court, in determining whether there is a case to answer;

(b) a judge, in deciding whether to grant an application made by the accused under paragraph 2 of Schedule 3 to the Crime and Disorder Act 1998 (applications for dismissal); and

(c) the court or jury, in determining whether that person is guilty of the offence charged,

may draw such inferences from the refusal as appear proper.

(14) Every annual report–

(a) under section 22 of the Police Act 1996; or

(b) made by the Commissioner of Police of the Metropolis,

shall contain information about searches under this section which have been carried out in the area to which the report relates during the period to which it relates.

(14A) [Repealed.]

(15) The information about such searches shall include–

(a) the total number of searches;

(b) the number of searches conducted by way of examination by a suitably qualified person;

(c) the number of searches not so conducted but conducted in the presence of such a person; and

(d) the result of the searches carried out.

(16) The information shall also include, as separate items–

(a) the total number of drug offence searches; and

(b) the result of those searches.

(17) In this section–

'the appropriate criminal intent' means an intent to commit an offence under–

(a) section 5(3) of the Misuse of Drugs Act 1971 (possession of controlled drug with intent to supply to another); or

(b) section 68(2) of the Customs and Excise Management Act 1979 (exportation etc with intent to evade a prohibition or restriction);

'appropriate officer' means–

(a) a constable,

(b) a person who is designated as a detention officer in pursuance of section 38 of the Police Reform Act 2002 if his designation applies paragraph 33D of Schedule 4 to that Act,

(c) [Repealed.]

'Class A drug' has the meaning assigned to it by section 2(1)(b) of the Misuse of Drugs Act 1971;

'drug offence search' means an intimate search for a Class A drug which an officer has authorised by virtue of subsection (1)(b) above; and
'suitably qualified person' means–
(a)  a registered medical practitioner; or
(b)  a registered nurse.

### X-rays and ultrasound scans

55A (1) If an officer of at least the rank of inspector has reasonable grounds for believing that a person who has been arrested for an offence and is in police detention–
(a)  may have swallowed a Class A drug, and
(b)  was in possession of it with the appropriate criminal intent before his arrest,
the officer may authorise that an x-ray is taken of the person or an ultrasound scan is carried out on the person (or both).

(2) An x-ray must not be taken of a person and an ultrasound scan must not be carried out on him unless the appropriate consent has been given in writing.

(3) If it is proposed that an x-ray is taken or an ultrasound scan is carried out, an appropriate officer must inform the person who is to be subject to it–
(a)  of the giving of the authorisation for it, and
(b)  of the grounds for giving the authorisation.

(4) An x-ray may be taken or an ultrasound scan carried out only by a suitably qualified person and only at–
(a)  a hospital,
(b)  a registered medical practitioner's surgery, or
(c)  some other place used for medical purposes.

(5) The custody record of the person must also state–
(a)  the authorisation by virtue of which the x-ray was taken or the ultrasound scan was carried out,
(b)  the grounds for giving the authorisation, and
(c)  the fact that the appropriate consent was given.

(6) The information required to be recorded by subsection (5) must be recorded as soon as practicable after the x-ray has been taken or ultrasound scan carried out (as the case may be).

(7) Every annual report–
(a)  under section 22 of the Police Act 1996, or
(b)  made by the Commissioner of Police of the Metropolis,
must contain information about x-rays which have been taken and ultrasound scans which have been carried out under this section in the area to which the report relates during the period to which it relates.

(8) The information about such x-rays and ultrasound scans must be presented separately and must include–
(a)  the total number of x-rays;
(b)  the total number of ultrasound scans;
(c)  the results of the x-rays;
(d)  the results of the ultrasound scans.

(9) If the appropriate consent to an x-ray or ultrasound scan of any person is refused without good cause, in any proceedings against that person for an offence–
(a)  the court, in determining whether there is a case to answer,
(b)  a judge, in deciding whether to grant an application made by the accused under paragraph 2 of Schedule 3 to the Crime and Disorder Act 1998 (applications for dismissal), and
(c)  the court or jury, in determining whether that person is guilty of the offence charged,
may draw such inferences from the refusal as appear proper.

(10) In this section 'the appropriate criminal intent', 'appropriate officer', 'Class A drug' and 'suitably qualified person' have the same meanings as in section 55 above.

### Right to have someone informed when arrested

56(1) Where a person has been arrested and is being held in custody in a police station or other premises, he shall be entitled, if he so requests, to have one friend or relative or other person who is known to him or who is likely to take an interest in his welfare told, as soon as is practicable except to the extent that delay is permitted by this section, that he has been arrested and is being detained there.

(2) Delay is only permitted–
 (a) in the case of a person who is in police detention for an indictable offence; and
 (b) if an officer of at least the rank of inspector authorises it.

(3) In any case the person in custody must be permitted to exercise the right conferred by subsection (1) above within 36 hours from the relevant time, as defined in section 41(2) above.

(4) An officer may give an authorisation under subsection (2) above orally or in writing but, if he gives it orally, he shall confirm it in writing as soon as is practicable.

(5) Subject to subsection (5A) below an officer may only authorise delay where he has reasonable grounds for believing that telling the named person of the arrest–
 (a) will lead to interference with or harm to evidence connected with an indictable offence or interference with or physical injury to other persons; or
 (b) will lead to the alerting of other persons suspected of having committed such an offence but not yet arrested for it; or
 (c) will hinder the recovery of any property obtained as a result of such an offence.

(5A) An officer may also authorise delay where he has reasonable grounds for believing that–
 (a) the person detained for the indictable offence has benefited from his criminal conduct, and
 (b) the recovery of the value of the property constituting the benefit will be hindered by telling the named person of the arrest.

(5B) For the purposes of subsection (5A) above the question whether a person has benefited from his criminal conduct is to be decided in accordance with Part 2 of the Proceeds of Crime Act 2002.

(6) If a delay is authorised–
 (a) the detained person shall be told the reason for it; and
 (b) the reason shall be noted on his custody record.

(7) The duties imposed by subsection (6) above shall be performed as soon as is practicable.

(8) The rights conferred by this section on a person detained at a police station or other premises are exercisable whenever he is transferred from one place to another; and this section applies to each subsequent occasion on which they are exercisable as it applies to the first such occasion.

(9) There may be no further delay in permitting the exercise of the right conferred by subsection (1) above once the reason for authorising delay ceases to subsist.

(10) Nothing in this section applies to a person arrested or detained under the terrorism provisions.

### Additional rights of children and young persons

57 The following subsections shall be substituted for section 34(2) of the Children and Young Persons Act 1933–

 '(2) Where a child or young person is in police detention, such steps as are practicable shall be taken to ascertain the identity of a person responsible for his welfare.

 (3) If it is practicable to ascertain the identity of a person responsible for the welfare of the child or young person, that person shall be informed, unless it is not practicable to do so–
  (a) that the child or young person has been arrested;
  (b) why he has been arrested; and
  (c) where he is being detained.

 (4) Where information falls to be given under subsection (3) above, it shall be given as soon as it is practicable to do so.

 (5) For the purposes of this section the persons who may be responsible for the welfare of a child or young person are–
  (a) his parent or guardian; or

(b) any other person who has for the time being assumed responsibility for his welfare.

(6) If it is practicable to give a person responsible for the welfare of the child or young person the information required by subsection (3) above, that person shall be given it as soon as it is practicable to do so.

(7) If it appears that at the time of his arrest a supervision order, as defined in section 11 of the Children and Young Persons Act 1969, is in force in respect of him, the person responsible for his supervision shall also be informed as described in subsection (3) above as soon it is reasonably practicable to do so.

(8) The reference to a parent or guardian in subsection (5) above is–
   (a) in the case of a child or young person in the care of a local authority, a reference to that authority; and
   (b) in the case of a child or young person in the care of a voluntary organisation in which parental rights and duties with respect to him are vested by virtue of a resolution under section 64(1) of the Child Care Act 1980, a reference to that organisation.

(9) The rights conferred on a child or young person by subsections (2) to (8) above are in addition to his rights under section 56 of the Police and Criminal Evidence Act 1984.

(10) The reference in subsection (2) above to a child or young person who is in police detention includes a reference to a child or young person who has been detained under the terrorism provisions; and in subsection (3) above 'arrest' includes such detention.

(11) In subsection (10) above 'the terrorism provisions' has the meaning assigned to it by section 65 of the Police and Criminal Evidence Act 1984.'

### Access to legal advice

58 (1) A person arrested and held in custody in a police station or other premises shall be entitled, if he so requests, to consult a solicitor privately at any time.

(2) Subject to subsection (3) below, a request under subsection (1) above and the time at which it was made shall be recorded in the custody record.

(3) Such a request need not be recorded in the custody record of a person who makes it at a time while he is at a court after being charged with an offence.

(4) If a person makes such a request, he must be permitted to consult a solicitor as soon as is practicable except to the extent that delay is permitted by this section.

(5) In any case he must be permitted to consult a solicitor within 36 hours from the relevant time, as defined in section 41(2) above.

(6) Delay in compliance with a request is only permitted–
   (a) in the case of a person who is in police detention for an indictable offence; and
   (b) if an officer of at least the rank of superintendent authorises it.

(7) An officer may give an authorisation under subsection (6) above orally or in writing but, if he gives it orally, he shall confirm it in writing as soon as is practicable.

(8) Subject to subsection (8A) below an officer may only authorise delay where he has reasonable grounds for believing that the exercise of the right conferred by subsection (1) above at the time when the person detained desires to exercise it–
   (a) will lead to interference with or harm to evidence connected with an indictable offence or interference with or physical injury to other persons; or
   (b) will lead to the alerting of other persons suspected of having committed such an offence but not yet arrested for it; or
   (c) will hinder the recovery of any property obtained as a result of such an offence.

(8A) An officer may also authorise delay where he has reasonable grounds for believing that–
   (a) the person detained for the indictable offence has benefited from his criminal conduct, and
   (b) the recovery of the value of the property constituting the benefit will be hindered by the exercise of the right conferred by subsection (1) above.

(8B) For the purposes of subsection (8A) above the question whether a person has

benefited from his criminal conduct is to be decided in accordance with Part 2 of the Proceeds of Crime Act 2002.
(9) If delay is authorised–
   (a) the detained person shall be told the reason for it; and
   (b) the reason shall be noted on his custody record.
(10) The duties imposed by subsection (9) above shall be performed as soon as is practicable.
(11) There may be no further delay in permitting the exercise of the right conferred by subsection (1) above once the reason for authorising delay ceases to subsist.
(12) Nothing in this section applies to a person arrested or detained under the terrorism provisions.
59 [Repealed.]

### Tape-recording of interviews
60(1) It shall be the duty of the Secretary of State–
   (a) to issue a code of practice in connection with the tape-recording of interviews of persons suspected of the commission of criminal offences which are held by police officers at police stations; and
   (b) to make an order requiring the tape-recording of interviews of persons suspected of the commission of criminal offences, or of such descriptions of criminal offences as may be specified in the order, which are so held, in accordance with the code as it has effect for the time being.
(2) An order under subsection (1) above shall be made by statutory instrument and shall be subject to annulment in pursuance of a resolution of either House of Parliament.

### Visual recording of interviews
60A(1) The Secretary of State shall have power–
   (a) to issue a code of practice for the visual recording of interviews held by police officers at police stations; and
   (b) to make an order requiring the visual recording of interviews so held, and requiring the visual recording to be in accordance with the code for the time being in force under this section.
(2) A requirement imposed by an order under this section may be imposed in relation to such cases or police stations in such areas, or both, as may be specified or described in the order.
(3) An order under subsection (1) above shall be made by statutory instrument and shall be subject to annulment in pursuance of a resolution of either House of Parliament.
(4) In this section–
   (a) references to any interview are references to an interview of a person suspected of a criminal offence; and
   (b) references to a visual recording include references to a visual recording in which an audio recording is comprised.

### Fingerprinting
61(1) Except as provided by this section no person's fingerprints may be taken without the appropriate consent.
(2) Consent to the taking of a person's fingerprints must be in writing if it is given at a time when he is at a police station.
(3) The fingerprints of a person detained at a police station may be taken without the appropriate consent if–
   (a) he is detained in consequence of his arrest for a recordable offence; and
   (b) he has not had his fingerprints taken in the course of the investigation of the offence by the police.
(3A) Where a person mentioned in paragraph (a) of subsection (3) or (4) has already had his fingerprints taken in the course of the investigation of the offence by the police, that fact shall be disregarded for the purposes of that subsection if–
   (a) the fingerprints taken on the previous occasion do not constitute a complete set of his fingerprints; or
   (b) some or all of the fingerprints taken on the previous occasion are not of sufficient

quality to allow satisfactory analysis, comparison or matching (whether in the case in question or generally).

(4) The fingerprints of a person detained at a police station may be taken without the appropriate consent if–

    (a) he has been charged with a recordable offence or informed that he will be reported for such an offence; and

    (b) he has not had his fingerprints taken in the course of the investigation of the offence by the police.

(4A) The fingerprints of a person who has answered to bail at a court or police station may be taken without the appropriate consent at the court or station if–

    (a) the court, or

    (b) an officer of at least the rank of inspector,

authorises them to be taken.

(4B) A court or officer may only give an authorisation under subsection (4A) if–

    (a) the person who has answered to bail has answered to it for a person whose fingerprints were taken on a previous occasion and there are reasonable grounds for believing that he is not the same person; or

    (b) the person who has answered to bail claims to be a different person from a person whose fingerprints were taken on a previous occasion.

(5) An officer may give an authorisation under subsection (4A) above orally or in writing but, if he gives it orally, he shall confirm it in writing as soon as is practicable.

(5A) The fingerprints of a person may be taken without the appropriate consent if (before or after the coming into force of this subsection) he has been arrested for a recordable offence and released and–

    (a) in the case of a person who is on bail, he has not had his fingerprints taken in the course of the investigation of the offence by the police; or

    (b) in any case, he has had his fingerprints taken in the course of that investigation but subsection (3A)(a) or (b) above applies.

(5B) The fingerprints of a person not detained at a police station may be taken without the appropriate consent if (before or after the coming into force of this subsection) he has been charged with a recordable offence or informed that he will be reported for such an offence and–

    (a) he has not had his fingerprints taken in the course of the investigation of the offence by the police; or

    (b) he has had his fingerprints taken in the course of that investigation but subsection (3A)(a) or (b) above applies.

(6) Subject to this section, the fingerprints of a person may be taken without the appropriate consent if (before or after the coming into force of this subsection)–

    (a) he has been convicted of a recordable offence,

    (b) he has been given a caution in respect of a recordable offence which, at the time of the caution, he has admitted, or

    (c) he has been warned or reprimanded under section 65 of the Crime and Disorder Act 1998 for a recordable offence, and

either of the conditions mentioned in subsection (6ZA) below is met.

(6ZA) The conditions referred to in subsection (6) above are–

    (a) the person has not had his fingerprints taken since he was convicted, cautioned or warned or reprimanded;

    (b) he has had his fingerprints taken since then but subsection (3A)(a) or (b) above applies.

(6ZB) Fingerprints may only be taken as specified in subsection (6) above with the authorisation of an officer of at least the rank of inspector.

(6ZC) An officer may only give an authorisation under subsection (6ZB) above if the officer is satisfied that taking the fingerprints is necessary to assist in the prevention or detection of crime.

(6A) A constable may take a person's fingerprints without the appropriate consent if–

    (a) the constable reasonably suspects that the person is committing or attempting to commit an offence, or has committed or attempted to commit an offence; and

    (b) either of the two conditions mentioned in subsection (6B) is met.

(6B) The conditions are that–
  (a) the name of the person is unknown to, and cannot be readily ascertained by, the constable;
  (b) the constable has reasonable grounds for doubting whether a name furnished by the person as his name is his real name.

(6BA) *A constable may take a person's fingerprints without the appropriate consent if the person is subject to a control order.*[19]

(6C) The taking of fingerprints by virtue of subsection (6A) *or (6BA)*[20] does not count for any of the purposes of this Act as taking them in the course of the investigation of an offence by the police.

(6D) Subject to this section, the fingerprints of a person may be taken without the appropriate consent if–
  (a) under the law in force in a country or territory outside England and Wales the person has been convicted of an offence under that law (whether before or after the coming into force of this subsection and whether or not he has been punished for it);
  (b) the act constituting the offence would constitute a qualifying offence if done in England and Wales (whether or not it constituted such an offence when the person was convicted); and
  (c) either of the conditions mentioned in subsection (6E) below is met.

(6E) The conditions referred to in subsection (6D)(c) above are–
  (a) the person has not had his fingerprints taken on a previous occasion under subsection (6D) above;
  (b) he has had his fingerprints taken on a previous occasion under that subsection but subsection (3A)(a) or (b) above applies.

(6F) Fingerprints may only be taken as specified in subsection (6D) above with the authorisation of an officer of at least the rank of inspector.

(6G) An officer may only give an authorisation under subsection (6F) above if the officer is satisfied that taking the fingerprints is necessary to assist in the prevention or detection of crime.

(7) Where a person's fingerprints are taken without the appropriate consent by virtue of any power conferred by this section–
  (a) before the fingerprints are taken, the person shall be informed of–
    (i)   the reason for taking the fingerprints;
    (ii)  the power by virtue of which they are taken; and
    (iii) in a case where the authorisation of the court or an officer is required for the exercise of the power, the fact that the authorisation has been given; and
  (b) those matters shall be recorded as soon as practicable after the fingerprints are taken.

(7A) If a person's fingerprints are taken at a police station, or by virtue of subsection (4A), (6A) *or (6BA)*[21] at a place other than a police station, whether with or without the appropriate consent–
  (a) before the fingerprints are taken, an officer (or, where by virtue of subsection (4A), (6A) or (6BA) the fingerprints are taken at a place other than a police station, the constable taking the fingerprints) shall inform him that they may be the subject of a speculative search; and
  (b) the fact that the person has been informed of this possibility shall be recorded as soon as is practicable after the fingerprints have been taken.

(8) If he is detained at a police station when the fingerprints are taken, the matters referred to in subsection (7)(a)(i) to (iii) above and, in the case falling within subsection (7A) above, the fact referred to in paragraph (b) of that subsection shall be recorded on his custody record.

19  Inserted by the Counter-Terrorism Act 2008 s10(1). Not yet in force: see the Counter-Terrorism Act 2008 s100(5).
20  Words 'or (6BA)' in italics inserted by the Counter-Terrorism Act 2008 s10(6)(a)(i). Not yet in force: see the Counter-Terrorism Act 2008 s100(5).
21  Words 'or (6BA)' in italics inserted by the Counter-Terrorism Act 2008 s10(6)(a)(iii). Not yet in force: see the Counter-Terrorism Act 2008 s100(5).

(8A) [Repealed.]

(8B) Any power under this section to take the fingerprints of a person without the appropriate consent, if not otherwise specified to be exercisable by a constable, shall be exercisable by a constable.

(9) Nothing in this section–

    (a) affects any power conferred by paragraph 18(2) of Schedule 2 to the Immigration Act 1971[*, section 141 of the Immigration and Asylum Act 1999 or regulations made under section 144 of that Act*[22]; or

    (b) applies to a person arrested or detained under the terrorism provisions.

(10) Nothing in this section applies to a person arrested under an extradition arrest power.

### Impressions of footwear

**61A** (1) Except as provided by this section, no impression of a person's footwear may be taken without the appropriate consent.

(2) Consent to the taking of an impression of a person's footwear must be in writing if it is given at a time when he is at a police station.

(3) Where a person is detained at a police station, an impression of his footwear may be taken without the appropriate consent if–

    (a) he is detained in consequence of his arrest for a recordable offence, or has been charged with a recordable offence, or informed that he will be reported for a recordable offence; and

    (b) he has not had an impression taken of his footwear in the course of the investigation of the offence by the police.

(4) Where a person mentioned in paragraph (a) of subsection (3) above has already had an impression taken of his footwear in the course of the investigation of the offence by the police, that fact shall be disregarded for the purposes of that subsection if the impression of his footwear taken previously is–

    (a) incomplete; or

    (b) is not of sufficient quality to allow satisfactory analysis, comparison or matching (whether in the case in question or generally).

(5) If an impression of a person's footwear is taken at a police station, whether with or without the appropriate consent–

    (a) before it is taken, an officer shall inform him that it may be the subject of a speculative search; and

    (b) the fact that the person has been informed of this possibility shall be recorded as soon as is practicable after the impression has been taken, and if he is detained at a police station, the record shall be made on his custody record.

(6) In a case where, by virtue of subsection (3) above, an impression of a person's footwear is taken without the appropriate consent–

    (a) he shall be told the reason before it is taken; and

    (b) the reason shall be recorded on his custody record as soon as is practicable after the impression is taken.

(7) The power to take an impression of the footwear of a person detained at a police station without the appropriate consent shall be exercisable by any constable.

(8) Nothing in this section applies to any person–

    (a) arrested or detained under the terrorism provisions;

    (b) arrested under an extradition arrest power.

### Intimate samples

**62** (1) Subject to section 63B below, an intimate sample may be taken from a person in police detention only–

    (a) if a police officer of at least the rank of inspector authorises it to be taken; and

    (b) if the appropriate consent is given.

(1A) An intimate sample may be taken from a person who is not in police detention but

---

22 Words from ', section 141' to '144 of that Act' in italics inserted by the Immigration and Asylum Act 1999 s169(1), Sch 14 para 80(1), (4). Not yet in force: see the Immigration and Asylum Act 1999 s170(4).

from whom, in the course of the investigation of an offence, two or more non-intimate samples suitable for the same means of analysis have been taken which have proved insufficient–
(a) if a police officer of at least the rank of inspector authorises it to be taken; and
(b) if the appropriate consent is given.
(2) An officer may only give an authorisation under subsection (1) or (1A) above if he has reasonable grounds–
(a) for suspecting the involvement of the person from whom the sample is to be taken in a recordable offence; and
(b) for believing that the sample will tend to confirm or disprove his involvement.
(2A) An intimate sample may be taken from a person where–
(a) two or more non-intimate samples suitable for the same means of analysis have been taken from the person under section 63(3E) below (persons convicted of offences outside England and Wales etc) but have proved insufficient;
(b) a police officer of at least the rank of inspector authorises it to be taken; and
(c) the appropriate consent is given.
(2B) An officer may only give an authorisation under subsection (2A) above if the officer is satisfied that taking the sample is necessary to assist in the prevention or detection of crime.
(3) An officer may give an authorisation under subsection (1) or (1A) or (2A) above orally or in writing but, if he gives it orally, he shall confirm it in writing as soon as is practicable.
(4) The appropriate consent must be given in writing.
(5) Before an intimate sample is taken from a person, an officer shall inform him of the following–
(a) the reason for taking the sample;
(b) the fact that authorisation has been given and the provision of this section under which it has been given; and
(c) if the sample was taken at a police station, the fact that the sample may be the subject of a speculative search.
(6) The reason referred to in subsection (5)(a) above must include, except in a case where the sample is taken under subsection (2A) above, a statement of the nature of the offence in which it is suspected that the person has been involved.
(7) After an intimate sample has been taken from a person, the following shall be recorded as soon as practicable–
(a) the matters referred to in subsection (5)(a) and (b) above;
(b) if the sample was taken at a police station, the fact that the person has been informed as specified in subsection (5)(c) above; and
(c) the fact that the appropriate consent was given.
(8) If an intimate sample is taken from a person detained at a police station, the matters required to be recorded by subsection (7) above shall be recorded in his custody record.
(9) In the case of an intimate sample which is a dental impression, the sample may be taken from a person only by a registered dentist.
(9A) In the case of any other form of intimate sample, except in the case of a sample of urine, the sample may be taken from a person only by–
(a) a registered medical practitioner; or
(b) a registered health care professional.
(10) Where the appropriate consent to the taking of an intimate sample from a person was refused without good cause, in any proceedings against that person for an offence–
(a) the court, in determining–
(i) whether to commit that person for trial; or
(ii) whether there is a case to answer; and
(aa) a judge, in deciding whether to grant an application made by the accused under–
[(i) section 6 of the Criminal Justice Act 1987 (application for dismissal of charge of serious fraud in respect of which notice of transfer has been given under section 4 of that Act); or

(ii) paragraph 5 of Schedule 6 to the Criminal Justice Act 1991 (application for dismissal of charge of violent or sexual offence involving child in respect of which notice of transfer has been given under section 53 of that Act); and paragraph 2 of Schedule 3 to the Crime and Disorder Act 1998 (applications for dismissal); and][23]

(b) the court or jury, in determining whether that person is guilty of the offence charged,

may draw such inferences from the refusal as appear proper.

(11) Nothing in this section applies to the taking of a specimen for the purposes of any of the provisions of sections 4 to 11 of the Road Traffic Act 1988 or of sections 26 to 38 of the Transport and Works Act 1992.

(12) Nothing in this section applies to a person arrested or detained under the terrorism provisions; and subsection (1A) shall not apply where the non-intimate samples mentioned in that subsection were taken under paragraph 10 of Schedule 8 to the Terrorism Act 2000.

### Other samples

63(1) Except as provided by this section, a non-intimate sample may not be taken from a person without the appropriate consent.

(2) Consent to the taking of a non-intimate sample must be given in writing.

(2A) A non-intimate sample may be taken from a person without the appropriate consent if two conditions are satisfied.

(2B) The first is that the person is in police detention in consequence of his arrest for a recordable offence.

(2C) The second is that–

(a) he has not had a non-intimate sample of the same type and from the same part of the body taken in the course of the investigation of the offence by the police, or

(b) he has had such a sample taken but it proved insufficient.

(3) A non-intimate sample may be taken from a person without the appropriate consent if–

(a) he is being held in custody by the police on the authority of a court; and

(b) an officer of at least the rank of inspector authorises it to be taken without the appropriate consent.

(3ZA) A non-intimate sample may be taken from a person without the appropriate consent if (before or after the coming into force of this subsection) he has been arrested for a recordable offence and released and–

(a) in the case of a person who is on bail, he has not had a non-intimate sample of the same type and from the same part of the body taken from him in the course of the investigation of the offence by the police; or

(b) in any case, he has had a non-intimate sample taken from him in the course of that investigation but–

(i) it was not suitable for the same means of analysis, or

(ii) it proved insufficient.

(3A) A non-intimate sample may be taken from a person (whether or not he is in police detention or held in custody by the police on the authority of a court) without the appropriate consent if he has been charged with a recordable offence or informed that he will be reported for such an offence and–

(a) he has not had a non-intimate sample taken from him in the course of the investigation of the offence by the police; or

(b) he has had a non-intimate sample taken from him in the course of that investigation but–

(i) it was not suitable for the same means of analysis, or

(ii) it proved insufficient; or

---

23 Subs (10)(aa)(i), (ii) repealed and subsequent words in square brackets substituted by the Criminal Justice Act 2003 s41, Sch 3 Pt 2 para 56(1), (2)(b). In force in relation to cases sent for trial under the Crime and Disorder Act 1998, ss51 or 51A(3)(d). Not yet in force for remaining purposes: see the Criminal Justice Act 2003 s336(3).

    (c) he has had a non-intimate sample taken from him in the course of that investigation and–

        (i) the sample has been destroyed pursuant to section 64ZA below or any other enactment, and

        (ii) it is disputed, in relation to any proceedings relating to the offence, whether a DNA profile relevant to the proceedings is derived from the sample.

(3B) Subject to this section, a non-intimate sample may be taken from a person without the appropriate consent if (before or after the coming into force of this subsection)–

    (a) he has been convicted of a recordable offence,

    (b) he has been given a caution in respect of a recordable offence which, at the time of the caution, he has admitted, or

    (c) he has been warned or reprimanded under section 65 of the Crime and Disorder Act 1998 for a recordable offence, and

either of the conditions mentioned in subsection (3BA) below is met.

(3BA) The conditions referred to in subsection (3B) above are–

    (a) a non-intimate sample has not been taken from the person since he was convicted, cautioned or warned or reprimanded;

    (b) such a sample has been taken from him since then but–

        (i) it was not suitable for the same means of analysis, or

        (ii) it proved insufficient.

(3BB) A non-intimate sample may only be taken as specified in subsection (3B) above with the authorisation of an officer of at least the rank of inspector.

(3BC) An officer may only give an authorisation under subsection (3BB) above if the officer is satisfied that taking the sample is necessary to assist in the prevention or detection of crime.

(3C) A non-intimate sample may also be taken from a person without the appropriate consent if he is a person to whom section 2 of the Criminal Evidence (Amendment) Act 1997 applies (persons detained following acquittal on grounds of insanity or finding of unfitness to plead).

*(3D) A non-intimate sample may also be taken from a person without the appropriate consent if the person is subject to a control order.*[24]

(3E) Subject to this section, a non-intimate sample may be taken without the appropriate consent from a person if–

    (a) under the law in force in a country or territory outside England and Wales the person has been convicted of an offence under that law (whether before or after the coming into force of this subsection and whether or not he has been punished for it);

    (b) the act constituting the offence would constitute a qualifying offence if done in England and Wales (whether or not it constituted such an offence when the person was convicted); and

    (c) either of the conditions mentioned in subsection (3F) below is met.

(3F) The conditions referred to in subsection (3E)(c) above are–

    (a) the person has not had a non-intimate sample taken from him on a previous occasion under subsection (3E) above;

    (b) he has had such a sample taken from him on a previous occasion under that subsection but–

        (i) the sample was not suitable for the same means of analysis, or

        (ii) it proved insufficient.

(3G) A non-intimate sample may only be taken as specified in subsection (3E) above with the authorisation of an officer of at least the rank of inspector.

(3H) An officer may only give an authorisation under subsection (3G) above if the officer is satisfied that taking the sample is necessary to assist in the prevention or detection of crime.

(4) An officer may only give an authorisation under subsection (3) above if he has reasonable grounds–

24 Inserted by the Counter-Terrorism Act 2008 s10(2). Not yet in force: see the Counter-Terrorism Act 2008 s100(5).

(a) for suspecting the involvement of the person from whom the sample is to be taken in a recordable offence; and

(b) for believing that the sample will tend to confirm or disprove his involvement.

(5) An officer may give an authorisation under subsection (3) above orally or in writing but, if he gives it orally, he shall confirm it in writing as soon as is practicable.

(5A) An officer shall not give an authorisation under subsection (3) above for the taking from any person of a non-intimate sample consisting of a skin impression if–

(a) a skin impression of the same part of the body has already been taken from that person in the course of the investigation of the offence; and

(b) the impression previously taken is not one that has proved insufficient.

(6) Where a non-intimate sample is taken from a person without the appropriate consent by virtue of any power conferred by this section–  ·

(a) before the sample is taken, an officer shall inform him of–

(i)   the reason for taking the sample;

(ii)  the power by virtue of which it is taken; and

(iii) in a case where the authorisation of an officer is required for the exercise of the power, the fact that the authorisation has been given; and

(b) those matters shall be recorded as soon as practicable after the sample is taken.

(7) The reason referred to in subsection (6)(a)(i) above must include, except in a case where the non-intimate sample is taken under subsection (3B) or (3E) above, a statement of the nature of the offence in which it is suspected that the person has been involved.

(8B) If a non-intimate sample is taken from a person at a police station *or by virtue of subsection (3D) at a place other than a police station,*[25] whether with or without the appropriate consent–

(a) before the sample is taken, an officer, *or, in a subsection (3D) case, a constable,*[26] shall inform him that it may be the subject of a speculative search; and

(b) the fact that the person has been informed of this possibility shall be recorded as soon as practicable after the sample has been taken.

(9) If a non-intimate sample is taken from a person detained at a police station, the matters required to be recorded by subsection (6) or (8B) above shall be recorded in his custody record.

(9ZA) The power to take a non-intimate sample from a person without the appropriate consent shall be exercisable by any constable.

(9A) Subsection (3B) above shall not apply to–

(a) any person convicted before 10th April 1995 unless he is a person to whom section 1 of the Criminal Evidence (Amendment) Act 1997 applies (persons imprisoned or detained by virtue of pre-existing conviction for sexual offence etc); or

(b) a person given a caution before 10th April 1995.

(10) Nothing in this section applies to a person arrested or detained under the terrorism provisions.

(11) Nothing in this section applies to a person arrested under an extradition arrest power.

### Fingerprints and samples: supplementary provisions

63A(1) Where a person has been arrested on suspicion of being involved in a recordable offence or has been charged with such an offence or has been informed that he will be reported for such an offence, fingerprints, impressions of footwear or samples or the information derived from samples taken under any power conferred by this Part of this Act from the person may be checked against–

(a) other fingerprints , impressions of footwear or samples to which the person seeking to check has access and which are held by or on behalf of any one or

25  Words 'or by virtue of subsection (3D) at a place other than a police station' in italics inserted by the Counter-Terrorism Act 2008 s10(6)(b)(ii). Not yet in force: see the Counter-Terrorism Act 2008 s100(5).

26  Words ', or, in a subsection (3D) case, a constable,' in italics inserted by the Counter-Terrorism Act 2008 s10(6)(b)(iii). Not yet in force: see the Counter-Terrorism Act 2008 s100(5).

more relevant law-enforcement authorities or which are held in connection with or as a result of an investigation of an offence;

(b) information derived from other samples if the information is contained in records to which the person seeking to check has access and which are held as mentioned in paragraph (a) above.

(1ZA) Fingerprints taken by virtue of section 61(6A) above may be checked against other fingerprints to which the person seeking to check has access and which are held by or on behalf of any one or more relevant law-enforcement authorities or which are held in connection with or as a result of an investigation of an offence.

(1A) In subsection (1) and (1ZA) above 'relevant law-enforcement authority' means–

(a) a police force;

(b) the Serious Organised Crime Agency;

(d) a public authority (not falling within paragraphs (a) to (c)) with functions in any part of the British Islands which consist of or include the investigation of crimes or the charging of offenders;

(e) any person with functions in any country or territory outside the United Kingdom which–

(i)  correspond to those of a police force; or

(ii) otherwise consist of or include the investigation of conduct contrary to the law of that country or territory, or the apprehension of persons guilty of such conduct;

(f)  any person with functions under any international agreement which consist of or include the investigation of conduct which is–

(i)   unlawful under the law of one or more places,

(ii)  prohibited by such an agreement, or

(iii) contrary to international law,

or the apprehension of persons guilty of such conduct.

(1B) The reference in subsection (1A) above to a police force is a reference to any of the following–

(a) any police force maintained under section 2 of the Police Act 1996 (police forces in England and Wales outside London);

(b) the metropolitan police force;

(c) the City of London police force;

(d) any police force maintained under or by virtue of section 1 of the Police (Scotland) Act 1967;

(e) the Police Service of Northern Ireland;

(f)  the Police Service of Northern Ireland Reserve;

(g) the Ministry of Defence Police;

(h) the Royal Navy Police;

(i)  the Royal Military Police;

(j)  the Royal Air Force Police;

(k) [Repealed.]

(l)  the British Transport Police;

(m)the States of Jersey Police Force;

(n) the salaried police force of the Island of Guernsey;

(o) the Isle of Man Constabulary.

(1C) Where–

(a) fingerprints, impressions of footwear or samples have been taken from any person in connection with the investigation of an offence but otherwise than in circumstances to which subsection (1) above applies, and

(b) that person has given his consent in writing to the use in a speculative search of the fingerprints, of the impressions of footwear or of the samples and of information derived from them,

the fingerprints or impressions of footwear or, as the case may be, those samples and that information may be checked against any of the fingerprints, impressions of footwear, samples or information mentioned in paragraph (a) or (b) of that subsection.

(1D) A consent given for the purposes of subsection (1C) above shall not be capable of being withdrawn.

(1E) Where fingerprints or samples have been taken from any person under section 61(6) or 63(3B) above (persons convicted etc), the fingerprints or samples, or information derived from the samples, may be checked against any of the fingerprints, samples or information mentioned in subsection (1)(a) or (b) above.

(1F) Where fingerprints or samples have been taken from any person under section 61(6D), 62(2A) or 63(3E) above (offences outside England and Wales etc), the fingerprints or samples, or information derived from the samples, may be checked against any of the fingerprints, samples or information mentioned in subsection (1)(a) or (b) above.

(2) Where a sample of hair other than pubic hair is to be taken the sample may be taken either by cutting hairs or by plucking hairs with their roots so long as no more are plucked than the person taking the sample reasonably considers to be necessary for a sufficient sample.

(3) Where any power to take a sample is exercisable in relation to a person the sample may be taken in a prison or other institution to which the Prison Act 1952 applies.

(3A) Where–

    (a) the power to take a non-intimate sample under section 63(3B) above is exercisable in relation to any person who is detained under Part III of the Mental Health Act 1983 in pursuance of–

        (i) a hospital order or interim hospital order made following his conviction for the recordable offence in question, or

        (ii) a transfer direction given at a time when he was detained in pursuance of any sentence or order imposed following that conviction, or

    (b) the power to take a non-intimate sample under section 63(3C) above is exercisable in relation to any person,

the sample may be taken in the hospital in which he is detained under that Part of that Act.

Expressions used in this subsection and in the Mental Health Act 1983 have the same meaning as in that Act.

(3B) Where the power to take a non-intimate sample under section 63(3B) above is exercisable in relation to a person detained in pursuance of directions of the Secretary of State under section 92 of the Powers of Criminal Courts (Sentencing) Act 2000 the sample may be taken at the place where he is so detained.

(4) Schedule 2A (fingerprinting and samples: power to require attendance at police station) shall have effect.

### Testing for presence of Class A drugs

63B(1) A sample of urine or a non-intimate sample may be taken from a person in police detention for the purpose of ascertaining whether he has any specified Class A drug in his body if–

    (a) either the arrest condition or the charge condition is met;

    (b) both the age condition and the request condition are met; and

    (c) the notification condition is met in relation to the arrest condition, the charge condition or the age condition (as the case may be).

(1A) The arrest condition is that the person concerned has been arrested for an offence but has not been charged with that offence and either–

    (a) the offence is a trigger offence; or

    (b) a police officer of at least the rank of inspector has reasonable grounds for suspecting that the misuse by that person of a specified Class A drug caused or contributed to the offence and has authorised the sample to be taken.

(2) The charge condition is either–

    (a) that the person concerned has been charged with a trigger offence; or

    (b) that the person concerned has been charged with an offence and a police officer of at least the rank of inspector, who has reasonable grounds for suspecting that the misuse by that person of any specified Class A drug caused or contributed to the offence, has authorised the sample to be taken.

(3) The age condition is–

    (a) if the arrest condition is met, that the person concerned has attained the age of 18;

    (b) if the charge condition is met, that he has attained the age of 14.

(4) The request condition is that a police officer has requested the person concerned to give the sample.

(4A) The notification condition is that—

    (a) the relevant chief officer has been notified by the Secretary of State that appropriate arrangements have been made for the police area as a whole, or for the particular police station, in which the person is in police detention, and

    (b) the notice has not been withdrawn.

(4B) For the purposes of subsection (4A) above, appropriate arrangements are arrangements for the taking of samples under this section from whichever of the following is specified in the notification—

    (a) persons in respect of whom the arrest condition is met;

    (b) persons in respect of whom the charge condition is met;

    (c) persons who have not attained the age of 18.

(5) Before requesting the person concerned to give a sample, an officer must—

    (a) warn him that if, when so requested, he fails without good cause to do so he may be liable to prosecution, and

    (b) in a case within subsection (1A)(b) or (2)(b) above, inform him of the giving of the authorisation and of the grounds in question.

(5A) In the case of a person who has not attained the age of 17—

    (a) the making of the request under subsection (4) above;

    (b) the giving of the warning and (where applicable) the information under subsection (5) above; and

    (c) the taking of the sample,

may not take place except in the presence of an appropriate adult.

(5B) If a sample is taken under this section from a person in respect of whom the arrest condition is met no other sample may be taken from him under this section during the same continuous period of detention but—

    (a) if the charge condition is also met in respect of him at any time during that period, the sample must be treated as a sample taken by virtue of the fact that the charge condition is met;

    (b) the fact that the sample is to be so treated must be recorded in the person's custody record.

(5C) Despite subsection (1)(a) above, a sample may be taken from a person under this section if—

    (a) he was arrested for an offence (the first offence),

    (b) the arrest condition is met but the charge condition is not met,

    (c) before a sample is taken by virtue of subsection (1) above he would (but for his arrest as mentioned in paragraph (d) below) be required to be released from police detention,

    (d) he continues to be in police detention by virtue of his having been arrested for an offence not falling within subsection (1A) above, and

    (e) the sample is taken before the end of the period of 24 hours starting with the time when his detention by virtue of his arrest for the first offence began.

(5D) A sample must not be taken from a person under this section if he is detained in a police station unless he has been brought before the custody officer.

(6) A sample may be taken under this section only by a person prescribed by regulations made by the Secretary of State by statutory instrument.

No regulations shall be made under this subsection unless a draft has been laid before, and approved by resolution of, each House of Parliament.

(6A) The Secretary of State may by order made by statutory instrument amend—

    (a) paragraph (a) of subsection (3) above, by substituting for the age for the time being specified a different age specified in the order, or different ages so specified for different police areas so specified;

    (b) paragraph (b) of that subsection, by substituting for the age for the time being specified a different age specified in the order.

(6B) A statutory instrument containing an order under subsection (6A) above shall not be made unless a draft of the instrument has been laid before, and approved by a resolution of, each House of Parliament.

(7) Information obtained from a sample taken under this section may be disclosed–
    (a) for the purpose of informing any decision about granting bail in criminal pro-ceedings (within the meaning of the Bail Act 1976) to the person concerned;
    (aa) for the purpose of informing any decision about the giving of a conditional caution under Part 3 of the Criminal Justice Act 2003 or a youth conditional caution under Chapter 1 of Part 4 of the Crime and Disorder Act 1998 to the person concerned;
    (b) where the person concerned is in police detention or is remanded in or com-mitted to custody by an order of a court or has been granted such bail, for the purpose of informing any decision about his supervision;
    (c) where the person concerned is convicted of an offence, for the purpose of informing any decision about the appropriate sentence to be passed by a court and any decision about his supervision or release;
    (ca) for the purpose of an assessment which the person concerned is required to attend by virtue of section 9(2) or 10(2) of the Drugs Act 2005;
    (cb) for the purpose of proceedings against the person concerned for an offence under section 12(3) or 14(3) of that Act;
    (d) for the purpose of ensuring that appropriate advice and treatment is made available to the person concerned.
(8) A person who fails without good cause to give any sample which may be taken from him under this section shall be guilty of an offence.
(9) [Repealed.]
(10) In this section–
    'appropriate adult', in relation to a person who has not attained the age of 17, means–
        (a) his parent or guardian or, if he is in the care of a local authority or voluntary organisation, a person representing that authority or organisation; or
        (b) a social worker of a local authority ; or
        (c) if no person falling within paragraph (a) or (b) is available, any responsible person aged 18 or over who is not a police officer or a person employed by the police;
    'relevant chief officer' means–
        (a) in relation to a police area, the chief officer of police of the police force for that police area; or
        (b) in relation to a police station, the chief officer of police of the police force for the police area in which the police station is situated.

### Testing for presence of Class A drugs: supplementary

63C(1) A person guilty of an offence under section 63B above shall be liable on summary conviction to imprisonment for a term not exceeding [three months] *51 weeks*[27], or to a fine not exceeding level 4 on the standard scale, or to both.
(2) A police officer may give an authorisation under section 63B above orally or in writ-ing but, if he gives it orally, he shall confirm it in writing as soon as is practicable.
(3) If a sample is taken under section 63B above by virtue of an authorisation, the authorisation and the grounds for the suspicion shall be recorded as soon as is practicable after the sample is taken.
(4) If the sample is taken from a person detained at a police station, the matters required to be recorded by subsection (3) above shall be recorded in his custody record.
(5) Subsections (11) and (12) of section 62 above apply for the purposes of section 63B above as they do for the purposes of that section; and section 63B above does not prejudice the generality of sections 62 and 63 above.
(6) In section 63B above–
    'Class A drug' and 'misuse' have the same meanings as in the Misuse of Drugs Act 1971;
    'specified' (in relation to a Class A drug) and 'trigger offence' have the same mean-ings as in Part III of the Criminal Justice and Court Services Act 2000.

27 Words 'three months' in square brackets repealed and subsequent words in italics substituted by the Criminal Justice Act 2003 s280(2), (3), Sch 26 para 35. Not yet in force: see the Criminal Justice Act 2003 s336(3).

**Destruction of fingerprints and samples**

**64**(1A) Where–

(a) fingerprints, impressions of footwear or samples are taken from a person in connection with the investigation of an offence, and

(b) subsection (3) below does not require them to be destroyed,

the fingerprints, impressions of footwear or samples may be retained after they have fulfilled the purposes for which they were taken but shall not be used by any person except for purposes related to the prevention or detection of crime, the investigation of an offence[, the conduct of a prosecution or the identification of a deceased person or of the person from whom a body part came.

(1B) In subsection (1A) above–

(a) the reference to using a fingerprint or an impression of footwear includes a reference to allowing any check to be made against it under section 63A(1) or (1C) above and to disclosing it to any person;

(b) the reference to using a sample includes a reference to allowing any check to be made under section 63A(1) or (1C) above against it or against information derived from it and to disclosing it or any such information to any person;

(c) the reference to crime includes a reference to any conduct which–

(i) constitutes one or more criminal offences (whether under the law of a part of the United Kingdom or of a country or territory outside the United Kingdom); or

(ii) is, or corresponds to, any conduct which, if it all took place in any one part of the United Kingdom, would constitute one or more criminal offences;

and

(d) the references to an investigation and to a prosecution include references, respectively, to any investigation outside the United Kingdom of any crime or suspected crime and to a prosecution brought in respect of any crime in a country or territory outside the United Kingdom.

(1BA) Fingerprints taken from a person by virtue of section 61(6A) above must be destroyed as soon as they have fulfilled the purpose for which they were taken.

(3) If–

(a) fingerprints, impressions of footwear or samples are taken from a person in connection with the investigation of an offence; and

(b) that person is not suspected of having committed the offence,

they must, except as provided in the following provisions of this section, be destroyed as soon as they have fulfilled the purpose for which they were taken.

(3AA) Samples, fingerprints and impressions of footwear are not required to be destroyed under subsection (3) above if–

(a) they were taken for the purposes of the investigation of an offence of which a person has been convicted; and

(b) a sample, fingerprint, (or as the case may be) an impression of footwear was also taken from the convicted person for the purposes of that investigation.

(3AB) Subject to subsection (3AC) below, where a person is entitled under subsection (1BA) or (3) above to the destruction of any fingerprint, impression of footwear or sample taken from him (or would be but for subsection (3AA) above), neither the fingerprint, nor the impression of footwear, nor the sample, nor any information derived from the sample, shall be used–

(a) in evidence against the person who is or would be entitled to the destruction of that fingerprint, impression of footwear or sample; or

(b) for the purposes of the investigation of any offence;

and subsection (1B) above applies for the purposes of this subsection as it applies for the purposes of subsection (1A) above.

(3AC) Where a person from whom a fingerprint, impression of footwear or sample has been taken consents in writing to its retention–

(a) that fingerprint, impression of footwear or sample need not be destroyed under subsection (3) above;

(b) subsection (3AB) above shall not restrict the use that may be made of the fingerprint, impression of footwear or sample or, in the case of a sample, of any information derived from it; and

(c) that consent shall be treated as comprising a consent for the purposes of section 63A(1C) above;

and a consent given for the purpose of this subsection shall not be capable of being withdrawn.

This subsection does not apply to fingerprints taken from a person by virtue of section 61(6A) above.

(3AD) For the purposes of subsection (3AC) above it shall be immaterial whether the consent is given at, before or after the time when the entitlement to the destruction of the fingerprint, impression of footwear or sample arises.

(4) [Repealed.]

(5) If fingerprints [or impressions of footwear] are destroyed–
 (a) any copies of the fingerprints or impressions of footwear shall also be destroyed; and
 (b) any chief officer of police controlling access to computer data relating to the fingerprints or impressions of footwear shall make access to the data impossible, as soon as it is practicable to do so.]

(6) A person who asks to be allowed to witness the destruction of his fingerprints or impressions of footwear or copies of them shall have a right to witness it.

(6A) If–
 (a) subsection (5)(b) above falls to be complied with; and
 (b) the person to whose fingerprints or impressions of footwear the data relate asks for a certificate that it has been complied with,

such a certificate shall be issued to him, not later than the end of the period of three months beginning with the day on which he asks for it, by the responsible chief officer of police or a person authorised by him or on his behalf for the purposes of this section.

(6B) In this section–
 . . .
 'the responsible chief officer of police' means the chief officer of police in whose polic] area the computer data were put on to the computer.

(7) Nothing in this section–
 (a) affects any power conferred by paragraph 18(2) of Schedule 2 to the Immigration Act 1971 or section 20 of the Immigration and Asylum Act 1999 (disclosure of police information to the Secretary of State for use for immigration purposes); or
 (b) applies to a person arrested or detained under the terrorism provisions.

**Photographing of suspects etc**

64A (1) A person who is detained at a police station may be photographed–
 (a) with the appropriate consent; or
 (b) if the appropriate consent is withheld or it is not practicable to obtain it, without it.

(1A) A person falling within subsection (1B) below may, on the occasion of the relevant event referred to in subsection (1B), be photographed elsewhere than at a police station–
 (a) with the appropriate consent; or
 (b) if the appropriate consent is withheld or it is not practicable to obtain it, without it.

(1B) A person falls within this subsection if he has been–
 (a) arrested by a constable for an offence;
 (b) taken into custody by a constable after being arrested for an offence by a person other than a constable;
 (c) made subject to a requirement to wait with a community support officer under paragraph 2(3) or (3B) of Schedule 4 to the Police Reform Act 2002 ('the 2002 Act');
 (ca) given a direction by a constable under section 27 of the Violent Crime Reduction Act 2006;
 (d) given a penalty notice by a constable in uniform under Chapter 1 of Part 1 of the Criminal Justice and Police Act 2001, a penalty notice by a constable under

- section 444A of the Education Act 1996, or a fixed penalty notice by a constable in uniform under section 54 of the Road Traffic Offenders Act 1988;
- (e) given a notice in relation to a relevant fixed penalty offence (within the meaning of paragraph 1 of Schedule 4 to the 2002 Act) by a community support officer by virtue of a designation applying that paragraph to him;
- (f) given a notice in relation to a relevant fixed penalty offence (within the meaning of paragraph 1 of Schedule 5 to the 2002 Act) by an accredited person by virtue of accreditation specifying that that paragraph applies to him; or
- (g) given a notice in relation to a relevant fixed penalty offence (within the meaning of Schedule 5A to the 2002 Act) by an accredited inspector by virtue of accreditation specifying that paragraph 1 of Schedule 5A to the 2002 Act applies to him.
- (2) A person proposing to take a photograph of any person under this section–
  - (a) may, for the purpose of doing so, require the removal of any item or substance worn on or over the whole or any part of the head or face of the person to be photographed; and
  - (b) if the requirement is not complied with, may remove the item or substance himself.
- (3) Where a photograph may be taken under this section, the only persons entitled to take the photograph are constables.
- (4) A photograph taken under this section–
  - (a) may be used by, or disclosed to, any person for any purpose related to the prevention or detection of crime, the investigation of an offence or the conduct of a prosecution or to the enforcement of a sentence; and
  - (b) after being so used or disclosed, may be retained but may not be used or disclosed except for a purpose so related.
- (5) In subsection (4)–
  - (a) the reference to crime includes a reference to any conduct which–
    - (i) constitutes one or more criminal offences (whether under the law of a part of the United Kingdom or of a country or territory outside the United Kingdom); or
    - (ii) is, or corresponds to, any conduct which, if it all took place in any one part of the United Kingdom, would constitute one or more criminal offences;

    and
  - (b) the references to an investigation and to a prosecution include references, respectively, to any investigation outside the United Kingdom of any crime or suspected crime and to a prosecution brought in respect of any crime in a country or territory outside the United Kingdom; and
  - (c) 'sentence' includes any order made by a court in England and Wales when dealing with an offender in respect of his offence.
- (6) References in this section to taking a photograph include references to using any process by means of which a visual image may be produced; and references to photographing a person shall be construed accordingly.
- (6A) In this section, a 'photograph' includes a moving image, and corresponding expressions shall be construed accordingly.
- (7) Nothing in this section applies to a person arrested under an extradition arrest power.

### Part V–supplementary
65(1) In this Part of this Act–
  'analysis', in relation to a skin impression, includes comparison and matching;
  'appropriate consent' means–
  - (a) in relation to a person who has attained the age of 17 years, the consent of that person;
  - (b) in relation to a person who has not attained that age but has attained the age of 14 years, the consent of that person and his parent or guardian; and
  - (c) in relation to a person who has not attained the age of 14 years, the consent of his parent or guardian;

'control order' has the same meaning as in the Prevention of Terrorism Act 2005;[28]
'extradition arrest power' means any of the following–
(a) a Part 1 warrant (within the meaning given by the Extradition Act 2003) in respect of which a certificate under section 2 of that Act has been issued;
(b) section 5 of that Act;
(c) a warrant issued under section 71 of that Act;
(d) a provisional warrant (within the meaning given by that Act);
'fingerprints', in relation to any person, means a record (in any form and produced by any method) of the skin pattern and other physical characteristics or features of–
(a) any of that person's fingers; or
(b) either of his palms;
'intimate sample' means–
(a) a sample of blood, semen or any other tissue fluid, urine or pubic hair;
(b) a dental impression;
(c) a swab taken from any part of a person's genitals (including pubic hair) or from a person's body orifice other than the mouth;
'intimate search' means a search which consists of the physical examination of a person's body orifices other than the mouth;
'non-intimate sample' means–
(a) a sample of hair other than pubic hair;
(b) a sample taken from a nail or from under a nail;
(c) a swab taken from any part of a person's body other than a part from which a swab taken would be an intimate sample;
(d) saliva;
(e) a skin impression;
'offence', in relation to any country or territory outside England and Wales, includes an act punishable under the law of that country or territory, however it is described;
'person subject to a control order' means a person who has become bound by a control order (see section 7(8) of the Prevention of Terrorism Act 2005) that remains in force;[29]
'registered dentist' has the same meaning as in the Dentists Act 1984;
'registered health care professional' means a person (other than a medical practitioner) who is–
(a) a registered nurse; or
(b) a registered member of a health care profession which is designated for the purposes of this paragraph by an order made by the Secretary of State;
'skin impression', in relation to any person, means any record (other than a fingerprint) which is a record (in any form and produced by any method) of the skin pattern and other physical characteristics or features of the whole or any part of his foot or of any other part of his body;
'speculative search', in relation to a person's fingerprints or samples, means such a check against other fingerprints or samples or against information derived from other samples as is referred to in section 63A(1) above;
'sufficient' and 'insufficient', in relation to a sample, means (subject to subsection (2) below) sufficient or insufficient (in point of quantity or quality) for the purpose of enabling information to be produced by the means of analysis used or to be used in relation to the sample;
'the terrorism provisions' means section 41 of the Terrorism Act 2000, and any provision of Schedule 7 to that Act conferring a power of detention; and
'terrorism' has the meaning given in section 1 of that Act;

28 Inserted by the Counter-Terrorism Act 2008 s10(5). Not yet in force: see the Counter-Terrorism Act 2008 s100(5).
29 Inserted by the Counter-Terrorism Act 2008 s10(5). Not yet in force: see the Counter-Terrorism Act 2008 s100(5).

*'terrorist investigation' has the meaning given by section 32 of the Terrorism Act 2000*[30]

(1A) A health care profession is any profession mentioned in section 60(2) of the Health Act 1999 other than the profession of practising medicine and the profession of nursing.

(1B) An order under subsection (1) shall be made by statutory instrument and shall be subject to annulment in pursuance of a resolution of either House of Parliament.

(2) References in this Part of this Act to a sample's proving insufficient include references to where, as a consequence of–

   (a) the loss, destruction or contamination of the whole or any part of the sample,

   (b) any damage to the whole or a part of the sample, or

   (c) the use of the whole or a part of the sample for an analysis which produced no results or which produced results some or all of which must be regarded, in the circumstances, as unreliable,

the sample has become unavailable or insufficient for the purpose of enabling information, or information of a particular description, to be obtained by means of analysis of the sample.

(3) For the purposes of this Part, a person has in particular been convicted of an offence under the law of a country or territory outside England and Wales if–

   (a) a court exercising jurisdiction under the law of that country or territory has made in respect of such an offence a finding equivalent to a finding that the person is not guilty by reason of insanity; or

   (b) such a court has made in respect of such an offence a finding equivalent to a finding that the person is under a disability and did the act charged against him in respect of the offence.

### 'Qualifying offence'

65A(1) In this Part, 'qualifying offence' means–

   (a) an offence specified in subsection (2) below, or

   (b) an ancillary offence relating to such an offence.

(2) The offences referred to in subsection (1)(a) above are–

   (a) murder;

   (b) manslaughter;

   (c) false imprisonment;

   (d) kidnapping;

   (e) an offence under section 4, 16, 18, 20 to 24 or 47 of the Offences Against the Person Act 1861;

   (f) an offence under section 2 or 3 of the Explosive Substances Act 1883;

   (g) an offence under section 1 of the Children and Young Persons Act 1933;

   (h) an offence under section 4(1) of the Criminal Law Act 1967 committed in relation to murder;

   (i) an offence under sections 16 to 18 of the Firearms Act 1968;

   (j) an offence under section 9 or 10 of the Theft Act 1968 or an offence under section 12A of that Act involving an accident which caused a person's death;

   (k) an offence under section 1 of the Criminal Damage Act 1971 required to be charged as arson;

   (l) an offence under section 1 of the Protection of Children Act 1978;

   (m) an offence under section 1 of the Aviation Security Act 1982;

   (n) an offence under section 2 of the Child Abduction Act 1984;

   (o) an offence under section 9 of the Aviation and Maritime Security Act 1990;

   (p) an offence under any of sections 1 to 19, 25, 26, 30 to 41, 47 to 50, 52, 53, 57 to 59, 61 to 67, 69 and 70 of the Sexual Offences Act 2003;

   (q) an offence under section 5 of the Domestic Violence, Crime and Victims Act 2004;

   (r) an offence for the time being listed in section 41(1) of the Counter-Terrorism Act 2008.

---

30 Inserted by the Counter-Terrorism Act 2008 s10(5). Not yet in force: see the Counter-Terrorism Act 2008 s100(5).

(3) The Secretary of State may by order made by statutory instrument amend subsection (2) above.

(4) A statutory instrument containing an order under subsection (3) above shall not be made unless a draft of the instrument has been laid before, and approved by resolution of, each House of Parliament.

(5) In subsection (1)(b) above 'ancillary offence', in relation to an offence, means–
  (a) aiding, abetting, counselling or procuring the commission of the offence;
  (b) an offence under Part 2 of the Serious Crime Act 2007 (encouraging or assisting crime) in relation to the offence (including, in relation to times before the commencement of that Part, an offence of incitement);
  (c) attempting or conspiring to commit the offence.

## PART VI:  CODES OF PRACTICE–GENERAL

### Codes of practice

66(1) The Secretary of State shall issue codes of practice in connection with–
  (a) the exercise by police officers of statutory powers–
    (i) to search a person without first arresting him;
    (ii) to search a vehicle without making an arrest; or
    (iii) to arrest a person;
  (b) the detention, treatment, questioning and identification of persons by police officers;
  (c) searches of premises by police officers; and
  (d) the seizure of property found by police officers on persons or premises.

(2) Codes shall (in particular) include provision in connection with the exercise by police officers of powers under section 63B above.

### Codes of practice–supplementary

67(1) In this section, 'code' means a code of practice under section 60, 60A or 66.

(2) The Secretary of State may at any time revise the whole or any part of a code.

(3) A code may be made, or revised, so as to–
  (a) apply only in relation to one or more specified areas,
  (b) have effect only for a specified period,
  (c) apply only in relation to specified offences or descriptions of offender.

(4) Before issuing a code, or any revision of a code, the Secretary of State must consult–
  (a) the Association of Police Authorities,
  (b) the Association of Chief Police Officers of England, Wales and Northern Ireland,
  (c) the General Council of the Bar,
  (d) the Law Society of England and Wales,
  (e) the Institute of Legal Executives, and
  (f) such other persons as he thinks fit.

(5) A code, or a revision of a code, does not come into operation until the Secretary of State by order so provides.

(6) The power conferred by subsection (5) is exercisable by statutory instrument.

(7) An order bringing a code into operation may not be made unless a draft of the order has been laid before Parliament and approved by a resolution of each House.

(7A) An order bringing a revision of a code into operation must be laid before Parliament if the order has been made without a draft having been so laid and approved by a resolution of each House.

(7B) When an order or draft of an order is laid, the code or revision of a code to which it relates must also be laid.

(7C) No order or draft of an order may be laid until the consultation required by subsection (4) has taken place.

(7D) An order bringing a code, or a revision of a code, into operation may include transitional or saving provisions.

(8) [Repealed.]

(9) Persons other than police officers who are charged with the duty of investigating offences or charging offenders shall in the discharge of that duty have regard to any relevant provision of . . . a code.

(9A) Persons on whom powers are conferred by–

  (a) any designation under section 38 or 39 of the Police Reform Act 2002 (police powers for police authority employees), or

  (b) any accreditation under section 41 of that Act (accreditation under community safety accreditation schemes),

shall have regard to any relevant provision of a code in the exercise or performance of the powers and duties conferred or imposed on them by that designation or accreditation.

(10) A failure on the part–

  (a) of a police office to comply with any provision of a code;

  (b) of any person other than a police officer who is charged with the duty of investigating offences or charging offenders to have regard to any relevant provision of a code in the discharge of that duty, or

  (c) of a person designated under section 38 or 39 or accredited under section 41 of the Police Reform Act 2002 (c 30) to have regard to any relevant provision of a code in the exercise or performance of the powers and duties conferred or imposed on him by that designation or accreditation,

shall not of itself render him liable to any criminal or civil proceedings.

(11) In all criminal and civil proceedings any code shall be admissible in evidence; and if any provision of . . . a code appears to the court or tribunal conducting the proceedings to be relevant to any question arising in the proceedings it shall be taken into account in determining that question.

(12) In subsection (11) 'criminal proceedings' includes service proceedings.

(13) In this section 'service proceedings' means proceedings before a court (other than a civilian court) in respect of a service offence; and 'service offence' and 'civilian court' here have the same meanings as in the Armed Forces Act 2006.

## PART VII: DOCUMENTARY EVIDENCE IN CRIMINAL PROCEEDINGS

68 [Repealed.]

69 [Repealed.]

70 [Repealed.]

### Microfilm copies

71 In any proceedings the contents of a document may (whether or not the document is still in existence) be proved by the production of an enlargement of a microfilm copy of that document or of the material part of it, authenticated in such manner as the court may approve.

[Where the proceedings concerned are proceedings before a magistrates' court inquiring into an offence as examining justices this section shall have effect with the omission of the words 'authenticated in such manner as the court may approve.][31]

### Part VII–supplementary

72(1) In this Part of this Act–

  'copy', in relation to a document, means anything onto which information recorded in the document has been copied, by whatever means and whether directly or indirectly, and 'statement' means any representation of fact, however made; and

  'proceedings' means criminal proceedings, including service proceedings.

(1A) In subsection (1) 'service proceedings' means proceedings before a court (other than a civilian court) in respect of a service offence; and 'service offence' and 'civilian court' here have the same meanings as in the Armed Forces Act 2006.

(2) Nothing in this Part of this Act shall prejudice any power of a court to exclude evidence (whether by preventing questions from being put or otherwise) at its discretion.

---

31 Words in square brackets repealed by the Criminal Justice Act (CJA) 2003 ss41, 332, Sch 3 Pt 2 para 56(1), (3), Sch 37 Pt 4. Not yet in force: see CJA 2003 s336(3).

## PART VIII: EVIDENCE IN CRIMINAL PROCEEDINGS—GENERAL

### *Convictions and acquittals*
### Proof of convictions and acquittals

73(1) Where in any proceedings the fact that a person has in the United Kingdom or any other member State been convicted or acquitted of an offence otherwise than by a Service court is admissible in evidence, it may be proved by producing a certificate of conviction or, as the case may be, of acquittal relating to that offence, and proving that the person named in the certificate as having been convicted or acquitted of the offence is the person whose conviction or acquittal of the offence is to be proved.

(2) For the purposes of this section a certificate of conviction or of acquittal—
   (a) shall, as regards a conviction or acquittal on indictment, consist of a certificate, signed by the proper officer of the court where the conviction or acquittal took place, giving the substance and effect (omitting the formal parts) of the indictment and of the conviction or acquittal; and
   (b) shall, as regards a conviction or acquittal on a summary trial, consist of a copy of the conviction or of the dismissal of the information, signed by the proper officer of the court where the conviction or acquittal took place or by the proper officer of the court, if any, to which a memorandum of the conviction or acquittal was sent; and
   (c) shall, as regards a conviction or acquittal by a court in a member State (other than the United Kingdom), consist of a certificate, signed by the proper officer of the court where the conviction or acquittal took place, giving details of the offence, of the conviction or acquittal, and of any sentence;
   and a document purporting to be a duly signed certificate of conviction or acquittal under this section shall be taken to be such a certificate unless the contrary is proved.

(3) In subsection (2) above 'proper officer' means—
   (a) in relation to a magistrates' court in England and Wales, the designated officer for the court; and
   (b) in relation to any other court in the United Kingdom, the clerk of the court, his deputy or any other person having custody of the court record, and
   (c) in relation to any court in another member State ('the EU court'), a person who would be the proper officer of the EU court if that court were in the United Kingdom.

(4) The method of proving a conviction or acquittal authorised by this section shall be in addition to and not to the exclusion of any other authorised manner of proving a conviction or acquittal.

### Conviction as evidence of commission of offence

74(1) In any proceedings the fact that a person other than the accused has been convicted of an offence by or before any court in the United Kingdom or any other member State or by a Service court outside the United Kingdom shall be admissible in evidence for the purpose of proving that that person committed that offence, where evidence of his having done so is admissible, whether or not any other evidence of his having committed that offence is given.

(2) In any proceedings in which by virtue of this section a person other than the accused is proved to have been convicted of an offence by or before any court in the United Kingdom or any other member State or by a Service court outside the United Kingdom, he shall be taken to have committed that offence unless the contrary is proved.

(3) In any proceedings where evidence is admissible of the fact that the accused has committed an offence, if the accused is proved to have been convicted of the offence—
   (a) by or before any court in the United Kingdom or any other member State; or
   (b) by a Service court outside the United Kingdom,
   he shall be taken to have committed that offence unless the contrary is proved.

(4) Nothing in this section shall prejudice—

(a) the admissibility in evidence of any conviction which would be admissible apart from this section; or

(b) the operation of any enactment whereby a conviction or a finding of fact in any proceedings is for the purposes of any other proceedings made conclusive evidence of any fact.

### Provisions supplementary to section 74

75(1) Where evidence that a person has been convicted of an offence is admissible by virtue of section 74 above, then without prejudice to the reception of any other admissible evidence for the purpose of identifying the facts on which the conviction was based–

(a) the contents of any document which is admissible as evidence of the conviction; and

(b) the contents of–

(i) the information, complaint, indictment or charge-sheet on which the person in question was convicted, or

(ii) in the case of a conviction of an offence by a court in a member State (other than the United Kingdom), any document produced in relation to the proceedings for that offence which fulfils a purpose similar to any document or documents specified in sub-paragraph (i),

shall be admissible in evidence for that purpose.

(2) Where in any proceedings the contents of any document are admissible in evidence by virtue of subsection (1) above, a copy of that document, or of the material part of it, purporting to be certified or otherwise authenticated by or on behalf of the court or authority having custody of that document shall be admissible in evidence and shall be taken to be a true copy of that document or part unless the contrary is shown.

(3) Nothing in any of the following–

(a) section 14 of the Powers of Criminal Courts (Sentencing) Act 2000 (under which a conviction leading to probation or discharge is to be disregarded except as mentioned in that section);

(aa) section 187 of the Armed Forces Act 2006 (which makes similar provision in respect of service convictions);

(b) section 247 of the Criminal Procedure (Scotland) Act 1995 (which makes similar provision in respect of convictions on indictment in Scotland); and

(c) section 8 of the Probation Act (Northern Ireland) 1950 (which corresponds to section 13 of the Powers of Criminal Courts Act 1973) or any legislation which is in force in Northern Ireland for the time being and corresponds to that section,

shall affect the operation of section 74 above; and for the purposes of that section any order made by a court of summary jurisdiction in Scotland under section 228 or section 246(3) of the said Act of 1995 shall be treated as a conviction.

(4) Nothing in section 74 above shall be construed as rendering admissible in any proceedings evidence of any conviction other than a subsisting one.

## Confessions

### Confessions

76(1) In any proceedings a confession made by an accused person may be given in evidence against him in so far as it is relevant to any matter in issue in the proceedings and is not excluded by the court in pursuance of this section.

(2) If, in any proceedings where the prosecution proposes to give in evidence a confession made by an accused person, it is represented to the court that the confession was or may have been obtained–

(a) by oppression of the person who made it; or

(b) in consequence of anything said or done which was likely, in the circumstances existing at the time, to render unreliable any confession which might be made by him in consequence thereof,

the court shall not allow the confession to be given in evidence against him except in so far as the prosecution proves to the court beyond reasonable doubt that the confession (notwithstanding that it may be true) was not obtained as aforesaid.

(3) In any proceedings where the prosecution proposes to give in evidence a confession made by an accused person, the court may of its own motion require the prosecution, as a condition of allowing it to do so, to prove that the confession was not obtained as mentioned in subsection (2) above.

(4) The fact that a confession is wholly or partly excluded in pursuance of this section shall not affect the admissibility in evidence–
   (a) of any facts discovered as a result of the confession; or
   (b) where the confession is relevant as showing that the accused speaks, writes or expresses himself in a particular way, of so much of the confession as is necessary to show that he does so.

(5) Evidence that a fact to which this subsection applies was discovered as a result of a statement made by an accused person shall not be admissible unless evidence of how it was discovered is given by him or on his behalf.

(6) Subsection (5) above applies–
   (a) to any fact discovered as a result of a confession which is wholly excluded in pursuance of this section; and
   (b) to any fact discovered as a result of a confession which is partly so excluded, if the fact is discovered as a result of the excluded part of the confession.

(7) Nothing in Part VII of this Act shall prejudice the admissibility of a confession made by an accused person.

(8) In this section 'oppression' includes torture, inhuman or degrading treatment, and the use or threat of violence (whether or not amounting to torture).

[(9) Where the proceedings mentioned in subsection (1) above are proceedings before a magistrates' court inquiring into an offence as examining justices this section shall have effect with the omission of
   (a) in subsection (1) the words 'and is not excluded by the court in pursuance of this section', and
   (b) subsections (2) to (6) and (8).][32]

### Confessions may be given in evidence for co-accused

76A(1) In any proceedings a confession made by an accused person may be given in evidence for another person charged in the same proceedings (a co-accused) in so far as it is relevant to any matter in issue in the proceedings and is not excluded by the court in pursuance of this section.

(2) If, in any proceedings where a co-accused proposes to give in evidence a confession made by an accused person, it is represented to the court that the confession was or may have been obtained–
   (a) by oppression of the person who made it; or
   (b) in consequence of anything said or done which was likely, in the circumstances existing at the time, to render unreliable any confession which might be made by him in consequence thereof,
the court shall not allow the confession to be given in evidence for the co-accused except in so far as it is proved to the court on the balance of probabilities that the confession (notwithstanding that it may be true) was not so obtained.

(3) Before allowing a confession made by an accused person to be given in evidence for a co-accused in any proceedings, the court may of its own motion require the fact that the confession was not obtained as mentioned in subsection (2) above to be proved in the proceedings on the balance of probabilities.

(4) The fact that a confession is wholly or partly excluded in pursuance of this section shall not affect the admissibility in evidence–
   (a) of any facts discovered as a result of the confession; or
   (b) where the confession is relevant as showing that the accused speaks, writes or expresses himself in a particular way, of so much of the confession as is necessary to show that he does so.

---

32 Subs (9) repealed by CJA 2003 ss41, 332, Sch 3 Pt 2 para 56(1), (4), Sch 37 Pt 4. Not yet in force: see the CJA 2003 s336(3).

(5) Evidence that a fact to which this subsection applies was discovered as a result of a statement made by an accused person shall not be admissible unless evidence of how it was discovered is given by him or on his behalf.

(6) Subsection (5) above applies–

(a) to any fact discovered as a result of a confession which is wholly excluded in pursuance of this section; and

(b) to any fact discovered as a result of a confession which is partly so excluded, if the fact is discovered as a result of the excluded part of the confession.

(7) In this section 'oppression' includes torture, inhuman or degrading treatment, and the use or threat of violence (whether or not amounting to torture).

### Confessions by mentally handicapped persons

77(1) Without prejudice to the general duty of the court at a trial on indictment with a jury to direct the jury on any matter on which it appears to the court appropriate to do so, where at such a trial–

(a) the case against the accused depends wholly or substantially on a confession by him; and

(b) the court is satisfied–

(i) that he is mentally handicapped; and

(ii) that the confession was not made in the presence of an independent person,

the court shall warn the jury that there is special need for caution before convicting the accused in reliance on the confession, and shall explain that the need arises because of the circumstances mentioned in paragraphs (a) and (b) above.

(2) In any case where at the summary trial of a person for an offence it appears to the court that a warning under subsection (1) above would be required if the trial were on indictment with a jury, the court shall treat the case as one in which there is a special need for caution before convicting the accused on his confession.

(2A) In any case where at the trial on indictment without a jury of a person for an offence it appears to the court that a warning under subsection (1) above would be required if the trial were with a jury, the court shall treat the case as one in which there is a special need for caution before convicting the accused on his confession.

(3) In this section–

'independent person' does not include a police officer or a person employed for, or engaged on, police purposes;

'mentally handicapped', in relation to a person, means that he is in a state of arrested or incomplete development of mind which includes significant impairment of intelligence and social functioning; and

'police purposes' has the meaning assigned to it by section 101(2) of the Police Act 1996.

### Miscellaneous

### Exclusion of unfair evidence

78(1) In any proceedings the court may refuse to allow evidence on which the prosecution proposes to rely to be given if it appears to the court that, having regard to all the circumstances, including the circumstances in which the evidence was obtained, the admission of the evidence would have such an adverse effect on the fairness of the proceedings that the court ought not to admit it.

(2) Nothing in this section shall prejudice any rule of law requiring a court to exclude evidence.

[(3) This section shall not apply in the case of proceedings before a magistrates' court inquiring into an offence as examining justices.][33]

### Time for taking accused's evidence

79 If at the trial of any person for an offence–

(a) the defence intends to call two or more witnesses to the facts of the case; and

---

33 Subs (3) repealed by CJA 2003 ss41, 332, Sch 3 Pt 2 para 56(1), (5), Sch 37 Pt 4. Not yet in force: see CJA 2003 s336(3).

(b) those witnesses include the accused,

the accused shall be called before the other witness or witnesses unless the court in its discretion otherwise directs.

### Compellability of accused's spouse or civil partner

80 (1) [Repealed.]

(2) In any proceedings the spouse or civil partner of a person charged in the proceedings shall, subject to subsection (4) below, be compellable to give evidence on behalf of that person.

(2A) In any proceedings the spouse or civil partner of a person charged in the proceedings shall, subject to subsection (4) below, be compellable–

(a) to give evidence on behalf of any other person charged in the proceedings but only in respect of any specified offence with which that other person is charged; or

(b) to give evidence for the prosecution but only in respect of any specified offence with which any person is charged in the proceedings.

(3) In relation to the spouse or civil partner of a person charged in any proceedings, an offence is a specified offence for the purposes of subsection (2A) above if–

(a) it involves an assault on, or injury or a threat of injury to, the spouse or civil partner or a person who was at the material time under the age of 16;

(b) it is a sexual offence alleged to have been committed in respect of a person who was at the material time under that age; or

(c) it consists of attempting or conspiring to commit, or of aiding, abetting, counselling, procuring or inciting the commission of, an offence falling within paragraph (a) or (b) above.

(4) No person who is charged in any proceedings shall be compellable by virtue of subsection (2) or (2A) above to give evidence in the proceedings.

(4A) References in this section to a person charged in any proceedings do not include a person who is not, or is no longer, liable to be convicted of any offence in the proceedings (whether as a result of pleading guilty or for any other reason).

(5) In any proceedings a person who has been but is no longer married to the accused shall be . . . compellable to give evidence as if that person and the accused had never been married.

(5A) In any proceedings a person who has been but is no longer the civil partner of the accused shall be compellable to give evidence as if that person and the accused had never been civil partners.

(6) Where in any proceedings the age of any person at any time is material for the purposes of subsection (3) above, his age at the material time shall for the purposes of that provision be deemed to be or to have been that which appears to the court to be or to have been his age at that time.

(7) In subsection (3)(b) above 'sexual offence' means an offence under the Sexual Offences Act 1956, the Indecency with Children Act 1960, the Protection of Children Act 1978 or Part 1 of the Sexual Offences Act 2003.

(8) [Repealed.]

(9) Section 1(d) of the Criminal Evidence Act 1898 (communications between husband and wife and section 43(1) of the Matrimonial Causes Act 1965 (evidence as to marital intercourse) shall cease to have effect.

### Rule where accused's spouse or civil partner

80A The failure of the spouse or civil partner of a person charged in any proceedings to give evidence in the proceedings shall not be made the subject of any comment by the prosecution.

### Advance notice of expert evidence in Crown Court

81 (1) Criminal Procedure Rules may make provision for–

(a) requiring any party to proceedings before the court to disclose to the other party or parties any expert evidence which he proposes to adduce in the proceedings; and

(b) prohibiting a party who fails to comply in respect of any evidence with any requirement imposed by virtue of paragraph (a) above from adducing that evidence without the leave of the court.

(2) Criminal Procedure Rules made by virtue of this section may specify the kinds of expert evidence to which they apply and may exempt facts or matters of any description specified in the rules.

### Part VIII—supplementary

### Part VIII—interpretation

82(1) In this Part of this Act–

'confession' includes any statement wholly or partly adverse to the person who made it, whether made to a person in authority or not and whether made in words or otherwise;

'proceedings' means criminal proceedings, including service proceedings; and

'Service court' means the Court Martial or the Service Civilian Court.

(1A) In subsection (1) 'service proceedings' means proceedings before a court (other than a civilian court) in respect of a service offence; and 'service offence' and 'civilian court' here have the same meanings as in the Armed Forces Act 2006.

(2) [Repealed.]

(3) Nothing in this Part of this Act shall prejudice any power of a court to exclude evidence (whether by preventing questions from being put or otherwise) at its discretion.

### Part IX:  Police Complaints and Discipline
[Repealed.]

### The Police Complaints Authority

[Repealed.]

### Establishment of the Police Complaints Authority

83(1) [Repealed.]

(2) [Repealed.]

(3) [Repealed.]

84-105 [Repealed.]

### PART X  POLICE–GENERAL

106 [Repealed.]

### Police officers performing duties of higher rank

107 (1) For the purpose of any provision of this Act or any other Act under which a power in respect of the investigation of offences or the treatment of persons in police custody is exercisable only by or with the authority of a police officer of at least the rank of superintendent, an officer of the rank of chief inspector shall be treated as holding the rank of superintendent if

(a) he has been authorised by an officer holding a rank above the rank of superintendent to exercise the power or, as the case may be, to give his authority for its exercise, or

(b) he is acting during the absence of an officer holding the rank of superintendent who has authorised him, for the duration of that absence, to exercise the power or, as the case may be, to give his authority for its exercise.

(2) For the purpose of any provision of this Act or any other Act under which such a power is exercisable only by or with the authority of an officer of at least the rank of inspector, an officer of the rank of sergeant shall be treated as holding the rank of inspector if he has been authorised by an officer of at least the rank of superintendent to exercise the power or, as the case may be, to give his authority for its exercise.

108-110[Repealed.]

### Regulations for Police Forces and Police Cadets–Scotland

111 (1) In section 26 to the Police (Scotland) Act 1967 (regulations as to government and administration of police forces)–

(a) after subsection (1) there shall be inserted the following subsection–
'(1A) Regulations under this section may authorise the Secretary of State, the police authority or the chief constable to make provision for any purpose specified in the regulations.'; and
(b) at the end there shall be inserted the following subsection–
'(10) Any statutory instrument made under this section shall be subject to annulment in pursuance of a resolution of either House of Parliament.'.
(2) In section 27 of the said Act of 1967 (regulations for police cadets) in subsection (3) for the word '(9)' there shall be substituted the words '(1A), (9) and (10)'.

112 [Repealed.]

## PART XI:  MISCELLANEOUS AND SUPPLEMENTARY

### Application of Act to Armed Forces

113 (1) The Secretary of State may by order make provision in relation to–
(a) investigations of service offences,
(b) persons arrested under a power conferred by or under the Armed Forces Act 2006,
(c) persons charged under that Act with service offences,
(d) persons in service custody, or
(e) persons convicted of service offences,
which is equivalent to that made by any provision of Part 5 of this Act (or this Part of this Act so far as relating to that Part), subject to such modifications as the Secretary of State considers appropriate.
(2) Section 67(9) above shall not have effect in relation to investigations of service offences.
(3) The Secretary of State shall issue a code of practice, or a number of such codes, for persons other than police officers who are concerned with–
(a) the exercise of powers conferred by or under Part 3 of the Armed Forces Act 2006; or
(b) investigations of service offences.
(3A) In subsections (4) to (10), 'code' means a code of practice under subsection (3).
(4) Without prejudice to the generality of subsection (3) above, a code may contain provisions, in connection with the powers mentioned in subsection (3)(a) above or the investigations mentioned in subsection (3)(b) above, as to the following matters–
(a) the tape-recording of interviews;
(b) searches of persons and premises; and
(c) the seizure of things found on searches.
(5) The Secretary of State may at any time revise the whole or any part of a code.
(6) A code may be made, or revised, so as to–
(a) apply only in relation to one or more specified areas,
(b) have effect only for a specified period,
(c) apply only in relation to specified offences or descriptions of offender.
(7) The Secretary of State must lay a code, or any revision of a code, before Parliament.
(8) A failure on the part of any person to comply with any provision of a code shall not of itself render him liable to any criminal or civil proceedings except those to which this subsection applies.
(9) Subsection (8) above applies to proceedings in respect of an offence under a provision of Part 1 of the Armed Forces Act 2006 other than section 42 (criminal conduct).
(10) In all criminal and civil proceedings any code shall be admissible in evidence and if any provision of a code appears to the court or tribunal conducting the proceedings to be relevant to any question arising in the proceedings it shall be taken into account in determining that question.
(11) [Repealed.]
(12) Parts VII and VIII of this Act have effect for the purposes of service proceedings, subject to any modifications which the Secretary of State may by order specify.

(12A) In this section—
'service offence' has the meaning given by section 50 of the Armed Forces Act 2006;
'criminal proceedings' includes service proceedings;
'service proceedings' means proceedings before a court (other than a civilian court) in respect of a service offence; and
'civilian court' has the meaning given by section 374 of the Armed Forces Act 2006;
and section 376(1) and (2) of that Act (meaning of 'convicted' in relation to summary hearings and the SAC) apply for the purposes of subsection (1)(e) above as they apply for the purposes of that Act.
(13) An order under this section shall be made by statutory instrument and shall be subject to annulment in pursuance of a resolution of either House of Parliament.
(14) Section 373(5) and (6) of the Armed Forces Act 2006 (supplementary provisions) apply in relation to an order under this section as they apply in relation to an order under that Act.

### Application of Act to Revenue and Customs

114 (1) 'Arrested', 'arresting', 'arrest' and 'to arrest' shall respectively be substituted for 'detained', 'detaining', 'detention' and 'to detain' wherever in the customs and excise Acts, as defined in section 1(1) of the Customs and Excise Management Act 1979, those words are used in relation to persons.
(2) The Treasury may by order direct—
(a) that any provision of this Act which relates to investigations of offences conducted by police officers or to persons detained by the police shall apply, subject to such modifications as the order may specify, to investigations conducted by officers of Revenue and Customs or to persons detained by officers of Revenue and Customs; and
(b) that, in relation to investigations of offences conducted by officers of Revenue and Customs—
(i) this Act shall have effect as if the following sections were inserted after section 14—

#### 'Exception for Revenue and Customs

14A Material in the possession of a person who acquired or created it in the course of any trade, business, profession or other occupation or for the purpose of any paid or unpaid office and which relates to a matter in relation to which Her Majesty's Revenue and Customs have functions, is neither excluded material nor special procedure material for the purposes of any enactment such as is mentioned in section 9(2) above.

#### Revenue and Customs: restriction on other powers to apply for production of documents

14B(1) An officer of Revenue and Customs may make an application for the delivery of, or access to, documents under a provision specified in subsection (3) only if the condition in subsection (2) is satisfied.
(2) The condition is that the officer thinks that an application under Schedule 1 would not succeed because the material required does not consist of or include special procedure material.
(3) The provisions are—
(a) section 20BA of, and Schedule 1AA to, the Taxes Management Act 1970 (serious tax fraud);
(b) paragraph 11 of Schedule 11 to the Value Added Tax Act 1994 (VAT);
(c) paragraph 4A of Schedule 7 to the Finance Act 1994 (insurance premium tax);
(d) paragraph 7 of Schedule 5 to the Finance Act 1996 (landfill tax);
(e) paragraph 131 of Schedule 6 to the Finance Act 2000 (climate change levy);

> > > (f) paragraph 8 of Schedule 7 to the Finance Act 2001 (aggregates levy);
> > > (g) Part 6 of Schedule 13 to the Finance Act 2003 (stamp duty land tax).'; and
> > (ii) section 55 above shall have effect as if it related only to things such as are mentioned in subsection (1)(a) of that section and
> (c) that in relation to Revenue and Customs detention (as defined in any order made under this subsection) the Bail Act 1976 shall have effect as if references in it to a constable were references to an officer of Revenue and Customs of such grade as may be specified in the order;
> (d) that where an officer of Revenue and Customs searches premises in reliance on a warrant under section 8 of, or paragraph 12 of Schedule 1 to, this Act (as applied by an order under this subsection) the officer shall have the power to search persons found on the premises–
> > (i) in such cases and circumstances as are specified in the order, and
> > (ii) subject to any conditions specified in the order; and
> (e) that powers and functions conferred by a provision of this Act (as applied by an order under this subsection) may be exercised only by officers of Revenue and Customs acting with the authority (which may be general or specific) of the Commissioners for Her Majesty's Revenue and Customs.

(2A) A certificate of the Commissioners that an officer of Revenue and Customs had authority under subsection (2)(e) to exercise a power or function conferred by a provision of this Act shall be conclusive evidence of that fact.

(3) An order under subsection (2)–
> (a) may make provision that applies generally or only in specified cases or circumstances,
> (b) may make different provision for different cases or circumstances,
> (c) may, in modifying a provision, in particular impose conditions on the exercise of a function, and
> (d) shall not be taken to limit a power under section 164 of the Customs and Excise Management Act 1979.

(4) [Repealed.]

(5) An order under this section shall be made by statutory instrument and shall be subject to annulment in pursuance of a resolution of either House of Parliament.

### Power to apply Act to officers of the Secretary of State etc

114A(1) The Secretary of State may by order direct that–
> (a) the provisions of Schedule 1 to this Act so far as they relate to special procedure material, and
> (b) the other provisions of this Act so far as they relate to the provisions falling within paragraph (a) above,

shall apply, with such modifications as may be specified in the order, for the purposes of investigations falling within subsection (2) as they apply for the purposes of investigations of offences conducted by police officers

(2) An investigation falls within this subsection if–
> (a) it is conducted by an officer of the department of the Secretary of State for Business, Innovation and Skills or by another person acting on that Secretary of State's behalf;
> (b) it is conducted by that officer or other person in the discharge of a duty to investigate offences; and
> (c) the investigation relates to an indictable offence or to anything which there are reasonable grounds for suspecting has involved the commission of an indictable offence.

(3) The investigations for the purposes of which provisions of this Act may be applied with modifications by an order under this section include investigations of offences committed, or suspected of having been committed, before the coming into force of the order or of this section.

578    *Defending suspects at police stations  /  appendix 1*

(4) An order under this section shall be made by statutory instrument and shall be subject to annulment in pursuance of a resolution of either House of Parliament.

### Expenses

115 Any expenses of a Minister of the Crown incurred in consequence of the provisions of this Act, including any increase attributable to those provisions in sums payable under any other Act, shall be defrayed out of money provided by Parliament.

116 [Repealed.]

### Power of constable to use reasonable force

117 Where any provision of this Act–

(a) confers a power on a constable; and

(b) does not provide that the power may only be exercised with the consent of some person, other than a police officer,

the officer may use reasonable force, if necessary, in the exercise of the power.

### General interpretation

118 (1) In this Act–

'British Transport Police Force' means the constables appointed under section 53 of the British Transport Commission Act 1949 (c xxix);

'designated police station' has the meaning assigned to it by section 35 above;

'document' means anything in which information of any description is recorded.;

'item subject to legal privilege' has the meaning assigned to it by section 10 above;

'parent or guardian' means–

(a) in the case of a child or young person in the care of a local authority, that authority;

(b) [Repealed.]

'premises' has the meaning assigned to it by section 23 above;

'recordable offence' means any offence to which regulations under section 27 above apply;

'vessel' includes any ship, boat, raft or other apparatus constructed or adapted for floating on water.

(2) Subject to subsection (2A) a person is in police detention for the purposes of this Act if–

(a) he has been taken to a police station after being arrested for an offence or after being arrested under section 41 of the Terrorism Act 2000, or

(b) he is arrested at a police station after attending voluntarily at the station or accompanying a constable to it,

and is detained there or is detained elsewhere in the charge of a constable, except that a person who is at a court after being charged is not in police detention for those purposes.

(2A) Where a person is in another's lawful custody by virtue of paragraph 22, 34(1) or 35(3) of Schedule 4 to the Police Reform Act 2002, he shall be treated as in police detention.

### Amendments and repeals

119 (1) The enactments mentioned in Schedule 6 to this Act shall have effect with the amendments there specified.

(2) The enactments mentioned in Schedule 7 to this Act (which include enactments already obsolete or unnecessary) are repealed to the extent specified in the third column of that Schedule.

(3) The repeals in Parts II and IV of Schedule 7 to this Act have effect only in relation to criminal proceedings.

### Extent

120 (1) Subject to the following provisions of this section, this Act extends to England and Wales only.

(2) The following extend to Scotland only–

section 111;

section 112(1); and

section 119(2), so far as it relates to the provisions of the Pedlars Act 1871 repealed by Part VI of Schedule 7.

(3) The following extend to Northern Ireland only–
section 6(4), and
section 112(2).

(4) The following extend to England and Wales and Scotland–
section 6(1) and (2);
section 7;
and
section 119(2), so far as it relates to section 19 of the Pedlars Act 1871.

(5) The following extend to England and Wales, Scotland and Northern Ireland–
section 6(3);
section 9(2A);
and
section 114(1).

(6) Nothing in subsection (1) affects–
(a) the extent of section 113(1) to (7) and (12) to (14);
(b) the extent of the relevant provisions so far as they relate to service proceedings.

(8) In this section 'the relevant provisions' means–
(a) section 67(11) to (13);
(c) Parts VII and VIII of this Act, except paragraph 10 of Schedule 3;
(d) section 113(8) to (10).

(8A) In this section 'service proceedings' means proceedings before a court (other than a civilian court) in respect of a service offence; and 'service offence' and 'civilian court' here have the same meanings as in the Armed Forces Act 2006.'

(8B) Section 384 of the Armed Forces Act 2006 (Channel Islands, Isle of Man and British overseas territories) applies in relation to the provisions mentioned in subsection (6)(a) and (b) above as it applies in relation to that Act.

(9A) Section 119(1), so far as it relates to any provision amended by Part II of Schedule 6, extends to any place to which that provision extends.

(10) Section 119(2), so far as it relates–
(a) to any provision contained in–
the Army Act 1955;
the Air Force Act 1955;
the Armed Forces Act 1981; or
the Value Added Tax Act 1983;
(b) to any provision mentioned in Part VI of Schedule 7, other than section 18 of the Pedlars Act 1871,
extends to any place to which that provision extends.

(11) So far as any of the following–
section 115;
in section 118, the definition of 'document';
this section;
section 121; and
section 122,
has effect in relation to any other provision of this Act, it extends to any place to which that provision extends.

### Commencement

121 (1) This Act, except section 120 above, this section and section 122 below, shall come into operation on such day as the Secretary of State may by order made by statutory instrument appoint, and different days may be so appointed for different provisions and for different purposes.

(2) Different days may be appointed under this section for the coming into force of section 60 above in different areas.

(3) When an order under this section provides by virtue of subsection (2) above that section 60 above shall come into force in an area specified in the order, the duty

imposed on the Secretary of State by that section shall be construed as a duty to make an order under it in relation to interviews in that area.

(4) An order under this section may make such transitional provision as appears to the Secretary of State to be necessary or expedient in connection with the provisions thereby brought into operation.

### Short title

122 This Act may be cited as the Police and Criminal Evidence Act 1984.

## SCHEDULE 1: SPECIAL PROCEDURE

Section 9

### Making of orders by circuit judge

1 If on an application made by a constable a [circuit judge] *judge*[34] is satisfied that one or other of the sets of access conditions is fulfilled, he may make an order under paragraph 4 below.

2 The first set of access conditions is fulfilled if–

(a) there are reasonable grounds for believing–
  (i) that an indictable offence has been committed;
  (ii) that there is material which consists of special procedure material or also includes special procedure material and does not also include excluded material on premises specified in the application, or on premises occupied or controlled by a person specified in the application (including all such premises on which there are reasonable grounds for believing that there is such material as it is reasonably practicable so to specify);
  (iii) that the material is likely to be of substantial value (whether by itself or together with other material) to the investigation in connection with which the application is made; and
  (iv) that the material is likely to be relevant evidence;

(b) other methods of obtaining the material–
  (i) have been tried without success; or
  (ii) have not been tried because it appeared that they were bound to fail; and

(c) it is in the public interest, having regard–
  (i) to the benefit likely to accrue to the investigation if the material is obtained; and
  (ii) to the circumstances under which the person in possession of the material holds it,

that the material should be produced or that access to it should be given.

3 The second set of access conditions is fulfilled if–

(a) there are reasonable grounds for believing that there is material which consists of or includes excluded material or special procedure material on premises specified in the application, or on premises occupied or controlled by a person specified in the application (including all such premises on which there are reasonable grounds for believing that there is such material as it is reasonably practicable so to specify);

(b) but for section 9(2) above a search of such premises for that material could have been authorised by the issue of a warrant to a constable under an enactment other than this Schedule; and

(c) the issue of such a warrant would have been appropriate.

4 An order under this paragraph is an order that the person who appears to the [circuit judge] *judge* to be in possession of the material to which the application relates shall[35]–

---

34 Words 'circuit judge' in square brackets repealed and subsequent word in italics substituted by the Courts Act 2003 s65, Sch 4 para 6(1). Not yet in force: see the Courts Act 2003 s110(1).

35 Words 'circuit judge' in square brackets repealed and subsequent word in italics substituted by the Courts Act 2003 s65, Sch 4 para 6(1). Not yet in force: see the Courts Act 2003 s110(1).

(a) produce it to a constable for him to take away; or

(b) give a constable access to it,

not later than the end of the period of seven days from the date of the order or the end of such longer period as the order may specify.

5 Where the material consists of information stored in any electronic form–

(a) an order under paragraph 4(a) above shall have effect as an order to produce the material in a form in which it can be taken away and in which it is visible and legible or from which it can readily be produced in a visible and legible form; and

(b) an order under paragraph 4(b) above shall have effect as an order to give a constable access to the material in a form in which it is visible and legible.

6 For the purposes of sections 21 and 22 above material produced in pursuance of an order under paragraph 4(a) above shall be treated as if it were material seized by a constable.

### Notices of applications for orders

7 An application for an order under paragraph 4 above shall be made inter partes.

8 Notice of an application for such an order may be served on a person either by delivering it to him or by leaving it at his proper address or by sending it by post to him in a registered letter or by the recorded delivery service.

9 Such a notice may be served–

(a) on a body corporate, by serving it on the body's secretary or clerk or other similar officer; and

(b) on a partnership, by serving it on one of the partners.

10 For the purposes of this Schedule, and of section 7 of the Interpretation Act 1978 in its application to this Schedule, the proper address of a person, in the case of secretary or clerk or other similar officer of a body corporate, shall be that of the registered or principal office of that body, in the case of a partner of a firm shall be that of the principal office of the firm, and in any other case shall be the last known address of the person to be served.

11 Where notice of an application for an order under paragraph 4 above has been served on a person, he shall not conceal, destroy, alter or dispose of the material to which the application relates except–

(a) with the leave of a judge; or

(b) with the written permission of a constable,

until–

(i) the application is dismissed or abandoned; or

(ii) he has complied with an order under paragraph 4 above made on the application.

### Issue of warrants by circuit judge

12 If on an application made by a constable a [circuit judge] *judge*[36]–

(a) is satisfied–

(i) that either set of access conditions is fulfilled; and

(ii) that any of the further conditions set out in paragraph 14 below is also fulfilled in relation to each set of premises specified in the application; or

(b) is satisfied–

(i) that the second set of access conditions is fulfilled; and

(ii) that an order under paragraph 4 above relating to the material has not been complied with,

he may issue a warrant authorising a constable to enter and search the premises or (as the case may be) all premises occupied or controlled by the person referred to in paragraph 2(a)(ii) or 3(a), including such sets of premises as are specified in the application (an 'all premises warrant').

12A The judge may not issue an all premises warrant unless he is satisfied–

---

36 Words 'circuit judge' in square brackets repealed and subsequent word in italics substituted by the Courts Act 2003 s65, Sch 4 para 6(1). Not yet in force: see the Courts Act 2003 s110(1).

(a) that there are reasonable grounds for believing that it is necessary to search premises occupied or controlled by the person in question which are not specified in the application, as well as those which are, in order to find the material in question; and

(b) that it is not reasonably practicable to specify all the premises which he occupies or controls which might need to be searched.

**13** A constable may seize and retain anything for which a search has been authorised under paragraph 12 above.

**14** The further conditions mentioned in paragraph 12(a)(ii) above are–

(a) that it is not practicable to communicate with any person entitled to grant entry to the premises;

(b) that it is practicable to communicate with a person entitled to grant entry to the premises but it is not practicable to communicate with any person entitled to grant access to the material;

(c) that the material contains information which–

(i) is subject to a restriction or obligation such as is mentioned in section 11(2)(b) above; and

(ii) is likely to be disclosed in breach of it if a warrant is not issued;

(d) that service of notice of an application for an order under paragraph 4 above may seriously prejudice the investigation.

**15**(1) If a person fails to comply with an order under paragraph 4 above, a [circuit judge] *judge*[37] may deal with him as if he had committed a contempt of the Crown Court.

(2) Any enactment relating to contempt of the Crown Court shall have effect in relation to such a failure as if it were such a contempt.

### Costs

**16** The costs of any application under this Schedule and of anything done or to be done in pursuance of an order made under it shall be in the discretion of the judge.

### Interpretation

**17** In this Schedule 'judge' means a [circuit judge] *judge*[38] of the High Court, a Circuit judge, a Recorder or a District Judge (Magistrates' Courts).

## SCHEDULE 1A

[Repealed.]

## SCHEDULE 2: PRESERVED POWERS OF ARREST

**Section 26**

| | | |
|---|---|---|
| 1952 | c 52 | Section 49 of the Prison Act 1952. |
| 1952 | c 67 | Section 13 of the Visiting Forces Act 1952. |
| 1969 | c 54 | Section 32 of the Children and Young Persons Act 1969. |
| 1971 | c 77 | Section 24(2) of the Immigration Act 1971 and paragraphs 17, 24 and 33 of Schedule 2 and paragraph 7 of Schedule 3 to that Act. |
| 1976 | c 63 | Section 7 of the Bail Act 1976. |
| 1983 | c 2 | Rule 36 in Schedule 1 to the Representation of the People Act 1983. |
| 1983 | c 20 | Sections 18, 35(10), 36(8), 38(7), 136(1) and 138 of the Mental Health Act 1983. |
| 1984 | c 47 | Section 5(5) of the Repatriation of Prisoners Act 1984. |

---

37 Words 'circuit judge' in square brackets repealed and subsequent word in italics substituted by the Courts Act 2003 s65, Sch 4 para 6(1). Not yet in force: see the Courts Act 2003 s110(1).

38 Words 'circuit judge' in square brackets repealed and subsequent word in italics substituted by the Courts Act 2003 s65, Sch 4 para 6(1). Not yet in force: see the Courts Act 2003 s110(1).

## SCHEDULE 2A: FINGERPRINTING AND SAMPLES: POWER TO REQUIRE ATTENDANCE AT POLICE STATION[39]

### Part 1: Fingerprinting

#### Persons arrested and released

1(1) A constable may require a person to attend a police station for the purpose of taking his fingerprints under section 61(5A).

(2) The power under sub-paragraph (1) above may not be exercised in a case falling within section 61(5A)(b) (fingerprints taken on previous occasion insufficient etc) after the end of the period of six months beginning with the day on which the appropriate officer was informed that section 61(3A)(a) or (b) applied.

(3) In sub-paragraph (2) above 'appropriate officer' means the officer investigating the offence for which the person was arrested.

#### Persons charged etc

2(1) A constable may require a person to attend a police station for the purpose of taking his fingerprints under section 61(5B).

(2) The power under sub-paragraph (1) above may not be exercised after the end of the period of six months beginning with–

(a) in a case falling within section 61(5B)(a) (fingerprints not taken previously), the day on which the person was charged or informed that he would be reported, or

(b) in a case falling within section 61(5B)(b) (fingerprints taken on previous occasion insufficient etc), the day on which the appropriate officer was informed that section 61(3A)(a) or (b) applied.

(3) In sub-paragraph (2)(b) above 'appropriate officer' means the officer investigating the offence for which the person was charged or informed that he would be reported.

#### Persons convicted etc of an offence in England and Wales

3(1) A constable may require a person to attend a police station for the purpose of taking his fingerprints under section 61(6).

(2) Where the condition in section 61(6ZA)(a) is satisfied (fingerprints not taken previously), the power under sub-paragraph (1) above may not be exercised after the end of the period of two years beginning with–

(a) the day on which the person was convicted, cautioned or warned or reprimanded, or

(b) if later, the day on which this Schedule comes into force.

(3) Where the condition in section 61(6ZA)(b) is satisfied (fingerprints taken on previous occasion insufficient etc), the power under sub-paragraph (1) above may not be exercised after the end of the period of two years beginning with–

(a) the day on which an appropriate officer was informed that section 61(3A)(a) or (b) applied, or

(b) if later, the day on which this Schedule comes into force.

(4) In sub-paragraph (3)(a) above 'appropriate officer' means an officer of the police force which investigated the offence in question.

(5) Sub-paragraphs (2) and (3) above do not apply where the offence is a qualifying offence (whether or not it was such an offence at the time of the conviction, caution or warning or reprimand).

#### Persons subject to a control order

4 *A constable may require a person to attend a police station for the purpose of taking his fingerprints under section 61(6BA).*[40]

---

39 Inserted by the Crime and Security Act 2010 s6(2). In force (for certain purposes): 7 March 2011 (SI 2011/414 art 2(d)). Date in force for remaining purposes: see CSA 2010 s59(1).

40 Words in italics not yet in force in force: see SI 2011/414 art 2(d) and the Crime and Security Act 2010 s59(1).

### Persons convicted etc of an offence outside England and Wales

5 A constable may require a person to attend a police station for the purpose of taking his fingerprints under section 61(6D).

### Multiple attendance

6(1) Where a person's fingerprints have been taken under section 61 on two occasions in relation to any offence, he may not under this Schedule be required to attend a police station to have his fingerprints taken under that section in relation to that offence on a subsequent occasion without the authorisation of an officer of at least the rank of inspector.

(2) Where an authorisation is given under sub-paragraph (1) above–
(a) the fact of the authorisation, and
(b) the reasons for giving it,
shall be recorded as soon as practicable after it has been given.

## Part 2: Intimate Samples
### Persons suspected to be involved in an offence

7 A constable may require a person to attend a police station for the purpose of taking an intimate sample from him under section 62(1A) if, in the course of the investigation of an offence, two or more non-intimate samples suitable for the same means of analysis have been taken from him but have proved insufficient.

### Persons convicted etc of an offence outside England and Wales

8 A constable may require a person to attend a police station for the purpose of taking a sample from him under section 62(2A) if two or more non-intimate samples suitable for the same means of analysis have been taken from him under section 63(3E) but have proved insufficient.

## Part 3: Non-intimate Samples[41]
### Persons arrested and released

9(1) A constable may require a person to attend a police station for the purpose of taking a non-intimate sample from him under section 63(3ZA).

(2) The power under sub-paragraph (1) above may not be exercised in a case falling within section 63(3ZA)(b) (sample taken on a previous occasion not suitable etc) after the end of the period of six months beginning with the day on which the appropriate officer was informed of the matters specified in section 63(3ZA)(b)(i) or (ii).

(3) In sub-paragraph (2) above, 'appropriate officer' means the officer investigating the offence for which the person was arrested.

### Persons charged etc

10(1) A constable may require a person to attend a police station for the purpose of taking a non-intimate sample from him under section 63(3A).

(2) The power under sub-paragraph (1) above may not be exercised in a case falling within section 63(3A)(a) (sample not taken previously) after the end of the period of six months beginning with the day on which he was charged or informed that he would be reported.

(3) The power under sub-paragraph (1) above may not be exercised in a case falling within section 63(3A)(b) (sample taken on a previous occasion not suitable etc) after the end of the period of six months beginning with the day on which the appropriate officer was informed of the matters specified in section 63(3A)(b)(i) or (ii).

(4) In sub-paragraph (3) above 'appropriate officer' means the officer investigating the offence for which the person was charged or informed that he would be reported.

### Persons convicted etc of an offence in England and Wales

11(1) A constable may require a person to attend a police station for the purpose of taking a non-intimate sample from him under section 63(3B).

41 Inserted by the Crime and Security Act 2010 s6(2). Date in force (for certain purposes): 7 March 2011: see SI 2011/414 art 2(d). Date in force (for remaining purposes): to be appointed: see the Crime and Security Act 2010 s59(1).

(2) Where the condition in section 63(3BA)(a) is satisfied (sample not taken previously), the power under sub-paragraph (1) above may not be exercised after the end of the period of two years beginning with–
  (a) the day on which the person was convicted, cautioned or warned or reprimanded, or
  (b) if later, the day on which this Schedule comes into force.
(3) Where the condition in section 63(3BA)(b) is satisfied (sample taken on a previous occasion not suitable etc), the power under sub-paragraph (1) above may not be exercised after the end of the period of two years beginning with–
  (a) the day on which an appropriate officer was informed of the matters specified in section 63(3BA)(b)(i) or (ii), or
  (b) if later, the day on which this Schedule comes into force.
(4) In sub-paragraph (3)(a) above 'appropriate officer' means an officer of the police force which investigated the offence in question.
(5) Sub-paragraphs (2) and (3) above do not apply where–
  (a) the offence is a qualifying offence (whether or not it was such an offence at the time of the conviction, caution or warning or reprimand), or
  (b) he was convicted before 10th April 1995 and is a person to whom section 1 of the Criminal Evidence (Amendment) Act 1997 applies.

### Persons subject to a control order[42]
12 *A constable may require a person to attend a police station for the purpose of taking a non-intimate sample from him under section 63(3D).*

### Persons convicted etc of an offence outside England and Wales
13 A constable may require a person to attend a police station for the purpose of taking a non-intimate sample from him under section 63(3E).

### Multiple exercise of power
14(1) Where a non-intimate sample has been taken from a person under section 63 on two occasions in relation to any offence, he may not under this Schedule be required to attend a police station to have another such sample taken from him under that section in relation to that offence on a subsequent occasion without the authorisation of an officer of at least the rank of inspector.
(2) Where an authorisation is given under sub-paragraph (1) above–
  (a) the fact of the authorisation, and
  (b) the reasons for giving it,
  shall be recorded as soon as practicable after it has been given.

### Part 4: General and Supplementary
### Requirement to have power to take fingerprints or sample
15 A power conferred by this Schedule to require a person to attend a police station for the purposes of taking fingerprints or a sample under any provision of this Act may be exercised only in a case where the fingerprints or sample may be taken from the person under that provision (and, in particular, if any necessary authorisation for taking the fingerprints or sample under that provision has been obtained).

### Date and time of attendance
16(1) A requirement under this Schedule–
  (a) shall give the person a period of at least seven days within which he must attend the police station; and
  (b) may direct him so to attend at a specified time of day or between specified times of day.
(2) In specifying a period or time or times of day for the purposes of sub-paragraph (1) above, the constable shall consider whether the fingerprints or sample could

42 Inserted by the Crime and Security Act 2010 s6(2). Date in force (in relation to paras 9–11, 13, 14): 7 March 2011: see SI 2011/414 art 2(d). Date in force (in relation to para 12): to be appointed: see SI 2011/414 art 2(d) and the Crime and Security Act 2010 s59(1).

reasonably be taken at a time when the person is for any other reason required to attend the police station.

(3) A requirement under this Schedule may specify a period shorter than seven days if–

  (a) there is an urgent need for the fingerprints or sample for the purposes of the investigation of an offence; and

  (b) the shorter period is authorised by an officer of at least the rank of inspector.

(4) Where an authorisation is given under sub-paragraph (3)(b) above–

  (a) the fact of the authorisation, and

  (b) the reasons for giving it,

shall be recorded as soon as practicable after it has been given.

(5) If the constable giving a requirement under this Schedule and the person to whom it is given so agree, it may be varied so as to specify any period within which, or date or time at which, the person must attend; but a variation shall not have effect unless confirmed by the constable in writing.

### Enforcement

**17** A constable may arrest without warrant a person who has failed to comply with a requirement under this Schedule.

## SCHEDULES 3–6

[Repealed.]

## SCHEDULE 7: REPEALS

Not reproduced.

# Criminal Justice and Public Order Act 1994 ss34–38

### *Inferences from accused's silence*
### Effect of accused's failure to mention facts when questioned or charged

34 (1) Where, in any proceedings against a person for an offence, evidence is given that the accused–

    (a) at any time before he was charged with the offence, on being questioned under caution by a constable trying to discover whether or by whom the offence had been committed, failed to mention any fact relied on in his defence in those proceedings; or

    (b) on being charged with the offence or officially informed that he might be prosecuted for it, failed to mention any such fact; or

    (c) at any time after being charged with the offence, on being questioned under section 22 of the Counter-Terrorism Act 2008 (post-charge questioning), failed to mention any such fact,[43]

being a fact which in the circumstances existing at the time the accused could reasonably have been expected to mention when so questioned, charged or informed, as the case may be, subsection (2) below applies.

  (2) Where this subsection applies–

    [(a) a magistrates' court inquiring into the offence as examining justices;][44]

    (b) a judge, in deciding whether to grant an application made by the accused under–

      [(i) section 6 of the Criminal Justice Act 1987 (application for dismissal of charge of serious fraud in respect of which notice of transfer has been given under section 4 of that Act); or

      (ii) paragraph 5 of Schedule 6 to the Criminal Justice Act 1991 (application for dismissal of charge of violent or sexual offence involving child in respect of which notice of transfer has been given under section 53 of that Act)][45] *paragraph 2 of Schedule 3 to the Crime and Disorder Act 1998;*

    (c) the court, in determining whether there is a case to answer; and

    (d) the court or jury, in determining whether the accused is guilty of the offence charged,

may draw such inferences from the failure as appear proper.

  (2A) Where the accused was at an authorised place of detention at the time of the failure, subsections (1) and (2) above do not apply if he had not been allowed an opportunity to consult a solicitor prior to being questioned, charged or informed as mentioned in subsection (1) above.

  (3) Subject to any directions by the court, evidence tending to establish the failure may be given before or after evidence tending to establish the fact which the accused is alleged to have failed to mention.

  (4) This section applies in relation to questioning by persons (other than constables) charged with the duty of investigating offences or charging offenders as it applies in relation to questioning by constables; and in subsection (1) above 'officially informed' means informed by a constable or any such person.

  (5) This section does not–

    (a) prejudice the admissibility in evidence of the silence or other reaction of the accused in the face of anything said in his presence relating to the conduct in

---

43 Subs (1)(c) and word '; or' immediately preceding it inserted by the Counter-Terrorism Act 2008 s22(9). Not yet in force: see the Counter-Terrorism Act 2008 s100(5).

44 Subs (2)(a) repealed by the Criminal Justice Act 2003 ss41, 332, Sch 3 Pt 2 para 64(1), (2)(a), Sch 37 Pt 4. Not yet in force: see the Criminal Justice Act 2003 s336(3).

45 Subs (2)(b)(i), (ii) repealed and subsequent words in italics substituted by the Criminal Justice Act 2003 s41, Sch 3 Pt 2 para 64(1), (2)(b). Date in force (in relation to cases sent for trial under the Crime and Disorder Act 1998 s51 or s51A(3)(d)): 9 May 2005: see SI 2005/1267 art 2(1), (2)(a), Schedule Pt 1 para 1(1)(p). Date in force (for remaining purposes): to be appointed: see the Criminal Justice Act 2003 s336(3).

respect of which he is charged, in so far as evidence thereof would be admissible apart from this section; or

(b) preclude the drawing of any inference from any such silence or other reaction of the accused which could properly be drawn apart from this section.

(6) This section does not apply in relation to a failure to mention a fact if the failure occurred before the commencement of this section.

(7) [Repealed.]

### Effect of accused's silence at trial

35(1) At the trial of any person for an offence, subsections (2) and (3) below apply unless–

(a) the accused's guilt is not in issue; or

(b) it appears to the court that the physical or mental condition of the accused makes it undesirable for him to give evidence;

but subsection (2) below does not apply if, at the conclusion of the evidence for the prosecution, his legal representative informs the court that the accused will give evidence or, where he is unrepresented, the court ascertains from him that he will give evidence.

(2) Where this subsection applies, the court shall, at the conclusion of the evidence for the prosecution, satisfy itself (in the case of proceedings on indictment [with a jury], in the presence of the jury) that the accused is aware that the stage has been reached at which evidence can be given for the defence and that he can, if he wishes, give evidence and that, if he chooses not to give evidence, or having been sworn, without good cause refuses to answer any question, it will be permissible for the court or jury to draw such inferences as appear proper from his failure to give evidence or his refusal, without good cause, to answer any question.

(3) Where this subsection applies, the court or jury, in determining whether the accused is guilty of the offence charged, may draw such inferences as appear proper from the failure of the accused to give evidence or his refusal, without good cause, to answer any question.

(4) This section does not render the accused compellable to give evidence on his own behalf, and he shall accordingly not be guilty of contempt of court by reason of a failure to do so.

(5) For the purposes of this section a person who, having been sworn, refuses to answer any question shall be taken to do so without good cause unless–

(a) he is entitled to refuse to answer the question by virtue of any enactment, whenever passed or made, or on the ground of privilege; or

(b) the court in the exercise of its general discretion excuses him from answering it.

(6) [Repealed.]

(7) This section applies–

(a) in relation to proceedings on indictment for an offence, only if the person charged with the offence is arraigned on or after the commencement of this section;

(b) in relation to proceedings in a magistrates' court, only if the time when the court begins to receive evidence in the proceedings falls after the commencement of this section.

### Effect of accused's failure or refusal to account for objects, substances or marks

36(1) Where–

(a) a person is arrested by a constable, and there is–

(i) on his person; or

(ii) in or on his clothing or footwear; or

(iii) otherwise in his possession; or

(iv) in any place in which he is at the time of his arrest,

any object, substance or mark, or there is any mark on any such object; and

(b) that or another constable investigating the case reasonably believes that the presence of the object, substance or mark may be attributable to the participation of the person arrested in the commission of an offence specified by the constable; and

(c) the constable informs the person arrested that he so believes, and requests him to account for the presence of the object, substance or mark; and

(d) the person fails or refuses to do so,

then if, in any proceedings against the person for the offence so specified, evidence of those matters is given, subsection (2) below applies.

(2) Where this subsection applies–

[(a) a magistrates' court inquiring into the offence as examining justices;][46]

(b) a judge, in deciding whether to grant an application made by the accused under–

[(i) section 6 of the Criminal Justice Act 1987 (application for dismissal of charge of serious fraud in respect of which notice of transfer has been given under section 4 of that Act); or

(ii) paragraph 5 of Schedule 6 to the Criminal Justice Act 1991 (application for dismissal of charge of violent or sexual offence involving child in respect of which notice of transfer has been given under section 53 of that Act)][47]
*paragraph 2 of Schedule 3 to the Crime and Disorder Act 1998;*

(c) the court, in determining whether there is a case to answer; and

(d) the court or jury, in determining whether the accused is guilty of the offence charged,

may draw such inferences from the failure or refusal as appear proper.

(3) Subsections (1) and (2) above apply to the condition of clothing or footwear as they apply to a substance or mark thereon.

(4) Subsections (1) and (2) above do not apply unless the accused was told in ordinary language by the constable when making the request mentioned in subsection (1)(c) above what the effect of this section would be if he failed or refused to comply with the request.

(4A) Where the accused was at an authorised place of detention at the time of the failure or refusal, subsections (1) and (2) above do not apply if he had not been allowed an opportunity to consult a solicitor prior to the request being made.

(5) This section applies in relation to officers of customs and excise as it applies in relation to constables.

(6) This section does not preclude the drawing of any inference from a failure or refusal of the accused to account for the presence of an object, substance or mark or from the condition of clothing or footwear which could properly be drawn apart from this section.

(7) This section does not apply in relation to a failure or refusal which occurred before the commencement of this section.

(8) [Repealed.]

**Effect of accused's failure or refusal to account for presence at a particular place**

37(1) Where–

(a) a person arrested by a constable was found by him at a place at or about the time the offence for which he was arrested is alleged to have been committed; and

(b) that or another constable investigating the offence reasonably believes that the presence of the person at that place and at that time may be attributable to his participation in the commission of the offence; and

(c) the constable informs the person that he so believes, and requests him to account for that presence; and

(d) the person fails or refuses to do so,

46 Subs (2)(a) repealed by CJA 2003 ss41, 332, Sch 3 Pt 2 para 64(1), (4)(a), Sch 37 Pt 4. Not yet in force: see the Criminal Justice Act 2003 s336(3).

47 Subs (2)(b)(i), (ii) repealed and subsequent words in italics substituted by CJA 2003 s41, Sch 3 Pt 2 para 64(1), (4)(b). In force (in relation to cases sent for trial under the Crime and Disorder Act 1998 ss51, 51A(3)(d)): 9 May 2005: see SI 2005/1267 art 2(1), (2)(a), Schedule Pt 1 para 1(1)(p). Date in force: to be appointed: see the Criminal Justice Act 2003 s336(3).

then if, in any proceedings against the person for the offence, evidence of those matters is given, subsection (2) below applies.

(2) Where this subsection applies–

[(a) a magistrates' court inquiring into the offence as examining justices;][48]

(b) a judge, in deciding whether to grant an application made by the accused under–

[(i) section 6 of the Criminal Justice Act 1987 (application for dismissal of charge of serious fraud in respect of which notice of transfer has been given under section 4 of that Act); or

(ii) paragraph 5 of Schedule 6 to the Criminal Justice Act 1991 (application for dismissal of charge of violent or sexual offence involving child in respect of which notice of transfer has been given under section 53 of that Act)][49]

*paragraph 2 of Schedule 3 to the Crime and Disorder Act 1998;*

(c) the court, in determining whether there is a case to answer; and

(d) the court or jury, in determining whether the accused is guilty of the offence charged,

may draw such inferences from the failure or refusal as appear proper.

(3) Subsections (1) and (2) do not apply unless the accused was told in ordinary language by the constable when making the request mentioned in subsection (1)(c) above what the effect of this section would be if he failed or refused to comply with the request.

(3A) Where the accused was at an authorised place of detention at the time of the failure or refusal, subsections (1) and (2) do not apply if he had not been allowed an opportunity to consult a solicitor prior to the request being made.

(4) This section applies in relation to officers of customs and excise as it applies in relation to constables.

(5) This section does not preclude the drawing of any inference from a failure or refusal of the accused to account for his presence at a place which could properly be drawn apart from this section.

(6) This section does not apply in relation to a failure or refusal which occurred before the commencement of this section.

(7) [Repealed.]

### Interpretation and savings for sections 34, 35, 36 and 37

38(1) In sections 34, 35, 36 and 37 of this Act–

'legal representative' means a person who, for the purposes of the Legal Services Act 2007, is an authorised person in relation to an activity which constitutes the exercise of a right of audience or the conduct of litigation (within the meaning of that Act); and

'place' includes any building or part of a building, any vehicle, vessel, aircraft or hovercraft and any other place whatsoever.

(2) In sections 34(2), 35(3), 36(2) and 37(2), references to an offence charged include references to any other offence of which the accused could lawfully be convicted on that charge.

(2A) In each of sections 34(2A), 36(4A) and 37(3A) 'authorised place of detention' means–

(a) a police station; or

(b) any other place prescribed for the purposes of that provision by order made by the Secretary of State;

and the power to make an order under this subsection shall be exercisable by statutory instrument which shall be subject to annulment in pursuance of a resolution of either House of Parliament.

---

48 Subs (2)(a) repealed by CJA 2003 ss41, 332, Sch 3 Pt 2 para 64(1), (4)(a), Sch 37 Pt 4. Not yet in force: see the Criminal Justice Act 2003 s336(3).

49 Subs (2)(b)(i), (ii) repealed and subsequent words in italics substituted by CJA 2003 s41, Sch 3 Pt 2 para 64(1), (4)(b). In force (in relation to cases sent for trial under the Crime and Disorder Act 1998 ss51, 51A(3)(d)): 9 May 2005: see SI 2005/1267 art 2(1), (2)(a), Schedule Pt 1 para 1(1)(p). Date in force: to be appointed: see the Criminal Justice Act 2003 s336(3).

(3) A person shall not have the proceedings against him transferred to the Crown Court for trial, have a case to answer or be convicted of an offence solely on an inference drawn from such a failure or refusal as is mentioned in section 34(2), 35(3), 36(2) or 37(2).

(4) A judge shall not refuse to grant such an application as is mentioned in section 34(2)(b), 36(2)(b) and 37(2)(b) solely on an inference drawn from such a failure as is mentioned in section 34(2), 36(2) or 37(2).

(5) Nothing in sections 34, 35, 36 or 37 prejudices the operation of a provision of any enactment which provides (in whatever words) that any answer or evidence given by a person in specified circumstances shall not be admissible in evidence against him or some other person in any proceedings or class of proceedings (however described, and whether civil or criminal).

In this subsection, the reference to giving evidence is a reference to giving evidence in any manner, whether by furnishing information, making discovery, producing documents or otherwise.

(6) Nothing in sections 34, 35, 36 or 37 prejudices any power of a court, in any proceedings, to exclude evidence (whether by preventing questions being put or otherwise) at its discretion.

# Police and Criminal Evidence Act 1984 (PACE) Codes

# POLICE AND CRIMINAL EVIDENCE ACT 1984

A

# CODE A

### CODE OF PRACTICE FOR THE EXERCISE BY:

### POLICE OFFICERS OF STATUTORY POWERS OF STOP AND SEARCH

### POLICE OFFICERS AND POLICE STAFF OF REQUIREMENTS TO RECORD PUBLIC ENCOUNTERS

### Commencement - Transitional Arrangements

This code applies to any search by a police officer and the recording of public encounters taking place after midnight on 06 March 2011.

**General**

This code of practice must be readily available at all police stations for consultation by police officers, police staff, detained persons and members of the public.

The notes for guidance included are not provisions of this code, but are guidance to police officers and others about its application and interpretation. Provisions in the annexes to the code are provisions of this code.

This code governs the exercise by police officers of statutory powers to search a person or a vehicle without first making an arrest. The main stop and search powers to which this code applies are set out in Annex A, but that list should not be regarded as definitive. [See Note 1] In addition, it covers requirements on police officers and police staff to record encounters not governed by statutory powers. This code does not apply to:

(a)    the powers of stop and search under;

    (i)    Aviation Security Act 1982, section 27(2);

    (ii)    Police and Criminal Evidence Act 1984, section 6(1) (which relates specifically to powers of constables employed by statutory undertakers on the premises of the statutory undertakers).

(b)    searches carried out for the purposes of examination under Schedule 7 to the Terrorism Act 2000 and to which the Code of Practice issued under paragraph 6 of Schedule 14 to the Terrorism Act 2000 applies.

**1    Principles governing stop and search**

1.1    Powers to stop and search must be used fairly, responsibly, with respect for people being searched and without unlawful discrimination. The Equality Act 2010 makes it unlawful for police officers to discriminate against, harass or victimise any person on the grounds of the 'protected characteristics' of age, disability, gender reassignment, race, religion or belief, sex and sexual orientation, marriage and civil partnership, pregnancy and maternity when using their powers. When police forces are carrying out their functions they also have a duty to have regard to the need to eliminate unlawful discrimination, harassment and victimisation and to take steps to foster good relations.

1.2    The intrusion on the liberty of the person stopped or searched must be brief and detention for the purposes of a search must take place at or near the location of the stop.

**A**

1.3   If these fundamental principles are not observed the use of powers to stop and search may be drawn into question.  Failure to use the powers in the proper manner reduces their effectiveness.  Stop and search can play an important role in the detection and prevention of crime, and using the powers fairly makes them more effective.

1.4   The primary purpose of stop and search powers is to enable officers to allay or confirm suspicions about individuals without exercising their power of arrest. Officers may be required to justify the use or authorisation of such powers, in relation both to individual searches and the overall pattern of their activity in this regard, to their supervisory officers or in court.  Any misuse of the powers is likely to be harmful to policing and lead to mistrust of the police.  Officers must also be able to explain their actions to the member of the public searched.  The misuse of these powers can lead to disciplinary action.

1.5   An officer must not search a person, even with his or her consent, where no power to search is applicable.  Even where a person is prepared to submit to a search voluntarily, the person must not be searched unless the necessary legal power exists, and the search must be in accordance with the relevant power and the provisions of this Code.  The only exception, where an officer does not require a specific power, applies to searches of persons entering sports grounds or other premises carried out with their consent given as a condition of entry.

## 2   Explanation of powers to stop and search

2.1   This code applies to powers of stop and search as follows:

(a)   powers which require reasonable grounds for suspicion, before they may be exercised; that articles unlawfully obtained or possessed are being carried, or under Section 43 of the Terrorism Act 2000 that a person is a terrorist;

(b)   authorised under section 60 of the Criminal Justice and Public Order Act 1994, based upon a reasonable belief that incidents involving serious violence may take place or that people are carrying dangerous instruments or offensive weapons within any locality in the police area or that it is expedient to use the powers to find such instruments or weapons that have been used in incidents of serious violence;

(c)   authorised under section 44(1) of the Terrorism Act 2000 based upon a consideration that the exercise of the power is necessary for the prevention of acts of terrorism (see paragraph 2.18A), and

(d)    powers to search a person who has not been arrested in the exercise of a power to search premises (see Code B paragraph 2.4).

**Searches requiring reasonable grounds for suspicion**

2.2    Reasonable grounds for suspicion depend on the circumstances in each case. There must be an objective basis for that suspicion based on facts, information, and/or intelligence which are relevant to the likelihood of finding an article of a certain kind or, in the case of searches under section 43 of the Terrorism Act 2000, to the likelihood that the person is a terrorist. Reasonable suspicion can never be supported on the basis of personal factors. It must rely on intelligence or information about, or some specific behaviour by, the person concerned. For example, unless the police have a description of a suspect, a person's physical appearance (including any of the 'protected characteristics' set out in the Equality Act 2010 (see paragraph 1.1), or the fact that the person is known to have a previous conviction, cannot be used alone or in combination with each other, or in combination with any other factor, as the reason for searching that person. Reasonable suspicion cannot be based on generalisations or stereotypical images of certain groups or categories of people as more likely to be involved in criminal activity.

2.3    Reasonable suspicion may also exist without specific information or intelligence and on the basis of the behaviour of a person. For example, if an officer encounters someone on the street at night who is obviously trying to hide something, the officer may (depending on the other surrounding circumstances) base such suspicion on the fact that this kind of behaviour is often linked to stolen or prohibited articles being carried. Similarly, for the purposes of section 43 of the Terrorism Act 2000, suspicion that a person is a terrorist may arise from the person's behaviour at or near a location which has been identified as a potential target for terrorists.

2.4    However, reasonable suspicion should normally be linked to accurate and current intelligence or information, such as information describing an article being carried, a suspected offender, or a person who has been seen carrying a type of article known to have been stolen recently from premises in the area. Searches based on accurate and current intelligence or information are more likely to be effective. Targeting searches in a particular area at specified crime problems increases their effectiveness and minimises inconvenience to law-abiding members of the public. It also helps in justifying the use of searches both to those who are searched and to the public. This does not however prevent stop and search powers being exercised in other locations where such powers may be exercised and reasonable suspicion exists.

**A**

2.5     Searches are more likely to be effective, legitimate, and secure public confidence when reasonable suspicion is based on a range of factors. The overall use of these powers is more likely to be effective when up to date and accurate intelligence or information is communicated to officers and they are well-informed about local crime patterns.

2.6     Where there is reliable information or intelligence that members of a group or gang habitually carry knives unlawfully or weapons or controlled drugs, and wear a distinctive item of clothing or other means of identification to indicate their membership of the group or gang, that distinctive item of clothing or other means of identification may provide reasonable grounds to stop and search a person. [See Note 9]

2.7     A police officer may have reasonable grounds to suspect that a person is in innocent possession of a stolen or prohibited article or other item for which he or she is empowered to search. In that case the officer may stop and search the person even though there would be no power of arrest.

2.8     Under section 43(1) of the Terrorism Act 2000 a constable may stop and search a person whom the officer reasonably suspects to be a terrorist to discover whether the person is in possession of anything which may constitute evidence that the person is a terrorist. These searches may only be carried out by an officer of the same sex as the person searched (see Annex F). An authorisation under section 44(1) of the Terrorism Act 2000 allows vehicles to be stopped and searched by a constable in uniform who reasonably suspects that articles which could be used in connection with terrorism will be found in the vehicle or in anything in or on that vehicle. See paragraph 2.18A below.

2.9     An officer who has reasonable grounds for suspicion may detain the person concerned in order to carry out a search. Before carrying out a search the officer may ask questions about the person's behaviour or presence in circumstances which gave rise to the suspicion. As a result of questioning the detained person, the reasonable grounds for suspicion necessary to detain that person may be confirmed or, because of a satisfactory explanation, be eliminated. [See Notes 2 and 3] Questioning may also reveal reasonable grounds to suspect the possession of a different kind of unlawful article from that originally suspected. Reasonable grounds for suspicion however cannot be provided retrospectively by such questioning during a person's detention or by refusal to answer any questions put.

2.10    If, as a result of questioning before a search, or other circumstances which come to the attention of the officer, there cease to be reasonable grounds for suspecting that an article is being carried of a kind for which there is a power to stop and search, no search may take place. [See Note 3] In the absence of any other lawful power to detain, the person is free to leave at will and must be so informed.

2.11    There is no power to stop or detain a person in order to find grounds for a search. Police officers have many encounters with members of the public which do not involve detaining people against their will. If reasonable grounds for suspicion emerge during such an encounter, the officer may search the person, even though no grounds existed when the encounter began. If an officer is detaining someone for the purpose of a search, he or she should inform the person as soon as detention begins.

**Searches authorised under section 60 of the Criminal Justice and Public Order Act 1994**

2.12    Authority for a constable in uniform to stop and search under section 60 of the Criminal Justice and Public Order Act 1994 may be given if the authorising officer reasonably believes:

(a)    that incidents involving serious violence may take place in any locality in the officer's police area, and it is expedient to use these powers to prevent their occurrence;

(b)    that persons are carrying dangerous instruments or offensive weapons without good reason in any locality in the officer's police area or

(c)    that an incident involving serious violence has taken place in the officer's police area, a dangerous instrument or offensive weapon used in the incident is being carried by a person in any locality in that police area, and it is expedient to use these powers to find that instrument or weapon.

2.13    An authorisation under section 60 may only be given by an officer of the rank of inspector or above and in writing, or orally if paragraph 2.12(c) applies and it is not practicable to give the authorisation in writing. The authorisation (whether written or oral) must specify the grounds on which it was given, the locality in which the powers may be exercised and the period of time for which they are in force. The period authorised shall be no longer than appears reasonably necessary to prevent, or seek to prevent incidents of serious violence, or to deal with the problem of carrying dangerous instruments or offensive weapons or to find a dangerous instrument or offensive weapon that has been used. It may not exceed 24 hours. An oral authorisation given where paragraph 2.12(c) applies must be recorded in writing as

A

soon as practicable.  [See Notes 10-13]

2.14  An inspector who gives an authorisation must, as soon as practicable, inform an officer of or above the rank of superintendent.  This officer may direct that the authorisation shall be extended for a further 24 hours, if violence or the carrying of dangerous instruments or offensive weapons has occurred, or is suspected to have occurred, and the continued use of the powers is considered necessary to prevent or deal with further such activity or to find a dangerous instrument or offensive weapon used that has been used.  That direction must be given in writing unless it is not practicable to do so, in which case it must be recorded in writing as soon as practicable afterwards.  [See Note 12]

2.14A  The selection of persons and vehicles under section 60 to be stopped and, if appropriate, searched should reflect an objective assessment of the nature of the incident or weapon in question and the individuals and vehicles thought likely to be associated with that incident or those weapons (see Notes 10 and 11).  The powers must not be used to stop and search persons and vehicles for reasons unconnected with the purpose of the authorisation.  When selecting persons and vehicles to be stopped in response to a specific threat or incident, officers must take care not to discriminate unlawfully against anyone on the grounds of any of the protected characteristics set out in the Equality Act 2010 (see paragraph 1.1).

2.14B  The driver of a vehicle which is stopped under section 60 and any person who is searched under section 60 are entitled to a written statement to that effect if they apply within twelve months from the day the vehicle was stopped or the person was searched.  This statement is a record which states that the vehicle was stopped or (as the case may be) that the person was searched under section 60 and it may form part of the search record or be supplied as a separate record.

**Powers to require removal of face coverings**

2.15  Section 60AA of the Criminal Justice and Public Order Act 1994 also provides a power to demand the removal of disguises.  The officer exercising the power must reasonably believe that someone is wearing an item wholly or mainly for the purpose of concealing identity.  There is also a power to seize such items where the officer believes that a person intends to wear them for this purpose.  There is no power to stop and search for disguises.  An officer may seize any such item which is discovered when exercising a power of search for something else, or which is being carried, and which the officer reasonably believes is intended to be used for concealing anyone's identity.  This power can only be used if an authorisation given under section 60 or under section 60AA, is in force.  [See Note 4]

2.16   Authority under section 60AA for a constable in uniform to require the removal of disguises and to seize them may be given if the authorising officer reasonably believes that activities may take place in any locality in the officer's police area that are likely to involve the commission of offences and it is expedient to use these powers to prevent or control these activities.

2.17   An authorisation under section 60AA may only be given by an officer of the rank of inspector or above, in writing, specifying the grounds on which it was given, the locality in which the powers may be exercised and the period of time for which they are in force.  The period authorised shall be no longer than appears reasonably necessary to prevent, or seek to prevent the commission of offences.  It may not exceed 24 hours.  [See Notes 10-13]

2.18   An inspector who gives an authorisation must, as soon as practicable, inform an officer of or above the rank of superintendent.  This officer may direct that the authorisation shall be extended for a further 24 hours, if crimes have been committed, or are suspected to have been committed, and the continued use of the powers is considered necessary to prevent or deal with further such activity.  This direction must also be given in writing at the time or as soon as practicable afterwards.  [See Note 12]

**Searches authorised under section 44 of the Terrorism Act 2000**

2.18A The European Court of Human Rights has ruled that the stop and search powers under sections 44 to 47 of the Terrorism Act 2000 are not compatible with the right to a private life under Article 8 of the European Convention on Human Rights.  Neither the European Court ruling nor the provisions of this Code can amend these statutory provisions.  However, in an oral statement made by the Home Secretary in the House of Commons on 8 July 2010, interim guidelines were announced pending a review (with a view to legislative amendment) of these provisions to ensure that police do not exercise any powers under section 44 in a way which would be incompatible with Convention rights.  Under these guidelines:

(i)   Authorisations under section 44(1) should be given, and may be confirmed by the Secretary of State, only:

   •   in relation to searches of vehicles and anything in or on vehicles, but not searches of drivers or passengers or anything being carried by a driver or passenger; and

   •   if such searches are considered necessary for the prevention of acts of terrorism.

Note: Section 44(3) provides that an authorising officer may give an authorisation when they consider it is 'expedient' for the prevention of acts of terrorism, but the test now to be applied is that of necessity – taking account of all of the circumstances.

(ii)    A search of a vehicle or of anything in or on a vehicle under section 44(1) should only be carried out if it is reasonably suspected that articles which could be used in connection with terrorism will be found in the vehicle or in anything in or on that vehicle.

Note: This now applies despite the provision in section 45(1)(b) which allows the power to be exercised whether or not the constable has grounds for suspecting the presence of such articles.

(iii)    Authorisations to search pedestrians, drivers of vehicles and passengers in vehicles and anything carried by a driver or passenger, are not to be given under section 44(1) or (2) and if given, will not be confirmed. For these searches police must rely on the power under section 43 which requires the person who may be searched to be reasonably suspected of being a terrorist, but does not authorise the removal of headgear or footwear in public.

The provisions of paragraphs 2.1, 2.8, 2.19 to 2.26, 3.5, Annex A paragraphs 15 and 16 and Annex C paragraph 1 are amended by this Code to reflect these guidelines:

2.19    An officer of the rank of assistant chief constable (or equivalent) or above, may give authority under section 44(1) of the Terrorism Act 2000 for a constable in uniform to exercise the power to stop and search any vehicle and anything in or on any vehicle, in the whole or any part or parts of the authorising officer's police area. An authorisation may only be given if the officer considers it is necessary for the prevention of acts of terrorism.

2.20    If an authorisation is given orally at first, it must be confirmed in writing by the officer who gave it as soon as reasonably practicable.

2.21    When giving an authorisation, the officer must specify the geographical area in which the power may be used, and the time and date that the authorisation ends (up to a maximum of 28 days from the time the authorisation was given). [See Notes 12 and 13]

2.22    The officer giving an authorisation under section 44(1) must cause the Secretary of State to be informed, as soon as reasonably practicable, that such an authorisation has been given. An authorisation which is not confirmed by the Secretary of State within 48 hours of its having been given, shall have effect up until the end of that 48 hour period or the end of the period specified in the authorisation (whichever is the earlier). [See Note 14]

2.23    Following notification of the authorisation, the Secretary of State may:

(i)    cancel the authorisation with immediate effect or with effect from such other time as he or she may direct;

(ii)    confirm it but for a shorter period than that specified in the authorisation; or

(iii)    confirm the authorisation as given.

2.24    When an authorisation under section 44(1) is given, a constable in uniform may exercise the power:

(a)    only for the purpose of stopping and searching a vehicle and anything in or on a vehicle for articles of a kind which could be used in connection with terrorism (see paragraph 2.25); and

(b)    only if there are reasonable grounds for suspecting the presence of such articles.  See paragraphs 2.2 to 2.11, "Searches requiring reasonable grounds for suspicion"

2.24A    When a Community Support Officer on duty and in uniform has been conferred powers under Section 44(1) of the Terrorism Act 2000 by a Chief Officer of their force, the exercise of this power must comply with the requirements of this Code of Practice, including the recording requirements.

2.25    Paragraphs 2.2 to 2.11 above ("Searches requiring reasonable grounds for suspicion") are to be applied to the stopping and searching of vehicles when an authorisation under section 44(1) is given.

2.26    The powers under sections 43 and 44(1) of the Terrorism Act 2000 allow a constable to search only for articles which could be used for terrorist purposes.  However, this would not prevent a search being carried out under other powers if, in the course of exercising these powers, the officer formed reasonable grounds for suspicion.

**Powers to search in the exercise of a power to search premises**

2.27    The following powers to search premises also authorise the search of a person, not under arrest, who is found on the premises during the course of the search:

(a)    section 139B of the Criminal Justice Act 1988 under which a constable may enter school premises and search the premises and any person on those premises for any bladed or pointed article or offensive weapon;

(b) under a warrant issued under section 23(3) of the Misuse of Drugs Act 1971 to search premises for drugs or documents but only if the warrant specifically authorises the search of persons found on the premises; and

(c) under a search warrant or order issued under paragraph 1, 3 or 11 of Schedule 5 to the Terrorism Act 2000 to search premises and any person found there for material likely to be of substantial value to a terrorist investigation.

2.28 Before the power under section 139B of the Criminal Justice Act 1988 may be exercised, the constable must have reasonable grounds to believe that an offence under section 139A of the Criminal Justice Act 1988 (having a bladed or pointed article or offensive weapon on school premises) has been or is being committed. A warrant to search premises and persons found therein may be issued under section 23(3) of the Misuse of Drugs Act 1971 if there are reasonable grounds to suspect that controlled drugs or certain documents are in the possession of a person on the premises.

2.29 The powers in paragraph 2.27 do not require prior specific grounds to suspect that the person to be searched is in possession of an item for which there is an existing power to search. However, it is still necessary to ensure that the selection and treatment of those searched under these powers is based upon objective factors connected with the search of the premises, and not upon personal prejudice.

## 3 Conduct of searches

3.1 All stops and searches must be carried out with courtesy, consideration and respect for the person concerned. This has a significant impact on public confidence in the police. Every reasonable effort must be made to minimise the embarrassment that a person being searched may experience. [See Note 4]

3.2 The co-operation of the person to be searched must be sought in every case, even if the person initially objects to the search. A forcible search may be made only if it has been established that the person is unwilling to co-operate or resists. Reasonable force may be used as a last resort if necessary to conduct a search or to detain a person or vehicle for the purposes of a search.

3.3 The length of time for which a person or vehicle may be detained must be reasonable and kept to a minimum. Where the exercise of the power requires reasonable suspicion, the thoroughness and extent of a search must depend on what is suspected of being carried, and by whom. If the suspicion relates to a particular article which is seen to be slipped into a person's pocket, then, in the absence of other grounds for suspicion or an opportunity for the article to be moved elsewhere, the search must be confined to that pocket. In the case of a small article which can readily be concealed, such as a drug, and which might be concealed anywhere on the person, a more extensive search may be necessary. In the case of searches mentioned in paragraph 2.1(b), (c), and (d), which do not require reasonable grounds for suspicion, officers may make any reasonable search to look for items for which they are empowered to search. [See *Note 5*]

3.4   The search must be carried out at or near the place where the person or vehicle was first detained. [See *Note 6*]

3.5   There is no power to require a person to remove any clothing in public other than an outer coat, jacket or gloves, except under section 60AA of the Criminal Justice and Public Order Act 1994 (which empowers a constable to require a person to remove any item worn to conceal identity). [See *Notes 4* and *6*] A search in public of a person's clothing which has not been removed must be restricted to superficial examination of outer garments. This does not, however, prevent an officer from placing his or her hand inside the pockets of the outer clothing, or feeling round the inside of collars, socks and shoes if this is reasonably necessary in the circumstances to look for the object of the search or to remove and examine any item reasonably suspected to be the object of the search. For the same reasons, subject to the restrictions on the removal of headgear, a person's hair may also be searched in public (see paragraphs 3.1 and 3.3).

3.6   Where on reasonable grounds it is considered necessary to conduct a more thorough search (e.g. by requiring a person to take off a T-shirt), this must be done out of public view, for example, in a police van unless paragraph 3.7 applies, or police station if there is one nearby. [See *Note 6*] Any search involving the removal of more than an outer coat, jacket, gloves, headgear or footwear, or any other item concealing identity, may only be made by an officer of the same sex as the person searched and may not be made in the presence of anyone of the opposite sex unless the person being searched specifically requests it. [See *Annex F* and *Notes 4, 7* and *8*]

3.7   Searches involving exposure of intimate parts of the body must not be conducted as a routine extension of a less thorough search, simply because nothing is found in the course of the initial search. Searches involving exposure of intimate parts of the body may be carried out only at a nearby police station or other nearby location which is out of public view (but not a police vehicle). These searches must be conducted in accordance with paragraph 11 of Annex A to Code C except that an intimate search mentioned in paragraph 11(f) of Annex A to Code C may not be authorised or carried out under any stop and search powers. The other provisions of Code C do not apply to the conduct and recording of searches of persons detained at police stations in the exercise of stop and search powers. [See *Note 7*]

**A**

### Steps to be taken prior to a search

3.8   Before any search of a detained person or attended vehicle takes place the officer must take reasonable steps, if not in uniform (see paragraph 3.9), to show their warrant card to the person to be searched or in charge of the vehicle to be searched and whether or not in uniform, to give that person the following information:

(a)   that they are being detained for the purposes of a search

(b)   the officer's name (except in the case of enquiries linked to the investigation of terrorism, or otherwise where the officer reasonably believes that giving his or her name might put him or her in danger, in which case a warrant or other identification number shall be given) and the name of the police station to which the officer is attached;

(c)   the legal search power which is being exercised; and

(d)   a clear explanation of:

    (i)   the object of the search in terms of the article or articles for which there is a power to search; and

    (ii)   in the case of:

- the power under section 60 of the Criminal Justice and Public Order Act 1994 (see *paragraph 2.1(b)*), the nature of the power, the authorisation and the fact that it has been given;

- the power under section 44 of the Terrorism Act 2000, the nature of the power, the authorisation and the fact that it has been given and the grounds for suspicion; (see *paragraph 2.1(c)* and *2.18A*.

- all other powers requiring reasonable suspicion (see *paragraph 2.1(a)*), the grounds for that suspicion.

(e)   that they are entitled to a copy of the record of the search if one is made (see section 4 below) if they ask within 3 months from the date of the search and:

    (i)   if they are not arrested and taken to a police station as a result of the search and it is practicable to make the record on the spot, that immediately after the search is completed they will be given, if they request, either:

- a copy of the record, or

- a receipt which explains how they can obtain a copy of the full record or access to an electronic copy of the record, or

(ii)    if they are arrested and taken to a police station as a result of the search, that the record will be made at the station as part of their custody record and they will be given, if they request, a copy of their custody record which includes a record of the search as soon as practicable whilst they are at the station. [See *Note 16*]

3.9    Stops and searches under the powers mentioned in paragraphs 2.1(b), and (c) may be undertaken only by a constable in uniform.

3.10    The person should also be given information about police powers to stop and search and the individual's rights in these circumstances.

3.11    If the person to be searched, or in charge of a vehicle to be searched, does not appear to understand what is being said, or there is any doubt about the person's ability to understand English, the officer must take reasonable steps to bring information regarding the person's rights and any relevant provisions of this Code to his or her attention. If the person is deaf or cannot understand English and is accompanied by someone, then the officer must try to establish whether that person can interpret or otherwise help the officer to give the required information.

**4    Recording requirements**

**(a)    Searches which do not result in an arrest**

4.1    When an officer carries out a search in the exercise of any power to which this Code applies and the search does not result in the person searched or person in charge of the vehicle searched being arrested and taken to a police station, a record must be made of it, electronically or on paper, unless there are exceptional circumstances which make this wholly impracticable (e.g. in situations involving public disorder or when the recording officer's presence is urgently required elsewhere). If a record is to be made, the officer carrying out the search must make the record on the spot unless this is not practicable, in which case, the officer must make the record as soon as practicable after the search is completed.    [See *Note 16.*]

4.2    If the record is made at the time, the person who has been searched or who is in charge of the vehicle that has been searched must be asked if they want a copy and if they do, they must be given immediately, either:

   •    a copy of the record, or

   •    a receipt which explains how they can obtain a copy of the full record or access to an electronic copy of the record

**A**

4.2A  An officer is not required to provide a copy of the full record or a receipt at the time if they are called to an incident of higher priority.  [See *Note 21*]

**(b)  Searches which result in an arrest**

4.2B  If a search in the exercise of any power to which this Code applies results in a person being arrested and taken to a police station, the officer carrying out the search is responsible for ensuring that a record of the search is made as part of their custody record.  The custody officer must then ensure that the person is asked if they want a copy of the record and if they do, that they are given a copy as soon as practicable. [See *Note 16*].

**(c)  Record of search**

4.3  The record of a search must always include the following information:

    (a)  A note of the self defined ethnicity, and if different, the ethnicity as perceived by the officer making the search, of the person searched or of the person in charge of the vehicle searched (as the case may be); [See *Note 18*]

    (b)  The date, time and place the person or vehicle was searched [See *Note 6*];

    (c)  The object of the search in terms of the article or articles for which there is a power to search;

    (d)  In the case of:

        •  the power under section 60 of the Criminal Justice and Public Order Act 1994 (see *paragraph 2.1(b)*), the nature of the power, the authorisation and the fact that it has been given;  [See *Note 17*]

        •  the power under section 44 of the Terrorism Act 2000, the nature of the power, the authorisation and the fact that it has been given and the grounds for suspicion; [see *paragraphs 2.1(c)* and *2.18A and Note 17*].

        •  all other powers requiring reasonable suspicion (see *paragraph 2.1(a)*), the grounds for that suspicion.

    (e)  subject to paragraph 3.8(b), the identity of the officer carrying out the search. [See *Note 15*]

4.3A  For the purposes of completing the search record, there is no requirement to record the name, address and date of birth of the person searched or the person in charge of a vehicle which is searched and the person is under no obligation to provide this information.

4.4   Nothing in paragraph 4.3 requires the names of police officers to be shown on the search record or any other record required to be made under this code in the case of enquiries linked to the investigation of terrorism or otherwise where an officer reasonably believes that recording names might endanger the officers. In such cases the record must show the officers' warrant or other identification number and duty station.

4.5   A record is required for each person and each vehicle searched. However, if a person is in a vehicle and both are searched, and the object and grounds of the search are the same, only one record need be completed. If more than one person in a vehicle is searched, separate records for each search of a person must be made. If only a vehicle is searched, the self-defined ethnic background of the person in charge of the vehicle must be recorded, unless the vehicle is unattended.

4.6   The record of the grounds for making a search must, briefly but informatively, explain the reason for suspecting the person concerned, by reference to the person's behaviour and/or other circumstances.

4.7   Where officers detain an individual with a view to performing a search, but the need to search is eliminated as a result of questioning the person detained, a search should not be carried out and a record is not required. [See *paragraph 2.10, Notes 3* and *22A*]

4.8   After searching an unattended vehicle, or anything in or on it, an officer must leave a notice in it (or on it, if things on it have been searched without opening it) recording the fact that it has been searched.

4.9   The notice must include the name of the police station to which the officer concerned is attached and state where a copy of the record of the search may be obtained and how (if applicable) an electronic copy may be accessed and where any application for compensation should be directed.

4.10   The vehicle must if practicable be left secure.

4.10A   *Not used*

4.10B   *Not used*

## Recording of encounters not governed by statutory powers

4.11   *Not used.*

4.12   There is no national requirement for an officer who requests a person in a public place to account for themselves, i.e. their actions, behaviour, presence in an area or possession of anything, to make any record of the encounter or to give the person a receipt. [See *Notes 22A* and *22B*]

A

4.12A  *Not used*

4.13   *Not used*

4.14   *Not used*

4.15   *Not used*

4.16   *Not used*

4.17   *Not used*

4.18   *Not used*

4.19   *Not used*

4.20   *Not used*

## 5  Monitoring and supervising the use of stop and search powers

5.1   Supervising officers must monitor the use of stop and search powers and should consider in particular whether there is any evidence that they are being exercised on the basis of stereotyped images or inappropriate generalisations. Supervising officers should satisfy themselves that the practice of officers under their supervision in stopping, searching and recording is fully in accordance with this Code. Supervisors must also examine whether the records reveal any trends or patterns which give cause for concern, and if so take appropriate action to address this.

5.2   Senior officers with area or force-wide responsibilities must also monitor the broader use of stop and search powers and, where necessary, take action at the relevant level.

5.3   Supervision and monitoring must be supported by the compilation of comprehensive statistical records of stops and searches at force, area and local level. Any apparently disproportionate use of the powers by particular officers or groups of officers or in relation to specific sections of the community should be identified and investigated.

5.4   In order to promote public confidence in the use of the powers, forces in consultation with police authorities must make arrangements for the records to be scrutinised by representatives of the community, and to explain the use of the powers at a local level. [See *Note 19*].

**Notes for Guidance**

*Officers exercising stop and search powers*

1    *This code does not affect the ability of an officer to speak to or question a person in the ordinary course of the officer's duties without detaining the person or exercising any element of compulsion. It is not the purpose of the code to prohibit such encounters between the police and the community with the co-operation of the person concerned and neither does it affect the principle that all citizens have a duty to help police officers to prevent crime and discover offenders. This is a civic rather than a legal duty; but when a police officer is trying to discover whether, or by whom, an offence has been committed he or she may question any person from whom useful information might be obtained, subject to the restrictions imposed by Code C. A person's unwillingness to reply does not alter this entitlement, but in the absence of a power to arrest, or to detain in order to search, the person is free to leave at will and cannot be compelled to remain with the officer.*

2    *In some circumstances preparatory questioning may be unnecessary, but in general a brief conversation or exchange will be desirable not only as a means of avoiding unsuccessful searches, but to explain the grounds for the stop/search, to gain co-operation and reduce any tension there might be surrounding the stop/search.*

3    *Where a person is lawfully detained for the purpose of a search, but no search in the event takes place, the detention will not thereby have been rendered unlawful.*

4    *Many people customarily cover their heads or faces for religious reasons - for example, Muslim women, Sikh men, Sikh or Hindu women, or Rastafarian men or women. A police officer cannot order the removal of a head or face covering except where there is reason to believe that the item is being worn by the individual wholly or mainly for the purpose of disguising identity, not simply because it disguises identity. Where there may be religious sensitivities about ordering the removal of such an item, the officer should permit the item to be removed out of public view. Where practicable, the item should be removed in the presence of an officer of the same sex as the person and out of sight of anyone of the opposite sex [see Annex F].*

5    *A search of a person in public should be completed as soon as possible.*

6    *A person may be detained under a stop and search power at a place other than where the person was first detained, only if that place, be it a police station or elsewhere, is nearby. Such a place should be located within a reasonable travelling distance using whatever mode of travel (on foot or by car) is appropriate. This applies to all searches under stop and search powers, whether or not they involve the removal of clothing or*

A

*exposure of intimate parts of the body (see paragraphs 3.6 and 3.7) or take place in or out of public view. It means, for example, that a search under the stop and search power in section 23 of the Misuse of Drugs Act 1971 which involves the compulsory removal of more than a person's outer coat, jacket or gloves cannot be carried out unless a place which is both nearby the place they were first detained and out of public view, is available. If a search involves exposure of intimate parts of the body and a police station is not nearby, particular care must be taken to ensure that the location is suitable in that it enables the search to be conducted in accordance with the requirements of paragraph 11 of Annex A to Code C.*

7     *A search in the street itself should be regarded as being in public for the purposes of paragraphs 3.6 and 3.7 above, even though it may be empty at the time a search begins. Although there is no power to require a person to do so, there is nothing to prevent an officer from asking a person voluntarily to remove more than an outer coat, jacket or gloves in public.*

8     *Not used*

9     *Other means of identification might include jewellery, insignias, tattoos or other features which are known to identify members of the particular gang or group.*

**Authorising officers**

10     The powers under section 60 are separate from and additional to the *normal stop and search powers which require reasonable grounds to suspect an individual of carrying an offensive weapon (or other article). Their overall purpose is to prevent serious violence and the widespread carrying of weapons which might lead to persons being seriously injured by disarming potential offenders or finding weapons that have been used in circumstances where other powers would not be sufficient. They should not therefore be used to replace or circumvent the normal powers for dealing with routine crime problems. A particular example might be an authorisation to prevent serious violence or the carrying of offensive weapons at a sports event by rival team supporters when the expected general appearance and age range of those likely to be responsible, alone, would not be sufficiently distinctive to support reasonable suspicion (see paragraph 2.6). The purpose of the powers under section 60AA is to prevent those involved in intimidatory or violent protests using face coverings to disguise identity.*

11     *Authorisations under section 60 require a reasonable belief on the part of the authorising officer. This must have an objective basis, for example: intelligence or relevant information such as a history of antagonism and violence between particular*

groups; previous incidents of violence at, or connected with, particular events or locations; a significant increase in knife-point robberies in a limited area; reports that individuals are regularly carrying weapons in a particular locality; information following an incident in which weapons were used about where the weapons might be found or in the case of section 60AA previous incidents of crimes being committed while wearing face coverings to conceal identity.

12    It is for the authorising officer to determine the period of time during which the powers mentioned in paragraph 2.1(b) and (c) may be exercised. The officer should set the minimum period he or she considers necessary to deal with the risk of violence, the carrying of knives or offensive weapons, or terrorism or to find dangerous instruments or weapons that have been used. A direction to extend the period authorised under the powers mentioned in paragraph 2.1(b) may be given only once. Thereafter further use of the powers requires a new authorisation. There is no provision to extend an authorisation of the powers mentioned in paragraph 2.1(c); further use of the powers requires a new authorisation.

13    It is for the authorising officer to determine the geographical area in which the use of the powers is to be authorised. In doing so the officer may wish to take into account factors such as the nature and venue of the anticipated incident or the incident which has taken place, the number of people who may be in the immediate area of that incident, their access to surrounding areas and the anticipated or actual level of violence. The officer should not set a geographical area which is wider than that he or she believes necessary for the purpose of preventing anticipated violence, the carrying of knives or offensive weapons, acts of terrorism, finding a dangerous instrument or weapon that has been used or, in the case of section 60AA, the prevention of commission of offences. It is particularly important to ensure that constables exercising such powers are fully aware of where they may be used. If the area specified is smaller than the whole force area, the officer giving the authorisation should specify either the streets which form the boundary of the area or a divisional boundary within the force area. If the power is to be used in response to a threat or incident that straddles police force areas, an officer from each of the forces concerned will need to give an authorisation.

14    An officer who has authorised the use of powers under section 44(1) of the Terrorism Act 2000 must take immediate steps to send a copy of the authorisation to the National Joint Unit, Metropolitan Police Special Branch, who will forward it to the Secretary of State. The Secretary of State should be informed of the reasons for the authorisation. The National Joint Unit will inform the force concerned, within 48 hours of the authorisation being made, whether the Secretary of State has confirmed or cancelled or altered the authorisation. See paragraph 2.18A.

### Recording

15    Where a stop and search is conducted by more than one officer the identity of all the officers engaged in the search must be recorded on the record.  Nothing prevents an officer who is present but not directly involved in searching from completing the record during the course of the encounter.

16    When the search results in the person searched or in charge of a vehicle which is searched being arrested, the requirement to make the record of the search as part of the person's custody record does not apply if the person is granted "street bail" after arrest (see section 30A of PACE) to attend a police station and is not taken in custody to the police station  An arrested person's entitlement to a copy of the search record which is made as part of their custody record does not affect their entitlement to a copy of their custody record or any other provisions of PACE Code C section 2 (Custody records).

17    It is important for monitoring purposes to specify whether the authority for exercising a stop and search power was given under section 60 of the Criminal Justice and Public Order Act 1994, or under section 44(1) of the Terrorism Act 2000.

18    Officers should record the self-defined ethnicity of every person stopped according to the categories used in the 2001 census question listed in Annex B.  The person should be asked to select one of the five main categories representing broad ethnic groups and then a more specific cultural background from within this group.  The ethnic classification should be coded for recording purposes using the coding system in Annex B.  An additional "Not stated" box is available but should not be offered to respondents explicitly.  Officers should be aware and explain to members of the public, especially where concerns are raised, that this information is required to obtain a true picture of stop and search activity and to help improve ethnic monitoring, tackle discriminatory practice, and promote effective use of the powers.  If the person gives what appears to the officer to be an "incorrect" answer (e.g. a person who appears to be white states that they are black), the officer should record the response that has been given and then record their own perception of the person's ethnic background by using the PNC classification system.  If the "Not stated" category is used the reason for this must be recorded on the form.

19    Arrangements for public scrutiny of records should take account of the right to confidentiality of those stopped and searched.  Anonymised forms and/or statistics generated from records should be the focus of the examinations by members of the public.

20    Not used

21    *In situations where it is not practicable to provide a written copy of the record or immediate access to an electronic copy of the record or a receipt of the search at the time (see paragraph 4.2A above), the officer should consider giving the person details of the station which they may attend for a copy of the record. A receipt may take the form of a simple business card which includes sufficient information to locate the record should the person ask for copy, for example, the date and place of the search, a reference number or the name of the officer who carried out the search (unless paragraph 4.4 applies).*

22    Not used

22A   *Where there are concerns which make it necessary to monitor any local disproportionality, forces have discretion to direct officers to record the self-defined ethnicity of persons they request to account for themselves in a public place or who they detain with a view to searching but do not search. Guidance should be provided locally and efforts made to minimise the bureaucracy involved. Records should be closely monitored and supervised in line with paragraphs 5.1 to 5.4 and forces can suspend or re-instate recording of these encounters as appropriate.*

22B   *A person who is asked to account for themselves should, if they request, be given information about how they can report their dissatisfaction about how they have been treated.*

**Definition of Offensive Weapon**

23    *'Offensive weapon' is defined as any article made or adapted for use for causing injury to the person, or intended by the person having it with him for such use or by someone else. There are three categories of offensive weapons: those made for causing injury to the person; those adapted for such a purpose; and those not so made or adapted, but carried with the intention of causing injury to the person. A firearm, as defined by section 57 of the Firearms Act 1968, would fall within the definition of offensive weapon if any of the criteria above apply.*

24    Not used

25    Not used

**ANNEX A SUMMARY OF MAIN STOP AND SEARCH POWERS**

THIS TABLE RELATES TO STOP AND SEARCH POWERS ONLY. INDIVIDUAL STATUTES BELOW MAY CONTAIN OTHER POLICE POWERS OF ENTRY, SEARCH AND SEIZURE

| Power | Object of Search | Extent of Search | Where Exercisable |
|---|---|---|---|
| **Unlawful articles general** | | | |
| 1. Public Stores Act 1875, s6 | HM Stores stolen or unlawfully obtained | Persons, vehicles and vessels | Anywhere where the constabulary powers are exercisable |
| 2. Firearms Act 1968, s47 | Firearms | Persons and vehicles | A public place, or anywhere in the case of reasonable suspicion of offences of carrying firearms with criminal intent or trespassing with firearms |
| 3. Misuse of Drugs Act 1971, s23 | Controlled drugs | Persons and vehicles | Anywhere |
| 4. Customs and Excise Management Act 1979, s163 | Goods: (a) on which duty has not been paid; (b) being unlawfully removed, imported or exported; (c) otherwise liable to forfeiture to HM Revenue and Customs | Vehicles and vessels only | Anywhere |
| 5. Aviation Security Act 1982, s27(1) | Stolen or unlawfully obtained goods | Airport employees and vehicles carrying airport employees or aircraft or any vehicle in a cargo area whether or not carrying an employee | Any designated airport |

| Power | Object of Search | Extent of Search | Where Exercisable |
|---|---|---|---|
| 6.  Police and Criminal Evidence Act 1984, s1 | Stolen goods; articles for use in certain Theft Act offences; offensive weapons, including bladed or sharply-pointed articles (except folding pocket knives with a bladed cutting edge not exceeding 3 inches); prohibited possession of a category 4 (display grade) firework, any person under 18 in possession of an adult firework in a public place. | Persons and vehicles | Where there is public access |
| | Criminal Damage: Articles made, adapted or intended for use in destroying or damaging property | Persons and vehicles | Where there is public access |
| 7.  Sporting events (Control of Alcohol etc.) Act 1985, s7 | Intoxicating liquor | Persons, coaches and trains | Designated sports grounds or coaches and trains travelling to or from a designated sporting event. |
| 8.  Crossbows Act 1987, s4 | Crossbows or parts of crossbows (except crossbows with a draw weight of less than 1.4 kilograms) | Persons and vehicles | Anywhere except dwellings |
| 9.  Criminal Justice Act 1988 s139B | Offensive weapons, bladed or sharply pointed article | Persons | School premises |
| **Evidence of game and wildlife offences** | | | |
| 10.  Poaching Prevention Act 1862, s2 | Game or poaching equipment | Persons and vehicles | A public place |
| 11. Deer Act 1991, s12 | Evidence of offences under the Act | Persons and vehicles | Anywhere except dwellings |
| 12. Conservation of Seals Act 1970, s4 | Seals or hunting equipment | Vehicles only | Anywhere |

**A**

| Power | Object of Search | Extent of Search | Where Exercisable |
| --- | --- | --- | --- |
| 13. Protection of Badgers Act 1992, s11 | Evidence of offences under the Act | Persons and vehicles | Anywhere |
| 14. Wildlife and Countryside Act 1981, s19 | Evidence of wildlife offences | Persons and vehicles | Anywhere except dwellings |
| **Other** | | | |
| 15. Terrorism Act 2000, s.43(1) | <u>Anything which may constitute evidence that the person is a terrorist</u> | Persons | Anywhere |
| 16. Terrorism Act 2000, s.44(1) | Articles of a kind which could be used in connection with terrorism | Vehicles, and anything in or on vehicles (See paragraph 2.18A) | Anywhere within the area or locality authorised under subsection (1) |
| 17. Not used | | | |
| 18. Paragraphs 7 and 8 of Schedule 7 to the Terrorism Act 2000 | Anything relevant to determining if a person being examined falls within section 40(1)(b) | Persons, vehicles, vessels etc.  (Note: These searches are subject to the Code of Practice issued under paragraph 6 of Schedule 14 to the Terrorism Act 2000) | Ports and airports |
| 19. Section 60 Criminal Justice and Public Order Act 1994 | Offensive weapons or dangerous instruments to prevent incidents of serious violence or to deal with the carrying of such items or find such items which have been used in incidents of serious violence | Persons and vehicles | Anywhere within a locality authorised under subsection (1) |

## ANNEX B   SELF-DEFINED ETHNIC CLASSIFICATION CATEGORIES

| | |
|---|---|
| *White* | *W* |
| A.   *White - British* | *W1* |
| B.   *White - Irish* | *W2* |
| C.   *Any other White background* | *W9* |
| | |
| *Mixed* | *M* |
| D.   *White and Black Caribbean* | *M1* |
| E.   *White and Black African* | *M2* |
| F.   *White and Asian* | *M3* |
| G.   *Any other Mixed Background* | *M9* |
| | |
| *Asian / Asian - British* | *A* |
| H.   *Asian - Indian* | *A1* |
| I.    *Asian - Pakistani* | *A2* |
| J.   *Asian - Bangladeshi* | *A3* |
| K.   *Any other Asian background* | *A9* |
| | |
| *Black / Black - British* | *B* |
| L.   *Black - Caribbean* | *B1* |
| M.   *Black African* | *B2* |
| N.   *Any other Black background* | *B9* |
| | |
| *Other* | *O* |
| O.   *Chinese* | *01* |
| P.   *Any other* | *09* |
| | |
| **Not Stated** | **NS** |

**A**

### ANNEX C   SUMMARY OF POWERS OF COMMUNITY SUPPORT OFFICERS TO SEARCH AND SEIZE

The following is a summary of the search and seizure powers that may be exercised by a community support officer (CSO) who has been designated with the relevant powers in accordance with Part 4 of the Police Reform Act 2002.

When exercising any of these powers, a CSO must have regard to any relevant provisions of this Code, including section 3 governing the conduct of searches and the steps to be taken prior to a search.

#### 1.  Power to stop and search not requiring consent

| Designation | Powers conferred | Object of Search | Extent of Search | Where Exercisable |
|---|---|---|---|---|
| 1. Police Reform Act 2002, Schedule 4, paragraph 15 | Terrorism Act 2000, s44(1)(a) and (d) and 45(2); *(See paragraph 2.18A)* | Items intended to be used in connection with terrorism. | a) Vehicles or anything carried in or on the vehicle | Anywhere within area of locality authorised and in the company and under the supervision of a constable. |

#### 2.  Powers to search requiring the consent of the person and seizure

A CSO may detain a person using reasonable force where necessary as set out in Part 1 of Schedule 4 to the Police Reform Act 2002.  If the person has been lawfully detained, the CSO may search the person provided that person gives consent to such a search in relation to the following:

| Designation | Powers conferred | Object of Search | Extent of Search | Where Exercisable |
|---|---|---|---|---|
| 1. Police Reform Act 2002, Schedule 4, paragraph 7A | (a) Criminal Justice and Police Act 2001, s12(2) | (a) Alcohol or a container for alcohol | (a) Persons | (a) Designated public place |
| | (b) Confiscation of Alcohol (Young Persons) Act 1997, s1 | (b) Alcohol | (b) Persons under 18 years old | (b) Public place |
| | (c) Children and Young Persons Act 1933, section 7(3) | (c) Tobacco or cigarette papers | (c) Persons under 16 years old found smoking | (c) Public place |

### 3. Powers to search not requiring the consent of the person and seizure

A CSO may detain a person using reasonable force where necessary as set out in Part 1 of Schedule 4 to the Police Reform Act 2002. If the person has been lawfully detained, the CSO may search the person without the need for that person's consent in relation to the following:

| Designation | Powers conferred | Object of Search | Extent of Search | Where Exercisable |
|---|---|---|---|---|
| Police Reform Act 2002, Schedule 4, paragraph 2A | Police and Criminal Evidence Act 1984, s.32 | a) Objects that might be used to cause physical injury to the person or the CSO.<br><br>b) Items that might be used to assist escape. | Persons made subject to a requirement to wait. | Any place where the requirement to wait has been made. |

### 4. Powers to seize without consent

This power applies when drugs are found in the course of any search mentioned above.

| Designation | Powers conferred | Object of Seizure | Where Exercisable |
|---|---|---|---|
| Police Reform Act 2002, Schedule 4, paragraph 7B | Police Reform Act 2002, Schedule 4, paragraph 7B | Controlled drugs in a person's possession. | Any place where the person is in possession of the drug. |

## ANNEX D – Deleted.

## ANNEX E – Deleted.

**ANNEX F   ESTABLISHING GENDER OF PERSONS FOR THE PURPOSE OF
SEARCHING**

1.   Certain provisions of this and other Codes explicitly state that searches and other
     procedures may only be carried out by, or in the presence of, persons of the same
     sex as the person subject to the search or other procedure.  (See *paragraphs 2.8
     and 3.6 and Note 4 of this Code, Code C paragraph 4.1 and Annex A paragraphs
     5, 6, 11 and 12 (searches, strip and intimate searches of detainees under sections
     54 and 55 of PACE), Code D paragraph 5.5 and Note 5F (searches, examinations
     and photographing of detainees under section 54A of PACE) and 6.9 (taking samples)
     and Code H paragraph 4.1 and Annex A paragraphs 6, 7 and 12 (searches, strip and
     intimate searches under sections 54 and 55 of PACE and 43(2) of the Terrorism Act of
     persons arrested under section 41 of the Terrorism Act 2000).*

2.   All searches should be carried out with courtesy, consideration and respect for the
     person concerned.  Police officers should show particular sensitivity when dealing
     with transsexual or transvestite persons *(see Notes F1 and F2).*  The following
     approach is designed to minimise embarrassment and secure the co-operation of the
     person subject to the search.

**(a)   Consideration**

3.   At law, the gender of an individual is their gender as registered at birth unless they
     possess a gender recognition certificate as issued under section 9 of the Gender
     Recognition Act 2004, in which case the person's gender is the acquired gender.

     (a)   If there is no doubt as to the sex of a person, or there is no reason to suspect
           that the person is not the sex that they appear to be, they should be dealt with
           as that sex.

     (b)   A person who possesses a gender recognition certificate must be treated as
           their acquired gender.

     (c)   If the police are not satisfied that the person possesses a gender recognition
           certificate and there is doubt as to a person's gender, the person should be
           asked what gender they consider themselves to be.  If the person expresses a
           preference to be dealt with as a particular gender, they should be asked to sign
           the search record, the officer's notebook or, if applicable, their custody record,
           to indicate and confirm their preference.  If appropriate, the person should be
           treated as being that gender.

(d)    If a person is unwilling to make such an election, efforts should be made to determine the predominant lifestyle of the person.  For example, if they appear to live predominantly as a woman, they should be treated as such.

(e)    If there is still doubt, the person should be dealt with according to the sex that they were born.

5.    Once a decision has been made about which gender an individual is to be treated as, where possible before an officer searches that person, the officer should be advised of the doubt as to the person's gender.  This is important so as to maintain the dignity of the officer(s) concerned.

**(b)    Documentation**

6.    Where the gender of the detainee is established under *paragraphs 2(b)* to *(e)* above the decision should be recorded either on the search record, in the officer's notebook or, if applicable, in the person's custody record.

7.    Where the person elects which gender they consider themselves to be under *paragraph 2(c)* but is not treated as their elected gender, the reason must be recorded in the search record, in the officer's notebook or, if applicable, in the person's custody record.

**Note for Guidance**

F1    *Transsexual means a person who is proposing to undergo, is undergoing or has undergone a process (or part of a process) for the purpose of gender reassignment which is a protected characteristic under the Equality Act 2010 (see paragraph 1.1) by changing physiological or other attributes of their sex.  It would apply to a woman making the transition to being a man and a man making the transition to being a woman as well as to a person who has only just started out on the process of gender reassignment and to a person who has completed the process.  Both would share the characteristic of gender reassignment with each having the characteristics of one sex, but with certain characteristics of the other sex.*

F2    *Transvestite means a person of one gender who dresses in the clothes of a person of the opposite gender.*

F3    *Similar principles will apply to police officers and police staff whose duties involve carrying out, or being present at, any of the searches and other procedures mentioned in paragraph 1.  Chief officers are responsible for providing corresponding operational guidance and instructions for the deployment of any transsexual officers and staff under their direction and control.*

# POLICE AND CRIMINAL EVIDENCE ACT 1984

B

# CODE B

## CODE OF PRACTICE FOR SEARCHES OF PREMISES BY POLICE OFFICERS AND THE SEIZURE OF PROPERTY FOUND BY POLICE OFFICERS ON PERSONS OR PREMISES

### Commencement - Transitional Arrangements

This code applies to applications for warrants made after midnight on 06 March 2011 and to searches and seizures taking place after midnight on 06 March 2011.

**1      Introduction**

1.1     This Code of Practice deals with police powers to:

- search premises

- seize and retain property found on premises and persons

1.1A   These powers may be used to find:

- property and material relating to a crime

- wanted persons

- children who abscond from local authority accommodation where they have been remanded or committed by a court

1.2     A justice of the peace may issue a search warrant granting powers of entry, search and seizure, e.g. warrants to search for stolen property, drugs, firearms and evidence of serious offences.  Police also have powers without a search warrant.  The main ones provided by the Police and Criminal Evidence Act 1984 (PACE) include powers to search premises:

- to make an arrest

- after an arrest

1.3     The right to privacy and respect for personal property are key principles of the Human Rights Act 1998.  Powers of entry, search and seizure should be fully and clearly justified before use because they may significantly interfere with the occupier's privacy.  Officers should consider if the necessary objectives can be met by less intrusive means.

1.3A   Powers to search and seize must be used fairly, responsibly, with respect for people who occupy premises being searched or are in charge of property being seized and without unlawful discrimination.  The Equality Act 2010 makes it unlawful for police officers to discriminate against, harass or victimise any person on the grounds of the 'protected characteristics' of age, disability, gender reassignment, race, religion or belief, sex and sexual orientation, marriage and civil partnership, pregnancy and maternity when using their powers.  When police forces are carrying out their functions they also have a duty to have regard to the need to eliminate unlawful discrimination, harassment and victimisation and to take steps to foster good relations.

1.4 In all cases, police should therefore:

- exercise their powers courteously and with respect for persons and property

- only use reasonable force when this is considered necessary and proportionate to the circumstances

1.5 If the provisions of PACE and this Code are not observed, evidence obtained from a search may be open to question.

**2 General**

2.1 This Code must be readily available at all police stations for consultation by:

- police officers

- police staff

- detained persons

- members of the public

2.2 The *Notes for Guidance* included are not provisions of this Code.

2.3 This Code applies to searches of premises:

(a) by police for the purposes of an investigation into an alleged offence, with the occupier's consent, other than:

- routine scene of crime searches;

- calls to a fire or burglary made by or on behalf of an occupier or searches following the activation of fire or burglar alarms or discovery of insecure premises;

- searches when *paragraph 5.4* applies;

- bomb threat calls;

(b) under powers conferred on police officers by PACE, sections 17, 18 and 32;

(c) undertaken in pursuance of search warrants issued to and executed by constables in accordance with PACE, sections 15 and 16. See *Note 2A*;

(d) subject to *paragraph 2.6*, under any other power given to police to enter premises with or without a search warrant for any purpose connected with the investigation into an alleged or suspected offence. See *Note 2B*.

For the purposes of this Code, 'premises' as defined in PACE, section 23, includes any place, vehicle, vessel, aircraft, hovercraft, tent or movable structure and any offshore installation as defined in the Mineral Workings (Offshore Installations) Act 1971, section 1.  See *Note 2D*

2.4    A person who has not been arrested but is searched during a search of premises should be searched in accordance with Code A.  See *Note 2C*

2.5    This Code does not apply to the exercise of a statutory power to enter premises or to inspect goods, equipment or procedures if the exercise of that power is not dependent on the existence of grounds for suspecting that an offence may have been committed and the person exercising the power has no reasonable grounds for such suspicion.

2.6    This Code does not affect any directions or requirements of a search warrant, order or other power to search and seize lawfully exercised in England or Wales that any item or evidence seized under that warrant, order or power be handed over to a police force, court, tribunal, or other authority outside England or Wales.  For example, warrants and orders issued in Scotland or Northern Ireland, see *Note 2B(f)* and search warrants and powers provided for in sections 14 to 17 of the Crime (International Co-operation) Act 2003.

2.7    When this Code requires the prior authority or agreement of an officer of at least inspector or superintendent rank, that authority may be given by a sergeant or chief inspector authorised to perform the functions of the higher rank under PACE, section 107.

2.8    Written records required under this Code not made in the search record shall, unless otherwise specified, be made:

- in the recording officer's pocket book ('pocket book' includes any official report book issued to police officers) or

- on forms provided for the purpose

2.9    Nothing in this Code requires the identity of officers, or anyone accompanying them during a search of premises, to be recorded or disclosed:

(a)    in the case of enquiries linked to the investigation of terrorism; or

(b)    if officers reasonably believe recording or disclosing their names might put them in danger.

In these cases officers should use warrant or other identification numbers and the name of their police station.  Police staff should use any identification number provided to them by the police force.  See *Note 2E*

2.10   The 'officer in charge of the search' means the officer assigned specific duties and responsibilities under this Code.  Whenever there is a search of premises to which this Code applies one officer must act as the officer in charge of the search.  See *Note 2F*

2.11   In this Code:

(a)   'designated person' means a person other than a police officer, designated under the Police Reform Act 2002, Part 4 who has specified powers and duties of police officers conferred or imposed on them.  See *Note 2G.*

(b)   any reference to a police officer includes a designated person acting in the exercise or performance of the powers and duties conferred or imposed on them by their designation.

(c)   a person authorised to accompany police officers or designated persons in the execution of a warrant has the same powers as a constable in the execution of the warrant and the search and seizure of anything related to the warrant. These powers must be exercised in the company and under the supervision of a police officer.  See *Note 3C.*

2.12   If a power conferred on a designated person:

(a)   allows reasonable force to be used when exercised by a police officer, a designated person exercising that power has the same entitlement to use force;

(b)   includes power to use force to enter any premises, that power is not exercisable by that designated person except:

(i)   in the company and under the supervision of a police officer; or

(ii)   for the purpose of:

- saving life or limb; or

- preventing serious damage to property.

2.13   Designated persons must have regard to any relevant provisions of the Codes of Practice.

**Notes for guidance**

2A    PACE sections 15 and 16 apply to all search warrants issued to and executed by constables under any enactment, e.g. search warrants issued by a:

(a)    justice of the peace under the:

- Theft Act 1968, section 26 - stolen property;

- Misuse of Drugs Act 1971, section 23 - controlled drugs;

- PACE, section 8 - evidence of an indictable offence;

- Terrorism Act 2000, Schedule 5, paragraph 1;

- Prevention of Terrorism Act 2005, section 7C – monitoring compliance with control order (see paragraph 10.1).

(b)    Circuit judge under:

- PACE, Schedule 1;

- Terrorism Act 2000, Schedule 5, paragraph 11.

2B    Examples of the other powers in paragraph 2.3(d) include:

(a)    Road Traffic Act 1988, section 6E(1) giving police power to enter premises under section 6E(1) to:

- require a person to provide a specimen of breath; or

- arrest a person following:

   ~    a positive breath test;

   ~    failure to provide a specimen of breath;

(b)    Transport and Works Act 1992, section 30(4) giving police powers to enter premises mirroring the powers in (a) in relation to specified persons working on transport systems to which the Act applies;

(c)    Criminal Justice Act 1988, section 139B giving police power to enter and search school premises for offensive weapons, bladed or pointed articles;

(d)    Terrorism Act 2000, Schedule 5, paragraphs 3 and 15 empowering a superintendent in urgent cases to give written authority for police to enter and search premises for the purposes of a terrorist investigation;

(e) *Explosives Act 1875, section 73(b) empowering a superintendent to give written authority for police to enter premises, examine and search them for explosives;*

(f) *search warrants and production orders or the equivalent issued in Scotland or Northern Ireland endorsed under the Summary Jurisdiction (Process) Act 1881 or the Petty Sessions (Ireland) Act 1851 respectively for execution in England and Wales.*

(g) *Sections 7A and 7B of the Prevention of Terrorism Act 2005, searches connected with the enforcement of control orders (see paragraph 10.1).*

2C *The Criminal Justice Act 1988, section 139B provides that a constable who has reasonable grounds to believe an offence under the Criminal Justice Act 1988, section 139A has or is being committed may enter school premises and search the premises and any persons on the premises for any bladed or pointed article or offensive weapon. Persons may be searched under a warrant issued under the Misuse of Drugs Act 1971, section 23(3) to search premises for drugs or documents only if the warrant specifically authorises the search of persons on the premises. Powers to search premises under certain terrorism provisions also authorise the search of persons on the premises, for example, under paragraphs 1, 2, 11 and 15 of Schedule 5 to the Terrorism Act 2000 and section 52 of the Anti-terrorism, Crime and Security Act 2001.*

2D *The Immigration Act 1971, Part III and Schedule 2 gives immigration officers powers to enter and search premises, seize and retain property, with and without a search warrant. These are similar to the powers available to police under search warrants issued by a justice of the peace and without a warrant under PACE, sections 17, 18, 19 and 32 except they only apply to specified offences under the Immigration Act 1971 and immigration control powers. For certain types of investigations and enquiries these powers avoid the need for the Immigration Service to rely on police officers becoming directly involved. When exercising these powers, immigration officers are required by the Immigration and Asylum Act 1999, section 145 to have regard to this Code's corresponding provisions. When immigration officers are dealing with persons or property at police stations, police officers should give appropriate assistance to help them discharge their specific duties and responsibilities.*

2E *The purpose of paragraph 2.9(b) is to protect those involved in serious organised crime investigations or arrests of particularly violent suspects when there is reliable information that those arrested or their associates may threaten or cause harm to the officers or anyone accompanying them during a search of premises. In cases of doubt, an officer of inspector rank or above should be consulted.*

2F   *For the purposes of paragraph 2.10, the officer in charge of the search should normally be the most senior officer present. Some exceptions are:*

(a)   *a supervising officer who attends or assists at the scene of a premises search may appoint an officer of lower rank as officer in charge of the search if that officer is:*

- *more conversant with the facts;*

- *a more appropriate officer to be in charge of the search;*

(b)   *when all officers in a premises search are the same rank. The supervising officer if available must make sure one of them is appointed officer in charge of the search, otherwise the officers themselves must nominate one of their number as the officer in charge;*

(c)   *a senior officer assisting in a specialist role. This officer need not be regarded as having a general supervisory role over the conduct of the search or be appointed or expected to act as the officer in charge of the search.*

*Except in (c), nothing in this Note diminishes the role and responsibilities of a supervisory officer who is present at the search or knows of a search taking place.*

2G   *An officer of the rank of inspector or above may direct a designated investigating officer not to wear a uniform for the purposes of a specific operation.*

## 3   Search warrants and production orders

### (a)   Before making an application

3.1   When information appears to justify an application, the officer must take reasonable steps to check the information is accurate, recent and not provided maliciously or irresponsibly. An application may not be made on the basis of information from an anonymous source if corroboration has not been sought.  See *Note 3A*

3.2   The officer shall ascertain as specifically as possible the nature of the articles concerned and their location.

3.3   The officer shall make reasonable enquiries to:

(i)   establish if:

- anything is known about the likely occupier of the premises and the nature of the premises themselves;

- the premises have been searched previously and how recently;

(ii)    obtain any other relevant information.

3.4    An application:

(a)    to a justice of the peace for a search warrant or to a Circuit judge for a search warrant or production order under PACE, Schedule 1 must be supported by a signed written authority from an officer of inspector rank or above:

Note: If the case is an urgent application to a justice of the peace and an inspector or above is not readily available, the next most senior officer on duty can give the written authority.

(b)    to a circuit judge under the Terrorism Act 2000, Schedule 5 for

- a production order;

- search warrant; or

- an order requiring an explanation of material seized or produced under such a warrant or production order

- must be supported by a signed written authority from an officer of superintendent rank or above.

3.5    Except in a case of urgency, if there is reason to believe a search might have an adverse effect on relations between the police and the community, the officer in charge shall consult the local police/community liaison officer:

- before the search; or

- in urgent cases, as soon as practicable after the search

**(b)    Making an application**

3.6    A search warrant application must be supported in writing, specifying:

(a)    the enactment under which the application is made, see *Note 2A;*

(b)    (i)    whether the warrant is to authorise entry and search of:

- one set of premises; or

- if the application is under PACE section 8, or Schedule 1, paragraph 12, more than one set of specified premises or all premises occupied or controlled by a specified person, and

(ii)    the premises to be searched;

(c)    the object of the search, see *Note 3B;*

(d)      the grounds for the application, including, when the purpose of the proposed search is to find evidence of an alleged offence, an indication of how the evidence relates to the investigation;

(da)    Where the application is under PACE section 8, or Schedule 1, paragraph 12 for a single warrant to enter and search:

   (i)      more than one set of specified premises, the officer must specify each set of premises which it is desired to enter and search

   (ii)     all premises occupied or controlled by a specified person, the officer must specify;

   •    as many sets of premises which it is desired to enter and search as it is reasonably practicable to specify

   •    the person who is in occupation or control of those premises and any others which it is desired to search

   •    why it is necessary to search more premises than those which can be specified

   •    why it is not reasonably practicable to specify all the premises which it is desired to enter and search

(db)    Whether an application under PACE section 8 is for a warrant authorising entry and search on more than one occasion, and if so, the officer must state the grounds for this and whether the desired number of entries authorised is unlimited or a specified maximum.

(e)      there are no reasonable grounds to believe the material to be sought, when making application to a:

   (i)      justice of the peace or a Circuit judge consists of or includes items subject to legal privilege;

   (ii)     justice of the peace, consists of or includes excluded material or special procedure material;

   Note: this does not affect the additional powers of seizure in the Criminal Justice and Police Act 2001, Part 2 covered in *paragraph 7.7*, see *Note 3B;*

(f)      if applicable, a request for the warrant to authorise a person or persons to accompany the officer who executes the warrant, see *Note 3C.*

3.7 A search warrant application under PACE, Schedule 1, paragraph 12(a), shall if appropriate indicate why it is believed service of notice of an application for a production order may seriously prejudice the investigation. Applications for search warrants under the Terrorism Act 2000, Schedule 5, paragraph 11 must indicate why a production order would not be appropriate.

3.8 If a search warrant application is refused, a further application may not be made for those premises unless supported by additional grounds.

**Notes for guidance**

*3A The identity of an informant need not be disclosed when making an application, but the officer should be prepared to answer any questions the magistrate or judge may have about:*

  - *the accuracy of previous information from that source*

  - *any other related matters*

*3B The information supporting a search warrant application should be as specific as possible, particularly in relation to the articles or persons being sought and where in the premises it is suspected they may be found. The meaning of 'items subject to legal privilege', 'excluded material' and 'special procedure material' are defined by PACE, sections 10, 11 and 14 respectively.*

*3C Under PACE, section 16(2), a search warrant may authorise persons other than police officers to accompany the constable who executes the warrant. This includes, e.g. any suitably qualified or skilled person or an expert in a particular field whose presence is needed to help accurately identify the material sought or to advise where certain evidence is most likely to be found and how it should be dealt with. It does not give them any right to force entry, but it gives them the right to be on the premises during the search and to search for or seize property without the occupier's permission.*

**4 Entry without warrant - particular powers**

**(a) Making an arrest etc**

*4.1 The conditions under which an officer may enter and search premises without a warrant are set out in PACE, section 17. It should be noted that this section does not create or confer any powers of arrest. See other powers in Note 2B(a).*

**(b) Search of premises where arrest takes place or the arrested person was immediately before arrest**

4.2    When a person has been arrested for an indictable offence, a police officer has power under PACE, section 32 to search the premises where the person was arrested or where the person was immediately before being arrested.

**(c)    *Search of premises occupied or controlled by the arrested person***

4.3    The specific powers to search premises which <u>are</u> occupied or controlled by a person arrested for an indictable offence are set out in PACE, section 18. They may not be exercised, except if section 18(5) applies, unless an officer of inspector rank or above has given written authority. That authority should only be given when the authorising officer is satisfied that the premises <u>are</u> occupied or controlled by the arrested person and that the necessary grounds exist. If possible the authorising officer should record the authority on the Notice of Powers and Rights and, subject to *paragraph 2.9*, sign the Notice. The record of the grounds for the search and the nature of the evidence sought as required by section 18(7) of the Act should be made in:

- the custody record if there is one, otherwise

- the officer's pocket book, or

- the search record

## 5    Search with consent

5.1    Subject to *paragraph 5.4*, if it is proposed to search premises with the consent of a person entitled to grant entry the consent must, if practicable, be given in writing on the Notice of Powers and Rights before the search. The officer must make any necessary enquiries to be satisfied the person is in a position to give such consent. See *Notes 5A* and *5B*

5.2    Before seeking consent the officer in charge of the search shall state the purpose of the proposed search and its extent. This information must be as specific as possible, particularly regarding the articles or persons being sought and the parts of the premises to be searched. The person concerned must be clearly informed they are not obliged to consent, that any consent given can be withdrawn at any time, including before the search starts or while it is underway and anything seized may be produced in evidence. If at the time the person is not suspected of an offence, the officer shall say this when stating the purpose of the search.

5.3    An officer cannot enter and search or continue to search premises under *paragraph 5.1* if consent is given under duress or withdrawn before the search is completed.

5.4    It is unnecessary to seek consent under *paragraphs 5.1* and *5.2* if this would cause disproportionate inconvenience to the person concerned. See *Note 5C*

**B**

## Notes for guidance

5A    *In a lodging house, hostel or similar accommodation, every reasonable effort should be made to obtain the consent of the tenant, lodger or occupier. A search should not be made solely on the basis of the landlord's consent.*

5B    *If the intention is to search premises under the authority of a warrant or a power of entry and search without warrant, and the occupier of the premises co-operates in accordance with paragraph 6.4, there is no need to obtain written consent.*

5C    *Paragraph 5.4 is intended to apply when it is reasonable to assume innocent occupiers would agree to, and expect, police to take the proposed action, e.g. if:*

- *a suspect has fled the scene of a crime or to evade arrest and it is necessary quickly to check surrounding gardens and readily accessible places to see if the suspect is hiding*

- *police have arrested someone in the night after a pursuit and it is necessary to make a brief check of gardens along the pursuit route to see if stolen or incriminating articles have been discarded*

## 6    Searching premises - general considerations

### (a)    Time of searches

6.1    Searches made under warrant must be made within three calendar months of the date of the warrant's issue.

6.2    Searches must be made at a reasonable hour unless this might frustrate the purpose of the search.

6.3    When the extent or complexity of a search mean it is likely to take a long time, the officer in charge of the search may consider using the seize and sift powers referred to in *section 7.*

6.3A    A warrant under PACE, section 8 may authorise entry to and search of premises on more than one occasion if, on the application, the justice of the peace is satisfied that it is necessary to authorise multiple entries in order to achieve the purpose for which the warrant is issued. No premises may be entered or searched on any subsequent occasions without the prior written authority of an officer of the rank of inspector who is not involved in the investigation. All other warrants authorise entry on one occasion only.

6.3B   Where a warrant under PACE section 8, or Schedule 1, paragraph 12 authorises entry to and search of all premises occupied or controlled by a specified person, no premises which are not specified in the warrant may be entered and searched without the prior written authority of an officer of the rank of inspector who is not involved in the investigation.

**(b)    *Entry other than with consent***

6.4    The officer in charge of the search shall first try to communicate with the occupier, or any other person entitled to grant access to the premises, explain the authority under which entry is sought and ask the occupier to allow entry, unless:

   (i)    the search premises are unoccupied;

   (ii)    the occupier and any other person entitled to grant access are absent;

   (iii)    there are reasonable grounds for believing that alerting the occupier or any other person entitled to grant access would frustrate the object of the search or endanger officers or other people.

6.5    Unless *sub-paragraph 6.4(iii)* applies, if the premises are occupied the officer, subject to *paragraph 2.9*, shall, before the search begins:

   (i)    identify him or herself, show their warrant card (if not in uniform) and state the purpose of and grounds for the search;

   (ii)    identify and introduce any person accompanying the officer on the search (such persons should carry identification for production on request) and briefly describe that person's role in the process.

6.6    Reasonable and proportionate force may be used if necessary to enter premises if the officer in charge of the search is satisfied the premises are those specified in any warrant, or in exercise of the powers described in *paragraphs 4.1* to *4.3*, and if:

   (i)    the occupier or any other person entitled to grant access has refused entry;

   (ii)    it is impossible to communicate with the occupier or any other person entitled to grant access; or

   (iii)    any of the provisions of *paragraph 6.4* apply.

**(c)    *Notice of Powers and Rights***

6.7    If an officer conducts a search to which this Code applies the officer shall, unless it is impracticable to do so, provide the occupier with a copy of a Notice in a standard format:

(i) specifying if the search is made under warrant, with consent, or in the exercise of the powers described in *paragraphs 4.1* to *4.3*. Note: the notice format shall provide for authority or consent to be indicated, see *paragraphs 4.3* and *5.1;*

(ii) summarising the extent of the powers of search and seizure conferred by PACE and other relevant legislation as appropriate;

(ii) explaining the rights of the occupier, and the owner of the property seized;

(iv) explaining compensation may be payable in appropriate cases for damages caused entering and searching premises, and giving the address to send a compensation application, see *Note 6A;*

(v) stating this Code is available at any police station.

6.8  If the occupier is:

- present, copies of the Notice and warrant shall, if practicable, be given to them before the search begins, unless the officer in charge of the search reasonably believes this would frustrate the object of the search or endanger officers or other people

- not present, copies of the Notice and warrant shall be left in a prominent place on the premises or appropriate part of the premises and endorsed, subject to *paragraph 2.9* with the name of the officer in charge of the search, the date and time of the search

The warrant shall be endorsed to show this has been done.

### *(d)   Conduct of searches*

6.9  Premises may be searched only to the extent necessary to achieve the purpose of the search, having regard to the size and nature of whatever is sought.

6.9A  A search may not continue under:

- a warrant's authority once all the things specified in that warrant have been found;

- any other power once the object of that search has been achieved.

6.9B  No search may continue once the officer in charge of the search is satisfied whatever is being sought is not on the premises. See *Note 6B*. This does not prevent a further search of the same premises if additional grounds come to light supporting a further application for a search warrant or exercise or further exercise of another power. For example, when, as a result of new information, it is believed articles previously not found or additional articles are on the premises.

6.10    Searches must be conducted with due consideration for the property and privacy of the occupier and with no more disturbance than necessary.  Reasonable force may be used only when necessary and proportionate because the co-operation of the occupier cannot be obtained or is insufficient for the purpose.  See *Note 6C*

6.11    A friend, neighbour or other person must be allowed to witness the search if the occupier wishes unless the officer in charge of the search has reasonable grounds for believing the presence of the person asked for would seriously hinder the investigation or endanger officers or other people.  A search need not be unreasonably delayed for this purpose.  A record of the action taken should be made on the premises search record including the grounds for refusing the occupier's request.

6.12    A person is not required to be cautioned prior to being asked questions that are solely necessary for the purpose of furthering the proper and effective conduct of a search, see Code C, *paragraph 10.1(c)*.  For example, questions to discover the occupier of specified premises, to find a key to open a locked drawer or cupboard or to otherwise seek co-operation during the search or to determine if a particular item is liable to be seized.

6.12A  If questioning goes beyond what is necessary for the purpose of the exemption in Code C, the exchange is likely to constitute an interview as defined by Code C, *paragraph 11.1A* and would require the associated safeguards included in Code C, *section 10*.

### (e)    *Leaving premises*

6.13    If premises have been entered by force, before leaving the officer in charge of the search must make sure they are secure by:

- arranging for the occupier or their agent to be present

- any other appropriate means

### (f)    *Searches under PACE Schedule 1 or the Terrorism Act 2000, Schedule 5*

6.14    An officer shall be appointed as the officer in charge of the search, see *paragraph 2.10*, in respect of any search made under a warrant issued under PACE Act 1984, Schedule 1 or the Terrorism Act 2000, Schedule 5.  They are responsible for making sure the search is conducted with discretion and in a manner that causes the least possible disruption to any business or other activities carried out on the premises.

6.15    Once the officer in charge of the search is satisfied material may not be taken from the premises without their knowledge, they shall ask for the documents or other records concerned.  The officer in charge of the search may also ask to see the index to files held on the premises, and the officers conducting the search may inspect any files which, according to the index, appear to contain the material sought. A more extensive search of the premises may be made only if:

- the person responsible for them refuses to:

    – produce the material sought, or

    – allow access to the index

- it appears the index is:

    – inaccurate, or

    – incomplete

    – for any other reason the officer in charge of the search has reasonable grounds for believing such a search is necessary in order to find the material sought

**Notes for guidance**

6A    *Whether compensation is appropriate depends on the circumstances in each case. Compensation for damage caused when effecting entry is unlikely to be appropriate if the search was lawful, and the force used can be shown to be reasonable, proportionate and necessary to effect entry.  If the wrong premises are searched by mistake everything possible should be done at the earliest opportunity to allay any sense of grievance and there should normally be a strong presumption in favour of paying compensation.*

6B    *It is important that, when possible, all those involved in a search are fully briefed about any powers to be exercised and the extent and limits within which it should be conducted.*

6C    *In all cases the number of officers and other persons involved in executing the warrant should be determined by what is reasonable and necessary according to the particular circumstances.*

**7   Seizure and retention of property**

*(a)   Seizure*

7.1   Subject to *paragraph 7.2*, an officer who is searching any person or premises under any statutory power or with the consent of the occupier may seize anything:

(a)   covered by a warrant

(b)   the officer has reasonable grounds for believing is evidence of an offence or has been obtained in consequence of the commission of an offence but only if seizure is necessary to prevent the items being concealed, lost, disposed of, altered, damaged, destroyed or tampered with

(c)   covered by the powers in the Criminal Justice and Police Act 2001, Part 2 allowing an officer to seize property from persons or premises and retain it for sifting or examination elsewhere

See *Note 7B*

7.2   No item may be seized which an officer has reasonable grounds for believing to be subject to legal privilege, as defined in PACE, section 10, other than under the Criminal Justice and Police Act 2001, Part 2.

7.3   Officers must be aware of the provisions in the Criminal Justice and Police Act 2001, section 59, allowing for applications to a judicial authority for the return of property seized and the subsequent duty to secure in section 60, see *paragraph 7.12(iii)*.

7.4   An officer may decide it is not appropriate to seize property because of an explanation from the person holding it but may nevertheless have reasonable grounds for believing it was obtained in consequence of an offence by some person.  In these circumstances, the officer should identify the property to the holder, inform the holder of their suspicions and explain the holder may be liable to civil or criminal proceedings if they dispose of, alter or destroy the property.

7.5   An officer may arrange to photograph, image or copy, any document or other article they have the power to seize in accordance with *paragraph 7.1*.  This is subject to specific restrictions on the examination, imaging or copying of certain property seized under the Criminal Justice and Police Act 2001, Part 2.  An officer must have regard to their statutory obligation to retain an original document or other article only when a photograph or copy is not sufficient.

**B**

7.6     If an officer considers information stored in any electronic form and accessible from the premises could be used in evidence, they may require the information to be produced in a form:

- which can be taken away and in which it is visible and legible; or

- from which it can readily be produced in a visible and legible form

*(b)     Criminal Justice and Police Act 2001:  Specific procedures for seize and sift powers*

7.7     The Criminal Justice and Police Act 2001, Part 2 gives officers limited powers to seize property from premises or persons so they can sift or examine it elsewhere. Officers must be careful they only exercise these powers when it is essential and they do not remove any more material than necessary.  The removal of large volumes of material, much of which may not ultimately be retainable, may have serious implications for the owners, particularly when they are involved in business or activities such as journalism or the provision of medical services.  Officers must carefully consider if removing copies or images of relevant material or data would be a satisfactory alternative to removing originals.  When originals are taken, officers must be prepared to facilitate the provision of copies or images for the owners when reasonably practicable.  See *Note 7C*

7.8     Property seized under the Criminal Justice and Police Act 2001, sections 50 or 51 must be kept securely and separately from any material seized under other powers. An examination under section 53 to determine which elements may be retained must be carried out at the earliest practicable time, having due regard to the desirability of allowing the person from whom the property was seized, or a person with an interest in the property, an opportunity of being present or represented at the examination.

7.8A    All reasonable steps should be taken to accommodate an interested person's request to be present, provided the request is reasonable and subject to the need to prevent harm to, interference with, or unreasonable delay to the investigatory process.  If an examination proceeds in the absence of an interested person who asked to attend or their representative, the officer who exercised the relevant seizure power must give that person a written notice of why the examination was carried out in those circumstances.  If it is necessary for security reasons or to maintain confidentiality officers may exclude interested persons from decryption or other processes which facilitate the examination but do not form part of it. See *Note 7D*

7.9     It is the responsibility of the officer in charge of the investigation to make sure property is returned in accordance with sections 53 to 55.  Material which there is no power to retain must be:

- separated from the rest of the seized property

- returned as soon as reasonably practicable after examination of all the seized property

7.9A Delay is only warranted if very clear and compelling reasons exist, e.g. the:

- unavailability of the person to whom the material is to be returned

- need to agree a convenient time to return a large volume of material

7.9B Legally privileged, excluded or special procedure material which cannot be retained must be returned:

- as soon as reasonably practicable

- without waiting for the whole examination

7.9C As set out in section 58, material must be returned to the person from whom it was seized, except when it is clear some other person has a better right to it. See *Note 7E*

7.10 When an officer involved in the investigation has reasonable grounds to believe a person with a relevant interest in property seized under section 50 or 51 intends to make an application under section 59 for the return of any legally privileged, special procedure or excluded material, the officer in charge of the investigation should be informed as soon as practicable and the material seized should be kept secure in accordance with section 61. See *Note 7C*

7.11 The officer in charge of the investigation is responsible for making sure property is properly secured. Securing involves making sure the property is not examined, copied, imaged or put to any other use except at the request, or with the consent, of the applicant or in accordance with the directions of the appropriate judicial authority. Any request, consent or directions must be recorded in writing and signed by both the initiator and the officer in charge of the investigation. See *Notes 7F* and *7G*

7.12 When an officer exercises a power of seizure conferred by sections 50 or 51 they shall provide the occupier of the premises or the person from whom the property is being seized with a written notice:

(i)    specifying what has been seized under the powers conferred by that section;

(ii)   specifying the grounds for those powers;

(iii)  setting out the effect of sections 59 to 61 covering the grounds for a person with a relevant interest in seized property to apply to a judicial authority for its return and the duty of officers to secure property in certain circumstances when an application is made;

(iv)     specifying the name and address of the person to whom:

- notice of an application to the appropriate judicial authority in respect of any of the seized property must be given;

- an application may be made to allow attendance at the initial examination of the property.

7.13    If the occupier is not present but there is someone in charge of the premises, the notice shall be given to them. If no suitable person is available, so the notice will easily be found it should either be:

- left in a prominent place on the premises

- attached to the exterior of the premises

*(c)     Retention*

7.14    Subject to *paragraph 7.15*, anything seized in accordance with the above provisions may be retained only for as long as is necessary.  It may be retained, among other purposes:

(i)     for use as evidence at a trial for an offence;

(ii)    to facilitate the use in any investigation or proceedings of anything to which it is inextricably linked, see *Note 7H*;

(iii)   for forensic examination or other investigation in connection with an offence;

(iv)    in order to establish its lawful owner when there are reasonable grounds for believing it has been stolen or obtained by the commission of an offence.

7.15    Property shall not be retained under *paragraph 7.14(i), (ii)* or *(iii)* if a copy or image would be sufficient.

*(d)     Rights of owners etc*

7.16    If property is retained, the person who had custody or control of it immediately before seizure must, on request, be provided with a list or description of the property within a reasonable time.

7.17    That person or their representative must be allowed supervised access to the property to examine it or have it photographed or copied, or must be provided with a photograph or copy, in either case within a reasonable time of any request and at their own expense, unless the officer in charge of an investigation has reasonable grounds for believing this would:

     (i)     prejudice the investigation of any offence or criminal proceedings; or

     (ii)    lead to the commission of an offence by providing access to unlawful material such as pornography;

A record of the grounds shall be made when access is denied.

### Notes for guidance

7A    *Any person claiming property seized by the police may apply to a magistrates' court under the Police (Property) Act 1897 for its possession and should, if appropriate, be advised of this procedure.*

7B    *The powers of seizure conferred by PACE, sections 18(2) and 19(3) extend to the seizure of the whole premises when it is physically possible to seize and retain the premises in their totality and practical considerations make seizure desirable. For example, police may remove premises such as tents, vehicles or caravans to a police station for the purpose of preserving evidence.*

7C    *Officers should consider reaching agreement with owners and/or other interested parties on the procedures for examining a specific set of property, rather than awaiting the judicial authority's determination. Agreement can sometimes give a quicker and more satisfactory route for all concerned and minimise costs and legal complexities.*

7D    *What constitutes a relevant interest in specific material may depend on the nature of that material and the circumstances in which it is seized. Anyone with a reasonable claim to ownership of the material and anyone entrusted with its safe keeping by the owner should be considered.*

7E    *Requirements to secure and return property apply equally to all copies, images or other material created because of seizure of the original property.*

7F    *The mechanics of securing property vary according to the circumstances; "bagging up", i.e. placing material in sealed bags or containers and strict subsequent control of access is the appropriate procedure in many cases.*

7G    *When material is seized under the powers of seizure conferred by PACE, the duty to retain it under the Code of Practice issued under the Criminal Procedure and Investigations Act 1996 is subject to the provisions on retention of seized material in PACE, section 22.*

7H    *Paragraph 7.14 (ii) applies if inextricably linked material is seized under the Criminal Justice and Police Act 2001, sections 50 or 51. Inextricably linked material is material it is not reasonably practicable to separate from other linked material without prejudicing*

B

*the use of that other material in any investigation or proceedings. For example, it may not be possible to separate items of data held on computer disk without damaging their evidential integrity. Inextricably linked material must not be examined, imaged, copied or used for any purpose other than for proving the source and/or integrity of the linked material.*

**8      Action after searches**

8.1    If premises are searched in circumstances where this Code applies, unless the exceptions in *paragraph 2.3(a)* apply, on arrival at a police station the officer in charge of the search shall make or have made a record of the search, to include:

   (i)    the address of the searched premises;

   (ii)   the date, time and duration of the search;

   (iii)  the authority used for the search:

   - if the search was made in exercise of a statutory power to search premises without warrant, the power which was used for the search:

   - if the search was made under a warrant or with written consent;

      - a copy of the warrant and the written authority to apply for it, *see paragraph 3.4*; or

      - the written consent;

      shall be appended to the record or the record shall show the location of the copy warrant or consent.

   (iv)   subject to *paragraph 2.9*, the names of:

   - the officer(s) in charge of the search;

   - all other officers and authorised persons who conducted the search;

   (v)    the names of any people on the premises if they are known;

   (vi)   any grounds for refusing the occupier's request to have someone present during the search, see *paragraph 6.11;*

   (vii)  a list of any articles seized or the location of a list and, if not covered by a warrant, the grounds for their seizure;

   (viii) whether force was used, and the reason;

(ix)    details of any damage caused during the search, and the circumstances;

(x)    if applicable, the reason it was not practicable;

    (a)    to give the occupier a copy of the Notice of Powers and Rights, see *paragraph 6.7*;

    (b)    before the search to give the occupier a copy of the Notice, see *paragraph 6.8*;

(xi)    when the occupier was not present, the place where copies of the Notice of Powers and Rights and search warrant were left on the premises, see *paragraph 6.8*.

8.2    On each occasion when premises are searched under warrant, the warrant authorising the search on that occasion shall be endorsed to show:

(i)    if any articles specified in the warrant were found and the address where found;

(ii)    if any other articles were seized;

(iii)    the date and time it was executed and if present, the name of the occupier or if the occupier is not present the name of the person in charge of the premises;

(iv)    subject to *paragraph 2.9*, the names of the officers who executed it and any authorised persons who accompanied them;

(v)    if a copy, together with a copy of the Notice of Powers and Rights was:

    •    handed to the occupier; or

    •    endorsed as required by *paragraph 6.8*; and left on the premises and where.

8.3    Any warrant shall be returned within three calendar months of its issue or sooner on completion of the search(es) authorised by that warrant, if it was issued by a:

    •    justice of the peace, to the designated officer for the local justice area in which the justice was acting when issuing the warrant; or

    •    judge, to the appropriate officer of the court concerned,

## 9    Search registers

9.1    A search register will be maintained at each sub-divisional or equivalent police station. All search records required under *paragraph 8.1* shall be made, copied, or referred to in the register.  See *Note 9A*

**Note for guidance**

*9A    Paragraph 9.1 also applies to search records made by immigration officers.  In these cases, a search register must also be maintained at an immigration office.  See also Note 2D*

**10      Searches under sections 7A, 7B and 7C of the Prevention of Terrorism Act 2005 in connection with control orders**

10.1    This Code applies to the powers under sections 7A, 7B and 7C of the Prevention of Terrorism Act 2005 to enter and search premises subject to the modifications in the following paragraphs.

10.2    In paragraph 2.3(d), the reference to the investigation into an alleged or suspected offence include the enforcement of obligations imposed by or under a control order made under the Prevention of Terrorism Act 2005.

10.3    References to the purpose and object of the search, the nature of articles sought and what may be seized and retained include (as appropriate):

- in relation section 7A (absconding), determining whether the controlled person has absconded and if it appears so, any material or information that may assist in the pursuit and arrest of the controlled person.

- in relation to section 7B (failure to grant access to premises), determining whether any control order obligations have been contravened and if it appears so, any material or information that may assist in determining whether the controlled person is complying with the obligations imposed by the control order or in investigating any apparent contravention of those obligations.

- in relation to section 7C (monitoring compliance), determining whether the controlled person is complying with their control order obligations, and any material that may assist in that determination.

- evidence in relation to an offence under section 9 of the Prevention of Terrorism Act 2005 (offences relating to control orders).

**B**

# POLICE AND CRIMINAL EVIDENCE ACT 1984 (PACE)

## CODE C

**C**

## CODE OF PRACTICE FOR THE DETENTION, TREATMENT AND QUESTIONING OF PERSONS BY POLICE OFFICERS

### Commencement – Transitional Arrangements

This Code applies to people in police detention after midnight on 31 January 2008, notwithstanding that their period of detention may have commenced before that time.

## 1    General

1.1    All persons in custody must be dealt with expeditiously, and released as soon as the need for detention no longer applies.

1.1A    A custody officer must perform the functions in this Code as soon as practicable. A custody officer will not be in breach of this Code if delay is justifiable and reasonable steps are taken to prevent unnecessary delay. The custody record shall show when a delay has occurred and the reason. See *Note 1H*

1.2    This Code of Practice must be readily available at all police stations for consultation by:

- police officers

- police staff

- detained persons

- members of the public.

1.3    The provisions of this Code:

- include the *Annexes*

- do not include the *Notes for Guidance*.

1.4    If an officer has any suspicion, or is told in good faith, that a person of any age may be mentally disordered or otherwise mentally vulnerable, in the absence of clear evidence to dispel that suspicion, the person shall be treated as such for the purposes of this Code. See *Note 1G*

1.5    If anyone appears to be under 17, they shall be treated as a juvenile for the purposes of this Code in the absence of clear evidence that they are older.

1.6    If a person appears to be blind, seriously visually impaired, deaf, unable to read or speak or has difficulty orally because of a speech impediment, they shall be treated as such for the purposes of this Code in the absence of clear evidence to the contrary.

1.7    'The appropriate adult' means, in the case of a:

(a)    juvenile:

(i)    the parent, guardian or, if the juvenile is in local authority or voluntary organisation care, or is otherwise being looked after under the Children Act 1989, a person representing that authority or organisation;

(ii)    a social worker of a local authority;

        (iii)    failing these, some other responsible adult aged 18 or over who is not a police officer or employed by the police.

    (b)    person who is mentally disordered or mentally vulnerable: See Note 1D

        (iv)    a relative, guardian or other person responsible for their care or custody;

        (v)    someone experienced in dealing with mentally disordered or mentally vulnerable people but who is not a police officer or employed by the police;

        (vi)    failing these, some other responsible adult aged 18 or over who is not a police officer or employed by the police.

1.8    If this Code requires a person be given certain information, they do not have to be given it if at the time they are incapable of understanding what is said, are violent or may become violent or in urgent need of medical attention, but they must be given it as soon as practicable.

1.9    References to a custody officer include any:-

- police officer; or

- designated staff custody officer acting in the exercise or performance of the powers and duties conferred or imposed on them by their designation,

    performing the functions of a custody officer. See *Note 1J*.

1.9A    When this Code requires the prior authority or agreement of an officer of at least inspector or superintendent rank, that authority may be given by a sergeant or chief inspector authorised to perform the functions of the higher rank under the Police and Criminal Evidence Act 1984 (PACE), section 107.

1.10    Subject to *paragraph 1.12*, this Code applies to people in custody at police stations in England and Wales, whether or not they have been arrested, and to those removed to a police station as a place of safety under the Mental Health Act 1983, sections 135 and 136. *Section 15* applies solely to people in police detention, e.g. those brought to a police station under arrest or arrested at a police station for an offence after going there voluntarily.

1.11    People detained under the Terrorism Act 2000, Schedule 8 and section 41 and other provisions of that Act are not subject to any part of this Code. Such persons are subject to the Code of Practice for detention, treatment and questioning of persons by police officers detained under that Act.

1.12    This Code's provisions do not apply to people in custody:

(i)    arrested on warrants issued in Scotland by officers under the Criminal Justice and Public Order Act 1994, section 136(2), or arrested or detained without warrant by officers from a police force in Scotland under section 137(2). In these cases, police powers and duties and the person's rights and entitlements whilst at a police station in England or Wales are the same as those in Scotland;

(ii)    arrested under the Immigration and Asylum Act 1999, section 142(3) in order to have their fingerprints taken;

(iii)    whose detention is authorised by an immigration officer under the Immigration Act 1971;

(iv)    who are convicted or remanded prisoners held in police cells on behalf of the Prison Service under the Imprisonment (Temporary Provisions) Act 1980;

(v)    not used

(vi)    detained for searches under stop and search powers except as required by Code A.

The provisions on conditions of detention and treatment in *sections 8* and *9* must be considered as the minimum standards of treatment for such detainees.

1.13    In this Code:

(a)    'designated person' means a person other than a police officer, designated under the Police Reform Act 2002, Part 4 who has specified powers and duties of police officers conferred or imposed on them;

(b)    reference to a police officer includes a designated person acting in the exercise or performance of the powers and duties conferred or imposed on them by their designation.

1.14    Designated persons are entitled to use reasonable force as follows:-

(a)    when exercising a power conferred on them which allows a police officer exercising that power to use reasonable force, a designated person has the same entitlement to use force; and

(b)    at other times when carrying out duties conferred or imposed on them that also entitle them to use reasonable force, for example:

- when at a police station carrying out the duty to keep detainees for whom they are responsible under control and to assist any other police officer or designated person to keep any detainee under control and to prevent their escape.

- when securing, or assisting any other police officer or designated person in securing, the detention of a person at a police station.

- when escorting, or assisting any other police officer or designated person in escorting, a detainee within a police station.

- for the purpose of saving life or limb; or

- preventing serious damage to property.

1.15 Nothing in this Code prevents the custody officer, or other officer given custody of the detainee, from allowing police staff who are not designated persons to carry out individual procedures or tasks at the police station if the law allows. However, the officer remains responsible for making sure the procedures and tasks are carried out correctly in accordance with the Codes of Practice. Any such person must be:

(a) a person employed by a police authority maintaining a police force and under the control and direction of the Chief Officer of that force;

(b) employed by a person with whom a police authority has a contract for the provision of services relating to persons arrested or otherwise in custody.

1.16 Designated persons and other police staff must have regard to any relevant provisions of the Codes of Practice.

1.17 References to pocket books include any official report book issued to police officers or other police staff.

### Notes for guidance

1A    *Although certain sections of this Code apply specifically to people in custody at police stations, those there voluntarily to assist with an investigation should be treated with no less consideration, e.g. offered refreshments at appropriate times, and enjoy an absolute right to obtain legal advice or communicate with anyone outside the police station.*

1B    *A person, including a parent or guardian, should not be an appropriate adult if they:*

- *are*

  - *suspected of involvement in the offence*

  - *the victim*

- – *a witness*

- – *involved in the investigation*

• received admissions prior to attending to act as the appropriate adult.

*Note: If a juvenile's parent is estranged from the juvenile, they should not be asked to act as the appropriate adult if the juvenile expressly and specifically objects to their presence.*

1C  *If a juvenile admits an offence to, or in the presence of, a social worker or member of a youth offending team other than during the time that person is acting as the juvenile's appropriate adult, another appropriate adult should be appointed in the interest of fairness.*

1D  *In the case of people who are mentally disordered or otherwise mentally vulnerable, it may be more satisfactory if the appropriate adult is someone experienced or trained in their care rather than a relative lacking such qualifications. But if the detainee prefers a relative to a better qualified stranger or objects to a particular person their wishes should, if practicable, be respected.*

1E  *A detainee should always be given an opportunity, when an appropriate adult is called to the police station, to consult privately with a solicitor in the appropriate adult's absence if they want. An appropriate adult is not subject to legal privilege.*

1F  *A solicitor or independent custody visitor (formerly a lay visitor) present at the police station in that capacity may not be the appropriate adult.*

1G  *'Mentally vulnerable' applies to any detainee who, because of their mental state or capacity, may not understand the significance of what is said, of questions or of their replies. 'Mental disorder' is defined in the Mental Health Act 1983, section 1(2) as 'mental illness, arrested or incomplete development of mind, psychopathic disorder and any other disorder or disability of mind'. When the custody officer has any doubt about the mental state or capacity of a detainee, that detainee should be treated as mentally vulnerable and an appropriate adult called.*

1H  *Paragraph 1.1A is intended to cover delays which may occur in processing detainees e.g. if:*

• a large number of suspects are brought into the station simultaneously to be placed in custody;

• interview rooms are all being used;

• there are difficulties contacting an appropriate adult, solicitor or interpreter.

*1I    The custody officer must remind the appropriate adult and detainee about the right to legal advice and record any reasons for waiving it in accordance with section 6.*

*1J    The designation of police staff custody officers applies only in police areas where an order commencing the provisions of the Police Reform Act 2002, section 38 and Schedule 4A, for designating police staff custody officers is in effect.*

*1K    This Code does not affect the principle that all citizens have a duty to help police officers to prevent crime and discover offenders. This is a civic rather than a legal duty; but when a police officer is trying to discover whether, or by whom, an offence has been committed he is entitled to question any person from whom he thinks useful information can be obtained, subject to the restrictions imposed by this Code. A person's declaration that he is unwilling to reply does not alter this entitlement.*

## 2    Custody records

2.1A   When a person is brought to a police station:

- under arrest

- is arrested at the police station having attended there voluntarily or

- attends a police station to answer bail

they should be brought before the custody officer as soon as practicable after their arrival at the station or, if appropriate, following arrest after attending the police station voluntarily. This applies to designated and non-designated police stations. A person is deemed to be "at a police station" for these purposes if they are within the boundary of any building or enclosed yard which forms part of that police station.

2.1    A separate custody record must be opened as soon as practicable for each person brought to a police station under arrest or arrested at the station having gone there voluntarily or attending a police station in answer to street bail. All information recorded under this Code must be recorded as soon as practicable in the custody record unless otherwise specified. Any audio or video recording made in the custody area is not part of the custody record.

2.2    If any action requires the authority of an officer of a specified rank, subject to *paragraph 2.6A*, their name and rank must be noted in the custody record.

2.3    The custody officer is responsible for the custody record's accuracy and completeness and for making sure the record or copy of the record accompanies a detainee if they are transferred to another police station. The record shall show the:

- time and reason for transfer;

- time a person is released from detention.

2.4   A solicitor or appropriate adult must be permitted to consult a detainee's custody record as soon as practicable after their arrival at the station and at any other time whilst the person is detained. Arrangements for this access must be agreed with the custody officer and may not unreasonably interfere with the custody officer's duties.

2.4A   When a detainee leaves police detention or is taken before a court they, their legal representative or appropriate adult shall be given, on request, a copy of the custody record as soon as practicable. This entitlement lasts for 12 months after release.

2.5   The detainee, appropriate adult or legal representative shall be permitted to inspect the original custody record after the detainee has left police detention provided they give reasonable notice of their request. Any such inspection shall be noted in the custody record.

2.6   Subject to *paragraph 2.6A*, all entries in custody records must be timed and signed by the maker. Records entered on computer shall be timed and contain the operator's identification.

2.6A   Nothing in this Code requires the identity of officers or other police staff to be recorded or disclosed:

(a)   not used;

(b)   if the officer or police staff reasonably believe recording or disclosing their name might put them in danger.

In these cases, they shall use their warrant or other identification numbers and the name of their police station. See *Note 2A*

2.7   The fact and time of any detainee's refusal to sign a custody record, when asked in accordance with this Code, must be recorded.

### Note for guidance

2A   *The purpose of paragraph 2.6A(b) is to protect those involved in serious organised crime investigations or arrests of particularly violent suspects when there is reliable information that those arrested or their associates may threaten or cause harm to those involved. In cases of doubt, an officer of inspector rank or above should be consulted.*

**3      Initial action**

*(a)     Detained persons – normal procedure*

3.1     When a person is brought to a police station under arrest or arrested at the station having gone there voluntarily, the custody officer must make sure the person is told clearly about the following continuing rights which may be exercised at any stage during the period in custody:

   (i)      the right to have someone informed of their arrest as in *section 5*;

   (ii)     the right to consult privately with a solicitor and that free independent legal advice is available;

   (iii)    the right to consult these Codes of Practice. See *Note 3D*

3.2     The detainee must also be given:

   •      a written notice setting out:

      –      the above three rights;

      –      the arrangements for obtaining legal advice;

      –      the right to a copy of the custody record as in *paragraph 2.4A*;

      –      the caution in the terms prescribed in *section 10*.

   •      an additional written notice briefly setting out their entitlements while in custody, see *Notes 3A* and *3B*.

   Note: The detainee shall be asked to sign the custody record to acknowledge receipt of these notices. Any refusal must be recorded on the custody record.

3.3     A citizen of an independent Commonwealth country or a national of a foreign country, including the Republic of Ireland, must be informed as soon as practicable about their rights of communication with their High Commission, Embassy or Consulate. See *section 7*

3.4     The custody officer shall:

   •      record the offence(s) that the detainee has been arrested for and the reason(s) for the arrest on the custody record. See *paragraph 10.3* and *Code G paragraphs 2.2* and *4.3*.

   •      note on the custody record any comment the detainee makes in relation to the arresting officer's account but shall not invite comment. If the arresting officer is not physically present when the detainee is brought to a police station, the arresting officer's account must be made available to the custody officer remotely or by a third party on the arresting officer's behalf. If the custody officer authorises a person's detention the detainee must be informed of the grounds as soon as practicable and before they are questioned about any offence;

- note any comment the detainee makes in respect of the decision to detain them but shall not invite comment;

- not put specific questions to the detainee regarding their involvement in any offence, nor in respect of any comments they may make in response to the arresting officer's account or the decision to place them in detention. Such an exchange is likely to constitute an interview as in *paragraph 11.1A* and require the associated safeguards in *section 11*.

See *paragraph 11.13* in respect of unsolicited comments.

3.5    The custody officer shall:

(a)    ask the detainee, whether at this time, they:

  (i)    would like legal advice, see *paragraph 6.5*;

  (iii)    want someone informed of their detention, see *section 5*;

(b)    ask the detainee to sign the custody record to confirm their decisions in respect of (a);

(c)    determine whether the detainee:

  (iii)    is, or might be, in need of medical treatment or attention, see *section 9*;

  (iv)    requires:

    - an appropriate adult;

    - help to check documentation;

    - an interpreter;

(d)    record the decision in respect of (c).

3.6    When determining these needs the custody officer is responsible for initiating an assessment to consider whether the detainee is likely to present specific risks to custody staff or themselves. Such assessments should always include a check on the Police National Computer, to be carried out as soon as practicable, to identify any risks highlighted in relation to the detainee. Although such assessments are primarily the custody officer's responsibility, it may be necessary for them to consult and involve others, e.g. the arresting officer or an appropriate health care professional, see *paragraph 9.13*. Reasons for delaying the initiation or completion of the assessment must be recorded.

3.7    Chief Officers should ensure that arrangements for proper and effective risk assessments required by *paragraph 3.6* are implemented in respect of all detainees at police stations in their area.

3.8    Risk assessments must follow a structured process which clearly defines the categories of risk to be considered and the results must be incorporated in the detainee's custody record. The custody officer is responsible for making sure those responsible for the detainee's custody are appropriately briefed about the risks. If no specific risks are identified by the assessment, that should be noted in the custody record. See *Note 3E* and *paragraph 9.14*

3.9    The custody officer is responsible for implementing the response to any specific risk assessment, e.g.:

- reducing opportunities for self harm;

- calling a health care professional;

- increasing levels of monitoring or observation.

3.10   Risk assessment is an ongoing process and assessments must always be subject to review if circumstances change.

3.11   If video cameras are installed in the custody area, notices shall be prominently displayed showing cameras are in use. Any request to have video cameras switched off shall be refused.

**(b)    Detained persons – special groups**

3.12   If the detainee appears deaf or there is doubt about their hearing or speaking ability or ability to understand English, and the custody officer cannot establish effective communication, the custody officer must, as soon as practicable, call an interpreter for assistance in the action under *paragraphs 3.1–3.5*. See *section 13*

3.13   If the detainee is a juvenile, the custody officer must, if it is practicable, ascertain the identity of a person responsible for their welfare. That person:

- may be:

    – the parent or guardian;

–    if the juvenile is in local authority or voluntary organisation care, or is otherwise being looked after under the Children Act 1989, a person appointed by that authority or organisation to have responsibility for the juvenile's welfare;

–    any other person who has, for the time being, assumed responsibility for the juvenile's welfare.

•    must be informed as soon as practicable that the juvenile has been arrested, why they have been arrested and where they are detained. This right is in addition to the juvenile's right in *section 5* not to be held incommunicado. See *Note 3C*

3.14  If a juvenile is known to be subject to a court order under which a person or organisation is given any degree of statutory responsibility to supervise or otherwise monitor them, reasonable steps must also be taken to notify that person or organisation (the 'responsible officer'). The responsible officer will normally be a member of a Youth Offending Team, except for a curfew order which involves electronic monitoring when the contractor providing the monitoring will normally be the responsible officer.

3.15  If the detainee is a juvenile, mentally disordered or otherwise mentally vulnerable, the custody officer must, as soon as practicable:

•    inform the appropriate adult, who in the case of a juvenile may or may not be a person responsible for their welfare, as in *paragraph 3.13*, of:

–    the grounds for their detention;

–    their whereabouts.

•    ask the adult to come to the police station to see the detainee.

3.16  It is imperative that a mentally disordered or otherwise mentally vulnerable person, detained under the Mental Health Act 1983, section 136, be assessed as soon as possible. If that assessment is to take place at the police station, an approved social worker and a registered medical practitioner shall be called to the station as soon as possible in order to interview and examine the detainee. Once the detainee has been interviewed, examined and suitable arrangements made for their treatment or care, they can no longer be detained under section 136. A detainee must be immediately discharged from detention under section 136 if a registered medical practitioner, having examined them, concludes they are not mentally disordered within the meaning of the Act.

3.17 If the appropriate adult is:

- already at the police station, the provisions of *paragraphs 3.1* to *3.5* must be complied with in the appropriate adult's presence;

- not at the station when these provisions are complied with, they must be complied with again in the presence of the appropriate adult when they arrive.

3.18 The detainee shall be advised that:

- the duties of the appropriate adult include giving advice and assistance;

- they can consult privately with the appropriate adult at any time.

3.19 If the detainee, or appropriate adult on the detainee's behalf, asks for a solicitor to be called to give legal advice, the provisions of *section 6* apply.

3.20 If the detainee is blind, seriously visually impaired or unable to read, the custody officer shall make sure their solicitor, relative, appropriate adult or some other person likely to take an interest in them and not involved in the investigation is available to help check any documentation. When this Code requires written consent or signing the person assisting may be asked to sign instead, if the detainee prefers. This paragraph does not require an appropriate adult to be called solely to assist in checking and signing documentation for a person who is not a juvenile, or mentally disordered or otherwise mentally vulnerable (see *paragraph 3.15*).

**(c)** **Persons attending a police station voluntarily**

3.21 Anybody attending a police station voluntarily to assist with an investigation may leave at will unless arrested. See *Note 1K*. If it is decided they shall not be allowed to leave, they must be informed at once that they are under arrest and brought before the custody officer, who is responsible for making sure they are notified of their rights in the same way as other detainees. If they are not arrested but are cautioned as in *section 10*, the person who gives the caution must, at the same time, inform them they are not under arrest, they are not obliged to remain at the station but if they remain at the station they may obtain free and independent legal advice if they want. They shall be told the right to legal advice includes the right to speak with a solicitor on the telephone and be asked if they want to do so.

3.22 If a person attending the police station voluntarily asks about their entitlement to legal advice, they shall be given a copy of the notice explaining the arrangements for obtaining legal advice. See *paragraph 3.2*

### (d)   Documentation

3.23   The grounds for a person's detention shall be recorded, in the person's presence if practicable.

3.24   Action taken under *paragraphs 3.12* to *3.20* shall be recorded.

### (e)   Persons answering street bail

3.25   When a person is answering street bail, the custody officer should link any documentation held in relation to arrest with the custody record. Any further action shall be recorded on the custody record in accordance with paragraphs 3.23 and 3.24 above.

### Notes for guidance

3A   *The notice of entitlements should:*

- *list the entitlements in this Code, including:*

    - *visits and contact with outside parties, including special provisions for Commonwealth citizens and foreign nationals;*

    - *reasonable standards of physical comfort;*

    - *adequate food and drink;*

    - *access to toilets and washing facilities, clothing, medical attention, and exercise when practicable.*

- *mention the:*

    - *provisions relating to the conduct of interviews;*

    - *circumstances in which an appropriate adult should be available to assist the detainee and their statutory rights to make representation whenever the period of their detention is reviewed.*

3B   *In addition to notices in English, translations should be available in Welsh, the main minority ethnic languages and the principal European languages, whenever they are likely to be helpful. Audio versions of the notice should also be made available.*

3C   *If the juvenile is in local authority or voluntary organisation care but living with their parents or other adults responsible for their welfare, although there is no legal obligation to inform them, they should normally be contacted, as well as the authority or organisation unless suspected of involvement in the offence concerned. Even if the juvenile is not living with their parents, consideration should be given to informing them.*

3D     *The right to consult the Codes of Practice does not entitle the person concerned to delay unreasonably any necessary investigative or administrative action whilst they do so. Examples of action which need not be delayed unreasonably include:*

- *procedures requiring the provision of breath, blood or urine specimens under the Road Traffic Act 1988 or the Transport and Works Act 1992;*

- *searching detainees at the police station;*

- *taking fingerprints, footwear impressions or non-intimate samples without consent for evidential purposes.*

3E     *Home Office Circular 32/2000 provides more detailed guidance on risk assessments and identifies key risk areas which should always be considered.*

**4**     **Detainee's property**

*(a)*     *Action*

4.1     The custody officer is responsible for:

    (a)     ascertaining what property a detainee:

       (i)     has with them when they come to the police station, whether on:

- arrest or re-detention on answering to bail;

- commitment to prison custody on the order or sentence of a court;

- lodgement at the police station with a view to their production in court from prison custody;

- transfer from detention at another station or hospital;

- detention under the Mental Health Act 1983, section 135 or 136;

- remand into police custody on the authority of a court

       (ii)     might have acquired for an unlawful or harmful purpose while in custody;

    (b)     the safekeeping of any property taken from a detainee which remains at the police station.

The custody officer may search the detainee or authorise their being searched to the extent they consider necessary, provided a search of intimate parts of the body or involving the removal of more than outer clothing is only made as in *Annex A*. A search may only be carried out by an officer of the same sex as the detainee. See *Note 4A*

4.2   Detainees may retain clothing and personal effects at their own risk unless the custody officer considers they may use them to cause harm to themselves or others, interfere with evidence, damage property, effect an escape or they are needed as evidence. In this event the custody officer may withhold such articles as they consider necessary and must tell the detainee why.

4.3   Personal effects are those items a detainee may lawfully need, use or refer to while in detention but do not include cash and other items of value.

**(b)   Documentation**

4.4   It is a matter for the custody officer to determine whether a record should be made of the property a detained person has with him or had taken from him on arrest. Any record made is not required to be kept as part of the custody record but the custody record should be noted as to where such a record exists. Whenever a record is made the detainee shall be allowed to check and sign the record of property as correct. Any refusal to sign shall be recorded.

4.5   If a detainee is not allowed to keep any article of clothing or personal effects, the reason must be recorded.

**Notes for guidance**

4A   *PACE, Section 54(1) and paragraph 4.1 require a detainee to be searched when it is clear the custody officer will have continuing duties in relation to that detainee or when that detainee's behaviour or offence makes an inventory appropriate. They do not require every detainee to be searched, e.g. if it is clear a person will only be detained for a short period and is not to be placed in a cell, the custody officer may decide not to search them. In such a case the custody record will be endorsed 'not searched', paragraph 4.4 will not apply, and the detainee will be invited to sign the entry. If the detainee refuses, the custody officer will be obliged to ascertain what property they have in accordance with paragraph 4.1.*

4B   *Paragraph 4.4 does not require the custody officer to record on the custody record property in the detainee's possession on arrest if, by virtue of its nature, quantity or size, it is not practicable to remove it to the police station.*

4C   *Paragraph 4.4 does not require items of clothing worn by the person be recorded unless withheld by the custody officer as in paragraph 4.2.*

## 5 Right not to be held incommunicado

### (a) Action

5.1 Any person arrested and held in custody at a police station or other premises may, on request, have one person known to them or likely to take an interest in their welfare informed at public expense of their whereabouts as soon as practicable. If the person cannot be contacted the detainee may choose up to two alternatives. If they cannot be contacted, the person in charge of detention or the investigation has discretion to allow further attempts until the information has been conveyed. See *Notes 5C* and *5D*

5.2 The exercise of the above right in respect of each person nominated may be delayed only in accordance with *Annex B.*

5.3 The above right may be exercised each time a detainee is taken to another police station.

5.4 The detainee may receive visits at the custody officer's discretion. See *Note 5B*

5.5 If a friend, relative or person with an interest in the detainee's welfare enquires about their whereabouts, this information shall be given if the suspect agrees and *Annex B* does not apply. See *Note 5D*

5.6 The detainee shall be given writing materials, on request, and allowed to telephone one person for a reasonable time, see *Notes 5A* and *5E*. Either or both these privileges may be denied or delayed if an officer of inspector rank or above considers sending a letter or making a telephone call may result in any of the consequences in:

    (a) *Annex B paragraphs 1* and *2* and the person is detained in connection with an indictable offence;

    (b) *Not used*

Nothing in this paragraph permits the restriction or denial of the rights in *paragraphs 5.1* and *6.1.*

5.7 Before any letter or message is sent, or telephone call made, the detainee shall be informed that what they say in any letter, call or message (other than in a communication to a solicitor) may be read or listened to and may be given in evidence. A telephone call may be terminated if it is being abused. The costs can be at public expense at the custody officer's discretion.

5.7A Any delay or denial of the rights in this section should be proportionate and should last no longer than necessary.

**(b)   Documentation**

5.8   A record must be kept of any:

   (a)   request made under this section and the action taken;

   (b)   letters, messages or telephone calls made or received or visit received;

   (c)   refusal by the detainee to have information about them given to an outside enquirer. The detainee must be asked to countersign the record accordingly and any refusal recorded.

**Notes for guidance**

5A   *A person may request an interpreter to interpret a telephone call or translate a letter.*

5B   *At the custody officer's discretion, visits should be allowed when possible, subject to having sufficient personnel to supervise a visit and any possible hindrance to the investigation.*

5C   *If the detainee does not know anyone to contact for advice or support or cannot contact a friend or relative, the custody officer should bear in mind any local voluntary bodies or other organisations who might be able to help. Paragraph 6.1 applies if legal advice is required.*

5D   *In some circumstances it may not be appropriate to use the telephone to disclose information under paragraphs 5.1 and 5.5.*

5E   *The telephone call at paragraph 5.6 is in addition to any communication under paragraphs 5.1 and 6.1.*

**6   Right to legal advice**

**(a)   Action**

6.1   Unless *Annex B* applies, all detainees must be informed that they may at any time consult and communicate privately with a solicitor, whether in person, in writing or by telephone, and that free independent legal advice is available. See *paragraph 3.1, Note 6B, 6B1, 6B2* and *Note 6J*

6.2   Not Used

6.3   A poster advertising the right to legal advice must be prominently displayed in the charging area of every police station. See *Note 6H*

6.4     No police officer should, at any time, do or say anything with the intention of dissuading a detainee from obtaining legal advice.

6.5     The exercise of the right of access to legal advice may be delayed only as in *Annex B*. Whenever legal advice is requested, and unless *Annex B* applies, the custody officer must act without delay to secure the provision of such advice. If, on being informed or reminded of this right, the detainee declines to speak to a solicitor in person, the officer should point out that the right includes the right to speak with a solicitor on the telephone. If the detainee continues to waive this right the officer should ask them why and any reasons should be recorded on the custody record or the interview record as appropriate. Reminders of the right to legal advice must be given as in *paragraphs 3.5, 11.2, 15.4, 16.4, 2B of Annex A, 3 of Annex K* and *16.5* and Code D, *paragraphs 3.17(ii)* and *6.3*. Once it is clear a detainee does not want to speak to a solicitor in person or by telephone they should cease to be asked their reasons. See *Note 6K*

6.5A    In the case of a juvenile, an appropriate adult should consider whether legal advice from a solicitor is required. If the juvenile indicates that they do not want legal advice, the appropriate adult has the right to ask for a solicitor to attend if this would be in the best interests of the person. However, the detained person cannot be forced to see the solicitor if he is adamant that he does not wish to do so.

6.6     A detainee who wants legal advice may not be interviewed or continue to be interviewed until they have received such advice unless:

    (a)     *Annex B* applies, when the restriction on drawing adverse inferences from silence in *Annex C* will apply because the detainee is not allowed an opportunity to consult a solicitor; or

    (b)     an officer of superintendent rank or above has reasonable grounds for believing that:

        (i)     the consequent delay might:

- lead to interference with, or harm to, evidence connected with an offence;

- lead to interference with, or physical harm to, other people;

- lead to serious loss of, or damage to, property;

- lead to alerting other people suspected of having committed an offence but not yet arrested for it;

- hinder the recovery of property obtained in consequence of the commission of an offence.

(ii)    when a solicitor, including a duty solicitor, has been contacted and has agreed to attend, awaiting their arrival would cause unreasonable delay to the process of investigation.

Note: In these cases the restriction on drawing adverse inferences from silence in *Annex C* will apply because the detainee is not allowed an opportunity to consult a solicitor.

(c)    the solicitor the detainee has nominated or selected from a list:

(i)    cannot be contacted;

(ii)    has previously indicated they do not wish to be contacted; or

(iii)    having been contacted, has declined to attend; and

the detainee has been advised of the Duty Solicitor Scheme but has declined to ask for the duty solicitor.

In these circumstances the interview may be started or continued without further delay provided an officer of inspector rank or above has agreed to the interview proceeding.

Note: The restriction on drawing adverse inferences from silence in Annex C will not apply because the detainee is allowed an opportunity to consult the duty solicitor;

(d)    the detainee changes their mind, about wanting legal advice.

In these circumstances the interview may be started or continued without delay provided that:

(i)    the detainee agrees to do so , in writing or on the interview record made in accordance with Code E or F; and

(ii)    an officer of inspector rank or above has inquired about the detainee's reasons for their change of mind and gives authority for the interview to proceed.

Confirmation of the detainee's agreement, their change of mind, the reasons for it if given and, subject to *paragraph 2.6A,* the name of the authorising officer shall be recorded in the written interview record or the interview record made in accordance with Code E or F. See *Note 6I.* Note: In these circumstances the restriction on drawing adverse inferences from silence in *Annex C* will not apply because the detainee is allowed an opportunity to consult a solicitor if they wish.

6.7    If *paragraph 6.6(b)(i)* applies, once sufficient information has been obtained to avert the risk, questioning must cease until the detainee has received legal advice unless *paragraph 6.6(a), (b)(ii), (c)* or *(d)* applies.

6.8    A detainee who has been permitted to consult a solicitor shall be entitled on request to have the solicitor present when they are interviewed unless one of the exceptions in *paragraph 6.6* applies.

6.9    The solicitor may only be required to leave the interview if their conduct is such that the interviewer is unable properly to put questions to the suspect. See *Notes 6D and 6E*

6.10   If the interviewer considers a solicitor is acting in such a way, they will stop the interview and consult an officer not below superintendent rank, if one is readily available, and otherwise an officer not below inspector rank not connected with the investigation. After speaking to the solicitor, the officer consulted will decide if the interview should continue in the presence of that solicitor. If they decide it should not, the suspect will be given the opportunity to consult another solicitor before the interview continues and that solicitor given an opportunity to be present at the interview. See *Note 6E*

6.11   The removal of a solicitor from an interview is a serious step and, if it occurs, the officer of superintendent rank or above who took the decision will consider if the incident should be reported to the Law Society. If the decision to remove the solicitor has been taken by an officer below superintendent rank, the facts must be reported to an officer of superintendent rank or above who will similarly consider whether a report to the Law Society would be appropriate. When the solicitor concerned is a duty solicitor, the report should be both to the Law Society and to the Legal Services Commission.

6.12   'Solicitor' in this Code means:

-   a solicitor who holds a current practising certificate

-   an accredited or probationary representative included on the register of representatives maintained by the Legal Services Commission.

6.12A  An accredited or probationary representative sent to provide advice by, and on behalf of, a solicitor shall be admitted to the police station for this purpose unless an officer of inspector rank or above considers such a visit will hinder the investigation and directs otherwise. Hindering the investigation does not include giving proper legal advice to a detainee as in *Note 6D*. Once admitted to the police station, *paragraphs 6.6 to 6.10* apply.

6.13  In exercising their discretion under *paragraph 6.12A*, the officer should take into account in particular:

- whether:

    –   the identity and status of an accredited or probationary representative have been satisfactorily established;

    –   they are of suitable character to provide legal advice, e.g. a person with a criminal record is unlikely to be suitable unless the conviction was for a minor offence and not recent.

- any other matters in any written letter of authorisation provided by the solicitor on whose behalf the person is attending the police station. See *Note 6F*

6.14  If the inspector refuses access to an accredited or probationary representative or a decision is taken that such a person should not be permitted to remain at an interview, the inspector must notify the solicitor on whose behalf the representative was acting and give them an opportunity to make alternative arrangements. The detainee must be informed and the custody record noted.

6.15  If a solicitor arrives at the station to see a particular person, that person must, unless *Annex B* applies, be so informed whether or not they are being interviewed and asked if they would like to see the solicitor. This applies even if the detainee has declined legal advice or, having requested it, subsequently agreed to be interviewed without receiving advice. The solicitor's attendance and the detainee's decision must be noted in the custody record.

### (b)    Documentation

6.16  Any request for legal advice and the action taken shall be recorded.

6.17  A record shall be made in the interview record if a detainee asks for legal advice and an interview is begun either in the absence of a solicitor or their representative, or they have been required to leave an interview.

### Notes for guidance

6A    *In considering if paragraph 6.6(b) applies, the officer should, if practicable, ask the solicitor for an estimate of how long it will take to come to the station and relate this to the time detention is permitted, the time of day (i.e. whether the rest period under paragraph 12.2 is imminent) and the requirements of other investigations. If the solicitor is on their way or is to set off immediately, it will not normally be appropriate to begin an interview before they arrive. If it appears necessary to begin an interview before the* solicitor's arrival, they should be given an indication of how long the police would be able to wait before 6.6(b) applies so there is an opportunity to make arrangements for someone else to provide legal advice.

6B    A detainee who asks for legal advice should be given an opportunity to consult a specific solicitor or another solicitor from that solicitor's firm or the duty solicitor. If advice is not available by these means, or they do not want to consult the duty solicitor, the detainee should be given an opportunity to choose a solicitor from a list of those willing to provide legal advice. If this solicitor is unavailable, they may choose up to two alternatives. If these attempts are unsuccessful, the custody officer has discretion to allow further attempts until a solicitor has been contacted and agrees to provide legal advice. Apart from carrying out these duties, an officer must not advise the suspect about any particular firm of solicitors. See Notes for Guidance 6B1 and 6B2 below.

6B1   **With effect from 1 February 2008**, Note for Guidance 6B above will cease to apply in the following forces areas:

Greater Manchester Police
West Midlands Police
West Yorkshire Police

and the following provisions will apply to those force areas:  a detainee who asks for legal advice to be paid for by himself should be given an opportunity to consult a specific solicitor or another solicitor from that solicitor's firm. If this solicitor is unavailable by these means, they may choose up to two alternatives. If these attempts are unsuccessful, the custody officer has discretion to allow further attempts until a solicitor has been contacted and agrees to provide legal advice. Otherwise, publicly funded legal advice shall in the first instance be accessed by telephoning a call centre authorised by the Legal Services Commission (LSC) to deal with calls from the police station. The Defence Solicitor Call Centre will determine whether legal advice should be limited to telephone advice or whether a solicitor should attend. Legal advice will be by telephone if a detainee is:

- detained for a non-imprisonable offence,

- arrested on a bench warrant for failing to appear and being held for production before the court (except where the solicitor has clear documentary evidence available that would result in the client being released from custody),

- arrested on suspicion of driving with excess alcohol (failure to provide a specimen, driving whilst unfit/drunk in charge of a motor vehicle), or

- detained in relation to breach of police or court bail conditions.

*An attendance by a solicitor for an offence suitable for telephone advice will depend on whether limited exceptions apply, such as:*

- *whether the police are going to carry out an interview or an identification parade,*

- *whether the detainee is eligible for assistance from an appropriate adult,*

- *whether the detainee is unable to communicate over the telephone,*

- *whether the detainee alleges serious maltreatment by the police.*

*Apart from carrying out these duties, an officer must not advise the suspect about any particular firm of solicitors. See Note for Guidance 6B2 below.*

6B2    **With effect from 21 April 2008**, *the contents of Notes for Guidance 6B and 6B1 above will be superseded by this paragraph in all police forces areas in England and Wales by the following. A detainee who asks for legal advice to be paid for by himself should be given an opportunity to consult a specific solicitor or another solicitor from that solicitor's firm. If this solicitor is unavailable by these means, they may choose up to two alternatives. If these attempts are unsuccessful, the custody officer has discretion to allow further attempts until a solicitor has been contacted and agrees to provide legal advice. Otherwise, publicly funded legal advice shall in the first instance be accessed by telephoning a call centre authorised by the Legal Services Commission (LSC) to deal with calls from the police station. The Defence Solicitor Call Centre will determine whether legal advice should be limited to telephone advice or whether a solicitor should attend. Legal advice will be by telephone if a detainee is:*

- *detained for a non-imprisonable offence,*

- *arrested on a bench warrant for failing to appear and being held for production before the court (except where the solicitor has clear documentary evidence available that would result in the client being released from custody),*

- *arrested on suspicion of driving with excess alcohol (failure to provide a specimen, driving whilst unfit/drunk in charge of a motor vehicle), or*

- *detained in relation to breach of police or court bail conditions.*

*An attendance by a solicitor for an offence suitable for telephone advice will depend on whether limited exceptions apply, such as:*

- *whether the police are going to carry out an interview or an identification parade,*

- *whether the detainee is eligible for assistance from an appropriate adult,*

- *whether the detainee is unable to communicate over the telephone,*

- *whether the detainee alleges serious maltreatment by the police.*

*Apart from carrying out these duties, an officer must not advise the suspect about any particular firm of solicitors.*

6C *Not Used*

6D *A detainee has a right to free legal advice and to be represented by a solicitor. Legal advice by telephone advice may be provided in respect of those offences listed in Note for Guidance 6B1 and 6B2 above. The Defence Solicitor Call Centre will determine whether attendance is required by a solicitor. The solicitor's only role in the police station is to protect and advance the legal rights of their client. On occasions this may require the solicitor to give advice which has t he effect of the client avoiding giving evidence which strengthens a prosecution case. The solicitor may intervene in order to seek clarification, challenge an improper question to their client or the manner in which it is put, advise their client not to reply to particular questions, or if they wish to give their client further legal advice. Paragraph 6.9 only applies if the solicitor's approach or conduct prevents or unreasonably obstructs proper questions being put to the suspect or the suspect's response being recorded. Examples of unacceptable conduct include answering questions on a suspect's behalf or providing written replies for the suspect to quote.*

6E *An officer who takes the decision to exclude a solicitor must be in a position to satisfy the court the decision was properly made. In order to do this they may need to witness what is happening.*

6F *If an officer of at least inspector rank considers a particular solicitor or firm of solicitors is persistently sending probationary representatives who are unsuited to provide legal advice, they should inform an officer of at least superintendent rank, who may wish to take the matter up with the Law Society.*

6G *Subject to the constraints of Annex B, a solicitor may advise more than one client in an investigation if they wish. Any question of a conflict of interest is for the solicitor under their professional code of conduct. If, however, waiting for a solicitor to give advice to one client may lead to unreasonable delay to the interview with another, the provisions of paragraph 6.6(b) may apply.*

6H *In addition to a poster in English, a poster or posters containing translations into Welsh, the main minority ethnic languages and the principal European languages should be displayed wherever they are likely to be helpful and it is practicable to do so.*

6I *Paragraph 6.6(d) requires the authorisation of an officer of inspector rank or above to the continuation of an interview when a detainee who wanted legal advice changes their mind. It is permissible for such authorisation to be given over the telephone, if the*

C

*authorising officer is able to satisfy themselves about the reason for the detainee's change of mind and is satisfied it is proper to continue the interview in those circumstances.*

6J    *Whenever a detainee exercises their right to legal advice by consulting or communicating with a solicitor, they must be allowed to do so in private. This right to consult or communicate in private is fundamental. If the requirement for privacy is compromised because what is said or written by the detainee or solicitor for the purpose of giving and receiving legal advice is overheard, listened to, or read by others without the informed consent of the detainee, the right will effectively have been denied. When a detainee chooses to speak to a solicitor on the telephone, they should be allowed to do so in private unless this is impractical because of the design and layout of the custody area or the location of telephones. However, the normal expectation should be that facilities will be available, unless they are being used, at all police stations to enable detainees to speak in private to a solicitor either face to face or over the telephone.*

6K    *A detainee is not obliged to give reasons for declining legal advice and should not be pressed to do so.*

## 7    Citizens of independent Commonwealth countries or foreign nationals

### (a)    *Action*

7.1    Any citizen of an independent Commonwealth country or a national of a foreign country, including the Republic of Ireland, may communicate at any time with the appropriate High Commission, Embassy or Consulate. The detainee must be informed as soon as practicable of:

- this right;

- their right, upon request, to have their High Commission, Embassy or Consulate told of their whereabouts and the grounds for their detention. Such a request should be acted upon as soon as practicable.

7.2    If a detainee is a citizen of a country with which a bilateral consular convention or agreement is in force requiring notification of arrest, the appropriate High Commission, Embassy or Consulate shall be informed as soon as practicable, subject to *paragraph 7.4*. The countries to which this applies as at 1 April 2003 are listed in *Annex F*.

7.3    Consular officers may visit one of their nationals in police detention to talk to them and, if required, to arrange for legal advice. Such visits shall take place out of the hearing of a police officer.

7.4    Notwithstanding the provisions of consular conventions, if the detainee is a political refugee whether for reasons of race, nationality, political opinion or religion, or is seeking political asylum, consular officers shall not be informed of the arrest of one of their nationals or given access or information about them except at the detainee's express request.

**(b)  Documentation**

7.5   A record shall be made when a detainee is informed of their rights under this section and of any communications with a High Commission, Embassy or Consulate.

**Note for guidance**

7A    *The exercise of the rights in this section may not be interfered with even though Annex B applies.*

**8    Conditions of detention**

**(a)  Action**

8.1   So far as it is practicable, not more than one detainee should be detained in each cell.

8.2   Cells in use must be adequately heated, cleaned and ventilated. They must be adequately lit, subject to such dimming as is compatible with safety and security to allow people detained overnight to sleep. No additional restraints shall be used within a locked cell unless absolutely necessary and then only restraint equipment, approved for use in that force by the Chief Officer, which is reasonable and necessary in the circumstances having regard to the detainee's demeanour and with a view to ensuring their safety and the safety of others. If a detainee is deaf, mentally disordered or otherwise mentally vulnerable, particular care must be taken when deciding whether to use any form of approved restraints.

8.3   Blankets, mattresses, pillows and other bedding supplied shall be of a reasonable standard and in a clean and sanitary condition. See *Note 8A*

8.4   Access to toilet and washing facilities must be provided.

8.5   If it is necessary to remove a detainee's clothes for the purposes of investigation, for hygiene, health reasons or cleaning, replacement clothing of a reasonable standard of comfort and cleanliness shall be provided. A detainee may not be interviewed unless adequate clothing has been offered.

8.6   At least two light meals and one main meal should be offered in any 24 hour period. See *Note 8B*. Drinks should be provided at meal times and upon reasonable request between meals. Whenever necessary, advice shall be sought from the appropriate health care professional, see *Note 9A,* on medical and dietary matters. As far as practicable, meals provided shall offer a varied diet and meet any specific dietary needs or religious beliefs the detainee may have. The detainee may, at the custody officer's discretion, have meals supplied by their family or friends at their expense. See *Note 8A*

8.7   Brief outdoor exercise shall be offered daily if practicable.

8.8   A juvenile shall not be placed in a police cell unless no other secure accommodation is available and the custody officer considers it is not practicable to supervise them if they are not placed in a cell or that a cell provides more comfortable accommodation than other secure accommodation in the station. A juvenile may not be placed in a cell with a detained adult.

### (b)   Documentation

8.9   A record must be kept of replacement clothing and meals offered.

8.10   If a juvenile is placed in a cell, the reason must be recorded.

8.11   The use of any restraints on a detainee whilst in a cell, the reasons for it and, if appropriate, the arrangements for enhanced supervision of the detainee whilst so restrained, shall be recorded. See *paragraph 3.9*

### Notes for guidance

8A   *The provisions in paragraph 8.3 and 8.6 respectively are of particular importance in the case of a person likely to be detained for an extended period. In deciding whether to allow meals to be supplied by family or friends, the custody officer is entitled to take account of the risk of items being concealed in any food or package and the officer's duties and responsibilities under food handling legislation.*

8B   *Meals should, so far as practicable, be offered at recognised meal times, or at other times that take account of when the detainee last had a meal.*

### 9   Care and treatment of detained persons

### (a)   General

9.1   Nothing in this section prevents the police from calling the police surgeon or, if appropriate, some other health care professional, to examine a detainee for the purposes of obtaining evidence relating to any offence in which the detainee is suspected of being involved. See *Note 9A*

9.2   If a complaint is made by, or on behalf of, a detainee about their treatment since their arrest, or it comes to notice that a detainee may have been treated improperly, a report must be made as soon as practicable to an officer of inspector rank or above not connected with the investigation. If the matter concerns a possible assault or the possibility of the unnecessary or unreasonable use of force, an appropriate health care professional must also be called as soon as practicable.

9.3    Detainees should be visited at least every hour. If no reasonably foreseeable risk was identified in a risk assessment, see *paragraphs 3.6 – 3.10*, there is no need to wake a sleeping detainee. Those suspected of being intoxicated through drink or drugs or having swallowed drugs, see *Note 9CA*, or whose level of consciousness causes concern must, subject to any clinical directions given by the appropriate health care professional, see *paragraph 9.13*:

- be visited and roused at least every half hour

- have their condition assessed as in *Annex H*

- and clinical treatment arranged if appropriate

See *Notes 9B, 9C* and *9H*

9.4    When arrangements are made to secure clinical attention for a detainee, the custody officer must make sure all relevant information which might assist in the treatment of the detainee's condition is made available to the responsible health care professional. This applies whether or not the health care professional asks for such information. Any officer or police staff with relevant information must inform the custody officer as soon as practicable.

**(b)    *Clinical treatment and attention***

9.5    The custody officer must make sure a detainee receives appropriate clinical attention as soon as reasonably practicable if the person:

(a)    appears to be suffering from physical illness; or

(b)    is injured; or

(c)    appears to be suffering from a mental disorder; or

(d)    appears to need clinical attention

9.5A   This applies even if the detainee makes no request for clinical attention and whether or not they have already received clinical attention elsewhere. If the need for attention appears urgent, e.g. when indicated as in *Annex H*, the nearest available health care professional or an ambulance must be called immediately.

9.5B   The custody officer must also consider the need for clinical attention as set out in Note for Guidance 9C in relation to those suffering the effects of alcohol or drugs.

9.6    *Paragraph 9.5* is not meant to prevent or delay the transfer to a hospital if necessary of a person detained under the Mental Health Act 1983, section 136. See *Note 9D*. When an assessment under that Act takes place at a police station, see *paragraph 3.16*, the custody officer must consider whether an appropriate health care professional should be called to conduct an initial clinical check on the detainee. This applies particularly when there is likely to be any significant delay in the arrival of a suitably qualified medical practitioner.

9.7    If it appears to the custody officer, or they are told, that a person brought to a station under arrest may be suffering from an infectious disease or condition, the custody officer must take reasonable steps to safeguard the health of the detainee and others at the station. In deciding what action to take, advice must be sought from an appropriate health care professional. See *Note 9E*. The custody officer has discretion to isolate the person and their property until clinical directions have been obtained.

9.8    If a detainee requests a clinical examination, an appropriate health care professional must be called as soon as practicable to assess the detainee's clinical needs. If a safe and appropriate care plan cannot be provided, the police surgeon's advice must be sought. The detainee may also be examined by a medical practitioner of their choice at their expense.

9.9    If a detainee is required to take or apply any medication in compliance with clinical directions prescribed before their detention, the custody officer must consult the appropriate health care professional before the use of the medication. Subject to the restrictions in *paragraph 9.10,* the custody officer is responsible for the safekeeping of any medication and for making sure the detainee is given the opportunity to take or apply prescribed or approved medication. Any such consultation and its outcome shall be noted in the custody record.

9.10   No police officer may administer or supervise the self-administration of medically prescribed controlled drugs of the types and forms listed in the Misuse of Drugs Regulations 2001, Schedule 2 or 3. A detainee may only self-administer such drugs under the personal supervision of the registered medical practitioner authorising their use. Drugs listed in Schedule 4 or 5 may be distributed by the custody officer for self-administration if they have consulted the registered medical practitioner authorising their use, this may be done by telephone, and both parties are satisfied self-administration will not expose the detainee, police officers or anyone else to the risk of harm or injury.

9.11 When appropriate health care professionals administer drugs or other medications, or supervise their self-administration, it must be within current medicines legislation and the scope of practice as determined by their relevant professional body.

9.12 If a detainee has in their possession, or claims to need, medication relating to a heart condition, diabetes, epilepsy or a condition of comparable potential seriousness then, even though *paragraph 9.5* may not apply, the advice of the appropriate health care professional must be obtained.

9.13 Whenever the appropriate health care professional is called in accordance with this section to examine or treat a detainee, the custody officer shall ask for their opinion about:

- any risks or problems which police need to take into account when making decisions about the detainee's continued detention;

- when to carry out an interview if applicable; and

- the need for safeguards.

9.14 When clinical directions are given by the appropriate health care professional, whether orally or in writing, and the custody officer has any doubts or is in any way uncertain about any aspect of the directions, the custody officer shall ask for clarification. It is particularly important that directions concerning the frequency of visits are clear, precise and capable of being implemented. See *Note 9F.*

## (c) Documentation

9.15 A record must be made in the custody record of:

(a) the arrangements made for an examination by an appropriate health care professional under *paragraph 9.2* and of any complaint reported under that paragraph together with any relevant remarks by the custody officer;

(b) any arrangements made in accordance with *paragraph 9.5*;

(c) any request for a clinical examination under *paragraph 9.8* and any arrangements made in response;

(d) the injury, ailment, condition or other reason which made it necessary to make the arrangements in (a) to (c), *see Note 9G*;

(e) any clinical directions and advice, including any further clarifications, given to police by a health care professional concerning the care and treatment of the detainee in connection with any of the arrangements made in (a) to (c), *see Note 9F*;

C

(f)    if applicable, the responses received when attempting to rouse a person using the procedure in *Annex H, see Note 9H.*

9.16  If a health care professional does not record their clinical findings in the custody record, the record must show where they are recorded. See *Note 9G.* However, information which is necessary to custody staff to ensure the effective ongoing care and well being of the detainee must be recorded openly in the custody record, see *paragraph 3.8* and *Annex G, paragraph 7.*

9.17  Subject to the requirements of *Section 4*, the custody record shall include:

- a record of all medication a detainee has in their possession on arrival at the police station;

- a note of any such medication they claim to need but do not have with them.

### Notes for guidance

9A    *A 'health care professional' means a clinically qualified person working within the scope of practice as determined by their relevant professional body. Whether a health care professional is 'appropriate' depends on the circumstances of the duties they carry out at the time.*

9B    *Whenever possible juveniles and mentally vulnerable detainees should be visited more frequently.*

9C    *A detainee who appears drunk or behaves abnormally may be suffering from illness, the effects of drugs or may have sustained injury, particularly a head injury which is not apparent. A detainee needing or dependent on certain drugs, including alcohol, may experience harmful effects within a short time of being deprived of their supply. In these circumstances, when there is any doubt, police should always act urgently to call an appropriate health care professional or an ambulance. Paragraph 9.5 does not apply to minor ailments or injuries which do not need attention. However, all such ailments or injuries must be recorded in the custody record and any doubt must be resolved in favour of calling the appropriate health care professional.*

9CA   *Paragraph 9.3 would apply to a person in police custody by order of a magistrates' court under the Criminal Justice Act 1988, section 152 (as amended by the Drugs Act 2005, section 8) to facilitate the recovery of evidence after being charged with drug possession or drug trafficking and suspected of having swallowed drugs. In the case of the healthcare needs of a person who has swallowed drugs, the custody officer subject to any clinical directions, should consider the necessity for rousing every half hour. This does not negate the need for regular visiting of the suspect in the cell.*

9D     *Whenever practicable, arrangements should be made for persons detained for assessment under the Mental Health Act 1983, section 136 to be taken to a hospital. There is no power under that Act to transfer a person detained under section 136 from one place of safety to another place of safety for assessment.*

9E     *It is important to respect a person's right to privacy and information about their health must be kept confidential and only disclosed with their consent or in accordance with clinical advice when it is necessary to protect the detainee's health or that of others who come into contact with them.*

9F     *The custody officer should always seek to clarify directions that the detainee requires constant observation or supervision and should ask the appropriate health care professional to explain precisely what action needs to be taken to implement such directions.*

**C**

9G     *Paragraphs 9.15 and 9.16 do not require any information about the cause of any injury, ailment or condition to be recorded on the custody record if it appears capable of providing evidence of an offence.*

9H     *The purpose of recording a person's responses when attempting to rouse them using the procedure in Annex H is to enable any change in the individual's consciousness level to be noted and clinical treatment arranged if appropriate.*

## 10    Cautions

### (a)    When a caution must be given

10.1   A person whom there are grounds to suspect of an offence, see *Note 10A*, must be cautioned before any questions about an offence, or further questions if the answers provide the grounds for suspicion, are put to them if either the suspect's answers or silence, (i.e. failure or refusal to answer or answer satisfactorily) may be given in evidence to a court in a prosecution. A person need not be cautioned if questions are for other necessary purposes, e.g.:

(a)    solely to establish their identity or ownership of any vehicle;

(b)    to obtain information in accordance with any relevant statutory requirement, see *paragraph 10.9*;

(c)    in furtherance of the proper and effective conduct of a search, e.g. to determine the need to search in the exercise of powers of stop and search or to seek co-operation while carrying out a search;

(d)    to seek verification of a written record as in *paragraph 11.13*;

(e)     Not used

10.2    Whenever a person not under arrest is initially cautioned, or reminded they are under caution, that person must at the same time be told they are not under arrest and are free to leave if they want to. See *Note 10C*

10.3    A person who is arrested, or further arrested, must be informed at the time, or as soon as practicable thereafter, that they are under arrest and the grounds for their arrest, see paragraph 3.4, *Note 10B* and *Code G, paragraphs 2.2 and 4.3.*.

10.4    As per *Code G, section 3*, a person who is arrested, or further arrested, must also be cautioned unless:

(a)     it is impracticable to do so by reason of their condition or behaviour at the time;

(b)     they have already been cautioned immediately prior to arrest as in *paragraph 10.1.*

## (b)     Terms of the cautions

10.5    The caution which must be given on:

(a)     arrest;

(b)     all other occasions before a person is charged or informed they may be prosecuted, see *section 16*,

should, unless the restriction on drawing adverse inferences from silence applies, see *Annex C*, be in the following terms:

"You do not have to say anything. But it may harm your defence if you do not mention when questioned something which you later rely on in Court. Anything you do say may be given in evidence."

Where the use of the Welsh Language is appropriate, a constable may provide the caution directly in Welsh in the following terms:

*"Does dim rhaid i chi ddweud dim byd. Ond gall niweidio eich amddiffyniad os na fyddwch chi'n sôn, wrth gael eich holi, am rywbeth y byddwch chi'n dibynnu arno nes ymlaen yn y Llys. Gall unrhyw beth yr ydych yn ei ddweud gael ei roi fel tystiolaeth."*

See *Note 10G*

10.6    *Annex C, paragraph 2* sets out the alternative terms of the caution to be used when the restriction on drawing adverse inferences from silence applies.

10.7 Minor deviations from the words of any caution given in accordance with this Code do not constitute a breach of this Code, provided the sense of the relevant caution is preserved. See *Note 10D*

10.8 After any break in questioning under caution, the person being questioned must be made aware they remain under caution. If there is any doubt the relevant caution should be given again in full when the interview resumes. See *Note 10E*

10.9 When, despite being cautioned, a person fails to co-operate or to answer particular questions which may affect their immediate treatment, the person should be informed of any relevant consequences and that those consequences are not affected by the caution. Examples are when a person's refusal to provide:

- their name and address when charged may make them liable to detention;

- particulars and information in accordance with a statutory requirement, e.g. under the Road Traffic Act 1988, may amount to an offence or may make the person liable to a further arrest.

**(c)  Special warnings under the Criminal Justice and Public Order Act 1994, sections 36 and 37**

10.10 When a suspect interviewed at a police station or authorised place of detention after arrest fails or refuses to answer certain questions, or to answer satisfactorily, after due warning, see *Note 10F*, a court or jury may draw such inferences as appear proper under the Criminal Justice and Public Order Act 1994, sections 36 and 37. Such inferences may only be drawn when:

(a) the restriction on drawing adverse inferences from silence, see *Annex C*, does not apply; and

(b) the suspect is arrested by a constable and fails or refuses to account for any objects, marks or substances, or marks on such objects found:

- on their person;

- in or on their clothing or footwear;

- otherwise in their possession; or

- in the place they were arrested;

(c) the arrested suspect was found by a constable at a place at or about the time the offence for which that officer has arrested them is alleged to have been committed, and the suspect fails or refuses to account for their presence there.

When the restriction on drawing adverse inferences from silence applies, the suspect may still be asked to account for any of the matters in (*b*) or (*c*) but the special warning described in *paragraph 10.11* will not apply and must not be given.

10.11 For an inference to be drawn when a suspect fails or refuses to answer a question about one of these matters or to answer it satisfactorily, the suspect must first be told in ordinary language:

(a)    what offence is being investigated;

(b)    what fact they are being asked to account for;

(c)    this fact may be due to them taking part in the commission of the offence;

(d)    a court may draw a proper inference if they fail or refuse to account for this fact;

(e)    a record is being made of the interview and it may be given in evidence if they are brought to trial.

**(d)    Juveniles and persons who are mentally disordered or otherwise mentally vulnerable**

10.12 If a juvenile or a person who is mentally disordered or otherwise mentally vulnerable is cautioned in the absence of the appropriate adult, the caution must be repeated in the adult's presence.

**(e)    Documentation**

10.13 A record shall be made when a caution is given under this section, either in the interviewer's pocket book or in the interview record.

**Notes for guidance**

10A   *There must be some reasonable, objective grounds for the suspicion, based on known facts or information which are relevant to the likelihood the offence has been committed and the person to be questioned committed it.*

10B   *An arrested person must be given sufficient information to enable them to understand that they have been deprived of their liberty and the reason they have been arrested, e.g. when a person is arrested on suspicion of committing an offence they must be informed of the suspected offence's nature, when and where it was committed. The suspect must also be informed of the reason or reasons why the arrest is considered necessary. Vague or technical language should be avoided.*

10C The restriction on drawing inferences from silence, see Annex C, paragraph 1, does not apply to a person who has not been detained and who therefore cannot be prevented from seeking legal advice if they want, see paragraph 3.21.

10D If it appears a person does not understand the caution, the person giving it should explain it in their own words.

10E It may be necessary to show to the court that nothing occurred during an interview break or between interviews which influenced the suspect's recorded evidence. After a break in an interview or at the beginning of a subsequent interview, the interviewing officer should summarise the reason for the break and confirm this with the suspect.

10F The Criminal Justice and Public Order Act 1994, sections 36 and 37 apply only to suspects who have been arrested by a constable or Customs and Excise officer and are given the relevant warning by the police or customs officer who made the arrest or who is investigating the offence. They do not apply to any interviews with suspects who have not been arrested.

10G Nothing in this Code requires a caution to be given or repeated when informing a person not under arrest they may be prosecuted for an offence. However, a court will not be able to draw any inferences under the Criminal Justice and Public Order Act 1994, section 34, if the person was not cautioned.

## 11    Interviews – general

### (a)    Action

11.1A An interview is the questioning of a person regarding their involvement or suspected involvement in a criminal offence or offences which, under *paragraph 10.1*, must be carried out under caution. Whenever a person is interviewed they must be informed of the nature of the offence, or further offence. Procedures under the Road Traffic Act 1988, section 7 or the Transport and Works Act 1992, section 31 do not constitute interviewing for the purpose of this Code.

11.1    Following a decision to arrest a suspect, they must not be interviewed about the relevant offence except at a police station or other authorised place of detention, unless the consequent delay would be likely to:

(a)    lead to:

- interference with, or harm to, evidence connected with an offence;
- interference with, or physical harm to, other people; or
- serious loss of, or damage to, property;

(b)    lead to alerting other people suspected of committing an offence but not yet arrested for it; or

(c)    hinder the recovery of property obtained in consequence of the commission of an offence.

Interviewing in any of these circumstances shall cease once the relevant risk has been averted or the necessary questions have been put in order to attempt to avert that risk.

11.2    Immediately prior to the commencement or re-commencement of any interview at a police station or other authorised place of detention, the interviewer should remind the suspect of their entitlement to free legal advice and that the interview can be delayed for legal advice to be obtained, unless one of the exceptions in *paragraph 6.6* applies. It is the interviewer's responsibility to make sure all reminders are recorded in the interview record.

11.3    Not Used

11.4    At the beginning of an interview the interviewer, after cautioning the suspect, see *section 10*, shall put to them any significant statement or silence which occurred in the presence and hearing of a police officer or other police staff before the start of the interview and which have not been put to the suspect in the course of a previous interview. See *Note 11A*. The interviewer shall ask the suspect whether they confirm or deny that earlier statement or silence and if they want to add anything.

11.4A A significant statement is one which appears capable of being used in evidence against the suspect, in particular a direct admission of guilt. A significant silence is a failure or refusal to answer a question or answer satisfactorily when under caution, which might, allowing for the restriction on drawing adverse inferences from silence, see *Annex C,* give rise to an inference under the Criminal Justice and Public Order Act 1994, Part III.

11.5    No interviewer may try to obtain answers or elicit a statement by the use of oppression. Except as in *paragraph 10.9*, no interviewer shall indicate, except to answer a direct question, what action will be taken by the police if the person being questioned answers questions, makes a statement or refuses to do either. If the person asks directly what action will be taken if they answer questions, make a statement or refuse to do either, the interviewer may inform them what action the police propose to take provided that action is itself proper and warranted.

11.6    The interview or further interview of a person about an offence with which that person has not been charged or for which they have not been informed they may be prosecuted, must cease when:

(a)    the officer in charge of the investigation is satisfied all the questions they consider relevant to obtaining accurate and reliable information about the offence have been put to the suspect, this includes allowing the suspect an opportunity to give an innocent explanation and asking questions to test if the explanation is accurate and reliable, e.g. to clear up ambiguities or clarify what the suspect said;

(b)    the officer in charge of the investigation has taken account of any other available evidence; and

(c)    the officer in charge of the investigation, or in the case of a detained suspect, the custody officer, see *paragraph 16.1*, reasonably believes there is sufficient evidence to provide a realistic prospect of conviction for that offence. See *Note 11B*

This paragraph does not prevent officers in revenue cases or acting under the confiscation provisions of the Criminal Justice Act 1988 or the Drug Trafficking Act 1994 from inviting suspects to complete a formal question and answer record after the interview is concluded.

### (b)   Interview records

11.7  (a)    An accurate record must be made of each interview, whether or not the interview takes place at a police station

      (b)    The record must state the place of interview, the time it begins and ends, any interview breaks and, subject to *paragraph 2.6A*, the names of all those present; and must be made on the forms provided for this purpose or in the interviewer's pocket book or in accordance with the Codes of Practice E or F;

      (c)    Any written record must be made and completed during the interview, unless this would not be practicable or would interfere with the conduct of the interview, and must constitute either a verbatim record of what has been said or, failing this, an account of the interview which adequately and accurately summarises it.

11.8  If a written record is not made during the interview it must be made as soon as practicable after its completion.

11.9  Written interview records must be timed and signed by the maker.

11.10  If a written record is not completed during the interview the reason must be recorded in the interview record.

11.11  Unless it is impracticable, the person interviewed shall be given the opportunity to read the interview record and to sign it as correct or to indicate how they consider it inaccurate. If the person interviewed cannot read or refuses to read the record or sign it, the senior interviewer present shall read it to them and ask whether they would like to sign it as correct or make their mark or to indicate how they consider it inaccurate. The interviewer shall certify on the interview record itself what has occurred. See *Note 11E*

11.12 If the appropriate adult or the person's solicitor is present during the interview, they should also be given an opportunity to read and sign the interview record or any written statement taken down during the interview.

11.13 A written record shall be made of any comments made by a suspect, including unsolicited comments, which are outside the context of an interview but which might be relevant to the offence. Any such record must be timed and signed by the maker. When practicable the suspect shall be given the opportunity to read that record and to sign it as correct or to indicate how they consider it inaccurate. See *Note 11E*

11.14 Any refusal by a person to sign an interview record when asked in accordance with this Code must itself be recorded.

### (c)   *Juveniles and mentally disordered or otherwise mentally vulnerable people*

11.15 A juvenile or person who is mentally disordered or otherwise mentally vulnerable must not be interviewed regarding their involvement or suspected involvement in a criminal offence or offences, or asked to provide or sign a written statement under caution or record of interview, in the absence of the appropriate adult unless *paragraphs 11.1, 11.18 to 11.20* apply. See *Note 11C*

11.16 Juveniles may only be interviewed at their place of education in exceptional circumstances and only when the principal or their nominee agrees. Every effort should be made to notify the parent(s) or other person responsible for the juvenile's welfare and the appropriate adult, if this is a different person, that the police want to interview the juvenile and reasonable time should be allowed to enable the appropriate adult to be present at the interview. If awaiting the appropriate adult would cause unreasonable delay, and unless the juvenile is suspected of an offence against the educational establishment, the principal or their nominee can act as the appropriate adult for the purposes of the interview.

11.17 If an appropriate adult is present at an interview, they shall be informed:

- they are not expected to act simply as an observer; and

- the purpose of their presence is to:

  - advise the person being interviewed;

–   observe whether the interview is being conducted properly and fairly;

–   facilitate communication with the person being interviewed.

**(d)    Vulnerable suspects – urgent interviews at police stations**

11.18 The following persons may not be interviewed unless an officer of superintendent rank or above considers delay will lead to the consequences in *paragraph 11.1(a) to (c),* and is satisfied the interview would not significantly harm the person's physical or mental state (see Annex G):

(a)    a juvenile or person who is mentally disordered or otherwise mentally vulnerable if at the time of the interview the appropriate adult is not present;

(b)    anyone other than in *(a)* who at the time of the interview appears unable to:

•    appreciate the significance of questions and their answers; or

•    understand what is happening because of the effects of drink, drugs or any illness, ailment or condition;

(c)    a person who has difficulty understanding English or has a hearing disability, if at the time of the interview an interpreter is not present.

11.19 These interviews may not continue once sufficient information has been obtained to avert the consequences in *paragraph 11.1(a) to (c).*

11.20 A record shall be made of the grounds for any decision to interview a person under *paragraph 11.18.*

**Notes for guidance**

*11A    Paragraph 11.4 does not prevent the interviewer from putting significant statements and silences to a suspect again at a later stage or a further interview.*

*11B    The Criminal Procedure and Investigations Act 1996 Code of Practice, paragraph 3.4 states 'In conducting an investigation, the investigator should pursue all reasonable lines of enquiry, whether these point towards or away from the suspect. What is reasonable will depend on the particular circumstances.' Interviewers should keep this in mind when deciding what questions to ask in an interview.*

*11C    Although juveniles or people who are mentally disordered or otherwise mentally vulnerable are often capable of providing reliable evidence, they may, without knowing or wishing to do so, be particularly prone in certain circumstances to provide information that may be unreliable, misleading or self-incriminating. Special care should always be taken when questioning such a person, and the appropriate adult should be involved if there is any doubt about a person's age, mental state or capacity. Because of the risk of unreliable evidence it is also important to obtain corroboration of any facts admitted whenever possible.*

11D   *Juveniles should not be arrested at their place of education unless this is unavoidable. When a juvenile is arrested at their place of education, the principal or their nominee must be informed.*

11E   *Significant statements described in paragraph 11.4 will always be relevant to the offence and must be recorded. When a suspect agrees to read records of interviews and other comments and sign them as correct, they should be asked to endorse the record with, e.g. 'I agree that this is a correct record of what was said' and add their signature. If the suspect does not agree with the record, the interviewer should record the details of any disagreement and ask the suspect to read these details and sign them to the effect that they accurately reflect their disagreement. Any refusal to sign should be recorded.*

## 12   Interviews in police stations

### (a)   Action

12.1   If a police officer wants to interview or conduct enquiries which require the presence of a detainee, the custody officer is responsible for deciding whether to deliver the detainee into the officer's custody.

12.2   Except as below, in any period of 24 hours a detainee must be allowed a continuous period of at least 8 hours for rest, free from questioning, travel or any interruption in connection with the investigation concerned. This period should normally be at night or other appropriate time which takes account of when the detainee last slept or rested. If a detainee is arrested at a police station after going there voluntarily, the period of 24 hours runs from the time of their arrest and not the time of arrival at the police station. The period may not be interrupted or delayed, except:

    (a)    when there are reasonable grounds for believing not delaying or interrupting the period would:

        (i)    involve a risk of harm to people or serious loss of, or damage to, property;

        (iii)    delay unnecessarily the person's release from custody;

        (iii)    otherwise prejudice the outcome of the investigation;

    (b)    at the request of the detainee, their appropriate adult or legal representative;

    (c)    when a delay or interruption is necessary in order to:

(i)     comply with the legal obligations and duties arising under *section 15*;

(ii)    to take action required under *section 9* or in accordance with medical advice.

If the period is interrupted in accordance with *(a)*, a fresh period must be allowed. Interruptions under *(b)* and *(c)*, do not require a fresh period to be allowed.

12.3    Before a detainee is interviewed the custody officer, in consultation with the officer in charge of the investigation and appropriate health care professionals as necessary, shall assess whether the detainee is fit enough to be interviewed. This means determining and considering the risks to the detainee's physical and mental state if the interview took place and determining what safeguards are needed to allow the interview to take place. See *Annex G*. The custody officer shall not allow a detainee to be interviewed if the custody officer considers it would cause significant harm to the detainee's physical or mental state. Vulnerable suspects listed at *paragraph 11.18* shall be treated as always being at some risk during an interview and these persons may not be interviewed except in accordance with *paragraphs 11.18* to *11.20*.

12.4    As far as practicable interviews shall take place in interview rooms which are adequately heated, lit and ventilated.

12.5    A suspect whose detention without charge has been authorised under PACE, because the detention is necessary for an interview to obtain evidence of the offence for which they have been arrested, may choose not to answer questions but police do not require the suspect's consent or agreement to interview them for this purpose. If a suspect takes steps to prevent themselves being questioned or further questioned, e.g. by refusing to leave their cell to go to a suitable interview room or by trying to leave the interview room, they shall be advised their consent or agreement to interview is not required. The suspect shall be cautioned as in *section 10*, and informed if they fail or refuse to co-operate, the interview may take place in the cell and that their failure or refusal to co-operate may be given in evidence. The suspect shall then be invited to co-operate and go into the interview room.

12.6    People being questioned or making statements shall not be required to stand.

12.7    Before the interview commences each interviewer shall, subject to *paragraph 2.6A*, identify themselves and any other persons present to the interviewee.

12.8    Breaks from interviewing should be made at recognised meal times or at other times that take account of when an interviewee last had a meal. Short refreshment breaks shall be provided at approximately two hour intervals, subject to the interviewer's discretion to delay a break if there are reasonable grounds for believing it would:

**C**

    (i)      involve a:

- risk of harm to people;

- serious loss of, or damage to, property;

    (ii)    unnecessarily delay the detainee's release;

    (iii)   otherwise prejudice the outcome of the investigation.

See *Note 12B*

12.9   If during the interview a complaint is made by or on behalf of the interviewee concerning the provisions of this Code, the interviewer should:

    (i)      record it in the interview record;

    (ii)    inform the custody officer, who is then responsible for dealing with it as in *section 9*.

**(b)   Documentation**

12.10 A record must be made of the:

- time a detainee is not in the custody of the custody officer, and why

- reason for any refusal to deliver the detainee out of that custody

12.11 A record shall be made of:

    (a)    the reasons it was not practicable to use an interview room; and

    (b)    any action taken as in *paragraph 12.5*.

The record shall be made on the custody record or in the interview record for action taken whilst an interview record is being kept, with a brief reference to this effect in the custody record.

12.12 Any decision to delay a break in an interview must be recorded, with reasons, in the interview record.

12.13 All written statements made at police stations under caution shall be written on forms provided for the purpose.

12.14 All written statements made under caution shall be taken in accordance with *Annex D*. Before a person makes a written statement under caution at a police station they shall be reminded about the right to legal advice. See *Note 12A*

### Notes for guidance

*12A*   *It is not normally necessary to ask for a written statement if the interview was recorded in writing and the record signed in accordance with paragraph 11.11 or audibly or visually recorded in accordance with Code E or F. Statements under caution should normally be taken in these circumstances only at the person's express wish. A person may however be asked if they want to make such a statement.*

*12B*   *Meal breaks should normally last at least 45 minutes and shorter breaks after two hours should last at least 15 minutes. If the interviewer delays a break in accordance with paragraph 12.8 and prolongs the interview, a longer break should be provided. If there is a short interview, and another short interview is contemplated, the length of the break may be reduced if there are reasonable grounds to believe this is necessary to avoid any of the consequences in paragraph 12.8(i) to (iii).*

### 13   Interpreters

#### (a)   General

13.1   Chief officers are responsible for making sure appropriate arrangements are in place for provision of suitably qualified interpreters for people who:

- are deaf;

- do not understand English.

Whenever possible, interpreters should be drawn from the National Register of Public Service Interpreters (NRPSI) or the Council for the Advancement of Communication with Deaf People (CACDP) Directory of British Sign Language/English Interpreters.

#### (b)   Foreign languages

13.2   Unless *paragraphs 11.1, 11.18* to *11.20* apply, a person must not be interviewed in the absence of a person capable of interpreting if:

(a)   they have difficulty understanding English;

(b)   the interviewer cannot speak the person's own language;

(c)   the person wants an interpreter present.

13.3   The interviewer shall make sure the interpreter makes a note of the interview at the time in the person's language for use in the event of the interpreter being called to give evidence, and certifies its accuracy. The interviewer should allow sufficient time for the interpreter to note each question and answer after each is put, given and interpreted.

The person should be allowed to read the record or have it read to them and sign it as correct or indicate the respects in which they consider it inaccurate. If the interview is audibly recorded or visually recorded, the arrangements in Code E or F apply.

13.4    In the case of a person making a statement to a police officer or other police staff other than in English:

   (a)    the interpreter shall record the statement in the language it is made;

   (b)    the person shall be invited to sign it;

   (c)    an official English translation shall be made in due course.

### (c)    Deaf people and people with speech difficulties

13.5    If a person appears to be deaf or there is doubt about their hearing or speaking ability, they must not be interviewed in the absence of an interpreter unless they agree in writing to being interviewed without one or *paragraphs 11.1, 11.18 to 11.20* apply.

13.6    An interpreter should also be called if a juvenile is interviewed and the parent or guardian present as the appropriate adult appears to be deaf or there is doubt about their hearing or speaking ability, unless they agree in writing to the interview proceeding without one or *paragraphs 11.1, 11.18 to 11.20* apply.

13.7    The interviewer shall make sure the interpreter is allowed to read the interview record and certify its accuracy in the event of the interpreter being called to give evidence. If the interview is audibly recorded or visually recorded, the arrangements in Code E or F apply.

### (d)    Additional rules for detained persons

13.8    All reasonable attempts should be made to make the detainee understand that interpreters will be provided at public expense.

13.9    If *paragraph 6.1* applies and the detainee cannot communicate with the solicitor because of language, hearing or speech difficulties, an interpreter must be called. The interpreter may not be a police officer or any other police staff when interpretation is needed for the purposes of obtaining legal advice. In all other cases a police officer or other police staff may only interpret if the detainee and the appropriate adult, if applicable, give their agreement in writing or if the interview is audibly recorded or visually recorded as in Code E or F.

13.10    When the custody officer cannot establish effective communication with a person charged with an offence who appears deaf or there is doubt about their ability to hear, speak or to understand English, arrangements must be made as soon as practicable for an interpreter to explain the offence and any other information given by the custody officer.

### (e)    Documentation

13.11 Action taken to call an interpreter under this section and any agreement to be interviewed in the absence of an interpreter must be recorded.

### 14    Questioning – special restrictions

14.1    If a person is arrested by one police force on behalf of another and the lawful period of detention in respect of that offence has not yet commenced in accordance with PACE, section 41 no questions may be put to them about the offence while they are in transit between the forces except to clarify any voluntary statement they make.

14.2    If a person is in police detention at a hospital they may not be questioned without the agreement of a responsible doctor. See *Note 14A*

### Note for guidance

14A    *If questioning takes place at a hospital under paragraph 14.2, or on the way to or from a hospital, the period of questioning concerned counts towards the total period of detention permitted.*

### 15    Reviews and extensions of detention

### (a)    Persons detained under PACE

15.1    The review officer is responsible under PACE, section 40 for periodically determining if a person's detention, before or after charge, continues to be necessary. This requirement continues throughout the detention period and except as in *paragraph 15.10*, the review officer must be present at the police station holding the detainee. See *Notes 15A* and *15B*

15.2    Under PACE, section 42, an officer of superintendent rank or above who is responsible for the station holding the detainee may give authority any time after the second review to extend the maximum period the person may be detained without charge by up to 12 hours. Further detention without charge may be authorised only by a magistrates' court in accordance with PACE, sections 43 and 44. See *Notes 15C, 15D* and *15E*

15.2A Section 42(1) of PACE as amended extends the maximum period of detention for indictable offences from 24 hours to 36 hours. Detaining a juvenile or mentally vulnerable person for longer than 24 hours will be dependent on the circumstances of the case and with regard to the person's:

(a)    special vulnerability;

(b)    the legal obligation to provide an opportunity for representations to be made prior to a decision about extending detention;

(c)    the need to consult and consider the views of any appropriate adult; and

(d)    any alternatives to police custody.

15.3    Before deciding whether to authorise continued detention the officer responsible under *paragraphs 15.1* or *15.2* shall give an opportunity to make representations about the detention to:

(a)    the detainee, unless in the case of a review as in *paragraph 15.1*, the detainee is asleep;

(b)    the detainee's solicitor if available at the time; and

(c)    the appropriate adult if available at the time.

15.3A Other people having an interest in the detainee's welfare may also make representations at the authorising officer's discretion.

15.3B Subject to *paragraph 15.10*, the representations may be made orally in person or by telephone or in writing. The authorising officer may, however, refuse to hear oral representations from the detainee if the officer considers them unfit to make representations because of their condition or behaviour. See *Note 15C*

15.3C The decision on whether the review takes place in person or by telephone or by video conferencing (see Note 15G) is a matter for the review officer. In determining the form the review may take, the review officer must always take full account of the needs of the person in custody. The benefits of carrying out a review in person should always be considered, based on the individual circumstances of each case with specific additional consideration if the person is:

(a)    a juvenile (and the age of the juvenile); or

(b)    mentally vulnerable; or

(c)    has been subject to medical attention for other than routine minor ailments; or

(d)    there are presentational or community issues around the person's detention.

15.4    Before conducting a review or determining whether to extend the maximum period of detention without charge, the officer responsible must make sure the detainee is reminded of their entitlement to free legal advice, see *paragraph 6.5,* unless in the case of a review the person is asleep.

15.5    If, after considering any representations, the officer decides to keep the detainee in detention or extend the maximum period they may be detained without charge, any comment made by the detainee shall be recorded. If applicable, the officer responsible under *paragraph 15.1 or 15.2* shall be informed of the comment as soon as practicable. See also *paragraphs 11.4 and 11.13*

15.6    No officer shall put specific questions to the detainee:

- regarding their involvement in any offence; or

- in respect of any comments they may make:

    – when given the opportunity to make representations; or

    – in response to a decision to keep them in detention or extend the maximum period of detention.

Such an exchange could constitute an interview as in *paragraph 11.1A* and would be subject to the associated safeguards in *section 11* and, in respect of a person who has been charged, *paragraph 16.5*. See also *paragraph 11.13*

15.7    A detainee who is asleep at a review, see *paragraph 15.1,* and whose continued detention is authorised must be informed about the decision and reason as soon as practicable after waking.

15.8    Not used

### (b)    Telephone review of detention

15.9    PACE, section 40A provides that the officer responsible under section 40 for reviewing the detention of a person who has not been charged, need not attend the police station holding the detainee and may carry out the review by telephone.

15.9A PACE, section 45A(2) provides that the officer responsible under section 40 for reviewing the detention of a person who has not been charged, need not attend the police station holding the detainee and may carry out the review by video conferencing facilities (See *Note 15G*).

15.9B A telephone review is not permitted where facilities for review by video conferencing exist and it is practicable to use them.

15.9C The review officer can decide at any stage that a telephone review or review by video conferencing should be terminated and that the review will be conducted in person. The reasons for doing so should be noted in the custody record.

See *Note 15F*

15.10 When a telephone review is carried out, an officer at the station holding the detainee shall be required by the review officer to fulfil that officer's obligations under PACE section 40 or this Code by:

(a)   making any record connected with the review in the detainee's custody record;

(b)   if applicable, making a record in (a) in the presence of the detainee; and

(c)   giving the detainee information about the review.

15.11 When a telephone review is carried out, the requirement in *paragraph 15.3* will be satisfied:

(a)   if facilities exist for the immediate transmission of written representations to the review officer, e.g. fax or email message, by giving the detainee an opportunity to make representations:

(i)    orally by telephone; or

(ii)   in writing using those facilities; and

(b)   in all other cases, by giving the detainee an opportunity to make their representations orally by telephone.

## (c)   Documentation

15.12 It is the officer's responsibility to make sure all reminders given under *paragraph 15.4* are noted in the custody record.

15.13 The grounds for, and extent of, any delay in conducting a review shall be recorded.

15.14 When a telephone review is carried out, a record shall be made of:

(a)   the reason the review officer did not attend the station holding the detainee;

(b)   the place the review officer was;

(c)   the method representations, oral or written, were made to the review officer, see *paragraph 15.11.*

15.15 Any written representations shall be retained.

15.16 A record shall be made as soon as practicable about the outcome of each review or determination whether to extend the maximum detention period without charge or an application for a warrant of further detention or its extension. If *paragraph 15.7* applies, a record shall also be made of when the person was informed and by whom. If an authorisation is given under PACE, section 42, the record shall state the number of hours and minutes by which the detention period is extended or further extended. If a warrant for further detention, or extension, is granted under section 43 or 44, the record shall state the detention period authorised by the warrant and the date and time it was granted.

### Notes for guidance

15A  *Review officer for the purposes of:*

- PACE, sections 40 and 40A means, in the case of a person arrested but not charged, an officer of at least inspector rank not directly involved in the investigation and, if a person has been arrested and charged, the custody officer;

15B  *The detention of persons in police custody not subject to the statutory review requirement in paragraph 15.1 should still be reviewed periodically as a matter of good practice. Such reviews can be carried out by an officer of the rank of sergeant or above. The purpose of such reviews is to check the particular power under which a detainee is held continues to apply, any associated conditions are complied with and to make sure appropriate action is taken to deal with any changes. This includes the detainee's prompt release when the power no longer applies, or their transfer if the power requires the detainee be taken elsewhere as soon as the necessary arrangements are made. Examples include persons:*

(a)  *arrested on warrant because they failed to answer bail to appear at court;*

(b)  *arrested under the Bail Act 1976, section 7(3) for breaching a condition of bail granted after charge;*

(c)  *in police custody for specific purposes and periods under the Crime (Sentences) Act 1997, Schedule 1;*

(d)  *convicted, or remand prisoners, held in police stations on behalf of the Prison Service under the Imprisonment (Temporary Provisions) Act 1980, section 6;*

(e)  *being detained to prevent them causing a breach of the peace;*

(f)  *detained at police stations on behalf of the Immigration Service.*

(g)    *detained by order of a magistrates' court under the Criminal Justice Act 1988, section 152 (as amended by the Drugs Act 2005, section 8) to facilitate the recovery of evidence after being charged with drug possession or drug trafficking and suspected of having swallowed drugs.*

*The detention of persons remanded into police detention by order of a court under the Magistrates' Courts Act 1980, section 128 is subject to a statutory requirement to review that detention. This is to make sure the detainee is taken back to court no later than the end of the period authorised by the court or when the need for their detention by police ceases, whichever is the sooner.*

15C    *In the case of a review of detention, but not an extension, the detainee need not be woken for the review. However, if the detainee is likely to be asleep, e.g. during a period of rest allowed as in paragraph 12.2, at the latest time a review or authorisation to extend detention may take place, the officer should, if the legal obligations and time constraints permit, bring forward the procedure to allow the detainee to make representations. A detainee not asleep during the review must be present when the grounds for their continued detention are recorded and must at the same time be informed of those grounds unless the review officer considers the person is incapable of understanding what is said, violent or likely to become violent or in urgent need of medical attention.*

15D    *An application to a Magistrates' Court under PACE, sections 43 or 44 for a warrant of further detention or its extension should be made between 10am and 9pm, and if possible during normal court hours. It will not usually be practicable to arrange for a court to sit specially outside the hours of 10am to 9pm. If it appears a special sitting may be needed outside normal court hours but between 10am and 9pm, the clerk to the justices should be given notice and informed of this possibility, while the court is sitting if possible.*

15E    *In paragraph 15.2, the officer responsible for the station holding the detainee includes a superintendent or above who, in accordance with their force operational policy or police regulations, is given that responsibility on a temporary basis whilst the appointed long-term holder is off duty or otherwise unavailable.*

15F    *The provisions of PACE, section 40A allowing telephone reviews do not apply to reviews of detention after charge by the custody officer When video conferencing is not required, they allow the use of a telephone to carry out a review of detention before charge. The procedure under PACE, section 42 must be done in person.*

15G    *The use of video conferencing facilities for decisions about detention under section 45A of PACE is subject to the introduction of regulations by the Secretary of State.*

## 16    Charging detained persons

### (a)    Action

16.1   When the officer in charge of the investigation reasonably believes there is sufficient evidence to provide a realistic prospect of conviction for the offence (see *paragraph 11.6)*, they shall without delay, and subject to the following qualification, inform the custody officer who will be responsible for considering whether the detainee should be charged. See *Notes 11B* and *16A*. When a person is detained in respect of more than one offence it is permissible to delay informing the custody officer until the above conditions are satisfied in respect of all the offences, but see *paragraph 11.6*. If the detainee is a juvenile, mentally disordered or otherwise mentally vulnerable, any resulting action shall be taken in the presence of the appropriate adult if they are present at the time. See *Notes 16B* and *16C*

16.1A  Where guidance issued by the Director of Public Prosecutions under section 37A is in force the custody officer must comply with that Guidance in deciding how to act in dealing with the detainee. See *Notes 16AA* and *16AB*.

16.1B  Where in compliance with the DPP's Guidance the custody officer decides that the case should be immediately referred to the CPS to make the charging decision, consultation should take place with a Crown Prosecutor as soon as is reasonably practicable. Where the Crown Prosecutor is unable to make the charging decision on the information available at that time, the detainee may be released without charge and on bail (with conditions if necessary) under section 37(7)(a). In such circumstances, the detainee should be informed that they are being released to enable the Director of Public Prosecutions to make a decision under section 37B.

16.2   When a detainee is charged with or informed they may be prosecuted for an offence, see *Note 16B,* they shall, unless the restriction on drawing adverse inferences from silence applies, see *Annex C*, be cautioned as follows:

> *'You do not have to say anything. But it may harm your defence if you do not mention now something which you later rely on in court. Anything you do say may be given in evidence.'*

Where the use of the Welsh Language is appropriate, a constable may provide the caution directly in Welsh in the following terms:

> *'Does dim rhaid i chi ddweud dim byd. Ond gall niweidio eich amddiffyniad os na fyddwch chi'n sôn, yn awr, am rywbeth y byddwch chi'n dibynnu arno nes ymlaen yn y llys. Gall unrhyw beth yr ydych yn ei ddweud gael ei roi fel tystiolaeth.'*

*Annex C, paragraph 2* sets out the alternative terms of the caution to be used when the restriction on drawing adverse inferences from silence applies.

16.3   When a detainee is charged they shall be given a written notice showing particulars of the offence and, subject to *paragraph 2.6A*, the officer's name and the case reference number. As far as possible the particulars of the charge shall be stated in simple terms, but they shall also show the precise offence in law with which the detainee is charged. The notice shall begin:

> *'You are charged with the offence(s) shown below.'* Followed by the caution.

If the detainee is a juvenile, mentally disordered or otherwise mentally vulnerable, the notice should be given to the appropriate adult.

16.4   If, after a detainee has been charged with or informed they may be prosecuted for an offence, an officer wants to tell them about any written statement or interview with another person relating to such an offence, the detainee shall either be handed a true copy of the written statement or the content of the interview record brought to their attention. Nothing shall be done to invite any reply or comment except to:

(a)   caution the detainee, *'You do not have to say anything, but anything you do say may be given in evidence.'*;

Where the use of the Welsh Language is appropriate, caution the detainee in the following terms:

> *'Does dim rhaid i chi ddweud dim byd, ond gall unrhyw beth yr ydych yn ei ddweud gael ei roi fel tystiolaeth.'*

and

(b)   remind the detainee about their right to legal advice.

16.4A  If the detainee:

- cannot read, the document may be read to them

- is a juvenile, mentally disordered or otherwise mentally vulnerable, the appropriate adult shall also be given a copy, or the interview record shall be brought to their attention

16.5   A detainee may not be interviewed about an offence after they have been charged with, or informed they may be prosecuted for it, unless the interview is necessary:

- to prevent or minimise harm or loss to some other person, or the public

- to clear up an ambiguity in a previous answer or statement

- in the interests of justice for the detainee to have put to them, and have an opportunity to comment on, information concerning the offence which has come to light since they were charged or informed they might be prosecuted

Before any such interview, the interviewer shall:

(a) caution the detainee, *'You do not have to say anything, but anything you do say may be given in evidence.'*

Where the use of the Welsh Language is appropriate, the interviewer shall caution the detainee, *'Does dim rhaid i chi ddweud dim byd, ond gall unrhyw beth yr ydych yn ei ddweud gael ei roi fel tystiolaeth.'*

(b) remind the detainee about their right to legal advice.

See *Note 16B*

16.6 The provisions of *paragraphs 16.2* to *16.5* must be complied with in the appropriate adult's presence if they are already at the police station. If they are not at the police station then these provisions must be complied with again in their presence when they arrive unless the detainee has been released.

See *Note 16C*

16.7 When a juvenile is charged with an offence and the custody officer authorises their continued detention after charge, the custody officer must try to make arrangements for the juvenile to be taken into the care of a local authority to be detained pending appearance in court unless the custody officer certifies it is impracticable to do so or, in the case of a juvenile of at least 12 years old, no secure accommodation is available and there is a risk to the public of serious harm from that juvenile, in accordance with PACE, section 38(6). See *Note 16D*

**(b) Documentation**

16.8 A record shall be made of anything a detainee says when charged.

16.9 Any questions put in an interview after charge and answers given relating to the offence shall be recorded in full during the interview on forms for that purpose and the record signed by the detainee or, if they refuse, by the interviewer and any third parties present. If the questions are audibly recorded or visually recorded the arrangements in Code E or F apply.

16.10 If it is not practicable to make arrangements for a juvenile's transfer into local authority care as in *paragraph 16.7,* the custody officer must record the reasons and complete a certificate to be produced before the court with the juvenile. See *Note 16D*

### Notes for guidance

16A   The custody officer must take into account alternatives to prosecution under the Crime and Disorder Act 1998, reprimands and warning applicable to persons under 18, and in national guidance on the cautioning of offenders, for persons aged 18 and over.

16AA   When a person is arrested under the provisions of the Criminal Justice Act 2003 which allow a person to be re-tried after being acquitted of a serious offence which is a qualifying offence specified in Schedule 5 to that Act and not precluded from further prosecution by virtue of section 75(3) of that Act the detention provisions of PACE are modified and make an officer of the rank of superintendent or above who has not been directly involved in the investigation responsible for determining whether the evidence is sufficient to charge.

16AB   Where Guidance issued by the Director of Public Prosecutions under section 37B is in force, a custody officer who determines in accordance with that Guidance that there is sufficient evidence to charge the detainee, may detain that person for no longer than is reasonably necessary to decide how that person is to be dealt with under PACE, section 37(7)(a) to (d), including, where appropriate, consultation with the Duty Prosecutor. The period is subject to the maximum period of detention before charge determined by PACE, sections 41 to 44. Where in accordance with the Guidance the case is referred to the CPS for decision, the custody officer should ensure that an officer involved in the investigation sends to the CPS such information as is specified in the Guidance.

16B   The giving of a warning or the service of the Notice of Intended Prosecution required by the Road Traffic Offenders Act 1988, section 1 does not amount to informing a detainee they may be prosecuted for an offence and so does not preclude further questioning in relation to that offence.

16C   There is no power under PACE to detain a person and delay action under paragraphs 16.2 to 16.5 solely to await the arrival of the appropriate adult. After charge, bail cannot be refused, or release on bail delayed, simply because an appropriate adult is not available, unless the absence of that adult provides the custody officer with the necessary grounds to authorise detention after charge under PACE, section 38.

16D   Except as in paragraph 16.7, neither a juvenile's behaviour nor the nature of the offence provides grounds for the custody officer to decide it is impracticable to arrange the juvenile's transfer to local authority care. Similarly, the lack of secure local authority accommodation does not make it impracticable to transfer the juvenile. The availability of secure accommodation is only a factor in relation to a juvenile aged 12 or over when the local authority accommodation would not be adequate to protect the public from serious harm from them. The obligation to transfer a juvenile to local authority accommodation *applies as much to a juvenile charged during the daytime as to a juvenile to be held overnight, subject to a requirement to bring the juvenile before a court under PACE, section 46.*

## 17 Testing persons for the presence of specified Class A drugs

### (a) Action

17.1 This section of Code C applies only in selected police stations in police areas where the provisions for drug testing under section 63B of PACE (as amended by section 5 of the Criminal Justice Act 2003 and section 7 of the Drugs Act 2005) are in force and in respect of which the Secretary of State has given a notification to the relevant chief officer of police that arrangements for the taking of samples have been made. Such a notification will cover either a police area as a whole or particular stations within a police area. The notification indicates whether the testing applies to those arrested or charged or under the age of 18 as the case may be and testing can only take place in respect of the persons so indicated in the notification. Testing cannot be carried out unless the relevant notification has been given and has not been withdrawn. See *Note 17F*

17.2 A sample of urine or a non-intimate sample may be taken from a person in police detention for the purpose of ascertaining whether he has any specified Class A drug in his body only where they have been brought before the custody officer and:

(a) either the arrest condition, see *paragraph 17.3*, or the charge condition, see *paragraph 17.4* is met;

(b) the age condition see *paragraph 17.5*, is met;

(c) the notification condition is met in relation to the arrest condition, the charge condition, or the age condition, as the case may be. (Testing on charge and/or arrest must be specifically provided for in the notification for the power to apply. In addition, the fact that testing of under 18s is authorised must be expressly provided for in the notification before the power to test such persons applies.). See *paragraph 17.1*; and

(d) a police officer has requested the person concerned to give the sample (the request condition).

17.3 The arrest condition is met where the detainee:

(a) has been arrested for a trigger offence, see *Note 17E*, but not charged with that offence; or

(b)      has been arrested for any other offence but not charged with that offence and a police officer of inspector rank or above, who has reasonable grounds for suspecting that their misuse of any specified Class A drug caused or contributed to the offence, has authorised the sample to be taken.

17.4   The charge condition is met where the detainee:

(a)      has been charged with a trigger offence, or

(b)      has been charged with any other offence and a police officer of inspector rank or above, who has reasonable grounds for suspecting that the detainee's misuse of any specified Class A drug caused or contributed to the offence, has authorised the sample to be taken.

17.5   The age condition is met where:

(a)      in the case of a detainee who has been arrested but not charged as in *paragraph 17.3*, they are aged 18 or over;

(b)      in the case of a detainee who has been charged as in *paragraph 17.4*, they are aged 14 or over.

17.6   Before requesting a sample from the person concerned, an officer must:

(a)      inform them that the purpose of taking the sample is for drug testing under PACE. This is to ascertain whether they have a specified Class A drug present in their body;

(b)      warn them that if, when so requested, they fail without good cause to provide a sample they may be liable to prosecution;

(c)      where the taking of the sample has been authorised by an inspector or above in accordance with *paragraph 17.3(b)* or *17.4(b)* above, inform them that the authorisation has been given and the grounds for giving it;

(d)      remind them of the following rights, which may be exercised at any stage during the period in custody:

(i)       the right to have someone informed of their arrest [see section 5];

(ii)      the right to consult privately with a solicitor and that free independent legal advice is available [see section 6]; and

(iii)     the right to consult these Codes of Practice [see section 3].

17.7  In the case of a person who has not attained the age of 17 —

    (a)    the making of the request for a sample under *paragraph 17.2(d)* above;

    (b)    the giving of the warning and the information under *paragraph 17.6* above; and

    (c)    the taking of the sample,

    may not take place except in the presence of an appropriate adult. (see Note 17G)

17.8  Authorisation by an officer of the rank of inspector or above within *paragraph 17.3(b)* or *17.4(b)* may be given orally or in writing but, if it is given orally, it must be confirmed in writing as soon as practicable.

17.9  If a sample is taken from a detainee who has been arrested for an offence but not charged with that offence as in *paragraph 17.3*, no further sample may be taken during the same continuous period of detention. If during that same period the charge condition is also met in respect of that detainee, the sample which has been taken shall be treated as being taken by virtue of the charge condition, see *paragraph 17.4*, being met.

17.10  A detainee from whom a sample may be taken may be detained for up to six hours from the time of charge if the custody officer reasonably believes the detention is necessary to enable a sample to be taken. Where the arrest condition is met, a detainee whom the custody officer has decided to release on bail without charge may continue to be detained, but not beyond 24 hours from the relevant time (as defined in section 41(2) of PACE), to enable a sample to be taken.

17.11  A detainee in respect of whom the arrest condition is met, but not the charge condition, see *paragraphs 17.3* and *17.4*, and whose release would be required before a sample can be taken had they not continued to be detained as a result of being arrested for a further offence which does not satisfy the arrest condition, may have a sample taken at any time within 24 hours after the arrest for the offence that satisfies the arrest condition.

## *(b)* *Documentation*

17.12  The following must be recorded in the custody record:

    (a)    if a sample is taken following authorisation by an officer of the rank of inspector or above, the authorisation and the grounds for suspicion;

    (b)    the giving of a warning of the consequences of failure to provide a sample;

    (c)    the time at which the sample was given; and

(d)    the time of charge or, where the arrest condition is being relied upon, the time of arrest and, where applicable, the fact that a sample taken after arrest but before charge is to be treated as being taken by virtue of the charge condition, where that is met in the same period of continuous detention. See *paragraph 17.9*

## (c)    General

17.13 A sample may only be taken by a prescribed person. See *Note 17C*.

17.14 Force may not be used to take any sample for the purpose of drug testing.

17.15 The terms "Class A drug" and "misuse" have the same meanings as in the Misuse of Drugs Act 1971. "Specified" (in relation to a Class A drug) and "trigger offence" have the same meanings as in Part III of the Criminal Justice and Court Services Act 2000.

17.16 Any sample taken:

(a)    may not be used for any purpose other than to ascertain whether the person concerned has a specified Class A drug present in his body; and

(b)    can be disposed of as clinical waste unless it is to be sent for further analysis in cases where the test result is disputed at the point when the result is known, or where medication has been taken, or for quality assurance purposes.

## (d)    Assessment of misuse of drugs

17.17 Under the provisions of Part 3 of the Drugs Act 2005, where a detainee has tested positive for a specified Class A drug under section 63B of PACE a police officer may, at any time before the person's release from the police station, impose a requirement on the detainee to attend an initial assessment of their drug misuse by a suitably qualified person and to remain for its duration. Where such a requirement is imposed, the officer must, at the same time, impose a second requirement on the detainee to attend and remain for a follow-up assessment. The officer must inform the detainee that the second requirement will cease to have effect if, at the initial assessment they are informed that a follow-up assessment is not necessary. These requirements may only be imposed on a person if:

(a)    they have reached the age of 18

(b)    notification has been given by the Secretary of State to the relevant chief officer of police that arrangements for conducting initial and follow-up assessments have been made for those from whom samples for testing have been taken at the police station where the detainee is in custody.

17.18 When imposing a requirement to attend an initial assessment and a follow-up assessment the police officer must:

    (a)    inform the person of the time and place at which the initial assessment is to take place;

    (b)    explain that this information will be confirmed in writing; and

    (c)    warn the person that they may be liable to prosecution if they fail without good cause to attend the initial assessment and remain for its duration and if they fail to attend the follow-up assessment and remain for its duration (if so required).

17.19 Where a police officer has imposed a requirement to attend an initial assessment and a follow-up assessment in accordance with *paragraph 17.17*, he must, before the person is released from detention, give the person notice in writing which:

    (a)    confirms their requirement to attend and remain for the duration of the assessments; and

    (b)    confirms the information and repeats the warning referred to in *paragraph 17.18*.

17.20 The following must be recorded in the custody record:

    (a)    that the requirement to attend an initial assessment and a follow-up assessment has been imposed; and

    (b)    the information, explanation, warning and notice given in accordance with *paragraphs 17.17* and *17.19*.

17.21 Where a notice is given in accordance with *paragraph 17.19*, a police officer can give the person a further notice in writing which informs the person of any change to the time or place at which the initial assessment is to take place and which repeats the warning referred to in *paragraph 17.18(c)*.

17.22 Part 3 of the Drugs Act 2005 also requires police officers to have regard to any guidance issued by the Secretary of State in respect of the assessment provisions.

**Notes for guidance**

17A    *When warning a person who is asked to provide a urine or non-intimate sample in accordance with paragraph 17.6(b), the following form of words may be used:*

    *"You do not have to provide a sample, but I must warn you that if you fail or refuse without good cause to do so, you will commit an offence for which you may be imprisoned, or fined, or both".*

*Where the Welsh language is appropriate, the following form of words may be used:*

*'Does dim rhaid i chi roi sampl, ond mae'n rhaid i mi eich rhybuddio y byddwch chi'n cyflawni trosedd os byddwch chi'n methu neu yn gwrthod gwneud hynny heb reswm da, ac y gellir, oherwydd hynny, eich carcharu, eich dirwyo, neu'r ddau.'*

17B   *A sample has to be sufficient and suitable. A sufficient sample is sufficient in quantity and quality to enable drug-testing analysis to take place. A suitable sample is one which by its nature, is suitable for a particular form of drug analysis.*

17C   *A prescribed person in paragraph 17.13 is one who is prescribed in regulations made by the Secretary of State under section 63B(6) of the Police and Criminal Evidence Act 1984. [The regulations are currently contained in regulation SI 2001 No. 2645, the Police and Criminal Evidence Act 1984 (Drug Testing Persons in Police Detention) (Prescribed Persons) Regulations 2001.]*

17D   *Samples, and the information derived from them, may not be subsequently used in the investigation of any offence or in evidence against the persons from whom they were taken.*

17E   *Trigger offences are:*

1.   *Offences under the following provisions of the Theft Act 1968:*

| | |
|---|---|
| *section 1* | *(theft)* |
| *section 8* | *(robbery)* |
| *section 9* | *(burglary)* |
| *section 10* | *(aggravated burglary)* |
| *section 12* | *(taking a motor vehicle or other conveyance without authority)* |
| *section 12A* | *(aggravated vehicle-taking)* |
| *section 22* | *(handling stolen goods)* |
| *section 25* | *(going equipped for stealing etc.)* |

2.   *Offences under the following provisions of the Misuse of Drugs Act 1971, if committed in respect of a specified Class A drug:–*

| | |
|---|---|
| *section 4* | *(restriction on production and supply of controlled drugs)* |
| *section 5(2)* | *(possession of a controlled drug)* |
| *section 5(3)* | *(possession of a controlled drug with intent to supply)* |

3.   Offences under the following provisions of the Fraud Act 2006:

   section 1          (fraud)

   section 6          (possession etc. of articles for use in frauds)

   section 7          (making or supplying articles for use in frauds)

3A.   An offence under section 1(1) of the Criminal Attempts Act 1981 if committed in respect of an offence under

(a)   any of the following provisions of the Theft Act 1968:

   section 1          (theft)

   section 8          (robbery)

   section 9          (burglary)

   section 22        (handling stolen goods)

(b)   section 1 of the Fraud Act 2006 (fraud)

4.   Offences under the following provisions of the Vagrancy Act 1824:

   section 3          (begging)

   section 4          (persistent begging)

17F   The power to take samples is subject to notification by the Secretary of State that appropriate arrangements for the taking of samples have been made for the police area as a whole or for the particular police station concerned for whichever of the following is specified in the notification:

(a)   persons in respect of whom the arrest condition is met;

(b)   persons in respect of whom the charge condition is met;

(c)   persons who have not attained the age of 18.

Note: Notification is treated as having been given for the purposes of the charge condition in relation to a police area, if testing (on charge) under section 63B(2) of PACE was in force immediately before section 7 of the Drugs Act 2005 was brought into force; and for the purposes of the age condition, in relation to a police area or police station, if immediately before that day, notification that arrangements had been made for the taking of samples from persons under the age of 18 (those aged 14-17) had been given and had not been withdrawn.

17G   Appropriate adult in paragraph 17.7 means the person's –

   (a)   parent or guardian or, if they arein the care of a local authority or voluntary organisation, a person representing that authority or organisation; or

   (b)   a social worker of a local authority; or

   (c)   if no person falling within (a) or (b) above is available, any responsible person aged 18 or over who is not a police officer or a person employed by the police.

## ANNEX A – INTIMATE AND STRIP SEARCHES

**A**    **Intimate search**

1.    An intimate search consists of the physical examination of a person's body orifices other than the mouth. The intrusive nature of such searches means the actual and potential risks associated with intimate searches must never be underestimated.

*(a)*    *Action*

2.    Body orifices other than the mouth may be searched only:

     (a)    if authorised by an officer of inspector rank or above who has reasonable grounds for believing that the person may have concealed on themselves:

         (i)    anything which they could and might use to cause physical injury to themselves or others at the station; or

         (ii)    a Class A drug which they intended to supply to another or to export;

         and the officer has reasonable grounds for believing that an intimate search is the only means of removing those items; and

     (b)    if the search is under *paragraph 2(a)(ii)* (a drug offence search), the detainee's appropriate consent has been given in writing.

2A.    Before the search begins, a police officer, designated detention officer or staff custody officer, must tell the detainee:-

     (a)    that the authority to carry out the search has been given;

     (b)    the grounds for giving the authorisation and for believing that the article cannot be removed without an intimate search.

2B    Before a detainee is asked to give appropriate consent to a search under *paragraph 2(a)(ii)* (a drug offence search) they must be warned that if they refuse without good cause their refusal may harm their case if it comes to trial, see *Note A6*. This warning may be given by a police officer or member of police staff. A detainee who is not legally represented must be reminded of their entitlement to have free legal advice, see Code C, *paragraph 6.5*, and the reminder noted in the custody record.

3.    An intimate search may only be carried out by a registered medical practitioner or registered nurse, unless an officer of at least inspector rank considers this is not practicable and the search is to take place under *paragraph 2(a)(i)*, in which case a police officer may carry out the search. See *Notes A1 to A5*

3A.    Any proposal for a search under *paragraph 2(a)(i)* to be carried out by someone other than a registered medical practitioner or registered nurse must only be considered as a last resort and when the authorising officer is satisfied the risks associated with allowing the item to remain with the detainee outweigh the risks associated with removing it. See *Notes A1* to *A5*

4.    An intimate search under:

   • *paragraph 2(a)(i)* may take place only at a hospital, surgery, other medical premises or police station

   • *paragraph 2(a)(ii)* may take place only at a hospital, surgery or other medical premises and must be carried out by a registered medical practitioner or a registered nurse

5.    An intimate search at a police station of a juvenile or mentally disordered or otherwise mentally vulnerable person may take place only in the presence of an appropriate adult of the same sex, unless the detainee specifically requests a particular adult of the opposite sex who is readily available. In the case of a juvenile the search may take place in the absence of the appropriate adult only if the juvenile signifies in the presence of the appropriate adult they do not want the adult present during the search and the adult agrees. A record shall be made of the juvenile's decision and signed by the appropriate adult.

6.    When an intimate search under *paragraph 2(a)(i)* is carried out by a police officer, the officer must be of the same sex as the detainee. A minimum of two people, other than the detainee, must be present during the search. Subject to *paragraph 5*, no person of the opposite sex who is not a medical practitioner or nurse shall be present, nor shall anyone whose presence is unnecessary. The search shall be conducted with proper regard to the sensitivity and vulnerability of the detainee.

## (b)    Documentation

7.    In the case of an intimate search, the following shall be recorded as soon as practicable, in the detainee's custody record:

   (a)    for searches under *paragraphs 2(a)(i)* and *(ii);*

   • the authorisation to carry out the search;

   • the grounds for giving the authorisation;

   • the grounds for believing the article could not be removed without an intimate search

- which parts of the detainee's body were searched

- who carried out the search

- who was present

- the result.

(b)    for searches under paragraph 2(a)(ii):

- the giving of the warning required by *paragraph 2B*;

- the fact that the appropriate consent was given or (as the case may be) refused, and if refused, the reason given for the refusal (if any).

8.    If an intimate search is carried out by a police officer, the reason why it was impracticable for a registered medical practitioner or registered nurse to conduct it must be recorded.

**B    Strip search**

9.    A strip search is a search involving the removal of more than outer clothing. In this Code, outer clothing includes shoes and socks.

*(a)    Action*

10.    A strip search may take place only if it is considered necessary to remove an article which a detainee would not be allowed to keep, and the officer reasonably considers the detainee might have concealed such an article. Strip searches shall not be routinely carried out if there is no reason to consider that articles are concealed.

**The conduct of strip searches**

11.    When strip searches are conducted:

(a)    a police officer carrying out a strip search must be the same sex as the detainee;

(b)    the search shall take place in an area where the detainee cannot be seen by anyone who does not need to be present, nor by a member of the opposite sex except an appropriate adult who has been specifically requested by the detainee;

(c)    except in cases of urgency, where there is risk of serious harm to the detainee or to others, whenever a strip search involves exposure of intimate body parts, there must be at least two people present other than the detainee, and if the search is of a juvenile or mentally disordered or otherwise mentally vulnerable person, one of the people must be the appropriate adult. Except in urgent cases as above, a search of a juvenile may take place in the absence of the appropriate adult only if the juvenile signifies in the presence of the appropriate adult that they do not want the adult to be present during the search and the adult agrees. A record shall be made of the juvenile's decision and signed by the appropriate adult. The presence of more than two people, other than an appropriate adult, shall be permitted only in the most exceptional circumstances;

(d)    the search shall be conducted with proper regard to the sensitivity and vulnerability of the detainee in these circumstances and every reasonable effort shall be made to secure the detainee's co-operation and minimise embarrassment. Detainees who are searched shall not normally be required to remove all their clothes at the same time, e.g. a person should be allowed to remove clothing above the waist and redress before removing further clothing;

(e)    if necessary to assist the search, the detainee may be required to hold their arms in the air or to stand with their legs apart and bend forward so a visual examination may be made of the genital and anal areas provided no physical contact is made with any body orifice;

(f)    if articles are found, the detainee shall be asked to hand them over. If articles are found within any body orifice other than the mouth, and the detainee refuses to hand them over, their removal would constitute an intimate search, which must be carried out as in *Part A*;

(g)    a strip search shall be conducted as quickly as possible, and the detainee allowed to dress as soon as the procedure is complete.

### *(b)    Documentation*

12.    A record shall be made on the custody record of a strip search including the reason it was considered necessary, those present and any result.

### *Notes for guidance*

*A1    Before authorising any intimate search, the authorising officer must make every reasonable effort to persuade the detainee to hand the article over without a search. If the detainee agrees, a registered medical practitioner or registered nurse should whenever possible be asked to assess the risks involved and, if necessary, attend to assist the detainee.*

*A2    If the detainee does not agree to hand the article over without a search, the authorising officer must carefully review all the relevant factors before authorising an intimate search.*

*In particular, the officer must consider whether the grounds for believing an article may be concealed are reasonable.*

A3 *If authority is given for a search under paragraph 2(a)(i), a registered medical practitioner or registered nurse shall be consulted whenever possible. The presumption should be that the search will be conducted by the registered medical practitioner or registered nurse and the authorising officer must make every reasonable effort to persuade the detainee to allow the medical practitioner or nurse to conduct the search.*

A4 *A constable should only be authorised to carry out a search as a last resort and when all other approaches have failed. In these circumstances, the authorising officer must be satisfied the detainee might use the article for one or more of the purposes in paragraph 2(a)(i) and the physical injury likely to be caused is sufficiently severe to justify authorising a constable to carry out the search.*

A5 *If an officer has any doubts whether to authorise an intimate search by a constable, the officer should seek advice from an officer of superintendent rank or above.*

A6 *In warning a detainee who is asked to consent to an intimate drug offence search, as in paragraph 2B, the following form of words may be used:*

*"You do not have to allow yourself to be searched, but I must warn you that if you refuse without good cause, your refusal may harm your case if it comes to trial."*

*Where the use of the Welsh Language is appropriate, the following form of words may be used:*

*'Nid oes rhaid i chi roi caniatâd i gael eich archwilio, ond mae'n rhaid i mi eich rhybuddio os gwrthodwch heb reswm da, y gallai eich penderfyniad i wrthod wneud niwed i'ch achos pe bai'n dod gerbron llys.'*

## ANNEX B – DELAY IN NOTIFYING ARREST OR ALLOWING ACCESS TO LEGAL ADVICE

### A    Persons detained under PACE

1. The exercise of the rights in *Section 5* or *Section 6,* or both, may be delayed if the person is in police detention, as in PACE, section 118(2), in connection with an indictable offence, has not yet been charged with an offence and an officer of superintendent rank or above, or inspector rank or above only for the rights in *Section 5*, has reasonable grounds for believing their exercise will:

   (i) lead to:

   • interference with, or harm to, evidence connected with an indictable offence; or

   • interference with, or physical harm to, other people; or

   (ii) lead to alerting other people suspected of having committed an indictable offence but not yet arrested for it; or

   (iii) hinder the recovery of property obtained in consequence of the commission of such an offence.

2. These rights may also be delayed if the officer has reasonable grounds to believe that:

   (i) the person detained for an indictable offence has benefited from their criminal conduct (decided in accordance with Part 2 of the Proceeds of Crime Act 2002); and

   (ii) the recovery of the value of the property constituting that benefit will be hindered by the exercise of either right.

3. Authority to delay a detainee's right to consult privately with a solicitor may be given only if the authorising officer has reasonable grounds to believe the solicitor the detainee wants to consult will, inadvertently or otherwise, pass on a message from the detainee or act in some other way which will have any of the consequences specified under *paragraphs 1 or 2*. In these circumstances the detainee must be allowed to choose another solicitor. See *Note B3*

4. If the detainee wishes to see a solicitor, access to that solicitor may not be delayed on the grounds they might advise the detainee not to answer questions or the solicitor was initially asked to attend the police station by someone else. In the latter case the detainee must be told the solicitor has come to the police station at another person's request, and must be asked to sign the custody record to signify whether they want to see the solicitor.

5. The fact the grounds for delaying notification of arrest may be satisfied does not automatically mean the grounds for delaying access to legal advice will also be satisfied.

6. These rights may be delayed only for as long as grounds exist and in no case beyond 36 hours after the relevant time as in PACE, section 41. If the grounds cease to apply within this time, the detainee must, as soon as practicable, be asked if they want to exercise either right, the custody record must be noted accordingly, and action taken in accordance with the relevant section of the Code.

7. A detained person must be permitted to consult a solicitor for a reasonable time before any court hearing.

**B** Not used

**C** *Documentation*

13. The grounds for action under this Annex shall be recorded and the detainee informed of them as soon as practicable.

14. Any reply given by a detainee under *paragraphs 6* or *11* must be recorded and the detainee asked to endorse the record in relation to whether they want to receive legal advice at this point.

**D** *Cautions and special warnings*

15. When a suspect detained at a police station is interviewed during any period for which access to legal advice has been delayed under this Annex, the court or jury may not draw adverse inferences from their silence.

### Notes for guidance

*B1 Even if Annex B applies in the case of a juvenile, or a person who is mentally disordered or otherwise mentally vulnerable, action to inform the appropriate adult and the person responsible for a juvenile's welfare if that is a different person, must nevertheless be taken as in paragraph 3.13 and 3.15.*

*B2 In the case of Commonwealth citizens and foreign nationals, see Note 7A.*

*B3 A decision to delay access to a specific solicitor is likely to be a rare occurrence and only when it can be shown the suspect is capable of misleading that particular solicitor and there is more than a substantial risk that the suspect will succeed in causing information to be conveyed which will lead to one or more of the specified consequences.*

**ANNEX C – RESTRICTION ON DRAWING ADVERSE INFERENCES FROM SILENCE AND TERMS OF THE CAUTION WHEN THE RESTRICTION APPLIES**

*(a)   The restriction on drawing adverse inferences from silence*

1.   The Criminal Justice and Public Order Act 1994, sections 34, 36 and 37 as amended by the Youth Justice and Criminal Evidence Act 1999, section 58 describe the conditions under which adverse inferences may be drawn from a person's failure or refusal to say anything about their involvement in the offence when interviewed, after being charged or informed they may be prosecuted. These provisions are subject to an overriding restriction on the ability of a court or jury to draw adverse inferences from a person's silence. This restriction applies:

(a)   to any detainee at a police station, see Note 10C who, before being interviewed, see *section 11* or being charged or informed they may be prosecuted, see section 16, has:

   (i)    asked for legal advice, see *section 6, paragraph 6.1*;

   (ii)   not been allowed an opportunity to consult a solicitor, including the duty solicitor, as in this Code; and

   (iii)  not changed their mind about wanting legal advice, see *section 6, paragraph 6.6(d)*

   Note the condition in (ii) will

   –   apply when a detainee who has asked for legal advice is interviewed before speaking to a solicitor as in *section 6, paragraph 6.6(a)* or *(b)*.

   –   not apply if the detained person declines to ask for the duty solicitor, see *section 6, paragraphs 6.6(c)* and *(d)*;

(b)   to any person charged with, or informed they may be prosecuted for, an offence who:

   (i)    has had brought to their notice a written statement made by another person or the content of an interview with another person which relates to that offence, see *section 16, paragraph 16.4*;

   (ii)   is interviewed about that offence, see *section 16, paragraph 16.5*; or

   (iii)  makes a written statement about that offence, see *Annex D paragraphs 4* and *9*.

**(b)** **Terms of the caution when the restriction applies**

2.    When a requirement to caution arises at a time when the restriction on drawing adverse inferences from silence applies, the caution shall be:

*'You do not have to say anything, but anything you do say may be given in evidence.'*

Where the use of the Welsh Language is appropriate, the caution may be used directly in Welsh in the following terms:

*'Does dim rhaid i chi ddweud dim byd, ond gall unrhyw beth yr ydych chi'n ei ddweud gael ei roi fel tystiolaeth.'*

3.    Whenever the restriction either begins to apply or ceases to apply after a caution has already been given, the person shall be re-cautioned in the appropriate terms. The changed position on drawing inferences and that the previous caution no longer applies shall also be explained to the detainee in ordinary language. See *Note C2*

### Notes for guidance

C1    *The restriction on drawing inferences from silence does not apply to a person who has not been detained and who therefore cannot be prevented from seeking legal advice if they want to, see paragraphs 10.2 and 3.15.*

C2    *The following is suggested as a framework to help explain changes in the position on drawing adverse inferences if the restriction on drawing adverse inferences from silence:*

   (a)    *begins to apply:*

   *'The caution you were previously given no longer applies. This is because after that caution:*

   (i)    *you asked to speak to a solicitor but have not yet been allowed an opportunity to speak to a solicitor. See paragraph 1(a); or*

   (ii)    *you have been charged with/informed you may be prosecuted. See paragraph 1(b).*

   *'This means that from now on, adverse inferences cannot be drawn at court and your defence will not be harmed just because you choose to say nothing. Please listen carefully to the caution I am about to give you because it will apply from now on. You will see that it does not say anything about your defence being harmed.'*

(b)    *ceases to apply before or at the time the person is charged or informed they may be prosecuted, see paragraph 1(a);*

> *'The caution you were previously given no longer applies. This is because after that caution you have been allowed an opportunity to speak to a solicitor. Please listen carefully to the caution I am about to give you because it will apply from now on. It explains how your defence at court may be affected if you choose to say nothing.'*

## ANNEX D – WRITTEN STATEMENTS UNDER CAUTION

### (a) *Written by a person under caution*

1. A person shall always be invited to write down what they want to say.

2. A person who has not been charged with, or informed they may be prosecuted for, any offence to which the statement they want to write relates, shall:

   (a) unless the statement is made at a time when the restriction on drawing adverse inferences from silence applies, see Annex C, be asked to write out and sign the following before writing what they want to say:

   *'I make this statement of my own free will. I understand that I do not have to say anything but that it may harm my defence if I do not mention when questioned something which I later rely on in court. This statement may be given in evidence.';*

   (b) if the statement is made at a time when the restriction on drawing adverse inferences from silence applies, be asked to write out and sign the following before writing what they want to say;

   *'I make this statement of my own free will. I understand that I do not have to say anything. This statement may be given in evidence.'*

3. When a person, on the occasion of being charged with or informed they may be prosecuted for any offence, asks to make a statement which relates to any such offence and wants to write it they shall:

   (a) unless the restriction on drawing adverse inferences from silence, see *Annex C*, applied when they were so charged or informed they may be prosecuted, be asked to write out and sign the following before writing what they want to say:

   *'I make this statement of my own free will. I understand that I do not have to say anything but that it may harm my defence if I do not mention when questioned something which I later rely on in court. This statement may be given in evidence.';*

   (b) if the restriction on drawing adverse inferences from silence applied when they were so charged or informed they may be prosecuted, be asked to write out and sign the following before writing what they want to say:

   *'I make this statement of my own free will. I understand that I do not have to say anything. This statement may be given in evidence.'*

4.    When a person, who has already been charged with or informed they may be prosecuted for any offence, asks to make a statement which relates to any such offence and wants to write it they shall be asked to write out and sign the following before writing what they want to say:

*'I make this statement of my own free will. I understand that I do not have to say anything. This statement may be given in evidence.';*

5.    Any person writing their own statement shall be allowed to do so without any prompting except a police officer or other police staff may indicate to them which matters are material or question any ambiguity in the statement.

### (b)    Written by a police officer or other police staff

6.    If a person says they would like someone to write the statement for them, a police officer, or other police staff shall write the statement.

7.    If the person has not been charged with, or informed they may be prosecuted for, any offence to which the statement they want to make relates they shall, before starting, be asked to sign, or make their mark, to the following:

(a)    unless the statement is made at a time when the restriction on drawing adverse inferences from silence applies, see Annex C:

*'I, ..........................., wish to make a statement. I want someone to write down what I say. I understand that I do not have to say anything but that it may harm my defence if I do not mention when questioned something which I later rely on in court. This statement may be given in evidence.';*

(b)    if the statement is made at a time when the restriction on drawing adverse inferences from silence applies:

*'I, ..........................., wish to make a statement. I want someone to write down what I say. I understand that I do not have to say anything. This statement may be given in evidence.'*

8.    If, on the occasion of being charged with or informed they may be prosecuted for any offence, the person asks to make a statement which relates to any such offence they shall before starting be asked to sign, or make their mark to, the following:

(a)    unless the restriction on drawing adverse inferences from silence applied, see Annex C, when they were so charged or informed they may be prosecuted:

*'I, ..........................., wish to make a statement. I want someone to write down what I say. I understand that I do not have to say anything but that it may harm*

*my defence if I do not mention when questioned something which I later rely on in court. This statement may be given in evidence.';*

(b)    if the restriction on drawing adverse inferences from silence applied when they were so charged or informed they may be prosecuted:

*'I, ..........................., wish to make a statement. I want someone to write down what I say. I understand that I do not have to say anything. This statement may be given in evidence.'*

9.    If, having already been charged with or informed they may be prosecuted for any offence, a person asks to make a statement which relates to any such offence they shall before starting, be asked to sign, or make their mark to:

*'I, ..........................., wish to make a statement. I want someone to write down what I say. I understand that I do not have to say anything. This statement may be given in evidence.'*

10.    The person writing the statement must take down the exact words spoken by the person making it and must not edit or paraphrase it. Any questions that are necessary, e.g. to make it more intelligible, and the answers given must be recorded at the same time on the statement form.

11.    When the writing of a statement is finished the person making it shall be asked to read it and to make any corrections, alterations or additions they want. When they have finished reading they shall be asked to write and sign or make their mark on the following certificate at the end of the statement:

*'I have read the above statement, and I have been able to correct, alter or add anything I wish. This statement is true. I have made it of my own free will.'*

12.    If the person making the statement cannot read, or refuses to read it, or to write the above mentioned certificate at the end of it or to sign it, the person taking the statement shall read it to them and ask them if they would like to correct, alter or add anything and to put their signature or make their mark at the end. The person taking the statement shall certify on the statement itself what has occurred.

C

**ANNEX E – SUMMARY OF PROVISIONS RELATING TO MENTALLY DISORDERED AND OTHERWISE MENTALLY VULNERABLE PEOPLE**

1.    If an officer has any suspicion, or is told in good faith, that a person of any age may be mentally disordered or otherwise mentally vulnerable, or mentally incapable of understanding the significance of questions or their replies that person shall be treated as mentally disordered or otherwise mentally vulnerable for the purposes of this Code. See *paragraph 1.4*

2.    In the case of a person who is mentally disordered or otherwise mentally vulnerable, 'the appropriate adult' means:

    (a)    a relative, guardian or other person responsible for their care or custody;

    (b)    someone experienced in dealing with mentally disordered or mentally vulnerable people but who is not a police officer or employed by the police;

    (c)    failing these, some other responsible adult aged 18 or over who is not a police officer or employed by the police.

    See *paragraph 1.7(b) and Note 1D*

3.    If the custody officer authorises the detention of a person who is mentally vulnerable or appears to be suffering from a mental disorder, the custody officer must as soon as practicable inform the appropriate adult of the grounds for detention and the person's whereabouts, and ask the adult to come to the police station to see them. If the appropriate adult:

    •    is already at the station when information is given as in *paragraphs 3.1* to *3.5* the information must be given in their presence

    •    is not at the station when the provisions of *paragraph 3.1* to *3.5* are complied with these provisions must be complied with again in their presence once they arrive.

    See *paragraphs 3.15* to *3.17*

4.    If the appropriate adult, having been informed of the right to legal advice, considers legal advice should be taken, the provisions of *section 6* apply as if the mentally disordered or otherwise mentally vulnerable person had requested access to legal advice. See *paragraph 3.19* and *Note E1*.

5.    The custody officer must make sure a person receives appropriate clinical attention as soon as reasonably practicable if the person appears to be suffering from a mental disorder or in urgent cases immediately call the nearest health care professional or an ambulance. It is not intended these provisions delay the transfer of a detainee to a

place of safety under the Mental Health Act 1983, section 136 if that is applicable. If an assessment under that Act is to take place at a police station, the custody officer must consider whether an appropriate health care professional should be called to conduct an initial clinical check on the detainee. See *paragraph 9.5* and *9.6*

6.     It is imperative a mentally disordered or otherwise mentally vulnerable person detained under the Mental Health Act 1983, section 136 be assessed as soon as possible. If that assessment is to take place at the police station, an approved social worker and registered medical practitioner shall be called to the station as soon as possible in order to interview and examine the detainee. Once the detainee has been interviewed, examined and suitable arrangements been made for their treatment or care, they can no longer be detained under section 136. A detainee should be immediately discharged from detention if a registered medical practitioner having examined them, concludes they are not mentally disordered within the meaning of the Act. See *paragraph 3.16*

7.     If a mentally disordered or otherwise mentally vulnerable person is cautioned in the absence of the appropriate adult, the caution must be repeated in the appropriate adult's presence. See *paragraph 10.12*

8.     A mentally disordered or otherwise mentally vulnerable person must not be interviewed or asked to provide or sign a written statement in the absence of the appropriate adult unless the provisions of *paragraphs 11.1* or *11.18* to *11.20* apply. Questioning in these circumstances may not continue in the absence of the appropriate adult once sufficient information to avert the risk has been obtained. A record shall be made of the grounds for any decision to begin an interview in these circumstances. See *paragraphs 11.1, 11.15* and *11.18* to *11.20*

9.     If the appropriate adult is present at an interview, they shall be informed they are not expected to act simply as an observer and the purposes of their presence are to:

   •     advise the interviewee

   •     observe whether or not the interview is being conducted properly and fairly

   •     facilitate communication with the interviewee

   See *paragraph 11.17*

10.    If the detention of a mentally disordered or otherwise mentally vulnerable person is reviewed by a review officer or a superintendent, the appropriate adult must, if available at the time, be given an opportunity to make representations to the officer about the need for continuing detention. See *paragraph 15.3*

11.    If the custody officer charges a mentally disordered or otherwise mentally vulnerable person with an offence or takes such other action as is appropriate when there is sufficient evidence for a prosecution this must be done in the presence of the appropriate adult. The written notice embodying any charge must be given to the appropriate adult. See *paragraphs 16.1 to 16.4A*

12.    An intimate or strip search of a mentally disordered or otherwise mentally vulnerable person may take place only in the presence of the appropriate adult of the same sex, unless the detainee specifically requests the presence of a particular adult of the opposite sex. A strip search may take place in the absence of an appropriate adult only in cases of urgency when there is a risk of serious harm to the detainee or others. See *Annex A, paragraphs 5 and 11(c)*

13.    Particular care must be taken when deciding whether to use any form of approved restraints on a mentally disordered or otherwise mentally vulnerable person in a locked cell. See *paragraph 8.2*

## Notes for guidance

E1    *The purpose of the provision at paragraph 3.19 is to protect the rights of a mentally disordered or otherwise mentally vulnerable detained person who does not understand the significance of what is said to them. If the detained person wants to exercise the right to legal advice, the appropriate action should be taken and not delayed until the appropriate adult arrives. A mentally disordered or otherwise mentally vulnerable detained person should always be given an opportunity, when an appropriate adult is called to the police station, to consult privately with a solicitor in the absence of the appropriate adult if they want.*

E2    *Although people who are mentally disordered or otherwise mentally vulnerable are often capable of providing reliable evidence, they may, without knowing or wanting to do so, be particularly prone in certain circumstances to provide information that may be unreliable, misleading or self-incriminating. Special care should always be taken when questioning such a person, and the appropriate adult should be involved if there is any doubt about a person's mental state or capacity. Because of the risk of unreliable evidence, it is important to obtain corroboration of any facts admitted whenever possible.*

E3    *Because of the risks referred to in Note E2, which the presence of the appropriate adult is intended to minimise, officers of superintendent rank or above should exercise their discretion to authorise the commencement of an interview in the appropriate adult's absence only in exceptional cases, if it is necessary to avert an immediate risk of serious harm. See paragraphs 11.1, 11.18 to 11.20*

**ANNEX F – COUNTRIES WITH WHICH BILATERAL CONSULAR CONVENTIONS OR AGREEMENTS REQUIRING NOTIFICATION OF THE ARREST AND DETENTION OF THEIR NATIONALS ARE IN FORCE AS AT 1 APRIL 2003**

Armenia

Austria

Azerbaijan

Belarus

Belgium

Bosnia-Herzegovina

Bulgaria

China*

Croatia

Cuba

Czech Republic

Denmark

Egypt

France

Georgia

German Federal Republic

Greece

Hungary

Italy

Japan

Kazakhstan

Macedonia

Mexico

Moldova

Mongolia

Norway

Poland

Romania

Russia

Slovak Republic

Slovenia

Spain

Sweden

Tajikistan

Turkmenistan

Ukraine

USA

Uzbekistan

Yugoslavia

\* Police are required to inform Chinese officials of arrest/detention in the Manchester consular district only. This comprises Derbyshire, Durham, Greater Manchester, Lancashire, Merseyside, North South and West Yorkshire, and Tyne and Wear.

**ANNEX G – FITNESS TO BE INTERVIEWED**

1.    This Annex contains general guidance to help police officers and health care professionals assess whether a detainee might be at risk in an interview.

2.    A detainee may be at risk in a interview if it is considered that:

      (a)    conducting the interview could significantly harm the detainee's physical or mental state;

      (b)    anything the detainee says in the interview about their involvement or suspected involvement in the offence about which they are being interviewed **might** be considered unreliable in subsequent court proceedings because of their physical or mental state.

3.    In assessing whether the detainee should be interviewed, the following must be considered:

      (a)    how the detainee's physical or mental state might affect their ability to understand the nature and purpose of the interview, to comprehend what is being asked and to appreciate the significance of any answers given and make rational decisions about whether they want to say anything;

      (b)    the extent to which the detainee's replies may be affected by their physical or mental condition rather than representing a rational and accurate explanation of their involvement in the offence;

      (c)    how the nature of the interview, which could include particularly probing questions, might affect the detainee.

4.    It is essential health care professionals who are consulted consider the functional ability of the detainee rather than simply relying on a medical diagnosis, e.g. it is possible for a person with severe mental illness to be fit for interview.

5.    Health care professionals should advise on the need for an appropriate adult to be present, whether reassessment of the person's fitness for interview may be necessary if the interview lasts beyond a specified time, and whether a further specialist opinion may be required.

6.    When health care professionals identify risks they should be asked to quantify the risks. They should inform the custody officer:

      •    whether the person's condition:

           –    is likely to improve

        –      will require or be amenable to treatment; and

        •      indicate how long it may take for such improvement to take effect

7.      The role of the health care professional is to consider the risks and advise the custody officer of the outcome of that consideration. The health care professional's determination and any advice or recommendations should be made in writing and form part of the custody record.

8.      Once the health care professional has provided that information, it is a matter for the custody officer to decide whether or not to allow the interview to go ahead and if the interview is to proceed, to determine what safeguards are needed. Nothing prevents safeguards being provided in addition to those required under the Code. An example might be to have an appropriate health care professional present during the interview, in addition to an appropriate adult, in order constantly to monitor the person's condition and how it is being affected by the interview.

**ANNEX H – DETAINED PERSON: OBSERVATION LIST**

1.  If any detainee fails to meet any of the following criteria, an appropriate health care professional or an ambulance must be called.

2.  When assessing the level of rousability, consider:

    *Rousability* – can they be woken?

    •   go into the cell

    •   call their name

    •   shake gently

    *Response to questions* – can they give appropriate answers to questions such as:

    •   What's your name?

    •   Where do you live?

    •   Where do you think you are?

    *Response to commands* – can they respond appropriately to commands such as:

    •   Open your eyes!

    •   Lift one arm, now the other arm!

3.  Remember to take into account the possibility or presence of other illnesses, injury, or mental condition, a person who is drowsy and smells of alcohol may also have the following:

    •   Diabetes

    •   Epilepsy

    •   Head injury

    •   Drug intoxication or overdose

    •   Stroke

**ANNEX I** – Not Used

**ANNEX J** – Not Used

**ANNEX K – X-RAYS AND ULTRASOUND SCANS**

*(a)  Action*

1.      PACE, section 55A allows a person who has been arrested and is in police detention to have an X-ray taken of them or an ultrasound scan to be carried out on them (or both) if:

      (a)      authorised by an officer of inspector rank or above who has reasonable grounds for believing that the detainee:

           (i)      may have swallowed a Class A drug; and

           (ii)     was in possession of that Class A drug with the intention of supplying it to another or to export; and

      (b)      the detainee's appropriate consent has been given in writing.

2.      Before an x-ray is taken or an ultrasound scan carried out, a police officer, designated detention officer or staff custody officer must tell the detainee:-

      (a)      that the authority has been given; and

      (b)      the grounds for giving the authorisation.

3.      Before a detainee is asked to give appropriate consent to an x-ray or an ultrasound scan, they must be warned that if they refuse without good cause their refusal may harm their case if it comes to trial, see *Notes K1* and *K2*. This warning may be given by a police officer or member of police staff. A detainee who is not legally represented must be reminded of their entitlement to have free legal advice, see Code C, *paragraph 6.5*, and the reminder noted in the custody record.

4.      An x-ray may be taken, or an ultrasound scan may be carried out, only by a registered medical practitioner or registered nurse, and only at a hospital, surgery or other medical premises.

*(b)*    **Documentation**

5.      The following shall be recorded as soon as practicable in the detainee's custody record:

(a)      the authorisation to take the x-ray or carry out the ultrasound scan (or both);

(b)      the grounds for giving the authorisation;

(c)      the giving of the warning required by *paragraph 3*; and

(d)      the fact that the appropriate consent was given or (as the case may be) refused, and if refused, the reason given for the refusal (if any); and

(e)      if an x-ray is taken or an ultrasound scan carried out:

•      where it was taken or carried out

•      who took it or carried it out

•      who was present

•      the result

6       Paragraphs 1.4 – 1.7 of this Code apply and an appropriate adult should be present when consent is sought to any procedure under this Annex.

**Notes for guidance**

*K1*     *If authority is given for an x-ray to be taken or an ultrasound scan to be carried out (or both), consideration should be given to asking a registered medical practitioner or registered nurse to explain to the detainee what is involved and to allay any concerns the detainee might have about the effect which taking an x-ray or carrying out an ultrasound scan might have on them. If appropriate consent is not given, evidence of the explanation may, if the case comes to trial, be relevant to determining whether the detainee had a good cause for refusing.*

*K2*     *In warning a detainee who is asked to consent to an X-ray being taken or an ultrasound scan being carried out (or both), as in paragraph 3, the following form of words may be used:*

*"You do not have to allow an x-ray of you to be taken or an ultrasound scan to be carried out on you, but I must warn you that if you refuse without good cause, your refusal may harm your case if it comes to trial."*

Where the use of the Welsh Language is appropriate, the following form of words may be provided in Welsh:

*'Does dim rhaid i chi ganiatáu cymryd sgan uwchsain neu belydr-x (neu'r ddau) arnoch, ond mae'n rhaid i mi eich rhybuddio os byddwch chi'n gwrthod gwneud hynny heb reswm da, fe allai hynny niweidio eich achos pe bai'n dod gerbron llys.'*

C

# POLICE AND CRIMINAL EVIDENCE ACT 1984

# CODE D

**D**

## CODE OF PRACTICE FOR THE IDENTIFICATION OF PERSONS BY POLICE OFFICERS

**Commencement - Transitional Arrangements**

This code has effect in relation to any identification procedure carried out after midnight on 06 March 2011.

## 1   Introduction

1.1   This Code of Practice concerns the principal methods used by police to identify people in connection with the investigation of offences and the keeping of accurate and reliable criminal records.  The powers and procedures in this code must be used fairly, responsibly, with respect for the people to whom they apply and without unlawful discrimination.  The Equality Act 2010 makes it unlawful for police officers to discriminate against, harass or victimise any person on the grounds of the 'protected characteristics' of age, disability, gender reassignment, race, religion or belief, sex and sexual orientation, marriage and civil partnership, pregnancy and maternity when using their powers.  When police forces are carrying out their functions they also have a duty to have regard to the need to eliminate unlawful discrimination, harassment and victimisation and to take steps to foster good relations.

1.2   In this code, identification by an eye-witness arises when a witness who has seen the offender committing the crime and is given an opportunity to identify a person suspected of involvement in the offence in a video identification, identification parade or similar procedure.  These eye-witness identification procedures (see Part A of section 3 below) are designed to:

- test the witness' ability to identify the suspect as the person they saw on a previous occasion

- provide safeguards against mistaken identification.

While this Code concentrates on visual identification procedures, it does not preclude the police making use of aural identification procedures such as a "voice identification parade", where they judge that appropriate.

1.2A  In this code, separate provisions in Part B of section 3 below apply when any person, including a police officer, is asked if they recognise anyone they see in an image as being someone they know and to test their claim that they recognise that person as someone who is known to them.  Except where stated, these separate provisions are not subject to the eye-witnesses identification procedures described in paragraph 1.2.

1.3   Identification by fingerprints applies when a person's fingerprints are taken to:

- compare with fingerprints found at the scene of a crime

- check and prove convictions

- help to ascertain a person's identity.

1.3A  Identification using footwear impressions applies when a person's footwear impressions are taken to compare with impressions found at the scene of a crime.

1.4  Identification by body samples and impressions includes taking samples such as blood or hair to generate a DNA profile for comparison with material obtained from the scene of a crime, or a victim.

1.5  Taking photographs of arrested people applies to recording and checking identity and locating and tracing persons who:

- are wanted for offences

- fail to answer their bail.

1.6  Another method of identification involves searching and examining detained suspects to find, e.g., marks such as tattoos or scars which may help establish their identity or whether they have been involved in committing an offence.

1.7  The provisions of the Police and Criminal Evidence Act 1984 (PACE) and this Code are designed to make sure fingerprints, samples, impressions and photographs are taken, used and retained, and identification procedures carried out, only when justified and necessary for preventing, detecting or investigating crime. If these provisions are not observed, the application of the relevant procedures in particular cases may be open to question.

## 2  General

2.1  This Code must be readily available at all police stations for consultation by:

- police officers and police staff

- detained persons

- members of the public

2.2  The provisions of this Code:

- include the *Annexes*

- do not include the *Notes for guidance*.

2.3  Code C, paragraph 1.4, regarding a person who may be mentally disordered or otherwise mentally vulnerable and the *Notes for guidance* applicable to those provisions apply to this Code.

2.4  Code C, paragraph 1.5, regarding a person who appears to be under the age of 17 applies to this Code.

2.5   Code C, paragraph 1.6, regarding a person who appears to be blind, seriously visually impaired, deaf, unable to read or speak or has difficulty communicating orally because of a speech impediment applies to this Code.

2.6   In this Code:

- 'appropriate adult' means the same as in Code C, paragraph 1.7

- 'solicitor' means the same as in Code C, paragraph 6.12

and the *Notes for guidance* applicable to those provisions apply to this Code.

- where a search or other procedure under this code may only be carried out or observed by a person of the same sex as the person to whom the search or procedure applies, the gender of the detainee and other persons present should be established and recorded in line with Annex F of Code A.

2.7   References to custody officers include those performing the functions of custody officer, see *paragraph 1.9* of Code C.

2.8   When a record of any action requiring the authority of an officer of a specified rank is made under this Code, subject to *paragraph 2.18,* the officer's name and rank must be recorded.

2.9   When this Code requires the prior authority or agreement of an officer of at least inspector or superintendent rank, that authority may be given by a sergeant or chief inspector who has been authorised to perform the functions of the higher rank under PACE, section 107.

2.10  Subject to *paragraph 2.18*, all records must be timed and signed by the maker.

2.11  Records must be made in the custody record, unless otherwise specified. References to 'pocket book' include any official report book issued to police officers or police staff.

2.12  If any procedure in this Code requires a person's consent, the consent of a:

- mentally disordered or otherwise mentally vulnerable person is only valid if given in the presence of the appropriate adult

- juvenile is only valid if their parent's or guardian's consent is also obtained unless the juvenile is under 14, when their parent's or guardian's consent is sufficient in its own right.  If the only obstacle to an identification procedure in *section 3* is that a juvenile's parent or guardian refuses consent or reasonable efforts to obtain it have failed, the identification officer may apply the provisions of *paragraph 3.21.* See *Note 2A*

2.13   If a person is blind, seriously visually impaired or unable to read, the custody officer or identification officer shall make sure their solicitor, relative, appropriate adult or some other person likely to take an interest in them and not involved in the investigation is available to help check any documentation. When this Code requires written consent or signing, the person assisting may be asked to sign instead, if the detainee prefers. This paragraph does not require an appropriate adult to be called solely to assist in checking and signing documentation for a person who is not a juvenile, or mentally disordered or otherwise mentally vulnerable (see *Note 2B* and Code C *paragraph 3.15*).

2.14   If any procedure in this Code requires information to be given to or sought from a suspect, it must be given or sought in the appropriate adult's presence if the suspect is mentally disordered, otherwise mentally vulnerable or a juvenile. If the appropriate adult is not present when the information is first given or sought, the procedure must be repeated in the presence of the appropriate adult when they arrive. If the suspect appears deaf or there is doubt about their hearing or speaking ability or ability to understand English, and effective communication cannot be established, the information must be given or sought through an interpreter.

2.15   Any procedure in this Code involving the participation of a suspect who is mentally disordered, otherwise mentally vulnerable or a juvenile must take place in the presence of the appropriate adult. See Code C paragraph 1.4.

2.15A  Any procedure in this Code involving the participation of a witness who is or appears to be mentally disordered, otherwise mentally vulnerable or a juvenile should take place in the presence of a pre-trial support person unless the witness states that they do not want a support person to be present. A support person must not be allowed to prompt any identification of a suspect by a witness. See *Note 2AB*.

2.16   References to:

•      'taking a photograph', include the use of any process to produce a single, still or moving, visual image

•      'photographing a person', should be construed accordingly

•      'photographs', 'films', 'negatives' and 'copies' include relevant visual images recorded, stored, or reproduced through any medium

•      'destruction' includes the deletion of computer data relating to such images or making access to that data impossible

**D**

2.17   Except as described, nothing in this Code affects the powers and procedures:

(i)   for requiring and taking samples of breath, blood and urine in relation to driving offences, etc, when under the influence of drink, drugs or excess alcohol under the:

- Road Traffic Act 1988, sections 4 to 11

- Road Traffic Offenders Act 1988, sections 15 and 16

- Transport and Works Act 1992, sections 26 to 38;

(ii)   under the Immigration Act 1971, Schedule 2, paragraph 18, for taking photographs and fingerprints from persons detained under that Act, Schedule 2, paragraph 16 (Administrative Controls as to Control on Entry etc.); for taking fingerprints in accordance with the Immigration and Asylum Act 1999; sections 141 and 142(3), or other methods for collecting information about a person's external physical characteristics provided for by regulations made under that Act, section 144;

(iii)   under the Terrorism Act 2000, Schedule 8, for taking photographs, fingerprints, skin impressions, body samples or impressions from people:

- arrested under that Act, section 41,

- detained for the purposes of examination under that Act, Schedule 7, and to whom the Code of Practice issued under that Act, Schedule 14, paragraph 6, applies ('the terrorism provisions')

See *Note 2C*;

(iv)   for taking photographs, fingerprints, skin impressions, body samples or impressions from people who have been:

- arrested on warrants issued in Scotland, by officers exercising powers under the Criminal Justice and Public Order Act 1994, section 136(2)

- arrested or detained without warrant by officers from a police force in Scotland exercising their powers of arrest or detention under the Criminal Justice and Public Order Act 1994, section 137(2), (Cross Border powers of arrest etc.).

Note: In these cases, police powers and duties and the person's rights and entitlements whilst at a police station in England and Wales are the same as if the person had been arrested in Scotland by a Scottish police officer.

2.18   Nothing in this Code requires the identity of officers or police staff to be recorded or disclosed:

   (a)   in the case of enquiries linked to the investigation of terrorism;

   (b)   if the officers or police staff reasonably believe recording or disclosing their names might put them in danger.

   In these cases, they shall use warrant or other identification numbers and the name of their police station. *See Note 2D*

2.19   In this Code:

   (a)   'designated person' means a person other than a police officer, designated under the Police Reform Act 2002, Part 4, who has specified powers and duties of police officers conferred or imposed on them;

   (b)   any reference to a police officer includes a designated person acting in the exercise or performance of the powers and duties conferred or imposed on them by their designation.

2.20   If a power conferred on a designated person:

   (a)   allows reasonable force to be used when exercised by a police officer, a designated person exercising that power has the same entitlement to use force;

   (b)   includes power to use force to enter any premises, that power is not exercisable by that designated person except:

      (i)   in the company, and under the supervision, of a police officer; or

      (ii)   for the purpose of:

         •   saving life or limb; or

         •   preventing serious damage to property.

2.21   Nothing in this Code prevents the custody officer, or other officer given custody of the detainee, from allowing police staff who are not designated persons to carry out individual procedures or tasks at the police station if the law allows. However, the officer remains responsible for making sure the procedures and tasks are carried out correctly in accordance with the Codes of Practice. Any such person must be:

   (a)   a person employed by a police authority maintaining a police force and under the control and direction of the Chief Officer of that force;

   (b)   employed by a person with whom a police authority has a contract for the provision of services relating to persons arrested or otherwise in custody.

2.22   Designated persons and other police staff must have regard to any relevant provisions of the Codes of Practice.

**Notes for guidance**

2A     *For the purposes of paragraph 2.12, the consent required from a parent or guardian may, for a juvenile in the care of a local authority or voluntary organisation, be given by that authority or organisation.  In the case of a juvenile, nothing in paragraph 2.12 requires the parent, guardian or representative of a local authority or voluntary organisation to be present to give their consent, unless they are acting as the appropriate adult under paragraphs 2.14 or 2.15.  However, it is important that a parent or guardian not present is fully informed before being asked to consent.  They must be given the same information about the procedure and the juvenile's suspected involvement in the offence as the juvenile and appropriate adult.  The parent or guardian must also be allowed to speak to the juvenile and the appropriate adult if they wish. Provided the consent is fully informed and is not withdrawn, it may be obtained at any time before the procedure takes place.*

2AB    *The Youth Justice and Criminal Evidence Act 1999 guidance "Achieving Best Evidence in Criminal Proceedings" indicates that a pre-trial support person should accompany a vulnerable witness during any identification procedure unless the witness states that they do not want a support person to be present.  It states that this support person should not be (or not be likely to be) a witness in the investigation.*

2B     *People who are seriously visually impaired or unable to read may be unwilling to sign police documents.  The alternative, i.e. their representative signing on their behalf, seeks to protect the interests of both police and suspects.*

2C     *Photographs, fingerprints, samples and impressions may be taken from a person detained under the terrorism provisions to help determine whether they are, or have been, involved in terrorism, as well as when there are reasonable grounds for suspecting their involvement in a particular offence.*

2D     *The purpose of paragraph 2.18(b) is to protect those involved in serious organised crime investigations or arrests of particularly violent suspects when there is reliable information that those arrested or their associates may threaten or cause harm to the officers.  In cases of doubt, an officer of inspector rank or above should be consulted.*

**3      Identification and recognition of suspects**

*(A)    Identification of a suspect by an eye-witness*

3.0    This part applies when an eye-witness has seen the offender committing the crime or in any other circumstances which tend to prove or disprove the involvement of the person they saw in the crime, for example, close to the scene of the crime, immediately before or immediately after it was committed.  It sets out the procedures to be used to test the ability of that eye-witness to identify a person suspected of involvement in the offence as the person they saw on the previous occasion.  Except where stated, this part does not apply to the procedures described in Part B and *Note 3AA.*

3.1    A record shall be made of the suspect's description as first given by a potential witness.  This record must:

(a)    be made and kept in a form which enables details of that description to be accurately produced from it, in a visible and legible form, which can be given to the suspect or the suspect's solicitor in accordance with this Code; and

(b)    unless otherwise specified, be made before the witness takes part in any identification procedures under *paragraphs 3.5 to 3.10, 3.21 or 3.23.*

A copy of the record shall where practicable, be given to the suspect or their solicitor before any procedures under *paragraphs 3.5 to 3.10, 3.21 or 3.23* are carried out.  See *Note 3E*

*(a)    Cases when the suspect's identity is not known*

3.2    In cases when the suspect's identity is not known, a witness may be taken to a particular neighbourhood or place to see whether they can identify the person they saw on a previous occasion.  Although the number, age, sex, race, general description and style of clothing of other people present at the location and the way in which any identification is made cannot be controlled, the principles applicable to the formal procedures under *paragraphs 3.5 to 3.10* shall be followed as far as practicable.  For example:

(a)    where it is practicable to do so, a record should be made of the witness' description of the suspect, as in paragraph 3.1 (a), before asking the witness to make an identification;

(b)    care must be taken not to direct the witness' attention to any individual unless, taking into account all the circumstances, this cannot be avoided.  However, this does not prevent a witness being asked to look carefully at the people around at the time or to look towards a group or in a particular direction, if this appears necessary to make sure that the witness does not overlook a possible suspect simply because the witness is looking in the opposite direction and also to enable the witness to make comparisons between any suspect and others who are in the area;  See *Note 3F*

(c)    where there is more than one witness, every effort should be made to keep them separate and witnesses should be taken to see whether they can identify a person independently;

(d)    once there is sufficient information to justify the arrest of a particular individual for suspected involvement in the offence, e.g., after a witness makes a positive identification, the provisions set out from paragraph 3.4 onwards shall apply for any other witnesses in relation to that individual.;

(e)    the officer or police staff accompanying the witness must record, in their pocket book, the action taken as soon as, and in as much detail, as possible. The record should include: the date, time and place of the relevant occasion the witness claims to have previously seen the suspect; where any identification was made; how it was made and the conditions at the time (e.g., the distance the witness was from the suspect, the weather and light); if the witness's attention was drawn to the suspect; the reason for this; and anything said by the witness or the suspect about the identification or the conduct of the procedure.

3.3    A witness must not be shown photographs, computerised or artist's composite likenesses or similar likenesses or pictures (including 'E-fit' images) if the identity of the suspect is known to the police and the suspect is available to take part in a video identification, an identification parade or a group identification.  If the suspect's identity is not known, the showing of such images to a witness to obtain identification evidence must be done in accordance with *Annex E.*

(b)    Cases when the suspect is known and available

3.4    If the suspect's identity is known to the police and they are available, the identification procedures set out in paragraphs 3.5 to 3.10 may be used.  References in this section to a suspect being 'known' mean there is sufficient information known to the police to justify the arrest of a particular person for suspected involvement in the offence. A suspect being 'available' means they are immediately available or will be within a reasonably short time and willing to take an effective part in at least one of the following which it is practicable to arrange:

- video identification;

- identification parade; or

- group identification.

**Video identification**

3.5　A 'video identification' is when the witness is shown moving images of a known suspect, together with similar images of others who resemble the suspect.  Moving images must be used unless:

- the suspect is known but not available (see paragraph 3.21 of this Code); or

- in accordance with paragraph 2A of Annex A of this Code, the identification officer does not consider that replication of a physical feature can be achieved or that it is not possible to conceal the location of the feature on the image of the suspect.

  The identification officer may then decide to make use of video identification but using **still** images.

3.6　Video identifications must be carried out in accordance with *Annex A*.

**Identification parade**

3.7　An 'identification parade' is when the witness sees the suspect in a line of others who resemble the suspect.

3.8　Identification parades must be carried out in accordance with *Annex B*.

**Group identification**

3.9　A 'group identification' is when the witness sees the suspect in an informal group of people.

3.10　Group identifications must be carried out in accordance with *Annex C*.

**Arranging eye-witness identification procedures**

3.11　Except for the provisions in *paragraph 3.19*, the arrangements for, and conduct of, the identification procedures in paragraphs 3.5 to 3.10 and circumstances in which an identification procedure must be held shall be the responsibility of an officer not below inspector rank who is not involved with the investigation, 'the identification officer'. Unless otherwise specified, the identification officer may allow another officer or police staff, see *paragraph 2.21*, to make arrangements for, and conduct, any of these identification procedures.  In delegating these procedures, the identification officer must be able to supervise effectively and either intervene or be contacted for advice. No officer or any other person involved with the investigation of the case against the suspect, beyond the extent required by these procedures, may take any part in these procedures or act as the identification officer. This does not prevent the identification officer from consulting the officer in charge of the investigation to determine which procedure to use. When an identification procedure is required, in the interest of fairness to suspects and witnesses, it must be held as soon as practicable.

**Circumstances in which an eye-witness identification procedure must be held**

3.12 Whenever:

(i) an eye witness has identified a suspect or purported to have identified them prior to any identification procedure set out in paragraphs 3.5 to 3.10 having been held; or

(ii) there is a witness available who expresses an ability to identify the suspect, or where there is a reasonable chance of the witness being able to do so, and they have not been given an opportunity to identify the suspect in any of the procedures set out in paragraphs 3.5 to 3.10,

and the suspect disputes being the person the witness claims to have seen, an identification procedure shall be held unless it is not practicable or it would serve no useful purpose in proving or disproving whether the suspect was involved in committing the offence, for example:

• where the suspect admits being at the scene of the crime and gives an account of what took place and the eye-witness does not see anything which contradicts that.

• when it is not disputed that the suspect is already known to the witness who claims to have recognised them when seeing them commit the crime.

3.13 An eye-witness identification procedure may also be held if the officer in charge of the investigation considers it would be useful.

**Selecting an eye-witness identification procedure**

3.14 If, because of paragraph 3.12, an identification procedure is to be held, the suspect shall initially be offered a video identification unless:

(a) a video identification is not practicable; or

(b)    an identification parade is both practicable and more suitable than a video identification; or

(c)    paragraph 3.16 applies.

The identification officer and the officer in charge of the investigation shall consult each other to determine which option is to be offered.  An identification parade may not be practicable because of factors relating to the witnesses, such as their number, state of health, availability and travelling requirements.  A video identification would normally be more suitable if it could be arranged and completed sooner than an identification parade.  Before an option is offered the suspect must also be reminded of their entitlement to have free legal advice, see Code C, *paragraph 6.5*.

3.15    A suspect who refuses the identification procedure first offered shall be asked to state their reason for refusing and may get advice from their solicitor and/or if present, their appropriate adult.  The suspect, solicitor and/or appropriate adult shall be allowed to make representations about why another procedure should be used.  A record should be made of the reasons for refusal and any representations made.  After considering any reasons given, and representations made, the identification officer shall, if appropriate, arrange for the suspect to be offered an alternative which the officer considers suitable and practicable.  If the officer decides it is not suitable and practicable to offer an alternative identification procedure, the reasons for that decision shall be recorded.

3.16    A group identification may initially be offered if the officer in charge of the investigation considers it is more suitable than a video identification or an identification parade and the identification officer considers it practicable to arrange.

**Notice to suspect**

3.17    Unless *paragraph 3.20* applies, before a video identification, an identification parade or group identification is arranged, the following shall be explained to the suspect:

(i)    the purposes of the video identification, identification parade or group identification;

(ii)    their entitlement to free legal advice; see Code C, paragraph 6.5;

(iii)    the procedures for holding it, including their right to have a solicitor or friend present;

(iv)    that they do not have to consent to or co-operate in a video identification, identification parade or group identification;

(v)     that if they do not consent to, and co-operate in, a video identification, identification parade or group identification, their refusal may be given in evidence in any subsequent trial and police may proceed covertly without their consent or make other arrangements to test whether a witness can identify them, see *paragraph 3.21;*

(vi)    whether, for the purposes of the video identification procedure, images of them have previously been obtained, see *paragraph 3.20*, and if so, that they may co-operate in providing further, suitable images to be used instead;

(vii)   if appropriate, the special arrangements for juveniles;

(viii)  if appropriate, the special arrangements for mentally disordered or otherwise mentally vulnerable people;

(ix)    that if they significantly alter their appearance between being offered an identification procedure and any attempt to hold an identification procedure, this may be given in evidence if the case comes to trial, and the identification officer may then consider other forms of identification, see *paragraph 3.21* and *Note 3C*;

(x)     that a moving image or photograph may be taken of them when they attend for any identification procedure;

(xi)    whether, before their identity became known, the witness was shown photographs, a computerised or artist's composite likeness or similar likeness or image by the police, see *Note 3B;*

(xii)   that if they change their appearance before an identification parade, it may not be practicable to arrange one on the day or subsequently and, because of the appearance change, the identification officer may consider alternative methods of identification, see *Note 3C;*

(xiii)  that they or their solicitor will be provided with details of the description of the suspect as first given by any witnesses who are to attend the video identification, identification parade, group identification or confrontation, see paragraph 3.1.

3.18   This information must also be recorded in a written notice handed to the suspect. The suspect must be given a reasonable opportunity to read the notice, after which, they should be asked to sign a second copy to indicate if they are willing to co-operate with the making of a video or take part in the identification parade or group identification. The signed copy shall be retained by the identification officer.

3.19  The duties of the identification officer under *paragraphs 3.17* and *3.18* may be performed by the custody officer or other officer not involved in the investigation if:

(a)  it is proposed to release the suspect in order that an identification procedure can be arranged and carried out and an inspector is not available to act as the identification officer, see *paragraph 3.11*, before the suspect leaves the station; or

(b)  it is proposed to keep the suspect in police detention whilst the procedure is arranged and carried out and waiting for an inspector to act as the identification officer, see *paragraph 3.11,* would cause unreasonable delay to the investigation.

The officer concerned shall inform the identification officer of the action taken and give them the signed copy of the notice.  See *Note 3C*

3.20  If the identification officer and officer in charge of the investigation suspect, on reasonable grounds that if the suspect was given the information and notice as in *paragraphs 3.17* and *3.18*, they would then take steps to avoid being seen by a witness in any identification procedure, the identification officer may arrange for images of the suspect suitable for use in a video identification procedure to be obtained before giving the information and notice.  If suspect's images are obtained in these circumstances, the suspect may, for the purposes of a video identification procedure, co-operate in providing new images which if suitable, would be used instead, see *paragraph 3.17(vi)*.

**(c)  Cases when the suspect is known but not available**

3.21  When a known suspect is not available or has ceased to be available, see *paragraph 3.4*, the identification officer may make arrangements for a video identification (see Annex A).  If necessary, the identification officer may follow the video identification procedures but using still images.  Any suitable moving or still images may be used and these may be obtained covertly if necessary.  Alternatively, the identification officer may make arrangements for a group identification.  See *Note 3D*.  These provisions may also be applied to juveniles where the consent of their parent or guardian is either refused or reasonable efforts to obtain that consent have failed.  (see *paragraph 2.12*).

3.22  Any covert activity should be strictly limited to that necessary to test the ability of the witness to identify the suspect.

3.23  The identification officer may arrange for the suspect to be confronted by the witness if none of the options referred to in paragraphs 3.5 to 3.10 or 3.21 are practicable. A "confrontation" is when the suspect is directly confronted by the witness.  A confrontation does not require the suspect's consent.  Confrontations must be carried out in accordance with Annex D.

**D**

3.24   Requirements for information to be given to, or sought from, a suspect or for the suspect to be given an opportunity to view images before they are shown to a witness, do not apply if the suspect's lack of co-operation prevents the necessary action.

**(d)   Documentation**

3.25   A record shall be made of the video identification, identification parade, group identification or confrontation on forms provided for the purpose.

3.26   If the identification officer considers it is not practicable to hold a video identification or identification parade requested by the suspect, the reasons shall be recorded and explained to the suspect.

3.27   A record shall be made of a person's failure or refusal to co-operate in a video identification, identification parade or group identification and, if applicable, of the grounds for obtaining images in accordance with *paragraph 3.20*.

**(e)   Showing films and photographs of incidents and information released to the media**

3.28   Nothing in this Code inhibits showing films, photographs or other images to the public through the national or local media, or to police officers for the purposes of recognition and tracing suspects. However, when such material is shown to obtain evidence of recognition, the procedures in Part B will apply. See *Note 3AA*.

3.29   When a broadcast or publication is made, see *paragraph 3.28*, a copy of the relevant material released to the media for the purposes of recognising or tracing the suspect, shall be kept. The suspect or their solicitor shall be allowed to view such material before any eye-witness identification procedures under *paragraphs 3.5* to *3.10*, *3.21* or *3.23* of Part A are carried out, provided it is practicable and would not unreasonably delay the investigation. Each eye-witness involved in the procedure shall be asked, after they have taken part, whether they have seen any film, photograph or image relating to the offence or any description of the suspect which has been broadcast or published in any national or local media or on any social networking site and if they have, they should be asked to give details of the circumstances, such as the date and place as relevant. Their replies shall be recorded. This paragraph does not affect any separate requirement under the Criminal Procedure and Investigations Act 1996 to retain material in connection with criminal investigations.

**(f)    Destruction and retention of photographs taken or used in eye-witness identification procedures**

3.30   PACE, section 64A, see *paragraph 5.12*, provides powers to take photographs of suspects and allows these photographs to be used or disclosed only for purposes related to the prevention or detection of crime, the investigation of offences or the conduct of prosecutions by, or on behalf of, police or other law enforcement and prosecuting authorities inside and outside the United Kingdom or the enforcement of a sentence.  After being so used or disclosed, they may be retained but can only be used or disclosed for the same purposes.

3.31   Subject to *paragraph 3.33,* the photographs (and all negatives and copies), of suspects not taken in accordance with the provisions in *paragraph 5.12* which are taken for the purposes of, or in connection with, the identification procedures in *paragraphs 3.5 to 3.10, 3.21 or 3.23* must be destroyed unless the suspect:

(a)    is charged with, or informed they may be prosecuted for, a recordable offence;

(b)    is prosecuted for a recordable offence;

(c)    is cautioned for a recordable offence or given a warning or reprimand in accordance with the Crime and Disorder Act 1998 for a recordable offence; or

(d)    gives informed consent, in writing, for the photograph or images to be retained for purposes described in *paragraph 3.30.*

3.32   When *paragraph 3.31* requires the destruction of any photograph, the person must be given an opportunity to witness the destruction or to have a certificate confirming the destruction if they request one within five days of being informed that the destruction is required.

3.33   Nothing in *paragraph 3.31* affects any separate requirement under the Criminal Procedure and Investigations Act 1996 to retain material in connection with criminal investigations.

**(B)    *Evidence of recognition by showing films, photographs and other images***

3.34   This Part of this section applies when, for the purposes of obtaining evidence of recognition, any person, including a police officer:

(a)    views the image of an individual in a film, photograph or any other visual medium; and

(b)    is asked whether they recognise that individual as someone who is known to them.

See *Notes 3AA* and *3G*

3.35 The films, photographs and other images shall be shown on an individual basis to avoid any possibility of collusion and to provide safeguards against mistaken recognition (see *Note 3G*), the showing shall as far as possible follow the principles for video identification if the suspect is known, see *Annex A*, or identification by photographs if the suspect is not known, see *Annex E.*

3.36 A record of the circumstances and conditions under which the person is given an opportunity to recognise the individual must be made and the record must include:

(a)   Whether the person knew or was given information concerning the name or identity of any suspect.

(b)   What the person has been told *before* the viewing about the offence, the person(s) depicted in the images or the offender and by whom.

(c)   How and by whom the witness was asked to view the image or look at the individual.

(d)   Whether the viewing was alone or with others and if with others, the reason for it.

(e)   The arrangements under which the person viewed the film or saw the individual and by whom those arrangements were made.

(f)   Whether the viewing of any images was arranged as part of a mass circulation to police and the public or for selected persons.

(g)   The date time and place images were viewed or further viewed or the individual was seen.

(h)   The times between which the images were viewed or the individual was seen.

(i)   How the viewing of images or sighting of the individual was controlled and by whom.

(j)   Whether the person was familiar with the location shown in any images or the place where they saw the individual and if so, why.

(k)   Whether or not on this occasion, the person claims to recognise any image shown, or any individual seen, as being someone known to them, and if they do:

   (i)   the reason

   (ii)   the words of recognition

(iii)   any expressions of doubt

(iv)   what features of the image or the individual triggered the recognition.

3.37   The record under paragraph 3.36 may be made by:

- the person who views the image or sees the individual and makes the recognition.

- the officer or police staff in charge of showing the images to the person or in charge of the conditions under which the person sees the individual.

### Notes for guidance

3AA   *The eye-witness identification procedures in Part A should not be used to test whether a witness can recognise a person as someone they know and would be able to give evidence of recognition along the lines that "On (describe date, time location) I saw an image of an individual who I recognised as AB." In these cases, the procedures in Part B shall apply.*

3A   *Except for the provisions of Annex E, paragraph 1, a police officer who is a witness for the purposes of this part of the Code is subject to the same principles and procedures as a civilian witness.*

3B   *When a witness attending an identification procedure has previously been shown photographs, or been shown or provided with computerised or artist's composite likenesses, or similar likenesses or pictures, it is the officer in charge of the investigation's responsibility to make the identification officer aware of this.*

3C   *The purpose of paragraph 3.19 is to avoid or reduce delay in arranging identification procedures by enabling the required information and warnings, see sub-paragraphs 3.17(ix) and 3.17(xii), to be given at the earliest opportunity.*

3D   *Paragraph 3.21 would apply when a known suspect deliberately makes themselves 'unavailable' in order to delay or frustrate arrangements for obtaining identification evidence. It also applies when a suspect refuses or fails to take part in a video identification, an identification parade or a group identification, or refuses or fails to take part in the only practicable options from that list. It enables any suitable images of the suspect, moving or still, which are available or can be obtained, to be used in an identification procedure. Examples include images from custody and other CCTV systems and from visually recorded interview records, see Code F Note for Guidance 2D.*

D

3E   *When it is proposed to show photographs to a witness in accordance with Annex E, it is the responsibility of the officer in charge of the investigation to confirm to the officer responsible for supervising and directing the showing, that the first description of the suspect given by that witness has been recorded.  If this description has not been recorded, the procedure under Annex E must be postponed.  See Annex E paragraph 2*

3F   *The admissibility and value of identification evidence obtained when carrying out the procedure under paragraph 3.2 may be compromised if:*

   (a)   before a person is identified, the witness' attention is specifically drawn to that person; or

   (b)   the suspect's identity becomes known before the procedure.

3G   *The admissibility and value of evidence of recognition obtained when carrying out the procedures in Part B may be compromised if before the person is recognised, the witness who has claimed to know them is given or is made, or becomes aware of, information about the person which was not previously known to them personally but which they have purported to rely on to support their claim that the person is in fact known to them.*

**4   Identification by fingerprints and footwear impressions**

   *(A)   Taking fingerprints in connection with a criminal investigation*

   **(a)   General**

4.1   References to 'fingerprints' means any record, produced by any method, of the skin pattern and other physical characteristics or features of a person's:

   (i)   fingers; or

   (ii)   palms.

   **(b)   Action**

4.2   A person's fingerprints may be taken in connection with the investigation of an offence only with their consent or if *paragraph 4.3* applies.  If the person is at a police station consent must be in writing.

4.3   PACE, section 61, provides powers to take fingerprints without consent from any person over the age of ten years:

   (a)   under section 61(3), from a person detained at a police station in consequence of being arrested for a recordable offence, see *Note 4A*, if they have not had their fingerprints taken in the course of the investigation of the offence unless those previously taken fingerprints are not a complete set or some or all of those fingerprints are not of sufficient quality to allow satisfactory analysis, comparison or matching.

(b)     under section 61(4), from a person detained at a police station who has been charged with a recordable offence, see *Note 4A*, or informed they will be reported for such an offence if they have not had their fingerprints taken in the course of the investigation of the offence unless those previously taken fingerprints are not a complete set or some or all of those fingerprints are not of sufficient quality to allow satisfactory analysis, comparison or matching.

(c)     under section 61(4A), from a person who has been bailed to appear at a court or police station if the person:

(i)      has answered to bail for a person whose fingerprints were taken previously and there are reasonable grounds for believing they are not the same person; or

(ii)     who has answered to bail claims to be a different person from a person whose fingerprints were previously taken;

and in either case, the court or an officer of inspector rank or above, authorises the fingerprints to be taken at the court or police station (an inspector's authority may be given in writing or orally and confirmed in writing, as soon as practicable);

(ca)    under section 61(5A) from a person who has been arrested for a recordable offence and released if the person:

(i)      is on bail and has not had their fingerprints taken in the course of the investigation of the offence, or;

(ii)     has had their fingerprints taken in the course of the investigation of the offence, but they do not constitute a complete set or some, or all, of the fingerprints are not of sufficient quality to allow satisfactory analysis, comparison or matching.

(cb)    under section 61(5B) from a person not detained at a police station who has been charged with a recordable offence or informed they will be reported for such an offence if they have not had their fingerprints taken in the course of the investigation or their fingerprints have been taken in the course of the investigation of the offence, but they do not constitute a complete set or some, or all, of the fingerprints are not of sufficient quality to allow satisfactory analysis, comparison or matching.

(d)    under section 61(6), from a person who has been:

    (i)    convicted of a recordable offence;

    (ii)    given a caution in respect of a recordable offence which, at the time of the caution, the person admitted; or

    (iii)    warned or reprimanded under the Crime and Disorder Act 1998, section 65, for a recordable offence,

if, since their conviction, caution, warning or reprimand their fingerprints have not been taken or their fingerprints which have been taken since then do not constitute a complete set or some, or all, of the fingerprints are not of sufficient quality to allow satisfactory analysis, comparison or matching, and in either case, an officer of inspector rank or above, is satisfied that taking the fingerprints is necessary to assist in the prevention or detection of crime and authorises the taking;

(e)    under section 61(6A) from a person a constable reasonably suspects is committing or attempting to commit, or has committed or attempted to commit, any offence if either:

- the person's name is unknown and cannot be readily ascertained by the constable; or

- the constable has reasonable grounds for doubting whether a name given by the person is their real name.

Note: fingerprints taken under this power are not regarded as having been taken in the course of the investigation of an offence.

[See *Note 4C*]

(f)    under section 61(6D) from a person who has been convicted outside England and Wales of an offence which if committed in England and Wales would be a qualifying offence as defined by PACE, section 65A (see *Note 4AB*) if:

    (i)    the person's fingerprints have not been taken previously under this power or their fingerprints have been so taken on a previous occasion but they do not constitute a complete set or some, or all, of the fingerprints are not of sufficient quality to allow satisfactory analysis, comparison or matching; and

(ii)    a police officer of inspector rank or above is satisfied that taking fingerprints is necessary to assist in the prevention or detection of crime and authorises them to be taken.

4.4    PACE, section 63A(4) and Schedule 2A provide powers to:

(a)    make a requirement (in accordance with Annex G) for a person to attend a police station to have their fingerprints taken in the exercise of certain powers in paragraph 4.3 above when that power applies at the time the fingerprints would be taken in accordance with the requirement. Those powers are:

(i)    section 61(5A) – Persons arrested for a recordable offence and released, see paragraph 4.3(ca): The requirement may not be made more than six months from the day the investigating officer was informed that the fingerprints previously taken were incomplete or below standard.

(ii)    section 61(5B) – Persons charged etc. with a recordable offence, see paragraph 4.3(cb): The requirement may not be made more than six months from:

- the day the person was charged or reported if fingerprints have not been taken since then; or

- the day the investigating officer was informed that the fingerprints previously taken were incomplete or below standard.

(iii)    section 61(6) – Person convicted, cautioned, warned or reprimanded for a recordable offence in England and Wales, see paragraph 4.3(d): Where the offence for which the person was convicted etc is also a qualifying offence (see *Note 4AB*), there is no time limit for the exercise of this power. Where the conviction etc. is for a recordable offence which is <u>not</u> a qualifying offence, the requirement may not be made more than two years from:

- the day the person was convicted, cautioned, warned or reprimanded, or the day Schedule 2A comes into force (if later), if fingerprints have not been taken since then; or

- the day an officer from the force investigating the offence was informed that the fingerprints previously taken were incomplete or below standard or the day Schedule 2A comes into force (if later).

(v)    section 61(6D) – A person who has been convicted of a qualifying offence (see *Note 4AB*) outside England and Wales, see paragraph 4.3(g): There is no time limit for making the requirement.

D

Note:  A person who has had their fingerprints taken under any of the powers in section 61 mentioned in paragraph 4.3 on two occasions in relation to any offence may not be required under Schedule 2A to attend a police station for their fingerprints to be taken again under section 61 in relation to that offence, unless authorised by an officer of inspector rank or above.  The fact of the authorisation and the reasons for giving it must be recorded as soon as practicable.

**(b)    arrest, without warrant, a person who fails to comply with the requirement.**

4.5    A person's fingerprints may be taken, as above, electronically.

4.6    Reasonable force may be used, if necessary, to take a person's fingerprints without their consent under the powers as in *paragraphs 4.3* and *4.4.*

4.7    Before any fingerprints are taken:

(a)    without consent under any power mentioned in *paragraphs 4.3* and *4.4* above, the person must be informed of:

(i)    the reason their fingerprints are to be taken;

(ii)    the power under which they are to be taken; and

(iii)    the fact that the relevant authority has been given if any power mentioned in *paragraph 4.3(c), (d)* or *(f)* applies

(b)    with or without consent at a police station or elsewhere, the person must be informed:

(i)    that their fingerprints may be subject of a speculative search against other fingerprints, see *Note 4B*; and

(ii)    that their fingerprints may be retained in accordance with *Annex F, Part (a)* unless they were taken under the power mentioned in paragraph 4.3(e) when they must be destroyed after they have being checked (See *Note 4C*).

**(c)    Documentation**

4.8A    A record must be made as soon as practicable after the fingerprints are taken, of:

•    the matters in paragraph 4.7(a)(i) to (iii) and the fact that the person has been informed of those matters; and

•    the fact that the person has been informed of the matters in paragraph 4.7(b) (i) and (ii).

The record must be made in the person's custody record if they are detained at a police station when the fingerprints are taken.

4.8    If force is used, a record shall be made of the circumstances and those present.

4.9    Not used

**(B)    Taking fingerprints in connection with immigration enquiries**

**Action**

4.10   A person's fingerprints may be taken and retained for the purposes of immigration law enforcement and control in accordance with powers and procedures other than under PACE and for which the UK Border Agency (not the police) are responsible.  Details of these powers and procedures which are under the Immigration Act 1971, Schedule 2 and Immigration and Asylum Act 1999, section 141, including modifications to the PACE Codes of Practice are contained in Chapter 24 of the Operational Instructions and Guidance manual which is published by the UK Border Agency (See *Note 4D).*

4.11   *Not used*

4.12   *Not used*

4.13   *Not used*

4.14   *Not used*

4.15   *Not used*

**(C)    Taking footwear impressions in connection with a criminal investigation**

**(a)    Action**

4.16   Impressions of a person's footwear may be taken in connection with the investigation of an offence only with their consent or if *paragraph 4.17* applies.  If the person is at a police station consent must be in writing.

4.17   PACE, section 61A, provides power for a police officer to take footwear impressions without consent from any person over the age of ten years who is detained at a police station:

(a)    in consequence of being arrested for a recordable offence, see *Note 4A*; or if the detainee has been charged with a recordable offence, or informed they will be reported for such an offence; and

(b)    the detainee has not had an impression of their footwear taken in the course of the investigation of the offence unless the previously taken impression is not complete or is not of sufficient quality to allow satisfactory analysis, comparison or matching (whether in the case in question or generally).

4.18    Reasonable force may be used, if necessary, to take a footwear impression from a detainee without consent under the power in *paragraph 4.17*.

4.19    Before any footwear impression is taken with, or without, consent as above, the person must be informed:

   (a)    of the reason the impression is to be taken;

   (b)    that the impression may be retained and may be subject of a speculative search against other impressions, see *Note 4B*, unless destruction of the impression is required in accordance with *Annex F, Part (a)*; and

   (c)    that if their footwear impressions are required to be destroyed, they may witness their destruction as provided for in *Annex F, Part (a)*.

**(b)    Documentation**

4.20    A record must be made as soon as possible, of the reason for taking a person's footwear impressions without consent. If force is used, a record shall be made of the circumstances and those present.

4.21    A record shall be made when a person has been informed under the terms of *paragraph 4.19(b),* of the possibility that their footwear impressions may be subject of a speculative search.

*Notes for guidance*

4A    *References to 'recordable offences' in this Code relate to those offences for which convictions, cautions, reprimands and warnings may be recorded in national police records. See PACE, section 27(4). The recordable offences current at the time when this Code was prepared, are any offences which carry a sentence of imprisonment on conviction (irrespective of the period, or the age of the offender or actual sentence passed) as well as the non-imprisonable offences under the Vagrancy Act 1824 sections 3 and 4 (begging and persistent begging), the Street Offences Act 1959, section 1 (loitering or soliciting for purposes of prostitution), the Road Traffic Act 1988, section 25 (tampering with motor vehicles), the Criminal Justice and Public Order Act 1994, section 167 (touting for hire car services) and others listed in the National Police Records (Recordable Offences) Regulations 2000 as amended.*

4AB    *A qualifying offence is one of the offences specified in PACE, section 65A. These indictable offences which concern the use or threat of violence or unlawful force against persons, sexual offences and offences against children include, for example, murder, manslaughter, false imprisonment, kidnapping and other offences such as:*

- *sections 4, 16, 18, 20 to 24 or 47 of the Offences Against the Person Act 1861;*

- *sections 16 to 18 of the Firearms Act 1968;*

- *sections 9 or 10 of the Theft Act 1968 or under section 12A of that Act involving an accident which caused a person's death;*

- *section 1 of the Criminal Damage Act 1971 required to be charged as arson;*

- *section 1 of the Protection of Children Act 1978 and;*

- *sections 1 to 19, 25, 26, 30 to 41, 47 to 50, 52, 53, 57 to 59, 61 to 67, 69 and 70 of the Sexual Offences Act 2003.*

4B    *Fingerprints, footwear impressions or a DNA sample (and the information derived from it) taken from a person arrested on suspicion of being involved in a recordable offence, or charged with such an offence, or informed they will be reported for such an offence, may be subject of a speculative search.  This means the fingerprints, footwear impressions or DNA sample may be checked against other fingerprints, footwear impressions and DNA records held by, or on behalf of, the police and other law enforcement authorities in, or outside, the UK, or held in connection with, or as a result of, an investigation of an offence inside or outside the UK.  Fingerprints, footwear impressions and samples taken from a person suspected of committing a recordable offence but not arrested, charged or informed they will be reported for it, may be subject to a speculative search only if the person consents in writing.  The following is an example of a basic form of words:*

> *"I consent to my fingerprints, footwear impressions and DNA sample and information derived from it being retained and used only for purposes related to the prevention and detection of a crime, the investigation of an offence or the conduct of a prosecution either nationally or internationally.*

> *I understand that my fingerprints, footwear impressions or DNA sample may be checked against other fingerprint, footwear impressions and DNA records held by or on behalf of relevant law enforcement authorities, either nationally or internationally.*

> *I understand that once I have given my consent for my fingerprints, footwear impressions or DNA sample to be retained and used I cannot withdraw this consent."*

**D**

*See Annex F regarding the retention and use of fingerprints and footwear impressions taken with consent for elimination purposes.*

4C   *The power under section 61(6A) of PACE described in paragraph 4.3(e) allows fingerprints of a suspect who has not been arrested to be taken in connection with any offence (whether recordable or not) using a mobile device and then checked on the street against the database containing the national fingerprint collection. Fingerprints taken under this power cannot be retained after they have been checked. The results may make an arrest for the suspected offence based on the name condition unnecessary (See Code G paragraph 2.9(a)) and enable the offence to be disposed of without arrest, for example, by summons/charging by post, penalty notice or words of advice. If arrest for a non-recordable offence is necessary for any other reasons, this power may also be exercised at the station. Before the power is exercised, the officer should:*

- *inform the person of the nature of the suspected offence and why they are suspected of committing it.*

- *give them a reasonable opportunity to establish their real name before deciding that their name is unknown and cannot be readily ascertained or that there are reasonable grounds to doubt that a name they have given is their real name.*

- *as applicable, inform the person of the reason why their name is not know and cannot be readily ascertained or of the grounds for doubting that a name they have given is their real name, including, for example, the reason why a particular document the person has produced to verify their real name, is not sufficient.*

4D   *Powers to take fingerprints without consent for immigration purposes are given to police and immigration officers under the:*

(a)   *Immigration Act 1971, Schedule 2, paragraph 18(2), when it is reasonably necessary for the purposes of identifying a person detained under the Immigration Act 1971, Schedule 2, paragraph 16 (Detention of person liable to examination or removal), and*

(b)   *Immigration and Asylum Act 1999, section 141(7) when a person:*

- *fails without reasonable excuse to produce, on arrival, a valid passport with a photograph or some other document satisfactorily establishing their identity and nationality;*

- *is refused entry to the UK but is temporarily admitted if an immigration officer reasonably suspects the person might break a residence or reporting condition;*

- *is subject to directions for removal from the UK;*

- *has been arrested under the Immigration Act 1971, Schedule 2, paragraph 17;*

- *has made a claim for asylum*

- *is a dependant of any of the above.*

*The Immigration and Asylum Act 1999, section 142(3), also gives police and immigration officers power to arrest without warrant, a person who fails to comply with a requirement imposed by the Secretary of State to attend a specified place for fingerprinting.*

## 5 Examinations to establish identity and the taking of photographs

### (A) Detainees at police stations

### (a) Searching or examination of detainees at police stations

5.1 PACE, section 54A(1), allows a detainee at a police station to be searched or examined or both, to establish:

(a) whether they have any marks, features or injuries that would tend to identify them as a person involved in the commission of an offence and to photograph any identifying marks, see *paragraph 5.5*; or

(b) their identity, see *Note 5A*.

A person detained at a police station to be searched under a stop and search power, see Code A, is not a detainee for the purposes of these powers.

5.2 A search and/or examination to find marks under section 54A (1) (a) may be carried out without the detainee's consent, see *paragraph 2.12*, only if authorised by an officer of at least inspector rank when consent has been withheld or it is not practicable to obtain consent, see *Note 5D*.

5.3 A search or examination to establish a suspect's identity under section 54A (1) (b) may be carried out without the detainee's consent, see *paragraph 2.12*, only if authorised by an officer of at least inspector rank when the detainee has refused to identify themselves or the authorising officer has reasonable grounds for suspecting the person is not who they claim to be.

5.4 Any marks that assist in establishing the detainee's identity, or their identification as a person involved in the commission of an offence, are identifying marks. Such marks may be photographed with the detainee's consent, see *paragraph 2.12*; or without their consent if it is withheld or it is not practicable to obtain it, see *Note 5D.*

5.5    A detainee may only be searched, examined and photographed under section 54A, by a police officer of the same sex.

5.6    Any photographs of identifying marks, taken under section 54A, may be used or disclosed only for purposes related to the prevention or detection of crime, the investigation of offences or the conduct of prosecutions by, or on behalf of, police or other law enforcement and prosecuting authorities inside, and outside, the UK. After being so used or disclosed, the photograph may be retained but must not be used or disclosed except for these purposes, see *Note 5B.*

5.7    The powers, as in *paragraph 5.1,* do not affect any separate requirement under the Criminal Procedure and Investigations Act 1996 to retain material in connection with criminal investigations.

5.8    Authority for the search and/or examination for the purposes of *paragraphs 5.2* and *5.3* may be given orally or in writing. If given orally, the authorising officer must confirm it in writing as soon as practicable.  A separate authority is required for each purpose which applies.

5.9    If it is established a person is unwilling to co-operate sufficiently to enable a search and/or examination to take place or a suitable photograph to be taken, an officer may use reasonable force to:

(a)    search and/or examine a detainee without their consent; and

(b)    photograph any identifying marks without their consent.

5.10   The thoroughness and extent of any search or examination carried out in accordance with the powers in section 54A must be no more than the officer considers necessary to achieve the required purpose. Any search or examination which involves the removal of more than the person's outer clothing shall be conducted in accordance with Code C, Annex A, paragraph 11.

5.11   An intimate search may not be carried out under the powers in section 54A.

**(b)    Photographing detainees at police stations and other persons elsewhere than at a police station**

5.12   Under PACE, section 64A, an officer may photograph:

(a)    any person whilst they are detained at a police station; and

(b)    any person who is elsewhere than at a police station and who has been:

(i)    arrested by a constable for an offence;

(ii)    taken into custody by a constable after being arrested for an offence by a person other than a constable;

(iii)    made subject to a requirement to wait with a community support officer under paragraph 2(3) or (3B) of Schedule 4 to the Police Reform Act 2002;

(iiia)    given a direction by a constable under section 27 of the Violent Crime Reduction Act 2006.

(iv)    given a penalty notice by a constable in uniform under Chapter 1 of Part 1 of the Criminal Justice and Police Act 2001, a penalty notice by a constable under section 444A of the Education Act 1996, or a fixed penalty notice by a constable in uniform under section 54 of the Road Traffic Offenders Act 1988;

(v)    given a notice in relation to a relevant fixed penalty offence (within the meaning of paragraph 1 of Schedule 4 to the Police Reform Act 2002) by a community support officer by virtue of a designation applying that paragraph to him;

(vi)    given a notice in relation to a relevant fixed penalty offence (within the meaning of paragraph 1 of Schedule 5 to the Police Reform Act 2002) by an accredited person by virtue of accreditation specifying that that paragraph applies to him; or

(vii)    given a direction to leave and not return to a specified location for up to 48 hours by a police constable (under section 27 of the Violent Crime Reduction Act 2006).

5.12A Photographs taken under PACE, section 64A:

(a)    may be taken with the person's consent, or without their consent if consent is withheld or it is not practicable to obtain their consent, see *Note 5E*; and

(b)    may be used or disclosed only for purposes related to the prevention or detection of crime, the investigation of offences or the conduct of prosecutions by, or on behalf of, police or other law enforcement and prosecuting authorities inside and outside the United Kingdom or the enforcement of any sentence or order made by a court when dealing with an offence. After being so used or disclosed, they may be retained but can only be used or disclosed for the same purposes. See *Note 5B*.

5.13    The officer proposing to take a detainee's photograph may, for this purpose, require the person to remove any item or substance worn on, or over, all, or any part of, their head or face.  If they do not comply with such a requirement, the officer may remove the item or substance.

5.14    If it is established the detainee is unwilling to co-operate sufficiently to enable a suitable photograph to be taken and it is not reasonably practicable to take the photograph covertly, an officer may use reasonable force, see *Note 5F*.

(a)    to take their photograph without their consent; and

(b)    for the purpose of taking the photograph, remove any item or substance worn on, or over, all, or any part of, the person's head or face which they have failed to remove when asked.

5.15    For the purposes of this Code, a photograph may be obtained without the person's consent by making a copy of an image of them taken at any time on a camera system installed anywhere in the police station.

**(c)    Information to be given**

5.16    When a person is searched, examined or photographed under the provisions as in *paragraph 5.1* and *5.12*, or their photograph obtained as in *paragraph 5.15*, they must be informed of the:

(a)    purpose of the search, examination or photograph;

(b)    grounds on which the relevant authority, if applicable, has been given; and

(c)    purposes for which the photograph may be used, disclosed or retained.

This information must be given before the search or examination commences or the photograph is taken, except if the photograph is:

(i)    to be taken covertly;

(ii)    obtained as in *paragraph 5.15*, in which case the person must be informed as soon as practicable after the photograph is taken or obtained.

**(d)    Documentation**

5.17    A record must be made when a detainee is searched, examined, or a photograph of the person, or any identifying marks found on them, are taken. The record must include the:

(a)    identity, subject to paragraph 2.18, of the officer carrying out the search, examination or taking the photograph;

(b)   purpose of the search, examination or photograph and the outcome;

(c)   detainee's consent to the search, examination or photograph, or the reason the person was searched, examined or photographed without consent;

(d)   giving of any authority as in *paragraphs 5.2* and *5.3*, the grounds for giving it and the authorising officer.

5.18   If force is used when searching, examining or taking a photograph in accordance with this section, a record shall be made of the circumstances and those present.

**(B)   *Persons at police stations not detained***

5.19   When there are reasonable grounds for suspecting the involvement of a person in a criminal offence, but that person is at a police station **voluntarily** and not detained, the provisions of *paragraphs 5.1* to *5.18* should apply, subject to the modifications in the following paragraphs.

5.20   References to the 'person being detained' and to the powers mentioned in *paragraph 5.1* which apply only to detainees at police stations shall be omitted.

5.21   Force may not be used to:

(a)   search and/or examine the person to:

(i)   discover whether they have any marks that would tend to identify them as a person involved in the commission of an offence; or

(ii)   establish their identity, see *Note 5A*;

(b)   take photographs of any identifying marks, see *paragraph 5.4*; or

(c)   take a photograph of the person.

5.22   Subject to *paragraph 5.24*, the photographs of persons or of their identifying marks which are not taken in accordance with the provisions mentioned in *paragraphs 5.1* or *5.12*, must be destroyed (together with any negatives and copies) unless the person:

(a)   is charged with, or informed they may be prosecuted for, a recordable offence;

(b)   is prosecuted for a recordable offence;

(c)   is cautioned for a recordable offence or given a warning or reprimand in accordance with the Crime and Disorder Act 1998 for a recordable offence; or

(d)   gives informed consent, in writing, for the photograph or image to be retained as in *paragraph 5.6*.

5.23    When *paragraph 5.22* requires the destruction of any photograph, the person must be given an opportunity to witness the destruction or to have a certificate confirming the destruction provided they so request the certificate within five days of being informed the destruction is required.

5.24    Nothing in *paragraph 5.22* affects any separate requirement under the Criminal Procedure and Investigations Act 1996 to retain material in connection with criminal investigations.

**Notes for guidance**

5A    *The conditions under which fingerprints may be taken to assist in establishing a person's identity, are described in Section 4.*

5B    *Examples of purposes related to the prevention or detection of crime, the investigation of offences or the conduct of prosecutions include:*

(a)    *checking the photograph against other photographs held in records or in connection with, or as a result of, an investigation of an offence to establish whether the person is liable to arrest for other offences;*

(b)    *when the person is arrested at the same time as other people, or at a time when it is likely that other people will be arrested, using the photograph to help establish who was arrested, at what time and where;*

(c)    *when the real identity of the person is not known and cannot be readily ascertained or there are reasonable grounds for doubting a name and other personal details given by the person, are their real name and personal details. In these circumstances, using or disclosing the photograph to help to establish or verify their real identity or determine whether they are liable to arrest for some other offence, e.g. by checking it against other photographs held in records or in connection with, or as a result of, an investigation of an offence;*

(d)    *when it appears any identification procedure in section 3 may need to be arranged for which the person's photograph would assist;*

(e)    *when the person's release without charge may be required, and if the release is:*

(i)    *on bail to appear at a police station, using the photograph to help verify the person's identity when they answer their bail and if the person does not answer their bail, to assist in arresting them; or*

(ii)    *without bail, using the photograph to help verify their identity or assist in locating them for the purposes of serving them with a summons to appear at court in criminal proceedings;*

(f)    *when the person has answered to bail at a police station and there are reasonable grounds for doubting they are the person who was previously granted bail, using the photograph to help establish or verify their identity;*

(g)    *when the person arrested on a warrant claims to be a different person from the person named on the warrant and a photograph would help to confirm or disprove their claim;*

(h)    *when the person has been charged with, reported for, or convicted of, a recordable offence and their photograph is not already on record as a result of (a) to (f) or their photograph is on record but their appearance has changed since it was taken and the person has not yet been released or brought before a court.*

5C    *There is no power to arrest a person convicted of a recordable offence solely to take their photograph. The power to take photographs in this section applies only where the person is in custody as a result of the exercise of another power, e.g. arrest for fingerprinting under PACE, section 27.*

5D    *Examples of when it would not be practicable to obtain a detainee's consent, see paragraph 2.12, to a search, examination or the taking of a photograph of an identifying mark include:*

    (a)    *when the person is drunk or otherwise unfit to give consent;*

    (b)    *when there are reasonable grounds to suspect that if the person became aware a search or examination was to take place or an identifying mark was to be photographed, they would take steps to prevent this happening, e.g. by violently resisting, covering or concealing the mark etc and it would not otherwise be possible to carry out the search or examination or to photograph any identifying mark;*

    (c)    *in the case of a juvenile, if the parent or guardian cannot be contacted in sufficient time to allow the search or examination to be carried out or the photograph to be taken.*

5E    *Examples of when it would not be practicable to obtain the person's consent, see paragraph 2.12, to a photograph being taken include:*

    (a)    *when the person is drunk or otherwise unfit to give consent;*

    (b)    *when there are reasonable grounds to suspect that if the person became aware a photograph, suitable to be used or disclosed for the use and disclosure described in paragraph 5.6, was to be taken, they would take steps to prevent it being taken, e.g. by violently resisting, covering or distorting their face etc, and it would not otherwise be possible to take a suitable photograph;*

**D**

(c)   *when, in order to obtain a suitable photograph, it is necessary to take it covertly; and*

(d)   *in the case of a juvenile, if the parent or guardian cannot be contacted in sufficient time to allow the photograph to be taken.*

5F   *The use of reasonable force to take the photograph of a suspect elsewhere than at a police station must be carefully considered. In order to obtain a suspect's consent and co-operation to remove an item of religious headwear to take their photograph, a constable should consider whether in the circumstances of the situation the removal of the headwear and the taking of the photograph should be by an officer of the same sex as the person. It would be appropriate for these actions to be conducted out of public view.*

## 6   Identification by body samples and impressions

### (A)   General

6.1   References to:

(a)   an 'intimate sample' mean a dental impression or sample of blood, semen or any other tissue fluid, urine, or pubic hair, or a swab taken from any part of a person's genitals or from a person's body orifice other than the mouth;

(b)   a 'non-intimate sample' means:

(i)   a sample of hair, other than pubic hair, which includes hair plucked with the root, see Note 6A;

(ii)   a sample taken from a nail or from under a nail;

(iii)   a swab taken from any part of a person's body other than a part from which a swab taken would be an intimate sample;

(iv)   saliva;

(v)   a skin impression which means any record, other than a fingerprint, which is a record, in any form and produced by any method, of the skin pattern and other physical characteristics or features of the whole, or any part of, a person's foot or of any other part of their body.

### (B)   Action

### (a)   Intimate samples

6.2    PACE, section 62, provides that intimate samples may be taken under:

(a)    section 62(1), from a person in police detention only:

(i)    if a police officer of inspector rank or above has reasonable grounds to believe such an impression or sample will tend to confirm or disprove the suspect's involvement in a recordable offence, see *Note 4A*, and gives authorisation for a sample to be taken; and

(ii)   with the suspect's written consent;

(b)    section 62(1A), from a person not in police detention but from whom two or more non-intimate samples have been taken in the course of an investigation of an offence and the samples, though suitable, have proved insufficient if:

(i)    a police officer of inspector rank or above authorises it to be taken; and

(ii)   the person concerned gives their written consent.  See *Notes 6B* and *6C*

(c)    section 62(2A), from a person convicted outside England and Wales of an offence which if committed in England and Wales would be qualifying offence as defined by PACE, section 65A (see *Note 4AB*) from whom two or more non-intimate samples taken under section 63(3E) (see paragraph 6.6(h) have proved insufficient if:

(i)    a police officer of inspector rank or above is satisfied that taking the sample is necessary to assist in the prevention or detection of crime and authorises it to be taken; and

(ii)   the person concerned gives their written consent.

6.2A   PACE, section 63A(4) and Schedule 2A provide powers to:

(a)    make a requirement (in accordance with Annex G) for a person to attend a police station to have an intimate sample taken in the exercise of one of the following powers in paragraph 6.2 when that power applies at the time the sample is to be taken in accordance with the requirement or after the person's arrest if they fail to comply with the requirement:

(i)    section 62(1A) – Persons from whom two or more non-intimate samples have been taken and proved to be insufficient, see paragraph 6.2(b): There is no time limit for making the requirement.

(ii)   section 62(2A) – Persons convicted outside England and Wales from whom two or more non-intimate samples taken under section 63(3E) (see paragraph 6.6(h) have proved insufficient, see *paragraph 6.2(c)*: There is no time limit for making the requirement.

6.3   Before a suspect is asked to provide an intimate sample, they must be:

(a)   informed:

   (i)   of the reason, including the nature of the suspected offence (except if taken under *paragraph 6.2(c)* from a person convicted outside England and Wales.

   (ii)   that authorisation has been given and the provisions under which given;

   (iii)   that a sample taken at a police station may be subject of a speculative search;

(b)   warned that if they refuse without good cause their refusal may harm their case if it comes to trial, see *Note 6D*. If the suspect is in police detention and not legally represented, they must also be reminded of their entitlement to have free legal advice, see Code C, *paragraph 6.5*, and the reminder noted in the custody record. If *paragraph 6.2(b)* applies and the person is attending a station voluntarily, their entitlement to free legal advice as in Code C, *paragraph 3.21* shall be explained to them.

6.4   Dental impressions may only be taken by a registered dentist. Other intimate samples, except for samples of urine, may only be taken by a registered medical practitioner or registered nurse or registered paramedic.

**(b)   Non-intimate samples**

6.5   A non-intimate sample may be taken from a detainee only with their written consent or if *paragraph 6.6* applies.

6.6   a non-intimate sample may be taken from a person without the appropriate consent in the following circumstances:

(a)   under section 63(2A) from a person who is in police detention as a consequence of being arrested for a recordable offence and who has not had a non-intimate sample of the same type and from the same part of the body taken in the course of the investigation of the offence by the police or they have had such a sample taken but it proved insufficient.

(b)   Under section 63(3) from a person who is being held in custody by the police on the authority of a court if an officer of at least the rank of inspector authorises it to be taken. An authorisation may be given:

    (i)    if the authorising officer has reasonable grounds for suspecting the person of involvement in a recordable offence and for believing that the sample will tend to confirm or disprove that involvement, and

    (ii)   in writing or orally and confirmed in writing, as soon as practicable;

but an authorisation may not be given to take from the same part of the body a further non-intimate sample consisting of a skin impression unless the previously taken impression proved insufficient

(c)   under section 63(3ZA) from a person who has been arrested for a recordable offence and released if the person:

    (i)    is on bail and has not had a sample of the same type and from the same part of the body taken in the course of the investigation of the offence, or;

    (ii)   has had such a sample taken in the course of the investigation of the offence, but it proved unsuitable or insufficient.

(d)   under section 63(3A), from a person (whether or not in police detention or held in custody by the police on the authority of a court) who has been charged with a recordable offence or informed they will be reported for such an offence if the person:

    (i)    has not had a non-intimate sample taken from them in the course of the investigation of the offence;

    (ii)   has had a sample so taken, but it proved unsuitable or insufficient, see *Note 6B*; or

    (iii)  has had a sample taken in the course of the investigation of the offence and the sample has been destroyed and in proceedings relating to that offence there is a dispute as to whether a DNA profile relevant to the proceedings was derived from the destroyed sample.

(e)   under section 63(3B), from a person who has been:

    (i)    convicted of a recordable offence;

    (ii)   given a caution in respect of a recordable offence which, at the time of the caution, the person admitted; or

    (iii)  warned or reprimanded under the Crime and Disorder Act 1998, section 65, for a recordable offence, if, since their conviction, caution, warning or reprimand a non-intimate sample has not been taken from them or a sample which has been taken since then has proved to be unsuitable or insufficient and in either case, an officer of inspector rank or above, is satisfied that taking the fingerprints is necessary to assist in the prevention or detection of crime and authorises the taking;

(f)     under section 63(3C) from a person to whom section 2 of the Criminal Evidence (Amendment) Act 1997 applies (persons detained following acquittal on grounds of insanity or finding of unfitness to plead).

(g)     under section 63(3E) from a person who has been convicted outside England and Wales of an offence which if committed in England and Wales would be a qualifying offence as defined by PACE, section 65A (see *Note 4AB*) if:

   (i)     a non-intimate sample has not been taken previously under this power or unless a sample was so taken but was unsuitable or insufficient; and

   (ii)    a police officer of inspector rank or above is satisfied that taking a sample is necessary to assist in the prevention or detection of crime and authorises it to be taken.

6.6A   PACE, section 63A(4) and Schedule 2A provide powers to:

(a)     make a requirement (in accordance with Annex G) for a person to attend a police station to have a non-intimate sample taken in the exercise of one of the following powers in paragraph 6.6 when that power applies at the time the sample would be taken in accordance with the requirement:

   (i)     section 63(3ZA) – Persons arrested for a recordable offence and released, see paragraph 6.6(c): The requirement may not be made more than six months from the day the investigating officer was informed that the sample previously taken was unsuitable or insufficient.

   (ii)    section 63(3A) – Persons charged etc. with a recordable offence, see paragraph 6.6(d): The requirement may not be made more than six months from:

   •    the day the person was charged or reported if a sample has not been taken since then; or

   •    the day the investigating officer was informed that the sample previously taken was unsuitable or insufficient.

(iii) section 63(3B) – Person convicted, cautioned, warned or reprimanded for a recordable offence in England and Wales, see paragraph 6.6(e): Where the offence for which the person was convicted etc is also a qualifying offence (see *Note 4AB*), there is no time limit for the exercise of this power. Where the conviction etc was for a recordable offence that is <u>not</u> a qualifying offence, the requirement may not be made more than two years from:

- the day the person was convicted, cautioned, warned or reprimanded, or the day Schedule 2A comes into force (if later), if a samples has not been taken since then; or

- the day an officer from the force investigating the offence was informed that the sample previously taken was unsuitable or insufficient or the day Schedule 2A comes into force (if later).

(iv) section 63(3E) – A person who has been convicted of qualifying offence (see *Note 4AB*) outside England and Wales, see paragraph 6.6(h): There is no time limit for making the requirement.

Note: A person who has had a non-intimate sample taken under any of the powers in section 63 mentioned in paragraph 6.6 on two occasions in relation to any offence may not be required under Schedule 2A to attend a police station for a sample to be taken again under section 63 in relation to that offence, unless authorised by an officer of inspector rank or above. The fact of the authorisation and the reasons for giving it must be recorded as soon as practicable.

**(b)    arrest, without warrant, a person who fails to comply with the requirement.**

6.7    Reasonable force may be used, if necessary, to take a non-intimate sample from a person without their consent under the powers mentioned in *paragraph 6.6.*

6.8    Before any non-intimate sample is taken:

(a) without consent under any power mentioned in paragraphs 6.6 and 6.6A, the person must be informed of:

(i) the reason for taking the sample;

(ii) the power under which the sample is to be taken;

(iii) the fact that the relevant authority has been given if any power mentioned in *paragraph 6.6(b), (e) or (h)* applies;

(b)     with or without consent at a police station or elsewhere, the person must be informed:

    (i)     that their sample or information derived from it may be subject of a speculative search against other samples and information derived from them, see *Note 6E* and

    (ii)    that their sample and the information derived from it may be retained in accordance with Annex F, Part (a).

**(c)     Removal of clothing**

6.9     When clothing needs to be removed in circumstances likely to cause embarrassment to the person, no person of the opposite sex who is not a registered medical practitioner or registered health care professional shall be present, (unless in the case of a juvenile, mentally disordered or mentally vulnerable person, that person specifically requests the presence of an appropriate adult of the opposite sex who is readily available) nor shall anyone whose presence is unnecessary. However, in the case of a juvenile, this is subject to the overriding proviso that such a removal of clothing may take place in the absence of the appropriate adult only if the juvenile signifies in their presence, that they prefer the adult's absence and they agree.

**(c)     Documentation**

6.10    A record must be made as soon as practicable after the sample is taken of:

- The matters in paragraph 6.8(a)(i) to (iii) and the fact that the person has been informed of those matters; and

- The fact that the person has been informed of the matters in paragraph 6.8(b) (i) and (ii).

6.10A If force is used, a record shall be made of the circumstances and those present.

6.11    A record must be made of a warning given as required by *paragraph 6.3*.

6.12    *Not used*

**Notes for guidance**

*6A     When hair samples are taken for the purpose of DNA analysis (rather than for other purposes such as making a visual match), the suspect should be permitted a reasonable choice as to what part of the body the hairs are taken from. When hairs are plucked, they should be plucked individually, unless the suspect prefers otherwise and no more should be plucked than the person taking them reasonably considers necessary for a sufficient sample.*

6B  (a)  *An insufficient sample is one which is not sufficient either in quantity or quality to provide information for a particular form of analysis, such as DNA analysis. A sample may also be insufficient if enough information cannot be obtained from it by analysis because of loss, destruction, damage or contamination of the sample or as a result of an earlier, unsuccessful attempt at analysis.*

(b)  *An unsuitable sample is one which, by its nature, is not suitable for a particular form of analysis.*

6C  *Nothing in paragraph 6.2 prevents intimate samples being taken for elimination purposes with the consent of the person concerned but the provisions of paragraph 2.12 relating to the role of the appropriate adult, should be applied. Paragraph 6.2(b) does not, however, apply where the non-intimate samples were previously taken under the Terrorism Act 2000, Schedule 8, paragraph 10.*

6D  *In warning a person who is asked to provide an intimate sample as in paragraph 6.3, the following form of words may be used:*

*'You do not have to provide this sample/allow this swab or impression to be taken, but I must warn you that if you refuse without good cause, your refusal may harm your case if it comes to trial.'*

6E  *Fingerprints or a DNA sample and the information derived from it taken from a person arrested on suspicion of being involved in a recordable offence, or charged with such an offence, or informed they will be reported for such an offence, may be subject of a speculative search. This means they may be checked against other fingerprints and DNA records held by, or on behalf of, the police and other law enforcement authorities in or outside the UK or held in connection with, or as a result of, an investigation of an offence inside or outside the UK. Fingerprints and samples taken from any other person, e.g. a person suspected of committing a recordable offence but who has not been arrested, charged or informed they will be reported for it, may be subject to a speculative search only if the person consents in writing to their fingerprints being subject of such a search. The following is an example of a basic form of words:*

*"I consent to my fingerprints/DNA sample and information derived from it being retained and used only for purposes related to the prevention and detection of a crime, the investigation of an offence or the conduct of a prosecution either nationally or internationally.*

*I understand that this sample may be checked against other fingerprint/DNA records held by or on behalf of relevant law enforcement authorities, either nationally or internationally.*

*I understand that once I have given my consent for the sample to be retained and used I cannot withdraw this consent."*

*See Annex F regarding the retention and use of fingerprints and samples taken with consent for elimination purposes.*

6F   *Samples of urine and non-intimate samples taken in accordance with sections 63B and 63C of PACE may not be used for identification purposes in accordance with this Code. See Code C note for guidance 17D.*

### Annex A - Video identification

#### (a)   General

1.   The arrangements for obtaining and ensuring the availability of a suitable set of images to be used in a video identification must be the responsibility of an identification officer, who has no direct involvement with the case.

2.   The set of images must include the suspect and at least eight other people who, so far as possible, resemble the suspect in age, general appearance and position in life. Only one suspect shall appear in any set unless there are two suspects of roughly similar appearance, in which case they may be shown together with at least twelve other people.

2A   If the suspect has an unusual physical feature, e.g., a facial scar, tattoo or distinctive hairstyle or hair colour which does not appear on the images of the other people that are available to be used, steps may be taken to:

   (a)   conceal the location of the feature on the images of the suspect and the other people; or

   (b)   replicate that feature on the images of the other people.

   For these purposes, the feature may be concealed or replicated electronically or by any other method which it is practicable to use to ensure that the images of the suspect and other people resemble each other.  The identification officer has discretion to choose whether to conceal or replicate the feature and the method to be used.  If an unusual physical feature has been described by the witness, the identification officer should, if practicable, have that feature replicated.  If it has not been described, concealment may be more appropriate.

2B   If the identification officer decides that a feature should be concealed or replicated, the reason for the decision and whether the feature was concealed or replicated in the images shown to any witness shall be recorded.

2C   If the witness requests to view an image where an unusual physical feature has been concealed or replicated without the feature being concealed or replicated, the witness may be allowed to do so.

3.   The images used to conduct a video identification shall, as far as possible, show the suspect and other people in the same positions or carrying out the same sequence of movements.  They shall also show the suspect and other people under identical conditions unless the identification officer reasonably believes:

**D**

(a)　because of the suspect's failure or refusal to co-operate or other reasons, it is not practicable for the conditions to be identical; and

(b)　any difference in the conditions would not direct a witness' attention to any individual image.

4.　The reasons identical conditions are not practicable shall be recorded on forms provided for the purpose.

5.　Provision must be made for each person shown to be identified by number.

6.　If police officers are shown, any numerals or other identifying badges must be concealed. If a prison inmate is shown, either as a suspect or not, then either all, or none of, the people shown should be in prison clothing.

7.　The suspect or their solicitor, friend, or appropriate adult must be given a reasonable opportunity to see the complete set of images before it is shown to any witness. If the suspect has a reasonable objection to the set of images or any of the participants, the suspect shall be asked to state the reasons for the objection. Steps shall, if practicable, be taken to remove the grounds for objection. If this is not practicable, the suspect and/or their representative shall be told why their objections cannot be met and the objection, the reason given for it and why it cannot be met shall be recorded on forms provided for the purpose.

8.　Before the images are shown in accordance with *paragraph 7,* the suspect or their solicitor shall be provided with details of the first description of the suspect by any witnesses who are to attend the video identification. When a broadcast or publication is made, as in *paragraph 3.28*, the suspect or their solicitor must also be allowed to view any material released to the media by the police for the purpose of recognising or tracing the suspect, provided it is practicable and would not unreasonably delay the investigation.

9.　The suspect's solicitor, if practicable, shall be given reasonable notification of the time and place the video identification is to be conducted so a representative may attend on behalf of the suspect. The suspect may not be present when the images are shown to the witness(es). In the absence of the suspect's solicitor, the viewing itself shall be recorded on video. No unauthorised people may be present.

*(b)　Conducting the video identification*

10.　The identification officer is responsible for making the appropriate arrangements to make sure, before they see the set of images, witnesses are not able to communicate with each other about the case, see any of the images which are to be shown, see, or be reminded of, any photograph or description of the suspect or be given any other indication as to the suspect's identity, or overhear a witness who has already seen the material.  There must be no discussion with the witness about the composition of the set of images and they must not be told whether a previous witness has made any identification.

11.   Only one witness may see the set of images at a time.  Immediately before the images are shown, the witness shall be told that the person they saw on a specified earlier occasion may, or may not, appear in the images they are shown and that if they cannot make a positive identification, they should say so.  The witness shall be advised that at any point, they may ask to see a particular part of the set of images or to have a particular image frozen for them to study.  Furthermore, it should be pointed out to the witness that there is no limit on how many times they can view the whole set of images or any part of them.  However, they should be asked not to make any decision as to whether the person they saw is on the set of images until they have seen the whole set at least twice.

12.   Once the witness has seen the whole set of images at least twice and has indicated that they do not want to view the images, or any part of them, again, the witness shall be asked to say whether the individual they saw in person on a specified earlier occasion has been shown and, if so, to identify them by number of the image.  The witness will then be shown that image to confirm the identification, see *paragraph 17.*

13.   Care must be taken not to direct the witness' attention to any one individual image or give any indication of the suspect's identity.  Where a witness has previously made an identification by photographs, or a computerised or artist's composite or similar likeness, the witness must not be reminded of such a photograph or composite likeness once a suspect is available for identification by other means in accordance with this Code.  Nor must the witness be reminded of any description of the suspect.

14.   After the procedure, each witness shall be asked whether they have seen any broadcast or published films or photographs, or any descriptions of suspects relating to the offence and their reply shall be recorded.

### (c)   *Image security and destruction*

15.   Arrangements shall be made for all relevant material containing sets of images used for specific identification procedures to be kept securely and their movements accounted for.  In particular, no-one involved in the investigation shall be permitted to view the material prior to it being shown to any witness.

16.   As appropriate, *paragraph 3.30 or 3.31* applies to the destruction or retention of relevant sets of images.

### (d)    Documentation

17.    A record must be made of all those participating in, or seeing, the set of images whose names are known to the police.

18.    A record of the conduct of the video identification must be made on forms provided for the purpose.  This shall include anything said by the witness about any identifications or the conduct of the procedure and any reasons it was not practicable to comply with any of the provisions of this Code governing the conduct of video identifications.

**Annex B - Identification parades**

### (a) General

1. A suspect must be given a reasonable opportunity to have a solicitor or friend present, and the suspect shall be asked to indicate on a second copy of the notice whether or not they wish to do so.

2. An identification parade may take place either in a normal room or one equipped with a screen permitting witnesses to see members of the identification parade without being seen. The procedures for the composition and conduct of the identification parade are the same in both cases, subject to *paragraph 8* (except that an identification parade involving a screen may take place only when the suspect's solicitor, friend or appropriate adult is present or the identification parade is recorded on video).

3. Before the identification parade takes place, the suspect or their solicitor shall be provided with details of the first description of the suspect by any witnesses who are attending the identification parade. When a broadcast or publication is made as in *paragraph 3.28*, the suspect or their solicitor should also be allowed to view any material released to the media by the police for the purpose of recognising or tracing the suspect, provided it is practicable to do so and would not unreasonably delay the investigation.

### (b) Identification parades involving prison inmates

4. If a prison inmate is required for identification, and there are no security problems about the person leaving the establishment, they may be asked to participate in an identification parade or video identification.

5. An identification parade may be held in a Prison Department establishment but shall be conducted, as far as practicable under normal identification parade rules. Members of the public shall make up the identification parade unless there are serious security, or control, objections to their admission to the establishment. In such cases, or if a group or video identification is arranged within the establishment, other inmates may participate. If an inmate is the suspect, they are not required to wear prison clothing for the identification parade unless the other people taking part are other inmates in similar clothing, or are members of the public who are prepared to wear prison clothing for the occasion.

### (c) Conduct of the identification parade

6. Immediately before the identification parade, the suspect must be reminded of the procedures governing its conduct and cautioned in the terms of Code C, paragraphs 10.5 or 10.6, as appropriate.

7.    All unauthorised people must be excluded from the place where the identification parade is held.

8.    Once the identification parade has been formed, everything afterwards, in respect of it, shall take place in the presence and hearing of the suspect and any interpreter, solicitor, friend or appropriate adult who is present (unless the identification parade involves a screen, in which case everything said to, or by, any witness at the place where the identification parade is held, must be said in the hearing and presence of the suspect's solicitor, friend or appropriate adult or be recorded on video).

9.    The identification parade shall consist of at least eight people (in addition to the suspect) who, so far as possible, resemble the suspect in age, height, general appearance and position in life. Only one suspect shall be included in an identification parade unless there are two suspects of roughly similar appearance, in which case they may be paraded together with at least twelve other people. In no circumstances shall more than two suspects be included in one identification parade and where there are separate identification parades, they shall be made up of different people.

10.   If the suspect has an unusual physical feature, e.g., a facial scar, tattoo or distinctive hairstyle or hair colour which cannot be replicated on other members of the identification parade, steps may be taken to conceal the location of that feature on the suspect and the other members of the identification parade if the suspect and their solicitor, or appropriate adult, agree. For example, by use of a plaster or a hat, so that all members of the identification parade resemble each other in general appearance.

11.   When all members of a similar group are possible suspects, separate identification parades shall be held for each unless there are two suspects of similar appearance when they may appear on the same identification parade with at least twelve other members of the group who are not suspects. When police officers in uniform form an identification parade any numerals or other identifying badges shall be concealed.

12.   When the suspect is brought to the place where the identification parade is to be held, they shall be asked if they have any objection to the arrangements for the identification parade or to any of the other participants in it and to state the reasons for the objection. The suspect may obtain advice from their solicitor or friend, if present, before the identification parade proceeds. If the suspect has a reasonable objection to the arrangements or any of the participants, steps shall, if practicable, be taken to remove the grounds for objection. When it is not practicable to do so, the suspect shall be told why their objections cannot be met and the objection, the reason given for it and why it cannot be met, shall be recorded on forms provided for the purpose.

13. The suspect may select their own position in the line, but may not otherwise interfere with the order of the people forming the line.  When there is more than one witness, the suspect must be told, after each witness has left the room, that they can, if they wish, change position in the line. Each position in the line must be clearly numbered, whether by means of a number laid on the floor in front of each identification parade member or by other means.

14. Appropriate arrangements must be made to make sure, before witnesses attend the identification parade, they are not able to:

    (i)    communicate with each other about the case or overhear a witness who has already seen the identification parade;

    (ii)   see any member of the identification parade;

    (iii)  see, or be reminded of, any photograph or description of the suspect or be given any other indication as to the suspect's identity; or

    (iv)   see the suspect before or after the identification parade.

15. The person conducting a witness to an identification parade must not discuss with them the composition of the identification parade and, in particular, must not disclose whether a previous witness has made any identification.

16. Witnesses shall be brought in one at a time.  Immediately before the witness inspects the identification parade, they shall be told the person they saw on a specified earlier occasion may, or may not, be present and if they cannot make a positive identification, they should say so.  The witness must also be told they should not make any decision about whether the person they saw is on the identification parade until they have looked at each member at least twice.

17. When the officer or police staff (see paragraph 3.11) conducting the identification procedure is satisfied the witness has properly looked at each member of the identification parade, they shall ask the witness whether the person they saw on a specified earlier occasion is on the identification parade and, if so, to indicate the number of the person concerned, see *paragraph 28*.

18. If the witness wishes to hear any identification parade member speak, adopt any specified posture or move, they shall first be asked whether they can identify any person(s) on the identification parade on the basis of appearance only.  When the request is to hear members of the identification parade speak, the witness shall be reminded that the participants in the identification parade have been chosen on the basis of physical appearance only.  Members of the identification parade may then

be asked to comply with the witness' request to hear them speak, see them move or adopt any specified posture.

19. If the witness requests that the person they have indicated remove anything used for the purposes of *paragraph 10* to conceal the location of an unusual physical feature, that person may be asked to remove it.

20. If the witness makes an identification after the identification parade has ended, the suspect and, if present, their solicitor, interpreter or friend shall be informed. When this occurs, consideration should be given to allowing the witness a second opportunity to identify the suspect.

21 After the procedure, each witness shall be asked whether they have seen any broadcast or published films or photographs or any descriptions of suspects relating to the offence and their reply shall be recorded.

22. When the last witness has left, the suspect shall be asked whether they wish to make any comments on the conduct of the identification parade.

### (d)   Documentation

23. A video recording must normally be taken of the identification parade. If that is impracticable, a colour photograph must be taken. A copy of the video recording or photograph shall be supplied, on request, to the suspect or their solicitor within a reasonable time.

24. As appropriate, *paragraph 3.30* or *3.31*, should apply to any photograph or video taken as in *paragraph 23*.

25. If any person is asked to leave an identification parade because they are interfering with its conduct, the circumstances shall be recorded.

26. A record must be made of all those present at an identification parade whose names are known to the police.

27. If prison inmates make up an identification parade, the circumstances must be recorded.

28. A record of the conduct of any identification parade must be made on forms provided for the purpose. This shall include anything said by the witness or the suspect about any identifications or the conduct of the procedure, and any reasons it was not practicable to comply with any of this Code's provisions.

**Annex C - Group identification**

*(a)      General*

1.      The purpose of this Annex is to make sure, as far as possible, group identifications follow the principles and procedures for identification parades so the conditions are fair to the suspect in the way they test the witness' ability to make an identification.

2.      Group identifications may take place either with the suspect's consent and co-operation or covertly without their consent.

3.      The location of the group identification is a matter for the identification officer, although the officer may take into account any representations made by the suspect, appropriate adult, their solicitor or friend.

4.      The place where the group identification is held should be one where other people are either passing by or waiting around informally, in groups such that the suspect is able to join them and be capable of being seen by the witness at the same time as others in the group.  For example people leaving an escalator, pedestrians walking through a shopping centre, passengers on railway and bus stations, waiting in queues or groups or where people are standing or sitting in groups in other public places.

5.      If the group identification is to be held covertly, the choice of locations will be limited by the places where the suspect can be found and the number of other people present at that time.  In these cases, suitable locations might be along regular routes travelled by the suspect, including buses or trains or public places frequented by the suspect.

6.      Although the number, age, sex, race and general description and style of clothing of other people present at the location cannot be controlled by the identification officer, in selecting the location the officer must consider the general appearance and numbers of people likely to be present.  In particular, the officer must reasonably expect that over the period the witness observes the group, they will be able to see, from time to time, a number of others whose appearance is broadly similar to that of the suspect.

7.      A group identification need not be held if the identification officer believes, because of the unusual appearance of the suspect, none of the locations it would be practicable to use, satisfy the requirements of *paragraph 6* necessary to make the identification fair.

8.    Immediately after a group identification procedure has taken place (with or without the suspect's consent), a colour photograph or video should be taken of the general scene, if practicable, to give a general impression of the scene and the number of people present. Alternatively, if it is practicable, the group identification may be video recorded.

9.    If it is not practicable to take the photograph or video in accordance with *paragraph 8,* a photograph or film of the scene should be taken later at a time determined by the identification officer if the officer considers it practicable to do so.

10.   An identification carried out in accordance with this Code remains a group identification even though, at the time of being seen by the witness, the suspect was on their own rather than in a group.

11.   Before the group identification takes place, the suspect or their solicitor shall be provided with details of the first description of the suspect by any witnesses who are to attend the identification.  When a broadcast or publication is made, as in *paragraph 3.28*, the suspect or their solicitor should also be allowed to view any material released by the police to the media for the purposes of recognising or tracing the suspect, provided that it is practicable and would not unreasonably delay the investigation.

12.   After the procedure, each witness shall be asked whether they have seen any broadcast or published films or photographs or any descriptions of suspects relating to the offence and their reply recorded.

### (b)    Identification with the consent of the suspect

13.   A suspect must be given a reasonable opportunity to have a solicitor or friend present. They shall be asked to indicate on a second copy of the notice whether or not they wish to do so.

14.   The witness, the person carrying out the procedure and the suspect's solicitor, appropriate adult, friend or any interpreter for the witness, may be concealed from the sight of the individuals in the group they are observing, if the person carrying out the procedure considers this assists the conduct of the identification.

15.   The person conducting a witness to a group identification must not discuss with them the forthcoming group identification and, in particular, must not disclose whether a previous witness has made any identification.

16.   Anything said to, or by, the witness during the procedure about the identification should be said in the presence and hearing of those present at the procedure.

17.     Appropriate arrangements must be made to make sure, before witnesses attend the group identification, they are not able to:

(i)      communicate with each other about the case or overhear a witness who has already been given an opportunity to see the suspect in the group;

(ii)     see the suspect; or

(iii)    see, or be reminded of, any photographs or description of the suspect or be given any other indication of the suspect's identity.

18.     Witnesses shall be brought one at a time to the place where they are to observe the group. Immediately before the witness is asked to look at the group, the person conducting the procedure shall tell them that the person they saw may, or may not, be in the group and that if they cannot make a positive identification, they should say so. The witness shall be asked to observe the group in which the suspect is to appear. The way in which the witness should do this will depend on whether the group is moving or stationary.

**Moving group**

19.     When the group in which the suspect is to appear is moving, e.g. leaving an escalator, the provisions of *paragraphs 20* to *24* should be followed.

20.     If two or more suspects consent to a group identification, each should be the subject of separate identification procedures. These may be conducted consecutively on the same occasion.

21.     The person conducting the procedure shall tell the witness to observe the group and ask them to point out any person they think they saw on the specified earlier occasion.

22.     Once the witness has been informed as in *paragraph 21* the suspect should be allowed to take whatever position in the group they wish.

23.     When the witness points out a person as in *paragraph 21* they shall, if practicable, be asked to take a closer look at the person to confirm the identification. If this is not practicable, or they cannot confirm the identification, they shall be asked how sure they are that the person they have indicated is the relevant person.

24.     The witness should continue to observe the group for the period which the person conducting the procedure reasonably believes is necessary in the circumstances for them to be able to make comparisons between the suspect and other individuals of broadly similar appearance to the suspect as in *paragraph 6*.

D

**Stationary groups**

25.    When the group in which the suspect is to appear is stationary, e.g. people waiting in a queue, the provisions of *paragraphs 26 to 29* should be followed.

26.    If two or more suspects consent to a group identification, each should be subject to separate identification procedures unless they are of broadly similar appearance when they may appear in the same group. When separate group identifications are held, the groups must be made up of different people.

27.    The suspect may take whatever position in the group they wish. If there is more than one witness, the suspect must be told, out of the sight and hearing of any witness, that they can, if they wish, change their position in the group.

28.    The witness shall be asked to pass along, or amongst, the group and to look at each person in the group at least twice, taking as much care and time as possible according to the circumstances, before making an identification.  Once the witness has done this, they shall be asked whether the person they saw on the specified earlier occasion is in the group and to indicate any such person by whatever means the person conducting the procedure considers appropriate in the circumstances. If this is not practicable, the witness shall be asked to point out any person they think they saw on the earlier occasion.

29.    When the witness makes an indication as in *paragraph 28,* arrangements shall be made, if practicable, for the witness to take a closer look at the person to confirm the identification.  If this is not practicable, or the witness is unable to confirm the identification, they shall be asked how sure they are that the person they have indicated is the relevant person.

**All cases**

30.    If the suspect unreasonably delays joining the group, or having joined the group, deliberately conceals themselves from the sight of the witness, this may be treated as a refusal to co-operate in a group identification.

31.    If the witness identifies a person other than the suspect, that person should be informed what has happened and asked if they are prepared to give their name and address. There is no obligation upon any member of the public to give these details. There shall be no duty to record any details of any other member of the public present in the group or at the place where the procedure is conducted.

32.    When the group identification has been completed, the suspect shall be asked whether they wish to make any comments on the conduct of the procedure.

33. If the suspect has not been previously informed, they shall be told of any identifications made by the witnesses.

   *(c)* *Identification without the suspect's consent*

34. Group identifications held covertly without the suspect's consent should, as far as practicable, follow the rules for conduct of group identification by consent.

35. A suspect has no right to have a solicitor, appropriate adult or friend present as the identification will take place without the knowledge of the suspect.

36. Any number of suspects may be identified at the same time.

   *(d)* *Identifications in police stations*

37. Group identifications should only take place in police stations for reasons of safety, security or because it is not practicable to hold them elsewhere.

38. The group identification may take place either in a room equipped with a screen permitting witnesses to see members of the group without being seen, or anywhere else in the police station that the identification officer considers appropriate.

39. Any of the additional safeguards applicable to identification parades should be followed if the identification officer considers it is practicable to do so in the circumstances.

   *(e)* *Identifications involving prison inmates*

40. A group identification involving a prison inmate may only be arranged in the prison or at a police station.

41. When a group identification takes place involving a prison inmate, whether in a prison or in a police station, the arrangements should follow those in *paragraphs 37* to *39*. If a group identification takes place within a prison, other inmates may participate. If an inmate is the suspect, they do not have to wear prison clothing for the group identification unless the other participants are wearing the same clothing.

   *(f)* *Documentation*

42. When a photograph or video is taken as in *paragraph 8* or *9,* a copy of the photograph or video shall be supplied on request to the suspect or their solicitor within a reasonable time.

43. *Paragraph 3.30* or *3.31*, as appropriate, shall apply when the photograph or film taken in accordance with *paragraph 8* or *9* includes the suspect.

44.    A record of the conduct of any group identification must be made on forms provided for the purpose.  This shall include anything said by the witness or suspect about any identifications or the conduct of the procedure and any reasons why it was not practicable to comply with any of the provisions of this Code governing the conduct of group identifications.

### Annex D - Confrontation by a witness

1. Before the confrontation takes place, the witness must be told that the person they saw may, or may not, be the person they are to confront and that if they are not that person, then the witness should say so.

2. Before the confrontation takes place the suspect or their solicitor shall be provided with details of the first description of the suspect given by any witness who is to attend.  When a broadcast or publication is made, as in *paragraph 3.28*, the suspect or their solicitor should also be allowed to view any material released to the media for the purposes of recognising or tracing the suspect, provided it is practicable to do so and would not unreasonably delay the investigation.

3. Force may not be used to make the suspect's face visible to the witness.

4. Confrontation must take place in the presence of the suspect's solicitor, interpreter or friend unless this would cause unreasonable delay.

5. The suspect shall be confronted independently by each witness, who shall be asked "Is this the person?".  If the witness identifies the person but is unable to confirm the identification, they shall be asked how sure they are that the person is the one they saw on the earlier occasion.

6. The confrontation should normally take place in the police station, either in a normal room or one equipped with a screen permitting a witness to see the suspect without being seen.  In both cases, the procedures are the same except that a room equipped with a screen may be used only when the suspect's solicitor, friend or appropriate adult is present or the confrontation is recorded on video.

7. After the procedure, each witness shall be asked whether they have seen any broadcast or published films or photographs or any descriptions of suspects relating to the offence and their reply shall be recorded.

D

**Annex E - Showing photographs**

*(a)    Action*

1.    An officer of sergeant rank or above shall be responsible for supervising and directing the showing of photographs.  The actual showing may be done by another officer or police staff, see *paragraph 3.11*.

2.    The supervising officer must confirm the first description of the suspect given by the witness has been recorded before they are shown the photographs.  If the supervising officer is unable to confirm the description has been recorded they shall postpone showing the photographs.

3.    Only one witness shall be shown photographs at any one time.  Each witness shall be given as much privacy as practicable and shall not be allowed to communicate with any other witness in the case.

4.    The witness shall be shown not less than twelve photographs at a time, which shall, as far as possible, all be of a similar type.

5.    When the witness is shown the photographs, they shall be told the photograph of the person they saw may, or may not, be amongst them and if they cannot make a positive identification, they should say so.  The witness shall also be told they should not make a decision until they have viewed at least twelve photographs.  The witness shall not be prompted or guided in any way but shall be left to make any selection without help.

6.    If a witness makes a positive identification from photographs, unless the person identified is otherwise eliminated from enquiries or is not available, other witnesses shall not be shown photographs.  But both they, and the witness who has made the identification, shall be asked to attend a video identification, an identification parade or group identification unless there is no dispute about the suspect's identification.

7.    If the witness makes a selection but is unable to confirm the identification, the person showing the photographs shall ask them how sure they are that the photograph they have indicated is the person they saw on the specified earlier occasion.

8.    When the use of a computerised or artist's composite or similar likeness has led to there being a known suspect who can be asked to participate in a video identification, appear on an identification parade or participate in a group identification, that likeness shall not be shown to other potential witnesses.

9.    When a witness attending a video identification, an identification parade or group identification has previously been shown photographs or computerised or artist's composite or similar likeness (and it is the responsibility of the officer in charge of the

investigation to make the identification officer aware that this is the case), the suspect and their solicitor must be informed of this fact before the identification procedure takes place.

10. None of the photographs shown shall be destroyed, whether or not an identification is made, since they may be required for production in court. The photographs shall be numbered and a separate photograph taken of the frame or part of the album from which the witness made an identification as an aid to reconstituting it.

### (b) Documentation

11. Whether or not an identification is made, a record shall be kept of the showing of photographs on forms provided for the purpose. This shall include anything said by the witness about any identification or the conduct of the procedure, any reasons it was not practicable to comply with any of the provisions of this Code governing the showing of photographs and the name and rank of the supervising officer.

12. The supervising officer shall inspect and sign the record as soon as practicable.

**D**

### Annex F - Fingerprints, footwear impressions and samples - destruction and speculative searches

*(a)   **Fingerprints, footwear impressions and samples taken in connection with a criminal investigation from a person suspected of committing the offence under investigation.***

1.    The retention and destruction of fingerprints, footwear impressions and samples taken in connection with a criminal investigation from a person suspected of committing the offence under investigation is subject to PACE, section 64.

*(b)   **Fingerprints, footwear impressions and samples taken in connection with a criminal investigation from a person not suspected of committing the offence under investigation.***

2.    When fingerprints, footwear impressions or DNA samples are taken from a person in connection with an investigation and the person is not suspected of having committed the offence, see *Note F1*, they must be destroyed as soon as they have fulfilled the purpose for which they were taken unless:

(a)   they were taken for the purposes of an investigation of an offence for which a person has been convicted; and

(b)   fingerprints, footwear impressions or samples were also taken from the convicted person for the purposes of that investigation.

However, subject to *paragraph 2*, the fingerprints, footwear impressions and samples, and the information derived from samples, may not be used in the investigation of any offence or in evidence against the person who is, or would be, entitled to the destruction of the fingerprints, footwear impressions and samples, see *Note F2*.

3.    The requirement to destroy fingerprints, footwear impressions and DNA samples, and information derived from samples, and restrictions on their retention and use in *paragraph 1* do not apply if the person gives their written consent for their fingerprints, footwear impressions or sample to be retained and used after they have fulfilled the purpose for which they were taken, see *Note F1*.

4.    When a person's fingerprints, footwear impressions or sample are to be destroyed:

(a)   any copies of the fingerprints and footwear impressions must also be destroyed;

(b)   the person may witness the destruction of their fingerprints, footwear impressions or copies if they ask to do so within five days of being informed destruction is required;

(c)    access to relevant computer fingerprint data shall be made impossible as soon as it is practicable to do so and the person shall be given a certificate to this effect within three months of asking; and

(d)    neither the fingerprints, footwear impressions, the sample, or any information derived from the sample, may be used in the investigation of any offence or in evidence against the person who is, or would be, entitled to its destruction.

5.    Fingerprints, footwear impressions or samples, and the information derived from samples, taken in connection with the investigation of an offence which are not required to be destroyed, may be retained after they have fulfilled the purposes for which they were taken but may be used only for purposes related to the prevention or detection of crime, the investigation of an offence or the conduct of a prosecution in, as well as outside, the UK and may also be subject to a speculative search.  This includes checking them against other fingerprints, footwear impressions and DNA records held by, or on behalf of, the police and other law enforcement authorities in, as well as outside, the UK.

**(b)    Fingerprints taken in connection with Immigration Service enquiries**

6.    See *paragraph 4.10.*

**Notes for guidance**

F1    *Fingerprints, footwear impressions and samples given voluntarily for the purposes of elimination play an important part in many police investigations.  It is, therefore, important to make sure innocent volunteers are not deterred from participating and their consent to their fingerprints, footwear impressions and DNA being used for the purposes of a specific investigation is fully informed and voluntary.  If the police or volunteer seek to have the fingerprints, footwear impressions or samples retained for use after the specific investigation ends, it is important the volunteer's consent to this is also fully informed and voluntary.*

*Examples of consent for:*

- *DNA/fingerprints/footwear impressions - to be used only for the purposes of a specific investigation;*

- *DNA/fingerprints/footwear impressions - to be used in the specific investigation and retained by the police for future use.*

*To minimise the risk of confusion, each consent should be physically separate and the volunteer should be asked to sign each consent.*

(a)    DNA:

    (i)      DNA sample taken for the purposes of elimination or as part of an intelligence-led screening and to be used only for the purposes of that investigation and destroyed afterwards:

        *"I consent to my DNA/mouth swab being taken for forensic analysis. I understand that the sample will be destroyed at the end of the case and that my profile will only be compared to the crime stain profile from this enquiry. I have been advised that the person taking the sample may be required to give evidence and/or provide a written statement to the police in relation to the taking of it".*

    (ii)     DNA sample to be retained on the National DNA database and used in the future:

        *"I consent to my DNA sample and information derived from it being retained and used only for purposes related to the prevention and detection of a crime, the investigation of an offence or the conduct of a prosecution either nationally or internationally."*

        *"I understand that this sample may be checked against other DNA records held by, or on behalf of, relevant law enforcement authorities, either nationally or internationally".*

        *"I understand that once I have given my consent for the sample to be retained and used I cannot withdraw this consent."*

(b)    Fingerprints:

    (i)      Fingerprints taken for the purposes of elimination or as part of an intelligence-led screening and to be used only for the purposes of that investigation and destroyed afterwards:

        *"I consent to my fingerprints being taken for elimination purposes. I understand that the fingerprints will be destroyed at the end of the case and that my fingerprints will only be compared to the fingerprints from this enquiry. I have been advised that the person taking the fingerprints may be required to give evidence and/or provide a written statement to the police in relation to the taking of it."*

    (ii)     Fingerprints to be retained for future use:

        *"I consent to my fingerprints being retained and used only for purposes related to the prevention and detection of a crime, the investigation of an offence or the conduct of a prosecution either nationally or internationally".*

"*I understand that my fingerprints may be checked against other records held by, or on behalf of, relevant law enforcement authorities, either nationally or internationally.*"

"*I understand that once I have given my consent for my fingerprints to be retained and used I cannot withdraw this consent.*"

(c) *Footwear impressions:*

(i) *Footwear impressions taken for the purposes of elimination or as part of an intelligence-led screening and to be used only for the purposes of that investigation and destroyed afterwards:*

"*I consent to my footwear impressions being taken for elimination purposes. I understand that the footwear impressions will be destroyed at the end of the case and that my footwear impressions will only be compared to the footwear impressions from this enquiry. I have been advised that the person taking the footwear impressions may be required to give evidence and/or provide a written statement to the police in relation to the taking of it.*"

(ii) *Footwear impressions to be retained for future use:*

"*I consent to my footwear impressions being retained and used only for purposes related to the prevention and detection of a crime, the investigation of an offence or the conduct of a prosecution, either nationally or internationally*".

"*I understand that my footwear impressions may be checked against other records held by, or on behalf of, relevant law enforcement authorities, either nationally or internationally.*"

"*I understand that once I have given my consent for my footwear impressions to be retained and used I cannot withdraw this consent.*"

F2 *The provisions for the retention of fingerprints, footwear impressions and samples in paragraph 1 allow for all fingerprints, footwear impressions and samples in a case to be available for any subsequent miscarriage of justice investigation.*

**D**

**Annex G –Requirement for a person to attend a police station for fingerprints and samples.**

1.    A requirement under Schedule 2A for a person to attend a police station to have fingerprints or samples taken:

(a)    must give the person a period of at least seven days within which to attend the police station; and

(b)    may direct them to attend at a specified time of day or between specified times of day.

2.    When specifying the period and times of attendance, the officer making the requirements must consider whether the fingerprints or samples could reasonably be taken at a time when the person is required to attend the police station for any other reason.  See Note G1.

3.    An officer of the rank of inspector or above may authorise a period shorter than 7 days if there is an urgent need for person's fingerprints or sample for the purposes of the investigation of an offence.  The fact of the authorisation and the reasons for giving it must be recorded as soon as practicable.

4.    The constable making a requirement and the person to whom it applies may agree to vary it so as to specify any period within which, or date or time at which, the person is to attend.  However, variation shall not have effect for the purposes of enforcement, unless it is confirmed by the constable in writing.

*Notes for Guidance*

G1    *The specified period within which the person is to attend need not fall within the period allowed (if applicable) for making the requirement.*

G2    *To justify the arrest without warrant of a person who fails to comply with a requirement, (see paragraph 4.4(b) above), the officer making the requirement, or confirming a variation, should be prepared to explain how, when and where the requirement was made or the variation was confirmed and what steps were taken to ensure the person understood what to do and the consequences of not complying with the requirement.*

# POLICE AND CRIMINAL EVIDENCE ACT 1984 (PACE)

# CODE E

# CODE OF PRACTICE ON AUDIO RECORDING INTERVIEWS WITH SUSPECTS

**E**

## Commencement - Transitional Arrangements

This code applies to interviews carried out after midnight on 1 May 2010, notwithstanding that the interview may have commenced before that time.

**1    General**

1.1    This Code of Practice must be readily available for consultation by:

- police officers

- police staff

- detained persons

- members of the public.

1.2    The *Notes for Guidance* included are not provisions of this Code.

1.3    Nothing in this Code shall detract from the requirements of Code C, the Code of Practice for the detention, treatment and questioning of persons by police officers.

1.4    This Code does not apply to those people listed in Code C, *paragraph 1.12.*

1.5    The term:

- 'appropriate adult' has the same meaning as in Code C, *paragraph 1.7*

- 'solicitor' has the same meaning as in Code C, *paragraph 6.12.*

1.5A    Recording of interviews shall be carried out openly to instil confidence in its reliability as an impartial and accurate record of the interview.

1.6    In this Code:

(aa)    'recording media' means any removable, physical audio recording medium (such as magnetic tape, optical disc or solid state memory) which can be played and copied.

(a)    'designated person' means a person other than a police officer, designated under the Police Reform Act 2002, Part 4 who has specified powers and duties of police officers conferred or imposed on them;

(b)    any reference to a police officer includes a designated person acting in the exercise or performance of the powers and duties conferred or imposed on them by their designation.

(c)    'secure digital network' is a computer network system which enables an original interview recording to be stored as a digital multi media file or a series of such files, on a secure file server which is accredited by the National Accreditor for Police Information Systems in the National Police Improvement Agency (NPIA) in accordance with the UK Government Protective Marking Scheme.  (see section 7 of this Code).

1.7 Sections 2 to 6 of this code set out the procedures and requirements which apply to all interviews together with the provisions which apply only to interviews recorded using removable media. Section 7 sets out the provisions which apply to interviews recorded using a secure digital network and specifies the provisions in sections 2 to 6 which do not apply to secure digital network recording.

1.8 Nothing in this Code prevents the custody officer, or other officer given custody of the detainee, from allowing police staff who are not designated persons to carry out individual procedures or tasks at the police station if the law allows. However, the officer remains responsible for making sure the procedures and tasks are carried out correctly in accordance with this Code. Any such police staff must be:

(a) a person employed by a police authority maintaining a police force and under the control and direction of the Chief Officer of that force; or

(b) employed by a person with whom a police authority has a contract for the provision of services relating to persons arrested or otherwise in custody.

1.9 Designated persons and other police staff must have regard to any relevant provisions of the Codes of Practice.

1.10 References to pocket book include any official report book issued to police officers or police staff.

1.11 References to a custody officer include those performing the functions of a custody officer as in *paragraph 1.9* of Code C.

## 2 Recording and sealing master recordings

2.1 Not used.

2.2 One recording, the master recording, will be sealed in the suspect's presence. A second recording will be used as a working copy. The master recording is either of the two recordings used in a twin deck/drive machine or the only recording in a single deck/drive machine. The working copy is either the second/third recording used in a twin/triple deck/drive machine or a copy of the master recording made by a single deck/drive machine. See *Notes 2A* and *2B [This paragraph does not apply to interviews recorded using a secure digital network, see paragraphs 7.4 to 7.6]*

2.3 Nothing in this Code requires the identity of officers or police staff conducting interviews to be recorded or disclosed:

(a) in the case of enquiries linked to the investigation of terrorism (see *paragraph 3.2*); or

(b)      if the interviewer reasonably believes recording or disclosing their name might put them in danger.

In these cases interviewers should use warrant or other identification numbers and the name of their police station. See *Note 2C*

### Notes for guidance

2A    *The purpose of sealing the master recording in the suspect's presence is to show the recording's integrity is preserved. If a single deck/drive machine is used the working copy of the master recording must be made in the suspect's presence and without the master recording leaving their sight. The working copy shall be used for making further copies if needed.*

2B    *Not used.*

2C    *The purpose of paragraph 2.3(b) is to protect those involved in serious organised crime investigations or arrests of particularly violent suspects when there is reliable information that those arrested or their associates may threaten or cause harm to those involved. In cases of doubt, an officer of inspector rank or above should be consulted.*

## 3      Interviews to be audio recorded

3.1    Subject to *paragraphs 3.3* and *3.4*, audio recording shall be used at police stations for any interview:

(a)      with a person cautioned under Code C, *section 10* in respect of any indictable offence, including an offence triable either way, see *Note 3A*

(b)      which takes place as a result of an interviewer exceptionally putting further questions to a suspect about an offence described in *paragraph 3.1(a)* after they have been charged with, or told they may be prosecuted for, that offence, see Code C, *paragraph 16.5*

(c)      when an interviewer wants to tell a person, after they have been charged with, or informed they may be prosecuted for, an offence described in *paragraph 3.1(a)*, about any written statement or interview with another person, see Code C, *paragraph 16.4*.

3.2    The Terrorism Act 2000 makes separate provision for a Code of Practice for the audio recording of interviews of those arrested under Section 41 of, or Schedule 7 to, the 2000 Act. The provisions of this Code do not apply to such interviews. [See *Note 3C*].

3.3   The custody officer may authorise the interviewer not to audio record the interview when it is:

(a)   not reasonably practicable because of equipment failure or the unavailability of a suitable interview room or recording equipment and the authorising officer considers, on reasonable grounds, that the interview should not be delayed; or

(b)   clear from the outset there will not be a prosecution.

Note: In these cases the interview should be recorded in writing in accordance with Code C, *section 11*. In all cases the custody officer shall record the specific reasons for not audio recording. See *Note 3B*

3.4   If a person refuses to go into or remain in a suitable interview room, see Code C *paragraph 12.5*, and the custody officer considers, on reasonable grounds, that the interview should not be delayed the interview may, at the custody officer's discretion, be conducted in a cell using portable recording equipment or, if none is available, recorded in writing as in Code C, *section 11*. The reasons for this shall be recorded.

3.5   The whole of each interview shall be audio recorded, including the taking and reading back of any statement.

3.6   A sign or indicator which is visible to the suspect must show when the recording equipment is recording.

E

### Notes for guidance

3A   *Nothing in this Code is intended to preclude audio recording at police discretion of interviews at police stations with people cautioned in respect of offences not covered by paragraph 3.1, or responses made by persons after they have been charged with, or told they may be prosecuted for, an offence, provided this Code is complied with.*

3B   *A decision not to audio record an interview for any reason may be the subject of comment in court. The authorising officer should be prepared to justify that decision.*

3C   *If, during the course of an interview under this Code, it becomes apparent that the interview should be conducted under one of the terrorism codes for recording of interviews the interview should only continue in accordance with the relevant code.*

**4    The interview**

*(a)    General*

4.1    The provisions of Code C:

- *sections 10 and 11*, and the applicable *Notes for Guidance* apply to the conduct of interviews to which this Code applies

- *paragraphs 11.7* to *11.14* apply only when a written record is needed.

4.2    Code C, *paragraphs 10.10, 10.11* and Annex C describe the restriction on drawing adverse inferences from a suspect's failure or refusal to say anything about their involvement in the offence when interviewed or after being charged or informed they may be prosecuted, and how it affects the terms of the caution and determines if and by whom a special warning under sections 36 and 37 of the Criminal Justice and Public Order Act 1994 can be given.

*(b)    Commencement of interviews*

4.3    When the suspect is brought into the interview room the interviewer shall, without delay but in the suspect's sight, load the recorder with new recording media and set it to record. The recording media must be unwrapped or opened in the suspect's presence. *[This paragraph does not apply to interviews recorded using a secure digital network, see paragraphs 7.4 and 7.5].*

4.4    The interviewer should tell the suspect about the recording process and point out the sign or indicator which shows that the recording equipment is activated and recording. See *paragraph 3.6.*  The interviewer shall:

(a)    say the interview is being audibly recorded

(b)    subject to *paragraph 2.3*, give their name and rank and that of any other interviewer present

(c)    ask the suspect and any other party present, e.g. a solicitor, to identify themselves

(d)    state the date, time of commencement and place of the interview

(e)    state the suspect will be given a notice about what will happen to the copies of the recording. *[This sub-paragraph does not apply to interviews recorded using a secure digital network, see paragraphs 7.4 and 7.6 to 7.7]*

See *Note 4A*

4.5    The interviewer shall:

- caution the suspect, see Code C, *section 10*

- remind the suspect of their entitlement to free legal advice, see Code C, *paragraph 11.2*.

4.6    The interviewer shall put to the suspect any significant statement or silence, see *Code C, paragraph 11.4*.

**(c)    Interviews with deaf persons**

4.7    If the suspect is deaf or is suspected of having impaired hearing, the interviewer shall make a written note of the interview in accordance with Code C, at the same time as audio recording it in accordance with this Code. See *Notes 4B* and *4C*

**(d)    Objections and complaints by the suspect**

4.8    If the suspect objects to the interview being audibly recorded at the outset, during the interview or during a break, the interviewer shall explain that the interview is being audibly recorded and that this Code requires the suspect's objections to be recorded on the audio recording. When any objections have been audibly recorded or the suspect has refused to have their objections recorded, the interviewer shall say they are turning off the recorder, give their reasons and turn it off. The interviewer shall then make a written record of the interview as in Code C, *section 11*. If, however, the interviewer reasonably considers they may proceed to question the suspect with the audio recording still on, the interviewer may do so. This procedure also applies in cases where the suspect has previously objected to the interview being visually recorded, see *Code F 4.8*, and the investigating officer has decided to audibly record the interview. See *Note 4D*

4.9    If in the course of an interview a complaint is made by or on behalf of the person being questioned concerning the provisions of this Code or Code C, the interviewer shall act as in Code C, *paragraph 12.9*. See *Notes 4E* and *4F*

4.10   If the suspect indicates they want to tell the interviewer about matters not directly connected with the offence and they are unwilling for these matters to be audio recorded, the suspect should be given the opportunity to tell the interviewer at the end of the formal interview.

**(e)    Changing recording media**

4.11   When the recorder shows the recording media only has a short time left, the interviewer shall tell the suspect the recording media are coming to an end and round off that part of the interview. If the interviewer leaves the room for a second set of recording media,

E

the suspect shall not be left unattended. The interviewer will remove the recording media from the recorder and insert the new recording media which shall be unwrapped or opened in the suspect's presence. The recorder should be set to record on the new media. To avoid confusion between the recording media, the interviewer shall mark the media with an identification number immediately after they are removed from the recorder. *[This paragraph does not apply to interviews recorded using a secure digital network as this does not use removable media, see paragraphs 1.6(c), 7.4 and 7.14 to 7.15.]*

**(f)   *Taking a break during interview***

4.12   When a break is taken, the fact that a break is to be taken, the reason for it and the time shall be recorded on the audio recording.

4.12A  When the break is taken and the interview room vacated by the suspect, the recording media shall be removed from the recorder and the procedures for the conclusion of an interview followed, see *paragraph 4.18*.

4.13   When a break is a short one and both the suspect and an interviewer remain in the interview room, the recording may be stopped. There is no need to remove the recording media and when the interview recommences the recording should continue on the same recording media. The time the interview recommences shall be recorded on the audio recording.

4.14   After any break in the interview the interviewer must, before resuming the interview, remind the person being questioned that they remain under caution or, if there is any doubt, give the caution in full again. See *Note 4G*.

*[Paragraphs 4.12 to 4.14 do not apply to interviews recorded using a secure digital network, see paragraphs 7.4 and 7.8 to 7.10]*

**(g)   *Failure of recording equipment***

4.15   If there is an equipment failure which can be rectified quickly, e.g. by inserting new recording media, the interviewer shall follow the appropriate procedures as in paragraph 4.11. When the recording is resumed the interviewer shall explain what happened and record the time the interview recommences. If, however, it will not be possible to continue recording on that recorder and no replacement recorder is readily available, the interview may continue without being audibly recorded. If this happens, the interviewer shall seek the custody officer's authority as in paragraph 3.3. See *Note 4H [This paragraph does not apply to interviews recorded using a secure digital network, see paragraphs 7.4 and 7.11]*

**(h)** **Removing recording media from the recorder**

4.16 When recording media is removed from the recorder during the interview, they shall be retained and the procedures in *paragraph 4.18* followed. *[This paragraph does not apply to interviews recorded using a secure digital network as this does not use removable media, see 1.6(c), 7.4 and 7.14 to 7.15.]*

**(i)** **Conclusion of interview**

4.17 At the conclusion of the interview, the suspect shall be offered the opportunity to clarify anything he or she has said and asked if there is anything they want to add.

4.18 At the conclusion of the interview, including the taking and reading back of any written statement, the time shall be recorded and the recording shall be stopped. The interviewer shall seal the master recording with a master recording label and treat it as an exhibit in accordance with force standing orders. The interviewer shall sign the label and ask the suspect and any third party present during the interview to sign it. If the suspect or third party refuse to sign the label an officer of at least inspector rank, or if not available the custody officer, shall be called into the interview room and asked, subject to *paragraph 2.3*, to sign it.

4.19 The suspect shall be handed a notice which explains:

- how the audio recording will be used

- the arrangements for access to it

- that if the person is charged or informed they will be prosecuted, a copy of the audio recording will be supplied as soon as practicable or as otherwise agreed between the suspect and the police or on the order of a court.

*[Paragraphs 4.17 to 4.19 do not apply to interviews recorded using a secure digital network, see paragraphs 7.4 and 7.12 to 7.13]*

**Notes for guidance**

4A *For the purpose of voice identification the interviewer should ask the suspect and any other people present to identify themselves.*

4B *This provision is to give a person who is deaf or has impaired hearing equivalent rights of access to the full interview record as far as this is possible using audio recording.*

4C *The provisions of Code C, section 13 on interpreters for deaf persons or for interviews with suspects who have difficulty understanding English continue to apply.*

4D    *The interviewer should remember that a decision to continue recording against the wishes of the suspect may be the subject of comment in court.*

4E    *If the custody officer is called to deal with the complaint, the recorder should, if possible, be left on until the custody officer has entered the room and spoken to the person being interviewed. Continuation or termination of the interview should be at the interviewer's discretion pending action by an inspector under Code C, paragraph 9.2.*

4F    *If the complaint is about a matter not connected with this Code or Code C, the decision to continue is at the interviewer's discretion. When the interviewer decides to continue the interview, they shall tell the suspect the complaint will be brought to the custody officer's attention at the conclusion of the interview. When the interview is concluded the interviewer must, as soon as practicable, inform the custody officer about the existence and nature of the complaint made.*

4G    *The interviewer should remember that it may be necessary to show to the court that nothing occurred during a break or between interviews which influenced the suspect's recorded evidence. After a break or at the beginning of a subsequent interview, the interviewer should consider summarising on the record the reason for the break and confirming this with the suspect.*

4H    *Where the interview is being recorded and the media or the recording equipment fails the officer conducting the interview should stop the interview immediately. Where part of the interview is unaffected by the error and is still accessible on the media, that media shall be copied and sealed in the suspect's presence and the interview recommenced using new equipment/media as required. Where the content of the interview has been lost in its entirety the media should be sealed in the suspect's presence and the interview begun again. If the recording equipment cannot be fixed or no replacement is immediately available the interview should be recorded in accordance with Code C, section 11.*

## 5    After the interview

5.1    The interviewer shall make a note in their pocket book that the interview has taken place, was audibly recorded, its time, duration and date and the master recording's identification number.

5.2    If no proceedings follow in respect of the person whose interview was recorded, the recording media must be kept securely as in *paragraph 6.1* and *Note 6A*.

*[This section (paragraphs 5.1, 5.2 and Note 5A) does not apply to interviews recorded using a secure digital network, see paragraphs 7.4 and 7.14 to 7.15]*

**Note for guidance**

5A    *Any written record of an audibly recorded interview should be made in accordance with national guidelines approved by the Secretary of State, and with regard to the advice contained in the Manual of Guidance for the preparation, processing and submission of prosecution files.*

**6      Media security**

6.1    The officer in charge of each police station at which interviews with suspects are recorded shall make arrangements for master recordings to be kept securely and their movements accounted for on the same basis as material which may be used for evidential purposes, in accordance with force standing orders. See *Note 6A*

6.2    A police officer has no authority to break the seal on a master recording required for criminal trial or appeal proceedings. If it is necessary to gain access to the master recording, the police officer shall arrange for its seal to be broken in the presence of a representative of the Crown Prosecution Service. The defendant or their legal adviser should be informed and given a reasonable opportunity to be present. If the defendant or their legal representative is present they shall be invited to reseal and sign the master recording. If either refuses or neither is present this should be done by the representative of the Crown Prosecution Service. See *Notes 6B* and *6C*

6.3    If no criminal proceedings result or the criminal trial and, if applicable, appeal proceedings to which the interview relates have been concluded, the chief officer of police is responsible for establishing arrangements for breaking the seal on the master recording, if necessary.

6.4    When the master recording seal is broken, a record must be made of the procedure followed, including the date, time, place and persons present.

*[This section (paragraphs 6.1 to 6.4 and Notes 6A to 6C) does not apply to interviews recorded using a secure digital network, see paragraphs 7.4 and 7.14 to 7.15]*

**Notes for guidance**

6A    *This section is concerned with the security of the master recording sealed at the conclusion of the interview. Care must be taken of working copies of recordings because their loss or destruction may lead to the need to access master recordings.*

6B    *If the recording has been delivered to the crown court for their keeping after committal for trial the crown prosecutor will apply to the chief clerk of the crown court centre for the release of the recording for unsealing by the crown prosecutor.*

6C    *Reference to the Crown Prosecution Service or to the crown prosecutor in this part of the Code should be taken to include any other body or person with a statutory responsibility for prosecution for whom the police conduct any audibly recorded interviews.*

## 7    Recording of Interviews by Secure Digital Network

7.1    A secure digital network does not use removable media and this section specifies the provisions which will apply when a secure digital network is used.

7.2    *Not used.*

7.3    The following requirements are solely applicable to the use of a secure digital network for the recording of interviews.

### (a)    Application of sections 1 to 6 of Code E

7.4    Sections 1 to 6 of Code E above apply except for the following paragraphs:

- Paragraph 2.2 under "Recording and sealing of master recordings"

- Paragraph 4.3 under "(b) Commencement of interviews"

- Paragraph 4.4 (e) under "(b) Commencement of interviews"

- Paragraphs 4.11 – 4.19 under "(e) Changing recording media", "(f) Taking a break during interview", "(g) Failure of recording equipment", "(h) Removing recording media from the recorder" and "(i) Conclusion of interview"

- Paragraphs 6.1 – 6.4 and Notes 6A to 6C under "Media security"

### (b)    Commencement of Interview

7.5    When the suspect is brought into the interview room, the interviewer shall without delay and in the sight of the suspect, switch on the recording equipment and enter the information necessary to log on to the secure network and start recording.

7.6    The interviewer must then inform the suspect that the interview is being recorded using a secure digital network and that recording has commenced.

7.7    In addition to the requirements of paragraph 4.4 (a – d) above, the interviewer must inform the person that:

- they will be given access to the recording of the interview in the event that they are charged or informed that they will be prosecuted but if they are not charged or informed that they will be prosecuted they will only be given access as agreed with the police or on the order of a court; and

- they will be given a written notice at the end of the interview setting out their rights to access the recording and what will happen to the recording.

**(c)    Taking a break during interview**

7.8    When a break is taken, the fact that a break is to be taken, the reason for it and the time shall be recorded on the audio recording. The recording shall be stopped and the procedures in paragraphs 7.12 and 7.13 for the conclusion of an interview followed.

7.9    When the interview recommences the procedures in paragraphs 7.5 to 7.7 for commencing an interview shall be followed to create a new file to record the continuation of the interview. The time the interview recommences shall be recorded on the audio recording.

7.10    After any break in the interview the interviewer must, before resuming the interview, remind the person being questioned that they remain under caution or, if there is any doubt, give the caution in full again. See *Note 4G*

**(d)    Failure of recording equipment**

7.11    If there is an equipment failure which can be rectified quickly, e.g. by commencing a new secure digital network recording, the interviewer shall follow the appropriate procedures as in *paragraphs 7.8 to 7.10*. When the recording is resumed the interviewer shall explain what happened and record the time the interview recommences. If, however, it is not possible to continue recording on the secure digital network the interview should be recorded on removable media as in *paragraph 4.3* unless the necessary equipment is not available. If this happens the interview may continue without being audibly recorded and the interviewer shall seek the custody officer's authority as in *paragraph 3.3*. See *Note 4H*.

**(e)    Conclusion of interview**

7.12    At the conclusion of the interview, the suspect shall be offered the opportunity to clarify anything he or she has said and asked if there is anything they want to add.

7.13    At the conclusion of the interview, including the taking and reading back of any written statement:

(a)    the time shall be orally recorded

(b)     the suspect shall be handed a notice which explains:

- how the audio recording will be used

- the arrangements for access to it

- that if they are charged or informed that they will be prosecuted, they will be given access to the recording of the interview either electronically or by being given a copy on removable recording media, but if they are not charged or informed that they will prosecuted, they will only be given access as agreed with the police or on the order of a court.

See *Note 7A*.

(c)     the suspect must be asked to confirm that he or she has received a copy of the notice at paragraph 7.13(b) above.  If the suspect fails to accept or to acknowledge receipt of the notice, the interviewer will state for the recording that a copy of the notice has been provided to the suspect and that he or she has refused to take a copy of the notice or has refused to acknowledge receipt.

(d)     the time shall be recorded and the interviewer shall notify the suspect that the recording is being saved to the secure network.  The interviewer must save the recording in the presence of the suspect.  The suspect should then be informed that the interview is terminated.

**(f)    After the interview**

7.14    The interviewer shall make a note in their pocket book that the interview has taken place, was audibly recorded, its time, duration and date and the original recording's identification number.

7.15    If no proceedings follow in respect of the person whose interview was recorded, the recordings must be kept securely as in *paragraphs 7.16* and *7.17*.

See Note 5A

**(g)    Security of secure digital network interview records**

7.16    Interview record files are stored in read only format on non-removable storage devices, for example, hard disk drives, to ensure their integrity.  The recordings are first saved locally to a secure non-removable device before being transferred to the remote network device.  If for any reason the network connection fails, the recording remains on the local device and will be transferred when the network connections are restored.

7.17 Access to interview recordings, including copying to removable media, must be strictly controlled and monitored to ensure that access is restricted to those who have been given specific permission to access for specified purposes when this is necessary. For example, police officers and CPS lawyers involved in the preparation of any prosecution case, persons interviewed if they have been charged or informed they may be prosecuted and their legal representatives.

### Note for Guidance

7A    *The notice at paragraph 7.13 above should provide a brief explanation of the secure digital network and how access to the recording is strictly limited. The notice should also explain the access rights of the suspect, his or her legal representative, the police and the prosecutor to the recording of the interview. Space should be provided on the form to insert the date and the file reference number for the interview.*

E

# POLICE AND CRIMINAL EVIDENCE ACT 1984 (PACE)

# CODE F

# CODE OF PRACTICE ON VISUAL RECORDING WITH SOUND OF INTERVIEWS WITH SUSPECTS

**F**

## Commencement

The contents of this code should be considered if an interviewing officer decides to make a visual recording with sound of an interview with a suspect after midnight on 1 May 2010.

There is no statutory requirement under PACE to visually record interviews

## 1   General

1.1   This code of practice must be readily available for consultation by police officers and other police staff, detained persons and members of the public.

1.2   The notes for guidance included are not provisions of this code. They form guidance to police officers and others about its application and interpretation.

1.3   Nothing in this code shall be taken as detracting in any way from the requirements of the Code of Practice for the Detention, Treatment and Questioning of Persons by Police Officers (Code C). [See *Note 1A*].

1.4   The interviews to which this Code applies are set out in paragraphs 3.1 - 3.3.

1.5   In this code, the term "appropriate adult", "solicitor" and "interview" have the same meaning as those set out in Code C. The corresponding provisions and Notes for Guidance in Code C applicable to those terms shall also apply where appropriate.

1.5A   The visual recording of interviews shall be carried out openly to instil confidence in its reliability as an impartial and accurate record of the interview.

1.6   Any reference in this code to visual recording shall be taken to mean visual recording with sound and in this code:

(aa)   'recording media' means any removable, physical audio recording medium (such as magnetic tape, optical disc or solid state memory) which can be played and copied.

(a)   'designated person' means a person other than a police officer, designated under the Police Reform Act 2002, Part 4 who has specified powers and duties of police officers conferred or imposed on them;

(b)   any reference to a police officer includes a designated person acting in the exercise or performance of the powers and duties conferred or imposed on them by their designation.

(c)   'secure digital network' is a computer network system which enables an original interview recording to be stored as a digital multi media file or a series of such files, on a secure file server which is accredited by the National Accreditor for Police Information Systems in the National Police Improvement Agency (NPIA) in accordance with the UK Government Protective Marking Scheme. (see section 7 of this Code).

1.7   References to "pocket book" in this Code include any official report book issued to police officers.

### Note for Guidance

1A    As in paragraph 1.9 of Code C, references to custody officers include those carrying out the functions of a custody officer.

### 2    Recording and sealing of master recordings

2.1    Not used

2.2    The camera(s) shall be placed in the interview room so as to ensure coverage of as much of the room as is practicably possible whilst the interviews are taking place. [See *Note 2A*].

2.3    The certified recording medium will be of a high quality, new and previously unused. When the certified recording medium is placed in the recorder and switched on to record, the correct date and time, in hours, minutes and seconds, will be superimposed automatically, second by second, during the whole recording. [See *Note 2B*]. See section 7 regarding the use of a secure digital network to record the interview.

2.4    One copy of the certified recording medium, referred to in this code as the master copy, will be sealed before it leaves the presence of the suspect. A second copy will be used as a working copy. [See *Note 2C* and *2D*].

2.5    Nothing in this code requires the identity of an officer to be recorded or disclosed if:

   (a)    the interview or record relates to a person detained under the Terrorism Act 2000 (see paragraph 3.2); or

   (b)    otherwise where the officer reasonably believes that recording or disclosing their name might put them in danger.

2.6    In these cases, the officer will have their back to the camera and shall use their warrant or other identification number and the name of the police station to which they are attached. Such instances and the reasons for them shall be recorded in the custody record. [See *Note 2E*]

### Notes for Guidance

2A    Interviewing officers will wish to arrange that, as far as possible, visual recording arrangements are unobtrusive. It must be clear to the suspect, however, that there is no opportunity to interfere with the recording equipment or the recording media.

2B    In this context, the certified recording media should be capable of having an image of the date and time superimposed upon them as they record the interview.

2C    *The purpose of sealing the master copy before it leaves the presence of the suspect is to establish their confidence that the integrity of the copy is preserved.*

2D    *The recording of the interview may be used for identification procedures in accordance with paragraph 3.21 or Annex E of Code D.*

2E    *The purpose of the paragraph 2.5(b) is to protect police officers and others involved in the investigation of serious organised crime or the arrest of particularly violent suspects when there is reliable information that those arrested or their associates may threaten or cause harm to the officers, their families or their personal property.*

**3    Interviews to be visually recorded**

3.1    Subject to paragraph 3.2 below, if an interviewing officer decides to make a visual recording these are the areas where it might be appropriate:

(a)    with a suspect in respect of an indictable offence (including an offence triable either way) [see *Notes 3A* and *3B*];

(b)    which takes place as a result of an interviewer exceptionally putting further questions to a suspect about an offence described in sub-paragraph (a) above after they have been charged with, or informed they may be prosecuted for, that offence [see *Note 3C*];

(c)    in which an interviewer wishes to bring to the notice of a person, after that person has been charged with, or informed they may be prosecuted for an offence described in sub-paragraph (a) above, any written statement made by another person, or the content of an interview with another person [see *Note 3D*]

(d)    with, or in the presence of, a deaf or deaf/blind or speech impaired person who uses sign language to communicate;

(e)    with, or in the presence of anyone who requires an "appropriate adult"; or

(f)    in any case where the suspect or their representative requests that the interview be recorded visually.

3.2    The Terrorism Act 2000 makes separate provision for a code of practice for the video recording of interviews in a police station of those detained under Schedule 7 or section 41 of the Act. The provisions of this code do not therefore apply to such interviews [see *Note 3E*].

3.3    The custody officer may authorise the interviewing officer not to record the interview visually:

(a) where it is not reasonably practicable to do so because of failure of the equipment, or the non-availability of a suitable interview room, or recorder, and the authorising officer considers on reasonable grounds that the interview should not be delayed until the failure has been rectified or a suitable room or recorder becomes available. In such cases the custody officer may authorise the interviewing officer to audio record the interview in accordance with the guidance set out in Code E;

(b) where it is clear from the outset that no prosecution will ensue; or

(c) where it is not practicable to do so because at the time the person resists being taken to a suitable interview room or other location which would enable the interview to be recorded, or otherwise fails or refuses to go into such a room or location, and the authorising officer considers on reasonable grounds that the interview should not be delayed until these conditions cease to apply.

In all cases the custody officer shall make a note in the custody records of the reasons for not taking a visual record. [See *Note 3F*].

3.4 When a person who is voluntarily attending the police station is required to be cautioned in accordance with Code C prior to being interviewed, the subsequent interview shall be recorded, unless the custody officer gives authority in accordance with the provisions of paragraph 3.3 above for the interview not to be so recorded.

3.5 The whole of each interview shall be recorded visually, including the taking and reading back of any statement.

3.6 A sign or indicator which is visible to the suspect must show when the visual recording equipment is recording.

### Notes for Guidance

3A *Nothing in the code is intended to preclude visual recording at police discretion of interviews at police stations with people cautioned in respect of offences not covered by paragraph 3.1, or responses made by interviewees after they have been charged with, or informed they may be prosecuted for, an offence, provided that this code is complied with.*

3B *Attention is drawn to the provisions set out in Code C about the matters to be considered when deciding whether a detained person is fit to be interviewed.*

3C *Code C sets out the circumstances in which a suspect may be questioned about an offence after being charged with it.*

3D   *Code C sets out the procedures to be followed when a person's attention is drawn after charge, to a statement made by another person. One method of bringing the content of an interview with another person to the notice of a suspect may be to play him a recording of that interview.*

3E   *If, during the course of an interview under this Code, it becomes apparent that the interview should be conducted under one of the terrorism codes for video recording of interviews the interview should only continue in accordance with the relevant code.*

3F   *A decision not to record an interview visually for any reason may be the subject of comment in court. The authorising officer should therefore be prepared to justify their decision in each case.*

## 4   The Interview

### (a)   General

4.1   The provisions of Code C in relation to cautions and interviews and the Notes for Guidance applicable to those provisions shall apply to the conduct of interviews to which this Code applies.

4.2   Particular attention is drawn to those parts of Code C that describe the restrictions on drawing adverse inferences from a suspect's failure or refusal to say anything about their involvement in the offence when interviewed, or after being charged or informed they may be prosecuted and how those restrictions affect the terms of the caution and determine whether a special warning under Sections 36 and 37 of the Criminal Justice and Public Order Act 1994 can be given.

### (b)   Commencement of interviews

4.3   When the suspect is brought into the interview room the interviewer shall without delay, but in sight of the suspect, load the recording equipment and set it to record. The recording media must be unwrapped or otherwise opened in the presence of the suspect. [See *Note 4A*]

4.4   The interviewer shall then tell the suspect formally about the visual recording and point out the sign or indicator which shows that the recording equipment is activated and recording. See *paragraph 3.6*. The interviewer shall:

(a)   explain the interview is being visually recorded;

(b)   subject to paragraph 2.5, give his or her name and rank, and that of any other interviewer present;

(c)    ask the suspect and any other party present (e.g. his solicitor) to identify themselves.

(d)    state the date, time of commencement and place of the interview; and

(e)    state that the suspect will be given a notice about what will happen to the recording.

4.5    The interviewer shall then caution the suspect, which should follow that set out in Code C, and remind the suspect of their entitlement to free and independent legal advice and that they can speak to a solicitor on the telephone.

4.6    The interviewer shall then put to the suspect any significant statement or silence (i.e. failure or refusal to answer a question or to answer it satisfactorily) which occurred before the start of the interview, and shall ask the suspect whether they wish to confirm or deny that earlier statement or silence or whether they wish to add anything. The definition of a "significant" statement or silence is the same as that set out in Code C.

### (c)    *Interviews with the deaf*

4.7    If the suspect is deaf or there is doubt about their hearing ability, the provisions of Code C on interpreters for the deaf or for interviews with suspects who have difficulty in understanding English continue to apply.

### (d)    *Objections and complaints by the suspect*

4.8    If the suspect raises objections to the interview being visually recorded either at the outset or during the interview or during a break in the interview, the interviewer shall explain the fact that the interview is being visually recorded and that the provisions of this code require that the suspect's objections shall be recorded on the visual recording.   When any objections have been visually recorded or the suspect has refused to have their objections recorded, the interviewer shall say that they are turning off the recording equipment, give their reasons and turn it off.  If a separate audio recording is being maintained, the officer shall ask the person to record the reasons for refusing to agree to visual recording of the interview.  Paragraph 4.8 of Code E will apply if the person objects to audio recording of the interview.  The officer shall then make a written record of the interview.  If the interviewer reasonably considers they may proceed to question the suspect with the visual recording still on, the interviewer may do so.  See *Note 4G*.

4.9    If in the course of an interview a complaint is made by the person being questioned, or on their behalf, concerning the provisions of this code or of Code C, then the interviewer shall act in accordance with Code C, record it in the interview record and inform the custody officer. [See *Notes 4B* and *4C*].

F

4.10   If the suspect indicates that they wish to tell the interviewer about matters not directly connected with the offence of which they are suspected and that they are unwilling for these matters to be recorded, the suspect shall be given the opportunity to tell the interviewer about these matters after the conclusion of the formal interview.

### (e) Changing the recording media

4.11   In instances where the recording medium is not of sufficient length to record all of the interview with the suspect, further certified recording medium will be used. When the recording equipment indicates that the recording medium has only a short time left to run, the interviewer shall advise the suspect and round off that part of the interview. If the interviewer wishes to continue the interview but does not already have further certified recording media with him, they shall obtain a set. The suspect should not be left unattended in the interview room. The interviewer will remove the recording media from the recording equipment and insert the new ones which have been unwrapped or otherwise opened in the suspect's presence. The recording equipment shall then be set to record. Care must be taken, particularly when a number of sets of recording media have been used, to ensure that there is no confusion between them. This could be achieved by marking the sets of recording media with consecutive identification numbers.

### (f)   Taking a break during the interview

4.12   When a break is to be taken during the course of an interview and the interview room is to be vacated by the suspect, the fact that a break is to be taken, the reason for it and the time shall be recorded. The recording equipment must be turned off and the recording media removed. The procedures for the conclusion of an interview set out in paragraph 4.19, below, should be followed.

4.13   When a break is to be a short one, and both the suspect and a police officer are to remain in the interview room, the fact that a break is to be taken, the reasons for it and the time shall be recorded on the recording media. The recording equipment may be turned off, but there is no need to remove the recording media. When the interview is recommenced the recording shall continue on the same recording media and the time at which the interview recommences shall be recorded.

4.14   When there is a break in questioning under caution, the interviewing officer must ensure that the person being questioned is aware that they remain under caution. If there is any doubt, the caution must be given again in full when the interview resumes. [See *Note 4D* and *4E*].

**(g) Failure of recording equipment**

4.15 If there is a failure of equipment which can be rectified quickly, the appropriate procedures set out in paragraph 4.12 shall be followed. When the recording is resumed the interviewer shall explain what has happened and record the time the interview recommences. If, however, it is not possible to continue recording on that particular recorder and no alternative equipment is readily available, the interview may continue without being recorded visually. In such circumstances, the procedures set out in paragraph 3.3 of this code for seeking the authority of the custody officer will be followed. [See *Note 4F*].

**(h) Removing used recording media from recording equipment**

4.16 Where used recording media are removed from the recording equipment during the course of an interview, they shall be retained and the procedures set out in paragraph 4.18 below followed.

**(i) Conclusion of interview**

4.17 Before the conclusion of the interview, the suspect shall be offered the opportunity to clarify anything he or she has said and asked if there is anything that they wish to add.

4.18 At the conclusion of the interview, including the taking and reading back of any written statement, the time shall be recorded and the recording equipment switched off. The master recording shall be removed from the recording equipment, sealed with a master recording label and treated as an exhibit in accordance with the force standing orders. The interviewer shall sign the label and also ask the suspect and any third party present during the interview to sign it. If the suspect or third party refuses to sign the label, an officer of at least the rank of inspector, or if one is not available, the custody officer, shall be called into the interview room and asked, subject to *paragraph 2.5*, to sign it.

4.19 The suspect shall be handed a notice which explains the use which will be made of the recording and the arrangements for access to it. The notice will also advise the suspect that a copy of the tape shall be supplied as soon as practicable if the person is charged or informed that he will be prosecuted.

**Notes for Guidance**

4A The interviewer should attempt to estimate the likely length of the interview and ensure that an appropriate quantity of certified recording media and labels with which to seal the master copies are available in the interview room.

*4B   Where the custody officer is called immediately to deal with the complaint, wherever possible the recording equipment should be left to run until the custody officer has entered the interview room and spoken to the person being interviewed. Continuation or termination of the interview should be at the discretion of the interviewing officer pending action by an inspector as set out in Code C.*

*4C   Where the complaint is about a matter not connected with this code of practice or Code C, the decision to continue with the interview is at the discretion of the interviewing officer. Where the interviewing officer decides to continue with the interview, the person being interviewed shall be told that the complaint will be brought to the attention of the custody officer at the conclusion of the interview. When the interview is concluded, the interviewing officer must, as soon as practicable, inform the custody officer of the existence and nature of the complaint made.*

*4D   In considering whether to caution again after a break, the officer should bear in mind that he may have to satisfy a court that the person understood that he was still under caution when the interview resumed.*

*4E   The officer should bear in mind that it may be necessary to satisfy the court that nothing occurred during a break in an interview or between interviews which influenced the suspect's recorded evidence. On the re-commencement of an interview, the officer should consider summarising on the record the reason for the break and confirming this with the suspect.*

*4F   If any part of the recording media breaks or is otherwise damaged during the interview, it should be sealed as a master copy in the presence of the suspect and the interview resumed where it left off. The undamaged part should be copied and the original sealed as a master tape in the suspect's presence, if necessary after the interview. If equipment for copying is not readily available, both parts should be sealed in the suspect's presence and the interview begun again.*

*4G   The interviewer should be aware that a decision to continue recording against the wishes of the suspect may be the subject of comment in court.*

## 5   After the Interview

5.1   The interviewer shall make a note in his or her pocket book of the fact that the interview has taken place and has been recorded, its time, duration and date and the identification number of the master copy of the recording media.

5.2 Where no proceedings follow in respect of the person whose interview was recorded, the recording media must nevertheless be kept securely in accordance with paragraph 6.1 and Note 6A.

**Note for Guidance**

5A *Any written record of a recorded interview shall be made in accordance with national guidelines approved by the Secretary of State, and with regard to the advice contained in the Manual of Guidance for the preparation, processing and submission of files.*

**6      Master Copy Security**

*(a)    General*

6.1 The officer in charge of the police station at which interviews with suspects are recorded shall make arrangements for the master copies to be kept securely and their movements accounted for on the same basis as other material which may be used for evidential purposes, in accordance with force standing orders [See *Note 6A*].

*(b)    Breaking master copy seal for criminal proceedings*

6.2 A police officer has no authority to break the seal on a master copy which is required for criminal trial or appeal proceedings. If it is necessary to gain access to the master copy, the police officer shall arrange for its seal to be broken in the presence of a representative of the Crown Prosecution Service. The defendant or their legal adviser shall be informed and given a reasonable opportunity to be present. If the defendant or their legal representative is present they shall be invited to reseal and sign the master copy. If either refuses or neither is present, this shall be done by the representative of the Crown Prosecution Service. [See *Notes 6B* and *6C*].

*(c)    Breaking master copy seal: other cases*

6.3 The chief officer of police is responsible for establishing arrangements for breaking the seal of the master copy where no criminal proceedings result, or the criminal proceedings, to which the interview relates, have been concluded and it becomes necessary to break the seal. These arrangements should be those which the chief officer considers are reasonably necessary to demonstrate to the person interviewed and any other party who may wish to use or refer to the interview record that the master copy has not been tampered with and that the interview record remains accurate. [See *Note 6D*]

F

6.4    Subject to paragraph 6.6, a representative of each party must be given a reasonable opportunity to be present when the seal is broken, the master copy copied and re-sealed.

6.5    If one or more of the parties is not present when the master copy seal is broken because they cannot be contacted or refuse to attend or paragraph 6.6 applies, arrangements should be made for an independent person such as a custody visitor, to be present. Alternatively, or as an additional safeguard, arrangement should be made for a film or photographs to be taken of the procedure.

6.6    Paragraph 6.5 does not require a person to be given an opportunity to be present when;

    (a)    it is necessary to break the master copy seal for the proper and effective further investigation of the original offence or the investigation of some other offence; and

    (b)    the officer in charge of the investigation has reasonable grounds to suspect that allowing an opportunity might prejudice any such an investigation or criminal proceedings which may be brought as a result or endanger any person.  [See *Note 6E*]

### (d)    Documentation

6.7    When the master copy seal is broken, copied and re-sealed, a record must be made of the procedure followed, including the date time and place and persons present.

### Notes for Guidance

*6A    This section is concerned with the security of the master copy which will have been sealed at the conclusion of the interview.  Care should, however, be taken of working copies since their loss or destruction may lead unnecessarily to the need to have access to master copies.*

*6B    If the master copy has been delivered to the Crown Court for their keeping after committal for trial the Crown Prosecutor will apply to the Chief Clerk of the Crown Court Centre for its release for unsealing by the Crown Prosecutor.*

*6C    Reference to the Crown Prosecution Service or to the Crown Prosecutor in this part of the code shall be taken to include any other body or person with a statutory responsibility for prosecution for whom the police conduct any recorded interviews.*

*6D    The most common reasons for needing access to master copies that are not required for criminal proceedings arise from civil actions and complaints against police and civil actions between individuals arising out of allegations of crime investigated by police.*

6E *Paragraph 6.6 could apply, for example, when one or more of the outcomes or likely outcomes of the investigation might be; (i) the prosecution of one or more of the original suspects, (ii) the prosecution of someone previously not suspected, including someone who was originally a witness; and (iii) any original suspect being treated as a prosecution witness and when premature disclosure of any police action, particularly through contact with any parties involved, could lead to a real risk of compromising the investigation and endangering witnesses.*

**7      Visual Recording of Interviews by Secure Digital Network**

7.1     This section applies if an officer wishes to make a visual recording with sound of an interview mentioned in section 3 of this Code using a secure digital network which does not use removable media (see *paragraph 1.6(c)* above.

7.3     The provisions of sections 1 to 6 of this Code which relate or apply only to removable media will not apply to a secure digital network recording.

7.4     The statutory requirement and provisions for the audio recording of interviews using a secure digital network set out in section 7 of Code E should be applied to the visual recording with sound of interviews mentioned in section 3 of this code as if references to audio recordings of interviews include visual recordings with sound.

F

**POLICE AND CRIMINAL EVIDENCE ACT 1984**

**CODE G**

**CODE OF PRACTICE FOR THE STATUTORY POWER OF ARREST
BY POLICE OFFICERS**

**Commencement**

This Code applies to any arrest made by a police officer after midnight on
31 December 2005

**G**

## 1.   Introduction

1.1   This Code of Practice deals with statutory power of police to arrest persons suspected of involvement in a criminal offence.

1.2   The right to liberty is a key principle of the Human Rights Act 1998. The exercise of the power of arrest represents an obvious and significant interference with that right.

1.3   The use of the power must be fully justified and officers exercising the power should consider if the necessary objectives can be met by other, less intrusive means. Arrest must never be used simply because it can be used. Absence of justification for exercising the powers of arrest may lead to challenges should the case proceed to court. When the power of arrest is exercised it is essential that it is exercised in a non-discriminatory and proportionate manner.

1.4   Section 24 of the Police and Criminal Evidence Act 1984 (as substituted by section 110 of the Serious Organised Crime and Police Act 2005) provides the statutory power of arrest. If the provisions of the Act and this Code are not observed, both the arrest and the conduct of any subsequent investigation may be open to question.

1.5   This code of practice must be readily available at all police stations for consultation by police officers and police staff, detained persons and members of the public.

1.6   The notes for guidance are not provisions of this code.

## 2   Elements of Arrest under section 24 PACE

2.1   A lawful arrest requires two elements:

A person's involvement or suspected involvement or attempted involvement in the commission of a criminal offence;

**AND**

Reasonable grounds for believing that the person's arrest is necessary.

2.2   Arresting officers are required to inform the person arrested that they have been arrested, even if this fact is obvious, and of the relevant circumstances of the arrest in relation to both elements and to inform the custody officer of these on arrival at the police station. See Code C paragraph 3.4.

*Involvement in the commission of an offence'*

2.3   A constable may arrest without warrant in relation to any offence, except for the single exception listed in Note for Guidance 1. A constable may arrest anyone:

- who is about to commit an offence or is in the act of committing an offence

- whom the officer has reasonable grounds for suspecting is about to commit an offence or to be committing an offence

- whom the officer has reasonable grounds to suspect of being guilty of an offence which he or she has reasonable grounds for suspecting has been committed

- anyone who is guilty of an offence which has been committed or anyone whom the officer has reasonable grounds for suspecting to be guilty of that offence.

### *Necessity criteria*

2.4 The power of arrest is only exercisable if the constable has reasonable grounds for believing that it is necessary to arrest the person. The criteria for what may constitute necessity are set out in paragraph 2.9. It remains an operational decision at the discretion of the arresting officer as to:

- what action he or she may take at the point of contact with the individual;

- the necessity criterion or criteria (if any) which applies to the individual; and

- whether to arrest, report for summons, grant street bail, issue a fixed penalty notice or take any other action that is open to the officer.

2.5 In applying the criteria, the arresting officer has to be satisfied that at least one of the reasons supporting the need for arrest is satisfied.

2.6 Extending the power of arrest to all offences provides a constable with the ability to use that power to deal with any situation. However applying the necessity criteria requires the constable to examine and justify the reason or reasons why a person needs to be taken to a police station for the custody officer to decide whether the person should be placed in police detention.

2.7 The criteria below are set out in section 24 of PACE as substituted by section 110 of the Serious Organised Crime and Police Act 2005. The criteria are exhaustive. However, the circumstances that may satisfy those criteria remain a matter for the operational discretion of individual officers. Some examples are given below of what those circumstances may be.

2.8 In considering the individual circumstances, the constable must take into account the situation of the victim, the nature of the offence, the circumstances of the suspect and the needs of the investigative process.

**G**

2.9    The criteria are that the arrest is necessary:

(a)    to enable the name of the person in question to be ascertained (in the case where the constable does not know, and cannot readily ascertain, the person's name, or has reasonable grounds for doubting whether a name given by the person as his name is his real name)

(b)    correspondingly as regards the person's address

an address is a satisfactory address for service of summons if the person will be at it for a sufficiently long period for it to be possible to serve him or her with a summons; or, that some other person at that address specified by the person will accept service of the summons on their behalf.

(c)    to prevent the person in question –

(i)    causing physical injury to himself or any other person;

(ii)    suffering physical injury ;

(iii)    causing loss or damage to property;

(iv)    committing an offence against public decency (only applies where members of the public going about their normal business cannot reasonably be expected to avoid the person in question); or

(v)    causing an unlawful obstruction of the highway;

(d)    to protect a child or other vulnerable person from the person in question

(e)    to allow the prompt and effective investigation of the offence or of the conduct of the person in question.

This may include cases such as:

(i)    Where there are reasonable grounds to believe that the person:

• has made false statements;

• has made statements which cannot be readily verified;

• has presented false evidence;

• may steal or destroy evidence;

• may make contact with co-suspects or conspirators;

• may intimidate or threaten or make contact with witnesses;

- where it is necessary to obtain evidence by questioning; or

(ii)   when considering arrest in connection with an indictable offence, there is a need to:

- enter and search any premises occupied or controlled by a person

- search the person

- prevent contact with others

- take fingerprints, footwear impressions, samples or photographs of the suspect

(iii)   ensuring compliance with statutory drug testing requirements.

(f)   to prevent any prosecution for the offence from being hindered by the disappearance of the person in question.

This may arise if there are reasonable grounds for believing that

- if the person is not arrested he or she will fail to attend court

- street bail after arrest would be insufficient to deter the suspect from trying to evade prosecution

**3      Information to be given on Arrest**

**(a)    *Cautions - when a caution must be given (taken from Code C section 10)***

3.1     A person whom there are grounds to suspect of an offence (see Note 2) must be cautioned before any questions about an offence, or further questions if the answers provide the grounds for suspicion, are put to them if either the suspect's answers or silence, (i.e. failure or refusal to answer or answer satisfactorily) may be given in evidence to a court in a prosecution.  A person need not be cautioned if questions are for other necessary purposes e.g.:

(a)    solely to establish their identity or ownership of any vehicle;

(b)    to obtain information in accordance with any relevant statutory requirement;

(c)    in furtherance of the proper and effective conduct of a search, e.g. to determine the need to search in the exercise of powers of stop and search or to seek co-operation while carrying out a search;

(d)    to seek verification of a written record as in *Code C paragraph 11.13*;

**G**

(e)   when examining a person in accordance with the Terrorism Act 2000, Schedule 7 and the Code of Practice for Examining Officers issued under that Act, Schedule 14, paragraph 6.

3.2   Whenever a person not under arrest is initially cautioned, or reminded they are under caution, that person must at the same time be told they are not under arrest and are free to leave if they want to.

3.3   A person who is arrested, or further arrested, must be informed at the time, or as soon as practicable thereafter, that they are under arrest and the grounds for their arrest, see *Note 3*.

3.4   A person who is arrested, or further arrested, must also be cautioned unless:

(a)   it is impracticable to do so by reason of their condition or behaviour at the time;

(b)   they have already been cautioned immediately prior to arrest as in *paragraph 3.1.*

(c)   Terms of the caution (Taken from Code C section 10)

3.5   The caution, which must be given on arrest, should be in the following terms:

"You do not have to say anything. But it may harm your defence if you do not mention when questioned something which you later rely on in Court. Anything you do say may be given in evidence."

See *Note 5*

3.6   Minor deviations from the words of any caution given in accordance with this Code do not constitute a breach of this Code, provided the sense of the relevant caution is preserved. See *Note 6*

3.7   When, despite being cautioned, a person fails to co-operate or to answer particular questions which may affect their immediate treatment, the person should be informed of any relevant consequences and that those consequences are not affected by the caution. Examples are when a person's refusal to provide:

•   their name and address when charged may make them liable to detention;

•   particulars and information in accordance with a statutory requirement, e.g. under the Road Traffic Act 1988, may amount to an offence or may make the person liable to a further arrest.

## 4      Records of Arrest

*(a) General*

4.1    The arresting officer is required to record in his pocket book or by other methods used for recording information:

- the nature and circumstances of the offence leading to the arrest

- the reason or reasons why arrest was necessary

- the giving of the caution

- anything said by the person at the time of arrest

4.2    Such a record should be made at the time of the arrest unless impracticable to do. If not made at that time, the record should then be completed as soon as possible thereafter.

4.3    On arrival at the police station, the custody officer shall open the custody record (see paragraph 1.1A and section 2 of Code C). The information given by the arresting officer on the circumstances and reason or reasons for arrest shall be recorded as part of the custody record.  Alternatively, a copy of the record made by the officer in accordance with paragraph 4.1 above shall be attached as part of the custody record. See *paragraph 2.2* and *Code C paragraphs 3.4 and 10.3.*

4.4    The custody record will serve as a record of the arrest.  Copies of the custody record will be provided in accordance with paragraphs 2.4 and 2.4A of Code C and access for inspection of the original record in accordance with paragraph 2.5 of Code C.

*(b) Interviews and arrests*

4.5    Records of interview, significant statements or silences will be treated in the same way as set out in sections 10 and 11 of Code C and in Code E (tape recording of interviews).

**G**

*Notes for guidance*

1      *The powers of arrest for offences under sections 4(1) and 5(1) of the Criminal Law Act 1967 require that the offences to which they relate must carry a sentence fixed by law or one in which a first time offender aged 18 or over could be sentenced to 5 years or more imprisonment*

2    *There must be some reasonable, objective grounds for the suspicion, based on known facts or information which are relevant to the likelihood the offence has been committed and the person to be questioned committed it.*

3    *An arrested person must be given sufficient information to enable them to understand they have been deprived of their liberty and the reason they have been arrested, e.g. when a person is arrested on suspicion of committing an offence they must be informed of the suspected offence's nature, when and where it was committed. The suspect must also be informed of the reason or reasons why arrest is considered necessary. Vague or technical language should be avoided.*

4    *Nothing in this Code requires a caution to be given or repeated when informing a person not under arrest they may be prosecuted for an offence. However, a court will not be able to draw any inferences under the Criminal Justice and Public Order Act 1994, section 34, if the person was not cautioned.*

5    *If it appears a person does not understand the caution, the people giving it should explain it in their own words.*

6    *The powers available to an officer as the result of an arrest – for example, entry and search of premises, holding a person incommunicado, setting up road blocks – are only available in respect of indictable offences and are subject to the specific requirements on authorisation as set out in the 1984 Act and relevant PACE Code of Practice.*

**POLICE & CRIMINAL EVIDENCE ACT 1984 (PACE)**

# CODE H

## CODE OF PRACTICE IN CONNECTION WITH THE DETENTION, TREATMENT AND QUESTIONING BY POLICE OFFICERS OF PERSONS UNDER SECTION 41 OF, AND SCHEDULE 8 TO, THE TERRORISM ACT 2000

### Commencement – Transitional Arrangements

This Code applies to people in police detention following their arrest under section 41 of the Terrorism Act 2000, after midnight (on 24 July 2006), notwithstanding that they may have been arrested before that time.

**1      General**

1.1    This Code of Practice applies to, and only to, persons arrested under section 41 of the Terrorism Act 2000 (TACT) and detained in police custody under those provisions and Schedule 8 of the Act. References to detention under this provision that were previously included in PACE Code C – Code for the Detention, Treatment, and Questioning of Persons by Police Officers, no longer apply.

1.2    The Code ceases to apply at any point that a detainee is:

(a)    charged with an offence

(b)    released without charge,or

(c)    transferred to a prison see *section 14.5*

1.3    References to an offence in this Code include being concerned in the commission, preparation or instigation of acts of terrorism.

1.4    This Code's provisions do not apply to detention of individuals under any other terrorism legislation. This Code does not apply to people:

(i)     detained under section 5(1) of the Prevention of Terrorism Act 2005.

(ii)    detained for examination under TACT Schedule 7 and to whom the Code of Practice issued under that Act, Schedule 14, paragraph 6 applies;

(iii)   detained for searches under stop and search powers.

The provisions for the detention, treatment and questioning by police officers of persons other than those in police detention following arrest under section 41 of TACT, are set out in Code C issued under section 66(1) of the Police & Criminal Evidence Act (PACE)1984 (PACE Code C).

1.5    All persons in custody must be dealt with expeditiously, and released as soon as the need for detention no longer applies.

1.6    There is no provision for bail under TACT prior to charge.

1.7    An officer must perform the assigned duties in this Code as soon as practicable. An officer will not be in breach of this Code if delay is justifiable and reasonable steps are taken to prevent unnecessary delay. The custody record shall show when a delay has occurred and the reason. See *Note 1H*

1.8    This Code of Practice must be readily available at all police stations for consultation by:

•      police officers

- police staff

- detained persons

- members of the public.

1.9    The provisions of this Code:

- include the *Annexes*

- do not include the *Notes for Guidance.*

1.10   If an officer has any suspicion, or is told in good faith, that a person of any age may be mentally disordered or otherwise mentally vulnerable, in the absence of clear evidence to dispel that suspicion, the person shall be treated as such for the purposes of this Code. See *Note 1G*

1.11   For the purposes of this Code, a juvenile is any person under the age of 17. If anyone appears to be under 17, and there is no clear evidence that they are 17 or over, they shall be treated as a juvenile for the purposes of this Code.

1.12   If a person appears to be blind, seriously visually impaired, deaf, unable to read or speak or has difficulty orally because of a speech impediment, they shall be treated as such for the purposes of this Code in the absence of clear evidence to the contrary.

1.13   'The appropriate adult' means, in the case of a:

(a)   juvenile:

(i)   the parent, guardian or, if the juvenile is in local authority or voluntary organisation care, or is otherwise being looked after under the Children Act 1989, a person representing that authority or organisation;

(ii)   a social worker of a local authority social services department;

(iii)   failing these, some other responsible adult aged 18 or over who is not a police officer or employed by the police.

(b)   person who is mentally disordered or mentally vulnerable: See *Note 1D*

(i)   a relative, guardian or other person responsible for their care or custody;

(ii)   someone experienced in dealing with mentally disordered or mentally vulnerable people but who is not a police officer or employed by the police;

(iii)   failing these, some other responsible adult aged 18 or over who is not a police officer or employed by the police.

1.14   If this Code requires a person be given certain information, they do not have to be given it if at the time they are incapable of understanding what is said, are violent or may become violent or in urgent need of medical attention, but they must be given it as soon as practicable.

1.15   References to a custody officer include any:-

- police officer; or

- designated staff custody officer acting in the exercise or performance of the powers and duties conferred or imposed on them by their designation,

performing the functions of a custody officer. See *Note 1J*.

1.16   When this Code requires the prior authority or agreement of an officer of at least inspector or superintendent rank, that authority may be given by a sergeant or chief inspector authorised by section 107 of PACE to perform the functions of the higher rank under TACT.

1.17   In this Code:

(a)   'designated person' means a person other than a police officer, designated under the Police Reform Act 2002, Part 4 who has specified powers and duties of police officers conferred or imposed on them;

(b)   reference to a police officer includes a designated person acting in the exercise or performance of the powers and duties conferred or imposed on them by their designation.

1.18   Designated persons are entitled to use reasonable force as follows:-

(a)   when exercising a power conferred on them which allows a police officer exercising that power to use reasonable force, a designated person has the same entitlement to use force; and

(b)   at other times when carrying out duties conferred or imposed on them that also entitle them to use reasonable force, for example:

- when at a police station carrying out the duty to keep detainees for whom they are responsible under control and to assist any other police officer or designated person to keep any detainee under control and to prevent their escape.

- when securing, or assisting any other police officer or designated person in securing, the detention of a person at a police station.

- when escorting, or assisting any other police officer or designated person in escorting, a detainee within a police station.

- for the purpose of saving life or limb; or

- preventing serious damage to property.

1.19 Nothing in this Code prevents the custody officer, or other officer given custody of the detainee, from allowing police staff who are not designated persons to carry out individual procedures or tasks at the police station if the law allows. However, the officer remains responsible for making sure the procedures and tasks are carried out correctly in accordance with the Codes of Practice. Any such person must be:

(a) a person employed by a police authority maintaining a police force and under the control and direction of the Chief Officer of that force;

(b) employed by a person with whom a police authority has a contract for the provision of services relating to persons arrested or otherwise in custody.

1.20 Designated persons and other police staff must have regard to any relevant provisions of this Code.

1.21 References to pocket books include any official report book issued to police officers or other police staff.

### Notes for guidance

1A *Although certain sections of this Code apply specifically to people in custody at police stations, those there voluntarily to assist with an investigation should be treated with no less consideration, e.g. offered refreshments at appropriate times, and enjoy an absolute right to obtain legal advice or communicate with anyone outside the police station.*

1B *A person, including a parent or guardian, should not be an appropriate adult if they:*

- *are*

  - *suspected of involvement in the offence or involvement in the commission, preparation or instigation of acts of terrorism*

  - *the victim*

  - *a witness*

  - *involved in the investigation*

- *received admissions prior to attending to act as the appropriate adult.*

H

*Note: If a juvenile's parent is estranged from the juvenile, they should not be asked to act as the appropriate adult if the juvenile expressly and specifically objects to their presence.*

1C    *If a juvenile admits an offence to, or in the presence of, a social worker or member of a youth offending team other than during the time that person is acting as the juvenile's appropriate adult, another appropriate adult should be appointed in the interest of fairness.*

1D    *In the case of people who are mentally disordered or otherwise mentally vulnerable, it may be more satisfactory if the appropriate adult is someone experienced or trained in their care rather than a relative lacking such qualifications. But if the detainee prefers a relative to a better qualified stranger or objects to a particular person their wishes should, if practicable, be respected.*

1E    *A detainee should always be given an opportunity, when an appropriate adult is called to the police station, to consult privately with a solicitor in the appropriate adult's absence if they want. An appropriate adult is not subject to legal privilege.*

1F    *A solicitor or independent custody visitor (formerly a lay visitor) present at the police station in that capacity may not be the appropriate adult.*

1G    *'Mentally vulnerable' applies to any detainee who, because of their mental state or capacity, may not understand the significance of what is said, of questions or of their replies. 'Mental disorder' is defined in the Mental Health Act 1983, section 1(2) as 'mental illness, arrested or incomplete development of mind, psychopathic disorder and any other disorder or disability of mind'. When the custody officer has any doubt about the mental state or capacity of a detainee, that detainee should be treated as mentally vulnerable and an appropriate adult called.*

1H    *Paragraph 1.7 is intended to cover delays which may occur in processing detainees e.g if:*

- *a large number of suspects are brought into the station simultaneously to be placed in custody;*

- *interview rooms are all being used;*

- *there are difficulties contacting an appropriate adult, solicitor or interpreter.*

1I    *The custody officer must remind the appropriate adult and detainee about the right to legal advice and record any reasons for waiving it in accordance with section 6.*

*1J*    *The designation of police staff custody officers applies only in police areas where an order commencing the provisions of the Police Reform Act 2002, section 38 and Schedule 4A, for designating police staff custody officers is in effect.*

*1K*    *This Code does not affect the principle that all citizens have a duty to help police officers to prevent crime and discover offenders. This is a civic rather than a legal duty; but when a police officer is trying to discover whether, or by whom, an offence has been committed he is entitled to question any person from whom he thinks useful information can be obtained, subject to the restrictions imposed by this Code. A person's declaration that he is unwilling to reply does not alter this entitlement.*

*1L*    *If a person is moved from a police station to receive medical treatment, or for any other reason, the period of detention is still calculated from the time of arrest under section 41 of TACT (or, if a person was being detained under TACT Schedule 7 when arrested, from the time at which the examination under Schedule 7 began).*

*1M*    Under Paragraph 1 of Schedule 8 to TACT, all police stations are designated for detention of persons arrested under section 41 of TACT. Paragraph 4 of Schedule 8 requires that the constable who arrests a person under section 41 takes him as soon as practicable to the police station which he considers is "most appropriate".

## 2    Custody records

2.1    When a person is brought to a police station:

*    under TACT section 41 arrest, or

*    is arrested under TACT section 41 at the police station having attended there voluntarily,

they should be brought before the custody officer as soon as practicable after their arrival at the station or, if appropriate, following arrest after attending the police station voluntarily *see Note 3H*. A person is deemed to be "at a police station" for these purposes if they are within the boundary of any building or enclosed yard which forms part of that police station.

2.2    A separate custody record must be opened as soon as practicable for each person brought to a police station under arrest or arrested at the station having gone there voluntarily. All information recorded under this Code must be recorded as soon as practicable in the custody record unless otherwise specified. Any audio or video recording made in the custody area is not part of the custody record.

2.3    If any action requires the authority of an officer of a specified rank, this must be noted in the custody record, subject to paragraph 2.8.

H

2.4   The custody officer is responsible for the custody record's accuracy and completeness and for making sure the record or copy of the record accompanies a detainee if they are transferred to another police station. The record shall show the:

- time and reason for transfer;

- time a person is released from detention.

2.5   A solicitor or appropriate adult must be permitted to consult a detainee's custody record as soon as practicable after their arrival at the station and at any other time whilst the person is detained. Arrangements for this access must be agreed with the custody officer and may not unreasonably interfere with the custody officer's duties or the justifiable needs of the investigation.

2.6   When a detainee leaves police detention or is taken before a court they, their legal representative or appropriate adult shall be given, on request, a copy of the custody record as soon as practicable. This entitlement lasts for 12 months after release.

2.7   The detainee, appropriate adult or legal representative shall be permitted to inspect the original custody record once the detained person is no longer held under the provisions of TACT section 41 and Schedule 8, provided they give reasonable notice of their request. Any such inspection shall be noted in the custody record.

2.8   All entries in custody records must be timed and identified by the maker. Nothing in this Code requires the identity of officers or other police staff to be recorded or disclosed in the case of enquiries linked to the investigation of terrorism. In these cases, they shall use their warrant or other identification numbers and the name of their police station *see Note 2A*. If records are entered on computer these shall also be timed and contain the operator's identification.

2.9   The fact and time of any detainee's refusal to sign a custody record, when asked in accordance with this Code, must be recorded.

### Note for guidance

2A   *The purpose of paragraph 2.8 is to protect those involved in terrorist investigations or arrests of terrorist suspects from the possibility that those arrested, their associates or other individuals or groups may threaten or cause harm to those involved.*

**3  Initial action**

*(a)  Detained persons – normal procedure*

3.1   When a person is brought to a police station under arrest or arrested at the station having gone there voluntarily, the custody officer must make sure the person is told clearly about the following continuing rights which may be exercised at any stage during the period in custody:

(i)   the right to have someone informed of their arrest as in *section 5*;

(ii)  the right to consult privately with a solicitor and that free independent legal advice is available;

(iii) the right to consult this Code of Practice. See *Note 3D*

3.2   The detainee must also be given:

- a written notice setting out:

  - the above three rights;

  - the arrangements for obtaining legal advice;

  - the right to a copy of the custody record as in *paragraph 2.6;*

  - the caution in the terms prescribed in *section 10.*

- an additional written notice briefly setting out their entitlements while in custody, see *Notes 3A* and *3B.*

Note: The detainee shall be asked to sign the custody record to acknowledge receipt of these notices. Any refusal must be recorded on the custody record.

3.3   A citizen of an independent Commonwealth country or a national of a foreign country, including the Republic of Ireland, must be informed as soon as practicable about their rights of communication with their High Commission, Embassy or Consulate. See *section 7*

3.4   The custody officer shall:

- record that the person was arrested under section 41 of TACT and the reason(s) for the arrest on the custody record. See *paragraph 10.2 and Note for Guidance 3G.*

- note on the custody record any comment the detainee makes in relation to the arresting officer's account but shall not invite comment. If the arresting officer is not physically present when the detainee is brought to a police station, the arresting officer's account must be made available to the custody officer remotely or by a third party on the arresting officer's behalf;

- note any comment the detainee makes in respect of the decision to detain them but shall not invite comment;

- not put specific questions to the detainee regarding their involvement in any offence, nor in respect of any comments they may make in response to the arresting officer's account or the decision to place them in detention *See paragraphs 14.1* and *14.2* and *Notes for Guidance 3H, 14A* and *14B*. Such an exchange is likely to constitute an interview as in *paragraph 11.1* and require the associated safeguards in *section 11*.

See *paragraph 5.9 of the Code of Practice issued under TACT Schedule 8 Paragraph 3* in respect of unsolicited comments.

If the first review of detention is carried out at this time, see paragraphs 14.1 and 14.2, and Part II of Schedule 8 to the Terrorism Act 2000 in respect of action by the review officer.

3.5   The custody officer shall:

(a)   ask the detainee, whether at this time, they:

   (vii)    would like legal advice, see *section 6*;

   (viii)   want someone informed of their detention, see *section 5*;

(b)   ask the detainee to sign the custody record to confirm their decisions in respect of (*a*);

(c)   determine whether the detainee:

   (i)    is, or might be, in need of medical treatment or attention, see *section 9*;

   (ii)   requires:

   - an appropriate adult;

   - help to check documentation;

   - an interpreter;

(d)   record the decision in respect of (*c*).

3.6   When determining these needs the custody officer is responsible for initiating an assessment to consider whether the detainee is likely to present specific risks to custody staff, any individual who may have contact with detainee (e.g. legal advisers, medical staff), or themselves. Such assessments should always include a check on the Police National Computer, to be carried out as soon as practicable, to identify any risks highlighted in relation to the detainee. Although such assessments are primarily the custody officer's responsibility, it will be necessary to obtain information from other sources, especially the investigation team *See Note 3E*, the arresting officer or an appropriate health care professional, see *paragraph 9.15*. Reasons for delaying the initiation or completion of the assessment must be recorded.

3.7     Chief Officers should ensure that arrangements for proper and effective risk assessments required by *paragraph 3.6* are implemented in respect of all detainees at police stations in their area.

3.8     Risk assessments must follow a structured process which clearly defines the categories of risk to be considered and the results must be incorporated in the detainee's custody record. The custody officer is responsible for making sure those responsible for the detainee's custody are appropriately briefed about the risks. The content of any risk assessment and any analysis of the level of risk relating to the person's detention is not required to be shown or provided to the detainee or any person acting on behalf of the detainee. If no specific risks are identified by the assessment, that should be noted in the custody record. See *Note 3F* and *paragraph 9.15*

3.9     Custody officers are responsible for implementing the response to any specific risk assessment, which should include for example:

• reducing opportunities for self harm;

• calling a health care professional;

• increasing levels of monitoring or observation;

• reducing the risk to those who come into contact with the detainee .

See Note for Guidance 3F

3.10    Risk assessment is an ongoing process and assessments must always be subject to review if circumstances change.

3.11    If video cameras are installed in the custody area, notices shall be prominently displayed showing cameras are in use. Any request to have video cameras switched off shall be refused.

3.12    A constable, prison officer or other person authorised by the Secretary of State may take any steps which are reasonably necessary for

(a)     photographing the detained person

**H**

(b)     measuring him, or

(c)     identifying him.

3.13   Paragraph 3.12 concerns the power in TACT Schedule 8 Paragraph 2. The power in TACT Schedule 8 Paragraph 2 does not cover the taking of fingerprints, intimate samples or non-intimate samples, which is covered in TACT Schedule 8 paragraphs 10-15.

### (b)    *Detained persons – special groups*

3.14   If the detainee appears deaf or there is doubt about their hearing or speaking ability or ability to understand English, and the custody officer cannot establish effective communication, the custody officer must, as soon as practicable, call an interpreter for assistance in the action under *paragraphs 3.1–3.5*. See *section 13*

3.15   If the detainee is a juvenile, the custody officer must, if it is practicable, ascertain the identity of a person responsible for their welfare. That person:

- may be:

    – the parent or guardian;

    – if the juvenile is in local authority or voluntary organisation care, or is otherwise being looked after under the Children Act 1989, a person appointed by that authority or organisation to have responsibility for the juvenile's welfare;

    – any other person who has, for the time being, assumed responsibility for the juvenile's welfare.

- must be informed as soon as practicable that the juvenile has been arrested, why they have been arrested and where they are detained. This right is in addition to the juvenile's right in *section 5* not to be held incommunicado. See *Note 3C*

3.16   If a juvenile is known to be subject to a court order under which a person or organisation is given any degree of statutory responsibility to supervise or otherwise monitor them, reasonable steps must also be taken to notify that person or organisation (the 'responsible officer'). The responsible officer will normally be a member of a Youth Offending Team, except for a curfew order which involves electronic monitoring when the contractor providing the monitoring will normally be the responsible officer.

3.17  If the detainee is a juvenile, mentally disordered or otherwise mentally vulnerable, the custody officer must, as soon as practicable:

- inform the appropriate adult, who in the case of a juvenile may or may not be a person responsible for their welfare, as in *paragraph 3.15,* of:

  - the grounds for their detention;

  - their whereabouts.

- ask the adult to come to the police station to see the detainee.

3.18  If the appropriate adult is:

- already at the police station, the provisions of *paragraphs 3.1* to *3.5* must be complied with in the appropriate adult's presence;

- not at the station when these provisions are complied with, they must be complied with again in the presence of the appropriate adult when they arrive.

3.19  The detainee shall be advised that:

- the duties of the appropriate adult include giving advice and assistance;

- they can consult privately with the appropriate adult at any time.

3.20  If the detainee, or appropriate adult on the detainee's behalf, asks for a solicitor to be called to give legal advice, the provisions of *section 6* apply.

3.21  If the detainee is blind, seriously visually impaired or unable to read, the custody officer shall make sure their solicitor, relative, appropriate adult or some other person likely to take an interest in them and not involved in the investigation is available to help check any documentation. When this Code requires written consent or signing the person assisting may be asked to sign instead, if the detainee prefers. This paragraph does not require an appropriate adult to be called solely to assist in checking and signing documentation for a person who is not a juvenile, or mentally disordered or otherwise mentally vulnerable (see *paragraph 3.17*).

**(c)  Documentation**

3.22  The grounds for a person's detention shall be recorded, in the person's presence if practicable.

3.23  Action taken under *paragraphs 3.14* to *3.22* shall be recorded.

H

### Notes for guidance

3A   The notice of entitlements should:

- list the entitlements in this Code, including:

  - visits and contact with outside parties where practicable, including special provisions for Commonwealth citizens and foreign nationals;

  - reasonable standards of physical comfort;

  - adequate food and drink;

  - access to toilets and washing facilities, clothing, medical attention, and exercise when practicable.

- mention the:

  - provisions relating to the conduct of interviews;

  - circumstances in which an appropriate adult should be available to assist the detainee and their statutory rights to make representation whenever the period of their detention is reviewed.

3B   In addition to notices in English, translations should be available in Welsh, the main minority ethnic languages and the principal European languages whenever they are likely to be helpful. Audio versions of the notice should also be made available.

3C   If the juvenile is in local authority or voluntary organisation care but living with their parents or other adults responsible for their welfare, although there is no legal obligation to inform them, they should normally be contacted, as well as the authority or organisation unless suspected of involvement in the offence concerned. Even if the juvenile is not living with their parents, consideration should be given to informing them.

3D   The right to consult this or other relevant Codes of Practice does not entitle the person concerned to delay unreasonably any necessary investigative or administrative action whilst they do so. Examples of action which need not be delayed unreasonably include:

- searching detainees at the police station;

- taking fingerprints or non-intimate samples without consent for evidential purposes.

3E   The investigation team will include any officer involved in questioning a suspect, gathering or analysing evidence in relation to the offences of which the detainee is suspected of *having committed. Should a custody officer require information from the investigation team, the first point of contact should be the officer in charge of the investigation.*

3F  *Home Office Circular 32/2000 provides more detailed guidance on risk assessments and identifies key risk areas which should always be considered. This should be read with the Guidance on Safer Detention & Handling of Persons in Police Custody issued by the National Centre for Policing Excellence in conjunction with the Home Office and Association of Chief Police Officers.*

3G  *Arrests under TACT section 41 can only be made where an officer has reasonable grounds to suspect that the individual concerned is a "terrorist". This differs from the PACE power of arrest in that it need not be linked to a specific offence. There may also be circumstances where an arrest under TACT is made on the grounds of sensitive information which can not be disclosed. In such circumstances, the grounds for arrest may be given in terms of the interpretation of a "terrorist" set out in TACT sections 40(1)(a) or 40(1)(b).*

3H  *For the purpose of arrests under TACT section 41, the review officer is responsible for authorising detention (see Paragraphs 14.1 and 14.2, and Notes for Guidance 14A and 14B). The review officer's role is explained in TACT Schedule 8 Part II. A person may be detained after arrest pending the first review, which must take place as soon as practicable after the person's arrest.*

## 4    Detainee's property

### (a)    Action

4.1    The custody officer is responsible for:

(a)    ascertaining what property a detainee:

    (i)    has with them when they come to the police station, either on first arrival at the police station or any subsequent arrivals at a police station in connection with that detention.

    (ii)    might have acquired for an unlawful or harmful purpose while in custody;

(b)    the safekeeping of any property taken from a detainee which remains at the police station.

The custody officer may search the detainee or authorise their being searched to the extent they consider necessary, provided a search of intimate parts of the body or involving the removal of more than outer clothing is only made as in *Annex A*. A search may only be carried out by an officer of the same sex as the detainee. See *Note 4A*

**H**

4.2   Detainees may retain clothing and personal effects at their own risk unless the custody officer considers they may use them to cause harm to themselves or others, interfere with evidence, damage property, effect an escape or they are needed as evidence. In this event the custody officer may withhold such articles as they consider necessary and must tell the detainee why.

4.3   Personal effects are those items a detainee may lawfully need, use or refer to while in detention but do not include cash and other items of value.

**(b)   Documentation**

4.4   It is a matter for the custody officer to determine whether a record should be made of the property a detained person has with him or had taken from him on arrest (see *Note for Guidance 4D)*. Any record made is not required to be kept as part of the custody record but the custody record should be noted as to where such a record exists. Whenever a record is made the detainee shall be allowed to check and sign the record of property as correct. Any refusal to sign shall be recorded.

4.5   If a detainee is not allowed to keep any article of clothing or personal effects, the reason must be recorded.

**Notes for guidance**

4A   *PACE, Section 54(1) and paragraph 4.1 require a detainee to be searched when it is clear the custody officer will have continuing duties in relation to that detainee or when that detainee's behaviour or offence makes an inventory appropriate. They do not require every detainee to be searched, e.g. if it is clear a person will only be detained for a short period and is not to be placed in a cell, the custody officer may decide not to search them. In such a case the custody record will be endorsed 'not searched', paragraph 4.4 will not apply, and the detainee will be invited to sign the entry. If the detainee refuses, the custody officer will be obliged to ascertain what property they have in accordance with paragraph 4.1.*

4B   *Paragraph 4.4 does not require the custody officer to record on the custody record property in the detainee's possession on arrest if, by virtue of its nature, quantity or size, it is not practicable to remove it to the police station.*

4C   *Paragraph 4.4 does not require items of clothing worn by the person be recorded unless withheld by the custody officer as in paragraph 4.2.*

4D   *Section 43(2) of TACT allows a constable to search a person who has been arrested under section 41 to discover whether he has anything in his possession that may constitute evidence that he is a terrorist.*

## 5    Right not to be held incommunicado

### (a)    *Action*

5.1    Any person arrested and held in custody at a police station or other premises may, on request, have one named person who is a friend, relative or a person known to them who is likely to take an interest in their welfare informed at public expense of their whereabouts as soon as practicable. If the person cannot be contacted the detainee may choose up to two alternatives. If they cannot be contacted, the person in charge of detention or the investigation has discretion to allow further attempts until the information has been conveyed. See *Notes 5D* and *5E*

5.2    The exercise of the above right in respect of each person nominated may be delayed only in accordance with *Annex B*.

5.3    The above right may be exercised each time a detainee is taken to another police station or returned to a police station having been previously transferred to prison. This Code does not afford such a right to a person on transfer to a prison, where a detainee's rights will be governed by Prison Rules *see paragraph 14.8.*

5.4    If the detainee agrees, they may receive visits from friends, family or others likely to take an interest in their welfare, at the custody officer's discretion. Custody Officers should liaise closely with the investigation team (see *Note 3E)* to allow risk assessments to be made where particular visitors have been requested by the detainee or identified themselves to police. In circumstances where the nature of the investigation means that such requests can not be met, consideration should be given, in conjunction with a representative of the relevant scheme, to increasing the frequency of visits from independent visitor schemes. See *Notes 5B* and *5C.*

5.5    If a friend, relative or person with an interest in the detainee's welfare enquires about their whereabouts, this information shall be given if the suspect agrees and *Annex B* does not apply. See *Note 5E*

5.6    The detainee shall be given writing materials, on request, and allowed to telephone one person for a reasonable time, see *Notes 5A* and *5F.* Either or both these privileges may be denied or delayed if an officer of inspector rank or above considers sending a letter or making a telephone call may result in any of the consequences in *Annex B paragraphs 1* and *2*, particularly in relation to the making of a telephone call in a language which an officer listening to the call (see paragraph 5.7) does not understand. See *note 5G.*

Nothing in this paragraph permits the restriction or denial of the rights in *paragraphs 5.1* and *6.1.*

**H**

5.7   Before any letter or message is sent, or telephone call made, the detainee shall be informed that what they say in any letter, call or message (other than in a communication to a solicitor) may be read or listened to and may be given in evidence. A telephone call may be terminated if it is being abused *see Note 5G*. The costs can be at public expense at the custody officer's discretion.

5.8   Any delay or denial of the rights in this section should be proportionate and should last no longer than necessary.

**(b)   Documentation**

5.9   A record must be kept of any:

   (a)   request made under this section and the action taken;

   (b)   letters, messages or telephone calls made or received or visit received;

   (c)   refusal by the detainee to have information about them given to an outside enquirer, or any refusal to see a visitor. The detainee must be asked to countersign the record accordingly and any refusal recorded.

**Notes for guidance**

5A   *A person may request an interpreter to interpret a telephone call or translate a letter.*

5B   *At the custody officer's discretion (and subject to the detainee's consent), visits from friends, family or others likely to take an interest in the detainee's welfare, should be allowed when possible, subject to sufficient personnel being available to supervise a visit and any possible hindrance to the investigation. Custody Officers should bear in mind the exceptional nature of prolonged TACT detention and consider the potential benefits that visits may bring to the health and welfare of detainees who are held for extended periods.*

5C   *Official visitors should be given access following consultation with the officer who has overall responsibility for the investigation provided the detainee consents, and they do not compromise safety or security or unduly delay or interfere with the progress of an investigation. Official visitors should still be required to provide appropriate identification and subject to any screening process in place at the place of detention. Official visitors may include:*

   •   *An accredited faith representative*

   •   *Members of either House of Parliament*

   •   *Public officials needing to interview the prisoner in the course of their duties*

- *Other persons visiting with the approval of the officer who has overall responsibility for the investigation*

- *Consular officials visiting a detainee who is a national of the country they represent subject to Annex F.*

*Visits from appropriate members of the Independent Custody Visitors Scheme should be dealt with in accordance with the separate Code of Practice on Independent Custody Visiting.*

5D  *If the detainee does not know anyone to contact for advice or support or cannot contact a friend or relative, the custody officer should bear in mind any local voluntary bodies or other organisations that might be able to help. Paragraph 6.1 applies if legal advice is required.*

5E  *In some circumstances it may not be appropriate to use the telephone to disclose information under paragraphs 5.1 and 5.5.*

5F  *The telephone call at paragraph 5.6 is in addition to any communication under paragraphs 5.1 and 6.1. Further calls may be made at the custody officer's discretion.*

5G  *The nature of terrorism investigations means that officers should have particular regard to the possibility of suspects attempting to pass information which may be detrimental to public safety, or to an investigation.*

## 6    Right to legal advice

### (a)   Action

6.1  Unless *Annex B* applies, all detainees must be informed that they may at any time consult and communicate privately with a solicitor, whether in person, in writing or by telephone, and that free independent legal advice is available from the duty solicitor. Where an appropriate adult is in attendance, they must also be informed of this right. See *paragraph 3.1, Note 1I, Note 6B* and *Note 6I*

6.2  A poster advertising the right to legal advice must be prominently displayed in the charging area of every police station. See *Note 6G*

6.3  No police officer should, at any time, do or say anything with the intention of dissuading a detainee from obtaining legal advice.

6.4  The exercise of the right of access to legal advice may be delayed exceptionally only as in *Annex B*. Whenever legal advice is requested, and unless *Annex B* applies, the custody officer must act without delay to secure the provision of such advice. If, on being informed or reminded of this right, the detainee declines to speak to a solicitor in person,

**H**

the officer should point out that the right includes the right to speak with a solicitor on the telephone (see *paragraph 5.6)*. If the detainee continues to waive this right the officer should ask them why and any reasons should be recorded on the custody record or the interview record as appropriate. Reminders of the right to legal advice must be given as in *paragraphs 3.5, 11.3,* and the PACE Code D on the Identification of Persons by Police Officers (PACE Code D), *paragraphs 3.19(ii)* and *6.2*. Once it is clear a detainee does not want to speak to a solicitor in person or by telephone they should cease to be asked their reasons. See *Note 6J*.

6.5   An officer of the rank of Commander or Assistant Chief Constable may give a direction under TACT Schedule 8 paragraph 9 that a detainee may only consult a solicitor within the sight and hearing of a qualified officer. Such a direction may only be given if the officer has reasonable grounds to believe that if it were not, it may result in one of the consequences set out in TACT Schedule 8 paragraphs 8(4) or 8(5)(c). See *Annex B paragraph 3* and *Note 6I*. A "qualified officer" means a police officer who:

(a)   is at least the rank of inspector;

(b)   is of the uniformed branch of the force of which the officer giving the direction is a member, and

(c)   in the opinion of the officer giving the direction, has no connection with the detained person's case

Officers considering the use of this power should first refer to Home Office Circular 40/2003.

6.6   In the case of a juvenile, an appropriate adult should consider whether legal advice from a solicitor is required. If the juvenile indicates that they do not want legal advice, the appropriate adult has the right to ask for a solicitor to attend if this would be in the best interests of the person. However, the detained person cannot be forced to see the solicitor if he is adamant that he does not wish to do so.

6.7   A detainee who wants legal advice may not be interviewed or continue to be interviewed until they have received such advice unless:

(a)   *Annex B* applies, when the restriction on drawing adverse inferences from silence in *Annex C* will apply because the detainee is not allowed an opportunity to consult a solicitor; or

(b)    an officer of superintendent rank or above has reasonable grounds for believing that:

    (i)    the consequent delay might:

- lead to interference with, or harm to, evidence connected with an offence;

- lead to interference with, or physical harm to, other people;

- lead to serious loss of, or damage to, property;

- lead to alerting other people suspected of having committed an offence but not yet arrested for it;

- hinder the recovery of property obtained in consequence of the commission of an offence.

    (ii)    when a solicitor, including a duty solicitor, has been contacted and has agreed to attend, awaiting their arrival would cause unreasonable delay to the process of investigation.

Note: In these cases the restriction on drawing adverse inferences from silence in *Annex C* will apply because the detainee is not allowed an opportunity to consult a solicitor.

(c)    the solicitor the detainee has nominated or selected from a list:

    (i)    cannot be contacted;

    (ii)    has previously indicated they do not wish to be contacted; or

    (iii)    having been contacted, has declined to attend; and

the detainee has been advised of the Duty Solicitor Scheme but has declined to ask for the duty solicitor.

In these circumstances the interview may be started or continued without further delay provided an officer of inspector rank or above has agreed to the interview proceeding.

Note: The restriction on drawing adverse inferences from silence in *Annex C* will not apply because the detainee is allowed an opportunity to consult the duty solicitor;

(d)   the detainee changes their mind, about wanting legal advice.

In these circumstances the interview may be started or continued without delay provided that:

(i)   the detainee agrees to do so , in writing or on the interview record made in accordance with the Code of Practice issued under TACT Schedule 8 Paragraph 3; and

(ii)   an officer of inspector rank or above has inquired about the detainee's reasons for their change of mind and gives authority for the interview to proceed.

Confirmation of the detainee's agreement, their change of mind, the reasons for it if given and, subject to *paragraph 2.8,* the name of the authorising officer shall be recorded in the written interview record or the interview record made in accordance with the Code of Practice issued under Paragraph 3 of Schedule 8 to the Terrorism Act. See *Note 6H.* Note: In these circumstances the restriction on drawing adverse inferences from silence in *Annex C* will not apply because the detainee is allowed an opportunity to consult a solicitor if they wish.

6.8   If *paragraph 6.7(a)* applies, where the reason for authorising the delay ceases to apply, there may be no further delay in permitting the exercise of the right in the absence of a further authorisation unless *paragraph 6.7 (b), (c)* or *(d)* applies.

6.9   A detainee who has been permitted to consult a solicitor shall be entitled on request to have the solicitor present when they are interviewed unless one of the exceptions in *paragraph 6.7* applies.

6.10   The solicitor may only be required to leave the interview if their conduct is such that the interviewer is unable properly to put questions to the suspect. See *Notes 6C* and *6D*

6.11   If the interviewer considers a solicitor is acting in such a way, they will stop the interview and consult an officer not below superintendent rank, if one is readily available, and otherwise an officer not below inspector rank not connected with the investigation. After speaking to the solicitor, the officer consulted will decide if the interview should continue in the presence of that solicitor. If they decide it should not, the suspect will be given the opportunity to consult another solicitor before the interview continues and that solicitor given an opportunity to be present at the interview. See *Note 6D*

6.12   The removal of a solicitor from an interview is a serious step and, if it occurs, the officer of superintendent rank or above who took the decision will consider if the incident should be reported to the Law Society. If the decision to remove the solicitor has been taken by an officer below superintendent rank, the facts must be reported to an officer of superintendent rank or above who will similarly consider whether a report to the Law Society would be appropriate. When the solicitor concerned is a duty solicitor, the report should be both to the Law Society and to the Legal Services Commission.

6.13   'Solicitor' in this Code means:

- a solicitor who holds a current practising certificate

- an accredited or probationary representative included on the register of representatives maintained by the Legal Services Commission.

6.14   An accredited or probationary representative sent to provide advice by, and on behalf of, a solicitor shall be admitted to the police station for this purpose unless an officer of inspector rank or above considers such a visit will hinder the investigation and directs otherwise. Hindering the investigation does not include giving proper legal advice to a detainee as in *Note 6C*. Once admitted to the police station, *paragraphs 6.7 to 6.11* apply.

6.15   In exercising their discretion under *paragraph 6.14*, the officer should take into account in particular:

- whether:

  – the identity and status of an accredited or probationary representative have been satisfactorily established;

  – they are of suitable character to provide legal advice,

  – any other matters in any written letter of authorisation provided by the solicitor on whose behalf the person is attending the police station. See *Note 6E*

6.16   If the inspector refuses access to an accredited or probationary representative or a decision is taken that such a person should not be permitted to remain at an interview, the inspector must notify the solicitor on whose behalf the representative was acting and give them an opportunity to make alternative arrangements. The detainee must be informed and the custody record noted.

6.17   If a solicitor arrives at the station to see a particular person, that person must, unless *Annex B* applies, be so informed whether or not they are being interviewed and asked if they would like to see the solicitor. This applies even if the detainee has declined legal advice or, having requested it, subsequently agreed to be interviewed without receiving advice. The solicitor's attendance and the detainee's decision must be noted in the custody record.

**H**

**(b)    Documentation**

6.18    Any request for legal advice and the action taken shall be recorded.

6.19    A record shall be made in the interview record if a detainee asks for legal advice and an interview is begun either in the absence of a solicitor or their representative, or they have been required to leave an interview.

**Notes for guidance**

6A    *If paragraph 6.7(b) applies, the officer should, if practicable, ask the solicitor for an estimate of how long it will take to come to the station and relate this to the time detention is permitted, the time of day (i.e. whether the rest period under paragraph 12.2 is imminent) and the requirements of other investigations. If the solicitor is on their way or is to set off immediately, it will not normally be appropriate to begin an interview before they arrive. If it appears necessary to begin an interview before the solicitor's arrival, they should be given an indication of how long the police would be able to wait so there is an opportunity to make arrangements for someone else to provide legal advice. Nothing within this section is intended to prevent police from ascertaining immediately after the arrest of an individual whether a threat to public safety exists (see paragraph 11.2).*

6B    *A detainee who asks for legal advice should be given an opportunity to consult a specific solicitor or another solicitor from that solicitor's firm or the duty solicitor. If advice is not available by these means, or they do not want to consult the duty solicitor, the detainee should be given an opportunity to choose a solicitor from a list of those willing to provide legal advice. If this solicitor is unavailable, they may choose up to two alternatives. If these attempts are unsuccessful, the custody officer has discretion to allow further attempts until a solicitor has been contacted and agrees to provide legal advice. Apart from carrying out these duties, an officer must not advise the suspect about any particular firm of solicitors.*

6C    *A detainee has a right to free legal advice and to be represented by a solicitor. The solicitor's only role in the police station is to protect and advance the legal rights of their client. On occasions this may require the solicitor to give advice which has the effect of the client avoiding giving evidence which strengthens a prosecution case. The solicitor may intervene in order to seek clarification, challenge an improper question to their client or the manner in which it is put, advise their client not to reply to particular questions, or if they wish to give their client further legal advice. Paragraph 6.9 only applies if the solicitor's approach or conduct prevents or unreasonably obstructs proper questions being put to the suspect or the suspect's response being recorded. Examples of unacceptable conduct include answering questions on a suspect's behalf or providing written replies for the suspect to quote.*

6D   An officer who takes the decision to exclude a solicitor must be in a position to satisfy the court the decision was properly made. In order to do this they may need to witness what is happening.

6E   If an officer of at least inspector rank considers a particular solicitor or firm of solicitors is persistently sending probationary representatives who are unsuited to provide legal advice, they should inform an officer of at least superintendent rank, who may wish to take the matter up with the Law Society.

6F   Subject to the constraints of Annex B, a solicitor may advise more than one client in an investigation if they wish. Any question of a conflict of interest is for the solicitor under their professional code of conduct. If, however, waiting for a solicitor to give advice to one client may lead to unreasonable delay to the interview with another, the provisions of paragraph 6.7(b) may apply.

6G   In addition to a poster in English, a poster or posters containing translations into Welsh, the main minority ethnic languages and the principal European languages should be displayed wherever they are likely to be helpful and it is practicable to do so.

6H   Paragraph 6.7(d) requires the authorisation of an officer of inspector rank or above to the continuation of an interview when a detainee who wanted legal advice changes their mind. It is permissible for such authorisation to be given over the telephone, if the authorising officer is able to satisfy themselves about the reason for the detainee's change of mind and is satisfied it is proper to continue the interview in those circumstances.

6I   Whenever a detainee exercises their right to legal advice by consulting or communicating with a solicitor, they must be allowed to do so in private. This right to consult or communicate in private is fundamental. Except as allowed by the Terrorism Act 2000, Schedule 8, paragraph 9, if the requirement for privacy is compromised because what is said or written by the detainee or solicitor for the purpose of giving and receiving legal advice is overheard, listened to, or read by others without the informed consent of the detainee, the right will effectively have been denied. When a detainee chooses to speak to a solicitor on the telephone, they should be allowed to do so in private unless a direction under Schedule 8, paragraph 9 of the Terrorism Act 2000 has been given or this is impractical because of the design and layout of the custody area, or the location of telephones. However, the normal expectation should be that facilities will be available, unless they are being used, at all police stations to enable detainees to speak in private to a solicitor either face to face or over the telephone.

6J   A detainee is not obliged to give reasons for declining legal advice and should not be pressed to do so.

H

**7      Citizens of independent Commonwealth countries or foreign nationals**

*(a)     Action*

7.1     Any citizen of an independent Commonwealth country or a national of a foreign country, including the Republic of Ireland, may communicate at any time with the appropriate High Commission, Embassy or Consulate. The detainee must be informed as soon as practicable of:

- this right;

- their right, upon request, to have their High Commission, Embassy or Consulate told of their whereabouts and the grounds for their detention. Such a request should be acted upon as soon as practicable.

7.2     If a detainee is a citizen of a country with which a bilateral consular convention or agreement is in force requiring notification of arrest, the appropriate High Commission, Embassy or Consulate shall be informed as soon as practicable, subject to *paragraph 7.4*. The countries to which this applies as at 1 April 2003 are listed in *Annex F*.

7.3     Consular officers may visit one of their nationals in police detention to talk to them and, if required, to arrange for legal advice. Such visits shall take place out of the hearing of a police officer.

7.4     Notwithstanding the provisions of consular conventions, if the detainee is a political refugee whether for reasons of race, nationality, political opinion or religion, or is seeking political asylum, consular officers shall not be informed of the arrest of one of their nationals or given access or information about them except at the detainee's express request.

*(b)     Documentation*

7.5     A record shall be made when a detainee is informed of their rights under this section and of any communications with a High Commission, Embassy or Consulate.

*Note for guidance*

7A      *The exercise of the rights in this section may not be interfered with even though Annex B applies.*

**8      Conditions of detention**

*(a)     Action*

8.1     So far as it is practicable, not more than one detainee should be detained in each cell.

8.2    Cells in use must be adequately heated, cleaned and ventilated. They must be adequately lit, subject to such dimming as is compatible with safety and security to allow people detained overnight to sleep. No additional restraints shall be used within a locked cell unless absolutely necessary and then only restraint equipment, approved for use in that force by the Chief Officer, which is reasonable and necessary in the circumstances having regard to the detainee's demeanour and with a view to ensuring their safety and the safety of others. If a detainee is deaf, mentally disordered or otherwise mentally vulnerable, particular care must be taken when deciding whether to use any form of approved restraints.

8.3    Blankets, mattresses, pillows and other bedding supplied shall be of a reasonable standard and in a clean and sanitary condition.

8.4    Access to toilet and washing facilities must be provided.

8.5    If it is necessary to remove a detainee's clothes for the purposes of investigation, for hygiene, health reasons or cleaning, replacement clothing of a reasonable standard of comfort and cleanliness shall be provided. A detainee may not be interviewed unless adequate clothing has been offered.

8.6    At least two light meals and one main meal should be offered in any 24 hour period. See *Note 8B*. Drinks should be provided at meal times and upon reasonable request between meals. Whenever necessary, advice shall be sought from the appropriate health care professional, see *Note 9A*, on medical and dietary matters. As far as practicable, meals provided shall offer a varied diet and meet any specific dietary needs or religious beliefs the detainee may have. Detainees should also be made aware that the meals offered meet such needs. The detainee may, at the custody officer's discretion, have meals supplied by their family or friends at their expense. See *Note 8A*

8.7    Brief outdoor exercise shall be offered daily if practicable. Where facilities exist, indoor exercise shall be offered as an alternative if outside conditions are such that a detainee can not be reasonably expected to take outdoor exercise (e.g., in cold or wet weather) or if requested by the detainee or for reasons of security, see *Note 8C*.

8.8    Where practicable, provision should be made for detainees to practice religious observance. Consideration should be given to providing a separate room which can be used as a prayer room. The supply of appropriate food and clothing, and suitable provision for prayer facilities, such as uncontaminated copies of religious books, should also be considered. *See Note 8D*.

8.9    A juvenile shall not be placed in a cell unless no other secure accommodation is available and the custody officer considers it is not practicable to supervise them if they are not placed in a cell or that cell provides more comfortable accommodation than

**H**

other secure accommodation in the station. A juvenile may not be placed in a cell with a detained adult.

8.10  Police stations should keep a reasonable supply of reading material available for detainees, including but not limited to, the main religious texts. *See Note 8D.* Detainees should be made aware that such material is available and reasonable requests for such material should be met as soon as practicable unless to do so would:

(i)  interfere with the investigation; or

(ii)  prevent or delay an officer from discharging his statutory duties, or those in this Code.

If such a request is refused on the grounds of (i) or (ii) above, this should be noted in the custody record and met as soon as possible after those grounds cease to apply.

### (b)  Documentation

8.11  A record must be kept of replacement clothing and meals offered.

8.12  The use of any restraints on a detainee whilst in a cell, the reasons for it and, if appropriate, the arrangements for enhanced supervision of the detainee whilst so restrained, shall be recorded. See *paragraph 3.9*

### Notes for guidance

8A  *In deciding whether to allow meals to be supplied by family or friends, the custody officer is entitled to take account of the risk of items being concealed in any food or package and the officer's duties and responsibilities under food handling legislation. If an officer needs to examine food or other items supplied by family and friends before deciding whether they can be given to the detainee, he should inform the person who has brought the item to the police station of this and the reasons for doing so.*

8B  *Meals should, so far as practicable, be offered at recognised meal times, or at other times that take account of when the detainee last had a meal.*

8C  *In light of the potential for detaining individuals for extended periods of time, the overriding principle should be to accommodate a period of exercise, except where to do so would hinder the investigation, delay the detainee's release or charge, or it is declined by the detainee.*

8D  *Police forces should consult with representatives of the main religious communities to ensure the provision for religious observance is adequate, and to seek advice on the appropriate storage and handling of religious texts or other religious items.*

## 9      Care and treatment of detained persons

### *(a)     General*

9.1     Notwithstanding other requirements for medical attention as set out in this section, detainees who are held for more than 96 hours must be visited by a healthcare professional at least once every 24 hours.

9.2     Nothing in this section prevents the police from calling the police surgeon or, if appropriate, some other health care professional, to examine a detainee for the purposes of obtaining evidence relating to any offence in which the detainee is suspected of being involved. See *Note 9A*

9.3     If a complaint is made by, or on behalf of, a detainee about their treatment since their arrest, or it comes to notice that a detainee may have been treated improperly, a report must be made as soon as practicable to an officer of inspector rank or above not connected with the investigation. If the matter concerns a possible assault or the possibility of the unnecessary or unreasonable use of force, an appropriate health care professional must also be called as soon as practicable.

9.4     Detainees should be visited at least every hour. If no reasonably foreseeable risk was identified in a risk assessment, see *paragraphs 3.6 – 3.10*, there is no need to wake a sleeping detainee. Those suspected of being intoxicated through drink or drugs or having swallowed drugs, see *Note 9C*, or whose level of consciousness causes concern must, subject to any clinical directions given by the appropriate health care professional, see *paragraph 9.15*:

*       be visited and roused at least every half hour

*       have their condition assessed as in *Annex H*

*       and clinical treatment arranged if appropriate

See *Notes 9B, 9C* and *9G*

9.5     When arrangements are made to secure clinical attention for a detainee, the custody officer must make sure all relevant information which might assist in the treatment of the detainee's condition is made available to the responsible health care professional. This applies whether or not the health care professional asks for such information. Any officer or police staff with relevant information must inform the custody officer as soon as practicable.

**H**

**(b)   *Clinical treatment and attention***

9.6   The custody officer must make sure a detainee receives appropriate clinical attention as soon as reasonably practicable if the person:

    (a)   appears to be suffering from physical illness; or

    (b)   is injured; or

    (c)   appears to be suffering from a mental disorder; or

    (d)   appears to need clinical attention

9.7   This applies even if the detainee makes no request for clinical attention and whether or not they have already received clinical attention elsewhere. If the need for attention appears urgent, e.g. when indicated as in *Annex H*, the nearest available health care professional or an ambulance must be called immediately.

9.8   The custody officer must also consider the need for clinical attention as set out in *Note 9C* in relation to those suffering the effects of alcohol or drugs.

9.9   If it appears to the custody officer, or they are told, that a person brought to a station under arrest may be suffering from an infectious disease or condition, the custody officer must take reasonable steps to safeguard the health of the detainee and others at the station. In deciding what action to take, advice must be sought from an appropriate health care professional. See *Note 9D*. The custody officer has discretion to isolate the person and their property until clinical directions have been obtained.

9.10   If a detainee requests a clinical examination, an appropriate health care professional must be called as soon as practicable to assess the detainee's clinical needs. If a safe and appropriate care plan cannot be provided, the police surgeon's advice must be sought. The detainee may also be examined by a medical practitioner of their choice at their expense.

9.11   If a detainee is required to take or apply any medication in compliance with clinical directions prescribed before their detention, the custody officer must consult the appropriate health care professional before the use of the medication. Subject to the restrictions in *paragraph 9.12*, the custody officer is responsible for the safekeeping of any medication and for making sure the detainee is given the opportunity to take or apply prescribed or approved medication. Any such consultation and its outcome shall be noted in the custody record.

9.12   No police officer may administer or supervise the self-administration of medically prescribed controlled drugs of the types and forms listed in the Misuse of Drugs Regulations 2001, Schedule 2 or 3. A detainee may only self-administer such drugs under the personal supervision of the registered medical practitioner authorising their use. Drugs listed in Schedule 4 or 5 may be distributed by the custody officer for self-administration if they have consulted the registered medical practitioner authorising their use, this may be done by telephone, and both parties are satisfied self-administration will not expose the detainee, police officers or anyone else to the risk of harm or injury.

9.13 When appropriate health care professionals administer drugs or other medications, or supervise their self-administration, it must be within current medicines legislation and the scope of practice as determined by their relevant professional body.

9.14 If a detainee has in their possession, or claims to need, medication relating to a heart condition, diabetes, epilepsy or a condition of comparable potential seriousness then, even though *paragraph 9.6* may not apply, the advice of the appropriate health care professional must be obtained.

9.15 Whenever the appropriate health care professional is called in accordance with this section to examine or treat a detainee, the custody officer shall ask for their opinion about:

- any risks or problems which police need to take into account when making decisions about the detainee's continued detention;

- when to carry out an interview if applicable; and

- the need for safeguards.

9.16 When clinical directions are given by the appropriate health care professional, whether orally or in writing, and the custody officer has any doubts or is in any way uncertain about any aspect of the directions, the custody officer shall ask for clarification. It is particularly important that directions concerning the frequency of visits are clear, precise and capable of being implemented. See *Note 9E.*

## (c) Documentation

9.17 A record must be made in the custody record of:

(a) the arrangements made for an examination by an appropriate health care professional under *paragraph 9.3* and of any complaint reported under that paragraph together with any relevant remarks by the custody officer;

(b) any arrangements made in accordance with *paragraph 9.6*;

(c) any request for a clinical examination under *paragraph 9.10* and any arrangements made in response;

**H**

(d)   the injury, ailment, condition or other reason which made it necessary to make the arrangements in (a) to (c), see *Note 9F;*

(e)   any clinical directions and advice, including any further clarifications, given to police by a health care professional concerning the care and treatment of the detainee in connection with any of the arrangements made in (a) to (c), see *Note 9E;*

(f)   if applicable, the responses received when attempting to rouse a person using the procedure in *Annex H,* see *Note 9G.*

9.18   If a health care professional does not record their clinical findings in the custody record, the record must show where they are recorded. See *Note 9F.* However, information which is necessary to custody staff to ensure the effective ongoing care and well being of the detainee must be recorded openly in the custody record, see *paragraph 3.8* and *Annex G, paragraph 7.*

9.19   Subject to the requirements of *Section 4*, the custody record shall include:

•   a record of all medication a detainee has in their possession on arrival at the police station;

•   a note of any such medication they claim to need but do not have with them.

### Notes for guidance

*9A   A 'health care professional' means a clinically qualified person working within the scope of practice as determined by their relevant professional body. Whether a health care professional is 'appropriate' depends on the circumstances of the duties they carry out at the time.*

*9B   Whenever possible juveniles and mentally vulnerable detainees should be visited more frequently.*

*9C   A detainee who appears drunk or behaves abnormally may be suffering from illness, the effects of drugs or may have sustained injury, particularly a head injury which is not apparent. A detainee needing or dependent on certain drugs, including alcohol, may experience harmful effects within a short time of being deprived of their supply. In these circumstances, when there is any doubt, police should always act urgently to call an appropriate health care professional or an ambulance. Paragraph 9.6 does not apply to minor ailments or injuries which do not need attention. However, all such ailments or injuries must be recorded in the custody record and any doubt must be resolved in favour of calling the appropriate health care professional.*

9D *It is important to respect a person's right to privacy and information about their health must be kept confidential and only disclosed with their consent or in accordance with clinical advice when it is necessary to protect the detainee's health or that of others who come into contact with them.*

9E *The custody officer should always seek to clarify directions that the detainee requires constant observation or supervision and should ask the appropriate health care professional to explain precisely what action needs to be taken to implement such directions.*

9F *Paragraphs 9.17 and 9.18 do not require any information about the cause of any injury, ailment or condition to be recorded on the custody record if it appears capable of providing evidence of an offence.*

9G *The purpose of recording a person's responses when attempting to rouse them using the procedure in Annex H is to enable any change in the individual's consciousness level to be noted and clinical treatment arranged if appropriate.*

**10 Cautions**

**(a) When a caution must be given**

10.1 A person whom there are grounds to suspect of an offence, see *Note 10A*, must be cautioned before any questions about an offence, or further questions if the answers provide the grounds for suspicion, are put to them if either the suspect's answers or silence, (i.e. failure or refusal to answer or answer satisfactorily) may be given in evidence to a court in a prosecution.

10.2 A person who is arrested, or further arrested, must be informed at the time, or as soon as practicable thereafter, that they are under arrest and the grounds for their arrest, see paragraph 3.4, *Note 3G* and *Note 10B*.

10.3 As per *section 3* of PACE Code G, a person who is arrested, or further arrested, must also be cautioned unless:

(a)   it is impracticable to do so by reason of their condition or behaviour at the time;

(b)   they have already been cautioned immediately prior to arrest as in *paragraph 10.1.*

**(b) Terms of the cautions**

10.4 The caution which must be given on:

(a)   arrest;

**H**

(b)    all other occasions before a person is charged or informed they may be prosecuted, see *PACE Code C*, section 16.

should, unless the restriction on drawing adverse inferences from silence applies, see *Annex C*, be in the following terms:

*"You do not have to say anything. But it may harm your defence if you do not mention when questioned something which you later rely on in Court. Anything you do say may be given in evidence."*

See *Note 10F*

10.5    *Annex C, paragraph 2* sets out the alternative terms of the caution to be used when the restriction on drawing adverse inferences from silence applies.

10.6    Minor deviations from the words of any caution given in accordance with this Code do not constitute a breach of this Code, provided the sense of the relevant caution is preserved. See *Note 10C*

10.7    After any break in questioning under caution, the person being questioned must be made aware they remain under caution. If there is any doubt the relevant caution should be given again in full when the interview resumes. See *Note 10D*

10.8    When, despite being cautioned, a person fails to co-operate or to answer particular questions which may affect their immediate treatment, the person should be informed of any relevant consequences and that those consequences are not affected by the caution. Examples are when a person's refusal to provide:

*    their name and address when charged may make them liable to detention;

*    particulars and information in accordance with a statutory requirement

**(c)    Special warnings under the Criminal Justice and Public Order Act 1994, sections 36 and 37**

10.9    When a suspect interviewed at a police station or authorised place of detention after arrest fails or refuses to answer certain questions, or to answer satisfactorily, after due warning, see *Note 10E*, a court or jury may draw such inferences as appear proper under the Criminal Justice and Public Order Act 1994, sections 36 and 37. Such inferences may only be drawn when:

(a)    the restriction on drawing adverse inferences from silence, see *Annex C*, does not apply; and

(b)     the suspect is arrested by a constable and fails or refuses to account for any objects, marks or substances, or marks on such objects found:

- on their person;

- in or on their clothing or footwear;

- otherwise in their possession; or

- in the place they were arrested;

(c)     the arrested suspect was found by a constable at a place at or about the time the offence for which that officer has arrested them is alleged to have been committed, and the suspect fails or refuses to account for their presence there.

When the restriction on drawing adverse inferences from silence applies, the suspect may still be asked to account for any of the matters in (*b*) or (*c*) but the special warning described in *paragraph 10.10* will not apply and must not be given.

10.10 For an inference to be drawn when a suspect fails or refuses to answer a question about one of these matters or to answer it satisfactorily, the suspect must first be told in ordinary language:

(a)     what offence is being investigated;

(b)     what fact they are being asked to account for;

(c)     this fact may be due to them taking part in the commission of the offence;

(d)     a court may draw a proper inference if they fail or refuse to account for this fact;

(e)     a record is being made of the interview and it may be given in evidence if they are brought to trial.

**(d)     *Juveniles and persons who are mentally disordered or otherwise mentally vulnerable***

10.11 If a juvenile or a person who is mentally disordered or otherwise mentally vulnerable is cautioned in the absence of the appropriate adult, the caution must be repeated in the adult's presence.

**(e)     *Documentation***

10.12 A record shall be made when a caution is given under this section, either in the interviewer's pocket book or in the interview record.

*Notes for guidance*

10A   *There must be some reasonable, objective grounds for the suspicion, based on known facts or information which are relevant to the likelihood the offence has been committed and the person to be questioned committed it.*

10B   *An arrested person must be given sufficient information to enable them to understand that they have been deprived of their liberty and the reason they have been arrested, e.g. when a person is arrested on suspicion of committing an offence they must be informed of the suspected offence's nature, when and where it was committed see Note 3G. The suspect must also be informed of the reason or reasons why the arrest is considered necessary. Vague or technical language should be avoided.*

10C   *If it appears a person does not understand the caution, the person giving it should explain it in their own words.*

10D   *It may be necessary to show to the court that nothing occurred during an interview break or between interviews which influenced the suspect's recorded evidence. After a break in an interview or at the beginning of a subsequent interview, the interviewing officer should summarise the reason for the break and confirm this with the suspect.*

10E   *The Criminal Justice and Public Order Act 1994, sections 36 and 37 apply only to suspects who have been arrested by a constable or Customs and Excise officer and are given the relevant warning by the police or customs officer who made the arrest or who is investigating the offence. They do not apply to any interviews with suspects who have not been arrested.*

10F   *Nothing in this Code requires a caution to be given or repeated when informing a person not under arrest they may be prosecuted for an offence. However, a court will not be able to draw any inferences under the Criminal Justice and Public Order Act 1994, section 34, if the person was not cautioned.*

**11   Interviews – general**

**(a)   Action**

11.1   An interview in this Code is the questioning of a person arrested on suspicion of being a terrorist which, under *paragraph 10.1*, must be carried out under caution. Whenever a person is interviewed they must be informed of the grounds for arrest *see Note 3G*.

11.2   Following a decision to arrest a suspect, they must not be interviewed about the relevant offence except at a place designated for detention under Schedule 8 paragraph 1 of the Terrorism Act 2000, unless the consequent delay would be likely to:

(a) lead to:

- interference with, or harm to, evidence connected with an offence;

- interference with, or physical harm to, other people; or

- serious loss of, or damage to, property;

(b) lead to alerting other people suspected of committing an offence but not yet arrested for it; or

(c) hinder the recovery of property obtained in consequence of the commission of an offence.

Interviewing in any of these circumstances shall cease once the relevant risk has been averted or the necessary questions have been put in order to attempt to avert that risk.

11.3 Immediately prior to the commencement or re-commencement of any interview at a designated place of detention, the interviewer should remind the suspect of their entitlement to free legal advice and that the interview can be delayed for legal advice to be obtained, unless one of the exceptions in *paragraph 6.7* applies. It is the interviewer's responsibility to make sure all reminders are recorded in the interview record.

11.4 At the beginning of an interview the interviewer, after cautioning the suspect, see *section 10*, shall put to them any significant statement or silence which occurred in the presence and hearing of a police officer or other police staff before the start of the interview and which have not been put to the suspect in the course of a previous interview. See *Note 11A*. The interviewer shall ask the suspect whether they confirm or deny that earlier statement or silence and if they want to add anything.

11.5 A significant statement is one which appears capable of being used in evidence against the suspect, in particular a direct admission of guilt. A significant silence is a failure or refusal to answer a question or answer satisfactorily when under caution, which might, allowing for the restriction on drawing adverse inferences from silence, see *Annex C*, give rise to an inference under the Criminal Justice and Public Order Act 1994, Part III.

11.6 No interviewer may try to obtain answers or elicit a statement by the use of oppression. Except as in *paragraph 10.8*, no interviewer shall indicate, except to answer a direct question, what action will be taken by the police if the person being questioned answers questions, makes a statement or refuses to do either. If the person asks directly what action will be taken if they answer questions, make a statement or refuse to do either, the interviewer may inform them what action the police propose to take provided that action is itself proper and warranted.

**H**

11.7    The interview or further interview of a person about an offence with which that person has not been charged or for which they have not been informed they may be prosecuted, must cease when:

(a)     the officer in charge of the investigation is satisfied all the questions they consider relevant to obtaining accurate and reliable information about the offence have been put to the suspect, this includes allowing the suspect an opportunity to give an innocent explanation and asking questions to test if the explanation is accurate and reliable, e.g. to clear up ambiguities or clarify what the suspect said;

(b)     the officer in charge of the investigation has taken account of any other available evidence; and

(c)     the officer in charge of the investigation, or in the case of a detained suspect, the custody officer, see *PACE Code C paragraph 16.1*, reasonably believes there is sufficient evidence to provide a realistic prospect of conviction for that offence. See *Note 11B*

### (b)    Interview records

11.8    Interview records should be made in accordance with the Code of Practice issued under Schedule 8 Paragraph 3 to the Terrorism Act where the interview takes place at a designated place of detention.

### (c)    Juveniles and mentally disordered or otherwise mentally vulnerable people

11.9    A juvenile or person who is mentally disordered or otherwise mentally vulnerable must not be interviewed regarding their involvement or suspected involvement in a criminal offence or offences, or asked to provide or sign a written statement under caution or record of interview, in the absence of the appropriate adult unless *paragraphs 11.2, 11.11 to 11.13* apply. See *Note 11C*

11.10   If an appropriate adult is present at an interview, they shall be informed:

•     they are not expected to act simply as an observer; and

•     the purpose of their presence is to:

–     advise the person being interviewed;

–     observe whether the interview is being conducted properly and fairly;

–     facilitate communication with the person being interviewed.

The appropriate adult may be required to leave the interview if their conduct is such that the interviewer is unable properly to put questions to the suspect.  This will include situations where the appropriate adult's approach or conduct prevents or unreasonably obstructs proper questions being put to the suspect or the suspect's responses being recorded.  If the interviewer considers an appropriate adult is acting in such a way, they will stop the interview and consult an officer not below superintendent rank, if one is readily available, and otherwise an officer not below inspector rank not connected with the investigation. After speaking to the appropriate adult, the officer consulted will decide if the interview should continue without the attendance of that appropriate adult.  If they decide it should not, another appropriate adult should be obtained before the interview continues, unless the provisions of paragraph 11.11 below apply.

### (d)    Vulnerable suspects – urgent interviews at police stations

11.11 The following persons may not be interviewed unless an officer of superintendent rank or above considers delay will lead to the consequences in *paragraph 11.2(a)* to *(c)*, and is satisfied the interview would not significantly harm the person's physical or mental state (see Annex G):

(a)    a juvenile or person who is mentally disordered or otherwise mentally vulnerable if at the time of the interview the appropriate adult is not present;

(b)    anyone other than in *(a)* who at the time of the interview appears unable to:

   •    appreciate the significance of questions and their answers; or

   •    understand what is happening because of the effects of drink, drugs or any illness, ailment or condition;

(c)    a person who has difficulty understanding English or has a hearing disability, if at the time of the interview an interpreter is not present.

11.12 These interviews may not continue once sufficient information has been obtained to avert the consequences in *paragraph 11.2(a)* to *(c)*.

11.13 A record shall be made of the grounds for any decision to interview a person under *paragraph 11.11*.

H

*Notes for guidance*

11A    *Paragraph 11.4 does not prevent the interviewer from putting significant statements and silences to a suspect again at a later stage or a further interview.*

11B    *The Criminal Procedure and Investigations Act 1996 Code of Practice, paragraph 3.4 states 'In conducting an investigation, the investigator should pursue all reasonable lines of enquiry, whether these point towards or away from the suspect. What is reasonable will depend on the particular circumstances.' Interviewers should keep this in mind when deciding what questions to ask in an interview.*

11C    *Although juveniles or people who are mentally disordered or otherwise mentally vulnerable are often capable of providing reliable evidence, they may, without knowing or wishing to do so, be particularly prone in certain circumstances to provide information that may be unreliable, misleading or self-incriminating. Special care should always be taken when questioning such a person, and the appropriate adult should be involved if there is any doubt about a person's age, mental state or capacity. Because of the risk of unreliable evidence it is also important to obtain corroboration of any facts admitted whenever possible.*

11D    *Consideration should be given to the effect of extended detention on a detainee and any subsequent information they provide, especially if it relates to information on matters that they have failed to provide previously in response to similar questioning see Annex G.*

11E    *Significant statements described in paragraph 11.4 will always be relevant to the offence and must be recorded. When a suspect agrees to read records of interviews and other comments and sign them as correct, they should be asked to endorse the record with, e.g. 'I agree that this is a correct record of what was said' and add their signature. If the suspect does not agree with the record, the interviewer should record the details of any disagreement and ask the suspect to read these details and sign them to the effect that they accurately reflect their disagreement. Any refusal to sign should be recorded.*

## 12    Interviews in police stations

### (a)    Action

12.1    If a police officer wants to interview or conduct enquiries which require the presence of a detainee, the custody officer is responsible for deciding whether to deliver the detainee into the officer's custody.

12.2    Except as below, in any period of 24 hours a detainee must be allowed a continuous period of at least 8 hours for rest, free from questioning, travel or any interruption in connection with the investigation concerned. This period should normally be at night or other appropriate time which takes account of when the detainee last slept or rested. If a detainee is arrested at a police station after going there voluntarily, the period of 24 hours runs from the time of their arrest (or, if a person was being detained under TACT Schedule 7 when arrested, from the time at which the examination under Schedule 7 began) and not the time of arrival at the police station. The period may not be interrupted or delayed, except:

(a)   when there are reasonable grounds for believing not delaying or interrupting the period would:

   (i)   involve a risk of harm to people or serious loss of, or damage to, property;

   (ii)   delay unnecessarily the person's release from custody;

   (iii)   otherwise prejudice the outcome of the investigation;

(b)   at the request of the detainee, their appropriate adult or legal representative;

(c)   when a delay or interruption is necessary in order to:

   (i)   comply with the legal obligations and duties arising under *section 14*;

   (ii)   to take action required under *section 9* or in accordance with medical advice.

If the period is interrupted in accordance with *(a)*, a fresh period must be allowed. Interruptions under *(b)* and *(c)*, do not require a fresh period to be allowed.

12.3   Before a detainee is interviewed the custody officer, in consultation with the officer in charge of the investigation and appropriate health care professionals as necessary, shall assess whether the detainee is fit enough to be interviewed. This means determining and considering the risks to the detainee's physical and mental state if the interview took place and determining what safeguards are needed to allow the interview to take place. The custody officer shall not allow a detainee to be interviewed if the custody officer considers it would cause significant harm to the detainee's physical or mental state. Vulnerable suspects listed at *paragraph 11.11* shall be treated as always being at some risk during an interview and these persons may not be interviewed except in accordance with *paragraphs 11.11* to *11.13*.

12.4   As far as practicable interviews shall take place in interview rooms which are adequately heated, lit and ventilated.

12.5   A suspect whose detention without charge has been authorised under TACT Schedule 8, because the detention is necessary for an interview to obtain evidence of the offence for which they have been arrested, may choose not to answer questions but police do not require the suspect's consent or agreement to interview them for this purpose. If a suspect takes steps to prevent themselves being questioned or further questioned, e.g. by refusing to leave their cell to go to a suitable interview room or by trying to leave the interview room, they shall be advised their consent or agreement to interview is not required. The suspect shall be cautioned as in *section 10*, and informed if they fail or refuse to co-operate, the interview may take place in the cell and that their failure or refusal to co-operate may be given in evidence. The suspect shall then be invited to co-operate and go into the interview room.

12.6   People being questioned or making statements shall not be required to stand.

12.7   Before the interview commences each interviewer shall, subject to the qualification at *paragraph 2.8,* identify themselves and any other persons present to the interviewee.

12.8   Breaks from interviewing should be made at recognised meal times or at other times that take account of when an interviewee last had a meal. Short refreshment breaks shall be provided at approximately two hour intervals, subject to the interviewer's discretion to delay a break if there are reasonable grounds for believing it would:

(i)      involve a:

- risk of harm to people;

- serious loss of, or damage to, property;

(ii)     unnecessarily delay the detainee's release;

(iii)    otherwise prejudice the outcome of the investigation.

See *Note 12B*

12.9   During extended periods where no interviews take place, because of the need to gather further evidence or analyse existing evidence, detainees and their legal representative shall be informed that the investigation into the relevant offence remains ongoing. If practicable, the detainee and legal representative should also be made aware in general terms of any reasons for long gaps between interviews. Consideration should be given to allowing visits, more frequent exercise, or for reading or writing materials to be offered *see paragraph 5.4, section 8* and *Note 12C.*

12.10  If during the interview a complaint is made by or on behalf of the interviewee concerning the provisions of this Code, the interviewer should:

(i)      record it in the interview record;

(ii)     inform the custody officer, who is then responsible for dealing with it as in *section 9*.

**(b)     Documentation**

12.11  A record must be made of the:

- time a detainee is not in the custody of the custody officer, and why

- reason for any refusal to deliver the detainee out of that custody

12.12  A record shall be made of:

(a)     the reasons it was not practicable to use an interview room; and

(b)     any action taken as in *paragraph 12.5*.

The record shall be made on the custody record or in the interview record for action taken whilst an interview record is being kept, with a brief reference to this effect in the custody record.

12.13  Any decision to delay a break in an interview must be recorded, with reasons, in the interview record.

12.14  All written statements made at police stations under caution shall be written on forms provided for the purpose.

12.15  All written statements made under caution shall be taken in accordance with *Annex D*. Before a person makes a written statement under caution at a police station they shall be reminded about the right to legal advice. See *Note 12A*

**Notes for guidance**

12A   *It is not normally necessary to ask for a written statement if the interview was recorded in writing and the record signed in accordance with the Code of Practice issued under TACT Schedule 8 Paragraph 3. Statements under caution should normally be taken in these circumstances only at the person's express wish. A person may however be asked if they want to make such a statement.*

12B   *Meal breaks should normally last at least 45 minutes and shorter breaks after two hours should last at least 15 minutes. If the interviewer delays a break in accordance with paragraph 12.8 and prolongs the interview, a longer break should be provided. If there is a short interview, and another short interview is contemplated, the length of the break may be reduced if there are reasonable grounds to believe this is necessary to avoid any of the consequences in paragraph 12.8(i) to (iii).*

**H**

12C   *Consideration should be given to the matters referred to in paragraph 12.9 after a period of over 24 hours without questioning. This is to ensure that extended periods of detention without an indication that the investigation remains ongoing do not contribute to a deterioration of the detainee's well-being.*

## 13   Interpreters

### (a)   General

13.1   Chief officers are responsible for making sure appropriate arrangements are in place for provision of suitably qualified interpreters for people who:

- are deaf;

- do not understand English.

Whenever possible, interpreters should be drawn from the National Register of Public Service Interpreters (NRPSI) or the Council for the Advancement of Communication with Deaf People (CACDP) Directory of British Sign Language/English Interpreters.

### (b)   Foreign languages

13.2   Unless *paragraphs 11.2, 11.11* to *11.13* apply, a person must not be interviewed in the absence of a person capable of interpreting if:

(a)   they have difficulty understanding English;

(b)   the interviewer cannot speak the person's own language;

(c)   the person wants an interpreter present.

13.3   The interviewer shall make sure the interpreter makes a note of the interview at the time in the person's language for use in the event of the interpreter being called to give evidence, and certifies its accuracy. The interviewer should allow sufficient time for the interpreter to note each question and answer after each is put, given and interpreted. The person should be allowed to read the record or have it read to them and sign it as correct or indicate the respects in which they consider it inaccurate. If the interview is audibly recorded or visually recorded with sound, the Code of Practice issued under paragraph 3 of Schedule 8 to the Terrorism Act 2000 will apply.

13.4   In the case of a person making a statement to a police officer or other police staff other than in English:

(a)   the interpreter shall record the statement in the language it is made;

(b)   the person shall be invited to sign it;

(c)     an official English translation shall be made in due course.

### (c)     *Deaf people and people with speech difficulties*

13.5   If a person appears to be deaf or there is doubt about their hearing or speaking ability, they must not be interviewed in the absence of an interpreter unless they agree in writing to being interviewed without one or *paragraphs 11.2, 11.11* to *11.13* apply.

13.6   An interpreter should also be called if a juvenile is interviewed and the parent or guardian present as the appropriate adult appears to be deaf or there is doubt about their hearing or speaking ability, unless they agree in writing to the interview proceeding without one or *paragraphs 11.2, 11.11* to *11.13* apply.

13.7   The interviewer shall make sure the interpreter is allowed to read the interview record and certify its accuracy in the event of the interpreter being called to give evidence. If the interview is audibly recorded or visually recorded, the Code of Practice issued under TACT Schedule 8 Paragraph 3 will apply.

### (d)     *Additional rules for detained persons*

13.8   All reasonable attempts should be made to make the detainee understand that interpreters will be provided at public expense.

13.9   If *paragraph 6.1* applies and the detainee cannot communicate with the solicitor because of language, hearing or speech difficulties, an interpreter must be called. The interpreter may not be a police officer or any other police staff when interpretation is needed for the purposes of obtaining legal advice. In all other cases a police officer or other police staff may only interpret if the detainee and the appropriate adult, if applicable, give their agreement in writing or if the interview is audibly recorded or visually recorded as in the Code of Practice issued under TACT Schedule 8 Paragraph 3.

13.10 When the custody officer cannot establish effective communication with a person charged with an offence who appears deaf or there is doubt about their ability to hear, speak or to understand English, arrangements must be made as soon as practicable for an interpreter to explain the offence and any other information given by the custody officer.

### (e)     *Documentation*

13.11 Action taken to call an interpreter under this section and any agreement to be interviewed in the absence of an interpreter must be recorded.

**H**

## 14    Reviews and Extensions of Detention

### *(a)    Reviews and Extensions of Detention*

14.1    The powers and duties of the review officer are in the Terrorism Act 2000, Schedule 8, Part II. See *Notes 14A* and *14B*. A review officer should carry out his duties at the police station where the detainee is held, and be allowed such access to the detainee as is necessary for him to exercise those duties.

14.2    For the purposes of reviewing a person's detention, no officer shall put specific questions to the detainee:

- regarding their involvement in any offence; or

- in respect of any comments they may make:

    - when given the opportunity to make representations; or

    - in response to a decision to keep them in detention or extend the maximum period of detention.

Such an exchange could constitute an interview as in *paragraph 11.1* and would be subject to the associated safeguards in *section 11* and, in respect of a person who has been charged see *PACE Code C Section 16.8*.

14.3    If detention is necessary for longer than 48 hours, a police officer of at least superintendent rank, or a Crown Prosecutor may apply for warrants of further detention under the Terrorism Act 2000, Schedule 8, Part III.

14.4    When an application for a warrant of further or extended detention is sought under Paragraph 29 or 36 of Schedule 8, the detained person and their representative must be informed of their rights in respect of the application. These include:

a)    the right to a written or oral notice of the warrant See *Note 14G.*

b)    the right to make oral or written representations to the judicial authority about the application.

c)    the right to be present and legally represented at the hearing of the application, unless specifically excluded by the judicial authority.

d)    their right to free legal advice (see section 6 of this Code).

### (b)   Transfer of detained persons to Prison

14.5   Where a warrant is issued which authorises detention beyond a period of 14 days from the time of arrest (or if a person was being detained under TACT Schedule 7, from the time at which the examination under Schedule 7 began), the detainee must be transferred from detention in a police station to detention in a designated prison as soon as is practicable, unless:

   a)   the detainee specifically requests to remain in detention at a police station and that request can be accommodated, or

   b)   there are reasonable grounds to believe that transferring a person to a prison would:

   i)   significantly hinder a terrorism investigation;

   ii)   delay charging of the detainee or his release from custody, or

   iii)   otherwise prevent the investigation from being conducted diligently and expeditiously.

   If any of the grounds in (b)(i) to (iii) above are relied upon, these must be presented to the judicial authority as part of the application for the warrant that would extend detention beyond a period of 14 days from the time of arrest (or if a person was being detained under TACT Schedule 7, from the time at which the examination under Schedule 7 began) *See Note 14J.*

14.6   If a person remains in detention at a police station under a warrant of further detention as described at section 14.5, they must be transferred to a prison as soon as practicable after the grounds at (b)(i) to (iii) of that section cease to apply.

14.7   Police should maintain an agreement with the National Offender Management Service (NOMS) that stipulates named prisons to which individuals may be transferred under this section. This should be made with regard to ensuring detainees are moved to the most suitable prison for the purposes of the investigation and their welfare, and should include provision for the transfer of male, female and juvenile detainees. Police should ensure that the Governor of a prison to which they intend to transfer a detainee is given reasonable notice of this. Where practicable, this should be no later than the point at which a warrant is applied for that would take the period of detention beyond 14 days.

14.8   Following a detained person's transfer to a designated prison, their detention will be governed by the terms of Schedule 8 and Prison Rules, and this Code of Practice will not apply during any period that the person remains in prison detention. The Code will once more apply if a detained person is transferred back from prison detention to police

**H**

detention. In order to enable the Governor to arrange for the production of the detainee back into police custody, police should give notice to the Governor of the relevant prison as soon as possible of any decision to transfer a detainee from prison back to a police station. Any transfer between a prison and a police station should be conducted by police, and this Code will be applicable during the period of transit See *Note 14K*. A detainee should only remain in police custody having been transferred back from a prison, for as long as is necessary for the purpose of the investigation.

14.9   The investigating team and custody officer should provide as much information as necessary to enable the relevant prison authorities to provide appropriate facilities to detain an individual. This should include, but not be limited to:

i)        medical assessments

ii)       security and risk assessments

iii)      details of the detained person's legal representatives

iv)      details of any individuals from whom the detained person has requested visits, or who have requested to visit the detained person.

14.10  Where a detainee is to be transferred to prison, the custody officer should inform the detainee's legal adviser beforehand that the transfer is to take place (including the name of the prison). The custody officer should also make all reasonable attempts to inform:

•        family or friends who have been informed previously of the detainee's detention; and

•        the person who was initially informed of the detainee's detention as at *paragraph 5.1*.

**(c)    Documentation**

14.11  It is the responsibility of the officer who gives any reminders as at *paragraph 14.4*, to ensure that these are noted in the custody record, as well any comments made by the detained person upon being told of those rights.

14.12  The grounds for, and extent of, any delay in conducting a review shall be recorded.

14.13  Any written representations shall be retained.

14.14  A record shall be made as soon as practicable about the outcome of each review or determination whether to extend the maximum detention period without charge or an application for a warrant of further detention or its extension.

14.15 Any decision not to transfer a detained person to a designated prison under paragraph *14.5*, must be recorded, along with the reasons for this decision. If a request under paragraph *14.5(a)* is not accommodated, the reasons for this should also be recorded.

### Notes for guidance

14A TACT Schedule 8 Part II sets out the procedures for review of detention up to 48 hours from the time of arrest under TACT section 41 (or if a person was being detained under TACT Schedule 7, from the time at which the examination under Schedule 7 began). These include provisions for the requirement to review detention, postponing a review, grounds for continued detention, designating a review officer, representations, rights of the detained person and keeping a record. The review officer's role ends after a warrant has been issued for extension of detention under Part III of Schedule 8.

14B Section 24(1) of the Terrorism Act 2006, amended the grounds contained within the 2000 Act on which a review officer may authorise continued detention. Continued detention may be authorised if it is necessary-

a) to obtain relevant evidence whether by questioning him or otherwise

b) to preserve relevant evidence

c) while awaiting the result of an examination or analysis of relevant evidence

d) for the examination or analysis of anything with a view to obtaining relevant evidence

e) pending a decision to apply to the Secretary of State for a deportation notice to be served on the detainee, the making of any such application, or the consideration of any such application by the Secretary of State

f) pending a decision to charge the detainee with an offence.

14C Applications for warrants to extend detention beyond 48 hours, may be made for periods of 7 days at a time (initially under TACT Schedule 8 paragraph 29, and extensions thereafter under TACT Schedule 8, Paragraph 36), up to a maximum period of 28 days from the time of arrest (or if a person was being detained under TACT Schedule 7, from the time at which the examination under Schedule 7 began). Applications may be made for shorter periods than 7 days, which must be specified. The judicial authority may also substitute a shorter period if he feels a period of 7 days is inappropriate.

14D Unless Note 14F applies, applications for warrants that would take the total period of detention up to 14 days or less should be made to a judicial authority, meaning a

**H**

District Judge (Magistrates' Court) designated by the Lord Chancellor to hear such applications.

14E   Any application for a warrant which would take the period of detention beyond 14 days from the time of arrest (or if a person was being detained under TACT Schedule 7, from the time at which the examination under Schedule 7 began), must be made to a High Court Judge.

14F   If an application has been made to a High Court judge for a warrant which would take detention beyond 14 days, and the High Court judge instead issues a warrant for a period of time which would not take detention beyond 14 days, further applications for extension of detention must also be made to a High Court judge, regardless of the period of time to which they refer.

14G   TACT Schedule 8 Paragraph 31 requires a notice to be given to the detained person if a warrant is sought for further detention. This must be provided before the judicial hearing of the application for that warrant and must include:

a)   notification that the application for a warrant has been made

b)   the time at which the application was made

c)   the time at which the application is to be heard

d)   the grounds on which further detention is sought.

A notice must also be provided each time an application is made to extend an existing warrant

14H   An officer applying for an order under TACT Schedule 8 Paragraph 34 to withhold specified information on which he intends to rely when applying for a warrant of further detention, may make the application for the order orally or in writing. The most appropriate method of application will depend on the circumstances of the case and the need to ensure fairness to the detainee.

14I   Where facilities exist, hearings relating to extension of detention under Part III of Schedule 8 may take place using video conferencing facilities provided that the requirements set out in Schedule 8 are still met. However, if the judicial authority requires the detained person to be physically present at any hearing, this should be complied with as soon as practicable. Paragraphs 33(4) to 33(9) of TACT Schedule 8 govern the relevant conduct of hearings.

14J   Transfer to prison is intended to ensure that individuals who are detained for extended periods of time are held in a place designed for longer periods of detention than police *stations. Prison will provide detainees with a greater range of facilities more appropriate to longer detention periods.*

14K *The Code will only apply as is appropriate to the conditions of detention during the period of transit. There is obviously no requirement to provide such things as bed linen or reading materials for the journey between prison and police station.*

## 15   Charging

15.1   Charging of detained persons is covered by PACE and guidance issued under PACE by the Director of Public Prosecutions. General guidance on charging can be found in section 16 of PACE Code C.

## 16   Testing persons for the presence of specified Class A drugs

16.1   The provisions for drug testing under section 63B of PACE (as amended by section 5 of the Criminal Justice Act 2003 and section 7 of the Drugs Act 2005), do not apply to detention under TACT section 41 and Schedule 8. Guidance on these provisions can be found in section 17 of PACE Code C.

**H**

**ANNEX A – INTIMATE AND STRIP SEARCHES**

*A    Intimate search*

1.    An intimate search consists of the physical examination of a person's body orifices other than the mouth. The intrusive nature of such searches means the actual and potential risks associated with intimate searches must never be underestimated.

*(a)    Action*

2.    Body orifices other than the mouth may be searched only if authorised by an officer of inspector rank or above who has reasonable grounds for believing that the person may have concealed on themselves anything which they could and might use to cause physical injury to themselves or others at the station and the officer has reasonable grounds for believing that an intimate search is the only means of removing those items.

3.    Before the search begins, a police officer, designated detention officer or staff custody officer, must tell the detainee:-

    (a)    that the authority to carry out the search has been given;

    (b)    the grounds for giving the authorisation and for believing that the article cannot be removed without an intimate search.

4.    An intimate search may only be carried out by a registered medical practitioner or registered nurse, unless an officer of at least inspector rank considers this is not practicable, in which case a police officer may carry out the search. See *Notes A1* to *A5*

5.    Any proposal for a search under *paragraph 2* to be carried out by someone other than a registered medical practitioner or registered nurse must only be considered as a last resort and when the authorising officer is satisfied the risks associated with allowing the item to remain with the detainee outweigh the risks associated with removing it. See *Notes A1 to A5*

6.    An intimate search at a police station of a juvenile or mentally disordered or otherwise mentally vulnerable person may take place only in the presence of an appropriate adult of the same sex, unless the detainee specifically requests a particular adult of the opposite sex who is readily available. In the case of a juvenile the search may take place in the absence of the appropriate adult only if the juvenile signifies in the presence of the appropriate adult they do not want the adult present during the search and the adult agrees. A record shall be made of the juvenile's decision and signed by the appropriate adult.

7.   When an intimate search under *paragraph 2* is carried out by a police officer, the officer must be of the same sex as the detainee. A minimum of two people, other than the detainee, must be present during the search. Subject to *paragraph 6*, no person of the opposite sex who is not a medical practitioner or nurse shall be present, nor shall anyone whose presence is unnecessary. The search shall be conducted with proper regard to the sensitivity and vulnerability of the detainee.

**(b)    Documentation**

8.   In the case of an intimate search under paragraph 2, the following shall be recorded as soon as practicable, in the detainee's custody record:

- the authorisation to carry out the search;

- the grounds for giving the authorisation;

- the grounds for believing the article could not be removed without an intimate search

- which parts of the detainee's body were searched

- who carried out the search

- who was present

- the result.

9.   If an intimate search is carried out by a police officer, the reason why it was impracticable for a registered medical practitioner or registered nurse to conduct it must be recorded.

**B    Strip search**

10.   A strip search is a search involving the removal of more than outer clothing. In this Code, outer clothing includes shoes and socks.

**(a)    Action**

11.   A strip search may take place only if it is considered necessary to remove an article which a detainee would not be allowed to keep, and the officer reasonably considers the detainee might have concealed such an article. Strip searches shall not be routinely carried out if there is no reason to consider that articles are concealed.

**H**

**The conduct of strip searches**

12.　When strip searches are conducted:

(a)　a police officer carrying out a strip search must be the same sex as the detainee;

(b)　the search shall take place in an area where the detainee cannot be seen by anyone who does not need to be present, nor by a member of the opposite sex except an appropriate adult who has been specifically requested by the detainee;

(c)　except in cases of urgency, where there is risk of serious harm to the detainee or to others, whenever a strip search involves exposure of intimate body parts, there must be at least two people present other than the detainee, and if the search is of a juvenile or mentally disordered or otherwise mentally vulnerable person, one of the people must be the appropriate adult. Except in urgent cases as above, a search of a juvenile may take place in the absence of the appropriate adult only if the juvenile signifies in the presence of the appropriate adult that they do not want the adult to be present during the search and the adult agrees. A record shall be made of the juvenile's decision and signed by the appropriate adult. The presence of more than two people, other than an appropriate adult, shall be permitted only in the most exceptional circumstances;

(d)　the search shall be conducted with proper regard to the sensitivity and vulnerability of the detainee in these circumstances and every reasonable effort shall be made to secure the detainee's co-operation and minimise embarrassment. Detainees who are searched shall not normally be required to remove all their clothes at the same time, e.g. a person should be allowed to remove clothing above the waist and redress before removing further clothing;

(e)　if necessary to assist the search, the detainee may be required to hold their arms in the air or to stand with their legs apart and bend forward so a visual examination may be made of the genital and anal areas provided no physical contact is made with any body orifice;

(f)　if articles are found, the detainee shall be asked to hand them over. If articles are found within any body orifice other than the mouth, and the detainee refuses to hand them over, their removal would constitute an intimate search, which must be carried out as in *Part A*;

(g)　a strip search shall be conducted as quickly as possible, and the detainee allowed to dress as soon as the procedure is complete.

**(b)    Documentation**

13.    A record shall be made on the custody record of a strip search including the reason it was considered necessary, those present and any result.

**Notes for guidance**

A1    *Before authorising any intimate search, the authorising officer must make every reasonable effort to persuade the detainee to hand the article over without a search. If the detainee agrees, a registered medical practitioner or registered nurse should whenever possible be asked to assess the risks involved and, if necessary, attend to assist the detainee.*

A2    *If the detainee does not agree to hand the article over without a search, the authorising officer must carefully review all the relevant factors before authorising an intimate search. In particular, the officer must consider whether the grounds for believing an article may be concealed are reasonable.*

A3    *If authority is given for a search under paragraph 2, a registered medical practitioner or registered nurse shall be consulted whenever possible. The presumption should be that the search will be conducted by the registered medical practitioner or registered nurse and the authorising officer must make every reasonable effort to persuade the detainee to allow the medical practitioner or nurse to conduct the search.*

A4    *A constable should only be authorised to carry out a search as a last resort and when all other approaches have failed. In these circumstances, the authorising officer must be satisfied the detainee might use the article for one or more of the purposes in paragraph 2 and the physical injury likely to be caused is sufficiently severe to justify authorising a constable to carry out the search.*

A5    *If an officer has any doubts whether to authorise an intimate search by a constable, the officer should seek advice from an officer of superintendent rank or above.*

**ANNEX B – DELAY IN NOTIFYING ARREST OR ALLOWING ACCESS TO LEGAL ADVICE FOR PERSONS DETAINED UNDER THE TERRORISM ACT 2000.**

*A    Delays under TACT Schedule 8*

1.    The rights as in *sections 5* or *6,* may be delayed if the person is detained under the Terrorism Act 2000, section 41, has not yet been charged with an offence and an officer of superintendent rank or above has reasonable grounds for believing the exercise of either right will have one of the following consequences:

(a)    interference with or harm to evidence of a serious offence,

(b)    interference with or physical injury to any person,

(c)    the alerting of persons who are suspected of having committed a serious offence but who have not been arrested for it,

(d)    the hindering of the recovery of property obtained as a result of a serious offence or in respect of which a forfeiture order could be made under section 23,

(e)    interference with the gathering of information about the commission, preparation or instigation of acts of terrorism,

(f)    the alerting of a person and thereby making it more difficult to prevent an act of terrorism, or

(g)    the alerting of a person and thereby making it more difficult to secure a person's apprehension, prosecution or conviction in connection with the commission, preparation or instigation of an act of terrorism.

2.    These rights may also be delayed if the officer has reasonable grounds for believing that:

(a)    the detained person has benefited from his criminal conduct (to be decided in accordance with Part 2 of the Proceeds of Crime Act 2002), and

(b)    the recovery of the value of the property constituting the benefit will be hindered by—

(i)    informing the named person of the detained person's detention (in the case of an authorisation under Paragraph 8(1)(a) of Schedule 8 to TACT, or

(ii)    the exercise of the right under paragraph 7 (in the case of an authorisation under Paragraph 8(1)(b) of Schedule 8 to TACT.

3.  Authority to delay a detainee's right to consult privately with a solicitor may be given only if the authorising officer has reasonable grounds to believe the solicitor the detainee wants to consult will, inadvertently or otherwise, pass on a message from the detainee or act in some other way which will have any of the consequences specified under *paragraph 8 of Schedule 8 to the Terrorism Act 2000.* In these circumstances the detainee must be allowed to choose another solicitor. See *Note B3*

4.  If the detainee wishes to see a solicitor, access to that solicitor may not be delayed on the grounds they might advise the detainee not to answer questions or the solicitor was initially asked to attend the police station by someone else. In the latter case the detainee must be told the solicitor has come to the police station at another person's request, and must be asked to sign the custody record to signify whether they want to see the solicitor.

5.  The fact the grounds for delaying notification of arrest may be satisfied does not automatically mean the grounds for delaying access to legal advice will also be satisfied.

6.  These rights may be delayed only for as long as is necessary but not beyond 48 hours from the time of arrest (or if a person was being detained under TACT Schedule 7, from the time at which the examination under Schedule 7 began). If the above grounds cease to apply within this time the detainee must as soon as practicable be asked if they wish to exercise either right, the custody record noted accordingly, and action taken in accordance with the relevant section of this Code.

7.  A person must be allowed to consult a solicitor for a reasonable time before any court hearing.

**B    Documentation**

8.  The grounds for action under this Annex shall be recorded and the detainee informed of them as soon as practicable.

9.  Any reply given by a detainee under *paragraph 6* must be recorded and the detainee asked to endorse the record in relation to whether they want to receive legal advice at this point.

**C    Cautions and special warnings**

10. When a suspect detained at a police station is interviewed during any period for which access to legal advice has been delayed under this Annex, the court or jury may not draw adverse inferences from their silence.

**H**

**Notes for guidance**

B1   *Even if Annex B applies in the case of a juvenile, or a person who is mentally disordered or otherwise mentally vulnerable, action to inform the appropriate adult and the person responsible for a juvenile's welfare if that is a different person, must nevertheless be taken as in paragraph 3.15 and 3.17.*

B2   *In the case of Commonwealth citizens and foreign nationals, see Note 7A.*

B3   *A decision to delay access to a specific solicitor is likely to be a rare occurrence and only when it can be shown the suspect is capable of misleading that particular solicitor and there is more than a substantial risk that the suspect will succeed in causing information to be conveyed which will lead to one or more of the specified consequences.*

## ANNEX C – RESTRICTION ON DRAWING ADVERSE INFERENCES FROM SILENCE AND TERMS OF THE CAUTION WHEN THE RESTRICTION APPLIES

### (a) *The restriction on drawing adverse inferences from silence*

1. The Criminal Justice and Public Order Act 1994, sections 34, 36 and 37 as amended by the Youth Justice and Criminal Evidence Act 1999, section 58 describe the conditions under which adverse inferences may be drawn from a person's failure or refusal to say anything about their involvement in the offence when interviewed, after being charged or informed they may be prosecuted. These provisions are subject to an overriding restriction on the ability of a court or jury to draw adverse inferences from a person's silence. This restriction applies:

   (a) to any detainee at a police station who, before being interviewed, see *section 11* or being charged or informed they may be prosecuted, see *section 15,* has:

      (i) asked for legal advice, see *section 6, paragraph 6.1*;

      (ii) not been allowed an opportunity to consult a solicitor, including the duty solicitor, as in this Code; and

      (iii) not changed their mind about wanting legal advice, see *section 6, paragraph 6.7(c)*

      Note the condition in (ii) will

      – apply when a detainee who has asked for legal advice is interviewed before speaking to a solicitor as in *section 6, paragraph 6.6(a)* or *(b).*

      – not apply if the detained person declines to ask for the duty solicitor, see *section 6, paragraphs 6.7(b)* and *(c)*;

   (b) to any person charged with, or informed they may be prosecuted for, an offence who:

      (i) has had brought to their notice a written statement made by another person or the content of an interview with another person which relates to that offence, see PACE Code C *section 16, paragraph 16.6*;

      (ii) is interviewed about that offence, see PACE Code C *section 16, paragraph 16.8*; or

      (iii) makes a written statement about that offence, see *Annex D paragraphs 4* and *9.*

**H**

### (b)    Terms of the caution when the restriction applies

2.    When a requirement to caution arises at a time when the restriction on drawing adverse inferences from silence applies, the caution shall be:

*'You do not have to say anything, but anything you do say may be given in evidence.'*

3.    Whenever the restriction either begins to apply or ceases to apply after a caution has already been given, the person shall be re-cautioned in the appropriate terms. The changed position on drawing inferences and that the previous caution no longer applies shall also be explained to the detainee in ordinary language. See *Note C1*

### Notes for guidance

C1    *The following is suggested as a framework to help explain changes in the position on drawing adverse inferences if the restriction on drawing adverse inferences from silence:*

(a)    *begins to apply:*

*'The caution you were previously given no longer applies. This is because after that caution:*

(i)    *you asked to speak to a solicitor but have not yet been allowed an opportunity to speak to a solicitor. See paragraph 1(a); or*

(ii)    *you have been charged with/informed you may be prosecuted. See paragraph 1(b).*

*'This means that from now on, adverse inferences cannot be drawn at court and your defence will not be harmed just because you choose to say nothing. Please listen carefully to the caution I am about to give you because it will apply from now on. You will see that it does not say anything about your defence being harmed.'*

(b)    *ceases to apply before or at the time the person is charged or informed they may be prosecuted, see paragraph 1(a);*

*'The caution you were previously given no longer applies. This is because after that caution you have been allowed an opportunity to speak to a solicitor. Please listen carefully to the caution I am about to give you because it will apply from now on. It explains how your defence at court may be affected if you choose to say nothing.'*

## ANNEX D – WRITTEN STATEMENTS UNDER CAUTION

### (a) Written by a person under caution

1. A person shall always be invited to write down what they want to say.

2. A person who has not been charged with, or informed they may be prosecuted for, any offence to which the statement they want to write relates, shall:

   (a) unless the statement is made at a time when the restriction on drawing adverse inferences from silence applies, see Annex C, be asked to write out and sign the following before writing what they want to say:

   *'I make this statement of my own free will. I understand that I do not have to say anything but that it may harm my defence if I do not mention when questioned something which I later rely on in court. This statement may be given in evidence.';*

   (b) if the statement is made at a time when the restriction on drawing adverse inferences from silence applies, be asked to write out and sign the following before writing what they want to say;

   *'I make this statement of my own free will. I understand that I do not have to say anything. This statement may be given in evidence.'*

3. When a person, on the occasion of being charged with or informed they may be prosecuted for any offence, asks to make a statement which relates to any such offence and wants to write it they shall:

   (a) unless the restriction on drawing adverse inferences from silence, see *Annex C*, applied when they were so charged or informed they may be prosecuted, be asked to write out and sign the following before writing what they want to say:

   *'I make this statement of my own free will. I understand that I do not have to say anything but that it may harm my defence if I do not mention when questioned something which I later rely on in court. This statement may be given in evidence.';*

   (b) if the restriction on drawing adverse inferences from silence applied when they were so charged or informed they may be prosecuted, be asked to write out and sign the following before writing what they want to say:

   *'I make this statement of my own free will. I understand that I do not have to say anything. This statement may be given in evidence.'*

**H**

4.    When a person, who has already been charged with or informed they may be prosecuted for any offence, asks to make a statement which relates to any such offence and wants to write it they shall be asked to write out and sign the following before writing what they want to say:

> *'I make this statement of my own free will. I understand that I do not have to say anything. This statement may be given in evidence.';*

5.    Any person writing their own statement shall be allowed to do so without any prompting except a police officer or other police staff may indicate to them which matters are material or question any ambiguity in the statement.

### (b)    Written by a police officer or other police staff

6.    If a person says they would like someone to write the statement for them, a police officer, or other police staff shall write the statement.

7.    If the person has not been charged with, or informed they may be prosecuted for, any offence to which the statement they want to make relates they shall, before starting, be asked to sign, or make their mark, to the following:

 (a)    unless the statement is made at a time when the restriction on drawing adverse inferences from silence applies, see *Annex C*:

> *'I, ..........................., wish to make a statement. I want someone to write down what I say. I understand that I do not have to say anything but that it may harm my defence if I do not mention when questioned something which I later rely on in court. This statement may be given in evidence.';*

 (b)    if the statement is made at a time when the restriction on drawing adverse inferences from silence applies:

> *'I, ..........................., wish to make a statement. I want someone to write down what I say. I understand that I do not have to say anything. This statement may be given in evidence.'*

8.    If, on the occasion of being charged with or informed they may be prosecuted for any offence, the person asks to make a statement which relates to any such offence they shall before starting be asked to sign, or make their mark to, the following:

 (a)    unless the restriction on drawing adverse inferences from silence applied, see *Annex C,* when they were so charged or informed they may be prosecuted:

'I, ............................, wish to make a statement. I want someone to write down what I say. I understand that I do not have to say anything but that it may harm my defence if I do not mention when questioned something which I later rely on in court. This statement may be given in evidence.';

(b)    if the restriction on drawing adverse inferences from silence applied when they were so charged or informed they may be prosecuted:

'I, ............................, wish to make a statement. I want someone to write down what I say. I understand that I do not have to say anything. This statement may be given in evidence.'

9.    If, having already been charged with or informed they may be prosecuted for any offence, a person asks to make a statement which relates to any such offence they shall before starting, be asked to sign, or make their mark to:

'I, ............................, wish to make a statement. I want someone to write down what I say. I understand that I do not have to say anything. This statement may be given in evidence.'

10.   The person writing the statement must take down the exact words spoken by the person making it and must not edit or paraphrase it. Any questions that are necessary, e.g. to make it more intelligible, and the answers given must be recorded at the same time on the statement form.

11.   When the writing of a statement is finished the person making it shall be asked to read it and to make any corrections, alterations or additions they want. When they have finished reading they shall be asked to write and sign or make their mark on the following certificate at the end of the statement:

'I have read the above statement, and I have been able to correct, alter or add anything I wish. This statement is true. I have made it of my own free will.'

12.   If the person making the statement cannot read, or refuses to read it, or to write the above mentioned certificate at the end of it or to sign it, the person taking the statement shall read it to them and ask them if they would like to correct, alter or add anything and to put their signature or make their mark at the end. The person taking the statement shall certify on the statement itself what has occurred.

**H**

**ANNEX E – SUMMARY OF PROVISIONS RELATING TO MENTALLY DISORDERED AND OTHERWISE MENTALLY VULNERABLE PEOPLE**

1.  If an officer has any suspicion, or is told in good faith, that a person of any age may be mentally disordered or otherwise mentally vulnerable, or mentally incapable of understanding the significance of questions or their replies that person shall be treated as mentally disordered or otherwise mentally vulnerable for the purposes of this Code. See *paragraph 1.10*

2.  In the case of a person who is mentally disordered or otherwise mentally vulnerable, 'the appropriate adult' means:

    (a)   a relative, guardian or other person responsible for their care or custody;

    (b)   someone experienced in dealing with mentally disordered or mentally vulnerable people but who is not a police officer or employed by the police;

    (c)   failing these, some other responsible adult aged 18 or over who is not a police officer or employed by the police.

    See *paragraph 1.13(b) and Note 1D*

3.  If the detention of a person who is mentally vulnerable or appears to be suffering from a mental disorder is authorised by the review officer (see *paragraphs 14.1* and *14.2* and *Notes for Guidance 14A* and *14B)* , the custody officer must as soon as practicable inform the appropriate adult of the grounds for detention and the person's whereabouts, and ask the adult to come to the police station to see them. If the appropriate adult:

    •   is already at the station when information is given as in *paragraphs 3.1* to *3.5* the information must be given in their presence

    •   is not at the station when the provisions of *paragraph 3.1* to *3.5* are complied with these provisions must be complied with again in their presence once they arrive.

    See *paragraphs 3.15* to *3.16*

4.  If the appropriate adult, having been informed of the right to legal advice, considers legal advice should be taken, the provisions of *section 6* apply as if the mentally disordered or otherwise mentally vulnerable person had requested access to legal advice. See *paragraph 3.20* and *Note E1.*

5.  The custody officer must make sure a person receives appropriate clinical attention as soon as reasonably practicable if the person appears to be suffering from a mental disorder or in urgent cases immediately call the nearest health care professional or an ambulance. It is not intended these provisions delay the transfer of a detainee to a

place of safety under the Mental Health Act 1983, section 136 if that is applicable. If an assessment under that Act is to take place at a police station, the custody officer must consider whether an appropriate health care professional should be called to conduct an initial clinical check on the detainee. See *paragraph 9.6* and *9.8*

6.    If a mentally disordered or otherwise mentally vulnerable person is cautioned in the absence of the appropriate adult, the caution must be repeated in the appropriate adult's presence. See *paragraph 10.11*

7.    A mentally disordered or otherwise mentally vulnerable person must not be interviewed or asked to provide or sign a written statement in the absence of the appropriate adult unless the provisions of *paragraphs 11.2* or *11.11* to *11.13* apply. Questioning in these circumstances may not continue in the absence of the appropriate adult once sufficient information to avert the risk has been obtained. A record shall be made of the grounds for any decision to begin an interview in these circumstances. See *paragraphs 11.2, 11.9* and *11.11* to *11.13*

8.    If the appropriate adult is present at an interview, they shall be informed they are not expected to act simply as an observer and the purposes of their presence are to:

   •    advise the interviewee

   •    observe whether or not the interview is being conducted properly and fairly

   •    facilitate communication with the interviewee

   See *paragraph 11.10*

9.    If the custody officer charges a mentally disordered or otherwise mentally vulnerable person with an offence or takes such other action as is appropriate when there is sufficient evidence for a prosecution this must be done in the presence of the appropriate adult. The written notice embodying any charge must be given to the appropriate adult. See *paragraphs PACE Code C Section 16.*

10.   An intimate or strip search of a mentally disordered or otherwise mentally vulnerable person may take place only in the presence of the appropriate adult of the same sex, unless the detainee specifically requests the presence of a particular adult of the opposite sex. A strip search may take place in the absence of an appropriate adult only in cases of urgency when there is a risk of serious harm to the detainee or others. See *Annex A, paragraphs 6* and *12(c)*

11.   Particular care must be taken when deciding whether to use any form of approved restraints on a mentally disordered or otherwise mentally vulnerable person in a locked cell. See *paragraph 8.2*

**H**

**Notes for guidance**

E1   *The purpose of the provision at paragraph 3.20 is to protect the rights of a mentally disordered or otherwise mentally vulnerable detained person who does not understand the significance of what is said to them. If the detained person wants to exercise the right to legal advice, the appropriate action should be taken and not delayed until the appropriate adult arrives. A mentally disordered or otherwise mentally vulnerable detained person should always be given an opportunity, when an appropriate adult is called to the police station, to consult privately with a solicitor in the absence of the appropriate adult if they want.*

E2   *Although people who are mentally disordered or otherwise mentally vulnerable are often capable of providing reliable evidence, they may, without knowing or wanting to do so, be particularly prone in certain circumstances to provide information that may be unreliable, misleading or self-incriminating. Special care should always be taken when questioning such a person, and the appropriate adult should be involved if there is any doubt about a person's mental state or capacity. Because of the risk of unreliable evidence, it is important to obtain corroboration of any facts admitted whenever possible.*

E3   *Because of the risks referred to in Note E2, which the presence of the appropriate adult is intended to minimise, officers of superintendent rank or above should exercise their discretion to authorise the commencement of an interview in the appropriate adult's absence only in exceptional cases, if it is necessary to avert an immediate risk of serious harm. See paragraphs 11.2, 11.11 to 11.13*

**ANNEX F – COUNTRIES WITH WHICH BILATERAL CONSULAR CONVENTIONS OR AGREEMENTS REQUIRING NOTIFICATION OF THE ARREST AND DETENTION OF THEIR NATIONALS ARE IN FORCE.**

| | |
|---|---|
| Armenia | Kazakhstan |
| Austria | Macedonia |
| Azerbaijan | Mexico |
| Belarus | Moldova |
| Belgium | Mongolia |
| Bosnia-Herzegovina | Norway |
| Bulgaria | Poland |
| China* | Romania |
| Croatia | Russia |
| Cuba | Slovak Republic |
| Czech Republic | Slovenia |
| Denmark | Spain |
| Egypt | Sweden |
| France | Tajikistan |
| Georgia | Turkmenistan |
| German Federal Republic | Ukraine |
| Greece | USA |
| Hungary | Uzbekistan |
| Italy | Yugoslavia |
| Japan | |

\* Police are required to inform Chinese officials of arrest/detention in the Manchester consular district only. This comprises Derbyshire, Durham, Greater Manchester, Lancashire, Merseyside, North South and West Yorkshire, and Tyne and Wear.

## ANNEX G – FITNESS TO BE INTERVIEWED

1.    This Annex contains general guidance to help police officers and health care professionals assess whether a detainee might be at risk in an interview.

2.    A detainee may be at risk in a interview if it is considered that:

(a)    conducting the interview could significantly harm the detainee's physical or mental state;

(b)    anything the detainee says in the interview about their involvement or suspected involvement in the offence about which they are being interviewed **might** be considered unreliable in subsequent court proceedings because of their physical or mental state.

3.    In assessing whether the detainee should be interviewed, the following must be considered:

(a)    how the detainee's physical or mental state might affect their ability to understand the nature and purpose of the interview, to comprehend what is being asked and to appreciate the significance of any answers given and make rational decisions about whether they want to say anything;

(b)    the extent to which the detainee's replies may be affected by their physical or mental condition rather than representing a rational and accurate explanation of their involvement in the offence;

(c)    how the nature of the interview, which could include particularly probing questions, might affect the detainee.

4.    It is essential health care professionals who are consulted consider the functional ability of the detainee rather than simply relying on a medical diagnosis, e.g. it is possible for a person with severe mental illness to be fit for interview.

5.    Health care professionals should advise on the need for an appropriate adult to be present, whether reassessment of the person's fitness for interview may be necessary if the interview lasts beyond a specified time, and whether a further specialist opinion may be required.

6.    When health care professionals identify risks they should be asked to quantify the risks. They should inform the custody officer:

•    whether the person's condition:

–    is likely to improve

        –     will require or be amenable to treatment; and

     •     indicate how long it may take for such improvement to take effect

7.     The role of the health care professional is to consider the risks and advise the custody officer of the outcome of that consideration. The health care professional's determination and any advice or recommendations should be made in writing and form part of the custody record.

8.     Once the health care professional has provided that information, it is a matter for the custody officer to decide whether or not to allow the interview to go ahead and if the interview is to proceed, to determine what safeguards are needed. Nothing prevents safeguards being provided in addition to those required under the Code. An example might be to have an appropriate health care professional present during the interview, in addition to an appropriate adult, in order constantly to monitor the person's condition and how it is being affected by the interview.

## ANNEX H – DETAINED PERSON: OBSERVATION LIST

1.   If any detainee fails to meet any of the following criteria, an appropriate health care professional or an ambulance must be called.

2.   When assessing the level of rousability, consider:

*Rousability* – can they be woken?

- go into the cell

- call their name

- shake gently

*Response to questions* – can they give appropriate answers to questions such as:

- What's your name?

- Where do you live?

- Where do you think you are?

*Response to commands* – can they respond appropriately to commands such as:

- Open your eyes!

- Lift one arm, now the other arm!

3.   Remember to take into account the possibility or presence of other illnesses, injury, or mental condition, a person who is drowsy and smells of alcohol may also have the following:

- Diabetes

- Epilepsy

- Head injury

- Drug intoxication or overdose

- Stroke

# APPENDIX 3

# Checklists

**Checklist 1: Instructions from a third party**

  1 Date and time of call
  2 Name of person taking the call

*Details of third party*
  3 Name
  4 Address
  5 Telephone number
  6 Relationship to person arrested

*Details of arrested person*
  7 Name
  8 Address
  9 Telephone number
10 Any aliases used
11 Any vulnerabilities, medication, etc
12 Whether the suspect requested legal advice

*Details of the incident*
13 Reason for the arrest
14 Time and place of arrest
15 Circumstances of the arrest
16 Involvement of the third party (if any)
17 Details of other persons arrested
18 Details of any other witnesses

*Details of the detention*
19 Police station suspect taken to
20 Name(s) of officer(s) involved

*Initial advice given*
21 Advice given to third party
22 Action taken in response to third party contact

A full and accurate note must be taken of all information obtained and advice given, which should be timed and dated.

## Checklist 2: Finding the client

1) Contact the custody officer at the police station where it is believed that the suspect has been taken. Where an enquiry about the whereabouts of a suspect is made by a person with an interest in the suspect's welfare, that information must normally be given, provided the suspect agrees (Code C, Code H para 5.5).

2) If the custody officer is not willing to give the required information, it may be that a decision has been made to hold the suspect incommunicado under Police and Criminal Evidence Act 1984 (PACE) s56 or the Terrorism Act (TA) 2000 Sch 8 para 8 (see para 2.117 above). This presents a difficulty, since from the police point of view disclosing to the lawyer that the person has been detained may defeat the purpose of the action they have taken. The lawyer may wish to give an undertaking not to disclose the whereabouts of the suspect to a third party. The lawyer should also ask whether a decision to delay access to legal advice under PACE s58 or TA 2000 Sch 8 has been taken (see paras 2.139 and 2.145 above), since if it has not, the police will be under a duty to inform the suspect of the lawyer's interest, although strictly only if the lawyer attends in person (see para 3.22 above).

3) If the custody officer says that the person is not detained at that police station, the custody officer should be asked whether the person has been at that station and, if so, where the person has been taken. If this still draws a blank, the custody officer should be asked whether he or she is aware of an arrest having taken place recently and whether he or she is expecting a suspect to be brought into the police station in the near future. It may assist if the names of any officers involved in the arrest are known.

4) If this still does not work, it is worth asking the custody officer to check the custody records, since although the custody officer should be aware of who is, or has been, in custody, there may have been a recent change of shift or there may be a temporary custody officer. If this still does not work, the custody officer should be asked to inform the lawyer if and when the person is brought in. If the suspect is not located but there is still reason to believe that the suspect is in custody, checks should be made at regular intervals.

5) If all of the above fail, the lawyer should consider telephoning other stations and going through the same process. Depending on the circumstances, the lawyer may also consider contacting HMRC offices or other police forces such as the British Transport Police.

A full and accurate note should be kept of all information sought and obtained, including the date, time and name and status of officers spoken to.

**Checklist 3: Obtaining information from the custody officer on the telephone**

*Details of the suspect*
1 Name
2 Address
3 Date of birth
4 Gender
5 Whether a risk assessment has been conducted, and its outcome
6 Whether juvenile/vulnerable/other special needs (for example, interpreter)
7 Identity of appropriate adult and whether contacted (if relevant)

*Police and investigation details*
8 Name of custody officer
9 Station where held and custody record number
10 Name of officer in case/arresting officer
11 Whether client arrested or a volunteer
12 Time and place of arrest
13 Time of arrival at station
14 Time detention authorised
15 Reason for and circumstances of arrest, and why arrest necessary
16 Details of alleged offence(s)
17 Whether an indictable offence
18 Any exceptional police procedure (delay in advice/delay in informing relative or friend/intimate body search/drug test/identification procedure)
19 Reason for detention
20 Time solicitor requested
21 Reason for delay in contacting solicitor (if relevant)
22 Reason for proceeding without solicitor (if relevant)
23 Whether interviewed yet (if so, why)
24 Whether and when interview likely to take place
25 Whether search made/proposed and/or samples taken/proposed, and result
26 Any significant statement or silence
27 Any other person(s) arrested/sought by police

*Charge/release (if relevant)*
28 If charged:
    time of charge
    nature of charge(s)
    bailed/detained in custody
29 If bailed following charge:
    date/time/place of court appearance
    any conditions attached to bail
30 If not bailed:
    reason for refusing bail
    date/time/place of court appearance
    police attitude to bail from the court

31 If not charged:
  whether released unconditionally/reported for summons/bailed
  if reported for summons, what offence(s) anticipated
32 If bailed without charge:
  reason for police bail
  date/time/place of surrender

*Action*
33 Arrange telephone access to client
34 Confirm with custody officer:
  expected time of arrival
  that the officer will contact the lawyer if plans change that the client
  will not be interviewed before the lawyer arrives
  that above will be noted on custody record

A full and accurate note must be taken of all information requested and obtained, and the source of that information, which should be timed and dated.

**Checklist 4: Initial telephone conversation with client**

1) Confirm that the suspect does want legal advice, and does want it from the lawyer concerned (or the lawyer's firm).
2) Inform the client of the lawyer's status, and confirm that legal advice is free (unless the client has chosen to instruct the lawyer privately).
3) If appropriate, inform the client of the lawyer's role and, in particular, that the lawyer's role is to act in the client's best interests.
4) Obtain initial information from the client, the client's understanding of the reason for the arrest, and any particular concerns or complaints that the client may have. The lawyer may at this stage be asked to contact a third party to inform him or her of the suspect's arrest. In principle, there is no reason why this should not be done, but care must be taken to ensure that this message is not used to pass on information to a person evading arrest or which might result in evidence or proceeds not being recovered or which might otherwise lead to interference with the course of justice. If in any doubt, the lawyer should agree to contact the third party only on the understanding that the lawyer will first tell the custody officer what is intended.
5) Decide whether, and when, to attend in person (see para 3.58 below).
6) Give initial advice to the suspect, including advice about whether it would be advisable for the lawyer to attend in person. If the lawyer does intend to attend, or to arrange for attendance, in person the lawyer should usually advise the suspect not to answer police questions, and not to sign any documents, until the suspect has received advice in person. However, in drink/driving cases the suspect should not normally be advised to refuse to give a sample pending arrival of the lawyer (see para 2.129 above). If attendance is to be delayed, the suspect should be warned of possible attempts by the police to persuade the suspect to proceed with an interview in the absence of the lawyer.

A full and accurate note should be taken of all information obtained and advice given, which should be timed and dated.

## Checklist 5: Deciding whether to attend the police station

1) The lawyer should normally attend if:

the suspect has been arrested for an offence and is going to be interviewed;

the police are intending to conduct an identification procedure;

the client complains of serious maltreatment by the police;

the client is a youth or a person at risk.

2) If 1) above does not apply, the lawyer should still consider attending if:

the client is apparently drunk or under the influence of drugs (unless satisfied that the police have taken all appropriate action);

the alleged offence (or circumstances, if the client has been arrested for other than an offence) is serious or may have serious consequences;

there are important issues concerning searches of person or property;

there are important issues concerning the taking of samples;

an interview has been conducted, but advice is necessary at the time of charge;

the circumstances of the client indicate that attendance is necessary – for example, the client is unfamiliar with police processes, or the client is particularly upset or nervous;

detention is likely to be lengthy;

the lawyer is not satisfied that advice by telephone can be given with sufficient confidentiality;

the lawyer is not satisfied that he or she can adequately communicate with the client by telephone;

representations need to be made to the police and these cannot adequately be made by telephone, e-mail or fax.

3) Attendance may not be necessary or justified where the client:

has been arrested for a road traffic offence (including excess alcohol);

has been arrested on warrant and no further offence is suspected;

has been arrested for breach of bail and no further offence is suspected;

has been arrested under a civil order or warrant.

Always consider whether attendance is mandatory and, if not, whether the sufficient benefit test is satisfied. Consider whether professional obligations to the client require attendance even though payment may not be made under the Standard Criminal Contract.

A full and accurate note must be taken of all information obtained, advice given, reason for not attending (where attendance is mandatory) and reason for attending (where attendance is not mandatory).

## Checklist 6: Reading the custody record

1) The custody record number
2) The name and address of the suspect
3) The grounds and reasons for arrest
   - Is this the same as the information already given to the lawyer?
   - What is the statutory or common law authority for the arrest?
   - Why was arrest necessary?
   - Is the arrest lawful?
   - Is it an indictable offence?
   - Is it indictable-only? This is relevant, in particular, to probationary representatives
4) The age of the suspect
   - If the suspect is under 17 years, what action has been taken in respect of an appropriate adult?
5) The time that a solicitor was requested
   - What time was this acted on by the police?
   - If there is a significant time lapse, why is this?
6) The time of arrest and the time of arrival at the police station
   - If there is a significant time difference, why is this?
7) The time detention was authorised and grounds for detention being authorised
   - Are the grounds for detention lawful?
   - Is there sufficient evidence to charge?
8) The property found on the suspect, if recorded. This may give an important indication of evidence in relation to the offence for which the suspect has been arrested (for example, large sums of money, bunches of keys, self-sealing bags, etc), or of other offences about which the police may want to question the suspect.
9) Any indication that the suspect is, or may be, mentally disordered or mentally vulnerable, and the results of the risk assessment conducted by the custody officer
   - If so, what action has been taken in respect of an appropriate adult?
   - Has a healthcare professional been called?
10) Any indication that the suspect is, or may be, unfit through drink or drugs
    - If so, has a healthcare practitioner been called?
    - If a healthcare practitioner has already examined the client, what was the purpose of the examination and what was the result?
11) Whether a property search been authorised
    - If so, on what authority and for what purpose?
    - What, if anything, has been seized?
12) Whether the suspect has been asked to sign a police officer's notebook
    - If so, why was the suspect asked to do so before the lawyer's arrival?
    - What was in the officer's notebook?
13) Whether an interview has been conducted
    - If so, why was an interview conducted at that stage?
    - Was it conducted contrary to Code C para 6.6 or para 11.1?
    - What was said in the interview?

14) Any authorities given or decisions taken in respect of the taking of samples, fingerprints, photographs or drugs-testing
    - Have these been conducted?
    - What was the result?
    - Why were they authorised/conducted before the arrival of the lawyer?
15) Actions taken in respect of the risk assessment required under Code C para 3.6
16) Any unusual entries – for example, late entries, deleted entries

A full and accurate note must be taken of all information obtained and further enquiries made, which should be timed and dated.

## Checklist 7: Information from the officer in the case

1) The reason for and circumstances of the arrest, and reason why arrest was necessary.
2) Details of the suspected offence(s) for which the client was originally arrested.
3) Details of any other suspected offence(s) and whether the client has been, or is to be, re-arrested under PACE s31 in respect of such offences.
4) Whether any other person has been arrested in connection with the offence(s), and whether that other person implicated the client.
5) Whether any other person is being sought in connection with the offence(s).
6) Whether the client has been interviewed and, if so, why and what was said.
7) Whether the client has made any admissions, or any significant statement or silence, outside the context of an interview.
8) Whether any question has been put to the client under CJPOA 1994 s36 or s37 and any reply made.
9) Details of the evidence the police have that allegedly implicates the client.
10) Whether a search of property has been conducted.
    - If so, whether anything of evidential significance has been found.
    - If not, whether and when it is proposed to carry out a search. In both cases, the legal authority for the search should be ascertained and checked against the offence for which the client has been arrested.
11) Whether it is intended to carry out any other procedure such as:
    - removal of clothing;
    - an intimate or non-intimate search;
    - taking an intimate or non-intimate sample;
    - taking a handwriting sample;
    - conducting an identification procedure;
    and the reasons for and legal authority for such procedures.
12) What other investigations are being conducted or are intended.
13) Whether the client has any previous convictions or other forms of previous misconduct.
14) The purpose of any forthcoming interview.
15) Whether the officer has any other relevant information that has not been disclosed to the lawyer and, if relevant, whether a strategy of phased disclosure is being used.
16) The officer's view of the client's fitness for interview and whether the client may come within the categories requiring an appropriate adult.
17) Whether the officer has sufficient evidence to charge (if relevant), and what is likely to happen after the interview.
18) (Where appropriate) The attitude of the officer to diversion from prosecution.
19) Whether the officer is aware of any indications that the client may present a risk to the safety of the lawyer.

A full and accurate note must be taken of all information sought and obtained, together with relevant times.

## Checklist 8: Summary of police evidence to be requested

1) A history of the case, or 'case narrative', including whether and how the case was reported to the police or whether and why the police initiated the investigation, how the client came to be arrested and what happened on arrest, and what has happened in the case so far from the officer's point of view.

2) What investigations have been made at the crime scene (if relevant), including who has attended (arresting and other officers, scene of crime officers, forensic specialists, etc).

3) What relevant communications have taken place (for example, between members of the public and the police, and between police officers), what was said, and how this has been recorded. Where appropriate, the lawyer should ask to see or hear records made.

4) Who has been interviewed in relation to the case, and who has made a statement. The lawyer should ask to see relevant statements. Where appropriate, a detailed note should be taken of descriptions given of relevant events and relevant people, especially possible suspects.

5) What searches have been conducted, samples taken, photographs or other recordings made. The lawyer should ask to see the product of such activities.

6) What relevant real evidence or objects the police have in their possession (for example, weapons, documents, clothing, CCTV recordings, etc). Again, where appropriate, the lawyer should ask to see such items.

7) What forensic examinations or tests have been conducted, and the results of such examinations or tests.

8) What other investigations, forensic tests, etc, are planned.

9) What information the officer has concerning the client's previous convictions or other forms of previous misconduct.

A full and accurate note must be taken of all information sought and obtained, together with relevant times.

**Checklist 9: Structure of initial consultation**

1) Explain who you are, your status, the fact that legal advice and assistance is free (if appropriate), and how the consultation will be conducted.

2) Seek out any immediate preoccupations or specific needs – for example, medication, food, concern about children, etc – and take appropriate action.

3) Take client's background details. This may help the client to settle down and develop confidence in you, and enables you to assess the client. However, it may be more appropriate to do this later in the interview, particularly if the client is known to you.

4) Tell the client what information you have obtained from the police, give an outline of what the prosecution would have to prove (if appropriate), and (where appropriate) an initial indication of the apparent strength of the police case.

5) Take the client's account of the relevant circumstances, including the circumstances of the arrest and whether the client has already said anything relevant to the police.

6) Give advice on the client's legal position.

7) Give advice on whether the client should answer questions in the police interview.

8) Give advice (as appropriate) on search, samples, identification procedures, etc.

9) Brief the client on the conduct of the police interview and your role during the interview.

10) Prepare the client for the police interview.

## Checklist 10: Initial consultation with client

*Confirm the following information*
1 Full name
2 Address
3 Date of birth/age
4 Telephone number (daytime and evening)

*Inform the client*
5 Name and status of the lawyer
6 The fact that legal advice is free
7 The role of the lawyer
8 What the lawyer has been told about the suspect and/or the alleged offence(s)
9 The power of the police to detain the client
10 What is likely to happen during police detention

*Give the client*
11 The 'client care' letter
12 A business card

*Ask the client*
13 What they know about the matter for which s/he has been arrested (including involvement of any co-accused)
14 Whether they have said anything relevant to the police and/or whether they have refused to answer any questions put to them by the police
15 Whether the police have found or removed any item:
   • on arrest
   • on detention
   • during any search of the person or property
   • from any other person
16 Whether the police have told them about evidence in their possession
17 What happened at the time of arrest
18 Whether they have received any injuries
19 Whether they are currently under the influence of drink/drugs
20 Whether they suffer from any other relevant disability (including name and address of doctor where relevant)
21 Whether there are previous convictions
22 Whether currently on police or court bail
23 Whether currently on licence or subject to return to prison
24 Information about personal circumstances:
   • marital/cohabitee status and whether any children or dependants
   • employment status
   • whether currently taking medication
   • any relevant medical condition
   • details of accommodation, including occupation status and length of residence
   • details of any probation officer or social worker involved
25 Whether they wish a friend or relative to be contacted

*Advise the client*

26 What the police have to prove
27 The client's legal position
28 Whether to answer questions in the police interview
29 How to handle the police interview
30 What is likely to happen after the police interview, including the possibility of police approaches in the absence of the lawyer.

**Checklist 11: Dealing with more than one client in respect of the same or a related offence**

1) Take instructions from Client 1. Tell him or her that you have also been asked to act for Client 2 and ask whether Client 1 is aware of any conflict or potential conflict of interests. If Client 1 says that there is, you cannot act for Client 2, although you should take action to ensure that Client 2 is able to secure access to legal advice.

2) If Client 1 says that he or she is aware of no conflict or potential conflict, consider for yourself whether the instructions given by Client 1 disclose a conflict or potential conflict, and if you conclude that they do, you cannot act for Client 2.

3) If you are satisfied that there is no conflict or potential conflict, advise Client 1 that if you receive information that is confidential to Client 1 but which is relevant to Client 2, you will have to disclose that information to Client 2, and will seek permission from Client 1 to disclose that information if the situation arises. If Client 1 does not agree to this, you cannot act for Client 2.

4) If Client 1 is content with this approach, see Client 2 and advise him or her that you are acting for Client 1, and that if there is a conflict or potential conflict of interests, you cannot act for Client 2. Ask Client 2 if he or she is aware of a conflict or a potential conflict with Client 1. If Client 2 says that there is, tell Client 2 that you cannot act for him or her, although you can take action to secure legal advice for him or her.

5) If Client 2 says that he or she is not aware of a conflict, or potential conflict, inform Client 2 that if he or she gives you any information, or you subsequently receive information, that is relevant to Client 1 you will have to disclose it to Client 1. If Client 2 does not agree to this, you cannot act for Client 2.

6) If Client 2 is content with this, take instructions from Client 2. In view of the danger of concoction, do not give any information to Client 2 that you have obtained from Client 1 before you have taken instructions from him or her.

7) Consider whether the instructions obtained from Client 2 disclose a conflict or potential conflict of interests. If they do, you cannot continue to act for Client 2, and must also consider whether you can continue to act for Client 1 having regard to the principles set out in paras 5.40 and 5.41 above.

8) Continue to keep the issue of conflict of interests under review, and if a conflict of interests becomes apparent, consider whether you should cease to act for either or both clients.

Keep a full and accurate note of what is said to the clients, and their responses, and consider asking them to endorse the notes.

**Checklist 12: Information for a bail application to custody officer or court**

1 Full name
2 Address
3 Date of birth/age

*Failure to surrender to custody*

4 Does the client have previous conviction(s) for Bail Act offences?
  If yes:
  • when?
  • penalty imposed?
  • what were the circumstances?
  • have they been granted bail since the last Bail Act offence?
5 Has the client previously surrendered to custody satisfactorily?
  If yes:
  • when?
  • in what circumstances?
  • penalty imposed for relevant offence(s)?
6 If the client is married/cohabiting:
  • how long have they been living together?
  • how stable is the relationship?
7 If the client has children or other dependants:
  • where do they live?
  • how often does the client see them?
  • in what way does he or she support them?
8 In respect of the client's accommodation:
  • how long have they lived there?
  • does s/he own/rent/squat it?
  • who pays the rent/mortgage?
  • if they cannot return there, do they have other available accommodation?
9 How long has the client lived in the area?
10 Where were they brought up?
11 If there are parents and/or siblings, where do they live and what contact does he or she have with them?
12 If the client is in employment:
  • where do they work?
  • what job does he or she do?
  • how long have they had the job?
  • is it a permanent job?
  • hat is the employer's reaction likely to be to the arrest and charge?
13 Possible sureties, securities and conditions:
  • where appropriate, the following information in respect of possible sureties:
    ○ name
    ○ address
    ○ telephone number
    ○ occupation
    ○ length of time known to the client
    ○ relationship to client

      ◦ any previous convictions
      ◦ likely financial circumstances [indent highlighted text]
- appropriate police station if reporting condition imposed
- any problems with a condition of residence
- if client has no, or unsuitable, accommodation, would s/he agree to stay in a bail hostel?
- does client have a passport?

If yes:
- would they agree to surrender it to the court?
- do they have any plans to travel abroad?
- would they be willing to deposit a security of money or valuables?

## Fear of further offences

14 Is client currently on bail?

If yes:
- date(s) imposed
- whether police or court bail
- alleged offence(s)
- how long on bail
- if court bail, whether conditional:

If yes:
- conditions already imposed
- whether conditions have changed since bail originally granted

15 Does client have previous convictions?

If yes:
- when, where, sentence(s) imposed
- were any of them committed whilst on bail?
- were any of them for similar offences to offence(s) now charged?
- have client's circumstances changed?

16 Have client's circumstances materially changed since current alleged offence(s)?

17 Possible conditions:
- if a curfew is appropriate, would client agree to it?
- if a condition is made not to go to scene of alleged crime, would client agree to it?
- are there other conditions that may be appropriate?

## Interference with witnesses

18 Does client have previous convictions for serious assault/perverting the course of justice?

19 Has the client made any threats against the witness(es) in the current case?

20 Possible conditions:
- if a condition was made not to contact the witness(es), would the client agree to it?

## Own protection

21 Does the client have access to accommodation away from the relevant area?

## Checklist 13: Identification parade checklist and report form

1 Is identification in dispute?                                        yes/no
2 Is an identification parade practicable, and would it serve a useful
  purpose, having regard to:
  • whether it could be held at a later time/date
  • whether the police have made sufficient effort
  • whether the lawyer should offer to help find persons to stand
    on the parade – any purported identification already made?   yes/no
3 Should the suspect ask for/agree to a parade, having regard to:
  • what is known about the initial view by the witness
  • what is known about other, non-identification evidence
  • what alternative method of identification is likely?          yes/no
4 Original description of identifying witness(es) provided?       yes/no
5 Any material released to the media and, if so, copies provided?
                                                                       yes/no
6 Arrangements for taking photograph or video of parade checked?
                                                                       yes/no
7 Arrangements for witnesses to attend the police station checked?
                                                                       yes/no
8 Arrangements for other members of the parade to attend the
  police station checked?                                          yes/no
9 Route taken by witnesses from waiting room to parade room
  checked?                                                          yes/no
10 Arrangements to keep witnesses who have viewed parade
   separate from other witnesses checked?                          yes/no
11 Location of officers in the case checked?                       yes/no
12 Suspect informed by the identification officer:
   • purpose of the parade?                                        yes/no
   • right to free legal advice?                                   yes/no
   • right to have lawyer present?                                 yes/no
   • whether any witnesses have been shown photographs, photofits,
     identikits or similar?                                        yes/no
   • fact that suspect does not have to agree to parade?           yes/no
   • fact that if suspect refuses parade, refusal may be given in
     evidence and police may proceed covertly to test whether
     witness makes an identification?                              yes/no
   • fact that if s/he significantly alters appearance between taking
     of photograph and ID parade, this may be given in evidence?
                                                                       yes/no
   • fact that a video/photograph may be taken of him/her?         yes/no
   • fact that if s/he changes his/her appearance other ID
     arrangements may be made?                                     yes/no
   • fact that s/he or his/her lawyer will be provided with original
     description given by identifying witness(es)?                 yes/no
13 Suspect given notice setting out the above, and asked to sign copy?
                                                                       yes/no
14 Suspect given advice by lawyer regarding parade, including:
   • how it will be conducted
   • stance

- where to look
- right to decide on where to stand
- not to speak while witness is in the room
- effect of one-way screens
- to tell lawyer if dissatisfied with conduct of parade?      yes/no
15 Whether other persons on the parade are satisfactory, including:
- number
- age
- height
- race
- position in life
- hair
- facial hair
- eyes
- build
- clothing
- distinguishing marks (eg, visible tattoos)
- any feature given in original description by witness(es)?
16 Suspect informed by identification officer:
- of conduct of the parade?      yes/no
- about caution?      yes/no
- to indicate whether s/he objects to any of the arrangements for the parade?      yes/no
(If yes, note what is said and any action taken to deal with the objection(s))
17 Suspect asked at end of parade whether s/he has any comments on the conduct of the parade?      yes/no
(If yes, note precisely what is said)
18 Any representations made by the lawyer?      yes/no
(If yes, note precisely what is said)
19 Time parade started and finished
20 Any other relevant comments
21 The conduct of the parade (complete one copy of this question for each witness)

| 1 | 2 | 3 | 4 | 5 | 6 | 7 | 8 | 9 | 10 | 11 | 12 | 13 | 14 | 15 | 16 |
|---|---|---|---|---|---|---|---|---|----|----|----|----|----|----|----|
|   |   |   |   |   |   |   |   |   |    |    |    |    |    |    |    |

(Note position of suspect with an X and give brief description of other persons on the parade)

Other persons present in the parade room?

Name of witness?

Suspect told he or she can choose where to stand?      yes/no

Time witness brought into parade room?

Number of officer bringing witness in?

Witness told:
- to look at each person on parade at least twice                    yes/no
- to take his/her time                                               yes/no
- that parade contains the suspect(s) and others who cannot
  have been involved                                                 yes/no
- that he or she will be asked if the person that he or she saw
  is on the parade and, if so, his/her number                       yes/no
- that the person he or she saw may not be on the parade, and
  that if he or she cannot make a positive identification he or
  she should say so                                                  yes/no

Note what the witness does and says (use diagram if helpful)

Any identification made by the witness                               yes/no
(If yes, note precisely what is said)

Any comment by the suspect while the witness is in the room
or after he or she leaves                                            yes/no
(If yes, note precisely what is said)

Time witness left the parade room

Any representations made by the lawyer                               yes/no
(If yes, note precisely what is said)

Was a photograph/video taken of the parade?                          yes/no

## Checklist 14: Video identification checklist and report form

1 Is identification in dispute?      yes/no
2 Is an identification parade or group identification more suitable?
     yes/no
3 Does the suspect consent to a video identification?      yes/no
4 Arrangements for witnesses to attend the police station checked
     yes/no
5 Arrangements for selection of video ID images checked?      yes/no
6 Route taken by witnesses from waiting room to viewing room
  checked?      yes/no
7 Arrangements to keep witnesses who have viewed film separate
  from other witnesses checked?      yes/no
8 Location of officers in the case checked?      yes/no
9 Suspect informed by the identification officer:
- purpose of the video procedure      yes/no
- right to free legal advice      yes/no
- right to have lawyer present      yes/no
- whether any witnesses have been shown photographs,
photofits, identikits or similar      yes/no
- fact that suspect does not have to co-operate with the video
identification      yes/no
- fact that if suspect refuses to co-operate, refusal may be given
in evidence and police may proceed covertly to test whether
witness makes an identification      yes/no
- fact that if s/he significantly alters appearance this may be
given in evidence      yes/no
- fact that a video/photograph may be taken of him/her      yes/no
- fact that ifs/he changes his/her appearance, other ID
arrangements may be made      yes/no
- fact that s/he or his/her lawyer will be provided with original
description given by identifying witness(es)      yes/no
10 Suspect given notice setting out the above, and asked to sign
  copy?      yes/no
11 Suspect given advice by lawyer regarding video identification
  procedure including:
- how it will be conducted
- to tell lawyer if dissatisfied with the arrangements      yes/no
12 Whether images for the video ID are satisfactory, including:
- number
- age
- height
- race
- position in life
- hair
- facial hair
- eyes
- build
- clothing
- distinguishing marks (eg, visible tattoos)

- any feature given in original description by witness(es)
- background
- lighting

13 Any objections made to the set of images before it is shown to the witness(es)?                                        yes/no
(If yes, note what is said and action taken to deal with objection)

14 The conduct of the video identification procedure (complete one copy of this question for each witness)

Other persons present in the viewing room?

Name of witness?

Time witness brought in to viewing room? Number of officer bringing witness in?

Witness told:
- that the person he or she saw may or may not be on the video
                                                          yes/no
- to refrain from making an identification or saying that he or she cannot make an identification until he or she has seen the entire film at least twice                                 yes/no
- that at any point he or she may ask to see a particular part of the film again, or to have a particular frame frozen for him/her to study                                                   yes/no
- that there is no limit to the number of times he or she may view the whole film or any part of it                         yes/no

Note what the witness does and says

Any identification made by the witness?                    yes/no
If yes, was the film of the person identified shown to the witness again?                                                        yes/no
(Note precisely what is said)

Time witness left the viewing room

Any representations made by the lawyer                     yes/no
(If yes, note precisely what is said)

15 Any representations made by the lawyer when all witnesses have viewed the video?                                          yes/no
(If yes, note precisely what is said)

16 Time viewing completed

17 Any other relevant comments

## Checklist 15: Questions to ask an immigration detainee

1. Full name including any aliases previously used.
2. Date of birth.
3. Nationality; and if different, country of birth.
4. Current address (other than detention), and addresses for last six months.
5. Contact details of relative or friend.
6. Date and place of most recent travel.
7. Whether travelling on own passport on arrival.
8. Were any questions asked at airport by immigration; and if so, details.
9. Were any answers given then inaccurate; and if so, details.
10. If the client had to apply for entry clearance, were answers given then inaccurate; and if so, details.
11. Has the client instructed previous lawyer or adviser; and if so, how recently?
12. If so, why does the client not wish to continue with previous adviser?
13. Has the client been served with any papers?
14. Does the client need interpreter; if so, what language and dialect?

*In-country clients with leave:*
15. If the client was given lawful leave, when does it/did it expire?
16. If the client made application for extension, what was the date submitted and does client have proof of sending?
17. Does the client have a UKBA reference number (usually letter of alphabet for surname followed by 6–7 digits)?
18. If not retained by immigration service, what is the whereabouts of the client's passport?

*If entered illegally or in breach of landing conditions:*
19. What are the client's present family circumstances, including long-term relationships?
20. Where relevant, what is the immigration status of family members?
21. If any children were born in the UK, what was the immigration status of the other parent at the time of birth?
22. Are immigration authorities aware of family circumstances; and if so, when were they told about them?
23. How has the client been supporting herself or himself to date?
24. If the client is returned, what does the client think will happen:
    a. to the family group in the UK?
    b. to the client themselves?
25. If the client expresses anxiety about what will happen to him or her, what evidence is there to justify the anxiety?
26. If the client has overstayed for less than 28 days, or if the client is in breach of the client's landing conditions, is it sensible to consider seeking to leave as soon as possible?
27. Is it likely that if removed the client would wish to return to the UK lawfully in the future?

*If an appeal right given exercisable prior to removal:*
28. Has the client already lodged an appeal notice?
29. Does the client have community ties other than as identified above?
30. Does the client have any physical or mental health issues?
31. Does the client have friends willing and able to stand surety?
32. If so, what is their immigration status?
33. If not already doing so before detention, could the client reside with surety?
34. Has the client ever failed to attend any court in the UK previously?

*If no present appeal right is available, but answers to 22–25 above indicate there may be asylum/human rights issues:*
35. Why were family details not disclosed to immigration authorities earlier?
36. If fear of serious ill harm/persecution on return exists, why was an application to the UKBA not made earlier?
37. What evidence can be gathered to support either asylum/human rights element, as it will be needed urgently?

## APPENDIX 4

# Specimen letters and statement

**1   Letter to client in police custody where access is denied**

[*Client's name*],
[*Name of*] Police station,
[*Address*]
                                                                    URGENT – BY HAND
                                                                              [*Date*]


Dear [*Client's name*],

[I am at the police station having been told that you asked for me to be contacted. I have now been told by the custody officer that you do not wish to see me.]

*Or, if appropriate,*
[I am at the police station having been asked to attend by [*name of third party from whom instructions received*], and have been told by the custody officer that you have not asked to see me.]

*Or, if appropriate,*
[I am at the police station, but the police are not allowing me to see you as they have decided to deny you access to legal advice under s58 of the Police and Criminal Evidence Act 1984 or Terrorism Act 2000 Sch 8.]

Unless you have asked to see another lawyer, I strongly suggest that you tell the police now that you want to see me straight away. Legal advice whilst you are at a police station is free. Please sign your name at the bottom of the letter to show whether or not you want to see me, and ask the police officer to return the letter to me straight away.

If you want to see me but the police do not let you, please read the following advice carefully:
1.  The police may ask you to sign a form stating that you do not want legal advice. I advise you not to sign it.
2.  Tell the police that you want to see me. If you are interviewed, tell the police at the beginning of the interview that you do not want to be interviewed until you have seen a lawyer.
3.  If the police tell you that they will not let you see me, but that they will let you see a duty solicitor, tell the police that you would prefer to see me, but that you would like to see the duty solicitor if you cannot see me.
4.  If you are interviewed without speaking to a lawyer, you have the right to remain silent and not to answer the questions the police put to you. I advise you to tell the police that you are not willing to answer their questions until you have spoken to a lawyer.
5.  If the police carry on with an interview, I advise you either to say nothing at all, or to say 'no comment' to each of the questions.
6.  If the police say that they want to carry out an intimate search of your body, or if they say they want to take samples from you, like a sample of your saliva, I advise you to tell the police that you do not wish to agree to a search or to give a sample until you have spoken to a lawyer. However, if the police tell you they intend to carry on anyway, I advise you to tell them that you do not give consent, but that you will not resist.
7.  The police cannot under any circumstances stop you from speaking to a lawyer for more than 36 hours [48 hours] starting with the time you arrived at the police station. If the police want to keep you at the police station longer than that they will have to take you before a court and must then allow you to see a lawyer.

If you want to see me but the police will not allow this, please rest assured that I will do all I can to obtain access so that I can see you.

Yours sincerely,

[*Name of lawyer*]

I want to see my lawyer straight away

(Sign here) _____

*or*

I do not want to see the lawyer who wrote this letter

(Sign here) _____

## 2   Letter to police where access to client is denied

The Custody Officer [*or Officer in Charge of the Station*]
[*Name of*] Police station,
[*Address*]                                                    URGENT – BY HAND
                                                                        [*Date*]


Dear Sir/Madam,

Re: [*Name of client*]
   [*Custody record number, if known*]

I am writing to you concerning my above-named client who is currently detained at your police station. I am at the police station and wish to see my client immediately.

[I have been told that my client no longer wishes to see me. Code of Practice C para 6.15 provides that in this situation the suspect must be informed that the lawyer is present and must be asked if s/he would like to see the lawyer. I would like to see my client now so that I may be satisfied whether or not they wish to obtain legal advice from me. I do not accept that it is lawful to deny me access, but if you intend to do so I want to know what your legal authority is for doing so. I also ask you to give the attached letter [*enclose specimen letter 1*] to my client straight away.]

*Or, if appropriate,*
[I have been instructed by a third party, [name of third party], but have been told that access to my client is denied because they have not asked for legal advice. I would remind you that Code of Practice C Annex B para 4 states that access to a lawyer may not be delayed on the grounds that the lawyer has been instructed to attend the police station by someone else provided that the suspect wishes to see the lawyer. Further, Code C para 6.15 provides that the suspect must be told of the lawyer's arrival and must be asked if they wish to see the lawyer. I would like to see my client now so that I may be satisfied whether or not they wish to obtain legal advice from me. I do not accept that it is lawful to deny me access, but if you intend to do so I would wish to know what is your legal authority for doing so. I would also ask you to give the attached letter [*enclose specimen letter 1*] to my client straight away.]

*Or, if appropriate,*
[I have been instructed to advise my above client, but have been informed that access is being denied under s58 or Terrorism Act 2000 Sch 8. I do not accept that denial of access to me is lawful because [*here set out the reasons why s58 or TA 2000 does not apply, eg, not an indictable offence, not properly authorised, no reasonable grounds to believe that legal advice will lead to one of the prohibited consequences*]. If you intend to deny me access to my client I want to know what your legal authority is and why you regard the criteria as being satisfied in relation to me. I also ask you to give the attached letter [*enclose specimen letter 1*] to my client straight away.]

I confirm that I do not consider the decision to deny me access to my client is lawful and [wish to make a formal complaint] or [will consider making a formal complaint in due course].

Yours faithfully,


[*Name of lawyer*]

**3 Letter confirming representations at review/regarding bail**

The Custody Officer,
[*Name of*] Police station,
[*Address*]

URGENT – BY HAND
[*Date*]

Dear Sir/Madam,

Re: [*Name of client*]
    [*Custody record number – if known*]

This letter confirms the representations made at [time] to [*person to whom representations were made*].

[Further detention of my client without charge is not justified because [*reasons given at review, eg, police have sufficient evidence to charge, maximum period of detention has expired, police are not acting expeditiously, grounds for detention are not satisfied*]. In such circumstances, further detention is unlawful, and I will advise my client regarding civil action against the police for false imprisonment in due course.]

*Or, if appropriate,*
[My client is entitled to bail pending their court appearance because [*reasons given, eg, the custody officer was given details of my client's address, there are no reasonable grounds for believing that my client would cause loss or damage to property if they were released, etc*]. There are no other grounds which would justify the further detention of my client.]

Please place this letter with my client's custody record so that it is available for production before a court if necessary.

Yours faithfully,


[*Name of lawyer*]

## 4   Client care letter

[*Client's name*]
[*Name of* ] Police station
[*Address*]

[*Date*]


Dear [*Client's name*],

This letter confirms that I am [*status of lawyer*] with [*name of firm*].

Whilst you are at the police station I will be dealing with your case personally. If it becomes necessary for another member of my firm to become involved, I will tell you before it happens.

The partner of this firm who has responsibility for your case is [*name of partner*]. They may be contacted if necessary, or if you are unhappy with the service we are providing.

Work done for you whilst you are at the police station is free. If you want us to act for you after you leave the police station, you may then be entitled to legal aid to cover any further work. We will talk to you about this if it becomes necessary.

Yours sincerely,


[*Name of lawyer*]

## 5 Formal complaint

The Custody Officer,
[*Name of*] Police station,
[*Address*]

URGENT – BY HAND
[*Date*]

Dear Sir/Madam,

Re: [*Client's name*]
    [*Custody record number, if known*]

We refer to our above client who is currently detained at [*name of*] Police station.

We are instructed by out client to make a formal complaint concerning police conduct. The complaint is that [*set out brief details of complaint*].

Our client [wishes] or [does not wish] to be interviewed about this complaint whilst they are detained by the police. When our client is interviewed, they wish to be accompanied by a lawyer from this firm. Please, therefore, give this firm prior notice of your intention to interview out client concerning this complaint.

[Our client appears to have suffered the following injuries [set out brief details of the apparent injuries]. Our client [wishes] or [does not wish] to be examined by a doctor.]

Please pass this letter to the inspector or other officer who is to be informed of the complaint under Code of Practice C para 9.2.

Yours faithfully,


[*Name of firm*]

## 6   Letter to police regarding intimate sample

The Custody Officer,
[*Name of*] Police station,
[*Address*]                                                    URGENT – BY HAND
                                                                          [*Date*]


Dear Sir/Madam,

Re: [*Client's name*]
    [*Custody record number, if known*]

We refer to the request made on [*date and time*] by [*name of officer making the request*] that our above client should provide a sample of [nature of sample requested]. We understand that it is agreed that the sample requested is an intimate sample and is governed by s62 of the Police and Criminal Evidence Act 1984 and Code of Practice D section 6.

In our view an intimate sample should not be taken because

[there are no reasonable grounds for suspecting our client's involvement in a recordable offence.]

*and/or*
[there are no reasonable grounds for believing that the sample will tend to confirm or disprove involvement in the offence concerned and/or insufficient information has been given to the me or my client to enable an assessment to be made as to whether there are reasonable grounds.]

*and/or*
[the client has not been informed of the grounds for the granting of authorisation.]

In these circumstances, we confirm that we have advised *[client's name]* that the conditions for taking an intimate sample have not been satisfied.

Yours faithfully,


[*Name of firm*]

## 7 Letter to police regarding intimate search

The Custody Officer,
[*Name of*] Police station,
[*Address*]

URGENT – BY HAND
[*Date*]


Dear Sir/Madam,

Re: [*Client's name*]
[*Custody record number, if known*]

We refer to the request made on [*date and time*] by [*name of officer making the request*] that our above client should allow a personal search to be carried out. In our view the proposed search is an intimate search under the provisions of s55 of the Police and Criminal Evidence Act 1984.

We acknowledge that a search can be conducted without our client's consent but in our view an intimate search would be unlawful in the present circumstances. The reasons for this are

[that it has not been authorised by an inspector or above as is required under s55(1) of the Police and Criminal Evidence Act 1984.]

*and/or*
[that there are no reasonable grounds for believing that our client [may have concealed on him or her anything that they could use to cause physical injury to him/herself or others] or [may have a Class A drug concealed on him or her and was in possession of it intending to supply it, etc]]

*and/or*
[the officer giving consent to the search cannot have been satisfied that the suspected item could not be found without an intimate search as is required under s55(2) of the Police and Criminal Evidence Act 1984 since they did not give adequate information to our client/ourselves to enable the suspected item to be produced voluntarily, if it exists.]

In these circumstances, an intimate search is unlawful and we hereby inform you that our client does not consent to it. We have advised our client not to resist such a search if, despite these representations, you intend to proceed but we shall advise out client that s/he may take civil action against the officers concerned and the chief constable.

Yours faithfully,


[*Name of firm*]

## 8   Specimen statement to be handed in during interview or at charge

Statement of [*Name of client*]

Handed to [*name of officer concerned*] at [*name of police station*] on [*date and time statement handed in*] in the presence of [*names of others present*].

I, [*name of client and address*] wish to make the following statement:

[I was advised by my lawyer to hand in this statement and not to answer questions in the police interview(s).]

*And/or, if appropriate*
[I have been advised by my lawyer to hand in a statement on being charged.]

The information that I have been given by the police regarding the alleged offence(s) is as follows. [*Here insert a summary of the information given.*]

I wish to state the following regarding the alleged offence(s). [*Here set out the facts which are to be made known at this stage.*]

This is my statement. I have read the statement [The statement has been read to me.] and I agree with its contents. I have not been told what to say.

Signed:                                    Date:

# Immigration appeal hearing centres

BELFAST
The Old Town Hall Building
80 Victoria Street
Belfast BT1 3GL
Tel: 0845 600 0877
Fax: 0141 242 7555

BIRMINGHAM
2nd Floor Sheldon Court
1 Wagon Lane, Sheldon
Birmingham B26 3DU
Tel: 0845 6000 877
Fax: 0121 742 4142

BRADFORD
Phoenix House
Rushton Avenue, Thornbury
Bradford BD3 7BH
Tel: 0845 6000 877
Fax: 01274 267 045

BRENTFORD
Brentford Magistrates Court
Market Place, Brentford
Middlesex TW8 8EN
Tel: 0208 700 9350 / 9360
Fax: 0208 917 3527

BROMLEY
Bromley Magistrates Court
1st Floor, 1 London Road, Bromley
Kent BR1 1RA
Tel: 0845 600 08

CARDIFF
(queries to Birmingham office)

DORKING
Dorking Magistrates Court
London Road, Dorking
Surrey RH4 1SZ
Tel: 01306 880888
**Fax:** 01306 742194

GLASGOW
4th Floor Eagle Building
215 Bothwell Street
Glasgow G2 7EZ
Tel: 0845 6000 877
Fax: 0141 242 7555

HARMONDSWORTH
Asylum & Immigration Tribunal
Colnbrook By pass
Harmondsworth
Middlesex UB7 0HD
Tel: 020 8750 7760
Fax: 020 8750 7771

HATTON CROSS
Asylum & Immigration Tribunal
York House
2–3 Dukes Green Avenue
Feltham TW14 0LS
Tel: 0845 600 0877
Fax: 020 8831 3500

HATTON CROSS
Asylum & Immigration Tribunal
Gloucester House
4 Dukes Green Avenue,
Feltham TW14 0LR
Tel: 0845 600 0877
Fax: 020 8831 3500

LEICESTER
Asylum and Immigration Tribunal
PO Box 6987
Leicester LE1 6ZX
Tel: 0845 600 0877

LONDON
Taylor House
88 Rosebery Avenue
London EC1R 4QU
Tel: 0845 6000 877
Fax: 020 7862 4211

London Tribunal Centre
Field House, 15 Bream's Buildings
London EC4A 1DZ
Tel: 020 7073 4200
Fax: 020 7073 4090/4091

York House
2/3 Dukes Green Avenue
Off Faggs Road, Feltham
Middlesex TW14 0LS
Tel: 0845 6000 877
Fax: 0208 8313 500

MANCHESTER
1st Floor Piccadilly Exchange
2 Piccadilly Plaza
Manchester M1 4AH
Tel: 0845 6000 877
Fax: 0161 234 2035/2036

NEWPORT
Asylum & Immigration Tribunal
Columbus House
Langstone Business Park
Chepstowe Road
Newport  NP18 2LX
Tel: 0845 600 0877
Fax: 01633 416734

NORTH SHIELDS
Kings Court
Royal Quays, Earl Grey Way
North Shields
Tyne & Wear NE29 6AR
Tel: 0845 6000 877
Fax: 0191 298 2247/2248

**Home Office Presenting Officers**

BIRMINGHAM
1st Floor 2308 Coventry Road
Sheldon
Birmingham B26 3JS
Tel: 0121 700 1616
Fax: 0121 706 1696

GLASGOW
10th Floor Eagle Building
215 Bothwell Street
Glasgow G2 7ED
Tel: 0141 221 4218
Fax: 0141 204 5987

HARMONDSWORTH
Harmondsworth Hearing Centre
Colnbrook By pass
Harmondsworth
Middlesex UB7 0HD
Tel: 020 8750 7760

NOTTINGHAM
Nottingham Magistrates Court
Carrington Street
Nottingham NG2 1EE
Tel: 0845 6000 877
Fax: 0115 955 8216

STOKE-ON-TRENT
Bennett House
Town Road, Hanley
Stoke-on-Trent ST1 2QB
Tel: 0845 6000 877
Fax: 0178 2200 144

SUTTON
Copthall House
9 The Pavement
Grove Road
Sutton
Surrey SM1 1DA
Tel: 020 8652 2300
Fax: 020 8652 2301

WALSALL
2nd Floor Bridge House
Bridge Street
Walsall WS1 1HZ
Tel: 0845 6000 877
Fax: 0192 2626 056

YARL'S WOOD
Hearing Centre A
Twinswood Business Park
Thurleigh Road
Bedfordshire MK44 1FD
Tel: 0300 123 1711

LEEDS
2nd Floor Springfield House
76 Wellington Street
Leeds LS1 2AY
Tel: 0113 244 4205
Fax: 0113 245 3472

LONDON
Hanover House
Plane Tree Crescent, Feltham
Middlesex TW13 7JJ
Tel: 020 8917 2039
Fax: 020 8890 6489

2nd Floor Building 1
Angel Square
1 Torrens Street
London EC1V 1SX
Tel: 020 7239 1701
Fax: 020 7239 1702

# Immigration sample forms

June 2011

**Form IAFT-1 – page1**

## APPEAL TO THE FIRST-TIER TRIBUNAL (IMMIGRATION AND ASYLUM CHAMBER) against your Home Office decision

| UKBA International Group: (for UKBAIG use only) | Appeal Lodged: (For FTT(IAC) use only) | Type of decision: *Tick one box* |
|---|---|---|
| | | Asylum ☐ |
| | | Non Asylum ☐ |

**Do you wish to have your appeal decided on the papers or at an oral hearing?**
*An **oral hearing** is a hearing at which you will have the opportunity to attend, but the hearing may go ahead if you fail to do so. An appeal **on the papers** means that the appeal will be decided on the information you provide on the appeal form and any other documents submitted as evidence.*

*Tick one box*

Oral Hearing ☐

Papers ☐

### Section 1 - Personal Information

A. Family Name or Surname
   (For instance as shown on your passport)

B. Given or First Name(s)
   (For instance as shown on your passport)

C. Title (Mr / Mrs / Miss / Ms or Other)

D. Date of birth (Day/Month/Year)            /            /

E. Gender         ☐ Male      ☐ Female

F. Address where you can be contacted.

*Notice: If you change your address, you **must** notify the First-tier Tribunal immediately in writing.*

                    Postcode

G. Prison Reference (if applicable)

H. Nationality (if more than one, state all)

I. If you have chosen to have an oral hearing, who will be attending?

   ☐ Yourself      ☐ Your representative
   ☐ Witnesses

J. Will anyone giving evidence at the hearing need an interpreter? *If more than one language or interpreter is required, you may wish to indicate on a separate sheet.*

   ☐ No      ☐ Yes – give details below

   | Who: |
   | Language: |
   | Dialect: |

K. If anyone attending the hearing has a disability, state any special requirements they have.

## If you are detained under the Immigration Acts or in prison serving a criminal sentence, please provide the following information:

L. Are removal directions currently set for you?  ☐ Yes   ☐ No

M. Time of removal (insert time & circle AM or PM)  ☐☐☐☐   AM / PM

N. Date of removal  ☐   /   /   ☐

O. Are you currently serving a criminal sentence?  ☐ Yes   ☐ No

P. If yes, what date is your sentence due to end?  ☐   /   /   ☐

Q. What category prisoner are you? (please circle as appropriate)  A    B    C    D

## Section 2 – Your Home Office Decision (refer to your Notice of Decision)

A. Home Office Reference Number  ☐☐☐☐☐☐ / ☐☐

B. Port Reference  ☐☐☐ / ☐☐☐☐☐

C. COHID Reference  ☐☐☐☐☐☐☐☐☐☐☐☐☐☐☐☐☐☐

D. Method of service of decision.  ☐ Post   ☐ Fax/Personal service
☐ Courier   ☐ Other (please specify)

E. Date of Service of Decision  ☐   /   /   ☐

F. Are you sending your Notice of Decision with this form?  ☐ Yes   ☐ No – please explain below

If you do not send the Notice of Decision with the appeal form, your appeal may be dealt with on the papers unless a satisfactory reason is given here.

## Applying for Anonymity

The tribunal will publish your name on documents relating to your case which can be viewed publically. You can apply to the tribunal for anonymity which, when granted, will result in the tribunal removing your name from all published documents.

The Application for Anonymity form can be found online at www.justice.gov.uk/global/forms/hmcts/tribunals/immigration-and-asylum/index.htm and should be completed and returned with this appeal form.

June 2011

## Section 3 – Your Appeal

A.  **Late appeal**

Your appeal must be received at the **Administrative Support Centre** within:

- **5 business days** after you have been served with the notice of decision if your are detained under the Immigration Acts or
- **10 business days** after you have been served with the notice of decision if you are not detained under the Immigration Acts.

If you know your appeal is late, or you are not sure if it will be received in time, you must apply for an extension of time. Explain why your appeal is late in the box below. Attach any evidence / additional sheets if necessary.

B. If you are sending any other documents with this form to support your appeal, they must be in English or a certified translation. Please list them here:

C. If you are **intending** to send other documents that are not yet available to you. Please list them here:

D. **Grounds of your appeal**

- You **must** let us know the reasons you disagree with the decision on the Notice of Decision document.
- Include any information that has not been mentioned in the Notice of Decision and say whether you have raised these issues before.
- You **must** give as much detail as possible as you may not be allowed to mention any further grounds at a later date. Attach any evidence / additional sheets of paper if necessary.
- If your appeal relates in whole or in part to an **Asylum decision**, complete all of **boxes 1 to 6** that apply to you.
- If you are not sure which boxes apply to you or there are other points of the refusal letter that you disagree with, write your grounds in **box 7**.
- If your appeal relates to a **Non Asylum** decision complete **box 8**.

**Asylum Decision**

*1.* If you disagree with the Home Office's interpretation of **the situation in your country**, please explain why in this box, and give reasons to support your point of view.

**2.** If the Home Office has suggested that you could **live safely in another part of the country of origin**, and you disagree, please explain why in this box.

**3.** If the Home Office has stated that your claim is **not credible,** and you disagree, please explain why in this box.

**4.** If the Home Office has stated that you do not qualify as a refugee on grounds of race, religion, nationality, membership of a particular social group or political opinion (under the criteria of the 1951 Geneva Convention), and you disagree, please explain why in this box.

June 2011

**Form IAFT-1 – page 5**

*5.* If the Home Office has stated that specific articles of the **European Convention on Human Rights** (ECHR) do not apply to your case, and you disagree, please explain why in this box.

*6.* If the Home Office has stated that you do not qualify as a person who is eligible for humanitarian protection (under the Refugee or Person in Need of International Protection Regulations 2006), and you disagree, please explain why in this box.

*7.* If there is anything else that you disagree with in the Home Office letter, please explain why in this box.

**Non-Asylum Decision**

*8.* If your appeal relates to a non-asylum decision with which you disagree, you must give your reasons below and refer to the paragraphs of the refusal letter (you may continue on a separate sheet if necessary).

**Statement of additional grounds**

If your notice of decision requires you to make a **Statement of additional grounds,** you should make the statement in the box below. If there are any **other reasons** why you think:
- you should be allowed to stay in the United Kingdom, including any reasons relating to the European Convention on Human Rights
- you should not be required to leave.

Do not repeat any grounds and reasons that you have already given in Section 3D.

|  |
|---|
|  |

E. Have you appealed against any other immigration decision in the United Kingdom or overseas?

☐ No      ☐ Yes – give details below:

| Date | Appeal number (if known) |
|---|---|
| / / |  |
| / / |  |
| / / |  |

F. To the best of your knowledge and belief has any member of your family, a Dependant or anyone planning to accompany you made an appeal or are they planning to appeal against a United Kingdom immigration decision?

☐ No      ☐ Yes – give details in the table below:

| Name | Relationship | Appeal number / Post reference number |
|---|---|---|
|  |  |  |
|  |  |  |
|  |  |  |

June 2011

## Section 4 - Your declaration

If you are the appellant and are completing this form yourself, you must sign and date this declaration.

**Declaration** - I, the appellant, believe the facts stated in this appeal form are true.

Signature:

Date

/       /

## Section 5 – Representative Details (refer to guidance notes)

A. Name of Representative

B. Name of Representative's Organisation (if any)

C. Postal address for correspondence

Postcode

D. Reference for correspondence

E. Telephone number

F. Mobile telephone number

G. Fax number

H. Email address

**Declaration by the representative - to be completed only when signing on behalf of the person named in Section 1 of this form**
I, the representative, am giving notice of appeal in accordance with the appellant's instructions and the appellant believes that the facts stated in this appeal form are true.

Representative's Signature:

Date

/       /

#### Notice to representatives
You must notify the First-tier Tribunal, and other parties, if you cease to represent the appellant. If the appellant changes representative, details of the new representative should be sent to the same address to which you are sending this form. Please give **the appellant's full name, address,** and **Post Reference number.**

**Data Protection statement**
Information, including personal details that you have provided in this form will not be used by the First-tier Tribunal, for any purpose other than the determination of your application. The information may be disclosed to other government departments and public authorities only, for related immigration or asylum purposes

| ASYLUM AND IMMIGRATION (TREATMENT OF CLAIMANTS ETC.) ACT 2004 | Application to be released on bail | Form B1 |

## Section 1 — Personal Information

| | | |
|---|---|---|
| **A** | Home Office reference number | |
| **B** | Your surname or family name. Please use CAPITAL LETTERS | |
| **C** | Your other names | |
| **D** | Address where you are detained | |
| | | Post code |
| **E** | Your date of birth **(Give as Day/Month/Year)** | (day) / (month) / (year) |
| **F** | Are you male or female? | Male ☐  Female ☐ |
| **G** | Nationality (or nationalities) or citizenship | |
| **H** | Date or arrival in the United Kingdom | (day) / (month) / (year) |
| **I** | Do you have a representative? | No ☐  Yes ☐  If yes, your representative should complete Section 7 on page 4. |

## Section 2 — About your application

| | | |
|---|---|---|
| **A** | Do you have an asylum or immigration appeal pending? | No ☐  Yes ☐  What is the appeal number, if you know it? |
| **B** | Have you lodged a bail application before? | No ☐  Yes ☐  What is the bail number, if you know it? |
| **C** | The address where you plan to live, if your bail application is granted. | Number/Street |
| | | Town |
| | | Post code |

Form B1 (Aug 2008), Application for bail: Rule 38, Asylum and Immigration Tribunal (Procedure) Rules 2005

| Section 3 | | Personal Information |
|---|---|---|
| A | **Recognisance** | I agree to be bound to a recognisance of **£** |
| B | **Deposit** – applies to bail applications in Scotland only | If bail is granted, I will pay a deposit of **£** |
| C | **Electronic monitoring** – if bail is granted and electronic monitoring is considered an appropriate condition of bail, the applicant will remain in detention until such times as UKBA have arranged for them to be electronically monitored, but not exceeding 2 working days after the date on which bail is granted.<br><br>If appropriate, does the applicant consent to the above? | No ☐    Yes ☐ |
| D | Applicant's signature and date | /          / |
| E | Name of the applicant. Please use CAPITAL LETTERS | |

| Section 4 | | About your sureties (if any) | |
|---|---|---|---|
| | | Surety 1 | Surety 2 |
| A | Surname or family name. Please use CAPITAL LETTERS. | | |
| B | Your other names | | |
| C | Address | | |
| | | Post code | Post code |
| D | Telephone number | | |
| E | Relationship to Applicant | | |
| F | Immigration Status | | |
| G | Occupation | | |
| H | Recognisance/Deposit | £ | £ |
| I | Date of birth | | |
| J | Nationality (or nationalities) or citizenship held | | |

| K | Passport numbers(s) (if more than one nationality is held) | | |
|---|---|---|---|
| **Notice to applicants** | Please ensure that you and your surety/ies bring to the bail hearing: passports, bank statements and other financial documents necessary for the grant of bail. | | |

| Section 5 | The grounds on which you are applying for bail |
|---|---|

- In this section you must set out all the reasons why you think you should be released.
- **If you have had a previous application for bail refused, you <u>must give full details</u> of any additional grounds or change in circumstances since then.**
- Give as much detail as possible: use additional sheets of paper if you need to, and attach them to this form.

In this box, give all the reasons why you think you should be released.

| Section 6 | At the hearing of your application |
|---|---|

| A | Will you or your surety need an interpreter? | No ☐  Yes ☐ | If yes, which language will be needed? |
|---|---|---|---|
| | | Language | |
| | | Dialect (if required) | |

| B | If you or your legal representative has a disability, please explain any special arrangements needed for the hearing. | | |
|---|---|---|---|

| C | The hearing in respect of this bail application may be conducted by a video link during which the applicant will remain in the place of detention. Where exceptional circumstances exist and it is considered that the Applicant is unable to use the video link medium, please provide those reasons in this box for consideration by the Resident Senior Immigration Judge. *An appropriate member of the judiciary will decide whether the application will be heard in person or by video link. Parties will be informed of this decision when the case is listed.* | |

| **Section 7** | **Representation** |
|---|---|
| | If you have a representative, he or she must complete this section. |

| A | **Declaration by the Representative** | I, the representative, am making this application in accordance with the applicant's instructions, and the applicant believes the facts stated in this application are true. |
|---|---|---|
| | Representative's signature and date. |        /    / |
| B | Name of the representative. Please use CAPITAL LETTERS. | |
| C | Name of the representative's organisation. | |
| D | Postal address of the organisation. | Number/Street |
| | | |
| | | |
| | | Town |
| | | Post code |
| E | Reference for correspondence | |
| F | Telephone number | |
| G | Mobile number | |
| H | Fax number | |

| I | Email address | | | |
|---|---|---|---|---|
| **J** | Are you an office regulated by the Office of the Immigration Services Commissioner (OISC)? | No ☐  Yes ☐ | Please provide OISC reference: | |
| **K** | Has the applicant been granted publicly funded legal representation? | No ☐  Yes ☐ | Please provide the LSC reference if applicable: | |
| **Notice to representatives** | You must notify the court in which the bail application is made, and other parties, if you cease to represent the applicant. If the applicant changes representative, details of the new representative should be sent to the same address to which you are sending this form. Please give the **applicant's full name, address,** and **Home Office reference number.** | | | |

| Section 8 | Declaration by applicant |
|---|---|
| | If you are the applicant and you are completing this form yourself, you must complete the declaration. |
| **A**  **Declaration by the Applicant** | I, the applicant, believe that the facts stated in this application are true. |
| Applicant's signature and date. | /    / |
| **B**  Name of the applicant. Please use CAPITAL LETTERS. | |

| Section 9 | When you have completed the form |
|---|---|
| What to do next | Keep a copy of this form for your own use. Send or deliver the original form to the court to which you intend to make your application for bail. |
| Data Protection statement | Information, including personal details, provided in this form will not be used by the Asylum and Immigration Tribunal for purpose other than the determination of your application. The information may be disclosed to other government departments and public authorities only, for related immigration or asylum purposes. |

# Index

**evidence** *continued*
surveillance 5.50
warrants of further detention 9.10, 9.18, 9.24
**evidence, exclusion of** 13.28–13.57
abuse of process, stay of proceedings as 13.28
access to legal advice 2.123, 2.130, 3.47, 13.43, 13.46–13.47
denial 2.147, 2.150, 13.10, 13.47
fairness 13.47
arrest 2.44
breaches of PACE and codes 13.30–13.32, 13.43–13.45
bugging interview rooms 13.56
cautions 4.27, 7.6, 10.31, 13.48
common law 13.28
confessions/admissions 13.28–13.29, 13.32–13.43, 13.46, 13.56–13.57
confrontation, identification by 8.67, 8.69
deception 13.56
denial of access to legal advice 2.147, 2.150, 13.10, 13.47
detention
reviews 2.95
time limits 2.79
enforcement 13.28–13.57
entrapment 13.53–13.55
European Convention on Human Rights 13.44
fair hearing, right to a 13.44, 13.47
fairness 5.55, 13.44, 13.47
false confessions 13.31, 13.33
false or misleading information 4.26
identification procedures 13.50–13.51
inducements 13.57
information on rights, withholding 13.46
intervention 13.32–13.33
interviews
bugging interview rooms 13.56
conduct 13.49
intervention 13.32–13.33
recording 13.49
signing records 7.8
subsequent 13.29
tainted 13.29
verballing 13.49
mental disabilities 13.28, 13.31–13.33
negotiations 13.29
notes of conduct, taking contemporaneous 13.30, 13.32
oppression 13.33
presence of lawyer 13.32–13.33, 13.43
private and family life, right to respect for 13.44
searches, questions during 13.52

seizure 13.52
signing records 7.8
silence, right to 13.43
verballing 13.49
visual identification 8.23, 13.51
**examination** *see* **search and examination to ascertain identity**
**excluded and special procedure material, access to** 2.52
**exclusion of evidence** *see* **evidence, exclusion of**
**exclusion of representatives**
access to legal advice, delay in 4.4–4.8
accredited or probationary representatives 4.4–4.9
consultation of another lawyer after exclusion, allowing 7.54
intervention during interviews 7.50–7.57
procedure 7.53–7.57
**expertise of lawyers** 1.33
**experts, names and addresses of** 1.47
**explanations of procedure to clients** 5.4, 5.10, 10.105–10.107
**extradition** 1.73

**face or head coverings, removal of** 6.11, 6.15
**face-to-face discussions on cases** 1.28
**fair hearing, right to a**
access to legal advice, delay in or denial of 2.119, 2.144, 13.10, 13.47
adverse inferences from silence 5.64, 13.10
breach of the peace 2.25
compulsory questioning 5.62
defences 5.58
evidence, exclusion of 13.44, 13.47
interviews 13.14
reprimands or warnings 11.33
**fairness** *see* **fair hearing, right to a; fairness of interviews**
**fairness of interviews** 7.35–7.36, 13.14
adverse inferences from silence 5.64, 5.125–5.127
ambiguous questions 7.64
bombastic and bullying style 7.63, 7.67
confessions/admissions
false 7.67
inducements 7.64
maximising and minimising consequences 7.67
oppression 7.61, 7.67
style of questioning 7.67